Brief Contents

List of Features

No Easy Answers

Research Report

The Real World

Policy Questions

Contents

5: Cognitive Development in Infancy 120

6: Social and Personality Development in Infancy 146

Part III: Early Childhood 175

7: Physical and Cognitive Development in Early Childhood 175

8: Social and Personality Development in Early Childhood 206

Part IV: Middle Childhood 244

9: Physical and Cognitive Development in Middle Childhood 244

10: Social and Personality Development in Middle Childhood 276

Part V: Adolescence 306

11: Physical and Cognitive Development in Adolescence 306

12: Social and Personality Development in Adolescence 339

Part VI: Early Adulthood 370

13: Physical and Cognitive Development in Early Adulthood 370

14: Social and Personality Development in Early Adulthood 403

Part VII: Middle Adulthood 434

15: Physical and Cognitive Development in Middle Adulthood 434

16: Social and Personality Development in Middle Adulthood 460

Part VIII: Late Adulthood and the End of Life 483

17: Physical and Cognitive Development in Late Adulthood 483

18: Social and Personality Development in Late Adulthood 512

19: Death, Dying, and Bereavement 540

To The Instructor

Having taught human development for many years, I know that teaching a course in lifespan development is one of the most difficult assignments an instructor can face. You must deal with the challenge of getting through all the necessary descriptive material in a single semester. At the same time, you have to cover theories of development, some of which are among the most complex and important theories in the behavioral sciences. In preparing the fifth edition of *Lifespan Development*, I hoped to support lifespan development instructors by producing a textbook that thoroughly addresses the basic facts of development, makes the more abstract material about theories understandable to students, and motivates them to read the book by presenting information in a way that is both engaging and relevant to real-world applications of developmental science.

New to the Fifth Edition

The fifth edition has been thoroughly revised and updated to reflect the latest research in the field of human development. Following are some highlights of the new edition:

Learning Objectives. Every section of the text now has a corresponding, numbered learning objective. These objectives are called out in the margin and repeated in the chapter summary to facilitate student review. In addition, the Instructor's Manual and Test Bank now correspond to these learning objectives, allowing you to assess your students' knowledge of key educational objectives.

End-of-chapter Practice Tests (Test Yourself). A multiple-choice practice test now appears after the chapter summary and the end of every chapter. The test questions are organized by section and answers are provided at the back of the text, allowing students to assess their knowledge and prepare for course quizzes and exams.

MyDevelopmentLab Study Plan. We have designed a two-page study plan for MyDevelopmentLab at the end of every chapter. This visual feature highlights some of the key resources available to students on MyDevelopmentLab, such as pre- and post-tests, customized study plans, and multimedia videos and simulations. The Test Bank includes questions specifically geared toward MyDevelopmentLab for your assessment needs.

Organizational Changes. The fifth edition is now organized around eight parts, including new, separate parts on Infancy; Early Childhood; Middle Childhood; Adolescence; Early Adulthood; and Middle Adulthood. A number of organizational changes have been made within chapters as well to reflect current research and to help make the content easier for students to understand. For instance, research methods are now covered prior to research designs (Chapter 1, "Basic Concepts and Methods"); Vygotsky's sociocultural approach is now covered in a section on cognitive theories (Chapter 2, "Theories of Development"); coverage of genetic and chromosomal disorders now appears directly after the material on conception and genetics (Chapter 3, "Prenatal Development and Birth"); material on emotional responsiveness is now covered in the context of caregivers and attachment (Chapter 6, "Social and Personality Development in Infancy"); to provide students with a solid foundation for family and peer relationships, coverage of personality and self-concept and gender development has been moved earlier in the chapter (Chapter 8, "Social and Personality Development in Early Childhood"); there is now earlier coverage of brain development and physical growth and separate coverage of anorexia nervosa and bulimia nervosa (Chapter 11, "Physical and Cognitive Development in Adolescence"); self-esteem in adolescence is now covered prior to gender roles (Chapter 12, "Social and Personality Development in Adolescence"); discussions of health and wellness now begin with personal factors affecting one's health rather than with

STDs (Chapter 13, "Physical and Cognitive Development in Early Adulthood"); evolutionary theory and social role theory are now covered in the context of intimate relationships (Chapter 14, "Social and Personality Development in Early Adulthood"); life expectancy and longevity are discussed together and now open the chapter on late adulthood (Chapter 17, "Physical and Cognitive Development in Late Adulthood"); family relationships and friendships, and timing and reasoning for retirement are now covered in a single section (Chapter 18, "Social and Personality Development in Late Adulthood"); and the theoretical perspectives on grieving are now discussed prior to the actual experience of grieving (Chapter 19, "Death, Dying, and Bereavement").

Updated Research. The fifth edition has been updated to include almost 500 new references. Some examples of this include:

- Revised discussion of Baltes' lifespan perspective and additional information on descriptive research methods (Chapter 1, "Basic Concepts and Methods")
- New coverage of studies connecting scaffolding during the preschool years with higher levels of achievement in elementary school (Chapter 2, "Theories of Development")
- Expanded coverage of the fetal stage, including new material on the fetal brain and updated discussion of teratogens, including new material on critical periods and prescription and over-the-counter drugs (Chapter 3, "Prenatal Development and Birth")
- Revised discussion of infant mortality (Chapter 4, "Physical, Sensory, and Perceptual Development in Infancy")
- Revised coverage of theoretical perspectives of language to include the interactionist view (Chapter 5, "Cognitive Development in Infancy")
- Updated research on infant temperament (Chapter 6, "Social and Personality Development in Infancy")
- New material on infantile amnesia and revised coverage of information-processing theories (Chapter 7, "Physical and Cognitive Development in Early Childhood")
- Updated discussion of temperament (Chapter 8, "Social and Personality Development in Early Childhood")
- New section on excessive weight gain in childhood; updated discussion of literacy to include second-language learners and the balance approach to reading; and new material on inclusive education (Chapter 9, "Physical and Cognitive Development in Middle Childhood")
- New section on the trait and social-cognitive perspectives; new coverage of self-efficacy; and new section on media influences, including television, computers, the Internet, and video games (Chapter 10, "Social and Personality Development in Middle Childhood")
- Updated coverage of puberty includes the secular trend and the effect of the timing of puberty on social development; new section on adolescent sexuality with cover-age of sexual minority youth (Chapter 11, "Physical and Cognitive Development in Adolescence")
- Updated coverage of ethnic identify includes new discussions of biracial and immigrant teens; section on romantic relationships now includes both heterosexual and homosexual relationships (Chapter 12, "Social and Personality Development in Adolescence")
- New discussion of intimate partner abuse in same-sex relationships; new section on substance abuse; and revised coverage of formal operations (Chapter 13, "Physical and Cognitive Development in Early Adulthood")
- New section on emerging adulthood; updated discussion of career development, including Donald Super's stages; new section on the quality of work life movement; and new discussion of women's work patterns (Chapter 14, "Social and Personality Development in Early Adulthood")
- Updated research on the secular trend in menopause and women's attitudes towards menopause across ethnic groups; new coverage of the Type D personality type; new material on alcoholism (Chapter 15, "Physical and Cognitive Development in Middle Adulthood")

- New discussion of Vaillant's revision of Erikson's theory; new coverage of the life events approach; new coverage of the Big Five personality traits; and updated research on burnout and sex differences in worker satisfaction (Chapter 16, "Social and Personality Development in Middle Adulthood")
- New discussion of glaucoma and macular degeneration; updated research on Alzheimer's disease and dementia (Chapter 17, "Physical and Cognitive Development in Late Adulthood")
- New coverage of the process of life review; new coverage of continuity theory; updated discussion of the protective nature of marriage for older adults (Chapter 18, "Social and Personality Development in Late Adulthood")
- Revised research on children's and adolescents' understanding of death; new coverage of the dual-process model of grieving and of the grieving process for those who have lost a loved one to a violent crime (Chapter 19, "Death, Dying, and Bereavement")

Themed Essays and Policy Questions

The fifth edition of *Lifespan Development* includes three kinds of thought-provoking themed essays in every chapter, plus social policy sections at the end of every part.

No Easy Answers. The No Easy Answers essays introduce students to the idea that there are many questions for which developmental psychologists cannot provide definitive answers. For example, the essay in Chapter 15 deals with hormone therapy and discusses the benefits and potential risks of this therapy. Students are asked to take a stand on whether they feel that, due to the risks involved, hormone therapy should be a last resort or that, since no medical treatment is entirely free of risk, women should feel free to take hormone therapy to help relieve some of their menopausal symptoms.

I developed these discussions in response to my own students' continuing difficulty in understanding that psychology is not a science that can offer straightforward recipes for perfect behavioral outcomes. My hope is that, by reading these discussions, students will become more sensitive to the complexity of human development and more tolerant of the ambiguities inherent in the behavioral and social sciences.

Research Report. Research Reports provide detailed accounts of specific research studies. For example, Chapter 5 discusses research on early gestural language in the children of deaf parents and Chapter 17 examines research on mild cognitive impairment and Alzheimer's disease. "Questions for Critical Analysis" appear at the end of each feature to help students assess the research and make connections between the research study and their daily lives.

The Real World. The Real World essays explore practical applications of developmental theory and research, in such areas as parenting, teaching, caregiving, aging, and working. For example, the essay in Chapter 5 discusses the importance of reading to toddlers and Chapter 11 examines crisis intervention for pregnant teenagers. Each of these essays opens with a real-life story and concludes with "Questions for Reflection."

Policy Question. Discussions of social policy issues relevant to human development appear at the end of each part in the fifth edition. The features discuss the following questions:

Part I: Should Pregnant Women Who Use Illicit Drugs Be Prosecuted?
Part II: Are "Safe Haven" Policies a Good Idea?
Part III: "Deadbeat Dads": Irresponsible Parents or Political Scapegoats?
Part IV: Has Test-Based Reform Improved Schools in the United States?
Part V: Should Video Games be Regulated by the Government?
Part VI: What Reforms are Needed in the Student Loan System?
Part VII: What Types of Couples Should be Sanctioned by Society?
Part VIII: How Should Stem Cell Research Be Funded and Regulated?

The first goal of these discussions is to acquaint students with a few social and political issues related to topics discussed in the text. The second goal is to encourage students to find out how these issues are being dealt with where they live. Each Policy Question feature ends with a list of suggestions that should help students find out more about the issue. My hope is that students will gain an understanding of the implications of developmental psychology for social policy as well as of the impact of social policies on human development.

Supplements for the Instructor

We have designed a collection of instructor resources for the fifth edition that will help you prepare for class, enhance your course presentations, and assess your students' understanding of the material. These are only available to qualified instructors using the text. Please contact your local publishing representative for more information.

- **MyDevelopmentLab.** This interactive and instructive multimedia resource can be used to supplement a traditional lecture course or to administer a course entirely online. It is an all-inclusive tool, a text-specific E-Book plus multimedia tutorials, audio, video, simulations, animations, and controlled assessments to completely engage students and reinforce learning. Fully customizable and easy to use, MyDevelopmentLab meets the individual teaching and learning needs of every instructor and every student. Visit the site at www.mydevelopmentlab.com.
- **Instructor's Classroom Kit Volume 1 and Volume 2 with CD-ROM.** The Instructor's supplements package for this book is organized into two volumes (Vol. 1 covering the first half of the book and Vol. 2 the remaining chapters). Each volume contains the following resources: Instructor's Manual, Test Bank, and both the Lecture Outline and Art Only PowerPoint® Presentations. Electronic versions of all files are available on the accompanying CD-ROM.
  - **Instructor's Manual.** The Instructor's Manual has been thoroughly revised and reorganized by Karen Saenz of Houston Community College to be even more user-friendly. Each chapter has the following resources: "At-a-Glance" grids, showcasing key supplemental resources available for instructors and students by chapter; a Chapter Overview; a list of the numbered Learning Objectives; and a complete table of the Key Terms with page references. New to this edition, each chapter also offers an extensive, detailed, and fully integrated Teaching Notes section with Discussion Launchers, Feature Box Activities, lists of available media to use in the classroom, Classroom Activity ideas, and Critical Thinking Questions. The Teaching Notes are closely tied to the numbered learning objectives from the text so you can easily connect the content of this manual to the corresponding learning objectives. For instructors looking to expand upon the textbook content, each chapter closes with an optional relevant Lecture Enhancer.
  - **Test Bank.** Prepared by Rod Fowers of Highline Community College, the Test Bank is composed of approximately 2,000 fully referenced multiple-choice, short-answer, and essay questions. The test questions are tied to the numbered learning objectives from the text, allowing you to assess knowledge of specific skills. In addition, questions may be viewed by level of difficulty and skill type. To help you follow through with the dynamic resources offered in MyDevelopmentLab in your assessments, this edition of the Test Bank offers five blended multiple-choice and completion questions and 1 to 2 essay questions for each chapter that test select MyDevelopmentLab assets. This supplement is also available in TestGen Computerized Test Bank version, an easy way to create polished, hard-copy tests.
  - **PowerPoint Presentations.** Prepared by Susan Carol Losh of Florida State University, the PowerPoint presentations include both a detailed lecture outline with select art from the text and a set of slides containing the complete art program from the book.

- **Interactive Lecture Questions for Clickers for Lifespan Development.** These lecture questions, developed by Denise Boyd, can be used to help jumpstart classroom discussions.
- **Insights into Developmental Psychology.** This video program highlights important high-interest topics across the lifespan. Ask your local sales representative how to obtain a copy.
- **Allyn and Bacon Human Development Transparency Package.** An extensive set of full-color transparencies is available through your sales representative.

To the Student

Most of the students who take a lifespan course do so because it is required for a degree in nursing, education, or another applied field. Others enroll in lifespan development because they are pursuing degrees in psychology or human development. Still others simply want to know more about the fascinating topic of age-related changes in psychological functioning. Whatever your reason for taking the course, you are likely to find that the theories and research that you read about in this text will help you better understand your own developmental path-where you've been, where you are, and where you're headed. At the same time, the practical applications of developmental principles that are woven into our discussions of theory and research will help you interact more effectively with others whose ages, cultures, and developmental concerns differ from you own. Be forewarned, though: Despite the intriguing nature of the topics that are covered in a lifespan course, the amount of information that you are expected to learn in such a course can be quite daunting unless you make a concerted effort to break it down into chunks that are both meaningful and manageable in size. This textbook has been designed to help you do just that.

The task of understanding and remembering the information in a developmental psychology textbook may seem overwhelming. However, when you finish reading this book, you will have a better understanding of yourself and of other people. So, all your hard work will be well worth the effort.

How to Work with This Book

Here is an overview of the book's features that should be helpful to you in accomplishing the task of learning as much as you can about human development in the next few weeks.

- **Chapter Outlines.** Before you read each chapter, read over the outline at its beginning. More information will stick in your mind if you have an idea of what to expect.
- **Chapter Introductions.** Each chapter opens with a real-life example of the psychological principles that will be covered in the chapter. For instance, Chapter 18: Social and Personality Development in Late Adulthood begins with stories of various couples who have been married for over 80 years. Reading these introductions will help you see how psychology connects to your life.
- **Learning Objectives.** Each chapter is structured around numbered learning objective questions, which correspond to the sections of the chapter. As you read through a section, the learning objective can help you focus your reading on the important concepts. The learning objective questions are answered in the end-of-chapter summary to help you review the major concepts from the chapter.

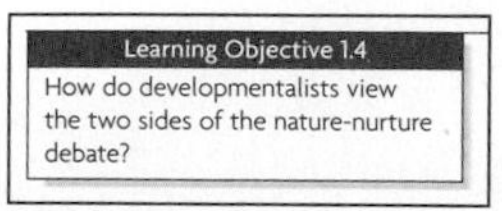

Learning Objective 1.4
How do developmentalists view the two sides of the nature-nurture debate?

- **Marginal Glossary.** Key terms are defined in the margin near where they are first used in the text. As you come to each boldface term in the text, stop and read its definition in the margin. Then go back and reread the sentence that introduced the key term. A complete list of the key terms with page references is included at the end of each chapter.

> **nature-nurture debate** the debate about the relative contributions of biological processes and experiential factors to development

- **Critical Thinking Questions.** These questions, which appear at the end of each major section, encourage you to relate material in the book to your own experiences. They can also help you remember the information in the text, because linking new information to things you already know is a highly effective memory strategy.

> *Critical Thinking*
>
> 1. How have culture, religion, and science shaped your views of development?

- **Chapter Summary.** Looking over the chapter summary can help you assess how much of the information you remember. Each summary is organized around the major sections of the chapter and includes answers to the numbered learning objective questions. A complete key terms list, including page references, is also included so that you can review your knowledge of the main chapter concepts and terminology.
- **Test Yourself Practice Tests.** Now located at the end of each chapter, these practice tests are organized by the major chapter sections and include multiple-choice; fill-in-the-blank; and matching questions. When you finish reading a chapter, take the practice test and find out what you've mastered and what you need to review. You can check your understanding of the major concepts in each chapter by referring to the answer key provided at the end of the book.
- **MyDevelopmentLab Study Plan.** In addition to the pedagogical features in the text itself, you will find additional study material on MyDevelopmentLab (www.mydevelopmentlab.com). After each chapter, you will find a two-page overview of the resources available to you on MyDevelopmentLab, including pre- and post-tests, customized study plans, and multimedia resources like videos and simulations that will help you strengthen your knowledge of the chapter. Using MyDevelopment Lab along with your textbook will improve your grade in the course.

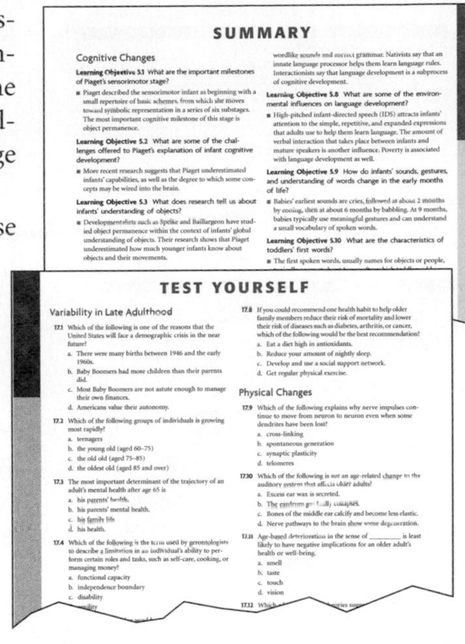

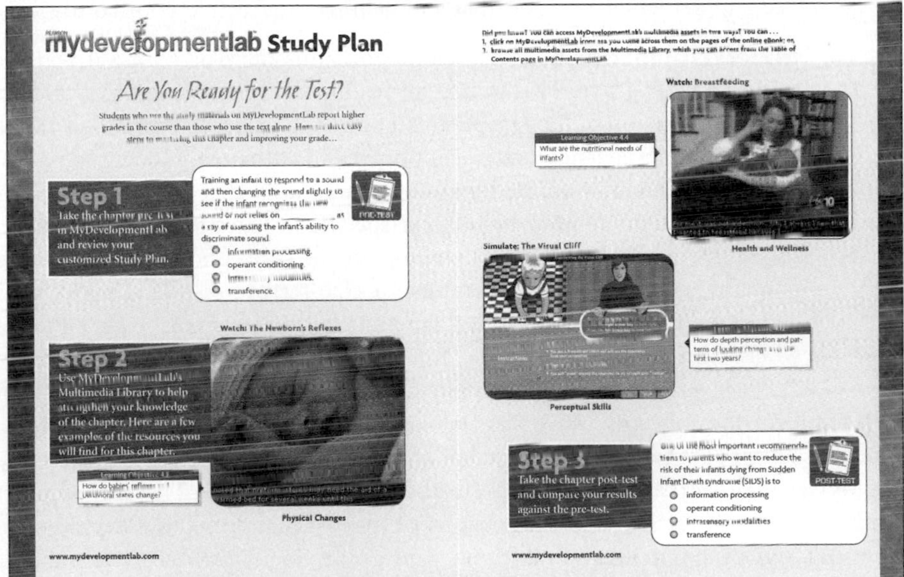

Chapter and Part Features

In additional to its pedagogical features, *Lifespan Development* offers a variety of features to help you examine concepts in more detail and relate what you've learned to your daily life.

- **No Easy Answers.** Often times in developmental psychology, there is no "correct" or easy answer to a problem. These features help you understand the complexities involved in trying to apply developmental theories and research to real life problems. For instance, one of the features examines what impact watching television has on infants. Every feature concludes with a "Take a Stand" section in which you are encouraged to offer your own view on the issue.

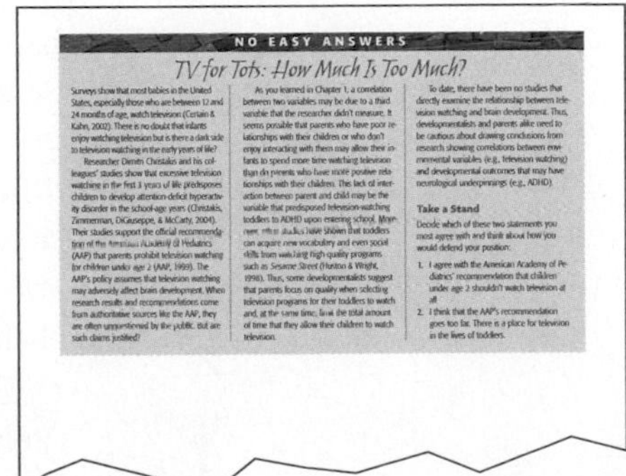

RESEARCH REPORT

Gender Differences in the Brain

THE REAL WORLD

Computers in Rehabilitation Programs

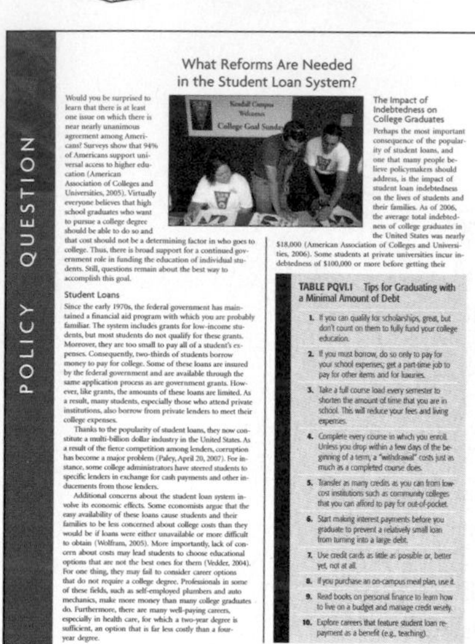
POLICY QUESTION

What Reforms Are Needed in the Student Loan System?

- **Research Reports.** These features, found in every chapter, recount the findings of important studies and allow you to take a more in-depth look at some of the research being done in developmental psychology today. For instance, one of the features examines the research being done on gender differences in the adult brain. Every feature concludes with "Questions for Critical Analysis" to help you sharpen your critical-thinking skills.
- **The Real World.** These features offer practical advice on parenting, teaching, caregiving, and other aspects of daily life to which developmental psychology is relevant. Every feature opens with a real-life situation before proceeding to discuss how developmental psychology impacts the situation. For instance, one of the features examines how computers are used in rehabilitation programs for older adults. "Questions for Reflection" conclude each feature, allowing you to consider how you would handle various situations.
- **Policy Questions.** Discussions of social policy issues relevant to human development appear at the end of each Part of the textbook. For example, the Policy Question at the end of Part 6 addresses what reforms are needed in the student loan program. These discussions will provide you with insight into how the findings of developmental research may be used to influence policy changes in the real world.

Supplements for the Student

In addition to all of the pedagogical features in the text, we have designed a number of supplemental products that will help you succeed in your course.

- **MyDevelopmentLab.** MyDevelopmentLab is the place to go if you want to improve your grade. This online all-in-one study resource offers a dynamic, electronic version of the *Lifespan* textbook with over 200 embedded video clips (2 to 4 minutes in length, close-captioned and with post-viewing activities) and over 60 embedded animations and simulations that dynamically illustrate chapter concepts. With over 100 text-specific practice test questions per chapter, MyDevelopmentLab helps you master the concepts from the text and prepare for exams. After you complete a chapter pre-test, MyDevelopmentLab generates a customized Study Plan that helps you focus your study efforts where you need it the most. You can then re-read those sections of the E-Book and view the accompanying videos, animations, and simulations to help reinforce the concepts. Once you feel confident in your knowledge of the chapter, take the chapter post-test and track your progress against the pre-test results. To help you use MyDevelopmentLab efficiently, this textbook contains a special MyDevelopmentLab Study Plan feature at the end of each chapter of the text that provides a step-by-step plan for using MyDevelopmentLab to improve your grade. To access MyDevelopmentLab or to take a tour of its features, visit www.mydevelopmentlab.com.
- **Grade Aid Study Guide.** The Grade Aid Study Guide for the fifth edition of *Lifespan Development* has been revised by Karen Saenz of Houston Community College. This guide is designed to be your go-to resource for preparing you for the material in the chapter, helping you retain the information you are gathering, testing what you remember, and finally, taking you deeper into the material. Each chapter guides you through the textbook chapter as follows:
  - "Before You Read" provides a brief chapter summary, a complete list of key terms, and a review of the chapter learning objectives.
  - "As You Read" offers a varied collection of demonstrations, activities, and exercises that help you practice and reinforce your skills while you work through the chapter.
  - "After You Read" consists of practice tests that help you assess areas of strength and areas that need some improvement in preparation for the real exam.
  - "When You Have Finished" helps you round out your knowledge with web links for further information and a crossword puzzle built with key terms from the text.

Acknowledgments

No one ever accomplishes much of anything alone. Therefore, I would like to thank a number of people for providing me with the support I needed to complete this project. First and foremost, my husband Jerry Boyd, my sons Matt and Chris Boyd, my daughter Marianne Meece, my son-in-law Michael Meece, and my granddaughters, Mackenzie and Madeleine Meece, are my most important cheerleaders. Likewise, a number of my colleagues at Houston Community College (Karen Saenz, Jane Cirillo, Madeleine Wright, Genevieve Stevens, David Gersh, and Saundra Boyd) acted as sounding boards for various ideas as I was preparing the fifth edition.

The fifth edition was supervised by Stephen Frail, who provided many ideas and words of encouragement. And, of course, developmental editors are essential to the process. I am indebted to Julie Swasey for pointing out digressions, improving the logical order of the topics in several chapters, and for her cogent summaries of reviewers' comments.

To Our Reviewers: Finally, I would like to thank the many colleagues who served as reviewers on both the fifth edition and prior editions of *Lifespan Development* for their thought-provoking comments and criticisms as well as their willingness to take time out of their busy schedules to help me improve this book.

Reviewers of the Fifth Edition:

Ted Barker, Okaloosa-Walton College
Saundra Y. Boyd, Houston Community College
Tony Fowler, Florence-Darlington Technical College
Terry R. Isbell, Northwestern State University
Rosalind Shorter, Jefferson Community College
Mojisola Tiamiyu, University of Toledo
Patricia Riely Twaddle, Moberly Area Community College
John D. Williams, Brookhaven College
Rebecca M. Wood, Central Connecticut State University
Pauline Davey Zeece, University of Nebraska at Lincoln

Past Reviewers:

Jeffrey Arnett, University of Maryland
Cynthia Avens, Daytona Beach Community College
Barbara E. Baker, Nashville State Tech
Troy E. Beckert, Utah State University
Laura Hess Brown, State University of New York at Oswego
Barbara DeFilippo, Lane Community College
Julie Felender, Fullerton College
Tina Footen, Boise State University
Loren Ford, Clackamas Community College
Kathleen V. Fox, Salisbury State University
Lynn Haller, Morehead State University
Debra L. Hollister, Valencia Community College
Scott L. Horton, University of Southern Maine
Suzy Horton, Mesa Community College
Shabana Kausar, Minnesota State University
John S. Klein, Castleton State College
David D. Kurz, Delmar College
Billie Laney, Central Texas Community College
Kathryn Levit, George Mason University
Susan Magun-Jackson, University of Memphis
April Mansfield, Long Beach City College
Carrie M. Margolin, The Evergreen State College
Joseph A. Mayo, Gordon College
Alan C. Miller, Santa Fe Community College
James E. Oliver, Henry Ford Community College
Regina K. Peters, Hawkeye Community College
Joe E. Price, San Diego State University
Celinda Reese, Oklahoma State University
Paul Roodin, State University of New York at Oswego
Jonathan Schwartz, Yeshiva University
Lynn Shelley, Westfield State College
Rosalind Shorter, Jefferson Community College
Stephanie Stein, Central Washington University
Kevin Sumrall, Montgomery College
Stephen Truhon, Winston-Salem State University
Bradley M. Waite, Central Connecticut State University
Eugene H. Wong, California State University—San Bernardino
Virginia V. Wood, University of Texas—Brownsville

Denise Boyd

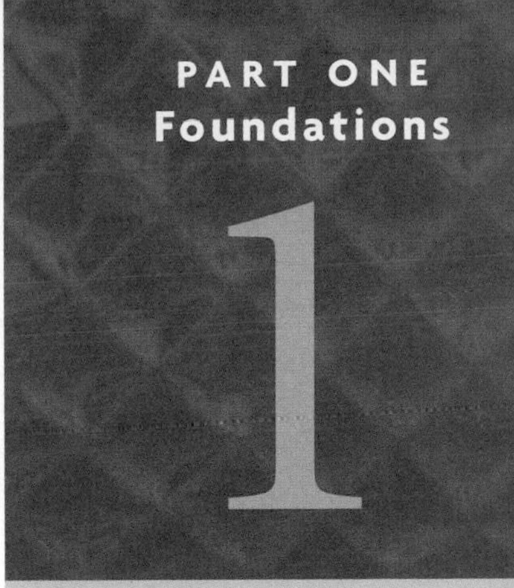

Basic Concepts and Methods

Suppose that you lived in a household that included five generations: you, your divorced older sister and her 2-year-old child, a middle-aged couple (your parents), an older couple (your grandparents), and your 90-year-old great-grandmother. Further, suppose that your family was asked to describe an ideal living space that could accommodate your multigenerational family. What kinds of features do you think your family would suggest?

Several years back, the editorial staffs of *Builder* and *Home* magazines carried out just such a study (Curry, 2005). Post-2000 census trends told them that multigenerational households are on the rise in the United States, so they decided to build a show house that was based on interviews with multigenerational families. The eight families who participated in the project represented the major ethnic and

income groups in the United States. Each had at least three generations living under one roof. Their reasons for choosing to live in multigenerational households varied from economic necessity to cultural traditions to the practical aspects of caring for a family member with a disability or for young children whose parents were working. Some also saw multigenerational living as a way of helping recent immigrants adjust to life in the United States.

The multigenerational families who participated in the "Reality House" project told the magazines' researchers that, like most families, they needed extra storage space for bulky items such as multipacks of paper towels and kitchens that were large enough to accommodate more than one cook at a time. But they also emphasized the need for private areas where individual family members could escape from the constant togetherness that is often a feature of multigenerational living. Important, too, were the contrasting needs of family members in different phases of the life cycle. Most of the multigenerational families wanted flexible spaces that could be easily modified to accommodate the changing physical needs of elderly family members. Still, most also wanted their homes to be child-friendly. And the young and middle-aged adults in these families requested spaces that could be used for studying, telecommuting, and running home-based businesses.

When you think about it, it's not surprising that multigenerational families have living space needs that are somewhat different from those of other families. After all, people who are in different phases of life have different needs. These needs arise from the physical, cognitive, and social characteristics that distinguish the various phases of life. Such needs, and the age-related characteristics that produce them, are what the study of human development is all about.

In this chapter, you will learn how the science of human development came into being. You will also learn about the key issues in the scientific study of development. In addition, when you finish reading the chapter, you will be acquainted with the research designs and methods used by developmentalists.

An Introduction to Human Development

human development the scientific study of age-related changes in behavior, thinking, emotion, and personality

The field of **human development** is the scientific study of age-related changes in behavior, thinking, emotion, and personality. Long before the scientific method was used to study development, though, philosophers offered a variety of explanations for differences they observed in individuals of different ages. In the 19th century, the scientific methods used by early pioneers in the study of human behavior were applied to questions about age-related change. Nevertheless, the term "development" was largely confined to childhood during the early years. However, in the second half of the twentieth century, behavioral scientists began to acknowledge that important age-related changes occur across the entire human lifespan. Their efforts led to useful ways of categorizing important issues in the study of development and revealed a wealth of data suggesting that human development is a highly complex process.

Philosophical and Scientific Roots

Learning Objective 1.1
What ideas about development were proposed by early philosophers and scientists?

Early philosophers based their ideas about development on spiritual authorities, general philosophical orientations, and deductive logic. In the 19th century, though, people who wanted to better understand human development turned to science.

Original Sin, the Blank Slate, and Innate Goodness Typically, philosophers' inquiries into the nature of development focused on why babies, who appear to be quite similar, grow up to vary widely. They were particularly concerned with the moral dimensions of development. For example, the Christian doctrine of *original sin*, often attributed to 4th-century philosopher Augustine of Hippo, taught that all humans are born with a selfish nature. To reduce the influence of this inborn tendency toward selfishness, Augustine taught, humans must seek spiritual rebirth and submit themselves to religious training. Thus, from this perspective, developmental outcomes, both good and bad, are the result of each individual's struggle to overcome an inborn tendency to act immorally when doing so somehow benefits the self.

By contrast, 17th-century English philosopher John Locke drew upon a broad philosophical approach known as *empiricism* when he claimed that the mind of a child is a *blank slate*. Empiricism is the view that humans possess no innate tendencies and that all differences among humans are attributable to experience. As such, the blank slate view suggests that adults can mold children into whatever they want them to be. Therefore, differences among adults can be explained in terms of differences in their childhood environments rather than as a result of a struggle to overcome any kind of inborn tendencies as the original sin view proposed.

Different still was the *innate goodness* view proposed by 18th-century Swiss philosopher Jean-Jacques Rousseau. He claimed that all human beings are naturally good and seek out experiences that help them grow (Ozman & Craver, 1986). Rousseau believed that children need only nurturing and protection to reach their full potential. Good developmental outcomes happen when a child's environment refrains from interfering in her attempts to nurture her own development. In contrast, poor outcomes occur when a child experiences frustration in her efforts to express the innate goodness with which she was born. Thus, the innate goodness and original sin approaches share the view that development involves a struggle between internal and external forces. In contrast to both, the blank slate view sees the child as a passive recipient of environmental influences.

This page from the *Huenshel's Complete Grammar*, published in 1895, illustrates the influence of the doctrine of original sin on education and child-rearing. Statements that promote religious and moral principles are embedded in this exercise on verbs. The idea was that the goals of teaching grammar to children and shaping their spiritual development could be, and should be, accomplished simultaneously.

LESSON XXXII.

VERBS.—REVIEW.

1. Name the mode of each verb in these sentences:

1. Bring me some flowers.
2. I must not be careless.
3. Who is the King of Glory?
4. Can that be the man?
5. The pupils have recited well.
6. Passionate men are easily irritated.
7. Do not walk so fast.
8. The prize cannot be obtained without labor.
9. Idleness often leads to vice.
10. Live for something.
11. In all climates, spring is beautiful.
12. I would have gone if I had known that I was needed.
13. If we would seem true, we must be true.

Early Scientific Theories The 19th century brought with it an explosion of interest in how scientific methods might be applied to questions that previously had been thought to belong within the domain of philosophy. Charles Darwin, for example, became well known for proposing the idea that the wide variety of life forms that exist on the Earth evolved gradually as a result of the interplay between environmental factors and genetic processes. More-

Charles Darwin, who fathered 10 children, initiated the scientific study of childhood. He used the same scientific methods that led to the discoveries on which he based his theory of evolution to make and record daily observations of his children's development.

over, Darwin proposed that studying children's development might help scientists better understand the evolution of the human species. To that end, Darwin and other like-minded scientists kept detailed records of their own children's early development (called *baby biographies*), in the hope of finding evidence to support the theory of evolution (Charlesworth, 1992). These were the first organized studies of human development, but critics claimed that studying children for the purpose of proving a theory might cause observers to misinterpret or ignore important information.

G. Stanley Hall of Clark University wanted to find more objective ways to study development. He used questionnaires and interviews to study large numbers of children. His 1891 article entitled "The Contents of Children's Minds on Entering School" represented the first scientific study of child development (White, 1992).

Hall agreed with Darwin that the milestones of childhood were similar to those that had taken place in the development of the human species. He thought that developmentalists should identify **norms**, or average ages at which developmental milestones are reached. Norms, Hall said, could be used to learn about the evolution of the species as well as to track the development of individual children.

Arnold Gesell's research suggested the existence of a genetically programmed sequential pattern of change (Gesell, 1925; Thelen & Adolph, 1992). Gesell used the term **maturation** to describe such a pattern of change. He thought that maturationally determined development occurred regardless of practice, training, or effort. For example, infants don't have to be taught how to walk—they begin to do so on their own once they reach a certain age. Because of his strong belief that many important developmental changes are determined by maturation, Gesell spent decades studying children and developing norms. He pioneered the use of movie cameras and one-way observation devices to study children's behavior. Gesell's findings became the basis for many tests that are used today to determine whether individual children are developing normally.

Learning Objective 1.2

What is the lifespan perspective?

The Lifespan Perspective

Until quite recently, psychologists thought of adulthood as a long period of stability followed by a short span of unstable years immediately preceding death. This view has changed because, for one thing, it has become common for adults to go through major life changes, such as divorce and career shifts. There has also been a significant increase in life expectancy that has occurred in the industrialized world. At the beginning of the 20th century, Americans' life expectancy at birth was only 49 years. By the century's end, the expected lifespan of someone born in the United States was about 76 years. As a result, older adults now constitute a larger proportion of the U.S. population than ever before. In fact, adults over the age of 100 are one of the most rapidly growing age groups in the industrialized world.

The changes outlined above have led to the adoption of a lifespan perspective. The **lifespan perspective** maintains that important changes occur during every period of development and that these changes must be interpreted in terms of the culture and context in which they occur (Baltes, Reese, & Lipsitt, 1980). Thus, understanding change in adulthood has become just as important as understanding change in childhood, and input from many disciplines is necessary to fully explain human development. This new perspective emphasizes these key elements:

- *Plasticity:* Individuals of all ages possess the capacity for positive change in response to environmental demands.
- *Interdisciplinary research:* Research from different kinds of disciplinary perspectives (e.g., anthropology, economics, psychology) is needed to fully understand lifespan development.

norms average ages at which developmental milestones are reached

maturation the gradual unfolding of a genetically programmed sequential pattern of change

lifespan perspective the current view of developmentalists that important changes occur throughout the entire human lifespan and that these changes must be interpreted in terms of the culture and context in which they occur; thus, interdisciplinary research is critical to understanding human development

- *Multi-contextual nature of development:* Individual development occurs within several interrelated contexts (e.g., family, neighborhood, culture).

Paul Baltes has been a leader in the development of a comprehensive theory of lifespan human development (Baltes, Staudinger, & Lindenberger, 1999). One of Baltes's most important contributions to the study of human development is his emphasis on the positive aspects of advanced age. He points out that, as human beings age, they adopt strategies that help them maximize gains and compensate for losses. For instance, one of Baltes's most often quoted examples is that of concert pianist Arthur Rubinstein, who was able to outperform much younger musicians well into his 80s (Cavanaugh & Whitbourne, 1999). Rubinstein reported that he maintained his performance capacity by carefully choosing pieces that he knew very well (maximizing gain) and by practicing these pieces more frequently than he had at earlier ages (compensating for the physical losses associated with age). You will read more about Baltes's theories and his research later, in the chapters devoted to late adulthood.

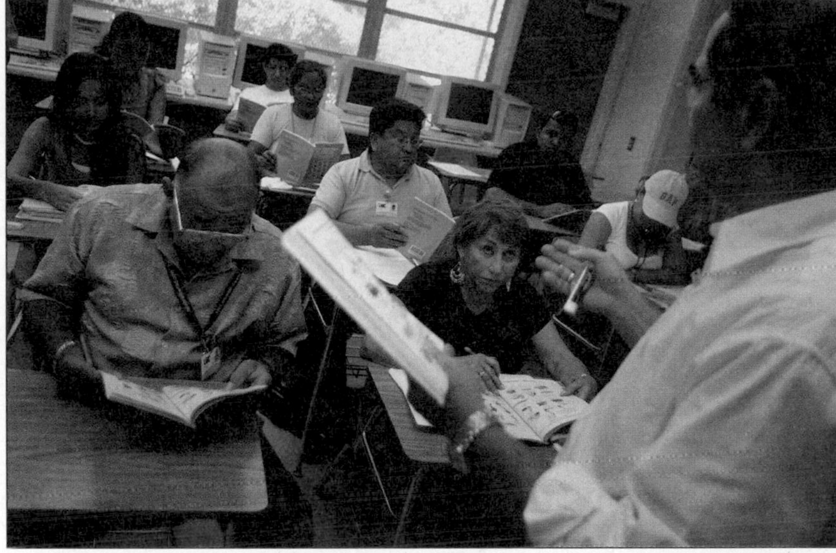
The lifespan perspective recognizes that important changes occur throughout life.

The Domains and Periods of Development

Learning Objective 1.3
What major domains and periods do developmental scientists use to organize their discussions of the human lifespan?

Scientists who study age-related changes often use three broad categories, called *domains of development*, to classify these changes. The **physical domain** includes changes in the size, shape, and characteristics of the body. For example, developmentalists study the physiological processes associated with puberty. Also included in this domain are changes in how individuals sense and perceive the physical world, such as the gradual development of depth perception over the first year of life.

Changes in thinking, memory, problem-solving, and other intellectual skills are included in the **cognitive domain**. Researchers working in the cognitive domain study topics as diverse as how children learn to read and why some memory functions deteriorate in old age. They also examine the ways in which individual differences among children and adults, such as intelligence test scores, are related to other variables within this domain.

The **social domain** includes changes in variables that are associated with the relationship of an individual to others. For instance, studies of children's social skills fall into the social domain, as does research on individual differences in personality. Individuals' beliefs about themselves are also usually classified within the social domain.

Using domain classifications helps to organize discussions of human development. However, it is always important to remember that the three domains do not function independently of one another. For instance, when a girl goes through puberty, a change in the physical domain, her ability to think abstractly (cognitive domain) and her feelings about potential romantic partners (social domain) change as well. In addition to categorizing developmental events according to domains, developmental scientists also use a system of age-related categories that are known as *periods of development*. The first of these phases, the *prenatal period*, is the only one that has clearly defined biological boundaries at its beginning and end in that it begins at conception and ends at birth. The next period, *infancy*, begins at birth and ends when children begin to use language to communicate, a milestone that marks the beginning of *early childhood*. Thus, while infancy begins at birth for all children, its end point can vary from one child to another. A social event, the child's entrance into school or some other kind of formal training, marks the transition from early to *middle childhood*. Consequently, cultures vary to some degree with regard to when early childhood ends and middle childhood begins.

physical domain changes in the size, shape, and characteristics of the body

cognitive domain changes in thinking, memory, problem-solving, and other intellectual skills

social domain change in variables that are associated with the relationship of an individual to others

By contrast, a biological milestone, puberty, signals the end of middle childhood and the beginning of *adolescence*. Still, the timing of this transition varies across individuals. And when does adolescence end? One way of answering this question is by noting that different cultures set different legal boundaries for the end of adolescence and the beginning of *early adulthood*. For instance, a person must be 18 years of age to join the military without parental permission in the United States, but 16 is the age of majority for military service in the United Kingdom. Even within one culture, such as the United States, legal adulthood is defined differently for different activities: 16 for driving, 17 or 18 for criminal accountability, 18 for signing contracts, 21 for buying alcohol, and 24 for economic independence with regard to college financial aid. Such variations highlight the social and psychological, rather than biological, nature of the transition to adulthood, the complexities of which have led some researchers to propose a new period of development called *emerging adulthood* that encompasses the late teens and early twenties.

The transition from early to *middle adulthood*, generally thought to occur around age 40, is even more arbitrary. The timing of biological milestones that are associated with middle age, such as menopause, varies widely from one person to another. Thus, there is no clear physical boundary between early and middle adulthood, and social boundaries are rapidly changing. For instance, childbirth, once thought of almost exclusively as an early adulthood event, is becoming increasingly common among middle-aged women. Likewise, *late adulthood*, though customarily described as beginning at age 60, is not distinguished by any biological or social events that clearly distinguish a middle-aged from an older adult.

Despite the difficulties involved in defining the various periods of development, they can still serve as a useful system for organizing the study of development. As a result, this textbook is organized around them. For our purposes, the first two years after birth constitute infancy. Early childhood is defined as the years between two and six. Our chapters on middle childhood discuss development between the ages of 6 and 12. Adolescence is defined as the years from 12 to 18, with early adulthood constituting those between 18 and 40. Finally, the period from 40 to 60 is middle adulthood, and the years from 60 to the end of life are late adulthood.

Critical Thinking

1. How have culture, religion, and science shaped your views of development?

Key Issues in the Study of Human Development

There are several key issues that cut across all of the domains and periods of development. These include the relative contributions to development of biological and environmental factors and the presence or absence of stages. In addition, one researcher might propose that a specific change is common to all human beings, while another might propose that the change in question occurs under some conditions but not others. Researchers debate, too, the degree to which the settings in which development occurs contribute to developmental outcomes.

Learning Objective 1.4
How do developmentalists view the two sides of the nature-nurture debate?

Nature versus Nurture

Some early developmentalists thought of change as resulting from *either* forces outside the person *or* forces inside the person. The debate about the relative contributions of biological processes and experiential factors to development is known as the **nature-nurture debate**. In struggling with this important issue, psychologists have moved away from either/or approaches toward more subtle ways of looking at both types of influences. For example, the concept of *inborn biases* is based on the notion that children are born with tendencies to respond in certain ways. Some of these inborn biases are shared by virtually all children. For instance, the sequence in which children acquire spoken language—single words precede two-word sentences, and so on—is virtually identical in all children no matter what language they are learning (Pinker, 2002). Moreover, babies seem to be equipped with a set of behaviors that entice others to care for them,

nature-nurture debate the debate about the relative contributions of biological processes and experiential factors to development

including crying, snuggling, and, very soon after birth, smiling, and they appear to be delighted when their efforts to arouse interest in others are successful.

Other inborn biases may vary from one individual to another. Even in the early days of life, for example, some infants are relatively easy to soothe when they become distressed, while others are more difficult to manage. Whether these inborn patterns are coded in the genes, are created by variations in the prenatal environment, or arise through some combination of the two, the basic point is that a baby is not a blank slate at birth. Babies seem to start life prepared to seek out and react to particular kinds of experiences.

Thinking on the nurture side of the issue is also more complex than in the past. For example, modern developmentalists have accepted the concept of *internal models of experience*. The key element to this concept is the idea that the effect of some experience depends not on any objective properties of the experience but rather on the individual's *interpretation* of it, the meaning the individual attaches to that experience. For instance, suppose a friend says to you, "Your new haircut looks great; it's a lot nicer when it's short like that." Your friend intends to pay you a compliment, but you also hear an implied criticism ("Your hair used to look awful"), so your reactions, your feelings, and even your relationship with your friend are affected by how you interpret the comment—not by what your friend meant or by the objective qualities of the remark.

Continuity versus Discontinuity

Learning Objective 1.5

What is the continuity-discontinuity debate?

Another key issue in the study of human development is the *continuity-discontinuity* issue. The question is whether age-related change is primarily a matter of amount or degree (the *continuity* side of the debate) or more commonly involves changes in type or kind (the *discontinuity* side). For example, a 2-year-old is likely to have no individual friends among her playmates, while an 8-year-old is likely to have several. We could think of this as a **quantitative change** (a change in amount) from zero friends to some friends. This view implies that the qualitative aspects of friendship are the same at every age—or, as developmentalists would express it, changes in friendship are *continuous* in nature. Alternatively, we could think of the difference in friendships from one age to another as a **qualitative change** (a change in kind or type)—from disinterest in peers to interest or from one sort of peer relationship to another. In other words, from this perspective, changes in friendships are *discontinuous*, in that each change represents a change in the quality of a child's relationships with peers. Thus, friendships at 2 are quite different from friendships at 8 and differ in ways that cannot be captured by describing them solely in terms of the number of friends a child has.

Of particular significance is the idea that, if development consists only of additions (quantitative change), then the concept of **stages**, qualitatively distinct periods of development, is not needed to explain it. However, if development involves reorganization or the emergence of wholly new strategies, qualities, or skills (qualitative change), then the concept of stages may be useful. As you'll learn in Chapter 2, one of the important differences among theories of development is whether they assume development occurs in stages or is primarily continuous in nature.

quantitative change a change in amount

qualitative change a change in kind or type

Three Kinds of Change

Learning Objective 1.6

How do the three kinds of age-related change differ?

Age-related changes are a part of our everyday lives, so much so that we often give them little thought. Yet, have you ever thought about the difference between a human being's first step and his or her first date? Clearly, both are related to age, but they represent fundamentally different kinds of change. Generally, developmental scientists think of each age-related change as representing one of three categories.

Normative age-graded changes are universal, that is, they are common to every individual in a species and are linked to specific ages. Some universal changes (like a baby's first step) happen because we are all biological organisms subject to a genetically programmed maturing process. The infant who shifts from crawling to walking and the older adult whose skin

stages qualitatively distinct periods of development

normative age-graded changes changes that are common to every member of a species

The biological clock obviously constrains the social clock to some extent at least. Virtually every culture emphasizes family formation in early adulthood because that is, in fact, the optimal biological time for child rearing.

becomes progressively more wrinkled are following a plan that is an intrinsic part of the physical body, most likely something in the genetic code itself.

However, some changes are universal because of shared experiences. A social clock also shapes all (or most) lives into shared patterns of change (Helson, Mitchell, & Moane, 1984). In each culture, the **social clock**, or a set of *age norms*, defines a sequence of normal life experiences, such as the right time to go out on a first date, the appropriate timing of marriage and childbearing, and the expected time of retirement.

Age norms can lead to **ageism**—a set of prejudicial attitudes about older adults, analogous to sexism or racism (Palmore, 1990). In U.S. culture, for example, older adults are very often perceived as incompetent. As a result, many are denied opportunities to work because employers believe that they are incapable of carrying out required job functions. Thus, social expectations about the appropriate age for retirement work together with ageism to shape individual lives, resulting in a pattern in which most people retire or significantly reduce their working hours in later adulthood.

Equally important as a source of variation in life experience are historical forces, which affect each generation somewhat differently. Such changes are called **normative history-graded changes**. Social scientists use the word *cohort* to describe a group of individuals who are born within some fairly narrow span of years and thus share the same historical experiences at the same times in their lives. Within any given culture, successive cohorts may have quite different life experiences (see the Research Report on page 10).

Finally, **nonnormative changes** result from unique, unshared events. One clearly unshared event in each person's life is conception; the combination of genes each individual receives at conception is unique. Thus, genetic differences—including physical characteristics such as body type and hair color as well as genetic disorders—represent one category of individual differences. Characteristics influenced by both heredity and environment, such as intelligence and personality, constitute another class of individual differences.

Other individual differences are the result of the timing of a developmental event. Child development theorists have adopted the concept of a **critical period**. The idea is that there may be specific periods in development when an organism is especially sensitive to the presence (or absence) of some particular kind of experience.

Most knowledge about critical periods comes from animal research. For baby ducks, for instance, the first 15 hours or so after hatching is a critical period for the development of a following response. Newly hatched ducklings will follow any duck or any other moving object that happens to be around them at that critical time. If nothing is moving at that critical point, they don't develop any following response at all (Hess, 1972).

The broader concept of a sensitive period is more common in the study of human development. A **sensitive period** is a span of months or years during which a child may be particularly responsive to specific forms of experience or particularly influenced by their absence. For example, the period from 6 to 12 months of age may be a sensitive period for the formation of parent-infant attachment.

In studies of adults, one important concept related to timing has been the idea of *on-time* and *off-time* events (Neugarten, 1979). The idea is that experiences occurring at the expected times for an individual's culture or cohort will pose fewer difficulties for the individual than will off-time experiences. Thus, being widowed at 30 is more likely to produce serious life disruption or forms of pathology such as depression than would being widowed at 70.

social clock a set of age norms defining a sequence of life experiences that is considered normal in a given culture and that all individuals in that culture are expected to follow

ageism a prejudicial view of older adults that characterizes them in negative ways

normative history-graded changes changes that occur in most members of a cohort as a result of factors at work during a specific, well-defined historical period

nonnormative changes changes that result from unique, unshared events

critical period a specific period in development when an organism is especially sensitive to the presence (or absence) of some particular kind of experience

sensitive period a span of months or years during which a child may be particularly responsive to specific forms of experience or particularly influenced by their absence

Atypical development is another kind of individual change. **Atypical development** (also known as *abnormal behavior*, *psychopathology*, or *maladaptive development*) refers to deviation from a typical, or "normal," developmental pathway in a direction that is harmful to an individual. Examples of atypical development include mental retardation, mental illness, and behavioral problems such as extreme aggressiveness in children and compulsive gambling in adults.

Contexts of Development

Learning Objective 1.7

How does consideration of the contexts in which change occurs improve scientists' understanding of human development?

In recent decades, developmental scientists have become increasingly aware of the importance of looking beyond a child's immediate family for explanations of development. According to this view, we must understand the context in which the child is growing: the neighborhood and school, the occupations of the parents and their level of satisfaction in these occupations, the parents' relationships with each other and their own families, and so on. For example, a child growing up in a neighborhood where drugs and violence are a part of everyday life is coping with a set of problems radically different from those of a child in a relatively safer neighborhood.

A good example of research that examines such a larger system of influences is Gerald Patterson's work on the origins of delinquency (Patterson, Capaldi, & Bank, 1991; Patterson, DeBarsyshe, & Ramsey, 1989). His studies show that parents who use poor discipline techniques and poor monitoring are more likely to have noncompliant children. Once established, such a behavior pattern has repercussions in other areas of the child's life, leading to both rejection by peers and difficulty in school. These problems, in turn, are likely to push the young person toward delinquency (Dishion, Patterson, Stoolmiller, & Skinner, 1991; Vuchinich, Bank, & Patterson, 1992). So a pattern that began in the family is maintained and exacerbated by interactions with peers and with the school system.

When considering the contexts of development, however, we have to keep in mind that all of the various contexts interact with each other and with the characteristics of the individuals who are developing within them. Along these lines, some developmentalists have found the concepts of *vulnerability* and *resilience* to be useful (Garmezy, 1993; Garmezy & Rutter, 1983; Masten, Best, & Garmezy, 1990; Moen & Erickson, 1995; Rutter, 1987; Werner, 1995). According to this view, each child is born with certain vulnerabilities, such as a tendency toward emotional irritability or alcoholism, a physical abnormality, an allergy, or whatever. Each child is also born with some protective factors, such as high intelligence, good physical coordination, an easy temperament, or a lovely smile, that tend to make her more resilient in the face of stress. These vulnerabilities and protective factors then interact with the child's environment, so the same environment can have quite different effects, depending on the qualities the child brings to the interaction.

atypical development development that deviates from the typical developmental pathway in a direction that is harmful to the individual

The combination of a highly vulnerable child and a poor or unsupportive environment produces by far the most negative outcomes (Horowitz, 1990). Either of these two negative conditions alone—a vulnerable child or a poor environment—can be overcome. A resilient child in a poor environment may do quite well, since she can find and take advantage of all the stimulation and opportunities available; similarly, a vulnerable child may do quite well in a highly supportive environment in which parents help the child overcome or cope with her vulnerabilities. The "double whammy"—being a vulnerable child in a poor environment—leads to really poor

The settings in which children grow up and adults age contribute to the developmental process. How do you think these older adults' experiences differ from those of people their age who live in industrialized cultures?

outcomes for the child. The characteristics of the larger society in which a child's family and neighborhood are embedded matter as well. The term *culture* has no commonly agreed-on definition, but in essence it describes some system of meanings and customs, including values, attitudes, goals, laws, beliefs, moral guidelines, and physical artifacts of various kinds, such as tools, forms of dwellings, and the like. Furthermore, to be called a culture, a system of meanings and customs must be shared by some identifiable group, whether that group is a subsection of some population or a larger unit, and must be transmitted from one generation of that group to the next (Betancourt & Lopez, 1993; Cole, 1992). Culture shapes not only the development of individuals, but also ideas about what normal development is.

For example, researchers interested in middle and late adulthood often study retirement: why people retire, how retirement affects their health, and so on. But their findings do not apply to older adults in nonindustrialized cultures, where adults gradually shift from one kind of work to another as they get older rather than giving up work altogether and entering a new phase of life called "retirement." Consequently, developmentalists must be aware that retirement-related phenomena do not constitute universal changes. Instead, they represent developmental experiences that are culturally specific.

One final aspect of the context within which an individual's development occurs involves gender. Two individuals can be quite similar with regard to their individual characteristics and the environment within which they grow up. However, if one is female and the other male, they will experience the interaction between their characteristics and their environment differently. As you will learn in a later chapter, for example, the effects of the earliness or lateness with which a child goes through puberty depend on gender. Thus, early and late puberty have different meanings for boys and girls.

Critical Thinking

1. How do your culture's behavioral expectations for 20-year-olds, 40-year-olds, and 60-year-olds differ?

RESEARCH REPORT

Children and Adolescents in the Great Depression: An Example of a Cohort Effect

Research involving children and adolescents who grew up during the Great Depression of the 1930s illustrates that the same historical event can have different effects on adjacent cohorts (Elder, 1974; 1978; Elder, Liker, & Cross, 1984). Glen Elder and his colleagues used several hundred participants who were born either in 1920 or in 1928 and who were also participants in the Berkeley/Oakland Growth Study, a long-term study of groups of participants from childhood through late adulthood. Those in the 1920 group were in their teens during the Depression; those born in 1928 were still young children during the worst economic times.

In each cohort, researchers compared participants whose families had lost more than 35% of their pre-Depression income with those whose economic condition was better. They found that economic hardship was largely beneficial to the cohort born in 1920, who were teenagers when the Depression struck full force, while it was generally detrimental to the cohort born in 1928. Most of those whose families experienced the worst economic hardship were pushed into assuming adult responsibilities prematurely. Many worked at odd jobs, earning money that was vitally important to the family's welfare. They felt needed by their families, and as adults, they had a strong work ethic and commitment to family.

Those who were born in 1928 had a very different Depression experience. Their families frequently suffered a loss of cohesion and warmth. The consequences were generally negative for the children, especially the boys. They were less hopeful and less confident than their less economically stressed peers; in adolescence, they did less well in school and completed fewer years of education; as adults, they were less ambitions and less successful.

Questions for Critical Analysis

1. In what ways do these findings illustrate the concepts of vulnerability and resilience that you read about on p. 9?
2. Individuals who were born in 1985 were in high school when the terrorist attacks of September 11, 2001 occurred. Those who were born a decade later, in 1995, were in the early elementary grades. Individuals in both cohorts probably remember the events, but, because they experienced them during different periods of development, the two groups might have been affected differently. What kinds of differences do you think might be found in these two groups' long-term reactions to the events of September 11, 2001?

Research Methods and Designs

The easiest way to understand research methods is to look at a specific question and the alternative ways we might answer it. For example, older adults frequently complain that they have more trouble remembering people's names than they did when they were younger. Suppose we wanted to find out whether memory really declines with age. How would we go about answering this question?

The Goals of Developmental Science

Learning Objective 1.8
What are the goals of scientists who study human development?

Researchers who study human development use the scientific method to achieve four goals: to describe, to explain, to predict, and to influence human development from conception to death. To *describe* development is simply to state what happens. A descriptive statement such as "Older adults make more memory errors than young and middle-aged adults" is an example of this first goal of human development. To meet this goal, all we would have to do is measure memory function in adults of various ages.

Explaining development involves telling why a particular event occurs. To generate explanations, developmentalists rely on *theories*—sets of statements that propose general principles of development. Students often say that they hate reading about theories; what they want are the facts. However, theories are important because they help us look at facts from different perspectives. For example, "Older adults make more memory mistakes because of changes in the brain that happen as people get older" is a statement that attempts to explain the fact of age-related memory decline from a biological perspective. Alternatively, we could explain memory decline from an experiential perspective and hypothesize that memory function declines with age because older adults don't get as much memory practice as younger adults do.

Useful theories produce *predictions* or *hypotheses*, that researchers can test, such as "If changes in the brain cause declines in memory function, then elderly adults whose brains show the most change should also make the greatest number of memory errors." To test this hypothesis about changes in the brain and memory, we would have to measure some aspects of brain structure or function as well as memory function. Then we would have to find a way to relate one to the other. Alternatively, we could test the experiential explanation by comparing the memories of older adults who presumably get the most memory practice, such as those who are still working, to the memories of those who get less practice. If the working adults do better on tests of memory, the experiential perspective gains support. Moreover, if both the biological and the experiential hypotheses are supported by research, we have far more insight into age-related memory decline than we would have from either kind of hypothesis alone. In this way, theories add tremendous depth to psychologists' understanding of the facts of human development and provide them with information they can use to influence development.

Finally, developmental scientists hope to use their findings to *influence* developmental outcomes. Let's say, for example, that an older adult is diagnosed with a condition that can affect the brain, such as high blood pressure. If we know that brain function and memory are related, we can use tests of memory to make judgments about how much the person's medical condition may have already influenced his brain. At the same time, because we know that experience affects memory as well, we may be able to provide him with training that will help prevent memory problems from developing or worsening (see No Easy Answers on page 15).

Descriptive Methods

Learning Objective 1.9
What descriptive methods are used by developmental scientists?

A researcher who is interested in age and memory ability must decide how to go about finding relationships between *variables*. To developmentalists, variables are characteristics that vary from person to person, such as physical size, intelligence,

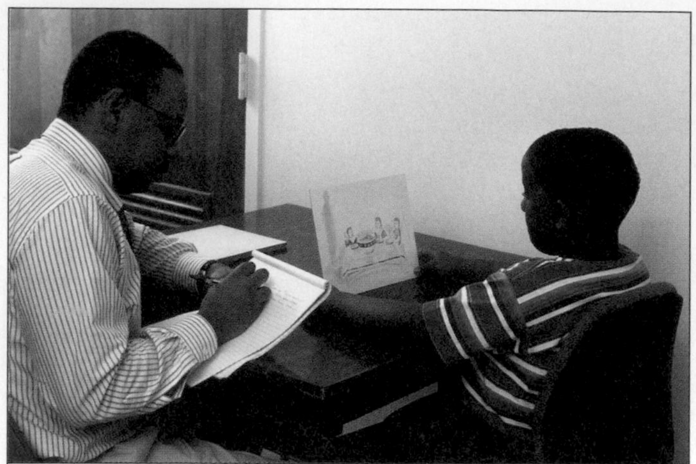

Psychologists who conduct case studies gather detailed information about a single individual. Their data often include the results of psychological tests.

and personality. When two or more variables vary together, there is some kind of relationship between them. The hypothesis that memory declines with age involves two variables, memory and age, and suggests a relationship between them. There are several ways of identifying such relationships.

Naturalistic Observation When psychologists use **naturalistic observation** as a research method, they observe people in their normal environments. For instance, to find out more about memory in older adults, a researcher could observe them in their homes or workplaces. Such studies provide developmentalists with information about psychological processes in everyday contexts.

The weakness of naturalistic observation, however, is *observer bias*. For example, if the researcher who is observing older adults is convinced that most of them have poor memories, he is likely to ignore any behavior that goes against this view. Because of observer bias, naturalistic observation studies often use "blind" observers who don't know what the research is about. In most cases, for the sake of accuracy, researchers use two or more observers so that the observations of each observer can be checked against those of the other(s).

Naturalistic observation studies are limited in the extent to which the results can be generalized. In addition, naturalistic observation studies are very time-consuming. They must be repeated in a variety of settings so that researchers can be sure people's behavior reflects development and not the influences of a specific environment.

Case Studies **Case studies** are in-depth examinations of single individuals. To test the hypothesis about memory and age, we could use a case study comparing one individual's scores on tests of memory in early and late adulthood. Such a study might tell us a lot about the stability or instability of memory in the individual studied, but we wouldn't know if our findings applied to others.

Still, case studies are extremely useful in making decisions about individuals. For example, to find out whether a child has mental retardation, a psychologist would conduct an extensive case study involving tests, interviews of the child's parents, behavioral observations, and so on. Case studies are also frequently the basis of important hypotheses about unusual developmental events, such as head injuries and strokes.

Laboratory Observation **Laboratory observation** differs from naturalistic observation in that the researcher exerts some degree of control over the environment. Suppose, for instance, that you volunteer to participate in a study in which you will have to take a computerized intelligence test. You go to the computer laboratory where the study will take place, and a researcher carrying a folder marked "Test Key" sits down with you in front of a computer. As she begins to explain the test's instructions, another person comes to the door and tells her that she must go to another room to take an important phone call. In her haste to leave, the researcher leaves the folder on the table next to the computer. A hidden video camera records your behavior while you are out of the room. (Do you think you would peek?) When the researcher returns, you complete the test that you believed was the purpose of the study. Later, the researcher and her colleagues will analyze the tapes of participants' responses in order to determine the frequency with which cheating occurs under such conditions. (Research ethics also requires that they inform you of the deceptive aspects of their study, as you will learn later.) As you can see, observing cheating behavior under controlled conditions offers many advantages over trying to identify and track it in an actual classroom.

Surveys Have you ever been questioned about which brand of soda you prefer or for whom you plan to vote in the next election? If so, then you have participated in a **survey**, a study in which researchers use interviews and/or questionnaires to collect data about atti-

naturalistic observation the process of studying people in their normal environments

case study an in-depth examination of a single individual

laboratory observation observation of behavior under controlled conditions

survey data collection method in which participants respond to questions

tudes, interests, values, and various kinds of behaviors. Surveys allow researchers to quickly gather information. They can also be used to track changes over time.

The value of any survey depends entirely on how representative the *sample* of participants is of the researcher's *population* of interest. A **population** is the entire group about which the researcher is attempting to learn something; a **sample** is a subset of that group. Thus, when voters are asked which candidate they prefer, the population of interest is all of the people who will vote in the election. The sample includes only the people who are actually questioned by the researchers. If the sample does not faithfully represent the population, that is, if it does not include the same proportions of males, females, Democrats, Republicans, and so forth, as the actual voting population does, then the survey's results will be inaccurate. Moreover, survey participants are sometimes influenced by the perceived *social desirability* of their answers. If they think that they should answer a question in a certain way to please the researchers, then they may not give truthful answers. Thus, whenever you hear a news report about a survey, you should remember that to judge whether the survey is valid or not, you need to know something about how the sample of participants was recruited and how the questions were asked.

Correlations A **correlation** is a relationship between two variables that can be expressed as a number ranging from –1.00 to +1.00. A zero correlation indicates that there is no relationship between the two variables. A positive correlation means that high scores on one variable are usually accompanied by high scores on the other. The closer a positive correlation is to +1.00, the stronger the relationship between the variables. Two variables that change in opposite directions have a negative correlation, and the nearer the correlation is to –1.00, the more strongly the two are connected.

To understand positive and negative correlations, think about the relationship between temperature and the use of air conditioners and heaters. Temperature and air conditioner use are positively correlated. As the temperature climbs, the number of air conditioners in use goes up. Conversely, temperature and heater use are negatively correlated. As the temperature decreases, the number of heaters in use goes up.

If we wanted to know whether age was related to memory, we could use a correlation. All that would be necessary would be to administer memory tests to adults of varying ages and calculate the correlation between test scores and ages. If there was a positive correlation between age and the number of memory errors people made—if older people made more errors—then we could say that our hypothesis had been supported. Conversely, if there was a negative correlation—if older people made fewer errors—then we would have to conclude that our hypothesis had not been supported.

Useful as they are, though, correlations have a major limitation: They do not indicate *causal* relationships. For example, even a high positive correlation between memory errors and age would tell us only that memory performance and age were connected in some way. It wouldn't tell us what caused the connection. It might be that younger adults understand the test instructions better. In order to identify a cause, we have to carry out experiments (See The Real World on page 19).

population the entire group that is of interest to a researcher

The Experimental Method

Learning Objective 1.10

What is the primary advantage of the experimental method?

An **experiment** is a study that tests a causal hypothesis. Suppose, for example, that we think age differences in memory are caused by older adults' failure to use memory techniques such as repeating a list mentally in order to remember it. We could test this hypothesis by providing memory technique training to one group of older adults and no training to another group. If the trained adults got higher scores on memory tests than they did before training and the no-training group showed no change, we could claim support for our hypothesis.

A key feature of an experiment is that participants are assigned *randomly* to one of two or more groups. In other words, chance determines which group each participant is placed in. When participants are randomly assigned to groups, the groups have equal amounts of variation with respect to characteristics such as intelligence, personality traits,

sample subset of a group that is of interest to a researcher who participates in a study

correlation a relationship between two variables that can be expressed as a number ranging from –1.00 to +1.00

experiment a study that tests a causal hypothesis

height, weight, and health status. Consequently, none of these variables can affect the outcome of the experiment.

Participants in the **experimental group** receive the treatment the experimenter thinks will produce a particular effect, while those in the **control group** receive either no special treatment or a neutral treatment. The presumed causal element in the experiment is called the **independent variable**, and the characteristic or behavior that the independent variable is expected to affect is called the **dependent variable**.

In a memory technique training experiment like the one suggested above, the group that receives the memory training is the experimental group, and the one that receives no instruction is the control group. Memory technique training is the variable that we, the experimenters, think will cause differences in memory function, so it is the independent variable. Performance on memory tests is the variable we are using to measure the effect of the memory technique training. Therefore, performance on memory tests is the dependent variable.

Experiments are essential for understanding many aspects of development. But two special problems in studying child or adult development limit the use of experiments. First, many of the questions researchers want to answer have to do with the effects of particular unpleasant or stressful experiences on individuals—abuse, prenatal influences of alcohol or tobacco, low birth weight, poverty, unemployment, widowhood. For obvious ethical reasons, researchers cannot manipulate these variables. For example, they cannot ask one set of pregnant women to have two alcoholic drinks a day and others to have none. To study the effects of such experiences, they must rely on nonexperimental methods, such as correlations.

experimental group the group in an experiment that receives the treatment the experimenter thinks will produce a particular effect

control group the group in an experiment that receives either no special treatment or a neutral treatment

independent variable the presumed causal element in an experiment

dependent variable the characteristic or behavior that is expected to be affected by the independent variable

cross-sectional design a research design in which groups of people of different ages are compared

longitudinal design a research design in which people in a single group are studied at different times in their lives

Second, the independent variable developmentalists are often most interested in is age itself, and researchers cannot assign participants randomly to age groups. They can compare 4-year-olds and 6-year-olds in their approach to some particular task, such as searching for a lost object, but the children differ in a host of ways other than their ages. Older children have had more and different experiences. Thus, unlike psychologists studying other aspects of behavior, developmental psychologists cannot systematically manipulate many of the variables they are most interested in.

To get around this problem, researchers can use any one of a series of strategies, sometimes called *quasi-experiments*, in which they compare groups without assigning the participants randomly. Cross-sectional studies are a form of quasi-experiment. So are studies in which researchers compare members of naturally occurring groups that differ in some dimension of interest, such as children whose parents choose to place them in day-care programs and children whose parents keep them at home.

Such comparisons have built-in problems, because groups that differ in one way are likely to differ in other ways as well. Compared with parents who keep their children at home, parents who place their children in day care are generally poorer, are more likely to be single parents, and tend to have different values or religious backgrounds. If researchers find that the two groups of children differ in some fashion, is it because they have spent their days in different environments or because of these other differences in their families? Researchers can make such comparisons a bit easier if they select comparison groups that are matched on those variables the researchers think might matter, such as income, marital status, or religion. But a quasi-experiment, by its very nature, will always yield more ambiguous results than will a fully controlled experiment.

Learning Objective 1.11

What are the pros and cons of cross-sectional, longitudinal, and sequential research designs?

Designs for Studying Age-Related Changes

In addition to deciding which method to use, developmental scientists must also determine how to incorporate age into their research design. There are three general strategies for doing so: (1) Study different groups of people of different ages, using what is called a **cross-sectional design**; (2) study the same people over a period of time, using a **longitudinal design**; (3) combine cross-sectional and longitudinal designs in some fashion, in a **sequential design**.

sequential design a research design that combines cross-sectional and longitudinal examinations of development

Cross-Sectional Designs Figure 1.1 is a good example of a cross-sectional study in which researchers examined age differences in people's ability to recognize facial expressions. As you

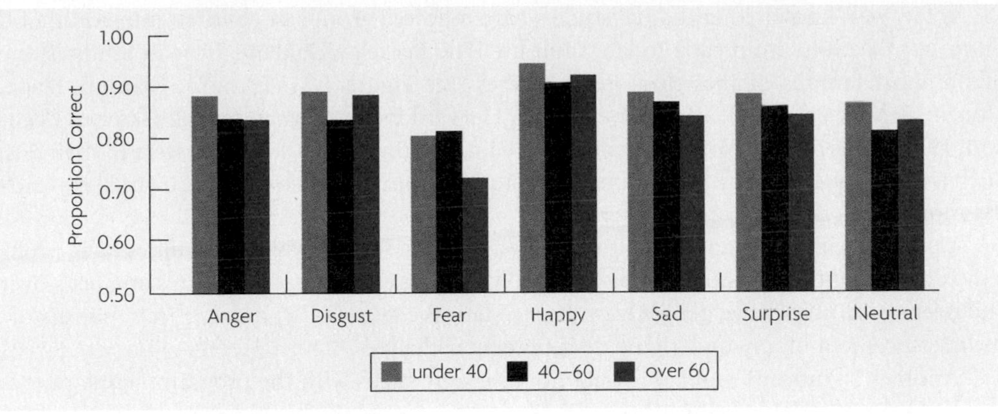

Figure 1.1
An Example of a Cross-Sectional Design

In this cross-sectional study, researchers compared the ability to recognize various kinds of facial expressions across young adult, middle-aged adult, and older adult groups. This study is cross-sectional because it measured the same variable at the same time in people of different ages.

(*Source*: Figure 1, "Age Differences in Recognition of Emotion in Lexical Stimuli and Facial Expressions" by Derek M. Isaacowitz et al, from *Psychology and Aging*, Vol. 22 (1), p. 147–159, Mar. 2007, American Psychological Association reprinted by permission.)

can see, younger adults outperformed those who were older in identifying anger. If these findings fit the researchers' hypothesis, they might be tempted to conclude that the ability to identify anger in facial expressions declines with age. But we cannot say this conclusively based on the cross-sectional data, because these adults differ in both age and cohort. Thus, the age differences in this study might reflect, for example, differences in education and not changes linked to age or development. Influences of this kind lead to **cohort effects**, findings that are the result of historical factors to which one age group in a cross-sectional study has been exposed.

Furthermore, cross-sectional studies cannot tell us anything about sequences of change with age or about the consistency of individual behavior over time, because each participant is tested only once. Still, cross-sectional research is very useful because it can be done relatively quickly and can reveal possible age differences or age changes.

cohort effects findings that are the result of historical factors to which one age group in a cross-sectional study has been exposed

Longitudinal Designs Longitudinal designs seem to solve the problems presented by cross-sectional designs, because they follow the same individuals over a period of time. Such studies allow psychologists to look at sequences of change and at individual consistency or inconsistency over time. And because longitudinal studies compare performance by the same people at different ages, they get around the obvious cohort problem.

NO EASY ANSWERS

It Depends . . .

Using research to improve people's lives is an important goal of scientists who study human development. In most cases, however, applying research to developmental problems isn't as simple as it might seem. Thus, one of the most important things you can learn about research is that the answers to many of the practical questions people ask about development begin with "It depends."

For example, when a parent discovers her son has been molested by a neighbor, she wants to know how the abuse will affect him in the future. But developmental psychologists don't have a concrete answer. They can tell the mother that the overwhelming majority of traumatized children show no long-term effects. They can also analyze the child and his particular situation and make an educated guess about what might happen in the future. In other words, the long-term outcomes depend on a variety of variables: how long the abuse lasted, at what age it began, the child's personality, the way the parents handled the situation when they learned of the abuse, and so on.

To further complicate matters, all of the relevant variables interact with one another. For example, counseling might benefit an outgoing child but be ineffective for a shy child who tends to keep his feelings to himself. Conversely, art therapy, a strategy that encourages children to express their feelings in drawings, might be effective with a shy child but have little impact on one who is outgoing. Because of such complexities, developmentalists can't tell the mother what she wants to hear: that if she follows a certain formula, her child will turn out fine.

Take a Stand

Decide which of these two statements you most agree with and think about how you would defend your position:

1. Relevant research findings should be the most important factor in the formation of social policies.
2. Research findings represent only one of several sources of information that ought to be considered in the formation of social policies.

A few well-known longitudinal studies have followed groups of children into adulthood or groups of adults from early to late adult life. The Berkeley/Oakland Growth Study is one of the most famous of these long-term studies (see Figure 1.2) (Eichorn, Clausen, Haan, Honzik, & Mussen, 1981). The Grant study of Harvard men is perhaps equally famous (Vaillant, 1977). This study followed several hundred men from age 18 until they were in their 60s. Such studies are extremely important in the study of human development, so you'll be reading more about them in later chapters.

Despite their importance, longitudinal designs have several major difficulties. One problem is that longitudinal studies typically involve giving each participant the same tests over and over again. Over time, people learn how to take the tests. Such *practice effects* may distort the measurement of any underlying developmental changes.

Another significant problem is that not everyone sticks with the program. Some participants drop out; others die or move away. As a general rule, the healthiest and best educated are most likely to stick it out, and that fact biases the results, particularly if the study covers the final decades of life. Each succeeding set of test results comes from proportionately more and more healthy adults, which may make it look as if there were less change or less decline than actually exists.

Longitudinal studies also don't really get around the cohort problem. For example, both the Grant study and the Berkeley/Oakland Growth Study observed and tested participants born in the same decade (1918–1928). Even if both studies showed the same pattern of change with age, we wouldn't know whether the pattern was unique to that cohort or reflected more basic developmental changes that would be observed in other cultures and other cohorts.

Sequential Designs One way to avoid the shortcomings of both cross-sectional and longitudinal designs is to use a sequential design. One group might include 25- to 30-year-olds, and the other 30- to 35-year-olds. We would then test each group several times over a number of years. In a sequential study, each testing point beyond the initial one allows researchers to make two types of comparisons. Age-group comparisons provide them with the same kind of information as a cross-sectional study. Comparison of each group to itself at an earlier testing point allows the researchers to collect longitudinal evidence at the same time.

Sequential designs also allow for comparisons of cohorts. If both groups demonstrate similar age-related patterns of change over time, researchers can conclude that the developmental pattern is not specific to any particular cohort. Finding the same developmental pattern in two cohorts provides psychologists with stronger evidence than either cross-sectional or longitudinal data alone. For example, Figure 1.3 illustrates a sequential study in which Baby Boomer women who were born between 1946 and 1964 were compared to women who

Figure 1.2
Example of a Longitudinal Design

These results are from a classic study in Berkeley and Oakland, California of a group of participants born either in 1920 or in 1928. They were tested frequently in childhood and adolescence, as well as three times in adulthood. Here you can see the sharp rise in self-confidence that occurred for both men and women in this group in their 30s—a pattern that may reflect a shared personality change, triggered by the common experiences of the social clock.

(*Source*: Adapted from Figures 1 and 2, p. 228, "As Time Goes By: Change and Stability in Personality Over Fifty Years" from *Psychology and Aging*, 1, Haan, N. et al. Copyright © 1986 by the American Psychological Association. Adapted by permission.)

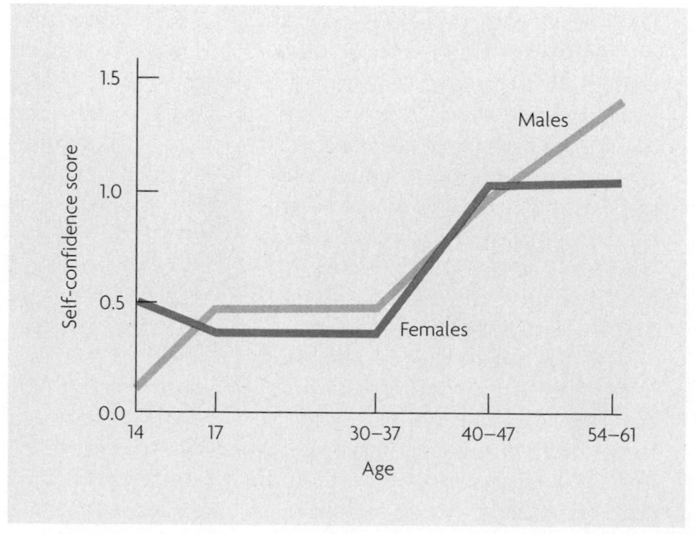

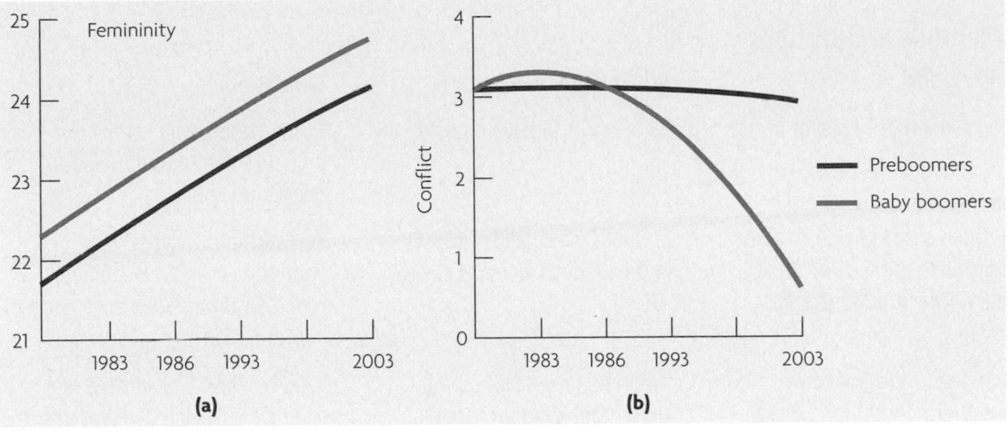

Figure 1.3
An Example of a Cross-Sequential Design

These findings illustrate the strengths of the cross-sequential design. Researchers tested more than 700 women in 1983, 1986, 1993, and 2003. Among the 700 were some women who were born during the "Baby Boom" (1946 to 1964) and some who were born earlier ("Preboomers"). Panel (a) shows that the tendency of women in both cohorts to describe themselves as "feminine" increased across all four testing points, but (b) shows that women's perceptions of conflict within their marriages remained stable across age for Preboomers but declined dramatically among Baby Boomers.

(*Source*: Adapted from Figure 1a, p. 950. Figure 6b, p. 953., from *Social Role and Birth Cohort Influenes on Gender-Linked Personality Traits in Women: A 20-Year Longitudinal Analysis*, by S. Kasen, et al. Journal of Personality and Social Psychology. 91 (5), Nov 2006, 944–958 Copyright © 2006 by the American Psychological Association. Adapted by permission.)

were born during the 1930s and early 1940s. Across four testing points, the two groups' self perceptions of femininity increased in parallel fashion, suggesting a true developmental change. By contrast, the relationship between age and reported frequency of marital conflict was different in each cohort, a finding that suggests that historical factors may have caused the two groups to vary in either actual marital conflict or in their perceptions of what constitutes conflict.

Cross-Cultural Research

Learning Objective 1.12

Why is cross-cultural research important to the study of human development?

Increasingly common in human development are studies comparing cultures or contexts, a task that researchers approach in several ways. One method of study, borrowed from the field of anthropology, is the ethnographic method. An **ethnography** is a detailed description of a single culture or context based on extensive observation. Often the observer lives in the culture or context for a period of time, perhaps as long as several years. Each ethnographic study is intended to stand alone, although it is sometimes possible to combine information from several different studies to see whether similar developmental patterns exist in the various cultures or contexts.

Alternatively, investigators may attempt to compare two or more cultures directly, by testing children or adults in each of the cultures with the same or comparable measures. Sometimes this involves comparing groups from different countries. Sometimes the comparisons are between subcultures within the same country; for example, increasingly common in the United States is research involving comparisons of children or adults living in different ethnic groups or communities, such as African Americans, Hispanic Americans, Asian Americans, and European Americans.

ethnography a detailed description of a single culture or context

Cross-cultural research is important to the study of human development for two reasons. First, developmentalists want to identify universal changes—that is, predictable events or processes experienced by individuals in all cultures. Developmentalists don't want to make a general statement about development—such as "Memory declines with age"—if the phenomenon in question happens only in certain cultures. Without cross-cultural research, it is impossible to know whether studies involving North Americans and Europeans apply to people in other parts of the world.

Second, one of the goals of developmentalists is to produce findings that can be used to improve people's lives. Cross-cultural research is critical to this goal as well. For example, developmentalists know that children in cultures that emphasize the community more than the individual are more cooperative than children in more individualistic cultures.

Ethnographers often interact in everyday settings with members of the cultures they study.

TABLE 1.1 Research Methods and Designs

Method	Description	Advantages	Limitations
Naturalistic Observation	Observation of behavior in natural settings	Participants behave naturally	Researchers expectations can influence results; little control over conditions
Case Studies	In-depth study of one or a few individuals using observation, interviews, or psychological testing	In-depth information; important in the study of unusual events	Results may not generalize beyond the case that is studied; time-consuming; subject to misinterpretation
Surveys	Interviews, questionnaires used to gather information quickly	Accurate information about large groups; track changes	Validity limited by sample representativeness; responses influenced by questions, social desirability
Correlational Studies	Determination of mathematical relationship between two variables	Assesses strength and direction of relationships	Cannot demonstrate cause and effect
Experiments	Random assignment of participants to control, experimental groups; manipulation of independent (causal) variable	Identification of cause-effect relationships	Results may not generalize to non-research settings; many variables cannot be studied in experiments
Cross-Sectional Designs	Participants of different ages studied at one time	Quick access to data about age differences	Ignores individual differences; cohort effects
Longitudinal Designs	Participants in one group studied several times	Track developmental changes in individuals and groups	Time-consuming; findings may apply only to the group that is studied
Sequential Designs	Study that combines both longitudinal and cross-sectional components	Cross-sectional and longitudinal data relevant to the same hypothesis	Time-consuming; different attrition rates across groups
Cross-Cultural Research	Research that either describes culture or includes culture as a variable	Information about universality and culture-specificity of age-related changes	Time consuming; difficult to construct tests and methods that are equally valid in different cultures

However, to use this information to help all children learn to cooperate, they need to know exactly how adults in such cultures teach their children to be cooperative. Cross-cultural research helps developmentalists identify specific variables that explain cultural differences. See Table 1.1 for a comparison of various research methods and designs.

Learning Objective 1.13

What are the ethical standards that developmental researchers must follow?

Research Ethics

Research ethics are the guidelines researchers follow to protect the rights of animals used in research and humans who participate in studies. Ethical guidelines are published by professional organizations such as the American Psychological Association, the American Educational Research Association, and the Society for Research in Child Development. Universities, private foundations, and government agencies have review committees that make sure all research sponsored by the institution is ethical. Guidelines for animal research include the requirement that animals be protected from unnecessary pain and suffering. Further, researchers must demonstrate that the potential benefits of their studies to either human or animal populations will be greater than any potential harm to animal subjects.

research ethics the guidelines researchers follow to protect the rights of animals used in research and humans who participate in studies

Ethical standards for research involving human participants address the following major concerns.

Protection from Harm It is unethical to do research that may cause participants permanent physical or psychological harm. Moreover, if the possibility of temporary harm exists, researchers must provide participants with some way of repairing the damage. For example, if the study will remind subjects of unpleasant experiences, like rape, researchers must provide them with counseling.

Informed Consent Researchers must inform participants of any possible harm and have them sign a consent form stating that they are aware of the risks of participating. In order for children to participate in studies, their parents must give permission after the researcher has informed them of possible risks. Children older than 7 must also give their own consent. If the research takes place in a school or day-care center, an administrator representing the institution must consent. In addition, both children and adults have the right to discontinue participation in a study at any time. Researchers are obligated to explain this right to children in language they can understand.

Confidentiality Participants have the right to confidentiality. Researchers must keep the identities of participants confidential and must report their data in such a way that no particular piece of information can be associated with any specific participant. The exception to confidentiality is when children reveal to researchers that they have been abused in any way by an adult. In most states, all citizens are required to report suspected cases of child abuse.

Knowledge of Results Participants, their parents, and the administrators of institutions in which research takes place have a right to a written summary of a study's results.

Deception If deception has been a necessary part of a study, participants have the right to be informed about the deception as soon as the study is over.

Critical Thinking

1. Researchers have found a positive correlation between a mother's age at the birth of her child and the child's later IQ: Very young mothers have children with lower IQs. How many different explanations of this correlation can you think of?

2. Suppose a cross-sectional study of sex-role attitudes reveals that adults between the ages of 20 and 50 have the most egalitarian attitudes, while teenagers and adults over 50 have more traditional attitudes. How might cohort differences influence your interpretation of these results?

THE REAL WORLD

Thinking Critically about Research

Three-year-old Mina loves to play with the other children at her day-care center and can't wait to get to "school" each morning. But her mother, Christina, is worried about reports that she has heard on the news about the possible harmful effects of day care on children's development. Like most parents, Christina wants what is best for her child, but she also needs to work. She wonders how to find a balance between Mina's need for quality time with Mom and her family's economic needs.

In today's information age, we are bombarded with research results that are relevant to one developmental period or another every day. One report may say that drinking grape juice will protect you from a heart attack, while another may tell you that drinking grape juice will increase your risk of developing Alzheimer's disease. Similarly, one study may say that day care helps children's cognitive development, while another is interpreted to mean that day care is harmful.

When research results appear to be in conflict or when results are at variance with our own personal values, many of us respond by saying either "I agree with that study" or "I don't agree with that study." A better approach is to learn to use your knowledge of research methods to become a "critical consumer" of research.

For example, suppose you read a newspaper report of a study "proving" that putting infants in day care causes behavior problems later in childhood. After reading this chapter, you should know that only an experiment can produce such proof. To demonstrate that day care causes behavior problems, researchers would have to randomly assign infants to day-care and home-care groups. You should be aware that such a study would be unethical and, therefore, impossible. Thus, a newspaper report may claim that a study showing a correlation between day care and behavior problems demonstrates that one causes the other—but you, the critical consumer, should know better. Once you have evaluated the scientific merit of a given research result, you can move forward with determining what it means to you in your own "real world."

Questions for Reflection

1. How would you explain the ideas in this discussion to a concerned parent who heard about a study "proving" that day care is harmful to young children?
2. If such a study were reported, what variables other than day care itself might explain the results?

SUMMARY

An Introduction to Human Development

Learning Objective 1.1 What ideas about development were proposed by early philosophers and scientists?

- The philosophical concepts of original sin, innate goodness, and the blank slate have influenced Western ideas about human development. Darwin studied child development to gain insight into evolution. G. Stanley Hall published the first scientific study of children and introduced the concepts of norms.

Learning Objective 1.2 What is the lifespan perspective?

- Today's developmentalists recognize that change happens throughout life. The lifespan perspective includes the notions that plasticity exists throughout the lifespan, information from a variety of disciplines are needed to understand development, and that development occurs in multiple contexts.

Learning Objective 1.3 What major domains and periods do developmental scientists use to organize their discussions of the human lifespan?

- Theorists and researchers classify age-related change according to three broad categories: the physical, cognitive, and social domains. They also refer to the major periods of development: prenatal, infancy, early childhood, middle childhood, adolescence, early adulthood, middle adulthood, and late adulthood.

Key Issues in the Study of Human Development

Learning Objective 1.4 How do developmentalists view the two sides of the nature-nurture debate?

- Historically, developmentalists have debated nature versus nurture, but now they believe that every developmental change is a product of both.

Learning Objective 1.5 What is the continuity-discontinuity debate?

- Developmentalists also differ with regard to the continuity-discontinuity issue. Some emphasize qualitative changes, while others focus on quantitative changes.

Learning Objective 1.6 How do the three kinds of age-related change differ?

- Normative age-graded changes are those that are experienced by all human beings. Normative history-graded changes are common to individuals who have similar cultural and historical experiences. Genetic factors and the timing of experiences are two important causes of nonnormative changes in development.

Learning Objective 1.7 How does consideration of the contexts in which change occurs improve scientists' understanding of human development?

- The contexts of development include both individual variables and the settings with which development occurs (e.g., family, neighborhood, culture). Individual traits and contexts interact in complex ways to influence development.

Research Methods and Designs

Learning Objective 1.8 What are the goals of scientists who study human development?

- Developmental psychologists use scientific methods to describe, explain, predict, and influence age-related changes and individual differences.

Learning Objective 1.9 What descriptive methods are used by developmental scientists?

- Case studies and naturalistic observation provide a lot of important information, but it usually isn't generalizable to other individuals or groups. Correlational studies measure relationships between variables. They can be done quickly, and the information they yield is more generalizable than that from case studies or naturalistic observation.

Learning Objective 1.10 What is the primary advantage of the experimental method?

- To test causal hypotheses, it is necessary to use experimental designs in which participants are assigned randomly to experimental or control groups.

Learning Objective 1.11 What are the pros and cons of cross-sectional, longitudinal, and sequential research designs?

- In cross-sectional studies, separate age groups are each tested once. In longitudinal designs, the same individuals are tested repeatedly over time. Sequential designs combine cross-sectional and longitudinal comparisons.

Learning Objective 1.12 Why is cross-cultural research important to the study of human development?

- Cross-cultural research helps developmentalists identify universal factors and cultural variables that affect development.

Learning Objective 1.13 What are the ethical standards that developmental researchers must follow?

- Ethical principles governing psychological research include protection from harm, informed consent, confidentiality, knowledge of results, and protection from deception.

KEY TERMS

ageism (*p. 8*)
atypical development (*p. 9*)
case study (*p. 12*)
cognitive domain (*p. 5*)
cohort effects (*p. 15*)
control group (*p. 14*)
correlation (*p. 13*)
critical period (*p. 8*)
cross-sectional design (*p. 14*)
dependent variable (*p. 14*)
ethnography (*p. 17*)
experiment (*p. 13*)
experimental group (*p. 14*)
human development (*p. 2*)
independent variable (*p. 14*)
laboratory observation (*p. 12*)
lifespan perspective (*p. 4*)
longitudinal design (*p. 14*)
maturation (*p. 4*)
naturalistic observation (*p. 12*)
nature-nurture debate (*p. 6*)
nonnormative changes (*p. 8*)
normative age-graded changes (*p. 7*)
normative history-graded changes (*p. 8*)
norms (*p. 4*)
physical domain (*p. 5*)
population (*p. 13*)
qualitative change (*p. 7*)
quantitative change (*p. 7*)
research ethics (*p. 18*)
sample (*p. 13*)
sensitive period (*p. 8*)
sequential design (*p. 14*)
social clock (*p. 8*)
social domain (*p. 5*)
stages (*p. 7*)
survey (*p. 12*)

TEST YOURSELF

An Introduction to Human Development

1.1 The philosophy that proposes that adults can mold children into whatever the adults want them to be is called

a. morality.
b. the blank slate.
c. original sin.
d. innate goodness.

1.2 Which of the following early theorists kept a baby biography of his children's development?

a. Charles Darwin
b. G. Stanley Hall
c. Arnold Gesell
d. Jean-Jacques Rousseau

1.3 The view that development from conception to death should be studied from multiple disciplinary perspectives is known as the ________________________.

1.4 ____________________ is the capacity for positive change in response to environmental demands.

1.5 Improvements in children's memory function fall within the ____________ domain of development.

1.6 Fill in the developmental milestones that mark the beginning and ending of each major period of development:

Period	Milestones
Prenatal	
Infancy	
Early Childhood	
Middle Childhood	
Adolescence	
Early Adulthood	
Middle Adulthood	
Late Adulthood	

Key Issues in the Study of Human Development

1.7 Which of the following is an example of an inborn bias that is charted for many infants?

a. crying and snuggling to entice others to care for them
b. sleeping through the night
c. not liking solid foods
d. being easy to sooth when they become distressed

1.8 By far the most negative outcomes for a child are the result of a

a. highly vulnerable child.
b. poor or unsupportive environment.
c. combination of high vulnerability and poor environment.
d. combination of low vulnerability and unsupportive environment.

1.9 When a caterpillar changes into a butterfly, this is an example of a

a. quantitative change.
b. continuous change.
c. universal change.
d. qualitative change.

1.10 The idea that experiences occurring at the expected times for an individual's culture or cohort will pose fewer difficulties for an individual than experiences occurring at unexpected times is called the concept of

a. the critical period.
b. the historical period.
c. the sensitive period.
d. on-time and off-time events.

1.11 Developmental scientists emphasize

a. the environmental hazards of the place where a person lives.

b. all of the different contexts in which the child is growing.

c. how much the individual likes his or her environment.

d. the child's temperament.

1.12 Give an example of each type of change in the chart below:

Type of Change	Example
Normative Age-Graded	
Normative History-Graded	
Nonnormative	

Research Methods and Designs

1.13 Sets of statements that propose general principles to explain development are called

a. theories.

b. the independent variables.

c. hypotheses.

d. the critical periods.

1.14 Nicole studies parents and their children by watching them interact at the zoo. This is an example of the

a. naturalistic observation method.

b. case study method.

c. experimental method.

d. correlational method.

1.15 Which of the following is the major limitation of the correlational method?

a. Observer bias is likely.

b. It studies only single individuals.

c. It does not tell us about causal relationships.

d. Research ethics prevent its use in most developmental studies.

1.16 An experiment is testing the effects of observed violence of children's behavior. One group of children views a violent cartoon. A second group views a humorous nonviolent cartoon. A third group is not exposed to any cartoon. The first group is the

a. experimental group.

b. control group.

c. comparison group.

d. observational group.

1.17 Because developmental psychologists cannot systematically manipulate many of the variables they are most interested in, they often use

a. case studies.

b. ethnography.

c. quasi-experiments.

d. panel studies.

1.18 In the cross-sectional method,

a. the same group of subjects is given the same test repeatedly over a 20-year period.

b. surveys are administered to samples of people from around the country.

c. groups of subjects of different ages are studied.

d. the behaviors of subjects in a laboratory environment are compared with their behaviors in their natural setting.

1.19 A study in which the intelligence test performance of the same group of children is assessed at different points in their lifetime is an example of which of the following designs?

a. sequential

b. longitudinal

c. cross-sectional

d. time-sampling

1.20 Which of the following is an advantage of a longitudinal study?

a. The research is completed in a short period of time.

b. The healthiest participants drop out.

c. The better-educated participants drop out.

d. It allows the researcher to compare performance by the same people at different ages.

1.21 Match the research methods and designs with their definitions.

(1) naturalistic observation	(A) One group studied over time
(2) case study	(B) Manipulated independent variable
(3) survey	(C) Questionnaires
(4) correlation	(D) In-depth study of single individual
(5) experiment	(E) Behavior in typical settings
(6) cross-sectional	(F) Two or more age groups studied at the same time
(7) longitudinal	(G) Mathematical relationship between two variables
(8) sequential	(H) Two or more age groups studied over time

1.22 A detailed description of a single culture or context based on extensive observation is called

a. the cohort effect.

b. ageism.

c. maturation.

d. an ethnography.

1.23 Which of the following ethical standards for research involves the right to a written summary of a study's results?

a. knowledge of results

b. deception

c. informed consent

d. confidentiality

mydevelopmentlab Study Plan

PEARSON

Are You Ready for the Test?

Students who use the study materials on MyDevelopmentLab report higher grades in the course than those who use the text alone. Here are three easy steps to mastering this chapter and improving your grade…

Step 1

Take the chapter pre-test in MyDevelopmentLab and review your customized Study Plan.

In an experiment that examines the effect of social skills training on peer acceptance, the independent variable would be the

- social skills training.
- age of the children.
- level of peer acceptance.
- way the children were assigned to the experimental and control group.

Step 2

Use MyDevelopmentLab's Multimedia Library to help strengthen your knowledge of the chapter.

Explore: Psychology Timeline

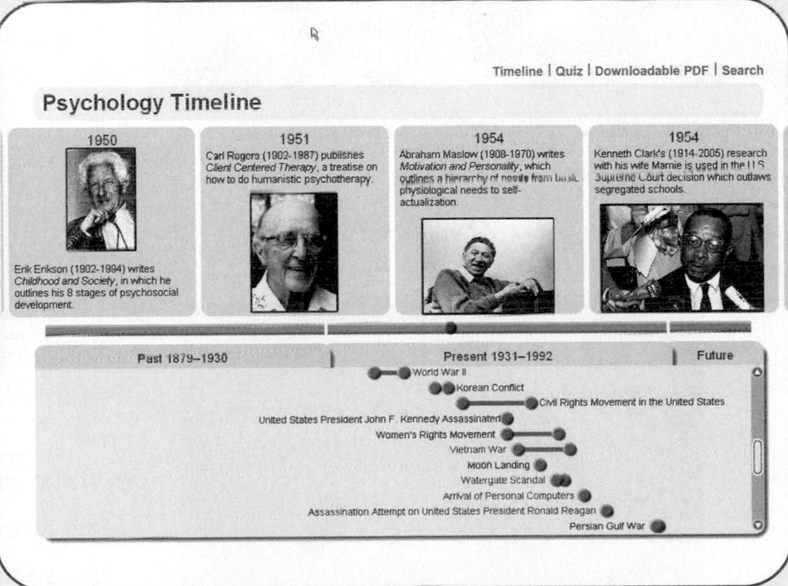

Learning Objective 1.1

What ideas about development were proposed by early philosophers and scientists?

www.mydevelopmentlab.com

continued on the next page

What is your learning style? Visit http://www.pearsonhighered.com/mypsychlab/learningstyles/MPL_LearnStartPage.htm to take our Learning Style Inventory and find out how MyDevelopmentLab can help you.

Explore: Race and Ethnicity in Psychological Inquiry

Diversity in Psychological Inquiry

At one time, participants in psychological research studies consisted primarily of only white male college students. Imagine a psychological study that looked at communication styles and whose participants were only white male college students. What variables can you identify in each of the following three photos that would be overlooked in such a study?

PLAY

Learning Objective 1.7

How does consideration of the contexts in which change occurs improve scientists' understanding of human development?

Simulate: Distinguishing Independent and Dependent Variables

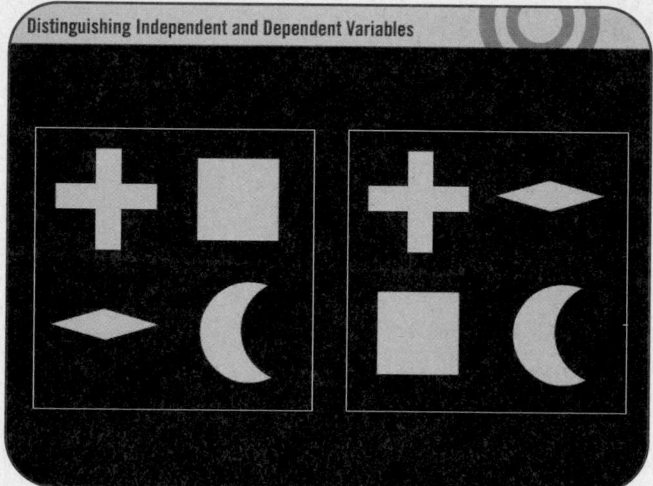

Learning Objective 1.10

What is the primary advantage of the experimental method?

Step 3

Take the chapter post-test and compare your results against the pre-test.

Scientists who study the changes in thinking, memory, problem-solving, and other intellectual skills are interested in the ____________ of development.

- interdisciplinary domain
- social domain
- cognitive domain
- psychosocial domain

Theories of Development

Suppose you were responsible for planning a birthday party for someone who was turning 70 and wanted to celebrate the milestone in a really big way. You might reserve a party room, order a cake, purchase 70 birthday candles, and hire an "oldies" band. But how likely would you be to plan an expedition to Nepal to climb one of the world's highest mountains on behalf of the celebrant? Mountaineering is probably not one of the activities that immediately springs to mind when you think about 70-year-olds. Consequently, you might be surprised to learn how Katsusuke Yanagisawa, a retired Japanese teacher, celebrated both his 70th and 71st birthdays (Gurubacharya, 2007).

For years Yanagisawa dreamed of climbing Cho Oyu, a 26,000-foot peak in the Himalayas, when he turned 70. So, the experienced climber did just that when he reached septuagenarian (person who is

70 or older) status in 2006. When Yanagisawa reached the summit of Cho Oyu, he felt a deep satisfaction at having achieved the goal he had dreamed of and planned for over several years. As he took in the beauty of the Himalayan peaks and valleys, he found himself drawn to the peak just next to Cho Oyu, the world's highest, Mount Everest. As he gazed at the majestic mountain, a new idea began to form in his mind. He contemplated the possibility of climbing Mount Everest to celebrate his 71st birthday. In doing so, he would become the oldest person ever to have climbed the 29,000-foot peak.

Although hundreds of climbers have made it to the summit of Mount Everest since the mountain was first scaled in 1953 by New Zealander Sir Edmund Hillary, it is still considered to be one of the most difficult treks a mountaineer can make. More than 200 people have died attempting to climb it. Consequently, Yanagisawa began his quest with a deep respect for the mountain and the arduous journey that he hoped would take him to the summit. After returning safely to the mountain's base on May 22, 2007, he reported that the climb had been far more difficult than he had anticipated. But the difficulty of his trek made it all the more satisfying when he reached the top. Once he reached the summit, Yanagisawa told reporters, he was overcome with emotion and immensely proud of the way he had handled the rigors of a climb that many experienced mountaineers never undertake.

Katsusuke Yanagisawa's mountaineering skills and his capacity for physical endurance are impressive, especially given his advanced age. But what do his feats have to do with the study of development? You may remember from Chapter 1 that developmental scientists *describe*, *explain*, *predict*, and *influence* behavior. What you have just read about Yanagisawa describes his behavior. A useful explanation of it will lead to predictions about the kinds of characteristics that predict such behavior in the general population of older adults. If these predictions hold true, then psychologists can use these findings to inform policies, programs, and individual interventions that support the developmental goals of elders. Thus, the long road that leads from descriptions of behavior to strategies for influencing it begins with an examination of how established theories of development might be used to explain it.

As you learned in Chapter 1, developmental psychologists use theories to formulate hypotheses, or testable answers, to "why" questions about behavior. At the broadest level are three very broad families of theories—psychoanalytic theory, learning theory, and cognitive-developmental theory. Theories within each of these families attempt to provide developmentalists with comprehensive explanations of just about every facet of human development. Theories that deal with the biological foundations of development and interactions between these factors and the environment extend developmentalists' understanding of age-related changes beyond the explanations that the three major theories provide. Thus, the most comprehensive explanations of developmental phenomena often include ideas from the psychoanalytic, learning, and cognitive approaches as well as those that are derived from biological and contextual theories.

This chapter will introduce you to the three major families of theories. These theories will come up again and again as you make your way through this book. This chapter will also acquaint you with other theoretical trends in the field of human development, and you will learn how developmental psychologists compare theories.

Psychoanalytic Theories

Every parent knows it's a constant struggle to keep babies from putting everything in their mouths. Why do babies exhibit this behavior? One way of explaining this seemingly odd phenomenon would be to suggest that infants derive more physical pleasure from mouthing objects than from manipulating them with other parts of their bodies. Such an approach would most likely belong to the family of **psychoanalytic theories**, a school of thought that originated with Viennese physician Sigmund Freud (1856–1939). Psychoanalytic theorists believe that developmental change happens because internal drives and emotions influence behavior.

Freud's Psychosexual Theory

Learning Objective 2.1

What are the main ideas of Freud's theory?

Most of Freud's ideas about development were derived from his work with adults who were suffering from serious mental disorders. These patients' memories of their early experiences constituted the primary source of data upon which Freud based his theory. One of his most important conclusions about his patients' memories was that behavior is governed by both conscious and unconscious processes. The most basic of these unconscious processes is an internal drive for physical pleasure that Freud called the *libido*. He believed the libido to be the motivating force behind most behavior.

Freud also argued that personality has three parts. The **id** contains the libido and operates at an unconscious level; the id is a person's basic sexual and aggressive impulses, which are present at birth. The **ego**, the conscious, thinking part of personality, develops in the first 2 to 3 years of life. One of the ego's jobs is to keep the needs of the id satisfied. For instance, when a person is hungry, it is the id that demands food immediately, and the ego is supposed to find a way to obtain it. The **superego**, the portion of the personality that acts as a moral judge, contains the rules of society and develops near the end of early childhood, at about age 6. Once the superego develops, the ego's task becomes more complex. It must satisfy the id without violating the superego's rules.

The ego is responsible for keeping the three components of personality in balance. According to Freud, a person experiences tension when any of the three components is in conflict with another. For example, if a person is hungry, the id may motivate her to do anything to find food, but the ego—her conscious self—may be unable to find any. Alternatively, food may be available, but the ego may have to violate one of the superego's moral rules to get it. In such cases, the ego may generate *defense mechanisms*, ways of thinking about a situation that reduce anxiety (see the No Easy Answers on page 29).

Many of Freud's patients had memories of sexual feelings and behavior in childhood. This led Freud to believe that sexual feelings are important to personality development. Based

psychoanalytic theories theories proposing that developmental change happens because of the influence of internal drives and emotions on behavior

id in Freud's theory, the part of the personality that comprises a person's basic sexual and aggressive impulses; it contains the libido and motivates a person to seek pleasure and avoid pain

ego according to Freud, the thinking element of personality

superego Freud's term for the part of personality that is the moral judge

on his patients' childhood memories, Freud proposed a series of **psychosexual stages** through which a child moves in a fixed sequence determined by maturation (see Table 2.1). In each stage, the libido is centered on a different part of the body. In the infant, the mouth is the focus of the drive for physical pleasure; the stage is therefore called the *oral stage*. As maturation progresses, the libido becomes focused on the anus (hence, the *anal stage*), and later on the genitals (the *phallic stage* and eventually the *genital stage*).

Optimum development, according to Freud, requires an environment that will satisfy the unique needs of each period. For example, the infant needs sufficient opportunity for oral stimulation. An inadequate early environment will result in *fixation*, characterized by behaviors that reflect unresolved problems and unmet needs. Thus, as you might guess from looking at the list of stages in Table 2.1, emphasis on the formative role of early experiences is a hallmark of psychoanalytic theories.

Freud's most controversial idea about early childhood is his assertion that children experience sexual attraction to the opposite-sex parent during the phallic stage (ages 3 to 6). Freud borrowed names for this conflict from Greek literature. Oedipus was a male character who was involved in a romantic relationship with his mother. Electra was a female character who had a similar relationship with her father. Thus, for a boy, the Oedipus complex involves a conflict between his affection for his mother and his fear of his father; for a girl, the Electra complex pits her bond with her father against her anxiety over the potential loss of her mother's love. In both genders, the complex is resolved by abandoning the quest to possess the opposite-sex parent in favor of identification with the same-sex parent. In other words, the phallic stage reaches a successful conclusion when boys develop a desire to be like their fathers and girls begin to view their mothers as role models.

psychosexual stages Freud's five stages of personality development through which children move in a fixed sequence determined by maturation; the libido is centered in a different body part in each stage

Learning Objective 2.2

What is the conflict associated with each of Erikson's psychosocial stages?

Erikson's Psychosocial Theory

Many of Freud's critics accepted his assertion that unconscious forces influence development, but they questioned his rather gloomy view that childhood trauma nearly always leads to emotional instability in adulthood. Later theorists, known as *neo-Freudians*, proposed ideas that built on the strengths of Freud's theory but tried to avoid its weaknesses.

Table 2.1 Freud's Psychosexual Stages

Stage	Approximate Ages	Focus of Libido	Major Developmental Task	Some Characteristics of Adults Fixated at This Stage
Oral	Birth to 1 year	Mouth, lips, tongue	Weaning	Oral behavior, such as smoking and overeating; passivity and gullibility
Anal	1 to 3 years	Anus	Toilet training	Orderliness, obstinacy or messiness, disorganization
Phallic	3 to 6 years	Genitals	Resolving Oedipus/ Electra complex	Vanity, recklessness, sexual dysfunction or deviancy
Latency*	6 to 12 years	None	Developing defense mechanisms; identifying with same-sex peers	None
Genital	12+	Genitals	Achieving mature sexual intimacy	Adults who have successfully integrated earlier stages should emerge with sincere interest in others and mature sexuality.

*Freud thought that the latency period is not really a psychosexual stage, because libido is not focused on the body during this period; therefore, fixation is impossible.

NO EASY ANSWERS

The Repressed Memory Controversy

Though they are removed from consciousness by the defense mechanisms of denial and repression, Freud claimed, traumatic events suffered in childhood, such as sexual abuse, lie smoldering in the unconscious. While hidden away, they cause distress in the personality and may even lead to serious mental illness. Consequently, Freud thought that the goal of psychotherapy was to uncover such events and help individuals learn to cope with them.

Memory researchers have investigated Freud's claim that childhood trauma is often forgotten in this way. It turns out that a few people who were crime victims or who were abused by their parents as children do forget the events for long periods of time, just as Freud predicted. However, most victims have vivid memories of traumatic events, even though they may forget minor details (Baddeley, 1998; Lindsay & Read, 1994). Moreover, those who commit crimes or abuse children are more likely to forget the incidents than are the victims (Taylor & Kopelman, 1984).

Memory experts also point out that therapists who directly suggest the possibility of repressed memories risk creating false memories in their clients' minds (Ceci & Bruck, 1993). However, repression does sometimes occur, and discovery of a repressed memory does sometimes improve a person's mental health. Thus, mental health professionals face a dilemma. Should they ignore the possibility of a repressed memory or risk creating a false one?

Therapists address the dilemma by obtaining training in techniques that can bring out repressed memories but don't directly suggest that such memories exist. For example, when clients believe they have recalled a repressed event, therapists help them look for concrete evidence. In the end, however, both therapist and client should recognize that they must often rely on flawed human judgment to decide whether a "recovered" memory was really repressed or was invented in the client's mind.

Take a Stand

Decide which of these two statements you most agree with and think about how you would defend your position:

1. If I thought that I had recovered a repressed memory of childhood abuse, I would prefer to have a skeptical therapist who would educate me about research findings showing that such memories are rarely forgotten.
2. If I thought that I had recovered a repressed memory of childhood abuse, I would prefer to have a supportive therapist who would help me search for evidence of the abuse.

Erik Erikson (1902–1994) is the neo-Freudian theorist who has had the greatest influence on the study of development (Erikson, 1950, 1959, 1980b, 1982; Erikson, Erikson, & Kivnick, 1986; Evans, 1969). Erikson thought development resulted from the interaction between internal drives and cultural demands; thus, his theory refers to **psychosocial stages** rather than to psycho*sexual* ones. Furthermore, Erikson thought that development continued through the entire lifespan.

In Erikson's view, to achieve a healthy personality, an individual must successfully resolve a crisis at each of the eight stages of development, as summarized in Table 2.2. Each crisis is defined by a pair of opposing possibilities, such as trust versus mistrust or integrity versus despair. Successful resolution of a crisis results in the development of the characteristic on the positive side of the dichotomy. A healthy resolution, however, does not mean moving totally to the positive side. For example, an infant needs to have experienced some mistrust in order to learn to identify people who are not trustworthy. But healthy development requires a favorable ratio of positive to negative. Of the eight stages described in Table 2.2, four have been the focus of the greatest amount of theorizing and research: trust in infancy, identity in adolescence, intimacy in early adulthood, and generativity in middle adulthood.

Erikson believed that the behavior of the major caregiver (usually the mother) is critical to the child's resolution of the first life crisis: *trust versus mistrust*. To ensure successful resolution of this crisis, the caregiver must be consistently loving and must respond to the child predictably and reliably. Infants whose early care has been erratic or harsh may develop mistrust. In either case, the child carries this aspect of personality throughout her development, and it affects the resolution of later tasks.

Adhering to group norms regarding which clothes are "in" and "out" is one of the ways that Erikson says teenagers begin to construct a sense of identity that distinguishes them from their parents.

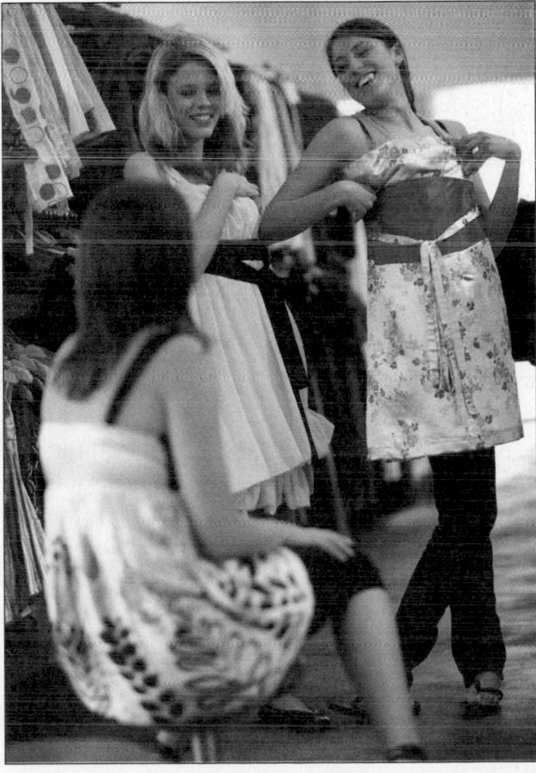

Table 2.2 Erikson's Psychosocial Stages

Approximate Ages	Stage	Positive Characteristics Gained and Typical Activities
Birth to 1 year	Trust versus mistrust	Hope; trust in primary caregiver and in one's own ability to make things happen (secure attachment to caregiver is key)
1 to 3	Autonomy versus shame and doubt	Will; new physical skills lead to demand for more choices, most often seen as saying "no" to caregivers; child learns self-care skills such as toileting
3 to 6	Initiative versus guilt	Purpose; ability to organize activities around some goal; more assertiveness and aggressiveness (Oedipus conflict with parent of same sex may lead to guilt)
6 to 12	Industry versus inferiority	Competence; cultural skills and norms, including school skills and tool use (failure to master these leads to sense of inferiority)
12 to 18	Identity versus role confusion	Fidelity; adaptation of sense of self to pubertal changes, consideration of future choices, achievement of a more mature sexual identity, and search for new values
18 to 30	Intimacy versus isolation	Love; person develops intimate relationships beyond adolescent love; many become parents
30 to late adulthood	Generativity versus stagnation	Care; people rear children, focus on occupational achievement or creativity, and train the next generation; turn outward from the self toward others
Late adulthood	Integrity versus despair	Wisdom; person conducts a life review, integrates earlier stages and comes to terms with basic identity; develops self-acceptance

Erikson's description of the central adolescent dilemma, *identity versus role confusion*, has been particularly influential. He argued that, in order to arrive at a mature sexual and occupational identity, every adolescent must examine his identity and the roles he must occupy. He must achieve an integrated sense of self, of what he wants to do and be, and of his appropriate sexual role. The risk is that the adolescent will suffer from confusion arising from the profusion of roles opening up to him at this age.

In the first of the three adult stages, the young adult builds on the identity established in adolescence to confront the crisis of *intimacy versus isolation*. Erikson defined intimacy as "the ability to fuse your identity with someone else's without fear that you're going to lose something yourself" (Erikson, in Evans, 1969). Many young people, Erikson thought, make the mistake of thinking they will find their identity in a relationship, but in his view it is only those who have already formed (or are well on the way to forming) a clear identity who can successfully enter this fusion of identities that he called *intimacy*. Young adults whose identities are weak or unformed will remain in shallow relationships and will experience a sense of isolation or loneliness.

The middle adulthood crisis is *generativity versus stagnation*, which is "primarily the concern in establishing and guiding the next generation" (Erikson, 1963, p. 267). The rearing of children is the most obvious way to achieve a sense of generativity. Doing creative work, giving service to an organization or to society, or serving as a mentor to younger colleagues can help the midlife adult achieve a sense of generativity. Failing that, the self-absorbed, nongenerative adult may feel a sense of stagnation.

psychosocial stages Erikson's eight stages, or crises, of personality development in which inner instincts interact with outer cultural and social demands to shape personality

The key idea underlying Erikson's theory is that each new crisis is thrust on the developing person because of changes in social demands that accompany changes in age. The fourth stage of industry versus inferiority, for example, begins when the child starts school and must learn to read and write. The child can't stay in elementary school until she does so. Even if she doesn't learn to read and write, she is pushed forward into middle school and high school, carrying the unresolved crisis with her as excess baggage. Thus, the childhood crises set the stage for those of adolescence and adulthood.

Evaluation of Psychoanalytic Theories

Learning Objective 2.3

What are the strengths and weaknesses of psychoanalytic theory?

Psychoanalytic theories such as Freud's and Erikson's, summarized in Table 2.3, have several attractive aspects. Most centrally, they highlight the importance of the child's earliest relationships with caregivers. Furthermore, they suggest that the child's needs change with age, so parents and other caregivers must continually adapt to the changing child. One of the implications of this is that we should not think of "good parenting" as an unchanging quality. Some people may be very good at meeting the needs of an infant but less capable of dealing with teenagers' identity struggles. The child's eventual personality and her overall mental health thus depend on the interaction pattern that develops in a particular family. The idea of changing needs is an extremely attractive element of these theories, because more and more of the research in developmental psychology is moving developmentalists toward just such a conception of the process.

Psychoanalytic theory has also given psychologists a number of helpful concepts, such as the unconscious, the ego, and identity, which have become a part of everyday language as well as theory. Moreover, psychologists are taking a fresh look at Freud's ideas about the importance of defense mechanisms in coping with anxiety (Cramer, 2000). Freud is also usually credited with the invention of psychotherapy, which is still practiced today. An additional strength of the psychoanalytic perspective is the emphasis on continued development during adulthood found in Erikson's theory. His ideas have provided a framework for a great deal of new research and theorizing about adult development.

The major weakness of psychoanalytic theories is the fuzziness of many of their concepts. For example, how could researchers detect the presence of the id, ego, superego, and so on? Without more precise definitions, it is extremely difficult to test these theories, despite their provocative explanations of development.

Critical Thinking

1. In which of Erickson's psychological stages would you place yourself? Does Erikson's description of it correspond to the challenges and concerns you are confronting?

Table 2.3 Psychoanalytic Theories

Theory	Main Idea	Evaluation: Strengths	Evaluation: Weaknesses
Freud's Psychosexual Theory	Personality develops in five stages from birth to adolescence; in each stage, the need for physical pleasure is focused on a different part of the body.	Emphasizes importance of experiences in infancy and early childhood; provides psychological explanations for mental illness	Sexual feelings are not as important in personality development as Freud claimed.
Erikson's Psychosocial Theory	Personality develops through eight life crises across the entire lifespan; a person finishes each crisis with either a good or a poor resolution.	Helps explain the role of culture in personality development; important in lifespan psychology; useful description of major themes of personality development at different ages	Describing each period in terms of a single crisis is probably an oversimplification.

Learning Theories

Psychologist John Watson (1878–1958) offered ideas about human development that were very different from those of Freud and other psychoanalysts. Watson believed that, through manipulation of the environment, children could be trained to be or do anything (Jones, 1924; Watson, 1930). To refer to this point of view, Watson coined the term **behaviorism**, which defines development in terms of behavior changes caused by environment influences. As Watson put it,

> Give me a dozen healthy infants, well-formed, and my own specified world to bring them up in and I'll guarantee to take any one at random and train him to become any type of specialist I might select—doctor, lawyer, merchant, chief, and yes, even beggerman and thief, regardless of his talents, penchants, abilities, vocations, and race of his ancestors. (1930, p. 104)

Watson's views represent a way of thinking about development that is common to all of the **learning theories**. These theories assert that development results from an accumulation of experiences. As you will see, however, each of the learning theories has a distinctive way of explaining how experience shapes development.

Learning Objective 2.4
How did Watson condition Little Albert to fear white, furry objects?

Classical Conditioning

Watson based many of his ideas about the relationship between learning and development on the work of Russian physiologist and Nobel prize winner Ivan Pavlov (1849–1936). Pavlov discovered that organisms can acquire new signals for existing responses (behaviors). The term **classical conditioning** refers to this principle. Each incidence of learning begins with a biologically programmed stimulus-response connection, or *reflex*. For example, salivation happens naturally when you put food in your mouth. In classical conditioning terms, the food is the *unconditioned (unlearned, natural) stimulus*; salivating is an *unconditioned (unlearned, natural) response.*

Stimuli presented just before or at the same time as the unconditioned stimulus are those that are likely to be associated with it. For example, most foods have odors, and to get to your mouth, food has to pass near your nose. Thus, you usually smell food before you taste it. Food odors eventually become *conditioned (learned) stimuli* that elicit salivation. In effect, they act as a signal to your salivary glands that food is coming. Once the connection between food odors and salivation has been established, smelling food triggers the salivation response even when you do not actually eat the food. When a response occurs reliably in connection with a conditioned stimulus in this way, it is known as a *conditioned (learned) response.*

For Watson, Pavlov's principles of classical conditioning held the key to understanding human development. He viewed developmental change as nothing more than the acquisition of connections between stimuli and responses. To prove his point, Watson set out to show that he could use the principles of classical conditioning to cause an infant to develop a new emotional response to a stimulus. Watson's hapless subject, 11-month-old "Little Albert," was exposed to loud noises while he played with a white rat, a stimulus that had fascinated him when it was first introduced. As a result of the pairing of the rat with the noises, however, Albert learned to fear the rat so thoroughly that he cried hysterically at the mere sight of the rodent. Moreover, he generalized his fear of the rat to other white, fuzzy objects such as a rabbit, a fur coat, and a Santa Claus mask.

As you might guess, Watson's experiment would be regarded as unethical by today's standards. Moreover, few developmentalists would agree with Watson's assertion that classical conditioning explains all of human development. Yet the Little Albert experiment demonstrated that classical conditioning may indeed be the source of developmental changes that involve emotional responses. For this reason, classical conditioning continues to have a place in the study of human development. It is especially important in infancy. Because a child's mother or father is present so often when nice things happen, such as when the child feels warm, comfortable, and cuddled, the mother and father usually serve as conditioned stimuli for pleasant feelings, a fact that makes it possible for the parents' presence to comfort a child.

behaviorism the view that defines development in terms of behavior changes caused by environmental influences

learning theories theories that assert that development results from an accumulation of experiences

classical conditioning learning that results from the association of stimuli

Skinner's Operant Conditioning

Learning Objective 2.5

How does operant conditioning occur?

Another behavioral approach to development may be found in a set of learning principles that are known collectively as **operant conditioning**, a term coined by B. F. Skinner (1904–1990), the most famous proponent of this theory (Skinner, 1953, 1980). Operant conditioning involves learning to repeat or stop behaviors because of the consequences they bring about. **Reinforcement** is anything that follows a behavior and causes it to be repeated. **Punishment** is anything that follows a behavior and causes it to stop.

A *positive reinforcement* is a consequence (usually involving something pleasant) that follows a behavior and increases the chances that the behavior will occur again. For example, if you buy a scratch-off lottery ticket and win $100, you will probably be more willing to buy another ticket in the future than you would if you hadn't won the money.

Negative reinforcement occurs when an individual learns to perform a specific behavior in order to cause something unpleasant to stop. For example, coughing is an unpleasant experience for most of us, and taking a dose of cough medicine usually stops it. As a result, when we begin coughing, we reach for the cough syrup. The behavior of swallowing a spoonful of cough syrup is reinforced by the cessation of coughing.

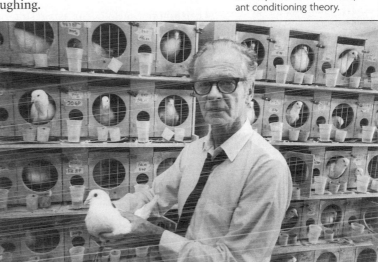

Laboratory research involving animals was important in the development of Skinner's operant conditioning theory.

Positive and negative reinforcement often interact in complex ways in real-life contexts. For example, most people understand that paying attention to a preschooler's whining is likely to increase it, an example of positive reinforcement. However, parents learn to attend to whining preschoolers because whining is irritating, and responding to it usually makes it stop. In other words, like taking cough syrup for an annoying cough, the parents' behavior of responding to whining is negatively reinforced by its consequence—namely, that the child *stops* whining.

In contrast to both kinds of reinforcement, punishment stops a behavior. Sometimes punishments involve eliminating nice things—taking away TV privileges, for example. However, punishment may also involve unpleasant things such as scolding. Like reinforcement, however, punishment is defined by its effect. Consequences that do not stop behavior can't be properly called punishments.

An alternative way to stop an unwanted behavior is **extinction**, which is the gradual elimination of a behavior through repeated nonreinforcement. If a teacher succeeds in eliminating a student's undesirable behavior by ignoring it, the behavior is said to have been *extinguished.*

Such examples illustrate the complex manner in which reinforcements and punishments operate in the real world. In laboratory settings, operant conditioning researchers usually work with only one participant or animal subject at a time; they needn't worry about the social consequences of behaviors or consequences. They can also control the situation so that a particular behavior is reinforced every time it occurs. In the real world, *partial reinforcement*—reinforcement of a behavior on some occasions but not others—is more common (see The Real World on page 34). Studies of partial reinforcement show that people take longer to learn a new behavior under partial reinforcement conditions; once established, however, such behaviors are very resistant to extinction.

operant conditioning learning to repeat or stop behaviors because of their consequences

reinforcement anything that follows a behavior and causes it to be repeated

punishment anything that follows a behavior and causes it to stop

extinction the gradual elimination of a behavior through repeated nonreinforcement

Bandura's Social-Cognitive Theory

Learning Objective 2.6

In what ways does social-cognitive theory differ from other learning theories?

Learning theorist Albert Bandura (b. 1925), whose ideas are more influential among developmental psychologists than those of the conditioning theorists, argues that learning does not always require reinforcement (1977a, 1982, 1989).

Modeling is an important source of learning for both children and adults. What behaviors have you learned by watching and copying others?

observational learning, or **modeling** learning that results from seeing a model reinforced or punished for a behavior

Learning may also occur as a result of watching someone else perform some action and experience reinforcement or punishment. Learning of this type, called **observational learning**, or **modeling**, is involved in a wide range of behaviors. For example, observant school children learn to distinguish between strict and lenient teachers by observing teachers' reactions to the misbehaviors of children who are risk-takers, that is, those who act out without having determined how teachers might react. As a result, when in the presence of strict teachers, observant children suppress forbidden behaviors such as talking out of turn and leaving their seats without permission. By contrast, when they are under the authority of lenient teachers, these children may display just as much misbehavior as their risk-taking peers.

THE REAL WORLD

Learning Principles in Real Life

Every night at bedtime, 5-year-old Keira uses every ploy she can think of to avoid going to sleep. Numerous trips to the bathroom, heart-rending pleas for just one more story, and seemingly endless requests for hugs and kisses, have all become a part of Keira's nightly routine. The final act of this family drama, which gets slightly longer each evening, repeats itself every night. Keira's parents reach their breaking point and say "no more" to all of the girl's requests, whereupon Keira initiates a frenzy of kicking, screaming, and crying in her bed until exhaustion finally puts her into sleep. Her parents have tried everything they can think of to shorten the process of putting Keira to bed, all to no avail. But they so hope that a new approach in which the girl earns stickers for going to bed without protesting will do the trick.

Virtually all parents try to reinforce some behaviors in their children by praising them or giving them material rewards. And most try to discourage unwanted behaviors through punishment. But it is easy to misapply learning principles or to create unintended consequences if you have not fully understood all the mechanisms involved.

For example, you want your children to stop climbing on a chair, so you scold them. You are conscientious and knowledgeable, and you carefully time your scolding and stop scolding when they stop climbing, so that the scolding operates as a negative reinforcer—but nothing works. They keep on leaving muddy footprints on your favorite chair. Why? Perhaps the children enjoy climbing on the chair, so the climbing is intrinsically reinforcing to them and outweighs the unpleasantness of your scolding. One way to deal with this might be to provide something else for them to climb on.

Another example: Suppose your 3-year-old son repeatedly demands your attention while you are fixing dinner. Because you don't want to reinforce this behavior, you ignore him the first six or eight times he calls you or tugs at your clothes. But after the ninth or tenth repetition, with his voice getting whinier each time, you can't stand it any longer and finally say something like "All right! What do you want?" Since you have ignored most of his demands, you might think you have not been reinforcing them. But what you have actually done is create a partial reinforcement schedule. You have rewarded only every tenth demand, and psychologists have established that this pattern of reinforcement helps create behavior that is very hard to extinguish. So your son may continue to be overly demanding for a very long time.

If such situations are familiar to you, it may pay to keep careful records for a while, noting each incident and your response. Then see whether you can figure out which principles are really at work and how you might change the pattern.

Questions for Reflection

1. If Keira's parents asked for your advice, how would you advise them to modify their plan for using reinforcement to change their daughter's nightly routine?
2. To what degree is partial reinforcement responsible for the pattern that has developed in Keira's family?

However, learning from modeling is not an entirely automatic process. Bandura points out that what an observer learns from watching someone else will depend on two cognitive elements: what she pays attention to and what she is able to remember. Moreover, to learn from a model, an observer must be physically able to imitate the behavior and motivated to perform it on her own. Because attentional abilities, memory, and physical capabilities change with age, what a child learns from any given modeled event may be quite different from what an adult learns from an identical event (Grusec, 1992).

As children, according to Bandura, we learn not only overt behavior, but also ideas, expectations, internal standards, and self-concepts, from models. At the same time, we acquire expectancies about what we can and cannot do—which Bandura (1997) calls *self-efficacy*. Once those standards and those expectancies or beliefs have been established, they affect the child's behavior in consistent and enduring ways. For example, you'll learn in Chapter 12 that self-efficacy beliefs influence our overall sense of well-being and even our physical health.

Evaluation of Learning Theories

Learning Objective 2.7
How well do the learning theories explain development?

Several implications of learning theories, summarized in Table 2.4, are worth emphasizing. First, learning theories can explain both consistency and change in behavior. If a child is friendly and smiling both at home and at school, learning theorists would explain the child's behavior by saying that the child is being reinforced for that behavior in both settings. It is equally possible to explain why a child is happy at home but miserable at school. We need only hypothesize that the home environment reinforces cheerful behavior but the school setting does not.

Learning theorists also tend to be optimistic about the possibility of change. Children's behavior can change if the reinforcement system—or their beliefs about themselves—change. So, problem behavior can be modified.

The great strength of learning theories is that they seem to give an accurate picture of the way in which many behaviors are learned. It is clear that both children and adults learn through conditioning and modeling. Furthermore, Bandura's addition of mental elements to learning theory adds further strength, since it allows an integration of learning models and other approaches.

Table 2.4 Learning Theories

		Evaluation	
Theory	**Main Idea**	**Strengths**	**Weaknesses**
Pavlov's Classical Conditioning	Learning happens when neutral stimuli become so strongly associated with natural stimuli that they elicit the same response.	Useful in explaining how emotional responses such as phobias are learned	Explanation of behavior change is too limited to serve as comprehensive theory of human development.
Skinner's Operant Conditioning Theory	Development involves behavior changes that are shaped by reinforcement and punishment.	Basis of many useful strategies for managing and changing human behavior	Humans are not as passive as Skinner claimed; the theory ignores hereditary, cognitive, emotional, and social factors in development.
Bandura's Social-Learning Theory	People learn from models; what they learn from a model depends on how they interpret the situation cognitively and emotionally.	Helps explain how models influence behavior; explains more about development than other learning theories do because of addition of cognitive and emotional factors	Does not provide an overall picture of development

Critical Thinking

1. Can you describe instances in your everyday life when your behavior is affected by classical conditioning, operant conditioning, and observational learning? How do you use these same principles to affect others' behavior?

However, the learning theorists' approach is not really developmental; it doesn't tell us much about change with age, either in childhood or in adulthood. Even Bandura's variation on learning theory does not tell us whether there are any changes with age in what a child can learn from modeling. Thus, learning theories help developmentalists understand how specific behaviors are acquired but do not contribute to an understanding of age-related change.

Cognitive Theories

The group of theories known as **cognitive theories** emphasizes mental aspects of development such as logic and memory. Have you ever watched a baby throw things out of her mother's shopping cart? No matter how many objects she drops, she watches each one intently as if she has no idea where it's going to land. Why do babies engage in repetitive actions of this kind? One reason might be that they use their motor skills (throwing things) and senses (watching them) to build mental pictures of the world around them. Thus, infants drop objects and watch them fall until they have learned all they can from this behavior; then they move on to a more mature way of interacting with the world.

Learning Objective 2.8

How does cognitive development progress, according to Piaget?

Piaget's Cognitive-Developmental Theory

cognitive theories theories that emphasize mental processes in development, such as logic and memory

scheme in Piaget's theory, an internal cognitive structure that provides an individual with a procedure to use in a specific circumstance

assimilation the process of using a scheme to make sense of an event or experience

One of the most influential theories in the history of developmental psychology is that of Swiss developmentalist Jean Piaget (1896–1980). Originally educated as a natural scientist, Piaget spent six decades studying the development of logical thinking in children. Because of the popularity of Watson's views, psychologists in the United States paid little attention to Piaget's work. During the late 1950s, however, American developmentalists "discovered" Piaget. From then on, developmental psychologists in the United States began to focus on children's thinking more than on how environmental stimuli influenced their behavior.

Piaget was struck by the fact that all children seem to go through the same sequence of discoveries about their world, making the same mistakes and arriving at the same solutions (Piaget, 1952, 1970, 1977; Piaget & Inhelder, 1969). For example, all 3- and 4-year-olds seem to think that if water is poured from a short, wide glass into a taller, narrower one, there is then more water, because the water level is higher in the narrow glass than it was in the wide glass. In contrast, most 7-year-olds realize that the amount of water has not changed. To explain such age differences, Piaget proposed several concepts that continue to guide developmental research.

A pivotal idea in Piaget's model is that of a **scheme**, an internal cognitive structure that provides an individual with a procedure to follow in a specific circumstance. For example, when you pick up a ball, you use your picking-up scheme. Piaget proposed that each of us begins life with a small repertoire of sensory and motor schemes, such as looking, tasting, touching, hearing, and reaching. As we use each scheme, it becomes better adapted to the world; in other words, it works better. During childhood and adolescence, mental schemes allow us to use symbols and think logically. Piaget proposed three processes to explain how children get from built-in schemes such as looking and touching to the complex mental schemes used in childhood, adolescence, and adulthood.

Piaget based many of his ideas on naturalistic observations of children of different ages on playgrounds and in schools.

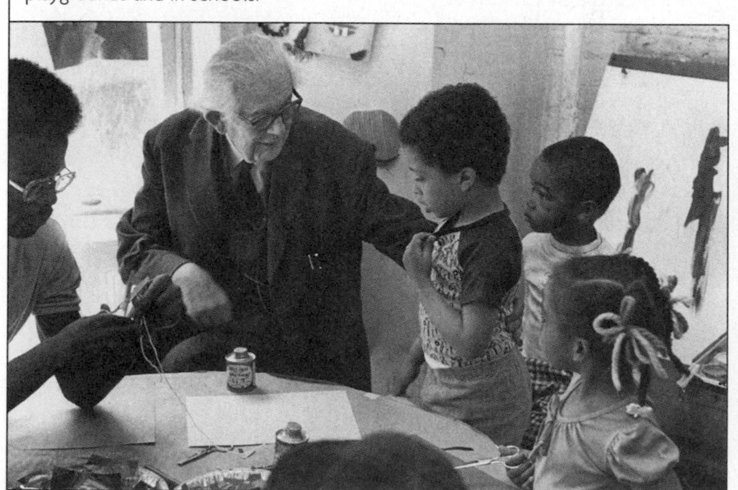

Assimilation is the process of using schemes to make sense of experiences. Piaget would say that a baby who grasps a toy is *assimilating* it to his grasping

scheme. The complementary process is **accommodation**, which involves changing the scheme as a result of some new information acquired through assimilation. When the baby grasps a square object for the first time, he will accommodate his grasping scheme; so the next time he reaches for a square object, his hand will be more appropriately bent to grasp it. Thus, the process of accommodation is the key to developmental change. Through accommodation, we improve our skills and reorganize our ways of thinking.

Equilibration is the process of balancing assimilation and accommodation to create schemes that fit the environment. To illustrate, think about infants' tendency to put things in their mouths. In Piaget's terms, they assimilate objects to their mouthing scheme. As they mouth each one, their mouthing scheme changes to include the instructions "*Do* mouth this" or "*Don't* mouth this." The accommodation is based on mouthing experiences. A pacifier feels good in the mouth, but a dead insect has an unpleasant texture. So, eventually, the mouthing scheme says it's okay to put a pacifier in the mouth, but it's not okay to mouth a dead insect. In this way, an infant's mouthing scheme attains a better fit with the real world.

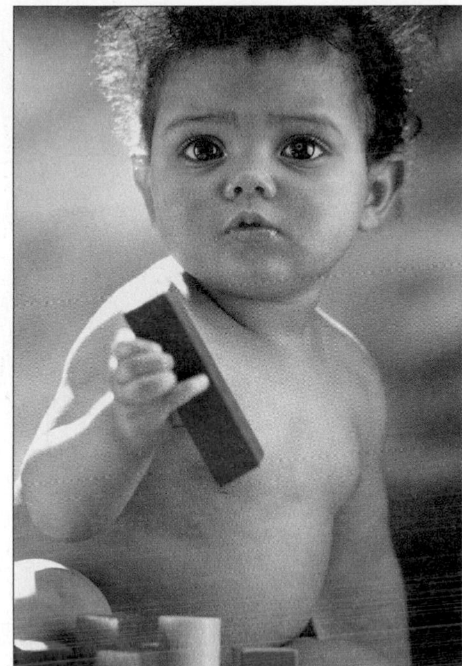

Using Piaget's terminology, we would say this infant is assimilating the object to her grasping scheme.

Piaget's research suggested to him that logical thinking evolves in four stages. During the *sensorimotor stage*, from birth to 18 months, infants use their sensory and motor schemes to act on the world around them. In the *preoperational stage*, from 18 months to about age 6, youngsters acquire symbolic schemes, such as language and fantasy, that they use in thinking and communicating. Next comes the *concrete operational stage*, during which 6- to 12-year-olds begin to think logically and become capable of solving problems such as the one illustrated in Figure 2.1.

The last phase is the *formal operational stage*, in which adolescents learn to think logically about abstract ideas and hypothetical situations.

Table 2.5 describes these stages more fully; you will read about each of them in detail later in the book. For now, it is important to understand that in Piaget's view, each stage grows out of the one that precedes it, and each involves a major restructuring of the child's way of thinking. It's also important to know that research has confirmed Piaget's belief that the sequence of the stages is fixed. However, children progress through them at different rates. In addition, some individuals do not attain the formal operational stage in adolescence or even in adulthood. Consequently, the ages associated with the stages are approximations.

accommodation changing a scheme as a result of some new information

equilibration the process of balancing assimilation and accommodation to create schemes that fit the environment

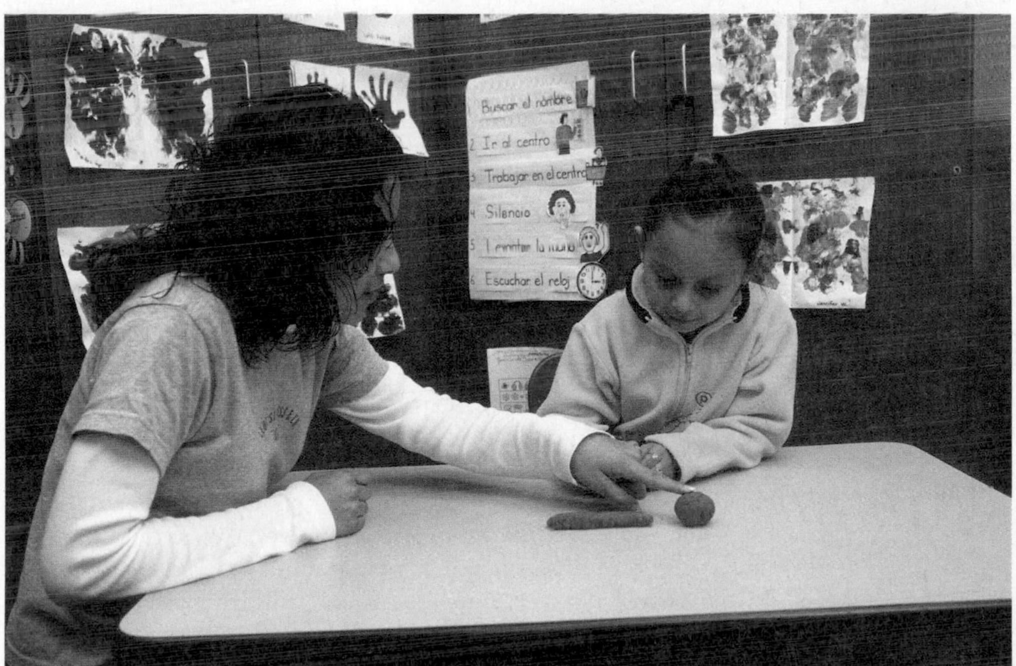

Figure 2.1
A Conservation Task

In one of the problems Piaget devised, a child is shown two clay balls of equal size and asked if they both contain the same amount of clay. Next, the researcher rolls one ball into a sausage shape and asks the child if the two shapes still contain the same amount of clay. A preoperational child will say that one now contains more clay than the other and will base his answer on their appearance: "The sausage has more because it's longer now." A concrete operational thinker will say that the two still contain the same amount of material because no clay was added or taken away from either. (Photo: Will Hart)

Table 2.5 Piaget's Cognitive-Developmental Stages

Approximate Ages	Stage	Description
Birth to 18 months	Sensorimotor	The baby understands the world through her senses and her motor actions; she begins to use simple symbols, such as single words and pretend play, near the end of this period.
18 months to 6 years	Preoperational	By age 2, the child can use symbols both to think and to communicate; he develops the abilities to take others' points of view, classify objects, and use simple logic by the end of this stage.
6 to 12	Concrete operational	The child's logic takes a great leap forward with the development of new internal operations, such as conservation and class inclusion, but is still tied to the known world; by the end of the period, he can reason about simple "what if" questions.
12+	Formal operational	The child begins to manipulate ideas as well as objects; she thinks hypothetically and, by adulthood, can easily manage a variety of "what if" questions; she greatly improves her ability to organize ideas and objects mentally.

Learning Objective 2.9

How did Vygotsky use the concepts of scaffolding and the zone of proximal development to explain cognitive development?

Vygotsky's Sociocultural Theory

Lev Vygotsky's **sociocultural theory** asserts that complex forms of thinking have their origins in social interactions rather than in the child's private explorations, as Piaget thought. According to Vygotsky, children's learning of new cognitive skills is guided by an adult (or a more skilled child, such as an older sibling), who structures the child's learning experience, a process Vygotsky called *scaffolding*. To create an appropriate scaffold, the adult must gain and keep the child's attention, model the best strategy, and adapt the whole process to the child's developmental level, or *zone of proximal development* (Landry, Garner, Swank, & Baldwin, 1996; Rogoff, 1990). Vygotsky used this term to signify tasks that are too hard for the child to do alone but that he can manage with guidance. For example, parents of a beginning reader provide a scaffold when they help him sound out new words.

Developmental psychologist Lev Vygotsky hypothesized that social interactions among children are critical to both cognitive and social development.

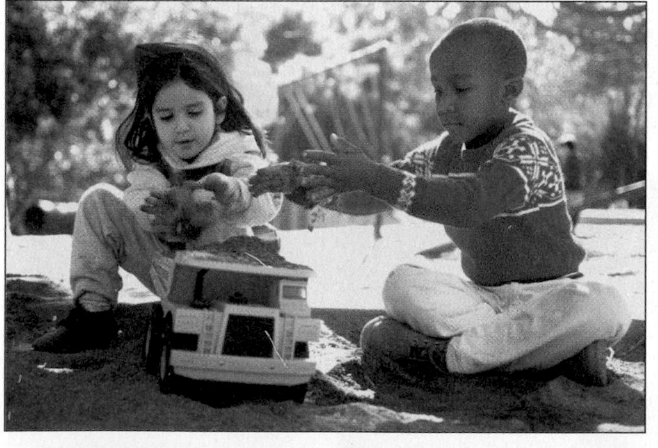

Vygotsky's ideas have important educational applications. Like Piaget's, Vygotsky's theory suggests the importance of opportunities for active exploration. But assisted discovery would play a greater role in a Vygotskian than in a Piagetian classroom; the teacher would provide the scaffolding for children's discovery, through questions, demonstrations, and explanations (Tharp & Gallimore, 1988). To be effective, the assisted discovery processes would have to be within the zone of proximal development of each child.

Learning Objective 2.10

How does information-processing theory explain the findings of developmental psychologists such as Piaget and Vygotsky?

Information-Processing Theory

The goal of **information-processing theory** is to explain how the mind manages information (Klahr, 1992). Theorizing about and studying memory processes are central to information-processing theory. Most memory research assumes that the human memory is made up of multiple components. The idea is that information moves through these components in an organized way (see Figure 2.2). The process of understanding a spoken word serves as a good example. First, you hear the word when the sounds enter your *sensory memory*. Your experiences with language allow you to recognize the pattern of sounds as a word. Next, the word moves into your *short-term memory*, the component of the memory system where all information is processed. Thus, short-

sociocultural theory Vygotsky's view that complex forms of thinking have their origins in social interactions rather than in an individual's private explorations

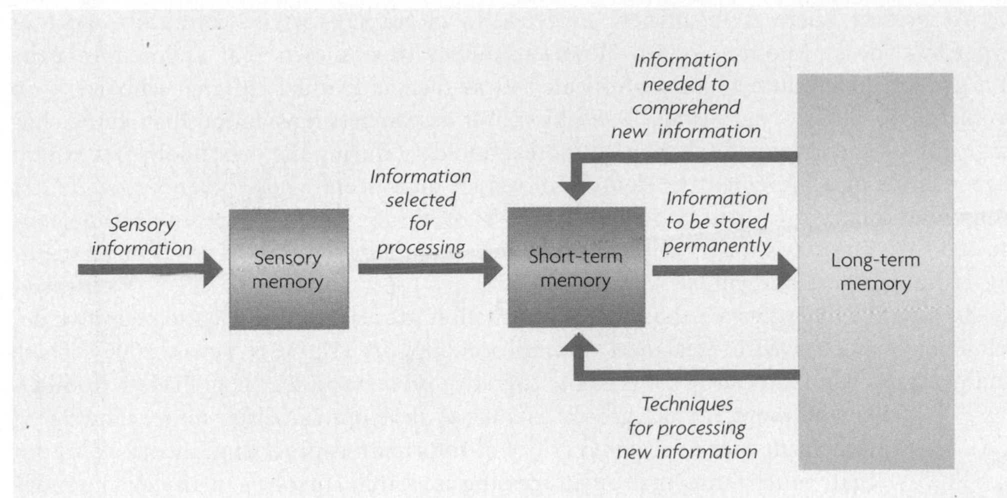

Figure 2.2 The Information-Processing System

Information-processing research on memory is based on the assumption that information moves into, out of, and through the sensory, short-term, and long-term memories in an organized way.

term memory is often called *working memory*. Knowledge of the word's meaning is then called up out of *long-term memory*, the component of the system where information is permanently stored, and placed in short-term memory, where it is linked to the word's sounds to enable you to understand it.

According to the information-processing model, children who are presented with problems such as Piaget's conservation tasks process the information they need to solve such problems in their short-term memories. As you will learn in Chapter 7, a great deal of research has shown that younger children's short-term memories are both more limited in capacity and less efficient than those of older children (Kail, 1990). Consequently, some developmentalists have used information processing theory to explain Piaget's stages. Their theories are called **neo-Piagetian theories** because they expand on Piaget's theory rather than contradict it (Case, 1985, 1997). As you'll learn in Chapter 7, according to neo-Piagetians, older children and adults can solve complex problems like those in Piaget's research because they can hold more pieces of information in their short-term memories at the same time than younger children can.

Evaluation of Cognitive Theories

Learning Objective 2.11

What are some of the important contributions and criticisms of the cognitive theories?

Research based on cognitive theories, especially the work of Piaget, has demonstrated that simplistic views, such as those of the conditioning theorists, cannot explain the development of the complex phenomenon that is logical thinking. Moreover, Piaget's research findings have been replicated in virtually every culture and in every cohort of children since his work was first published in the 1920s. Thus, not only did he formulate a theory that forced psychologists to think about child development in a new way, he also provided a set of findings that were impossible to ignore and difficult to explain. In addition, he developed innovative methods of studying children's thinking that continue to be important today (see the Research Report on page 41).

Nevertheless, Piaget turned out to be wrong about some of the ages at which children develop particular skills. As you will see in later chapters, researchers have found that children develop some intellectual skills at earlier ages than Piaget's findings suggested. Furthermore, Piaget was probably wrong about the generality of the stages themselves. Most 8-year-olds, for example, show concrete operational thinking on some tasks but not on others, and they are more likely to show complex thinking on familiar than on unfamiliar tasks. Thus, the whole process seems to be a great deal less stagelike than Piaget proposed.

information-processing theory a theoretical perspective that uses the computer as a model to explain how the mind manages information

neo-Piagetian theory an approach that uses information-processing principles to explain the developmental stages identified by Piaget

At present, there is insufficient evidence to either support or contradict most of Vygotsky's ideas (Thomas, 2000). However, studies have shown that children in pairs and groups do produce more sophisticated ideas than individual children who work on problems alone (Tan-Niam et al., 1998). Moreover, researchers have found that young children whose parents provide them with more scaffolding during the preschool years exhibit higher levels of achievement in elementary school than peers whose parents provide less support of this kind (Neitzel & Stright, 2003). Thus, future research may support the conclusion that Vygotsky's theory constitutes an important contribution to a full understanding of human development.

In contrast to Vygotsky's theory, the information processing approach to cognitive development has received a great deal of empirical support (Lamb & Lewis, 2005). These findings have helped to clarify some of the cognitive processes underlying Piaget's findings. Furthermore, it has greatly enhanced developmentalists' understanding of human memory. However, critics of information-processing theory point out that much information-processing research involves artificial memory tasks such as learning lists of words. Therefore, say critics, research based on the information-processing approach doesn't always accurately describe how memory works in the real world. Consequently, as Piaget did, information-processing theorists may underestimate children's capabilities with regard to real-world tasks.

Piagetians claim that information-processing theory emphasizes explanations of single cognitive tasks at the expense of a comprehensive picture of development. Finally, critics of both cognitive theories say that they ignore the role of emotions in development. The cognitive theories are summarized in Table 2.6.

Critical Thinking

1. What are the pros and cons of educating parents and teachers about Piaget's stages of cognitive development, that is, to what extent might parents and educators who learn about Piaget's stages overestimate or underestimate children's abilities?

Table 2.6 Cognitive Theories

Theory	Main Idea	Evaluation: Strengths	Evaluation: Weaknesses
Piaget's Theory of Cognitive Development	Reasoning develops in four universal stages from birth through adolescence; in each stage, the child builds a different kind of scheme.	Helps explain how children of different ages think about and act on the world	Stage concept may cause adults to underestimate children's reasoning abilities; there may be additional stages in adulthood.
Information-Processing Theory	The computer is used as a model for human cognitive functioning; encoding, storage, and retrieval processes change with age, causing changes in memory function; these changes happen because of both brain maturation and practice.	Helps explain how much information people of different ages can manage at one time and how they process it; provides a useful framework for studying individual differences in people of the same age	Human information processing is much more complex than that of a computer; the theory doesn't provide an overall picture of development.
Vygotsky's Sociocultural Theory	Emphasizes linguistic and social factors in cognitive development	Incorporates group learning processes into explanations of individual cognitive development	Insufficient evidence to support most ideas

RESEARCH REPORT

Piaget's Clever Research

Piaget not only proposed a novel and provocative theory; he also devised creative strategies for testing children's understanding. Probably the most famous of all Piaget's clever techniques is his method for studying conservation, the understanding that matter does not change in quantity when its appearance changes. As shown in Figure 2.1, Piaget began with two balls of clay of equal size; he showed them to a child and let the child hold and manipulate them until she agreed that they had the same amount of clay. Then in full view of the child, Piaget rolled one of the balls into a sausage shape. Then he asked the child whether there was still the same amount of clay in the sausage and the ball or whether one had more. Children of 4 and 5 consistently said that the ball contained more clay; children of 6 and 7 consistently said that the shapes still had the same amount. Thus, the older children understood that the quantity of clay was conserved even though its appearance changed.

In another study, Piaget explored children's understanding that objects can belong to multiple categories. (For example, Fido is both a dog and an animal; a high chair is both a chair and furniture.) Piaget usually studied this by first having children create their own classes and subclasses and then asking them questions about these. One 5-year-old child, for example, played with a set of flowers and had made two heaps, one large group of primroses and a smaller group of other mixed flowers. Piaget then had this conversation with the child (Piaget & Inhelder, 1959, p. 108):

PIAGET: If I make a bouquet of all the primroses and you make one of all the flowers, which will be bigger?

CHILD: Yours.

PIAGET: If I gather all the primroses in a meadow, will any flowers remain?

CHILD: Yes.

The child understood that there are flowers other than primroses but did not yet understand that all primroses are flowers—that the smaller, subordinate class is included in the larger class. Piaget's term for this concept was class inclusion.

In these conversations with children, Piaget was always trying to understand how the child thought, rather than trying to see whether the child could come up with the right answer. So he used an investigative method in which he followed the child's lead, asking probing questions or creating special exploratory tests to try to discover the child's logic. In the early days of Piaget's work, many American researchers were critical of this method, since Piaget did not ask precisely the same questions of each child. Still, the results were so striking, and so surprising, that they couldn't be ignored. And when stricter research techniques were devised, more often than not the investigators confirmed Piaget's observations.

Questions for Critical Analysis

1. To what extent were Piaget's methods influenced by children's language skills?
2. How might older children's more highly developed capacity for reflecting on and explaining their thought processes have influenced Piaget's inferences about younger children's capacity for logical thinking?

Biological and Ecological Theories

Theories that propose links between physiological processes and development represent one of the most important current trends in developmental psychology (Parke, 2004). Some of these theories focus on individual differences, while others deal with universal aspects of development. Moreover, all of them, to varying degrees, address the manner in which environmental factors interact with physiological processes.

Behavior Genetics

Learning Objective 2.12
How do behavior geneticists explain individual differences?

Behavior genetics focuses on the effect of heredity on individual differences. Traits or behaviors are believed to be influenced by genes when those of related people, such as children and their parents, are more similar than those of unrelated people. Behavior geneticists have shown that heredity affects a broad range of traits and behaviors, including intelligence, shyness, and aggressiveness.

Furthermore, the contributions of heredity to individual differences are evident throughout the lifespan. For example, researchers in the Netherlands have been studying a number of variables in identical and fraternal twins for several decades. As you'll learn in Chapter 3, identical twins are particularly important in genetic research because they have exactly the same genes. Moreover, it's useful to compare them to twins who are nonidentical because these individuals share the same environment but do not have the same genes. As you can see in

behavior genetics the study of the role of heredity in individual differences

Figure 2.3
IQs of Fraternal and Identical Twins

This figure illustrates the combined findings of several longitudinal and cross-sectional studies of Dutch twins (Posthuma, de Geus, & Boomsma, 2003). You will notice that in childhood, when fraternal twins share the same environment, their IQ scores are more strongly correlated than in adulthood, when they presumably no longer live together. By contrast, the IQ scores of identical twins are even more strongly correlated in adulthood than during the childhood years. This pattern suggests conclusions about both heredity and environment. Specifically, at least with regard to IQ scores, the influence of heredity appears to increase with age, while that of the environment declines.

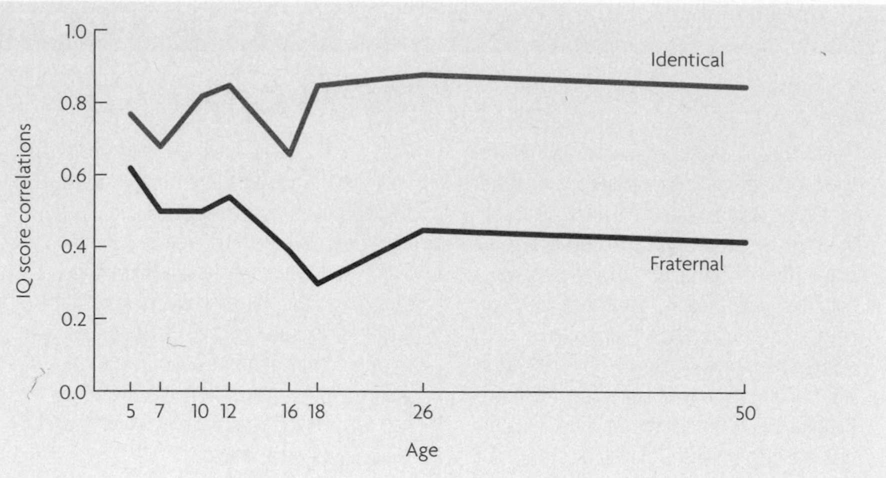

Figure 2.3, the Dutch researchers have found that IQ scores of identical twins are more strongly correlated than those of fraternal (nonidentical) twins from early childhood until middle age. Interestingly, too, such findings show that the environment affects IQ scores as well, but that its effects may be transient. This conclusion is suggested by the fact that the IQ scores of fraternal twins are more strongly correlated in childhood, when they are living together, than in adulthood, when they do not share the same environment.

Behavior geneticists also study how individuals' genetic makeup influences the environments in which they are developing, a phenomenon that could occur via either or both of two routes. First, the child inherits his genes from his parents, who also create the environment in which he is growing up. So a child's genetic heritage may predict something about his environment. For example, parents who themselves have higher IQ scores are not only likely to pass their "good IQ" genes on to their children, they are also likely to create a richer, more stimulating environment for those children. Similarly, children who inherit a tendency toward aggression or hostility from their parents are likely to live in a family environment that is higher in criticism and negativity—because those are expressions of the parents' own genetic tendencies toward aggressiveness or hostility (Reiss, 1998).

Second, each child's unique pattern of inherited qualities affects the way she behaves with other people, which in turn affects the way adults and other children respond to her. A cranky or temperamentally difficult baby may receive fewer smiles and more scolding than a placid, even-tempered one; a genetically brighter child may demand more personal attention, ask more questions, or seek out more complex toys than would a less bright child (Saudino & Plomin, 1997). Furthermore, children's interpretations of their experiences are affected by all their inherited tendencies, including not only intelligence but also temperament or pathology (Plomin, Reiss, Hetherington, & Howe, 1994).

Learning Objective 2.13
What kinds of behaviors are of interest to ethologists and sociobiologists?

Ethology and Sociobiology

The relationship between individuals and the settings in which they develop is the emphasis of *ecological theories*, perspectives that view development as resulting from the degree to which genes help or hinder individuals' efforts to adapt to their environments. One such theory, known as **ethology**, focuses on the study of animals in their natural environments. Ethologists emphasize genetically determined survival behaviors that are assumed to have evolved through natural selection. For example, nests are necessary for the survival of young birds. Therefore, ethologists say, evolution has equipped birds with nest-building genes.

ethology a perspective on development that emphasizes genetically determined survival behaviors presumed to have evolved through natural selection

Likewise, the young of many species are vulnerable to predators. Consequently, their genes direct them to form a relationship with a more mature member of the species very early in life. One such relationship results from a process called *imprinting* in which newborns of some species learn to recognize the characteristics of a protective organism within the first hours of life. Ethologist Konrad Lorenz (1903–1989) studied imprinting among animals extensively (Lorenz, 1935). He learned that young ducklings and geese, for example, imprint on any moving object to which they are exposed during the critical period for imprinting (24 to 48 hours after hatching). In fact, one of the best-known images in the field of ethology is that of Lorenz himself being followed by several goslings who had imprinted on him.

Lorenz found that once a gaggle of newly hatched geese had imprinted on him, they followed him wherever he went.

Similarly, ethologists believe that emotional relationships are necessary to the survival of human infants (Bowlby, 1969, 1980). They claim that evolution has produced genes that cause humans to form these relationships. For example, most people feel irritated when they hear a newborn crying. Ethologists say the baby is genetically programmed to cry in a certain way, and adults are genetically programmed to get irritated when they hear it. The caretaker responds to a crying baby's needs in order to remove the irritating stimulus of the noise. As the caretaker and infant interact, an emotional bond is created between them. Thus, genes for crying in an irritating manner increase infants' chances of survival.

Sociobiology is the study of society using the methods and concepts of biological science. When applied to human development, sociobiology emphasizes genes that aid group survival. Sociobiologists claim individual humans have the best chance for survival when they live in groups. Therefore, they claim, evolution has provided humans with genetic programming that helps us cooperate.

To support their views, sociobiologists look for social rules and behaviors that exist in all cultures. For example, every society has laws against murder. Sociobiologists believe that humans are genetically programmed to create rules based on respect for other people's lives. Evolution has selected these genes, they claim, because people need to respect each other's lives and to be able to cooperate.

Critics of ethology and sociobiology claim that these theories underestimate the impact of the environment. Moreover, these theories are difficult to test. How can researchers test ethological theorists' claim that infant-caregiver attachment is universal because it has survival value, for example? Finally, critics say that these theories ignore the fact that societies invent ways of enhancing whatever behaviors might be influenced by universal genetic programming. For instance, as sociobiologists hypothesize, genes may be involved in the universal prohibition of murder, but societies invent strategies for preventing it. Moreover, these strategies differ across societies and in their effectiveness.

Bronfenbrenner's Bioecological Theory

Learning Objective 2.14

What is the main idea of Bronfenbrenner's bioecological theory?

Another approach gaining interest in developmental psychology is Urie Bronfenbrenner's **bioecological theory**, which explains development in terms of relationships between people and their environments, or *contexts*, as Bronfenbrenner calls them (Bronfenbrenner, 1979, 1993). Bronfenbrenner attempts to classify all the individual and contextual variables that affect development and to specify how they interact.

According to Bronfenbrenner, the contexts of development are like circles within circles (see Figure 2.4 on page 44). The outermost circle, the *macrosystem* (the cultural context), contains the values and beliefs of the culture in which a child is growing up. For example, a society's beliefs about the importance of education exist in the cultural context.

The next level, the *exosystem* (the socioeconomic context), includes the institutions of the culture that affect children's development indirectly. For example, funding for education exists in the socioeconomic context. The citizens of a specific nation may strongly believe that all children should be educated (cultural context), but their ability to provide universal education may be limited by the country's wealth (socioeconomic context).

sociobiology the study of society using the methods and concepts of biology; when used by developmentalists, an approach that emphasizes genes that aid group survival

bioecological theory Bronfenbrenner's theory that explains development in terms of relationships between individuals and their environments, or interconnected contexts

Figure 2.4
Bronfenbrenner's Contexts of Development

Bronfenbrenner's ecological theory proposes that people are exposed to interconnected contexts that interact in complex ways to influence development.

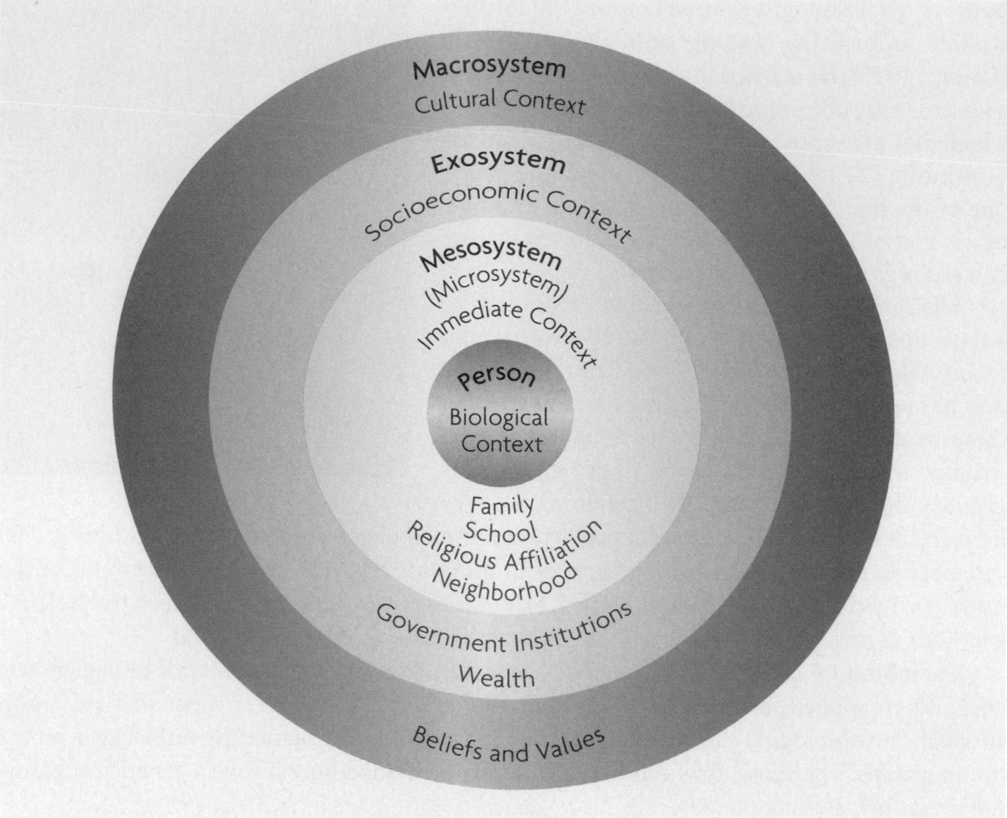

The *microsystem* (the immediate context) includes those variables to which people are exposed directly, such as their families, schools, religious institutions, and neighborhoods. The *mesosystem* is made up of the interconnections between these components. For example, the specific school a child attends and her own family are part of the microsystem. Her parents' involvement in her school and the response of the school to their involvement are part of the mesosystem. Thus, the culture a child is born into may strongly value quality education. Moreover, her nation's economy may provide ample funds for schooling. However, her own education will be more strongly affected by the particular school she attends and the connections—or lack thereof—between her school and her family. Thus, the child's immediate context may be either consistent with the cultural and socioeconomic contexts or at odds with them.

Finally, the child's genetic makeup and developmental stage—her *biological context*—also influence her development. For example, a student who hasn't mastered the skill of reading isn't likely to benefit from an enriched literature program. Thus, her culture, the socioeconomic situation, the school she attends, and her own family may all be geared toward providing a quality education. However, her ability to benefit from it will be determined by the degree to which her education fits her individual needs.

Bronfenbrenner's bioecological theory provides a way of thinking about development that captures the complexity of individual and contextual variables. To date, its greatest contribution to developmental psychology has been its emphasis on the need for research examining interactions among these variables (Thomas, 2000). For example, ecological theory has helped developmentalists understand that studies of infant day care can't just compare infants in day care to infants in home care. Such studies must also consider family variables, such as parents' educational level, and day-care variables, such as the ratio of caretakers to infants. Since the 1980s, an increasing number of such studies have appeared.

Critical Thinking

1. Like the learning theories you read about earlier in the chapter, behavior genetics, ethology, sociobiology, and bioecological theories, to varying degrees, consider the role of the environment in development. But what are some of the important differences between learning theories and the perspectives that are described in this section?

Comparing Theories

After learning about theories, students usually want to know which one is right. However, developmentalists don't think of theories in terms of right or wrong but, instead, compare theories on the basis of their assumptions and how useful they are in promoting understanding of development. Today's developmentalists often don't adhere to a single theory but take an approach that taps the strengths of each of the major theoretical perspectives.

Assumptions about Development

Learning Objective 2.15

What assumptions do the three families of theories make about development?

When we say that a theory assumes something about development, we mean that it holds some general perspective to be true. We can think of a theory's assumptions in terms of its answers to three questions about development.

One question addresses the *active or passive* issue: *Is a person active in shaping his own development, or is he a passive recipient of environmental influences?* Theories that claim a person's actions on the environment are the most important determinants of development are on the active side. Cognitive theories, for example, typically view development this way. In contrast, theories on the passive side, such as those of Pavlov and Skinner, maintain that development results from the environment acting on the individual.

As you learned in Chapter 1, the *nature versus nurture* question—*How do nature and nurture interact to produce development?*—is one of the most important in developmental psychology. All developmental theories, while admitting that both nature and nurture are involved in development, make assumptions about their relative importance. Theories claiming that biology contributes more to development than does environment are on the nature side of the question. Those that view environmental influences as most important are on the nurture side. Other theories assume that nature and nurture are equally important, and that it is impossible to say which contributes more to development.

Ethologists assert that the first 2 years of life are a critical period for the establishment of relationships between infants and caregivers.

You may also recall from Chapter 1 that the *continuity versus discontinuity* issue is a source of debate among developmentalists. Here, the question is *Does development happen continuously or in stages?* Theories that do not refer to stages assert that development is a stable, continuous process. Stage theories, on the other hand, emphasize change more than stability. They claim that development happens in leaps from lower to higher steps.

For the three major families of theories you have read about in this chapter, Table 2.7 on page 46 lists the assumptions each individual theory makes regarding these issues. Because each theory is based on different assumptions, each implies a different approach to studying development. Consequently, research derived from each theory tells us something different about development. Moreover, a theory's assumptions shape the way it is applied in the real world.

For example, a teacher who approached instruction from the cognitive perspective would create a classroom in which children could experiment to some degree on their own. He would also recognize that children differ in ability, interests, developmental level, and other internal characteristics. He would believe that structuring the educational environment is important, but would assume that what each student ultimately learns will be determined by his own actions on the environment.

Alternatively, a teacher who adopted the learning perspective would guide and reinforce children's learning very carefully. Such a teacher would place little importance on ability differences among children. Instead, she would try to accomplish the same instructional goals for all children through proper manipulation of the environment.

Usefulness

Learning Objective 2.16

On what criteria do developmentalists compare the usefulness of theories?

Developmentalists also compare theories with respect to their usefulness. You should be aware that there is a fair amount of disagreement among psychologists

Table 2.7 How Theories Answer Three Questions about Development

Theories	Active or Passive?	Nature or Nurture?	Stability or Change?
Psychoanalytic Theories			
Psychosexual Theory	Passive	Nature	Change (stages)
Psychosocial Theory	Passive	Both	Change
Learning Theories			
Classical Conditioning	Passive	Nurture	Stability (no stages)
Operant Conditioning	Passive	Nurture	Stability
Social-Learning Theory	Active	Nurture	Stability
Cognitive Theories			
Cognitive-Developmental Theory	Active	Both	Change
Sociocultural Theory	Active	Both	Change
Information-Processing Theory	Active	Both	Both

on exactly how useful each theory is. Nevertheless, there are a few general criteria most psychologists use to evaluate the usefulness of a theory.

One way to evaluate usefulness is to assess a theory's ability to generate predictions that can be tested using scientific methods. For example, as you learned earlier in this chapter, one criticism of Freud's theory is that many of his claims are difficult to test. In contrast, when Piaget claimed that most children can solve concrete operational problems by age 7, he made an assertion that is easily tested. Thus, Piaget's theory is viewed by many developmentalists as more useful in this sense than Freud's. Vygotsky, learning theorists, and information-processing theorists also proposed many testable ideas. By contrast, according to some developmental psychologists, current biological and ecological theories are weak because they are difficult to test (Thomas, 2000).

Another criterion by which to judge the usefulness of a theory is its *heuristic* value, the degree to which it stimulates thinking and research. In terms of heuristic value, Freud's and Piaget's theories earn equally high marks. Both are responsible for an enormous amount of theorizing and research on human development, often by psychologists who strongly disagree with them. In fact, all of the theories in this chapter are important heuristically.

Yet another way of evaluating a theory's usefulness, though, is in terms of practical value. In other words, a theory may be deemed useful if it provides solutions to problems. Based on this criterion, the learning and information-processing theories seem to stand out because they provide tools that can be used to influence behavior. A person who suffers from anxiety attacks, for example, can learn to use biofeedback, a technique derived from conditioning theories, to manage anxiety. Similarly, a student who needs to learn to study more effectively can get help from study skills courses based on information-processing research.

Ultimately, of course, no matter how many testable hypotheses or practical techniques a theory produces, it has little or no usefulness to developmentalists if it doesn't explain the basic facts of development. Based on this criterion, learning theories, especially classical and operant conditioning, are regarded by many developmentalists as somewhat less useful than other perspectives (Thomas, 2000). Although they explain how specific behaviors may be learned, they cannot account for the complexity of human development, which can't be reduced to connections between stimuli and responses or between behaviors and reinforcers.

As you can see, the point of comparing theories is not to conclude which one is true. Instead, such comparisons help to reveal the unique contribution each can make to a comprehensive understanding of human development.

Eclecticism

Learning Objective 2.17
What is eclecticism?

Today's developmental scientists try to avoid the kind of rigid adherence to a single theoretical perspective that was characteristic of theorists such as Freud, Piaget, and Skinner. Instead, they emphasize **eclecticism**, the use of multiple theoretical perspectives to explain and study human development (Parke, 2004). The interdisciplinary nature of the study of human development you read about in Chapter 1 is reflected in this trend as well.

To better understand the eclectic approach, think about how ideas drawn from several sources might help us better understand a child's disruptive behavior in school. Observations of the child's behavior and her classmates' reactions may suggest that her behavior is being rewarded by the other children's responses (a behavioral explanation). Deeper probing of the child's family situation may indicate that her acting-out behavior may be an emotional reaction to a family event such as divorce (a psychoanalytic explanation).

eclecticism the use of multiple theoretical perspectives to explain and study human development

The interdisciplinary nature of today's developmental science also contributes to eclecticism. For instance, an anthropologist might suggest that the rapid-fire communication media found in almost every home nowadays (e.g., television) require children to develop attention strategies that differ from those that are appropriate for classroom environments. As a result, children today exhibit more disruptive behavior in school than children in past generations because of the mismatch between the kinds of information delivery to which they are accustomed and those which are found in school.

By adopting an eclectic approach, developmentalists can devise more comprehensive theories from which to derive questions and hypotheses for further research. In other words, their theories and studies may more closely match the behavior of real people in real situations.

Critical Thinking

1. Which of the many theories in this chapter do you find to be most useful to your own efforts to understand development? What are the theory's assumptions, and how do they compare to the criteria for usefulness? Finally, what other theories could be used along with them to broaden your understanding of development?

SUMMARY

Psychoanalytic Theories

Learning Objective 2.1 What are the main ideas of Freud's theory?

- Freud emphasized that behavior is governed by both conscious and unconscious motives and that the personality develops in steps: The id is present at birth; the ego and the superego develop in childhood. Freud proposed psychosexual stages: the oral, anal, phallic, latency, and genital stages.

Learning Objective 2.2 What is the conflict associated with each of Erikson's psychosocial stages?

- Erikson proposed that personality develops in eight psychosocial stages over the course of the lifespan: trust versus mistrust; autonomy versus shame and doubt; initiative versus guilt; industry versus inferiority; identity versus role confusion; intimacy versus isolation; generativity versus stagnation; and integrity versus despair.

Learning Objective 2.3 What are the strengths and weaknesses of psychoanalytic theory?

- Psychoanalytic concepts, such as the unconscious and identity, have contributed to psychologists' understanding of development. However, these theories propose many ideas that are difficult to test.

Learning Theories

Learning Objective 2.4 How did Watson condition Little Albert to fear white, furry objects?

- Classical conditioning—learning through association of stimuli—helps explain the acquisition of emotional responses. Watson used these principles to condition a fear of white rats in an infant called "Little Albert," who generalized his fear to other white, furry objects.

Learning Objective 2.5 How does operant conditioning occur?

- Operant conditioning involves learning to repeat or stop behaviors because of their consequences. However, consequences often affect behavior in complex ways in the real world.

Learning Objective 2.6 In what ways does social-cognitive theory differ from other learning theories?

- Bandura's social-cognitive theory places more emphasis on mental elements than other learning theories do and assumes a more active role for the individual.

Learning Objective 2.7 How well do the learning theories explain development?

- Learning theories provide useful explanations of how behaviors are acquired but fall short of a truly comprehensive picture of human development.

Cognitive Theories

Learning Objective 2.8 How does cognitive development progress, according to Piaget?

- Piaget focused on the development of logical thinking. He discovered that such thinking develops across four childhood and adolescent stages: the sensorimotor, preoperational, concrete operational, and formal operational stages. He proposed that movement from one stage to another is the result of changes in mental frameworks called *schemes*.

Learning Objective 2.9 How did Vygotsky use the concepts of scaffolding and the zone of proximal development to explain cognitive development?

- Vygotsky's socio-cultural theory has become important to developmentalists' attempts to explain how culture affects development.

Learning Objective 2.10 How does information-processing theory explain the findings of developmental psychologists such as Piaget and Vygotsky?

- Information-processing theory uses the computer as a model to explain intellectual processes such as memory and problem-solving. It suggests that there are both age differences and individual differences in the efficiency with which humans use their information-processing systems.

Learning Objective 2.11 What are some of the important contributions and criticisms of the cognitive theories?

- Research has confirmed the sequence of skill development Piaget proposed but suggests that young children are more capable of logical thinking than he believed. Information-processing theory has been important in explaining Piaget's findings and memory processes.

Biological and Ecological Theories

Learning Objective 2.12 How do behavior geneticists explain individual differences?

- Behavior geneticists study the influence of heredity on individual differences and the ways in which individuals' genes influence their environments.

Learning Objective 2.13 What kinds of behaviors are of interest to ethologists and sociobiologists?

- What kinds of behaviors are of interest to ethologists and sociobiologists? Ethologists study genetically determined traits and behaviors that help animals adapt to their environments. Sociobiologists emphasize the genetic basis of behaviors that promote the development and maintenance of social organizations in both animals and humans.

Learning Objective 2.14 What is the main idea of Bronfenbrenner's bioecological theory?

- Bronfenbrenner's bioecological theory has helped developmental psychologists categorize environmental factors and think about the ways in which they influence individuals.

Comparing Theories

Learning Objective 2.15 What assumptions do the three families of theories make about development?

- Theories vary in how they answer three basic questions about development: Are individuals active or passive in their own development? How do nature and nurture interact to produce development? Does development happen continuously or in stages?

Learning Objective 2.16 On what criteria do developmentalists compare the usefulness of theories?

- Useful theories allow psychologists to devise hypotheses to test their validity, are heuristically valuable, provide practical solutions to problems, and explain the facts of development.

Learning Objective 2.17 What is eclecticism?

- Developmentalists who take an eclectic approach use theories derived from all the major families, as well as those of many disciplines, to explain and study human development.

KEY TERMS

accommodation *(p. 37)*
assimilation *(p. 36)*
behavior genetics *(p. 41)*
behaviorism *(p. 32)*
bioecological theory *(p. 43)*
classical conditioning *(p. 32)*
cognitive theories *(p. 36)*
eclecticism *(p. 47)*
ego *(p. 27)*
equilibration *(p. 37)*
ethology *(p. 42)*
extinction *(p. 33)*
id *(p. 27)*
information-processing theory *(p. 39)*
learning theories *(p. 32)*
neo-Piagetian theory *(p. 39)*
observational learning, or modeling *(p. 34)*
operant conditioning *(p. 33)*
psychoanalytic theories *(p. 27)*
psychosexual stages *(p. 28)*
psychosocial stages *(p. 30)*
punishment *(p. 33)*
reinforcement *(p. 33)*
scheme *(p. 36)*
sociobiology *(p. 43)*
sociocultural theory *(p. 38)*
superego *(p. 27)*

TEST YOURSELF

Psychoanalytic Theories

2.1 Which of the following parts of personality is entirely in our unconscious?
- a. ego
- b. superego
- c. id
- d. Oedipus

2.2 Which term best describes Freud's theory of development?
- a. psychosocial stages
- b. ego development
- c. id integrity
- d. psychosexual stages

2.3 Erikson's theory differed from Freud's in that Erikson
- a. emphasized instincts more heavily than Freud.
- b. believed that our urges are primarily destructive.
- c. believed that development continued throughout the lifespan.
- d. is considered more pessimistic than Freud.

2.4 Which of the following accurately summarizes Erikson's theory?
- a. A poor interpersonal relationship can cause individuals to fixate on problems.
- b. The superego is a more powerful force than the id and drives most behavior.
- c. Without societal pressures to conform to, we would be overly destructive.
- d. Healthy development requires confronting and resolving crises throughout the lifespan.

2.5 Identify each of the following concepts as belonging to Freud's or Erikson's theory:
- a. libido
- b. lifespan stages
- c. defense mechanisms
- d. Oedipus complex
- e. emphasis on early childhood
- f. identity crisis
- g. generativity

Learning Theories

2.6 Whenever the eye doctor puffs air in your eye, you blink. Now, before she puffs the air, she says "ready"; then she puffs the air, and you blink. After doing this several times, you begin to blink as soon as she says "ready." In this example, what kind of learning has taken place?
- a. classical conditioning
- b. sensitization
- c. operant conditioning
- d. habituation

2.7 A consequence that increases behavior is a __________, while one that decreases behavior is a __________.

2.8 Bandura suggests that learning can take place without direct reinforcement. What is this type of learning called?
- a. positive reinforcement
- b. modeling
- c. instrumental conditioning
- d. classical conditioning

2.9 Together, people's beliefs about what they can and cannot do form their
- a. identity.
- b. self-efficacy.
- c. self-esteem.
- d. self-image.

2.10 Which of the following is a weakness of learning theories?
- a. They give an accurate picture of the way many behaviors are learned.
- b. They are not really developmental theories.
- c. They tend to be optimistic about the possibility of changing behavior.
- d. They can explain both consistency and change in behavior.

Cognitive Theories

2.11 Piaget proposed that children develop cognitively by acquiring more complex schemes. How did he define schemes?

a. the action of categorizing items into groups
b. scientific theories about human development
c. cognitive structures that provide a procedure to follow in a specific situation
d. ideas we have about how to get what we want

2.12 You learn how to drive a car with an automatic transmission; then you try to drive a car with standard transmission. The adjustment you make is an example of the process of

a. equilibration.
b. assimilation.
c. accommodation.
d. hierarchical categorizing.

2.13 Chris is in elementary school and has learned to solve problems logically. Which of Piaget's stages best describes her level of cognitive development?

a. concrete operational
b. sensorimotor
c. preoperational
d. formal operational

2.14 In Vygotsky's theory, what does scaffolding mean?

a. building new schemes
b. developing a firm sense of self-identity
c. acquiring new emotional experiences through direct experience
d. modeling and structuring a child's learning experience

2.15 Information processing theorists explain Piaget's findings as the result of inefficiencies in children's __________.

2.16 Which of the following is a weakness of Piaget's theory?

a. He developed innovative methods of studying children's thinking.
b. He was wrong about the ages at which children develop specific skills.
c. His theory forced psychologists to think about child development in a new way.
d. His findings have been replicated in virtually every culture and every cohort of children since the 1920s.

Biological and Ecological Theories

2.17 Individuals' behavior

a. is completely fixed by their genetic inheritance.
b. is based totally on their relationships with their mothers.
c. will always be a joint product of the genetic pattern and the environment.
d. is based on their socioeconomic status.

2.18 __________ is the study of genetically determined behaviors that help animals adapt to their environments.

2.19 An emphasis on genetically determined behaviors that help animals and humans create and maintain social organizations is the main idea of __________.

2.20 Arrange the following contexts of Bronfenbrenner's bioecological theory in the proper order, from the largest circle to the smallest.

a. macrosystem, exosystem, microsystem, biological context
b. microsystem, biological context, macrosystem, exosystem
c. biological context, exosystem, microsystem, macrosystem
d. macrosystem, biological context, microsystem, exosystem

2.21 A child's school is a part of her

a. microsystem.
b. macrosystem.
c. exosystem.
d. mesosystem.

Comparing Theories

2.22 In which of the following theories is a person most likely to be an active participant in his own environment?

a. Freud's psychosexual theory
b. classical conditioning
c. operant conditioning
d. Piaget's cognitive-developmental theory

2.23 In which of the following theories does development happen continuously?

a. Erikson's psychosocial theory
b. classical conditioning
c. social-cognitive theory
d. cognitive developmental

2.24 According to __________, a person is more likely to be influenced by nature than by nurture.

a. Freud's psychosexual theory
b. classical conditioning
c. operant conditioning
d. Piaget's cognitive developmental theory

2.25 Which of the following is *not* one of the criteria of usefulness listed in the text?

a. Does it stimulate thinking and research?
b. Does it explain the basic facts of development?
c. Does it explain a person's motivation for his or her behavior?
d. Does it generate predictions that can be tested with scientific methods?

2.26 When developmentalists incorporate multiple theoretical perspectives into explanations of age-related change, they are using an approach known as __________.

PEARSON

mydevelopmentlab Study Plan

Are You Ready for the Test?

Students who use the study materials on MyDevelopmentLab report higher grades in the course than those who use the text alone. Here are three easy steps to mastering this chapter and improving your grade...

Step 1

Take the chapter pre-test in MyDevelopmentLab and review your customized Study Plan.

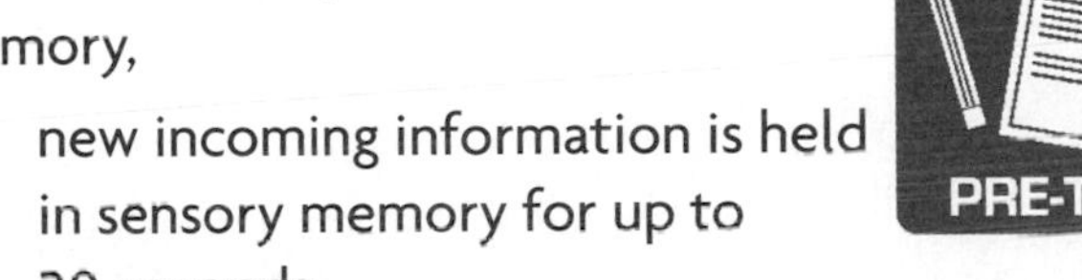

PRE-TEST

In the information-processing model of memory,

- new incoming information is held in sensory memory for up to 20 seconds.
- when you need to use information from long-term memory, it is retrieved by your sensory memory.
- Information moves from sensory memory to short-term memory.
- information is transferred from short-term memory to sensory memory for processing.

Step 2

Use MyDevelopmentLab's Multimedia Library to help strengthen your knowledge of the chapter.

Explore: Three Stages of Classical

The Three Stages of Classical Conditioning

The response made to the conditioned stimulus is termed the conditioned response.

What animals learn in classical conditioning is that the conditioned stimulus predicts the delivery of the unconditioned stimulus.

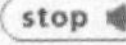

back | stop | start over

Learning Objective 2.4

How did Watson condition Little Albert to fear white, furry objects?

www.mydevelopmentlab.com

continued on the next page

Students who regularly complete MyDevelopmentLab activities score two grades higher, on average, on exams compared with students who do not use MyDevelopmentLab.

Explore: Piaget's Stages of Cognitive Development

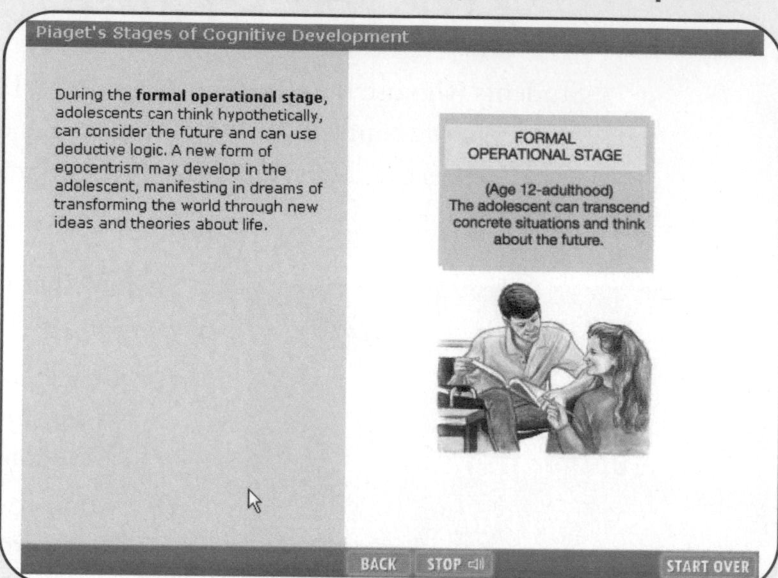
Piaget's Stages of Cognitive Development
During the formal operational stage, adolescents can think hypothetically, can consider the future and can use deductive logic. A new form of egocentrism may develop in the adolescent, manifesting in dreams of transforming the world through new ideas and theories about life.
FORMAL OPERATIONAL STAGE
(Age 12-adulthood)
The adolescent can transcend concrete situations and think about the future.
BACK
STOP
START OVER

Learning Objective 2.8

How does cognitive development progress, according to Piaget?

Explore: Human Development: No Man is an Island

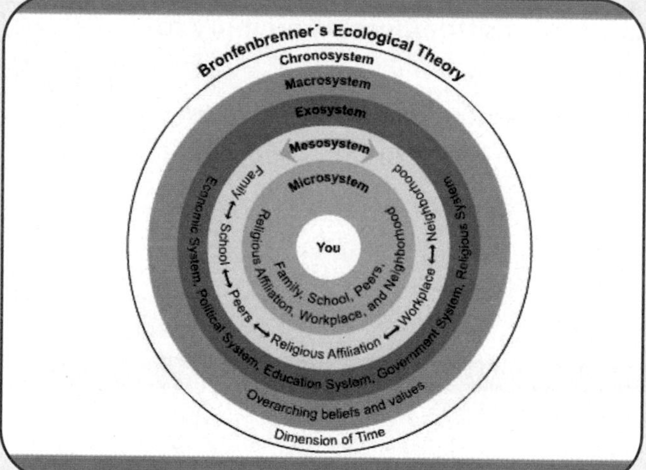
Bronfenbrenner's Ecological Theory
Chronosystem
Macrosystem
Exosystem
Mesosystem
Microsystem
You
Family, School, Peers, Religious Affiliation, Workplace, and Neighborhood
Family ⟷ School ⟷ Peers ⟷ Religious Affiliation ⟷ Workplace ⟷ Neighborhood
Economic System, Political System, Education System, Government System, Religious System
Overarching beliefs and values
Dimension of Time

Learning Objective 2.14

What is the main idea of Bronfenbrenner's bioecological theory?

Step 3

Take the chapter post-test and compare your results against the pre-test.

POST-TEST

Erikson's theory is known as a psychosocial theory because he thought that

- people could not deal with psychological demands unless they had the support of their friends.
- psychological forces were more important for development than social forces.
- internal sexual drives needed to be shaped by social forces for there to be successful adjustment.
- development resulted from the interaction between internal drives and cultural demands.

Prenatal Development and Birth

How many different kinds of twins are there? A simple answer to this question is standard content in human development textbooks: Identical twins, two individuals that develop from a single fertilized egg, and fraternal twins, two individuals who develop from separate fertilized eggs. But did you know that there is a third type of twins in which the two individuals develop from a single egg that has been fertilized by two sperm? Such twins are known as "semi-identical" because they are identical with respect to the genes they received from their mother but are not identical with regard to their father's genes.

Like many scientific discoveries, the revelation that twins can be semi-identical as well as identical and fraternal occurred accidentally (Whitfield, 2007). Genetic researchers at Good Samaritan Hospital in Phoenix, Arizona, were presented with the puzzling case of two

infants who appeared to be identical twins but who differed in genital anatomy. One of the infants appeared to be a normal male, but the other child had genitals that were neither clearly male nor female. Tests showed that the body of the twin with ambiguous genitalia possessed both male and female tissue. Although the twin with normal genitalia did not have any actual female tissues, DNA analysis revealed that both boys' bodies were carrying male and female genes. Further testing showed that the boys had developed from a single egg and two sperm, one of which was male and the other of which was female. Moreover, each boy received a different mix of genes from the two sperm. It was this different combination of genes from their father that led to the anatomical difference between the two boys' genitalia. (By the way, the boys are completely normal in every other way.)

Although rare, such cases point out that scientists' understanding of much of human development relies on reason rather than on direct observation. With modern reproductive technology, conception can be directly observed in laboratories, but no one knows whether what happens in laboratory test tubes generalizes to conception that happens naturally inside a woman's body. Indeed, laboratory studies of conception would lead scientists to logically conclude that an embryo could not possibly develop from one egg and two sperm. Yet, the semi-identical twins who were studied by the Good Samaritan researchers are living proof that scientists still have a great deal to learn about conception and prenatal development.

A photographer snapped this amazing photo showing the tiny hand of a 21-week-old fetus grasping the finger of the surgeon who had just completed an operation to correct a serious malformation of the fetus's spine. New technologies have not only allowed for the development of prenatal treatment strategies for correcting birth defects, but they have also revealed many features of prenatal development that were unimaginable just a few decades ago.

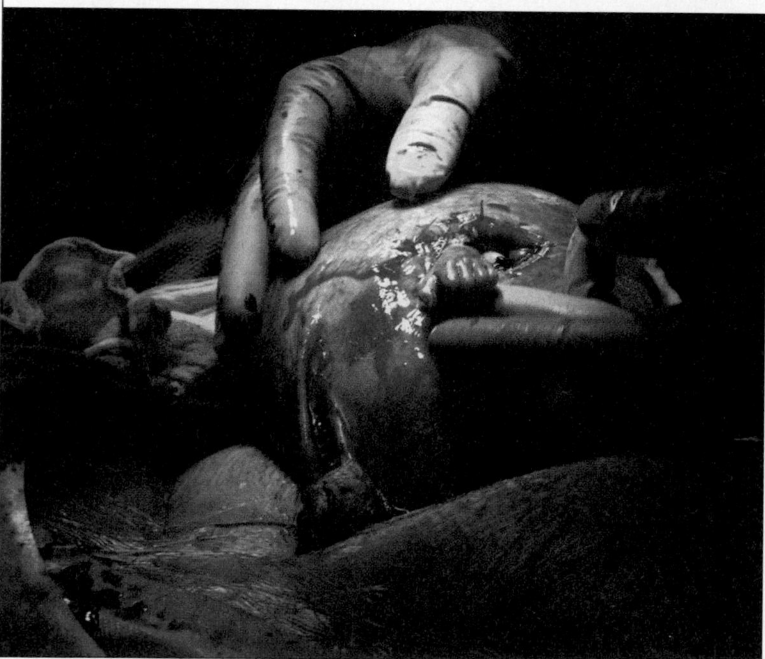

New technologies that are evolving at a breathtaking pace enabled the Good Samaritan researchers to trace each gene in the twins' body to the parent from whom it originated and to the two sperm that were involved in the boys' conception. Thanks to these technologies, scientists are gaining insight into prenatal developmental processes that were shrouded in mystery just a few decades ago. In this chapter, you will become acquainted with some of these insights and, we hope, gain a greater appreciation for the amazing process of prenatal development. You will also learn about the beginning of the developmental process: conception, prenatal development, and birth.

Conception and Genetics

The first step in the development of an individual human being happens at conception, when each of us receives a combination of genes that will shape our experiences throughout the rest of our lives.

The Process of Conception

Learning Objective 3.1
What are the characteristics of the zygote?

Ordinarily, a woman produces one *ovum* (egg cell) per month from one of her two ovaries, roughly midway between menstrual periods. If the ovum is not fertilized, it travels from the ovary down the *fallopian tube* toward the *uterus*, where it gradually disintegrates and is expelled as part of the menstrual fluid. However, if a couple has intercourse during the crucial few days when the ovum is in the fallopian tube, one of the millions of sperm ejaculated as part of each male orgasm may travel the full distance through the woman's vagina, cervix, uterus, and fallopian tube and penetrate the wall of the ovum.

Chromosomes, DNA, and Genes As you probably know, every cell in the human body contains 23 pairs of **chromosomes**, or strings of genetic material. However, sperm and ovum, collectively called **gametes**, contain 23 single (unpaired) chromosomes. At conception, chromosomes in the ovum and the sperm combine to form 23 pairs in an entirely new cell called a **zygote**.

Chromosomes are composed of molecules of **deoxyribonucleic acid (DNA)**. Each chromosome can be further subdivided into segments, called **genes**, each of which influences a particular feature or developmental pattern. A gene controlling some specific characteristic always appears in the same place (the *locus*) on the same chromosome in every individual of the same species. For example, the locus of the gene that determines whether a person's blood is type A, B, or O is on chromosome 9.

chromosomes strings of genetic material in the nuclei of cells

gametes cells that unite at conception (ova in females; sperm in males)

zygote single cell created when sperm and ovum unite

deoxyribonucleic acid (DNA) chemical material that makes up chromosomes and genes

genes pieces of genetic material that control or influence traits

gonads sex glands (ovaries in females; testes in males)

Determination of Sex Twenty-two pairs of chromosomes, called *autosomes*, contain most of the genetic information for the new individual. The twenty-third pair, the *sex chromosomes*, determine the sex. One of the two sex chromosomes, the *X chromosome*, is one of the largest chromosomes in the body and carries a large number of genes. The other, the *Y chromosome*, is quite small and contains only a few genes. Zygotes containing two X chromosomes develop into females, and those containing one X and one Y chromosome develop into males. Since the cells in a woman's body contain only X chromosomes, all her ova carry X chromosomes. Half of a man's sperm contain X chromosomes; the other half contain Y chromosomes. Consequently, the sex of the new individual is determined by the sex chromosome in the sperm.

How do chromosomal differences become physical differences between males and females? Sometime between the 4 and 8 weeks following conception, the *SRY* gene on the Y chromosome signals the male embryo's body to begin secreting hormones called *androgens*. These hormones cause male genitals to develop. If androgens are not present, female genitals develop no matter what the embryo's chromosomal status is. Likewise, female embryos that are exposed to androgens, either via medications that the mother is taking or a genetic disorder called *congenital adrenal hyperplasia*, can develop male-appearing external genitalia. Development of the **gonads**, testes in males and ovaries in females, also depends upon the presence or absence of androgens. Prenatal androgens also influence the developing brain and may play a role in the development of sex differences in cognitive functioning and in the development of sexual orientation (Lippa, 2005). (We will explore these topics in greater detail in later chapters.)

Each cell in the human body has 23 pairs of chromosomes in its nucleus. The 23 single chromosomes in a female gamete, or egg, combine with the 23 single chromosomes in a male gamete, or sperm, to create a new, genetically unique array of 23 pairs of chromosomes that contain all of the instructions needed to guide the development of a human being from conception forward and which will influence him or her throughout life.

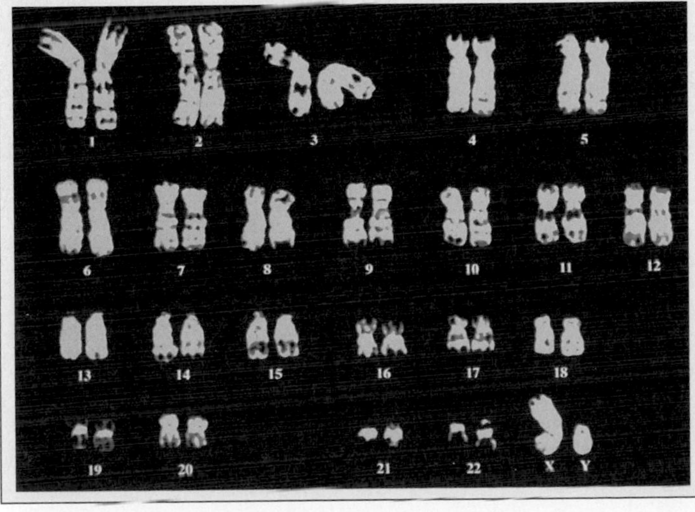

Male

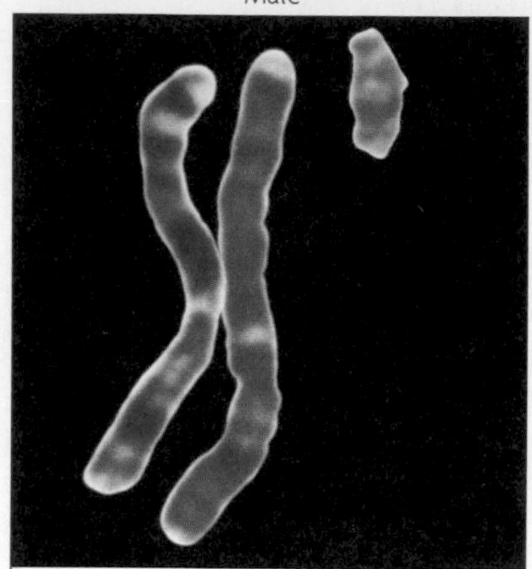

Female

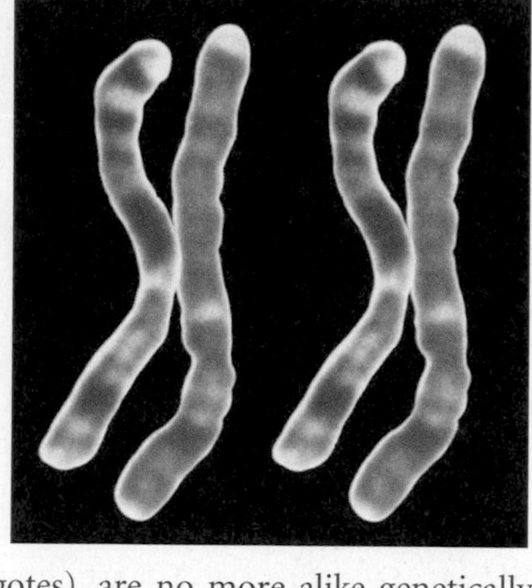

The X chromosomes are quite large and carry thousands of genes. By contrast, the Y chromosome is very small and carries little genetic information. The mismatch between the genetic material on the X and Y chromosomes leaves males more vulnerable to some genetic disorders than females are. That's because if a female has a harmful gene on one of her X chromosomes, it is likely to be balanced by a corresponding gene on her other X chromosome that either blocks or minimizes the effects of the harmful gene.

Multiple Births In most cases, human infants are conceived and born one at a time. However, in about 4 out of every 100 births, more than one baby is born, usually twins. As noted in the discussion at the outset of the chapter, the phenomenon of semi-identical twinning is very rare. Experts estimate that it occurs in less than 1% of all conceptions, and the resulting zygotes rarely survive (Whitfield, 2007). In most cases, as many as two-thirds of twins are *fraternal twins*, or twins that come from two sets of ova and sperm. Such twins, also called *dizygotic twins* (meaning that they originate from two zygotes), are no more alike genetically than any other pair of siblings, and need not even be of the same sex.

The remaining one-third of twins are *identical twins* (*monozygotic*, or arising from one zygote). Identical twins result when a single zygote, for unknown reasons, separates into two parts, each of which develops into a separate individual. Because identical twins develop from the same zygote, they have identical genes. Research involving identical twins is one of the major investigative strategies in the field of behavior genetics (see the Research Report).

Over the past 30 years, the annual number of multiple births has increased about 66% in the United States (National Center for Health Statistics [NCHS], Martin et al., 2005). One reason for the increase is that the number of women over 35 giving birth for the first time has grown. There are two factors that underlie the association between multiple births and ma-

RESEARCH REPORT

Twins in Genetic Research

Researchers interested in the role of heredity in human development have been comparing identical and fraternal twins since the earliest days of developmental psychology. The logic is this: If identical twins (whose genes are exactly the same) who are raised apart are more similar than fraternal twins or non-twin siblings (whose genes are similar, but not identical) who are raised together, heredity must be important in the trait being studied. For example, the numbers below are correlations based on several studies of twins' intelligence test scores (Bouchard & McGue, 1981, p. 1056, Fig. 1). Recall from Chapter 1 that the closer to 1.00 a correlation is, the stronger the relationship.

Identical twins reared together	.85
Identical twins reared apart	.67
Fraternal twins reared together	.58
Non-twin siblings reared apart	.24

As you can see, intelligence test scores are more strongly correlated in identical twins than in fraternal twins or non-twin siblings, even when the identical twins are raised in different families. Such findings are taken to be evidence for the heritability of intelligence.

Developmentalists have also studied emotional characteristics in identical and fraternal twins. For example, researchers in Sweden examined 99 pairs of identical twins and 229 pairs of fraternal twins reared apart, and then compared these to twins reared together (Bergeman et al., 1993). Identical twins, whether raised together or apart, were found to be more similar than fraternal twins on measures of emotionality, activity, and sociability.

Taken together, the findings of these studies point to strong genetic components in both intelligence and emotional characteristics. However, what these studies reveal about environment may be even more significant. If psychological characteristics such as intelligence, emotionality, activity, and sociability were determined solely by heredity, identical twins would be *exactly* alike, and researchers would find correlations of +1.00. The correlations twin researchers have found are less than +1.00, even for identical twins who grow up in the same home. Moreover, the correlations for identical twins raised apart are lower than those for identical twins raised together.

To see the point more clearly, think about blood type. An individual's blood type *is* determined by the genes. Thus, identical twins always have the same blood type; that is, there is a correlation of +1.00, a perfect correlation, between the blood types of identical twins. Identical twin studies offer strong evidence that psychological traits, though clearly influenced by heredity, are not determined by the genes to the same extent as physical traits such as blood type.

Questions for Critical Analysis

1. Fraternal twins are no more genetically similar than non-twin siblings, yet the IQs of fraternal twins are more strongly correlated than those of non-twin brothers and sisters. What explanations can you think of to explain this difference?
2. The term *environment* is extremely broad. What are some of the individual variables that comprise an individual's environment?

ternal age (Reynolds, Schieve, Martin, Jeng, & Macaluso, 2003). First, for reasons that researchers don't yet understand, women are far more likely to naturally conceive twins and other multiples after age 35. Second, women over 35 are more likely than younger women to experience difficulty becoming pregnant and, thus, are more likely to be treated with fertility-enhancing drugs. Women of all ages who use these drugs are more likely to deliver multiples than women who conceive naturally.

How Genes Influence Development

Learning Objective 3.2
In what ways do genes influence development?

At conception, the genes from the father contained in the sperm and those from the mother in the ovum combine to create a unique genetic blueprint—the **genotype**—that characterizes the new individual. The **phenotype** is the individual's whole set of actual characteristics. One way to remember the distinction is that the phenotype can be identified by directly observing the individual. For example, you can easily see that a woman has brown eyes, which are part of her phenotype. Her genotype, though, can't be so easily determined. In many cases, you have to know her parents' and offsprings' eye color to find out whether she carries genes for another eye color, because complex rules govern the way genotypes influence phenotypes.

Dominant and Recessive Genes The simplest genetic rule is the **dominant-recessive pattern,** in which a single dominant gene strongly influences phenotype. (Table 3.1 lists several normal phenotypical traits and indicates whether they arise from dominant or recessive genes.) People whose chromosomes carry either two dominant or two recessive genes are referred to as *homozygous*. Those with one dominant and one recessive gene are said to be *heterozygous*.

If a child receives a single dominant gene for a trait from one parent, the child's phenotype will include the trait determined by that gene. In contrast, a child's phenotype will include a recessive trait only if she inherits a recessive gene from both parents. For example, geneticists have found that the curliness of hair is controlled by a single pair of genes (see Figure 3.1, page 58). The gene for curly hair is dominant; therefore, if a man has curly hair, his genotype includes at least one gene for curly hair and half of his sperm carry this gene. Conversely, straight hair is recessive, so a straight-haired man's genotype must include two straight-hair genes for his phenotype to include straight hair. Geneticists also know that the only kind of hair type a straight-haired father can pass on to his children is straight hair, because all his sperm carry recessive, straight-hair genes.

Table 3.1 Genetic Sources of Normal Traits

Dominant Genes	Recessive Genes	Polygenic (many genes)
Freckles	Flat feet	Height
Coarse hair	Thin lips	Body type
Dimples	Rh-negative blood	Eye color
Curly hair	Fine hair	Skin color
Nearsightedness	Red hair	Personality
Broad lips	Blond hair	
Rh-positive blood	Type O blood	
Types A and B blood		
Dark hair		

(*Source*: Tortora & Grabowski, 1993.)

genotype the unique genetic blueprint of each individual

phenotype an individual's particular set of observed characteristics

dominant-recessive pattern pattern of inheritance in which a single dominant gene influences a person's phenotype but two recessive genes are necessary to produce an associated trait

Figure 3.1
The Genetics of Hair Type

Examples of how the genes for curly and straight hair pass from parents to children.

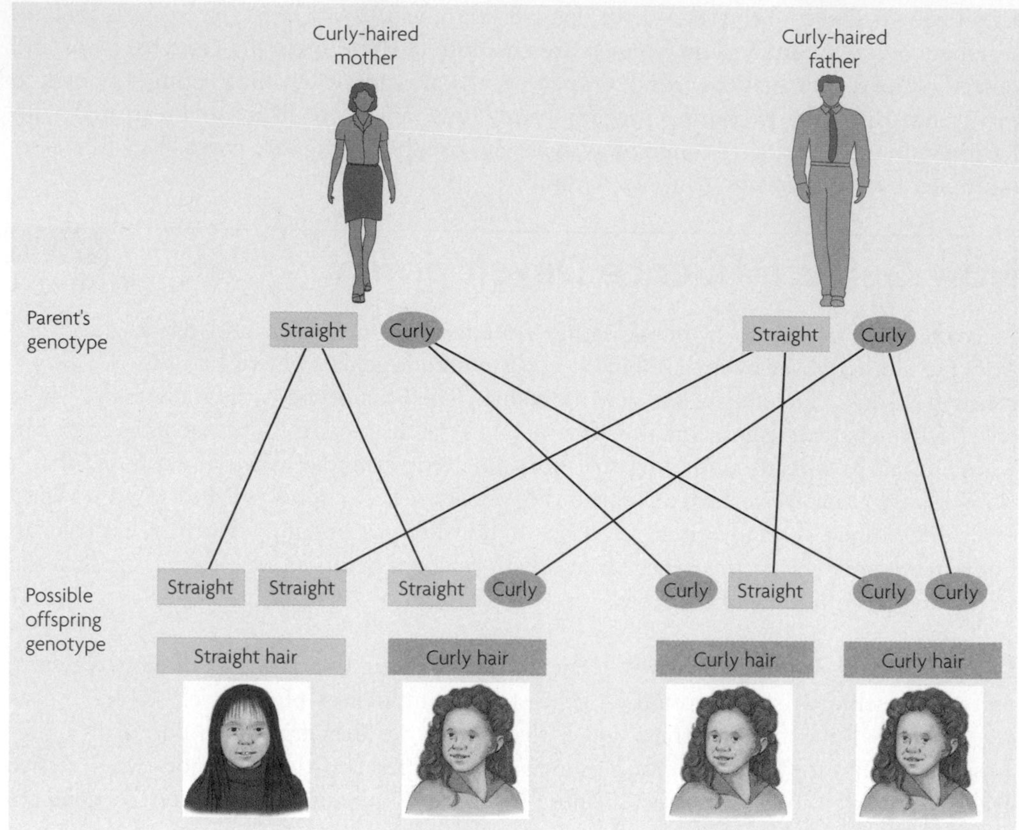

In addition, human geneticists have learned that both dominant and recessive genes differ in *expressivity*, meaning that the degree to which any gene influences phenotypes varies from person to person. For example, all individuals who have the gene for curly hair don't have equally curly hair. So, even when a child receives a dominant gene for curly hair from her father, the amount and type of curl in her hair probably won't be exactly the same as his.

Blood type is also determined by a dominant-recessive pattern of inheritance. Because a person must have two recessive genes to have type O blood, the genotype of every person who has this type is clear. However, the genotype of people with type A or B blood is not obvious because types A and B are dominant. Thus, when a person's phenotype includes either type A or type B blood, one of the person's blood type genes must be for that type, but the other could be for some other type. However, if a type A father and a type B mother produce a child with type O, each of them carries a gene for type O, because the child must receive one such gene from each parent to have the type O phenotype.

Polygenic Inheritance With **polygenic inheritance**, many genes influence the phenotype. There are many polygenic traits in which the dominant-recessive pattern is also at work. For example, geneticists believe that children get three genes for skin color from each parent (Tortora & Grabowski, 1993). Dark skin is dominant over light skin, but the skin colors also blend together. Thus, when one parent is dark-skinned and the other is fair-skinned, the child will have skin that is somewhere between the two. The dark-skinned parent's dominant genes will ensure that the child will be darker than the fair parent, but the fair-skinned parent's genes will prevent the child from having skin as dark as that of the dark-skinned parent.

Eye color is another polygenic trait with a dominant-recessive pattern (Tortora & Grabowski, 1993). Scientists don't know for sure how many genes influence eye color. They do know, however, that these genes don't cause specific colors. Instead, they cause the colored part of the eye to be dark or light. Dark colors (black, brown, hazel, and green) are dominant over light colors (blue and gray). However, blended colors are also possible. People whose chromosomes carry a combination of genes for green, blue, and gray eyes can have blue-gray,

polygenic inheritance pattern of inheritance in which many genes influence a trait

green-blue, or blue-green eyes. Likewise, genes that cause different shades of brown can combine their effects to make children's eye color phenotypes different from those of their brown-eyed parents.

Many genes influence height, and they are not subject to a dominant-recessive pattern of inheritance. Most geneticists believe that each height gene has a small influence over a child's size (Tanner, 1990).

Other Types of Inheritance You probably learned about dominant and recessive traits in high school biology and came away with the impression that they represented the only rules that govern how genotypes are expressed as phenotypes. But there are several other modes of genetic transmission; two of them have gained an increasing amount of attention in recent years.

Geneticists have been aware of the process of *genomic imprinting* for some time, but recent technological advances have enabled them to more fully study its impact on development. A genomic imprint is a chemical label that identifies each gene in a person's body as having come from his father or mother. Research indicates that some genes are harmful only if they are tagged as having come from the father and others cause disorders only if they originated from the mother (Jirtle & Weidman, 2007). Scientists don't yet fully understand the process of genomic imprinting and how it affects development. It could be that genomic imprints "turn on" an atypical developmental process or "turn off" a normal one. Alternatively, the imprints may evoke responses in other genes or tissues in the developing individual's body that set the process of atypical development in motion. Some studies suggest that age-related deterioration of genomic imprints may be particularly important in diseases that appear later in life, including several kinds of cancer, Type II diabetes, and heart disease (Jirtle & Weidman, 2007).

Studies involving genetic material that is found in the mitochondria, rather than the nucleus, of a woman's eggs have gained importance in recent years as well. In *mitochrondrial inheritance*, children inherit genes that are carried in structures called *mitochondria* which are found in the fluid that surrounds the nucleus of the ovum before it is fertilized. Consequently, mitochondrial genes are passed only from mother to child. Geneticists have learned that several serious disorders, including some types of blindness, are transmitted in this way. In most such cases, the mother herself is unaffected by the harmful genes (Amato, 1998).

Multi-Factorial Inheritance There are many physical traits that are influenced by both genes and environment, a pattern known as **multi-factorial inheritance**. Height is one example. If a child is ill, poorly nourished, or emotionally neglected, he may be smaller than others his age. Thus, when a child is shorter than 97% of his agemates, doctors try to determine whether he is short because of his genes or because something is causing him to grow poorly (Sulkes, 1998; Tanner, 1990).

As discussed in Chapter 1 and in the Research Report on page 10, psychological traits such as intelligence and personality are influenced by both heredity and environment. Thus, they result from multi-factorial inheritance. But just how do genes and environment work together to produce variations in such traits? A set of five general principles proposed by Michael Rutter and his colleagues (1997) can help organize our thinking about this question:

- *"Individuals differ in their reactivity to the environment"* (p. 338). Some individuals are highly reactive, highly sensitive to stress or strangeness; others react with much less volatility.
- *"There is a two-way interplay between individuals and their environments"* (p. 338). It is important not to think of this process as a one-way street. Influences go back and forth.
- *"The interplay between persons and their environments needs to be considered within an ecological framework"* (p. 339). Although our research nearly always treats environmental events—such as divorce—as if they were constant, they are not. Such events vary as a function of culture, poverty, family structure, and a whole host of other variables.

multi-factorial inheritance inheritance affected by both genes and the environment

- *"People process their experiences rather than just serve as passive recipients of environmental forces"* (p. 339). It is the meaning each person attaches to an experience that governs the effect, not the experience itself. Thus, the "same" experience can have widely differing effects, depending on how the individual interprets it.
- *"People act on their environment so as to shape and select their experiences"* (p. 339). For instance, a child with a genetic predisposition toward shyness may choose not to play organized sports. As a result, he will not have the same opportunity to gain information about his athletic (and presumably genetic) talents as a more outgoing child who enjoys being in groups. Because of his choice, the shy child will have fewer opportunities than the outgoing child to learn and practice athletic skills.

Critical Thinking

1. In what ways have genetic and environmental influences interacted to influence your development?

Genetic and Chromosomal Disorders

Did you know that the chances that a pregnancy will end with the birth of a healthy baby are about 97%? Of the 3% of births in which the health of a newborn is impaired or seriously threatened, about 30% are the result of harmful genes or errors in the process of early development that have altered a child's chromosomal makeup (CDC, 2005).

Learning Objective 3.3

What are the effects of the major dominant, recessive, and sex-linked diseases?

Genetic Disorders

Many disorders appear to be transmitted through the operation of dominant and recessive genes (see Table 3.2). *Autosomal disorders* are caused by genes located on the autosomes (chromosomes other than sex chromosomes). The genes that cause *sex-linked* disorders are found on the X chromosome.

Autosomal Disorders Most disorders caused by recessive genes are diagnosed in infancy or early childhood. For example, a recessive gene causes a baby to have problems digesting the amino acid phenylalanine. Toxins build up in the baby's brain and cause mental retardation. This condition, called *phenylketonuria (PKU)*, is found in about 1 in every 10,000 babies (Nicholson, 1998). If a baby consumes no foods containing phenylalanine, however, he will not develop mental retardation. Milk is one of the foods PKU babies can't have, so early diagnosis is critical. For this reason, most states require all babies to be tested for PKU soon after birth.

Like many recessive disorders, PKU is associated with ethnicity. Caucasian babies are more likely to have the disorder than infants in other groups. Similarly, West African and

Table 3.2 Some Genetic Disorders

Autosomal Dominant Disorders	Autosomal Recessive Disorders	Sex-Linked Recessive Disorders
Huntington's disease	Phenylketonuria	Hemophilia
High blood pressure	Sickle-cell disease	Fragile-X syndrome
Extra fingers	Cystic fibrosis	Red-green color blindness
Migraine headaches	Tay-Sachs disease	Missing front teeth
Schizophrenia	Kidney cysts in infants	Night blindness
	Albinism	Some types of muscular dystrophy
		Some types of diabetes

(*Sources*: Amato, 1998; Tortora & Grabowski, 1993.)

African American infants are more likely to suffer from *sickle-cell disease*, a recessive disorder that causes red blood cell deformities (Scott, 1998). In sickle-cell disease, the blood can't carry enough oxygen to keep the body's tissues healthy. Few children with sickle-cell disease live past the age of 20, and most who survive to adulthood die before they are 40 (Scott, 1998).

Almost one-half of West Africans have either sickle-cell disease or *sickle-cell trait* (Amato, 1998). Persons with sickle-cell trait carry a single recessive gene for sickle-cell disease, which causes a few of their red blood cells to be abnormal. Thus, doctors can identify carriers of the sickle-cell gene by testing their blood for sickle-cell trait. Once potential parents know they carry the gene, they can make informed decisions about future childbearing. In the United States, about 1 in 650 African Americans has sickle-cell disease, and 1 in 8 has sickle-cell trait. The disease and trait also occur more frequently in Americans of Mediterranean, Caribbean, Indian, Arab, and Latin American ancestry than in those of European ancestry (Wong, 1993).

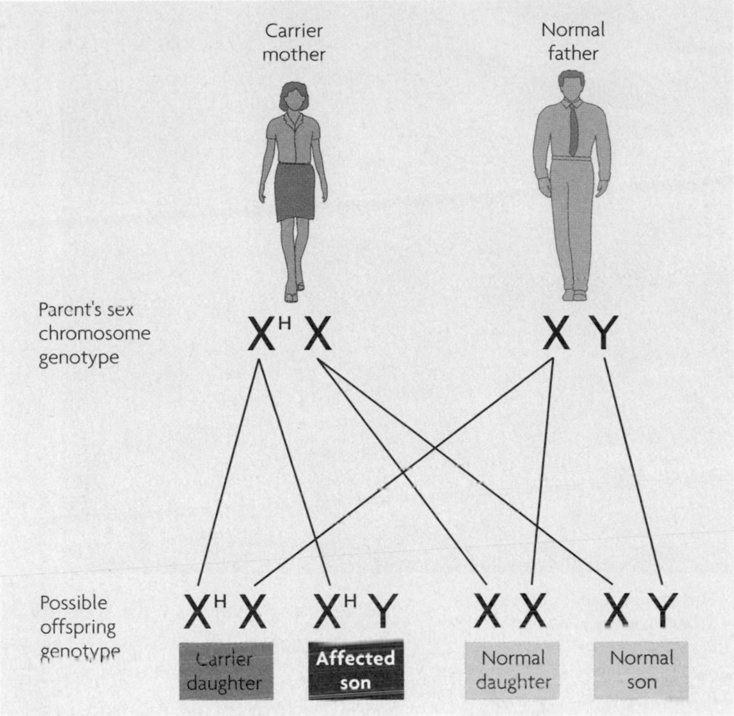

Figure 3.2
Sex-Linked Inheritance

Compare this pattern of sex-linked transmission of a recessive disease (hemophilia) with the pattern shown in Figure 3.2.

About 1 in every 3,000 babies born to Jewish couples of Eastern European ancestry suffers from another recessive disorder, *Tay-Sachs disease*. By the time she is 1 to 2 years old, a Tay-Sachs baby is likely to have severe mental retardation and be blind. Very few survive past the age of 3 (Painter & Bergman, 1998).

Disorders caused by dominant genes, such as *Huntington's disease*, are usually not diagnosed until adulthood (Amato, 1998). This disorder causes the brain to deteriorate and affects both psychological and motor functions. Until recently, children of Huntington's disease sufferers had to wait until they became ill themselves to know for sure that they carried the gene. There is now a blood test to identify the Huntington's gene. Thus, people who have a parent with this disease can now make better decisions about their own childbearing, as well as prepare themselves to live with a serious disorder when they get older.

Sex-Linked Disorders Most sex-linked disorders are caused by recessive genes (see Figure 3.2). One fairly common sex-linked recessive disorder is *red green color blindness*. People with this disorder have difficulty distinguishing between the colors red and green when these colors are adjacent. About 1 in 800 men and 1 in 400 women have this disorder. Most learn ways of compensating for the disorder and thus live perfectly normal lives.

A more serious sex-linked recessive disorder is *hemophilia*. The blood of people with hemophilia lacks the chemical components that cause blood to clot. Thus, when a person with hemophilia bleeds, the bleeding doesn't stop naturally. Approximately 1 in 5,000 baby boys is born with this disorder, which is almost unknown in girls (Scott, 1998).

About 1 in every 1,500 males and 1 in every 2,500 females have a sex-linked disorder called *fragile-X syndrome* (Amato, 1998). A person with this disorder has an X chromosome with a "fragile," or damaged, spot. Fragile-X syndrome can cause mental retardation that becomes progressively worse as a child gets older (Adesman, 1996). In fact, experts estimate that 5–7% of all males with mental retardation have fragile-X syndrome (Zigler & Hodapp, 1991).

Chromosomal Errors

Learning Objective 3.4

How do trisomies and other disorders of the autosomes and sex chromosomes affect development?

A variety of problems can be caused when a child has too many or too few chromosomes, a condition referred to as a *chromosomal error*, or *chromosomal anomaly*. Like genetic disorders, these are distinguished by whether they involve autosomes or sex chromosomes.

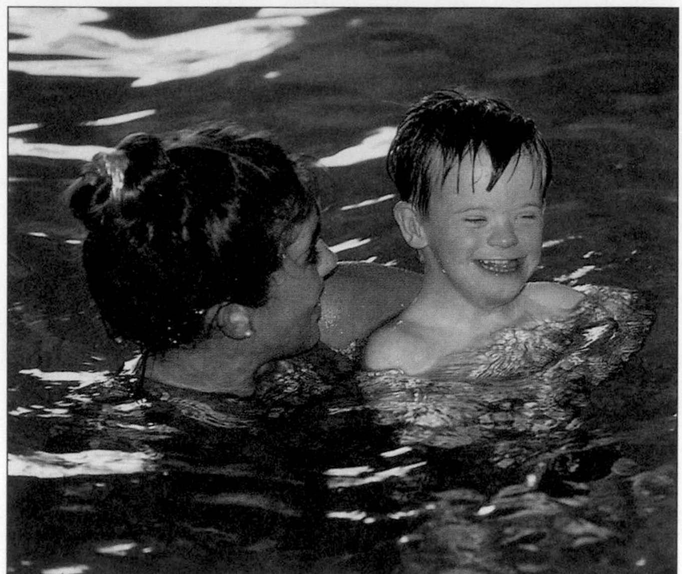

This child shows the distinctive facial features of a child with Down syndrome.

Trisomies A *trisomy* is a condition in which a child has three copies of a specific autosome. The most common is *trisomy 21*, or *Down syndrome*, in which the child has three copies of chromosome 21. Roughly 1 in every 800–1,000 infants is born with this abnormality (Nightingale & Goodman, 1990). These children have mental retardation and have distinctive facial features, smaller brains, and often other physical abnormalities such as heart defects (Haier et al., 1995).

The risk of bearing a child with trisomy 21 is greatest for mothers over 35. Among women aged 35–39, the incidence of Down syndrome is about 1 in 280 births. Among those over 45, it is as high as 1 in 50 births (D'Alton & DeCherney, 1993).

Scientists have identified children with trisomies in the 13th and 18th pairs of chromosomes as well (Amato, 1998). These disorders have more severe effects than trisomy 21. Few trisomy 13 or trisomy 18 children live past the age of 1 year. As with trisomy 21, the chances of having a child with one of these disorders increase with a woman's age.

Sex-Chromosome Anomalies A second class of anomalies is associated with the sex chromosomes. The most common is an XXY pattern, called *Klinefelter's syndrome*, that occurs in 1 or 2 out of every 1,000 males (Amato, 1998). Affected boys usually look normal but have underdeveloped testes and, as adults, very low sperm production. Many have language and learning disabilities. At puberty, these boys experience both male and female changes. For example, their penises enlarge and their breasts develop.

A single-X pattern (X0), called *Turner's syndrome*, may also occur. Individuals with Turner's syndrome are anatomically female but show stunted growth and are usually sterile. Without hormone therapy, they do not menstruate or develop breasts at puberty. About one-fourth have serious heart defects (Amato, 1998). These girls also show an imbalance in their cognitive skills: They often perform particularly poorly on tests that measure spatial ability but usually perform at or above normal levels on tests of verbal skill (Golombok & Fivush, 1994).

Neither Klinefelter's nor Turner's syndrome is associated with the mother's age. However, older mothers are more likely to produce normal-appearing girls with an extra X chromosome and boys with an extra Y chromosome (Amato, 1998). Females with an XXX pattern, about 1 in every 1,000 female births, are usually of normal size but develop more slowly than their peers (Amato, 1998). Many, though not all, have poor verbal abilities, score low on intelligence tests, and do more poorly in school than other groups with sex chromosome anomalies (Bender, Harmon, Linden, & Robinson, 1995).

Approximately 1 in 1,000 boys has an extra Y chromosome. Most are taller than average and have large teeth. They usually experience normal puberty, and they have no difficulty fathering children (Amato, 1998). Developmentalists now know that it is only a myth that an extra Y chromosome causes below-average intelligence and high aggression (Tortora & Grabowski, 1993).

Critical Thinking

1. In your view, what are the advantages and disadvantages of genetic counseling for couples who want to have a child but who are concerned about genetic or chromosomal disorder that runs in one or both of their families?

Pregnancy and Prenatal Development

Pregnancy is a physical condition in which a woman's body is nurturing a developing embryo or fetus. *Prenatal development*, or *gestation*, is the process that transforms a zygote into a newborn. Thus, the process that ends with the birth of a baby involves two sets of experiences: those of the pregnant woman, and those of the developing zygote, embryo, and fetus.

The Mother's Experience

Learning Objective 3.5

What are the characteristics of each of the trimesters of pregnancy?

Pregnancy is customarily divided into trimesters, three periods of 3 months each (see Table 3.3).

First Trimester Pregnancy begins when the zygote implants itself in the lining of the woman's uterus (also called the *womb*). The zygote then sends out chemical messages that cause the woman's menstrual periods to stop. Some of these chemicals are excreted in her urine, making it possible to diagnose pregnancy within a few days after conception. Other chemicals cause physical changes, such as breast enlargement.

The *cervix* (the narrow, lower portion of the uterus, which extends into the vagina) thickens and secretes mucus that serves as a barrier to protect the developing embryo from harmful organisms that might enter the womb through the vagina. The uterus begins to shift position and put pressure on the woman's bladder, causing her to urinate more often. This and other symptoms, like fatigue and breast tenderness, may interfere with sleep. Another common early symptom of pregnancy is *morning sickness*—feelings of nausea, often accompanied by vomiting, that usually occur in the morning.

Table 3.3 Milestones of Pregnancy

Trimester	Events	Prenatal Care	Serious Problems
First trimester: From first day of last menstrual period (LMP) to 12 weeks	Missed period Breast enlargement Abdominal thickening	Confirmation of pregnancy Calculation of due date Blood and urine tests (and other tests if needed) Monthly doctor visits to monitor vital functions, uterine growth, weight gain, sugar and protein in urine	Ectopic pregnancy Abnormal urine or blood tests Increased blood pressure Malnutrition Bleeding Miscarriage
Second trimester: From 12 weeks after LMP to 24 weeks after LMP	Weight gain "Showing" Fetal movements felt Increased appetite	Monthly doctor visits continue Ultrasound to measure fetal growth and locate placenta	Gestational diabetes Excessive weight gain Increased blood pressure Rh incompatibility of mother and fetus Miscarriage 13 to 20 weeks Premature labor 21+ weeks
Third trimester: From 25 weeks after LMP to beginning of labor	Weight gain Breast discharge	Weekly visits beginning at 32nd week Ultrasound to assess position of fetus Treatment of Rh incompatibility if needed Pelvic exams to check for cervical dilation	Increased blood pressure Bleeding Premature labor Bladder infection

(*Sources*: Hobbs & Ferth, 1993; Kliegman, 1998; Tortora & Grabowski, 1993.)

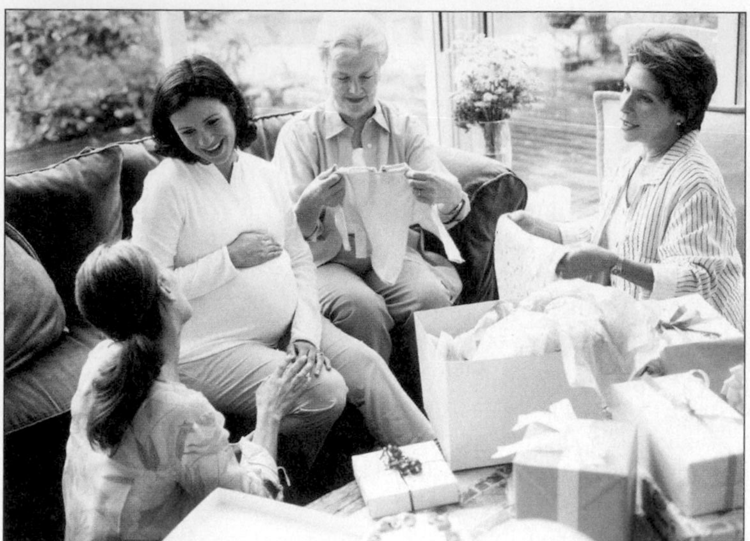

Supportive partners, friends, and relatives can help third-trimester mothers-to-be maintain positive attitudes and balance negative emotions, which often accompany their feelings of physical awkwardness, against the anticipated joy of birth.

Prenatal care during the first trimester is critical to prevent birth defects, because all of the baby's organs form during the first 8 weeks. Early prenatal care can identify maternal conditions, such as sexually transmitted diseases, that may threaten prenatal development. Doctors and nurses can also urge women to abstain from drugs and alcohol early in prenatal development, when such behavior changes may prevent birth defects.

Early prenatal care can also be important to the pregnant woman's health. For example, a small number of zygotes implant in one of the fallopian tubes instead of in the uterus, a condition called *ectopic pregnancy*. Early surgical removal of the zygote is critical to the woman's future ability to have children.

About 15% of pregnancies end in miscarriage, or *spontaneous abortion*. From the woman's point of view, an early miscarriage is similar to a menstrual period, although feelings of discomfort and blood loss are usually greater. Medical care is always necessary after a miscarriage because the woman's body may fail to completely expel the embryo.

Second Trimester During the second trimester of pregnancy, from the end of week 12 through week 24, morning sickness usually disappears, resulting in increases in appetite. The pregnant woman gains weight, and the uterus expands to accommodate a fetus that is growing rapidly. Consequently, the woman begins to "show" sometime during the second trimester. She also begins to feel the fetus's movements, usually at some point between the 16th and 18th weeks.

At monthly clinic visits, doctors monitor both the mother's and the baby's vital functions and keep track of the growth of the baby in the womb. Ultrasound tests are usually performed, and the sex of the baby can be determined after about the 13th week. Monthly urine tests check for *gestational diabetes*, a kind of diabetes that happens only during pregnancy. Women who have any kind of diabetes, including gestational diabetes, have to be carefully monitored during the second trimester because their babies may grow too rapidly, leading to premature labor or a baby that is too large for vaginal delivery. The risk of miscarriage drops in the second trimester. However, a few fetuses die between the 13th and 20th weeks of pregnancy.

Third Trimester At 25 weeks, the pregnant woman enters her third trimester. Weight gain and abdominal enlargement are the main experiences of this period. In addition, the woman's breasts may begin to secrete a substance called *colostrum* in preparation for nursing.

Most women begin to feel more emotionally connected to the fetus during the third trimester. Individual differences in fetal behavior, such as hiccupping or thumb-sucking, sometimes become obvious during the last weeks of pregnancy. These behaviors may be observed during ultrasound tests that produce increasingly clear images of the fetus. In addition, most women notice that the fetus has regular periods of activity and rest.

Monthly prenatal doctor visits continue in the third trimester until week 32, when most women begin visiting the doctor's office or clinic once a week. Monitoring of blood pressure is especially important, as some women develop a life-threatening condition called *toxemia of pregnancy* during the third trimester. This condition is signaled by a sudden increase in blood pressure and can cause a pregnant woman to have a stroke.

cephalocaudal pattern growth that proceeds from the head downward

Learning Objective 3.6

What happens in each of the stages of prenatal development?

Prenatal Development

In contrast to the trimesters of pregnancy, the three stages of prenatal development are defined by specific developmental milestones and are not of equal length. Moreover, the entire process follows two developmental patterns you can see at work in the photographs in Table 3.4. With the **cephalocaudal pattern**, development proceeds

Table 3.4 Milestones in Prenatal Development

	Stage/Time Frame	Milestones	
GERMINAL	Day 1: Conception	Sperm and ovum unite, forming a zygote containing genetic instructions for the development of a new and unique human being.	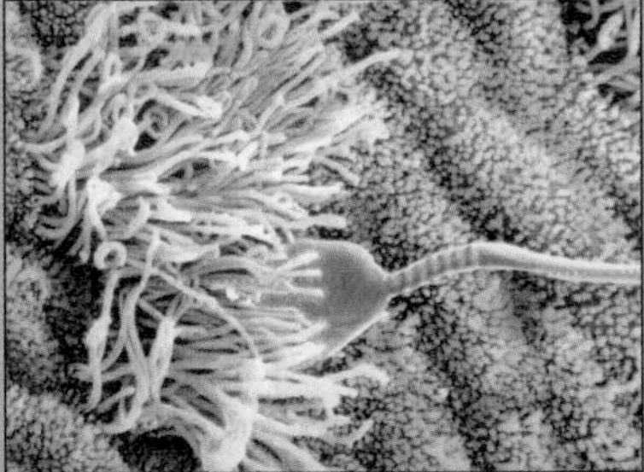 Sperm and egg
GERMINAL	Days 10 to 14: Implantation	The zygote burrows into the lining of the uterus. Specialized cells that will become the placenta, umbilical cord, and embryo are already formed.	 Zygote
EMBRYONIC	Weeks 3 to 8: Organogenesis	All of the embryo's organ systems form during the 6-week period following implantation.	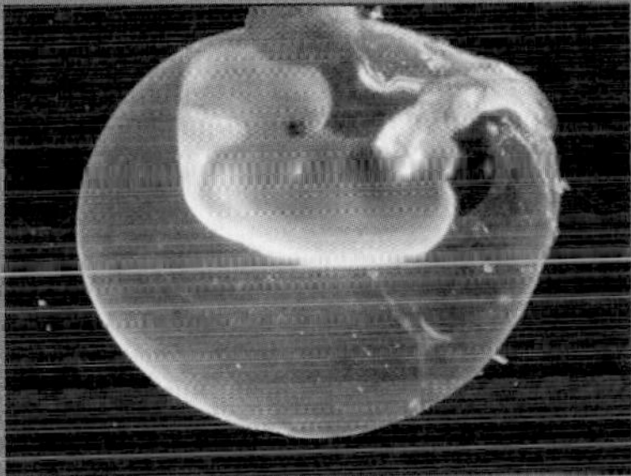 6-week embryo
FETAL	Weeks 9 to 38: Growth and Organ Refinement	The fetus grows from 1 inch long and ¼ ounce, to a length of about 20 inches and a weight of 7–9 pounds. By week 12, most fetuses can be identified as male or female. Changes in the brain and lungs make viability possible by week 24; optimum development requires an additional 14 to 16 weeks in the womb. Most neurons form by week 28, and connections among them begin to develop shortly thereafter. In the last 8 weeks, the fetus can hear and smell, is sensitive to touch, and responds to light. Learning is also possible.	

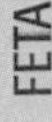

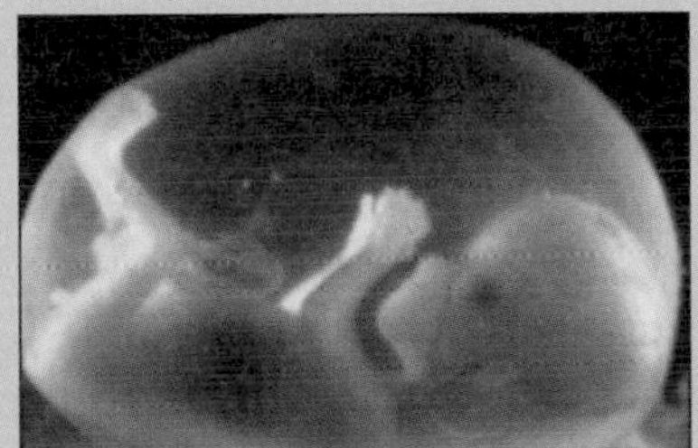
12-week fetus

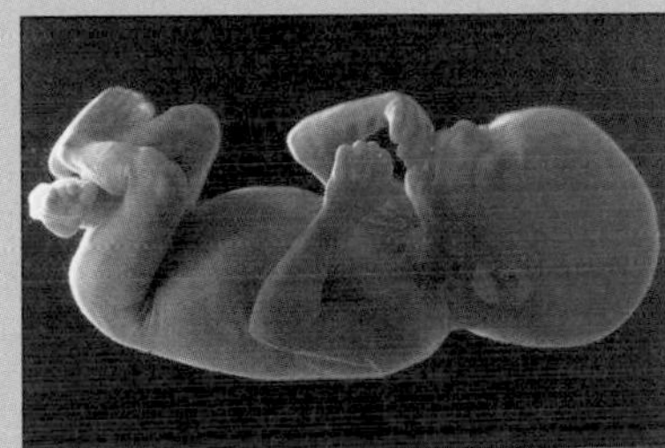
14-week fetus

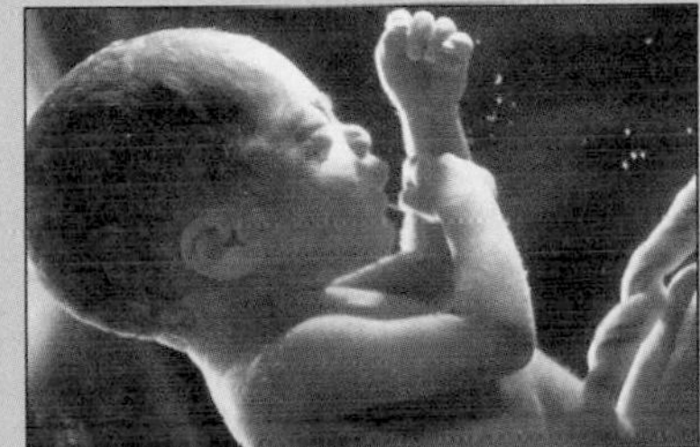
Well developed fetus (age not given)

(*Sources*: Kliegman, 1998; Tortora & Grabowski, 1993.)

from the head down. For example, the brain is formed before the reproductive organs. With the **proximodistal pattern**, development happens in an orderly way from the center of the body outward to the extremities. In other words, structures closer to the center of the body, such as the rib cage, develop before the fingers and toes.

The Germinal Stage The first 2 weeks of gestation, from conception to *implantation*, constitute the **germinal stage**. During this stage, cells specialize into those that will become the fetus's body and those that will become the structures needed to support its development. Cell division happens rapidly, and by the 4th day, the zygote contains dozens of cells.

On day 5, the cells become a hollow, fluid-filled ball called a *blastocyst*. Inside the blastocyst, cells that will eventually become the embryo begin to clump together. On day 6 or 7, the blastocyst comes into contact with the uterine wall, and by the 12th day, it is completely buried in the uterine tissue, a process called **implantation**. Some of the cells of the blastocyst's outer wall combine with cells of the uterine lining to begin creating the **placenta**, an organ that allows oxygen, nutrients, and other substances to be transferred between the mother's and baby's blood. The placenta's specialized structures bring the mother's and baby's blood close to each other without allowing them to mix.

Like the zygote, the placenta secretes chemical messages (hormones) that stop the mother's menstrual periods and keep the placenta connected to the uterus. Other placental hormones allow the bones of the woman's pelvis to become more flexible, induce breast changes, and increase the mother's metabolism rate. At the same time, the blastocyst's inner cells begin to specialize. One group of cells will become the **umbilical cord**, the organ that connects the embryo to the placenta. Vessels in the umbilical cord carry blood from the baby to the mother and back again. Other cells will form the *yolk sac*, a structure that produces blood cells until the embryo's blood-cell-producing organs are formed. Still others will become the **amnion**, a fluid-filled sac in which the baby floats until just before it is born. By the 12th day, the cells that will become the embryo's body are also formed.

The Embryonic Stage The **embryonic stage** begins at implantation, approximately 2 weeks after conception, and continues until the end of week 8. By the time many women first suspect a pregnancy, usually 3 weeks after conception, the embryo's cells are starting to specialize and come together to form the foundations of all the body's organs. For example, the cells of the nervous system, the **neurons**, form a structure called the *neural tube*, from which the brain and spinal cord will develop. A primitive heart and the forerunners of the kidneys also develop during week 3, along with three sacs that will become the digestive system.

In week 4, the end of the embryo's neural tube swells to form the brain. Spots that will become the eyes appear on the embryo's head, and its heart begins to beat. The backbone and ribs become visible as bone and muscle cells move into place. The face starts to take shape, and the endocrine system begins to develop.

By week 5, the embryo is about ¼ inch long, 10,000 times larger than the zygote. Its arms and legs are developing rapidly. Five fingers are visible on its hands. Its eyes have corneas and lenses, and its lungs are beginning to develop.

In week 6, the embryo's brain begins to produce patterns of electrical activity and it moves in response to stimuli. During week 7 embryos begin to move spontaneously (Joseph, 2000). They have visible skeletons and fully developed limbs. The bones are beginning to harden and the muscles are maturing; by this point, the embryo can maintain a semi-upright posture. The eyelids seal shut to protect the developing eyes. The ears are completely formed, and x-rays can detect tooth buds in the jawbones.

During the last week of the embryonic stage, week 8, the liver and spleen begin to function. These organs allow the embryo to make and filter its own blood cells. Its heart is well developed and efficiently pumps blood to every part of the body. The embryo's movements increase as the electrical activity in its brain becomes more organized. Connections between the brain and the rest of the body are also well established. The embryo's digestive and urinary systems are functioning. By the end of week 8, **organogenesis**, the technical term for organ development, is complete.

proximodistal pattern growth that proceeds from the middle of the body outward

germinal stage the first stage of prenatal development, beginning at conception and ending at implantation (approximately 2 weeks)

implantation attachment of the blastocyst to the uterine wall

placenta specialized organ that allows substances to be transferred from mother to embryo and from embryo to mother, without their blood mixing

umbilical cord organ that connects the embryo to the placenta

amnion fluid-filled sac in which the fetus floats until just before it is born

embryonic stage the second stage of prenatal development, from week 2 through week 8, during which the embryo's organ systems form

neurons specialized cells of the nervous system

organogenesis process of organ development

The Fetal Stage The final phase is the **fetal stage**, beginning at the end of week 8 and continuing until birth. The fetus grows from a weight of about ¼ ounce and a length of 1 inch to a baby weighing about 7 pounds and having a length of about 20 inches, who is ready to be born. In addition, this stage involves refinements of the organ systems that are essential to life outside the womb (see Table 3.5).

By the end of week 23, a small number of babies have attained **viability**, the ability to live outside the womb (Moore & Persaud, 1993). However, most babies born this early die, and those who do survive struggle for many months. Remaining in the womb just 1 week longer, until the end of week 24, greatly increases a baby's chances of survival. The extra week probably allows time for lung function to become more efficient. In addition, most brain structures are completely developed by the end of the 24th week. For these reasons, most experts accept 24 weeks as the average age of viability.

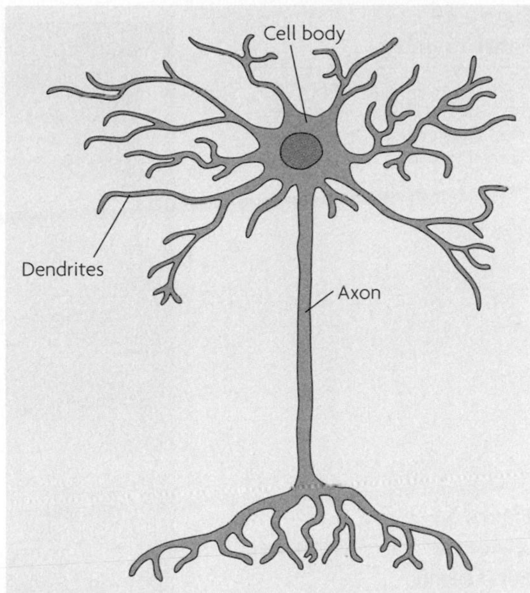

Figure 3.3
Parts of the Neuron

The structure of a single developed neuron. The cell bodies are the first to be developed, primarily between weeks 12 and 24. Axons and dendrites develop later, especially during the final 12 weeks, and continue to increase in size and complexity for several years after birth.

The Fetal Brain As you learned earlier, the foundational structures of all of the body's organ systems are formed during the embryonic stage. Yet most of the formation and fine-tuning of the brain take place during the fetal stage. Recall that neurons, the specialized cells of the nervous system, begin developing during the embryonic stage in week 3. But the pace of neural formation picks up dramatically between the 10th and 18th weeks, a process known as *neuronal proliferation.*

Between the 13th and 21st weeks, the newly formed neurons migrate to the parts of the brain where they will reside for the rest of the individual's life (Chong et al., 1996). While migrating, neurons consist only of **cell bodies**, the part of the cell that contains the nucleus and in which all the cell's vital functions are carried out (see Figure 3.3). Once they have reached their final destinations in the fetal brain, the neurons begin to develop connections. These connections are called **synapses**, tiny spaces between neurons across which neural impulses travel from one neuron to the next. Several changes in fetal behavior signal that the process

Table 3.5 Milestones of the Fetal Stage

Period	What Develops
Weeks 9–12	Fingerprints; grasping reflex; facial expressions; swallowing and rhythmic "breathing" of amniotic fluid; urination; genitalia appear; alternating periods of physical activity and rest
Weeks 13–16	Hair follicles; responses to mother's voice and loud noises; 8–10 inches long; weighs 6 ounces
Weeks 17–20	Fetal movements felt by mother; heartbeat detectable with stethoscope; lanugo (hair) covers body; eyes respond to light introduced into the womb; eyebrows; fingernails; 12 inches long
Weeks 21–24	Vernix (oily substance) protects skin; lungs produce surfactant (vital to respiratory function); viability becomes possible, although most born now do not survive
Weeks 25–28	Recognition of mother's voice; regular periods of rest and activity; 14–15 inches long; weighs 2 pounds; good chance of survival if born now
Weeks 29–32	Very rapid growth; antibodies acquired from mother; fat deposited under skin; 16–17 inches long; weighs 4 pounds; excellent chance of survival if delivered now
Weeks 32–36	Movement to head-down position for birth; lungs mature; 18 inches long; weighs 5–6 pounds; virtually 100% chance of survival if delivered
Week 37+	Full-term status; 19–21 inches long; weighs 6–9 pounds

fetal stage the third stage of prenatal development, from week 9 to birth, during which growth and organ refinement take place

viability ability of the fetus to survive outside the womb

cell body The part of a neuron that contains the cell body and is the site of vital cell functions

synapses Tiny spaces across which neural impulses flow from one neuron to the next

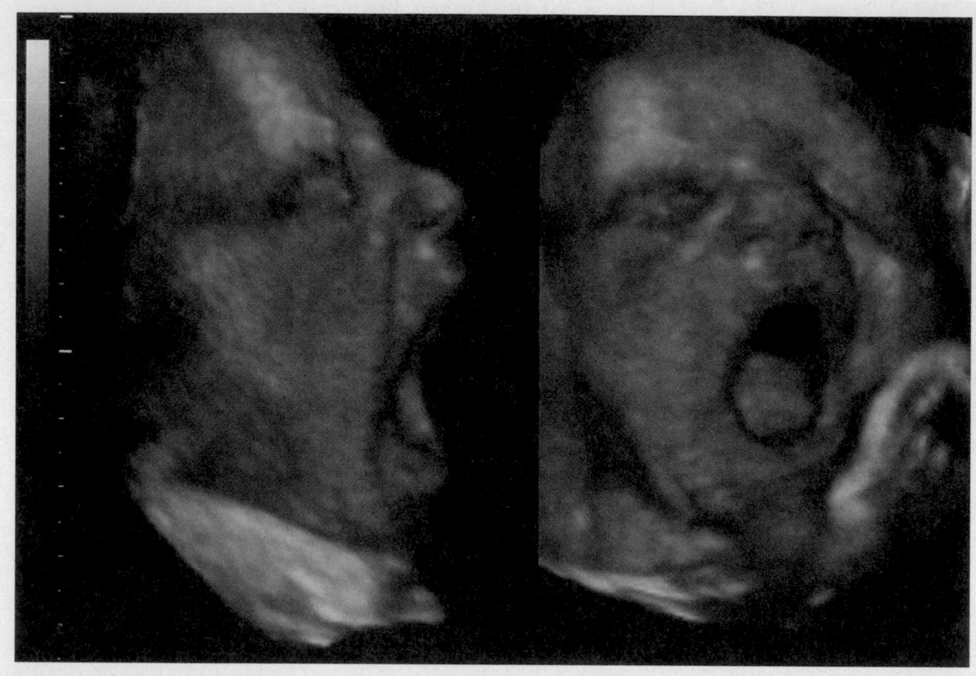

Figure 3.4
Fetal Yawning

Fetal yawning appears between the 10th and 15th week. Its presence signals the beginning of sleep stages in the fetal brain.

Figure 3.5
A Normal Third-Trimester Fetal Brain

Glial cells that develop during the last few months of prenatal development hold neurons together and give form and structure to the fetal brain.

(*Source:* Brown, Estroff, & Barnenott, 2004)

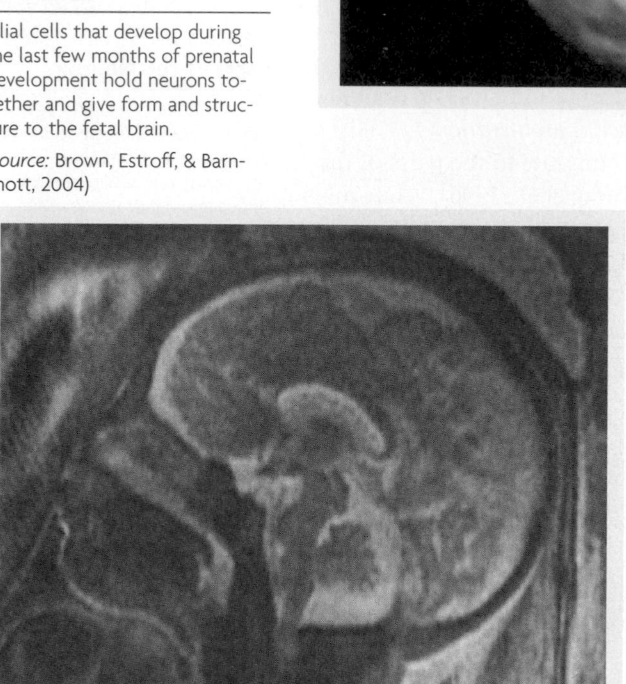

of synapse formation is underway. For instance, the fetus exhibits alternating periods of activity and rest and begins to yawn (Walusinski et al., 2005; see Figure 3.4). When observed, these changes tell physicians that fetal brain development is proceeding normally.

Synapse formation requires the growth of two neuronal structures. **Axons** are tail-like extensions that can grow to be several feet in length. **Dendrites** are tentacle-like branches that extend out from the cell body (see Figure 3.3). Dendrite development is thought to be highly sensitive to adverse environmental influences such as maternal malnutrition and defects in placental functioning (Dieni & Rees, 2003).

Simultaneously with neuronal migration, **glial cells** begin to develop. These cells are the "glue" that hold the neurons together to give shape to the brain's major structures. As glial cells develop, the brain begins to assume a more mature appearance, one that can be observed using *magnetic resonance imaging (MRI)* and other modern technologies that you will read more about later in the chapter (see Figure 3.5).

Learning Objective 3.7

How do male and female fetuses differ?

Sex Differences

Because prenatal development is strongly influenced by maturational codes that are the same for both males and females, there are only a few sex differences in prenatal development. One fairly well-documented difference is that male fetuses, on average, are more physically active (DiPietro, Hodgson, Costigan, & Johnson, 1996; DiPietro, Hodgson, Costigan, Hilton, & Johnson, 1996). Further, activity level is fairly stable from the fetal stage through childhood (Accardo et al., 1997). This means that the sex differences in children's activity level you'll read about in later chapters probably begin in the womb.

Subtle sex differences in prenatal brain development probably contribute to different patterns of growth hormone secretions in adolescence as well. Researchers have linked prenatal hormones to sex differences in the dominance of the right and left hemispheres of the

axons Tail-like extensions of neurons

dendrites Branchlike protrusions from the cell bodies of neurons

brain, physical aggression, and connections between brain and motor patterns (Pressman, DiPietro, Costigan, Shupe, & Johnson, 1998; Todd, Swarzenski, Rossi, & Visconti, 1995).

Developmentalists aren't sure why, but female fetuses appear to be more sensitive to external stimulation and to advance more rapidly in skeletal development (Groome et al., 1999; Tanner, 1990). Female infants are about 1–2 weeks ahead in bone development at birth, even though newborn boys are typically longer and heavier. Female superiority in skeletal development persists through childhood and early adolescence, causing girls to acquire many coordinated movements and motor skills, especially those involving the hands and wrists, earlier than boys. The gap between the sexes gets wider every year until the mid-teens, when boys catch up and surpass girls in general physical coordination.

Boys are more vulnerable to all kinds of prenatal problems. Many more boys than girls are conceived—from 120 to 150 male embryos to every 100 female ones—but more of the males are spontaneously aborted. At birth, there are about 105 boys for every 100 girls. Male fetuses also appear to be more sensitive to variables such as marijuana and maternal stress, which may negatively affect prenatal development (Bethus, Lemaire, Lhomme, & Goodall, 2005; Wang, Dow-Edwards, Anderson, Minkoff, & Hurd, 2004).

Prenatal Behavior

Learning Objective 3.8

What behaviors have scientists observed in fetuses?

In recent years, techniques such as ultrasound imaging have provided researchers with a great deal of information about fetal behavior. Some researchers suggest that establishing norms for fetal behavior would help health-care providers better assess fetal health (Nijhuis, 2003). Thus, in recent years, the number of research studies examining fetal behavior has increased significantly. These studies have revealed some rather remarkable findings, some of which are shown in Figure 3.6.

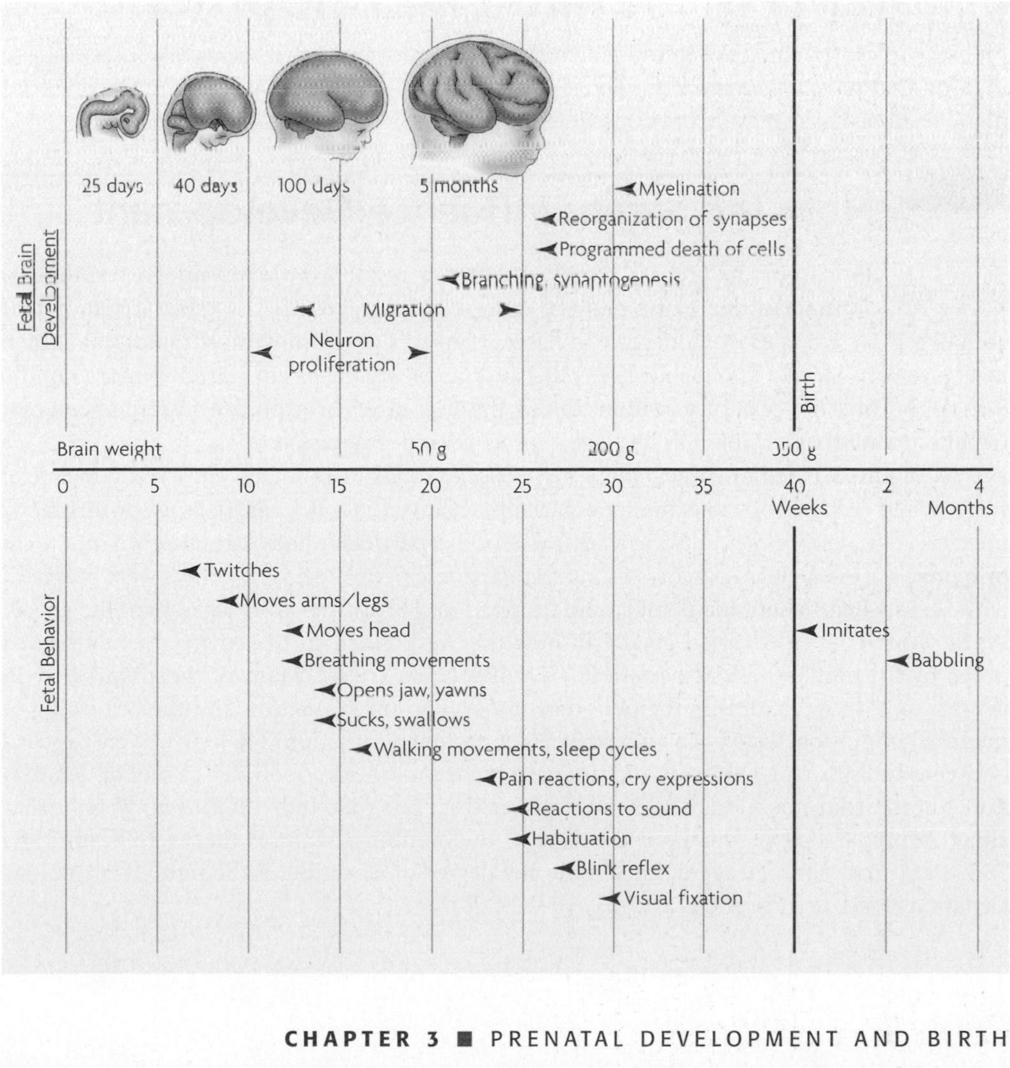

Figure 3.6
Correlations between Fetal Behavior and Brain Development

Researchers have discovered numerous correlations between fetal brain development and behavior.

(*Source*: Walusinski, O., Kurjak, A., Andonotopo, W., & Azumendi, G. (2005). Fetal yawning: A behavior's birth with 4D US revealed. *The Ultrasound Review of Obstetrics & Gynecology, 5,* 210–217.)

glial cells The "glue" that holds neurons together to give form to the structures of the nervous system

For one thing, researchers have discovered that the fetus can distinguish between familiar and novel stimuli by the 32nd or 33rd week (Sandman, Wadhwa, Hetrick, Porto, & Peeke, 1997). In one study, pregnant women recited a short children's rhyme out loud each day from week 33 through week 37. In week 38, researchers played a recording of either the rhyme the mother had been reciting or a different rhyme and measured the fetal heart rate. Fetal heart rates dropped during the familiar rhyme, but not during the unfamiliar rhyme, suggesting that the fetuses had learned the sound patterns of the rhyme recited by their mothers (DeCasper, Lecaneut, Busnel, Granier-DeFerre, & Maugeais, 1994).

Evidence for fetal learning also comes from studies in which newborns appear to remember stimuli to which they were exposed prenatally. In a classic study of prenatal learning, pregnant women read Dr. Seuss's classic children's story *The Cat in the Hat* out loud each day for the final 6 weeks of their pregnancies. After the infants were born, they were allowed to suck on special pacifiers that turned a variety of sounds off and on. Each kind of sound required a special type of sucking. Researchers found that the babies quickly adapted their sucking patterns in order to listen to the familiar story, but did not increase their sucking in order to listen to an unfamiliar story (DeCasper & Spence, 1986). In other words, babies preferred the sound of the story they had heard *in utero* (in the womb).

Stable individual differences in behavior are also identifiable in fetuses. Longitudinal studies have shown that very active fetuses tend to become children who are very active. Moreover, these children are more likely to be labeled "hyperactive" by parents and teachers. In contrast, fetuses that are less active than average are more likely to become children who have mental retardation (Accardo et al., 1997).

Critical Thinking

1. Why do you think most expectant mothers become emotionally attached to their unborn children during the third trimester?

Problems in Prenatal Development

Prenatal development is not immune to outside influences, as you'll see in this section. Keep in mind that most of the problems you'll read about are very rare, many are preventable, and many need not have permanent consequences for the child.

Learning Objective 3.9

How do teratogens affect prenatal development?

How Teratogens Influence Development

Deviations in prenatal development can result from exposure to **teratogens**, substances that cause damage to an embryo or fetus. The general rule is that each organ system is most vulnerable to harm when it is developing most rapidly, as shown in Figure 3.7 (Moore & Persaud, 1993). Because most organ systems develop most rapidly during the first 8 weeks of gestation, this is the period when exposure to teratogens carries the greatest risk. Table 3.6 on page 72 lists several teratogens.

As Figure 3.7 demonstrates, there are *critical periods* in both the embryonic and fetal stages when certain body systems are especially sensitive to teratogens. If drugs or infections interfere with development during a critical period, a particular body structure will not form properly. For example, researchers found that Japanese people whose mothers were pregnant with them when the atomic bombs were dropped on Hiroshima and Nagasaki at the end of World War II in 1945 varied greatly in how they responded to the environmental hazard posed by the bombs' radioactive fallout (Schull & Otake, 1997). Many of those who were in the 8th to 15th week, during the period of rapid neuronal formation and the beginning of neuronal migration, were born with irreversible mental retardation. Those who were exposed between the 16th and 25th week did not have higher-than-expected rates of mental retardation, but they did exhibit higher levels of seizure disorders than individuals who were further along in prenatal development at the time of the bombings. Fetuses that were beyond the 25th week in gestational age did not show any degree of elevation in the rates of mental retardation or seizure disorders.

teratogens substances, such as viruses and drugs, that can cause birth defects

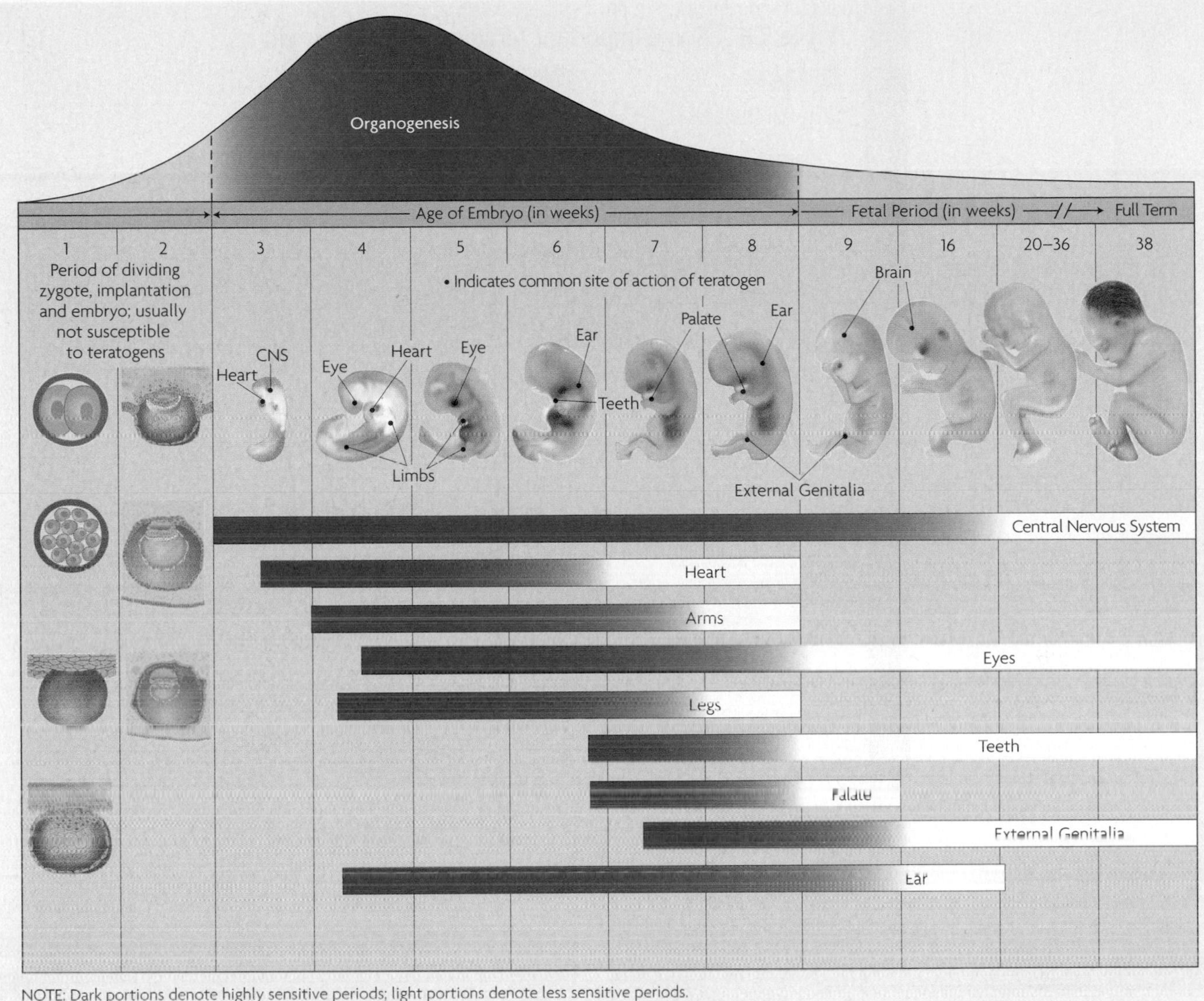

Figure 3.7
The Timing of Teratogen Exposure

The timing of teratogen exposure is crucial. Notice that teratogens have the most impact during the embryonic stage, except on certain body parts such as the brain and ears, which continue to be at risk for teratogenic effects because they continue to grow and develop during the fetal period.

(*Source*: Moore, 1998.)

Despite the trends that were found among Hiroshima and Nagasaki survivors, remarkably, many individuals who experienced prenatal exposure to radiation, even during the critical periods, were born without defects of any kind. Such cases demonstrate that there are many factors that contribute to the effects that a particular teratogen has on prenatal development. Two such factors are the duration and intensity of teratogen exposure. A single, brief exposure to even the most powerful teratogen may have little or no impact on development. However, if a single exposure is particularly intense, that is, if the "dose" of the teratogen is high, then it may be sufficient to cause damage. Among the Japanese atomic bomb survivors, the farther a person's mother was from the actual impact sites of the two bombs, the less likely he or she was to develop mental retardation or a seizure disorder. However, exposures of low intensity may be harmful if they occur over an extended period of time. For this reason, special precautions must be taken by pregnant women who are likely to be exposed to even minimal doses of radiation or other potentially harmful substances that are a part of their everyday working environments.

Finally, researchers have hypothesized that fetuses vary widely in their susceptibility to teratogens. These differences are thought to arise from genes that moderate or block the effects of some kinds of harmful substances. For instance, studies involving various strains of laboratory mice have shown that some strains are completely immune to teratogens that cause serious facial deformities in others (Syska, Schmidt, & Schubert, 2004).

Table 3.6 Some Important Teratogens and Their Effects

Teratogens	Possible Effects on Fetus
Maternal Diseases	
Cancer	Fetal or placental tumor
Toxoplasmosis	Brain swelling, spinal abnormalities
Chicken pox	Scars, eye damage
Parvovirus	Anemia
Hepatitis B	Hepatitis
Chlamydia	Conjunctivitis, pneumonia
Tuberculosis	Pneumonia or tuberculosis
Drugs	
Inhalants	Problems similar to those of fetal alcohol syndrome; premature labor
Accutane/Vitamin A	Facial, ear, heart deformities
Streptomycin	Deafness
Penicillin	Skin disorders
Tetracycline	Tooth deformities
Diet pills	Low birth weight

(*Sources:* Amato, 1998; Kliegman, 1998.)

Learning Objective 3.10

What are the potential adverse effects of tobacco, alcohol, and other drugs on prenatal development?

Drugs

Any drug, including many whose safety we take for granted (e.g., antibiotics), can be teratogenic. That is why doctors always ask women of childbearing age whether they might be pregnant before prescribing medication for them. Unless a drug is absolutely necessary to a woman's health, doctors recommend avoiding drugs of any kind during pregnancy. However, sorting out the effects of drugs (prescription and nonprescription, legal and illegal) on prenatal development has proven to be an immensely challenging task because many pregnant women take multiple drugs. Other factors, such as maternal stress, lack of social support, or poverty and poor prenatal care, also often accompany illegal drug use (Johnson, Nusbaum, Bejarano, & Rosen, 1999). Nevertheless, there are several drugs that seem to affect infant development, independent of other variables.

Children with fetal alcohol syndrome have distinctive features.

Prescription and Over-the-Counter Drugs You may have heard about the thalidomide tragedy that occurred in the 1960s. The drug involved was a mild tranquilizer that doctors prescribed to pregnant women who were experiencing severe symptoms of morning sickness. Sadly, the drug caused serious malformations of the limbs in thousands of fetuses that were exposed to it (Vogin, 2005).

In general, doctors advise against taking any unnecessary medicines during pregnancy. Nevertheless, some pregnant women must take drugs in order to treat health conditions that may be threatening to their own and to their unborn child's life. For instance, pregnant women with epilepsy must take anti-seizure medication because the seizures themselves are potentially harmful to the unborn child. Other drugs that pregnant women may have to risk taking, even though they can be harmful, include medications that treat heart conditions and diabetes, those that control asthma symptoms, and some kinds of psychiatric drugs. In all such cases, physicians weigh the benefits of medication against potential teratogenic effects and look for a combination of drug and dosage that will effectively treat the mother's health condition while placing her unborn child at minimal risk.

In contrast to prescription drugs, most people, pregnant or otherwise, take over-the-counter medicines on a casual, as-needed, basis without consulting a doctor. Many of these drugs, such as acetaminophen, are safe for pregnant women unless taken to excess (Organization of Teratology Information Specialists, 2005). However, experts advise pregnant women to discuss the medicines they usually take with physicians at the outset of their pregnancies. These discussions should deal with both drugs and any vitamins or supplements that the pregnant woman usually takes. Their doctors will advise them as to which of the substances are safe and which are risky. Often, too, physicians can suggest safer alternatives. Typically, most look to older drugs that have been thoroughly tested (Vogin, 2005).

Illegal Drugs Significant numbers of pregnant women the world over take various illegal drugs. The drug most frequently used is marijuana. The infants of twice-weekly marijuana smokers suffer from tremors and sleep problems. They seem to have little interest in their surroundings for up to 2 weeks after birth (Brockington, 1996). Moreover, at age 6, children who had experienced prenatal exposure to marijuana are shorter on average than 6-year-olds whose mothers did not use marijuana during pregnancy (Cornelius, Goldschmidt, Day, & Larkby, 2002).

Both heroin and methadone, a drug often used in treating heroin addiction, can cause miscarriage, premature labor, and early death (Brockington, 1996). Further, 60–80% of babies born to heroin- or methadone-addicted women are addicted to these drugs as well. Addicted babies have high-pitched cries and suffer from withdrawal symptoms, such as irritability, uncontrollable tremors, vomiting, convulsions, and sleep problems. These symptoms may last as long as 4 months.

The degree to which heroin and methadone affect development depends on the quality of the environment in which babies are raised. Babies who are cared for by mothers who continue to be addicted themselves usually don't do as well as those whose mothers stop using drugs or who are raised by relatives or foster families (Schuler, Nair, & Black, 2002). By age 2, most heroin- or methadone-addicted babies in good homes are developing normally.

Use of cocaine, in either powder or "crack" form, by pregnant women is linked to many kinds of developmental problems in their children (Chatlos, 1997; Ornoy, 2002). However, most cocaine-using pregnant women are poor and abuse multiple substances, making it difficult to separate the effects of cocaine from those of poverty and other drugs. Some studies suggest that cocaine alone has no long-term effects on cognitive or social development (Kilbride, Castor, Hoffman, & Fuger, 2000; Phelps, Wallace, & Bontrager, 1997; Richardson, Conroy, & Day, 1996). However, other research has demonstrated that prenatal exposure to cocaine, especially when women use it several times a week, leads to a variety of developmental problems in infants (Brown, Bakeman, Coles, Sexson, & Demi, 1998; Madison, Johnson, Seikel, Arnold, & Schultheis, 1998; Mayes, Cicchetti, Acharyya, & Zhang, 2003; Schuler & Nair, 1999). Still other studies indicate that cocaine-exposed infants' problems may seem to be minimal when the children are assessed individually in researchers' laboratories. However, in complex environments such as school classrooms, their difficulties become more apparent (Betancourt et al., 1999).

The mixed findings on prenatal exposure to cocaine probably mean that this drug interacts with other environmental factors to produce a complex set of effects. For example, a cocaine-exposed infant who receives good follow-up care and whose mother discontinues her drug use may be less likely to suffer than another who receives little or no such care and is raised by a drug-using mother. Consequently, health professionals suggest that the development of cocaine-exposed babies should be closely monitored and that interventions should be tailored to fit the individual circumstances and characteristics of each infant (Kilbride et al., 2000).

Tobacco The correlation between smoking during pregnancy and an infant's birth weight has been well documented by researchers. Infants of mothers who smoke are on average about half a pound lighter at birth than infants of nonsmoking mothers (Fourn, Ducic, & Seguin, 1999; Mohsin, Wong, Bauman, & Bai, 2003). Prenatal exposure to tobacco may also have long-term effects on children's development. Some studies suggest that there are higher rates of learning problems and antisocial behavior among children whose mothers smoked during pregnancy (Fergusson, Horwood, & Lynskey, 1993; Tomblin, Smith, & Zhang, 1997; Visscher, Feder, Burns, Brady, & Bray, 2003). Moreover, children of women who smoked during pregnancy are more likely than their schoolmates to be diagnosed with attention-deficit hyperactivity disorder (Linnet et al., 2003; Thapar et al., 2003).

Alcohol In the face of mounting evidence documenting the detrimental effects of alcohol on prenatal development, the safest course for pregnant women is to drink no alcohol at all. For example, researchers have found that 6-year-olds who were prenatally exposed to alcohol are smaller than their non-alcohol-exposed peers (Cornelius, Goldschmidt, Day, & Larkby, 2002). In fact, studies show that alcohol can even adversely affect an ovum prior to ovulation or during its journey down the fallopian tube to the uterus. Likewise, a zygote can be affected by alcohol even before it has been implanted in the uterine lining (Kaufman, 1997).

Mothers who are heavy drinkers or alcoholics are at significant risk of delivering infants with *fetal alcohol syndrome (FAS)*. These children are generally smaller than normal, with smaller brains. They frequently have heart defects and hearing losses, and their faces are distinctive, with a somewhat flattened nose and often an unusually long space between nose and mouth (Church, Eldis, Blakley, & Bawle, 1997; Ornoy, 2002). As children, adolescents, and adults, they are shorter than normal and have smaller heads, and their intelligence test scores indicate mild mental retardation. Indeed, FAS is one of the most frequent causes of retardation in the United States, exceeding even trisomy 21 according to some studies (Streissguth et al., 1991). FAS children who do not have mental retardation often have learning and behavior difficulties (Mattson & Riley, 1999; Mattson, Riley, Gramling, Delis, & Jones, 1998; Meyer, 1998; Uecker & Nadel, 1996). Moreover, these problems can persist into adolescence and adulthood (Kerns, Don, Mateer, & Streissguth, 1997; Olson, Feldman, Streissguth, Sampson, & Bookstein, 1998; Ornoy, 2002).

Learning Objective 3.11

What are the risks associated with teratogenic maternal diseases?

Maternal Diseases

Several viruses pass through the placental filters and attack the embryo or fetus directly. For example, *rubella*, or *German measles*, causes a short-lived mild reaction in adults but may be deadly to a fetus. Most infants exposed to rubella in the first 4–5 weeks show some abnormality, compared with only about 10% of those exposed in the final 6 months of pregnancy (Moore & Persaud, 1993). Deafness, cataracts, and heart defects are the most common abnormalities. Because the possible effects of rubella are so severe, doctors now recommend that all women of childbearing age be vaccinated against the disease (American College of Obstetrics and Gynecology [ACOG], 2002). However, the vaccine may also be teratogenic. For this reason, the American College of Obstetrics and Gynecology suggests that women wait at least one month after receiving the vaccine before they begin trying to conceive.

HIV, the virus that causes AIDS, is one of many sexually transmitted organisms that can be passed directly from mother to fetus. The virus may cross the placenta and enter the fetus's bloodstream, or the infant may contract the virus in the birth canal during delivery.

Only about a quarter of infants born to HIV-infected mothers become infected, although scientists don't yet know how to predict which infants will contract the virus (Abrams et al., 1995; Annunziato & Frenkel, 1993). Transmission appears to be more likely when the mother has AIDS than when she is HIV-positive but not yet ill (Abrams et al., 1995). In addition, HIV-positive pregnant women who take the drug AZT have a markedly lower risk of transmitting the disease to their children—as low as 8% (Prince, 1998).

Infants who acquire HIV from their mothers typically become ill within the first 2 years of life (Prince, 1998). The virus weakens children's immune systems, allowing a host of other infectious agents, such as the bacteria that cause pneumonia and meningitis, to attack their bodies. Even children who remain symptom-free must restrict their exposure to viruses and bacteria. For example, HIV-positive children cannot be immunized with vaccines that utilize live viruses, such as the polio vaccine (Prince, 1998).

Other sexually transmitted diseases (STDs), including *syphilis, genital herpes, gonorrhea,* and *cytomegalovirus,* cause a variety of birth defects. Unlike most teratogens, the bacterium that causes syphilis is most harmful during the last 26 weeks of prenatal development and causes eye, ear, and brain defects. Genital herpes is usually passed from mother to infant during birth. One-third of infected babies die, and another 25–30% suffer blindness or brain damage. Thus, doctors usually deliver the babies of women who have herpes surgically. Gonorrhea, which can cause the infant to be blind, is also usually transmitted during birth. For this reason, doctors usually treat the eyes of newborns with a special ointment that prevents damage from gonorrhea.

A much less well-known sexually transmitted virus is *cytomegalovirus (CMV),* which is in the herpes group. As many as 60% of *all* women carry CMV, but most have no recognizable symptoms. Of babies whose mothers are infected with CMV, 1–2% become infected prenatally. When the mother's disease is in an active phase, the transmission rate is more like 40–50% (Blackman, 1990). About 2,500 babies born each year in the United States display symptoms of CMV and have a variety of serious problems, including deafness, central nervous system damage, and mental retardation (Blackman, 1990).

Other Maternal Influences on Prenatal Development

Learning Objective 3.12
What other maternal factors influence prenatal development?

Other maternal characteristics that can adversely affect prenatal development include the mother's diet, her age, and her mental and physical health.

Diet Some specific nutrients are vital to prenatal development. One is folic acid, a B vitamin found in beans, spinach, and other foods. Inadequate amounts of this nutrient are linked to neural tube defects, such as *spina bifida* (Daly, Kirke, Molloy, Weir, & Scott, 1995). The potential negative effects of insufficient folic acid occur in the very earliest weeks of pregnancy, before a woman may know she is pregnant. So it is important for women who plan to become pregnant to obtain at least 400 micrograms of this vitamin daily, the minimum required level.

It is also important for a pregnant woman to take in sufficient overall calories and protein to prevent malnutrition. A woman who experiences malnutrition during pregnancy, particularly during the final 3 months, has an increased risk of delivering a low-birth-weight infant who will have intellectual difficulties in childhood (Mutch, Leyland, & McGee, 1993). In addition, researchers have recently identified prenatal malnutrition, along with a variety of obstetrical complications, as an important risk factor in the development of mental illnesses in adulthood (Neugebauer, Hoek, & Susser, 1999; Susser & Lin, 1992).

The impact of maternal malnutrition appears to be greatest on the developing nervous system—a pattern found in studies of both humans and other mammals. For example, rats whose caloric intake has been substantially restricted during the fetal and early postnatal periods show a pattern described as *brain stunting,* in which both the weight and the volume of the brain are reduced. They also develop fewer dendrites and show less rich synaptic formation (Pollitt & Gorman, 1994). In human studies of cases in which prenatal malnutrition has been severe enough to cause the death of the fetus or newborn, effects very similar to those seen in the rat studies have been observed. That is, these infants had smaller brains and fewer and smaller brain cells (Georgieff, 1994).

Age Have you heard sensationalized media reports about women giving birth in their 50s and even into their 60s? Such late-in-life births are very rare, but it is nonetheless the case that the average age at which women give birth for the first time has increased over the past few decades. In 1970, the average age at which a woman delivered her first child was 21.4 years in

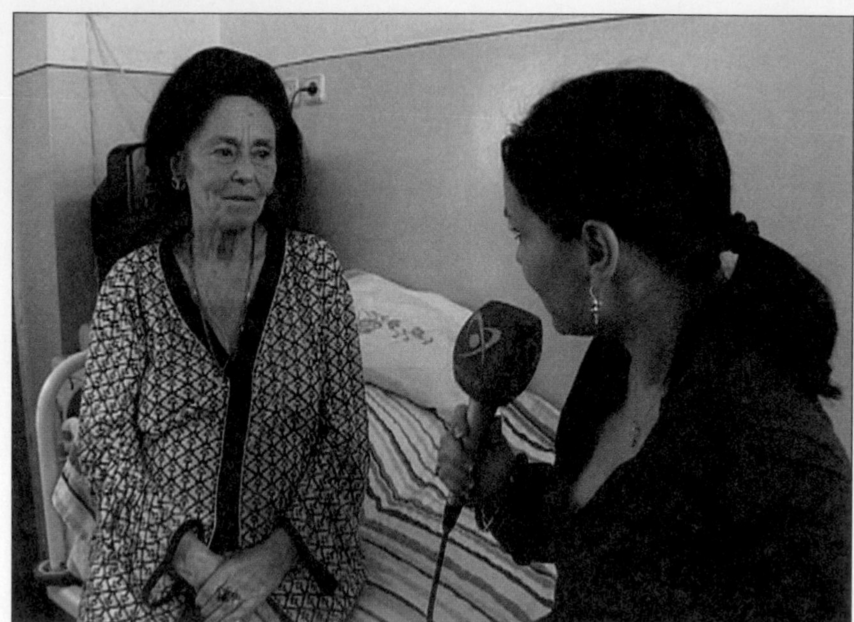

Reproductive technology has enabled women who are well past their childbearing years to give birth. After 10 years of fertility treatments, this 67-year-old Romanian woman delivered twin girls and became the world's oldest first-time mother.

the United States. By contrast, in 2003, the average was 25.1 years (Martin et al., 2005). One effect of this trend, as you have already learned, is that the number of multiple births each year has increased dramatically.

In most cases, older mothers have uncomplicated pregnancies and deliver healthy babies, but the risks associated with pregnancy do increase somewhat as women get older (Martin et al., 2005). Their babies are also at greater risk of weighing less than 5.5 pounds at birth, a finding that is partly explained by the greater incidence of multiple births among older mothers. Still, infants born to women over the age of 35, whether single or multiple birth, are at higher risk of having problems such as heart malformations and chromosomal disorders.

At the other end of the age continuum, when comparing the rates of problems seen in teenage mothers with those among mothers in their 20s, almost all researchers find higher rates among the teens. However, teenage mothers are also more likely to be poor and less likely to receive adequate prenatal care, so it is very hard to sort out the causal factors (Martin et al., 2005). Nevertheless, researchers have found higher rates of adverse pregnancy outcomes even among middle-class teenage mothers who received good prenatal care (Fraser, Brockert, & Ward, 1995). Moreover, the children of teenage mothers are more likely than children of women who are older to exhibit learning and behavior problems in school (Levine, Pollack, & Comfort, 2001).

Chronic Illnesses Chronic illnesses, whether emotional or physical, can also affect prenatal development. For example, long-term severe depression and other mood disorders can lead to slow fetal growth and premature labor (Weinstock, 1999). Moreover, developmentalists have learned that depressed mothers are less likely to feel attached to their fetuses. At least one study suggested that infants whose mothers do not develop a prenatal attachment to them are less socially responsive than other infants of the same age (Oates, 1998).

Conditions such as heart disease, diabetes, lupus, hormone imbalances, and epilepsy can also affect prenatal development negatively (Kliegman, 1998; McAllister et al., 1997; Sandman, Wadhwa, Chicz-DeMet, Porto, & Garite, 1999). In fact, one of the most important goals of the new specialty of *fetal-maternal medicine* is to manage the pregnancies of women who have such conditions in ways that will support the health of both mother and fetus. For example, pregnancy often makes it impossible for a diabetic woman to keep her blood sugar levels under control. In turn, erratic blood sugar levels may damage the fetus's nervous system or cause it to grow too rapidly (Allen & Kisilevsky, 1999; Kliegman, 1998). To prevent such complications, a fetal-maternal specialist must find a diet, a medication, or a combination of the two that will stabilize the mother's blood sugar but will not harm the fetus. Similarly, fetal-maternal specialists help women who have epilepsy balance their own need for anticonvulsant medication against possible harm to the fetus.

Environmental Hazards There are a number of substances found in the environment that may have detrimental effects on prenatal development. For example, women who work with mercury (e.g., dentists, dental technicians, semiconductor manufacturing workers) are advised to limit their exposure to this potentially teratogenic substance (March of Dimes, 2004). Consuming large amounts of fish may also expose pregnant women to high levels of mercury (because of industrial pollution of the oceans and waterways.) Fish may also contain elevated levels of another problematic industrial pollutant known as polychlorinated biphenyls, or PCBs. For these reasons, researchers recommend that pregnant women limit their consumption of fish, especially fresh tuna, shark, swordfish, and mackerel (March of Dimes, 2004).

There are several other environmental hazards that pregnant women are advised to avoid (March of Dimes, 2004):

- *Lead*, found in painted surfaces in older homes, pipes carrying drinking water, lead crystal glassware, and some ceramic dishes
- *Arsenic*, found in dust from pressure-treated lumber
- *Cadmium*, found in semiconductor manufacturing facilities
- *Anesthetic gases*, found in dental offices, outpatient surgical facilities, and hospital operating rooms
- *Solvents*, such as alcohol and paint thinners
- *Parasite-bearing substances*, such as animal feces and undercooked meat, poultry, or eggs

Maternal Emotions Some psychologists have suggested that maternal emotions can affect prenatal development. Their rationale is that stressful psychological states such as anxiety and depression lead to changes in body chemistry. In a pregnant woman, these changes result in both qualitative and quantitative differences in the hormones and other chemicals to which the fetus is exposed.

As persuasive as this idea may be, the question of whether maternal emotional states such as anxiety and depression affect prenatal development remains open. For example, one study found children of mothers who reported high levels of psychological distress during pregnancy to be more emotionally negative at both 6 months and 5 years of age than children of nondistressed mothers (Martin, Noyes, Wisenbaker, & Huttunen, 1999). But critics claim that the real connection is a matter of maternal genes and/or parenting style: Emotionally negative mothers may simply be more likely to have children who are less emotionally positive than their peers.

One fairly consistent finding, however, is that the fetuses of severely distressed mothers tend to grow more slowly than others (Linnet et al., 2003; Paarlberg, Vingerhoets, Passchier, Dekker, & van Geign, 1995). Developmentalists do not really know whether this effect results directly from emotion-related hormones or is an indirect effect of the mother's emotional state. A stressed or depressed mother may eat less, or her weakened immune system may limit her ability to fight off viruses and bacteria—either of these situations may retard fetal growth. Consequently, many psychologists suggest that providing stressed and/or depressed pregnant women with social support and counseling may lead to improvements in both maternal and fetal health (Brockington, 1996).

Fetal Assessment and Treatment

Learning Objective 3.13

How do physicians assess and manage fetal health?

Ultrasonography has become a routine part of prenatal care in the United States because of its usefulness in monitoring fetal growth. (Ultrasound images are produced by the echoes that result from bouncing sound waves off of internal tissues.) Other tests, including *chorionic villus sampling (CVS)* and *amniocentesis*, can be used to identify chromosomal errors and many genetic disorders prior to birth (see Figure 3.8 on page 78). With CVS, cells are extracted from the placenta and used in a variety of laboratory tests during the early weeks of prenatal development. With amniocentesis, which is done between weeks 14 and 16 of a woman's pregnancy, a needle is used to extract amniotic fluid containing fetal cells. Fetal cells filtered out of the fluid are then tested in a variety of ways to diagnose chromosomal and genetic disorders. Both tests are associated with an increased risk of miscarriage. CVS is used most often when a medical condition in the mother necessitates early diagnosis of fetal abnormalities (Curry, 2002). In general, amniocentesis carries a lower risk of miscarriage and fetal injury than CVS does. Thus, it is usually the preferred prenatal diagnostic technique and is routinely recommended as a screening tool for Down syndrome and other chromosomal abnormalities in pregnant women over age 35.

There are also many laboratory tests that use maternal blood, urine, and/or samples of amniotic fluid to help health-care providers monitor fetal development. For example, the presence of a substance called *alpha-fetoprotein* in a pregnant woman's blood is associated

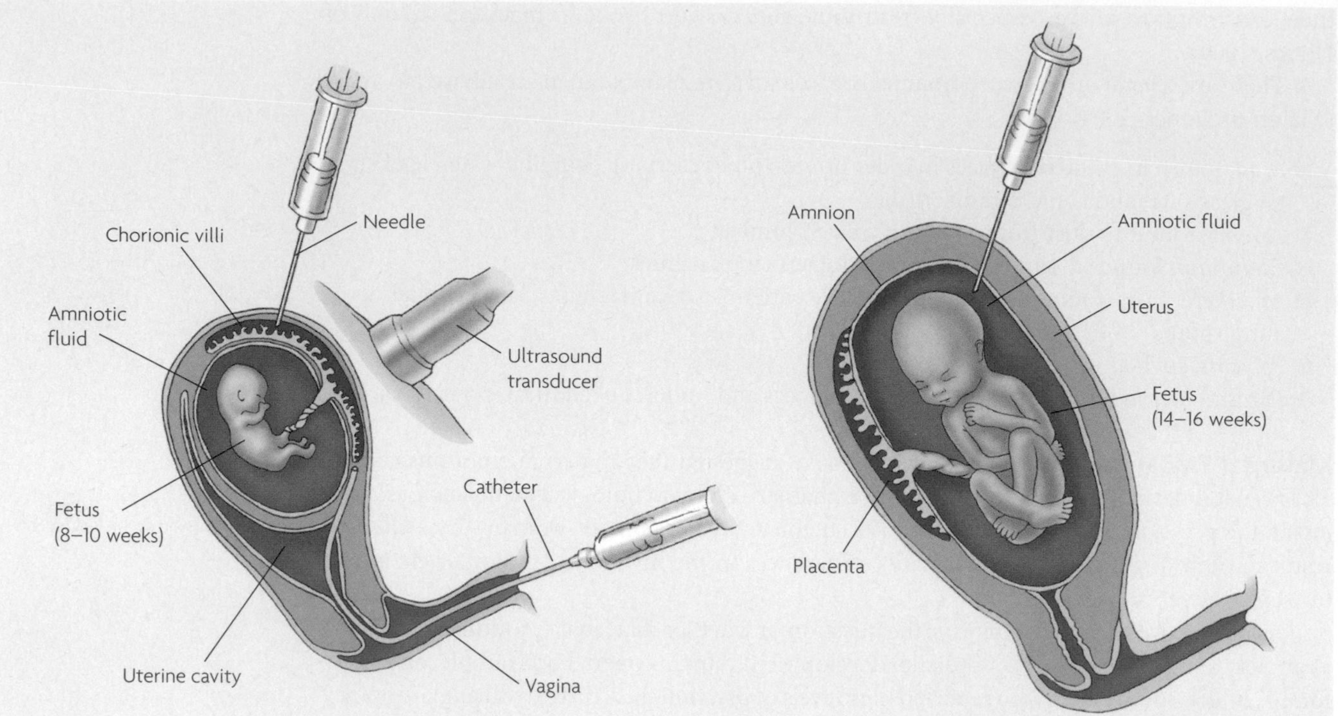

Figure 3.8
Two Methods of Prenatal Diagnosis

In chorionic villus sampling (left), placental cells are extracted through a hollow needle inserted in the mother's abdomen. These cells can then be used in a variety of laboratory analyses to determine whether the fetus is healthy. In amniocentesis, a similar technique is used to extract cells from the fluid that surrounds the fetus. These cells are used to create a chromosomal map that can help physicians identify several different kinds of birth defects.

with a number of prenatal defects, including abnormalities in the brain and spinal cord. Doctors can also use a laboratory test to assess the maturity of fetal lungs (Kliegman, 1998). This test is critical when doctors have to deliver a baby early because of the mother's health.

Fetoscopy involves insertion of a tiny camera into the womb to directly observe fetal development. Fetoscopy makes it possible for doctors to correct some kinds of defects surgically (Kliegman, 1998). Likewise, fetoscopy has made such techniques as fetal blood transfusions and bone marrow transplants possible. Specialists also use fetoscopy to take samples of blood from the umbilical cord. Laboratory tests performed on fetal blood samples can assess fetal organ function, diagnose genetic and chromosomal disorders, and detect fetal infections (Curry, 2002). For example, fetal blood tests can help doctors identify a bacterial infection that is causing a fetus to grow too slowly. Once diagnosed, the infection can be treated by injecting antibiotics into the amniotic fluid (so that they will be swallowed by the fetus) or into the umbilical cord (Kliegman, 1998).

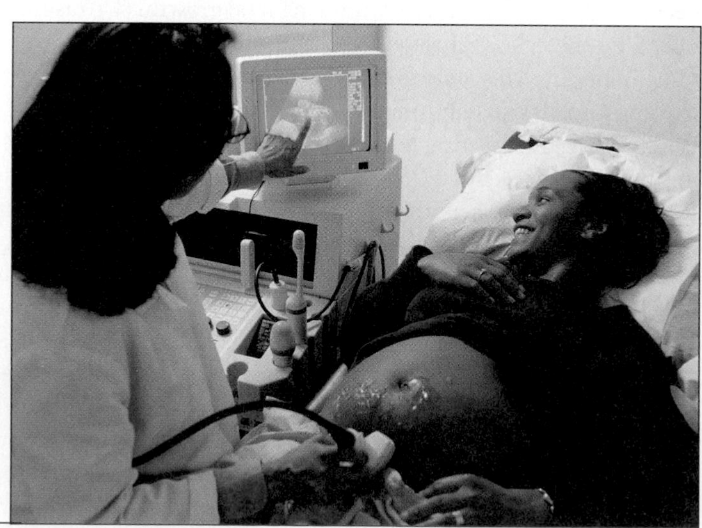

During the second trimester of pregnancy, ultrasound tests allow doctors to identify the fetus's sex, to diagnose fetal deformities and growth problems, and to determine the fetus's position in the uterus.

Researchers have examined how prenatal diagnosis affects parents-to-be. Compared to parents who did not know prior to birth about the disabilities their 1-year-olds would have, parents whose infants' difficulties were diagnosed prenatally report greater feelings of stress and depression (Hunfeld et al., 1999). However, specialists in fetal medicine suggest that the negative emotional effects of prenatal diagnosis can be moderated by providing parents-to-be with counseling and specific information about treatment at the time the diagnosis is made, rather than waiting until after the birth.

Critical Thinking

1. With the advent of antiretroviral drugs, the rate of mother-to-fetus transmission of HIV has been greatly reduced. Do you think that these findings justify mandatory testing and treatment of pregnant women who are at high risk of having HIV/AIDS?

Birth and the Neonate

Once gestation is complete, the fetus must be born—an event that holds some pain as well as a good deal of joy for most parents.

Birth Choices

Learning Objective 3.14
What kinds of birth choices are available to expectant parents?

In most places around the world, tradition dictates how babies are delivered. However, in industrialized countries, especially the United States, hospital deliveries became routine in the second half of the 20th century. Today, however, parents in such societies have several choices as to who will attend their baby's birth, whether medication will be used to manage the physical discomforts of labor and delivery, and where the birth will take place.

The Location of Birth and Birth Attendants One choice parents must make is where the baby is to be born. In most of the industrialized world, women deliver their babies in specialized maternity clinics. However, in the United States, there are four alternatives in most communities:

- A traditional hospital maternity unit
- A birth center or birthing room located within a hospital, which provides a more homelike setting for labor and delivery and often allows family members to be present throughout
- A free-standing birth center, like a hospital birth center except that it is located apart from the hospital, with delivery typically attended by a midwife rather than (or in addition to) a physician
- The mother's home

More than 99% of babies in the United States are born in hospitals (Martin et al., 2005). Thus, much of what researchers know about out-of-hospital births comes from studies in Europe. For example, in the Netherlands, a third of all deliveries occur at home (Eskes, 1992). Home deliveries are encouraged for uncomplicated pregnancies during which the woman has received good prenatal care. When these conditions are met, with a trained birth attendant present at delivery, the rate of delivery complications or infant problems is no higher than for hospital deliveries.

Certified nurse-midwives are registered nurses who have specialized training that allows them to care for pregnant women and deliver babies. *Certified midwives* have training in midwifery but are not nurses. Instead, most received training in other health-care professions, such as physical therapy, before becoming certified midwives. In Europe and Asia, nurse-midwives and certified midwives have been the primary caretakers of pregnant women and newborns for many years. By contrast, in the United States, physicians provide prenatal care and deliver babies for 91% of women (Martin et al., 2005).

Drugs During Labor and Delivery One key decision for expectant mothers concerns whether to use drugs during labor and delivery. *Analgesics* may be given during labor to

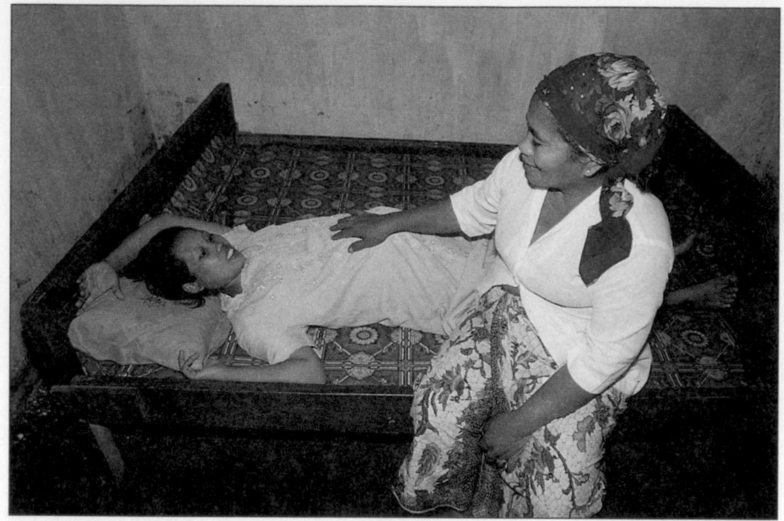

In the developing world, tradition determines where a baby is born and who attends the birth. Hospital deliveries are common in the United States, but many hospitals offer parents the option of delivering their babies in non-surgical settings such as the birthing room pictured below.

reduce pain. *Sedatives* or *tranquilizers* can be administered to reduce anxiety. *Anesthesia*, when used, is usually given later in labor to block pain, either totally (general anesthesia) or in certain portions of the body (local anesthesia such as an epidural).

Studying the causal links between drug use during labor and delivery and the baby's later behavior or development has proven to be difficult. First, it's clear that nearly all drugs given during labor pass through the placenta, enter the fetal bloodstream, and may remain there for several days. Not surprisingly, then, infants whose mothers have received any type of drug are typically slightly more sluggish, gain a little less weight, and spend more time sleeping in the first few weeks than do infants of nondrugged mothers (Maurer & Maurer, 1988).

Second, there are no consistently observed effects from analgesics and tranquilizers beyond the first few days, and only hints from a few studies of long-term effects of anesthesia (Rosenblith, 1992). Given such contradictory findings, only one specific piece of advice seems warranted: If you are a new mother who received medication during childbirth, bear in mind that your baby is also drugged, and that this will affect her behavior in the first few days. If you allow for this effect and realize that it will wear off, your long-term relationship with your child is likely to be unaffected.

Nevertheless, many women choose to avoid drugs altogether. The general term *natural childbirth* is commonly used to refer to this particular choice. This approach is also often called the *Lamaze method*, after the physician who popularized the notion of natural childbirth and devised a variety of pain management techniques. In natural childbirth, women rely on psychological and behavioral methods of pain management rather than on pain-relieving drugs.

Natural childbirth involves several components. First, a woman selects someone, usually the baby's father, to serve as a labor coach. *Prepared childbirth classes* psychologically prepare the woman and her labor coach for the experience of labor and delivery. For example, they learn to use the term *contraction* instead of *pain*. Further, believing that her baby will benefit from natural childbirth provides the woman with the motivation she needs to endure labor without the aid of pain-relieving medication. Finally, relaxation and breathing techniques provide her with behavioral responses that serve to replace the negative emotions that typically result from the physical discomfort of contractions. Aided by her coach, the woman focuses attention on her breathing rather than on the pain.

Learning Objective 3.15

What happens in each of the three stages of labor?

The Physical Process of Birth

Labor is typically divided into three stages (see Figure 3.9). Stage 1 covers the period during which two important processes occur: dilation and effacement. The cervix (the opening at the bottom of the uterus) must open up like the lens of a camera (*dilation*) and also flatten out (*effacement*). At the time of actual delivery, the cervix must normally be dilated to about 10 centimeters (about 4 inches).

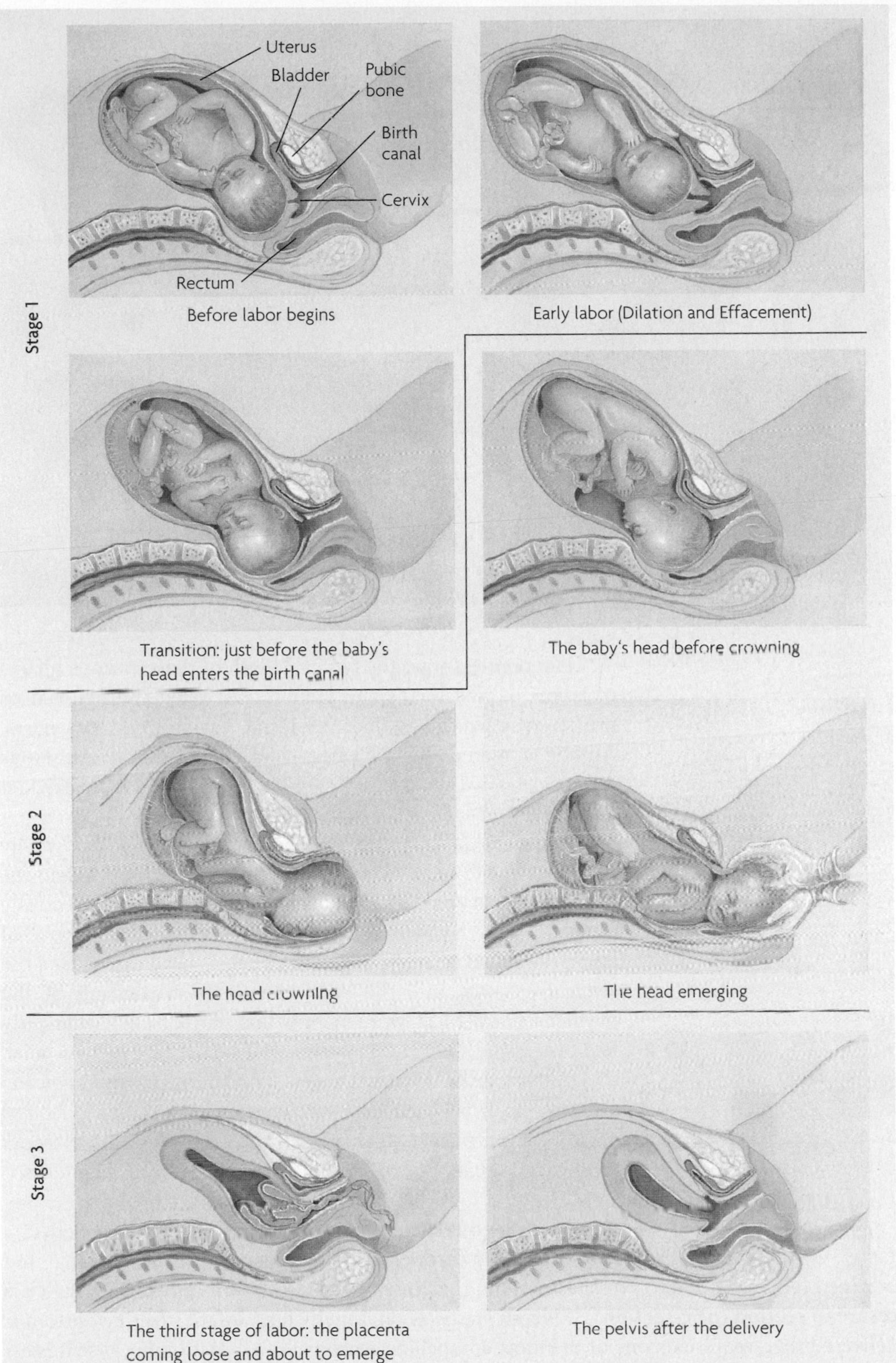

Figure 3.9
The Three Stages of Labor

The sequence of steps during delivery is shown clearly in these drawings.

Customarily, stage 1 is itself divided into phases. In the *early* (or *latent*) phase, contractions are relatively far apart and typically are not too uncomfortable. In the *active* phase, which begins when the cervix is 3 to 4 centimeters dilated and continues until dilation has reached 8 centimeters, contractions are closer together and more intense. The last 2 centimeters of dilation are achieved during a phase usually called *transition*. It is this phase, when contractions are closely spaced and strong, that women typically find the most painful. Fortunately, transition is also ordinarily the shortest phase.

Many fathers take prenatal classes like this one so that they can provide support to their partners during labor.

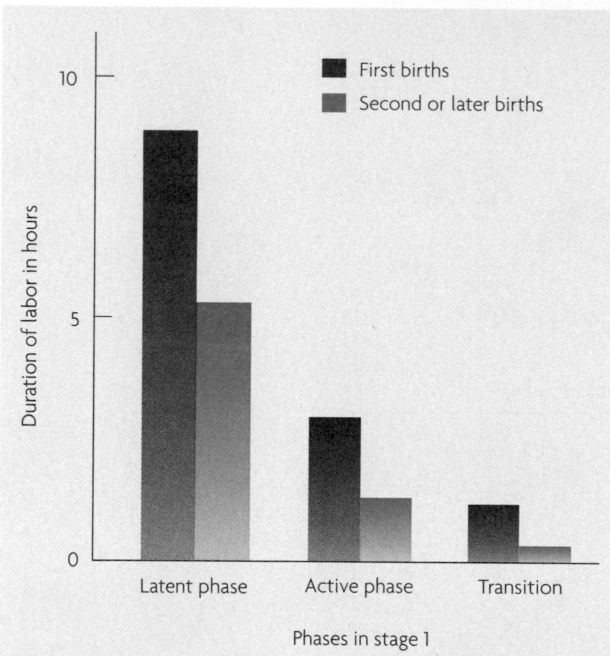

Figure 3.10
Duration of Labor in First and Second Births

Typical pattern of the stages of labor for first births and subsequent births.

(*Source*: Based on Biswas & Craigo, 1994, from Figures 10–16, p. 216, and 10–17, p. 217.)

Figure 3.10 shows the typical length of these various phases of labor for first births and later births. What the figure does not convey is the wide individual variability that exists. Among women delivering a first child, stage 1 may last as few as 3 hours or as many as 20 (Biswas & Craigo, 1994; Kilpatrick & Laros, 1989).

At the end of the transition phase, the mother will normally have the urge to help the infant emerge by "pushing." When the birth attendant (physician or midwife) is sure the cervix is fully dilated, she or he will encourage this pushing, and stage 2 of labor, the actual delivery, begins. The baby's head moves past the stretched cervix, into the birth canal, and finally out of the mother's body. Most women find this part of labor markedly less distressing than the transition phase because at this point they can assist the delivery process by pushing. Stage 2 typically lasts less than an hour and rarely takes longer than 2 hours. Stage 3, also typically quite brief, is the delivery of the placenta (also called the *afterbirth*) and other material from the uterus.

Cesarean Deliveries Sometimes it is necessary to deliver a baby surgically through incisions made in the abdominal and uterine walls. There are several situations that justify the use of this operation, called a **cesarean section (or c-section)**. A *breech presentation*, in which an infant's feet or bottom is delivered first, represents one of the most compelling reasons for a c-section because it is associated with collapse of the umbilical cord (ACOG, 2001). Other factors that call for the procedure include fetal distress during labor, labor that fails to progress in a reasonable amount of time, a fetus that is too large to be delivered vaginally, and maternal health conditions that may be aggravated by vaginal delivery (e.g., cardiovascular disease, spinal injury) or may be dangerous to a vaginally delivered fetus (e.g., herpes).

cesarean section (c-section) delivery of an infant through incisions in the abdominal and uterine walls

Many observers claim that the current rate of cesarean deliveries in the United States is too high. The National Center for Health Statistics (Martin et al., 2005) reports that just over 27% of all deliveries in 2003 in the United States involved a cesarean section. Critics of the frequency with which c-sections occur say that many of these operations are unnecessary. Are their claims justified?

THE REAL WORLD

Singing to Your Newborn

One of the first things that Dana did when she got her first chance to be alone with her newborn baby girl was to gently rock her while softly singing a lullaby that she remembered from her own childhood. As such, Dana was following an impulse that is common to parents, grandparents, and others who hold a newborn baby all over the world.

Singing to newborns is a behavior that has been found everywhere in the world. Just as they do when speaking to a newborn or an older infant, both mothers and fathers sing to infants with a unique singing style that includes a high-pitched tone and exaggerated rhythms (Bergeson & Trehub, 1999; Trainor, Clark, Huntley, & Adams, 1997; Trehub et al., 1997). Remarkably, researchers have found that newborns as young as 2 days old can distinguish among videotaped adults who are singing to babies, to other adults, or to no audience (Masataka, 1999). These findings suggest that the characteristics of the infant-directed singing style, as well as the ability to recognize it, may be inborn.

Researchers have identified two universal categories of songs for newborns: lullabies and playsongs. Songs of even tempo that are composed of smoothly connected notes are classified as lullabies. A good example in English is "Rock-a-Bye Baby." Songs that feature sharp disconnections between notes, often accompanied by gestures, are playsongs. The English song "The Itsy-Bitsy Spider" is such a song.

Lullabies and playsongs elicit different responses from infants. Babies respond to lullabies by turning their attention toward themselves and playing with their hands or sucking their thumbs (Rock, Trainor, & Addison, 1999). In contrast, they display externally directed responses to playsongs. Infants listening to playsongs wriggle, smile, and behave in ways that seem to encourage adults to continue singing (Rock et al., 1999). Adults seem to have an intuitive understanding of infants' responses to the two types of songs and can easily determine which type of song a videotaped baby is hearing (Rock et al., 1999). Thus, it isn't surprising that parents the world over use the two types of songs to regulate infant behavior. Lullabies help calm them, and playsongs entertain them.

However, being sung to may make important contributions to babies' development as well. One study found that preterm newborns in a neonatal intensive care nursery who were sung to three times a day for 20 minutes over a 4-day period ate more, gained weight faster, and were discharged from the hospital earlier than infants who were not sung to (Coleman, Pratt, Stoddard, Gerstmann, & Abel, 1997). Remarkably, too, the physiological functioning of babies who were sung to (as measured by variables such as oxygen saturation levels in their bloodstreams) was superior.

Some developmentalists speculate that singing to infants is linked to language development because important milestones in singing and speech—the first songs and the first words—appear at the same time (Chen-Hafteck, 1997). Others theorize that stimulation of the part of the brain used to perceive songs may enhance intellectual development. However, the greatest effect of parents' singing and babies' reactions to it may be communication of a mutual "I love you" message that helps to establish a lasting emotional bond between parent and child (Bergeson & Trehub, 1999).

Questions for Reflection

1. How could the research on singing to preemies be put into practice in neonatal intensive care units in non-disruptive ways?
2. If you were responsible for helping parents of newborns understand the value of singing to their babies, how would you explain the relevant research to them?

One factor behind current c-section statistics is that, as you learned earlier, more older women are having babies (Joseph et al., 2003). These women are more likely to conceive twins and other multiples. In such cases, surgical delivery almost always increases the odds in favor of the babies' postnatal health. Thus, the benefits of cesarean delivery outweigh its risks.

By contrast, a recent survey of hospital records found that nearly one-fourth of c-sections performed in 2002 in the United States were entirely elective (Hall, 2003). In these cases, women who had no medical problems, and who were carrying healthy fetuses, requested a surgical delivery, and their physicians complied. The ethics committee of the American College of Obstetrics and Gynecology (2004a) has ruled that elective surgical deliveries are ethical as long as the practitioner is certain that, for the patients who request them, vaginal deliveries carry equal risk. Advocates of elective cesareans say that the surgery spares women from future problems associated with vaginal delivery, such as uterine prolapse and urinary incontinence.

But should cesarean delivery be thought of as just another birth option? Critics say that the possible benefits of elective cesareans do not justify exposing women to their risks (Hall, 2003). They claim that many obstetric patients do not realize that a c-section is major surgery and carries the same risks as other abdominal operations. These risks include allergic reactions to anesthetic, infection, accidental injuries to other organs (as well as to the fetus), and excessive blood loss. Consequently, these critics believe that elective cesarean delivery represents a poorly informed choice on the part of the patient, and an irresponsible practice on the part of the physician.

Birth Complications During the process of birth, some babies go into *fetal distress*, signaled by a sudden change in heart rate. In most cases, doctors don't know why a baby experiences fetal distress. However, one cause of distress is pressure on the umbilical cord. For example, if the cord becomes lodged between the baby's head and the cervix, each contraction will push the baby's head against the cord. The collapsed blood vessels can no longer carry blood to and from the baby. When this happens, the baby experiences **anoxia**, or oxygen deprivation. Anoxia can result in death or brain damage, but doctors can prevent long-term effects by acting quickly to surgically deliver infants who experience distress (Handley-Derry et al., 1997).

Infants may also dislocate their shoulders or hips during birth. Some experience fractures, and in others, nerves that control facial muscles are compressed, causing temporary paralysis on one side of the face. Such complications are usually not serious and resolve themselves with little or no treatment.

If a laboring woman's blood pressure suddenly increases or decreases, a cesarean delivery may be indicated. In addition, some women's labor progresses so slowly that they remain in stage 1 for more than 24 hours. This can happen if the infant's head is in a position that prevents it from exerting enough pressure on the cervix to force it open. In such cases, surgery is indicated, because continuing labor can cause permanent damage to the mother's body.

After birth, most women require a period of a month or so to recover. During this time, the mother's body experiences a variety of hormonal changes including those required for nursing and for returning to the normal menstrual cycle. A few women experience a period of depression after giving birth (a potential problem that you will read more about in the chapters on early adulthood). However, most recover quickly, both physically and emotionally, from the ordeal of pregnancy and birth.

Learning Objective 3.16

What do physicians learn about a newborn from the Apgar and Brazelton scales?

Assessing the Neonate

A baby is referred to as a **neonate** for the first month of life. The health of babies born in hospitals and birthing centers, as well as most who are delivered at home by professional midwives, is usually assessed with the *Apgar scale* (Apgar, 1953). The baby receives a score of 0, 1, or 2 on each of five criteria, listed in Table 3.7. A maximum score of 10 is fairly unusual immediately after birth, because most infants are still somewhat blue in the fingers and toes at that stage. At a second assessment, usually 5 minutes after birth, however, 85–90% of infants score 9 or 10. A score of 7 or better indicates that the baby is in no danger. A score of 4, 5, or 6 usually means that the baby needs help establishing normal breathing patterns; a score of 3 or below indicates a baby in critical condition.

Health professionals often use the *Brazelton Neonatal Behavioral Assessment Scale* to track a newborn's development over about the first 2 weeks following birth (Brazelton, 1984).

Table 3.7 The Apgar Scale

	Score Assigned		
Aspect Observed	0	1	2
Heart rate	Absent	< 100 beats per minute	> 100 beats per minute
Respiratory rate	No breathing	Weak cry and shallow breathing	Good cry and regular breathing
Muscle tone	Flaccid	Some flexion of extremities	Well-flexed extremities
Response to stimulation of feet	None	Some motion	Crying
Color	Blue; pale	Body pink, extremities blue	Completely pink

(*Source*: Francis, Self, & Horowitz, 1987, pp. 731–732.)

anoxia oxygen deprivation experienced by a fetus during labor and/or delivery

neonate term for babies between birth and 1 month of age

A health professional examines the neonate's responses to stimuli, reflexes, muscle tone, alertness, cuddliness, and ability to quiet or soothe herself after being upset. Scores on this test can be helpful in identifying children who may have significant neurological problems. (See The Real World on page 83.)

Low Birth Weight and Preterm Birth

Learning Objective 3.17

Which infants are categorized as low birth weight and what risks are associated with this?

Classification of a neonate's weight is another important factor in assessment. All neonates below 2,500 grams (about 5.5 pounds) are classified as having **low birth weight (LBW)**. Most LBW infants are *preterm*, or born before the 38th week of gestation. The proportion of LBW infants is particularly high in the United States, where about 12% of newborns are preterm and 8% of newborns weigh less than 2,500 grams (Martin et al., 2005). Multiple fetuses—which, as you learned earlier in the chapter, are increasing in frequency in the industrialized world—are especially likely to result in preterm birth.

However, it is possible for an infant to have completed 37 weeks or more of gestation and still be an LBW baby. In addition, some preterm babies weigh the right amount for their gestational age, while others are smaller than expected. These *small-for-date neonates* appear to have suffered from retarded fetal growth and, as a group, have poorer prognoses than do infants who weigh an appropriate amount for their gestational age.

low birth weight (LBW) newborn weight below 5.5 pounds

NO EASY ANSWERS

When Do Preterm Infants Catch Up with Full-Term Infants?

Developmentalists who compare preterm infants to babies born at term often describe premature infants in terms of their "corrected age." For example, a 12-month-old who was born 2 months early would have a corrected age of 10 months. Thus, the brain functions, reflexes, and sensory skills of most 12-month-olds who were born 2 months early are very similar to those of full-term 10-month-olds (Fearon, Hains, Muir, & Kisilevsky, 2002; Sola, Rogido, & Partridge, 2002; Stolarova et al., 2003).

But when can parents and health care professionals expect to no longer have to rely on a child's corrected age to assess her development? The good news for most parents is that two-thirds to three-fourths of premature infants are no longer distinguishable from peers of the same chronological age by the time they go to school (Bowen, Gibson, & Hand, 2002; Foulder-Hughes & Cooke, 2003a). Despite this rosy prognosis, most developmentalists agree that the development of preterm children is best assessed on a case-by-case basis.

Several factors predict development in preterm infants for many years following birth. Lower birth weight and earlier gestational age are associated with long-term developmental delays (Foulder-Hughes & Cooke, 2003b; McGrath & Sullivan, 2002). Premature infants who experienced breathing problems, infectious illnesses, or brain injuries during the first few weeks of life are more likely to experience long-term developmental delays than premature infants who did not have such difficulties (McGrath & Sullivan, 2002). Gender matters as well; premature boys are more likely to display developmental delays than premature girls (Aylward, 2002). Thus, parents and health care professionals must take these factors into account when assessing an individual child's development.

However, it is also important for parents to know that their responses to the child contribute to how rapidly she develops (White-Traut et al., 2002). For example, a relatively recent innovation in the care of preterm newborns is an intervention called "kangaroo care" in which parents are shown how to increase the amount of skin-to-skin contact infants engage in with them. An important part of the intervention involves allowing parents to hold these tiny newborns for very long periods of time. Researchers have found that babies who receive kangaroo care grow and develop more rapidly than preterm infants given conventional neonatal care (Feldman & Eidelman, 2003; Tessier et al., 2003).

Other researchers have noted that parents' expectations for a preterm infant's development and their confidence in their ability to care for an at-risk child shape their responses to the infant's needs (Bugental & Happaney, 2004). Training appears to be of help to parents in both of these areas. Preterm infants whose families participate in parenting skills training programs display better neurobehavioral functioning during the first years of life than preterm infants whose families don't participate in such programs (Heidelise et al., 2004).

As you can see, the answer to the question of when a preterm child will catch up to his peers is, like so many other questions in the study of human development, "It depends."

Take a Stand

Decide which of these two statements would be the best advice that could be given to parents of a premature infant and think about how you would defend your position:

1. Two-thirds to three-quarters of premature infants catch up to their peers by the time they go to school, so it's best to adopt a "wait and see" attitude toward your child's development before attempting to influence it in order to avoid pushing the child beyond his or her limits.
2. Both parental responses and realistic expectations are important in parenting a child who was born prematurely, so it's best to do everything possible to enhance your child's development without expecting him or her to develop in exactly the same way as a child who was born at term.

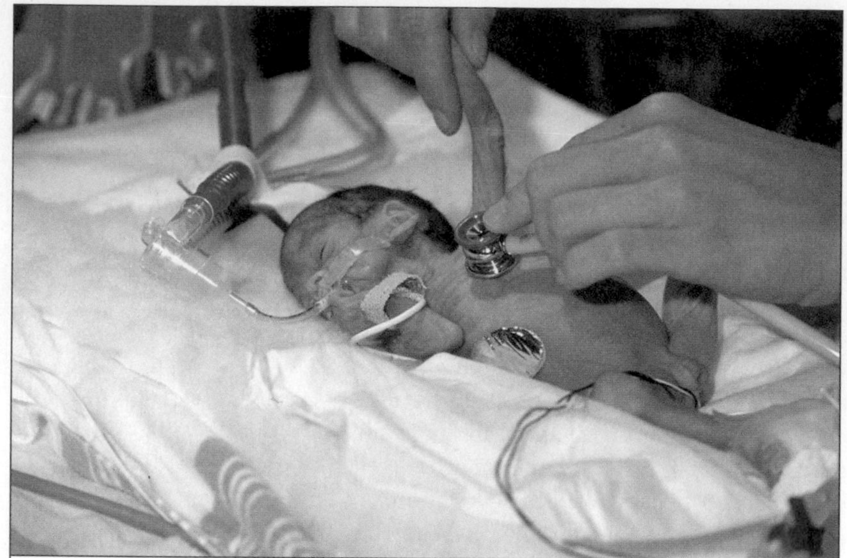

LBW infants' chances of survival are better when they receive care in a neonatal intensive care unit.

LBW infants display markedly lower levels of responsiveness at birth and in the early months of life. Those born more than 6 weeks early also often suffer from *respiratory distress syndrome* (also referred to as *hyaline membrane disease*). Their poorly developed lungs cause serious breathing difficulties. In 1990, physicians began treating this problem by administering surfactant (the chemical that makes it possible for the lungs to exchange oxygen and carbon dioxide in the blood) to preterm neonates, a therapy that has reduced the rate of death among very-low-birth-weight infants by about 30% (Corbet, Long, Schumacher, Gerdes, & Cotton, 1995; Schwartz, Anastasia, Scanlon, & Kellogg, 1994).

With adequate parental and educational support, the majority of LBW babies who weigh more than 1,500 grams (about 3 pounds) and who are not small-for-date catch up to their normal peers within the first few years of life although they do so at widely varying rates (see No Easy Answers on page 85). (Hill, Brooks-Gunn, & Waldfogel, 2003). But those below 1,500 grams remain smaller than normal and have significantly higher rates of long-term health problems, lower intelligence test scores, and more problems in school (Breslau et al., 1994; Breslau, Johnson, & Lucia, 2001; Hack et al., 1994; Weindrích, Jennen-Steínmetz, Laucht, & Schmidt, 2003). In fact, 40–50% of such babies show some kind of significant problem later.

An LBW neonate's general health also makes a difference. For example, LBW babies who experience bleeding in the brain immediately after birth are more likely to have later problems (Bendersky & Lewis, 1994). The economic circumstances of an LBW infant's family matter as well. Children in low-income families are more likely to suffer from long-term effects of low birth weight, such as attention problems, than are those who grow up in more affluent homes (Breslau & Chilcoat, 2000).

Boys are more likely than girls to show long-term effects of low birth weight. In fact, one recent study involving more than 700 6-year-olds found a higher rate of learning disabilities and other problems in LBW boys than among their normal-birth-weight (NBW) peers (Johnson & Breslau, 2000). By contrast, LBW girls did not differ at all from their NBW counterparts. The difference between LBW and NBW boys persisted when they were examined again at age 11.

Critical Thinking

1. What three pieces of advice would you give a pregnant friend after reading this chapter?

SUMMARY

Conception and Genetics

Learning Objective 3.1 What are the characteristics of the zygote?

- At conception, the 23 chromosomes from the sperm join with the 23 chromosomes from the ovum to make up the set of 46 that will be reproduced in each cell of the new individual.

Learning Objective 3.2 In what ways do genes influence development?

- Geneticists distinguish between the genotype (the pattern of inherited genes) and the phenotype (the individual's observable characteristics). Genes are transmitted from parents to children according to complex rules that include the dominant-recessive pattern, the polygenic pattern, and multi-factorial inheritance.

Genetic and Chromosomal Disorders

Learning Objective 3.3 What are the effects of the major dominant, recessive, and sex-linked diseases?

- Genes for specific diseases can cause a variety of disorders at conception.

Learning Objective 3.4 How do trisomies and other disorders of the autosomes and sex chromosomes affect development?

- Abnormal numbers of chromosomes and damage to chromosomes cause a number of serious disorders, including Down syndrome.

Pregnancy and Prenatal Development

Learning Objective 3.5 What are the characteristics of each of the trimesters of pregnancy?

- Pregnancy is divided into three approximately equal trimesters.

Learning Objective 3.6 What happens in each of the stages of prenatal development?

- Prenatal development occurs in three stages of unequal length (germinal, embryonic, fetal) that are marked by specific developmental milestones.

Learning Objective 3.7 How do male and female fetuses differ?

- Male fetuses are more active than their female counterparts. They also develop more slowly and are more vulnerable to most of the potentially negative influences on prenatal development.

Learning Objective 3.8 What behaviors have scientists observed in fetuses?

- The fetus is responsive to stimuli and appears to learn in the womb. Prenatal temperamental differences (for example, activity level) persist into infancy and childhood, and some aspects of the prenatal sensory environment may be important to future development.

Problems in Prenatal Development

Learning Objective 3.9 How do teratogens affect prenatal development?

- Teratogens exert greater effects on development during critical periods when specific organ systems are developing. The duration and intensity of exposure to a teratogen, as well as variations in genetic vulnerability, also contribute to teratogenic effects.

Learning Objective 3.10 What are the potential adverse effects of tobacco, alcohol, and other drugs on prenatal development?

- Drugs such as alcohol and nicotine appear to have harmful effects on the developing fetus; effects of drugs depend on the timing of exposure and the dosage.

Learning Objective 3.11 What are the risks associated with teratogenic maternal diseases?

- Some diseases contracted by the mother may cause abnormalities or disease in the child. These include rubella, AIDS, syphilis, gonorrhea, genital herpes, and CMV.

Learning Objective 3.12 What other maternal factors influence prenatal development?

- If the mother suffers from poor nutrition, her fetus faces increased risks of stillbirth, low birth weight, and death during the first year of life. Older mothers and very young mothers run increased risks, as do their infants. Long-term, severe depression or chronic physical illnesses in the mother may also increase the risk of complications of pregnancy or difficulties in the infant.

Learning Objective 3.13 How do physicians assess and manage fetal health?

- Several methods of prenatal diagnosis and treatment of birth defects or fetal abnormalities have become available in recent years.

Birth and the Neonate

Learning Objective 3.14 What kinds of birth choices are available to expectant parents?

- In the United States, most babies are delivered by physicians. For uncomplicated, low-risk pregnancies, delivery at home or in a birthing center is as safe as hospital delivery.

Learning Objective 3.15 What happens in each of the three stages of labor?

- The normal birth process has three parts: dilation and effacement, delivery, and placental delivery. Most drugs given to the mother during delivery pass through to the infant's bloodstream and have short-term effects on infant responsiveness and feeding patterns.

Learning Objective 3.16 What do physicians learn about a newborn from the Apgar and Brazelton scales?

- Doctors, nurses, and midwives use the Apgar scale to assess a neonate's health immediately after birth and the Brazelton Neonatal Behavioral Assessment Scale to track a newborn's development over the first 2 weeks of life.

Learning Objective 3.17 Which infants are categorized as low birth weight and what risks are associated with this?

- Neonates weighing less than 2,500 grams are designated as having low birth weight. The lower the weight, the greater the risk of significant lasting problems, such as low intelligence test scores or learning disabilities.

KEY TERMS

amnion (*p. 66*)
anoxia (*p. 84*)
axons (*p. 68*)
cell body (*p. 67*)
cephalocaudal pattern (*p. 64*
cesarean section (c-section) (*p. 82*)
chromosomes (*p. 55*)
dendrites (*p. 68*)
deoxyribonucleic acid (DNA) (*p. 55*)
dominant-recessive pattern (*p. 57*)
embryonic stage (*p. 66*)
fetal stage (*p. 67*)
gametes (*p. 55*)
genes (*p. 55*)
genotype (*p. 57*)
germinal stage (*p. 66*)
glial cells (*p. 68*)
gonads (*p. 55*)
implantation (*p. 66*)
low birth weight (LBW) (*p. 85*
multi-factorial inheritance (*p. 59*)
neonate (*p. 84*)
neurons (*p. 66*)
organogenesis (*p. 66*)
phenotype (*p. 57*)
placenta (*p. 66*)
polygenic inheritance (*p. 58*)
proximodistal pattern (*p. 66*)
synapses (*p. 67*)
teratogens (*p. 70*)
umbilical cord (*p. 66*)
viability (*p. 67*)
zygote (*p. 55*)

TEST YOURSELF

Conception and Genetics

3.1 Conception occurs when
a. the zygote implants in the uterine wall.
b. a sperm penetrates an ovum.
c. an ovum is released from the ovary.
d. gametes are produced.

3.2 Why do identical twins have identical genes?
a. because they develop from a single zygote that separates into two parts
b. because their genes are homozygous, not heterozygous
c. because both ova were released from the same ovary
d. because their phenotypes are identical

3.3 Why has the number of multiple births increased over the past 25 years?
a. The number of women over age 35 who are giving birth for the first time has grown.
b. Health care has improved, thus improving twins' chances of surviving.
c. The number of men fathering children after age 35 has grown.
d. The use of fertility drugs is declining.

3.4 The unique genetic blueprint from the mother and the father that characterizes a specific individual is called a
a. phenotype.
b. chromosome.
c. gamete.
d. genotype.

3.5 Two sisters, Carol and Kathy, have the same genes for obesity. Carol is severely overweight, and Kathy is only slightly heavy. The fact that the sisters' physical appearances are different, despite the similarity of their genes, is due to differences in
a. codominance.
b. genomic imprinting.
c. expressivity.
d. mitochrondrial inheritance.

Genetic and Chromosomal Abnormalities

3.6 Of the following genetic disorders, which does *not* belong with the others?
a. sickle-cell disease
b. hemophilia
c. Huntington's disease
d. Tay-Sachs disease

3.7 Where are the genes that cause sex-linked disorders found?
a. on the X chromosome
b. on the Y chromosome
c. on the multi-factorial chromosomes
d. on co-dominant chromosomes

3.8 Which of the following factors would put a couple at risk for having a child with trisomy 21?
a. the woman being under age 21
b. the couple being in a higher-SES group
c. the woman being over age 45
d. the man being over age 45

Pregnancy and Prenatal Development

3.9 Why is prenatal care during the first trimester important?
a. It can help identify women with gestational diabetes.
b. It can ensure that the pregnant woman is gaining enough weight to nourish the growing fetus.
c. It can identify ectopic pregnancies.
d. It can identify women at risk for toxemia of pregnancy.

3.10 The three stages of prenatal development, in order, are
a. germinal, embryonic, fetal.
b. viability, organogenesis, germinal.
c. embryonic, fetal, viability.
d. embryonic, germinal, fetal.

3.11 Which of the following is *not* an aspect of prenatal development that occurs in the germinal stages?

a. development of the cells that form the placenta

b. formation of the external genitalia

c. formation of the blastocyst

d. implantation of the cluster of cells into the uterine tissue

3.12 The ______ begins with implantation of the blastocyst into the uterine wall and continues through organogenesis.

a. germinal stage

b. embryonic stage

c. fetal stage

d. multi-factorial stage

3.13 Although survival rates are low, infants born at ______ may survive.

a. 12 weeks

b. 16 weeks

c. 20 weeks

d. 23 weeks

3.14 If the male fetus does not secrete androgens between the ages of 4 and 8 weeks,

a. the fetus will become female.

b. the unborn person will become homosexual.

c. the male fetus will fail to develop male genitalia.

d. the male fetus will grow more rapidly.

3.15 Which statement is true about the behavior of fetuses?

a. Newborns do not remember stimuli to which they were exposed prenatally.

b. Fetuses can distinguish between familiar and novel stimuli as early as the 20th week.

c. Prenatal behavior is stable in male fetuses but not in female fetuses.

d. Fetuses respond to sounds and vibrations with heart rate changes, head turns, and body movements.

Problems in Prenatal Development

3.16 Which period of prenatal development is the time of greatest risk for the influence of most teratogens?

a. the first 8 weeks of gestation

b. the beginning of the fetal period

c. the 29th week to the 38th week of development

d. the time of conception

3.17 Which of the following is *not* a typical characteristic of children who have fetal alcohol syndrome?

a. mild mental retardation

b. heart defects

c. learning and behavior difficulties

d. limb deformities

3.18 Of the following developing systems of an embryo/fetus, which would be most severely and negatively affected by maternal malnutrition?

a. musculo-skeletal

b. reproductive

c. nervous

d. cardiovascular

3.19 Which of the following prenatal diagnostic techniques is usually done during the first trimester of pregnancy and involves extracting cells for laboratory testing?

a. chronionic villus sampling

b. amniocentesis

c. ultrasonography

d. fetoscopy

Birth and the Neonate

3.20 Which of the following is *not* a typical difference between infants who are exposed to maternal birth medication and infants who are not exposed to birth medication?

a. more sluggish

b. more piercing or shrill crying

c. a little less weight gain

d. more time spent sleeping

3.21 The flattening out of the cervix is called

a. dilation.

b. transition.

c. fetal distress.

d. effacement.

3.22 Which period of birth is the shortest and the most painful?

a. stage 1, when the cervix effaces and dilates

b. transition, when the contractions are closely spaced and strong

c. stage 2, when the mother is pushing the baby down the birth canal

d. stage 3, when the placenta is delivered

3.23 Which of the following would be true of an infant who has received a score of 10 on the Apgar scale?

a. The infant is most likely one to two minutes old.

b. The infant is most likely five minutes old.

c. The infant is in need of immediate resuscitation to establish a normal breathing pattern.

d. The infant is in critical condition.

3.24 Neonates weighing below 5.5 pounds are classified as

a. low-birth-weight.

b. preterm infants.

c. breech presentation infants.

d. fetal distress infants.

3.25 Which statement is true about low-birth-weight babies?

a. Low-birth-weight girls are more likely to show long-term effects than low-birth-weight boys.

b. Most low-birth-weight babies never catch up to their normal peers.

c. Low birth weight is not related to the neonate's health.

d. Low-birth-weight infants show markedly lower levels of responsiveness.

PEARSON

mydevelopmentlab™ Study Plan

Are You Ready for the Test?

Students who use the study materials on MyDevelopmentLab report higher grades in the course than those who use the text alone. Here are three easy steps to mastering this chapter and improving your grade…

Step 1

Take the chapter pre-test in MyDevelopmentLab and review your customized Study Plan.

The proximodistal principle guides development so that development

- forms the sensory organs before it forms the digestive system.
- progresses at the same pace throughout the body.
- moves from the center of the body out toward the extremities.
- starts in the head region and moves down through the body.

Step 2

Use MyDevelopmentLab's Multimedia Library to help strengthen your knowledge of the chapter.

Explore: Building Blocks of Genetics

Building Blocks of Genetics

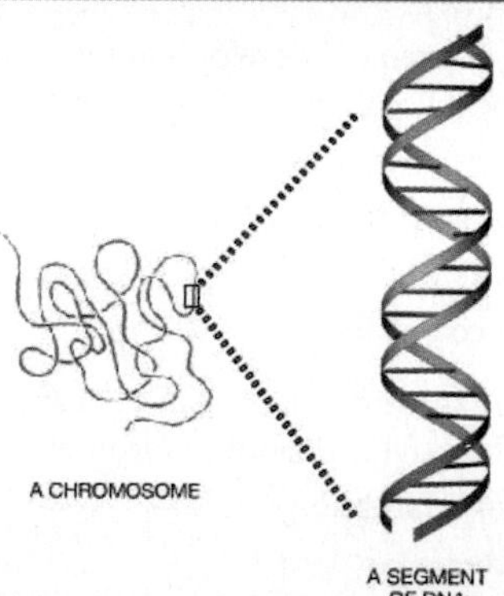

Each chromosome is essentially a long, threadlike strand of DNA, a giant molecule consisting of two spiraling and cross-linked chains. Resembling a twisted ladder and referred to as a double helix, each DNA molecule carries thousand of genes—the basic building blocks of the genetic code—which direct the synthesis of all the body's proteins.

back | stop | start over

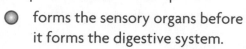

Learning Objective 3.1

What are the characteristics of the zygote?

"Each time I used MyDevelopmentLab my grade improved. It was obvious what chapters I studied for using the program and which ones I did not. MyDevelopmentLab was a very beneficial and key element in helping me understand this class."

—Student, University of North Carolina—Charlotte

Simulate: Teratogens and Their Effects

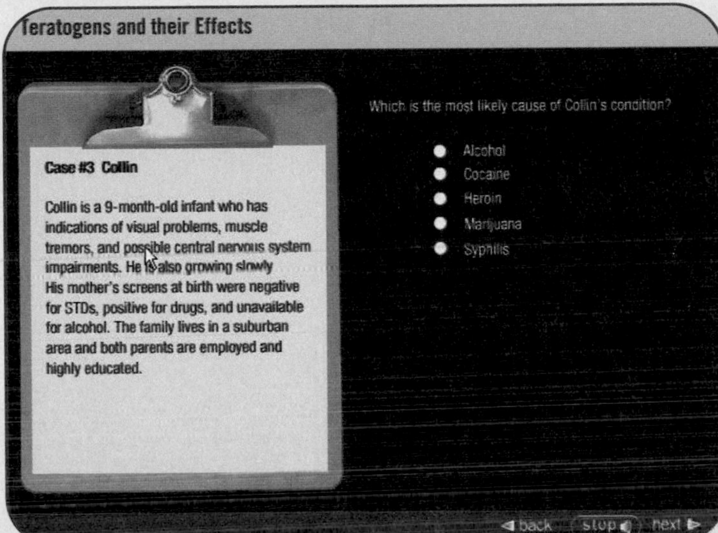

Teratogens and their Effects
Case #3 Collin
Collin is a 9-month-old infant who has indications of visual problems, muscle tremors, and possible central nervous system impairments. He is also growing slowly
His mother's screens at birth were negative for STDs, positive for drugs, and unavailable for alcohol. The family lives in a suburban area and both parents are employed and highly educated.
Which is the most likely cause of Collin's condition?
Alcohol
Cocaine
Heroin
Marijuana
Syphilis
back
stop
next

Learning Objective 3.9

How do teratogens affect prenatal development?

Watch: Drug-Free Deliveries

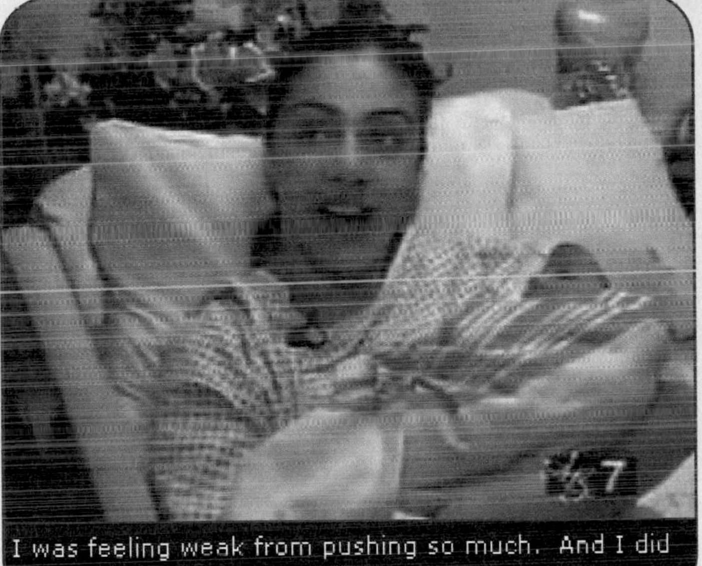

I was feeling weak from pushing so much. And I did
- I just gave up on it. I didn't want

Learning Objective 3.14

What kinds of birth choices are available to expectant parents?

Step 3

Take the chapter post-test and compare your results against the pre-test.

All of the organ systems form during the ________________ stage of prenatal development.

- fetal
- embryonic
- blastocyst
- germinal

www.mydevelopmentlab.com

POLICY QUESTION

Should Pregnant Women Who Use Illicit Drugs Be Prosecuted?

AN INNER VOICE
TELLS YOU
NOT TO DRINK
OR USE OTHER DRUGS
For information, contact:
National Clearinghouse for
Alcohol and Drug Information
P.O. Box 2345, Rockville, MD 20847-2345
1-800-729-6686

Given the potential damaging effects of drugs on prenatal development, everyone agrees that preventing pregnant women from using them is an important goal. But what is the best way to achieve this objective? In the United States, some have drawn a parallel between drug use during pregnancy and physical abuse of an infant after birth, suggesting that pregnant drug users should be criminally prosecuted.

Prosecution advocates argue that injecting a newborn with a drug is a crime. Even if no damage is done to the child, "delivering drugs to a minor" (the terminology used in most jurisdictions) is a crime in and of itself. When damage does occur, an additional crime, called "injury to a child" in most areas, may also have been committed. Thus, prosecution advocates argue that any woman who knowingly and deliberately administers drugs through her own bloodstream to the fetus she is carrying is guilty of the same crime as a parent who injects a newborn with a substance such as cocaine or heroin. They further suggest that prosecution will motivate drug-using pregnant women to stop. As persuasive as these arguments might seem, they raise numerous difficult issues.

Legal Status of the Fetus

One problem is that it isn't clear whether a fetus can be considered legally equivalent to a child. This is a critical point, because unless fetuses and children are legally equal, present laws against child abuse and delivery of drugs to children can't be applied to fetuses. In fact, the Hawaii State Supreme Court overturned the murder conviction of a woman whose habitual smoking of crystal methamphetamine while pregnant reportedly led to the death of her newborn son on precisely this premise (Barayuga, 2005). The justices stated that the woman could not be charged with murder because, under the law, a fetus is not a person.

However, some legal experts disagree with the position taken by the Hawaii court. They point out that recent U.S. Supreme Court rulings have introduced the issue of fetal viability into abortion law. These rulings allow states to outlaw abortions of viable fetuses and suggest using 24 weeks as the age of viability, based on current research on prenatal development. Thus, it would seem that states could also use existing laws against child abuse and giving drugs to children to prosecute women after the 24th week of pregnancy.

In addition, doctors often seek judicial intervention in cases where pregnant women make medical decisions that are potentially damaging to their fetuses. For example, in one case, a Utah woman was charged with murder in the stillbirth of one of her twin children because she had refused to undergo a cesarean earlier in her pregnancy (CBS News, 2004). Thus, precedents exist that would allow authorities to prosecute a drug-using pregnant woman strictly on the basis of the interests of a fetus.

Which Drugs?

Even if it is legally possible to use existing laws to prosecute pregnant drug users, fairness would seem to demand that women who use legal drugs be treated in the same way as those who use illegal drugs. As you learned in Chapter 3, many legal drugs, including alcohol and tobacco, are teratogenic. Further, giving such drugs to a child is a crime. If pregnant women are to be prosecuted for using illegal drugs, then shouldn't they be held legally responsible for exposing their fetuses to potentially harmful legal drugs as well?

Based on the logic outlined above, the answer must be yes. However, critics of the prosecution approach point out that prosecuting pregnant women for legal drug use undermines their right under the U.S. Constitution to equal protection under the law. Adults are legally entitled to use alcohol and tobacco despite evidence that it is dangerous or unwise to do so. Thus, criminalizing such behavior only for pregnant women places them in a special class and takes away their legal status as adults.

What Kind of Evidence Will Be Required?

If women are to be prosecuted for delivering drugs to their fetuses, as happened to two Texas women in 2004 ("Court Reverses Convictions," 2006), how will judges and jurors know that delivery has actually occurred? It might seem that hospitals could test newborns for various drugs and that positive test results would constitute evidence of delivery. The difficulty is that, while many drugs pass through the placenta, they don't always do so in sufficient amounts to be identifiable in a newborn's blood or urine. In addition, some drugs, including marijuana, remain in the system for a long time, making it possible to test for them several days after birth. But others, such as cocaine and alcohol, are excreted from the newborn's body within hours of birth. Thus, drug testing must be carried out almost immediately after birth to determine whether the newborn has been prenatally exposed to potentially harmful drugs (Centers for Disease Control [CDC], 1996).

An additional difficulty is that drug testing at birth usually reveals little or nothing about drug exposure earlier in pregnancy. Consequently, a pregnant woman could "deliver" a drug to her viable fetus during, for example, the 25th week of pregnancy (a potential crime according to logic of the prosecution approach), but no concrete evidence of this behavior would be available at the time of birth.

Which Behavior Will Be Deterred?

To get around the difficulty of identifying drug exposure at birth, some prosecution advocates have suggested that doctors be required to report drug use by their pregnant patients to the police, just as they are required to report suspected child abuse. However, critics say such policies may cause pregnant women to delay prenatal care or to deliver their babies alone (Harris, 2003). Thus, fear of prosecution might damage the health of more fetuses than drug use itself.

Alternatives to Prosecution

Rather than prosecuting pregnant drug users, most public health officials recommend a strategy that combines universal access to early prenatal care, education, and drug treatment (Foley, 2002). Access to early prenatal care is critical because it provides a context for educating individual pregnant women. In addition, health care providers can provide pregnant drug users with treatment information.

Prosecution foes also claim that education in the public schools and through the mass media about the link between drug use and birth defects will create an informed population. Among those receiving the information will be drug-using women who are or will be pregnant. Moreover, informed potential fathers and friends and family members may be able to exert social pressure on women to stop using drugs, at least during pregnancy. However, widespread education about the teratogenic effects of drugs already exists and justifies prosecution, advocates argue. They say that women who continue to use drugs even though they know they may harm a fetus are even more accountable for their behavior, in a moral sense, than those who are ignorant of the dangers of prenatal drug exposure.

What Is the Situation in Your Area?

Policies addressing drug use during pregnancy are different in every state. In March, 2001, the U.S. Supreme Court introduced some consistency when it ruled that pregnant women cannot be tested for drug use without their permission if the primary purpose of testing is to obtain evidence that will be used in a criminal trial ("Court Curbs Drug Tests," 2001). However, the Court left open the possibility of testing pregnant women without their permission for other reasons, such as for referral to drug treatment programs, and did not address the issue of drug testing for newborns. Thus, local authorities continue to approach this problem in different ways. With a little investigation, you can find out what the relevant government and institutional policies are in your area.

Your Turn

- Do the hospitals in your area routinely test newborns for drug exposure? If so, how?
- What do doctors in your area do when they suspect a baby's problems are caused by prenatal drug exposure?
- Does your state require doctors to report pregnant women who use drugs to the police or to a state agency?
- Are there drug rehabilitation programs specifically for pregnant women in your area?
- Has your state prosecuted any women for using drugs while pregnant? What were the details of the case(s)?
- Do you agree or disagree with the way this issue is addressed in your state and city? Why?

PART TWO
Infancy

4

Physical, Sensory, and Perceptual Development in Infancy

Have you ever tried to water ski? If you spent more time treading water than you did gliding over its surface, you might feel somewhat embarrassed to learn about the skiing prowess of 3-year-old Cole Marsolek of Menomonie, Wisconsin. Skiing at the age of 3 would be remarkable enough, but Cole was already an old hand at the sport by his third birthday. In fact, two months shy of his second birthday, he became something of a local celebrity when a Minneapolis television station featured video of the tyke happily perched on his training ski on Wisconsin's Tainter Lake and waving to his admirers on shore. But why would parents even consider allowing a toddler to water ski?

Cole's parents, Chad and Lissa Marsolek, report that "Ski, please!" were among Cole's first words. He expressed so much enthusiasm for the

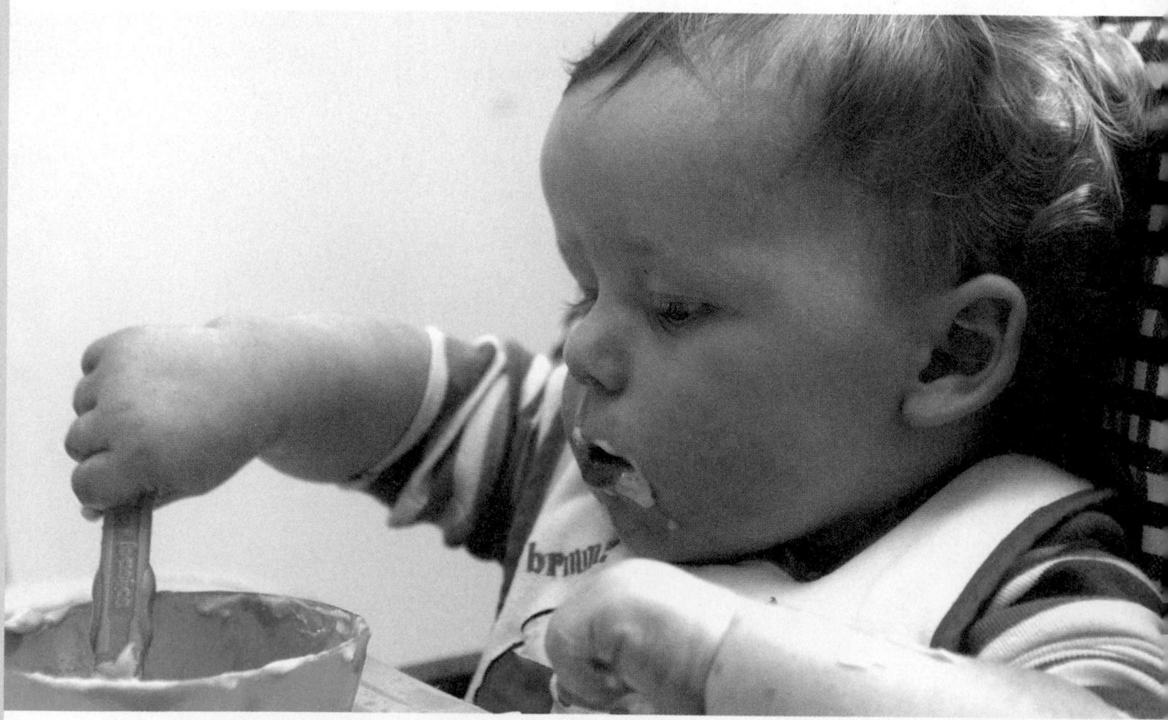

idea of skiing with them that they decided to let him give it a try. First they taught him how to float and maneuver in the water while wearing a life jacket. They also taught him how to hold his breath under water. When he mastered these two skills, Cole's parents allowed him to ride in an inner tube that was pulled along by the family boat. Although he loved tubing, Cole seemed to know that he wasn't really skiing and pleaded with his parents to let him ski. When Lissa saw a child-sized training ski for sale online, she purchased it immediately. Although Cole was just 22 months old at the time and was still in diapers, he was able to stand up and maintain his balance on the training ski the first time he tried it. His joyful facial expression seemed to say that he had finally gotten what he wanted, a chance to ski just like Mom and Dad.

If you are a skier or have ever tried the sport, you know how much coordination and balance it requires. How was a mere toddler able to do it? Consider that both of Cole's parents, Chad and Lissa Marsolek are skiers. In fact, the family goes skiing every evening in the summer. Moreover, Cole's mother was an early skier herself, having taken up the sport at the tender age of 3. Of course, mastering any sport requires more than physical ability and opportunities to practice. In Cole's case, the essential ingredient of high interest was evident from the time that he uttered his first "Ski, please!" The athletic ability Cole inherited from his parents and his own interest in the sport, together with opportunities to observe and practice the sport, all worked together to produce a remarkable outcome.

As students of human development, the case of the skiing toddler shows us that physical accomplishments result from a complex interaction of internal and external factors. As you will learn in this chapter, interactive influences are at work in the acquisition of everyday skills such as walking, just as they are in cases in which toddlers demonstrate skills that seem to be far beyond their years. Likewise, a number of variables influence infants' health and the development of their sensory and perceptual skills.

Physical Changes

What comes to mind when you think about the first two years of life? If you take the time to reflect on this period, you will realize that, apart from prenatal development, it is the period during which the greatest degree of physical change occurs. Although their senses work well, newborns have very limited physical skills. In contrast, 2-year-olds can not only move about independently, but they can also feed themselves and, to the dismay of many parents, get themselves into all kinds of precarious situations. Nevertheless, a 2-year-old still has a long way to go before she reaches physical maturity. But her brain is racing ahead of the rest of her body, a developmental pattern that accounts for the typical "top-heavy" appearance of toddlers (see The Real World on page 97).

Learning Objective 4.1

What important changes in the brain take place during infancy?

The Brain and Nervous System

The brain and the nervous system develop rapidly during the first 2 years. Figure 4.1 shows the main structures of the brain. At birth, the midbrain and the medulla are the most fully developed. These two parts, both in the lower part of the skull and connected to the spinal cord, regulate vital functions such as heartbeat and respiration, as well as attention, sleeping, waking, elimination, and movement of the head and neck—all actions a newborn can perform at least moderately well. The least-developed part of the brain at birth is the cortex, the convoluted gray matter that wraps around the midbrain and is involved in perception, body movement, thinking, and language.

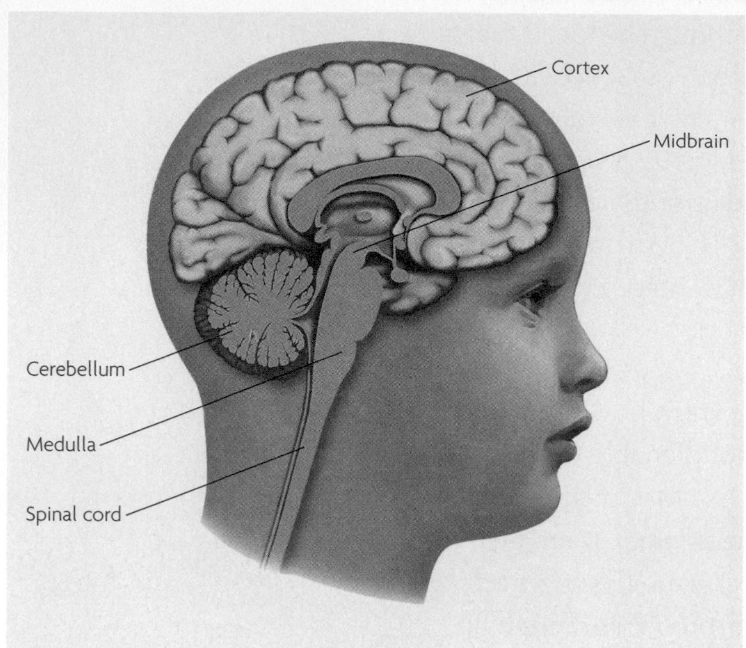

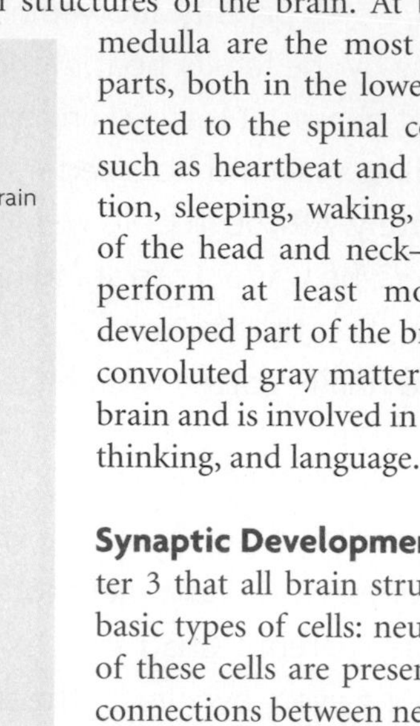

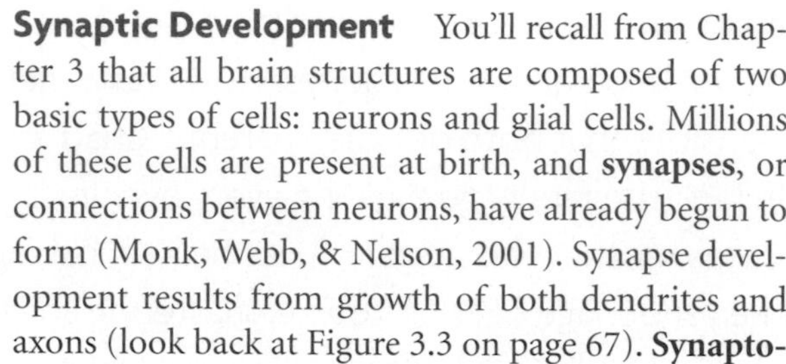

Figure 4.1
Parts of the Brain

The medulla and the midbrain are largely developed at birth. In the first 2 years after birth, it is primarily the cortex that develops, with each neuron going through an enormous growth of dendrites and a vast increase in synapses.

Synaptic Development You'll recall from Chapter 3 that all brain structures are composed of two basic types of cells: neurons and glial cells. Millions of these cells are present at birth, and **synapses**, or connections between neurons, have already begun to form (Monk, Webb, & Nelson, 2001). Synapse development results from growth of both dendrites and axons (look back at Figure 3.3 on page 67). **Synaptogenesis**, the creation of synapses, occurs rapidly in the cortex during the first few years after birth, resulting in a quadrupling of the overall weight of the brain by age 4 (Spreen, Risser, & Edgell, 1995). However, synaptogenesis is not smooth and continuous. Instead, it happens in spurts.

Typically, each synaptic growth spurt generates many more connections between neurons than the individual actually needs. Thus, each burst of synaptogenesis is followed by a period of **pruning** in which unnecessary pathways and connections are eliminated (Huttenlocher, 1994). For example, each muscle cell seems to develop synaptic connections with several motor neurons (nerve cells that carry impulses to muscles) in the spinal cord. As the infant works to gain control over his movements, some of these connections are used repeatedly, while others are ignored. Soon, the unused connections die off, or get "pruned" by the system. Once the pruning process is completed, each muscle fiber is connected to only one motor neuron.

This cycle of synaptogenesis followed by pruning continues through the lifespan. With each cycle, the brain becomes more efficient. Consequently, a 1-year-old actually has denser dendrites and synapses than an adult does, but the 1-year-old's network operates far less efficiently than that of the adult. However, efficiency comes at a price. Because infants have more unused synapses than adults, they can bounce back from a host of insults to the brain (e.g., malnutrition, head injury) much more easily than an adult. Neuroscientists use the term **plasticity** to refer to the brain's ability to change in response to experience.

Developmentalists draw several important implications from the cyclical synaptogenesis–pruning feature of neurological development. First, it seems clear that brain development follows the old dictum "Use it or lose it." A child growing up in a rich or intellectually challenging environment will retain a more complex network of synapses than one growing up with fewer forms of stimulation. The evidence to support this proposal comes from several kinds of research, including work with animals. For example, rat infants reared in highly stimulating environments have a denser network of neurons, dendrites, and synaptic connections in adulthood than rats not raised in such settings (e.g., Escorihuela, Tobena, & Fernández-Teruel, 1994). Animal studies also show that enriched environments help the young brain overcome damage caused by teratogens such as alcohol (Hannigan, O'Leary-Moore, & Berman, 2007).

synapses connections between neurons

synaptogenesis the process of synapse development

pruning the process of eliminating unused synapses

plasticity the ability of the brain to change in response to experience

In addition, as mentioned earlier, the brains of infants possess greater plasticity than those of older children and adults. Paradoxically, though, the period of greatest plasticity is also the period in which the child may be most vulnerable to major deficits—just as a fetus is most vulnerable to teratogens during the time of most rapid growth of any body system (Uylings, 2006). Thus, a young infant needs sufficient stimulation and order in his environment to maximize the early period of rapid growth and plasticity (de Haan, Luciana, Maslone, Matheny, & Richards, 1994). A really inadequate diet or a serious lack of stimulation in the early months may thus have subtle but long-range effects on the child's later cognitive progress. Some have even argued that watching too much television in the early months may impede brain development, as discussed in No Easy Answers on page 98.

Finally, new information about the continuation of synaptogenesis and pruning throughout the lifespan has forced developmental psychologists to change their ideas about the links between brain development and behavior. If the brain were almost completely organized by age 2, as most developmentalists believed until recently, it would seem logical to assume that whatever developments occurred after that age were largely the product of experience. But researchers now know that changes in psychological functioning are linked to changes in the brain throughout the entire human lifespan.

THE REAL WORLD

A Day in the Life of a Baby

Six-month-old Keisha's father, Jamal, is a stay-at-home dad who often feels frustrated. For one thing, his goal of maintaining his career via a telecommuting arrangement with his employer seems to always take a back seat to the minute-by-minute demands of taking care of little Keisha. He worries, too, about his list of undone household tasks—the laundry, cooking, yard work, and so on—that seems to get longer each day. And by the time Keisha's mother comes home from work each evening, he is often too tired to truly enjoy being with her. Despite his frustrations, Jamal values the time he spends with Keisha and wouldn't trade the opportunity to observe his daughter's development first-hand for anything. Jamal has learned something that all new parents do, something that cannot be fully appreciated until a person has actually done it: Caring for an infant is one of the most demanding, and most rewarding, tasks in life. Here's some insight into what Jamal and Keisha's days are like:

6:30 a.m.: Wakes up; takes bottle; diaper change; back to sleep
9:00 a.m.: Wakes up; diaper change; eats cereal and fruit; gets dressed; watches television; plays in walker until bored; moves to playpen; out of playpen onto floor; crawls and practices pulling up on furniture; chews on everything in sight
10:30 a.m.: Gets fussy; takes bottle; naps for 30 minutes
11:45 a.m.: Wakes up; plays outside in walker
12:00 p.m.: Eats meat and vegetables; tries to drink from cup; same play routine as earlier in the day
2:00 p.m.: Takes bottle; repeats play routine
4:00 p.m.: Gets fussy; naps for 1 hour
5:30 p.m.: Eats cereal and fruit; takes bottle
6:30 p.m.: Has bath; plays in tub for 20 minutes; gets dressed for bed; watches television with older brother and sister; plays, snuggles, and jabbers with siblings, Mom, and Dad
9:00 p.m.: Takes bottle; listens to Mom read a story; goes to sleep
2:00 a.m.: Wakes up; diaper change; takes bottle
4:00 a.m.: Wakes up; diaper change; takes bottle
6:30 a.m.: Daily cycle starts again

Considering Jamal and Keisha's daily routine, it's easy to see why parents sometimes get so caught up in the hour-by-hour struggles associated with taking care of an infant that they forget to stop and reflect on just how short, and fascinating, infancy is. After all, who hasn't heard a parent of a grown child say, "I don't know where the time went." This familiar declaration reminds parents that they should focus on appreciating the uniqueness

of each phase of their child's development rather than on longing for a future time when they won't be so busy.

Questions for Reflection

1. If Jamal asked for your advice, what suggestions would you give him for managing his time more effectively?
2. Based on what we know about infant sleep patterns (see page 99), is Keisha's awakening for 2:00 and 4:00 a.m. feedings typical? When would you expect her to be sleeping through the night?

Myelinization Another crucial process in the development of neurons is the creation of sheaths, or coverings, around individual axons, which insulate them from one another electrically and improve their conductivity. These sheaths are made of a substance called myelin; the process of developing the sheath is called **myelinization**.

The sequence of myelinization follows both cephalocaudal and proximodistal patterns (these were defined in Chapter 3). For example, nerves serving muscle cells in the neck and shoulders are myelinized earlier than those serving the abdomen. As a result, babies can control their head movements before they can roll over. Myelinization is most rapid during the first 2 years after birth, but it continues at a slower pace throughout childhood and adolescence. For example, the parts of the brain that are involved in vision reach maturity by the second birthday (Lippé, Perchet, & Lassonde, 2007). By contrast, those that govern motor movements are not fully myelinized until a child is about 6 years old (Todd, Swarzenski, Rossi, & Visconti, 1995).

myelinization a process in neuronal development in which sheaths made of a substance called myelin gradually cover individual axons and electrically insulate them from one another to improve the conductivity of the nerve

reticular formation the part of the brain that regulates attention

Other structures take even longer to become myelinized. For example, the **reticular formation** is the part of the brain responsible for keeping your attention on what you're doing and for helping you sort out important and unimportant information. Myelinization of the reticular formation begins in infancy but continues in spurts across childhood and adolescence. In fact, the process isn't complete until a person is in her mid-20s (Spreen, Risser, & Edgell, 1995). Consequently, during the first 2 years, infants improve their ability to focus on a task. Likewise, a 12-year-old is much better at concentrating than an infant but is still fairly inefficient when compared to an adult.

Learning Objective 4.2

How do babies' reflexes and behavioral states change?

Reflexes and Behavioral States

Changes in the brain result in predictable changes in babies' reflexes, sensory capacities, and patterns of waking and sleeping. In fact, such changes—or their lack—can be important indicators of nervous system health.

NO EASY ANSWERS

TV for Tots: How Much Is Too Much?

Surveys show that most babies in the United States, especially those who are between 12 and 24 months of age, watch television (Certain & Kahn, 2002). There is no doubt that infants enjoy watching television but is there a dark side to television watching in the early years of life?

Researcher Dimitri Christakis and his colleagues' studies show that excessive television watching in the first 3 years of life predisposes children to develop attention-deficit hyperactivity disorder in the school-age years (Christakis, Zimmerman, DiGiuseppe, & McCarty, 2004). Their studies support the official recommendation of the American Academy of Pediatrics (AAP) that parents prohibit television watching for children under age 2 (AAP, 1999). The AAP's policy assumes that television watching may adversely affect brain development. When research results and recommendations come from authoritative sources like the AAP, they are often unquestioned by the public. But are such claims justified?

As you learned in Chapter 1, a correlation between two variables may be due to a third variable that the researcher didn't measure. It seems possible that parents who have poor relationships with their children or who don't enjoy interacting with them may allow their infants to spend more time watching television than do parents who have more positive relationships with their children. This lack of interaction between parent and child may be the variable that predisposed television-watching toddlers to ADHD upon entering school. Moreover, other studies have shown that toddlers can acquire new vocabulary and even social skills from watching high-quality programs such as *Sesame Street* (Huston & Wright, 1998). Thus, some developmentalists suggest that parents focus on quality when selecting television programs for their toddlers to watch and, at the same time, limit the total amount of time that they allow their children to watch television.

To date, there have been no studies that directly examine the relationship between television watching and brain development. Thus, developmentalists and parents alike need to be cautious about drawing conclusions from research showing correlations between environmental variables (e.g., television watching) and developmental outcomes that may have neurological underpinnings (e.g., ADHD).

Take a Stand

Decide which of these two statements you most agree with and think about how you would defend your position:

1. I agree with the American Academy of Pediatrics' recommendation that children under age 2 shouldn't watch television at all.
2. I think that the AAP's recommendation goes too far. There is a place for television in the lives of toddlers.

Reflexes Humans are born with many **adaptive reflexes** that help them survive. Some, such as automatically sucking any object that enters the mouth, disappear in infancy or childhood. Others protect us against harmful stimuli over the whole lifespan. These include withdrawal from a painful stimulus and the opening and closing of the pupil of the eye in response to variations in brightness. Weak or absent adaptive reflexes in neonates suggest that the brain is not functioning properly and that the baby requires additional assessment.

This 4-week-old baby is using the inborn adaptive reflex of sucking.

The purposes of **primitive reflexes**, so called because they are controlled by the less sophisticated parts of the brain (the medulla and the midbrain), are less clear. For example, if you make a loud noise or startle a baby in some other way, you'll see her throw her arms outward and arch her back, a pattern that is part of the Moro, or startle, reflex. Stroke the bottom of her foot and she will splay out her toes and then curl them in, a reaction called the Babinski reflex. By 6 to 8 months of age, primitive reflexes begin to disappear. If such reflexes persist past this age, the baby may have some kind of neurological problem (DiMario, 2002).

Behavioral States Researchers have described five different states of sleep and wakefulness in neonates. Most infants move through these states in the same sequence: from deep sleep to lighter sleep and then to alert wakefulness and fussing. After they are fed, they become drowsy and drop back into deep sleep. The cycle repeats itself about every 2 hours.

Neonates sleep as much as 80% of the time, as much in the daytime as at night (Sola, Rogido, & Partridge, 2002). By 8 weeks of age, the total amount of sleep per day has dropped somewhat and signs of day/night sleep rhythms (called circadian rhythms) become evident. Babies of this age begin to sleep through two or three 2-hour cycles in sequence without coming to full wakefulness, and thus are often said to have started to "sleep through the night." By 6 months, babies are still sleeping a bit over 14 hours per day, but sleep is more regular and predictable. Most have clear nighttime sleep patterns and nap during the day at more predictable times.

Of course, babies vary a lot around these averages. Of the 6-week-old babies in one study, there was one who slept 22 hours per day and another who slept only 8.8 hours per day (Bamford et al., 1990). (Now, that must have been one tired set of parents!) And some babies do not develop a long nighttime sleep period until late in the first year of life. Moreover, cultural beliefs play an important role in parents' responses to infants' sleep patterns. For example, parents in the United States typically see a newborn's erratic sleep cycle as a behavior problem that requires "fixing" through parental intervention (Harkness, 1998). As a result, they focus a great deal of attention on trying to force babies to sleep through the night. In contrast, European parents are more likely to regard newborns' patterns of sleeping as manifestations of normal development and tend to expect babies to acquire stable sleep patterns naturally, without parental intervention, during the first 2 years.

Infants have different cries for pain, anger, and hunger. The basic cry, which often signals hunger, usually has a rhythmical pattern: cry, silence, breath, cry, silence, breath, with a kind of whistling sound often accompanying the in-breath. An anger cry is typically louder and more intense, and the pain cry normally has a very abrupt onset—unlike the other two kinds of cries, which usually begin with whimpering or moaning.

Cross-cultural studies suggest that crying increases in frequency over the first 6 weeks and then tapers off (St. James-Roberts, Bowyer, Varghese, & Sawdon, 1994). Moreover, parents across a variety of cultures use very similar techniques to soothe crying infants. Most babies stop crying when they are picked up, held, and talked or sung to. Getting a baby to suck on a pacifier also usually helps. Some parents worry that picking up a crying baby will lead to even more crying. But research suggests that prompt attention to a crying baby during the first 3 months actually leads to less crying later in infancy (Sulkes, 1998).

adaptive reflexes reflexes, such as sucking, that help newborns survive

primitive reflexes reflexes, controlled by "primitive" parts of the brain, that disappear during the first year of life

For the 15–20% of infants who develop **colic**, a pattern involving intense bouts of crying totaling 3 or more hours a day, for no immediately apparent reason such as hunger or a wet diaper, nothing seems to help. Typically, colic appears at about 2 weeks of age and then disappears spontaneously at 3 to 4 months (Coury, 2002). The crying is generally worst in late afternoon or early evening. Neither psychologists nor physicians know why colic begins or why it stops without any intervention. It is a difficult pattern to live with, but the good news is that it does go away.

On average, neonates are awake and alert for a total of only 2 to 3 hours each day, and this time is unevenly distributed over a 24-hour period. In other words, the baby may be awake for 15 minutes at 6:00 a.m., another 30 minutes at 1:00 p.m., another 20 minutes at 4:00 p.m., and so on. Over the first 6 months, advances in neurological development enable infants to remain awake and alert for longer periods of time as their patterns of sleeping, crying, and eating become more regular.

Learning Objective 4.3

How do infants' bodies change, and what is the typical pattern of motor skill development in the first 2 years?

Growth, Motor Skills, and Developing Body Systems

Did you know that half of all the growing you would ever do in your life happened before you were two years old? In other words, a two-year-old's height is approximately half of what her height will be when she reaches physical maturity, a remarkable rate of growth considering that attainment of the second half of her adult height will be spread over a period of 10 to 12 years. But infants' bodies don't just change in size. There are many qualitative changes, such as those that involve motor skills, that happen during this period as well. As you read about them, recall from Chapter 3 that physical development proceeds from the head downward (*cephalocaudal* pattern) and from the center of the body outward (*proximodistal* pattern).

Growth and Motor Skills Babies grow 10–12 inches and triple their body weight in the first year of life. By age 2 for girls and about 2½ for boys, toddlers are half as tall as they will be as adults. This means a 2- to 2½-year-old's adult height can be reliably predicted by doubling his or her current height. But 2-year-olds have proportionately much larger heads than do adults—which they need to hold their nearly full-sized brains.

colic an infant behavior pattern involving intense daily bouts of crying totaling 3 or more hours a day

Table 4.1 Milestones of Motor Development in the First 2 Years

Age (in months)	Gross Motor Skills	Fine Motor Skills
1	Stepping reflex; lifts head slightly	Holds object if placed in hand
2–3	Lifts head up to 90-degree angle when lying on stomach	Begins to swipe at objects in sight
4–6	Rolls over; sits with support; moves on hands and knees ("creeps"); holds head erect while in sitting position	Reaches for and grasps objects
7–9	Sits without support; crawls	Transfers objects from one hand to the other
10–12	Pulls self up and walks grasping furniture; then walks alone; squats and stoops; plays pat-a-cake	Shows some signs of hand preference; grasps a spoon across palm but has poor aim when moving food to mouth
13–18	Walks backward, sideways; runs (14–20 mos.); rolls ball to adult; claps	Stacks two blocks; puts objects into small container and dumps them out
19–24	Walks up and down stairs, two feet per step; jumps with both feet off ground	Uses spoon to feed self; stacks 4 to 10 blocks

(*Sources:* Capute et al., 1984; Den Ouden et al., 1991; Overby, 2002.)

Children acquire an impressive array of motor skills in the first 2 years. *Gross motor skills* include abilities such as crawling that enable the infant to get around in the environment. *Fine motor skills* involve use of the hands, as when a 1-year-old stacks one block on top of another. Table 4.1 summarizes developments in each of these areas over the first 24 months.

Throughout infancy, girls are ahead of boys in some aspects of physical maturity. For example, the separate bones of the wrist appear earlier in girls than in boys (Tanner, 1990). This means that female infants may have a slight advantage in the development of fine motor skills such as self-feeding. Typically, boys are found to be more physically active and acquire gross motor skills faster than girls do.

The striking improvements in motor development in the early months are easy to illustrate. Between 6 and 12 months of age, babies progress from sitting alone, to crawling, to walking.

Explaining Motor Skill Development Despite gender differences in the rate of physical development, the sequence of motor skill development is virtually the same for all children, even those with serious physical or mental handicaps. Children with mental retardation, for example, move through the various motor milestones more slowly than normal children do, but they do so in the same sequence. Such consistencies support the view that motor development is controlled by an inborn biological timetable (Thelen, 1995).

The late Esther Thelen (1941–2004) suggested that the inborn timetable for motor skills development interacts with other aspects of physical development (Thelen, 1996). She often cited the disappearance of the *stepping reflex*, the tendency for very young infants to attempt to take steps when they are placed in an upright position with their feet touching a flat surface, at 4 months of age as an example of her **dynamic systems theory**, the notion that several factors interact to influence development. Thelen noted that infants gain a proportionately substantial amount of weight at about the same time that they no longer show the stepping reflex. Consequently, claimed Thelen, infants no longer exhibit the stepping reflex because their muscles are not yet strong enough to handle the increased weight of their legs. True walking, according to Thelen, emerges both as a result of a genetic plan for motor skills development and because of a change in the ratio of muscle strength and weight in infants' bodies. This latter change is strongly influenced by environmental variables, especially nutrition. Thus, the streams of influence that are incorporated into dynamic systems theory include inborn genetic factors and environmental variables such as the availability of adequate nutrition.

Wayne Dennis's (1960) classic early study of children raised in Iranian orphanages presaged Thelen's theory. His work demonstrated that babies who were routinely placed on their backs in cribs learned to walk eventually, but they did so about a year later than babies in less restrictive settings. Research involving infants living in normal environments supports the notion that experience influences motor development. In one such study, very young babies who were given more practice sitting were able to sit upright longer than those without such practice (Zelazo, Zelazo, Cohen, & Zelazo, 1993). Opportunities to practice motor skills seem to be particularly important for young children who have disorders such as cerebral palsy that impair motor functioning (Kerr, McDowell, & McDonough, 2007). Consequently, developmentalists are fairly certain that severely restricting a baby's movement slows down acquisition of motor skills, and many are beginning to accept the idea that a baby's movement experiences in normal environments may also influence motor skill development.

dynamic systems theory the view that several factors interact to influence development

Developing Body Systems During infancy, bones change in size, number, and composition. Changes in the number and density of bones in particular parts of the body are responsible for improvements in coordinated movement. For example, at birth, the wrist contains a single mass of cartilage; by 1 year of age, the cartilage has developed into three separate bones. The progressive separation of the wrist bones is one of the factors behind gains in fine motor skills over the first 2 years. Wrist bones continue to differentiate over the next several years until eventually, in adolescence, the wrist has nine separate bones (Tanner, 1990).

The process of bone hardening, called *ossification*, occurs steadily, beginning in the last weeks of prenatal development and continuing through puberty. Bones in different parts of the body harden in a sequence that follows the typical proximodistal and cephalocaudal patterns. Motor development depends to a large extent on ossification. Standing, for example, is impossible if an infant's leg bones are too soft, no matter how well developed the muscles and nervous system are.

The body's full complement of muscle fibers is present at birth, although the fibers are initially small and have a high ratio of water to muscle (Tanner, 1990). In addition, a newborn's muscles contain a fairly high proportion of fat. By 1 year of age, the water content of an infant's muscles is equal to that of an adult's, and the ratio of fat to muscle tissue has begun to decline (Tershakovec & Stallings, 1998). Changes in muscle composition lead to increases in strength that enable 1-year-olds to walk, run, jump, climb, and so on.

Critical Thinking

1. Animal research plays a prominent role in developmentalists' understanding of early physical development. What are the problems with generalizing from the results of laboratory studies of animals to infants who are developing in the real world?

The lungs also grow rapidly and become more efficient during the first 2 years (Kercsmar, 1998). Improvements in lung efficiency, together with the increasing strength of heart muscles, give a 2-year-old greater *stamina*, or ability to maintain activity, than a newborn. Consequently, by the end of infancy, children are capable of engaging in fairly long periods of sustained motor activity without rest (often exhausting their parents in the process!).

Health and Wellness

Babies depend on the adults in their environments to help them stay healthy. Specifically, they need the right foods in the right amounts, and they need regular medical care.

Learning Objective 4.4

What are the nutritional needs of infants?

Nutrition

After several decades of extensive research in many countries, experts agree that, for most infants, breastfeeding is substantially superior nutritionally to bottle-feeding (Taveras et al., 2004). Breastfeeding is associated with a number of benefits. For one, breast milk contributes to more rapid weight and size gain (Prentice, 1994). On average, breastfed infants are less likely to suffer from such problems as diarrhea, gastroenteritis, bronchitis, ear infections, and colic, and they are less likely to die in infancy (Barness & Curran, 1996; Beaudry, Dufour, & Marcoux, 1995; Golding, Emmett, & Rogers, 1997a, 1997b; López-Alarcón, Villapando, & Fajardo, 1997). Breast milk also appears to stimulate better immune system function (Pickering et al., 1998). For these reasons, physicians strongly recommend breastfeeding if it is at all possible, even if the mother can nurse for only a few weeks after birth or if her breast milk must be supplemented with formula feedings (Tershakovec & Stallings, 1998).

Surprisingly, though, there are situations in which breast milk is not sufficient to meet babies' nutritional needs. For instance, preterm babies' intestinal tracts are not as mature as those of full-term infants. As a result, preterm babies require diets supplemented with amino acids and fats that fullterm infants' bodies can manufacture on their own (Guesry, 1998; Kliegman, 1998). However, these babies also need the immunological benefits of breast milk. Thus, physicians typically recommend feeding preterm babies a combination of breast milk and a supplemental formula that contains exactly the proteins, fats, vitamins, and minerals their bodies need.

There are also cases in which breastfeeding is impossible. For example, drugs are often present in the breast milk of mothers who are substance abusers or who depend on medications to maintain their own health. Many of these drugs can negatively affect infant development. Consequently, doctors recommend that these women avoid breastfeeding. In such cases, babies who are fed high-quality infant formula, prepared according to the manufacturer's instructions and properly sterilized, usually thrive on it (Tershakovec & Stallings, 1998).

Up until 4 to 6 months, babies need only breast milk or formula accompanied by appropriate supplements (Taveras et al., 2004). For example, pediatricians usually recommend iron supplements for most babies over 4 months of age and vitamin B12 supplements for infants whose nursing mothers are vegetarians (Tershakovec & Stallings, 1998). Likewise, doctors may recommend supplemental formula feeding for infants who are growing poorly.

There is no evidence to support the belief that solid foods encourage babies to sleep through the night. In fact, early introduction of solid food can interfere with nutrition. Pediatricians usually recommend withholding solid foods until a baby is 4 to 6 months old. The first solids should be single-grain cereals, such as rice cereal, with added iron. Parents should introduce a baby to no more than one new food each week. By following a systematic plan, parents can easily identify food allergies (Tershakovec & Stallings, 1998).

Malnutrition

Learning Objective 4.5

How does malnutrition affect infants' development?

Malnutrition in infancy can seriously impair a baby's brain because the nervous system is the most rapidly developing body system during the first 2 years of life. *Macronutrient malnutrition* results from a diet that contains too few calories. Macronutrient malnutrition is the world's leading cause of death among children under the age of 5 (Tershakovec & Stallings, 1998).

When the calorie deficit is severe, a disease called *marasmus* results. Infants with marasmus weigh less than 60% of what they should at their age, and many suffer permanent neurological damage from the disease. Most also suffer from parasitic infections that lead to chronic diarrhea. This condition makes it very difficult to treat marasmus by simply increasing an infant's intake of calories. However, a program of dietary supplementation with formula combined with intravenous feedings and treatment for parasites can reverse marasmus (Tershakovec & Stallings, 1998).

Some infants' diets contain almost enough calories, but not enough protein. Diets of this type lead to a disease called *kwashiorkor*, which is common in countries where infants are weaned too early to low-protein foods. Kwashiorkor-like symptoms are also seen in children who are chronically ill because of their bodies' inability to use the protein from the foods they eat. Like marasmus, kwashiorkor can lead to a variety of health problems as well as permanent brain damage (Tershakovec & Stallings, 1998).

Growth rate studies of poor children in the United States suggest that a small number of them suffer from macronutrient malnutrition (Tanner, 1990). In addition, a small proportion of infants have feeding problems, such as a poorly developed sucking reflex, that place them at risk for macronutrient malnutrition (Wright & Birks, 2000). However, most nutritional problems in industrialized societies involve *micronutrient malnutrition*, a deficiency of certain vitamins and/or minerals. For example, about 65% of infants and children in the United States have diets that are low enough in iron to cause anemia (Tershakovec & Stallings, 1998). Calcium deficiency, which results in poor bone health, is also becoming more common in the United States (Tershakovec & Stallings, 1998). Such deficiencies, although more common among the poor, are found in children of all economic levels.

Micronutrient malnutrition in infancy, especially when it leads to iron-deficiency anemia, may impede both social and language development (Guesry, 1998; Josse et al., 1999). Interestingly, researchers found that supplementing anemic

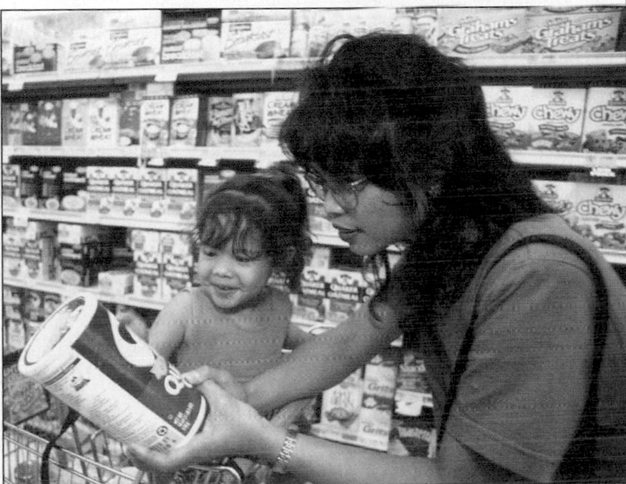

The goal of nutritional support programs for low-income mothers and children, such as the WIC program in the United States, is to prevent infant malnutrition. These programs may save taxpayers money in the long run, because malnutrition interferes with early brain development, thereby increasing the likelihood of learning problems and the need for special education services later in childhood.

infants' diets with iron led to improved scores on measures of social development but not language development, suggesting that the cognitive effects of anemia may be irreversible. Consequently, most public health officials support efforts to educate parents about the micronutritional needs of infants and children.

Learning Objective 4.6

What are infants' health care and immunization needs?

Health Care and Immunizations

Infants need frequent medical check-ups. Much of well baby care may seem routine, but it is extremely important to development. For example, during routine visits to the doctor's office or health clinic, babies' motor skills are usually assessed. An infant whose motor development is less advanced than expected for his age may require additional screening for developmental problems such as mental retardation (Sulkes, 1998).

One of the most important elements of well baby care is vaccination of the infant against a variety of diseases. Although immunizations later in childhood provide good protection, the evidence suggests that immunization is most effective when it begins in the first month of life and continues through childhood and adolescence (Umetsu, 1998). Even adults need occasional "booster" shots to maintain immunity.

In the United States, the average baby has seven respiratory illnesses in the first year of life. Interestingly, research in a number of countries shows that babies in day-care centers have about twice as many infections as those reared entirely at home, with those in small-group day care falling somewhere in between, presumably because babies cared for in group settings are exposed to a wider range of germs and viruses (Collet et al., 1994; Hurwitz, Gunn, Pinsky, & Schonberger, 1991; Lau, Uba, & Lehman, 2002). In general, the more people a baby is exposed to, the more often she is likely to be sick.

Neuropsychologists have suggested that the timing of respiratory illnesses that can lead to ear infections is important. Many note that infants who have chronic ear infections are more likely than their peers to have learning disabilities, attention disorders, and language deficits during the school years (Asbjornsen et al., 2005). These psychologists hypothesize that, because ear infections temporarily impair hearing, they may compromise the development of brain areas that are essential for language learning during the first 2 years of life (Spreen, Risser, & Edgell, 1995). Thus, most pediatricians emphasize the need for effective hygiene practices in day-care centers, such as periodic disinfection of all toys, as well as prompt treatment of infants' respiratory infections.

As recently as 1992, only 55% of children in the United States had received the full set of immunizations—a schedule that includes three separate injections of hepatitis vaccine, four of diphtheria/tetanus/pertussis, three of influenza, three of polio, and one each of measles/rubella and varicella zoster virus vaccines (Committee on Infectious Diseases, 1996). Vaccination against hepatitis A is also recommended in some cities (Centers for Disease Control [CDC] National Immunization Program, 2000). In 1995, an intensive media campaign sponsored by the federal government and the American Academy of Pediatrics (AAP) was put into place. As a result, the U.S. vaccination rate rose to more than 90% by 1999 and continued to rise in the early years of the 21st century (CDC National Immunization Program, 2000; Rosenthal et al., 2004). Public health officials believe that continued educational efforts, both in the media and by health care professionals who work directly with infants and their families, are necessary to prevent the immunization rate from returning to pre-campaign levels.

Critical Thinking

1. How would you go about raising public awareness of the dangers of micronutrient malnutrition, the importance of early immunizations, and the developmental risks associated with ear infections?

Infant Mortality

Researchers formally define **infant mortality** as death within the first year after birth. In the United States, about 7 babies out of every 1,000 die before age 1 (Kochanek & Martin, 2004). The rate has been declining steadily for the past several decades (down from 30 per 1,000 in 1950), but the United States continues to have a higher infant mortality rate than other industrialized nations. Almost two-thirds of these infant deaths occur in the first month of life

infant mortality death within the first year of life

and are directly linked to either congenital anomalies or low birth weight (Kochanek & Martin, 2004).

Sudden Infant Death Syndrome

Learning Objective 4.7

What have researchers learned about sudden infant death syndrome?

Deaths after the first month of life are most often the result of SIDS. **Sudden infant death syndrome (SIDS)**, in which an apparently healthy infant dies suddenly and unexpectedly, is the leading cause of death in the United States among infants between 1 month and 1 year of age (Task Force on Sudden Infant Death Syndrome, 2005). Physicians have not yet uncovered the basic cause of SIDS. But there are a few clues. For one thing, it is more common in the winter when babies may be suffering from viral infections that cause breathing difficulties. In addition, babies with a history of *apnea*—brief periods when their breathing suddenly stops—are more likely to die from SIDS (Kercsmar, 1998). Episodes of apnea may be noticed by medical personnel in the newborn nursery, or a nonbreathing baby may be discovered by her parents in time to be resuscitated. In such cases, physicians usually recommend using electronic breathing monitors that will sound an alarm if the baby stops breathing again while asleep.

SIDS is also more frequent among babies who sleep on their stomachs or sides, especially on a soft or fluffy mattress, pillow, or comforter (Task Force on Sudden Infant Death Syndrome, 2005). The American Academy of Pediatrics, along with physicians' organizations in many other countries, recommends that healthy infants be positioned on their backs to sleep. During the first 2 years after this recommendation was introduced, there was a 12% overall drop in SIDS cases in the United States, with even more dramatic declines of as much as 50% in areas where the recommendation was widely publicized (Spiers & Guntheroth, 1994). In England, Wales, New Zealand, and Sweden, major campaigns to discourage parents from placing their babies in the prone position (on their stomachs) have also been followed by sharp drops in SIDS rates (Gilman, Cheng, Winter, & Scragg, 1995).

Another important contributor is smoking by the mother during pregnancy or by anyone in the home after the child's birth. Babies exposed to such smoke are about four times as likely to die of SIDS as are babies with no smoking exposure (CDC, 2006).

Imaging studies of the brains of infants at high risk for SIDS, such as those who display apnea in the early days of life, suggest that myelination progresses at a slower rate in these children than in others who do not exhibit such risk factors (Morgan et al., 2002). Babies' patterns of sleep reflect these neurological differences and also predict SIDS risk. Infants who show increasingly lengthy sleep periods during the early months are at lower risk of dying from SIDS than babies whose sleep periods do not get much longer as they get older (Cornwell & Feigenbaum, 2006). Likewise, autopsies of SIDS babies have revealed that their brains often show signs of delayed myelination.

Group Differences in Infant Mortality

Learning Objective 4.8

How do infant mortality rates vary across groups?

Infant mortality rates, including deaths attributable both to congenital abnormalities and to SIDS, vary widely across racial groups in the United States, as shown in Figure 4.2 on page 106 (Kochanek & Smith, 2004; Matthews, 2005). Rates are lowest among Asian American infants; about 5 of every 1,000 such infants die each year. Among White babies, the rate is 5.9 per 1,000. The groups with the highest rates of infant death are Native Americans (9.1 per 1,000), Native Hawaiians (9 per 1,000), and African Americans (13.9 per 1,000). One reason for these differences is that infants in these groups are two to three times more likely to suffer from congenital abnormalities and low birth weight—the two leading causes of infant death in the first month of life—than babies in other groups. Furthermore, SIDS is also two to three times as common in these groups.

Because babies born into poor families are more likely to die than those born into families that are better off economically, some observers have suggested that poverty explains the higher rates of infant death among Native Americans (including Native Hawaiians) and African Americans, the groups with the highest rates of poverty. However, infant mortality

sudden infant death syndrome (SIDS) a phenomenon in which an apparently healthy infant dies suddenly and unexpectedly

Figure 4.2
Group Differences in Infant Mortality

As you can see, infant mortality rates vary widely across U.S. ethnic groups.

(*Source:* MacDorman & Atkinson, 1999; Matthews, 2005.)

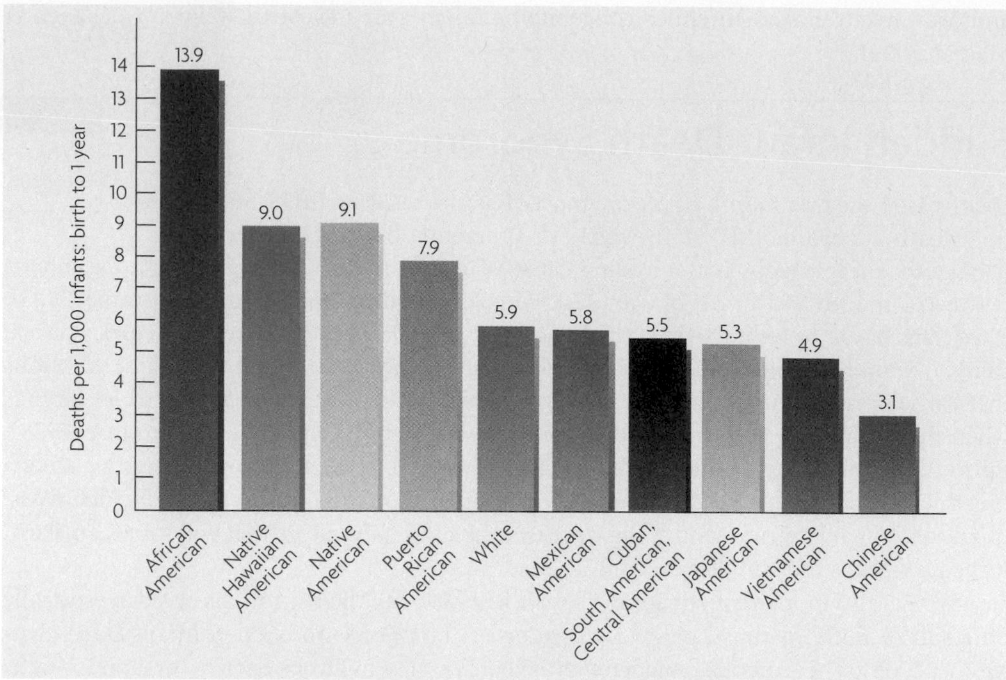

rates among Hispanic groups suggest that the link between poverty and infant mortality is complex. The average infant mortality rate among Mexican American, Cuban American, and South and Central American populations is only about 5.6 per 1,000 (MacDorman & Atkinson, 1999). These groups are almost as likely to be poor as African Americans and Native Americans. By contrast, Americans of Puerto Rican ancestry are no more likely to be poor than other Hispanic American groups, but the infant mortality rate in this group is 7.9 per 1,000.

Interestingly, mortality rates among the babies of immigrants of all groups are lower than those of U.S.-born infants. This finding also challenges the poverty explanation for group differences in infant mortality, because immigrant women are more likely to be poor and less likely to receive prenatal care than are women born in the United States (MacDorman & Atkinson, 1999; NCHS, 2006). Many researchers suggest that lower rates of tobacco and alcohol use among women born outside the United States may be an important factor.

Access to prenatal care is another factor that distinguishes ethnic groups in the United States (NCHS, 2006). As you can see in Figure 4.3, the two groups with the highest infant

Figure 4.3
Early Prenatal Care and Ethnicity

Wide disparities exist across ethnic groups with regard to access to prenatal care. Note that Native Americans and African Americans, the two groups with the highest rates of infant mortality, are least likely of all ethnic groups in the United States to obtain prenatal care in the first trimester.

(*Source:* National Center for Health Statistics (NCHS). (2006). *Health, United States, 2006.* Hyattsville, MD: Author.)

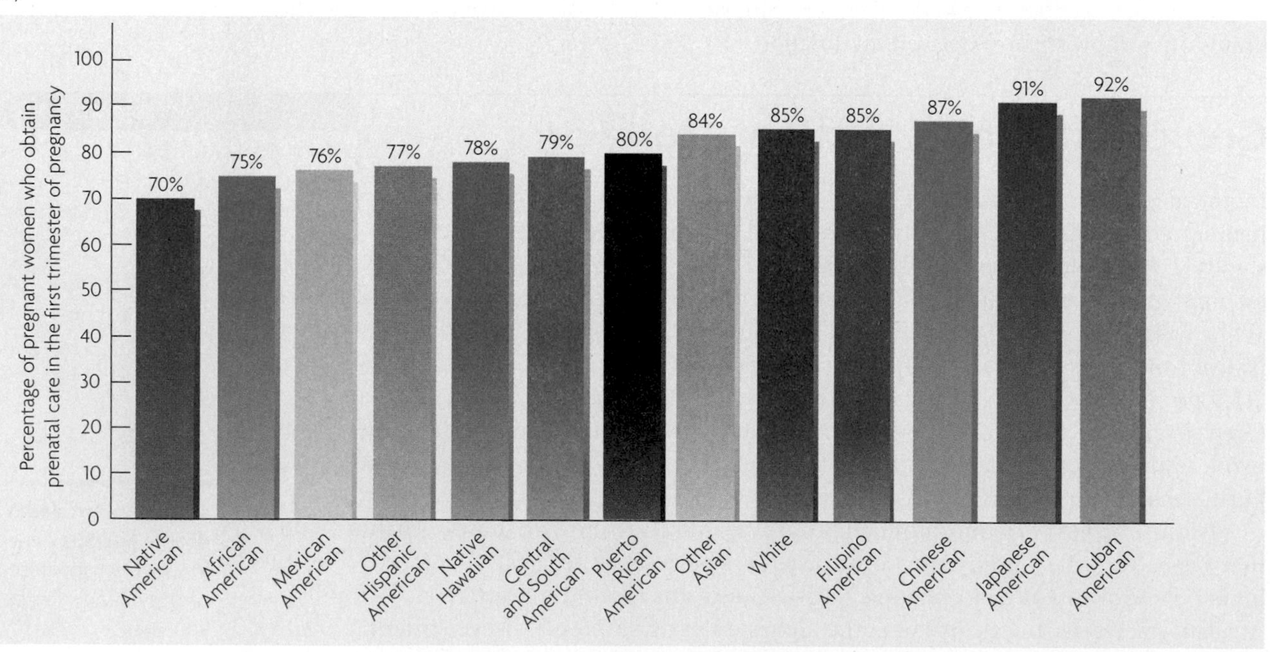

mortality rates, African Americans and Native Americans, are also those who are least likely to obtain prenatal care in the first trimester of pregnancy. Thus, the links among poverty, ethnicity, and infant mortality may be partly explained by access to prenatal care.

Critical Thinking

1. Generate your own hypothesis to explain group differences in infant mortality. What kind of information would you need to test your hypothesis?

Sensory Skills

When we study sensory skills, we are asking just what information the sensory organs receive. Does the structure of the eye permit infants to see color? Are the structures of the ear and the cortex such that a very young infant can discriminate among different pitches? The common theme running through all of what you will read in this section is that newborns and young infants have far more sensory capacity than physicians or psychologists thought even as recently as a few decades ago.

Vision

Learning Objective 4.9

How do infants' visual abilities change across the first months of life?

If you have ever had the chance to spend some time with a newborn, you probably noticed that, while awake, she spent a lot of time looking at things. But what, exactly, can a newborn see, and how well does she see it? The usual standard for **visual acuity** in adults is "20/20" vision. This means that you can see and identify something 20 feet away that the average person can also see at 20 feet. A person with 20/100 vision, in contrast, has to be as close as 20 feet to see something that the ordinary person can see at 100 feet. In other words, the higher the second number, the poorer the person's visual acuity. At birth, the infant's acuity is in the range of 20/200 to 20/400, but it improves rapidly during the first year as a result of synaptogenesis, pruning, and myelination in the neurons that serve the eyes and the brain's vision processing centers. Experts believe that most children reach the level of 20/20 vision by about 2 years of age (Keech, 2002). However, it's difficult to determine an infant's true visual acuity because children can't be tested with conventional eye exams until they are old enough to respond verbally to the examiner, typically at 4 to 5 years of age.

Newborns are pretty nearsighted, so they can focus very well at about 8 to 10 inches—just the distance between a parent's face and the baby's eyes when the baby is held for feeding.

Researchers have established that the types of cells in the eye (cones) necessary for perceiving red and green are clearly present by 1 month (and perhaps present at birth); those required for perceiving blue are probably present by then as well (Bornstein et al., 1992). Thus, infants can and do see and discriminate among various colors. Indeed, researchers have determined that infants' ability to sense color, even in the earliest weeks of life, is almost identical to that of adults (Pereverzeva, Hui-Lin Chien, Palmer, & Teller, 2002).

The process of following a moving object with your eyes is called **tracking**, and you do it every day in a variety of situations. You track the movement of other cars when you are driving; you track as you watch a friend walk toward you across the room; a baseball outfielder tracks the flight of the ball so that he can catch it. Because a newborn infant can't yet move independently, a lot of her experiences with objects are with things that move toward her or away from her. If she is to have any success in recognizing objects, she has to be able to keep her eyes on them as they move; she must be able to track. Classic research by Richard Aslin (1987) and others shows that tracking is initially fairly inefficient but improves quite rapidly. Infants younger than 2 months show some tracking for brief periods if the target is moving very slowly, but somewhere around 6 to 10 weeks a shift occurs, and babies' tracking becomes skillful rather quickly.

visual acuity how well one can see details at a distance

tracking the smooth movements of the eye used to follow the track of a moving object

Learning Objective 4.10

How do infants' senses of hearing, smell, taste, touch, and motion compare to those of older children and adults?

Hearing and Other Senses

As you learned in Chapter 2, babies can hear long before they are born. However, like vision, hearing improves considerably in the early months of life. The other senses follow a similar course.

Hearing Although children's hearing improves up to adolescence, newborns' **auditory acuity** is actually better than their visual acuity. Research evidence suggests that, within the general range of pitch and loudness of the human voice, newborns hear nearly as well as adults do (Ceponiene et al., 2002). Only with high-pitched sounds is their auditory skill less than that of an adult; such a sound needs to be louder to be heard by a newborn than to be heard by older children or adults (Werner & Gillenwater, 1990).

Another basic auditory skill that exists at birth but improves with age is the ability to determine the location of a sound. Because your two ears are separated from each other, sounds arrive at one ear slightly before the other, which allows you to judge location. Only if a sound comes from a source equidistant from the two ears (the "midline") does this system fail. In this case, the sound arrives at the same time to the two ears and you know only that the sound is somewhere on your midline. We know that newborns can judge at least the general direction from which a sound has come because they will turn their heads in roughly the right direction toward some sound. Finer-grained location of sounds, however, is not well developed at birth. For example, Barbara Morrongiello has observed babies' reactions to sounds played at the midline and then sounds coming from varying degrees away from the midline. Among infants 2 months old, it takes a shift of about 27 degrees off of midline before the baby shows a changed response; among 6-month-olds, only a 12-degree shift is needed; by 18 months, discrimination of a 4-degree shift is possible—nearly the skill level seen in adults (Morrongiello, 1988; Morrongiello, Fenwick, & Chance, 1990).

Smelling and Tasting The senses of smell and taste have been studied much less than vision and hearing, but we do have some basic knowledge. The two senses are intricately related in infants, just as they are in adults—that is, if you cannot smell for some reason (for example, because you have a cold), your taste sensitivity is also significantly reduced. Taste is detected by the taste buds on the tongue, which register four basic flavors: sweet, sour, bitter, and salty. Smell is registered in the mucous membranes of the nose and has nearly unlimited variations.

Newborns appear to respond differentially to all four of the basic flavors (Crook, 1987). Some of the clearest demonstrations of this come from an elegantly simple set of early studies by Jacob Steiner (Ganchrow, Steiner, & Daher, 1983; Steiner, 1979). Newborn infants who had never been fed were photographed before and after flavored water was put into their mouths. By varying the flavor, Steiner could determine whether the babies reacted differently to different tastes. As you can see in Figure 4.4, babies responded quite differently to sweet, sour, and bitter flavors. Newborns can also taste *umami*, the characteristic flavor that comes from adding monosodium glutamate (MSG) to food and which is typical of high-protein foods that are high in glutamates (e.g., meat, cheese). Generally, newborns express pleasure when researchers test them for umami sensitivity (Nicklaus, Boggio, & Issanchou, 2005). Some researchers speculate that newborns' preferences for umami-flavored and sweet foods explain their attraction to breast milk, a substance that is naturally rich in sugars and glutamates.

auditory acuity how well one can hear

Critical Thinking

1. In what ways do babies' sensory skills contribute to the development of parent-infant relationships?

Senses of Touch and Motion The infant's senses of touch and motion may well be the best developed of all. Certainly these senses are sufficiently well developed to get the baby fed. If you think back to the discussion of reflexes earlier in the chapter, you'll realize that the rooting reflex relies on a touch stimulus to the cheek while the sucking reflex relies on touch in the mouth. Babies appear to be especially sensitive to touches on the mouth, the face, the hands, the soles of the feet, and the abdomen, with less sensitivity in other parts of the body (Reisman, 1987).

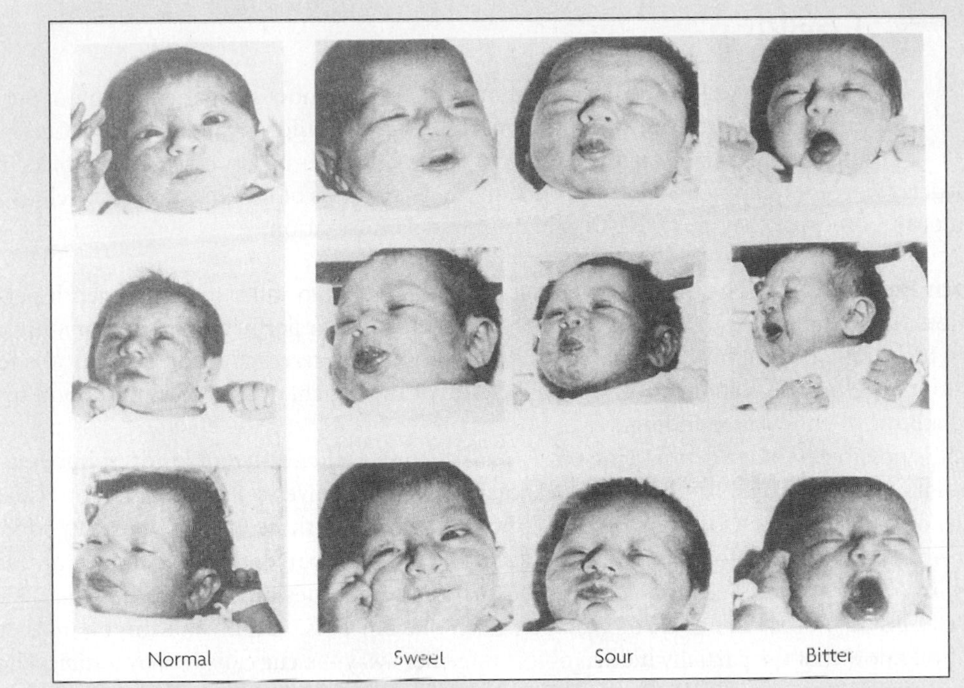

Figure 4.4
Taste Responses in Newborns

These are three of the newborns Steiner observed in his experiments on taste response. The left-hand column shows the babies' normal expressions; the remaining columns show the change in expression when they were given sweet, sour, and bitter tastes. What is striking is how similar the expressions are for each taste.

(*Source*: This figure was published in *Advances in Child Development and Behavior*, Vol. 13, H. W. Reese and L. P. Lipsitt, "Human Facial Expressions in Response to Taste and Smell Stimulation", Copyright Academic Press, 1979. Reprinted by permission.)

Perceptual Skills

When we turn to studies of perceptual skills, we are asking what the individual does with the sensory information—how it is interpreted or combined. Researchers have found that very young infants are able to make remarkably fine discriminations among sounds, sights, and feelings, and they pay attention to and respond to patterns, not just to individual events.

Studying Perceptual Development

Learning Objective 4.11
How do researchers study perceptual development?

Babies can't talk and can't respond to ordinary questions, so how are we to decipher just what they can see, hear, or discriminate? Researchers use three basic methods that allow them to "ask" a baby about what he experiences (Bornstein, Arterberry, & Mash, 2005). In the **preference technique**, devised by Robert Fantz (1956), the baby is simply shown two pictures or two objects, and the researcher keeps track of how long the baby looks at each one. If many infants shown the same pair of pictures consistently look longer at one picture than the other, this not only tells us that babies see some difference between the two but also may reveal something about the kinds of objects or pictures that capture babies' attention.

Another strategy takes advantage of the processes of **habituation**, or getting used to a stimulus, and its opposite, **dishabituation**, responding to a somewhat familiar stimulus as if it were new. Researchers first present the baby with a particular sight, sound, or object over and over until he habituates—that is, until he stops looking at it or showing interest in it. Then the researchers present another sight, sound, or object that is slightly different from the original one and watch to see whether the baby shows renewed interest (dishabituation). If the baby does show renewed interest, you know he perceives the slightly changed sight, sound, or object as "different" in some way from the original.

The third option is to use the principles of *operant conditioning*, described in Chapter 2. For example, an infant might be trained to turn her head when she hears a particular sound, with the sight of an interesting moving toy used as a reinforcement. After the learned response is well established, the experimenter can vary the sound in some systematic way to see whether or not the baby still turns her head.

preference technique a research method in which a researcher keeps track of how long a baby looks at each of two objects shown

habituation a decline in attention that occurs because a stimulus has become familiar

dishabituation responding to a somewhat familiar stimulus as if it were new

Learning Objective 4.12

How do depth perception and patterns of looking change over the first two years?

Looking

One important question to ask about visual perception is whether the infant perceives his environment in the same way as older children and adults do. Can he judge how far away an object is by looking at it? Does he visually scan an object in an orderly way? Developmentalists believe that infants' patterns of looking at objects tell us a great deal about what they are trying to gain from visual information.

Depth Perception One of the perceptual skills that has been most studied is depth perception. An infant needs to be able to judge depth in order to perform all kinds of simple tasks, including judging how far away an object is so that he can reach for it, how far it is to the floor if he has ideas about crawling off the edge of the couch, or how to aim a spoon toward a bowl of chocolate pudding.

It is possible to judge depth using any (or all) of three rather different kinds of information: First, *binocular cues* involve both eyes, each of which receives a slightly different visual image of an object; the closer the object is, the more different these two views are. In addition, of course, information from the muscles of the eyes tells you something about how far away an object may be. Second, pictorial information, sometimes called *monocular cues*, requires input from only one eye. For example, when one object is partially in front of another one, you know that the partially hidden object is farther away—a cue called *interposition*. The relative sizes of two similar objects, such as two telephone poles or two people you see in the distance, may also indicate that the smaller-appearing one is farther away. *Linear perspective* (like the impression that railroad lines are getting closer together as they get farther away) is another monocular cue. Third, *kinetic cues* come from either your own motion or the motion of some object: If you move your head, objects near you seem to move more than objects farther away (a phenomenon called *motion parallax*). Similarly, if you see objects moving, such as a person walking across a street or a train moving along a track, closer objects appear to move over larger distances in a given period of time.

In an experiment using a "visual cliff" apparatus, like the one used by Gibson and Walk, mom tries to entice her baby out onto the "cliff" side. But because the infant can perceive depth, he fears that he will fall if he comes toward her, so he stays put, looking concerned.

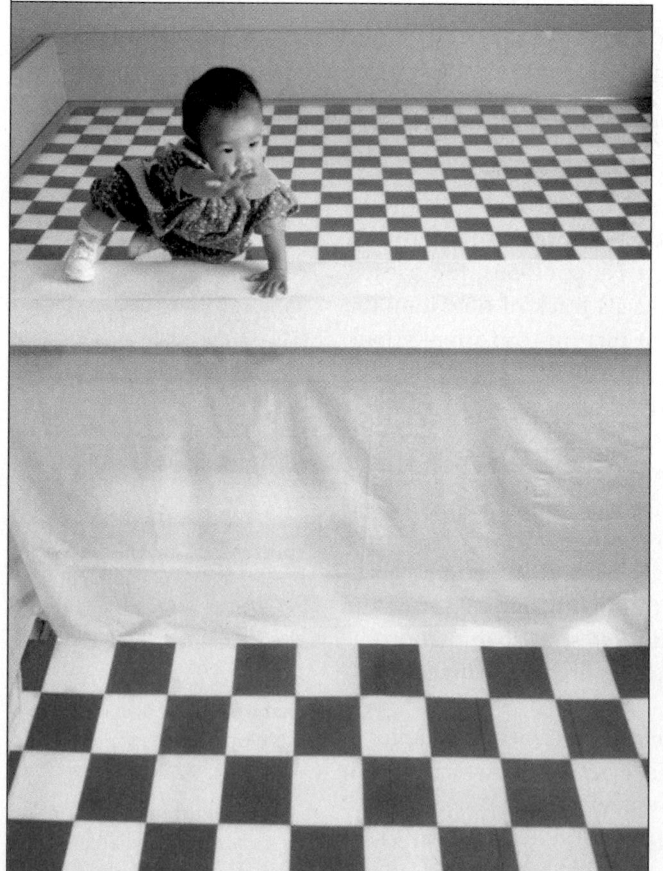

How early can an infant judge depth, and which of these cues does he use? This is still an active area of research, so the answer is not final. The best conclusion at the moment seems to be that kinetic information is used first, perhaps by about 3 months of age; binocular cues are used beginning at about 4 months; and linear perspective and other pictorial (monocular) cues are used last, perhaps at 5 to 7 months (Bornstein, 1992; Yonas, Elieff, & Arterberry, 2002).

In a remarkably clever early study, Eleanor Gibson and Richard Walk (1960) devised an apparatus called a visual cliff. You can see from the photograph that it consists of a large glass table with a sort of runway in the middle. On one side of the runway is a checkerboard pattern immediately below the glass; on the other side—the "cliff" side—the checkerboard is several feet below the glass. The baby could judge depth here by several means, but it is primarily kinetic information that is useful, since the baby in motion would see the nearer surface move more than the farther surface. If a baby has no depth perception, she should be equally willing to crawl on either side of the runway, but if she can judge depth, she should be reluctant to crawl out on the cliff side.

Since an infant had to be able to crawl in order to be tested in the Gibson and Walk procedure, the original subjects were all 6 months old or older. Most of these infants did not crawl out on the cliff side but were quite willing to crawl out on the shallow side. In other words, 6-month-old babies have depth perception.

What about younger infants? The traditional visual cliff procedure can't give us the answer, since the baby must be able to crawl in order to "tell" us whether he can judge depth. With younger babies, researchers have studied kinetic cues by watching babies react to apparently looming objects. Most often, the baby observes a film of an object moving toward him, apparently on a collision course. If the infant has some depth perception, he should flinch, move to one side, or blink as the object appears to come very close. Such flinching has been observed in 3-month-olds (Yonas & Owsley, 1987). Most experts now agree that this is about the lower age limit of depth perception.

What Babies Look At In the first 2 months, a baby's visual attention is guided by a search for meaningful patterns (Bornstein, Arterberry, & Mash, 2005). Babies scan the world around them until they come to a sharp light-dark contrast, which typically signals the edge of some object. Once she finds such an edge, the baby stops searching and moves her eyes back and forth across and around the edge. Motion also captures a baby's attention at this age, so she will look at things that move as well as things with large light-dark contrast. Between 2 and 3 months, the cortex has developed more fully, and the baby's attention seems to shift from *where* an object is to *what* an object is. Babies this age begin to scan rapidly across an entire figure rather than getting stuck on edges. As a result, they spend more time looking for patterns.

One early study that illustrates this point particularly well comes from the work of Albert Caron and Rose Caron (1981), who used stimuli like those in Figure 4.5 in a habituation procedure. The babies were first shown a series of pictures that shared some particular relationship—for example, a small figure positioned above a larger version of the same figure (small over big). After the baby stopped being interested in these training pictures (that is, after he habituated), the Carons showed him another figure (the test stimulus) that either followed the same pattern or followed some other pattern. If the baby had really habituated to the pattern of the original pictures (small over big), he should show little interest in stimuli like test stimulus A in Figure 4.5 ("Ho hum, same old boring small over big thing"), but he should show renewed interest in test stimulus B ("Hey, here's something new!"). Caron and Caron found that 3- and 4-month-old children did precisely that. So even at this early age, babies find and pay attention to patterns, not just specific stimuli.

Although there is little indication that faces are uniquely interesting patterns to infants, that is, babies do not systematically choose to look at faces rather than at other complex patterns, babies clearly prefer some to others. They prefer attractive faces (an intriguing result,

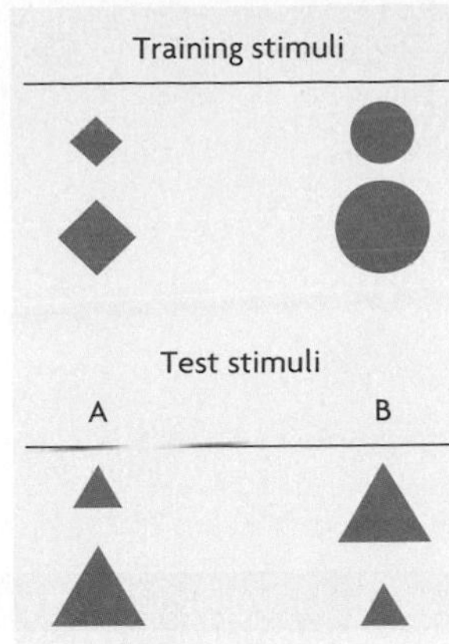

Figure 4.5
Pattern Recognition in Infants

In the Carons' study, the researchers first habituated each baby to a set of training stimuli (all "small over large" in this case). Then they showed each baby two test stimuli: one that had the same pattern as the training stimuli (A) and one that had a different pattern (B). Babies aged 3 and 4 months showed renewed interest in stimulus B but not stimulus A, indicating that they were paying attention to the pattern and not just specific stimuli.

(*Source*: This figure was published in *Pre-Term Birth and Psychological Development*, by S. Friedman and M. Sigman, "Processing of Relational Information as an Index of Infant Risk," by A.J. Caron and R.F. Caron pp. 227–228, Copyright Academic Press, 1981. Reprinted by permission.)

RESEARCH REPORT

Langlois's Studies of Babies' Preferences for Attractive Faces

A large number of current studies on infant perception seem to point toward the conclusion that many more perceptual rules are built in than we had supposed. One such rule appears to be a preference for attractive faces. In the first study in a classic series of experiments, Langlois and her colleagues (1987) tested 2- to 3-month-olds and 6- to 8-month-olds. Each baby was shown color slides of adult Caucasian women, half rated by adult judges as attractive, and half rated as unattractive. On each trial, the baby was shown two slides simultaneously, with each face approximately life-size, while the experimenter peeked through a hole in the screen to count the number of seconds the baby looked at each picture. Each baby saw some attractive/attractive pairs, some unattractive/unattractive pairs, and some mixed pairs. With mixed pairs, even the 2- and 3-month-old babies consistently looked longer at the attractive faces. Several later studies, including some in which pictures of individuals of different races were used, produced similar findings (Langlois, Roggman, & Rieser-Danner, 1990; Langlois et al., 1991).

More recent research has extended Langlois's findings. These studies show that infants prefer to look at images of other infants who have been rated as attractive by adults (Van Duuren, Kendell-Scott, & Stark, 2003). It is hard to imagine what sort of learning experiences could account for such preferences in a 2-month-old. Instead, these findings raise the possibility that there is some inborn template for the "correct" or "most desired" shape and configuration for members of our species, and that we simply prefer those who best match this template.

Questions for Critical Analysis

1. If there is an inborn template against which faces are compared, how might such a template affect adults' interactions with others?
2. How would researchers determine the degree to which attractiveness affects adults' perceptions of infants' faces? Why would such research be unable to tell us whether the concept of attractiveness is inborn?

discussed in the Research Report on page 111). They also prefer their mother's face from the earliest hours of life, a finding that has greatly surprised psychologists, although it may not surprise you.

Beyond the issue of preference, we also have the question of just what it is that babies are looking at when they scan a face. Before about 2 months of age, babies seem to look mostly at the edges of faces (the hairline and the chin), a conclusion buttressed by the finding by Pascalis and his colleagues (1995) that newborns could not discriminate Mom's face from a stranger's if the hairline was covered. After 4 months, however, covering the hairline did not affect the baby's ability to recognize Mom. In general, babies appear to begin to focus on the internal features of a face, particularly the eyes, at about 2 to 3 months.

Learning Objective 4.13

How do infants perceive human speech, recognize voices, and recognize sound patterns other than speech?

Listening

When we turn from looking to listening, we find similarly intriguing indications that very young infants not only make remarkably fine discriminations among individual sounds but also pay attention to patterns. Early studies established that as early as 1 month, babies can discriminate between speech sounds like *pa* and *ba* (Trehub & Rabinovitch, 1972). Studies using conditioned head-turning responses have shown that by perhaps 6 months of age, babies can discriminate between two-syllable "words" like *bada* and *baga* and can even respond to a syllable that is hidden inside a string of other syllables, like *tibati* or *kobako* (Fernald & Kuhl, 1987; Goodsitt, Morse, Ver Hoeve, & Cowan, 1984; Morse & Cowan, 1982). Even more remarkable, the quality of the voice making the sound doesn't seem to matter. By 2 or 3 months of age, babies respond to individual sounds as the same, whether they are spoken by a male or a female or by an adult or a child (Marean, Werner, & Kuhl, 1992). Research also indicates that infants can rapidly learn to discriminate between words and nonwords in artificial languages researchers invent strictly for the purpose of such experiments (Aslin, Saffran, & Newport, 1998).

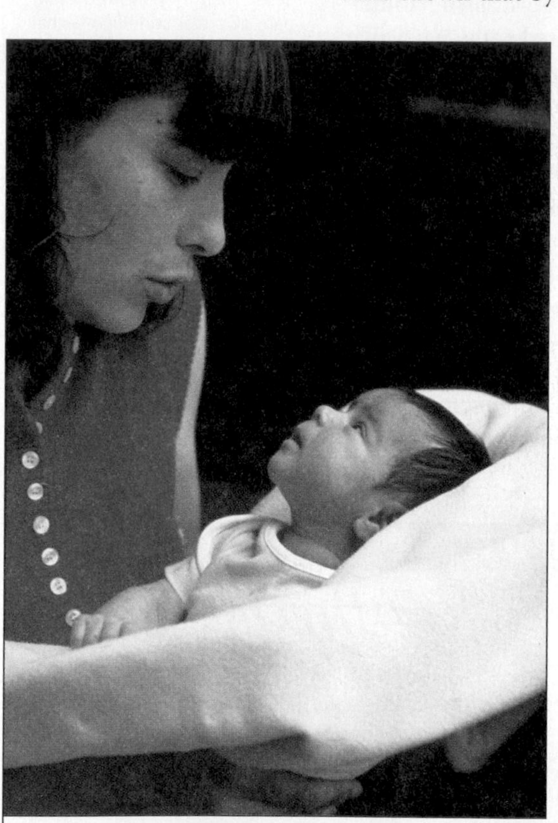

Newborns recognize their mother's voice and by one month of age can discriminate between syllables such as ba and pa.

Even more striking is the finding that babies are actually better at discriminating some kinds of speech sounds than adults are. Each language uses only a subset of all possible speech sounds. Japanese, for example, does not use the *l* sound that appears in English; Spanish makes a different distinction between *d* and *t* than occurs in English. It turns out that up to about 6 months of age, babies can accurately discriminate all sound contrasts that appear in any language, including sounds they do not hear in the language spoken to them. At about 6 months of age, they begin to lose the ability to distinguish pairs of vowels that do not occur in the language they are hearing; by age 1, the ability to discriminate nonheard consonant contrasts begins to fade (Polka & Werker, 1994).

Newborns also seem to be able to discriminate between individual voices. DeCasper and Fifer (1980) found that the newborn can tell the mother's voice from another female voice (but not the father's voice from another male voice) and prefers the mother's voice. Moreover, there is a correlation between gestational age and maternal voice recognition: Premature infants are less likely to recognize their mother's voice than are babies born at term (DeRegnier, Wewerka, Georgieff, Mattia, & Nelson, 2002). Thus, *in utero* learning appears to be responsible for newborns' preference for the maternal voice.

Learning Objective 4.14

What is intermodal perception?

Combining Information from Several Senses

If you think about the way you receive and use perceptual information, you'll realize that you rarely have information from only one sense at a time. Psychologists have been interested in knowing how early an infant can combine such information. Even more complex, how early can a baby learn something via one sense and transfer that information to another sense (for example, recognize solely by feel a toy he has seen but never before felt)? This skill is usually called **intermodal perception.**

Research findings show that intermodal perception is possible as early as 1 month and becomes common by 6 months (Rose & Ruff, 1987). Moreover, research comparing these skills in children born prematurely and those born at term suggests that basic maturational processes play an important role in their development (Espy et al., 2002).

Research also suggests that intermodal perception is important in infant learning. One group of researchers found that babies who habituated to a combined auditory-visual stimulus were better able to recognize a new stimulus than infants who habituated to either the auditory or the visual stimulus alone (Bahrick & Lickliter, 2000). For example, suppose you played a videotape of someone singing for one baby, played the videotape without the sound for another, and played an audio recording of the song for a third. Research suggests that the first baby would recognize a change in either the singer (visual stimulus) or the song (auditory stimulus) more quickly than would either of the other two infants.

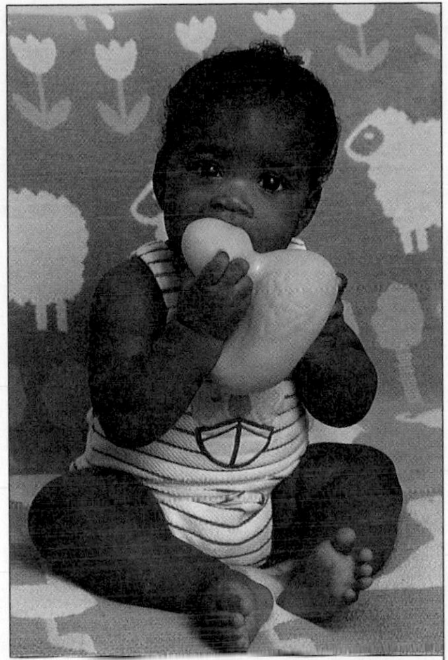

Even though 7-month-old Leslie is not looking at this toy while she chews on it, she is nonetheless learning something about how it ought to look based on how it feels in her mouth and in her hands—an example of intermodal perception.

In older infants, intermodal perception can be readily demonstrated, not only between touch and sight but between other modalities such as sound and sight. For instance, in several delightfully clever early experiments, Elizabeth Spelke (1979) showed that 4-month-old infants can connect sound rhythms with movement. She showed babies two films simultaneously, one depicting a toy kangaroo bouncing up and down and the other a donkey bouncing up and down, with one of the animals bouncing at a faster rate. Out of a loudspeaker located between the two films, the infant heard a tape recording of a rhythmic bouncing sound that matched the bounce pattern of one of the two animals. In this situation, babies showed a preference for looking at the film showing the bounce rate that matched the sound.

An even more striking illustration of the same basic process comes from the work of Jeffery Pickens (1994). He showed 5-month-old babies two films side by side, each displaying a train moving along a track. Then out of a loudspeaker he played engine sounds of various types, such as that of an engine getting gradually louder (thus appearing to come closer) or gradually fainter (thus appearing to be moving away). The babies in this experiment looked longer at a picture of a train whose movement matched the pattern of engine sounds. That is, they appeared to have some understanding of the link between the pattern of sound and the pattern of movement—knowledge that demonstrates not only intersensory integration but also a surprisingly sophisticated understanding of the accompaniments of motion.

Explaining Perceptual Development

Learning Objective 4.15

What arguments do nativists and empiricists offer in support of their theories of perceptual development?

The study of perceptual development has been significant because it has been a key battleground for the dispute about nature versus nurture. **Nativists** claim that most perceptual abilities are inborn, while **empiricists** argue that these skills are learned.

There are strong arguments for a nativist position on perceptual development. As researchers have become more and more clever in devising ways to test infants' perceptual skills, they have found more and more skills already present in newborns or very young infants: Newborns have good auditory acuity, poor but adequate visual acuity, excellent tactual and taste perception. They have at least some color vision and at least rudimentary ability to locate the source of sounds around them. More impressive still, they are capable of making quite sophisticated discriminations from the earliest days of life, including identifying their mother by sight, smell, or sound.

On the other side of the ledger, however, we find evidence from research with other species that some minimum level of experience is necessary to support the development of the perceptual systems. For example, animals deprived of light show deterioration of the

intermodal perception formation of a single perception of a stimulus that is based on information from two or more senses

nativists theorists who claim that perceptual abilities are inborn

empiricists theorists who argue that perceptual abilities are learned

whole visual system and a consequent decrease in perceptual abilities (Hubel & Weisel, 1963). Likewise, animals deprived of auditory stimuli display delayed or no development of auditory perceptual skills (Dammeijer, Schlundt, Chenault, Manni, & Anteunis, 2002).

Critical Thinking

1. If the empiricists are correct, and much of early perceptual learning depends on experience, what kinds of objects and activities do you think would be helpful in supporting an infant's visual and auditory perceptual development?

We can best understand the development of perceptual skills by thinking of it as the result of an interaction between inborn and experiential factors. A child is able to make visual discriminations between people or among objects within the first few days or weeks of life. The specific discriminations she learns and the number of separate objects she learns to recognize, however, will depend on her experience. A perfect example of this is the newborn's ability to discriminate her mother's face from a very similar woman's face. Such a discrimination must be the result of experience, yet the capacity to make the distinction must be built in. Thus, as is true of virtually all dichotomous theoretical disputes, both sides are correct. Both nature and nurture are involved.

SUMMARY

Physical Changes

Learning Objective 4.1 What important changes in the brain take place during infancy?

- Changes in the nervous system are extremely rapid in the first 2 years. In most parts of the brain, development of dendrites and synapses reaches its first peak between 12 and 24 months, after which "pruning" of synapses occurs. Myelinization of nerve fibers also occurs rapidly in the first 2 years.

Learning Objective 4.2 How do babies' reflexes and behavioral states change?

- Adaptive reflexes include such essential responses as sucking; primitive reflexes include the Moro (startle) and Babinski reflexes, which disappear within a few months. Neonates move through a series of states of consciousness in a cycle that lasts about 2 hours.

Learning Objective 4.3 How do infants' bodies change, and what is the typical pattern of motor skill development in the first 2 years?

- During infancy, bones increase in number and density; muscle fibers become larger and contain less water. Stamina improves as the lungs grow and the heart gets stronger. Motor skills improve rapidly in the first 2 years, as the baby moves from creeping to crawling to walking to running and becomes able to grasp objects.

Health and Wellness

Learning Objective 4.4 What are the nutritional needs of infants?

- Breastfeeding has been shown to be better for a baby nutritionally than bottle-feeding.

Learning Objective 4.5 How does malnutrition affect infants' development?

- Macronutrient malnutrition results from a diet that contains too few calories, while micronutrient malnutrition is caused by a diet that has sufficient calories but lacks specific nutrients, vitamins, or minerals.

Learning Objective 4.6 What are infants' health care and immunization needs?

- Babies need regular check-ups and a variety of immunizations.

Infant Mortality

Learning Objective 4.7 What have researchers learned about sudden infant death syndrome?

- Sudden infant death syndrome is the most common cause of death in the first year.

Learning Objective 4.8 How do infant mortality rates vary across groups?

- African American, Hawaiian American, and Native American children are more likely to die in the first year of life than those in other U.S. racial groups. Poverty seems a likely explanation, but the relationship between low income and infant mortality is complex.

Sensory Skills

Learning Objective 4.9 How do infants' visual abilities change across the first months of life?

- Color vision is present at birth, but visual acuity and visual tracking skill are relatively poor at birth and then develop rapidly during the first few months.

Learning Objective 4.10 How do infants' senses of hearing, smell, taste, touch, and motion compare to those of older children and adults?

- Basic auditory skills are more fully developed at birth; acuity is good for the range of the human voice, and the newborn can locate at least the approximate direction of sounds. The sensory capacities for smelling, tasting, and the senses of touch and motion are also well developed at birth.

Perceptual Skills

Learning Objective 4.11 How do researchers study perceptual development?

- In the preference technique, researchers track how long babies look at each of a pair of stimuli. Habituation involves exposing babies to stimuli until they are no longer interested in them. The purpose is to see whether the babies will then respond to a new stimulus that is only slightly different from the original one (dishabituation). By using operant conditioning, researchers train babies to perform behaviors such as turning their heads in response to specific stimuli. Then the researchers vary the stimulus slightly; if babies do not respond as they have been trained to do, then the researchers know that they can tell the difference between the original and the new stimulus.

Learning Objective 4.12 How do depth perception and patterns of looking change over the first two years?

- Depth perception is present in at least rudimentary form by 3 months. Babies initially use kinetic cues, then binocular cues, and finally pictorial (monocular) cues by about 5 to 7 months. Visual attention appears to follow definite rules, even in the first hours of life. Babies can discriminate the mother's face from other faces, and the mother's voice from other voices, almost immediately after birth.

Learning Objective 4.13 How do infants perceive human speech, recognize voices, and recognize sound patterns other than speech?

- From the beginning, babies appear to attend to and discriminate among speech contrasts present in all possible languages; by the age of 1 year, the infant makes fine discriminations only among speech sounds salient in the language he is actually hearing. By 6 months, babies also attend to and discriminate among different patterns of sounds, such as melodies or speech inflections.

Learning Objective 4.14 What is intermodal perception?

- Studies show that infants can learn something via one sense and transfer it to another sense.

Learning Objective 4.15 What arguments do nativists and empiricists offer in support of their theories of perceptual development?

- A central issue in the study of perceptual development continues to be the nativism-empiricism controversy. Many basic perceptual abilities, including strategies for examining objects, appear to be built into the system at birth or to develop as the brain develops over the early years. But specific experience is required both to maintain the underlying system and to learn fundamental discriminations and patterns.

KEY TERMS

adaptive reflexes *(p. 99)*
auditory acuity *(p. 108)*
colic *(p. 100)*
dishabituation *(p. 109)*
dynamic systems theory *(p. 101)*
empiricists *(p. 113)*
habituation *(p. 109)*
infant mortality *(p. 104)*
intermodal perception *(p. 113)*
myelinization *(p. 98)*
nativists *(p. 113)*
plasticity *(p. 96)*
preference technique *(p. 109)*
primitive reflexes *(p. 99)*
pruning *(p. 96)*
reticular formation *(p. 98)*
sudden infant death syndrome (SIDS) *(p. 105)*
synapses *(p. 96)*
synaptogenesis *(p. 96)*
tracking *(p. 107)*
visual acuity *(p. 107)*

TEST YOURSELF

Physical Changes

4.1 What is pruning as it relates to development?

a. a surgical technique for compensating for brain damage
b. elimination of redundant neural pathways
c. slowly easing the child off the bottle and onto solid food
d. a surgery that may alleviate epileptic seizures

4.2 Why can infants bounce back from head injury more easily than adolescents and adults can?

a. They have not yet experienced pruning.
b. Their brains have greater plasticity.
c. Their brains operate more efficiently.
d. They have fewer dendrites and synapses to lose.

4.3 Baby Jake is a week old. He is likely to be _____ most of the time.

a. actively awake
b. quietly awake
c. asleep
d. eating

4.4 One of the reasons that fine motor skills improve in the first 2 years is that

a. the wrist bones progressively separate.
b. infants' musculature is further developed.
c. bones harden during that time.
d. the bones have not grown long enough until that time.

4.5 During infancy, females appear to be ahead of boys in the development of

a. gross motor skills.
b. fine motor skills.
c. ossification.
d. physical activity.

4.6 What concept explains the fact that the sequences of motor development are virtually the same for all children?

a. an inborn timetable
b. growth
c. accommodation
d. genotypical influence

Health and Wellness

4.7 Which of the following is not a benefit of breastfeeding?

a. lower risk of infant mortality
b. lower risk of intestinal difficulties
c. better immune system functioning
d. slower weight gain

4.8 Which statement about feeding solid foods to infants is true?

a. Solids help babies sleep through the night.
b. Doctors recommend introducing solids between 4 and 6 months of age.
c. Solids help a baby's digestive system get ready for table food.
d. Newborns who are given solid foods grow faster than those who receive only breast milk or formula.

4.9 Macronutrient malnutrition results from a diet that contains

a. too little iron
b. too much vitamin A
c. too few calories
d. only breast milk

4.10 Which of the following is most likely to be lacking in a diet that produces micronutrient malnutrition?

a. protein
b. fat
c. carbohydrates
d. iron

4.11 Which of the following would not be included in the full set of children's immunizations in the United States?

a. hepatitis immunization
b. diphtheria/tetanus/pertussis immunization
c. smallpox vaccine
d. varicella zoster virus vaccine

Infant Mortality

4.12 Which of the following factors or influences is not associated with sudden infant death syndrome?

a. a history of physical abuse
b. a history of apnea
c. sleeping on the stomach on a soft, fluffy item of bedding
d. smoking by the mother during pregnancy

4.13 Sudden infant death syndrome (SIDS) is

a. a rare genetic disease
b. the most common cause of infant death in the United States
c. a possible outcome of infant abuse
d. a common chromosomal disorder that leads to early death

4.14 Which group has the lowest rate of infant mortality?

a. African Americans
b. Asian Americans
c. Caucasian Americans
d. Native Americans

4.15 Which of the following has NOT been proposed as an explanation for group differences in infant mortality?

a. variations in attentiveness to infant needs
b. variations in poverty rates
c. variations in access to prenatal care
d. variations in the rates of congenital abnormalities

4.16 Group differences in access to prenatal care and group differences in infant mortality

a. are unrelated.
b. are positively correlated.
c. are the result of random variation.
d. show similar patterns.

Sensory Skills

4.17 Which of the following visual abilities appears to be almost identical in newborns and adults?

a. tracking
b. visual acuity
c. color sensation
d. scanning of objects

4.18 There appears to be a drastic improvement in visual abilities at approximately

a. one month of age.
b. two months of age.
c. six months of age.
d. one year of age.

4.19 At what age do researchers find the ability to hear?

a. prenatally

b. first day of life

c. first week of life

d. first month of life

4.20 _____ are able to distinguish between their mothers and other women based on smell.

a. Postmature infants

b. Breastfed infants

c. Two-month-olds

d. Male infants

Perceptual Skills

4.21 Which of the following can be used to test an infant's perceptual abilities?

a. visual cliff

b. cross-modal transfer

c. tracking device

d. preference technique

4.22 Apparently infants first use _____ to judge depth perception at approximately 3 months of age.

a. binocular cues

b. linear perspective

c. interposition

d. kinetic cues

4.23 Newborn Alexa is most likely to focus her attention on which of the following?

a. a pastel watercolor picture of Pooh

b. her ceiling fan, when it is on

c. the pink blanket that her grandmother made for her

d. the picture of her parents sitting next to her crib

4.25 Which of the following faces would infants prefer?

a. an attractive face

b. a woman's face

c. a man's face

d. their father's face

4.25 Nativists' arguments are supported by the fact that

a. newborns have so many sensory abilities early in life.

b. animals deprived of light show a decrease in perceptual abilities.

c. animals deprived of auditory stimuli have limited auditory perceptual skills.

d. infants from Iranian orphanages were retarded in the development of perceptual skills.

Are You Ready for the Test?

Students who use the study materials on MyDevelopmentLab report higher grades in the course than those who use the text alone. Here are three easy steps to mastering this chapter and improving your grade…

Step 1

Take the chapter pre-test in MyDevelopmentLab and review your customized Study Plan.

Training an infant to respond to a sound and then changing the sound slightly to see if the infant recognizes the new sound or not relies on ____________ as a way of assessing the infant's ability to discriminate sound.

- information processing
- operant conditioning
- intrasensory modalities
- transference

Step 2

Use MyDevelopmentLab's Multimedia Library to help strengthen your knowledge of the chapter.

Learning Objective 4.2
How do babies' reflexes and behavioral states change?

Watch: The Newborn's Reflexes

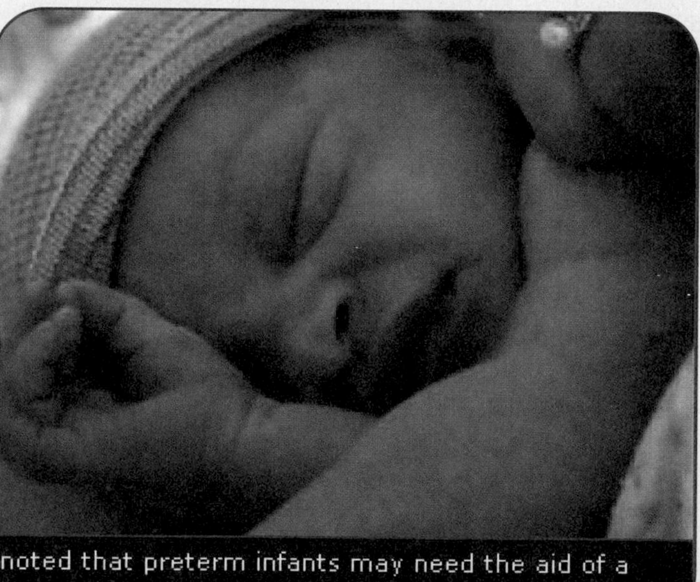

noted that preterm infants may need the aid of a
warmed bed for several weeks until this

Did you know? You can access MyDevelopmentLab's multimedia assets in two ways? You can . . .

1. **click on MyDevelopmentLab icons as a you come across them on the pages of the online eBook;**
2. **browse all multimedia assets from the Multimedia Library, which you can access from the Table of Contents page in MyDevelopmentLab.**

Watch: Breastfeeding

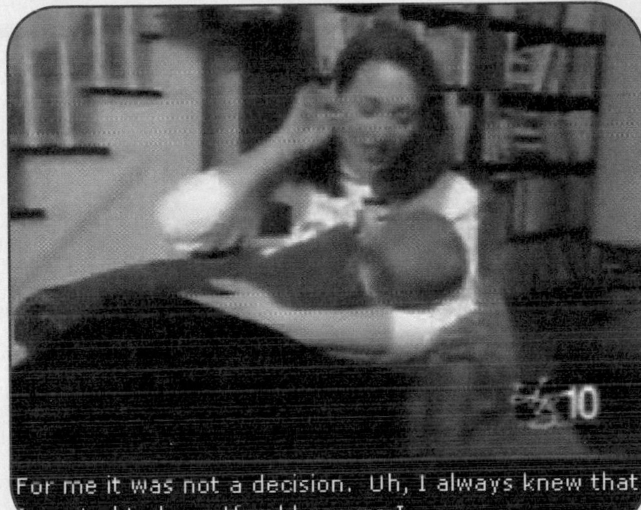

For me it was not a decision. Uh, I always knew that
wanted to breastfeed because I

Learning Objective 4.4

What are the nutritional needs of infants?

Simulate: The Visual Cliff

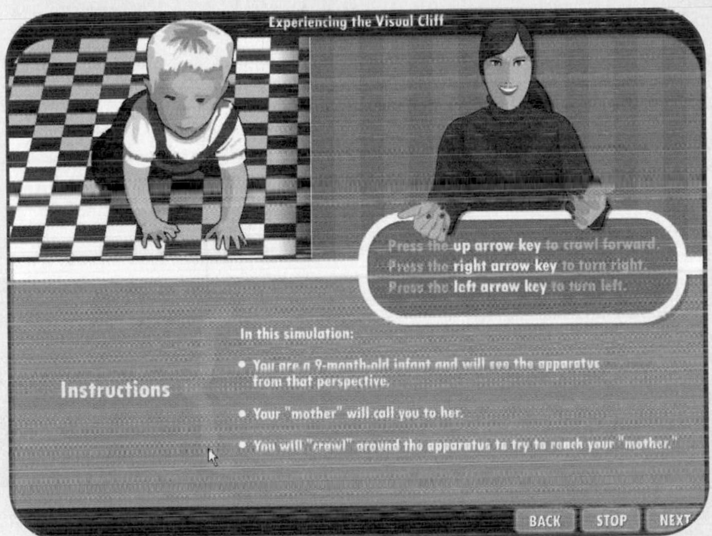

Learning Objective 4.12

How do depth perception and patterns of looking change over the first two years?

Step 3

Take the chapter post-test and compare your results against the pre-test.

One of the most important recommendations to parents who want to reduce the risk of their infants dying from Sudden Infant Death Syndrome (SIDS) is to

- introduce solid foods into the infant's diet at the earliest possible age.
- get rid of any household pets.
- put their babies to sleep lying on their side or their backs.
- keep the windows in their home closed to cut down on airborne allergens.

5

Cognitive Development in Infancy

Have you ever heard that listening to classical music can enhance an infant's intellectual development? This idea has been completely debunked by researchers, yet many people continue to believe it (Krakovsky, 2005). Why is that? Stanford University researchers Adrian Bangerter and Chip Heath have written about how this popular belief took root in the United States (Bangerter & Heath, 2004). According to their research, here is how it happened.

In 1993, the news media touted a study published in the scientific journal *Nature* (Rauscher, Shaw, & Ky, 1993) in which researchers reported that listening to a Mozart sonata appeared to *temporarily* raise college students' scores on intelligence tests. Almost immediately, the results of this study were dubbed the "Mozart effect" (ME) and were

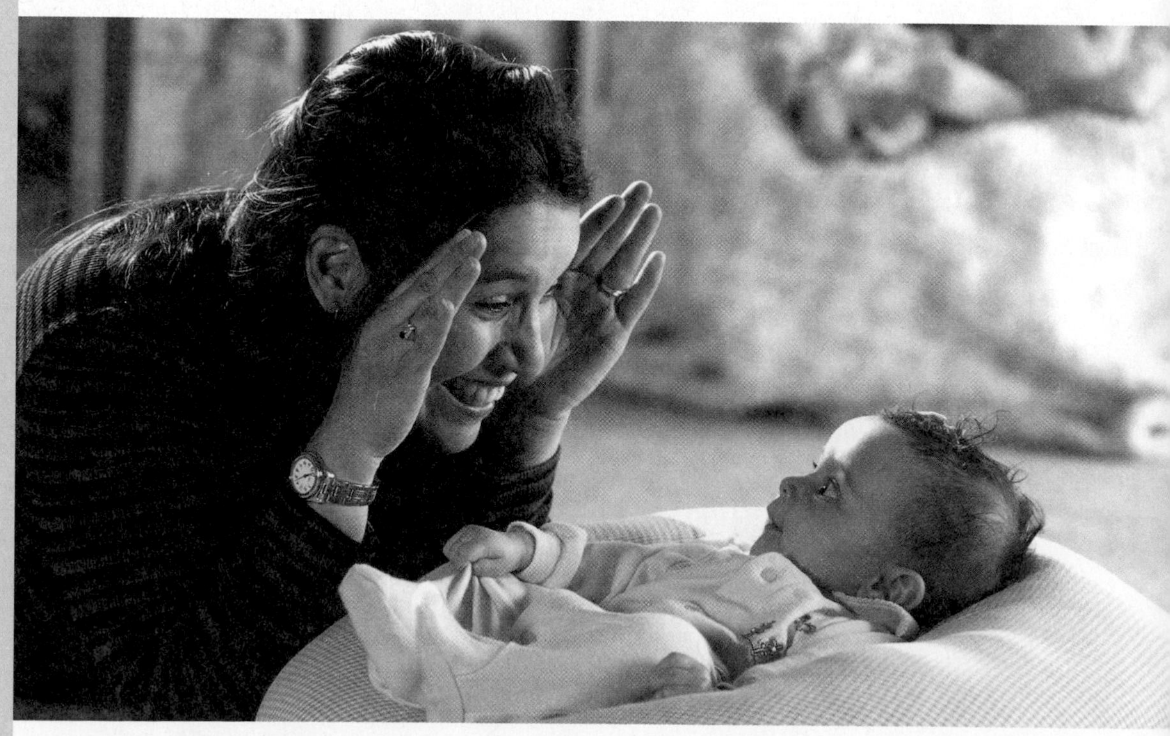

generalized to infants in the popular press. In hundreds of newspaper articles and other media reports that appeared between 1993 and 2001, Bangerter and Heath found that discussions of the ME eventually lost all connection to the original study, and the idea that Mozart sonatas can increase infants' scores on intelligence tests later in childhood came to be accepted as fact. Over the same period, the news media ignored numerous carefully designed research studies debunking the ME that were published in scientific journals (e.g., Chabris, 1999; Steele, Bass, & Crook, 1999). Policy makers in some jurisdictions even went so far as to provide parents of newborns with free CDs and to require publicly funded infant daycare programs to include music by Mozart in their curricula. As a result, the ME was perceived by the public as being endorsed by the government, lending further weight to the assumption that it must be real.

Today, it is widely known among developmental scientists that there is no empirical support for the ME (Crncec, Wilson, & Prior, 2006; Jones & Zigler, 2002; McKelvie & Low, 2002). Nevertheless, many popular books and Internet sites devoted to parenting and teaching continue to promote the idea that listening to music by Mozart raises infants' intelligence test scores (Krakovsky, 2005). Bangerter and Heath say that believing in the ME helps parents manage their worries about nurturing children's intellectual development. Consequently, anxious parents and teachers heed recommendations that are consistent with their beliefs and turn a deaf ear to others that go against them.

Wolfgang Amadeus Mozart composed some of the world's most beautiful and memorable music. However, there is no scientific support for the idea that listening to it will increase infants' intelligence.

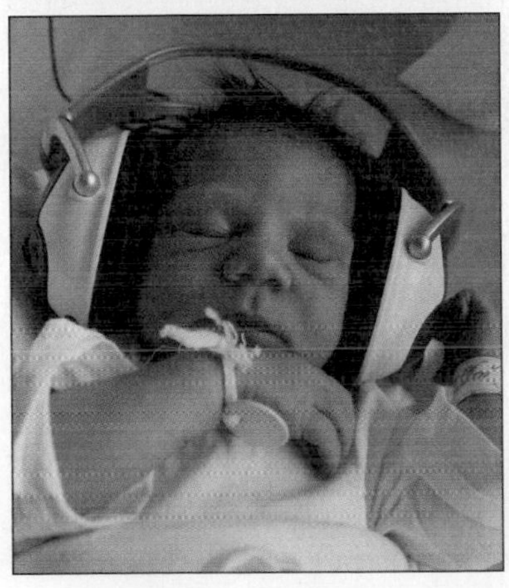

The influence of experience on cognitive development is most evident in cases in which a rather dramatic disruption in environmental support—malnourishment, child abuse, lead poisoning, and the like—impedes intellectual development. However, researchers have known for some time that extraordinary amounts of intellectual stimulation do little, if anything, to enhance cognitive development in healthy infants (Bruer, 1999). Thus, anxious parents can rest easy knowing that research shows that what babies need to fulfill their intellectual potential are caretakers who respond to all of their needs and who avoid narrowly focusing on a specific developmental outcome, such as increasing the odds that an infant will be able to get high scores on intelligence tests when she starts school.

In this chapter, you will learn about Piaget's explanation of the universal changes in thinking that happen in the first 2 years of life as well as how other theorists explain his research findings. You will also read about learning and memory during these years and about the beginnings of language. Individual differences in intelligence among infants will be discussed as well.

Cognitive Changes

The remarkable cognitive advances that happen in infancy are highly consistent across environments. Of course, 2-year-olds are still a long way from cognitive maturity, but some of the most important steps toward that goal are taken in the first 2 years of life.

Learning Objective 5.1

What are the important milestones of Piaget's sensorimotor stage?

Piaget's View of the First 2 Years

Recall from Chapter 2 that Piaget assumed that a baby *assimilates* incoming information to the limited array of schemes she is born with—looking, listening, sucking, grasping—and *accommodates* those schemes based on her experiences. He called this form of thinking *sensorimotor intelligence*. Thus, the **sensorimotor stage** is the period during which infants develop and refine sensorimotor intelligence. (See Table 5.1)

sensorimotor stage Piaget's first stage of development, in which infants use information from their senses and motor actions to learn about the world

primary circular reactions Piaget's phrase to describe a baby's simple repetitive actions in substage 2 of the sensorimotor stage, organized around the baby's own body

Sensorimotor Stage In Piaget's view, the newborn who is in Substage 1 of the sensorimotor stage is entirely tied to the immediate present, responding to whatever stimuli are available. She forgets events from one encounter to the next and does not appear to plan. Substage 2 (from roughly 1 to 4 months) is marked by the beginning of the coordinations between looking and listening, between reaching and looking, and between reaching and sucking that are such central features of the 2-month-old's means of exploring the world. The technique that distinguishes substage 2, **primary circular reactions**, refers to the many simple repetitive actions seen at this time, each organized around the infant's own body. For example, the baby may accidentally suck his thumb one day, find it pleasurable, and repeat the action.

Table 5.1 Substages of Piaget's Sensorimotor Stage

Substage	Average Age (in months)	Primary Technique	Characteristics
1	0–1	Reflexes	Use of built-in schemes or reflexes such as sucking or looking. Primitive schemes begin to change through very small steps of accommodation. Limited imitation, no ability to integrate information from several senses.
2	1–4	Primary circular reactions	Further accommodation of basic schemes, as the baby practices them endlessly–grasping, listening, looking, sucking. Beginning coordination of schemes from different senses, so that the baby now looks toward a sound and sucks on anything he can reach and bring to his mouth. But the baby does not yet link his body actions to results outside of his body.
3	4–8	Secondary circular reactions	The baby becomes much more aware of events outside her own body and makes them happen again in a kind of trial-and-error learning. Scientists are unsure whether babies this young understand the causal links yet, however. Imitation may occur, but only of schemes already in the baby's repertoire. Beginning understanding of the "object concept" can also be detected in this period.
4	8–12	Coordination of secondary schemes	Clear intentional means-end behavior. The baby not only goes after what he wants but he may combine two schemes to do so, such as moving a pillow aside to reach a toy. Imitation of novel behavior occurs, as does transfer of information from one sense to the other (cross-modal perception).
5	12–18	Tertiary circular reactions	"Experimentation" begins, in which the infant tries out new ways of playing with or manipulating objects. Very active, very purposeful trial-and-error exploration.
6	18–24	Beginning of mental representation	Development of use of symbols to represent object or events. The child understands that the symbol is separate from the object. As a result, infants in this stage are able to solve problems by thinking about them. Moreover, deferred imitation becomes possible because it requires ability to represent internally the event to be imitated.

In substage 3 (from about 4 to 8 months), the baby repeats some action in order to trigger a reaction outside her own body, a **secondary circular reaction**. The baby coos and Mom smiles, so the baby coos again to get Mom to smile again. These initial connections between body actions and external consequences seem to be simple, almost mechanical, links between stimuli and responses. However, in substage 4, the 8- to 12-month-old baby shows the beginnings of understanding causal connections, at which point she moves into exploratory high gear. One consequence of this new drive to explore is **means-end behavior**, or the ability to keep a goal in mind and devise a plan to achieve it. Babies show this kind of behavior when they move one toy out of the way to gain access to another. The end is the toy they want; the means to the end is moving the other toy.

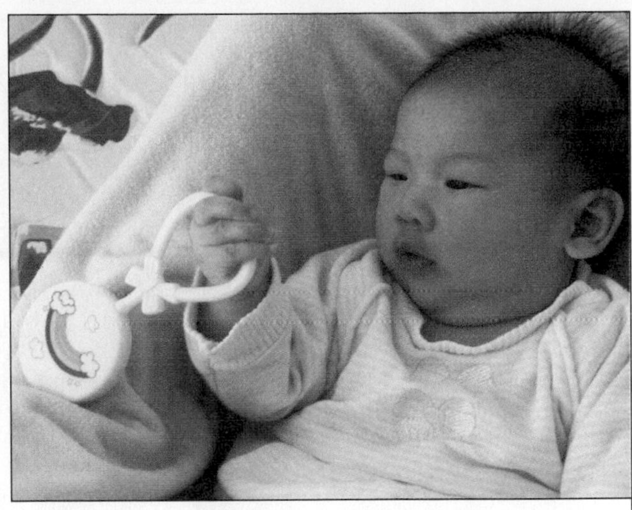

Three-month-old Andrea may be showing a secondary circular reaction here, shaking her hand repeatedly to hear the sound of the rattle. A learning theorist would say that the pleasure she experiences from hearing the sound is reinforcing her hand-shaking behavior.

In substage 5 from about 12 to 18 months, exploration of the environment becomes more focused, with the emergence of **tertiary circular reactions**. In this pattern, the baby doesn't merely repeat the original behavior but tries out variations. He may try out many sounds or facial expressions to see if they will trigger Mom's smile, or he may try dropping a toy from several heights to see if it makes different sounds or lands in different places. At this stage, the baby's behavior has a purposeful, experimental quality. Nonetheless, Piaget thought that the baby still did not have mental symbols to stand for objects in this substage.

The ability to manipulate mental symbols, such as words or images, marks substage 6, which lasts from roughly 18 months to 24 months of age. This new capacity allows the infant to generate solutions to problems simply by thinking about them, without the trial-and-error behavior typical of substage 5. As a result, means-end behavior becomes far more sophisticated than in earlier stages. For example, a 24-month-old who knows there are cookies in the cookie jar can figure out how to get one. Furthermore, she can find a way to overcome just about any obstacle placed in her path (Bauer, Schwade, Wewerka, & Delaney, 1999). If her parents respond to her climbing on the kitchen counter in pursuit of a cookie by moving the cookie jar to the top of the refrigerator, the substage 6 toddler's response will likely be to find a way to climb to the top of the refrigerator. Thus, changes in cognition are behind the common impression of parents and other caregivers that 18- to 24-month-olds cannot be left unsupervised, even for very short periods of time.

Object Permanence You know that this book continues to exist even when you are unable to see it—an understanding that Piaget called **object permanence**. In a series of studies, many of which involved his own children, Piaget discovered that babies acquire this understanding gradually during the sensorimotor period. According to his observations, replicated frequently by later researchers, the first sign that a baby is developing object permanence comes at about 2 months of age (in substage 2). Suppose you show a toy to a child of this age and then put a screen in front of the toy and remove the toy. When you then remove the screen, the baby will show some indication of surprise, as if he knows that something should still be there. The child thus seems to have a rudimentary expectation about the permanence of an object. But infants of this age show no signs of searching for a toy that has fallen over the side of the crib or that has disappeared beneath a blanket or behind a screen.

In substage 3 (at about 6–8 months), however, babies will look over the edge of the crib for dropped toys or on the floor for food that was spilled. (In fact, babies of this age may drive their parents nuts playing "dropsy" from the high chair.) Infants this age will also search for partially hidden objects. If you put a baby's favorite toy under a cloth but leave part of it sticking out, the infant will reach for the toy, which indicates that in some sense she "recognizes" that the whole object is there even though she can see only part of it. But if you cover the toy completely with the cloth or put it behind a screen, the infant will stop looking for it and will not reach for it, even if she has seen you put the cloth over it.

This behavior changes again between 8 and 12 months, in substage 4. Infants of this age will reach for or search for a toy that has been covered completely by a cloth or hidden by a

secondary circular reactions repetitive actions in substage 3 of the sensorimotor period, oriented around external objects

means-end behavior purposeful behavior carried out in pursuit of a specific goal

tertiary circular reactions The deliberate experimentation with variations of previous actions that occurs in substage 5 of the sensorimotor period

object permanence the understanding that objects continue to exist when they can't be seen

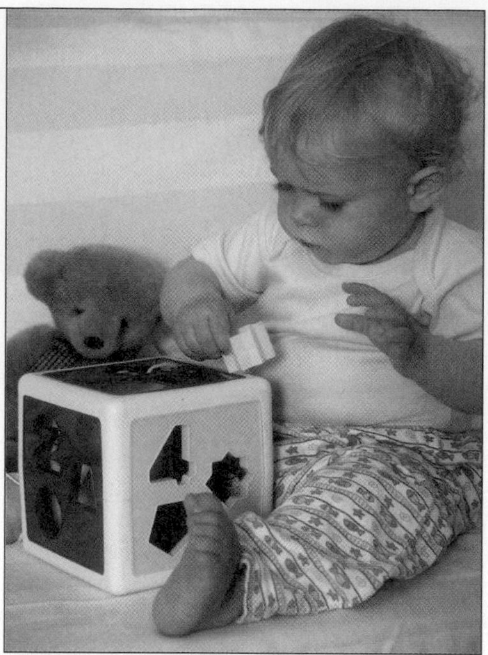

After babies acquire object permanence, they become fascinated with activities that involve putting objects into containers that partially or fully obscure the objects from view. This fascination goes far beyond toys such as the shape-sorter pictured here and extends to all kinds of things that hold objects and can be opened and closed—purses, closets, drawers, cabinets, shopping bags, garbage cans, pet crates, and a wide variety of other things that parents probably don't want their babies to get into.

screen. Thus, by 12 months, most infants appear to grasp the basic fact that objects continue to exist even when they are no longer visible. However, substage 4 infants' understanding of where a hidden object might be found is limited by the **A-not-B error.** This flaw in logic leads infants to look for an object in the place where it was last seen (position A) rather than in the place to which they have seen a researcher move it (position B) (Flavell, 1963). In substage 5, infants' searching strategies are somewhat more logical. For instance, if they see a researcher hide an object in her hand and immediately move the hand behind screen A, dropping the object out of view, they will persist in searching for the object in the researcher's hand just as substage 4 infants do. However, if they see the researcher move a hidden object from behind screen A to behind screen B, they will immediately look for it behind screen B. This error is not resolved until substage 6. Thus, infants' full understanding of the behavior objects and their connections to the spaces in which they appear and can possibly appear does not emerge until near the end of the second year of life.

Imitation Piaget also studied infants' ability to imitate the actions of others. He observed that as early as the first few months of life, infants could imitate actions they could see themselves make, such as hand gestures. But he found that they could not imitate other people's facial gestures until substage 4 (8–12 months). This second form of imitation seems to require some kind of intermodal perception, combining the visual cues of seeing the other's face with the kinesthetic cues (perceptions of muscle motion) from one's own facial movements. Piaget argued that imitation of any action that wasn't already in the child's repertoire did not occur until about 1 year, and that **deferred imitation**—a child's imitation of some action at a later time—was possible only in substage 6, since deferred imitation requires some kind of internal representation.

Learning Objective 5.2

What are some of the challenges offered to Piaget's explanation of infant cognitive development?

Challenges to Piaget's View

Many studies since Piaget's time have suggested that he underestimated the cognitive capacity of infants. By changing the methods used to measure object permanence, for instance, researchers have found that younger infants better understand object movements than Piaget suggested. Moreover, studies have shown that imitation appears at younger ages than Piaget's research implied.

Object Permanence In Piaget's studies of object permanence, infants were judged as having object permanence if they moved a blanket in order to retrieve a hidden object. You may recall from Chapter 4 that infants are unable to grasp and move objects in this way until they are 7 to 8 months old. Thus, Piaget's methods made it impossible to tell whether younger infants failed to exhibit object permanence because they were physically unable to perform the task of moving the blanket.

Thanks to the advent of computers, researchers have been able to measure infants' understanding of objects in ways that do not depend on motor skill development. In many post-Piagetian studies of object permanence, researchers use computer technology to keep track of how infants' eyes respond when researchers move objects from one place to another. These "looking" studies have demonstrated that babies as young as 4 months show clear signs of object permanence if a visual response rather than a reaching response is used to test it (Bail-

A-not-B error substage 4 infants' tendency to look for an object in the place where it was last seen (position A) rather than in the place to which they have seen a researcher move it (position B)

deferred imitation imitation that occurs in the absence of the model who first demonstrated it

largeon, 1987, 1994; Baillargeon & DeVos, 1991; Baillargeon, Spelke, & Wasserman, 1985). Moreover, many studies have examined how infants respond to a moving object that temporarily disappears behind a screen (e.g., Rosander & von Hofsten, 2004). In these studies, most 5-month-olds immediately looked to the other side of the screen when the moving object disappeared behind it and were delighted when it reappeared. These findings indicate that infants are holding some kind of representation of the hidden object in mind when it is behind the screen, the essence of object permanence. Nevertheless, such studies typically show that younger infants' understanding of object permanence is tied to the specific experimental situation. By contrast, babies who are nearing or past their first birthday understand object permanence sufficiently to use it across all kinds of situations, such as when they playfully hide objects from themselves and delight in "finding" them.

Findings like these have sparked renewed discussion of the nature-versus-nurture issue (e.g., Diamond, 1991; Fischer & Bidell, 1991; Karmiloff-Smith, 1991). Piaget assumed that a baby came equipped with a repertoire of sensorimotor schemes, but his most fundamental theoretical proposal was that the child constructed an understanding of the world, based on experience. In contrast, recent theorizing suggests that the development of object permanence is more a process of elaboration than one of discovery. Newborns may have considerable awareness of objects as separate entities that follow certain rules (Valenza, Leo, Gava, & Simion, 2006). Certainly, all the research on the perception of patterns suggests that babies pay far more attention to relationships between events than Piaget's model supposed. Still, no one would argue that a baby came equipped with a full-fledged knowledge of objects or a well-developed ability to experiment with the world.

Imitation With respect to imitation, Piaget's proposed sequence has been supported. Imitation of someone else's hand movement or an action with an object seems to improve steadily, starting at 1 or 2 months of age; imitation of two-part actions develops much later, perhaps around 15–18 months (Poulson, Nunes, & Warren, 1989). Yet there are two important exceptions to this general confirmation of Piaget's theory: Infants imitate some facial gestures in the first weeks of life, and deferred imitation seems to occur earlier than Piaget proposed.

Several researchers have found that newborn babies will imitate certain facial gestures—particularly tongue protrusion, as shown in Figure 5.1 (Anisfeld, 1991). This seems to happen only if the model sits with his tongue out looking at the baby for a fairly long period of time, perhaps as long as a minute. But the fact that newborns imitate at all is striking—although it is entirely consistent with the observation that quite young babies are capable of tactile visual intermodal transfer, or perception.

Most studies of deferred imitation also support Piaget's model. However, some research indicates that infants as young as 6 weeks of age can defer imitation for at least a few min-

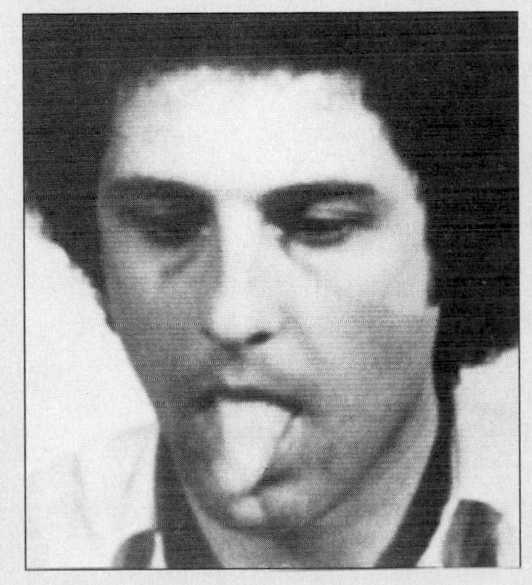

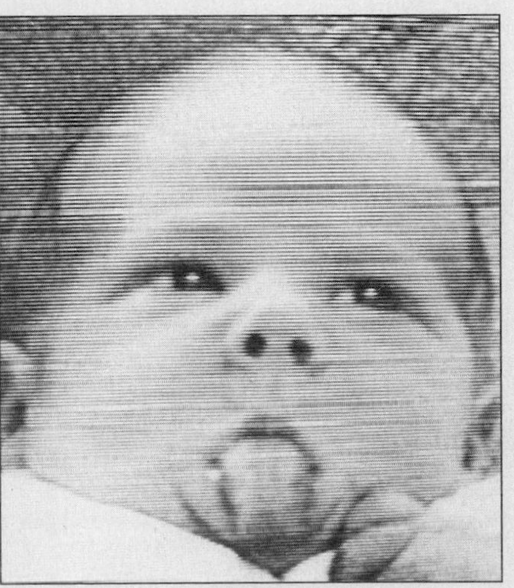

Figure 5.1
Imitation in Newborns

Although researchers still disagree on just how much newborns will imitate, everyone agrees that they will imitate the gesture of tongue protrusion, demonstrated here by Andrew Meltzoff from the earliest study of this kind.

(*Source:* Meltzoff & Moore, 1977. Copyright 1997 by the AAAS.)

utes (Bremner, 2002). Moreover, studies show that babies as young as 9 months can defer their imitation for as long as 24 hours (Meltzoff, 1988; Herbert, Gross, & Hayne, 2006). By 14 months, toddlers can recall and imitate someone's actions as much as 2 days later (Hanna & Meltzoff, 1993).

These findings are significant for several reasons. First, they make it clear that infants can and do learn specific behaviors through modeling, even when they have no chance to imitate the behavior immediately. In addition, these results suggest that babies may be more skillful than Piaget thought. Clearly, too, more abilities than he suggested may be built in from the beginning and develop continuously, rather than in stages, throughout infancy (Courage & Howe, 2002).

Learning Objective 5.3

What does research tell us about infants' understanding of objects?

Alternative Approaches

The many challenges to Piaget's characterization of infant thinking discussed above have led some developmental researchers to investigate object permanence within the more general context of infants' understanding of what objects are and how they behave. Researchers use the term **object concept** to refer to this understanding. The most thorough and clever work on the development of the object concept has been done by Elizabeth Spelke and her colleagues (Spelke, 1982; 1985; Spelke, von Hofsten, & Kestenbaum, 1989). Spelke believes that babies are born with certain built-in assumptions that guide their interactions with objects. One of these is the assumption that when two surfaces are connected to each other, they belong to the same object; Spelke calls this the connected surface principle. For instance, you know that all sides of your textbook are connected together in a single, solid object.

object concept an infant's understanding of the nature of objects and how they behave

violation of expectations method a research strategy in which researchers move an object in one way after having taught an infant to expect it to move in another

In Spelke's early studies of this phenomenon (e.g., Spelke, 1982), she first habituated some 3-month-old babies to a series of displays of two objects; other babies were habituated to the sight of one-object displays. Then the babies were shown two objects touching each other, such as two square blocks placed next to each other so that they created a rectangle. Under these conditions, the babies who had been habituated to two-object displays showed

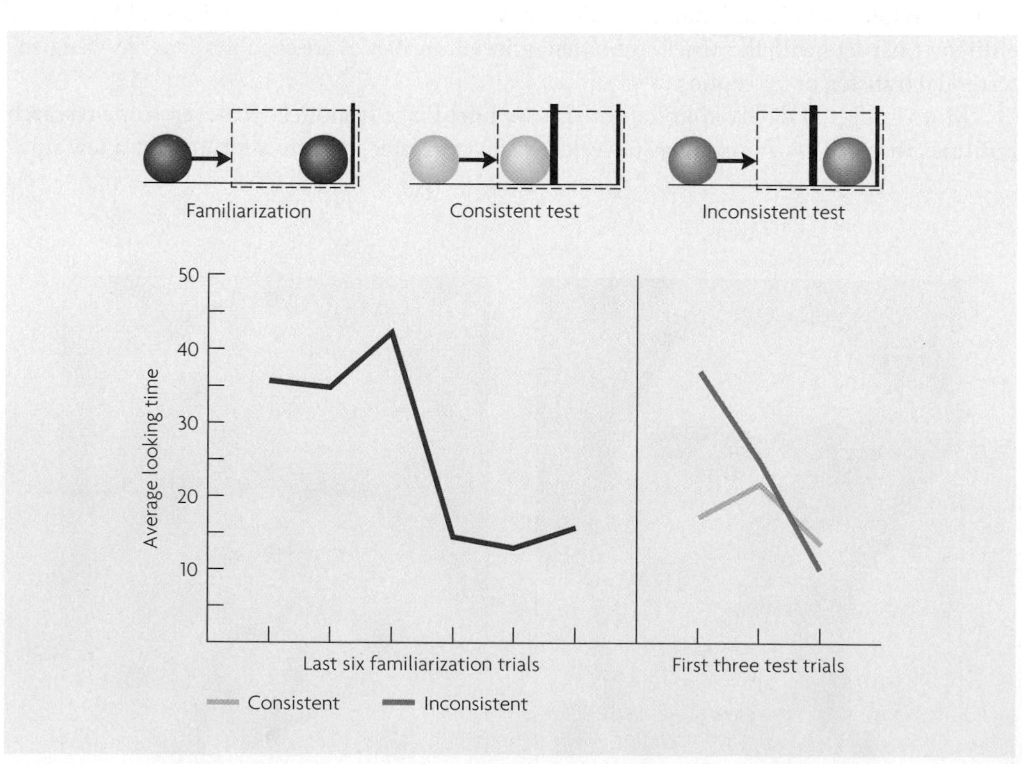

Figure 5.2
Spelke's Classic Study of Object Perception

The top part of the figure shows a schematic version of the three conditions Spelke used. The graph below shows the actual results. You can see that the babies stopped looking at the ball and screen after a number of familiarization trials, but they showed renewed interest in the inconsistent version—a sign that the babies saw this as somehow different or surprising. The very fact that the babies found the inconsistent trial surprising is evidence that infants as young as 2 months have far more knowledge about objects and their behavior than most developmentalists had thought.

(*Source*: Copyright © 1991 From "Physical Knowledge in Infancy: Reflections of Piaget's Theory" by E.S. Spelke, in *The Epigenesis of Mind: Essays on Biology and Cognition*, S. Carey and R. Gelman (eds.). Reproduced by permission of Lawrence Erlbaum Associates Inc, a division of Taylor & Francis Group.)

renewed interest, clearly indicating that they "saw" this display as different, presumably as a single object. Babies who had seen the one-object displays during habituation showed no renewed interest.

In later experiments, Spelke (1991) used the **violation of expectations method**, a research strategy in which an infant is habituated to a display that depicts the movement of an object and then is shown another display in which the object moves in a way that goes against what the infant expects to happen. An example of a violation of expectation procedure is shown schematically in the upper part of Figure 5.2 to demonstrate that babies as young as 2 and 3 months old are remarkably aware of what kinds of movements objects are capable of. Two-month-old babies were repeatedly shown a series of events like that in the "familiarization" section of the figure: A ball starting on the left-hand side was rolled to the right and disappeared behind a screen. The screen was then taken away, and the baby could see that the ball was stopped against the wall on the right. After the baby got bored looking at this sequence (habituated), he or she was tested with two variations, one "consistent" and one "inconsistent." In the consistent variation, a second wall was placed behind the screen and the sequence run as before, except now when the screen was removed, the ball could be seen resting up against the nearer wall. In the inconsistent variation, the ball was surreptitiously placed on the far side of the new wall. When the screen was removed, the ball was visible in this presumably impossible place. Babies in this experiment were quite uninterested in the consistent condition but showed sharply renewed interest in the inconsistent condition, as you can see in the lower part of Figure 5.2, which shows the actual results of this experiment.

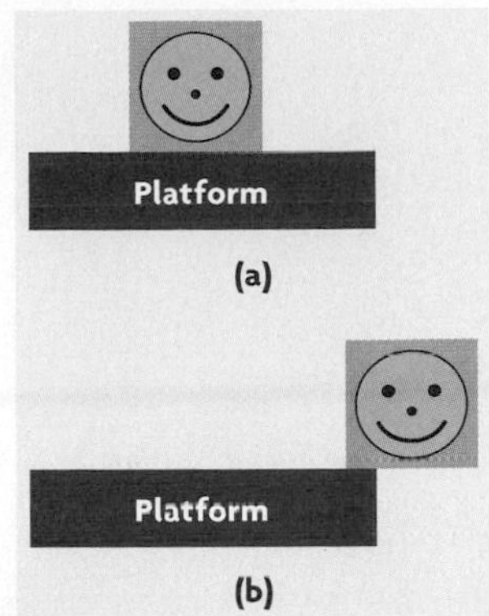

Figure 5.3
Baillergeon's Study of Object Stability Perception

Renée Baillargeon's research suggests that 2- and 3-month-old babies think that the smiling-face block will not fall under either of these conditions, but by 5 months, they realize that only the condition shown in (a) is stable. In condition (b), the block will fall.

(*Source*: From "How Do Infants Learn About the Physical World?" by Renée Baillargeon's, *Current Directions in Psychological Science*, Vol. 3, No. 5 (October 1994), p. 134, Fig 1. Reprinted by permission.)

Other researchers, such as Renée Baillargeon (1994), argue that knowledge about objects is not built in, but that strategies for learning are innate. According to this view, infants initially develop basic hypotheses about the way objects function—how they move, how they connect to one another. Then these early basic hypotheses are quite rapidly modified, based on the baby's experience with objects. For example, Baillargeon finds 2- to 3-month-old infants are already operating with a basic hypothesis that an object will fall if it isn't supported by something, but they have no notion of how much support is required. By about 5 months of age, this basic hypothesis has been refined, so they understand that the smiling-face block in the arrangement in the middle of Figure 5.3 (a) will stay supported, but the block in the arrangement on the bottom (b) will not (Baillargeon, 1994).

However, other psychologists question Baillargeon's conclusions. For example, developmental psychologist Leslie Cohen and his associates have conducted similar experiments with 8-month-olds and argue that infants respond to the stimuli used in such studies on the basis of novelty, rather than because of an understanding of stable and unstable block arrangements (Cashon & Cohen, 2000). Such varying interpretations demonstrate just how difficult it is to make inferences about infants' thinking from their interactions with physical objects.

Recent research has also examined the degree to which infants can make practical use of their understanding of objects and object movements. For example, several studies have shown that 2-year-olds experience difficulty when they are required to use this understanding to search for a hidden object (Keen, 2003). In one study, 2-, 2.5-, and 3-year-olds were shown a display similar to that in the top portion of Figure 5.2 and responded in exactly the same way as younger infants to the consistent and inconsistent displays (Berthier, DeBlois, Poirier, Novak, & Clifton, 2000). Next, a board in which there were several doors took the place of the screen; however, the barrier protruded several inches above this board (see Figure 5.4 on page 128). Across several trials, children were shown the ball rolling behind the board and were asked to open the door behind which they thought the ball would be found. Even though the children could clearly see behind which door the barrier was placed in every trial, none of the 2-year-olds and only a few of the 2.5-year-olds were able to succeed on this task, in contrast to the large majority of 3-year-olds. Developmentalists interpret such results to mean that young infants' understanding of objects is the foundation upon which the object concept is gradually constructed and applied to real-world interaction with objects over the first 3 years of life (Keen, 2003).

Critical Thinking

1. How would you explain an infant's habit of throwing things out of her crib to a parent who viewed it as misbehavior that needed to be corrected?

Figure 5.4
Toddlers' Understanding of Object Movement

Researchers use devices such as this one to find out whether toddlers can predict that a moving object will be stopped by the barrier that protrudes above the wall of doors. Children younger than 3 typically fail to identify the door behind which the object will be found.

Learning, Categorizing, and Remembering

Generally, the term *learning* is used to denote permanent changes in behavior that result from experience. From the first moments following birth, babies exhibit evidence of learning—that is, environmental forces change their behaviors. However, babies also actively organize their interactions with these forces, as research examining categorization and memory clearly shows.

Learning Objective 5.4

How do infants learn through conditioning and modeling?

Conditioning and Modeling

Learning of emotional responses through classical conditioning processes may begin as early as the first week of life. For example, in classic research, pediatrician Mavis Gunther (1955, 1961) found that inexperienced mothers often held nursing newborns in ways that caused the babies' nostrils to be blocked by the breast. Predictably, the babies reflexively turned away from the breast in response to the sensation of smothering. During future nursing sessions, babies who had experienced the smothering sensation while nursing at their mother's right breast refused to nurse on the right side; babies who had associated the smothering sensation with the left breast displayed the opposite pattern of refusal. Gunther hypothesized that classical conditioning was at work in such cases. She developed an intervention based on principles of stimulus-response learning to help babies "unlearn" the response of turning away from the breast they had learned to associate with the sensation of smothering.

Newborns also clearly learn by operant conditioning. Both the sucking response and head turning have been successfully increased by the use of reinforcements such as sweet liquids or the sound of the mother's voice or heartbeat (Moon & Fifer, 1990). At the least, the fact that conditioning of this kind can take place means that whatever neurological wiring is needed for operant learning is present at birth. Results like these also tell developmentalists something about the sorts of reinforcements that are effective with very young children; it is surely highly significant for the whole process of mother-infant interaction that the mother's voice is an effective reinforcer for virtually all babies.

Infants can also learn by watching models, especially in the second year. In one study, 10- and 12-month-olds were randomly assigned to two learning groups (Provasi, Dubon, & Bloch, 2001). "Observers" first watched an adult demonstrate how to find a toy by lifting the lids of various containers and then were allowed to play with the containers. "Actors" played with the containers on their own. Researchers found that observers were more proficient at finding the toy than actors in both age groups. However, the effect was much more pronounced among the older infants.

Schematic Learning

Learning Objective 5.5
How does categorical understanding change over the first 2 years?

Schematic learning is the organizing of experiences into expectancies, or "known" combinations. These expectancies, often called schemas, are built up over many exposures to particular experiences. Once formed, they help the baby to distinguish between the familiar and the unfamiliar.

One kind of schematic learning involves categories. Research suggests that by 7 months of age, and perhaps even earlier, infants actively use categories to process information (Pauen, 2000). For example, a 7-month-old is likely to habituate to a sequence of ten animal pictures and, if the next picture is of another animal, will not show surprise or look at it any longer than the first ten. If, however, researchers show the baby a picture of a human after ten animal pictures, the baby will look surprised and gaze at the picture longer. The same thing is likely to happen if researchers show an infant several pictures of humans and then switch to an animal picture.

Such findings suggest that infants build and use categories as they take in information. However, categorical organization as a cognitive tool is clearly not well developed in 7-month-olds. For one thing, infants of this age clearly do not understand the difference between lower-level and higher-level categories. "Dogs" and "animals," for example, can both be thought of as categories, but the higher-level one ("animals") includes the lower-level one. Thus, categories such as "animals" are referred to as *superordinates*. Researchers have found that infants respond to superordinate categories before they display reactions to basic-level categories (Pauen, 2002). In other words, 7- or 8-month-olds view "animals" and "furniture" as different categories, but not "dogs" and "birds." By contrast, 12-month-olds appear to understand both types of categories.

Still, 12-month-olds don't yet know that basic-level categories such as "dogs" and "birds" are nested within the superordinate category "animals." The concept that smaller categories are nested within larger ones, or *hierarchical categorization*, is demonstrated to some degree by 2-year-olds (Diesendruck & Shatz, 2001). However, full understanding of this kind of categorization is not typical until age 5 or so and is linked to language development and experiences with using words as category labels (Malabonga & Pasnak, 2002; Omiya & Uchida, 2002).

Memory

Learning Objective 5.6
How does memory function in the first 2 years?

You have probably heard that it is impossible to form memories while you are sleeping, so playing tapes of your textbook while you sleep is not likely to help you perform well on your next exam. However, newborns *do* appear to be able to remember auditory stimuli to which they are exposed while sleeping (Cheour et al., 2002). This is just one of several interesting characteristics of infant memory.

An ingenious series of studies by Carolyn Rovee-Collier and her colleagues has shown that babies as young as 3 months of age can remember specific objects and their own actions with those objects over periods as long as a week (Bhatt & Rovee-Collier, 1996; Bhatt, Wilk, Hill, & Rovee-Collier, 2004; Gerhardstein, Liu, & Rovee-Collier, 1998; Hayne & Rovee-Collier, 1995; Rovee-Collier, 1993). A researcher first hangs an attractive mobile over a baby's crib, as shown in Figure 5.5, and watches to see how the baby responds, noting how often he kicks his legs while looking at the mobile. After 3 minutes of this "baseline" observation, a string is used to connect the mobile to the baby's leg, so that each time the baby kicks his leg, the mobile

schematic learning organization of experiences into expectancies, called schemas, which enable infants to distinguish between familiar and unfamiliar stimuli

Figure 5.5
Rovee-Collier's Study of Infant Memory

This 3-month-old baby in one of Rovee-Collier's memory experiments will quickly learn to kick her foot in order to make the mobile move. And several days later, she will remember this connection between kicking and the mobile.

(*Source:* Rovee-Collier, 1993, p. 131.)

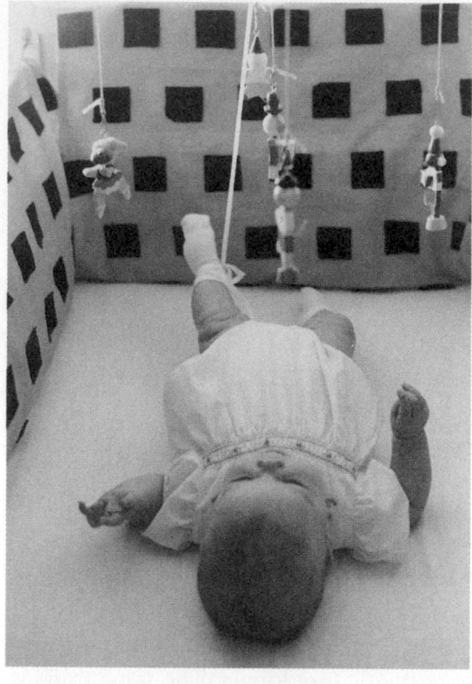

moves. Babies quickly learn to kick repeatedly in order to make this interesting action occur. Within 3–6 minutes, 3-month-olds double or triple their kick rates, clearly showing that learning has occurred. The researcher next tests the baby's memory of this learning by coming back some days later and hanging the same mobile over the crib but not attaching the string to the baby's foot. The crucial issue is whether the baby kicks rapidly at the mere sight of the mobile. If the baby remembers the previous occasion, he should kick at a higher rate than he did when he first saw the mobile, which is precisely what 3-month-old babies do, even after a delay of as long as a week.

Such findings demonstrate that the young infant is more cognitively sophisticated than developmentalists (and Piaget) had supposed. At the same time, these studies support Piaget's view that infants show systematic gains in the ability to remember over the months of infancy. Two-month-olds can remember their kicking action for only 1 day, 3-month-olds can remember it for over a week, and 6-month-olds can remember it longer than 2 weeks.

However, early infant memories are strongly tied to the specific context in which the original experience occurred (Barr, Marrott, & Rovee-Collier, 2003; Bhatt et al., 2004; Houston & Jusczyk, 2003). Even 6-month-olds do not recognize or remember the mobile if the context is changed even slightly—for example, by hanging a different cloth around the crib in which the infant is tested. However, Rovee-Collier and her colleagues have also learned that lost infant memories can be "reactivated" with the use of cues that remind the baby of the association between a behavior, such as kicking, and a stimulus, such as a mobile (Bearce & Rovee-Collier, 2006). Thus, babies do remember more than Piaget believed, but their memories are highly specific. With age, their memories become less and less tied to specific cues or contexts.

Critical Thinking

1. In what ways do conditioning, modeling, categorical learning, and memory contribute to the development of social relationships between infants and their caregivers?

The Beginnings of Language

Most of us think of "language" as beginning when the baby uses her first words, at about 12 months of age. But all sorts of important developments precede the first words. Before we look at these developments, though, we'll look at the various theoretical perspectives that try to explain them.

Learning Objective 5.7

What are the behaviorist, nativist, and interactionist explanations of language development?

Theoretical Perspectives

The nature-nurture debate is alive and well in discussions of language development. The child's amazing progress in this domain in the early years of life has been explained from both behaviorist and nativist points of view and as part of the larger process of cognitive development.

The Behaviorist View In the late 1950s, B. F. Skinner, the scientist who formulated operant conditioning theory, suggested a behaviorist explanation of language development (Skinner, 1957). He claimed that language development begins with babbling. While babbling, babies accidentally make sounds that somewhat resemble real words as spoken by their parents. Parents hear the wordlike sounds and respond to them with praise and encouragement, which serve as reinforcers. Thus, wordlike babbling becomes more frequent, while utterances that do not resemble words gradually disappear from babies' vocalizations. Skinner further hypothesized that parents and others respond to grammatical uses of words and do not respond to nongrammatical ones. As a result, correct grammar is reinforced and becomes more frequent, but incorrect grammar is extinguished through nonreinforcement.

At first glance, Skinner's theory might appear to make sense. However, systematic examination of the interactions between infants and parents reveals that adults do not reinforce babies' vocalizations in this manner. Instead, parents and others respond to all of a baby's vocalizations, and even sometimes imitate them—a consequence that, according to operant conditioning theory, should prolong babbling rather than lead to the development of grammatical language. Skinner's mistake was that his theory was not based on observations of language development but rather on his assumption that the principles of operant conditioning underlie all human learning and development.

The Nativist View Have you ever heard a child say "I breaked it" instead of "I broke it" or "foots" instead of "feet"? Such utterances are the biggest challenge of all for behaviorists' explanations of language development, because there is no way that they could be acquired through imitation. Moreover, when parents correct these errors, children often persist in using them, or they further *overregularize* them (e.g., "I broked it" or "feets"). Linguist Noam Chomsky used examples such as these to refute Skinner's theory (Chomsky, 1959). Chomsky argued that the only possible explanation for such errors was that children acquire grammar rules before they master the exceptions to them. Further, Chomsky proposed a nativist explanation for language development: Children's comprehension and production of language are guided by an innate language processor that he called the **language acquisition device (LAD)**, which contains the basic grammatical structure of all human language. In effect, the LAD tells infants what characteristics of language to look for in the stream of speech to which they are exposed. Simply put, the LAD tells babies that there are two basic types of sounds—consonants and vowels—and enables them to properly divide the speech they hear into the two categories so that they can analyze and learn the sounds that are specific to the language they are hearing. Chomsky supported the existence of the LAD with evidence compiled over hundreds of years by field linguists, which demonstrated that all human languages have the same grammatical forms. He also argued that the LAD is species-specific—that is, nonhuman species do not have one and, therefore, cannot learn grammatical language.

Another influential nativist, Dan Slobin (1985a, 1985b), proposes that babies are preprogrammed to pay attention to the beginnings and endings of strings of sounds and to stressed sounds—a hypothesis supported by research (e.g., Morgan, 1994). Together, these operating principles would help to explain some of the features of children's early grammars. In English, for example, the stressed words in a sentence are normally the verb and the noun—precisely the words that English-speaking children use in their earliest sentences. In Turkish, on the other hand, prefixes and suffixes are stressed, and Turkish-speaking children learn both very early. Both of these patterns make sense if we assume that the preprogrammed rule is not "verbness" or "nounness" or "prefixness" but "pay attention to stressed sounds."

The Interactionist View Clearly, nativist explanations like those of Chomsky and Slobin are more consistent than Skinner's view with both research findings and our everyday communication experiences with young children. Even so, some theorists argue that language development is part of the broader process of cognitive development and is influenced by both internal and external factors. These theorists are known as **interactionists**. There are two common threads that run through the interactionists' theories. First, infants are born with some kind of biological preparedness to pay more attention to language than to other kinds of information. Second, the interactionists argue that, rather than having a neurological module that is specific to language (i.e., an LAD), the infant's brain has a generalized set of tools that it employs across all of the sub-domains of cognitive development. These tools allow infants to extract general principles from all kinds of specific experiences, including those that they have with language. Consequently, some interactionists argue that the nativists have paid too little attention to the role that the social context plays in language development (Tomasello, 1999),

language acquisition device (LAD) an innate language processor, theorized by Chomsky, that contains the basic grammatical structure of all human language

interactionists theorists who argue that language development is a subprocess of general cognitive development and is influenced by both internal and external factors

while others point out that nativist theories fail to capture the degree to which language and cognition develop interdependently (Bowerman, 1985).

One prominent proponent of this view, Melissa Bowerman, puts the proposition this way: "When language starts to come in, it does not introduce new meanings to the child. Rather, it is used to express only those meanings the child has already formulated independently of language" (1985, p. 372). Even more broadly, Lois Bloom argues that from the beginning of language, the child's intent is to communicate, to share the ideas and concepts in his head. He does this as best he can with the gestures or words he knows, and he learns new words when they help him communicate his thoughts and feelings (1993; 1997; 2004).

One type of evidence in support of this argument comes from the observation that it is children and not mothers who initiate the majority of verbal exchanges (Bloom, 1997). Further evidence comes from studies showing links between achievements in language development and the child's broader cognitive development. For example, symbolic play, such as drinking from an empty cup, and imitation of sounds and gestures both appear at about the same time as the child's first words, suggesting some broad "symbolic" understanding that is reflected in a number of behaviors. In children whose language is significantly delayed, both symbolic play and imitation are usually delayed as well (Bates, O'Connell, & Shore, 1987; Ungerer & Sigman, 1984).

A second example occurs later: At about the point at which two-word sentences appear, we also see children begin to combine several gestures into a sequence in their pretend play, such as pouring imaginary liquid, drinking, and then wiping the mouth. Those children who are the first to show this sequencing in their play are also the first to show two- or three-word sentences in their speech (e.g., McCune, 1995; Shore, 1986).

Learning Objective 5.8

What are some of the environmental influences on language development?

Influences on Language Development

Developmentalists better understand how the environment influences language development than they did when Skinner and Chomsky began their historic debate in the 1950s. Moreover, the increasing emphasis on the interactionist approach has led researchers to examine the kinds of environmental influences to which children are exposed during different phases of language development. For example, adults and older children speak differently to infants than they do to preschoolers, a way of speaking that researchers call **infant-directed speech (IDS)**. This pattern of speech is characterized by a higher pitch than that which is exhibited by adults and children when they are not speaking to an infant. Moreover, adults speaking to infants and young children also repeat a lot, introducing minor variations ("Where is the ball? Can you see the ball? Where is the ball? There is the ball!"). They may also repeat the child's own sentences but in slightly longer, more grammatically correct forms—a pattern referred to as an expansion or a recasting. For example, if a child said "Mommy sock," the mother might recast it as "Yes, this is Mommy's sock," or if a child said "Doggie not eating," the parent might say "The doggie is not eating."

We also know that babies as young as a few days old can discriminate between IDS and adult-directed speech and that they prefer to listen to IDS, whether it is spoken by a female or a male voice (Cooper & Aslin, 1994; Pegg, Werker, & McLeod, 1992). This preference exists even when the IDS is being spoken in a language other than the one normally spoken to the child. Janet Werker and her colleagues (1994), for example, have found that both English and Chinese infants prefer to listen to infant-directed speech, whether it is spoken in English or in Cantonese (one of the major languages of China). Other studies by Werker indicate that IDS helps infants identify the sounds in their mothers' speech that are specific to the language that they are learning (e.g., the English schwa, the Spanish rolled *r*) by emphasizing those sounds more than others (Werker et al., 2007).

Infant-directed speech may also be important to grammar development. The quality of IDS that seems to be particularly attractive to babies is its higher pitch. Once the child's attention is drawn by this special tone, the very simplicity and repetitiveness of the adult's speech may help the child to pick out repeating grammatical forms. Children's attention also seems to be drawn to recast sentences. For example, Farrar (1992) found that a 2-year-old was two or

infant-directed speech the simplified, higher-pitched speech that adults use with infants and young children

THE REAL WORLD

The Importance of Reading to Toddlers

At bedtime, 20-month-old Lucy's mother has learned what to expect. "Moon," Lucy says, referring to the classic children's book *Goodnight Moon*. A ritual has developed in which her mother must read through the book at least twice before Lucy will consent to being put to bed. The little girl knows the story so well that her mother often stops reading in the middle of a sentence, and Lucy gleefully completes it. Although she is getting a bit tired of *Goodnight Moon*, Lucy's mother enjoys the nightly reading sessions, but she is curious as to whether her daughter is deriving cognitive benefits from them.

In this era of computers and video, books may seem rather old-fashioned. However, researchers have found that toddlers remember and understand a story better when an adult reads it to them than when they hear an electronic version of the same story read by a computer (de Jong & Bus, 2002). Moreover, a classic series of studies by G. J. Whitehurst and his colleagues suggests that interactive reading can have powerful effects on a child's language development.

In their first study, Whitehurst's team of researchers trained some parents to read picture books to their toddlers and to interact with them using a strategy Whitehurst calls *dialogic reading*, which involves the use of questions that can't be answered by pointing (Whitehurst et al., 1988). For example, a mother reading a story about Winnie the Pooh might say, "There's Eeyore. What's happening to him?" Other parents were encouraged to read to their children, but were given no special instructions about how to read. After a month, the children who had experienced dialogic reading showed a larger gain in vocabulary than did the children in the comparison group. Whitehurst later replicated this study in day-care centers for poor children in both Mexico and New York City and in a large number of Head Start classrooms (Valdez-Menchaca & Whitehurst, 1992; Whitehurst et al., 1994; Whitehurst et al., 1995).

Whitehurst's research strengthens the argument that richer interactive language between adult and child, the kind that comes from a shared experience with an information source (book, video, computer game, or whatever) is one important ingredient in fostering the child's language growth. Moreover, researchers have found that one of the best ways to help kindergarteners who are behind their peers in prereading skills is to teach their parents how to engage them in dialogic reading (Chow & McBride-Chang, 2003; Fielding-Barnsley & Purdie, 2003). Thus, the bedtime story that many parents enjoy each evening with their toddlers appears to be much more than just a transition to a peaceful night's sleep. It may also represent an important bridge between spoken and written language for a child who will face the developmental task of acquiring literacy in just a few short years.

Questions for Reflection

1. What would you say to a person who claimed that reading to an infant or toddler is a waste of time because of their limited language skills?
2. If a toddler doesn't want to be read to, do you think his parents should try to get him interested in books? If so, how do you think they should go about it?

three times more likely to imitate a correct grammatical form after he heard his mother recast his own sentences than when the mother used that same correct grammatical form in her normal conversation. Experimental studies confirm this effect of recastings. Children who are deliberately exposed to higher rates of specific types of recast sentences seem to learn the modeled grammatical forms more quickly than do those who hear no recastings (Nelson, 1977).

Developmentalists also know that children whose parents talk to them often, read to them regularly, and use a wide range of words in their speech differ from children whose parents do not. These children begin to talk sooner, develop larger vocabularies, use more complex sentences, and learn to read more readily when they reach school age (Hart & Risley, 1995; Huttenlocher, 1995; Snow, 1997). Thus, the sheer quantity of language a child hears is a significant factor.

Finally, poverty is related to language development. By age 4, the difference in vocabulary between poor and better-off children is already substantial, and the gap only widens over the school years. Similarly, Catherine Snow (1997) found that 4-year-old children reared in poverty use shorter and less complex sentences than do their better-off peers. Many factors no doubt contribute to these differences, but the richness and variety of the language a child hears is obviously highly significant. Of all these factors, being read to less often may be one of the most critical, as you can see from the Real World discussion about reading to toddlers.

Early Milestones of Language Development

Learning Objective 5.9
How do infants' sounds, gestures, and understanding of words change in the early months of life?

From birth to about 1 month of age, the most common sound an infant makes is a cry, although she also produces other fussing, gurgling, and satisfied sounds. Over the next few months, the number of ways in which a baby can express herself expands tremendously. Although some of these may seem to be of little consequence,

Gestures are just one of several skills in infants' repertoire of communicative skills.

each of the early milestones of language development makes a unique contribution to the language skills that all healthy children achieve in the first few years of life.

First Sounds and Gestures At about 1 or 2 months, the baby begins to make some laughing and **cooing** vowel sounds. Sounds like this are usually signals of pleasure and may show quite a lot of variation in tone, running up and down in volume or pitch. Consonant sounds appear at about 6 or 7 months, frequently combined with vowel sounds to make a kind of syllable. Babies of this age seem to play with these sounds, often repeating the same sound over and over (such as *babababababa* or *dahdahdah*). This sound pattern is called **babbling**, and it makes up about half of babies' noncrying sounds from about 6 to 12 months of age (Mitchell & Kent, 1990).

Any parent can tell you that babbling is a delight to listen to. It also seems to be an important part of the preparation for spoken language. For one thing, infants' babbling gradually acquires some of what linguists call the intonational pattern of the language they are hearing—a process one developmental psychologist refers to as "learning the tune before the words" (Bates et al., 1987). At the very least, infants do seem to develop at least two such "tunes" in their babbling. Babbling with a rising intonation at the end of a string of sounds seems to signal a desire for a response; a falling intonation requires no response.

A second important thing about babbling is that when babies first start babbling, they typically babble all kinds of sounds, including some that are not part of the language they are hearing. But at about 9 or 10 months, their sound repertoire gradually begins to narrow down to the set of sounds they are listening to, with the nonheard sounds dropping out (Oller, 1981). Findings like these do not prove that babbling is necessary for language development, but they certainly make it look as if babbling is part of a connected developmental process that begins at birth.

These little girls probably haven't yet spoken their first words, but chances are they already understand quite a few. Receptive language usually develops before expressive language.

Another part of that process appears to be a kind of gestural language that develops at around 9 or 10 months. At this age, babies begin "demanding" or "asking" for things using gestures or combinations of gestures and sound. A 10-month-old baby who apparently wants you to hand her a favorite toy may stretch and reach for it, opening and closing her hand while making whining or whimpering sounds. Interestingly, infants of this age use gestures in this way whether they are exposed to spoken language or sign language (see the Research Report). At about the same age, babies enter into those gestural games much loved by parents: "pat-a-cake," "soooo big," and "wave bye-bye" (Bates, O'Connell, & Shore, 1987).

Word Recognition Recent research has shown that babies are beginning to store individual words in their memories at around 8 months of age (Jusczyk & Hohne, 1997). By 9 or 10 months, most can understand the meanings of 20–30 words; this ability to understand words is known as **receptive language**. In the next few months, the number of words understood increases dramatically. In one investigation, researchers asked hundreds of mothers about their babies' understanding of various words. Reportedly, 10-month-olds understood an average of about 30 words; for 13-month-olds, the number was nearly 100 words (Fenson et al., 1994).

But how do babies separate a single word from the constant flow of speech to which they are exposed? Many linguists have proposed that a child can cope with the monumentally complex task of word learning only because he applies some built in biases or constraints (Baldwin, 1995; Golinkoff, Mervis, & Hirsh-Pasek, 1994; Jusczyk & Hohne 1997; Markman, 1992; Waxman & Kosowski, 1990). For example, the child may have a built in assumption that words refer to objects or actions but not both.

cooing making repetitive vowel sounds, particularly the *uuu* sound

babbling the repetitive vocalizing of consonant-vowel combinations by an infant

receptive language comprehension of spoken language

RESEARCH REPORT

Early Gestural Language in the Children of Deaf Parents

Gestures play an important communicative role in the lives of babies, both hearing and deaf (Goldin-Meadow, 2002). For deaf children, however, gestural language is especially important because most of them are quite limited in the ability to acquire speech. Moreover, studying how deaf children acquire sign language can provide developmentalists with insight into the process of language development in hearing children.

Deaf children of deaf parents are a particularly interesting group to study. The children do not hear oral language, but many are exposed to language—sign language. And, these children show the same early steps in language development as do hearing children. Deaf children show a kind of "sign babbling" that emerges between 5 and 7 months of age, much as hearing children begin to babble sounds in these same months (Takei, 2001). Then, at 8 or 9 months of age, deaf children begin using simple gestures, such as pointing, which is just about the same time that we see such gestures in hearing babies of hearing parents. At about 12 months of age, deaf babies seem to display their first referential signs (that is, signs in which a gesture appears to stand for some object or event)—for example, signaling that they want a drink by making a motion of bringing a cup to the mouth (Petitto, 1988).

Researchers have also studied an equally interesting group—hearing children of deaf parents. These babies are exposed to sign language from their parents and to hearing language from their contacts with others in their world, including TV, teachers, other relatives, and playmates. In one such study, involving a small sample of nine babies, the first sign appeared at an average age of 8 months, the first referential sign at 12.6 months, and the first spoken word at 12.2 months (Folven & Bonvillian, 1991). In another study, researchers found that hearing babies of deaf parents exhibited hand movements while babbling that were very similar to those of babies whose parents have normal hearing; remarkably, too, these hand movements were quite distinct from the infants' attempts to imitate their parents' sign language (Petitto et al., 2001). What is striking here is that the first referential signs and the first spoken words appear at such similar times, and that the spoken words appear at such a completely normal time, despite the fact that these children of deaf parents hear comparatively little spoken language.

This marked similarity in the sequence and timing of the steps of early language in the deaf and the hearing child provides strong support for the argument that the baby is somehow primed to learn language in some form, be it spoken or gestural.

Questions for Critical Analysis

1. Why do comparisons of deaf and hearing children of deaf parents provide evidence in favor of the view that language development is strongly influenced by an inborn plan of some kind?
2. In your view, what are the benefits and risks associated with being the hearing child of deaf parents?

Learning a language's patterns of word stress may also help babies identify words. Recent research suggests that infants discriminate between stressed and unstressed syllables fairly early—around 7 months of age—and use syllable stress as a cue to identify single words (Jusczyk, Houston, & Newsome, 1999). For example, first-syllable stress, such as in the word *market*, is far more common in English than second syllable stress, such as in the word *garage*. Thus, when English-learning infants hear a stressed syllable, they may assume that a new word is beginning. This strategy would help them single out a very large number of individual English words.

All of this information reveals a whole series of changes that seem to converge by 9 or 10 months: the beginning of meaningful gestures, the drift of babbling toward the heard language sounds, imitative gestural games, and the first comprehension of individual words. It is as if the child now understands something about the process of communication and is intending to communicate to adults.

The First Words

Learning Objective 5.10

What are the characteristics of toddlers' first words?

If you have ever studied another language, you probably understood the language before you could produce it yourself. Likewise, the 9- to 10-month-old infant understands far more words than she can say. **Expressive language**—the ability to produce, as well as understand and respond to, meaningful words—typically appears at about 12 or 13 months (Fenson et al., 1994). The baby's first word is an event that parents eagerly await, but it's fairly easy to miss. A word, as linguists usually define it, is any sound or set of sounds that is used consistently to refer to some thing, action, or quality. This means that a child who uses *ba* consistently to refer to her bottle is using a word, even though it isn't considered a word in English.

expressive language the ability to use sounds, signs, or symbols to communicate meaning

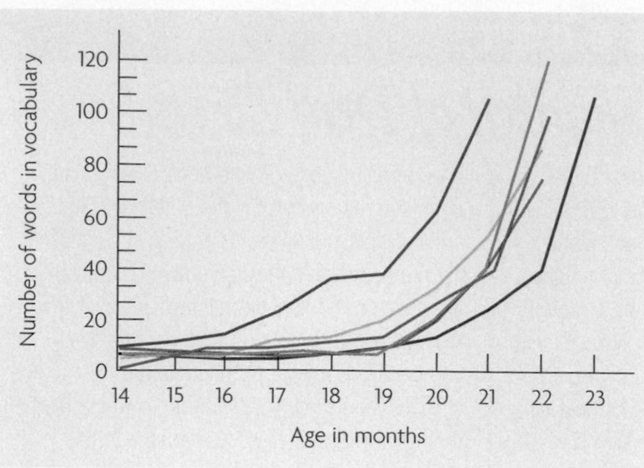

Figure 5.6
Vocabulary Growth in the Second Year

Each of the lines in this figure represents the vocabulary growth of one of the children studied longitudinally by Goldfield and Reznick. The six children shown here each acquired new words in the most common pattern: slow initial growth followed by a fairly rapid spurt.

(*Source*: Adaptation of Table 3, "Early Lexical Acquisition: Rate, Content, and the Vocabulary Spurt," by B. Goldfield & J. Reznick, in *Journal of Child Language*, 17, pp. 171–183. Reprinted with the permission of Cambridge University Press.)

Often, a child's earliest words are used in specific situations and in the presence of many cues. The child may say "bow-wow" or "doggie" only in response to such promptings as "How does the doggie go?" or "What's that?" Typically, this early word learning is very slow, requiring many repetitions for each word. In the first 6 months of word usage, children may learn as few as 30 words. Most linguists have concluded that this earliest word-use phase involves learning each word as something connected to a set of specific contexts. What the child has apparently not yet grasped is that words are symbolic—they refer to objects or events.

Very young children often combine a single word with a gesture to create a "two-word meaning" before they use two words together in their speech. For example, a child may point to his father's shoe and say "Daddy," as if to convey "Daddy's shoe" (Bates et al., 1987). In such cases, meaning is conveyed by the use of gesture and body language combined with a word. Linguists call these word-and-gesture combinations **holophrases**, and children use them frequently between 12 and 18 months of age.

Between 16 and 24 months, after the early period of very slow word learning, most children begin to add new words rapidly, as if they have figured out that things have names. Developmentalists refer to this period as the **naming explosion**. In this period, children seem to learn new words with very few repetitions, and they generalize these words to many more situations. According to one large cross-sectional study based on mothers' reports, the average 16-month-old has a speaking vocabulary of about 50 words; for a 24-month-old, the total has grown to about 320 words (Fenson et al., 1994).

For most children, the naming explosion is not a steady, gradual process; instead, vocabulary "spurts" begin at about the time the child has acquired 50 words. This pattern, observed by several researchers, is illustrated in Figure 5.6, which shows the vocabulary growth curves of six children studied longitudinally (Bloom, 1993; Goldfield & Reznick, 1990). Not all children show precisely this pattern, but a rapid increase over a period of a few months is typical.

Most observers agree that the bulk of new words learned during this early period of rapid vocabulary growth are names for things or people: *ball, car, milk, doggie, he*. Action words tend to appear later (Gleitman & Gleitman, 1992). One study involving a large group of children suggested that as many as two-thirds of the words children knew by age 2 were nouns, and only 8.5% were verbs (Fenson et al., 1994). It appears that infants lack the ability to consistently associate words with actions until about 18 months of age (Casasola & Cohen, 2000). Recent cross-linguistic research also suggests that, compared to Korean-speaking parents, English-speaking parents emphasize nouns more than verbs in speaking and reading to infants (Choi, 2000). Thus, the pattern of learning nouns before verbs may be influenced by the characteristics of the language being learned, as well as by the behavior of mature speakers as they speak to infants.

holophrases combinations of gestures and single words that convey more meaning than just the word alone

naming explosion the period when toddlers experience rapid vocabulary growth, typically beginning between 16 and 24 months

Learning Objective 5.11

What kinds of sentences do children produce between 18 and 24 months of age?

The First Sentences

Research suggests that sentences appear when a child has reached a threshold vocabulary of around 100 to 200 words (Fenson et al., 1994). For most children, this threshold is crossed at between 18 and 24 months of age.

The first sentences have several distinguishing features: They are short, generally two or three words, and they are simple. Language development researcher Roger Brown coined the term **telegraphic speech** to refer to this pattern (Brown & Bellugi, 1964). Nouns, verbs, and adjectives are usually included, but virtually all grammatical markers (which linguists call **inflections**) are missing. At the beginning, for example, children learning English do not normally use the *-s* ending for plurals or put the *-ed* ending on verbs to make the past tense.

It is also clear that even at this earliest stage children create sentences following rules—not adult rules, to be sure, but rules nonetheless. They focus on certain types of words and

telegraphic speech simple two-word sentences that usually include a noun and a verb

inflections additions to words that change their meaning (e.g., the *s* in toys, the *ed* in waited)

NO EASY ANSWERS

One Language or Two?

Knowing two languages is clearly a social and economic benefit to an adult. However, research suggests that there are cognitive advantages *and* disadvantages to growing up bilingual. In preschool and school-age children, bilingualism is associated with a clear advantage in *metalinguistic ability*, or the capacity to think about language (Bialystok, Shenfield, & Codd, 2000; Mohanty & Perregaux, 1997). In addition, most bilingual children display greater ability to focus attention on language tasks than do monolingual children (Bialystock & Majumder, 1998). These two advantages enable bilingual children to more easily grasp the connection between sounds and symbols in the beginning stages of learning to read if the languages being learned (e.g., Spanish and English) are similar in this regard (Bialystock, 1997; Oller, Cobo-Lewis, & Eilers, 1998).

On the negative side, infants in bilingual homes reach some milestones later than those learning a single language. For example, bilingual infants' receptive and expressive vocabularies are as large as those of monolingual infants, but the words they know are divided between two languages (Patterson, 1998). Consequently, they are behind monolingual infants in word knowledge no matter which language is considered, a difference that persists into the school years. In addition, children growing up in bilingual homes in which two languages vary greatly in how they are written (e.g., English and Chinese) may acquire reading skills in both languages more slowly than peers in monolingual homes (Bialystok, Majumder, & Martin, 2003). Even in adulthood, bilingualism is sometimes associated with decreased efficiency in memory tasks involving words (Gollan & Silverberg, 2001; McElree, Jia, & Litvak, 2000). However, bilinguals appear to develop compensatory strategies that allow them to overcome these obstacles.

Research indicates that bilingual children who are equally fluent in both languages encounter few, if any, learning problems in school (Vuorenkoski, Kuure, Moilanen, & Peninkilampi, 2000). However, most children do not attain equal fluency in both languages (Hakansson, Salameh, & Nettelbladt, 2003). As a result, they tend to think more slowly in the language in which they have less fluency (Chincotta & Underwood, 1997). When the language in which they are less fluent is the language in which they are schooled, they are at risk for learning problems (Anderson, 1998; Thorn & Gathercole, 1999). Therefore, parents who choose bilingualism should probably take into account their ability to fully support children's acquisition of fluency in both languages.

Clearly, the advantages in adulthood of being bilingual are substantial and may outweigh any disadvantages experienced in childhood. Thus, bilingual parents need to balance the various advantages and disadvantages of bilingualism, as well as their long-term parenting goals, to reach an informed decision about the kind of linguistic environment to provide for their babies.

Take a Stand

Decide which of these two statements you most agree with and think about how you would defend your position:

1. Parents who are fluent in more than one language should raise their children to be bilingual.
2. Parents who speak more than one language should decide on which language to speak most often in the home, and they should ensure that their children become fully fluent in that language.

put them together in particular orders. They also manage to convey a variety of different meanings with their simple sentences.

For example, young children frequently use a sentence made up of two nouns, such as *Mommy sock* or *sweater chair* (Bloom, 1973). The child who says "Mommy sock" may mean either *This is Mommy's sock* or *Mommy is putting a sock on my foot* (Bloom, 1973). Thus, to understand what a child means by a two-word sentence, it is necessary to know the context in which it occurred.

Individual Differences in Language Development

Learning Objective 5.12
What kinds of individual differences are evident in language development?

The sequences of development of language you've read about, and which are shown in Table 5.2 on page 138, are accurate on the average, but the speed with which children acquire language skill varies widely. One factor influencing this rate is the number of languages to which a child has daily exposure (see No Easy Answers). There also seem to be important style differences.

Differences in Rate Some children begin using individual words at 8 months, others not until 18 months; some do not use two-word sentences until 3 years or even later. You can see the range of normal variation in sentence construction very clearly in Figure 5.7 on page 138), which shows the average sentence length (referred to by linguists as the **mean length of utterance** [MLU]) of ten children, each studied longitudinally. Eve, Adam, and Sarah were studied by Roger Brown (1973); Jane, Martin, and Ben (all African American children) by Ira Blake (1994); and Eric, Gia, Kathryn, and Peter by Lois Bloom (1991). The figure includes a

mean length of utterance (MLU) the average number of meaningful units in a sentence

Table 5.2 Language Development in the First Two Years

Age	Milestone
2–3 months	Makes cooing sounds when alone; responds with smiles and cooing when talked to
20 weeks	Makes various vowel and consonant sounds with cooing
6 months	Babbles; utters phonemes of all languages
8–9 months	Focuses on the phonemes, rhythm, and intonation of language spoken in the home; has receptive vocabulary of 20 to 30 words
12 months	Expressive language emerges; says single words
12–18 months	Uses word-gesture combinations combined with variations in intonation (holophrases)
18–20 months	Uses two-word sentences (telegraphic speech); has expressive vocabulary of 100 to 200 words

line at the MLU level that normally accompanies a switch from simple, uninflected two-word sentences to more complex forms. You can see that Eve was the earliest to make this transition, at about 21 months; Adam and Sarah passed over this point about a year later.

More than half of children who talk late eventually catch up. The subset of those who do not catch up is made up primarily of children who also have poor receptive language (Bates, 1993; Thal, Tobias, & Morrison, 1991). This group appears to remain behind in language development and perhaps in cognitive development more generally. In practical terms, this means that if your child—or a child you care for—is significantly delayed in understanding as well as speaking language, you should seek professional help to try to diagnose the problem and begin appropriate intervention.

expressive style a style of word learning characterized by low rates of nounlike terms and high use of personal-social words and phrases

Differences in Style Katherine Nelson (1973) was the first developmentalist to point out that some toddlers use an **expressive style** when learning language. Such children's early vo-

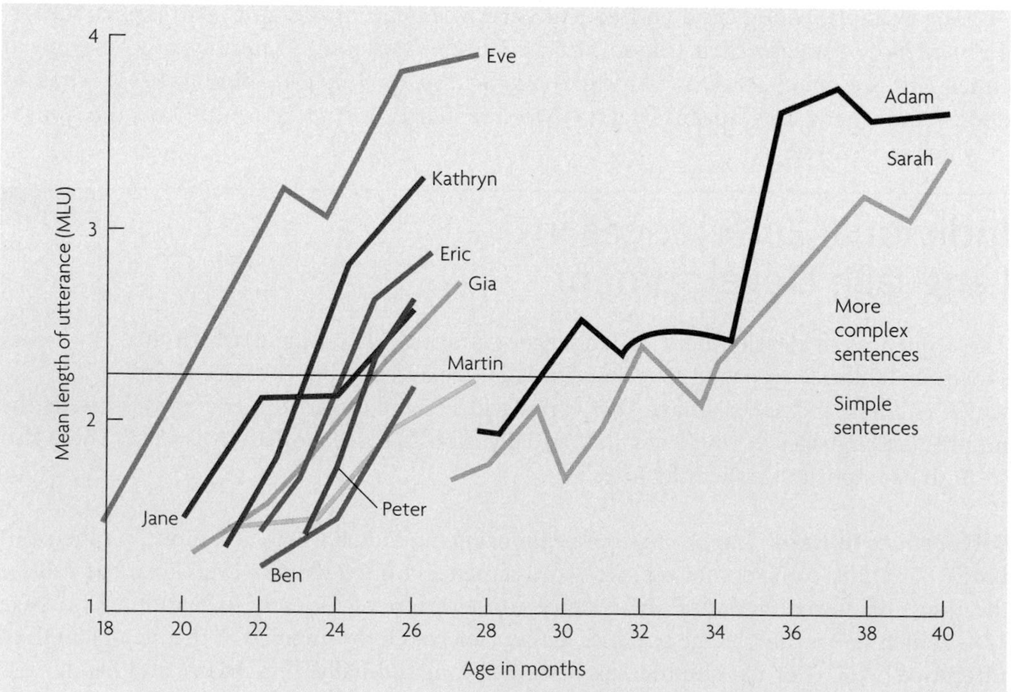

Figure 5.7 Variations in the Rate of Language Acquisition

The 10 children whose language is charted here, studied by three different linguists, moved at markedly different times from simple one- and two-word sentences to more complex sentences.

(*Sources:* Adapted from *A First Language: The Early Stages*, p. 55, Fig. 1, by Roger Brown; copyright © 1973 by the President and Fellows of Harvard College, reprinted by permission of Harvard University Press. Lois Bloom, *Language Development from Two to Three*, p. 92, Table 3.1; Cambridge, England: Cambridge University Press, 1991. I. K. Blake, "Language Development and Socialization in Young African-American Children," *Cross-Cultural Roots of Minority Children*, Greenfield and Cocking, Eds., p. 169, Table 9.1 and p. 171, Fig. 9.1; Hillsdale, NJ: Lawrence Erlbaum Associates, Inc., 1994.)

cabulary is not made up predominantly of nounlike words. Instead, most of their early words are linked to social relationships rather than objects. They often learn pronouns (*you, me*) early and use many more of what Nelson calls "personal-social" words, such as *no, yes, want,* or *please*. Their early vocabulary may also include some multiword strings, like *love you* or *do it* or *go away*. This is in sharp contrast to the children who use what Nelson calls a **referential style**, whose early vocabulary is made up predominantly of names for things or people.

Elizabeth Bates and her colleagues (1988; Thal & Bates, 1990) argue that referential-style children are, in some sense, more cognitively oriented. They are drawn to objects, spend more of their time in solitary play with objects, and interact with other people more often around objects. They are much more likely to show a clear spurt in vocabulary development in the early stages, adding many object names in a very short space of time, as if they—more than expressive children—have understood the basic principle that things have names. Such children are also advanced in their ability to understand complex adult language.

Expressive-style toddlers, on the other hand, are oriented more toward people and toward social interactions. Their early words and sentences include a lot of strings of words that are involved in common interactions with adults. Since many such strings include grammatical inflections, expressive children's early language often sounds more advanced than that of referential children, but their vocabularies are typically smaller, with no obvious spurt in vocabulary growth.

Just how these differences come about is still not clear. The most obvious possibility is that a child's early language is a reflection of the type of language she is hearing. There is some evidence, for example, that referential-style children, more than expressive-style children, have mothers who spend time naming objects and describing the child's environment (e.g., Furrow & Nelson, 1984; Goldfield, 1993). Yet it is also likely that the quality of the mother's speech is at least partially a response to the child's own language quality or style rather than—or in addition to—being a cause of it. Thus, referential children appear to elicit much more noun naming and equivalent referential speech from the mother than do expressive-style children (Pine, Lieven, & Rowland, 1997).

Language Development across Cultures

Learning Objective 5.13

How does language development vary across cultures?

Studies in a wide variety of language communities, including Turkish, Serbo-Croatian, Hungarian, Hebrew, Japanese, a New Guinean language called Kaluli, German, and Italian, have revealed important similarities in language development (Maitel, Dromi, Sagi, & Bornstein, 2000). Babies the world over coo before they babble; all babies understand language before they can speak it; babies in all cultures begin to use their first words at about 12 months.

Moreover, holophrases appear to precede telegraphic speech in every language, with the latter beginning at about 18 months. However, the specific word order that a child uses in early sentences is not the same for all children in all languages. In some languages, a noun/verb sequence is fairly common; in others, a verb/noun sequence may be heard. In addition, particular inflections are learned in highly varying orders from one language to another. Japanese children, for example, begin very early to use a special kind of marker, called a pragmatic marker, that tells something about the feeling or the context. In Japanese, the word *yo* is used at the end of a sentence when the speaker is experiencing some resistance from the listener; the word *ne* is used when the speaker expects approval or agreement. Japanese children begin to use these markers very early, much earlier than children whose languages contain other types of inflections.

Most strikingly, there are languages in which there seems to be no simple two-word-sentence stage in which the children use no inflections. Children learning Turkish, for example, use essentially the full set of noun and verb inflections by age 2 and never go through a stage of using uninflected words. Their language is simple, but it is rarely ungrammatical from the adult's point of view (Aksu-Koc & Slobin, 1985; Maratsos, 1998).

referential style a style of word learning characterized by emphasis on things and people and their naming and description

Critical Thinking

1. What would you say to someone who claimed that speaking to infants in "babytalk" interfered with their language development?

Learning Objective 5.14

How is intelligence measured in infancy?

Measuring Intelligence in Infancy

As you will learn in Chapter 7, psychologists have designed many instruments that measure **intelligence** in children and adults, an individual's ability to take in information and use it to adapt to the environment. However, it is quite difficult to create a test that can effectively measure intelligence in infants. Tests that measure intelligence in infancy, including the widely used **Bayley Scales of Infant Development**, measure primarily sensory and motor skills (Bayley, 1969, revised 1993). For example, 3-month-old infants are challenged to reach for a dangling ring; older babies are observed as they attempt to put cubes in a cup (9 months) or build a tower of three cubes (17 months). Some more clearly cognitive items are also included; for example, uncovering a toy hidden by a cloth is a test item used with 8-month-old infants to measure an aspect of object permanence.

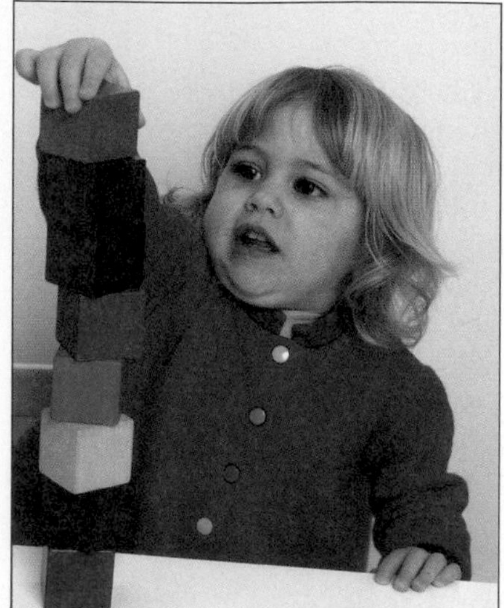

At 22 months, Katherine would clearly pass the 17-month item on the Bayley Scales of Infant Development that calls for the child to build a tower of three blocks.

Bayley's test and others like it have proven to be helpful in identifying infants and toddlers with serious developmental delays (Dezoete, MacArthur, & Tuck, 2003; Gardner et al., 2006). But as more general predictive tools for forecasting later IQ or school performance, such tests have not been nearly as useful as many had hoped. For example, the typical correlation between a Bayley test score at 12 months old and an intelligence test score at 4 years old is only about .20 to .30 (e.g., Bee et al., 1982)—hardly substantial enough to be used for predicting intellectual performance at later ages. On the whole, it appears that what is being measured on typical infant intelligence tests is not the same as what is tapped by the commonly used childhood or adult intelligence tests (Colombo, 1993). The most recent version of the test, the Bayley-III (Bayley, 2006), includes items that address cognitive and language development in addition to those that assess sensory and motor skills. Future research will determine whether it better predicts future intellectual performance than previous versions of the test have been found to.

Recent research has indicated that habituation tasks have potential as measures of infant intelligence. For example, if a baby is shown an object or a picture over and over, how many exposures does it take before the infant stops showing interest? The speed with which such habituation/recognition takes place may reveal something about the efficiency of the baby's perceptual/cognitive system and its neurological underpinnings. And if such efficiency lies behind some of the characteristics that psychologists call intelligence, then individual differences in rate of habituation in the early months of life may predict later intelligence test scores. That is exactly what some of the research examining links between measures of habituation in infants has found (Rose & Feldman, 1995; Rose, Feldman, & Jankowski, 2004; Slater, 1995).

Might such findings provide developmentalists with a useful test of infant intelligence? Some developmentalists believe that they will. For example, psychologist Joseph Fagan has developed a standardized test of habituation rate known as the Fagan Test of Infant Intelligence (Fagan & Detterman, 1992). Fagan argues that tests of habituation rate—also known as *novelty preference* and *visual recognition*—are particularly appropriate for individuals who are incapable of responding to conventional tests such as the Bayley scales (Fagan, 2000). For example, infants who suffer from cerebral palsy can't perform many of the tasks required by the Bayley scales. However, they are fully capable of viewing visual stimuli and exhibiting habituation to them. Fagan's research and that of others has shown that the Fagan test is a useful measure of cognitive function among such special populations (Fagan & Detterman, 1992; Smith, Fagan, & Ulvund, 2002; Gaultney & Gingras, 2005).

intelligence the ability to take in information and use it to adapt to the environment

Bayley Scales of Infant Development the best-known and most widely used test of infant "intelligence"

However, research examining the usefulness of the Fagan test with normal infants has produced mixed results. Some studies have shown that infants' scores on the test are correlated with later measures of intelligence and specific cognitive skills such as language comprehension (Andersson, 1996; Thompson, Fagan, & Fulker, 1991). Others have found that the Fagan test is poorly correlated with later measures of such variables (Cardon & Fulker, 1991; Tasbihsazan, Nettelbeck, & Kirby, 2003). Thus, the final determination as to the usefulness of habituation rate as a standardized measure of intelligence in infancy has yet to be made.

Critical Thinking

1. Think of contrasting "nature" and "nurture" explanations for individual differences in habituation rates.

SUMMARY

Cognitive Changes

Learning Objective 5.1 What are the important milestones of Piaget's sensorimotor stage?

- Piaget described the sensorimotor infant as beginning with a small repertoire of basic schemes, from which she moves toward symbolic representation in a series of six substages. The most important cognitive milestone of this stage is object permanence.

Learning Objective 5.2 What are some of the challenges offered to Piaget's explanation of infant cognitive development?

- More recent research suggests that Piaget underestimated infants' capabilities, as well as the degree to which some concepts may be wired into the brain.

Learning Objective 5.3 What does research tell us about infants' understanding of objects?

- Developmentalists such as Spelke and Baillargeon have studied object permanence within the context of infants' global understanding of objects. Their research shows that Piaget underestimated how much younger infants know about objects and their movements.

Learning, Categorizing, and Remembering

Learning Objective 5.4 How do infants learn through conditioning and modeling?

- Within the first few weeks of life, babies are able to learn through classical conditioning, operant conditioning, and observing models.

Learning Objective 5.5 How does categorical understanding change over the first 2 years?

- From an early age, infants use categories to organize information. The sophistication of these categories, and an understanding of how they relate to each other, increases over the first 2 years of life.

Learning Objective 5.6 How does memory function in the first 2 years?

- Three- and 4 month-old infants show signs of remembering specific experiences over periods of as long as a few days or a week, a sign that they must have some form of internal representation well before Piaget supposed.

The Beginnings of Language

Learning Objective 5.7 What are the behaviorist, nativist, and interactionist explanations of language development?

- Behaviorist theories of language development claim that infants learn language through parental reinforcement of wordlike sounds and correct grammar. Nativists say that an innate language processor helps them learn language rules. Interactionists say that language development is a subprocess of cognitive development.

Learning Objective 5.8 What are some of the environmental influences on language development?

- High-pitched infant-directed speech (IDS) attracts infants' attention to the simple, repetitive, and expanded expressions that adults use to help them learn language. The amount of verbal interaction that takes place between infants and mature speakers is another influence. Poverty is associated with language development as well.

Learning Objective 5.9 How do infants' sounds, gestures, and understanding of words change in the early months of life?

- Babies' earliest sounds are cries, followed at about 2 months by cooing, then at about 6 months by babbling. At 9 months, babies typically use meaningful gestures and can understand a small vocabulary of spoken words.

Learning Objective 5.10 What are the characteristics of toddlers' first words?

- The first spoken words, usually names for objects or people, typically occur at about 1 year, after which toddlers add words slowly for a few months and then rapidly.

Learning Objective 5.11 What kinds of sentences do children produce between 18 and 24 months of age?

- Simple two-word sentences appear in children's expressive language at about 18 months.

Learning Objective 5.12 What kinds of individual differences are evident in language development?

- The rate of language development varies from one child to another. In addition, some toddlers display an expressive style in early word learning while others show a referential style.

Learning Objective 5.13 How does language development vary across cultures?

- Early word learning seems to follow similar patterns in all cultures. However, the word order of a child's telegraphic speech depends on which language he is learning.

Measuring Intelligence in Infancy

Learning Objective 5.14 How is intelligence measured in infancy?

- Infant intelligence tests are not strongly related to later measures of intelligence. Measures of basic information processing skills in infancy, such as rate of habituation at 4 months, may be better correlated with later intelligence test scores.

KEY TERMS

A-not-B error *(p. 124)*
babbling *(p. 134)*
Bayley Scales of Infant Development *(p. 140)*
cooing *(p. 134)*
deferred imitation *(p. 124)*
expressive language *(p. 135)*
expressive style *(p. 138)*
holophrases *(p. 136)*
infant-directed speech (IDS) *(p. 132)*
inflections *(p. 136)*
intelligence *(p. 140)*
interactionists *(p. 131)*
language acquisition device (LAD) *(p. 131)*
mean length of utterance (MLU) *(p. 137)*
means-end behavior *(p. 123)*
naming explosion *(p. 136)*
object concept *(p. 126)*
object permanence *(p. 123)*
primary circular reactions *(p. 122)*
receptive language *(p. 134)*
referential style *(p. 139)*
schematic learning *(p. 129)*
secondary circular reactions *(p. 123)*
sensorimotor stage *(p. 122)*
telegraphic speech *(p. 136)*
tertiary circular reactions *(p. 123)*
violation of expectations method *(p. 126)*

TEST YOURSELF

Cognitive Changes

5.1 What is sensorimotor intelligence?
- a. utilizing innate schemes to process incoming information
- b. manipulating symbols to develop more sophisticated schemes
- c. a type of intelligence that is genetically determined
- d. using basic logic to categorize the world

5.2 Which of the following is an example of a tertiary circular reaction?
- a. You touch the child's cheek, and he turns his head in the opposite direction.
- b. The child verbally imitates the actions of others.
- c. The child repeatedly throws food on the floor, and then the walls, and then his sister, to see what will happen.
- d. The child no longer needs a pacifier to be comforted.

5.3 In which substage of the sensorimotor stage does the understanding of causal connections emerge?
- a. 1
- b. 2
- c. 4
- d. 6

5.4 An infant sees a toy disappear under a blanket and does not search for it. In fact, the infant acts as though the toy never existed. This is because the infant has not yet developed
- a. object permanence.
- b. intersensory transference.
- c. primary circular reactions.
- d. visual tracking.

5.5 According to Piaget, deferred imitation cannot begin until the sixth substage of the sensorimotor stage because it requires ______, which does not begin until this point.
- a. causal reasoning
- b. internal representation
- c. object permanence
- d. habituation

5.6 Which of the following is a criticism of Piaget's theory?
- a. Piaget overestimated children's abilities.
- b. Piaget did not use all of the advanced techniques that were available to him.
- c. Development occurs in stages, unlike the quantitative changes that Piaget proposed.
- d. Piaget underestimated children's abilities.

Learning, Categorizing, and Remembering

5.7 Researchers have increased newborns' head turning through the use of reinforcements such as the sound of the mother's voice. This is an example of
- a. classical conditioning.
- b. operant conditioning.
- c. habituation.
- d. schematic learning.

5.8 Schematic learning assumes that
- a. babies attempt to categorize their experiences.
- b. children cannot learn unless the information is organized for them.
- c. babies will learn only if they are reinforced for exploring.
- d. learning is sequential and orderly.

5.9 Which of the following is an accurate statement about infant memory?
- a. Infants younger than 6 months do not retain memories.
- b. The expansion of memory is preprogrammed.
- c. Infants develop very general memories for information.
- d. Early infant memory is specific to the context in which it was learned.

The Beginnings of Language

5.10 The theory of language development that proposes that infants learn language because they are reinforced is called the

a. holophrase acquisition.
b. nativist explanation.
c. behaviorist explanation.
d. language acquisition device.

5.11 According to Chomsky, the language acquisition device contains

a. most of the words in an infant's vocabulary.
b. the basic grammatical structure of all human language.
c. the innate ability to learn most of the words in an infant's first language.
d. the ability to distinguish sounds in an infant's first language from those in other languages.

5.12 Which of the following research findings supports the interactionist view?

a. the finding that newborns segment the sounds of speech into vowel and consonant categories
b. the finding that all languages share the same grammatical forms
c. the finding that infants pay attention to sound rhythm
d. the finding that when language is significantly delayed, so are symbolic play and imitation

5.13 Infant-directed speech, is characterized by

a. complex sentence structure.
b. a lower pitch.
c. grammatically incorrect speech.
d. simplicity.

5.14 What can parents do to increase their children's language development?

a. have their hearing tested
b. use only a limited number of words
c. use a lower pitched voice
d. read to them regularly

5.15 Impoverished children

a. typically learn to speak earlier than other children.
b. use longer sentences than other children.
c. use less complex sentences than other children.
d. have the same language skills as other children.

5.16 What is the baby's first communicative sound?

a. ma-ma
b. cooing
c. crying
d. laughing

5.17 A child's ability to understand a word that is spoken before she can say the word is called

a. expressive language.
b. receptive language.
c. imitation.
d. innate vocalization.

5.18 A child points to Daddy's shoe and says "Daddy." This is an example of a(n)

a. referential style.
b. expressive style.
c. holophrase.
d. personification.

5.19 Which of the following is an example of telegraphic speech?

a. "Daddy" (while pointing to Daddy's shoe)
b. "Ma-ma"
c. "Me fall"
d. "The cookie is good."

5.20 Most children who are late to talk

a. also have cognitive delays.
b. eventually catch up.
c. are above average in intelligence.
d. are girls.

5.21 Most of Max's speech involves naming objects. Max might be described as using

a. telegraphic speech.
b. a referential style.
c. an expressive style.
d. holophrases.

Measuring Intelligence in Infancy

5.22 The Bayley Scales of Infant Development are most useful for

a. identifying children with developmental delays.
b. predicting children's school performance in later years.
c. predicting children's later IQs.
d. assessing children's language skills.

5.23 Which of the following is an accurate statement about infant intelligence tests?

a. Some studies indicate that babies who habituate quickly when they are 4 or 5 months old are likely to have higher intelligence test scores at later ages.
b. The Bayley Scales of Infant Development accurately predict a child's intelligence at age 10.
c. None of the infant intelligence test scores correlate with intelligence test scores at later ages.
d. Infant intelligence tests are based on individual differences in cognitive abilities.

5.24 The Fagan Test of Infant Intelligence is especially useful at predicting later intelligence for

a. normal 18-month-olds.
b. children with cerebral palsy.
c. male infants.
d. normal 3-month-olds.

PEARSON

mydevelopmentlab Study Plan

Are You Ready for the Test?

Students who use the study materials on MyDevelopmentLab report higher grades in the course than those who use the text alone. Here are three easy steps to mastering this chapter and improving your grade...

Step 1

Take the chapter pre-test in MyDevelopmentLab and review your customized Study Plan.

PRE-TEST

Research has found that children reared in poverty use shorter and less complex sentences than more advantaged peers. One of the factors that contributes to this difference is that poorer children

- have more people who talk to them, so they need to use language less.
- are read to less often than more advantaged children.
- have less complex ideas that they are trying to express through langauge.
- often have been malnourished so they have little interest in learning to speak.

Step 2

Use MyDevelopmentLab's Multimedia Library to help strengthen your knowledge of the chapter.

Learning Objective 5.1

What are the important milestones of Piaget's sensorimotor stage?

Watch: The Sensorimotor Stage

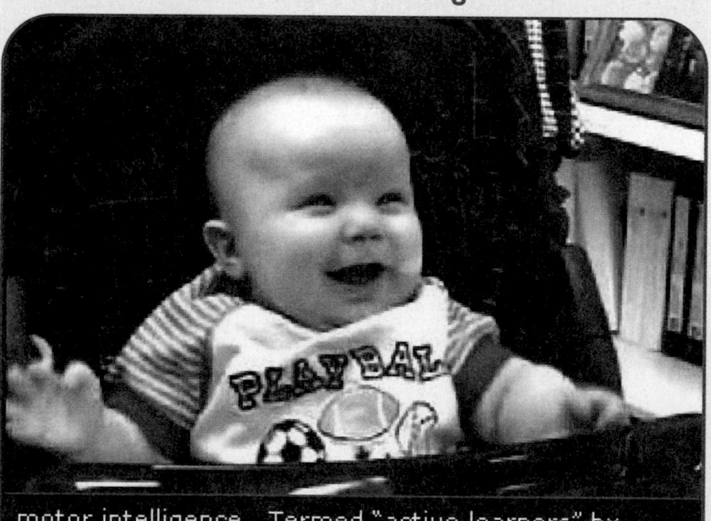
PLAYBAL
motor intelligence. Termed "active learners" by
researcher Jean Piaget, infants and

"Not only is MyDevelopmentLab easy to use, it also keeps me interested in the material. I have used the pre- and post-tests for every chapter thus far."

—Sarah, Northern Essex Community College

Explore: Physical Knowledge in Infancy

Learning Objective 5.3

What does research tell us about infants' understanding of objects?

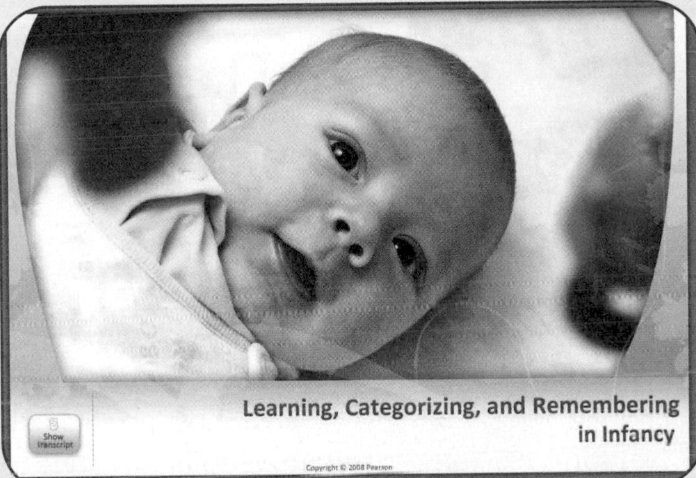
Learning, Categorizing, and Remembering in Infancy

Watch: Child-Directed Speech

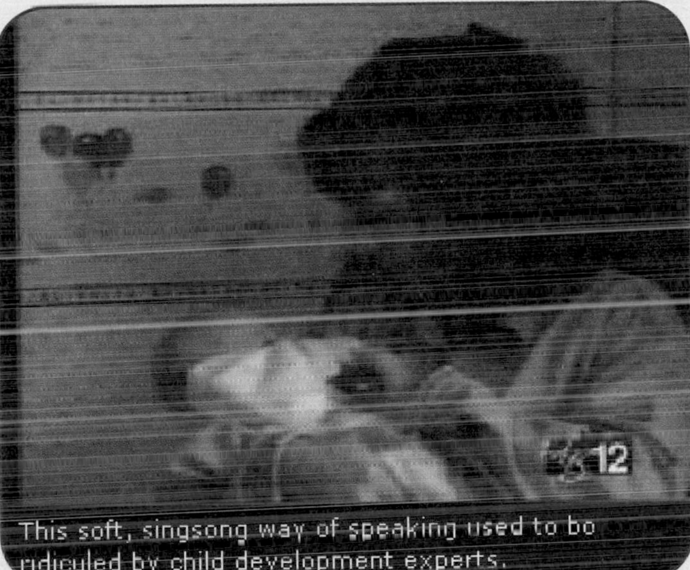
This soft, singsong way of speaking used to be ridiculed by child development experts.

Learning Objective 5.8

What are some of the environmental influences on language development?

Step 3

Take the chapter post-test and compare your results against the pre-test.

POST-TEST

Young infants can learn to kick their legs to make a mobile move, but

- such learning is strongly tied to the specific context in which it is learned.
- this type of learning takes a great deal of practice before it occurs.
- whether or not they will remember this experience is unpredictable.
- their memory for such events has a very brief duration.

www.mydevelopmentlab.com

6

Social and Personality Development in Infancy

Have you ever watched as preschoolers and their families wait in line at a fast food restaurant where there is an attractive play area? When children ask to go to the play area, most parents follow a script that goes something like this: "You have to finish eating before you can play." In response, some children look longingly at the play area but remain steadfastly at their parents' side. Others whine a bit but soon distract themselves by focusing on their anticipation of the toy they will get with their food. Still others behave as if they have just been told the world as they know it is coming to an end. They cry loudly and may even scream in frustration. Others defiantly run to the play area, seemingly oblivious to their parents' instructions to stay in line. Remarkably, too, these variations often occur among children from the same family.

Where do such differences come from? You probably won't be surprised to learn that they don't begin in early childhood. In fact, they

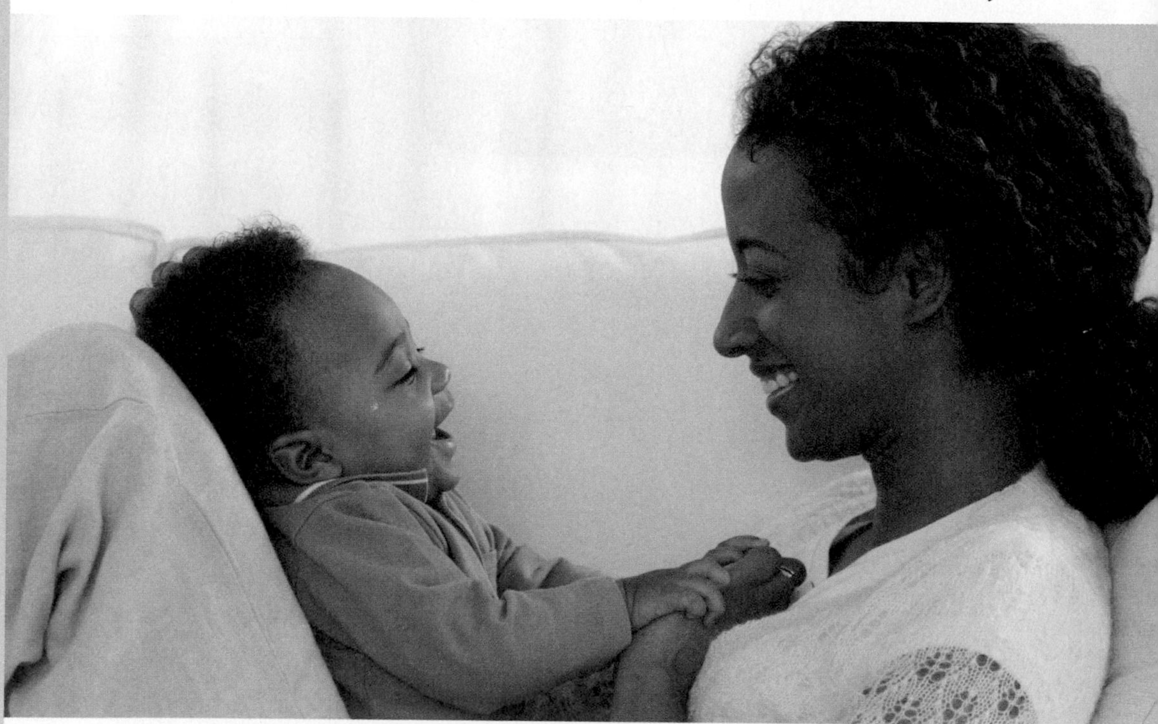

are evident from the earliest days of life. And when we look for answers to this question, we inevitably encounter the debate that pervades every discussion of human development, the nature-nurture controversy.

Psychiatrist Stanley Turecki (2000) argues that children who are difficult to manage are born, not made. Turecki's views were shaped by the challenges he faced in raising his own child, Jillian, who, even in infancy, appeared to be in a permanent state of discontent. She displayed fits of temper in response to every transition, even those as commonplace as transitioning from indoor to outdoor play and back again. In public, Jillian's tantrums were so loud and embarrassing that, by the time the child was 2 years old, Turecki and his wife were forced to carefully plan each outing so as to avoid any situation that might trigger one of them. They were concerned about the effect that living in a family that was ruled by the whims of a 2-year-old might have on their older daughters. In search of answers, Turecki turned to developmental science and formulated a plan for managing his daughter's behavior. He told his story and outlined the strategies he used to help his impossible infant blossom into a delightful child and teenager in a popular book called *The Difficult Child* (1985/2000).

When *The Difficult Child* was published, many parents of children like Jillian regarded it as a godsend, but the notion of "the difficult child" whose difficultness is the result of inborn traits is not without its critics. A noted pediatrician, Dr. Lawrence Diller (2001), for instance, has argued that books such as Turecki's may encourage parents to regard every troublesome behavior their child exhibits as a manifestation of an inborn, unchangeable trait and to abdicate their responsibility to discipline their children. When children become too out-of-control to live with, such parents turn to physicians who have become all too willing to prescribe medications that make children's behavior more manageable, argues Diller. Instead of turning to pharmacological solutions, says Diller, parents need to better understand how their parenting strategies and the environments they create for children influence their personalities.

Diller and others who have expressed similar ideas point out that it is the interaction between a child's inborn traits and the characteristics of his environment that determines personality. You will read about these interactions in this chapter. You will also learn that developmentalists of diverse theoretical orientations agree that the formation of a strong emotional connection to a primary caregiver early in life is critical to healthy child development and has important implications across the entire human lifespan. In this chapter, you will learn how such relationships develop. This chapter will also address the effects of nonparental care and a variety of other variables on infant development.

Theories of Social and Personality Development

Psychologists have used all of the theoretical perspectives you learned about in Chapter 2 to formulate hypotheses about infant social and personality development. However, the two most influential perspectives on these issues are the psychoanalytic and the ethological perspectives.

Learning Objective 6.1

How do Freud's and Erikson's views of personality development in the first 2 years differ?

Psychoanalytic Perspectives

You may remember from Chapter 2 that Freud proposed a series of psychosexual stages that extend from birth through adolescence, during which individuals attempt to satisfy certain basic drives in different ways. In the oral stage, from birth to age 2, infants derive satisfaction through the mouth. Freud further believed that the weaning process should be managed in such a way that the infant's need to suck is neither frustrated nor overgratified. The consequences of either, Freud claimed, would be fixation at this stage of development. Fixation would manifest itself, in Freud's view, in oral behaviors such as nail-biting and swearing.

Harlow's ingenious research demonstrated that infant monkeys became attached to a terrycloth-covered "mother" and would cling to it rather than to a wire mother that provided them with food.

Freud also emphasized the *symbiotic* relationship between the mother and young infant, in which the two behave as if they were one. He believed that the infant did not understand herself to be separate from her mother. Thus, another result of a gratifying nursing period followed by a balanced weaning process, Freud thought, was the infant's development of a sense of both attachment to and separation from the mother.

Erikson went beyond Freud's view. Nursing and weaning are important, he conceded, but they are only one aspect of the overall social environment. Erikson claimed that responding to the infant's other needs by talking to him, comforting him, and so on, was just as important. He proposed that the first 2 years comprise a period during which the infant learns to trust the world around him or becomes cynical about the social environment's ability to meet his needs—the *trust versus mistrust* stage.

One of the best-known studies in developmental psychology demonstrated that Erikson's view of infant development was more accurate than Freud's (Harlow & Zimmerman, 1959). In this study, infant monkeys were separated from their mothers at birth. The experimenters placed two different kinds of "surrogate" mothers in their cages. The monkeys received all their feedings from a wire mother with a nursing bottle attached. The other mother was covered with soft terrycloth. The researchers found that the monkeys approached the wire mother only when hungry. Most of the time, they cuddled against the cloth mother and ran to it whenever they were frightened or stressed. Subsequent studies with human infants correlating maternal feeding practices with infant adjustment suggested that the infant's social relationships are not based solely on either nursing or weaning practices (Schaffer & Emerson, 1964).

Learning Objective 6.2

What are the main ideas of attachment theory?

Ethological Perspectives

attachment theory the view that infants are biologically predisposed to form emotional bonds with caregivers and that the characteristics of those bonds shape later social and personality development

You may recall from Chapter 2 that the *ethological perspective* claims that all animals, including humans, possess innate predispositions that strongly influence their development. Thus, the ethological approach to social and personality development proposes that evolutionary forces have endowed infants with genes that predispose them to form emotional bonds with their caregivers, an approach known as **attachment theory**. Consequently, in contrast to the psychoanalysts, ethologists view the infant's capacity for forming social relationships as highly resistant to environmental forces such as variations in the quality of parenting. However, ethologists do claim that the first two years of life constitute a sen-

NO EASY ANSWERS

Adoption and Development

Most people who adopt a child assume that if they provide enough love and support, the child will develop both cognitively and emotionally pretty much the way their biological child would. However, adoptive parents need to take into account the child's circumstances prior to the adoption in order to form a realistic set of expectations. Children adopted before the age of 6 months, who have no history of institutionalization or abuse, are generally indistinguishable from nonadopted children in security of attachment, cognitive development, and social adjustment. This is true whether adoptive parents and children are of the same or different races and/or nationalities (Juffer & Rosenboom, 1997).

In contrast, children who are adopted later, who have histories of abuse and/or neglect, or who have lived in institutions for long periods tend to have more problems, both cognitive and emotional, than nonadopted children (Castle et al., 1999; Howe & Fearnley, 2003; Marcovitch, Goldberg, Gold, & Washington, 1997; O'Connor, Bredenkamp, & Rutter, 1999; Roy, Rutter, & Pickles, 2000; Verhulst & Versluis-Den Bieman, 1995). One study found that 91% of children who had been adopted after being abused, neglected, or institutionalized suffered from emotional problems even after having been in their adoptive families for an average of 9 years (Smith, Howard, & Monroe, 1998). Not surprisingly, parents of such children reported experiencing more parenting-related stress than did parents of either adoptees from more positive backgrounds or biological children (Mainemer, Gilman, & Ames, 1998). Consequently, people who adopt such children should expect that parenting them will not be easy.

The task of raising high-risk children can be made more manageable with parent training (Juffer, Hoksbergen, Riksen-Walraven, & Kohnstamm, 1997). Thus, adoptive parents should take advantage of any training offered by the institutions through which the adoption was arranged. If none is available, they should look for training elsewhere, perhaps at a local community college. Finally, at the first sign of difficulty, adoptive parents should seek help from a social worker or psychologist who specializes in treating children. Therapists can help with everyday tasks such as toilet-training and teach parents strategies for dealing with behavior that reflects severe emotional disturbance, such as self-injury.

Take a Stand

Decide which of these two statements you most agree with and think about how you would defend your position:

1. Raising an adopted child differs little from raising one's own biological child.
2. Raising an adopted child is more complex than raising one's own biological child.

sitive period for the formation of such relationships. They say that infants who fail to form a close relationship with a caregiver before the age of 2 are at risk for future social and personality problems. See No Easy Answers.

Because they hypothesize that early emotional bonds influence later social and personality development, ethological perspectives have been very influential in the study of development in this domain across the entire lifespan. In John Bowlby's terminology, infants create different *internal models* of their relationships with parents and other key adults (Bowlby, 1969). These models include such elements as the child's confidence (or lack of it) that the attachment figure will be available or reliable, the child's expectation of rebuff or affection, and the child's sense of assurance that the other is really a safe base for exploration. The internal model begins to be formed late in the child's first year of life and becomes increasingly elaborated and better established through the first 4 or 5 years. By age 5, most children have a clear internal model of the mother (or other primary caregiver), a self model, and a model of relationships. Once formed, such models shape and explain experiences and affect memory and attention. Children notice and remember experiences that fit their models and miss or forget experiences that don't match. As Piaget might say, a child more readily *assimilates* data that fit the model. More importantly, the model affects the child's behavior: The child tends to re-create, in each new relationship, the pattern with which he is familiar. This tendency to recreate the parent infant relationship in each new relationship, says Bowlby and other ethologists, continues into adulthood. For this reason, ethologists believe that, for example, poor communication between adult romantic partners may result from maladaptive communication patterns that developed between one of the individuals and his or her early caregivers.

Critical Thinking

1. How would learning theorists' explanations of early social relationships and their influences on later relationships differ from those of the psychoanalysts and the ethologists?

Attachment

Somehow, in the midst of endless diaper changes, food preparation, baths, and periods of exhaustion that exceed anything they have ever experienced before, the overwhelming majority of parents manage to respond to their infants in ways that foster the development of an **attachment** relationship. An attachment is an emotional bond in which a person's sense of security is bound up in the relationship. As the research discussed in the *No Easy Answers* feature suggests, it is not necessary for a child to be biologically related to his or her parents in order to develop such a relationship. In fact, the development of attachment relationships depends on the quantity and quality of the interactions that take place between infants and parents. To understand attachment between parent and infant, it is necessary to look at both sides of the equation—at the development of both the parents' bond to the child and the child's attachment to the parents.

Learning Objective 6.3

How does synchrony affect parent-infant relations?

The Parents' Attachment to the Infant

Contact between mother and infant immediately after birth does not appear to be either necessary or sufficient for the formation of a stable long-term bond between them (Wong, 1993). What is essential in the formation of that bond is the opportunity for mother and infant to develop a mutual, interlocking pattern of attachment behaviors, called **synchrony** (Moore, 2007). Synchrony is like a conversation. The baby signals his needs by crying or smiling; he responds to being held by quieting or snuggling; he looks at the parents when they look at him. The mother, in turn, enters into the interaction with her own repertoire of caregiving behaviors.

Fathers engage in physical play with infants more often than mothers do.

The father's bond with the infant, like the mother's, seems to depend more on the development of synchrony than on contact immediately after birth. Aiding the development of such mutuality is the fact that fathers seem to have the same repertoire of attachment behaviors as do mothers. In the early weeks of the baby's life, fathers touch, talk to, and cuddle their babies in the same ways that mothers do (Parke & Tinsley, 1981).

After the first weeks of the baby's life, however, signs of a kind of specialization of parental behaviors begin to emerge. Fathers spend more time playing with the baby, with more physical roughhousing; mothers spend more time in routine caregiving and also talk to and smile at the baby more (Walker, Messinger, Fogel, & Karns, 1992).

By 6 months, infants display distinctive patterns of responding to these mother-father differences (Feldman, 2003). Signs of positive emotional states, such as smiling, appear gradually and subtly when babies are interacting with their mothers. In contrast, babies laugh and wriggle with delight in short, intense bursts in interactions with their fathers. This isn't a matter of babies' preference for one parent or the other. Instead, such results mean that infants recognize the same behavioral differences in mothers and fathers that developmental scientists do when they observe parental behavior. In fact, some researchers have noted that measures of attachment behaviors based on typical mother-infant interactions may cause researchers to inappropriately conclude that fathers are less involved with babies than mothers and, therefore, less important to infants' development (Lewis & Lamb, 2003). To the contrary, research clearly indicates that babies benefit tremendously when both kinds of interaction are available to them.

attachment the emotional tie to a parent experienced by an infant, from which the child derives security

Learning Objective 6.4

What are the four phases of attachment and the behaviors associated with them?

The Infant's Attachment to the Parents

Like the parent's bond to the baby, the baby's attachment emerges gradually and is based on her ability to discriminate between her parents and other people. As you learned in Chapters 3 and 4, an infant can recognize her mother's voice prior to birth. By the time the baby is a few days old, she recognizes her mother by sight and smell as well (Cernoch & Porter, 1985; Walton, Bower, & Bower, 1992). Thus, the cognitive foundation for attachment is in place within days after birth.

synchrony a mutual, interlocking pattern of attachment behaviors shared by a parent and child

Establishing Attachment Bowlby suggested four phases in the development of the infant's attachment (Bowlby, 1969). Bowlby and other ethologists claim that these phases appear in a fixed sequence over the first 24 to 36 months of life that is strongly influenced by genes that are present in all healthy human infants. The infant exhibits a distinctive set of attachment-related behaviors and interaction patterns in each phase:

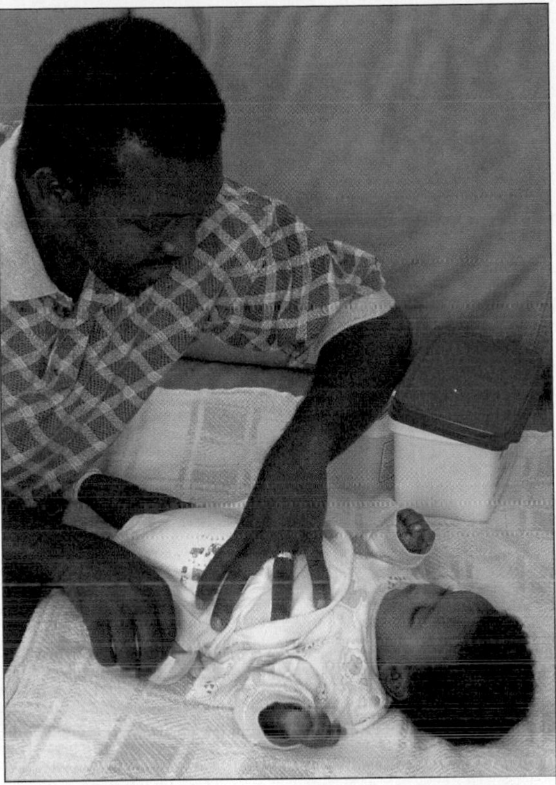

Dads like this one, who get involved with the day-to-day care of their babies, seem to develop stronger attachment relationships with their babies.

- *Phase 1: Nonfocused orienting and signaling (birth to 3 months).* Babies exhibit behaviors, such as crying, smiling, and making eye contact, that draw the attention of others and signal their needs. They direct these signals to everyone with whom they come into contact.
- *Phase 2: Focus on one or more figures (3 to 6 months).* Babies direct their "come here" signals to fewer people, typically those with whom they spend the most time, and are less responsive to unfamiliar people.
- *Phase 3: Secure base behavior (6 to 24 months).* True attachment emerges. Babies show "proximity-seeking" behaviors such as following and clinging to caregivers whom they regard as "safe bases," especially when they are anxious, injured, or have physical needs such as hunger. Most direct these behaviors to a primary caregiver when that person is available and to others only when the primary caregiver, for some reason, cannot or will not respond to them or is absent (Lamb, 1981).
- *Phase 4: Internal model (24 months and beyond).* An internal model of the attachment relationship allows children older than 2 to imagine how an anticipated action might affect the bonds they share with their caregivers (van IJzendoorn, 2005). The internal model plays a role in later relationships with early caregivers (i.e., adult children and their parents) and in other significant relationships (i.e., romantic partnerships) throughout life.

Attachment Behaviors Once the child has developed a clear attachment, at about 6 to 8 months of age, several related behaviors also begin appearing. *Stranger anxiety* and *separation*

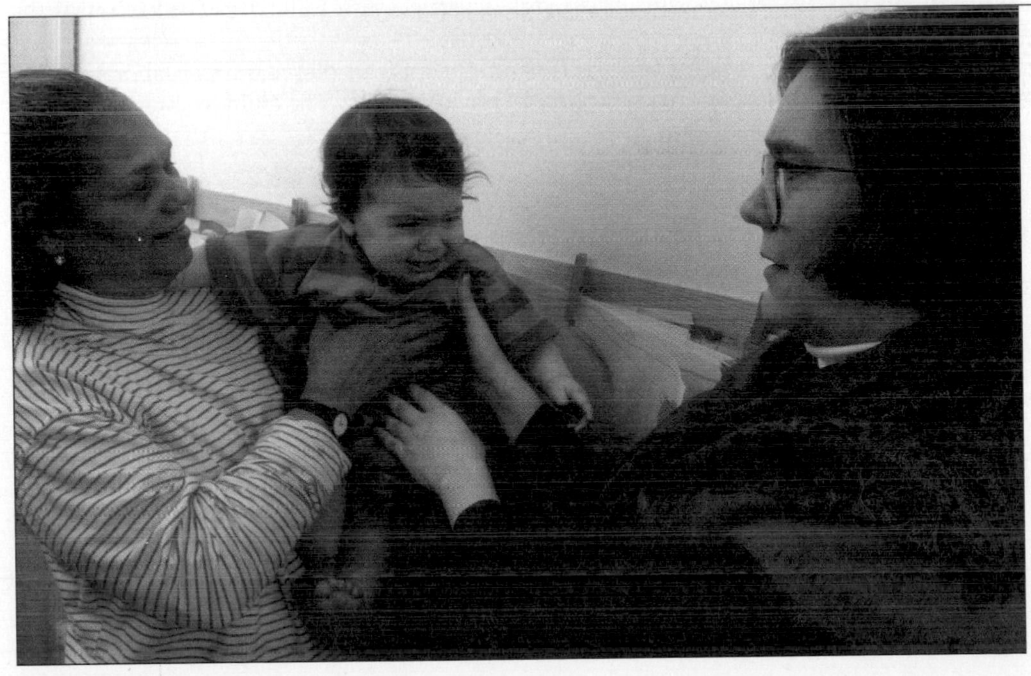

Separation anxiety signifies the formation of a true attachment relationship between an infant and her primary caregiver. Once the parent has actually left, this child will probably be content to play with the other children and will respond positively to her temporary caregivers.

anxiety, attachment behaviors that are rare before 5 or 6 months, rise in frequency until about 12 to 16 months, and then decline. Infants express **stranger anxiety** with behaviors such as clinging to their mothers when strangers are present. **Separation anxiety** is evident when infants cry or protest being separated from the mother. The research findings are not altogether consistent, but fear of strangers apparently emerges first. Separation anxiety starts a bit later but continues to be visible for a longer period. Such an increase in fear and anxiety has been observed in children from a number of different cultures, and in both home-reared children and children in day care in the United States.

stranger anxiety expressions of discomfort, such as clinging to the mother, in the presence of strangers

separation anxiety expressions of discomfort, such as crying, when separated from an attachment figure

social referencing an infant's use of others' facial expressions as a guide to his or her own emotions

secure attachment a pattern of attachment in which an infant readily separates from the parent, seeks proximity when stressed, and uses the parent as a safe base for exploration

Another attachment behavior is **social referencing** (Walden, 1991). Infants use cues from the facial expressions and the emotional tone of voice used by their attachment figures to help them figure out what to do in novel situations, such as when a stranger comes to visit (Flom & Bahrick, 2007; Hertenstein & Campos, 2004). Babies this age will first look at Mom's or Dad's face to check for the adult's emotional expression. If Mom looks pleased or happy, the baby is likely to explore a new toy with more ease or to accept a stranger with less fuss. If Mom looks concerned or frightened, the baby responds to those cues and reacts to the novel situation with equivalent fear or concern.

Social referencing also helps babies learn to regulate their own emotions. For example, an infant who is angry because an enjoyable activity is no longer available may use his caregiver's pleasant, comforting emotional expressions to transition himself into a more pleasant emotional state. By contrast, a baby whose caregiver responds to his anger with more anger may experience an escalation in the level of his own angry feelings. Most developmentalists think that the quality of the emotional give-and-take in interactions between an infant and his caregivers is important to the child's ability to control emotions such as anger and frustration in later years (Cole, Martin, & Dennis, 2004).

Learning Objective 6.5

What are the variables that contribute to the development and stability of the four types of attachment?

Variations in Attachment Quality

Virtually all babies seem to go through the four phases of attachment first identified by Bowlby, but the quality of the attachments they form differs from one infant to the next.

Secure and Insecure Attachments Variations in the quality of the first attachment relationship are now almost universally described using Ainsworth's category system (Ainsworth et al., 1978). The Ainsworth system distinguishes between secure attachment and two types of insecure attachment, which psychologists assess using a procedure called the *Strange Situation.*

insecure/avoidant attachment a pattern of attachment in which an infant avoids contact with the parent and shows no preference for the parent over other people

insecure/ambivalent attachment a pattern of attachment in which the infant shows little exploratory behavior, is greatly upset when separated from the mother, and is not reassured by her return or efforts to comfort him

insecure/disorganized attachment a pattern of attachment in which an infant seems confused or apprehensive and shows contradictory behavior, such as moving toward the mother while looking away from her

The Strange Situation consists of a series of eight episodes played out in a laboratory setting, typically with children between 12 and 18 months of age. The child is observed in each of the following situations:

- With the mother
- With the mother and a stranger
- Alone with the stranger
- Completely alone for a few minutes
- Reunited with the mother
- Alone again
- With the stranger again
- Reunited with the mother

Ainsworth suggested that children's reactions in these situations—particularly to the reunion episodes—showed attachment of one of three types: **secure attachment**, **insecure/avoidant attachment**, and **insecure/ambivalent attachment**. More recently, developmentalists have suggested a fourth type: **insecure/disorganized attachment** (Main & Solomon, 1990). The characteristics of each type are listed in Table 6.1.

Table 6.1 Categories of Secure and Insecure Attachment in Ainsworth's Strange Situation

Category	Behavior
Secure attachment	Child readily separates from caregiver and easily becomes absorbed in exploration; when threatened or frightened, child actively seeks contact and is readily consoled; child does not avoid or resist contact if mother initiates it. When reunited with mother after absence, child greets her positively or is easily soothed if upset. Clearly prefers mother to stranger.
Insecure/avoidant attachment	Child avoids contact with mother, especially at reunion after an absence. Does not resist mother's efforts to make contact, but does not seek much contact. Shows no preference for mother over stranger.
Insecure/ambivalent attachment	Child shows little exploration and is wary of stranger. Greatly upset when separated from mother, but not reassured by mother's return or her efforts at comforting. Child both seeks and avoids contact at different times. May show anger toward mother at reunion, and resists both comfort from and contact with stranger.
Insecure/disorganized attachment	Dazed behavior, confusion, or apprehension. Child may show contradictory behavior patterns simultaneously, such as moving toward mother while keeping gaze averted.

(*Sources:* Ainsworth et al., 1978; Carlson & Sroufe, 1995; Main & Solomon, 1990.)

Whether a child cries when he is separated from his mother is not a helpful indicator of the security of his attachment. Some securely attached infants cry then, others do not; the same is true of insecurely attached infants. It is the entire pattern of the child's response to the Strange Situation that is critical, not any one response. These attachment types have been observed in studies in many different countries, and secure attachment is the most common pattern in every country.

Stability of Attachment Classification Researchers have found that the quality of a child's attachment can be either consistent or changeable. It seems that, when a child's family environment or life circumstances are reasonably consistent, the security or insecurity of her attachment also seems to remain consistent, even over many years (Hamilton, 1995; Wartner, Grossman, Fremmer-Bombik, & Suess, 1994; Weinfield & Egeland, 2004). However, when a child's circumstances change in some major way—such as when the parents divorce or the family moves—the security of the child's attachment may change as well, either from secure to insecure or the reverse. For example, in one important study, developmentalists followed one group of middle-class White children from age 1 to age 21 (Waters, Treboux, Crowell, Merrick, & Albersheim, 1995). Those whose attachment classification changed over this long interval had nearly all experienced some major upheaval, such as the death of a parent, physical or sexual abuse, or a serious illness.

The fact that the security of a child's attachment can change over time does not refute the notion of attachment as arising from an internal model. Bowlby suggested that for the first 2 or 3 years, the particular pattern of attachment a child shows is in some sense a property of each specific relationship. For example, studies of toddlers' attachments to mothers and fathers show that about 30% of the children are securely attached to one parent and insecurely attached to the other, with both possible combinations equally likely (Fox, Kimmerly, & Schafer, 1991). It is the quality of each relationship that determines the security of the child's attachment to that specific adult. If the relationship changes markedly, the security of attachment may change, too. But, Bowlby argued, by age 4 or 5, the internal model becomes more a property of the child, more generalized across relationships, and thus more resistant to change. At that point, the child tends to impose the model on new relationships, including relationships with teachers or peers.

Learning Objective 6.6

What variables might affect a parent's ability to establish an attachment relationship with an infant?

Caregiver Characteristics and Attachment

Researchers have found that several characteristics of caregivers influence the attachment process. These characteristics include the caregivers' emotional responses to the infant, their marital and socioeconomic status, and their mental health.

Emotional Responsiveness Studies of parent-child interactions suggest that one crucial ingredient for secure attachment is *emotional availability* on the part of the primary caregiver (Biringen, 2000). An emotionally available caregiver is one who is able and willing to form an emotional attachment to the infant. For example, economically or emotionally distressed parents may be so distracted by their own problems that they can't invest emotion in the parent-infant relationship. Such parents may be able to meet the baby's physical needs but unable to respond emotionally.

Contingent responsiveness is another key ingredient of secure attachment (Isabella, 1995; Pederson & Moran, 1995; Pederson et al., 1990; Seifer, Schiller, Sameroff, Resnick, & Riordan, 1996). Parents who demonstrate contingent responsiveness are sensitive to the child's cues and respond appropriately. They smile when the baby smiles, talk to the baby when he vocalizes, pick him up when he cries, and so on (Ainsworth & Marvin, 1995). Infants of parents who display contingent responsiveness in the early months are more likely to be securely attached at age 12 months (Heinicke et al., 2000).

A low level of parental responsiveness thus appears to be an ingredient in any type of insecure attachment. However, each of the several subvarieties of insecure attachment is affected by additional distinct factors. For example, if the mother rejects the infant or regularly withdraws from contact with her, the baby is more likely to show an avoidant pattern of attachment, although the pattern also seems to occur when the mother is overly intrusive or overly stimulating toward the infant (Isabella, 1995). An ambivalent pattern is more common when the primary caregiver is inconsistently or unreliably available to the child. A disorganized pattern seems especially likely when the child has been abused, and in families in which either parent had some unresolved trauma in his or her own childhood, such as abuse or a parent's early death (Cassidy & Berlin, 1994; Main & Hesse, 1990). One caregiver variable that predicts attachment quality is marital status.

Marital Status and SES Researchers have found that infants whose parents are married are more likely to be securely attached than babies whose parents are either cohabiting or single (e.g., Rosenkrantz, Aronson, & Huston, 2004). However, the effects of marital status may be due to other characteristics of parents who choose to marry, cohabit, or remain single. Married parents typically have more education and are less likely to be poor than parents in the other groups.

Married parents are also, on average, older than parents in the other two groups (Rosenkrantz et al., 2004). Most of the information about the influence of maternal age on the attachment process comes from studies comparing adolescent to older mothers. These studies suggest that, with increasing age, mothers become less likely to describe their babies as "difficult" (Miller, Eisenberg, Fabes, & Shell, 1996). Moreover, older mothers display more sensitive caregiving behaviors than teenagers. Of course, teenaged mothers are likely to have less education and fewer economic resources than older mothers. Thus, it's hard to say whether age or maturity is responsible for the associations between maternal age and parenting characteristics. Finally, marital conflict poses risks for the development of attachment. Researchers have found that 6-month-olds who are exposed to parental arguments, especially those in which parents are verbally aggressive toward each other, are more likely to display signs of emotional withdrawal than babies who are not so exposed (Crockenberg, Leerkes, & Lekka, 2007). Emotional withdrawal on the part of the infant interferes with synchrony, thereby lessening the chances that she will develop a secure attachment to her primary caregiver.

Mental Health Psychiatric illness is another caregiver characteristic that appears to be related to attachment quality (Murray et al., 1999; Teti, Gelfand, Messinger, & Isabella, 1995). Developmentalists have found that babies who interact regularly with a depressed mother express more negative and fewer positive emotions. Some even resist their mother's efforts to nurse them; others refuse to eat altogether (Coulthard & Harris, 2003). As a result, compared with infants of nondepressed mothers, a higher proportion of the infants of depressed mothers are undernourished (Rahman, Lovel, Bunn, Igbal, & Harrington, 2004). All of these effects interfere with synchrony and can predispose the infant of a depressed mother to develop an insecure attachment. As a result, infants of depressed mothers are at higher risk for later problems. For example, they are more likely than other children to exhibit either heightened aggression or social withdrawal in school (Cummings & Davies, 1994). They also are at higher risk of developing psychiatric illnesses themselves in adulthood (Maki et al., 2004).

It is important to note that maternal depression itself doesn't necessarily doom an infant to an insecure attachment. The critical factors appear to be how and to what extent depression affects mother-infant interactions. There seem to be three problematic behavior patterns in depressed mothers. In one pattern, mothers are withdrawn and detached; they look at, touch, or talk to their babies less often and are less affectionate toward their infants than are nondepressed mothers (Field, 1995; Hart, Jones, Field, & Lundy, 1999). In the second pattern, mothers are overly involved with their infants, often interrupting and overstimulating them (Hart et al., 1999). The third group of depressed mothers overreact and respond angrily to babies' undesirable behaviors (O'Leary, Smith Slep, & Reid, 1999).

Of course, there are many depressed mothers who are just as sensitive and responsive to their babies' needs as mothers who do not suffer from depression. And, as you might expect, infants whose depressed mothers exhibit sensitive parenting behaviors are less likely to display long-term negative effects than babies of less sensitive depressed mothers (NICHD Early Child Care Research Network, 1999). In other words, when depressed mothers exhibit the same kinds of parenting behaviors as most nondepressed mothers, their emotional status doesn't appear to have negative effects on their babies' development.

Studies involving many mothers with panic disorder have shown that these mothers, like mothers with depression, exhibit behaviors that may interfere with synchrony (Warren et al., 2003). Because it is through behavior that maternal psychiatric illnesses affect infants, parent training may provide an avenue through which the potential negative effects of this caregiver characteristic can be moderated. Indeed, several studies have shown that training can increase the frequency of sensitive behaviors in depressed mothers and, as a result, lead to changes in infants' attachment status (van den Boom, 1994, 1995). Moreover, appropriate medications may positively affect many aspects of psychiatrically ill mothers' behaviors (e.g., Kaplan, Bachorowski, Smoski, & Zinser, 2001).

Long-Term Consequences of Attachment Quality

Learning Objective 6.7

What are the long-term consequences of attachment quality?

As we noted earlier, attachment theory proposes that early emotional relationships shape later ones. Thus, researchers have examined the links between Ainsworth's classification system and a wide range of other behaviors in infants, children, adolescents, and adults. Dozens of studies show that children rated as securely attached to their mothers in infancy are later more sociable, more positive in their behavior toward friends and siblings, less clinging and dependent on teachers, less aggressive and disruptive, more empathetic, and more emotionally mature in their interactions in school and other settings outside the home (e.g., Booth-LaForce et al., 2006; Carlson, Sampson, & Sroufe, 2003; Jacobsen, Husa, Fendrich, Kruesi, & Ziegenhain, 1997; Leve & Fagot, 1995).

Adolescents who were rated as securely attached in infancy or who are classed as secure on the basis of interviews in adolescence are also more socially skilled, have more intimate friendships, are more likely to be rated as leaders, and have higher self-esteem and better grades (Black & McCartney, 1995; Jacobsen & Hofmann, 1997; Lieberman, Doyle, & Markiewicz, 1995; Ostoja, McCrone, Lehn, Reed, & Sroufe, 1995). Those with insecure attachments—particularly those with avoidant attachments—not only have less positive and supportive friendships in adolescence but also are more likely to become sexually active early and to practice riskier sex (Carlson, Sroufe, Egeland, 2004; O'Beirne & Moore, 1995; Sroufe, Carlson, & Schulman, 1993; Urban, Carlson, Egeland, & Sroufe, 1991).

Quality of attachment in infancy also predicts sociability through early, middle, and late adulthood (Van Lange, DeBruin, Otten, & Joireman, 1997). Moreover, one study found a link between attachment history and sexual dysfunction in adult males (Kinzl, Mangweth, Traweger, & Biebl, 1996). In fact, that investigation found that quality of attachment in infancy predicted sexual dysfunction in adulthood better than a history of sexual abuse did.

Developmentalists have also found that an adult's internal model of attachment affects his or her parenting behaviors (Crittenden, Partridge, & Clausesen, 1991; Steele, Hodges, Kaniuk, Hillman, & Henderson, 2003). For example, mothers who are themselves securely attached are more responsive and sensitive in their behavior toward their infants or young children (Hammond, Landry, Swank, & Smith, 2000; van IJzendoorn, 1995). Attachment history affects parental attitudes as well. Some studies have shown that parents with a history of insecure attachment are more likely to view their infants negatively (Pesonen, Raikkonnen, Strandberg, Kelitikangas-Jarvinen, & Jarvenpaa, 2004). Such parents may also lack confidence in their ability to perform effectively in the parenting role (Huth-Bocks, Levendosky, Bogat, & von Eye, 2004).

Examinations of the long-term consequences of quality of attachment suggest that both psychoanalysts and ethologists are correct in their assumption that the attachment relationship becomes the foundation for future social relationships. Certainly, it appears to be critical to the relationship most similar to it—the relationship an individual ultimately develops with her or his own child.

Learning Objective 6.8

In what ways do patterns of attachment vary across cultures?

Cross-Cultural Research on Attachment

Studies in a variety of countries (e.g., Posada et al., 1995) support Ainsworth's contention that some form of "secure base behavior" occurs in every child, in every culture. But there is also some evidence suggesting that secure attachments may be more likely in certain cultures than in others. The most thorough analyses have come from some Dutch psychologists who have examined the results of 32 separate studies in eight different countries. Figure 6.1 presents the percentage of babies classified in each category for each country (van IJzendoorn & Kroonenberg, 1988). It is important to avoid overinterpret-

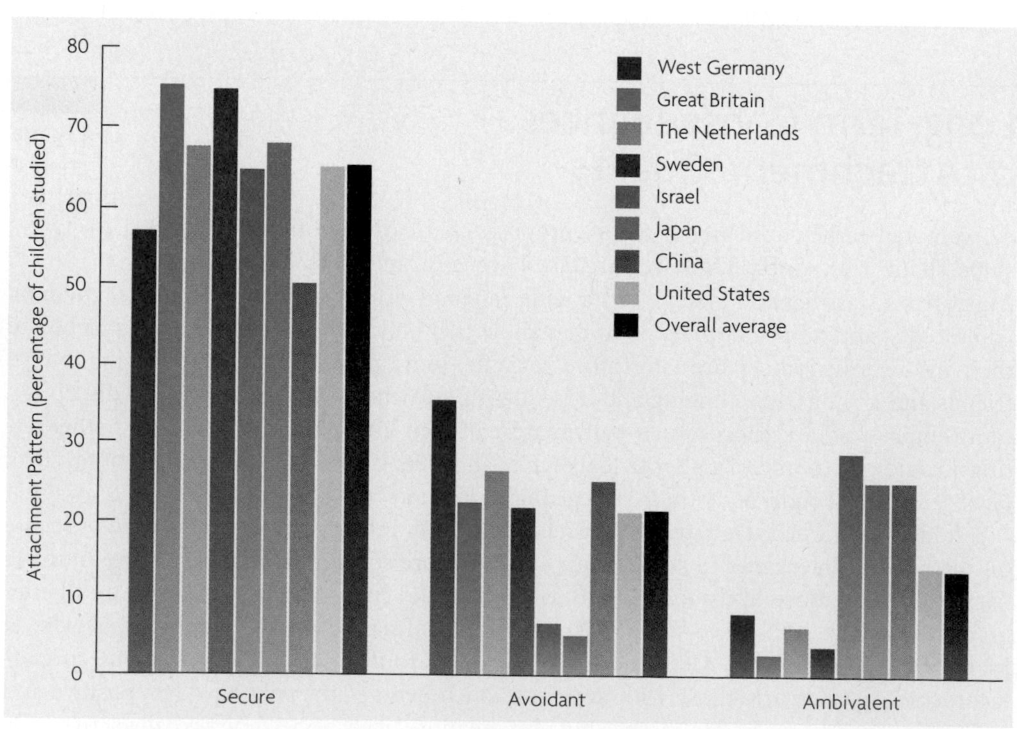

Figure 6.1 Cross-Cultural Comparisons of Attachment Categories

Although the percentage of infants in each of the attachment categories varies somewhat across cultures, secure attachment is the most common type of relationship between infants and caregivers in all societies.

(*Source:* Based on Table 1 of van IJzendoorn & Kroonenberg, 1988, pp. 150–151.)

ing the information in this figure, because in most cases there are only one or two studies from a given country, normally with quite small samples. The single study from China, for example, included only 36 babies. Still, the findings are thought-provoking. The most striking thing about them is their consistency. In each of the eight countries, secure attachment is the most common pattern, found in more than half of all babies studied. In all of the countries van Ijzendoorn studied, infants typically have one caregiver, usually the mother. What would researchers find in a culture in which the child's early care was more communal? To find out, developmentalists studied a group called the Efe, who forage in the forests of Zaire (Tronick, Morelli, & Ivey, 1992). The Efe live in camps, in small groups of perhaps 20 individuals, each group consisting of several extended families, often brothers and their wives. Infants in these communities are cared for communally in the early months and years of life. They are carried and held by all the adult women and interact regularly with many different adults. If they have needs, they are tended to by whichever adult or older child is nearby; they may even be nursed by women other than the mother, although they normally sleep with the mother. The researchers reported two things of particular interest about early attachment in this group. First, Efe infants seem to use virtually any adult or older child in their group as a safe base, which suggests that they may have no single central attachment. But, beginning at about 6 months, the Efe infants nonetheless seem to insist on being with their mother more and to prefer her over other women, although other women continue to help with caregiving responsibilities. Thus, even in an extremely communal rearing arrangement, some sign of a central attachment is evident, though perhaps less dominant.

At the moment, the most plausible hypothesis is that the same factors involving mother-infant interaction contribute to secure and insecure attachments in all cultures, and that these patterns reflect similar internal models. But it will take more research in which long-term outcomes for individuals in the various categories are studied before researchers will know whether this is correct.

Critical Thinking

1. Look back at the discussion of synchrony at the beginning of this section. How do you think it is manifested in adult relationships, and in what way do you think synchrony, or the lack thereof, influences those relationships?

Personality, Temperament, and Self-Concept

Psychologists typically use the word **personality** to describe patterns in the way children and adults relate to the people and objects in the world around them. Individual differences in personality appear to develop throughout childhood and adolescence, based on a basic set of behavioral and emotional predispositions present at birth (McCrae, Costa, Ostendord, & Angleitner, 2000). These predispositions are usually referred to as **temperament** (Rothbart, Ahadi, & Evans, 2000).

Dimensions of Temperament

Learning Objective 6.9
On which dimensions of temperament do most developmentalists agree?

Psychologists who study infant temperament have yet to agree on a basic set of temperament dimensions. One influential early theory, proposed by Thomas and Chess, two authors of one of the best-known longitudinal studies in developmental science, the New York Longitudinal Study, listed nine dimensions: activity level, rhythmicity, approach/withdrawal, adaptability to new experience, threshold of responsiveness, intensity of reaction, quality of mood (positive or negative), distractibility, and persistence (Thomas & Chess, 1977). Thomas and Chess further proposed that variations in these nine qualities tended to cluster into three types that can be applied to about 75% of infants. The remaining infants exhibit combinations of two or three of the main types of temperament.

- *Easy children (40% of infants).* These children approach new events positively, display predictable sleeping and eating cycles, are generally happy, and adjust easily to change.

personality a pattern of responding to people and objects in the environment

temperament inborn predispositions, such as activity level, that form the foundations of personality

- *Difficult children (10% of infants).* Patterns that include irregular sleeping and eating cycles, emotional negativity and irritability, and resistance to change characterize children in this category.
- *Slow-to-warm-up children (15% of infants).* Children in this group display few intense reactions, either positive or negative, and appear nonresponsive to unfamiliar people.

Other researchers have examined temperament from a trait perspective rather than a categorical perspective. These developmentalists view an individual infant's temperament as a function of how much or how little of various characteristics she possesses. For example, an infant in whom a high level of physical activity was combined with emotional irritability would have a different temperamental profile than an infant in whom high activity was combined with a more easygoing nature. There is some disagreement among developmentalists who have adopted the trait perspective as to what the component characteristics of temperament are, but their research has revealed a few key dimensions (Ahadi & Rothbart, 1994; Belsky, Hsieh, & Crnic, 1996; Kagan, 1994; Martin, Wisenbaker, & Huttunen, 1994). *Activity level* refers to an infant's tendency to either move often and vigorously or remain passive or immobile. *Approach/positive emotionality* is a tendency to move toward rather than away from new people, things, or objects, usually accompanied by positive emotion. (This dimension is similar to what others call *sociability.*) *Inhibition*—a tendency to respond with fear or withdrawal to new people, new situations, or new objects—is the flip side of approach. *Negative emotionality* is a tendency to respond to frustrating circumstances with anger, fussing, loudness, or irritability. Finally, *effortful control/task persistence* is an ability to stay focused, to manage attention and effort.

Learning Objective 6.10

What are the roles of heredity, neurological processes, and environment in the formation of temperament?

Origins and Stability of Temperament

Because temperamental differences appear so early in life, even during the prenatal period (see Chapter 3), it may seem that genes are entirely responsible for them. However, research suggests that both nature and nurture contribute to individual differences in temperament.

Heredity Studies of twins in many countries show that identical twins are more alike in their temperament than are fraternal twins (Rose, 1995; Stilberg, 2005). For example, one group of researchers studied 100 pairs of identical twins and 100 pairs of fraternal twins at both 14 and 20 months. At each age, the children's temperaments were rated by their mothers using the Buss and Plomin categories. In addition, each child's level of behavioral inhibition was measured by observing how the child reacted to strange toys and a strange adult in a special laboratory playroom. Did the child approach the novel toys quickly and eagerly or hang back or seem fearful? Did the child approach the strange adult or remain close to the mother? The correlations between temperament scores on all four of these dimensions were consistently higher for identical than for fraternal twins, indicating a strong genetic effect (Emde et al., 1992; Plomin et al., 1993).

Long-Term Stability Research showing that temperament is stable across infancy and into children's later years supports the view that temperament is strongly influenced by heredity. There is growing evidence of consistency in temperamental ratings over rather long periods of infancy and childhood (Kajan & Herschkowitz, 2005). For example, Australian researchers studying a group of 450 children found that mothers' reports of children's irritability, cooperation/manageability, inflexibility, rhythmicity, persistence, and tendency to approach rather than avoid contact were all quite consistent from infancy through age 8 (Pedlow, Sanson, Prior, & Oberklaid, 1993). Similarly, in an American longitudinal study of a group of children from age 1 through 12, psychologists found strong consistency in parents' reports of their children's overall "difficultness," as well as approach versus withdrawal, positive versus negative mood, and activity level (Guerin & Gottfried, 1994a, 1994b). Other research suggests that temperamental differences are stable from the preschool years into adulthood (Caspi, 2000).

Researchers have also found considerable consistency at various ages in Kagan's measure of inhibition, which is based on direct observation of the child's behavior rather than on the mother's ratings of the child's temperament. In one study, for example, children who had been classified as inhibited at 4 months were less socially responsive to both adults and children at age 2 than uninhibited peers (Young, Fox & Zahn-Waxler, 1999). In Kagan's own longitudinal study, half of the children who had shown high levels of crying and motor activity in response to a novel situation when they were 4 months old were still classified as highly inhibited at age 8, and three-fourths of those rated as uninhibited at 4 months remained in that category 8 years later (Kagan et al., 1993). Subsequent studies showed that these trends continued into the children's teen and early adulthood years (Kagan & Herschkowitz, 2005).

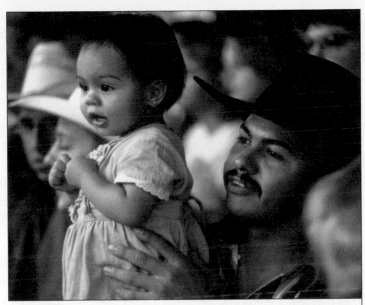
As long as securely attached infants remain physically close to their parents, they can easily manage the stresses associated with being in a large group of unfamiliar people.

Neurological Processes Many temperament theorists take the heredity argument a step further and trace the basic differences in behavior to variations in underlying physiological patterns (e.g., Gunnar, 1994; Rothbart, Derryberry, & Posner, 1994). For example, studies examining the genes that control the functions of two important neurotransmitters, *dopamine* and *serotonin*, support Kagan's hypothesis (Lakatos et al., 2003). These neurotransmitters regulate the brain's responses to new information and unusual situations, precisely the kinds of stimuli that appear to overstimulate shy children in Kagan's research.

Another important neurological variable that has been found to be associated with shyness is *frontal lobe asymmetry* (Kagan & Herschkowitz, 2005). In most people, the left and right hemispheres of the frontal lobes respond similarly to new stimuli; in other words, they exhibit *symmetry*. In shy infants, however, the two hemispheres respond differently—that is, *asymmetrically*—to such stimuli. Specifically, these children exhibit higher levels of arousal in the right hemisphere than in the left (Fox, Henderson, Rubin, Calkins, & Schmidt, 2001; Henderson, Marshall, Fox, & Rubin, 2004). Such findings make it tempting to conclude that temperamental differences are based in neurological processes. Research, however, suggests that it is difficult to say whether neurological differences are a cause or an effect of temperament. Developmentalists have found that shy infants whose temperaments change over the first 4 years of life—that is, those who become more outgoing—also become less likely to exhibit the asymmetrical pattern of arousal (Fox et al., 2001).

Environment Critics of neurological studies point out that it is impossible to know whether such findings are causes or effects (Johnson, 2003). They argue that behavior shapes the brain. Thus, shy children may exhibit different neurological patterns than outgoing children because their exhibition of shy behavior contributes to the neural networks that developmental processes in the brain, such as pruning, allow to develop and those that are shut down due to lack of use.

Consistent with these critics' claims, researchers have found that temperament-environment interactions tend to strengthen built-in qualities. For one thing, people of all ages choose their experiences, a process Sandra Scarr refers to as **niche-picking** (Scarr & McCartney, 1983). Our choices reflect our temperaments. For example, highly sociable children seek out contact with others; children low on the activity dimension are more likely to choose sedentary activities, such as puzzles or board games, than baseball.

Parents may also be able to either increase or decrease the effects of an infant's inborn temperamental tendencies. In one longitudinal study, researchers videotaped play sessions in which Chinese parents interacted with their 4-year-old children (Hou, Chen, & Chen, 2005). When the children were 7 years old, the researchers found that parent behavior at age 4 predicted behavioral inhibition (shyness) at age 7. Specifically, the more controlling parents were during the play sessions, the more likely their children were to be rated as more behaviorally

niche-picking the process of selecting experiences on the basis of temperament

inhibited at age 7 than they had been at age 4. Such findings suggest that, perhaps contrary to what you might expect, parents who accept an inhibited child's temperament may contribute more to the child's ability to overcome shyness later in life than parents who try to force a child to be more outgoing. Some experts suggest that parental influences may be greatest for children who are at the extremes of a given temperamental continuum. That is, children who are extremely inhibited may be more subject to parental influence than those who are moderately so (Buss & Plomin, 1984).

Developmentalists argue that the **goodness-of-fit** between children's temperaments and their environments influences how inborn temperamental characteristics are manifested later in life (Thomas & Chess, 1977). For example, if the parents of an irritable baby boy are good at tolerating his irritability and persist in establishing a synchronous relationship with him, then his irritability doesn't lead to the development of an insecure attachment. An infant's gender may also influence how the environment responds to his temperament, as discussed in the Research Report on page 161.

goodness-of-fit the degree to which an infant's temperament is adaptable to his or her environment, and vice versa

Learning Objective 6.11

How do the subjective self, the objective self, and the emotional self develop during the first 2 years?

Self-Concept

During the same months when a baby is creating an internal model of attachment and expressing her own unique temperament, she is also developing an internal model of self. Freud suggested that the infant needed to develop a sense of separateness from her mother before she could form a sense of self. Piaget emphasized that the infant's understanding of the basic concept of object permanence was a necessary precursor for the child's attaining self-permanence. Both of these aspects of early self-development reappear in more recent descriptions of the emergence of the sense of self (Lewis, 1990, 1991).

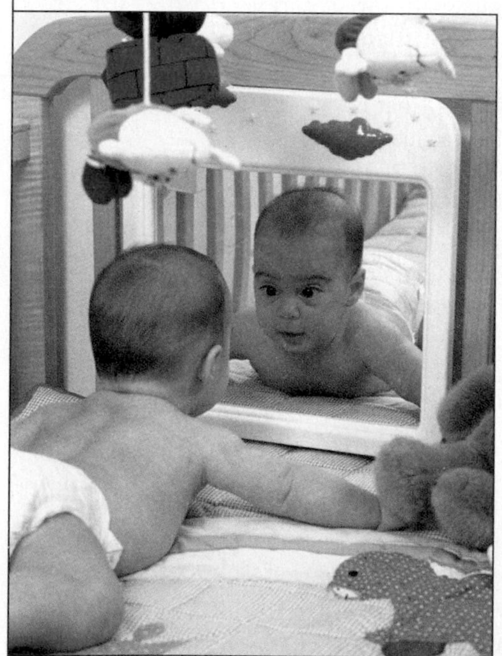

Research that has examined babies' ability to recognize themselves suggests that self-awareness develops in the middle of the second year.

The Subjective Self The child's first task is to figure out that he is separate from others and that this separate self endures over time and space. Developmentalists call this aspect of the self-concept the **subjective self**, or sometimes the *existential self*, because the key awareness seems to be "I exist." The roots of this understanding lie in the myriad everyday interactions the baby has with the objects and people in his world that lead him to understand, during the first 2 to 3 months of life, that he can have effects on things (Thompson & Goodvin, 2005). For example, when the child touches a mobile, it moves; when he cries, someone responds; when he smiles, his mother smiles back. Through this process, the baby separates self from everything else and a sense of "I" begins to emerge.

By the time the infant has constructed a fairly complete understanding of object permanence, at about 8–12 months, the subjective self has fully emerged. Just as he is figuring out that Mom and Dad continue to exist when they are out of sight, he is figuring out—at least in some preliminary way—that he exists separately and has some permanence.

The Objective Self The second major task is for the toddler to come to understand that she is also an object in the world (Thompson & Goodvin, 2005). Just as a ball has properties—roundness, the ability to roll, a certain feel in the hand—so the "self" has qualities or properties, such as gender, size, a name, shyness or boldness, coordination or clumsiness. It is this self-awareness that is the hallmark of the second aspect of identity, the **objective self,** sometimes called the **categorical self** because once the child achieves self-awareness the process of defining the self involves placing oneself in a whole series of categories.

It has not been easy to determine just when a child has developed the initial self-awareness that delineates the formation of the objective self. The most commonly used procedure involves a mirror. First, the baby is placed in front of a mirror, just to see how she behaves. Most infants between about 9 and 12 months old will look at their own image, make faces, or try to interact with the baby in the mirror in some way. After allowing this free ex-

subjective self an infant's awareness that she or he is a separate person who endures through time and space and can act on the environment

objective (categorical) self the toddler's understanding that she or he is defined by various categories such as gender or qualities such as shyness

RESEARCH REPORT

Gender Differences in Temperament

What kinds of temperamental differences come to mind when you think about boys and girls? You may think of boys as more irritable and girls as more fearful. But are these differences real, or are they simply stereotypes?

In some studies, researchers have found that boys are more emotionally intense and less fearful than girls and that girls are generally more sociable (Calkins, Dedmon, Gill, Lomax, & Johnson, 2002; Gartstein & Rothbart, 2003). Nevertheless, temperamental differences between boys and girls are much smaller than the differences *perceived* by parents and other adults. In one classic study, researchers found that adults viewing a videotape of an infant interpreted the baby's behavior differently depending on the gender label experimenters provided. Participants who were told the baby was a girl interpreted a particular behavior as expressing "fear." Amazingly, participants who believed the infant was a boy labeled the same behavior "anger" (Condry & Condry, 1976).

Research on another dimension of temperament—emotionality—provides further examples of how perceived differences in temperament may affect parental responses to children's behavior. Most studies have found that, even in infancy, girls are more responsive to others' facial expressions (McClure, 2000). This difference often leads to the perception that girls are more emotionally sensitive. However, studies of actual behavior reveal that boys are just as affectionate and empathetic as girls during infancy (Melson, Peet, & Sparks, 1991; Zahn-Waxler, Radke-Yarrow, Wagner, & Chapman, 1992).

Temperamental stereotyping may affect the quality of the parent-infant relationship. For example, parents of a calm, quiet girl may respond positively to her because they perceive her behavior to be consistent with their concept of "girlness." In contrast, parents of a physically active girl may develop a rejecting, disapproving attitude of her because they view her behavior as excessively masculine. These differences in parental responses may affect all aspects of parent-child relationships such that parents display higher levels of affection for a girl whom they perceive to be "feminine" than they do toward a daughter whom they view as "masculine."

You should recognize these questions as yet another example of the nature-nurture debate. The findings of behavioral geneticists seem to argue strongly that these differences are inborn. Yet it is also clear that parents treat boys and girls differently beginning very early in infancy. Thus, as children get older, gender differences in temperament are likely to be the result of both their inborn characteristics and the gender-based expectations and response patterns exhibited by their parents.

Questions for Critical Analysis

1. In what ways might stereotypes influence the methods that researchers use to study gender differences in temperament?
2. How do differences between men and women, which have evolved over many years, contribute to expectations about how male and female infants differ in temperament? In other words, in your view, do adults engage in what might be called "backward generalization" from adults to infants with regard to their opinions about the existence of gender differences early in life?

ploration for a time, the experimenter, while pretending to wipe the baby's face with a cloth, puts a spot of rouge on the baby's nose, and then lets the baby look in the mirror again. The crucial test of self-recognition, and thus of awareness of the self, is whether the baby reaches for the spot on her own nose, rather than the nose on the face in the mirror.

The results of a classic study using this procedure are graphed in Figure 6.2 (on page 162). As you can see, few of the 9- to 12-month-old children in this study touched their own nose, but three-quarters of the children aged 21 months showed that level of self-recognition, a result confirmed in a variety of other research studies, including studies in Europe (Asendorpf, Warkentin, & Baudonniere, 1996; Lewis & Brooks, 1978). Figure 6.2 also shows the rate at which children refer to themselves by name when they are shown a picture of themselves, which is another commonly used measure of self-awareness. You can see that this development occurs at almost exactly the same time as self-recognition in a mirror. Both are present by about the middle of the second year of life, a finding confirmed by other investigators (Bullock & Lütkenhaüs, 1990). At this point, toddlers begin to show a newly proprietary attitude ("Mine!") toward toys or other treasured objects.

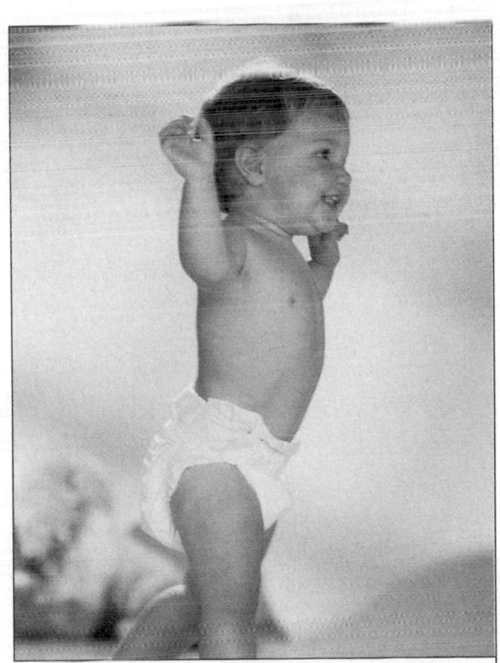

This baby's emotional reaction is best described as joy or delight rather than pride; her sense of self is not yet well-enough developed that she can feel pride in learning to walk.

As self-awareness develops, infants begin to refer to themselves by name and, near the end of the second year, to label themselves as boys or girls. In addition, infants recognize that they belong to the "child" category. They also use categorical terms such as "good" and "big" to describe themselves. For example, a girl might say "good girl" when she obeys her parent or "big girl" when she is successful at a task like using the toilet (Stipek, Gralinski, & Kopp, 1990).

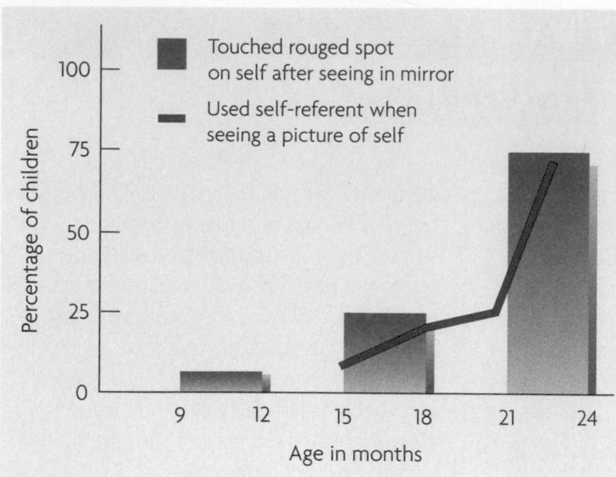

Figure 6.2
The Rouge Test

Mirror recognition and self-naming develop at almost exactly the same time.

(*Source:* Lewis & Brooks, 1978, pp. 214–215.)

The Emotional Self Development of the *emotional self* begins when babies learn to identify changes in emotion expressed in others' faces, at 2 to 3 months of age. Initially, they discriminate emotions best when they receive information on many channels simultaneously—such as when they see a particular facial expression and hear the same emotion expressed in the adult's voice (Walker-Andrews, 1997). Moreover, in these early weeks, infants are much better at discerning the emotional expressions of a familiar face than those of an unfamiliar face (Kahana-Kalman & Walker-Andrews, 2001). By 5 to 7 months, babies can begin to "read" one channel at a time, responding to facial expression alone or vocal expression alone, even when the emotions are displayed by a stranger rather than Mom or Dad (Balaban, 1995). They also respond to a much wider variety of emotions than younger infants do and can distinguish among happy, surprised, angry, fearful, interested, and sad faces (Soken & Pick, 1999; Walker-Andrews & Lennon, 1991).

Near the end of the first year, infants' perceptions of others' emotions help them anticipate others' actions and guide their own behavior (Phillips, Wellman, & Spelke, 2002). For instance, they react to another infant's neutral facial expression by actively trying to elicit an emotional expression from that child (Striano & Rochat, 1999). Just as adults often work at getting a baby to smile at them, babies seem to be following the same sort of script by 8 to 10 months of age.

As the infant's understanding of others' emotions advances, it is matched by parallel progression in expression of emotions. At birth, infants have different facial expressions for interest, pain, and disgust, and an expression that conveys enjoyment develops very quickly. By the time a baby is 2 to 3 months old, adult observers can also distinguish expressions of anger and sadness, with expressions of fear appearing by 6 or 7 months (Izard et al., 1995; Izard & Harris, 1995). At about the same time, infants begin to smile more to human faces than to a doll's face or another inanimate object, suggesting that at this early stage the baby is already responding to the added social signals available in the human face (Ellsworth, Muir, & Hains, 1993; Legerstee, Pomerleau, Malcuit, & Feider, 1987).

Over the next several months, the infant's emotional expressions, and the behaviors that arise from them, become more sophisticated. For example, as you learned earlier in the chapter, infants who have formed an attachment to a caregiver (typically in the last few months of the first year) use the caregiver's emotions to guide their own feelings. Moreover, by this age, babies have learned to calm themselves when their caregivers behave in expected ways (Cole et al., 2004). For example, a baby who is frustrated by hunger will calm down when she sees her caregiver preparing to nurse her or to provide her with some other kind of nourishment. Finally, near the middle of the second year, at about the same time that a child shows self-recognition in the mirror, such self-conscious emotional expressions as embarrassment, pride, and shame emerge (Lewis, Allesandri, & Sullivan, 1992; Lewis, Sullivan, Stanger, & Weiss, 1989; Mascolo & Fischer, 1995).

Critical Thinking

1. How do you think your genes and environment interacted to produce the temperamental characteristics and self-concept that you have today?

Effects of Nonparental Care

Since the late 1970s, women in virtually every industrialized country in the world have been entering the workforce in great numbers. In the United States, the change has been particularly rapid and massive: In 1970, only 18% of U.S. married women with children under age 6 were in the labor force; at the beginning of the 21st century, 61% of such women (and more than half of women with children under age 1) were working outside the home at least part-time (NICHD Early Child Care Research Network, 2003). The younger children are, the less likely they are to receive nonparental care. However, even among U.S. infants under the age of 2 years, half are cared for by someone other than a parent at least part-time (FIFCFS, 2005). The key question for psychologists is "What effect does such nonparental care have on infants and young children?"

Difficulties in Studying Nonparental Care

Learning Objective 6.12

Why is it difficult to study the effects of nonparental care on development?

It might seem that the effect on infant development of this trend toward nonparental care could easily be determined by comparing babies receiving nonparental care to those cared for by their parents. However, both "nonparental care" and "parental care" are really complex interactions among numerous variables rather than single factors whose effects can be studied independently. Thus, interpretation of research on nonparental care has to take into account a variety of issues.

To begin with, in many studies an enormous range of different care arrangements are all lumped under the general title of "nonparental care" (see Figure 6.3). Infants who are cared for by grandparents in their own homes, as well as those who are enrolled in day-care centers, receive nonparental care. In addition, infants enter these care arrangements at different ages, and they remain in them for varying lengths of time. Some have the same nonparental caregiver over many years; others shift often from one care setting to another. Moreover, nonparental care varies widely in quality.

According to recent surveys, the most common pattern is for a child to be cared for by a family member in the child's or family member's home (FIFCFS, 2005). Nevertheless, a majority of 3- to 6-year-olds who are cared for by relatives or in family day care are also enrolled at least part-time in some kind of child care center or preschool. Thus, another problem with studying the effects of nonparental care is that many children receive care in multiple settings.

To further complicate matters, families who place their children in nonparental care are different in a whole host of ways from those who care for their children primarily at home. How can researchers be sure that effects attributed to nonparental care are not instead the result of these other family differences?

Half of all infants in the United States now experience at least some nonparental care.

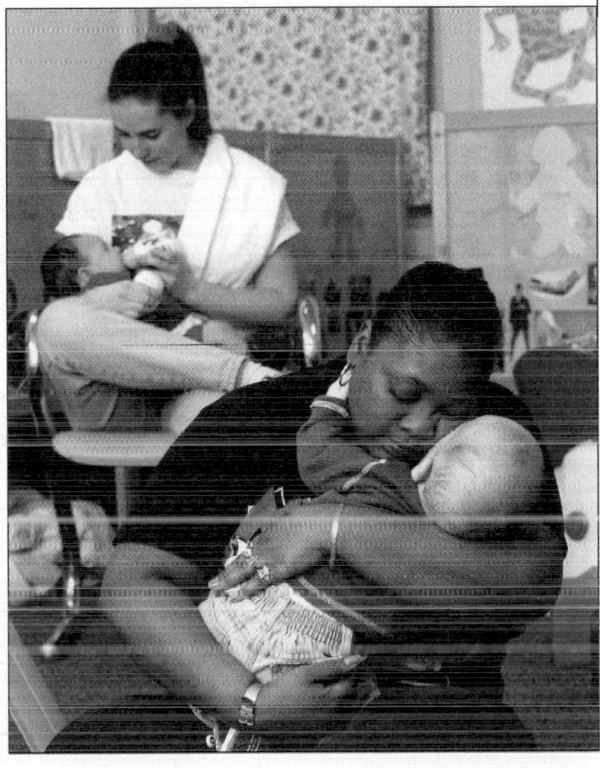

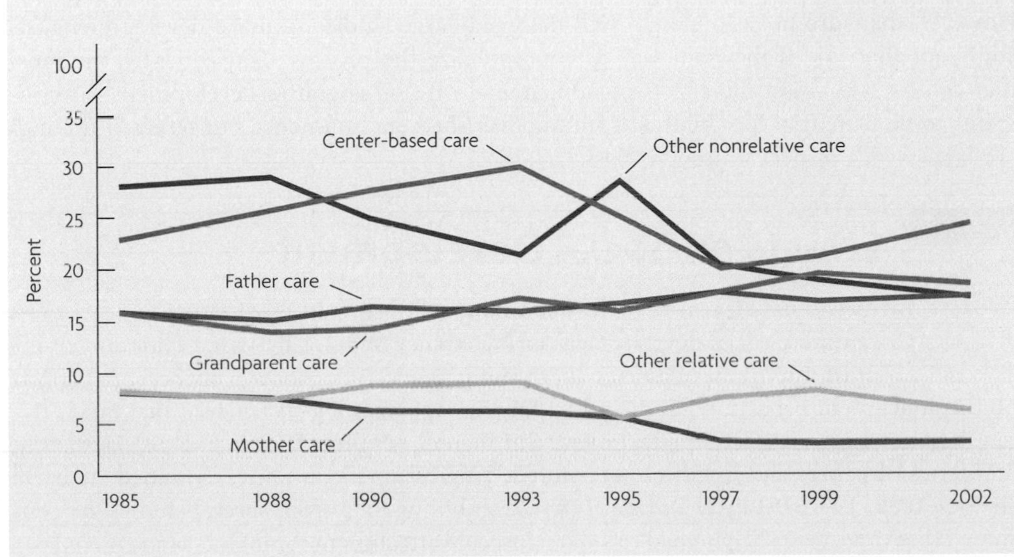

Figure 6.3
Nonparental Care Arrangements for Children under 6 in the United States

Children younger than 6 years whose mothers are employed are cared for in a variety of different settings in the United States.

(*Source:* Federal Interagency Forum on Child and Family Statistics. (2005). *America's Children in Brief: Key national indicators of well being, 2005.* Retrieved May 18, 2007 from http://www.childstats.gov/pubs.asp.)

Mothers also differ in their attitudes toward the care arrangements they have made. Some mothers with children in nonparental care would far rather be at home taking care of their children; others are happy to be working. Similarly, some mothers who are at home full-time would rather be working, and some are delighted to be at home. Studies of the effects of nonparental care rarely offer any information at all about the mother's level of satisfaction with her situation.

Most of the research on nonparental versus parental care has not taken these complexities into account. Researchers have frequently compared children "in day care" with those "reared at home" and assumed that any differences between the two groups were attributable to the day-care experience. Some recent studies are better, but clear answers to even the most basic questions about the impact of nonparental care on children's development are still not available. Nonetheless, because the issue is so critical, you need to be aware of what is and is not yet known.

Learning Objective 6.13

What might be the effects of nonparental care on cognitive development?

Effects on Cognitive Development

There is a good deal of evidence that high-quality day care has beneficial effects on many children's overall cognitive development (NICHD, 2006). This effect is particularly strong for children from poor families, who show significant and lasting gains in IQ and later school performance after attending highly enriched day care throughout infancy and early childhood (Campbell & Ramey, 1994; Loeb, Fuller, Kagan, & Carrol, 2003; Love et al., 2004; Ramey, 1993). Even middle-class children show some cognitive benefit when they are in high-quality day care (Peisner-Feinberg, 1995).

However, the picture is not entirely rosy. Several studies in the United States point to possible negative effects of day-care experience on cognitive development in some children, perhaps middle-class children especially. For example, in one large study of over 1,000 preschoolers, researchers found that White children—but not African American children—who had entered day care in the first year of life had lower vocabulary scores than those who had entered after age 1 (Baydar & Brooks-Gunn, 1991). Conversely, in a large study of 5- and 6-year-olds, researchers found that children from poor families who began day care before age 1 had higher reading and math scores at the start of school than did children from middle-class families who entered day care in infancy (Caughy, DiPietro, & Strobino, 1994).

How can these conflicting findings be reconciled? One fairly straightforward possibility is that the crucial issue is the discrepancy between the level of stimulation the child would receive at home and the quality of the child care. When a particular day-care setting for a given child provides more enrichment than the child would have received at home, day-care attendance has some beneficial cognitive effects; when day care is less stimulating than full-time home care would be for that child, day care has negative effects. However, there are not yet enough well-designed, large studies to make developmentalists confident that this is the right way to conceptualize the process. Consequently, the most that can be said about the effects of nonparental care on cognitive development is that it seems to be beneficial for children from impoverished environments, but research findings are mixed with respect to middle-class children.

Learning Objective 6.14

What does research suggest about the risks of nonparental care with respect to social development?

Effects on Social Development

As you have learned, the formation of an attachment relationship appears to be central to social development during infancy and in later years. Thus, one of the most important questions about nonparental care concerns its potential effects on the attachment process. Until the mid-1980s, most psychologists believed that infant day care had no negative effect on attachment. But then developmental psychologist Jay Belsky, in a series of papers and in testimony before a congressional committee, sounded an alarm (Belsky, 1985, 1992; Belsky & Rovine, 1988). Combining data from several studies, he concluded that there was a heightened risk of an insecure attachment for infants who entered day care before their first birthday.

Since that time, a number of other researchers have analyzed the combined results of large numbers of studies and confirmed Belsky's original conclusion. For example, a summary of the findings of 13 different studies involving 897 infants revealed that 35% of infants who had experienced at least 5 hours per week of nonparental care were insecurely attached, compared to 29% of infants with exclusively maternal care (Lamb, Sternberg, & Prodromidis, 1992).

Another study, involving more than 1,000 infants, demonstrated that infants whose parents exhibit behaviors associated with insecure attachment, such as poor sensitivity to the child's needs, are more likely to be negatively affected by nonparental care. When all of the infants were considered together, researchers found no differences in attachment quality between those who were in nonparental care and those who were cared for at home, regardless of the age at which they entered outside care or how many hours per week they were cared for there (NICHD Early Child Care Research Network, 1998). However, when researchers looked at only those babies whose parents displayed behaviors associated with insecure attachment, such as insensitivity to the child's needs, they found that children who were home-reared were more likely to be securely attached to their caregivers than those who were enrolled in nonparental care.

How does nonparental care affect other social relationships? Belsky argues that, when children reach school age, those who entered nonparental care during the early months of life and who have spent 20 or more hours per week in such care throughout early childhood are at greater risk for social problems than children who have spent less time in nonparental care (Belsky, 2001, 2002). A number of studies support Belsky's view (Kim, 1997; NICHD, 2006). In fact, some research indicates that Belsky's hypothesis may have been overly optimistic with regard to the amount of nonparental care that may be harmful. One study showed that kindergartners who had spent as little as 10 hours per week in nonparental care during infancy and early childhood were more likely to display aggressiveness toward peers and disobedience toward teachers than peers who were entirely home-reared (NICHD Early Child Care Research Network, 2003). However, other studies suggest that the negative effects of nonparental care are no longer evident in children over the age of 7 (Van Beijsterveldt, Hudziak, & Boomsma, 2005).

Interpreting Research on Nonparental Care

Learning Objective 6.15
What variables should be taken into account in interpretations of research on nonparental care?

What is it about nonparental care that predisposes infants to become aggressive, disobedient kindergartners? Studies of infants' psychological responses to nonparental care may hold a clue. Researchers have found that levels of the stress hormone *cortisol* increase from morning to afternoon in infants who are enrolled in center-based care (Watamura, Donzella, Alwin, & Gunnar, 2003; Vermeer & van IJzendoorn, 2006). By contrast, cortisol levels decrease over the course of the day in home-reared infants. Interestingly, cortisol levels of home-reared and center-care infants are identical on weekends and holidays. Thus, some developmentalists argue that the higher levels of cortisol experienced by center-care infants affect their rapidly developing brains in ways that lead to problem behaviors. However, there is no direct evidence yet to support this hypothesis.

Some developmentalists argue that nonparental care arrangements probably vary in the degree to which they induce stress in infants and young children. In other words, they say, quality of care may be just as important as quantity of care (Maccoby & Lewis, 2003). For example, some researchers have found that, when infants are cared for in high-quality centers, the amount of time they spend in such care is unrelated to social behavior (Love et al., 2003). Thus, developmentalists urge parents, especially those who must leave their infants in center-based care for extended periods of time, to make every effort to ensure that the arrangement they choose has the characteristics discussed in the Real World on page 166.

Another point to keep in mind is that individual and gender differences have been found to interact with nonparental care. For example, infants who are behaviorally inhibited, in Jerome Kagan's terms, may be more sensitive to the stresses associated with center-based care (Watamura et al., 2003). Moreover, boys in nonparental care are more likely than girls in similar care settings to be insecurely attached to their caregivers (Crockenberg, 2003). For these

THE REAL WORLD

Choosing a Day-Care Center

Rey is a single father who needs to find someone to care for his 14-month-old son while he is at work. Up until now, Rey's mother has been caring for the boy, but she has decided to return to work herself. Rey has heard about studies showing that high-quality care can enhance children's development, but he isn't exactly sure what is meant by the term "high-quality." Here are a few pointers Rey could use to find a high-quality child care center (Clarke-Stewart, 1992; Howes, Phillips, & Whitebook, 1992; Scarr & Eisenberg, 1993):

- *A low teacher/child ratio.* For children younger than 2, the ratio should be no higher than 1:4; for 2- to 3-year-olds, ratios between 1:4 and 1:10 appear to be acceptable.
- *A small group size.* The smaller the number of children cared for together—whether in one room in a day-care center or in a home—the better for the child. For infants, a maximum of 6 to 8 per group appears best; for 1- to 2-year-olds, between 6 and 12 per group; for older children, groups as large as 15 or 20 appear to be acceptable.
- *A clean, colorful space, adapted to child play.* It is not essential to have lots of expensive toys, but the center must offer a variety of activities that children find engaging, organized in a way that encourages play.
- *A daily plan.* The daily curriculum should include some structure, some specific teaching, and some supervised activities. However, too much regimentation is not ideal.
- *Sensitive caregivers.* The adults in the day-care setting should be positive, involved, and responsive to the children, not merely custodial.
- *Knowledgeable caregivers.* Training in child development and infant curriculum development helps caregivers provide a day-care setting that meets criteria for good quality.

Questions for Reflection

1. What do you think Rey should do to ease his son's transition from family care to a child care center?
2. One of the criteria is "sensitive caregivers." What kinds of caregiver behaviors might be indicative of this criterion?

reasons, more research that takes both temperament and gender into account is needed before we can say for certain that nonparental care has uniformly negative effects on children's social development (Crockenberg, 2003).

Finally, it is important to understand that, on average, the differences between children in nonparental care and their home-reared peers, both positive and negative, are very small (NICHD Early Child Care Research Network, 2006). Moreover, studies that have attempted to examine all of the complex variables associated with parental and nonparental care, such as parents' level of education, have shown that family variables are more important than the type of day-care arrangements a family chooses (NICHD Early Child Care Research Network, 2003). Developmental psychologist Sandra Scarr, a leading day-care researcher, has suggested that the kind of day care parents choose is an extension of their own characteristics and parenting styles (Scarr, 1997). For example, poorly educated parents may choose day-care arrangements that do not emphasize infant learning. Similarly, parents whose focus is on intellectual development may not place a high priority on the emotional aspects of a particular day-care arrangement. Thus, Scarr claims, day-care effects are likely to be parenting effects in disguise.

Critical Thinking

1. An experimental study could answer cause-and-effect questions about the effects of nonparental care, but why would such a study be unethical?

SUMMARY

Theories of Social and Personality Development

Learning Objective 6.1 How do Freud's and Erikson's views of personality development in the first 2 years differ?

- Freud suggested that individual differences in personality originated in the nursing and weaning practices of infants' mothers. Erikson emphasized the roles of both mothers and fathers, as well as other adults in the infant's environment, in providing for all the infant's needs, thereby instilling a sense of trust concerning the social world.

Learning Objective 6.2 What are the main ideas of attachment theory?

- Ethologists hypothesize that early emotional bonds are the foundation of later personality and social development. They further suggest that the first 2 years of life are a sensitive, or critical, period for the development of attachment.

Attachment

Learning Objective 6.3 How does synchrony affect parent-infant relations?

- For parents to form a strong attachment relationship with an infant, what is most crucial is the development of synchrony, a set of mutually reinforcing and interlocking behaviors that characterize most interactions between parent and infant. Fathers as well as mothers form strong bonds with their infants, but fathers show more physically playful behaviors with their children than do mothers.

Learning Objective 6.4 What are the four phases of attachment and the behaviors associated with them?

- Bowlby proposed that the child's attachment to a caregiver develops in three phases, beginning with rather indiscriminate aiming of attachment behaviors toward anyone within reach, through a focus on one or more figures, and finally to "secure base behavior," beginning at about 6 months of age, which signals the presence of a clear attachment.

Learning Objective 6.5 What are the variables that contribute to the development and stability of the four types of attachment?

- Children differ in the security of their first attachments, and thus in the internal models of relationships that they develop. The secure infant uses the parent as a safe base for exploration and can be readily consoled by the parent.

Learning Objective 6.6 What variables might affect a parent's ability to establish an attachment relationship with an infant?

- Caregiver characteristics such as marital status, age, education level, and income can affect infants' attachment quality. Also, infants whose parents have psychiatric illnesses are more likely to form insecure attachments than babies whose parents do not suffer from these disorders.

Learning Objective 6.7 What are the long-term consequences of attachment quality?

- The security of the initial attachment is reasonably stable; later in childhood, securely attached children appear to be more socially skillful, more curious and persistent in approaching new tasks, and more mature. The internal model of attachment that individuals develop in infancy affects how they parent their own babies.

Learning Objective 6.8 In what ways do patterns of attachment vary across cultures?

- Studies in many countries suggest that secure attachment is the most common pattern everywhere, but cultures differ in the frequency of different types of insecure attachment.

Personality, Temperament, and Self-Concept

Learning Objective 6.9 On which dimensions of temperament do most developmentalists agree?

- Temperament theorists generally agree on the following basic temperament dimensions: activity level, approach/positive emotionality, inhibition, negative emotionality, and effortful control/task persistence.

Learning Objective 6.10 What are the roles of heredity, neurological processes, and environment in the formation of temperament?

- There is strong evidence that temperamental differences have a genetic component, and that they are at least somewhat stable over infancy and childhood. However, temperament is not totally determined by heredity or neurological processes. The "fit" between children's temperaments and their environments may be more important than temperament itself.

Learning Objective 6.11 How do the subjective self, the objective self, and the emotional self develop during the first 2 years?

- The infant also begins to develop a sense of self, including the awareness of a separate self and the understanding of self-permanence (which may be collectively called the subjective self) and awareness of herself as an object in the world (the objective self). An emotional self also develops in the first year. The range of emotions babies experience—as well as their ability to make use of information about emotions, such as facial expressions—increases dramatically over the first year.

Effects of Nonparental Care

Learning Objective 6.12 Why is it difficult to study the effects of nonparental care on development?

- Comparing parental to nonparental care is difficult because there are so many types of nonparental care arrangements.

Learning Objective 6.13 What might be the effects of nonparental care on cognitive development?

- Day care often has positive effects on the cognitive development of less advantaged children, but it may have negative effects on that of more advantaged children if there is a large discrepancy between the home environment and the level of stimulation in day care.

Learning Objective 6.14 What does research suggest about the risks of nonparental care with respect to social development?

- The impact of day care on children's social development is unclear. Some studies show a small difference in security of attachment between children in day care and those reared at home; others suggest that home-care and day-care children do not differ with respect to attachment. Some studies show children who spend more time in day care to be more aggressive; others show them to be more socially skillful.

Learning Objective 6.15 What variables should be taken in to account in interpretations of research on non-parental care?

- Infants' physiological responses to the stresses associated with nonparental care may underlie its association with developmental outcomes. The quality of nonparental care a child receives may be as important as the quantity of nonparental care. Individual differences and gender may interact with the quality of a care arrangement, the quantity of outside-the-home care a child receives, or both. Average differences between children who receive nonparental care and those who are cared for entirely in their own home are small.

KEY TERMS

attachment *(p. 150)*
attachment theory *(p. 148)*
goodness-of-fit *(p. 160)*
insecure/ambivalent attachment *(p. 152)*
insecure/avoidant attachment *(p. 152)*
insecure/disorganized attachment *(p. 152)*
niche-picking *(p. 159)*
objective (categorical) self *(p. 160)*
personality *(p. 157)*
secure attachment *(p. 152)*
separation anxiety *(p. 152)*
social referencing *(p. 152)*
stranger anxiety *(p. 152)*
subjective self *(p. 160)*
synchrony *(p. 150)*
temperament *(p. 157)*

TEST YOURSELF

Theories of Social and Personality Development

6.1 The theorist who believed that the weaning process needed to be managed in such a way that the infant's need to suck was neither frustrated nor overgratified was

a. Ainsworth.
b. Bowlby.
c. Erikson.
d. Freud.

6.2 Harlow's research demonstrated that, within a monkey population,

a. the infant-mother relationship is based solely on nursing practices.
b. the infant-mother relationship is based solely on weaning practices.
c. the infant-mother relationship is not as important as the infant-father relationship.
d. the infant-mother relationship is based on the mother's ability to comfort and cuddle the infant when the infant is frightened or stressed.

6.3 Which of the following is *not* a claim that is made by ethologists?

a. The first two years constitute a sensitive period for the development of an emotional bond with a caregiver.
b. Early emotional bonds are templates for later relationships across the entire lifespan.
c. Failure to form an emotional bond causes an infant to develop fixation.
d. Evolution has equipped infants with genes that drive the development of emotional bonds with their caregivers.

Attachment

6.4 Of the following parent-infant interactive behaviors, which is *not* an example of synchrony?

a. Greta chooses a book of nursery rhymes to read to her drowsy infant.
b. Tom smiles, raises his eyebrows, and opens his eyes wide as he bends to speak to his infant.
c. Tovah's voice is high-pitched and lilting as she shows her baby a new toy.
d. Elena imitates her baby's babbling and pauses for the baby's response.

6.5 Which of the following statements best describes fathers' attachments to their infants?

a. Fathers do not seem to have as many attachment behaviors as do mothers.
b. Fathers' attachments to their children seem to depend more on contact immediately after birth.
c. Fathers' attachments to their infants depend more on the development of synchrony.
d. Fathers' attachments to their children are not as important as mothers' attachments.

6.6 The amount of give and take between an infant and his parent has been linked to

a. later intelligence.
b. the ability to control emotions later in life.
c. the child's emotional availability.
d. the child's language development.

6.7 As an employee of a day-care facility, you have observed that 1-year-old Timmy is very upset when he is left by his mother in the morning. When she returns in the evening, however, her presence does not comfort him. He will greet his mother but then immediately push her away or resist her efforts to comfort him. Timmy might be categorized as having a(n) ______ attachment relationship with his mother.

a. difficult
b. insecure/ambivalent
c. insecure/disorganized
d. resistant

6.8 Which of the following is *not* an accurate statement about the long-term consequences of attachment quality?

a. Securely attached infants become children who are more sociable and positive in their behavior toward friends and siblings.
b. Securely attached infants become adolescents who have more intimate friendships.
c. Securely attached infants become adolescents who have more liberal sexual attitudes.
d. The quality of infant attachment predicts sociability in adulthood.

6.9 You are a teacher of children who are approximately 12 years old. Which of the following characteristics would you be most likely to observe among your pupils who had been classified as securely attached when they were infants?

a. social competence
b. higher levels of intelligence
c. motor skill superiority
d. a wide range of hobbies

Personality, Temperament, and Self-Concept

6.10 How do temperament and personality differ?

a. Temperament is an emotional foundation for personality.
b. They mean essentially the same thing.
c. Personality develops first; temperament develops later.
d. Temperament disappears in early life and is replaced by personality.

6.11 Which concept is *not* similar in meaning to the others?

a. behavioral and emotional predispositions present at birth
b. temperament
c. how a child tends to react
d. intelligence

6.12 Which of the following is *not* a dimension of temperament described by many of the key researchers?

a. activity level
b. emotional maturity
c. inhibition
d. negative emotionality

6.13 Baby Nathan has a difficult time with his reactions to new things. He tends to react strongly to both positive and negative happenings. In addition, he does not have regular body functions. According to Chess and Thomas, Nathan would be a ______ child.

a. slow-to-warm-up
b. difficult
c. easy
d. sociable

6.14 Carrie tends to be an irritable, fussy child. She has a low threshold of frustration, and when she is hungry or wishes to be picked up, she very quickly becomes loudly angry. How would developmentalists describe this aspect of Carrie's temperament?

a. persistence
b. inhibition
c. negative emotionality
d. vigorous demand level

6.15 How are shy children different neurologically from other children?

a. The corpus callosum is thicker.
b. The frontal lobes respond asymmetrically.
c. There is excess dopamine.
d. There is a lower level of arousal in the right hemisphere.

6.16 Margaret has always been a highly sociable child. She has always surrounded herself with friends, and she has assumed several leadership positions at school and in the community. A developmentalist would say that Margaret's choice of experiences that are consistent with her temperament is an example of

a. intelligence.
b. locus of control.
c. resilience.
d. niche-picking.

6.17 What is the general conclusion of research that has examined the consistency of temperament over time?

a. Temperament is stable and consistent only through infancy and the preschool years and becomes highly variable once the child is exposed to school and peer influences.
b. Researchers have found consistency and stability of temperament, including qualities of inhibition and difficultness, across infancy and childhood.
c. Inhibition is the only quality of temperament that shows stability across infancy and childhood.
d. Temperament is useful for understanding how infants respond to their environment, but the construct is not valid for understanding reactions or behaviors beyond infancy.

6.18 What cognitive skill seems linked to the child's understanding of his or her subjective self?

a. object permanence
b. conservation
c. reversible thinking
d. transformative thinking

6.19 As children develop self-awareness, they also

a. begin to refer to themselves by name.
b. label themselves as "boys" or "girls."
c. use categorical words to describe themselves.
d. do all of the above.

Effects of Nonparental Care

6.20 Which of the following is *not* one of the difficulties in studying nonparental care?

a. Infants enter these care arrangements at different ages.
b. Nonparental care varies hugely in quality.
c. Most nonparental care occurs in day-care centers.
d. An enormous variety of arrangements are all lumped under the title nonparental care.

6.21 What has been discovered about the effects of day care on cognitive development?

a. Children spending time in day care exhibit more emotional problems.
b. Children from poorer families are especially disadvantaged by day care.
c. There are no consistent findings about the effects of day care.
d. Cognitively enriched day-care experiences tend to positively affect children.

6.22 Which of the following seems to strongly influence the effects of day care?

a. the age at which a child begins day care
b. the gender of the child and the gender of the day-care personnel
c. the number of hours per week that the child spends in care
d. whether the day-care personnel have children of their own

6.23 Suppose you were asked to help a friend select a day-care situation for his child. Which of the following would *not* be good advice to give him, based on what is currently known about the factors that affect developmental outcomes in children?

a. There should be a low teacher/child ratio, with no more than four infants for one teacher.
b. Children should have a range of unstructured activities, and staff should minimize their interference in the children's interactions.
c. Staff should be involved with and respond to children in an interactive fashion, not merely supervise them.
d. Training in child development and infant curriculum development will help the staff deliver a good quality of life.

PEARSON mydevelopmentlab™ Study Plan

Are You Ready for the Test?

Students who use the study materials on MyDevelopmentLab report higher grades in the course than those who use the text alone. Here are three easy steps to mastering this chapter and improving your grade…

Step 1

Take the chapter pre-test in MyDevelopmentLab and review your customized Study Plan.

In the early weeks of life, fathers

- have the same repertoire of attachment behaviors as mothers do.
- are awkward in handling their infants and interacting with them.
- have difficulty establishing the same sense of synchrony that mothers establish.
- talk with and smile at their infants more than mothers do.

PRE-TEST

Step 2

Use MyDevelopmentLab's Multimedia Library to help strengthen your knowledge of the chapter.

Learning Objective 6.3

How does synchrony affect parent-infant relations?

Watch: Attachment in Infants

or a lasting, enduring, long-term emotional tie. You will hear from a university student

www.mydevelopmentlab.com

continued on the next page

80% of students responding to a national user survey agree that MyDevelopmentLab helps them prepare for exams.

Watch: Self Awareness

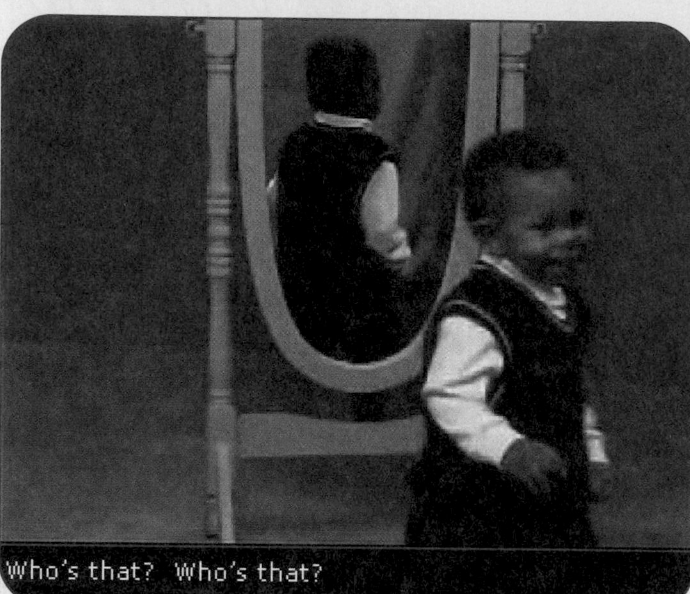

Who's that? Who's that?

Learning Objective 6.11

How do the subjective self, the objective self, and the emotional self develop during the first 2 years?

Watch: Day Care

At one end of the building, toddlers play happily with their toys. Only a few feet away,

Learning Objective 6.15

What variables should be taken into account in interpretations of research on nonparental care?

Step 3

Take the chapter post-test and compare your results against the pre-test.

POST-TEST

The development of the emotional self begins

- at 5 to 7 months, when the infant recognizes changes in emotions in the voices he hears.
- at the end of the first year, when the infant can use others' actions to guide his behavior.
- when the child can first express embarrassment, pride, and shame.
- at 2 to 3 months of age, when the infant can identify emotions expressed in the faces of others.

Are "Safe Haven" Policies a Good Idea?

Like many entering freshmen, 18-year-old Twyana Davis looked forward to the independence that living in a campus dorm would give her. Nevertheless, Davis's happiness was tempered by another reality: She was pregnant. When the time for the child's birth arrived, Davis delivered the child in her dorm room and placed it in a trash bin just outside her window. Pangs of guilt prompted her to call the campus police and to report "strange noises" coming from the bin in the hope that officers would rescue her baby. Thankfully, they did, and Davis ultimately came forward and claimed her child. In an effort to help other young women, Davis put her story into a book called *Sacred Womb* (Davis, 2003) and retold it on *Oprah* and other television programs.

Signs like this one inform the public about safe haven policies and alert them to locations where mothers can drop off their babies.

Explaining Infant Abandonment

Why would anyone abandon a newborn? Law professor Michelle Oberman, an expert in maternal/fetal law, has written extensively about cases such as Davis's (Meyer & Oberman, 2001). Her research shows that mothers who kill or abandon their newborns are young, typically in their late teens. Most are academically successful high school or college students who fear the embarrassment of having a child outside of marriage. Consequently, instead of seeking abortions, they deny their pregnancies and avoid situations in which their condition might be detected. Such girls won't be found, says Oberman, wearing a bikini at a beach party or visiting their doctors' offices for help with an upper respiratory infection. Giving birth confronts them with the reality of the pregnancy, but their commitment to continuing the denial motivates them to kill or abandon the baby.

Safe Haven Laws

Oberman's explanation might make it seem that infant abandonment is just another of the many poor decisions that young people are at risk of making as a result of the unique stresses of living in a world that values academic and economic success above all else. However, history clearly shows that infant abandonment is a problem that has plagued human society for as long as it has existed (Williams-Mbengue, 2003). In response, along with laws against abandonment and infant abuse, most societies have created legally sanctioned ways of helping young women relinquish their infants without fear of prosecution.

Over the past decade, such concerns have prompted the passage of *safe haven* laws in the United States that allow mothers to legally abandon their babies under certain circumstances. These laws vary a great deal from one state to another, but they all have certain features in common (Williams-Mbengue, 2003). One such feature is that all such laws limit the age at which a baby can be abandoned anonymously ranging from 3 days to 12 months. The laws also specify that the infant be free from signs of abuse or neglect. They also restrict legal abandonment to places at which a newborn is likely to receive immediate care, such as a hospital or a fire station; a mother who leaves her baby in a place where the baby is exposed to the elements or unlikely to receive care can be prosecuted for abandonment. Safe haven laws also state that the parental rights of a mother who abandons an infant will be terminated if she does not act to prevent such termination within a specified period of time.

Safe haven laws enjoy wide public approval. After all, what is more heart-rending than the story of an abandoned baby? Emotions aside, however, safe haven laws have many critics (Wiltenburg, 2003). Governor Linda Lingle of Hawaii has sparked controversy in her state because she is the only state chief executive in the United States to veto safe haven legislation, and she has done so more than once (Niesse, 2007). Lingle claims a careful review of the relevant evidence has convinced her that such laws do more harm than good (Honolulu Star-Bulletin, August 1, 2003). Is Governor Lingle right?

Criticisms of Safe Have Laws

Critics of safe haven laws say that society ought not to sanction an act as irresponsible and as morally indefensible as abandonment of an infant. Moreover, they claim that these policies violate infants' rights. Numerous treatises on the rights of children, such as the United Nations Commission on the Rights of the Child, state that the right of an individual to know who his or her biological parents are is a fundamental human right. The constitution of the European Union contains such a provision. In 2007, this provision was the basis of a lawsuit filed by a man whose mother abandoned him under France's safe haven law, a policy that dates back to the 18th century, by the way. However, he ultimately lost his case when EU courts ruled that the right of his mother to anonymity superseded his right to identify her. Many human rights advocates disagree and say that safe haven laws should be modified such that mothers have to identify themselves.

In addition to generating thorny moral dilemmas, safe haven laws create many practical problems. For one thing, an abandoned infant has no medical records, and there is no way for officials or for the child's adoptive parents to find out whether she is at risk of developing a genetic disorder. In addition, there is no way to know whether the infant was actually abandoned by her mother. Safe haven laws expressly forbid anyone other than the biological mother, or an agent to whom the mother has delegated her rights, from abandoning an infant. However, because of the "no questions asked" policy embodied in most safe haven laws, it is possible for a baby to be abandoned without the mother assenting to the abandonment or even knowing about it.

Anonymity presents additional challenges when officials terminate the rights of an abandoned infant's parents as well. Child protective laws require that both biological parents be given legal notice that their rights are subject to termination and that they can file a motion to prevent such termination from taking place. In the case of abandoned infants, there is no effective way of fulfilling these requirements. Critics argue that concerns for the rights of fathers and other relatives who may want to raise these children demand that safe haven laws be modified to require mothers to provide officials with contact information. Children's advocates point out that, as a result of the inconsistencies between safe haven laws and those that govern parental rights, abandoned babies spend far more time in temporary homes than do babies who are given up under adoption laws that require both mothers and fathers, whose paternity must be established with DNA tests, to voluntarily relinquish their parental rights.

Yet another shortcoming of safe haven laws was brought to light when Twyana Davis confessed to having conceived her child with a 12-year-old cousin (Cadwallader, 2006). Because Davis was 17 at the time, the relationship she had with her cousin violated laws against sexual exploitation of minors. Thus, safe haven laws may provide the perpetrators of sexual abuse with a convenient way to hide their crimes. Moreover, critics point out that the abandonment and killing of infants has not been stopped by safe haven laws. Babies continue to be found in dumpsters, and horrific cases of neonaticide continue to appear in the daily headlines.

Advocates' Responses to Critics

For their part, advocates of safe haven policies argue that these laws fulfill society's moral obligation to protect the lives of those who cannot protect themselves even when doing so leads to a host of practical problems. Thus, many states have enacted laws that better integrate safe haven policies with those that govern adoption and foster care. In addition, proponents say that safe haven laws can be made more effective by increasing public awareness of them. To that end, some states have established and widely advertised hotlines which women who are contemplating abandonment can call to find out where to take their babies. Many states have also mandated the inclusion of information about safe haven laws in sex education programs, and some have allocated funds for installing informational signs at fire stations and other safe havens.

Your Turn

You can learn more about the safe haven laws in your area by answering the following questions.

- How have legislators in your state modified safe haven policies in response to practical issues that have arisen since the original laws were passed?
- How do officials in your state publicize safe haven laws?
- How many women at your college are aware of safe haven laws? You can conduct a survey to find out.
- Does your college's health center provide students with information about safe haven policies and other options for students who are pregnant?
- As of this writing, there are no safe haven laws in Hawaii, Nebraska or the District of Columbia. However, there are many private agencies in these states and in the District that take in abandoned babies. If you live in one of these places, find out more about these agencies and about efforts to enact safe haven legislation.

PART THREE
Early Childhood

7

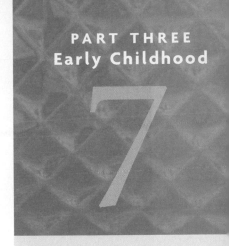

Physical and Cognitive Development in Early Childhood

It was a beautiful sunny day, so the two-year-old boy's nanny decided to take him out for a walk. Ever the conscientious caregiver, she securely strapped him into his stroller before heading for a nearby park. As the pair made their way through the park, a man suddenly accosted the nanny, separating her from the stroller and knocking her to the ground. His goal, it appeared, was to kidnap the child, but the strap that had been so carefully secured by the nanny foiled his attempt at a quick get-away. The nanny collected herself, got up off the ground, and attacked the man with all her might. As she pummeled him with her fists, he grabbed her arms to stop the attack, leaving several deep scratches in her forearms. Just then, a police officer came to the rescue, captured the would-be kidnapper, and carried him off to jail. The nanny comforted the boy, who was crying, and then hurried home. That evening, she recounted

the story to the boy's parents who were so grateful that they gave the nanny an expensive wristwatch as a reward.

Over the years, the story became standard family fare, the kind of story that is retold whenever relatives get together or when a new person enters the family who needs to be advised of the critical events of a family's history. Each time the story was retold, the boy assured the listeners that, despite his tender age at the time, he had a vivid memory of the event. The kidnapper's face, he said, was emblazoned in his memory, as was his nanny's valiant struggle to save him.

Several years later, the nanny, who had moved on to another position, had a religious experience that would change both her life and that of the family whose child she had saved. Consumed by the urge to relieve herself of the guilt she felt over her past wrongdoings, the nanny set out to correct each of them one by one. Eventually, she made her way to the family of the almost-kidnapped boy. By then, the boy was 15 years old, and the kidnapping episode was firmly rooted in his sense of personal history. Thus, he was shocked when he learned from the morally burdened former nanny that the entire story had been a fabrication. Moreover, she had given herself the scratches in order to make her story more convincing. The ex-nanny implored the family to forgive her, which they graciously did, and returned the watch.

The young man, still troubled by the fear associated with the "memory" of his near-kidnapping, found himself fascinated with the workings of the human mind. How, he wondered, was it possible that the mind could construct such a vivid memory of an event that had never actually occurred? His search for answers to his questions about cognitive functioning would lead him to a career in human development. By the time the young man reached the age of 30, he would be credited with having made some of the most important discoveries in the history of the field. That young man was Jean Piaget (Piaget, 1962).

In Chapter 2, we acquainted you with the general principles of Piaget's theory, and in Chapter 5 you read about his view of the sensorimotor stage. In this chapter, you will learn about his discoveries of the strengths and weaknesses of children's thinking during the early childhood period, and you will read about the efforts of other psychologists to challenge them and to find better explanations for them. But Piaget's work doesn't provide us with a full account of cognitive development in early childhood, so you will also read about momentous changes in memory functioning and language development that occur during this period. We will also acquaint you with the issues involved in the measurement of individual differences in cognitive functioning.

Physical Changes

Chapter 4 chronicled the many rapid changes in the infant's body. The physical changes between ages 2 and 6 are less dramatic. Subtle though they may be, the physical changes of the early childhood period provide children with an apt foundation for the cognitive and social leaps that lie ahead of them.

Growth and Motor Development

Learning Objective 7.1

What are the major milestones of growth and motor development between 2 and 6?

Changes in height and weight happen far more slowly in the preschool years than in infancy. Each year, the child adds about 2–3 inches in height and about 6 pounds in weight. At the same time, the young child makes steady progress in motor development. The changes are not as dramatic as the beginning of walking, but they enable the child to acquire skills that markedly increase his independence and exploratory ability.

Table 7.1 lists the major motor skills that emerge in these preschool years. What are most striking are the impressive gains the child makes in large-muscle skills. By age 5 or 6, children are running, jumping, hopping, galloping, climbing, and skipping. They can ride a tricycle; some can ride a two-wheeled bike. The degree of confidence with which the 5-year-old uses her body for these movements is impressive, particularly in contrast to the somewhat unsteady movements of the 18-month-old.

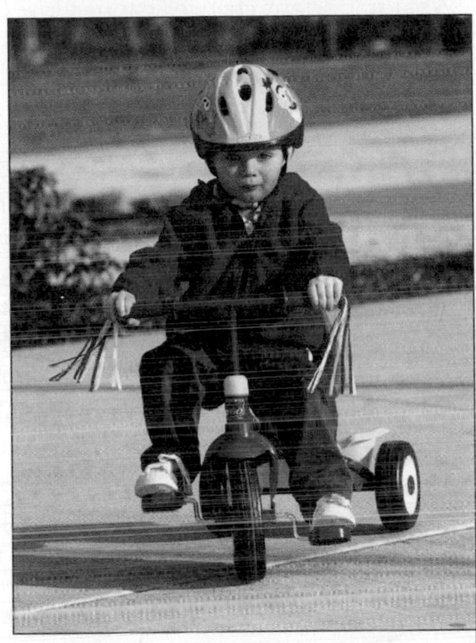

Off he goes, into greater independence. A child this age, especially one with secure attachment, is far more confident about being at a distance from his safe base.

Fine motor skills also improve in these years, but not to the same level of confidence. Three-year-olds can indeed pick up Cheerios, and 5-year-olds can thread beads on a string. But even at age 5 or 6, children are not highly skilled at such fine-motor tasks as using a pencil or crayon or cutting accurately with scissors. When a young child uses a crayon or a pencil, he uses his whole body—the tongue is moving and the whole arm and back are involved in the writing or drawing motion.

These are important facts for teachers of young children to understand. It is the rare kindergartner who is really skilled at such fine-motor tasks as writing letters. Younger preschoolers, of course, are even less skilled at these tasks. However, a "wait and see" strategy isn't the best approach to helping children learn to write letters and draw simple forms. Researchers have found that early training, beginning at about age 2½, can accelerate the rate at which young children acquire school-related fine-motor skills such as writing letters (Callaghan & Rankin, 2002).

Table 7.1 Milestones of Motor Development from Age 2 to Age 6

Age	Gross Motor Skills	Fine Motor Skills
18–24 months	Runs awkwardly; climbs stairs with both feet on each step; pushes and pulls boxes or wheeled toys	Shows clear hand preference; stacks four to six blocks; turns pages one at a time; picks up things without overbalancing; unscrews lid on a jar
2–3	Runs easily; climbs on furniture unaided; hauls and shoves big toys around obstacles	Picks up small objects; throws small ball while standing
3–4	Walks up stairs one foot per step; skips on two feet; walks on tiptoe; pedals and steers tricycle; walks in any direction pulling large toys	Catches large ball between outstretched arms; cuts paper with scissors; holds pencil between thumb and fingers
4–5	Walks up and down stairs one foot per step; stands, runs, and walks on tiptoe	Strikes ball with bat; kicks and catches ball; threads beads on a string; grasps pencil properly
5–6	Skips on alternate feet; walks on a line; slides, swings	Plays ball games well; threads needle and sews large stitches

(*Sources:* Connolly & Dalgleish, 1989; The Diagram Group, 1977; Fagard & Jacquet, 1989; Mathew & Cook, 1990; Thomas, 1990.)

Training effects are evident in studies of children's drawing as well (Callaghan & Rankin, 2002). Nevertheless, drawing appears to follow the developmental sequence shown in Figure 7.1, even when accelerated by training (Toomela, 1999). Moreover, the effectiveness of training seems to depend on how well young children understand the figures that experimenters attempt to teach them how to draw. That is, a child who has some grasp of what letters are will be more responsive to training in letter-writing (Callaghan, 1999). Thus, older preschoolers—those beyond age 3—benefit more from training than younger children. Moreover, learning to write letters appears to help children more fully understand them (Callaghan & Rankin, 2002). Thus, research examining young children's writing demonstrates that, in some cases, physical and cognitive development are interactive processes.

Learning Objective 7.2

What important changes happen in the brain during these years?

The Brain and Nervous System

Brain growth, synapse formation, and myelinization continue in early childhood, although at a slower pace than in infancy. However, the slower rate of growth should not be taken to mean that brain development is nearly complete. Indeed, a number of important neurological milestones are reached between the ages of 2 and 6. It is likely that these milestones represent the neurological underpinnings of the remarkable advances in thinking and language that occur during this period.

corpus callosum the membrane that connects the right and left hemispheres of the cerebral cortex

lateralization the process through which brain functions are divided between the two hemispheres of the cerebral cortex

Lateralization The **corpus callosum**, the brain structure through which the left and right sides of the cerebral cortex communicate, grows and matures more during the early childhood years than in any other period of life. The growth of this structure accompanies the functional specialization of the left and right hemispheres of the cerebral cortex. This process is called **lateralization.** Figure 7.2 shows how brain functions are lateralized in most people.

Neuroscientists suspect that our genes dictate which functions will be lateralized and which will not be. However, experience shapes the pace at which lateralization occurs. For example, in 95% of humans, language functions that enable us to understand the mean-

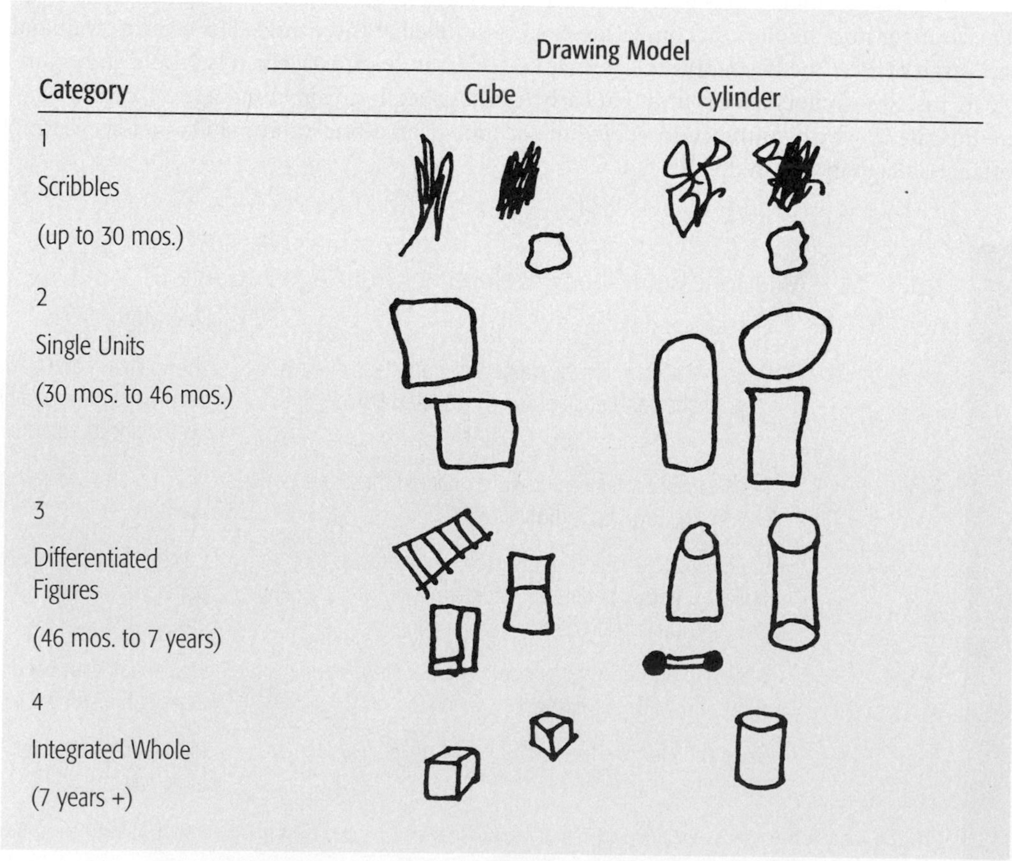

Figure 7.1
Stages in Children's Drawing

Examples of drawings in each category of two object forms.

(*Source*: From "Drawing development: Stages in the representation of a cube and a cylinder" by A. Toomela from *Child Development*, Vol. 70, No. 5, Page 1141. Sept/Oct 1999. Reprinted by permission.)

ings of words and the structure of sentences are carried out in the left hemisphere. Studies of fetal responses to different kinds of sounds (i.e., language and music) show that this pattern is evident even before we are born (de Lacoste, Horvath, & Woodward, 1991). The fact that left-side processing of language appears so early in life suggests that lateralization of these functions is dictated by our genes.

Nevertheless, language functions are not as fully lateralized in fetuses as they are in children and adults. Moreover, research indicates that the degree to which these language functions are relegated to the left side of the brain is linked to language production. Preschoolers who display the most advanced language skills in their everyday speech, as well as on standardized tests, show the highest levels of left-side lateralization of these functions (Mills, Coffey-Corina, & Neville, 1994). Of course, we don't know whether children acquire language more rapidly *because* their brains are lateralizing at a faster pace. It seems that the reverse is just as likely to be true—namely, that some children's brains are lateralizing language functions more rapidly because they are learning language faster. But such findings suggest that maturation and experience are both at work in the lateralization process.

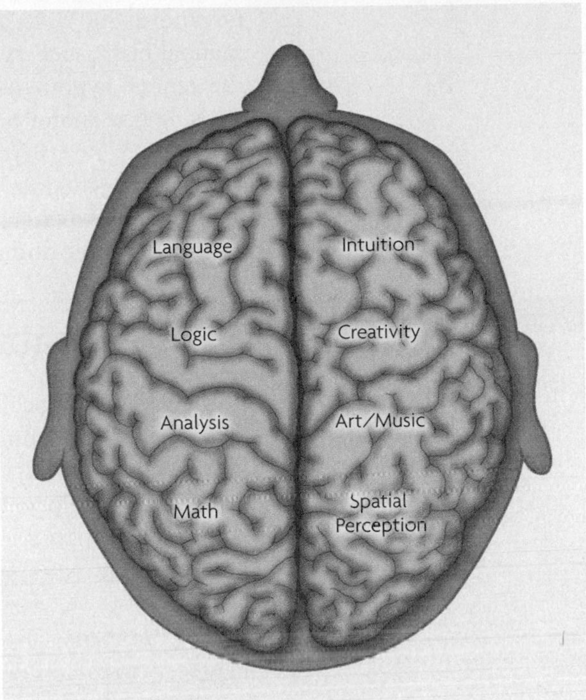

Figure 7.2
Lateralization of Brain Functions

Brain functions are lateralized as shown in the figure. Neurologists think that the basic outline of lateralization is genetically determined, whereas the specific timing of the lateralization of each function is determined by an interaction of genes and experiences.

The Reticular Formation and the Hippocampus Myelinization of the neurons of the reticular formation, which you will remember from Chapter 4 is the brain structure that regulates attention and concentration, is another important milestone of early childhood brain development. Neurons in other parts of the brain, such as the *hippocampus*, are also myelinated during this period (Tanner, 1990). The **hippocampus** is involved in the transfer of information to long term memory. Maturation of this brain structure probably accounts for improvements in memory function across the preschool years (Rolls, 2000). Moreover, maturation of the connections between the hippocampus and the cerebral cortex are probably responsible for our inability to remember much about the first three years of life, a phenomenon called *infantile amnesia* (Zola & Squire, 2003). Note that infantile amnesia does not involve a complete absence of early memories; thus, some people do have legitimate memories of very early experiences. Typically, though, memories of events that were laid down in the brain prior to age 3 are small in number and fragmentary in character. And, as Piaget's early memory experience suggests, children's early memories are strongly influenced by the verbal recollections of adults that children hear later in their lives, even when those "recollections" turn out to be entirely false.

Handedness **Handedness**, the tendency to rely primarily on the right or left hand, is another neurological milestone of the 2- to 6-year-old period (Tanner, 1990). Scientists used to assume that right-handedness increased among humans along with literacy. The idea was that parents and teachers encouraged children to use their right hands when teaching them how to write. In this way, right-handedness became a custom that was passed on from one generation to the next through instruction.

By examining skeletons that predate the invention of writing, archaeologists have determined that the proportions of right- and left-handers were about the same in illiterate ancient populations as among modern humans (83% right-handed, 14% left-handed, and 3% ambidextrous) (Steele & Mayes, 1995). These findings suggest that the prevalence of right-handedness is likely to be the result of genetic inheritance. Moreover, geneticists at the National Cancer Institute (NCI) have recently identified a dominant gene for right-handedness, which they believe to be so common in the human population that most people receive a copy of it from both parents (Talan, 1998).

Further evidence for the genetic hypothesis can be found in studies demonstrating that handedness appears very early in life—often before the first birthday—although it doesn't become well established until the preschool years (Stroganova, Posikera, Pushina, &

hippocampus a brain structure that is important in learning

handedness a strong preference for using one hand or the other that develops between 3 and 5 years of age

Orekhova, 2003). Research comparing children's right-hand and left-hand performance on manual tasks, such as moving pegs from one place to another on a pegboard, also supports the genetic hypothesis. Most of these studies show that older children are better at accomplishing fine-motor tasks with the nondominant hand than younger children are (Dellatolas et al., 2003; Roy, Bryden, & Cavill, 2003). Findings from studies comparing nondominant hand use in children and adults follow the same pattern (Annett, 2003; Cavill & Bryden, 2003). Thus, experience in using the hands appears to moderate, rather than strengthen, the advantage of the dominant over the nondominant hand.

Learning Objective 7.3
What are the nutritional and health care needs of young children?

Health and Wellness

Young children continue to require periodic medical check-ups as well as a variety of immunizations. Just as they do with infants, doctors monitor preschoolers' growth and motor development. At the same time, doctors and nurses often serve as parents' first source of help with children who have sensory or developmental disabilities that were not diagnosed in infancy (Sulkes, 1998). Further, health care professionals can help parents deal with everyday issues, such as the kinds of sleep problems discussed in the Real World feature.

Eating Patterns Because children grow more slowly during the early childhood years, they may seem to eat less than when they were babies. Moreover, food aversions often develop during the preschool years. For example, a child who loved carrots as an infant may refuse to eat them at age 2 or 3. Consequently, conflicts between young children and their parents often focus on eating behavior (Wong, 1993).

Nutritionists point out that it is important that parents not become so concerned about the quantity of food a child consumes that they cater to his preferences for sweets and other high-calorie or high-fat foods (Wong, 1993). Many children acquire eating habits during these years that lead to later weight problems. Surveys show that 15% of children aged 2 to 5 are overweight and another 16% are at risk of becoming so by the time they reach school age (Pediatric Nutrition Surveillance, 2005). Thus, nutritionists recommend keeping a variety of nutritious foods on hand and allowing a child's appetite to be a good guide to how much food he should eat. Of course, this approach works only if young children's access to sweets and other attractive, but nonnutritious, foods is limited.

Immunizing young children against a variety of diseases is an important goal of routine health care for this age group.

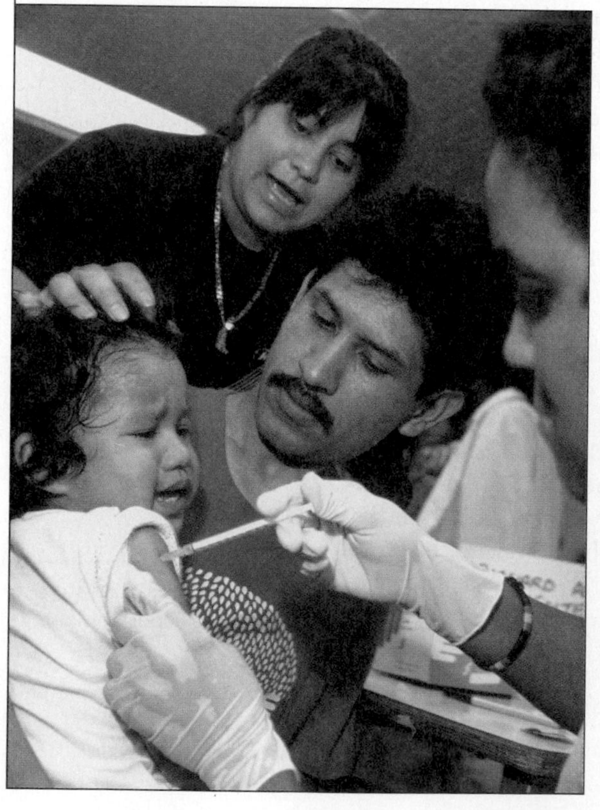

Parents should also keep in mind that young children eat only about half as much food as adults, and, unlike adults, many don't consume the majority of their daily calories at regular meals (Wong, 1993). Nutritionists suggest that concerned parents keep a daily record of what their children are actually eating for a week. In most cases, parents will find that children are consuming plenty of food.

Illnesses and Accidents In the United States, the average preschooler has four to six brief bouts of sickness each year, most often colds or the flu (Sulkes, 1998). Children who are experiencing high levels of stress or family upheaval are more likely to become ill. For example, a large nationwide study in the United States showed that children living in single-parent homes have more asthma, more headaches, and a generally higher vulnerability to illnesses of many types than do those living with both biological parents (Dawson, 1991).

Another danger for children is accidents. In any given year, about a quarter of all children under 5 in the United States have at least one accident that requires some kind of medical attention, and accidents are the major cause of death in preschool and school-age children (Fein, Darbin, & Selbst, 2002). At every age, accidents are more common among boys than among girls, presumably because of their more active and daring styles of play. The majority of acci-

THE REAL WORLD

A Good Night's Sleep for Kids (and Parents, Too!)

Every night Luis and Ramona go through the same ordeal when they put their 3-year-old son, Manny, to bed. The boy begs to sleep with them, but they always refuse. After four or five cycles of begging and sobbing, usually spread over at least an hour, Manny finally becomes so exhausted that he can no longer stay awake. Despite his parents' consistency, Manny often gets his way. He wakes up every night around 2:00 a.m. and attempts to slip into his parents' bed without their noticing. Sometimes Luis or Ramona awaken and take him back to bed, and, in the process, initiate another round of the begging-sobbing cycle that Manny exhibits at bedtime. Other times, they are sleeping so soundly that Manny's late-night invasion goes unnoticed, and they awaken to find him in their bed the next morning.

Manny's nighttime behavior is all too familiar to many parents of preschoolers. In operant conditioning terms, the experience of getting to sleep with parents reinforces the child's awakening. Often, too, the reinforcement occurs on a variable schedule, that is, just as Manny does, the child gets to sleep with the parents some nights but not others. Behavior that is reinforced on a variable schedule is extremely difficult to suppress. Consequently, pediatricians (e.g., Coury, 2002) recommend that parents work to prevent such patterns from becoming established by adopting effective bedtime practices that include the following:

- Provide the child with a structured, predictable daytime schedule, and stick to it as closely as possible every day.
- Set a regular bedtime that is 8 to 10 hours before the desired waking time.
- Discontinue daytime naps for a child who has difficulty getting to sleep or who awakens too early in the morning.
- Establish a routine set of "settling activities" such as a bath, story book, and goodnight kiss, and resist the child's efforts to prolong or modify the routine.
- Provide the child with a transitional object such as a doll or stuffed animal that is reserved especially for bedtime.

Making such adjustments can be challenging, especially when the child actively resists them. However, research confirms that these kinds of changes can significantly reduce sleep-related conflicts (Borkowski, Hunter, & Johnson, 2001). Thus, a few days or even weeks of persistence on the parents' part may pay off in years of undisturbed sleep for parents and children alike.

Questions for Reflection

1. If you were Manny's parent, what strategies would you use to try to prevent him from awakening at night and getting into your bed?
2. How might you explain how variable reinforcement contributes to the behavior of nighttime awakening in preschoolers to a parent by using gambling (i.e., sometimes you win, sometime you lose) as an analogy?

dents among children in this age range—falls, cuts, accidental poisonings, and the like—occur at home. Automobile accidents are the second greatest source of injuries among preschoolers. However, they are the leading cause of death in this age group (Fein, Durbin, & Selbst, 2002). Experts point out that, while parents obviously can't keep preschoolers entirely free from injuries, many are preventable. Children can wear protective gear while riding tricycles and bicycles, and the proper use of car seats and restraint systems greatly reduces death rates that are due to auto accidents.

Abuse and Neglect

Learning Objective 7.4
What factors contribute to abuse and neglect, and how do these traumas affect children's development?

Legally, *child abuse* is defined as physical or psychological injury that results from an adult's intentional exposure of a child to potentially harmful physical stimuli, sexual acts, or neglect (Sulkes, 1998). *Neglect* is the failure of caregivers to provide emotional and physical support for a child. However, it is fairly difficult to define child abuse and neglect in a practical sense. For example, if a parent allows a 2-year-old to play outdoors alone and the child falls and breaks her arm, has the injury resulted from an accident or from neglect? Such are the dilemmas confronting medical professionals, who are bound by law to report suspected cases of abuse and neglect to authorities. Doctors and nurses are reluctant to accuse parents of abuse in such situations, but they are also concerned about protecting children from further injury (Sulkes, 1998). In addition, cultural values concerning acceptable and unacceptable treatment of children make it extremely difficult to define abuse so that it is possible to study child maltreatment cross-culturally. What is abusive in one culture may not be so regarded in another.

Prevalence In the United States, most cases of abuse and neglect that result in serious injury or death involve children under age 4 (CDC, 2006). Because of the inherent difficulties in defining abuse, it is difficult to say just how many children suffer abuse. However, research suggests that 1–5% of U.S. children are treated by medical professionals for injuries resulting from abuse every year (CDC, 2006). Moreover, physicians estimate that abuse and/or neglect are responsible for about 10% of emergency room visits involving children under age 5 (Sulkes, 1998). Sadly, about 2,000 infants and children die as a result of abuse and/or neglect each year in the United States (CDC, 2006).

The majority of child abuse cases involve physical injuries (Sulkes, 1998). Others involve sexual abuse or are the result of neglect, such as underfeeding an infant. Other kinds of abuse include failure to obtain medical attention for an illness or injury, providing inadequate supervision, and drugging or poisoning children.

Risk Factors One useful model for explaining abuse classifies its causes into four broad categories: sociocultural factors, characteristics of the child, characteristics of the abuser, and family stresses (Bittner & Newberger, 1981). The main idea of this model is that episodes of abuse are typically precipitated by everyday interactions between parents and children—for example, when a parent reprimands a young child for spilling a glass of milk. At the time of the episode, several causal factors work together to produce abusive responses in parents. Thus, what differentiates abusive from nonabusive parents, according to this model, is the presence of a number of risk factors that shape how they respond to the ordinary stresses of parenting.

Sociocultural factors include personal or cultural values that regard physical abuse of children as morally acceptable. Parents are more likely to be abusive if they believe that there are few, if any, moral limits on what they can do to their children physically. Sociologists suggest that such beliefs stem from cultural traditions that regard children as property rather than human beings with individual rights (Mooney, Knox, & Schacht, 2000). Moreover, parents who live in communities where others share and act on these beliefs are more likely to be abusive.

Several characteristics of children or parents may set the stage for child abuse. For example, children with physical or mental disabilities or those who have difficult temperaments are more likely to be abused than others (Sulkes, 1998). Parents who are depressed, lack parenting skills and knowledge, have a history of abuse themselves, or are substance abusers are more likely to abuse or neglect their children (Eiden, Foote & Schuetze, 2007; Emery & Laumann-Billings, 1998). Research also shows that, compared to nonabusers, parents who are abusive are limited in their ability to empathize with others and to control their emotional reactions to others' behavior (Wiehe, 2003). In addition, mothers' live-in male partners who are not biologically related to the children in a household are more likely than biological fathers to be abusers (Daly & Wilson, 1996). Family stressors include factors such as poverty, unemployment, and interparental conflict (CDC, 2006; Sulkes, 1998). Keep in mind that no single factor produces abuse, but the presence of several of these variables in a particular family significantly increases the chances that the children will experience abuse.

Consequences of Abuse Some children who are frequently or severely abused develop *post-traumatic stress disorder (PTSD)* (Kendall-Tackett, Williams, & Finkelhor, 1993; Margolin & Gordis, 2000; Morrissette, 1999; Pynoos, Steinberg, & Wraith, 1995). This disorder involves extreme levels of anxiety, flashback memories of episodes of abuse, nightmares, and other sleep disturbances. Abused children are also more likely than nonabused peers to exhibit delays in all domains of development (Cicchetti, Rogosch, Maughan, Toth, & Bruce, 2003; Glaser, 2000; Malinosky-Rummell & Hansen, 1993; Rogosch, Cicchetti, & Aber, 1995).

On the positive side, children who are physically neglected typically recover rapidly once the abuse stops. In studies involving abused and/or neglected children who were placed in foster care, developmentalists have found that differences between abused and nonabused children in physical, cognitive, and social development disappear within 1 year (Olivan, 2003). As you might suspect, though, these studies suggest that the critical factor in the catching-up process is the quality of the post-abuse environment.

Prevention Preventing abuse begins with education. Informing parents about the potential consequences of some physical acts, such as the link between shaking an infant and brain damage, may help. In addition, parents need to know that injuring children is a crime, even if the intention is to discipline them. Parenting classes, perhaps as a required part of high school curricula, can help inform parents or future parents about principles of child development and appropriate methods of discipline (Mooney et al., 2000).

Another approach to prevention of abuse involves identification of families at risk. Physicians, nurses, and other professionals who routinely interact with parents of infants and young children have a particularly important role to play in this kind of prevention. Parents who seem to have problems attaching to their children can sometimes be identified during medical office visits. These parents can be referred to parenting classes or to social workers for help. Similarly, parents may ask doctors or nurses how to discipline their children. Such questions provide professionals with opportunities to discuss which practices are appropriate and which are not.

Finally, children who are abused must be protected from further injury. This can be accomplished through vigorous enforcement of existing child abuse laws. As noted, health professionals must report suspected abuse. However, in most states, ordinary citizens are also legally required to report suspected abuse. And reporting is only part of the picture. Once abuse is reported, steps must be taken to protect injured children from suspected abusers.

Critical Thinking

1. Ask your friends and fellow students to estimate the age at which brain development is complete. How do you think people's assumptions about the completeness of brain development affect their attitudes and behavior toward children?

Cognitive Changes

If you were to visit a preschool and go from classroom to classroom observing children in free play, what kind of activities do you think you would see? If you visited the classrooms in "chronological" order, you would see a progression of activities ranging from simple forms of constructive and pretend play among the 2-year-olds to sophisticated role-play and debates about the rules of board games among the 5- and 6-year-olds (see the Research Report on page 184). Forms of play change over the early childhood years because children's thinking changes. At the beginning of the period, children are just beginning to learn how to accomplish goals. By the time they reach age 5 or 6, they are proficient at manipulating symbols and can make accurate judgments about others' thoughts, feelings, and behavior.

Piaget's Preoperational Stage

Learning Objective 7.5

List the characteristics of children's thought during Piaget's preoperational stage.

According to Piaget, children acquire the **semiotic (symbolic) function** between the ages of 18 and 24 months. The semiotic function is the understanding that one object or behavior can represent another—a picture of a chair represents a real chair, a child's pretending to feed a doll stands for a parent's feeding a baby, and so on. Once this understanding has been achieved, children are in Piaget's **preoperational stage**.

During the preoperational stage, children become proficient at using symbols for thinking and communicating but still have difficulty thinking logically. At age 2 or 3, children begin to pretend in their play (Walker-Andrews & Kahana-Kalman, 1999). A broom may become a horse, or a block may become a train. Cross-cultural research suggests that this kind of object use by 2- to 3-year-olds in pretend play is universal (Haight et al., 1999). Young children also show signs of increasing proficiency at symbol use in their growing ability to understand models, maps, and graphic symbols such as letters (Callaghan, 1999; DeLoache, 1995).

Although young children are remarkably good at using symbols, their reasoning about the world is often flawed. For example, Piaget described the preoperational child's tendency to look at things entirely from her own point of view, a characteristic Piaget called **egocentrism** (Piaget, 1954). This term does not suggest that the young child is a self-centered egomaniac. It simply means that she assumes that everyone sees the world as she does. For example, while riding in the back seat of a car, a 3- or 4-year-old may suddenly call out "Look at that, Mom!"—not realizing that Mom can't see the object she's talking about. Moreover, the child doesn't realize that the car's motion prevents Mom from ever seeing the object in question. As a result, the youngster may become frustrated in her attempts to communicate with her mother about what she saw.

semiotic (symbolic) function the understanding that one object or behavior can represent another

preoperational stage Piaget's second stage of cognitive development, during which children become proficient in the use of symbols in thinking and communicating but still have difficulty thinking logically

egocentrism the young child's belief that everyone sees and experiences the world the way she does

RESEARCH REPORT

Children's Play and Cognitive Development

Careful observation of young children's play behaviors can provide preschool teachers and parents with useful information about cognitive development, because the forms of play change in very obvious ways during the years from 1 to 6, following a sequence that closely matches Piaget's stages (Rubin, Fein, & Vandenberg, 1983).

Constructive Play. By age 2 or so, children use objects to build or construct things, as the child in the photo below is doing. Piaget hypothesized that this kind of play is the foundation of children's understanding of the rules that govern physical reality. For example, through block play, they come to understand that a tower that is broad at the top and narrow at the bottom will be unstable.

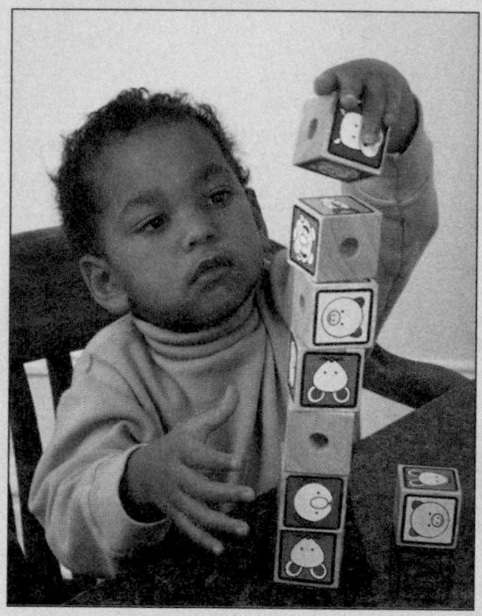

First Pretend Play. Piaget believed that pretend play was an important indicator of a child's capacity to use symbols. The first instances of such pretending are usually simple, like pretending to drink from a toy cup. Most children exhibit some pretending at around 12 months. Between 15 and 21 months, the recipient of the pretend action becomes another person or a doll. This change signals a significant movement away from sensorimotor and toward true symbolic thinking.

Substitute Pretend Play. Between 2 and 3 years of age, children begin to use objects to stand for something altogether different. For

example, the 30-month-old boy in the photo above is using a carrot as an imaginary violin and a stick as a bow. Children this age may use a broom as a horse or make "trucks" out of blocks.

Sociodramatic Play. In the preschool years, children engage in mutual pretense. For example, in playing doctor, as the children in the photo below are doing, participants fill roles such as "doctor," "nurse," and "patient." At first, children simply take up these roles; later, they name the various roles and may give each other explicit instructions about the right way to pretend a particular role. By age 4, virtually all children engage in some play of this type (Howes & Matheson, 1992).

Rule-Governed Play. By age 5 or 6, children prefer rule-governed pretending and formal games. For example, children of this age use rules such as "Whoever is smallest has to be the baby" when playing "house" and play simple games such as Red Rover and Red Light, Green Light. Younger children play these games as well, but 5- and 6-year-olds better understand their rules and will follow them for longer periods of time. Piaget suggested that older preschoolers' preference for rule-governed play indicates that they are about to make the transition to the next stage of cognitive development, *concrete operations*, in which they will acquire an understanding of rules (Piaget & Inhelder, 1969).

Questions for Critical Analysis

1. Which of the research methods discussed in Chapter 1 is best suited to the study of age-related changes in children's play activities?
2. Many children have imaginary friends (a phenomenon that is considered to be entirely normal by child psychologists). In which of the stages of play would you expect to first see children inventing imaginary playmates?

Figure 7.3 illustrates a classic experiment in which most young children demonstrate this kind of egocentrism. The child is shown a three-dimensional scene with mountains of different sizes and colors. From a set of drawings, she picks out the one that shows the scene the way she sees it. Most preschoolers can do this without much difficulty. Then the examiner asks the

child to pick out the drawing that shows how someone else sees the scene, such as a doll or the examiner. At this point, most preschoolers choose the drawing that shows their own view of the mountains (Flavell, Everett, Croft, & Flavell, 1981; Gzesh & Surber, 1985).

Piaget also pointed out that the preschool-aged child's thinking is guided by the appearance of objects—a theme that still dominates the research on children of this age. Children may believe, for example, that any moving object is an animal of some kind. This kind of thinking reflects the child's tendency to think of the world in terms of one variable at a time, a type of thought Piaget called **centration**. Because of centration, the child reaches the conclusion that all moving objects are animals through a series of false conclusions. The premise on which these conclusions are based is the fact that it is evident in everyday interactions with the world that all animals move—or, as scientists put it, have the capacity for *locomotion* (self-movement). But the preoperational thinker isn't capable of thinking of objects in terms of both their motion and their capacity for self-movement. Thus, movement, without regard to any other relevant characteristic of objects, becomes the sole criterion for distinguishing between living and nonliving objects. As a result, a child may fear a leaf that blows across the playground because he believes that the leaf is trying to follow him. Piaget used the term *animism* to refer to this particular product of preoperational logic.

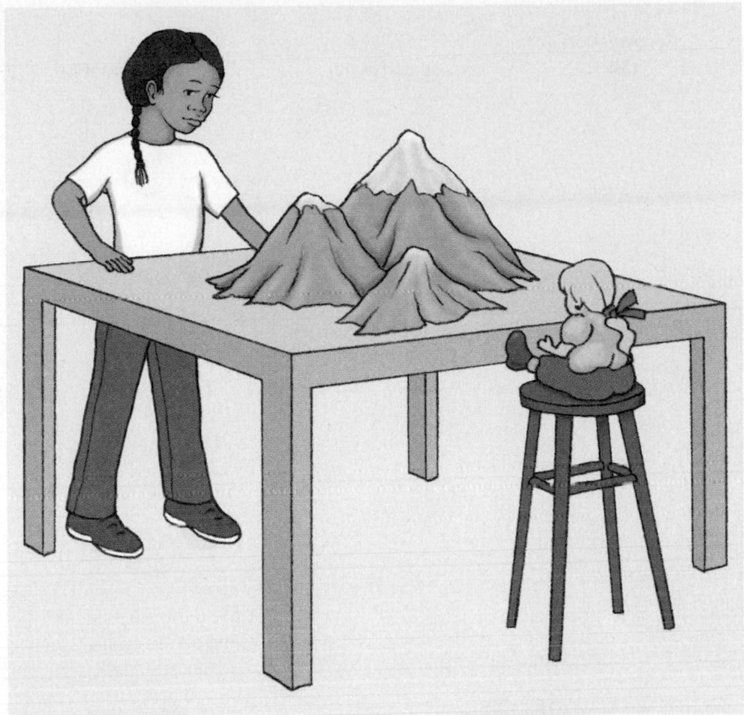

Figure 7.3
Piaget's Three Mountains Task

The experimental situation shown here is similar to one Piaget used to study egocentrism in children. The child is asked to pick out a picture that shows how the mountains look to her and then to pick out a picture that shows how the mountains look to the doll.

As you learned in the Research Report in Chapter 2, some of Piaget's most famous experiments deal with a cognitive process called **conservation**, the understanding that matter can change in appearance without changing in quantity. Because of centration and irreversibility, children rarely show any kind of conservation before age 5. When they do begin to understand this concept, they demonstrate their understanding with arguments based on three characteristics of appearance-only transformations of matter. The first of these is *identity*, the knowledge that quantities are constant unless matter is added to or subtracted from them. The second is *compensation*, the understanding that all relevant characteristics of the appearance of a given quantity of matter must be taken into account before reaching a conclusion about whether the quantity has changed. The third is *reversibility*, the capacity to mentally compare the transformed appearance of a given quantity of matter to its original appearance. Some of the conservation tasks Piaget used, along with children's typical responses to them, are shown in Figure 7.4 (on page 186). As you can see, assessing a child's stage of cognitive development involves finding out how she arrived at her answer to a question, not just evaluating the answer as right or wrong.

Challenges to Piaget's View

Learning Objective 7.6
How has recent research challenged Piaget's view of this period?

Studies of conservation have generally confirmed Piaget's observations (e.g., Ciancio et al., 1999; Gelman, 1972; Sophian, 1995; Wellman, 1982). Although younger children can demonstrate some understanding of conservation if the task is made very simple, most children cannot consistently solve conservation and other kinds of logical problems until at least age 5. However, evidence suggests that preschoolers are a great deal more cognitively sophisticated than Piaget thought.

Despite their egocentrism, children as young as 2 and 3 appear to have at least some ability to understand that another person sees things or experiences things differently than they do. For example, children this age adapt their speech or their play to the demands of a companion. They play differently with older and younger playmates and talk differently to a younger child (Brownell, 1990; Guralnik & Paul-Brown, 1984).

centration the young child's tendency to think of the world in terms of one variable at a time

conservation the understanding that matter can change in appearance without changing in quantity

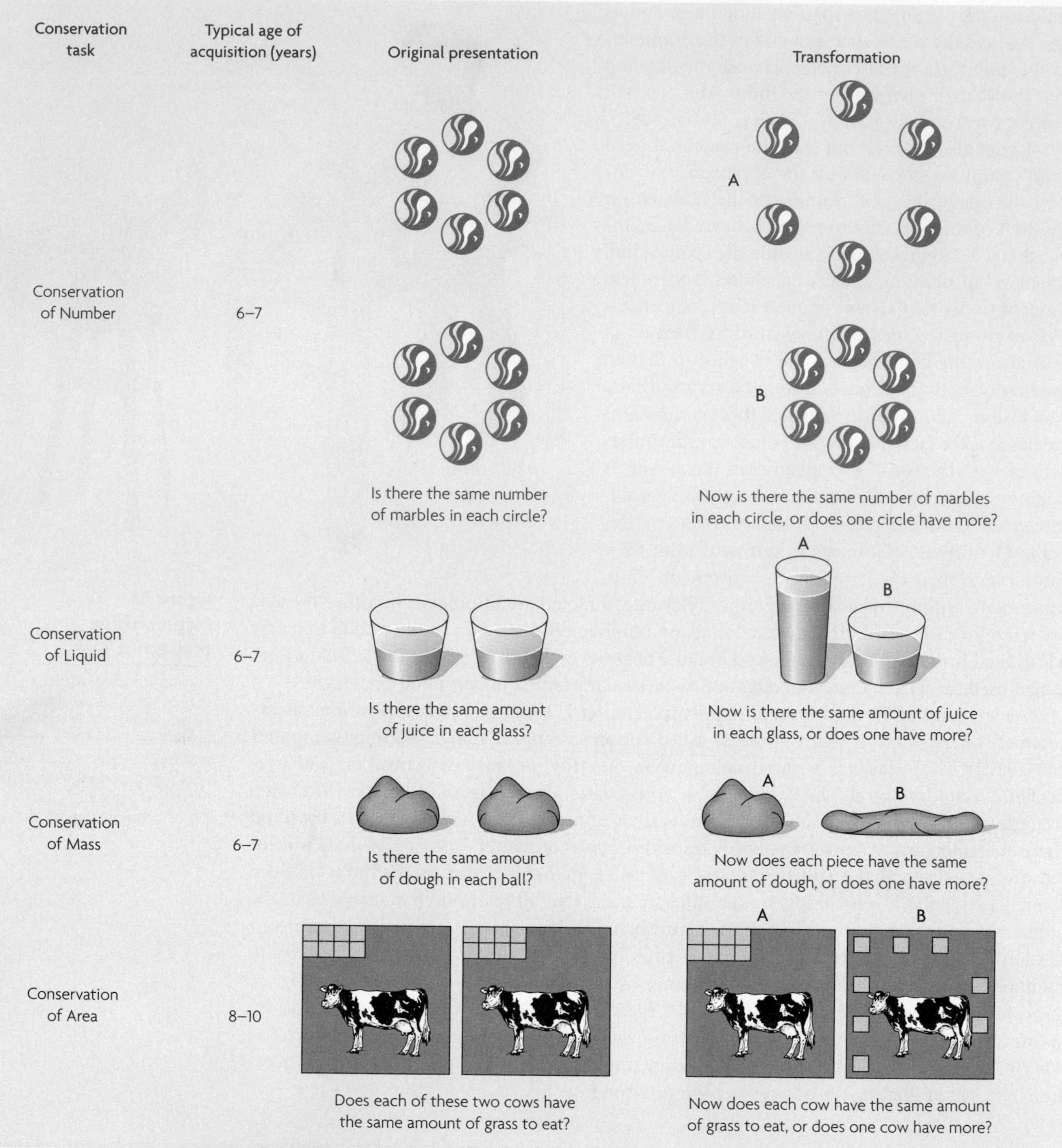

Conservation task
Typical age of acquisition (years)
Original presentation
Transformation
Conservation of Number
6–7
A
B
Is there the same number of marbles in each circle?
Now is there the same number of marbles in each circle, or does one circle have more?
Conservation of Liquid
6–7
A
B
Is there the same amount of juice in each glass?
Now is there the same amount of juice in each glass, or does one have more?
Conservation of Mass
6–7
A
B
Is there the same amount of dough in each ball?
Now does each piece have the same amount of dough, or does one have more?
Conservation of Area
8–10
A
B
Does each of these two cows have the same amount of grass to eat?
Now does each cow have the same amount of grass to eat, or does one cow have more?

Figure 7.4
Piaget's Conservation Tasks

Piaget's research involved several kinds of conservation tasks. He classified children's thinking as concrete operational with respect to a particular task if they could correctly solve the problem and provide a concrete operational reason for their answer. For example, if a child said, "The two circles of marbles are the same because you didn't add any or take any away when you moved them," the response was judged to be concrete operational. Conversely, if a child said, "The two circles are the same, but I don't know why," the response was not classified as concrete operational.

However, such understanding is clearly not perfect at this young age. Developmental psychologist John Flavell has proposed two levels of perspective-taking ability. At level 1, the child knows that other people experience things differently. At level 2, the child develops a whole series of complex rules for figuring out precisely what the other person sees or experiences (Flavell, Green, & Flavell, 1990). At 2 and 3 years old, children have level 1 knowledge but not level 2; level 2 knowledge begins to be evident in 4- and 5-year-olds.

For example, a child of 4 or 5 understands that another person feels sad if she fails or happy if she succeeds. The preschool child also begins to figure out that unpleasant emotions occur in situations in which there is a gap between desire and reality. Sadness, for example, normally occurs when someone loses something that is valued or fails to acquire some desired object (Harris, 1989).

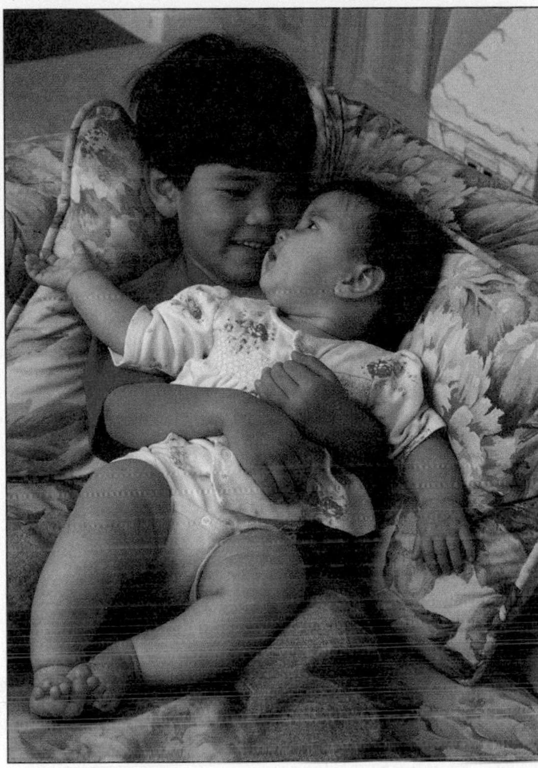
This young child is able to adapt his speech to the needs of his younger sibling, one of many indications that preschoolers are less egocentric than Piaget thought.

Studies of preschoolers' understanding of emotion have also challenged Piaget's description of the young child's egocentrism. For example, between 2 and 6, children learn to regulate or modulate their expressions of emotion to conform to others' expectations (Dunn, 1994). In addition, preschool children use emotional expressions such as crying or smiling to get things they want. These behaviors are obviously based at least in part on a growing awareness that other people judge your feelings by what they see you expressing. These behaviors wouldn't occur if children were completely incapable of looking at their own behavior from another person's perspective, as Piaget's assertions about egocentrism would suggest.

The young child's movement away from egocentrism seems to be part of a much broader change in her understanding of appearance and reality. Flavell has studied this understanding in a variety of ways (Flavell, Green, & Flavell, 1989; Flavell, Green, Wahl, & Flavell, 1987). In the most famous Flavell procedure, the experimenter shows the child a sponge that has been painted to look like a rock. Three-year-olds will say either that the object looks like a sponge and is a sponge or that it looks like a rock and is a rock. But 4- and 5-year-olds can distinguish between appearance and reality; they realize that the item looks like a rock but is a sponge (Flavell, 1986). Thus, the older children understand that the same object can be represented differently, depending on one's point of view.

Theories of Mind

Learning Objective 7.7
What is a theory of mind, and how does it develop?

Evidence like that described in the previous section has led a number of theorists to propose that the 4- or 5-year-old has developed a new and quite sophisticated **theory of mind**, or a set of ideas that explains other people's ideas, beliefs, desires, and behavior (Flavell, 1999).

Understanding Thoughts, Desires, and Beliefs The theory of mind does not spring forth full-blown at age 4. Toddlers as young as 18 months have some beginning understanding of the fact that people (but not inanimate objects) operate with goals and intentions (Meltzoff, 1995). By age 3, children understand some aspects of the link between people's thinking or feeling and their behavior. For example, they know that a person who wants something will try to get it. They also know that a person may still want something even if she can't have it (Lillard & Flavell, 1992). But they do not yet understand the basic principle that each person's actions are based on her or his own representation of reality, which may differ from what is "really" there. It is this new aspect of the theory of mind that clearly emerges between 3 and 5.

Studies that examine the **false belief principle** illustrate 3-year-olds' shortcomings in this area (Flavell, 1999). In one such study, children were presented with a box on which there were pictures of different kinds of candy. The experimenter shook the box to demonstrate that there was something inside and then asked 3- and 4-year-olds to guess what they would find if they opened it. Regardless of age, the children guessed that the box contained candy. Upon opening the box, though, the children discovered that it actually contained crayons. The experimenter then asked the children to predict what another child who saw the closed box would believe was in it. Three-year-olds thought that the child would believe that the box contained crayons, but the 4-year-olds realized that the pictures of candy on the box would lead the child to have a false belief that the box contained candy.

theory of mind a set of ideas constructed by a child or adult to explain other people's ideas, beliefs, desires, and behavior

false belief principle an understanding that enables a child to look at a situation from another person's point of view and determine what kind of information will cause that person to have a false belief

Still, there is much that the 4- or 5-year-old doesn't yet grasp about other people's thinking. The child of this age understands that other people think, but does not yet understand that other people can think about him. The 4-year-old understands "I know that you know." But he does not yet fully understand that this process is reciprocal—namely, "You know that I know."

Understanding of the reciprocal nature of thought seems to develop between age 5 and age 7 for most children. This would seem to be a particularly important understanding, because it is probably necessary for the creation of genuinely reciprocal friendships, which begin to emerge in the elementary school years (Sullivan, Zaitchik, & Tager-Flusberg, 1994). In fact, the rate at which an individual preschooler develops a theory of mind is a good predictor of her social skills both later in early childhood and during the school years (Moore, Barresi, & Thompson, 1998; Watson, Nixon, Wilson, & Capage, 1999).

Furthermore, it is not until about age 6 that most children realize that knowledge can be derived through inference. For example, researchers in one study showed 4- and 6-year-olds two toys of different colors (Pillow, 1999). Next, they placed the toys in separate opaque containers. They then opened one of the containers and showed the toy to a puppet. When asked whether the puppet now knew which color toy was in each container, only the 6-year-olds said yes.

Influences on the Development of a Theory of Mind Developmentalists have found that a child's theory of mind is correlated with his performance on Piaget's tasks, as well as on more recently developed problems designed to assess egocentrism and appearance/reality (Melot & Houde, 1998; Yirmiya & Shulman, 1996). In addition, pretend play seems to contribute to theory of mind development. Shared pretense with other children, in particular, is strongly related to theory of mind (Dockett & Smith, 1995; Schwebel, Rosen, & Singer, 1999). Furthermore, children whose parents discuss emotion-provoking past events with them develop a theory of mind more rapidly than do their peers who do not have such conversations (Welch-Ross, 1997).

Language skills—such as knowledge of words like *want*, *need*, *think*, or *remember*, which express feelings, desires, and thoughts—are also related to theory of mind development (Astington & Jenkins, 1995; Green, Pring, & Swettenham, 2004; Tardif, So, & Kaciroti, 2007). Indeed, some level of language facility may be a necessary condition for the development of a theory of mind. Developmentalists have found that children in this age range simply do not succeed at false-belief tasks until they have reached a certain threshold of general language skill (Astington & Jenkins, 1999; Jenkins & Astington, 1996; Watson et al., 1999).

Further support for the same point comes from the finding that children with disabilities that affect language development, such as congenital deafness or mental retardation, develop a theory of mind more slowly than others (Peterson & Siegal, 1995; Sicotte & Stemberger, 1999). Research has also demonstrated that, for children with mental disabilities, progress toward a fully developed theory of mind is better predicted by language skills than by type of disability (Bauminger & Kasari, 1999; Peterson & Siegal, 1999; Yirmiya, Eriel, Shaked, & Solomonica-Levi, 1998; Yirmiya, Solomonica-Levi, Shulman, & Pilowsky, 1996).

Theory of Mind across Cultures Cross-cultural psychologists claim that theory of mind research in the United States and Europe may not apply to children in other cultures and have produced some preliminary evidence to support this contention (Lillard, 1998). However, research also suggests that certain aspects of theory of mind development may be universal. For example, similar sequences of theory of mind development have been found in the United States, China, Japan, Europe, and India (Flavell, Zhang, Zou, Dong, & Qi, 1983; Jin et al., 2002; Joshi & MacLean, 1994; Tardif & Wellman, 2000; Tardif, So, & Kaciroti, 2007; Wellman, Cross, & Watson, 2001). Moreover, participation in shared pretending has been shown to contribute to theory of mind development cross-culturally (Tan-Niam, Wood, & O'Malley, 1998). Critics, however, argue that most of the societies where these results have been found are industrialized and that very different findings might emerge in studies of nonindustrialized societies.

In response to this argument, developmentalists presented false-belief tasks to a group called the Baka, who live in Cameroon (Avis & Harris, 1991). The Baka are hunter-gatherers who live together in camps. Each child was tested in his or her own hut, using materials with which the child was completely familiar. The child watched one adult, named Mopfana (a member of the Baka), put some mango kernels into a bowl with a lid. Mopfana then left the hut, and a second adult (also a group member) told the child they were going to play a game with Mopfana: They were going to hide the kernels in a cooking pot. Then he asked the child what Mopfana was going to do when he came back. Would he look for the kernels in the bowl or in the pot? Children between 2 and 4 years old were likely to say that Mopfana would look for the kernels in the pot; 4- and 5-year-olds were nearly always right. Even in very different cultures, then, something similar seems to be occurring between age 3 and age 5. In these years, all children seem to develop a theory of mind.

short-term storage space (STSS) neo-Piagetian theorist Robbie Case's term for the working memory

operational efficiency a neo-Piagetian term that refers to the maximum number of schemes that can be processed in working memory at one time

Alternative Theories of Early Childhood Thinking

Learning Objective 7.8

How do information-processing and sociocultural theorists explain changes in young children's thinking?

In recent years, a number of interesting theoretical approaches have attempted to explain both Piaget's original results and the more recent findings that contradict them.

Neo-Piagetian Theories One set of alternative proposals is based on the idea that children's performance on Piaget's tasks can be explained in terms of working memory limitations (Case, 1985, 1992). For example, the late Robbie Case (1944–2000), one of the best known neo-Piagetian theorists, used the term **short-term storage space (STSS)** to refer to the child's working memory. According to Case, there is a limit on how many schemes can be attended to in STSS. He refers to the maximum number of schemes that may be put into STSS at one time as **operational efficiency**. Improvements in operational efficiency occur through both practice (doing tasks that require memory use, such as learning the alphabet) and brain maturation as the child gets older. Thus, a 7-year-old is better able to handle the processing demands of conservation tasks than is a 4-year-old because of improvements in operational efficiency of the STSS.

A good example of the function of STSS may be found by examining *matrix classification*, a task Piaget often used with both young and school-aged children (see Figure 7.5). Matrix classification requires the child to place a given stimulus in two categories at the same time. Young children fail such tasks, according to neo-Piagetian theory, because they begin by processing the stimulus according to one dimension (either shape or color) and then either fail to realize that it is necessary to re-process it along the second dimension or forget to do so.

However, researchers have trained young children to perform correctly on such problems by using a two-step strategy. The children are taught to think of a red triangle, for example, in terms of shape first and color second. Typically, instruction involves a number of training tasks in which researchers remind children repeatedly to remember to re-classify stimuli with respect to the second variable. According to Case, both children's failure prior to instruction and the type of strategy training to which they respond illustrate the constraints imposed on problem solving by the limited operational efficiency of the younger child's STSS. There is only room for one scheme at a time in the child's STSS, either shape or color. The training studies show that younger children *can* learn to perform correctly, but their approach is qualitatively different from that of older children. The older child's more efficient STSS allows her to think about shape and color at the same time and, therefore, perform successfully without any training.

Figure 7.5 Neo-Piagetian Matrix Task

Neo-Piagetians have used Piaget's matrix classification task in strategy training studies with young children. Before training, most preschoolers say that a blue triangle or red circle belongs in the box with the question mark. After learning a two-step strategy in which they are taught to classify each object first by shape and then by color, children understand that a red triangle is the figure that is needed to complete the matrix.

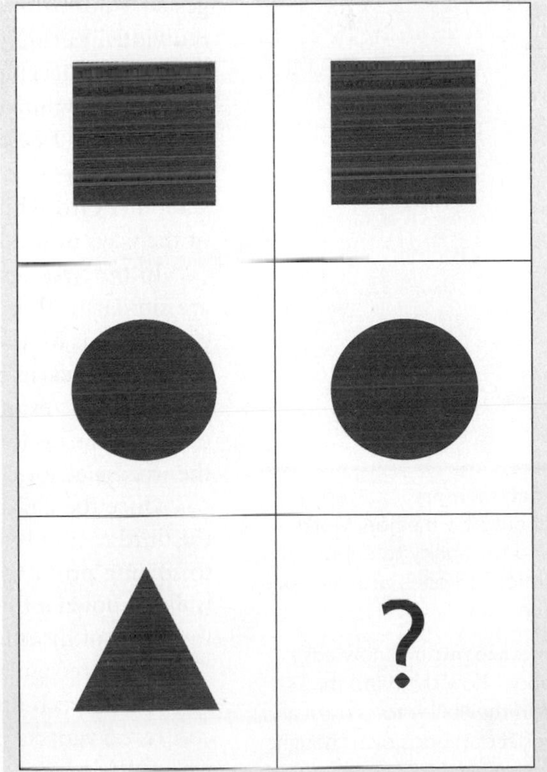

Information-Processing Theories Information-processing theorists also maintain that children's ability to make efficient use of their memory system influences their performance on problem-solving tasks. For instance, *scripts*, cognitive structures that underlie behaviors that are often repeated, emerge during early childhood. They are especially useful for managing the memory demands of tasks that involve sequential steps. For example, to brush his teeth, a preschooler must first get his toothbrush. Next, he must apply toothpaste to the brush, and so on. Establishment of a tooth-brushing script frees up the preschooler's information-processing resources so that he can focus on the quality of his brushing rather than the procedure itself.

Information processing theorists emphasize the importance of metamemory and metacognition. **Metamemory** is knowledge about and control of memory processes. For example, young children know that it takes longer to memorize a list of ten words than a list of five words but still aren't very good at coming up with strategies to apply to more difficult memory tasks (Kail, 1990). **Metacognition** is knowledge about and control of thought processes. For example, a child listening to a story may realize he has forgotten the main character's name and ask the reader what it is. Both knowing that the character's name has been forgotten and knowing that the character's name will make the story easier to understand are forms of metacognition.

Children's metamemory and metacognition improve during the early childhood period. Between age 3 and age 5, for example, children figure out that in order to tell whether a sponge painted like a rock is really a sponge or a rock, a person needs to touch or hold it. Just looking at it doesn't give someone enough information (Flavell, 1993; O'Neill, Astington, & Flavell, 1992). Thus, by about age 4 or 5, children seem to have some beginning grasp of these processes, but they still have a long way to go. As a result, their ability to solve complex problems such as those Piaget used is limited compared to that of older children.

Vygotsky's Sociocultural Theory In Chapter 2 you learned that psychologists' interest in Russian psychologist Lev Vygotsky's views on development has grown recently. Vygotsky's theory differs from both Piagetian and information-processing theory in its emphasis on the role of social factors in cognitive development. For example, two preschoolers working on a puzzle together discuss where the pieces belong. After a number of such dialogues, the participants internalize the discussion. It then becomes a model for an internal conversation the child uses to guide himself through the puzzle-solving process. In this way, Vygotsky suggested, solutions to problems are socially generated and learned. Vygotsky did not deny that individual learning takes place. Rather, he suggested that group learning processes are central to cognitive development. Consequently, from Vygotsky's perspective, social interaction is required for cognitive development (Thomas, 2000).

Chapter 2 described two important general principles of Vygotsky's theory: *the zone of proximal development* and *scaffolding*. Vygotsky also proposed specific stages of cognitive development from birth to age 7. Each stage represents a step toward the child's internalization of the ways of thinking used by the adults around him.

In the first period, called the *primitive stage*, the infant possesses mental processes that are similar to those of lower animals. He learns primarily through conditioning, until language begins to develop in the second year. At that point, he enters the *naive psychology stage*, in which he learns to use language to communicate but still does not understand its symbolic character. For example, he doesn't realize that any collection of sounds could stand for the object "chair" as long as everyone agreed—that is, if all English speakers agreed to substitute the word *blek* for *chair*, we could do so because we would all understand what *blek* meant.

Once the child begins to appreciate the symbolic function of language, near the end of the third year of life, he enters the *private speech stage*. In this stage, he uses language as a guide to solving problems. In effect, he tells himself how to do things. For example, a 3-year-old walking down a flight of stairs might say "Be careful" to himself. Such a statement would be the result of his internalization of statements made to him by adults and older children.

Piaget recognized the existence and importance of private speech. However, he believed that such speech disappeared as the child approached the end of the preoperational stage. In contrast, Vygotsky claimed that private speech becomes completely internalized at age 6 or 7, when children enter the final period of cognitive development, the *ingrowth stage*. Thus, he

metamemory knowledge about how memory works and the ability to control and reflect on one's own memory function

metacognition knowledge about how the mind thinks and the ability to control and reflect on one's own thought processes suggested that the logical thinking Piaget ascribed to older children results from their internalization of speech routines they acquire from older children and adults in the social world rather than from schemes the children construct for themselves through interaction with the physical world.

At present, there is insufficient evidence to either support or contradict most of Vygotsky's ideas (Thomas, 2000). However, studies have shown that young children whose parents provide them with more cognitive scaffolding during the preschool years exhibit higher levels of achievement in the early elementary grades than peers whose parents provide less support of this kind (Neitzel & Stright, 2003). Some intriguing research on children's construction of theory of mind during social interactions lends weight to Vygotsky's major propositions. It seems that children in pairs and groups do produce more sophisticated ideas than individual children who work on problems alone. However, the sophistication of a group's ideas appears to depend on the presence of at least one fairly advanced individual child in the group (Tan-Niam et al., 1998). However, studies strongly support Vygotsky's hypothesis that private speech helps children solve problems (Montero & De Dios, 2006).

Critical Thinking

1. Overcoming the egocentrism of early childhood is the foundation of many cognitive tasks later in life. For example, students who are writing research papers have to be able to look at their work from their professor's point of view in order to determine whether what they have written is understandable and in line with the requirements of the assignment. What other situations or tasks can you think of that require taking another person's perspective?

Changes in Language

To his credit, Piaget recognized that the overriding theme of cognitive development in the early childhood years is language acquisition. Of course, the process begins much earlier, as you learned in Chapter 5. Amazingly, though, children enter this period producing only a limited number of words and simple sentences, but leave it as accomplished, fluent speakers of at least one language.

Fast-Mapping

Learning Objective 7.9
How does fast mapping help children learn new words?

The average 2½-year-old's vocabulary of about 600 words is fairly impressive when we compare it to the dozen or so words most 1-year-olds know (E. Bates et al., 1994). This amounts to one or two new words every day between the ages of 12 and 24 months. Impressive though this feat is, it pales in comparison to the rate of vocabulary growth among preschoolers. By the time a child goes to school at age 5 or 6, total vocabulary has risen to perhaps 15,000 words—an astonishing increase of ten words a day (Anglin, 1995; Pinker, 1994). Moreover word learning appears to be the engine that drives the whole process of language development. That is, the more words a child knows, the more advanced she is with regard to grammar and other aspects of language (McGregor, Sheng, & Smith, 2005). What is the impetus behind word learning?

Researchers have found that a momentous shift in the way children approach new words happens around age 3. As a result of this shift, children begin to pay attention to words in whole groups, such as words that name objects in a single class (e.g., types of dinosaurs or kinds of fruit) or words with similar meanings. In a sense, understanding of the categorical nature of words helps children develop what we might think of as mental "slots" for new words. Once the slots are in place, they seem to automatically organize the linguistic input children receive from parents, teachers, peers, books, television programs, advertisements, and every other source of language to extract new words and fill the slots as quickly as possible.

Psychologists use the term **fast-mapping** to refer to this ability to categorically link new words to real-world objects or events (Carey & Bartlett, 1978). At the core of fast-mapping, say researchers, is a rapidly formed hypothesis about a new word's meaning (Behrend, Scofield, & Kleinknecht, 2001). The hypothesis is based on information derived from children's prior knowledge of words and word categories and from the context in which the word is used. Once formed, the hypothesis is tested through use of the word in the child's own speech, often immediately after learning it. The feedback children receive in response to use of the word helps them judge the accuracy of the hypothesis and the appropriateness of the category to which they

fast-mapping the ability to categorically link new words to real-world referents

have assumed that the word belongs. Perhaps this helps explain why preschoolers do so much talking and why they are so persistent at getting their listeners to actively respond to them.

Learning Objective 7.10

What happens during the grammar explosion?

The Grammar Explosion

Just as the vocabulary explosion you read about in Chapter 5 begins slowly, so the grammar explosion of the 2- to 6-year-old period starts with several months of simple sentences such as "Mommy sock." These utterances lack *inflections*, additions such as *'s* that would tell a child's listeners that she is trying to say that the sock belongs to Mommy. Within each language community, children seem to add inflections and more complex word orders in fairly predictable sequences (Legendre, 2006). In a classic early study, Roger Brown found that the earliest inflection used among children learning English is typically *-ing* added to a verb, as in "I playing" or "Doggie running," expressions that are common in the speech of 2½- to 3-year-olds (Brown, 1973). Over the next year or so come (in order) prepositions such as "on" and "in," the plural *-s* on nouns, irregular past tenses (such as "broke" or "ran"), possessives, articles ("a" and "the" in English), the *-s* added to third-person verbs (such as "He wants"), regular past tenses (such as "played" and "wanted"), and various forms of auxiliary verbs, as in "I *am* going."

These 2- to 3-year-olds probably speak to each other in short sentences that include uninflected nouns and verbs.

There are also predictable sequences in the child's developing use of questions and negatives. In each case, the child seems to go through periods when he creates types of sentences that he has not heard adults use, but that are consistent with the particular set of rules he is using. For example, in the development of questions there is a point at which the child can put a *wh-* word ("who," "what," "when," "where," "why") at the front end of a sentence, but doesn't yet put the auxiliary verb in the right place, as in "Where you are going now?" Similarly, in the development of negatives, children go through a stage in which they put in *not* or *n't* or *no* but omit the auxiliary verb, as in "I not crying."

Another intriguing phenomenon, noted in Chapter 5, is **overregularization**, or overgeneralization. No language is perfectly regular; every language includes some irregularly conjugated verbs or unusual forms of plurals. What 3- to 4-year-olds do is apply the basic rule to all these irregular instances, thus making the language more regular than it really is (Maratsos, 2000). In English, this is especially clear in children's creation of past tenses such as "wented," "blowed," and "sitted" or plurals such as "teeths" and "blockses" (Fenson et al., 1994).

After children have figured out inflections and the basic sentence forms using negatives and questions, they soon begin to create remarkably complex sentences, using a conjunction such as "and" or "but" to combine two ideas or using embedded clauses. Here are some examples from children aged 30 to 48 months (de Villiers & de Villiers, 1992, p. 379):

I didn't catch it but Teddy did!
I'm gonna sit on the one you're sitting on.
Where did you say you put my doll?
Those are punk rockers, aren't they?

overregularization attachment of regular inflections to irregular words such as the substitution of "goed" for "went"

When you remember that only about 18 months earlier these children were using sentences little more complex than "See doggie," you can appreciate how far they have come in a short time.

Learning Objective 7.11

What is phonological awareness, and why is it important?

Phonological Awareness

Certain aspects of early childhood language development, such as rate of vocabulary growth, predict how easily a child will learn to read and write when she enters school (Wood & Terrell, 1998). However, one specific component of early childhood language development, phonological awareness, seems to be especially important. **Phonological awareness** is a child's sensitivity to the sound patterns that are specific to the language being acquired. It also includes the child's knowledge of that particular language's system for representing sounds with letters. Researchers measure English-speaking children's phonological awareness with questions like these: "What would *bat* be if you took away the *b*? What would *bat* be if you took away the *b* and put *r* there instead?"

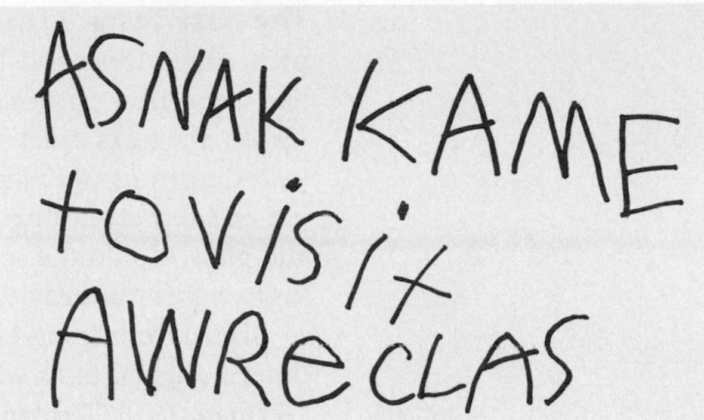

Figure 7.6 Invented Spelling

Translation: *A snake came to visit our class.* A 5-year-old used a strategy called invented spelling to write this sentence about a snake's visit (accompanied by an animal handler, we hope!) to her kindergarten class. Invented spelling requires a high level of phonological awareness. Research suggests that children who have well-developed phonological awareness skills by the time they reach kindergarten learn to read more quickly.

(Courtesy of Jerry and Denise Boyd. Used with permission.)

A child doesn't have to acquire phonological awareness in early childhood. It can be learned in elementary school through formal instruction (Ball, 1997; Bus & van IJzendoorn, 1999). However, numerous studies have shown that the greater a child's phonological awareness *before* he enters school, the faster he learns to read (Christensen, 1997; Gilbertson & Bramlett, 1998; Schatschneider, Francis, Foorman, Fletcher, & Mehta, 1999; Wood & Terrell, 1998). In addition, phonological awareness in the early childhood years is related to rate of literacy learning in languages as varied as Korean, English, Punjabi, and Chinese (Chiappe, Glaeser, & Ferko, 2007; Chiappe & Siegel, 1999; Ho & Bryant, 1997; Huang & Hanley, 1997; McBride-Chang & Ho, 2000).

Phonological awareness appears to develop primarily through word play. For example, among English-speaking children, learning and reciting nursery rhymes contributes to phonological awareness (Bryant, MacLean, & Bradley, 1990; Bryant, MacLean, Bradley, & Crossland, 1990; Layton, Deeny, Tall, & Upton, 1996). For Japanese children, a game called *shiritori*, in which one person says a word and another comes up with a word that begins with its ending sound, helps children develop these skills (Norboru, 1997; Serpell & Hatano, 1997). Educators have also found that using such games to teach phonological awareness skills to preschoolers is just as effective as more formal methods such as flash cards and worksheets (Brennan & Ireson, 1997). *Shared*, or *dialogic*, *reading* (recall the Real World feature in Chapter 5) has also been found to contribute to growth in phonological awareness (Burgess, 1997).

Preschoolers with good phonological awareness skills—those who have learned a few basic sound-letter connections informally, from their parents or from educational TV programs or videos—often use a strategy called **invented spelling** when they attempt to write (see Figure 7.6). In spite of the many errors they make, children who use invented spelling strategies before receiving school based instruction in reading and writing are more likely to become good spellers and readers later in childhood (McBride-Chang, 1998). Thus, the evidence suggests that one of the best ways parents and preschool teachers can help young children prepare for formal instruction in reading is to engage them in activities that encourage word play and invented spelling.

Critical Thinking

1. Suppose you knew a parent who was thrilled that her 5-year-old was beginning to write words but was concerned about the little girl's spelling errors. How would you explain the errors to the mother, and what would you advise her to do about them?

Differences in Intelligence

Thanks to advances in language skills, intelligence testing is far more reliable among preschoolers than among infants. Psychologists can devise tests of intelligence for preschoolers to measure their vocabulary, reasoning skills, and other cognitive processes that depend on language. Consequently, a large number of standardized tests have been developed for use with young children. However, widespread use of these tests has led to an ongoing debate about the origins of score differences and the degree to which scores can be modified.

phonological awareness children's understanding of the sound patterns of the language they are acquiring

invented spelling a strategy young children with good phonological awareness skills use when they write

Measuring Intelligence

Learning Objective 7.12
What are the strengths and weaknesses of IQ tests?

An important assumption in studying differences in intelligence is that these differences can be measured. Thus, it's important to understand something about the tests psychologists use to measure intelligence, as well as the meaning and stability of the scores the tests generate.

The First Tests The first modern intelligence test was published in 1905 by two Frenchmen, Alfred Binet and Theodore Simon (Binet & Simon, 1905). From the beginning, the test had a practical purpose—to identify children who might have difficulty in school. For this reason, the tasks Binet and Simon devised for the test were very much like some school tasks, including measures of vocabulary, comprehension of facts and relationships, and mathematical and verbal reasoning. For example, could the child describe the difference between wood and glass? Could the young child identify his nose, his ear, his head? Could he tell which of two weights was heavier?

Lewis Terman and his associates at Stanford University modified and extended many of Binet's original tasks when they translated and revised the test for use in the United States (Terman, 1916; Terman & Merrill, 1937). The Stanford-Binet, the name by which the test is still known, initially described a child's performance in terms of a score called an **intelligence quotient,** later shortened to **IQ**. This score was computed by comparing the child's chronological age (in years and months) with his mental age, defined as the level of questions he could answer correctly. For example, a child who could solve the problems for a 6-year-old but not those for a 7-year-old would have a mental age of 6. The formula used to calculate the IQ was

$$\text{mental age/chronological age} \times 100 = \text{IQ}$$

This formula results in an IQ above 100 for children whose mental age is higher than their chronological age and an IQ below 100 for children whose mental age is below their chronological age.

This system for calculating IQ is no longer used. Instead, IQ scores for the Stanford-Binet and all other intelligence tests are now based on a direct comparison of a child's performance with the average performance of a large group of other children of the same age. But the scoring is arranged so that an IQ of 100 is still average.

As you can see in Figure 7.7, about two-thirds of all children achieve scores between 85 and 115; roughly 96% of scores fall between 70 and 130. Children who score above 130 are often called *gifted*; those who score below 70 are normally referred to as *retarded*, although this label should not be applied unless the child also has problems with "adaptive behavior," such as an inability to dress or feed himself, a problem getting along with others, or a significant problem adapting to the demands of a regular school classroom. Some children with IQ scores in this low range are able to function in a regular schoolroom and should not be labeled retarded.

intelligence quotient (IQ) the ratio of mental age to chronological age; also, a general term for any kind of score derived from an intelligence test

Modern Intelligence Tests The tests used most frequently by psychologists today are those that were developed by David Wechsler. On all the Wechsler tests, the child is tested with several different types of problems, each ranging from very easy to very hard, that are

Figure 7.7
The Normal Curve

IQ scores form what mathematicians call a normal distribution—the famous "bell curve" you may have heard about. The two sides of a normal distribution curve are mirror images of each other. Thus, 34% of children score between 85 and 100, and another 34% score between 100 and 115. Likewise, 13% score between 70 and 85, and another 13% between 115 and 130. A few other human characteristics, such as height, are normally distributed as well.

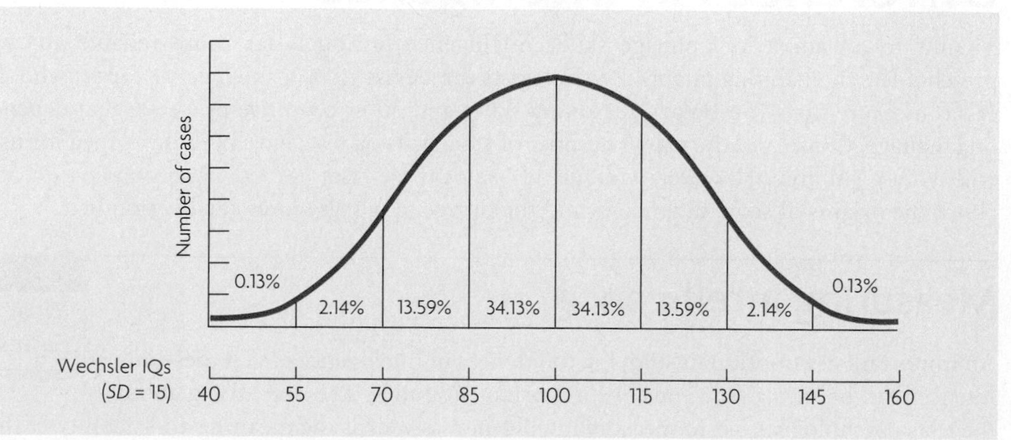

divided into subgroups. *Verbal scales* include tasks measuring vocabulary, understanding of similarities between objects, and general knowledge about the world. *Performance scales* involve nonverbal tasks such as arranging pictures in an order that tells a story or copying a pattern using a set of colored blocks. *Working memory scales* provide psychologists with information about a child's short-term memory capacity, and *processing speed scales* provide them with insight into how efficiently a child processes information. Many psychologists find the Wechsler approach to be helpful, because significant differences in a child's skills across scales may indicate particular kinds of learning problems.

Stability and Predictive Value of IQ Scores The correlation between a child's test score and her current or future grades in school is about .50–.60 (Brody, 1992; Carver, 1990; Neisser et al., 1996). This is a strong, but by no means perfect, correlation. It indicates that on the whole, children with high IQ scores will be among the high achievers in school, and those who score low will be among the low achievers. But success in school also depends on many factors other than IQ, including motivation, interest, and persistence. Because of this, some children with high IQ scores don't shine in school, while some lower-IQ children do.

The relationship between school performance and IQ scores holds within each social class and racial group in the United States, as well as in other countries and cultures. Among both the poor and the middle class, and among African Americans and Hispanic Americans as well as Whites, children with higher IQs are more likely to get good grades, complete high school, and go on to college (Brody, 1992). Such findings have led a number of theorists to argue that intelligence adds to the child's resilience—a concept mentioned in Chapter 1. Numerous studies show that poor children—whether they are White, Hispanic, African American, or from another minority group—are far more likely to develop the kind of self-confidence and personal competence it takes to move out of poverty if they have higher IQs (Luthar & Zigler, 1992; Masten & Coatsworth, 1998; Werner & Smith, 1992).

At the other end of the scale, low intelligence is associated with a number of negative long-term outcomes, including delinquency in adolescence, adult illiteracy, and criminal behavior in adulthood (Baydar, Brooks-Gunn, & Furstenberg, 1993; Stattin & Klackenberg-Larsson, 1993). This is not to say that all lower-IQ individuals are illiterates or criminals—that is clearly not the case. But low IQ makes a child more vulnerable, just as high IQ increases the child's resilience.

IQ scores are also quite stable. If two tests are given a few months or a few years apart, the scores are likely to be very similar. The correlations between IQ scores from adjacent years in middle childhood, for example, are typically in the range of .80 (Honzik, 1986). Yet this high level of predictability masks an interesting fact: Many children show quite wide fluctuations in their scores. In fact, about half of all children show noticeable changes from one testing to another and over time (McCall, 1993). Some show steadily rising scores, and some have declining ones; some show a peak in middle childhood and then a decline in adolescence. In rare cases, the shifts may cover a range as large as 40 points.

Such wide fluctuations are more common in young children. The general rule of thumb is that the older the child, the more stable the IQ score—although even in older children, scores may still fluctuate in response to major stresses such as parental divorce, a change of schools, or the birth of a sibling.

Limitations of IQ Tests Before moving on to the question of the possible origins of differences in IQ, it is important to emphasize a few key limitations of IQ tests and the scores derived from them. IQ tests do not measure underlying competence. An IQ score cannot tell you (or a teacher or anyone else) that your child has some specific, fixed, underlying capacity. Traditional IQ tests also do not measure a whole host of skills that are likely to be highly significant for getting along in the world. Originally, IQ tests were designed to measure only the specific range of skills that are needed for success in school. This they do quite well. What they do *not* do is indicate anything about a particular person's creativity, insight, street-smarts, ability to read social cues, or understanding of spatial relationships (Gardner, 1983; Sternberg & Wagner, 1993).

Learning Objective 7.13

What kinds of evidence support the nature and nurture explanations for individual differences in IQ?

Origins of Individual Differences in Intelligence

If a couple whom you perceive to be smart conceive a child, what would you predict about their offspring's IQ scores? Most people know that differences in intelligence run in families. But why do related people seem to be alike in this regard? Is it nature or nurture that is responsible?

Evidence for Heredity Both twin studies and studies of adopted children show strong hereditary influences on IQ, as you already know from the Research Report in Chapter 3. Identical twins are more like each other in IQ than are fraternal twins, and the IQs of adopted children are better predicted from the IQs of their natural parents than from those of their adoptive parents (Brody, 1992; Loehlin, Horn, & Willerman, 1994; Scarr, Weinberg, & Waldman, 1993). These are precisely the findings researchers would expect if a strong genetic element were at work.

Evidence for Family Influences Adoption studies also provide some strong support for an environmental influence on IQ scores, because the IQ scores of adopted children are clearly affected by the environment in which they have grown up. The clearest evidence for this comes from a study of 38 French children, all adopted in infancy (Capron & Duyme, 1989). Roughly half the children had been born to better-educated parents from a higher social class, while the other half had been born to working-class or poverty-level parents. Some of the children in each group had then been adopted by parents in a higher social class, while the others grew up in poorer families. The effect of rearing conditions was evident in that the children reared in upper-class homes had IQs 15–16 points higher than those reared in lower-class families, regardless of the social class level or education of the birth parents. A genetic effect was evident in that the children born to upper-class parents had higher IQs than those from lower-class families, no matter what kind of environment they were reared in.

When developmentalists observe how individual families interact with their infants or young children and then follow the children over time to see which ones later have high or low IQs, they begin to get some sense of the kinds of specific family interactions that foster higher scores. For one thing, parents of higher-IQ children provide them with an interesting and complex physical environment, including play materials that are appropriate for the child's age and developmental level (Bradley et al., 1989; Pianta & Egeland, 1994). They also respond warmly and appropriately to the child's behavior, smiling when the child smiles, answering the child's questions, and in myriad ways reacting to the child's cues (Barnard et al., 1989; Lewis, 1993). These kinds of parental behaviors may even help to limit the effects of poverty and other sources of family stress on children's intellectual development (Robinson, Lanzi, Weinberg, Ramey, & Ramey, 2002).

Children who attend enrichment programs like this Head Start program typically do not show lasting gains in IQ, but they are more likely to succeed in school.

Parents of higher-IQ children also talk to them often, using language that is descriptively rich and accurate (Hart & Risley, 1995; Sigman et al., 1988). And when they play with or interact with their children, they operate in what Vygotsky referred to as the *zone of proximal development* (described in Chapter 2), aiming their conversation, their questions, and their assistance at a level that is just above the level the children could manage on their own, thus helping the children to master new skills (Landry et al., 1996).

In addition, parents who appear to foster intellectual development try to avoid being excessively restrictive, punitive, or controlling, instead giving children room to explore, and even opportunities to make mistakes (Bradley et al., 1989; Olson, Bates, & Kaskie, 1992). In a similar vein, these parents ask questions rather than giving commands (Hart & Risley, 1995). Most also expect their children to do well and to develop rapidly. They emphasize and press for school achievement (Entwisle & Alexander, 1990).

Nevertheless, developmentalists can't be sure that these environmental characteristics are causally important, because parents provide both the genes and the environment. Perhaps these are simply the environmental features provided by brighter parents, and it is the genes and not the environment that cause the higher IQs in their children. However, the research on adopted children's IQs cited earlier suggests that these aspects of environment have a very real impact on children's intellectual development beyond whatever hereditary influences may affect them.

Evidence for Preschool Influences Home environments and family interactions are not the only sources of environmental influence. Children's experiences in formal educational programs are also associated with IQ scores. As a result, many government programs for economically disadvantaged children (such as Head Start) are based on the assumption that a family's economic resources can limit their ability to provide their children with such experiences and that such experiences are vital to supporting children's intellectual development. Typically, these programs provide children with the same kinds of intellectual stimulation that are common in the private preschools attended by most middle-class children. Children are encouraged to acquire new vocabulary, new knowledge about the world, and skills that are vital to reading, such as phonological awareness. The goal behind such programs is to enable all children to enter school with an equal chance of success. Children in these programs normally show a gain of about 10 IQ points while enrolled in them, but this IQ gain typically fades and then disappears within the first few years of school (Zigler & Styfco, 1993).

However, on other kinds of measures, a residual effect of enriched preschool experiences can clearly be seen some years later. Children who go through Head Start or another quality preschool experience are less likely to be placed in special education classes, less likely to repeat a grade, and more likely to graduate from high school (Barnett, 1995; Darlington, 1991). They also have better health, better immunization rates, and better school adjustment than their peers (Zigler & Styfco, 1993). One very long-term longitudinal study even suggested that the impact of enriched programs may last well into adulthood. This study found that young adults who had attended a particularly good experimental preschool program, the Perry Preschool Project in Milwaukee, had higher rates of high school graduation, lower rates of criminal behavior, lower rates of unemployment, and a lower probability of being on welfare than did their peers who had not attended such a preschool (Barnett, 1993).

When the enrichment program is begun in infancy rather than at age 3 or 4, even IQ scores remain elevated into adulthood (Campbell, Ramey, Pungello, Sparling, & Miller-Johnson, 2002; Ramey & Ramey, 1998). One very well-designed and meticulously reported infancy intervention was called the Abecedarian project (Campbell & Ramey, 1994; Ramey, 1993; Ramey & Campbell, 1987). Infants from poverty-level families whose mothers had low IQs were randomly assigned either to a special day-care program or to a control group that received nutritional supplements and medical care but no special enriched day care. The special day care program began when the infants were 6–12 weeks old and lasted until they started kindergarten.

Figure 7.8 on page 198 graphs the average IQ scores of the children in each of these two groups from age 2 to age 12. You can see that the IQs of the children who had been enrolled in the special program were higher at every age. Fully 44% of the control group children had IQ scores classified as borderline or retarded (scores below 85), compared with only 12.8% of the children who had been in the special program. In addition, the enriched day-care group had significantly higher scores on both reading and mathematics tests at age 12 and were only half as likely to have repeated a grade (Ramey, 1992, 1993).

Combining the Information Virtually all psychologists would agree that heredity is a highly important influence on IQ scores. Studies around the world consistently yield estimates that roughly half the variation in IQ within a given population is due to heredity (Neisser et al., 1996; Plomin & Rende, 1991; Rogers, Rowe, & May, 1994). The remaining half is clearly due to environment or to interactions between environment and heredity.

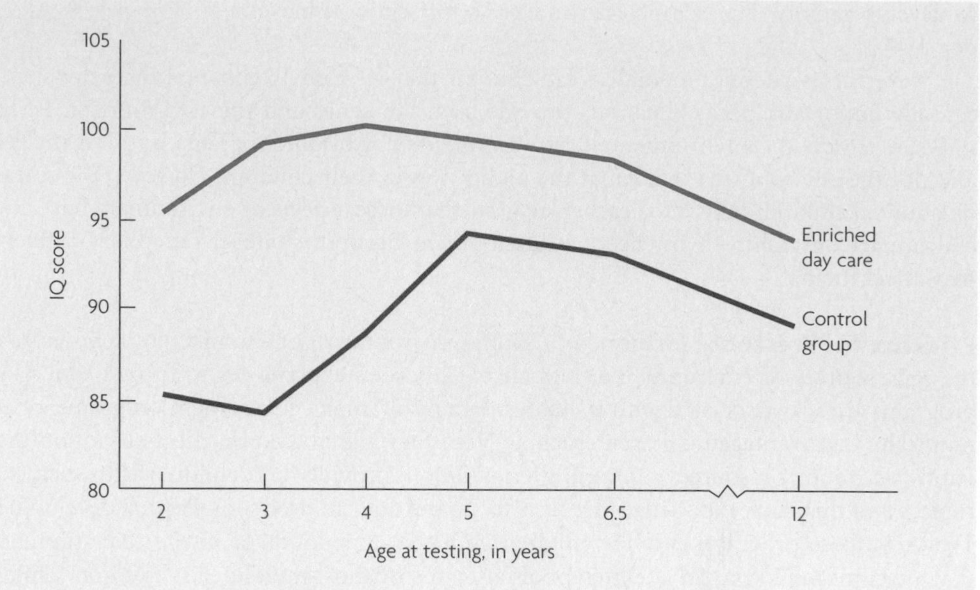

Figure 7.8 Early Education and IQ Scores

In Ramey's study, children from poverty-level families were randomly assigned in infancy to an experimental group that received special day care or to a control group, with the intervention lasting until age 5. At kindergarten, both groups entered public school. The difference in IQ between the experimental and control groups remained statistically significant even at age 12, seven years after the intervention had ended.

(*Source:* Ramey & Campbell, 1987, Figure 3, p. 135, with additional data from Ramey, 1993, Figure 2, p. 29.)

One useful way to think about this interaction is to use the concept of **reaction range**, a range between some upper and lower boundary of functioning established by one's genetic heritage; exactly where a child will fall within those boundaries is determined by environment. Some developmental psychologists estimate that the reaction range for IQ is about 20–25 points (Weinberg, 1989). That is, given a specific genetic heritage, a child's actual IQ test performance may vary by as much as 20 or 25 points, depending on the richness or poverty of the environment in which he grows up. When the child's environment is changed for the better, the child moves closer to the upper end of his reaction range. When the environment becomes worse, the child's effective intellectual performance falls toward the lower end of his reaction range. Thus, even though intelligence as measured on an IQ test is highly heritable and falls within the reaction range, the absolute IQ score is determined by environment.

Learning Objective 7.14

What theories and evidence have been offered in support of genetic and cultural explanations of group differences in IQ scores?

Group Differences in Intelligence Test Scores

There appear to be a number of consistent group differences in IQ test scores and other measures of intellectual performance. For instance, Chinese and Japanese children consistently demonstrate higher performance on achievement tests—particularly math and science tests (Geary, Bow-Thomas, Fan, & Siegler, 1993; Stevenson et al., 1990; Sue & Okazaki, 1990). But the finding that has been most troublesome for researchers and theorists is that in the United States, African American children consistently score lower than White children on measures of IQ. Some theorists have suggested that this difference can be traced to anatomical and physiological variations across groups (Mackintosh, 2007; Rushton & Rushton, 2003). However, this difference, which is on the order of 6 to 15 IQ points, is not found on infant tests of intelligence or on measures of infant habituation rate; it becomes apparent by the time children are 2 or 3 years old and persists through adolescence and adulthood (Brody, 1992; Fagan & Singer, 1983; Peoples, Fagan, & Drotar, 1995; Rowe, 2002; Rushton, Skuy, & Fridjhon, 2003). There is some indication that the size of the difference between African American and White children has been declining for several decades, but a noticeable difference persists (Neisser et al., 1996; Rushton & Jensen, 2006).

reaction range a range, established by one's genes, between upper and lower boundaries for traits such as intelligence; one's environment determines where, within those limits, one will be

While granting that IQ is highly heritable, many developmentalists point out that the difference between average African American and White IQ scores falls well within the presumed reaction range of IQ. They emphasize that the environments in which African American and White children are typically reared differ sufficiently to account for the average difference in scores (Brody, 1992). Specifically, African American children in the United

States are more likely to be born with low birth weight, to suffer from poor nutrition, and to have high blood levels of lead and are less likely to be read to or to receive a wide range of intellectual stimulation. And each of these environmental characteristics is known to be linked to lower IQ scores. Studies showing that African American and White adults who differ in IQ do not differ in performance on new verbal learning tasks support this view (Fagan & Holland, 2002).

Some of the most convincing research supporting such an environmental explanation comes from mixed-race adoption studies (Scarr & Weinberg, 1983; Weinberg, Scarr, & Waldman, 1992). For example, researchers have found that African American children adopted at an early age into White middle-class families scored only slightly lower on IQ tests than did White children adopted into the same families. Similarly, regardless of race, the more education parents have, the higher their children's IQs (Sellers, Burns, & Guyrke, 2002). Thus, IQ differences in African American and White children may reflect their parents' differing amounts of experience with formal education.

Another recent entry into the debate on group differences in IQ scores is the finding that, during the 19th and 20th centuries, average IQ scores increased in every racial group throughout the industrialized world. This phenomenon is known as the *Flynn effect* because it was discovered by psychologist James Flynn (Flynn, 1999, 2003). Flynn's analyses of IQ data over several generations suggest that individuals of average IQ born in the late 19th century would have mental retardation by today's standards. If IQ is largely genetic, Flynn argues, there should be a great deal of stability in any group's average score. Because IQ scores have changed so much in a relatively short period of time, Flynn suggests that cultural changes explain the effect that bears his name. Similarly, Flynn suggests that his cross-generational studies demonstrate that cultural factors are a likely explanation for cross-group differences as well. He points out that theorists from a variety of fields—from anthropology to medicine—have posited causes for cross-generational gains in IQ such as improved nutrition, greater access to media, and universal literacy. Flynn suggests that all of these factors vary across racial as well as generational groups.

Flynn further points out that many theorists have neglected to consider cultural beliefs in their search for a hereditary basis for intelligence. For example, some psychologists have argued that the differences between Asian and American children in performance on mathematics achievement tests result not from genetic differences in capacity but from differences in cultural beliefs (Stevenson & Lee, 1990). Specifically, Asian societies place little or no value on inborn talent. Instead, they believe that hard work can modify whatever talents a person was born with. Consequently, Asian parents and teachers require students to expend a great deal of effort trying to improve themselves intellectually and do not resort to ability-based explanations of failure. This means that an individual child does not simply accept academic failure as a sign of intellectual deficit but is encouraged by adults to keep on trying. As a result, Asian children spend more time on homework and other academic activities than do children in other cultures.

In contrast, U.S. schools emphasize ability through the routine use of IQ tests to place students in high-, average-, or low-ability classes. This approach reflects American society's greater acceptance of the idea that people are limited by the amount of ability they possess and that it is unfair to ask them to do more than tests suggest they are capable of. It is likely that these complex cultural variables affect children's environments in ways that lead to differences in IQ and achievement test scores (Chang & Murray, 1995; Schneider, Hieshima, Lee, & Plank, 1994; Stevenson & Lee, 1990; Stigler, Lee, & Stevenson, 1987).

Of course, the fact that group differences in IQ or achievement test performance may be explained by appealing to the concept of reaction range and to cultural beliefs does not make the differences disappear, nor does it make them trivial. Moreover, it's important to remember that there is the same amount of variation in IQ scores in all groups; there are many highly gifted African American children, just as there are many White children with mental retardation. Finally, the benefits of having a high IQ, as well as the risks associated with low IQ, are the same in every racial group (see No Easy Answers on page 200).

Critical Thinking

1. In which of Bronfenbrenner's contexts (see Chapter 2, p. 44) would you find cultural beliefs about ability? How might these beliefs be manifested in each of the other contexts, and how might they ultimately influence individual development?

NO EASY ANSWERS

To Test or Not to Test?

One of the questions that students often ask at this point is "Given all the factors that can affect a test score, is it worth bothering with IQ tests at all?" The answer is "yes": As long as the tests are used properly, intelligence testing can be very beneficial to children.

IQ tests are important tools for identifying children who have special educational needs, such as those who suffer from mental retardation. There are other methods for selecting children for special programs, such as teacher recommendations, but none of the alternatives is as reliable or as valid as an IQ test for measuring that set of cognitive abilities that are demanded by school. Even when a child's physical characteristics can be used to make a general diagnosis of mental retardation, as in cases of Down syndrome, an intelligence test can reveal to what degree the child is affected. This is important, because effective educational interventions are based on an understanding of how an individual's disability has affected the capacity to learn. Thus, IQ tests are a critical tool in the development of individual educational plans for children with disabilities.

More controversial is routine testing of young children who have no disabilities. Most testing experts agree that using IQ tests to classify normal young children is of little value because their test scores tend to be far less reliable than those of older children. Moreover, labels based on IQ testing at an early age may be detrimental to young children's future development. Test-based labels may lead teachers and parents to make inappropriate assumptions about children's ability to learn. For example, parents of a high-IQ preschooler may expect her to act like a miniature adult, while the family of a young child whose IQ score is average may limit her opportunities to learn because they are afraid she will fail.

In summary, comprehensive intelligence testing with individual tests can be beneficial to any child who is known to have or is suspected of having a disability of any kind. However, labeling nondisabled young children on the basis of IQ scores should be avoided.

Take a Stand

Decide which of these two statements you most agree with and think about how you would defend your position:

1. School children should not be given IQ tests unless there is some reason to suspect that they have a disability.
2. Using IQ tests to screen all school children for potential learning problems is a good practice.

SUMMARY

Physical Changes

Learning Objective 7.1 What are the major milestones of growth and motor development between 2 and 6?

- Physical development is slower from age 2 to age 6 than it is in infancy, but it nevertheless progresses steadily. Motor skills continue to improve gradually, with marked improvement in gross motor skills (running, jumping, galloping) and slower advances in fine motor skills.

Learning Objective 7.2 What important changes happen in the brain during these years?

- Significant changes in brain lateralization occur in early childhood. Handedness is another neurological milestone of this period.

Learning Objective 7.3 What are the nutritional and health care needs of young children?

- Slower rates of growth contribute to declines in appetite. Stress is a factor in early childhood illnesses such as colds and flu.

Learning Objective 7.4 What factors contribute to abuse and neglect, and how do these traumas affect children's development?

- Children between the ages of 2 and 9 are more likely to be abused or neglected than are infants or older children. Certain characteristics of both children and parents increase the risk of abuse. Long-term consequences of abuse have been found across all domains of development.

Cognitive Changes

Learning Objective 7.5 List the characteristics of children's thought during Piaget's preoperational stage.

- Piaget marked the beginning of the preoperational period at about 18–24 months, at the point when the child begins to use mental symbols. Despite this advance, the preschool child still lacks many sophisticated cognitive skills. In Piaget's view, such children are still egocentric, lack understanding of conservation, and are often fooled by appearances.

Learning Objective 7.6 How has recent research challenged Piaget's view of this period?

- Research challenging Piaget's findings makes it clear that young children are less egocentric than Piaget thought. By age 4, they can distinguish between appearance and reality in a variety of tasks.

Learning Objective 7.7 What is a theory of mind, and how does it develop?

- By the end of early childhood, children have a well-developed theory of mind. They understand that other people's actions are based on their thoughts and beliefs.

Learning Objective 7.8 How do information-processing and sociocultural theorists explain changes in young children's thinking?

- Neo-Piagetian and information-processing theories explain early childhood cognitive development in terms of limitations on young children's memory systems. Vygotsky's sociocultural theory asserts that children's thinking is shaped by social interaction through the medium of language.

Changes in Language

Learning Objective 7.9 How does fast-mapping help children learn new words?

- Fast-mapping, the use of categories to learn new words, enables young children to acquire new words rapidly.

Learning Objective 7.10 What happens during the grammar explosion?

- During the grammar explosion (ages 3 to 4), children make large advances in grammatical fluency.

Learning Objective 7.11 What is phonological awareness, and why is it important?

- Development of an awareness of the sound patterns of a particular language during early childhood is important in learning to read during the school years. Children seem to acquire this skill through word play.

Differences in Intelligence

Learning Objective 7.12 What are the strengths and weaknesses of IQ tests?

- Scores on early childhood intelligence tests are predictive of later school performance and are at least moderately consistent over time.

Learning Objective 7.13 What kinds of evidence support the nature and nurture explanations for individual differences in IQ?

- Differences in IQ have been attributed to both heredity and environment. Twin and adoption studies make it clear that at least half the variation in IQ scores is due to genetic differences; the remainder is attributable to environment and the interaction of heredity and environment.

Learning Objective 7.14 What theories and evidence have been offered in support of genetic and cultural explanations of group differences in IQ scores?

- Several kinds of group differences in IQ or other test scores have been found consistently. Such differences seem most appropriately attributed to environmental variation, rather than to genetics.

KEY TERMS

centration *(p. 185)*
conservation *(p. 185)*
corpus callosum *(p. 178)*
egocentrism *(p. 183)*
false belief principle *(p. 187)*
fast-mapping *(p. 191)*
handedness *(p. 179)*
hippocampus *(p. 179)*
intelligence quotient (IQ) *(p. 194)*
invented spelling *(p. 193)*
lateralization *(p. 178)*
metacognition *(p. 190)*
metamemory *(p. 180)*
operational efficiency *(p. 189)*
overregularization *(p. 192)*
phonological awareness *(p. 193)*
preoperational stage *(p. 183)*
reaction range *(p. 198)*
semiotic (symbolic) function *(p. 183)*
short-term storage space (STSS) *(p. 189)*
theory of mind *(p. 187)*

TEST YOURSELF

Physical Changes

7.1 Fine motor skills

a. are completely developed by the kindergarten year.
b. improve during the preschool years, but are not completely developed by age 6.
c. are not influenced by training.
d. all develop at the same time.

7.2 When does the left-side processing of language appear?

a. prenatally
b. in the preschool years
c. in the elementary-school years
d. in adolescence

7.3 The fact that handedness appears _____ supports the genetic hypothesis.

a. prenatally
b. in the first year
c. by age 4
d. in the school years

7.4 Parents should be concerned with

a. the quantity of food that children eat, even if this means that they eat high-fat foods.
b. the quality of food that children eat, since food preferences are often established during the preschool years.
c. the quantity of food that children eat, because obesity is prevalent during the preschool years.
d. neither the quality nor the quantity of food that children eat.

7.5 Which of the following is *not* one of the reasons parents report an increase in problems with children's sleep patterns after the child's second birthday?

a. Parents' expectations of 2-year-olds are often greater than their expectations of infants.

b. Temperamental differences in infants are manifested in their sleep patterns in early childhood.

c. Nightmares and night terrors begin appearing at about age 3.

d. There are changes in children's brains at about age 3.

7.6 Which of the following is *not* something parents can do to prevent bedtime and middle-of-the-night struggles?

a. Provide children with a transitional object such as a doll or stuffed animal.

b. Discontinue daytime naps.

c. Let the child go to bed whenever he or she is very tired.

d. Provide the child with a predictable daytime schedule.

7.7 Which of the following variables influences how often children get sick?

a. the amount of stress in their lives

b. how well they eat

c. whether or not they go to preschool

d. their intelligence

7.8 What is the most prevalent form of abuse of children?

a. sexual assault

b. neglect

c. inadequate supervision

d. physical injury

7.9 Which of the following is *not* a risk factor for child abuse and neglect?

a. physical disabilities

b. poverty

c. parental depression

d. being the oldest in a family

Cognitive Changes

7.10 A child is offered a choice between six pieces of candy laid out in a row and four pieces of candy spread father apart to form a longer row. If the child chooses the longer row with four pieces, we know that the child has not achieved

a. preoperational thought.

b. conservation.

c. a principle of false belief.

d. a theory of mind.

7.11 A set of ideas that explains other people's ideas, beliefs, desires, and behaviors is called a

a. false belief principle.

b. theory of mind.

c. metamemory.

d. matrix classification.

7.12 Knowledge about and control of thought processes is called

a. metacognition.

b. theory of mind.

c. cognitive dissonance.

d. self-concept.

7.13 According to Vygotsky, ______ is required for cognitive development.

a. social interaction

b. formal education

c. strong parent-child attachment

d. metacognition

7.14 Which of the following would be typical in Vygotsky's private speech stage?

a. The infant learns to use language to communicate.

b. The infant begins to make sounds.

c. The child uses language as a guide to problem-solving.

d. The child learns to take turns in conversation.

Changes in Language

7.15 Which of the following is the most developmentally advanced use of inflections?

a. "I playing."

b. "horsies"

c. "It breaked."

d. "I played."

7.16 What explains a child's use of expressions such as "I sitted down," "goed," or "mouses"?

a. The child is underextending the verb class.

b. The child has had insufficient practice with inflections.

c. The child is recasting language heard in the environment.

d. The child is overregularizing the rules of language.

7.17 What is phonological awareness?

a. the process by which children actively infer and use rules to create language

b. combinations of single words with gestures in order to communicate

c. children's understanding of the sound patterns of the language they are acquiring

d. verbal markers that convey information about feeling or context

7.18 What is the primary source of children's phonological awareness?

a. word play

b. exposure to a variety of languages

c. communication between parent and child

d. being read to

Differences in Intelligence

7.19 Which of the following would *not* be a typical task on a modern-day IQ test for children?

a. understanding similarities between objects
b. creating a poem
c. arranging pictures in an order that tells a story
d. defining vocabulary

7.20 Research indicates that IQ scores

a. are not related to later school performance.
b. are predictive of school performance only among White Americans.
c. are not stable.
d. are stable if tests are given only a few months or a few years apart.

7.21 Which of the following statements about the effects of Head Start and other quality preschool experiences is *not* true?

a. Children show a gain of about 10 points while enrolled in these programs.
b. Children maintain the IQ gains they make in these programs throughout adolescence.
c. Children in these programs are less likely to repeat a grade and are more likely to graduate from high school.
d. Children in these programs may have lower rates of criminal behavior and unemployment.

7.22 The concept of the reaction range suggests that the upper and lower boundaries of a child's intelligence are established by ______ and the child's actual level of intelligence is determined by ______.

a. her genes; environment
b. her parents' IQs; social experiences
c. a neurological substrate; the quality of formal education
d. the rate of habituation; hereditary influences

7.23 The research on group differences in IQ suggests that there are

a. no consistent group differences.
b. consistent group differences that are most likely due to environment.
c. consistent group differences but they disappear by age 2.
d. small group differences that are primarily genetic.

7.24 Across the 19th and 20th centuries, average IQ scores increased in every racial group throughout the industrialized world. This phenomenon is known as the

a. secular effect.
b. intelligence quotient.
c. reaction range.
d. Flynn effect.

7.25 Which of the following statements about IQ testing is true?

a. IQ testing is seldom beneficial to any child.
b. IQ testing of children is always reliable.
c. IQ tests are important tools for identifying children who have special educational needs.
d. Labeling nondisabled young children on the basis of IQ scores is strongly recommended.

PEARSON mydevelopmentlab™ **Study Plan**

Are You Ready for the Test?

Students who use the study materials on MyDevelopmentLab report higher grades in the course than those who use the text alone. Here are three easy steps to mastering this chapter and improving your grade…

Step 1

Take the chapter pre-test in MyDevelopmentLab and review your customized Study Plan.

One of the cognitive limitations of the preoperational stage, according to Piaget, is the

- inability to understand that one object or behavior can represent another.
- tendency to look at things entirely from the child's own point of view.
- inability to understand that people and objects continue to exist even when they are out of sight.
- difficulty of coordinating sensory inputs with their motor activities.

Step 2

Use MyDevelopmentLab's Multimedia Library to help strengthen your knowledge of the chapter.

Learning Objective 7.1

What are the major milestones of growth and motor development between 2 and 6?

Watch: Motor Development in Infants and Toddlers: Karen Adolph

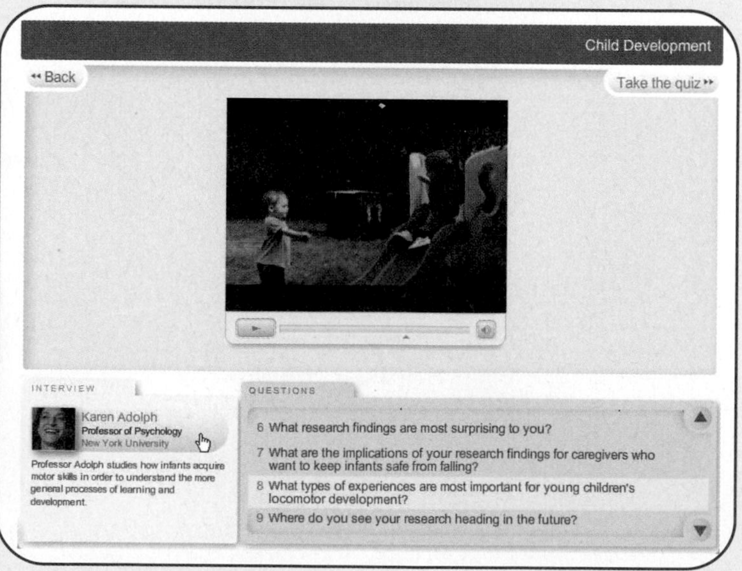

"I like the fact that there are activities (like the simulations) and practice tests. They help you better understand the concepts and prepare you for the actual exam. This is definitely better than using a regular textbook."

—Alyssa, Boston College

Watch: Conservation of Liquids

Learning Objective 7.5

List the characteristics of children's thought during Piaget's preoperational stage.

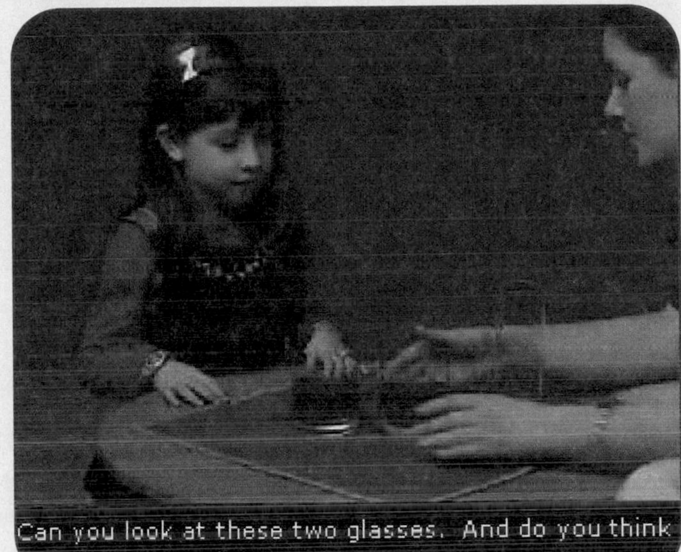

Can you look at these two glasses. And do you think
hat they have the same amount

Explore: Corrrelations Between IQ Scores of Persons of Varying Relationships

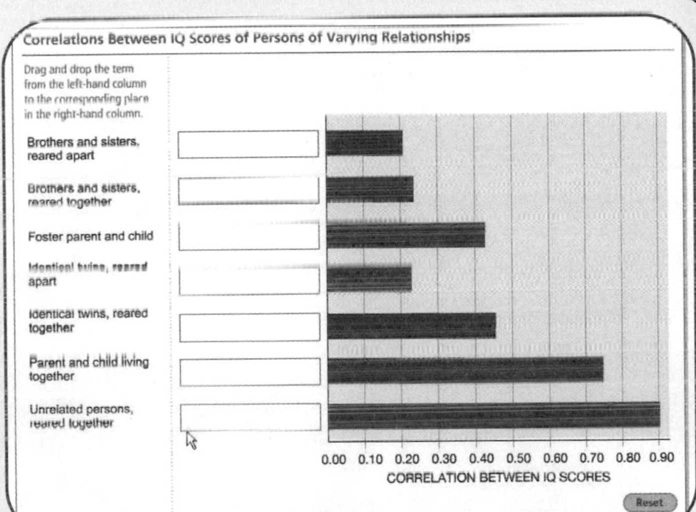

Learning Objective 7.13

What kinds of evidence support the nature and nurture explanations for individual differences in IQ?

Step 3

Take the chapter post-test and compare your results against the pre-test.

POST-TEST

The IQs of adopted children

- typical decrease following their adoption.
- more strongly resemble the IQs of their biological parents than their adoptive parents.
- are more similar to the IQs of their siblings than their parents.
- more strongly resemble the IQs of their adopted parents than their biological parents.

www.mydevelopmentlab.com

Social and Personality Development in Early Childhood

By all accounts, 2-year-old Remi was a bright and happy child who was attaining each of the milestones of early development right on time. As she progressed through her third year, however, her parents began to notice subtle differences between Remi and the other children in her preschool class. For one, Remi's peers were making impressive advances in the social use of language. They used expressions like "please" and "thank you" and were sometimes able to solve their conflicts with other children through verbal negotiations. Remi knew the same words that they did, and the grammatical features of her language were equal to theirs. What was missing from Remi's utterances, though, was the social sense of how her words were interpreted by others. At times, she reached out to others by repeating the same phrase over and over, only to abandon the effort to communicate altogether when she

failed to make others understand her. At others, she sat alone, clutching a rag doll from which she was inseparable, and talked to herself. Still, her parents, teachers, and pediatrician believed that, eventually, she would catch up.

Despite the optimism of the adults in her life, when Remi turned 4, the differences in social behavior that distinguished her from her peers became even more apparent. Not only was her language socially insensitive, but she did not form relationships with other children. Remi's teachers were somewhat comforted when she became fascinated with books. Their enthusiasm soon waned, though, when they realized that Remi wanted to count the letters in the books rather than try to read the words. After a few weeks, Remi was able to tell her teachers exactly how many letters were in each of the books in her classroom. Her behavioral idiosyncrasies seemed to be completely at odds with her cognitive and language development, which were humming along at an impressive rate.

Desperate to help their daughter, Remi's parents consulted a child psychologist. They learned that Remi was suffering from *Asperger's disorder*. Youngsters with this disorder have age-appropriate language and cognitive skills (Raja, 2006). However, they have difficulty interacting with others and often engage in self-stimulating, repetitive behaviors such as Remi's fascination with counting letters. Because of their normal language and cognitive skills, most children with Asperger's disorder are assumed to be "late bloomers" or "going through a phase." As the years go by, though, differences between children with Asperger's disorder and their peers become impossible to dismiss as a "phase." Nevertheless, with the support of special educators who are trained in the treatment of this disorder, children who suffer from Asperger's can attain high levels of achievement and lead happy lives.

The unique pattern of behaviors that is seen in Asperger's disorder demonstrates that early childhood development should be thought of as a foundation for future adaptive functioning that has four interlocking pieces: physical development, cognitive development, language development, and social development. Take away any individual piece, and the entire structure of human development is at risk, just as removing the cornerstone from the foundation of a building can cause it to collapse. Thus, in this chapter, you will become acquainted with the fourth, but critical, component of the foundation of human development, social and personality development. We begin by reminding you of how the psychoanalysts viewed this period and introducing you to an entirely different way of thinking about it.

Theories of Social and Personality Development

What is the period of early childhood all about? One way to describe it would be to call it the "stepping out" phase, because that's precisely what 2- to 6-year-olds do. They "step out" from the safety of the strong emotional bonds that they share with their parents into the risky world of relationships with others. How do they do it? The psychoanalysts outlined the broad themes of this foundational time of life, and the work of more recent theorists has provided us with a few details about the skills that children develop in the process of stepping out. Before we get into the details, let's look at the themes.

Learning Objective 8.1

What major themes of development did the psychoanalytic theorists propose for the early childhood period?

Psychoanalytic Perspectives

You may remember that Freud described two stages during these preschool years. The developmental task of the *anal stage* (1 to 3 years) is toilet training. That of the *phallic stage*, you may remember, is to establish a foundation for later gender and moral development by identifying with the same-sex parent. We might sum up Freud's view of the early childhood period as the time in life when young children, first, gain control of their bodily functions and, second, renegotiate their relationships with their parents to prepare for stepping out into the world of peers.

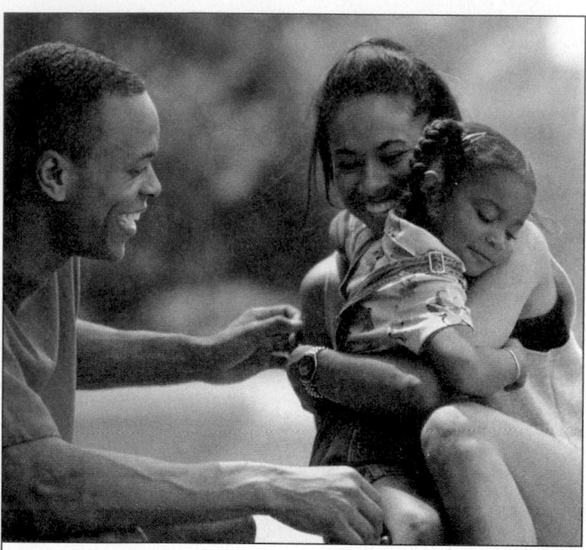

"Stepping out" is the major theme of social and personality development in early childhood. Maintaining strong bonds of affection with parents helps them feel secure enough to do so.

Erikson agreed with Freud's views on bodily control and parental relationships during the preschool years, but he placed the emphasis somewhat differently. Both of the stages he identified in the preschool period (see Table 2.3, page 31) are triggered by children's growing physical, cognitive, and social skills. The stage Erikson called *autonomy versus shame and doubt*, for example, is centered around the toddler's new mobility and the accompanying desire for autonomy. The stage of *initiative versus guilt* is ushered in by new cognitive skills, particularly the preschooler's ability to plan, which accentuates his wish to take the initiative. However, his developing conscience dictates the boundaries within which this initiative may be exercised (Evans & Erikson, 1967). For example, think about a situation in which one child wants to play with another child's toy. His sense of initiative might motivate him to simply take it, but his conscience will likely prompt him to find a more socially acceptable way to gain the toy. If he fails to achieve the kind of self-control that is required to maintain conformity to his conscience, the child is likely to be hampered by excessive guilt and defensiveness in future psychosocial crises.

The key to healthy development during this period, according to Erikson, is striking a balance between the child's emerging skills and desire for autonomy and the parents' need to protect the child and control the child's behavior. Thus, the parents' task changes rather dramatically after infancy. In the early months of life, the parents' primary task is to provide enough warmth, predictability, and responsiveness to foster a secure attachment and to support basic physiological needs. But once the child becomes physically, linguistically, and cognitively more independent, the need to control becomes a central aspect of the parents' task. Too much control and the child will not have sufficient opportunity to explore; too little control and the child will become unmanageable and fail to learn the social skills she will need to get along with peers as well as adults.

social-cognitive theory the theoretical perspective that asserts that social and personality development in early childhood is related to improvements in the cognitive domain

Learning Objective 8.2

What are the findings of social-cognitive theorists with respect to young children's understanding of the social world?

Social-Cognitive Perspectives

In contrast to the psychoanalytic tradition, **social-cognitive theory** assumes that social and emotional changes in the child are the result of—or at least are facilitated by—the enormous growth in cognitive abilities that happens during the preschool years (Macrae & Bodenhausen, 2000). Over the past three decades, psychologists have devoted a great deal of theoretical and empirical attention to determining just how the two domains are connected.

Person Perception Have you ever heard a child describe a peer as "nice" or "not nice"? Preschoolers' emerging capacity for applying categories to people is called **person perception**, or the ability to classify others. For example, by kindergarten age, children make judgments very similar to those of adults when asked to identify the most intelligent child in their class or play group (Droege & Stipek, 1993). Moreover, they describe their peers in terms of traits such as "grumpy" and "mean" (Yuill, 1997). They also make statements about other people's patterns of behavior—"Grandma always lets me pick the cereal at the grocery store." They use these observations to classify others into groups such as "people I like" and "people I don't like."

However, young children's observations and categorizations of people are far less consistent than those of older children. A playmate they judge to be "nice" one day may be referred to as "mean" the next. Developmentalists have found that young children's judgments about others are inconsistent because they tend to base them on their most recent interactions with those individuals (Ruble & Dweck, 1995). In other words, a 4-year-old girl describes one of her playmates as "nice" on Monday because she shares a cookie, but as "mean" on Tuesday because she refuses to share a candy bar. Or the child declares "I don't like Grandma any more because she made me go to bed early."

Preschoolers also categorize others on the basis of observable characteristics such as race, age, and gender. For example, the *cross-race effect*, a phenomenon in which individuals are more likely to remember the faces of people of their own race than those of people of a different race, is established by age 5 (Pezdek, Blandon-Gitlin, & Moore, 2003). Similarly, they talk about "big kids" (school-age children) and "little kids" (their agemates), and they seem to know that they fit in best with the latter. Self-segregation by gender—a topic you'll read more about later in the chapter—begins as early as age 2. Likewise, young children sometimes segregate themselves according to race (see the Research Report on page 210).

Understanding Rule Categories If you attended a formal dinner at which the forks were on the right side of the plates rather than on the left, would you be upset? Probably not, because *social conventions*, such as customs that govern where to place flatware, are rules that have nothing to do with our fundamental sense of right and wrong. Consequently, most of us are not troubled when they are violated and take a dim view of people who are bothered by such trifles. By contrast, we have little tolerance for the breaking of rules that we view as having a basis in morality, such as laws that forbid stealing and unwritten rules like the one that prohibits you from flirting with your best friend's romantic partner (or with your romantic partner's best friend!). When and how did we learn to make such distinctions?

Social-cognitive theorists have found that children begin to respond differently to violations of different kinds of rules between 2 and 3 (Smetana, Schlagman, & Adams, 1993). For example, they view taking another child's toy without permission as a more serious violation of rules than forgetting to say "thank you." They also say, just as adults would in response to similar questions, that stealing and physical violence are wrong, even if their particular family or preschool has no explicit rule against them. This kind of understanding seems to develop both as a consequence of preschoolers' increasing capacity for classification and as a result of adults' tendency to emphasize transgressions that have moral overtones more than violations of customs and other arbitrary rules when punishing children (Nucci & Smetana, 1996).

Understanding Others' Intentions Would you feel differently about a person who deliberately smashed your car's windshield with a baseball bat than you would about someone else who accidentally broke it while washing your car for you? Chances are you would be far more forgiving of the person who unintentionally broke your windshield, because we tend to

person perception the ability to classify others according to categories such as age, gender, and race

base our judgments of others' behavior and our responses to them on what we perceive to be their intentions. Working from his assumptions about young children's egocentrism, Piaget suggested that young children were incapable of such discriminations.

However, more recent research has demonstrated that young children do understand intentions to some degree (Zhang & Yu, 2002). For one thing, it's quite common for preschoolers to say "It was an accident . . . I didn't mean to do it" when they are punished. Such protests suggest that children understand that intentional wrongdoing is punished more severely than unintentional transgressions of the rules.

Several studies suggest that children can make judgments about actors' intentions both when faced with abstract problems and when personally motivated by a desire to avoid punishment. For example, in a classic study, 3-year-olds listened to stories about children playing ball (Nelson, 1980). Pictures were used to convey information about intentions (see Figure 8.1). The children were more likely to label as "bad" or "naughty" the child who intended to harm a playmate than the child who accidentally hit another child in the head with the ball. However, the children's judgments were also influenced by outcomes. In other words, they were more likely to say a child who wanted to hurt his playmate was "good" if he failed to hit the child with the ball. These results suggest that children know more about intentions than Piaget thought, but they are still limited in their ability to base judgments entirely on intentions.

Critical Thinking

1. How might the psychoanalytic and social-cognitive perspectives on early childhood development be integrated into a comprehensive explanation of age-related changes during this period?

RESEARCH REPORT

Racism in the Preschool Classroom

The preschool classroom or day-care center is often the only setting in which children of different races come together. Consequently, these classrooms are likely to be important to the development of racial attitudes. Preschool teachers, then, need to be aware of how such attitudes are formed.

Research suggests that, once young children form race schemas, they use them to make judgments about others. These early judgments probably reflect young children's egocentric thinking. Essentially, children view those like themselves as desirable companions and those who are unlike them—in gender, race, and other categorical variables—as undesirable (Doyle & Aboud, 1995). Thus, like the understanding of race itself, race-based playmate preferences probably result from immature cognitive structures rather than true racism.

Of course, cognitive development doesn't happen in a social vacuum, and by age 5, most White children in English-speaking countries have acquired an understanding of their culture's racial stereotypes and prejudices (Bigler & Liben, 1993). Likewise, African American, Hispanic American, and Native American children become sensitive very early in life to the fact that people of their race are viewed negatively by many Whites. Some studies suggest that this early awareness of racial stereotypes negatively influences minority children's self-esteem (Jambunathan & Burts, 2003). Moreover, White preschool teachers may not notice race-based behavior in their classrooms, but research suggests that minority children report a significant number of such events to their parents (Bernhard, Lefebvre, Kilbride, Chud, & Lange, 1998).

Psychologists speculate that the combination of immature cognitive development, acquisition of cultural stereotypes, and preschool teachers' insensitivity to racial incidents may foster racist attitudes. The key to preventing racial awareness from developing into racism, they say, is for preschool teachers to discuss race openly and to make conscious efforts to help children acquire non-prejudiced attitudes (Cushner, McClelland, & Safford, 1993). For example, they can make young children aware of historical realities such as slavery, race segregation, and minority groups' efforts to achieve equal rights. Teachers can also assign children of different races to do projects together. In addition, they can make children aware of each other's strengths as individuals, since both children and adults seem to perceive individual differences only within their own racial group (Ostrom, Carpenter, Sedikides, & Li, 1993).

Ideally, all children should learn to evaluate their own and others' behavior according to individual criteria rather than group membership, and minority children need to be especially encouraged to view their race positively. Preschool teachers are in a position to provide young children with a significant push toward these important goals.

Questions for Critical Analysis

1. How would you explain a White preschooler teachers' failure to notice race-based behaviors in their classrooms?
2. How would information-processing theory explain the role that historical knowledge regarding slavery, discrimination, and the civil rights movement might influence the development of preschoolers' ideas about race?

Figure 8.1
A Test of Children's Understanding of Intentionality

Pictures like these have been used to assess young children's understanding of an actor's intentions.

Personality and Self-Concept

As young children gain more understanding of the social environment, their distinctive personalities begin to emerge. At the same time, their self-concepts become more complex, allowing them to exercise greater control over their own behavior.

From Temperament to Personality

Learning Objective 8.3
How does temperament change in early childhood?

Are you familiar with the children's game "Duck, Duck, Goose"? For the benefit of readers who are unfamiliar with the game, here's how it goes. A child who has been assigned the role of "it" walks around the outside of a circle of children who are seated on the floor. As "it" passes by, he touches the head of each child and calls out "duck" until he comes to the child that he chooses to be the "goose." The "goose" then has to chase "it" around the circle and try to prevent him from taking goose's seat. If "goose" fails to beat "it," then she becomes "it" for the next round of the game. The difficult part of the game for many young children is waiting to be chosen to be the "goose."

Activities such as "Duck, Duck, Goose" may seem frivolous, but they contribute to the process through which temperament becomes modified into personality during the early childhood years. A child whose temperament includes a low ranking on the dimension of effortful control, for instance, may not be able to tolerate waiting for his turn in a game of "Duck, Duck, Goose" (Li-Grining, 2007). If he obeys his impulse to chase "it" and jumps up from his seat before he is declared the "goose," he will undoubtedly be scolded by his playmates. If his frustration leads him to withdraw from the game with the protest, "I *never* get to be the goose!", he will miss out on the fun of participating. Either way, he will learn that controlling his impulses is more beneficial to him than submitting to them. A few such experiences will teach him to moderate the effects of his lack of effortful control on his social behavior. As a result, his lack of effortful control will become less prominent in the profile of characteristics that constitute his personality and will change how his peers respond to him. Their approval of his modified profile will encourage him to keep his impulses in check.

Similarly, children with difficult temperaments learn that the behaviors associated with difficultness, such as complaining, often result in peer rejection. As a result, many of them change their behavior to gain social acceptance. Similarly, some shy toddlers are encouraged by their parents to be more sociable (Rubin, Burgess, & Hastings, 2002). Thus, personality represents the combination of the temperament with which children are probably born and the knowledge they gain about temperament-related behavior during childhood (McCrae et al., 2000; Svrakic, Svrakic, & Cloninger, 1996).

The transition from temperament to personality is also influenced by parental responses to the young child's temperament. If the parents reject the difficult child, the child is likely to emerge from the preschool years with a personality that puts him at risk for developing serious problems in social relationships, and he may suffer from cognitive deficits as well (Bates, 1989; Fish, Stifter, & Belsky, 1991). However, parents can moderate the risks associated with a difficult temperament by helping these children learn to regulate their emotions and behavior more effectively (Coplan, Bowker, & Cooper, 2003). Thus, infant temperament doesn't necessarily dictate the kind of personality a child will develop. Instead, it is one factor among many that shape an individual child's personality.

Learning Objective 8.4

What changes take place in the young child's categorical, emotional, and social selves during the preschool years?

Self-Concept

Ask a preschooler to describe herself, and you are likely to get an answer such as "I'm a girl." Pressed for more information, the child will add her hair color or some other physical characteristic, tell you who her friends are, or reveal who her favorite cartoon character is. These answers show that the categorical self, which first emerged during infancy, is becoming more mature. Likewise, the emotional self grows by leaps and bounds during these years, and a new component of self-concept, the *social self* emerges.

emotional regulation the ability to control emotional states and emotion-related behavior

The Emotional Self In recent years, research examining development of the emotional self during the early childhood years has focused on the acquisition of **emotional regulation**, or the ability to control emotional states and emotion-related behavior (Hoeksma, Oosterlaan, & Schipper, 2004). For example, children exhibit emotional regulation when they find a way to cheer themselves up when they are feeling sad, or when they divert their attention to a different activity when they get frustrated with something. Recent research has shown that emotional regulation in early childhood is linked to a variety of social variables. One study showed that level of emotional regulation at age 2 predicted level of aggressive behavior at age 4 in both boys and girls (Rubin, Burgess, Dwyer, & Hastings, 2003). Predictably, preschoolers who display high levels of emotional regulation are more popular with their peers than those who are less able to regulate their emotional behavior (Denham et al., 2003; Fantuzzo, Sekino, & Cohen, 2004). Emotional regulation skills appear to be particularly important for children whose temperaments include high levels of anger proneness (Diener & Kim, 2004). Further, longitudinal research has demonstrated that emotional regulation in early childhood is related to children's ability to obey moral rules and to think about right and wrong during the school years (Kochanska, Murray, & Coy, 1997).

All children get upset from time to time, but they vary widely in how well they manage distressing feelings.

The process of acquiring emotional regulation is one in which control shifts slowly from the parents to the child (Houck & Lecuyer-Maus, 2004). Here again, the child's temperament is a factor. For example, preschoolers who have consistently exhibited difficult behavior since infancy are more likely to have self-control problems in early childhood (Schmitz et al., 1999). Similarly, preschoolers who were born prematurely or who were delayed in language development in the second year of life experience more difficulties with self-control during early childhood (Carson, Klee, & Perry, 1998; Schothorst & van Engeland, 1996).

Another aspect of the emotional self involves **empathy**, the ability to identify with another person's emotional state. Empathy has two aspects: apprehending another person's emotional state or condition and then matching that emotional state oneself. An empathizing person experiences either the same feeling he imagines the other person to feel or a highly similar feeling. Empathy is negatively associated with aggression in the early childhood years; the more advanced preschoolers' capacity for empathy is, the less aggression they display (Findlay, Girardi, & Coplan, 2006; Strayer & Roberts, 2004). Moreover, the development of empathy in early childhood appears to provide the foundation on which a more sophisticated emotion, *sympathy* (a general feeling of sorrow or concern for another person), is built in later childhood and adolescence. The most thorough analysis of the development of empathy and sympathy has been offered by Martin Hoffman (1982, 1988), who describes four broad stages, summarized in Table 8.1.

In addition to empathy, young children's emotional selves include an awareness of emotional states that are linked to their culture's definitions of right and wrong. These feelings, which are sometimes called the *moral emotions*, include guilt, shame, and pride (Eisenberg, 2000). Guilt is usually thought of as the emotional state that is induced when a child breaks a rule. Consequently, a child who takes a forbidden cookie will experience guilt. Feelings of shame arise when she fails to live up to expectations. For instance, most parents and teachers urge young children to share their toys. Thus, when a child behaves selfishly and is reminded about the sharing rule, it is likely that he feels shame. By contrast, children feel pride when they succeed at meeting such expectations.

Research suggests that the interplay among these three emotions, and young children's awareness of them, influence the development of behavior that children's cultures regard as morally acceptable (Eisenberg, 2000). Thus, they form the foundation of later moral development. Studies suggest that these feelings evolve in the context of parent-child relationships. Young children who do not have warm, trusting relationships with their parents are at risk of failing to develop moral emotions or of developing feelings of guilt, shame, and pride that are too weak to influence their behavior (Koenig, Cicchetti, & Rogosch, 2004).

The Social Self Another facet of the child's emerging sense of self is an increasing awareness of herself as a player in the social game. By age 2, the toddler has already learned a variety of social "scripts"—routines of play or interaction with others. The toddler now begins to

empathy the ability to identify with another person's emotional state

Table 8.1 Stages in Development of Empathy Proposed by Hoffman

Stage	Description
Stage 1: Global empathy	Observed during the first year. If the infant is around someone expressing a strong emotion, he may match that emotion—for example, by beginning to cry when he hears another infant crying.
Stage 2: Egocentric empathy	Beginning at about 12 to 18 months of age, when children have developed a fairly clear sense of their separate selves, they respond to another's distress with some distress of their own, but they may attempt to "cure" the other person's problem by offering what they themselves would find most comforting. They may, for example, show sadness when they see another child hurt, and go get their own mother to help.
Stage 3: Empathy for another's feelings	Beginning as young as age 2 or 3 and continuing through elementary school, children note others' feelings, partially match those feelings, and respond to the other's distress in nonegocentric ways. Over these years, children become able to distinguish a wider (and more subtle) range of emotions.
Stage 4: Empathy for another's life condition	In late childhood or adolescence, some children develop a more generalized notion of others' feelings and respond not just to the immediate situation but to the other individual's general situation or plight. Thus, a young person at this level may become more distressed by another person's sadness if she knows that the sadness is chronic or that the person's general situation is particularly tragic than if she sees it as a momentary problem.

Sources: Hoffman, 1982, 1988.

Critical Thinking

1. If parents received a description of their child's temperament at birth (sort of like the owner's manual you get with a new appliance), do you think it would help them to be better parents? Conversely, do you think it would cause them to be overly tolerant of temperamental characteristics that might need to be modified for the child's own benefit, such as irritability?

develop some implicit understanding of her own roles in these scripts (Case, 1991). So she may begin to think of herself as a "helper" in some situations or as "the boss" when she is telling some other child what to do.

You can see this clearly in children's sociodramatic play, as they begin to take explicit roles: "I'll be the daddy and you be the mommy," or "I'm the boss." As part of the same process, the young child also gradually comes to understand her place in the network of family roles. She has sisters, brothers, father, mother, and so forth.

Moreover, role scripts help young children become more independent. For example, assuming the "student" role provides a preschooler with a prescription for appropriate behavior in the school situation. Students listen when the teacher speaks to the class, get out materials and put them away at certain times, help their classmates in various ways, and so on. Once a preschooler is familiar with and adopts the student role, he can follow the role script and is no longer dependent on the teacher to tell him what to do every minute of the day.

Gender Development

We noted earlier that preschoolers who are asked to describe themselves are likely to begin by stating whether they are boys or girls. In psychologists' terms, their tendency to do so suggests that "boy-ness" and "girl-ness" are *salient*, or important, categories for young children. Thus, one of the most fascinating developmental processes of the preschool period is the one that involves children's evolving sense of **gender**, the psychological and social associates and implications of biological sex.

Learning Objective 8.5

How do the major theoretical orientations explain gender development?

Explaining Gender Development

Developmentalists have proposed several explanations of gender development.

Psychoanalytic Explanations As you remember from Chapter 2, Freud suggested that 3- to 6-year-olds overcome the anxiety they feel about their desires for the opposite-sex parent (the Oedipus or Electra conflict) through identification with the same-sex parent. In order to identify with the parent, the child must learn and conform to his or her sex-role concepts. Thus, according to Freud, children acquire gender through the process of identification.

The difficulty with Freud's theory is that toddlers seem to understand far more about gender than the theory would predict. For example, many 18-month-olds accurately label themselves and others as boys or girls. Likewise, clearly sex-typed behavior appears long before age 4 or 5, when psychoanalytic theories claim identification occurs.

Social-Learning Explanations Social-learning theorists have emphasized the role of parents in shaping children's gender development (Bandura, 1977a; Mischel, 1966, 1970). This notion has been far better supported by research than have Freud's ideas. Parents do seem to reinforce sex-typed activities in children as young as 18 months, not only by buying different kinds of toys for boys and girls but also by responding more positively when their sons play with blocks or trucks or when their daughters play with dolls (Fagot & Hagan, 1991; Lytton & Romney, 1991). Such differential reinforcement is particularly clear with boys, especially from fathers (Siegal, 1987).

Still, helpful as it is, a social-learning explanation is probably not sufficient. In particular, parents differentially reinforce boys' and girls' behavior less than you'd expect, and probably not enough to account for the very early and robust discrimination children seem to make on the basis of gender. Even young children whose parents seem to treat their sons and daughters in highly similar ways nonetheless learn gender labels and prefer same-sex playmates.

gender the psychological and social associates and implications of biological sex

Social-Cognitive Explanations A third alternative, social-cognitive theory, suggests that children's understanding of gender is linked to gender-related behavior. For example, one such view, based strongly on Piagetian theory, is Lawrence Kohlberg's suggestion that the crucial aspect of the process is the child's understanding of the gender concept (Kohlberg, 1966; Kohlberg & Ullian, 1974). Once the child realizes that he is a boy or she is a girl forever, he or she becomes highly motivated to learn how to behave in the way that is expected or appropriate for that gender. Specifically, Kohlberg's theory predicts that systematic same-sex imitation will become evident only after the child has shown full gender constancy. **Gender constancy** is the understanding that gender is an innate characteristic that can't be changed. Most studies designed to test this hypothesis have supported Kohlberg. Children do seem to become much more sensitive to same-sex models after they understand gender constancy (Frey & Ruble, 1992). Kohlberg's theory allows developmentalists to make highly reliable predictions about the development of children's knowledge about gender.

However, social-cognitive theory is less accurate in predicting behavior. Specifically, it can't explain the obvious fact that children show clearly different behavior, such as toy preferences, long before they have achieved full understanding of the gender concept. A newer social-cognitive theory derived from the information-processing approach is usually called *gender schema theory* (Bem, 1981; Martin, 1991; Martin & Halverson, 1981). This approach includes many of Kohlberg's ideas about how gender constancy develops, but it does a better job of predicting behavior.

Gender Schema Theory You'll remember from Chapter 7 that a great deal of *schematic* learning happens in early childhood. A schema is a mental pattern or model that is used to process information. Just as the self concept can be thought of as a schema, so the child's understanding of gender can be seen in the same way. According to **gender schema theory**, the gender schema begins to develop as soon as the child notices the differences between male and female, knows his own gender, and can label the two groups with some consistency—all of which happens by age 2 or 3 (Bem, 1981; Martin & Ruble, 2002). Perhaps because gender is clearly an either/or category, children seem to understand very early that this is a key distinction, so the category serves as a kind of magnet for new information. Once the child has established even a primitive gender schema, a great many experiences can be assimilated to it. Thus, as soon as this schema begins to be formed, children may begin to show preference for same-sex playmates or for gender-stereotyped activities (Martin & Little, 1990).

Preschoolers first learn some broad distinctions about what kinds of activities or behavior "go with" each gender, both by observing other children and through the reinforcements they receive from parents. They also learn a few gender *scripts*—whole sequences of events that are normally associated with a given gender, such as "fixing dinner" or "building with tools"—just as they learn other social scripts at about this age (Levy & Fivush, 1993). Then, between age 4 and age 6, the child learns a more subtle and complex set of associations for his own gender—what children of his own gender like and don't like, how they play, how they talk, what kinds of people they associate with. Only between the ages of 8 and 10 does the child develop an equivalently complex view of the opposite gender (Martin, Wood, & Little, 1990).

The key difference between this theory and Kohlberg's gender constancy theory is that gender schema theory asserts that children need not understand that gender is permanent to form an initial gender schema. When they do begin to understand gender constancy, at about 5 or 6, children develop a more elaborate rule, or schema, of "what people who are like me do" and treat this rule the same way they treat other rules—as an absolute. Later, the child's application of the gender rule becomes more flexible. She knows, for example, that most boys don't play with dolls, but that they can do so if they like.

Biological Approaches For a long time, developmentalists dismissed the idea that biological differences between males and females were responsible for psychological differences between them. Today, though, they are taking another look at decades-old experimental studies with animals showing that prenatal exposure to male hormones such as *testosterone* powerfully influences behavior after birth (Lippa, 2005). Female animals exposed to testosterone

gender constancy the understanding that gender is a component of the self that is not altered by external appearance

gender schema theory an information-processing approach to gender concept development that asserts that people use a schema for each gender to process information about themselves and others

behave more like male animals; for instance, they are more aggressive than females who do not experience prenatal exposure to testosterone. Similarly, when experimenters block the release of testosterone during prenatal development of male animal embryos, the animals exhibit behavior that is more typical of the females of their species.

Hormonal influences have been proposed to explain the outcomes of cases involving boys who carry a genetic defect that causes them to develop deformed genitalia. Decades ago, a few such boys were subjected to plastic surgery to give them female-appearing genitals and were raised as girls. At that time, however, doctors did not realize that the genetic defect in question interferes only with testosterone's effects on the sex organs; the brains of these fetuses were exposed to normal amounts of testosterone throughout prenatal development (Rosenthal & Gitelman, 2002). Follow-up studies found that many of these children, when they learned of their status, sought surgery to masculinize their bodies. Moreover, even those who elected to retain the feminine identities they had been given in infancy possessed many attributes and behaviors that are more typical of males than of females (Reiner & Gearhardt, 2004). Such findings support the view that hormones play some role in gender development.

Learning Objective 8.6

Describe the development of gender identity, gender stability, and gender constancy.

The Gender Concept

Children seem to develop gender constancy in three steps. First comes **gender identity**, which is simply a child's ability to label his or her own sex correctly and to identify other people as men or women, boys or girls. By 9–12 months, babies already treat male and female faces as different categories (Fagot & Leinbach, 1993). Within the next year, they begin to learn the verbal labels that go with these categories. By age 2, most children correctly label themselves as boys or girls, and within 6–12 months, most can correctly label others as well.

Accurate labeling, though, does not signify complete understanding. The second step is **gender stability**, which is the understanding that you stay the same gender throughout life. Researchers have measured this by asking children such questions as "When you were a little baby, were you a little girl or a little boy?" or "When you grow up, will you be a mommy or a daddy?" Most children understand the stability of gender by about age 4 (Slaby & Frey, 1975) (see Figure 8.2).

gender identity the ability to correctly label oneself and others as male or female

gender stability the understanding that gender is a stable, life-long characteristic

The final step is the development of true gender constancy, the recognition that someone stays the same gender even though he may appear to change by wearing different clothes or changing his hair length. For example, boys don't change into girls by wearing dresses. It may seem odd that a child who understands that he will stay the same gender throughout life (gender stability) can nonetheless be confused about the effect of changes in dress or appearance on gender. But numerous studies, including studies of children growing up in other cultures such as Kenya, Nepal, Belize, and Samoa, show that children go through this sequence (Munroe, Shimmin, & Munroe, 1984). Moreover, it is related to general cognitive development (Trautner, Gervai, & Nemeth, 2003).

Figure 8.2
Gender Stereotyping in a Child's Drawing

In describing this self-portrait, the 5-year-old artist said, "This is how I will look when I get married to a boy. I am under a rainbow, so beautiful with a bride hat, a belt, and a purse." The girl knows she will always be female and associates gender with externals such as clothing (gender stability). She is also already quite knowledgeable about gender role expectations. (Courtesy of Jerry and Denise Boyd. Used with permission.)

The underlying logic of this sequence may be a bit clearer if you think of a parallel between gender constancy and the concept of conservation. Conservation involves recognition that an object remains the same in some fundamental way even though it changes externally.

Gender constancy is thus a kind of "conservation of gender" and is not typically understood until about 5 or 6, when children understand other conservations (Marcus & Overton, 1978).

Sex-Role Knowledge

Learning Objective 8.7

What are the characteristics of young children's sex-role knowledge?

Figuring out your gender and understanding that it stays constant are only part of the story. Learning what goes with being a boy or a girl in a given culture is also a vital part of the child's task. Researchers have studied this in two ways—by asking children what boys and girls (or men and women) like to do and what they are like (which is an inquiry about gender stereotypes) and by asking children if it is okay for boys to play with dolls or girls to climb trees or do equivalent cross-sex things (an inquiry about roles).

In every culture, adults have clear gender stereotypes. Indeed, the content of those stereotypes is remarkably similar in cultures around the world. Psychologists who have studied gender stereotypes in many different countries, including non-Western countries such as Thailand, Pakistan, and Nigeria, find that the most clearly stereotyped traits are weakness, gentleness, appreciativeness, and soft-heartedness for women, and aggression, strength, cruelty, and coarseness for men (Williams & Best, 1990). In most cultures, men are also seen as competent, skillful, assertive, and able to get things done, while women are seen as warm and expressive, tactful, quiet, gentle, aware of others' feelings, and lacking in competence, independence, and logic (Williams & Best, 1990).

As gender develops, children change their views about whether it is acceptable for boys to play with dolls or for girls to play sports such as baseball.

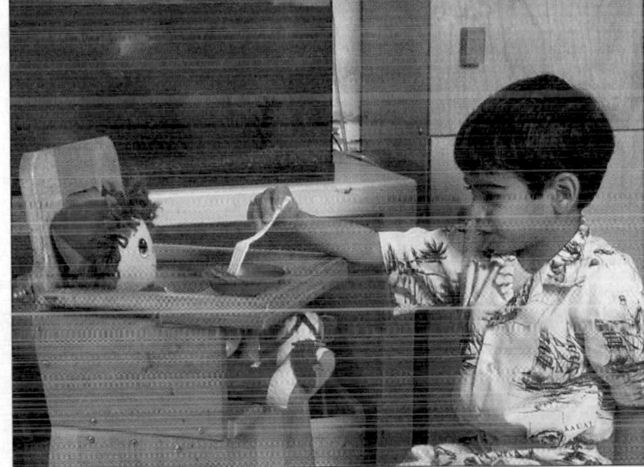

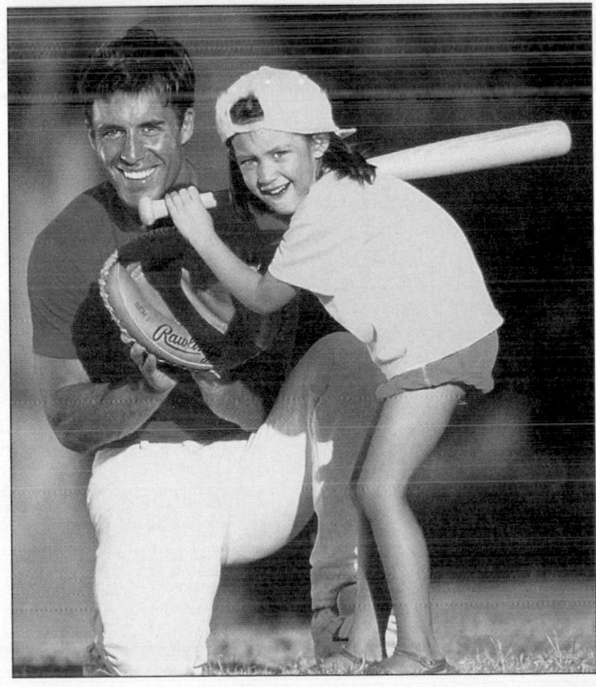

Studies of children show that these stereotyped ideas develop early. It would not be uncommon to hear a 3-year-old in the United States say "Mommies use the stove, and Daddies use the grill." A 4-year-old might define gender roles in terms of competencies: "Daddies are better at fixing things, but Mommies are better at tying bows and decorating." Even 2-year-olds in the United States already associate certain tasks and possessions with men and women, such as vacuum cleaners and food with women and cars and tools with men. By age 3 or 4, children can assign stereotypic occupations, toys, and activities to each gender. By age 5, children begin to associate certain personality traits, such as assertiveness and nurturance, with males or females (Martin, 1993; Serbin, Powlishta, & Gulko, 1993).

Studies of children's ideas about how men and women (or boys and girls) ought to behave add an interesting further element. For example, in an early study, a psychologist told a story to children aged 4–9 about a little boy named George who liked to play with dolls (Damon, 1977). George's parents told him that only little girls play with dolls; little boys shouldn't. The children were then asked questions about the story, such as "Why do people tell George not to play with dolls?" or "Is there a rule that boys shouldn't play with dolls?"

Four-year-olds in this study thought it was okay for George to play with dolls. There was no rule against it and he should do it if he wanted to. Six-year-olds, in contrast, thought it was wrong for George to play with dolls. By about age 9, children had differentiated between what boys and girls usually do and what is "wrong." One boy said, for example, that breaking windows was wrong and bad, but that playing with dolls was not bad in the same way: "Breaking windows you're not supposed to do. And if you play with dolls, well, you can, but boys usually don't."

What this study appeared to reveal is that the 5- to 6-year-old, having figured out that gender is permanent, is searching for a rule about how boys and girls behave (Martin & Halverson, 1981). The child picks up information from watching adults, from television, from listening to the labels that are attached to different activities (e.g., "Boys don't cry"). Initially, children treat these as absolute, moral rules. Later, they understand that these are social conventions; at this point, gender concepts become more flexible and stereotyping declines somewhat (Katz & Ksansnak, 1994).

Learning Objective 8.8

How is the behavior of young children sex-typed?

Sex-Typed Behavior

The final element in the development of gender is the actual behavior children show with those of the same and the opposite sex. An unexpected finding is that **sex-typed behavior**, or different patterns of behavior among girls and boys, develops earlier than ideas about gender (Campbell, Shirley, & Candy, 2004). By 18–24 months, children begin to show some preference for sex-stereotyped toys, such as dolls for girls or trucks or building blocks for boys, which is some months before they can consistently identify their own gender (Campbell, Shirley, & Caygill, 2002; O'Brien, 1992; Serbin, Poulin-Dubois, Colbourne, Sen, & Eichstedt, 2001). By age 3, children begin to show a preference for same-sex friends and are much more sociable with playmates of the same sex—at a time when they do not yet have a concept of gender stability (Corsaro, Molinari, Hadley, & Sugioka, 2003; Maccoby, 1988, 1990; Maccoby & Jacklin, 1987) (see Figure 8.3).

Not only are preschoolers' friendships and peer interactions increasingly sex-segregated; it is also clear that boy-boy interactions and girl-girl interactions differ in quality, even in these early years. One important part of same-sex interactions seems to involve instruction in and modeling of sex-appropriate behavior. In other words, older boys teach younger boys how to be "masculine," and older girls teach younger girls how to be "feminine" (Danby & Baker, 1998).

However, these "lessons" in sex-typed behavior are fairly subtle. Eleanor Maccoby, one of the leading theorists in this area, describes the girls' pattern as an *enabling style* (Maccoby, 1990). Enabling includes such behaviors as supporting the friend, expressing agreement, and making suggestions. All these behaviors tend to foster a greater equality and intimacy in the relationship and keep the interaction going. In contrast, boys are more likely to show what Maccoby calls a *constricting, or restrictive, style.* "A restrictive style is one that tends to derail the interaction—to inhibit the partner or cause the partner to withdraw, thus shortening the interaction or bringing it to an end" (1990, p. 517). Contradicting, interrupting, boasting, and other forms of self-display are all aspects of this style. Rough-and-tumble play and play fight-

sex-typed behavior different patterns of behavior exhibited by boys and girls

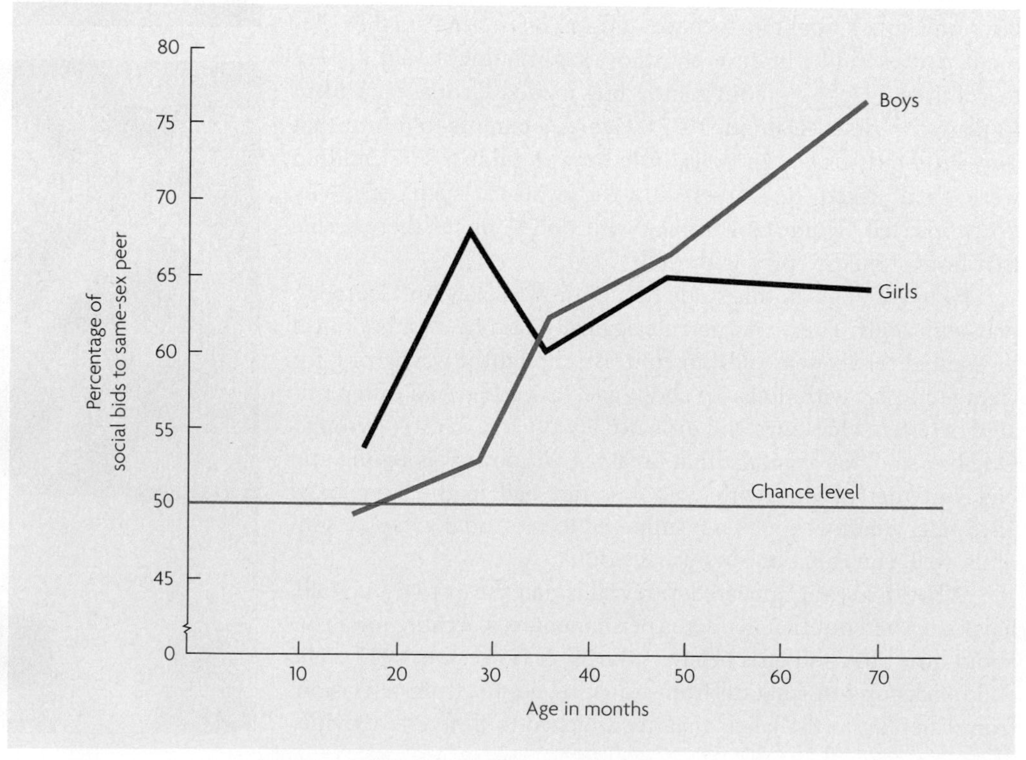

Figure 8.3
Gender and Playmate Preferences

In one classic study of playmate preferences, researchers counted how often preschool children played with same-sex and opposite-sex playmates. Children as young as 2 ½ already showed at least some preference for same-sex playmates.

(*Source*: Adaptation from *Child Development* by P. La Freniere, F. Strayer, & R. Gauthier. Figure 1, p. 1961, 1984. Reprinted by permission of Society for Research in Child Development.)

ing are other manifestations of boys' restrictive interaction style.

These two patterns begin to be visible in the preschool years. For example, beginning as early as age 3, boys and girls use quite different strategies in their attempts to influence each other's behavior (Maccoby, 1990). Girls generally ask questions or make requests; boys are much more likely to make demands or phrase things using imperatives ("Give me that!"). The really intriguing finding is that even at this early age, boys simply don't respond to the girls' enabling style. Thus, playing with boys yields little positive reinforcement for girls, and they begin to avoid such interactions and band together.

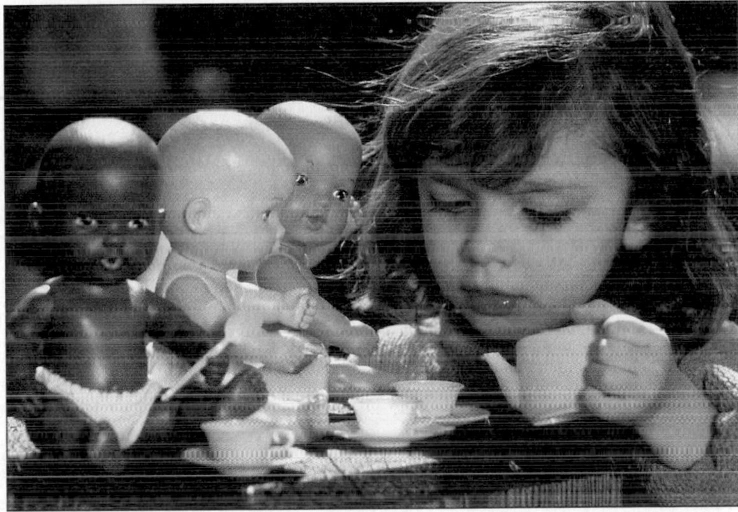

Play may provide children with opportunities to learn about gender expectations.

Another kind of learning opportunity happens when children exhibit **cross-gender behavior**, behavior that is atypical in their culture for their gender. For example, *tomboyishness*, girls' preference for activities that are more typical for boys, is a kind of cross-gender behavior. Generally, tomboyishness is tolerated by adults and peers (Sandnabba & Ahlberg, 1999). Not surprisingly, then, cross-gender behavior is far more common among girls than boys (Etaugh & Liss, 1992). Tomboyishness does not appear to interfere with the development of a "feminine" personality in adulthood, and it may allow girls to acquire positive characteristics such as assertiveness (Burn, O'Neil, & Nederend, 1996).

In contrast, both peers and adults actively discourage boys from engaging in cross-gender behavior. Specifically, boys who play with dolls or behave in an effeminate manner are likely to elicit expressions of disapproval—or even ridicule—from children, parents, and teachers (Martin, 1991). Many adults' reactions to boys' cross-gender behavior appear to be related to the fear that it may lead to homosexuality (Sandnabba & Ahlberg, 1999).

However, it cannot be assumed that the prevalence of sex-typed play among boys is strictly the result of adult and peer influence. For one thing, sex-typed play preferences appear earlier and are more consistent in male infants, which suggests that these preferences begin to develop before environmental forces have had much chance to influence them (Blakemore, LaRue, & Olejnik, 1979). Further, by age 3, boys are likely to show an actual aversion to girls' activities—for example, by saying "yuck" when experimenters offer them toys like dolls (Bussey & Bandura, 1992). In addition, boys may prefer the company of a girl who is a tomboy to that of a boy who engages in cross-gender activity (Alexander & Hines, 1994). Finally, researchers have found that it is very difficult to change boys' play preferences with modeling and reinforcement (Paley, 1986; Weisner & Wilson-Mitchell, 1990). These findings suggest that, at least for boys, sex-typed behavior is part of a complex process of identity development and not just the result of cultural modeling and reinforcement.

Critical Thinking

1. To what degree do you think the enabling and constrictive interaction styles are exhibited in adults' social interactions?

Family Relationships and Structure

Psychologists agree that family relationships constitute one of the most, if not *the* most, influential factors in early childhood development. These relationships reflect both continuity and change. The preschooler is no less attached to her family than the infant but, at the same time, is struggling to establish independence.

cross-gender behavior behavior that is atypical for one's own sex but typical for the opposite sex

Learning Objective 8.9

How does attachment change during the early childhood years?

Attachment

You'll remember from Chapter 6 that by 12 months of age, a baby has normally established a clear attachment to at least one caregiver. By age 2 or 3, the attachment is just as strong, but many attachment behaviors have become less visible. Three-year-olds still want to sit on Mom's or Dad's lap; they are still likely to seek some closeness when Mom returns from an absence. But when she is not afraid or under stress, the 3-year-old is able to wander farther and farther from her safe base without apparent distress. She can also deal with her potential anxiety due to separation by creating shared plans with the parents. For example, a parent might say "I'll be home after your naptime," to which the child may respond "Can we watch a movie then?" (Crittenden, 1992).

Off he goes, into greater independence. A child this age, especially one with secure attachment, is far more confident about being at a distance from his safe base.

Attachment quality also predicts behavior during the preschool years. Children who are securely attached to parents experience fewer behavior problems. Specifically, those who are insecurely attached display more anger and aggression toward both peers and adults in social settings such as day care and preschool (DeMulder, Denham, Schmidt, & Mitchell, 2000; Schmidt, DeMulder, & Denham, 2002).

For most children, the attachment relationship, whether secure or not, seems to change at about age 4. Bowlby described this new stage, or level, as a *goal-corrected partnership*. Just as the first attachment probably requires the baby to understand that his mother will continue to exist when she isn't there, so the preschooler grasps that the *relationship* continues to exist even when the partners are apart. Also at about age 4, the child's internal model of attachment appears to generalize. Bowlby argued that the child's model becomes less a specific property of an individual relationship and more a general property of all the child's social relationships. Thus, it's not surprising that 4- and 5-year-olds who are securely attached to their parents are more likely than their insecurely attached peers to have positive relationships with their preschool teachers (DeMulder et al., 2000).

At the same time, advances in the internal working model lead to new conflicts. In contrast to infants, 2-year-olds realize that they are independent contributors to the parent-child relationship. This heightened sense of autonomy brings them into more and more situations in which parents want one thing and children another. However, contrary to popular stereotypes, 2-year-olds actually comply with parents' requests more often than not. They are more likely to comply with safety requests ("Don't touch that, it's hot!") or with prohibitions about care of objects ("Don't tear up the book") than they are with requests to delay ("I can't talk to you now, I'm on the phone") or with instructions about self-care ("Please wash your hands now"). On the whole, however, children of this age comply fairly readily (Gralinski & Kopp, 1993). When they resist, it is most likely to be passive resistance—simply not doing what is asked rather than saying "no."

Learning Objective 8.10

How do parenting styles affect children's development?

Parenting Styles

Earlier we discussed the fact that temperamental differences lead children to respond differently to situations. Parents differ in temperament themselves, so, just like their children, they vary in how they respond to situations. Consider the situation in which a child resists going to bed, for example. One parent takes the nightly going-to-bed battle in stride and calmly insists that the child go to bed even when she throws a temper tantrum. Another parent responds to the child's emotional escalation by increasing the emotional intensity of his demands, leading to all-out warfare in which the parent assures his own victory by exploiting the physical, social, and emotional control he has over the child. Yet another parent may respond permissively and allow the child to go to bed whenever she wants to. Researchers call these differences **parenting styles**, or the characteristic strategies that parents use to manage children's behavior.

parenting styles the characteristic strategies that parents use to manage children's behavior

Of course, families vary in their responses to preschoolers' increasing demands for independence. Psychologists have struggled over the years to identify the best ways of defining parenting style. At present, the most fruitful conceptualization is one offered by developmentalist Diana Baumrind, who focuses on four aspects of family functioning: (1) warmth or nurturance; (2) clarity and consistency of rules; (3) level of expectations, which she describes in terms of "maturity demands;" and (4) communication between parent and child (Baumrind, 1972).

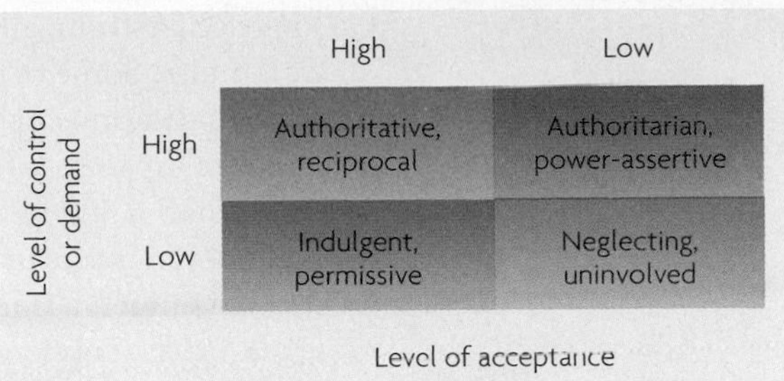

Figure 8.4
Control, Acceptance, and Parenting Style

Maccoby and Martin expanded on Baumrind's categories in this two-dimensional category system.

(*Source*: Adapted from E.E. Maccoby & J.A. Martin, 1983. "Socialization in the context of the family: parent-child interaction". In E.M. Hetherington (Ed.), *Handbook of Child Psychology*, Fig 2, p. 39. New York: Wiley. Reprinted by permission of the publisher.)

Each of these four dimensions has been independently shown to be related to various child behaviors. Children with nurturant and warm parents are more securely attached in the first 2 years of life than those with more rejecting parents; they also have higher self-esteem and are more empathetic, more altruistic, and more responsive to others' hurts or distress; they have higher IQs, are more compliant in preschool and elementary school, do better in school, and are less likely to show delinquent behavior in adolescence or criminal behavior in adulthood (Maccoby, 1980; Maughan, Pickles, & Quinton, 1995; Simons, Robertson, & Downs, 1989; Stormshak et al., 2000).

High levels of affection can even buffer a child against the negative effects of otherwise disadvantageous environments. Several studies of children and teens growing up in poor, tough neighborhoods show that parental warmth is associated with both social and academic competence (Masten & Coatsworth, 1998). In contrast, parental hostility is linked to declining school performance and higher risk of delinquency among poor children and adolescents (Melby & Conger, 1996).

The degree and clarity of the parents' control over the child are also significant. Parents with clear rules, consistently applied, have children who are much less likely to be defiant or noncompliant. Such children are also more competent and sure of themselves and less aggressive (Kurdek & Fine, 1994; Patterson, 1980).

Equally important is the form of control the parents use. The most optimal outcomes for the child occur when the parents are not overly restrictive, explain things to the child, and avoid the use of physical punishments. Children whose parents have high expectations (high "maturity demands," in Baumrind's language) also fare better. Such children have higher self-esteem and show more generosity and altruism toward others.

Finally, open and regular communication between parent and child has been linked to more positive outcomes. Listening to the child is as important as talking to him. Ideally, parents need to convey to the child that what the child has to say is worth listening to, that his ideas are important and should be considered in family decisions. Children of such parents have been found to be more emotionally and socially mature (Baumrind, 1971; Bell & Bell, 1982).

While each of these characteristics of families may be significant individually, they do not occur in isolation but in combinations and patterns. In her early research, Baumrind identified three patterns, or styles, of parenting (Baumrind, 1967). The **permissive parenting style** is high in nurturance but low in maturity demands, control, and communication. The **authoritarian parenting style** is high in control and maturity demands but low in nurturance and communication. The **authoritative parenting style** is high in all four dimensions.

permissive parenting style a style of parenting that is high in nurturance and low in maturity demands, control, and communication

authoritarian parenting style a style of parenting that is low in nurturance and communication, but high in control and maturity demands

authoritative parenting style a style of parenting that is high in nurturance, maturity demands, control, and communication

uninvolved parenting style a style of parenting that is low in nurturance, maturity demands, control, and communication

Eleanor Maccoby and John Martin have proposed a variation of Baumrind's category system, shown in Figure 8.4 (Maccoby & Martin, 1983). They categorize families on two dimensions: the degree of demand or control and the amount of acceptance versus rejection. The intersection of these two dimensions creates four types, three of which correspond quite closely to Baumrind's authoritarian, authoritative, and permissive types. Maccoby and Martin's conceptualization adds a fourth type, the **uninvolved parenting style**.

The Authoritarian Type The parent who responds to a child's refusal to go to bed by asserting physical, social, and emotional control over the child is exhibiting the authoritarian style. Children growing up in authoritarian families—with high levels of demand and control but relatively low levels of warmth and communication—do less well in school, have lower self-esteem, and are typically less skilled with peers than are children from other types of families. Some of these children appear subdued; others may show high aggressiveness or other indications of being out of control. These effects are not restricted to preschool-aged children. In a series of large studies of high school students, including longitudinal studies of more than 6,000 teens, developmentalists found that teenagers from authoritarian families had poorer grades in school and more negative self-concepts than did teenagers from authoritative families, a finding that has been replicated in more recent cohorts of teens (Steinberg et al., 1994; Steinberg, Blatt-Eisengart, & Cauffman, 2006).

The Permissive Type The permissive type of parent responds to a child's refusal to go to bed by allowing the child to go to bed whenever she wants to. Children growing up with indulgent or permissive parents also show some negative outcomes. Researchers have found that these children do slightly worse in school during adolescence and are likely to be both more aggressive (particularly if the parents are specifically permissive toward aggressiveness) and somewhat immature in their behavior with peers and in school. They are less likely to take responsibility and are less independent.

The Authoritative Type Authoritative parents respond to undesirable behaviors such as a child's refusal to go to bed by firmly sticking to their demands without resorting to asserting their power over the child. The most consistently positive outcomes have been associated with an authoritative pattern in which the parents are high in both control and acceptance—setting clear limits but also responding to the child's individual needs. Children reared in such families typically show higher self-esteem and are more independent, but are also more likely to comply with parental requests and may show more altruistic behavior as well. They are self-confident and achievement-oriented in school and get better grades than do children whose parents have other parenting styles (Crockenberg & Litman, 1990; Dornbusch et al., 1987; Steinberg, Elmen, & Mounts, 1989).

The Uninvolved Type Uninvolved parents do not bother to set bedtimes for children or even to tell them to go to bed. They appear to be totally indifferent to children's behavior and to the responsibilities of parenting. The most consistently negative outcomes are associated with the fourth pattern, the uninvolved, or neglecting, parenting style. You may remember from the discussion of secure and insecure attachments in Chapter 6 that one of the family characteristics often found in infants rated as insecure/avoidant is the "psychological unavailability" of the mother. The mother may be depressed or may be overwhelmed by other problems in her life and may simply not have made any deep emotional connection with the child. Likewise, a parent may be distracted from parenting by more attractive activities. Whatever the reason, such children continue to show disturbances in their social relationships for many years. In adolescence, for example, youngsters from neglecting families are more impulsive and antisocial, less competent with their peers, and much less achievement oriented in school (Block, 1971; Lamborn et al., 1991; Pulkkinen, 1982).

Figure 8.5 Parenting Style and Grades

Grades varied with parenting style in Steinberg and Dornbusch's study.

(*Source*: Steinberg et al., 1994, from Table 5, p. 762.)

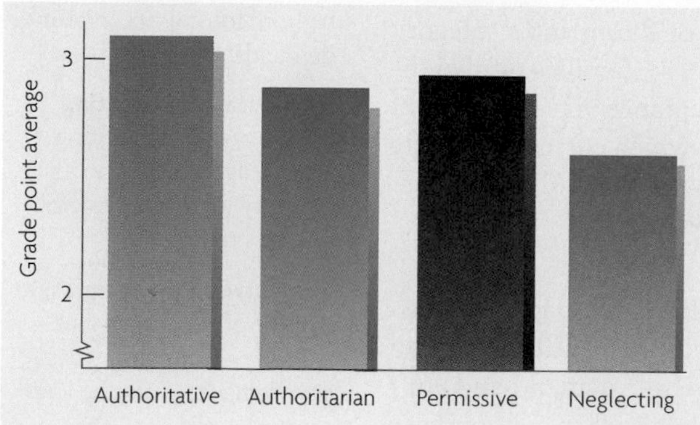

Effects of Parenting Styles Figure 8.5 illustrates the contrasting outcomes in the longitudinal study of adolescents you read about a few paragraphs back; it graphs variations in grade point average as a function of family style. In a longitudinal analysis, these same researchers found that students who described their parents as most authoritative at the beginning of the study showed more improvement in academic competence and self-reliance and the smallest increases in psychological symptoms and delinquent behavior over the succeeding 2 years. So these effects persist.

However, the effects of the family system are more complex than the figure shows. For example, authoritative parents are much more likely to be involved with their child's school, attending school functions and talking to teachers, and this involvement seems to play a crucial role in their children's better school performance. When an authoritative parent is not involved with the school, the academic outcome for the student is not so clearly positive. Similarly, a teenager whose parent is highly involved with the school but is not authoritative shows a less optimal outcome. It is the combination of authoritativeness and school involvement that is associated with the best results (Steinberg et al., 1992).

Another set of complexities is evident in the interaction between parenting style and child temperament. For example, authoritative parents often use **inductive discipline**, a discipline strategy in which parents explain to children why a punished behavior is wrong (Hoffman, 1970). Inductive discipline helps most preschoolers gain control of their behavior and learn to look at situations from perspectives other than their own. Likewise, the majority of preschool-aged children of parents who respond to demonstrations of poor self-control, such as temper tantrums, by asserting their social and physical power—as often happens when parents physically punish children—have poorer self-control than preschoolers whose parents use inductive discipline (Houck & Lecuyer-Maus, 2003; Kochanska, 1997b; Kochanska, Murray, Jacques, Koenig, & Vandegeest, 1996). For this and other reasons, most developmentalists are opposed to physical punishment, as discussed in the Real World feature on page 224.

However, research on inductive discipline suggests that it is not equally effective for all children. Those who have difficult temperaments or who are physically active and who seem to enjoy risk-taking—such as children who like to climb on top of furniture and jump off—seem to have a greater need for firm discipline and to benefit less from inductive discipline than do their peers whose temperamental make-up is different (Kochanska, 1997a). In fact, assumptions about the superiority of inductive discipline, as well as authoritative parenting in general, have been criticized by developmentalists who claim that correlations between discipline strategy and child behavior may arise simply because parents adapt their techniques to their children's behavior. Thus, parents of poorly behaved children may be more punitive or authoritarian because they have discovered that this is the kind of parenting their children need.

Ethnicity, Socioeconomic Status, and Parenting Styles

Learning Objective 8.11
How are ethnicity and socioeconomic status related to parenting style?

Ethnicity and socioeconomic variables also interact with parenting styles. In an important, large-scale, cross-sectional study involving roughly 10,000 9th- through 12th-grade students representing four ethnic groups (White, African American, Hispanic, and Asian), students answered questions about the acceptance, control, and autonomy they received from their parents (Steinberg, Mounts, Lamborn, & Dornbusch, 1991). When an adolescent described his family as above the average on all three dimensions, the family was classed as authoritative. Figure 8.6 on page 225 shows the percentages of families that were classed in this way in the four ethnic groups, broken down further by the social class and intactness of the family.

You can see that the authoritative pattern was most common among White families and least common among Asian Americans, but in each ethnic group, authoritative parenting was more common among the middle class and (with one exception) more common among intact families than among single-parent or step-parent families. Furthermore, these researchers found some relationship between authoritative parenting and positive outcomes in all ethnic groups. In all four groups, for example, teenagers from authoritative families showed more self-reliance and less delinquency than did those from nonauthoritative families. However, this study, like others, found strong links between authoritative parenting style and positive outcomes only for Whites and Hispanics. For Asian Americans and African Americans, the researchers found stronger connections between authoritarian style and variables such as school performance and social competence.

Studies in which children provide information about their parents' style as well as those in which researchers conduct direct observation of parents have consistently found that, in general, Asian American parents display an authoritarian style (Chao, 1994; Wang & Phinney,

inductive discipline a discipline strategy in which parents explain to children why a punished behavior is wrong

THE REAL WORLD

To Spank or Not to Spank?

Marie is at her wits end as to what to do about her 4-year-old daughter's whining. "What that child needs is a good spanking," Marie's grandmother declared one afternoon while the three were out shopping. Before she had children, Marie thought that she would never consider spanking them, but she now finds herself wondering whether her grandmother is right. Is Marie right to be reluctant to spank her daughter?

Surveys show that most parents believe that spanking can be an effective form of discipline if it is used sparingly and is reserved for situations in which all other disciplinary strategies have failed to achieve the desired result (Barkin et al., 2007). In the short term, spanking usually does get the child to stop an undesirable behavior and temporarily reduces the likelihood that the child will repeat it (Gershoff, 2002). In the long term, however, the effects of spanking are clearly negative (American Academy of Pediatrics, 1998). Research indicates that spanking (1) models infliction of pain as a means of getting someone to do what you want them to do, (2) associates the parent who spanks with the child's experience of physical pain, (3) leads to a family climate that is characterized by emotional rejection, and (4) is associated with higher levels of aggression among children who are spanked than among those who are not spanked.

For these reasons, developmentalists recommend that spanking, if it is used at all, be reserved for behaviors that are potentially harmful to the child or others (Namka, 2002). In addition, spanking, like other forms of punishment, should always be accompanied by an explanation of why the child was punished and an assurance that she is loved. Finally, experts agree that physical punishment should *never under any circumstances* be used to discipline children younger than 2 years of age (DYG Inc., 2004).

Thinking back to the question we posed at the outset of this discussion, we must conclude that Marie's reservations about spanking her daughter are on target. Moreover, although Marie's grandmother recommended spanking, she probably told her own children, "If you don't stop whining, I won't let you watch TV" before she started searching for a paddle. Unbeknownst to her, Marie's grandmother, like generations of parents before her, was using an everyday variation of a behavior management technique that psychologists call the *Premack principle* after researcher David Premack who demonstrated its effectiveness in a classic series of studies with primates and children (Premack, 1959). Thus, parents who employ the Premack principle instead of resorting to spanking can be assured of the support of grandmothers and psychologists alike.

Questions for Reflection

1. Look back at the operant conditioning principle of extinction in Chapter 1. How might it be used to diminish Marie's daughter's whining?
2. In what ways does having been spanked as a child influence an adult's views about the acceptability of spanking as a form of discipline?

1998). The finding that Asian American children score higher than their White counterparts on almost all measures of cognitive competence argues against the assumption that authoritative parenting is best. In fact, developmentalists have found a link between Asian American children's achievement and authoritarian parenting—that is, parents who have the most authoritarian parenting style have the highest-scoring children (Wang & Phinney, 1998). Similarly, authoritarian parenting has been shown to reduce the likelihood of substance abuse in both White and African American children (Broman, Reckase, & Freedman-Doan, 2006).

However, the key variable in these findings may not be ethnicity. Many studies have shown that parenting styles are grounded in parenting goals (e.g., Cheay & Rubin, 2004). Parenting goals are influenced by cultural values and by the immediate context in which parents are raising children. Consequently, it's important to know that many Asian American participants in studies comparing their parenting behaviors to those of European Americans have been recent immigrants to the United States. Thus, Asian American parents may be authoritarian in response to living in an environment that is different from the one in which they grew up, not because they are Asian. Authoritarian parenting may help them achieve two important goals: to help their children succeed economically and to enable them to maintain a sense of ethnic identity. Evidence supporting this interpretation also comes from studies of families who have emigrated to Israel, France, and Norway (Camilleri & Malewska-Peyre, 1997; Javo, Ronning, Heyerdahl, & Rudmin, 2004; Roer-Strier & Rivlis, 1998).

The same link between parenting goals and parenting style may help explain the greater incidence of authoritarian behavior on the part of African American parents. Specifically, African American parents are keenly aware of the degree to which social forces such as racism may impede their children's achievement of educational, economic, and social success. Consequently, they may adopt an authoritarian style because they believe it will enhance their children's potential for success. In fact, the correlation between authoritarian parenting and variables such as self-control among African American children suggests that they may be right (Baumrind, 1980; Broman, Reckase, & Freedman-Doan, 2006).

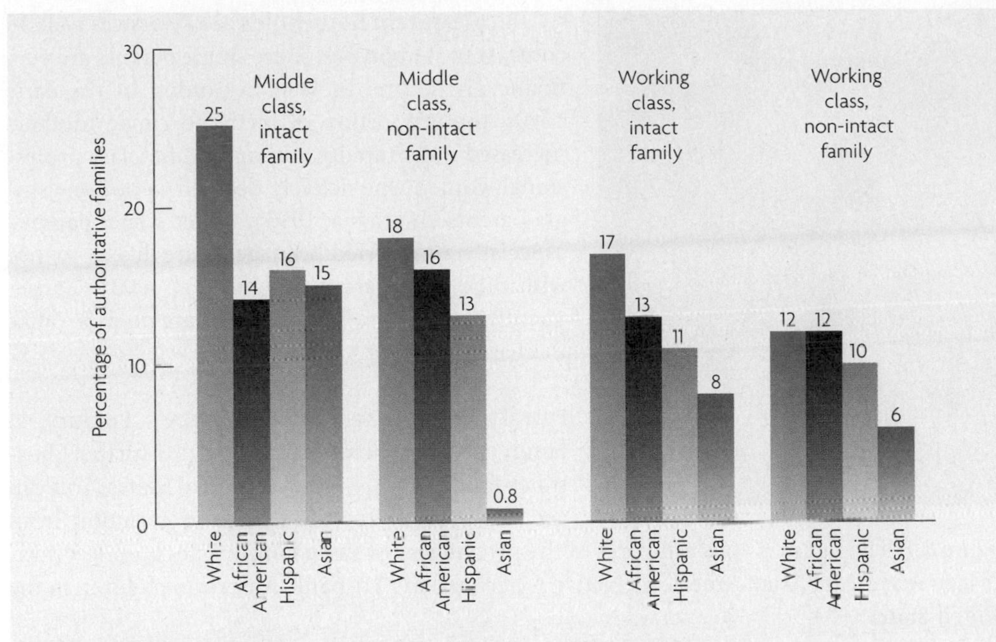

Figure 8.6 Social Class, Ethnicity, and Parenting Style

As this figure suggests, authoritative parenting is more common among middle-class parents as well as in intact families (in which the child lives with both natural parents) of all ethnicities.

(*Source:* Steinberg et al., 1991.)

Another reason that authoritarian parenting may be more common in African American families is that they are more likely to be poor. As Figure 8.6 shows, authoritative parenting is generally less common among poor parents than among middle-class parents in all four major U.S. ethnic groups. It seems likely that the reason for this pattern is similar to the one mentioned above for African Americans—that is, poor parents believe authoritarian parenting will help their children attain important goals.

Family Structure

Learning Objective 8.12

How is family structure related to children's development?

Despite increases in the number of single-parent households, the two-parent family continues to be the dominant structure in the United States. In 1970, almost 95% of children lived in such families, but by 2000, only 76% of children were living in two-parent homes (U.S. Bureau of the Census, 2003). Moreover, the proportion of single-parent families in the United States far exceeds that in other industrialized countries. For example, in Korea, Japan, and other Asian nations, only 4–8% of children live with a single parent (Martin, 1995).

Diversity in Two-Parent and Single-Parent Families The two-parent family, though still the most common living arrangement for children in the United States, is far more diverse than in the past or in other industrialized nations. Only about half of all children in the United States live with both their biological parents (Hernandez, 1997). From 20% to 30% of two-parent families were created when a divorced or never-married single parent married another single parent or a nonparent (Ganong & Coleman, 1994). Thus, many children in two-parent households have experienced single-parenting at one time or another while growing up.

However, it's important to keep in mind that any set of statistics is like a snapshot of a single moment in time—it fails to capture the number of changes in family structure many children experience across their early years. For example, in some two-parent households, the "parents" are actually the child's grandparents. In most cases, custodial grandparents are caring for the children of a daughter who has some kind of significant problem such as criminal behavior or substance abuse (Jendrek, 1993). These children are likely to have experienced a variety of living arrangements before coming to live with their grandparents. Likewise, many married parents once were single parents who had relationships with one or more live-in partners.

Some "two-parent" households in the United States are actually those in which a child is being raised by her grandparents.

Single-parent households are diverse as well. In contrast to stereotypes, some single parents are very financially secure. In fact, beginning in the early 1990s, the proportion of births to single mothers increased most rapidly among middle-class professional women who actively decided to become single parents (Ingrassia, 1993). Other single parents, especially unmarried teenagers, are likely to live with their own parents (Jorgenson, 1993). Consequently, single-parent households are no more alike than are two-parent households.

Family Structure and Ethnicity Looking at family structure across ethnic groups further illustrates family diversity in the United States. You can get some feeling for the degree of variation from Figure 8.7. The figure graphs estimates of the percentages of three family types among White, African American, Asian American, Native American, and Hispanic American children in the United States.

You can see that single-parent families are far more common among African Americans and Native Americans than among other groups. A difference in the proportion of births to unmarried women is one contributing factor. As Figure 8.8 shows, births to single women have increased rather dramatically across all racial and ethnic groups in the United States in the past few decades. However, the rates of such births are much higher among African American and Native American women than in other groups. (By the way, in all groups, more than three-quarters of single women giving birth are over the age of 20. Thus, teenage pregnancy contributes very little to the statistics on single motherhood.)

A second factor is that, although many African American and Native American single mothers eventually marry, adults in these groups—whether parents or not—are less likely to marry. Approximately 37% of African American adults and 27% of Native American adults have never been married. Among Whites, only 18% remain single throughout their lives (U.S. Bureau of the Census, 1998).

Figure 8.7
Ethnicity and Family Structure

Household types for U.S. children under 18 years of age.

(*Source:* U.S. Bureau of the Census, 2003.)

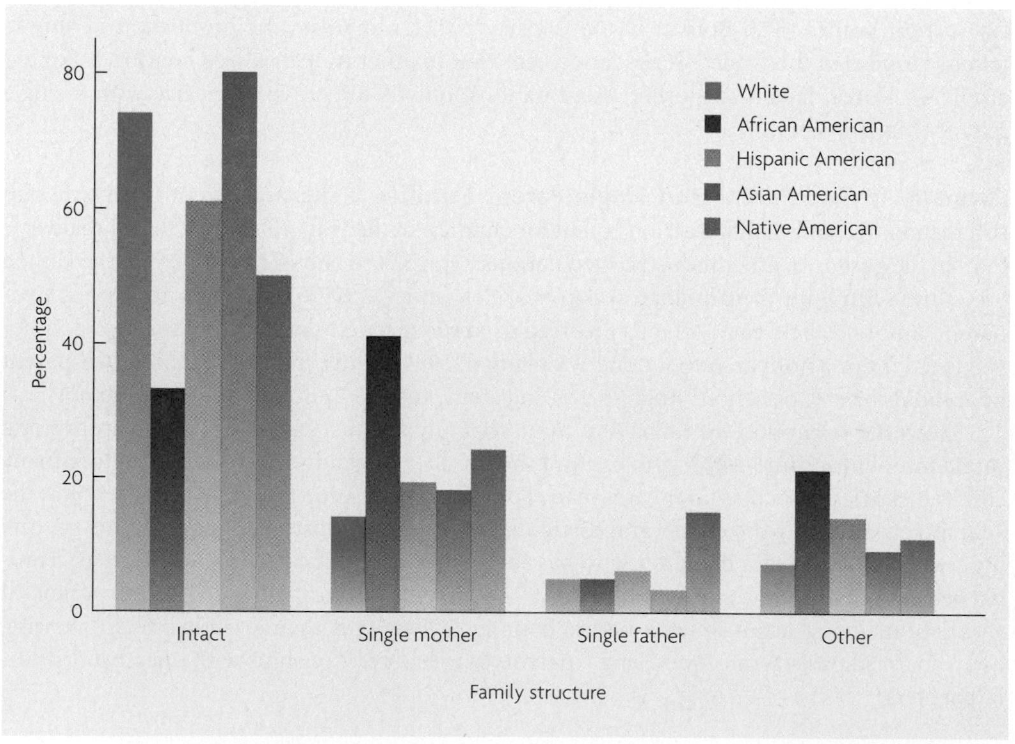

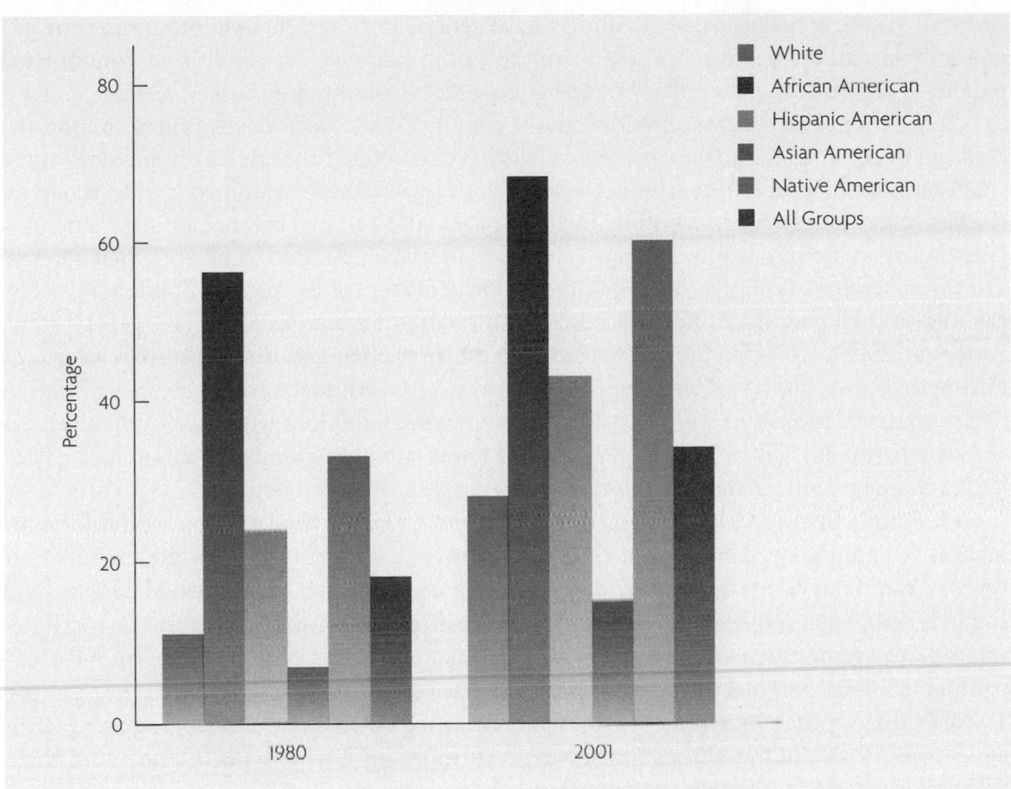

Figure 8.8
Ethnicity and Births to Unmarried Women

Percentage of births to unmarried women across racial/ethnic groups in the United States. The rate of births to unmarried women has increased across all groups in the United States over recent decades. These statistics are one reason for the growing number of school-aged and teenaged children who live in single-parent homes.

(*Source:* National Center for Health Statistics (NCHS), 2003.)

Of course, statistics can't explain why African American and Native American families are more likely than those of other groups to be headed by single parents. Sociologists speculate that, in the case of African Americans, lack of economic opportunities for men renders them less able to take on family responsibilities (Cherlin, 1992). Others add that grandparents and other relatives in both groups traditionally help support single mothers. For in stance, among Native Americans, a traditional cultural value sociologists call *kin orientation* views parenting as the responsibility of a child's entire family, including grandparents and aunts and uncles. As a result, Native American single parents, especially those who live in predominantly Native American communities, receive more material and emotional support than do single parents in other groups and may feel less pressure to marry (Ambert, 2001).

Other Types of Family Structures In contrast to the amount of research comparing two-parent and single-parent families, there are relatively few studies of the effects of other kinds of family structures. For example, research on custodial grandparenting tends to focus on the effects of the parenting experience on aging adults. Consequently, researchers know that grandparents' responses to children's problems are quite similar to those of parents (Daly & Glenwick, 2000). However, the stresses of parenting combined with the physical effects of aging are likely to cause older adults to feel more anxious and depressed than younger adults in similar situations (Burton, 1992; Jendrek, 1993). Thus, developmentalists know something about how parenting affects older adults but very little about how children raised by grandparents fare.

Similarly, concerns about children's sex-role identity and sexual orientation have dominated research on gay and lesbian parenting (Bailey,

Most gay and lesbian parents are raising children who were conceived in prior heterosexual relationships. However, a growing number of couples are choosing to be parents through artificial insemination or adoption. Research suggests that the variables that contribute to effective parenting and positive developmental outcomes for children are the same regardless of the sexual orientation of a child's parents.

Brobow, Wolfe, & Mikach, 1995). Studies have generally shown that children raised by gay and lesbian parents develop sex-role identities in the same way as children of heterosexual parents. They are also just as likely to be heterosexual (Golombok & Tasker, 1996).

To help answer general questions about cognitive and social development among the children of gay and lesbian parents, researchers have conducted comprehensive reviews of the small number of studies that have been done. Such reviews have examined a wide variety of studies of gay and lesbian parenting, including case studies, correlational studies, and comparisons of children in gay and lesbian families to those being raised by heterosexual parents. These reviews have typically found that the majority of studies suggest that children raised by gay and lesbian parents do not differ from those raised by heterosexuals (Fitzgerald, 1999; Patterson, 2006). However, most of the gay and lesbian participants in these studies have been raising their own biological children, who were conceived while the parents were involved in heterosexual relationships. Very few studies have involved children who have been raised exclusively by openly gay or lesbian parents, and fewer still have compared children of gay or lesbian parents with partners to those raised by single gays or lesbians.

One study involved 80 school-aged children who had been conceived by artificial insemination (Chan, Raboy, & Patterson, 1998). Researchers compared these children across four types of family structures: lesbian couples, single lesbian mothers, heterosexual couples, and single heterosexual mothers. The study found no differences in either cognitive or social development among them. However, they did find that the same variables—parenting stress, parental conflict, parental affection—predicted developmental outcomes in all four groups. These findings, much like those of research contrasting two-parent and single-parent families, suggest that children's development depends more on how parents interact with them than on any particular family configuration.

Learning Objective 8.13

How does divorce affect children's behavior in early childhood and in later years?

Divorce

There can be little doubt that divorce is traumatic for children. It's important to note, however, that some of the negative effects of divorce are due to factors that were present *before* the divorce, such as difficult temperament in the child or excessive marital conflict between the parents (Cherlin, Chase-Lansdale, & McRae, 1998). It's also important to keep in mind that divorce is not a single variable; children are probably affected by a multitude of divorce-related factors—parental conflict, poverty, disruptions of daily routine, involvement of the noncustodial parent, and so on (Bailey & Zvonkovic, 2003). For this reason, children whose parents separate or stay in conflict-ridden marriages may experience many of the same effects as children whose parents actually divorce (Ingoldsby, Shaw, Owens, & Winslow, 1999).

In the first few years after a divorce, children typically exhibit declines in school performance and show more aggressive, defiant, negative, or depressed behavior (Greene et al., 2006). By adolescence, the children of divorced parents are more likely than their peers to engage in criminal behavior (Price & Kunz, 2003). Children living in step-parent families also have higher rates of delinquency, more behavior problems in school, and lower grades than do those in intact families (Jeynes, 2006).

The negative effects of divorce seem to persist for many years. For example, children whose parents divorce have a higher risk of mental health problems in adulthood (Chase-Lansdale, Cherlin, & Kiernan, 1995; Cherlin et al., 1998; Wallerstein & Lewis, 1998). Many young adults whose parents are divorced lack the financial resources and emotional support necessary to succeed in college, and a majority report that they struggle with fears of intimacy in relationships (Cartwright, 2006). Not surprisingly, adults whose parents divorced are themselves more likely to divorce.

As a general rule, these negative effects are more pronounced for boys than for girls. However, some researchers have found that the effects are delayed in girls, making it more difficult to associate the effects with the divorce. Consequently, longitudinal studies often find that girls show equal or even greater negative effects (Amato, 1993; Hetherington, 1991a, 1991b). Age differences in the severity of the reaction have been found in some studies but

Many single parents manage to overcome substantial obstacles to give their children the support and supervision they need.

not others. For example, one longitudinal study found that the effects of divorce were most severe in a group of 12-year-olds who experienced parental divorce in early childhood rather than during their school years (Pagani et al., 1997).

Ethnicity, incidentally, does not appear to be a causal factor here. Yes, a larger percentage of African American children grow up in single-parent families. But the same negative outcomes occur in White single-parent families, and the same positive outcomes are found in two-parent minority families. For example, the school dropout rate for White children from single-parent families is higher than the dropout rate for Hispanic or African American children reared in two-parent families (McLanahan & Sandefur, 1994).

Understanding the Effects of Family Structure and Divorce

Learning Objective 8.14

What are some possible reasons for the relationship between family structure and development?

The broadest statement psychologists can make about the effects of family structure is that, at least in the United States, research suggests that the optimum situation for children appears to be one that includes two natural parents. Never-married mothers, divorced mothers or fathers who have not remarried, and step-parents are frequently linked to less positive outcomes. Factors associated with single-parenthood, such as poverty, may help explain its negative effects on development. Still, the differences between children who never experience single-parenting and those who do are too large to be completely explained by other variables. This means that at least part of the difference is connected to the family structure itself. Thus, it's important to know just what the differences are.

Children growing up in single-parent families are about twice as likely to drop out of high school, twice as likely to have a child before age 20, and less likely to have a steady job in their late teens or early 20s (McLanahan & Sandefur, 1994). Children of adolescent mothers are particularly at risk. Differences between children of teenagers and those whose mothers are older are evident in early childhood. Preschoolers whose mothers are single teenagers display less advanced cognitive and social development than their peers (Coley & Chase-Lansdale, 1998).

How are we to understand these various findings? First, single parenthood or divorce reduces the financial and emotional resources available to support the child. With only one parent, the household typically has only one income and only one adult to respond to the child's emotional needs. Data from the United States indicate that a woman's income drops an average of 40–50% after a divorce (Bradbury & Katz, 2002; Smock, 1993).

Second, any family transition involves upheaval. Both adults and children adapt slowly and with difficulty to subtraction from or addition of new adults to the family system (Hetherington & Stanley-Hagan, 1995). The period of maximum disruption appears to last several years, during which the parents often find it difficult to monitor their children and maintain control over them.

Perhaps most importantly, single-parenthood, divorce, and step-parenthood all increase the likelihood that the family climate or style will shift away from authoritative parenting. This shift is not uncommon in the first few years after a divorce, when the custodial parent (usually the mother) is distracted or depressed and less able to manage warm control; it occurs in step-families as well, where rates of authoritative parenting are lower than in intact families.

extended family a social network of grandparents, aunts, uncles, cousins, and so on

Remember, authoritarian or neglecting parenting is linked to poor outcomes whether it is triggered by a divorce, a stressful remarriage, the father's loss of a job, or any other stress (Goldberg, 1990). Ultimately, it is the parenting style, rather than any particular type of disruption, that is significant for the child (see No Easy Answers). Many families also construct a social network called an **extended family**, a family structure that includes parents, grandparents, aunts, uncles, cousins, and so on. Extended families seem to serve a protective function for children who are growing up in single-parent homes (Wilson, 1995). Grandmothers, for example, appear to be important sources of emotional warmth for the children of teenaged mothers (Coley & Chase-Lansdale, 1998). And, as mentioned earlier, extended family members often help single and divorced mothers with financial and emotional support as well as with child care. In the United States, such networks are more common among minorities than among Whites (Harrison, Wilson, Pine, Chan, & Buriel, 1990).

Critical Thinking

1. In what ways do you think parenting styles and family structure interact to affect development? For instance, might there be differences in how authoritarian parenting influences children in two-parent versus single-parent families?

NO EASY ANSWERS

When Divorce Is Unavoidable

Most parents know that divorce is traumatic for children and do their best to avoid it. However, as we all know, there are situations in which there is no alternative. In such cases, parents often turn to counselors and psychologists for advice on how to prevent the negative effects of divorce. Like so many other important challenges, helping a child overcome the trauma of divorce is not one for which there is a simple—or even complex—formula parents can follow.

It's important for divorcing parents to realize that they cannot eliminate all the short-term disruptive effects of this event on children. However, there are some specific things they can do that are likely to soften or lessen the effects:

- *Try to keep the number of separate changes the child has to cope with to a minimum*. If at all possible, keep the children in the same school or day-care setting and in the same house or apartment.
- *If the children are teenagers, consider having each child live with the parent of the same gender.* The data are not totally consistent, but it looks as if this may be a less stressful arrangement (Lee et al., 1994).
- *The custodial parent should help children stay in touch with the noncustodial parent.* Likewise, the noncustodial parent should maintain as much contact as possible with the children, calling and seeing them regularly, attending school functions, and so on.
- *Keep the open conflict to a minimum.* Most of all, try not to fight in front of the children. Open conflict has negative effects on children whether the parents are divorced or not (Boyan & Termini, 2005). Thus, divorce is not the only culprit; divorce combined with open conflict between the adults has worse effects.
- *Do not use the children as go-betweens or talk disparagingly about the ex-spouse to them.* Children who feel caught in the middle between the two parents are more likely to show various kinds of negative symptoms, such as depression or behavior problems (Buchanan, Maccoby, & Dornbusch, 1991).
- *Do not expect the children to provide emotional support.* Parents should maintain their own network of support, and use that network liberally. They should stay in touch with friends, seek out others in the same situation, join a support group.

In the midst of the emotional upheaval that accompanies divorce, these prescriptions are not easy to follow. However, if divorcing parents are able to do so, their children will probably suffer less.

Take a Stand

Decide which of these two statements you most agree with and think about how you would defend your position.

1. Given that divorce is traumatic for children, courts should require parents with children who want to divorce to go through counseling aimed at determining whether reconciliation is possible.
2. Courts should not require parents with children who want to divorce to go through counseling aimed at determining whether reconciliation is possible because a conflict-ridden marriage may be just as harmful to children as divorce is.

Peer Relationships

What is the first thought that springs to mind when you think about 2- to 6-year-olds? Perhaps it is the phenomenon of play. Certainly, people of all ages enjoy playing, although they obviously define it differently, but it is in the early childhood period that playing is the predominant form of behavior. In the context of play, children learn the skills they need to relate to others, and they learn that relationships have both negative and positive aspects.

Relating to Peers Through Play

Learning Objective 8.15
What are the various kinds of play that are exhibited by preschoolers?

In Chapter 7, you learned about the cognitive aspects of play. But what about the social features of children's play activities? The social dimensions of play were outlined in a classic observational study conducted by Mildred Parten (1932). If you observe young children who are engaged in free play, you will see that Parten's stages of play continue to be useful today.

At every age, children are likely to spend at least some of their time playing alone—a pattern known as *solitary play*. They may also exhibit *onlooker play*, a pattern in which they watch another child playing. However, children first begin to show some positive interest in playing with others as early as 6 months of age. If you place two babies that age on the floor facing each other, they will look at each other, touch, pull each other's hair, imitate each other's actions, and smile at each other.

By 14–18 months, two or more children play together with toys—sometimes cooperating, but more often simply playing side by side with different toys. Developmentalists refer to this as *parallel play*. Toddlers this age express interest in one another and gaze at or make noises at one another. However, it isn't until around 18 months that children engage in *associative play*. In associative play, toddlers pursue their own activities but also engage in spontaneous, though short-lived, social interactions. For example, one toddler may put down a toy to spend a few minutes chasing another, or one may imitate another's action with a toy.

By 3 or 4, children begin to engage in *cooperative play*, a pattern in which several children work together to accomplish a goal. Cooperative play can be either constructive or symbolic. A group of children may cooperate to build a city out of blocks, or they may assign roles such as "mommy," "daddy," and "baby" to one another to play house.

As you learned in Chapter 7, play is related to cognitive development. Play is also related to the development of **social skills**, a set of behaviors that usually lead to being accepted as a play partner or friend by others. For example, many researchers have focused on the social skill of *group entry*. Children who are skilled in group entry spend time observing others to find out what they're doing and then try to become a part of it. Children who have poor group-entry skills try to gain acceptance through aggressive behavior or by interrupting the group. Developmentalists have found that children with poor group-entry skills are often rejected by peers (Fantuzzo, Coolahan, & Mendez, 1998). Peer rejection, in turn, is an important factor in future social development.

According to recent studies, there appear to be sex differences in the reasons for and consequences of poor group-entry skills. For example, one study found that 3-year-old girls with poorly developed group-entry skills spent more time in parallel play than in cooperative play (Sims, Hutchins, & Taylor, 1997). In contrast, girls with better group-entry skills engaged in more cooperative than parallel play. Thus, the unskilled 3-year-old girls' patterns of play placed them at risk for future developmental problems, because age-appropriate play experience in the preschool years is related to social development later in childhood (Howes & Matheson, 1992; Maguire & Dunn, 1997).

The same study found that 3-year-old boys with poor group-entry skills tended to be aggressive and were often actively rejected

social skills a set of behaviors that usually lead to being accepted as a play partner or friend by peers

Developmentalists distinguish between true aggression (intentional harm) and the accidental injuries that often occur during normal rough-and-tumble play.

by peers. They typically responded to rejection by becoming even more aggressive and disruptive (Sims et al., 1997). Thus, the boys in this study seemed to be caught in a cycle: Aggressive behavior led to peer rejection, which, in turn, led to more aggression. This pattern may place boys at risk for developing an internal working model of relationships that includes aggressive behavior and, as a result, lead them to routinely respond aggressively to others in social situations.

Because of the risks associated with poor social skills, developmentalists have turned their attention to social-skills training as a preventive measure. For example, in one study, socially withdrawn 4- and 5-year-olds were taught specific verbal phrases to use when trying to gain acceptance by a group of peers (Doctoroff, 1997). In addition, their socially accepted peers were taught to remind the trained children to use their new skills. For the most part, social-skills interventions like this one lead to immediate gains in social acceptance. However, the degree to which early childhood social-skills training can prevent later social difficulties is unknown at present.

Learning Objective 8.16

What is the difference between instrumental and hostile aggression, and which is more prevalent during early childhood?

Aggression

Suppose you were the parent of two boys, a 4-year-old and a 6-year-old, and saw them laughing with delight while they were wrestling. What do you think might happen? You may remember a sequence of events like this one from your own childhood: First, one child "accidentally" punches the other too hard. Next, the victim's nascent sense of justice dictates that he respond in kind. Soon what started out as fun escalates into a full-blown fight.

Interactions of this kind are common in the early childhood period and even into the early adolescent years. **Aggression** is defined as behavior that is intended to injure another person or damage an object. The emphasis on intentionality helps separate true aggression from rough-and-tumble play in which children sometimes accidentally hurt one another. Every young child shows at least some aggressive behavior, but the form and frequency of aggression change over the preschool years, as you can see in the summary in Table 8.2.

When 2- or 3-year-old children are upset or frustrated, they are most likely to throw things or hit each other. As their verbal skills improve, however, they shift away from such overt physical aggression toward greater use of verbal aggression, such as taunting or name calling, just as their defiance of their parents shifts from physical to verbal strategies.

The decline in physical aggression over these years also undoubtedly reflects the preschooler's declining egocentrism and increasing understanding of other children's thoughts and feelings. Yet another factor in the decline of physical aggression is the emergence of *dominance hierarchies.* As early as age 3 or 4, groups of children arrange themselves in well-understood *pecking orders* of leaders and followers (Strayer, 1980). They know who will win a fight and who will lose one, which children they dare attack and which ones they must submit to—knowledge that serves to reduce the actual amount of physical aggression.

aggression behavior intended to harm another person or an object

Table 8.2 Changes in the Form and Frequency of Aggression from Age 2 to Age 8

	2- to 4-Year-Olds	4- to 8-Year-Olds
Physical aggression	At its peak	Declines
Verbal aggression	Relatively rare at 2; increases as child's verbal skills improve	Dominant form of aggression
Goal of aggression	Mostly instrumental	Mostly hostile
Occasion for aggression	Most often after conflicts with parents	Most often after conflicts with peers

(*Sources:* Cummings, Hollenbeck, Iannotti, Radke-Yarrow, & Zahn-Waxler, 1986; Goodenough, 1931; Hartup, 1974.)

A second change in the quality of aggression during the preschool years is a shift from *instrumental aggression* to *hostile aggression.* **Instrumental aggression** is aimed at gaining or damaging some object; the purpose of **hostile aggression** is to hurt another person or gain an advantage. Thus, when 3-year-old Sarah pushes aside her playmate Lucetta in the sandbox and grabs Lucetta's bucket, she is showing instrumental aggression. When Lucetta in turn gets angry at Sarah and calls her a dummy, she is displaying hostile aggression.

Psychologists have suggested several key factors in aggressive behavior. For example, one early group of American psychologists argued that aggression was always preceded by frustration, and that frustration was always followed by aggression (Dollard, Doob, Miller, Mowrer, & Sears, 1939). The frustration-aggression hypothesis turned out to be too broadly stated; not all frustration leads to aggression, but frustration does make aggression more likely. Toddlers and preschoolers are often frustrated—because they cannot always do what they want, and because they cannot express their needs clearly—and they often express that frustration through aggression. As the child acquires greater ability to communicate, plan, and organize her activities, her frustration level declines, and overt aggression drops.

Other developmentalists argue that reinforcement and modeling are important. For instance, when Sarah pushes Lucetta away and grabs her toy, Sarah is reinforced for her aggression because she gets the toy. This straightforward effect of reinforcement clearly plays a vital role in children's development of aggressive patterns of behavior. Moreover, when parents give in to their young child's tantrums or aggression, they are reinforcing the very behavior they deplore, and they thereby help to establish a long-lasting pattern of aggression and defiance.

Modeling, too, plays a key role in children's learning of aggressive behaviors. In a classic series of studies, psychologist Albert Bandura found that children learn specific forms of aggression, such as hitting, by watching other people perform them (Bandura, Ross, & Ross, 1961, 1963). Clearly, entertainment media offer children many opportunities to observe aggressive behavior, but real-life aggressive models may be more influential. For example, children learn that aggression is an acceptable way of solving problems by watching their parents, siblings, and others behave aggressively. Indeed, parents who consistently use physical punishment have children who are more aggressive than those of parents who do not model aggression in this way (Eron, Huesmann, & Zelli, 1991). It should not be surprising that when children have many different aggressive models, especially if those aggressive models appear to be rewarded for their aggression, they learn aggressive behavior.

Whatever the cause, most children become less aggressive during the preschool years. There are a few children, however, whose aggressive behavior pattern in early childhood becomes quite literally a way of life, a finding that has been supported by cross-cultural research (Hart, Olsen, Robinson, & Mandleco, 1997; Henry, Caspi, Moffitt, & Silva, 1996; Newman, Caspi, Moffitt, & Silva, 1997). Researchers have searched for causes of this kind of aggression, which some psychologists refer to as *trait aggression*, to distinguish it from developmentally normal forms of aggression.

Psychologists looking for a genetic basis for trait aggression have produced some supportive data (Hudziak et al., 2003; Plomin, 1990; vanBeijsterveldt, Bartels, Hudziak, & Boomsma, 2003). Others suggest that trait aggression is associated with being raised in an aggressive environment, such as an abusive family (Dodge, 1993). Family factors other than abuse, such as lack of affection and the use of coercive discipline techniques, also appear to be related to trait aggression, especially in boys (Chang, Schwartz, Dodge, & McBride-Chang, 2003; McFayden-Ketchumm, Bates, Dodge, & Pettit, 1996).

Still other developmentalists have discovered evidence that aggressive children may shape their environments in order to gain continuing reinforcement for their behavior. For example, aggressive boys as young as 4 years old tend to prefer other aggressive boys as playmates and to form stable peer groups. Boys in these groups develop their own patterns of interaction and reward each other with social approval for aggressive acts (Farver, 1996). This pattern of association among aggressive boys continues through middle childhood and adolescence.

Finally, social-cognitivists have produced a large body of research suggesting that highly aggressive children lag behind their peers in understanding others' intentions (Crick & Dodge, 1994). Research demonstrating that teaching aggressive children how to think about others' intentions reduces aggressive behavior also supports this conclusion (Crick & Dodge,

instrumental aggression aggression used to gain or damage an object

hostile aggression aggression used to hurt another person or gain an advantage

1996; Webster-Stratton & Reid, 2003). Specifically, these studies suggest that aggressive school-aged children seem to reason more like 2- to 3-year-olds about intentions. For example, they are likely to perceive a playground incident (say, one child accidentally tripping another during a soccer game) as an intentional act that requires retaliation. Training, which also includes anger management techniques, helps aggressive school-aged children acquire an understanding of others' intentions that most children learn between the ages of 3 and 5.

Similar results have been obtained in studies examining aggressive children's ability to engage in other kinds of social reasoning (Harvey, Fletcher, & French, 2001). However, developmentalists have found that, like their reasoning about intentions, aggressive children's social reasoning can be improved with training. In one study, for example, researchers successfully used videotapes of children engaging in rough-and-tumble play to teach aggressive children how to recognize the difference between "play fighting" and aggressive acts that can cause physical pain (Smith, Smees, & Pelligrini, 2004). Thus, trait aggression may originate in some kind of deviation from the typical social-cognitive developmental path during the early childhood period, and it may be reduced with interventions aimed at returning children to that path.

Learning Objective 8.17

How do prosocial behavior and friendship patterns change during early childhood?

Prosocial Behavior and Friendships

At the other end of the spectrum of peer relationships is a set of behaviors psychologists call **prosocial behavior**. Like aggression, prosocial behavior is intentional and voluntary, but its purpose is to help another person in some way (Eisenberg, 1992). In everyday language, such behavior is called *altruism*, and it changes with age, just as other aspects of peer behavior change.

Development of Prosocial Behavior Altruistic behaviors first become evident in children of about 2 or 3—at about the same time as real interest in playing with other children arises. They will offer to help another child who is hurt, share a toy, or try to comfort another person (Marcus, 1986; Zahn-Waxler & Radke-Yarrow, 1982; Zahn-Waxler et al., 1992). As you read in Chapter 7, children this young are only beginning to understand that others feel differently than they do—but they obviously understand enough about the emotions of others to respond in supportive and sympathetic ways when they see other children or adults hurt or sad.

prosocial behavior behavior intended to help another person

Beyond these early years, changes in prosocial behavior show a mixed pattern. Some kinds of prosocial behavior, such as taking turns, seem to increase with age. If you give children an opportunity to donate some treat to another child who is described as needy, older children donate more than younger children do. Helpfulness, too, seems to increase with age, through adolescence. But not all prosocial behaviors show this pattern. Comforting another child, for example, seems to be more common among preschoolers and children in early elementary grades than among older children (Eisenberg, 1992).

Prosocial behaviors, such as sharing, are influenced by cognitive development and by the deliberate efforts of parents and teachers to teach children to behave in such ways.

Children vary a lot in the amount of altruistic behavior they show, and young children who show relatively more empathy and altruism are also those who regulate their own emotions well. They show positive emotions readily and negative emotions less often (Eisenberg et al., 1996). They are also more popular with peers (Mayeux & Cillissen, 2003). These variations among childrens' levels of empathy or altruism seem to be related to specific kinds of child-rearing. In addition, longitudinal studies indicate that children who display higher levels of prosocial behavior in the preschool years continue to demonstrate higher levels of such behavior in adulthood (Eisenberg et al., 1999).

Parental Influences on Prosocial Behavior Research suggests that parental behavior contributes to the development of prosocial behavior (Eisenberg, 1992). Specifically, parents of altruistic children create a loving and warm family climate. If such warmth is combined with clear explanations and rules about what to do as well as what not to do, the children are even more likely to behave altruistically. Such parents also often explain the consequences of the child's action in terms of its effects on others—for example, "If you hit Susan, it will hurt her." Stating rules or guidelines positively rather than negatively also appears to be important; for example, "It's always good to be helpful to other people" is more effective guidance than "Don't be so selfish!"

Providing prosocial *attributions*—positive statements about the underlying cause for helpful behavior—also helps. For example, a parent might praise a child by saying "You're such a helpful child!" or "You certainly do a lot of nice things for other people." Having heard such statements often during early childhood helps children incorporate them into their self-concepts later in childhood. In this way, parents may help create a generalized, internalized pattern of altruistic behavior in the child.

Parents of altruistic children also look for opportunities for them to do helpful things. For example, they allow children to help cook, take care of pets, make toys to give away, teach younger siblings, and so forth. Finally, parental modeling of thoughtful and generous behavior—that is, parents demonstrating consistency between what they say and what they do—is another contributing factor.

Friendships Beginning at about 18 months, a few toddlers show early hints of playmate preferences or individual friendships (Howes, 1983, 1987). However, by age 3, about 20% of children have a stable playmate. By 4, more than half spend 30% or more of their time with one other child (Hinde, Titmus, Easton, & Tamplin, 1985). Thus, one important change in social behavior during early childhood is the formation of stable friendships (Hay, Payne, & Chadwick, 2004).

To be sure, these early peer interactions are still quite primitive. However, it is noteworthy that preschool friend pairs nonetheless show more mutual liking, more reciprocity, more extended interactions, more positive and less negative behavior, and more supportiveness in a novel situation than do nonfriend pairs at this same age—all signs that these relationships are more than merely passing fancies. Moreover, having had a friend in early childhood is related to social competence (Maguire & Dunn, 1997; Sebanc, 2003).

Critical Thinking

1. Do you think that peer relationships are necessary to social development in early childhood? That is, do you think that young children who have no exposure to children other than their own siblings are just as likely to emerge from early childhood with adequate social skills as those who have opportunities to interact with peers?

SUMMARY

Theories of Social and Personality Development

Learning Objective 8.1 What major themes of development did the psychoanalytic theorists propose for the early childhood period?

- Freud and Erikson each described two stages of personality development during the preschool years: the anal and phallic stages in Freud's theory and the stages in which autonomy and initiative are developed in Erikson's theory. Both theories, but especially Freud's, place primary importance on the parent-child relationship. More recent psychoanalytic approaches emphasize the importance of relationships with peers and siblings.

Learning Objective 8.2 What are the findings of social-cognitive theorists with respect to young children's understanding of the social world?

- Social-cognitive theorists assert that advances in social and personality development are associated with cognitive development. Three topics of interest to such theorists are person perception, understanding of others' intentions, and understanding of different kinds of rules.

Personality and Self-Concept

Learning Objective 8.3 How does temperament change in early childhood?

- During early childhood, children's temperaments are modified by social experiences both within and outside of the family to form their personalities.

Learning Objective 8.4 What changes take place in the young child's categorical, emotional, and social selves during the preschool years?

- The preschooler continues to define himself along a series of objective dimensions but does not yet have a global sense of self. Children make major strides in self-control and in their understanding of their own social roles in the preschool years, as parents gradually turn over the job of control to the child.

Gender Development

Learning Objective 8.5 How do the major theoretical orientations explain gender development?

- Freud's explanation of gender development has not received much support from researchers. Social-learning explanations are more persuasive but ignore the role of cognitive development. Social-cognitive theories explain and predict gender-related understanding and behavior better than psychoanalytic or learning theories.

Learning Objective 8.6 Describe the development of gender identity, gender stability, and gender constancy.

- Between ages 2 and 6, most children move through a series of steps in their understanding of gender constancy: first labeling their own and others' gender, then understanding the stability of gender, and finally comprehending the constancy of gender at about age 5 or 6.

Learning Objective 8.7 What are the characteristics of young children's sex-role knowledge?

- At about age 2, children begin to learn what is appropriate behavior for their gender. By age 5 or 6, most children have developed fairly rigid rules about what boys or girls are supposed to do and be.

Learning Objective 8.8 How is the behavior of young children sex-typed?

- Children display sex-typed behavior as early as 18–24 months of age. Some theorists think children play in gender-segregated groups because same-sex peers help them learn about sex-appropriate behavior.

Family Relationships and Structure

Learning Objective 8.9 How does attachment change during the early childhood years?

- The young child's attachment to the parent(s) remains strong, but except in stressful situations, attachment behaviors become less visible as the child gets older. Preschoolers refuse or defy parental influence attempts more than infants do. Outright defiance, however, declines from age 2 to age 6. Both these changes are clearly linked to the child's language and cognitive gains.

Learning Objective 8.10 How do parenting styles affect children's development?

- Authoritative parenting, which combines warmth, clear rules, and communication with high maturity demands, is associated with the most positive outcomes for children. Authoritarian parenting has some negative effects on development. However, permissive and uninvolved parenting seem to be the least positive styles.

Learning Objective 8.11 How are ethnicity and socioeconomic status related to parenting style?

- Ethnicity and socioeconomic class are linked to parenting style. Asian American and African American parents are more authoritarian than those in other ethnic groups, and poor parents in all ethnic groups tend to be authoritarian. Studies of parenting style and developmental outcomes in ethnic groups suggest that, in some situations, authoritative parenting may not be the best style.

Learning Objective 8.12 How is family structure related to children's development?

- Family structure affects early childhood social and personality development. Data from U.S. studies suggest that any family structure other than one that includes two biological parents is linked to more negative outcomes.

Learning Objective 8.13 How does divorce affect children's behavior in early childhood and in later years?

- Following a divorce, children typically show disrupted behavior for several years. Parenting styles also change, becoming less authoritative. However, many effects of divorce on children are associated with problems that existed before the marriage ended.

Learning Objective 8.14 What are some possible reasons for the relationship between family structure and development?

- To understand the influence of family structure on development, a number of variables, such as poverty, associated with differences in family structure must be taken into account. However, these variables alone are insufficient to explain differences in children that are correlated with variations in family make-up.

Peer Relationships

Learning Objective 8.15 What are the various kinds of play that are exhibited by preschoolers?

- Play with peers is evident before age 2 and becomes increasingly important through the preschool years.

Learning Objective 8.16 What is the difference between instrumental and hostile aggression, and which is more prevalent during early childhood?

- Physical aggression toward peers increases and then declines during these years, while verbal aggression increases among older preschoolers. Some children develop a pattern of aggressive behavior that continues to cause problems for them throughout childhood and adolescence.

Learning Objective 8.17 How do prosocial behavior and friendship patterns change during early childhood?

- Children as young as 2 show prosocial behavior toward others, and this behavior seems to become more common as the child's ability to take another's perspective increases. Stable friendships develop between children in this age range.

KEY TERMS

aggression *(p. 232)*
authoritarian parenting style *(p. 221)*
authoritative parenting style *(p. 221)*
cross-gender behavior *(p. 219)*
emotional regulation *(p. 212)*
empathy *(p. 213)*
extended family *(p. 230)*
gender *(p. 214)*
gender constancy *(p. 215)*
gender identity *(p. 216)*
gender schema theory *(p. 215)*
gender stability *(p. 216)*
hostile aggression *(p. 233)*
inductive discipline *(p. 223)*
instrumental aggression *(p. 233)*
parenting styles *(p. 220)*
permissive parenting style *(p. 221)*
person perception *(p. 209)*
prosocial behavior *(p. 234)*
sex-typed behavior *(p. 218)*
social-cognitive theory *(p. 208)*
social skills *(p. 231)*
uninvolved parenting style *(p. 221)*

TEST YOURSELF

Theories of Social and Personality Development

8.1 The text suggests that both Freud and Erikson believed that the key to the social development of 2- to 6-year-olds is
a. striking a balance between the child's emerging skills and parents' need for control.
b. the successful development of peer relationships.
c. whether potty training goes smoothly.
d. the ability of the parents to give the child freedom to grow.

8.2 Which of the following represents a complementary relationship?
a. becoming friends with someone who is older than we are
b. developing attachments with people who are our equals
c. an increase in attachment
d. developing an attachment to someone who has greater social power than we do

8.3 The ability to classify others is called
a. social-cognitive perception.
b. the Oedipus conflict.
c. complementary perception.
d. person perception.

8.4 A child who classifies a peer as "nice" or who can describe another's typical behavior patterns, such as by saying "she always eats all her cereal," has developed
a. social referencing.
b. person perception.
c. a gender concept.
d. prosocial behavior.

8.5 How do children's observations and categorizations of people change as they grow older?
a. They become more consistent.
b. They become more superficial.
c. They become more inconsistent.
d. They become more emotional.

Personality and Self-Concept

8.6 If you asked preschooler Mariana to describe herself, which of the following answers might you expect?
a. "I am good at drawing."
b. "I am a kind person."
c. "I am happy."
d. "I am smart."

8.7 The process of acquiring self-control requires
a. the ability to role-play.
b. sensorimotor thought.
c. shifting control from the parents to the child.
d. a rapid shift in the maturity level of the child.

8.8 Which of the following is an example of emotional self-regulation?
a. Judy is sad, so she turns on the television to watch a favorite cartoon.
b. Ray gives up on a puzzle that is too difficult for him.
c. Carol gets angry at her mother and storms out of the room.
d. When Dorothy pushes her off a swing, Kathy kicks Dorothy.

Gender Development

8.9 A little boy chooses a toy that he believes is for boys and rejects a shirt based on its color, saying "That's for girls!" He is using _____ to process information about gender.
a. gender identity
b. a gender schema
c. cross-gender comparison
d. a gender chromosome

8.10 Which of the following is the most accurate description of gender identity?

a. the understanding that you stay the same gender throughout life
b. a child's ability to label his or her sex correctly and to identify other people as women or men and girls or boys
c. the recognition that a woman continues to be a woman even if she wears a man's clothes and cuts her hair short
d. the choice of a pattern of behaviors that is typical or expected for one's sex

8.11 Choose the correct combination of gender understanding and the earliest age at which it is present in children.

a. gender identity—3 years old
b. gender constancy—4 years old
c. gender concept—7 years old
d. gender stability—4 years old

8.12 The interaction of a group of 4-year-old boys playing together most likely would *not* include

a. efforts to derail the interaction.
b. contradicting or interrupting.
c. boasting and forms of self-display.
d. behaviors that foster equality and connectedness.

8.13 Which of the following is *not* a true statement about children's cross-gender behavior?

a. Sex-typed behavior appears earlier in girls than in boys.
b. Tomboyism does not appear to interfere with the development of a feminine personality in adulthood.
c. Cross-gender behavior is far more common among girls than boys.
d. Many adults' reactions to boys' cross-gender play appear to be related to the fear that this form of play may lead to homosexuality.

Family Relationships and Structure

8.14 A child of 4 or 5 may have an internal model of attachment that

a. gradually fades as the child becomes more independent from his/her parents.
b. comes to be applied to new relationships, such as that with a preschool teacher.
c. develops into an external model of attachment as social relationships are developed.
d. is applied only to relationships with family members.

8.15 Lateefah's father has very high standards and expectations and requires Lateefah to comply with his wishes without discussion. He does not show affection, but he tells Lateefah that he has her best interests at heart. What is the best description of this parental style?

a. authoritative
b. permissive
c. authoritarian
d. inductive

8.16 Which parenting style has been associated with higher levels of self-esteem, better school performance, and more compliance with parents?

a. authoritarian
b. authoritative
c. permissive
d. complementary

8.17 When Sammy misbehaves, his parents explain what he has done wrong and why he is being punished. What discipline strategy is this?

a. authoritative discipline
b. complementary discipline
c. inductive discipline
d. reciprocal discipline

8.18 According to research studies, which of the following is an accurate statement about the interrelationships of parenting styles, socioeconomic status, and ethnicity?

a. Authoritative parenting was preferred by Asian American families.
b. Families of lower socioeconomic status typically used authoritative parenting strategies.
c. Single-parent families typically used authoritative parenting strategies.
d. Teenagers from authoritative families showed more self-reliance and less delinquency than did those from nonauthoritative families.

8.19 Spanking is an ineffective method of punishment for all but which one of the following reasons?

a. It models inappropriate behavior.
b. By pairing the parent repeatedly with spanking, it undermines the parents' positive value for the child.
c. It creates a family atmosphere of rejection.
d. Children who were spanked are less likely to be aggressive.

8.20 Which of the following is *not* a change in family processes typically experienced by families after divorce?

a. reduced financial and emotional resources to support the children
b. disruption and transition of the family system
c. increased violence
d. a shift away from authoritative parenting

Peer Relationships

8.21 One-year-old James is stacking his blocks and 14-month-old Yousef is pushing his car, but the two children pay no attention to each other as they play on the floor. What type of play is this?

a. sensorimotor
b. solitary
c. associative
d. parallel

That's enough high.
wall. But with big

8.22 What is the most dominant form of aggression among 4- to 8-year-old children?

a. verbal
b. physical
c. instrumental
d. hostile

8.23 Which of the following is a social-cognitive explanation for children's aggression?

a. Highly aggressive children may misunderstand others' intentions and perceive accidents as deliberate acts that require an aggressive response.
b. Aggression may have a genetic basis.
c. Aggression is always preceded by frustration, and frustration is always followed by aggression.
d. When parents reinforce their children's aggression, the children develop patterns of aggressive behavior.

8.24 Altruism is defined as

a. an emotional affection for others.
b. a desire to be good and helpful.
c. a willingness to delay gratification.
d. intentional behavior to benefit others.

8.25 During preschool, friends show all of the following except

a. more reciprocity.
b. more extended interactions.
c. more conflicts.
d. more supportiveness in novel situations.

PART FOUR
Middle Childhood

9

Physical and Cognitive Development in Middle Childhood

When you were eleven years old, could you have devised an investment plan that would assure your family of having sufficient funds to pay for your college education? That's exactly what Samantha Gorny did when she was in the fifth grade. How did an 11-year-old acquire such impressive financial planning skills?

Samantha is one of thousands of students in the United States who have participated in the *Stock Market Game (SMG)*, a 10-week program sponsored by the Foundation for Investor Education. SMG students at the elementary, middle-, and high-school levels learn the principles of investing along with basic financial skills, such as budgeting and credit management. Working in teams, students apply these principles to a virtual portfolio that is valued at $100,000 at the beginning of the game. Team members complete SMG assignments and follow the daily financial news in order to determine what

"There is a positive correlation between my students' use of MyDevelopmentLab tools and them having a better attitude about the course and being better prepared for the exams."
—Sean Reilley, Assistant Professor of Psychology, Morehead State University

Simulate: Baumrind's Parenting Styles

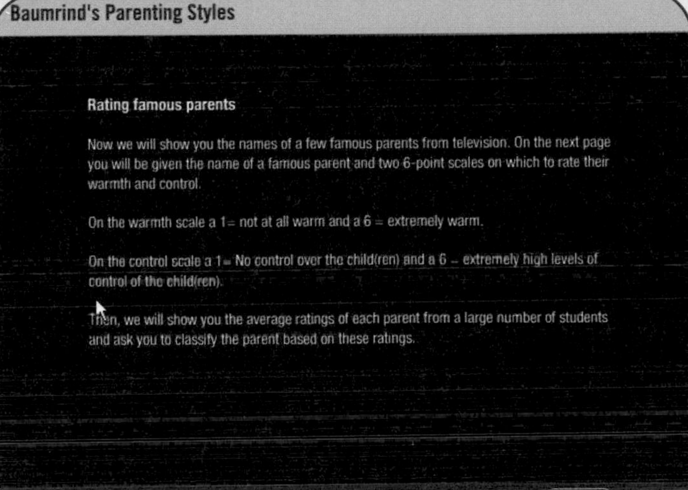

Baumrind's Parenting Styles
Rating famous parents
Now we will show you the names of a few famous parents from television. On the next page you will be given the name of a famous parent and two 6-point scales on which to rate their warmth and control.
On the warmth scale a 1 = not at all warm and a 6 = extremely warm.
On the control scale a 1 = No control over the child(ren) and a 6 = extremely high levels of control of the child(ren).
Then, we will show you the average ratings of each parent from a large number of students and ask you to classify the parent based on these ratings.
back
stop
next

Learning Objective 8.10
How do parenting styles affect children's development?

Watch: Parten's Play Categories: Onlooker, Parallel, Associative, and Cooperative

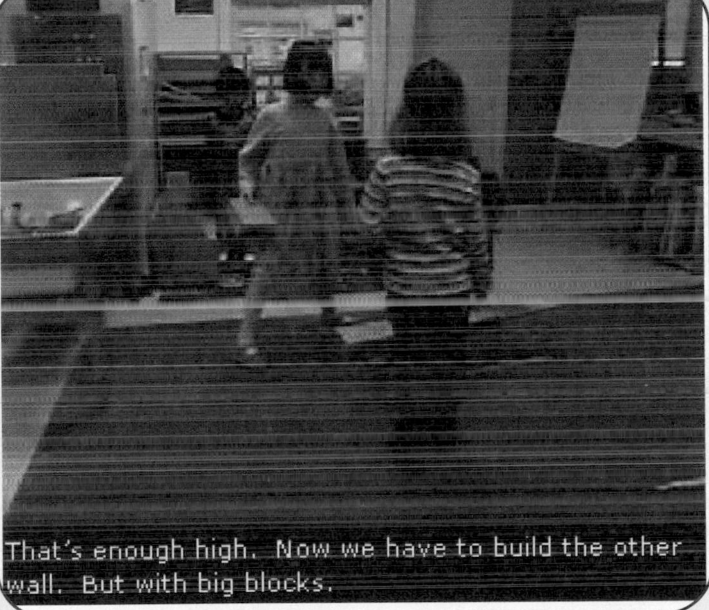

That's enough high. Now we have to build the other wall. But with big blocks.

Learning Objective 8.15
What are the various kinds of play that are exhibited by preschoolers?

Step 3

Take the chapter post-test and compare your results against the pre-test.

POST-TEST

Children who are reared with a permissive parenting style

- are somewhat immature with peers, less likely to take responsibility, and less independent.
- are impulsive and antisocial, and often assume the leadership position within peer groups.
- show higher self-esteem, are independent, and are more likely to comply with parental requests.
- have lower self-esteem and are quiet and subdued.

www.mydevelopmentlab.com

POLICY QUESTION

"Deadbeat Dads": Irresponsible Parents or Political Scapegoats?

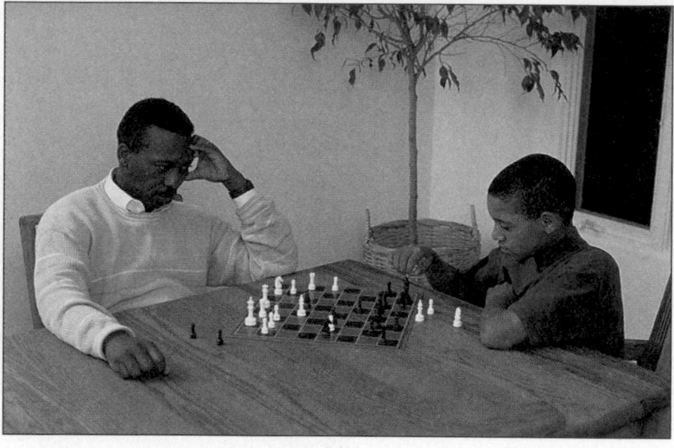

Developmental psychologists and policy makers alike have traditionally focused on the mother-child relationship. In recent years, however, attention has turned to the contributions fathers make to children's development. In general, research has shown that involvement of their father in their lives is associated with a number of benefits for children (Lamb & Lewis, 2005). For example, low-income African American children who have strong attachments to and regular contact with their fathers have been found to exhibit dramatically lower rates of early sexual activity and depression (Furstenberg & Harris, 1992). They are also more likely to be employed or enrolled in college as young adults. Thus, a number of policy initiatives to increase fathers' involvement in families have been implemented by governments around the world, but such policies have been especially common in the United States (Engle & Breaux, 1998). For the most part, these policies have emphasized the father's economic contribution to the family.

The Politics of Enforcement

Policies aimed at tracking down deadbeat dads enjoy wide public support, and they have proliferated at both the federal and state levels in recent years. One consequence of these policies has been that the FBI now investigates child support cases, because it is a federal crime to move from one state to another to avoid complying with a child support order. Another consequence is that, in many states, noncustodial parents can lose their driver's license and even professional credentials, such as a license to practice medicine, when they fail to pay child support (Administration for Children & Families, 2006).

However, deadbeat dads aren't the only targets of child support enforcement efforts. These policies are also aimed at forcing custodial mothers to cooperate with government officials. For example, women who receive welfare payments or financial support for making the transition from welfare to work must identify their children's fathers to government officials and help law enforcement officers find them. If women claim they do not know who their children's fathers are, they must identify all their sexual partners and submit themselves and their children to DNA testing (Monson, 1997). They must also cooperate in obtaining court orders compelling their sexual partners to obtain DNA testing. The penalty for failing to cooperate is denial of benefits.

The general public has also been enlisted in efforts to find deadbeat dads. Numerous Internet sites—some operated by law enforcement agencies and others by private concerns—contain lists of the names of alleged deadbeat dads, as well as addresses, last known location, and amount of support owed. (See, for example, www.scattorneygeneral.com and www.deadbeatlocators.com.) Many sites include photos, and some offer rewards for "tips" regarding the whereabouts of deadbeat dads.

Criticisms of Deadbeat Dad Policies

One important criticism of deadbeat dad policies concerns the rhetoric itself. The term "deadbeat dad" unnecessarily denigrates fathers and men in general, some critics say. Further, many claim that the assumption that the father is more able than the mother to provide for the child financially is sexist and does not match the realities of many child support cases. Critics point to two facts as proof that courts are already biased against fathers, without the additional effects of a politically inspired public frenzy over deadbeat dads: First, only about 10% of divorced fathers gain custody of their children (Fathers' Rights Coalition, 1999). Second, less than 30% of custodial fathers who go to court win child support awards from their children's mothers, whereas more than 80% of custodial mothers succeed in obtaining child support orders against their children's fathers (Fathers' Rights Coalition, 1999). Further, as a consequence of the zeal with which deadbeat dad policies are implemented in many areas, some men have spent thousands of dollars defending themselves against support orders based solely on a woman's claim that a particular man is the father of her child (Welch, 2004). To be sure, DNA testing eventually exonerates the men who are unjustly accused; nevertheless, many claim that their reputations have been irreparably harmed.

Critics of deadbeat dad policies point out that the ways in which child support orders are handled in the court system actually undermine attainment of their goals. For example, an alleged deadbeat dad can lose his driver's and professional licenses simply for failing to appear in court when ordered. If he loses his professional license as a result of missing the court date, his ability to pay child support will be severely reduced. And even if he retains his license, to make the court date, the father has to take time off from work, which usually results in a loss of income—which, in turn, reduces his ability to pay child support. Thus, fathers' rights organizations claim that "Deadbeat Dad" policies unfairly target "dead-broke dads" (Young, 2002).

It is the ability to pay, according to both fathers' rights organizations and empirical research, that lies at the heart of the child support issue. In spite of the stereotype created by political rhetoric, most noncustodial fathers consistently meet their child support obligations as long as they are financially able to do so (Meyer & Bartfield, 1998). However, research has shown that child support awards given to custodial mothers by judges in the United States often far exceed what a noncustodial father can realistically pay. Fathers are far less likely to pay child support when the amount of the award exceeds 35% of their gross income (Meyer & Bartfield, 1996). Awards are also highly inconsistent. Two noncustodial fathers with the same income may be ordered to pay very different amounts of support. Moreover, surveys have demonstrated that even minimal acceptable levels of support established in state guidelines exceed what most Americans think is fair (Coleman, Ganong, Killian, & McDaniel, 1999).

Even when an initial award is reasonable, noncustodial fathers who lose their jobs or suffer other kinds of financial setbacks rarely succeed in obtaining even temporary court-ordered reductions in the amount of child support they must pay (Young, 2002). Courts also frequently fail to realize that fathers' financial difficulties may be the result of substance abuse problems or mental illness (Dion, Braver, Wolchik, & Sandler, 1997). To make matters worse, to petition a court for a reduction, the father must be able to afford to hire an attorney to represent him. In addition, noncustodial fathers are not entitled to a reduction in child support when their children's mothers marry or obtain employment. In fact, in many cases, a custodial mother's standard of living is much higher than that of the noncustodial father, yet the father must continue to pay the same amount of support. Thus, it is not surprising that noncustodial fathers report that financial matters are the biggest source of stress in their lives (Lawson & Thompson, 1996).

Alternatives to Deadbeat Dad Policies

Critics of deadbeat dad policies say that one essential step in improving child support compliance in the United States is to reform the judicial process. First, standards should be set for child support awards so that there is more consistency among cases. Second, legislation that contains more specific criteria for changing child support levels and that takes both noncustodial and custodial parents' current economic circumstances into account is needed. Third, joint custody should be considered more often; fathers who share custody with their children's mothers are more likely to be involved in their children's daily lives and to pay child support (Arditti, 1991).

In addition to judicial reforms, many observers suggest that the issue of child support be embedded in a broader approach to increasing father involvement, one that recognizes that a father's contribution to his children goes far beyond the money he provides for them. Indeed, some critics suggest that the grief and despair many fathers experience when they lose daily contact with their children because of separation or divorce have been completely ignored in the debate over deadbeat dad policies (Knox, 1998). Policy makers also need to increase efforts to reduce the number of out of wedlock births, because never-married fathers are far less likely than divorced fathers to make support payments (Caputo, 1996).

What Is the Situation in Your State?

Every state takes steps to improve enforcement of child support orders. Use your Internet skills to find out information about your state's policies.

Your Turn

- What are the penalties in your state for nonpayment of child support?
- What efforts have been made by officials in your state to locate deadbeat dads?
- Can an alleged deadbeat dad or a noncustodial father who is seeking a reduction in child support award represent himself in court in your state? If not, are there agencies that provide low cost legal assistance to such men?
- Does your state have policies requiring custodial mothers to cooperate in identifying their children's fathers?
- Do welfare statistics in your state indicate that deadbeat dad policies have reduced the welfare rolls?
- Do you agree with your state's current approach to the deadbeat dad issue? Why or why not?

PART FOUR Middle Childhood

9

Physical and Cognitive Development in Middle Childhood

When you were eleven years old, could you have devised an investment plan that would assure your family of having sufficient funds to pay for your college education? That's exactly what Samantha Gorny did when she was in the fifth grade. How did an 11-year-old acquire such impressive financial planning skills?

Samantha is one of thousands of students in the United States who have participated in the *Stock Market Game (SMG)*, a 10-week program sponsored by the Foundation for Investor Education. SMG students at the elementary, middle-, and high-school levels learn the principles of investing along with basic financial skills, such as budgeting and credit management. Working in teams, students apply these principles to a virtual portfolio that is valued at $100,000 at the beginning of the game. Team members complete SMG assignments and follow the daily financial news in order to determine what

to invest their money in. Using SMG virtual trading computer software, they execute stock trades just as they would if they had an actual brokerage account. At the end of the ten weeks, prizes are awarded at the local and state levels to students whose portfolios increase the most in value. Teachers report that students love the program, and many become just as absorbed in following the stock market as some of their peers are in keeping up with their favorite sports teams.

SMG team members who participate in *InvestWrite* go a step further. At the conclusion of the SMG program, InvestWrite participants write essays in which they outline an investment plan that they have designed with a specific objective in mind. Students' essays are judged by their teachers who then submit the five best compositions in their classes to a panel of investment experts at the Foundation for Investor Education. National winners are given college scholarships and are treated to a trip to New York City where they participate in a daily opening ceremony at the New York Stock Exchange. Samantha's InvestWrite essay, *College Money 101*, explained her plan for using three different kinds of income-generating stocks to ensure that she and her parents would have enough money to pay for her college education. Her plan included a well-designed family budget that was structured to include regular contributions to an investment account. Samantha also took into account what options the family would have for financing her education if their investment strategies didn't work out. The foundation's expert panel proclaimed Samantha to be the 2007 InvestWrite National Grand Champion at the elementary level.

Does the idea of teaching elementary school students about the stock market seem a bit extreme to you? It shouldn't, because the middle childhood period is the time when every society begins to teach children the skills they will need to participate in adult society. In a world in which we are constantly enticed to spend our money foolishly and to put our money into investments that may not help us meet our financial goals, economic education is vital. Thus, the skills that are embodied in SMG are analogous to those that young people learned in the days when agriculture was people's primary means of earning a living. Children learned the cycle of planting, tending, and harvesting crops by participating in it with adults, just as today's children can learn financial skills through the hands-on experiences that are a part of SMG.

Why does every society begin to formally educate children at around the age of 6? As you will learn in this chapter, children of this age are just beginning to acquire the physical and cognitive skills that are needed for academic learning. Furthermore, when they enter school, their cognitive abilities are enhanced by learning experiences that are unique to formal educational environments.

Physical Changes

Imagine a foot race between a 6-year-old and a 12-year-old. Although there certainly could be exceptions to this generalization, the odds definitely favor the older child. In all likelihood, the 12-year-old will not only surpass the 6-year-old in speed, but will also display greater strength, agility, and endurance. Such differences arise from a host of hidden, qualitative changes that take place in the major systems of children's bodies between the ages of 6 and 12. Likewise, cognitive contests that involve children at either age of this age range, such as a game of checkers, also bear witness to the qualitative changes in the brain that occur across these years. As you will see, these changes underlie improvements in both motor and cognitive skills.

Learning Objective 9.1

What kinds of physical changes occur during middle childhood?

Growth and Motor Development

Between 6 and 12, children grow 2 to 3 inches and add about 6 pounds each year. Large-muscle coordination continues to improve, and children become increasingly adept at skills like bike riding; both strength and speed also increase. Hand-eye coordination improves as well (Thomas, Yan, & Stelmach, 2000). As a result, school-aged children perform more skillfully in activities requiring coordination of vision with body movements, such as shooting a basketball or playing a musical instrument.

Perhaps even more significant is the school-aged child's improving fine-motor coordination. Improvements in fine-motor coordination make writing possible, as well as the playing of most musical instruments, drawing, cutting, and many other tasks and activities. Such accomplished uses of the hands are made possible by maturation of the wrist, which occurs more rapidly in girls than in boys (Tanner, 1990).

Girls in this age range are ahead of boys in their overall rate of growth as well. By 12, girls have attained about 94% of their adult height, while boys have reached only 84% of theirs (Tanner, 1990). Girls also have slightly more body fat and slightly less muscle tissue than boys. Sex differences in skeletal and muscular maturation cause girls to be better coordinated but slower and somewhat weaker than boys. Thus, girls outperform boys in activities requiring coordinated movement, and boys do better when strength and speed are advantages. Still, the overall sex differences in joint maturation, strength, and speed are small at this age.

Learning Objective 9.2

In what ways does the brain change during these years?

The Brain and Nervous System

Two major growth spurts happen in the brain during middle childhood (Spreen, Risser, & Edgell, 1995). In most healthy children, the first takes place between ages 6 and 8, and the second between ages 10 and 12. Both spurts involve development of new synapses as well as increases in the thickness of the cerebral cortex.

The primary sites of brain growth during the first spurt are the sensory and motor areas. Growth in these areas may be linked to the striking improvements in fine-motor skills and eye-hand coordination that usually occur between 6 and 8. During the second spurt of brain growth, the frontal lobes of the cerebral cortex become the focus of developmental processes (van der Molen & Molenaar, 1994). Predictably, the areas of the brain that govern logic and planning, two cognitive functions that improve dramatically during this period, are located primarily in the frontal lobes.

When school-aged boys and girls participate in co-ed sports, boys' superior speed and strength are balanced by girls' advantage in coordination.

Myelinization also continues through middle childhood. Of particular importance is the continued myelinization of the frontal lobes, the reticular formation, and the nerves that link the reticular formation to the frontal lobes (Sowell et al., 2003). These connections are essential if the child is to be able to take full advantage of improvements in frontal lobe functions because, as you may recall, the reticular formation controls attention. It is well documented that the ability to control attention increases significantly during middle childhood (Lin, Hsiao & Chen, 1999).

It seems likely that myelinization allows the linkages between the frontal lobes and the reticular formation to work together so that 6- to 12-year-olds are able to develop a particular kind of concentration called *selective attention*. **Selective attention** is the ability to focus cognitive activity on the important elements of a problem or situation. For example, suppose your psychology instructor, who usually copies tests on white paper, gives you a test printed on blue paper. You won't spend a lot of time thinking about why the test is blue instead of white; this is an irrelevant detail. Instead, your selective attention skills will prompt you to ignore the color of the paper and focus on the test questions. In contrast, some younger elementary school children might be so distracted by the unusual color of the test paper that their test performance would be affected. As the nerves connecting the reticular formation and the frontal lobes become more fully myelinated between ages 6 and 12, children begin to function more like adults in the presence of such distractions.

The neurons of the **association areas**—parts of the brain where sensory, motor, and intellectual functions are linked—are myelinized to some degree by the time children enter middle childhood. However, from 6 to 12, the nerve cells in these areas achieve nearly complete myelinization. Neuroscientists believe that this advance in the myelinization process contributes to increases in information-processing speed. For example, suppose you were to ask a 6-year-old and a 12-year-old to identify pictures of common items—a bicycle, an apple, a desk, a dog—as rapidly as possible. Both children would know the items' names, but the 12-year-old would be able to produce the names of the items much more rapidly than the 6-year-old. Such increases in processing speed probably contribute to improvements in memory function, which you'll read about later in the chapter (Kail, 1990; Li, Lindenberger, Aschersleben, Prinz, & Baltes, 2004).

Another important advance in middle childhood occurs in the right cerebral hemisphere, with the lateralization of **spatial perception**, the ability to identify and act on relationships between objects in space. For example, when you imagine how a room would look with a different arrangement of furniture, you are using spatial perception. Perception of objects such as faces actually lateralizes before age 6. However, complex spatial perception, such as map-reading, isn't strongly lateralized until about age 8.

A behavioral test of the lateralization of spatial perception often used by neuroscientists involves **relative right-left orientation**, the ability to identify right and left from multiple perspectives. Such a test usually shows that most children younger than 8 know the difference between their own right and left. Typically, though, only children older than 8 understand the difference between statements like "It's on *your* right" and "It's on *my* right." Lateralization of spatial perception may also be related to the increased efficiency with which older children learn math concepts and problem-solving strategies. In addition, it is somewhat correlated to performance on Piaget's conservation tasks (van der Molen & Molenaar, 1994).

However, the development of spatial perception is more than just a physiological process. Developmentalists know this because this function lateralizes much more slowly in blind children than in those who have sight. Thus, it appears that visual experience plays an important role in this aspect of brain development.

Furthermore, some researchers propose that differences in visual experiences explain sex differences in spatial perception and the related function of **spatial cognition**, the ability to infer rules from and make predictions about the movement of objects in space. For example, when you are driving on a two-lane road and you make a judgment about whether you have enough room to pass a car ahead of you, you are using spatial cognition. From an early age, boys score much higher than girls, on average, on such spatial tasks (Halpern, 1986; Voyer, Voyer, & Bryden, 1995). Some researchers suggest that boys' play preferences, such as their greater interest in constructive activities like building with blocks, help them develop more acute spatial perception and cognition.

selective attention the ability to focus cognitive activity on the important elements of a problem or situation

association areas parts of the brain where sensory, motor, and intellectual functions are linked

spatial perception the ability to identify and act on relationships between objects in space

relative right-left orientation the ability to identify right and left from multiple perspectives

spatial cognition the ability to infer rules from and make predictions about the movement of objects in space

Learning Objective 9.3

What are the three most important health hazards for 6- to 12-year-olds?

Health and Wellness

Generally speaking, most school-aged children are very healthy. However, they continue to benefit from regular medical care, and there are a few serious health concerns for this age group.

Head Injuries Head injuries accompanied by some kind of change in level of consciousness (ranging from mild lethargy to a total loss of consciousness) are more common among school-aged children than any other age group (Fein, Durbin, & Selbst, 2002). In fact, about 10% of all children experience at least one such injury between the ages of 6 and 12. Motor vehicle accidents are the most common cause of head injuries in children, but bicycle accidents are another important cause. Research suggests that helmets could prevent about 85% of bicycle-related head injuries (National Center for Injury Prevention and Control, 2000).

Fortunately, the vast majority of children who experience head injuries recover fully and experience no long-term effects. However, these effects can be subtle and may not be apparent immediately after the injury. Thus, physicians say that every child who experiences a trauma to the head should receive medical attention and be monitored for several days (Fein, Durbin, & Selbst, 2002).

Asthma The most frequent cause of school absence for 6- to 12-year-olds is **asthma**, a chronic lung disease in which individuals experience sudden, potentially fatal attacks of breathing difficulty. According to health officials, asthma is responsible for more than 11 million school absences each year in the United States (Overby, 2002). The disease typically appears between ages 5 and 7 and is believed to be caused by hypersensitivity to allergens such as dust and animal hair. When a child who has asthma encounters these irritants, her bronchial tube linings become inflamed. In response, large amounts of mucus are produced, the airways become blocked, and the child has to gasp for air.

Doctors use a "step" approach to treating asthma, in which education is the first line of defense against the disease. The purpose of the educational intervention is to help children and parents identify and avoid irritants that trigger attacks. If these measures fail to control asthma symptoms, physicians move the child to the next step, one that involves daily medication. However, the medicines used at this step can have detrimental effects on children's cognitive development (Naude & Pretorius, 2003). For this reason, most health professionals who treat asthma try to avoid using them (Overby, 2002); they want to be certain that parents and children have fully complied with lower-level treatment strategies before moving to more intense approaches.

As children grow and their lung capacity increases, asthma attacks decrease in both intensity and frequency (Overby, 2002). However, about half of children with asthma continue to experience symptoms throughout their lives.

Excessive Weight Gain You may have heard about the British mother who was investigated by child protective officials because her average-height 8-year-old son weighed more than 200 pounds (Associated Press, February 27, 2007). The case sparked an international debate about whether a parent who allows a child to become so much heavier than he should be is guilty of child abuse. Such cases raise public awareness of the fact that **excessive weight gain** is the most serious long-term health risk of the middle childhood period. Excessive weight gain is a pattern in which children gain more weight in a year than is appropriate for their height, age, and sex. If a child gains excessive amounts of weight over a number of years, she is at risk of having weight problems and a number of serious health problems in adulthood.

To simplify the process of determining whether an individual child's weight gain is appropriate, health care professionals use a measure called **BMI-for-age**, a variation on the *body mass index (BMI)* that applies to adults (discussed in Chapter 15). The BMI estimates a person's proportion of body fat (NCHS, 2000a). A child's BMI-for-age is determined by calculating her BMI and comparing it to others her age. Age-based comparisons are needed because, in healthy children, the BMI itself naturally increases with age as the ratios of fat and

asthma a chronic lung disease, characterized by sudden, potentially fatal attacks of breathing difficulty

excessive weight gain a pattern in which children gain more weight in a year than is appropriate for their age and height

BMI-for-age comparison of an individual child's BMI against established norms for his or her age group and sex

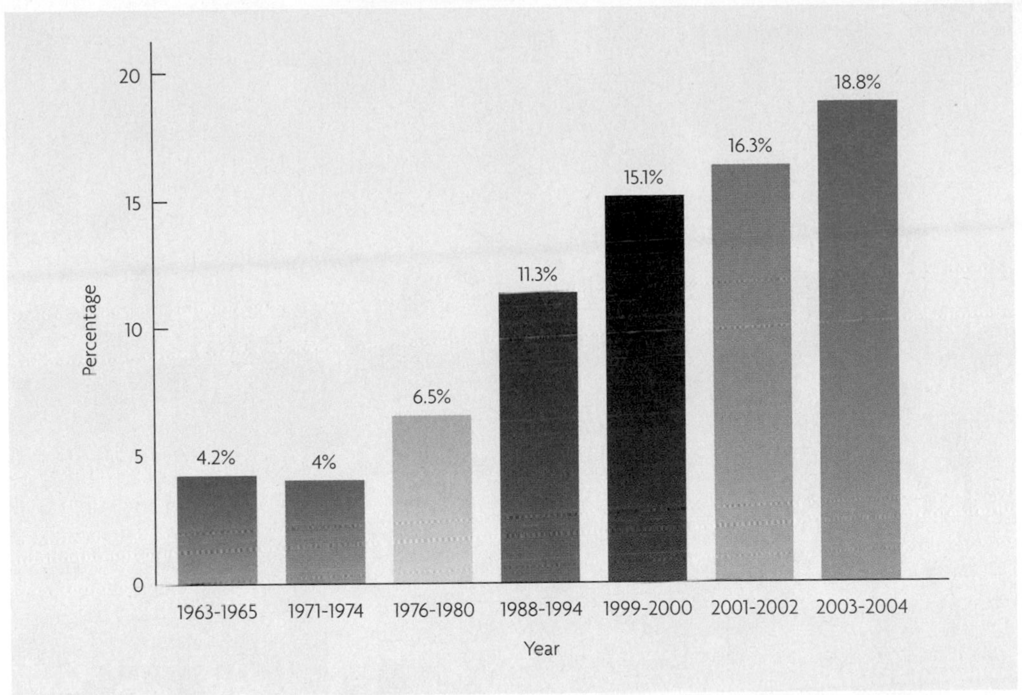

Figure 9.1 Prevalence of Overweight among 6- to 11-Year-Olds in the United States

The prevalence of overweight (BMI > 95th percentile) has increased dramatically in the United States over the past 40 years.

(*Source*: NCHS, 2007)

muscle change. Moreover, different standards are needed for boys and girls, because their BMIs do not increase at the same rate.

Children whose BMIs fall at the 95th percentile (the top 5%) are considered **overweight**, and those whose BMIs fall between the 85th and 95th percentiles are classified as **at-risk-for-overweight**. Because of growth spurts and the inherent instability of physical variables in childhood, multiple assessments are required before a child is actually classified as either, however. As you can see in Figure 9.1, the numbers of overweight and at-risk children in the United States have grown at an alarming rate over the past two decades. Currently, almost 1 in 5 children between the ages of 6 and 11 is overweight (NCHS, 2007). Similar increases have been documented in every country in the world that tracks the prevalence of overweight among children (Wang & Lobstein, 2006).

overweight a child whose BMI is at the 95th percentile

at risk-for-overweight a child whose BMI is between the 85th and 95th percentiles

Assessments of weight gain are a vitally important part of well-child care during middle childhood, because the older a child gets without stopping the pattern of excessive weight gain, the more likely the child is to be obese into the adult years (Magarey, Daniels, Boulton, & Cockington, 2003; NCHS, 2000b). Only a fifth of overweight babies become overweight adults, but half of those who were overweight in elementary school continue to be overweight in adulthood (Serdula et al., 1993). In addition, more than half of overweight children have one or more risk factors, such as elevated levels of cholesterol or high blood pressure, that predispose them to heart disease later in life (National Center for Chronic Disease Prevention and Health Promotion [NCCDPHP], 2000).

Many children in the industrialized world are overweight. One reason is that they consume snacks and beverages that contain a lot of sugar.

As you might suspect, overeating or eating too much of the wrong foods causes excessive weight gain in children just as it does in adults (NCCDPHP, 2000). However, both twin and adoption studies suggest that obesity probably results from an interaction between a genetic predisposition for obesity and environmental factors that promote overeating or low levels of activity (Stunkard, Harris, Pedersen, & McClearn, 1990). Whatever the genetic contribution might be, research suggests that a cultural pattern of decreases in physical activity and increases in the consumption of high-calorie convenience foods has led to the current epidemic of overweight children and adults (Arluk et al., 2003; Hood & Ellison, 2003; NCCDPHP, 2000; Vandewater, Shim, & Caplovitz, 2004).

Children who are overweight are often teased by their peers. Moreover, television programs make light of the problem of excessive weight gain in childhood. However, it is a serious health problem throughout the industrialized world.

It's important to keep in mind, though, that weight-loss diets for children can be fairly risky. Because they are still growing, the nutritional needs of overweight children differ from those of overweight adults (Tershakovec & Stallings, 1998). Consequently, overweight children require special diets developed and supervised by nutritional experts. Moreover, increasing the amount of exercise children get is just as important as changing their eating habits (NCCDPHP, 2000). Experts on weight management in childhood recommend that parents of overweight and at-risk children take the following steps (CDC, 2007):

- Provide plenty of vegetables, fruits, and whole-grain products
- Include low-fat or non-fat milk or dairy products
- Choose lean meats, poultry, fish, lentils, and beans for protein
- Serve reasonably sized portions
- Encourage everyone in the family to drink lots of water
- Limit sugar-sweetened vegetables
- Limit consumption of sugar and saturated fat
- Limit children's TV, video game, and computer time
- Involve the whole family in physical activities such as walking and bicycling

Critical Thinking

1. How do you think changes in children's frontal lobes during middle childhood affect their ability to manage health issues such as injuries, asthma, and overweight? What do these changes suggest about the need for parental monitoring with regard to these concerns?

Cognitive Changes

Along with impressive gains in physical development, children acquire some of the important hallmarks of mature thinking between ages 6 and 12.

Learning Objective 9.4

How do vocabulary and other aspects of language change during middle childhood?

Language

By age 5 or 6, virtually all children have mastered the basic grammar and pronunciation of their first language, but children of this age still have a fair distance to go before reaching adult levels of fluency. During middle childhood, children become skilled at managing the finer points of grammar (Prat-Sala, Shillcock, & Sorace,

2000; Ragnarsdottir, Simonsen, & Plunkett, 1999). For example, by the end of middle childhood, most children understand various ways of saying something about the past, such as "I went," "I was going," "I have gone," "I had gone," "I had been going," and so on. Moreover, they correctly use such tenses in their own speech. Across the middle childhood years, children also learn how to maintain the topic of conversation, how to create unambiguous sentences, and how to speak politely or persuasively (Anglin, 1993). All of these improvements contribute to the school-aged child's emerging mastery of conversation. By the age of 9 years, most children are fully capable of engaging in fluent conversation with speakers of any age, and their speech rates approach those of adults (Sturm & Seery, 2007).

Between 6 and 12, children also continue to add new vocabulary at a fairly astonishing rate of from 5,000 to 10,000 words per year. This estimate comes from several careful studies by developmental psychologist Jeremy Anglin, who estimates children's total vocabularies by testing them on a sample of words drawn at random from a large dictionary (Anglin, 1993, 1995; Skwarchuk & Anglin, 2002). Figure 9.2 shows Anglin's estimates for first, third, and fifth grade. Anglin finds that the largest gain between third and fifth grades occurs in knowledge of the type of words he calls *derived words*—words that have a basic root to which some prefix or suffix is added, such as "happily" or "unwanted."

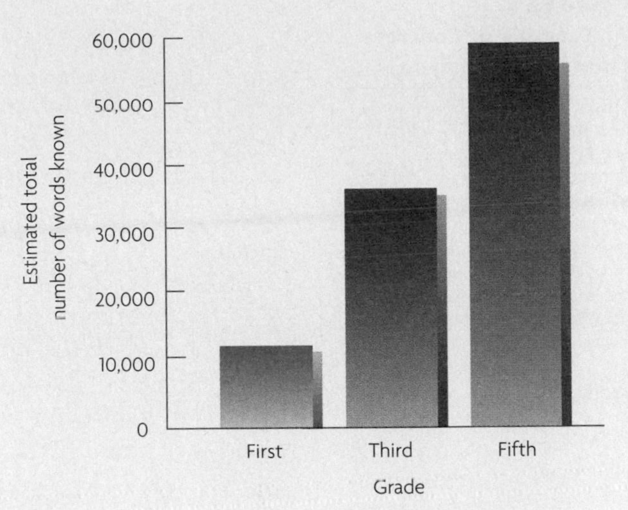

Figure 9.2 Vocabulary Growth in Middle Childhood

Anglin's estimates of the total vocabulary of first-, third-, and fifth-graders.

(*Source:* Anglin, 1995, from Figure 6, p. 7.)

Anglin argues that at age 8 or 9, the child shifts to a new level of understanding of the structure of language, figuring out relationships between whole categories of words, such as between adjectives and adverbs ("happy" and "happily," "sad" and "sadly") and between adjectives and nouns ("happy" and "happiness"). Once he grasps these relationships, the child can understand and create a whole class of new words, and his vocabulary thereafter increases rapidly.

Piaget's Concrete Operational Stage

Learning Objective 9.5
What cognitive advantages do children gain as they move through Piaget's concrete operational stage?

Have you watched a group of children being entertained by a magician? If so, then you may have noticed that younger children, preoperational thinkers in Piaget's terms, don't find magic tricks to be all that interesting. Why? Because, as you'll recall from Chapter 7, preoperational thinkers don't really understand the rules that govern physical reality. In middle childhood, children overcome this limitation and, as a result, they know that rabbits cannot be hidden in hats, and birds don't hide in the sleeves of a magician's jacket and fly out on cue. Knowing that the magician is appearing to do something that is physically impossible is what makes his performance interesting. Like adults, the school-aged child wonders "What's the trick?"

There is no better device for demonstrating the school-aged child's capacity for distinguishing between appearance and reality than Piaget's classic conservation tasks (see Figure 7.5 on page 189). By age 6, most children have begun to show some signs of the **concrete operational stage** and can quickly figure out that the a lump of clay has the same mass no matter how its appearance is changed. Thus, this stage is devoted to the construction of schemes that enable children to think logically about objects and events in the real world.

The stage takes its name from a set of immensely powerful schemes Piaget called *concrete operations*. These operations include mental processes such as *decentration*. You learned about its opposite, *centration* (thinking in terms of single variables), in the discussion of preoperational thinking in Chapter 7. **Decentration** is thinking that takes multiple variables into account. As a result, the school-aged child can see that a clay ball rolled into a sausage shape is wider than it was before, but also shorter. Decentration leads him to conclude that the reduced height of the sausage shape compensates for its increased width and that it still has the same amount of clay.

concrete operational stage Piaget's third stage of cognitive development, during which children construct schemes that enable them to think logically about objects and events in the real world

decentration thinking that takes multiple variables into account

Figure 9.3
An Example of Concrete Operational Thinking

This 5th-grader's composition illustrates the difficulty school-aged children have with deductive logic. His response to a hypothetical premise is to reinvent the world as he knows it through his own experiences or through stories about real people, places, and things. True deductive logic goes beyond what is already known.

(Courtesy of Jerry and Denise Boyd. Used with permission.)

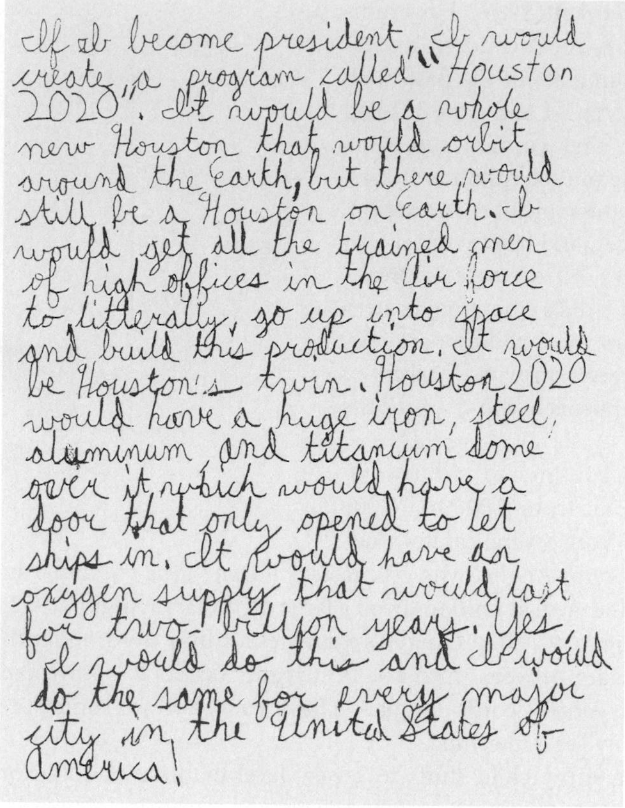

If I become president, I would create a program called "Houston 2020". It would be a whole new Houston that would orbit around the Earth, but there would still be a Houston on Earth. I would get all the trained men of high offices in the Air Force to litterally go up into space and build this production. It would be Houston's twin. Houston 2020 would have a huge iron, steel, aluminum and titanium dome over it which would have a door that only opened to let ships in. It would have an oxygen supply that would last for two-billion years. Yes I would do this and I would do the same for every major city in the United States of America!

As was mentioned in Chapter 7, preoperational children exhibit *irreversibility*, which is the inability to think of some transformed object as it was prior to the transformation. In contrast, concrete operational thinkers display its opposite, **reversibility**—the ability to mentally undo some kind of physical or mental transformation. Piaget thought that reversibility was the most critical of all the concrete operations. The clay sausage in a conservation experiment can be made back into a ball; the water can be poured back into the shorter, wider glass. Understanding of the basic reversibility of actions lies behind many of the gains made during the middle childhood period. For example, if a child has mastered reversibility, then knowing that A is larger than B also tells him that B is smaller than A. The ability to understand hierarchies of classes (such as Fido, spaniel, dog, and animal) also rests on this ability to move both ways in thinking about relationships.

Piaget also proposed that during this stage the child develops the ability to use **inductive logic**. She can go from her own experience to a general principle. For example, she can move from the observation "when a toy is added to a set of toys, it has one more than it did before" to the general principle "adding always makes more."

Elementary school children are fairly good observational scientists, and they enjoy cataloging, counting species of trees or birds, or figuring out the nesting habits of guinea pigs. But they are not yet good at **deductive logic** based on hypothetical premises, which requires starting with a general principle and then predicting some outcome or observation—like going from a theory to a hypothesis. For example, in the composition in Figure 9.3, a fifth-grader responded to the question "What would you do if you were President of the United States?" Responding to such a question requires deductive, not inductive, logic; this kind of task is difficult for 6- to 12-year-olds because they must imagine things they have not experienced. The concrete operations child is good at dealing with things she can see and manipulate or can imagine seeing or manipulating—that is, she is good with *concrete* things; she does not do well with manipulating ideas or possibilities. Thus, as the composition illustrates, children respond to deductive problems by generating ideas that are essentially copies of the things they know about in the concrete world.

reversibility the understanding that both physical actions and mental operations can be reversed

inductive logic a type of reasoning in which general principles are inferred from specific experiences

Learning Objective 9.6

What is horizontal decalage, and how does Siegler explain concrete operational thinking?

Direct Tests of Piaget's View

Piaget understood that it took children some years to apply their new cognitive skills to all kinds of problems, a phenomenon he called *horizontal decalage* (Feldman, 2004). (The French word *decalage* means "a shift.") However, other developmentalists have explained both consistencies and inconsistencies in school-aged children's reasoning as a result of their ability to use rules to solve problems.

deductive logic a type of reasoning, based on hypothetical premises, that requires predicting a specific outcome from a general principle

Horizontal Decalage Researchers have generally found that Piaget was right in his assertion that concrete operational schemes are acquired gradually across the 6- to 12-year-old period. Studies of conservation, for example, consistently show that children grasp conservation of mass or substance by about age 7. That is, they understand that the amount of clay is the same whether it is in a pancake or a ball or some other shape. They generally understand conservation of weight at about age 8, but they don't understand conservation of volume until age 11 (Tomlinson-Keasey, Eisert, Kahle, Hardy-Brown, & Keasey, 1979).

Studies of classification skills show that at about age 7 or 8 the child first grasps the principle of **class inclusion**, the understanding that subordinate classes are included in larger, superordinate classes. Bananas are included in the class of fruit, fruit is included in the class of food, and so forth. Preschool children understand that bananas are also fruit, but they do not yet fully understand the relationship between the classes.

A good illustration of all these changes comes from an early longitudinal study of concrete operational tasks conducted by Carol Tomlinson-Keasey and her colleagues (Tomlinson-Keasey et al., 1979). They followed a group of 38 children from kindergarten through third grade, testing them with five traditional concrete operational tasks each year: conservation of mass, conservation of weight, conservation of volume, class inclusion, and hierarchical classification. (As you recall from Chapter 7, *conservation* is the understanding that matter can change in appearance without changing in quantity.) You can see from Figure 9.4 that the children got better at all five tasks over the 3-year period, with a spurt between the end of kindergarten and the beginning of first grade (at about the age Piaget thought that concrete operations really arose) and another spurt during second grade.

Concrete Operations as Rules for Problem-Solving Other psychologists have conceptualized performance on concrete operational tasks in terms of rules for problem-solving. For example, Robert Siegler's approach is a kind of cross between Piagetian theory and information-processing theory. He argues that cognitive development consists of acquiring a set of basic rules that are then applied to a broader and broader range of problems on the basis of experience. There are no stages, only sequences. Siegler proposes that problem-solving rules emerge from experience—from repeated trial and error and experimentation (Siegler, 1994).

class inclusion the understanding that subordinate classes are included in larger, superordinate classes

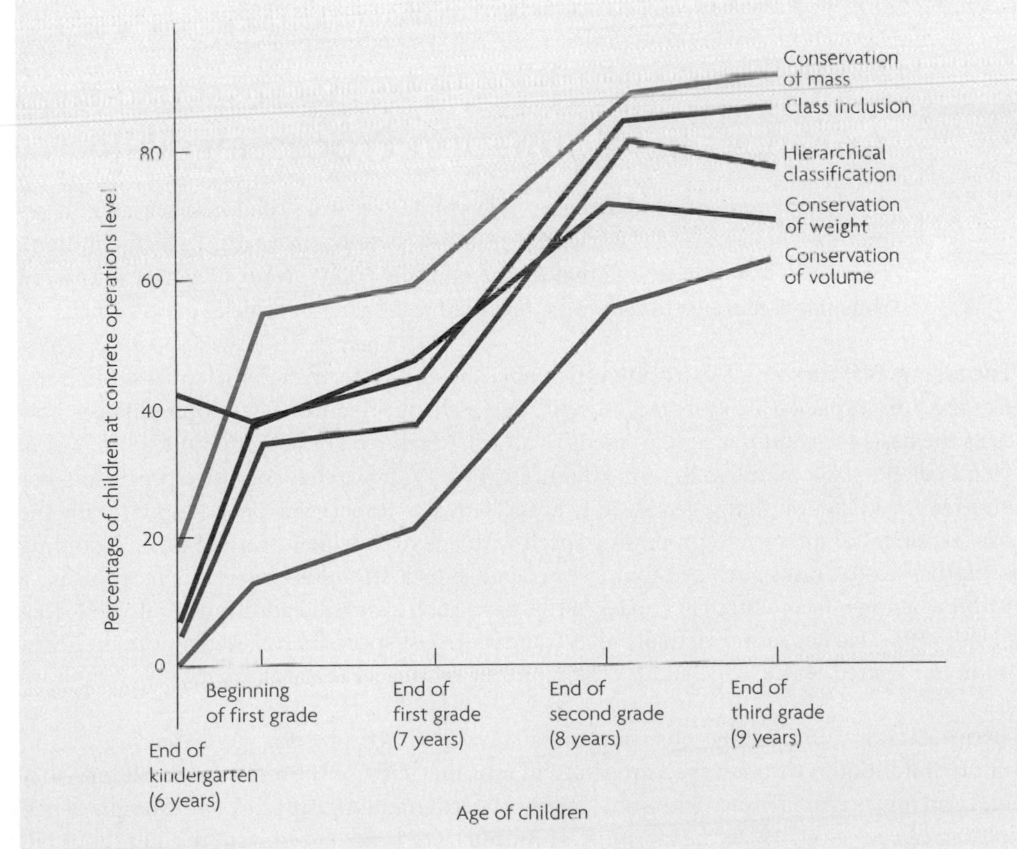

Figure 9.4
Within-Stage Development in Concrete Operations

In this classic longitudinal study, children were given the same set of concrete operational tasks five times, beginning in kindergarten and ending in third grade.

(*Source*: Tomlinson-Keasey et al., 1979, adapted from Table 2, p. 1158.)

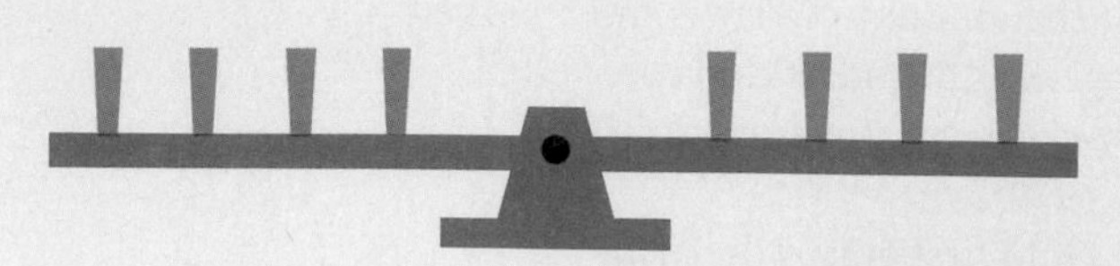

Figure 9.5
Siegler's Balance Task

This balance scale is similar to what Siegler used in his experiments.

Some of Siegler's own work on the development of rules illustrates how they may be acquired (Siegler & Chen, 2002). In one test, Siegler used a balance scale with a series of pegs on each side of the center, like the one in Figure 9.5. The child is asked to predict which way the balance will fall, depending on the location and number of disk-shaped weights placed on the pegs. A complete solution requires the child to take into account both the number of disks on each side and the specific location of the disks.

Children do not develop such a complete solution immediately. Instead, Siegler suggests that they develop four rules, in this order: Rule I is basically a preoperational rule, taking into account only one dimension, the number of weights. Children using this rule will predict that the side with more disks will go down, no matter which peg they are placed on. Rule II is a transitional rule. The child still judges on the basis of number, except when the same number of weights appears on each side; in that case, the child takes distance from the fulcrum into account. Rule III is basically a concrete operational rule; the child tries to take both distance and weight into account simultaneously, except that when the information is conflicting (such as when the side with weights closer to the fulcrum has more weights), the child simply guesses. Rule IV involves understanding the actual formula for calculating the combined effect of weight and distance for each side of the balance.

Siegler has found that almost all children perform on this and similar tasks as if they are following one or another of these rules, and that the rules seem to develop in the given order. Very young children behave as if they don't have a rule (they guess or behave randomly); when they do seem to begin using a rule, it is always Rule I that comes first. But progression from one rule to the next depends heavily on experience. If children are given practice with the balance scale so that they can make predictions and then check which way the balance actually falls, many rapidly develop the next rules in the sequence.

Thus, Siegler is attempting to describe a logical sequence children follow, not unlike the basic sequence of stages that Piaget described—but Siegler's research shows that a particular child's position in the sequence depends not so much on age as on the child's specific experience with a given set of materials. In Piaget's terminology, this is rather like saying that when accommodation of some scheme occurs, it always occurs in a particular sequence, but the rate at which the child moves through that sequence depends on experience.

Learning Objective 9.7

How do children's information-processing skills improve during these years?

Advances in Information-Processing Skills

As they progress through the middle childhood years, children are able to remember longer and longer lists of numbers, letters, or words. In fact, children's memories function so well that their testimony about events they have witnessed is usually accurate enough to be regarded as reliable in judicial proceedings.

Processing Efficiency **Processing efficiency**, the ability to make efficient use of short-term memory capacity, increases steadily with age, a change that most developmentalists now see as the basis for cognitive development (Halford, Maybery, O'Hare, & Grant, 1994; Kuhn, 1992; Li et al., 2004; Swanson & Kim, 2007). The best evidence that cognitive processing becomes more efficient is that it gets steadily faster with age. Robert Kail has found virtually the same exponential increase in processing speed with age for a wide variety of tasks, including perceptual-motor tasks such as tapping in response to a stimulus (for example, pressing a button when you hear a buzzer) and cognitive tasks such as mental addition (Kail, 1991; Kail & Hall, 1994). He has found virtually identical patterns of speed increases in studies in Korea and in the United States, which adds cross-cultural validity to the argument.

processing efficiency the ability to make efficient use of short-term memory capacity

automaticity the ability to recall information from long-term memory without using short-term memory capacity

Automaticity One of the most important ways in which processing efficiency grows in middle childhood is through the acquisition of **automaticity**, or the ability to recall information from long-term memory without using short-term memory capacity. For example, when children can respond "49" to the question "How much is 7 times 7?" without thinking about it, they have achieved automaticity with respect to that particular piece of information.

Automaticity is critical to efficient information-processing because it frees up short-term memory space for more complex processing. Thus, the child who knows "7 times 7" automatically can use that fact in a complex multiplication or division problem without giving up any of the short-term memory space he is using to solve the problem. As a result, he is better able to concentrate on the "big picture" instead of expending effort trying to recall a simple multiplication fact. Not surprisingly, researchers have found that elementary school children who have *automatized* basic math facts in this way learn complex computational skills more rapidly (Jensen & Whang, 1994).

Unless they are rank novices, these school-aged chess players will remember a series of chess moves or an arrangement of chess pieces far better than adults who don't play chess.

Automaticity is achieved primarily through practice. For example, when babies first learn to walk, they must focus all their mental effort on the act of walking. After a few weeks of practice, walking becomes automatic, and they can think about chasing the family cat or retrieving a ball that has rolled away. Likewise, adults can think about the grocery list while driving to the supermarket, because driving skills and the routes they routinely use to get from place to place are automatized. Thus, automaticity is important to information-processing throughout the lifespan. It is in middle childhood, however, that children seem to begin automatizing large quantities of information and skills at a fairly rapid rate.

Executive and Strategic Processes If you wanted to recall a list of everyday items (chair, pencil, spaghetti, tree . . .), you might consciously consider the various alternative strategies for remembering and then select the best one. You could also explain some things about how your mind works, such as which kinds of mental tasks you find most difficult. These are examples of *metacognition*—knowing about knowing or thinking about thinking—a set of skills first mentioned in Chapter 7. Metacognition is part of a large group of skills known as **executive processes**—information-processing skills that allow a person to devise and carry out alternative strategies for remembering and solving problems. Executive processes are based on a basic understanding of how the mind works. Such skills improve a great deal during middle childhood. For example, 10-year-olds are more likely than 8-year-olds to understand that attending to a story requires effort (Parault & Schwanenflugel, 2000).

One of the advantages of having good metacognitive and executive processing skills is that they help the individual devise methods for remembering information, or **memory strategies.** Although many people possess their own unique methods for remembering, Table 9.1 on page 256 lists a few common memory strategies. For the most part, these memory techniques first appear between the ages of 6 and 12.

Expertise There is a great deal of research showing that the amount of knowledge a person possesses makes a huge difference in how efficiently her information-processing system works. Children and adults who know a lot about a topic (dinosaurs, baseball cards, mathematics, or whatever it may be) categorize information about that topic in highly complex and hierarchical ways. They are also better at remembering and logically analyzing new information on that topic (Ni, 1998). In addition, children's capacity for creativity appears to greatly depend on how much knowledge they have about a topic (Sak & Maker, 2006).

Even typical age differences in strategy use or memory ability disappear when the younger group has more expertise than the older group. For example, psychologist Michelene Chi, in her now-classic early study, showed that expert chess players could remember the placement of chess pieces on a board much more quickly and accurately than novice chess players, even when the expert chess players were children and the novices were adults (Chi, 1978).

However, using advanced information-processing skills in their areas of expertise doesn't seem to help children's general memory and reasoning abilities (Ericsson & Crutcher, 1990).

executive processes information-processing skills that involve devising and carrying out strategies for remembering and solving problems

memory strategies learned methods for remembering information

Table 9.1 Some Common Information-Processing Strategies Used in Remembering

Strategy	Description
Rehearsal	Either mental or vocal repetition; may occur in children as young as 2 years under some conditions and is common in older children and adults
Organization	Grouping ideas, objects, or words into clusters to help in remembering them, such as "all animals," "the ingredients in the lasagna recipe," or "the chess pieces involved in the move called *castling*." This strategy is more easily applied to something a person has experience with or particular knowledge about. Two-year-olds use primitive clustering strategies.
Elaboration	Finding shared meaning or a common referent for two or more things that need to be remembered
Mnemonic	A device to assist memory; the phrase for the notes of the lines on the musical staff ("Every Good Boy Does Fine") is a mnemonic.
Systematic Searching	"Scanning" one's memory for the whole domain in which a piece of information might be found. Three- and 4-year-old children can begin to do this when they search for actual objects in the real world, but they are not good at doing this in memory. So search strategies may first be learned in the external world and then applied to inner searches.

(*Source:* Flavell, 1985.)

Critical Thinking

1. In what ways do advances in language, reasoning, and information-processing skills help children succeed in school? How do you think schooling influences these skills?

For this reason, many information-processing psychologists now believe that an individual's information-processing skills may depend entirely on the quantity and quality of relevant information stored in long-term memory. Thus, they say, to be able to learn scientific reasoning skills, for example, children must first acquire a body of knowledge about scientific topics (Zimmerman, 2000). To paraphrase developmental psychologist John Flavell, expertise makes any of us, including children, look very smart; lack of expertise makes us look very dumb (Flavell, 1985).

Schooling

For children all over the world, formal education is well under way by the time they reach the age of 6 or 7. Consequently, every society endeavors to find effective ways of teaching children the skills that they will need in adulthood. In general, studies show that teachers who display a teaching style that is similar to the approach that authoritative parents take to raising children—an approach that combines clear goals, good control, good communication, and high nurturance—are the most effective (MacIver, Reuman, & Main, 1995). In addition, at least in the United States, there is evidence that elementary schools with smaller classes, less than 20 pupils or so, are more effective than those with larger classes (Ecalle, Magnan, & Gibert, 2007). Still, quality considerations aside, because of its academic focus and the amount of time that children spend in school, formal education is one of the most important influences on the cognitive development of 6- to 12-year-olds.

Learning Objective 9.8

What should be included in an effective literacy curriculum?

Literacy

In the industrialized world, *literacy*, the ability to read and write, is the focus of education in the 6- to 12-year-old period. As you learned in Chapter 7, the skills children bring to school from their early childhood experiences may influence early reading as much as formal instruction (Crone & Whitehurst, 1999). Especially significant among these skills is the set known as *phonological awareness* (Anthony & Lonigan, 2004; Parrila, Kirby, & McQuarrie, 2004; Schatschneider, Fletcher, Francis, Carlson, & Foorman, 2004). Across the early elementary years, phonological awareness skills continue to increase (Shu,

Children's experiences in school are similar the world over. The similarities help explain why cognitive-developmental research involving 6- to 12-year-olds yields pretty much the same results in all cultures where children attend school.

Anderson, & Wu, 2000). Thus, children who lack such expertise at the start of school are likely to fall behind unless some systematic effort is made by teachers to provide them with a base of phonological knowledge (Torgesen et al., 1999). However, all beginning readers, both those who have high levels of phonological awareness and those who know less about sounds and symbols, seem to benefit from specific instruction in sound-letter correspondences (Adams & Henry, 1997). Moreover, beginning readers gain a significant advantage when they develop automaticity with respect to letter-sound correspondences and can effectively sound out words, or have "cracked the code" as some researchers put it.

Nevertheless, advocates of the **balanced approach** to reading instruction point out that teachers must move beyond basic phonics. In *guided reading* sessions, for instance, teachers work with small groups of children on reading books that are somewhat challenging for them (recall Vygotsky's zone of proximal development) (Iaquinta, 2006). When a child makes an error, the teacher uses the opportunity to explain a reading strategy or one of the many idiosyncrasies of written English to all of the children in the group. Proponents of the balanced approach also point to studies showing that, in the later elementary grades, attainment of reading fluency requires that children learn about meaningful word parts, such as prefixes and suffixes (Adams & Henry, 1997; McBride-Chang, Shu, Zhou, & Wagner, 2004; Nagy, Berninger, Abbott, Vaughan, & Vermeulen, 2004). At the same time it also appears that beginning readers gain a significant advantage when they achieve automaticity with respect to identifying sound-symbol connections (Samuels & Flor, 1997).

Once children have learned the basic reading process, learning about meaningful word parts, such as prefixes and suffixes, helps them become more efficient readers and better understand what they read (Adams & Henry, 1997; McBride-Chang, Shu, Zhou, & Wagner, 2004; Nagy, Berninger, Abbott, Vaughan, & Vermeulen, 2004). At the same time, instruction in comprehension strategies, such as identifying the main idea and purpose of a particular text, also helps (Pressley & Wharton-McDonald, 1997; Van den Broek, Lynch, Naslund, Ievers-Landis, & Verduin, 2004). Of course, all along the way, children need to be exposed to good literature, both in their own reading and in what teachers and parents read to them.

Some of the strategies used to teach reading also help children learn writing, the other component of literacy. For example, instruction in sound-symbol connections helps children

balanced approach reading instruction that combines explicit phonics instruction with other strategies for helping children acquire literacy

learn to spell as well as to read. Of course, good writing is far more than just spelling; it requires instruction and practice, just as reading does. Specifically, children need to learn about writing techniques, such as outlining and paragraph development, to become good writers. They also need to learn about language mechanics, such as grammar and appropriate uses of words, as well as how to edit their own and others' written work (Graham & Harris, 1997).

Despite educators' best efforts, many children fall behind their classmates in literacy during the early school years. In general, reading researchers have found that poor readers have problems with sound-letter combinations (Agnew, Dorn, & Eden, 2004; Gonzalez & Valle, 2000; Mayringer & Wimmer, 2000). Thus, many children who have reading difficulties benefit from highly specific phonics approaches that provide a great deal of practice in translating letters into sounds and vice versa (Berninger et al., 1999; Koppenhaver, Hendrix & Williams, 2007).

However, curriculum flexibility is also important in programs for poor readers. Some do not improve when exposed to phonics approaches. In fact, programs that combine sound-letter and comprehension training, such as the Reading Recovery program, have proven to be highly successful in helping poor readers catch up, especially when the programs are implemented in the early elementary years (Klein & Swartz, 1996). Consequently, teachers need to be able to assess the effectiveness of whatever approach they are using and change it to fit the needs of individual students.

Learning Objective 9.9

How do bilingual and ESL approaches to second-language instruction differ?

Second-Language Learners

Worldwide patterns of population growth and movement have led to tremendous increases in the number of children attending school in the United States, Canada, Great Britain, and Australia whose first language is not English. About two-thirds of these children speak English well enough to function in school, but the rest essentially do not speak English. Educators in English-speaking countries use the term *limited English proficient (LEP)* to refer to non–English-speaking children—either immigrant children or native-born children.

The number of LEP school children in the United States increased from 2.5 million in 1991 to nearly 5 million in 2001 (NCELA, 2002). As a result, at the beginning of the 21st century, 46% of all U.S. classrooms had at least one LEP student, and there continues to be a shortage of qualified teachers to help these students benefit from English-only instruction (Barron & Menken, 2002). In California, Florida, Illinois, New Jersey, New York, and Texas, more than 75% of schools offer special programs for LEP students. Most such students live in large cities. For example, more than 100 languages are spoken by school children in New York City, Chicago, Los Angeles, and the suburbs of Washington, DC. Educators in these cities face a particularly difficult task in dealing not only with the large number of LEP children but also with the staggering number of languages they and their parents speak.

Some LEP children, mostly those whose first language is Spanish, participate in **bilingual education**, in which instruction is given in two languages (NCES, 1997). Such programs have been developed for Spanish-speaking children because they constitute by far the largest group of LEP students in U.S. schools. Other English-speaking countries offer bilingual education to children from large non–English-speaking groups as well. For example, schools in Canada have provided both English- and French-speaking students in Quebec, a province whose residents primarily speak French, with bilingual education for decades.

bilingual education an approach to second-language education in which children receive instruction in two different languages

English-as-a-second-language (ESL) program an approach to second-language education in which children attend English classes for part of the day and receive most of their academic instruction in English

However, bilingual education is logistically impossible for most school districts that include LEP children. For one thing, if a school system has only a handful of students who speak a particular language, it is not financially feasible to establish a separate curriculum for them. In addition, it may be impossible to find bilingual teachers for children whose language is spoken by very few people outside of their country of origin. For these reasons, about 76% of LEP 6- to 12-year-olds in the United States are enrolled in **English-as-a-second-language (ESL) programs** (NCES, 1997a). In ESL programs, children spend part of the day in classes to learn English and part in academic classes that are conducted entirely in English.

Research has shown that no particular approach to second-language learning is more successful than any other (Mohanty & Perregaux, 1997). There is some indication that programs that include a home-based component, such as those that encourage parents to learn the new language along with their children, may be especially effective (Koskinen et al., 2000). But it seems that any structured program, whether bilingual education or ESL, fosters higher achievement among non–English-speaking children than simply integrating them into English-only classes, an approach called *submersion*. Although most children in submersion programs eventually catch up to their English-speaking peers, many educators believe that instruction that supports children's home language and culture as well as their English-language skills enhances their overall development (Cushner, McClelland, & Safford, 1992).

With respect to achievement, LEP students' performance in school is very similar to that of English-speaking children (NCES, 1997a). In fact, in U.S. schools, native-born English-speaking children are more likely to fail one or more grades than are children whose home language is either Asian or European. Spanish-speaking children fail in U.S. schools at about the same rate as English speakers. Thus, there is no evidence that a child who enters school with limited English skills has any greater risk of failure than native-born students.

A cautionary note is necessary, however: An LEP student does not have an increased risk of failure as long as the school provides some kind of transition to English-only instruction and school officials take care to administer all standardized tests in the language with which the child is most familiar (Cushner et al., 1992). Providing a transition to English-only instruction is necessary to optimize the LEP child's potential for achievement. Testing children in their native languages ensures that non–English-speaking children will not be misclassified as having mental retardation or learning disabled because of their limited English skills. Beyond these requirements, LEP students represent no particular burden to U.S. schools. Moreover, in all likelihood, their presence enriches the educational experience of children whose first language is English.

Achievement and Intelligence Tests

Learning Objective 9.10
Why do schools administer achievement tests, and what kinds of items do they include?

Perhaps you remember taking standardized tests during your elementary school years. The term *standardized* simply means that each individual's performance is determined by comparing his or her score to the average score attained by a large sample of similar individuals. For instance, an achievement test for first-graders compares each child's score to the average achieved by a large group of first graders who took the test prior to its publication. Most school systems in the United States administer standardized tests to students many times during their educational careers. The tests are generally of two types: *achievement tests* and *intelligence tests*.

Types of Tests **Achievement tests** are designed to assess specific information learned in school, using items like those in Table 9.2 on page 260. Scores are based on comparison of an individual child's performance to those of other children in the same grade across the country. Critics of achievement tests point out that, although educators and parents may think of achievement tests as indicators of what children learn in school, they are actually very similar to IQ tests. For example, suppose an achievement test contains the math problem "4 × 4." A bright child who hasn't yet learned multiplication may reason his way to the correct answer of 16. Another child may give the correct answer because she has learned it in school. Still another may know the answer because he learned to multiply from his parents. Thus, critics suggest that comprehensive portfolios of children's school work may be better indicators of actual school learning than standardized achievement tests (Neill, 1998).

Most U.S. schools also require students to take intelligence tests at various points in their educational careers. These tests are usually paper-and-pencil multiple-choice tests that can be given to large numbers of children at the same time. Some critics of routine IQ testing say that such tests aren't as accurate as the individual tests you read about in Chapter 7. Others object to the use of IQ tests because they often result in misclassification of

achievement test a test designed to assess specific information learned in school

Table 9.2 Some Sample Items from a Fourth-Grade Achievement Test

Vocabulary	Reference Skills	Mathematics Computation
jolly old man 1. angry 2. fat 3. merry 4. sorry	Which of these words would be first in ABC order? 1. pair 2. point 3. paint 4. polish	79 +14 149 −87 62 ×3
Language Expression	**Spelling**	**Mathematics**
Who wants ____ books? 1. that 2. these 3. them 4. this	Jason took the *cleanest* glass. right ____ wrong ____	What does the 3 in 13 stand for? 1. 3 ones 2. 13 ones 3. 3 tens 4. 13 tens

(*Source*: From *Comprehensive Tests of Basic Skills*, Form S. Reprinted by permission of the publisher, CTB/McGraw-Hill, Del Monte Research Park, Monterey, CA 93940. Copyright © 1973 by McGraw-Hill, Inc. All rights reserved. Printed in the USA.)

children in minority groups. Nevertheless, IQ tests are often used to group children for instruction because they are strongly correlated with achievement test scores.

Theories of Intelligence Some developmentalists say that the problem with relying on IQ tests to predict achievement is that they fail to provide a complete picture of mental abilities. For example, psychologist Howard Gardner proposed a theory of *multiple intelligences* (Gardner, 1983). This theory claims there are eight types of intelligence:

- *Linguistic*—the ability to use language effectively.
- *Logical/mathematical*—facility with numbers and logical problem-solving.
- *Musical*—the ability to appreciate and produce music.
- *Spatial*—the ability to appreciate spatial relationships.
- *Bodily kinesthetic*—the ability to move in a coordinated way, combined with a sense of one's body in space.
- *Naturalist*—the ability to make fine discriminations among the plants and animals of the natural world or the patterns and designs of human artifacts.
- *Interpersonal*—sensitivity to the behavior, moods, and needs of others.
- *Intrapersonal*—the ability to understand oneself.

Gardner's theory is based on observations of people with brain damage, mental retardation, and other severe mental handicaps. He points out that brain damage usually causes disruption of functioning in very specific mental abilities rather than a general decline in intelligence. He also notes that many individuals with mental deficits have remarkable talents. For example, some are gifted in music, while others can perform complex mathematical computations without using a calculator or pencil and paper. However, critics claim that Gardner's view, although intuitively appealing, has little empirical support (Aiken, 1997).

Robert Sternberg's *triarchic theory of intelligence* proposes three components of human intelligence (Sternberg, 1988). *Contextual intelligence* has to do with knowing the right behavior for a specific situation. For example, South American street vendors, most of whom are of elementary school age but are unschooled, are good at doing practical calculations but perform poorly on more abstract, written math problems. These children are highly "intelligent" in their daily context, but in the school context they appear to lack intellectual ability.

Experiential intelligence, according to Sternberg involves learning to give specific responses without thinking about them. For example, you can probably respond without thinking to the question "How much is 7 times 7?" Experiential intelligence also enables you to come up with novel solutions to everyday problems that you haven't quite been able to solve and to recognize when a tried-and-true solution is appropriate for a new problem.

Componential intelligence is a person's ability to come up with effective strategies. To Sternberg, this is the most important component of intelligence. He claims that intelligence tests are limited in their ability to identify gifted children because they put more emphasis on "correctness" of answers than on the quality of the strategies people use to arrive at them (Sternberg, 2002).

In general, Sternberg says, IQ tests measure how familiar a child is with "school" culture. Thus, children whose cultural background does not include formal schooling perform poorly because they are unfamiliar with the context of the test. Unfortunately, their poor performance is often mistakenly interpreted to mean that they lack intelligence (Sternberg & Grigorenko, 2006). Sternberg believes that intelligence tests should measure all three components of intelligence, and he has produced some research evidence suggesting that testing procedures based on his theory yield better performance predictions than conventional IQ tests (Sternberg, Wagner, Williams, & Horvath, 1995).

Emotional Intelligence Both Gardner's and Sternberg's theories have become important in helping educators understand the weaknesses of IQ tests. Moreover, psychologist Daniel Goleman's theory of *emotional intelligence* has also added to scientists' understanding of intelligence and achievement (Goleman, 1995). Emotional intelligence has three components:

NO EASY ANSWERS

IQ Testing in the Schools

Although IQ tests are frequently used in U.S. schools, they are very controversial. Everyone agrees that these tests have legitimate uses. For example, if a child is having difficulty learning to read, an IQ test can help determine the source of the problem. The arguments about IQ tests center on whether they ought to be used routinely to group elementary school children for instruction. Several strong reasons are usually given against such use.

First, as you may remember from earlier discussions, IQ tests do not measure all the facets of a child's functioning that may be relevant. For example, clinicians have found that some children with IQs below 70, who would be considered as mentally retarded if the score alone were used for classification, nonetheless have sufficient social skills to enable them to function well in a regular classroom. Second, there is the problem of the self-fulfilling prophecy that an IQ test score may establish. Because many parents and teachers still believe that IQ scores are a permanent feature of a child, once a child is labeled as "having" a particular IQ, that label tends to be difficult to remove. Psychologist Robert Rosenthal, in a series of famous studies, has shown that a teacher's belief about a given student's ability and potential has a small but significant effect on her behavior toward that student and on the student's eventual achievement (Rosenthal, 1994).

Another negative argument is that tests are biased in such a way that some groups of children are more likely to score high or low, even though their underlying ability is the same. For example, the tests may contain items that are not equally familiar to minorities and Whites; taking such tests and doing well may also require certain test-taking skills, motivations, or attitudes less common among some minority children, especially African American children (Kaplan, 1985; Reynolds & Brown, 1984). Researchers have devised *culturally reduced tests,* also called *culture-fair tests,* that minimize the impact of verbal knowledge, presumably the most culture-laden aspect of intelligence testing, on children's scores (Sattler, 2001). However, these tests do not correlate well with academic achievement, so they are not useful in the diagnosis of learning problems.

There is no quick or easy solution to this dilemma. It is certainly true that schools in the United States reflect the dominant middle-class White culture, with all of its values and assumptions. But it is also true that succeeding in these schools is essential if a child is to acquire the basic skills needed to cope with the complexities of life in an industrialized country. For a host of reasons, including poorer prenatal care, greater poverty rates, and different familial patterns, more African American children appear to need special classes in order to acquire the skills they lack.

Yet it is also true that placing a child in a special class may create a self-fulfilling prophecy. Expectations are typically lower in such classes, so the children—who were already learning slowly—are challenged even less and proceed even more slowly. However, to offer no special help to children who come to school lacking the skills needed to succeed seems equally unacceptable to many observers. Likewise, some bright children may benefit from acceleration. Thus, many developmentalists have concluded that IQ tests are more reliable and valid for grouping children than other alternatives such as teacher rating scales (Alvidrez & Weinstein, 1999).

Take a Stand

Decide which of these two statements you most agree with and think about how you would defend your position:

1. IQ testing should be considered only when a child has demonstrated some kind of difficulty with learning or appears to be exceptionally bright.
2. Using routine IQ testing as a means of screening children for possible learning problems and for identifying gifted children is a good idea and ought to be continued.

awareness of one's own emotions, the ability to express one's emotions appropriately, and the capacity to channel emotions into the pursuit of worthwhile goals. Without emotional intelligence, Goleman claims, it is impossible to achieve one's intellectual potential. However, research has yet to provide support for Goleman's hypothesis (Humphrey et al., 2007). Still, research on the relationship between self-control (the third component of emotional intelligence) in early childhood and achievement in adolescence suggests that Goleman's view is correct. Children's ability to exercise control over their emotions in early childhood is strongly related to measures of academic achievement in high school (Denham, 2006.)

Learning Objective 9.11

What kinds of group differences in achievement have educational researchers found?

Group Differences in Achievement

Although intelligence testing is a prominent feature of the educational environment, teachers and administrators are usually more concerned about what children actually learn than they are about their abilities. For this reason, a good deal of educational research focuses on finding explanations for group differences in achievement. These differences have been found across gender, ethnic groups, and cultures. See The Real World.

Sex Differences in Achievement Comparisons of total IQ test scores for boys and girls do not reveal consistent differences. It is only when the total scores are broken down into several separate skills that some patterns of sex differences emerge. On average, studies in the United States show that girls do slightly better on verbal tasks and at arithmetic computation and that boys do slightly better at numerical reasoning. For example, more boys than girls test as gifted in mathematics (Benbow, 1988; Lubinski & Benbow, 1992).

THE REAL WORLD

Homeschooling

The Johnson family is concerned about their son's progress in second grade. Although Michael struggled somewhat in first grade, he was eventually able to meet the minimum requirements for promotion to second grade. Now, however, he is beginning to fall seriously behind his classmates. Michael's teachers have suggested that he might benefit from special education services, but the Johnsons are exploring the possibility of homeschooling for Michael, an option that has been enthusiastically embraced by several of their neighbors. The Johnsons' neighbors have created a variety of opportunities for their children to interact so that they do not miss out on any of the social skills that children usually learn in school. But why would a parent want to take on the daunting task of educating a child at home?

Surveys show that the most frequent reason for homeschooling is parents' belief that they can do a better job of educating their children than public or private schools can (Basham, 2001). About 8% of homeschool parents have children with disabilities and prefer teaching them at home to having them receive special-education services from local schools (Basham, 2001). The one-on-one teaching these children get at home often helps them achieve more than their disabled peers in public schools are able to (Duvall, Delquadri, & Ward, 2004; Ensign, 1998). In addition, children with disabilities who are homeschooled don't have to deal with teasing from peers. In addition, many homeschool parents want to be sure that their own religious and moral values are included in their children's education. Many also want to protect their children from negative peer influences or school-based crime.

Research on homeschooling is sparse. Advocates point to a small number of studies showing that homeschooled children are socially competent and emotionally well adjusted and score above average on standardized achievement tests (Ray, 1999). They further argue that homeschooled children have the opportunity to become closer to their parents than children who attend school do (Jonsson, 2003). The growing prevalence of homeschooling, which includes about 2.4% of all children in the United States, has led to the creation of a variety of extracurricular organizations, such as musical groups and athletic leagues, that exclusively serve homeschoolers. Thus, today's homeschoolers have many opportunities for interacting with peers that are highly similar to those that are available to children who are enrolled in school.

However, opponents of homeschooling, a group that includes most professional educators, claim that comparisons of homeschooling and public education are misleading. They point out that researchers have studied only homeschooled children whose families volunteered to participate in research studies. In contrast, most public school achievement test data are based on representative samples or on populations of entire schools.

Questions for Reflection

1. What factors would motivate you to consider homeschooling your child, and what are some reasons that you would be reluctant to do so?
2. If you were discussing homeschooling with a classmate who cited research showing that homeschoolers get higher achievement test scores than children who are enrolled in public school, how would you explain the shortcomings of such research?

Where might such differences come from? The explanatory options should be familiar by now. As you learned earlier in this chapter, brain processes that underlie spatial perception and cognition are often argued to be the cause of sex differences in math achievement. To date, however, neurological research has failed to find sex differences in brain function large enough to explain sex differences in math achievement (Spreen et al., 1995).

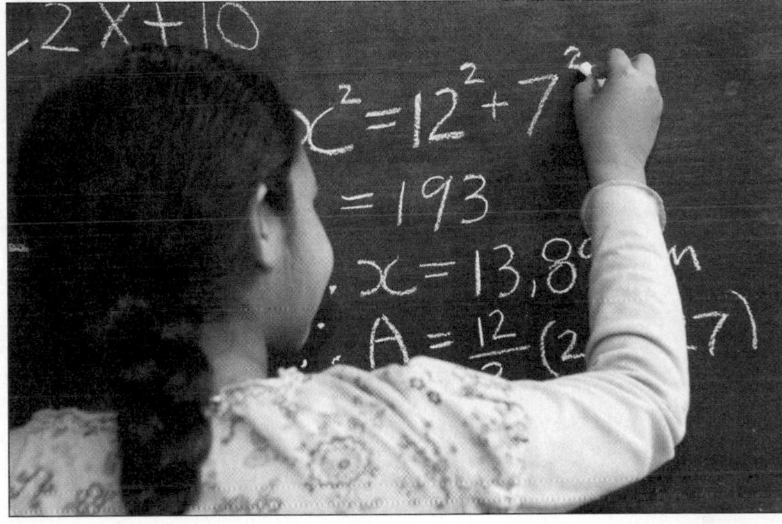

Encouragement from teachers and parents that is equal to that given to boys may help girls narrow the mathematics achievement gap.

So far, environmental explanations have proven to be more useful than biological theories in discussions of the sex differences in mathematical or verbal reasoning. Especially in the case of mathematics, there is considerable evidence that girls' and boys' skills are systematically shaped by a series of environmental factors.

For one thing, both teachers and parents seem to believe that boys have more math ability than girls (Jussim & Eccles, 1992; Tiedemann, 2000). Thus, they are more likely to attribute a girl's success in mathematics to effort or good teaching; poor performance by a girl is attributed to lack of ability. In contrast, teachers and parents attribute a boy's success to ability and his failure to lack of application (Jussim & Eccles, 1992). Moreover, children appear to internalize these beliefs, which, in turn, influence their interest in taking math courses and their beliefs about their likelihood of achieving success in math (Eccles, Jacobs, & Harold, 1990). The cumulative effects of these differences in expectations and treatment show up in high school, when sex differences on standardized math tests usually become evident. In part, then, the sex differences in math achievement test scores appear to be perpetuated by subtle family and school influences on children's attitudes.

Ethnic Differences in Achievement In the United States, there are ethnic group differences in achievement test scores similar to the differences in IQ test scores you read about in Chapter 7. Most developmentalists believe that the same factors that contribute to IQ score differences—economic status, access to prenatal care, family stability, and so on—also produce ethnic differences in measures of school performance such as grades and achievement test scores.

For example, psychologists have learned that children who use an **analytical style** define learning goals and follow a set of orderly steps to reach them. These children are well organized, are good at learning details, and think of information in terms of "right" and "wrong." Other children use a **relational style.** These children focus attention on "the big picture" instead of on individual bits of information.

For example, Ayana, who has an analytical style, and Richard, who uses a relational style, both listen carefully as their fourth-grade teacher gives instructions for a complicated project. Ayana lists every detail of the teacher's instructions and how many points each part is worth. In contrast, Richard writes down his general impression of each part of the project.

In working on the project, Ayana concentrates her effort on the parts that are worth the most points. Richard pays more attention to the aspects of the project he finds interesting. When it is finished, Ayana's project conforms more exactly to the teacher's instructions than Richard's does, and she receives a higher grade. Ayana's way of approaching school work—her cognitive style—better fits school expectations, giving her an advantage over Richard. In addition, Ayana's way of learning helps her get high scores on achievement tests, which require detailed knowledge of specific information and skills.

analytical style a tendency to focus on the details of a task

relational style a tendency to ignore the details of a task in order to focus on the "big picture"

Ethnic groups in the United States differ in the percentages of children who use each style. A higher percentage of Asian American and European American students are analyticals. In contrast, a higher percentage of African American, Hispanic American, and Native American children are relationals. Thus, differences among these groups in achievement test scores and school grades may be due to the different percentages of analyticals and relationals (Serpell & Hatano, 1997).

Achievement differences may also be due to philosophical beliefs that characterize some racial and ethnic groups in the United States. For example, American culture tends to be *individualistic*. In other words, it emphasizes the achievements of individuals and encourages competition rather than cooperation. However, some U.S. subcultures place more emphasis on interdependence, an outlook that sociologists and anthropologists usually refer to as *collectivist* (Serpell & Hatano, 1997). In Hawaii, educators tried changing their curriculum and teaching methods to better fit with the collectivist emphasis of Native Hawaiian children and families. The new approach involved more group work and cooperation among students, and it apparently helped children learn more (Cushner et al., 1992). The success of such interventions suggests that educational practices in the United States may be well adapted to some groups but not others, thereby producing differences in achievement between groups for whom the educational system is a good cultural "fit" and those for whom it is not.

Feelings of hopelessness on the part of some disadvantaged students may also be a factor. For example, some African American students in the United States, discouraged by racism and lack of opportunity, believe that they won't be able to succeed economically no matter how much they learn in school (Baranchik, 2002; Ogbu, 1990). Some research suggests that these feelings influence minority children's scores on standardized tests, as discussed in the Research Report. Educators believe schools can affect these students' beliefs by making sure textbooks and other materials accurately reflect the contributions of African Americans to American culture (Cushner et al., 1992).

Cross-Cultural Differences in Achievement Differences in math and science achievement between Asian children and North American children have been the focus of much study and debate. Over a 20-year period, studies have repeatedly shown that U.S. school children are significantly behind their peers in other industrialized nations (Caslyn, Gonzales, &

RESEARCH REPORT

Stereotype Threat

Suppose that on the first day of class, your professor had said that women usually get higher grades than men in human development courses. Do you think such a statement would cause male students to slack off? If so, you would be in agreement with the central hypothesis of *stereotype threat theory*.

Psychologists Claude Steele and Joshua Aronson (Steele & Aronson, 1995) define stereotype threat as a subtle sense of pressure members of a particular group feel when they are attempting to perform well in an area in which their group is characterized by a negative stereotype. According to Steele and Aronson, African American students experience stereotype threat whenever they are faced with an important cognitive test, such as a college entrance exam or an IQ test, because of the general cultural stereotype that African Americans are less intellectually able than members of other groups. In order to avoid confirming the stereotype, says the theory, African Americans avoid putting forth their best effort because to fail after having put forth one's best effort would mean that the stereotype is true.

Numerous studies have confirmed the existence of stereotype threat among both children and adults (McKown & Weinstein, 2003; Nussbaum & Steele, 2007; Steele & Aronson, 2004; Suzuki & Aronson, 2005). However, stereotype threat appears to have a smaller effect on children's test performance than it does on that of adults. Consequently, while the power of stereotype threat to influence adults' performance on cognitive tests has been well established by researchers, the jury is still out with regard to its importance in explaining group differences among children.

In addition, psychologist Paul Sackett points out that removing stereotype threat does not cause groups who are unequal to perform equally (Sackett, Hardison, & Cullen, 2004a, 2005). Sackett has also raised concerns about the degree to which the importance of stereotype threat has been misinterpreted in the popular press (Sackett, Hardinson, & Cullen, 2004b). Often, they say, Steele and Aronson's findings are presented in ways that cause naive individuals to believe that ethnic group differences would disappear if stereotype threat could be eliminated somehow. In some cases, the inference has been drawn that scientists should refrain from publishing or even discussing racial group differences so as not to engender feelings of stereotype threat among members of minority groups. By contrast, they argue that continued discussion of these differences serves to accentuate the need for more research on the topic.

Questions for Critical Analysis

1. If discussion of group differences in intelligence test scores contributes to racial prejudice, do you think society would be better off if researchers stopped trying to discover the causes for them? Why or why not?
2. How might parents and teachers moderate the effects of stereotype threat on children's test performance?

Frase, 1999). Yet studies show that underlying cognitive developmental processes are very similar in Asian and North American children (Zhou & Boehm, 2004). Developmentalists speculate that the differences result from variations in both cultural beliefs and teaching methods.

Across all cultures, parent involvement is associated with high achievement.

With respect to cultural beliefs, developmentalists have found that North American parents and teachers emphasize innate ability, which they assume to be unchangeable, more than effort. For Asians, the emphasis is just the opposite: They believe that people can become more capable by working harder (Serpell & Hatano, 1997). Because of these differences in beliefs, this theory claims, Asian parents and teachers have higher expectations for children and are better at finding ways to motivate them to do school work. Presumably for these same reasons, Asian families spend more time teaching their children specific academic skills than North American parents do (Sijuwade, 2003).

However, teaching methods in the two cultures also vary. For example, in one important set of studies, educational psychologists James Stigler and Harold Stevenson observed teaching strategies in 120 classrooms in Japan, Taiwan, and the United States, and they are convinced that Asian teachers have devised particularly effective modes of teaching mathematics and science (Stevenson, 1994; Stigler & Stevenson, 1991).

Japanese and Chinese teachers approach mathematics and science by crafting a series of "master lessons," each organized around a single theme or idea and each involving specific forms of student participation. These lessons are like good stories, with a beginning, a middle, and an end. In U.S. classrooms, by contrast, it is extremely uncommon for teachers to spend 30 or 60 minutes on a single coherent math or science lesson involving the whole class of children and a single topic. Instead, teachers shift often from one topic to another during a single math or science "lesson." They might do a brief bit on addition, then talk about measurement, then about telling time, and finally back to addition. Stigler and Stevenson also found striking differences in the amount of time teachers spend actually leading instruction for the whole class. In the U.S. classrooms, teachers spent 49% of their time instructing the entire class. By contrast, group instruction occurred 74% and 90% of the time, respectively, in Japan and Taiwan.

Asian and North American math instruction also differs in the emphasis on *computational fluency*, the degree to which an individual can automatically produce solutions to simple calculation problems. A number of mathematicians and professors of mathematics have claimed that math instruction in the United States has been influenced more by "fads" than by a sound understanding of the role of computational fluency in mathematical problem-solving (Murray, 1998). They point out that research has demonstrated that computational fluency is related both to calculation skills and to facility in solving word problems (Geary et al., 1999; Kail & Hall, 1999). Moreover, calculators are not commonly used in Asian schools. Many math educators suggest that, by the time they get to high school, U.S. students have learned to depend on calculators and, as a result, have a more difficult time learning algebra than their Asian counterparts do (Judson & Nishimori, 2005). These differences in algebra learning carry over into more advanced classes such as geometry and calculus. As a result, U.S. teens are often found to perform equally as well as their Asian peers with regard to mathematics concepts but fall short of them in problem-solving.

The high levels of achievement that are attained by Asian students may be best explained by the fact that Asian teachers and parents regard instruction in computational skills as a parental responsibility and instruction in conceptual understanding as the responsibility of the school (Office of Educational Research and Improvement, 1998). Thus, by the time children enter school, they have already spent a good deal of time rehearsing basic computational facts and are ready to think more deeply about mathematical concepts. Many are taught to use an *abacus*, the ancient Chinese calculating device. Others begin studying mathematics in the internationally popular *Kumon* program at the age of 3 years, and about a quarter of Japanese students continue to take Kumon classes throughout their school careers (OERI, 1998). The home-based approach to mathematics education that is common in Asian societies is effective because the amount of time that is needed to master computational skills varies widely from one child to another. Parents and individualized programs such as Kumon can more easily adapt their curricula to each child's unique pace of learning than schools can.

Another difference between U.S. and Asian schools, especially at the elementary level, involves the use of rewards. Because of the influence of Skinner's operant conditioning theory on education in the United States, teachers commonly use material rewards, such as stickers, to motivate children. Such rewards are effective only when they are tied to high standards, yet teachers in the United States often use them to reward students for less than optimal performance (Deci, Koestner, & Ryan, 1999; Eisenberger, Pierce, & Cameron, 1999).

In response to these criticisms, many educators say that achievement differences between North American and Asian students have been exaggerated to make U.S. schools look worse than they actually are (Berliner & Biddle, 1997). Moreover, more than 70% of American parents give grades of A or B to the nation's public schools (ABC News, 2000). Educators and parents alike often claim that Asian schools teach students to value conformity, while American schools place more emphasis on creativity. Indeed, some Asian educators agree that their schools have sacrificed creativity in order to attain high achievement test scores (Hatano, 1990).

Critical Thinking

1. How did your elementary school experiences shape the rest of your life?

Children with Special Needs

Some children are born with or develop differences that may significantly interfere with their education unless they receive some kind of special instruction (see Table 9.3). In the United States, 14% of all school children receive such services (National Center for Education Statistics [NCES] 2006). The categories listed in Table 9.3 are defined by law, and public schools are legally obligated to provide special education services for all children who qualify.

Learning Objective 9.12

Why is the term "learning disability" controversial?

Learning Disabilities

The largest group served by U.S. special educators has some kind of **learning disability**, or difficulty in mastering a specific academic skill—most often reading—despite possessing normal intelligence and no physical or sensory handicaps. When reading is the problem skill, the term **dyslexia** is often used (even though, technically speaking, *dyslexia* refers to a total absence of reading). Most children with reading disabilities can read, but not as well as others their age. Moreover, it appears that their skill deficits are specific to reading—such as an inability to automatize sound-letter correspondences—rather than the result of a general cognitive dysfunction (Wimmer, Mayringer, & Landerl, 1998).

How common such learning disabilities may be is still a matter of considerable dispute. Some experts in the field argue that up to 80% of all children classified by school systems as having learning disabilities are misclassified. They claim that only about 5 out of every 1,000 children have genuine neurologically based learning disabilities (Farnham-Diggory, 1992). The remainder who are so classified are more appropriately called *slow learners* or are suffering from some other problem, perhaps temporary emotional distress or poor teaching. Practically speaking, however, the term learning disability is used very broadly within school systems (at least within the United States) to label children who have unexpected or otherwise unexplainable difficulty with school work.

Explanations of the problem are just as subject to disagreement as its definition. One difficulty is that children labeled as having learning disabilities rarely show any signs of major brain damage on any standard neurological tests. So, if a learning disability results from a neurological problem, the neurological problem must be a subtle one. Some researchers have suggested that a large number of small abnormalities may develop in the brain during prena-

learning disability a disorder in which a child has difficulty mastering a specific academic skill, even though she possesses normal intelligence and no physical or sensory handicaps

dyslexia problems in reading or the inability to read

TABLE 9.3 Disabilities for Which U.S. Children Receive Special Education Services

Disability Category	Percentage of Special Education Students in the Category	Description of Disability
Learning Disability	43%	Achievement 2 or more years behind expectations based on intelligence tests Example: A fourth-grader with an average IQ who is reading at a first-grade level
Communication Disorder in Speech or Language	22%	A disorder of speech or language that affects a child's education; can be a problem with speech or an impairment in the comprehension or use of any aspect of language Example: A first-grader who makes errors in pronunciation like those of a 4-year-old and can't connect sounds and symbols
Mental Retardation	9%	IQ significantly below average intelligence, together with impairments in adaptive functions Example: A school-aged child with an IQ lower than 70 who is not fully toilet-trained and who needs special instruction in both academic and self-care skills
Serious Emotional Disturbance	7%	An emotional or behavior disorder that interferes with a child's education Example: A child whose severe temper tantrums cause him to be removed from the classroom every day
Other Health Impairments	7%	A health problem that interferes with a child's education Example: A child with severe asthma who misses several weeks of school each year. (Children with ADHD are included in this category.)
Autistic Disorders	3%	A group of disorders in which children's language and social skills are impaired Example: A child with autism who needs special training to acquire the capacity for verbal communication
Multiple Disabilities	2%	Need for special instruction and ongoing support in two or more areas to benefit from education Example: A child with cerebral palsy who is also deaf, thus requiring both physical and instructional adaptations
Hearing Impairment	1%	A hearing problem that interferes with a child's education Example: A child who needs a sign-language interpreter in the classroom
Orthopedic Impairment	1%	An orthopedic handicap that requires special adaptations Example: A child in a wheelchair who needs a special physical education class
Visual Impairment	.4%	Impaired visual acuity or a limited field of vision that interferes with education Example: A blind child who needs training in the use of Braille to read and write

(*Sources*: Kirk, Gallagher, & Anastasiow, 1993; NCES, 2006.)

tal life, such as some irregularity of neuron arrangement, or clumps of immature brain cells, or scars, or congenital tumors. The growing brain compensates for these problems by "rewiring" around the problem areas. These rewirings, in turn, may scramble normal information-processing pathways just enough to make reading or calculation or some other specific task very difficult (Farnham-Diggory, 1992). Other experts argue that there may not be any underlying neurological problem at all. Instead, children with learning disabilities (especially reading disabilities) may simply have a more general problem with understanding the sound and structure of language (Carroll & Snowling, 2004; Share & Leiken, 2004;

Torgesen et al., 1999). There is also some evidence that learning disabilities, especially dyslexia, may have a genetic basis (Gallagher, Frith, & Snowling, 2000; Turic et al., 2003).

These disagreements about both definition and explanation are (understandably) reflected in confusion at the practical level. Children are labeled as having learning disabilities and assigned to special classes, but a program that works well for one child may not work at all for another. Some parents of children with disabilities choose to homeschool (see The Real World on page 262). One type of school intervention that shows promise is an approach called *reciprocal teaching*. In reciprocal teaching programs, children with learning disabilities work in pairs or groups. Each child takes a turn summarizing and explaining the material to be learned to the others in the group. A number of studies have found that, after participating in reciprocal teaching, children with learning disabilities improved in summarization skills and memory strategies (e.g., Lederer, 2000).

Current special education laws rest most centrally on the philosophical view that children with disabilities have a right to participate in normal school environments (e.g., Stainback & Stainback, 1985). Proponents have further argued that such **inclusive education** aids the child with disabilities by integrating him into the nondisabled world, thus facilitating the development of important social skills as well as providing more appropriate academic challenges than are often found in separate classrooms or special programs for the disabled (Siegel, 1996). Advocates of inclusion are convinced that children with mild retardation and those with learning disabilities will show greater academic achievement if they are in regular classrooms.

Schools and school districts differ widely in the specific model of inclusion they use, although virtually all models involve a team of educators, including the classroom teacher, one or more special education teachers, classroom aides, and sometimes volunteers. Some schools follow a plan called a *pull-out program*, in which the student with the disability is placed in a regular classroom only part of each day, with the remainder of the time spent working with a special education teacher in a special class or resource room. More common are full-inclusion systems in which the child spends the entire school day in a regular class but receives help from volunteers, aides, or special education teachers who come to the classroom to work with the child there. In some districts, a group of children with disabilities may be assigned to a single regular classroom: in others, no more than one such child is normally assigned to any one class (Baker & Zigmond, 1995).

Learning Objective 9.13

How does attention-deficit hyperactivity disorder affect a child's development?

Attention-Deficit Hyperactivity Disorder

Some children experience learning difficulties that don't seem to fit the typical special education categories. For example, as many as 18% of U.S. school children have a mental disorder called **attention-deficit hyperactivity disorder (ADHD)** (CDC, 2007). Children with ADHD are more physically active and/or less attentive than their peers. These characteristics often lead to both academic and behavioral problems in school.

Application of the special education classification to a child with ADHD depends on how the disorder has affected his education and how it is being treated. For example, a child whose ADHD has caused him to fall more than 2 years behind other children in his grade will be classified as learning disabled. The point is that ADHD is not itself a legally recognized special-education category in the United States. Rather, it is a mental disorder that may cause a child to develop school problems so severe that he qualifies for services under one of the legally defined categories.

inclusive education general term for education programs in which children with disabilities are taught in regular classrooms

attention-deficit hyperactivity disorder (ADHD) a mental disorder that causes children to have difficulty attending to and completing tasks

Causes of ADHD The cause of ADHD is unknown. However, some developmentalists suggest that children with ADHD are neurologically different from their peers. Specifically, some have asserted that children with ADHD have functional deficits in the right hemisphere of the brain (Sandson, Bachna, & Morin, 2000). Others say that serotonin function is impaired in children with ADHD (Kent et al., 2002). Some type of biological factor does seem to be involved, as children who were born at 24–31 weeks of gestation are four to six times as likely to suffer from the symptoms of ADHD as their peers who were full-term infants (Barlow & Lewandowski, 2000). Other developmentalists hypothesize that children with ADHD require more sensory stimulation than their peers; thus, they move around more in order to get the stimulation they need (Antrop, Roeyers, Van Oost, & Buysse, 2000).

School can be a discouraging and frustrating place for a child with a learning disability.

Cultural factors may also be important in ADHD, as the disorder is rare outside of the United States (NIMH, 2006). Critics of using medication to control ADHD symptoms suggest that this cross-national difference is the result of overuse of the diagnosis in the United States. However, some developmentalists assert that educators and mental health professionals in other nations have failed to recognize the degree to which ADHD may be prevalent in their children (Overmeyer & Taylor, 1999). Others suggest that there is a real cross-cultural difference in the incidence of ADHD. For example, a study comparing African American and South African 6-year-olds who were similar in family structure and socioeconomic status found that a larger proportion of African American children, especially boys, scored higher on scales measuring hyperactivity (Barbarin, 1999).

Psychologists are fairly sure that diet, environmental toxins, or brain damage is not the cause of ADHD, despite what some promoters of "cures" claim (Spreen, Risser, & Edgell, 1995). At present, most experts believe that each individual case of ADHD is caused by a complex interaction of factors unique to the specific child. These factors may include genetics, temperament, parenting styles, peer relations, the type and quality of the school a child attends, and stressors in the child's life such as poverty, family instability, and parental mental illness.

Characteristics of ADHD On many kinds of attention tasks, children with ADHD do not differ at all from normal children (Lawrence et al., 2004). They seem to vary from their normal peers in activity level, the ability to sustain attention (especially with boring and repetitive tasks), and the ability to control impulses. However, the degree of hyperactivity children with ADHD exhibit is unrelated to their performance on attention tasks. That is, a child can be very physically active and still be good at controlling his attention. Likewise, a child can be very calm yet have little ability to sustain attention. For this reason, there are now two types of ADHD: (1) the hyperactive/impulsive type, in which a high activity level is the main problem, and (2) the inattentive type, in which an inability to sustain attention is the major difficulty (APA, 1994).

Most children with ADHD are successful in learning academic skills (Chadwick et al., 1999). However, their hyperactivity and/or inattentiveness often cause other kinds of problems. For one thing, children with both types of ADHD usually produce school work that is messy and filled with errors, causing them to get poor grades (Cahn et al., 1996). They may be disruptive in class and are often rejected by other children.

Treating and Managing ADHD By the time their children are diagnosed with ADHD, usually upon entering school, many parents have lost confidence in their ability to control them (Barkley, 1990). Some cope with their difficult child by being extremely permissive. Others respond by becoming excessively harsh and, out of frustration, sometimes treat the child with ADHD abusively. Thus, parent training can be useful in helping parents cope with children who have ADHD.

The goal of such parenting programs is to help parents regain a sense of control (Barkley, 1990). For example, experts recommend that teachers provide parents with daily reports of their children's work in the various school subjects—language, math, social studies, and so on. Parents can then use the information to enforce a standing rule that the child must have completed all school work before watching television or doing other desired activities. Such approaches, when applied consistently, can help parents of children with ADHD manage their children's difficulties, as well as their own emotional reactions, more effectively.

Many children with ADHD take stimulant medications, such as methylphenidate (Ritalin). Most of those who do are calmer and can concentrate better (Demb & Chang, 2004;

Mehta, Goodyer, & Sahakian, 2004). However, some studies show that many children's "response to the medication" may actually be due to changes in expectations on the part of their teachers and parents—sort of a self-fulfilling prophecy (Spreen et al., 1995). In addition, studies suggest that the concentration skills of children with ADHD can be improved with training. For example, one study found that, after an intensive 18-week training program, the attention skills of a group of children with ADHD were similar to those of a control group of children without attention difficulties (Semrud-Clikeman et al., 1999).

It's also important to note that medication doesn't always improve the grades of children with ADHD. For the most part, it seems that stimulant medications reduce such children's activity levels, help them control their impulses, and somewhat improve their social behavior. These effects usually result in improvements in classroom behavior and peer acceptance. Medications such as methylphenidate have the greatest effect on school grades among children whose ADHD symptoms are so severe that they interfere with actual learning (Spreen, Risser, & Edgell, 1995). For this reason, the use of stimulant medications for children who have mild or moderate ADHD symptoms is controversial. Moreover, recent studies show that many of the newer drugs that are used to treat ADHD (e.g., Adderall) are associated with changes in thinking that may increase a child's risk of developing a more serious psychological disorder (Gardner, 2007). Moreover, many of these drugs, including methylphenidate, have been found to increase the risk of cardiovascular events such as strokes and heart attacks in adults.

Critical Thinking

1. If you were the parent of a child with special needs, what reasons would you have for wanting your child to be placed in a special class and what factors would motivate you to prefer that she be taught in a regular class? How would the nature of the child's disability affect your preference?

SUMMARY

Physical Changes

Learning Objective 9.1 What kinds of physical changes occur during middle childhood?

- Physical development from age 6 to age 12 is steady and slow. Sex differences in skeletal and muscular maturation may lead boys and girls to pursue different activities.

Learning Objective 9.2 In what ways does the brain change during these years?

- Major brain growth spurts occur in 6- to 8-year-olds and in 10- to 12-year-olds. Neurological development leads to improvements in selective attention, information-processing speed, and spatial perception.

Learning Objective 9.3 What are the three most important health hazards for 6- to 12-year-olds?

- School-aged children are healthy but benefit from regular medical care. Head injuries, asthma, and excessive weight gain are the most prevalent health problems of this age group.

Cognitive Changes

Learning Objective 9.4 How do vocabulary and other aspects of language change during middle childhood?

- Language development continues in middle childhood with vocabulary growth, improvements in grammar, and understanding of the social uses of language.

Learning Objective 9.5 What cognitive advantages do children gain as they move through Piaget's concrete operational stage?

- Piaget proposed that a major change in the child's thinking occurs at about age 6, when the child begins to understand powerful operations such as reversibility and decentration. The child also learns to use inductive logic, but does not yet use deductive logic.

Learning Objective 9.6 What is horizontal decalage, and how does Siegler explain concrete operational thinking?

- Children do not master all of Piaget's concrete operational tasks at the same time, a pattern he called horizontal decalage. Moreover, Siegler's research suggests that the "operations" he observed may actually be rules for solving specific types of problems.

Learning Objective 9.7 How do children's information-processing skills improve during these years?

- Most information-processing theorists conclude that there are no age-related changes in children's information-processing capacity, but there are clearly improvements in speed and efficiency.

Schooling

Learning Objective 9.8 What should be included in an effective literacy curriculum?

- To become literate, children need specific instruction in sound-symbol correspondences, word parts, and other aspects of written language. They also need to be exposed to good literature and to have lots of opportunities to practice their reading and writing skills.

Learning Objective 9.9 How do bilingual and ESL approaches to second-language instruction differ?

- Children who participate in bilingual education receive academic instruction in their first language until they develop sufficient English skills to be taught in English. Those in ESL classes attend language classes in which they learn English and are instructed in English in their academic classes.

Learning Objective 9.10 Why do schools administer achievement tests, and what kind of items do they include?

- Children's school progress is assessed with both IQ tests and achievement tests. Both types of tests may ignore important aspects of intellectual functioning.

Learning Objective 9.11 What kinds of group differences in achievement have educational researchers found?

- Boys typically do better on tests of advanced mathematical ability. Girls do somewhat better on verbal tasks. Although poverty and other social factors may play a role, ethnic differences in achievement may also result from differences in learning styles, philosophy, or attitudes toward school. Differences in both cultural beliefs and teaching practices are probably responsible for cross-cultural variations in math and science achievement.

Children with Special Needs

Learning Objective 9.12 Why is the term "learning disability" controversial?

- There is considerable dispute about how to identify a genuine learning disability, and some children who are labeled as such have been misclassified. Practically speaking, "learning disability" serves as a catch-all term to describe children who, for unknown reasons, do not learn as quickly as their intelligence test scores suggest they should.

Learning Objective 9.13 How does attention-deficit hyperactivity disorder affect a child's development?

- Children with ADHD have problems with both academic learning and social relationships. Medication, parent training, and behavior modification are useful in helping children with ADHD overcome these difficulties.

KEY TERMS

achievement test *(p. 259)*
analytical style *(p. 263)*
association areas *(p. 247)*
asthma *(p. 248)*
at-risk for overweight *(p. 249)*
attention-deficit hyperactivity disorder (ADHD) *(p. 268)*
automaticity *(p. 254)*
balanced approach *(p. 257)*
bilingual education *(p. 258)*
BMI-for-age *(p. 248)*
class inclusion *(p. 253)*
concrete operational stage *(p. 251)*
decentration *(p. 251)*
deductive logic *(p. 252)*
dyslexia *(p. 266)*
English-as-a-second-language (ESL) program *(p. 258)*
excessive weight gain *(p. 248)*
executive processes *(p. 255)*
inclusive education *(p. 268)*
inductive logic *(p. 252)*
learning disability *(p. 266)*
memory strategies *(p. 255)*
overweight *(p. 249)*
processing efficiency *(p. 254)*
relational style *(p. 263)*
relative right-left orientation *(p. 247)*
reversibility *(p. 252)*
selective attention *(p. 247)*
spatial cognition *(p. 247)*
spatial perception *(p. 247)*

TEST YOURSELF

Physical Changes

9.1 During middle childhood, growth in the brain and nervous system results in all of the following advances in development except

a. improvements in logic and planning.
b. increased ability to think hypothetically and reason abstractly.
c. ability to control attention.
d. lateralization of spatial perception.

9.2 Map-reading is an example of which of the following cognitive skills?

a. spatial perception
b. relative right-left orientation
c. metacognition
d. inductive logic

9.3 Which of the following is *not* a significant health risk of middle childhood?

a. motor vehicle accidents

b. bicycle accidents

c. infectious diseases

d. overweight

9.4 Which of the following is a strategy that parents of an overweight child should *not* utilize?

a. Have the child follow a strict weight-loss diet.

b. Limit the amount of time the child spends on television, computers, and video games.

c. Help the child develop good eating habits without overemphasizing cultural norms for thinness.

d. Encourage the child to be physically active.

Cognitive Changes

9.5 A derived word is one that

a. was slang but is now considered acceptable.

b. has a basic root to which a prefix or suffix is added.

c. means dramatically different things in different cultures.

d. is offensive to individuals of particular cultural groups.

9.6 Which of the following correctly illustrates inductive logic?

a. understanding that adding to a set always makes the set have more

b. thinking up examples that illustrate the concept of equality

c. knowing how to take a general principle and predict a specific outcome

d. demonstrating an ability to process abstract ideals

9.7 Which of the following correctly illustrates an understanding of class inclusion?

a. understanding that cats and dogs are not the same

b. understanding that a rose is a flower and that flowers are plants

c. understanding that not all objects are alive

d. understanding that objects stay the same even if their appearance changes

9.8 According to Robert Siegler's explanation of children's cognitive development, a child who takes into account only one dimension of a problem is using ________ in the solution sequence.

a. Rule I

b. Rule II

c. Rule III

d. Rule IV

9.9 In information-processing explanations of children's cognitive development, the central development that supports children's advances in cognition is

a. lateralization of the lobes of the cerebral hemisphere.

b. accommodation of new schemes.

c. opportunities to solve new problems.

d. increased processing efficiency.

9.10 Which of the following is *not* a memory strategy that first emerges during middle childhood?

a. using a mnemonic

b. rehearsal

c. making a list

d. systematic searching

9.11 When Maria has to learn the capitals of all the states, she groups them into an alphabetized list in order to remember them. This is an example of which information-processing strategy?

a. mnemonics

b. organization

c. elaboration

d. systematic searching

Schooling

9.12 Which of the following skills is most significant for developing the ability to read well during middle childhood?

a. spatial cognition

b. class inclusion

c. mnemonics

d. phonological awareness

9.13 The term used to describe both non–English-speaking immigrant children and native-born children who do not speak English is

a. English-as-a-second-language (ESL).

b. submersion.

c. limited English proficient (LEP).

d. bilingual education.

9.14 The largest group of limited English-proficient children in the U.S. ________ have as their first language.

a. French

b. Japanese

c. Cantonese

d. Spanish

9.15 According to Howard Gardner's theory of multiple intelligences, an individual who produces works of art such as paintings or sculptures very likely has a high degree of ________ intelligence.

a. bodily kinesthetic

b. spatial

c. naturalist

d. intrapersonal

9.16 According to Robert Sternberg's triarchic theory of intelligence, an individual who can respond to a series of questions without having to think about the answers most likely has a high degree of ________ intelligence.

a. perceptual

b. componential

c. experiential

d. contextual

9.17 The most frequent reason for homeschooling is
- a. concerns about violence in the schools.
- b. to allow children the flexibility to travel with parents.
- c. to meet the child's special needs.
- d. parents' belief that they can do a better job than schools can.

9.18 On which of the following do boys appear to do better than girls?
- a. mathematics
- b. reading comprehension
- c. vocabulary skills
- d. speed of information processing

9.19 A child who approaches a school assignment by focusing on "the big picture" instead of on specific subtasks of the assignment is using a/an ________ learning style.
- a. analytical
- b. relational
- c. inductive
- d. deductive

9.20 Collectivist cultures
- a. emphasize individual achievement.
- b. have more private than public schools.
- c. focus on interdependence.
- d. encourage competition.

9.21 In a study that compared teaching methods in 120 classrooms in Taiwan, Japan, and the United States, Stigler and Stevenson found that
- a. Japanese and Chinese teachers teach mathematics and science by using lessons that are organized around a single theme or unit.
- b. American teachers emphasize computational fluency in math instruction.
- c. Asian teachers use material rewards, such as stickers, to motivate children.
- d. American teachers spend more time in whole-group instruction than Asian teachers do.

9.22 The degree to which an individual can automatically produce solutions to simple calculation problems is called
- a. computational fluency.
- b. executive processes.
- c. horizontal decalage.
- d. metacognition.

Children with Special Needs

9.23 What is the most prevalent disability for which U.S. children receive special education services?
- a. communication disorder
- b. mental retardation
- c. serious emotional disturbance
- d. learning disability

9.24 A child who has attention-deficit hyperactivity disorder may receive special education services for a learning disability if
- a. the teacher is unqualified to handle the child's special needs in the classroom environment.
- b. the child is a distraction or disturbance to other children.
- c. the child has fallen more than two grade levels behind other children of the same age.
- d. the child has difficulty with basic reading and writing skills.

mydevelopmentlab Study Plan

PEARSON

Are You Ready for the Test?

Students who use the study materials on MyDevelopmentLab report higher grades in the course than those who use the text alone. Here are three easy steps to mastering this chapter and improving your grade…

Step 1

Take the chapter pre-test in MyDevelopmentLab and review your customized Study Plan.

Howard Gardner has criticized the use of IQ tests to predict achievement because he maintains that

- they fail to provide a complete picture of mental abilities.
- the tests do not include enough material to adequately assess verbal abilities.
- they cannot identify the separate contribution that nature and nurture make to intelligence.
- the tests have not been standardized on appropriate subgroups in the population.

Step 2

Use MyDevelopmentLab's Multimedia Library to help strengthen your knowledge of the chapter.

Watch: Deductive Reasoning

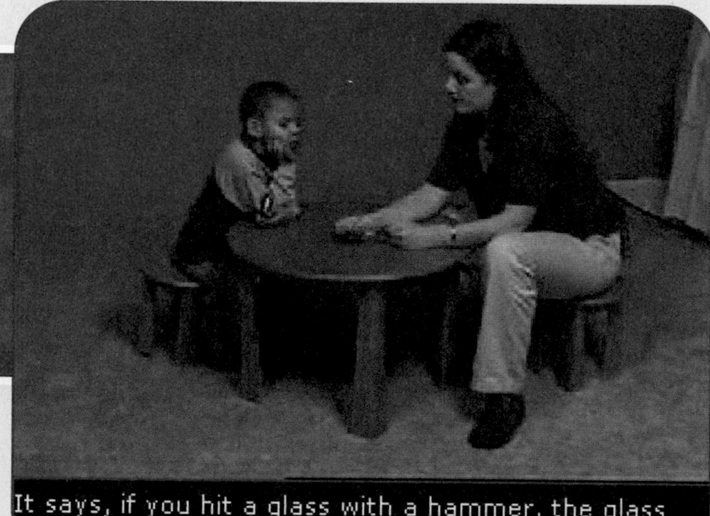

It says, if you hit a glass with a hammer, the glass will break.

Learning Objective 9.5

What cognitive advantages do children gain as they move through Piaget's concrete operational stage?

Did you know? MyDevelopmentLab provides a wealth of media and sensory tools that can help regardless of your learning ability or style. You can hear words pronounced in the audio glossary and watch close-captioned videos.

Simulate: Gardner's Theory of Intelligence

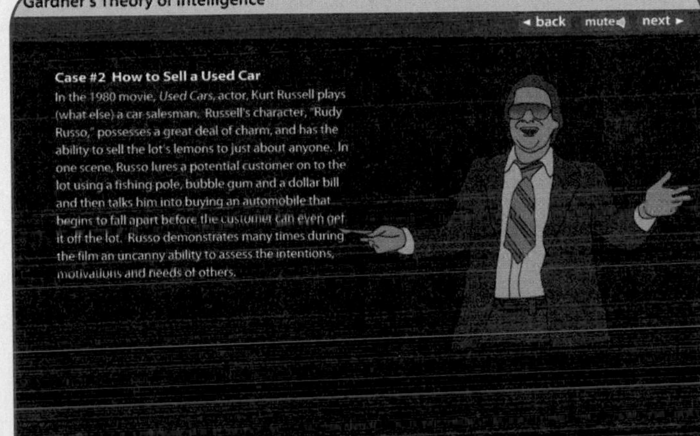

Gardner's Theory of Intelligence
◂ back
mute
next ▸
Case #2 How to Sell a Used Car
In the 1980 movie, Used Cars, actor, Kurt Russell plays (what else) a car salesman. Russell's character, "Rudy Russo," possesses a great deal of charm, and has the ability to sell the lot's lemons to just about anyone. In one scene, Russo lures a potential customer on to the lot using a fishing pole, bubble gum and a dollar bill and then talks him into buying an automobile that begins to fall apart before the customer can even get it off the lot. Russo demonstrates many times during the film an uncanny ability to assess the intentions, motivations and needs of others.

Learning Objective 9.10

Why do schools administer achievement tests, and what kind of items do they include?

Watch: Dyslexia Detector

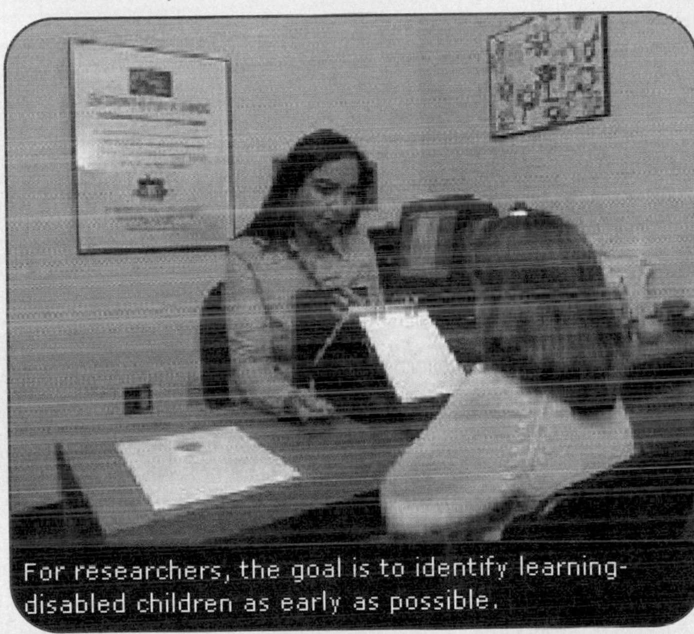

For researchers, the goal is to identify learning-disabled children as early as possible.

Learning Objective 9.12

Why is the term "learning disability" controversial?

Step 3

Take the chapter post-test and compare your results against the pre-test.

A child who has a relational style approaches a learning task by

- asking the teacher what need to be done next.
- looking at the "big picture."
- systematically planning the steps to reach a final goal.
- considering all the details before beginning to work.

www.mydevelopmentlab.com

10 Social and Personality Development in Middle Childhood

Do you remember when you learned to ride a bicycle? Perhaps your experience was similar to Leticia's. When she was 6 years old, Leticia's parents bought her a small bicycle with training wheels. Leticia loved to ride up and down her street and felt incredibly grown-up when the "big kids" allowed her to ride along with them.

One day, Leticia and her new-found "bike buddies" challenged each other to ride to the top of a dirt hill at the end of their street. Their game had one simple rule, if you couldn't make it to the top you were out. Leticia waited patiently for her turn and cheered along with the other children as each of her friends made it to the top. Finally, it was her turn. She made her way to the base of the hill and started to climb. To her dismay, though, her training wheels kept

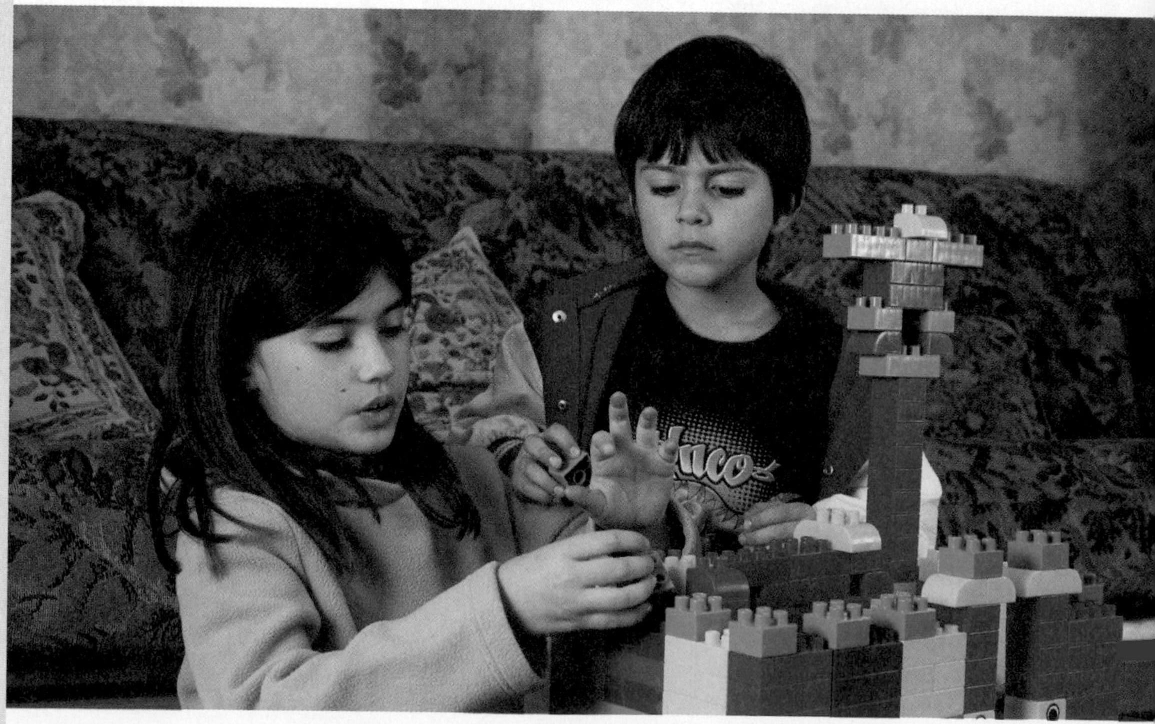

getting stuck. Each time she would jar them loose and start over but, soon, the other children were yelling "You're out! Get off the hill! You have to go home now."

Feeling lower than she ever had in her life, Leticia rode home as fast as she could and begged her father to take the training wheels off her bike. Leticia's father wasn't sure that she was ready, but, touched by the intensity of his daughter's plea, he reluctantly removed the training wheels. "I'll help you learn to balance," he said. "No, I can do it myself," Leticia replied confidently. But on her first attempt, she tipped over sideways, and the bike landed on top of her. Humbled by her first experience, the girl agreed to accept her father's assistance.

Leticia got back on her bike and started to ride, but this time her father ran alongside and nudged her back into an upright position each time her balance started to falter. After ten days of practicing with her father, Leticia was at last able to make it all the way to the end of the driveway without falling. At the end of her fourth trip from the garage to the end of the driveway, she cautiously ventured out into the street. To her delight, Leticia found that she was at last a true "big kid" who could ride her bicycle without training wheels. Leticia couldn't wait to play "ride up the hill" with her friends.

At this point in your study of human development, you probably recognize that Leticia's story represents the intersection of several developmental pathways. Advances in physical development are vital to the acquisition of her bicycle-riding skills. Cognitive development is at work in her understanding of rule-based games such as the one that she and her friends invented in the vacant lot. But what makes Leticia's experiences unique are the emotional and behavioral responses that her personality, self-concept, and relationship history contribute to the developmental equation. These are the topics of the present chapter. We begin with a consideration of the major themes of development that uniquely mark social and personality development in the middle childhood years and the different ways in which developmentalists have explained them.

Theories of Social and Personality Development

Leticia's story shows us that the development of self-perceived competence is the overarching theme of social and personality development in the middle childhood years. How do children develop this critical attribute? Developmentalists representing different theoretical perspectives emphasize different sets of factors in their explanations of the development of self-perceived competence in these years.

Learning Objective 10.1

How did the psychoanalytic theorists characterize the middle childhood years?

Psychoanalytic Perspectives

When you think back to your middle childhood years, what kinds of experiences stand out? Most likely, you remember interacting with your peers and siblings. If Freud were called upon to explain how your feelings about your own competence developed, he would appeal to the emotional qualities of these interactions. To illustrate, think back to how Leticia responded when her peers taunted her after she failed to make it up the hill. She was disappointed and embarrassed, but these difficult emotions motivated her to learn to ride her bicycle without training wheels. According to the psychoanalytic perspective, and in line with our everyday experiences with children, children vary greatly in the ways that they respond to such situations. Some become angry and lash out at those who reject them. Others withdraw and develop a general fear of social interactions. Parents, as Leticia's father did, contribute to these responses. However, Freud thought that the challenge of the middle childhood years was to form emotional bonds with peers and to move beyond those that were developed with parents in earlier years. Thus, much of the modern-day research on peer rejection and other emotional features of middle childhood find their roots in Freud's psychoanalytic approach.

Erik Erikson accepted Freud's view of the central role of peer relationships and the emotions that accompany them in middle childhood. He went beyond Freud's perspective, though, when he further characterized middle childhood as the period during which children experience the crisis of *industry versus inferiority*. During this stage, Erikson said, children develop a sense of their own competence through the achievement of culturally defined learning goals (see Table 2.3 on page 31). The psychosocial task of the 6- to 12-year-old is development of industry, or the willingness to work to accomplish goals. To develop industry, the child must be able to achieve the goals her culture sets for all children her age. In most countries, 6- to 12-year-olds must learn to read and write. If they fail to do so, Erikson's view claims, they will enter adolescence and adulthood with feelings of inferiority. These feelings of inferiority constitute an emotional mindset that can hamper an individual's ability to achieve for the rest of her life.

Contemporary studies that stress the child's need to feel competent are in tune with Erikson's views. Many of them suggest that he was right about the link between school experiences and an emerging sense of competence. It seems that most 6- to 12-year-olds gradually develop a view of their own competence as they succeed or fail at academic tasks such as reading and arithmetic (Chapman & Tunmer, 1997; Skaalvik & Valas, 1999). Thus, their self-assessments and actual achievements are strongly correlated; that is, those who are most successful judge themselves to be competent, while those who have difficulty perceive themselves as less so. However, individual differences in children's responses to success and failure moderate the effects of the experiences themselves. Some of these differences are found in the emotional realm, as suggested earlier.

Erikson also argued that children who lack success in school can develop it by participating in culturally valued pursuits outside of academic settings. A child who is a mediocre student, for instance, may channel his need to develop self-perceived competence into athletics. Another child who gets poor grades may do so because she spends most of her time reading books that she finds to be more interesting than her school work. Outsiders may worry about her sense of competence, but, internally, she has no doubts about her abilities.

Learning Objective 10.2

What are the main ideas of the trait and social-cognitive theorists?

The Trait and Social-Cognitive Perspectives

Psychoanalytic theorists have given us some compelling ideas about how individual differences in emotional responses to childhood experiences shape development and self-perceived competence. However, they tell us little about the origins of those differences. The primary goal of *trait theories*, by contrast, is to do just that. A **trait** is a stable pattern of responding to situations. This definition should remind you of our discussions of temperament in earlier chapters because the study of infant and early childhood tempera-

trait a stable pattern of responding to situations

ment is grounded in trait theory. By middle childhood, trait theorists argue that the various dimensions of temperament have evolved into five dimension's of personality (the so-called *Big Five*) that are shown in Table 10.1.

Research suggests that trait theorists are right about the emergence of stable traits in middle childhood. Moreover, these traits are known to contribute to the development of feelings of competence. For instance, a child who is reasonably *extraverted*, or outgoing, as Leticia appears to be, responds to peer rejection by becoming more determined to be accepted by the group. One who is *introverted*, or shy, would likely be so emotionally distraught by the taunts of her playmates that she would actively avoid social situations in the future. Still, children are not simply driven by personality-generated impulses in a mechanistic way, and trait theory leaves us wondering why extraversion doesn't always lead to social competence, and some people overcome their tendency toward introversion to become competent in the social arena.

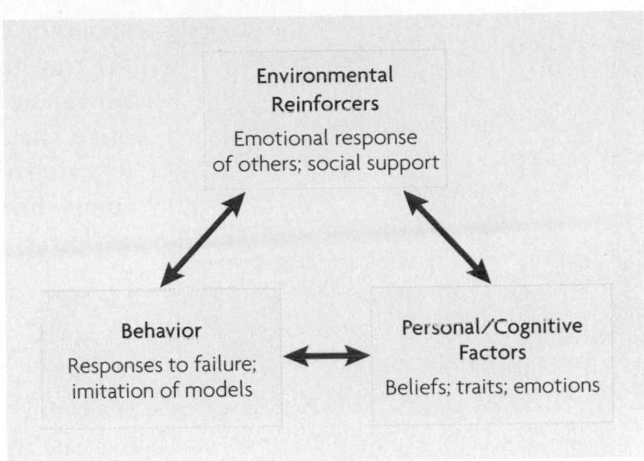

Figure 10.1
Bandura's Reciprocal Determinism

Bandura takes a social-cognitive view of personality. He suggests that three components—the external environment, individual behaviors, and cognitive factors, such as beliefs, expectancies, and personal dispositions—are all influenced by each other and play reciprocal roles in determining personality.

From the social-cognitive perspective, both the psychoanalytic theorists and the trait perspective focus on only one set of factors that shape the development of self-perceived competence in middle childhood. Albert Bandura, for instance, proposed that the emotions described by psychoanalytic theorists and the stable patterns of responding that have been identified by trait theorists, together with cognitive factors, constitute one of three interactive components that influence social and personality development (see Figure 10.1). Bandura used the term *person component* to refer to this emotional/cognitive component. The other components of his model were the developing person's *behavior* and the responses of the *environment*.

Bandura proposed that the personal, behavioral, and environmental components interact in a pattern he termed **reciprocal determinism**. Each of the three components influences, and is influenced by, the other two. For example, Leticia's emotional reaction to her failure to make it up the hill and her conclusion that removing the training wheels from her bike would solve her dilemma (the personal component) motivated her to head home and ask her father to remove the training wheels (the behavioral component). Her father responded by removing the wheels (the environmental component). His agreeing to do so affected Leticia's emotional state (the personal component) and led her to attempt to ride the bike without her father's help (the behavioral component).

reciprocal determinism Bandura's model in which personal, behavioral, and environmental factors interact to influence personality development

By organizing the various interactive influences in the way that it does, Bandura's model provides a more comprehensive explanation of how school-aged children develop ideas

Table 10.1 The Big Five Personality Traits

Trait	Qualities of Individuals Who Show the Trait	Possible Temperament Components
Extraversion	Active, assertive, enthusiastic, outgoing	High activity level; sociability; positive emotionality; talkativeness
Agreeableness	Affectionate, forgiving, generous, kind, sympathetic, trusting	Perhaps high approach/positive emotionality; perhaps effortful control
Conscientiousness	Efficient, organized, prudent, reliable, responsible	Effortful control/task persistence
Neuroticism (also called emotional instability)	Anxious, self-pitying, tense, touchy, unstable, worrying	Negative emotionality; irritability
Openness/Intellect	Artistic, curious, imaginative, insightful, original, wide interests	Approach; low inhibition

(*Sources*: Ahadi & Rothbart, 1994; John, Caspi, Robins, Moffitt, & Stouthamer-Loeber, 1994, Table 1, p. 161; McCrae & Costa, 1990.)

> **Critical Thinking**
>
> 1. How might you use Bandura's three-part model to create an explanation of how an event in your childhood influenced your development in the domain and personality development? What role did your emotional responses and personality traits play in the event?

about the degrees of competence they possess than either the psychoanalytic or the trait theorists do. Thus, Bandura's social-cognitive approach provides us with a way of taking into account the valuable insights of the psychoanalytic theorists relative to children's emotions with those of the trait theorists. And by integrating both into the three-part model that Bandura proposed, we gain a more comprehensive understanding of the mechanisms that drive the development of self-perceived competence in the middle childhood years.

Self-Concept

How much insight does a school-aged child really have into her own personality? The answer to this question depends on whether we look at the child at the beginning of this period or near the end of it. Across the years from 6 to 12, children's understanding of themselves improves quite a bit and, by the end of the middle childhood period, children's self-concepts include two new components, a *psychological self* and a *valued self*.

> **Learning Objective 10.3**
> What are the features of the psychological self?

The Psychological Self

The **psychological self** is a person's understanding of his or her enduring psychological characteristics. It first appears during the transition from early to middle childhood and becomes increasingly complex as the child approaches adolescence. It includes both basic information about the child's unique characteristics and self-judgments of competency.

Personality Traits Children don't use the same terminology as the trait theories that you read about earlier in the chapter, but they do describe their own personalities with increasing degrees of precision across the middle childhood years. For example a 6-year-old might use simple psychological self-descriptors such as "smart" or "dumb." By 10, a child is more likely to use comparisons in self-descriptions: "I'm smarter than most other kids" or "I'm not as talented in art as my friend" (Rosenberg, 1986; Ruble, 1987).

This developmental trend was illustrated in the results of an older study of the self-concepts of 9- to 18-year-olds (Montemayor & Eisen, 1977). Children who participated were asked to give 20 answers to the question "Who am I?" The researchers found that the younger children were still using mostly surface qualities to describe themselves, as in this description by a 9-year-old:

> My name is Bruce C. I have brown eyes. I have brown hair. I have brown eyebrows. I am nine years old. I LOVE! Sports. I have seven people in my family. I have great! eye site. I have lots! of friends. I live on 1923 Pinecrest Dr. I am going on 10 in September. I'm a boy. I have a uncle that is almost 7 feet tall. My school is Pinecrest. My teacher is Mrs. V. I play Hockey! I'm almost the smartest boy in the class. I LOVE! food. I love fresh air. I LOVE school. (Montemayor & Eisen, 1977, p. 317)

In contrast, consider the self-description of this 11-year-old girl in the sixth grade:

> My name is A. I'm a human being. I'm a girl. I'm a truthful person. I'm not very pretty. I do so-so in my studies. I'm a very good cellist. I'm a very good pianist. I'm a little bit tall for my age. I like several boys. I like several girls. I'm old-fashioned. I play tennis. I am a very good swimmer. I try to be helpful. I'm always ready to be friends with anybody. Mostly I'm good, but I lose my temper. I'm not well-liked by some girls and boys. I don't know if I'm liked by boys or not. (Montemayor & Eisen, 1977, pp. 317–318)

This girl, like the other 11-year-olds in the study, describes her external qualities, but she also emphasizes psychological factors such as personality traits.

Thus, as a child moves through the concrete operational period, her psychological self becomes more complex, more comparative, less tied to external features, and more centered on feelings and ideas.

psychological self an understanding of one's stable, internal traits

Self-Efficacy As we noted earlier in the chapter, middle childhood is the time when children develop perceptions of the degree to which they are competent. Albert Bandura has greatly advanced developmentalists' understanding of this crucial aspect of the psychological self. He defines **self-efficacy** as an individual's belief in her capacity to cause an intended event to occur (Bandura, 1997). How does it develop?

Bandura proposed that peer models are a primary source of self-efficacy beliefs (Bandura, 1997). Bandura would predict that, when Leticia observed her friends riding up the hill, she probably concluded that she could do likewise. Bandura further argued that, in order to believe that she could follow her peers' example, Leticia had to see herself as similar to them. (Recall the joy she experienced from thinking of herself as a "big kid.") Thus, *social comparisons*, or the process of drawing conclusions about the self based on comparisons to others, play an integral role in the degree to which children gain insight into their own self-efficacy from observing peers. Thus, simply watching other children model success at a task is insufficient for the development of self-efficacy in a child whom outsiders see as similar to the models. The child herself must perceive that similarity in order to be influenced by the models.

Encouragement from sources of information that children value also contribute to self-efficacy. Leticia's father's willingness to let her try to ride without training wheels played a role in her feelings of self-efficacy. However, nothing influences self-efficacy more than an individual's actual experiences (Britner & Pajares, 2006). In other words, believing that you can do something is less powerful, emotionally and cognitively, than really doing it. Consequently, the final hurdle in Leticia's development of self-efficacy for bicycle-riding was surmounted when she succeeded in learning to ride on her own.

The Valued Self

Learning Objective 10.4
How does self-esteem develop?

A child can have an accurate view of her personality traits, and even have a solid sense of self-efficacy, but still fail to value herself as an individual. To find out why, developmentalists have studied another aspect of self-concept development in middle childhood, the emergence of the *valued self*.

The Nature of Self-Esteem A child's evaluative judgments have several interesting features. First of all, over the years of elementary school and high school, children's evaluations of their own abilities become increasingly differentiated, with quite separate judgments about academic or athletic skills, physical appearance, social acceptance, friendships, romantic appeal, and relationships with parents (Harter, 1990; Marsh, Craven, & Debus, 1999). Paradoxically, however, it is when they reach school age—around age 7—that children first develop a global self-evaluation. Seven- and eight-year-olds (but not younger children) readily answer questions about how well they like themselves as people, how happy they are, or how well they like the way they are leading their lives. It is this global evaluation of one's own worth that is usually referred to as **self-esteem**, and it is not merely the sum of all the separate assessments a child makes about his skills in different areas. How stable are self-esteem judgments? A number of longitudinal studies of elementary school–aged children and teenagers show that self-esteem is quite stable in the short term but somewhat less so over periods of several years. The correlation between two self-esteem scores obtained a few months apart is generally about .60. Over several years, this correlation drops to about .40 (Alsaker & Olweus, 1992; Block & Robins, 1993). So, a child with high self-esteem at age 8 or 9 is likely to have high self-esteem at age 10 or 11. But it is also true that self-esteem is subject to a good deal of variation. To some degree, self-esteem is more stable in girls than in boys (Heinonen, Raikkonen, & Keltikangas-Jarvinen, 2003).

How Self-Esteem Develops Developmental psychologist Susan Harter (1987; 1990) has studied the development of self-esteem extensively. She has found that self-esteem is strongly influenced by mental comparisons of children's ideal selves and their actual experiences. For example, social self-esteem, the assessment of one's own social skills, is higher in popular

self-efficacy belief in one's capacity to cause an intended event to occur or to perform a task

self-esteem a global evaluation of one's own worth

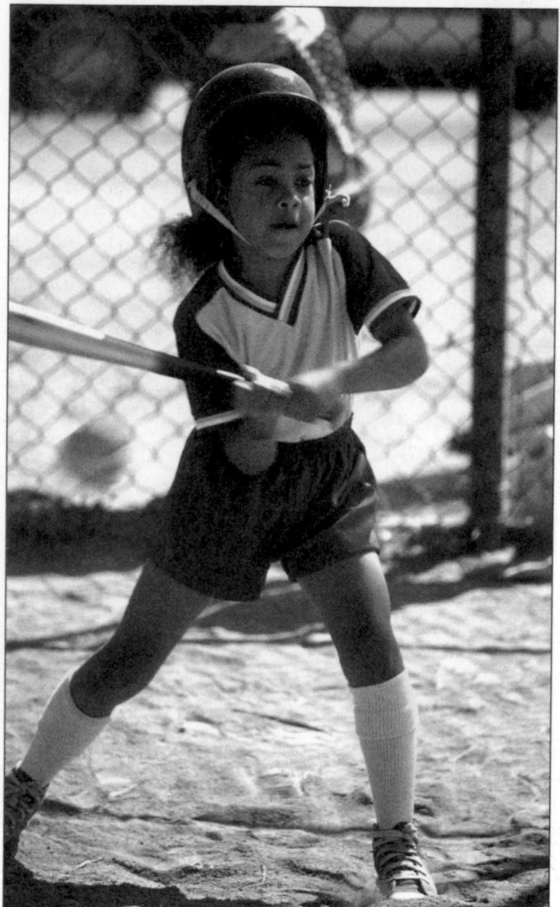

Hitting a home run will raise this girl's self-esteem only if she places a high value on being good at sports or at baseball specifically.

children than in those who are rejected by their peers (Jackson & Bracken, 1998). However, each component of self-esteem is valued differently by different children. Thus, a child who perceives herself to have poor social skills because she is unpopular may not necessarily have low self-esteem. The degree to which her social self-assessment affects her self-esteem is influenced by how much she values social skills and popularity. In addition, she may see herself as very competent in another area—such as academic skills—that balances her lack of social skills.

The key to self-esteem, then, is the amount of discrepancy between what the child desires and what the child thinks he has achieved. Thus, a child who values sports prowess but who isn't big enough or coordinated enough to be good at sports will have lower self-esteem than will an equally small or uncoordinated child who does not value sports skill so highly. Similarly, being good at something, such as singing or playing chess, won't raise a child's self-esteem unless the child values that particular skill.

The second major influence on a child's self-esteem is the overall support the child feels she is receiving from the important people around her, particularly parents and peers (Franco & Levitt, 1998). Apparently, to develop high self-esteem, children must first acquire the sense that they are liked and accepted in their families, by both parents and siblings. Next, they need to be able to find friends with whom they can develop stable relationships. Since childhood friendships begin with shared interests and activities, children need to be in an environment in which they can find others who like the same things they do and are similarly skilled. Athletic children need other athletic children to associate with; those who are musically inclined need to meet peers who are also musical; and so on.

The separate influences of the perceived discrepancy between the ideal and actual self and the amount of social support are clear in the results of Harter's research on self-esteem. She asked third-, fourth-, fifth-, and sixth-graders how important it was to them to do well in each of five domains, and how well they thought they actually did in each. The total discrepancy between these sets of judgments constituted the discrepancy score. A high discrepancy score indicates that the child didn't feel he was doing well in areas that mattered to him. The social support score was based on children's replies to a set of questions about whether they thought others (parents and peers) liked them as they were, treated them as a person, or felt that they were important. Figure 10.2 shows the results for the third- and fourth-graders; the findings for the fifth- and sixth-graders are virtually identical to these. Both sets of data support Harter's hypothesis, as does other research, including studies of African American children (Luster & McAdoo, 1995). Note that a low discrepancy score alone does not protect a child completely from low self-esteem if she lacks sufficient social support. Similarly, a loving and accepting family and peer group do not guarantee high self-esteem if the youngster does not feel that she is living up to her own standards.

Figure 10.2
Social Support, Domain Values, and Self-Esteem

For these third- and fourth-graders in Harter's studies, self-esteem was about equally influenced by the amount of support the children saw themselves receiving from parents and peers and the degree of discrepancy between the values the children placed on various domains and the skill they thought they had in each of those domains.

(*Source:* Harter, 1987, Figure 9.2, p. 227.)

Self-worth score: 3.75, 3.50, 3.25, 3.00, 2.75, 2.50, 2.25, 2.00, 1.75, 1.50
Social support: Low, Medium, High
Low discrepancy
Medium
High

The criteria by which children learn to evaluate themselves vary considerably from one society to another (Miller, Wang, Sandel, & Cho, 2002; Wang & Ollendick, 2001). In individualistic cultures, like that of the United States, parents focus on helping children develop a sense of self-esteem that is based in the children's own interests and abilities. In collectivist cultures, such as China's, children are taught to value themselves based on cultural ideals about what a "good" person is.

From all of these sources, the child fashions her ideas (her internal model) about what she should be and what she is. Like the internal model of attachment, self-esteem is not fixed in stone. It is responsive to changes in others' judgments as well as to changes in the child's own experience of success or failure. But once created, the model does tend to persist, both because the child tends to choose experiences that will confirm and support it and because the social environment—including the parents' evaluations of the child—tends to be at least moderately consistent.

Critical Thinking

1. How might Bandura's reciprocal determinism model be applied to explaining how a child could have a good understanding of her personality and strong self-efficacy and yet still have low self-esteem?

Advances in Social Cognition

To what extent did Leticia understand her peers' motivations for yelling at her when she couldn't make it to the top of the hill? Do you think she had any insight into why her father was reluctant to remove the training wheels from her bicycle? Children's ability to understand motivation is enhanced by the development of a theory of mind in early childhood. But by the end of the middle childhood period, children have developed a much broader understanding of others than they possessed at its beginning. Moreover, they are beginning to understand the moral aspects of social relationships.

The Child as Psychologist

Learning Objective 10.5

How does children's understanding of others change in middle childhood?

A number of early ground-breaking social-cognitive studies demonstrated that the child of this age looks beyond appearances and searches for deeper consistencies that will help him to interpret both his own and other people's behavior. Thus, like their understanding of the physical world, 6- to 12-year-olds' descriptions of other people move from the concrete to the abstract. If you ask a 6- or 7-year-old to describe others, he will focus almost exclusively on external features—what the person looks like, where he lives, what he does. This description by a 7-year-old boy, taken from a classic study of social cognitive development, is typical:

> He is very tall. He has dark brown hair, he goes to our school. I don't think he has any brothers or sisters. He is in our class. Today he has a dark orange [sweater] and gray trousers and brown shoes. (Livesley & Bromley, 1973, p. 213)

When young children do use internal or evaluative terms to describe people, they are likely to use quite global ones, such as "nice" or "mean," "good" or "bad." Further, young children do not seem to see these qualities as lasting or general traits of the individual, applicable in all situations or over time (Rholes & Ruble, 1984). In other words, the 6- or 7-year-old has not yet developed a concept that might be called "conservation of personality."

Beginning at about age 7 or 8, a rather dramatic shift occurs in children's descriptions of others. The child begins to focus more on the inner traits or qualities of another person and to assume that those traits will be visible in many situations (Gnepp & Chilamkurti, 1988). Children this age still describe others' physical features, but their descriptions are now used as examples of more general points about internal qualities. You can see the change when you compare the 7-year-old's description given above with this description by a child nearly 10 years old:

> He smells very much and is very nasty. He has no sense of humour and is very dull. He is always fighting and he is cruel. He does silly things and is very stupid. He has brown hair and cruel eyes. He is sulky and 11 years old and has lots of sisters. I think he is the most horrible boy in the class. He has a croaky voice and always chews his pencil and picks his teeth and I think he is disgusting. (Livesley & Bromley, 1973, p. 217)

This description still includes many external physical features but goes beyond such concrete surface qualities to the level of personality traits, such as lack of humor and cruelty.

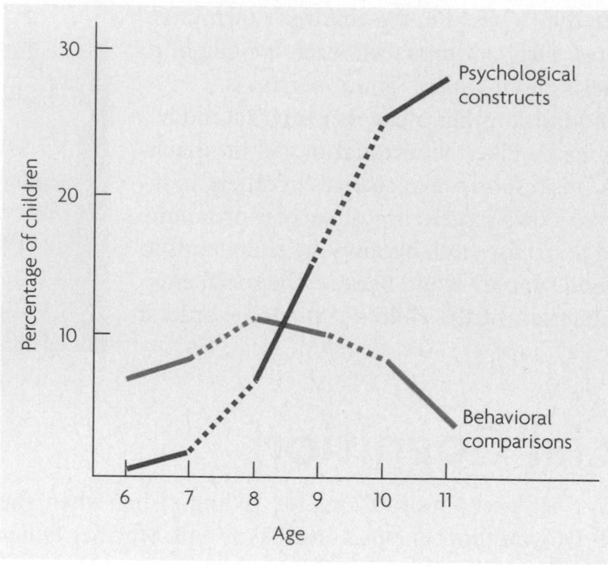

Figure 10.3
Changes in Children's Descriptions of Others

These data from Barenboim's study show the change in children's descriptions of their peers during the years of middle childhood. The solid lines represent longitudinal data, the dashed lines cross-sectional comparisons.

(*Source*: Adapted from *Child Development* by Barenboim, Figure 1, p. 134, 1981. Reprinted by permission of the Society for Research in Child Development.)

The movement from externals to internals in descriptions of others is well documented by research. For example, in one important early study, researchers asked 6-, 8-, and 10-year-olds to describe three other children; a year later, they asked them to do the same thing again (Barenboim, 1981). Figure 10.3 shows the results for two of the categories used in the study's data analysis. A *behavioral comparison* was any description that involved comparing a child's behaviors or physical features with those of another child or with a norm—for example, "Billy runs a lot faster than Jason" or "She draws the best in our whole class." Any statement that involved some internal personality trait—such as "Sarah is so kind" or "He's a real stubborn idiot!"—was referred to as a *psychological construct*. You can see that behavioral comparisons peaked at around age 8 but psychological constructs increased steadily throughout middle childhood.

School-aged children also understand family roles and relationships much better than younger children do. For example, by about age 9, children who live in two-parent homes understand that their parents' roles as parents are distinct from their roles as partners or spouses (Jenkins & Buccioni, 2000). Thus, a 9-year-old is better able than a 5-year-old to understand when divorcing parents say that their love for the child hasn't changed, even though their relationship with each other has ended. Emotionally, the divorce experience may be just as difficult, but school-aged children are more capable of understanding it cognitively.

moral realism stage the first of Piaget's stages of moral development, in which children believe rules are inflexible

Learning Objective 10.6

How do children in Piaget's moral realism and moral relativism stages reason about right and wrong?

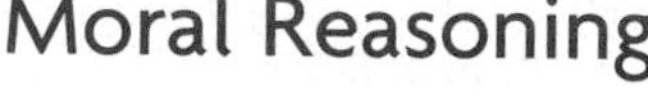

Moral Reasoning

Children's growing understanding of the internal experiences of other people helps them develop a better understanding of how they and others think about actions that have moral implications. *Moral reasoning* is the process of making judgments about the rightness or wrongness of specific acts. As you learned in Chapter 8, children learn to discriminate between intentional and unintentional acts between age 2 and age 6. However, using this understanding to make moral judgments is another matter. Piaget claimed that the ability to use reasoning about intentions to make judgments about the moral dimensions of behavior appears to emerge along with concrete operational reasoning.

Piaget suggested that there is a connection between children's understanding of the rules by which games are played and their reasoning about moral issues.

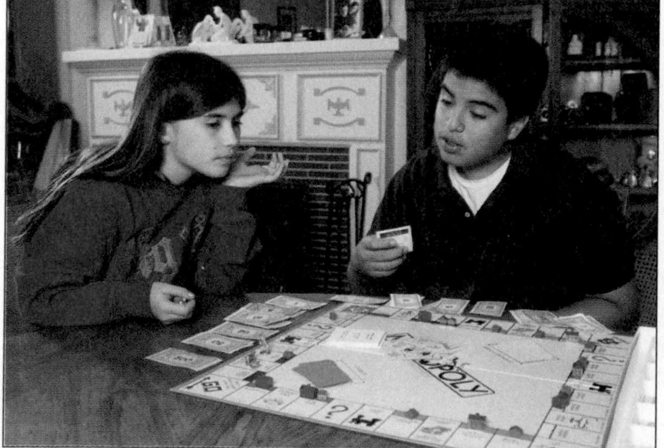

Piaget's Moral Realism and Moral Relativism Piaget studied moral development by observing children playing games. As he watched them play, Piaget noticed that younger children seemed to have less understanding of the games' rules. Following up on these observations, Piaget questioned children of different ages about rules. Their answers led him to propose a two-stage theory of moral development (Piaget, 1932).

At the beginning of the middle childhood period, children are in what Piaget termed the **moral realism stage**. They believe that the rules of games can't be changed because they come from authorities, such as parents, government officials, or religious figures. For example, one 6-year-old told Piaget that the game of marbles was invented on Noah's ark. He went on to explain that the rules can't be changed because the "big ones," meaning adults and older children, wouldn't like it (Piaget, 1965, p. 60).

Moral realists also believe that all rule violations eventually result in punishment. For example, Piaget told children a story about a child who fell into a stream when he tried to use a rotten piece of wood as a bridge. Children younger than 8 told him that the child was being punished for something "naughty" he had done in the past.

After age 8, Piaget proposed, children move into the **moral relativism stage**, in which they learn that people can agree to change rules if they want to. They realize that the important thing about a game is that all the players follow the same rules, regardless of what those are. For example, 8- to 12-year-olds know that a group of children playing baseball can decide to give each batter four strikes rather than three. They understand that their agreement doesn't change the game of baseball and that it doesn't apply to other people who play the game. At the same time, children of this age get better at following the rules of games.

Eight- to 12-year-olds also know that you don't get punished for rule violations unless you get caught. As a result, they view events like the one in which the child fell into the stream as accidents. They understand that accidents are not caused by "naughty" behavior. Children older than 8 also understand the relationship between punishment and intentions. For example, Piaget's research suggests that children over 8 can distinguish between a child who unintentionally left a store without paying for a candy bar and another who deliberately took one. Older children are likely to say that both children should return or pay for the candy, but only the one who intentionally stole it should be punished.

Research supports Piaget's claim that children over 8 give more weight to intentions than consequences when making moral judgments (Zelazo, Helwig, & Lau, 1996). However, although their thinking is more mature than that of preschoolers, 6- to 12-year-olds' moral reasoning is still highly egocentric. For example, every parent has heard the exclamation "It's not fair!" when a child fails to receive the same treat or privilege as a sibling. It is rare, if not

moral relativism stage the second of Piaget's stages of moral development, in which children understand that many rules can be changed through social agreement

THE REAL WORLD

Encouraging Moral Reasoning

Eight-year-old Marisol, much to the surprise of her mother, Andrea, was caught stealing a package of candy from a convenience store that she passed every day when she walked home from school. The manager called Marisol's mother to report what the girl had done, and by the time Andrea arrived, the little girl was crying and pledging never to steal again. "You still have to be punished," Andrea explained and told Marisol that she was taking away all of the girl's privileges for two weeks. However, like most parents, Andrea wants to be sure that Marisol understands why what she did was wrong. How can parents help children learn to reason about issues of right and wrong?

In his book *Raising Good Children*, developmental psychologist Thomas Lickona reminds readers that the development of mature moral reasoning takes many years (Lickona, 1983). At the same time, he offers parents and teachers several suggestions that will help them help their 6- to 12-year-olds prepare for movement to more mature levels. Following are some of his suggestions:

- Require kids to give reasons for what they want.
- Play developmentally appropriate games with them.
- Praise them for observing social conventions such as saying "please" and "thank you."
- When punishment is necessary, provide them with an explanation, advice on how to avoid punishment in the future, and a way of repairing any damage their misbehavior has caused.
- Teach them about reciprocity: "We do nice things for you, so you should be willing to help us."
- Give them meaningful chores so they will think of themselves as important family and community members.
- Help and encourage them to base obedience on love and respect rather than fear.
- Teach them religious and philosophical values, including the idea that some actions are right and others are wrong, regardless of circumstances.
- Challenge their egocentrism by asking questions such as, "How would you feel if someone did that to you?" when they violate others' rights.
- Include them in charitable projects, such as food drives, to extend the idea of love and caring beyond their own families.

Questions for Reflection

1. Which of Lickona's suggestions are most relevant to the situation in which Marisol's mother found herself?
2. Do you agree with Andrea that it was necessary to punish the girl? If so, what additional steps do you think Andrea should take to help Marisol learn the importance of respecting others' property?

Critical Thinking

1. Children's understanding of others' traits and behaviors and their understanding of moral dilemmas advances dramatically after age 8. How does each of these important domains of development support the other?

completely unknown, for a 6- to 12-year-old to protest the fairness of receiving something that a sibling didn't. Thus, school-aged children still have a long way to go with respect to mature moral reasoning, and we will return to this topic in the chapters on adolescent development (see The Real World on page 285).

The Social World of the School-Aged Child

School-aged children's growing ability to understand others changes their social relationships in important ways. Children continue to be attached to parents, but they are becoming more independent. Relationships with peers become more stable and many ripen into long-term friendships. In fact, the quality of 6- to 12-year-olds' peer relationships shapes their futures in many important ways.

Learning Objective 10.7

How does self-regulation affect school-aged children's relationships with their parents?

Relationships with Parents

Middle childhood is a period of increasing independence of child from family. Yet attachments to parents continue to be important, and relationships with siblings add another dimension to the social worlds of 6- to 12-year-olds who have them (see the Research Report). What does change, though, is the agenda of issues between parent and child. The parent-child agenda changes because parents of 6- to 12-year-olds recognize their children's growing capacity for **self-regulation**, the ability to conform to parental standards of behavior without direct supervision. As a result, as children get older, parents are more likely to allow them to engage in activities such as bicycle riding and skateboarding without supervision (Soori & Bhopal, 2002). However, cultures vary to some degree in the specific age at

self-regulation children's ability to conform to parental standards of behavior without direct supervision

RESEARCH REPORT

Birth Order and Children's Development

People often speculate that only children, those without siblings, are deprived of an important developmental experience and may be "spoiled" by their parents. Most research shows that only children grow up to be just as well adjusted as those who have brothers and sisters (Wang et al., 2000). Moreover, some studies have shown that only children may actually have an advantage over those who have siblings, at least with regard to cognitive development and academic achievement (Doh & Falbo, 1999; Falbo, 1992). Other studies suggest that the cognitive advantage enjoyed by only children may actually be due to birth order. First-borns, or the oldest surviving child in a family in which a first-born died in infancy, get higher scores, on average, on cognitive tests than later-borns do (Holmgren, Molander, & Nilsson, 2006; Kristensen & Bjerkedal, 2007). The *resource dilution* hypothesis explains these findings as the result of the progressive "watering down" of the parents' material and psychological resources with each additional birth (Downey, 2001). Thus, from this perspective, parents have the greatest influence on the oldest child, an advantage that is shared by only children and the oldest child in a multi-child family.

Critics of the resource dilution hypothesis point out that it places too much emphasis on what later-borns take away from the family and ignores the relationship-building opportunities that these children contribute to their older siblings' development (Gillies & Lucey, 2006). In support of their argument, critics cite research which suggests that later-borns have an advantage over their older siblings with regard to a variety of social skills, including the ability to negotiate solutions to interpersonal conflicts (Ross, Ross, Stein, & Trabasso, 2006). Likewise, first-borns who have siblings outperform only children on measures of social negotiation. First-borns with younger siblings also appear to gain self-reliance skills from serving as surrogate parents for younger siblings (Brody, Kim, Murry, & Brown, 2003). Regardless of birth order, too, affectionate sibling relationships moderate the effects of stressful life events such as parental divorce, and they enable children to advance more rapidly than only children do with regard to understanding others' mental states and behaviors (Gass, Jenkins, & Dunn, 2007; McAlister & Peterson, 2006). Thus, only and firstborn children may get more of the kind of attention from parents that is critical to cognitive development, but sibling relationships appear to make positive contributions to children's social and emotional development.

Questions for Critical Analysis

1. What kinds of sibling relationships would harm rather than help a child's social and emotional development?
2. In what kinds of situations might you expect only children to show social skills that are superior to those of children who have siblings?

which they expect this to occur. For example, White and Hispanic parents in the United States differ in their beliefs about the average age at which school-aged children can carry out specific tasks on their own (Savage & Gauvain, 1998). It appears that Hispanic American parents have less confidence in the self-regulatory abilities of younger school-aged children than White parents do. In general, though, most cultures expect 6- to 12-year-olds to be able to supervise their own behavior at least part of the time.

Some studies suggest that there are sex differences in parents' expectations with respect to self-regulatory behavior. For example, mothers make different kinds of demands on boys and girls. They appear to provide both with the same types of guidance, but are likely to give boys more autonomy over their own behavior than they give girls. Nevertheless, they are likely to hold daughters to a higher standard of accountability for failure than they do sons (Pomerantz & Ruble, 1998). Developmentalists speculate that this difference may lead to stronger standards of behavior for girls in later developmental periods.

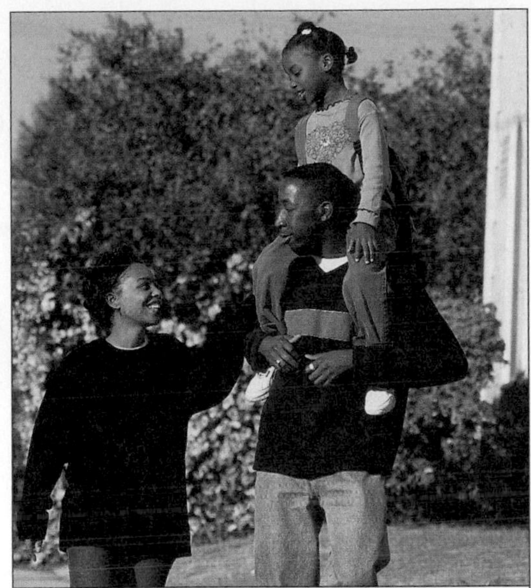

Research suggests that only children are just as well adjusted as those who have siblings.

Researchers have learned that there are several parenting variables that contribute to the development of self-regulation. First, the parents' own ability to self-regulate is important, perhaps because they are providing the child with models of good or poor self-regulation (Prinstein & La Greca, 1999). Also, the degree of self-regulation expected by parents influences the child's self-regulatory behavior. Higher expectations, together with parental monitoring to make certain the expectations are met, are associated with greater self-regulatory competence (Rodrigo, Janssens, & Ceballos, 1999).

You should recall that such parental behaviors are associated with the authoritative style of parenting. Longitudinal research has demonstrated that school-aged children whose parents have been consistently authoritative since they were toddlers are the most socially competent (Baumrind, 1991). Children rated "competent" were seen as both assertive and responsible in their relationships; those rated "partially competent" typically lacked one of these skills; those rated "incompetent" showed neither. In Baumrind's (1991) study, the majority of children from authoritative families were rated as fully competent, while most of those from neglecting families were rated as incompetent.

Friendships

Learning Objective 10.8

What changes occur in children's understanding of friendships during this period?

The biggest shift in relationships during middle childhood is the increasing importance of peers. One frequent manifestation of this trend is the appearance of "best-friend" relationships. Cross-cultural studies show that best-friend relationships, and the belief that having a best friend is important, are universal features of school-aged children's social development (Schraf & Hertz-Lazarowitz, 2003). Younger children, often as early as 3 years of age, express playmate preferences (Hay, Payne, & Chadwick, 2004). Among older school-aged children, however, a best friend is much more than a playmate, reflecting these children's better understanding of the characteristics that distinguish friendships from other kinds of relationships.

Social-cognitive researcher Robert Selman was one of the first to study children's understanding of friendships. He found that if you ask preschoolers and young school-aged children how people make friends, the answer is usually that they "play together" or spend time physically near each other (Damon, 1977, 1983; Selman, 1980).

In the later years of middle childhood, at around age 10, this view of friendship gives way to one in which the key concept seems to be reciprocal trust (Chen, 1997). Older children see friends as special people who possess desired qualities other than mere proximity, who are generous with each other, who help and trust each other, and so on. Figure 10.4 on page 288 is a 10-year-old boy's definition of a friend. His characterization of a friend—as someone "you can trust," who "will always be there for you when you are feeling down in the dumps" and "always sits by you at lunch"—illustrates the older child's understanding of dimensions of friendships such as trust, emotional support, and loyalty.

Figure 10.4
A 10-Year-Old's Explanation of Friendship

This essay on friendship written by a 10-year-old illustrates the way older school-aged children think about friends.

(Courtesy of Denise Boyd. Used with permission.)

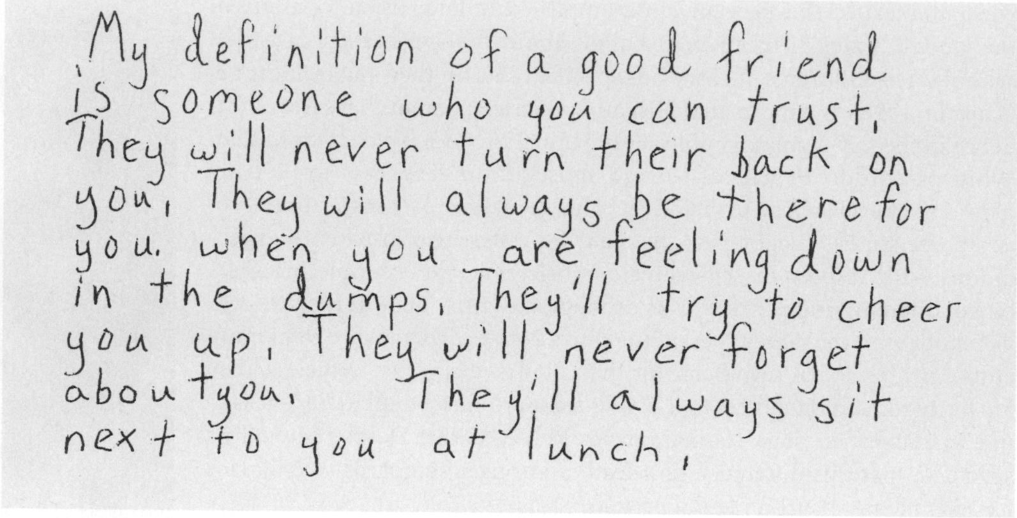

My definition of a good friend is someone who you can trust, They will never turn their back on you, They will always be there for you. when you are feeling down in the dumps, They'll try to cheer you up, They will never forget about you, They'll always sit next to you at lunch,

Researchers have examined the relationship between children's understanding of friendship and the quantity and quality of their friendships. In one such study, researchers Amanda Rose and Steven Asher (2004) presented fifth-graders with hypothetical situations in which one friend might have an opportunity to help another. For instance, in one scenario, the researchers described a child who was teased by her classmates. Rose and Asher found that children who expressed the view that children should not help others in such situations, in order to avoid putting themselves at risk of being treated similarly by peers, had fewer friends than did children who expressed the view that friends should place their relationships above concerns about how their helping behavior would affect their own social status.

Evidence of the centrality of friends to social development in middle childhood also comes from studies of children's behavior within friendships. Children are more open and more supportive when with their chums, smiling at, looking at, laughing with, and touching one another more than they do when they are with nonfriends; they talk more with friends and cooperate and help one another more. Pairs of friends are also more successful than nonfriends are in solving problems or performing some task together. Yet school-aged children are also more critical of friends and have more conflicts with them; they are more polite with strangers (Hartup, 1996). At the same time, when conflicts with friends occur, children are more concerned about resolving them than they are about settling disagreements with nonfriends. Thus, friendship seems to represent an arena in which children can learn how to manage conflicts (Newcomb & Bagwell, 1995).

Learning Objective 10.9

In what ways do boys and girls interact during the middle childhood years?

Gender Segregation

Possibly the most striking thing about peer group interactions in the elementary school years is how gender-segregated they are. This pattern seems to occur in every culture in the world and is frequently visible in children as young as 3 or 4. Boys play with boys and girls play with girls, each in their own areas and at their own kinds of games (Cairns & Cairns, 1994; Harkness & Super, 1985). In fact, gender seems to be more important than age, race, or any other categorical variable in 6- to 12-year-olds' selection of friends; in addition, the strength of children's preference for same-sex associates increases substantially across middle childhood (Graham, Cohen, Zbikowski, & Secrist, 1998). Moreover, gender segregation is unrelated to sex differences in parenting, suggesting that it is a feature of 6- to 12-year-olds' social relationships that they construct for reasons of their own (McHale, Crouter, & Tucker, 1999).

Shared interests and activities are a critical part of friendship in the early years of middle childhood. For example, rough-and-tumble play is common in boy-boy interactions but is typically avoided by girls. Thus, based on activity preferences, boys gravitate to other boys in social situations. In so doing, they learn how to socialize with other boys, but acquire few of the skills used by girls in their interactions, skills such as self-disclosure (Phillipsen, 1999). Thus, boys establish stable peer groups with dominance hierarchies that are based on rough-and-tumble play skills (Pelligrini & Smith, 1998). A similar pattern exists for girls: Gender segregation begins with shared activity preferences but leads to the development of social skills that are more useful in interactions with other girls than in interactions with boys.

However, there are some ritualized "boundary violations" between boys' and girls' groups, such as chasing games. For example, in one universal series of interactions, a girl taunts a boy with a statement like "You can't catch me, nyah nyah." Next, a boy chases and catches her, to the delight of both of their fully supportive same-sex peer groups (Thorne, 1986). As soon as the brief cross-gender encounter ends, both girl and boy return to their respective groups. On the whole, however, girls and boys between the ages of 6 and 12 actively avoid interacting with one another and show strong favoritism toward their own gender and negative stereotyping of the opposite gender (Powlishta, 1995).

In middle childhood, boys play with boys and girls play with girls. In fact, children's play groups are more sex-segregated at this age than at any other

Gender segregation patterns are even more pronounced in friendships during middle childhood. For example, when researchers ask children to describe the kind of playmate a fictional child would prefer, school-aged children's predictions are largely gender-based (Halle, 1999). Girls' and boys' friendships also differ in quality in intriguing ways. Boys' friendship groups are larger and more accepting of newcomers than are girls'. Boys play more outdoors and roam over a larger area in their play. Girls are more likely to play in pairs or in small, fairly exclusive groups, and they spend more playtime indoors or near home or school (Benenson, 1994; Gottman, 1986).

Sex differences also characterize the interaction between a pair of friends. Boys' friendships appear to be focused more on competition and dominance than are girls' friendships (Maccoby, 1995). In fact, among school-aged boys, researchers see higher levels of competition between pairs of friends than between strangers—the opposite of what is observed among girls. Friendships between girls include more agreement, more compliance, and more self-disclosure than is true between boys. For example, "controlling" speech—a category that includes rejecting comments, ordering, manipulating, challenging, defiance, refutation, or resistance of another's attempts to control—is twice as common among pairs of 7- and 8-year-old male friends as among pairs of female friends of that age (Leaper, 1991). Among the 4- and 5-year-olds in Leaper's study, there were no sex differences in controlling speech, suggesting that these differences in interaction pattern arise during middle childhood.

Why do you think competition is such a strong feature of friendship interactions among boys? Do you think this is true in every culture?

None of this information should obscure the fact that the interactions of male and female friendship pairs have much in common. For example, collaborative and cooperative exchanges are the most common forms of communication in both boys' and girls' friendships in middle childhood. And it is not necessarily the case that boys' friendships are less important to them than girls' are to them. Nevertheless, it seems clear that there are gender differences in form and style that may well have enduring implications for patterns of friendship over the lifespan.

Furthermore, school-aged children appear to evaluate the role of gender in peer relationships in light of other variables. For example, when asked whether a fictitious boy would prefer to play with a boy who is a stranger or with a girl who has been his friend for a while, most school-aged children say the boy would prefer to play with the friend (Halle, 1999). Such results suggest that, even though gender is clearly important in school-aged children's peer relationships, they are beginning to understand that other factors may be more important. This is yet another example of how children's growing cognitive abilities—specifically, their ability to think about more than one variable at a time—influence their ideas about the social world.

Learning Objective 10.10

What types of aggression are most common among school-aged children?

Patterns of Aggression

You may remember from Chapter 8 that physical aggression declines over the preschool years, while verbal aggression increases. In middle childhood, physical aggression becomes even less common as children learn the cultural rules about when it is acceptable to display anger or aggression and how much of a display is acceptable. In most cultures, this means that anger is increasingly disguised and aggression is increasingly controlled as children get older (Underwood, Coie, & Herbsman, 1992).

One interesting exception to this general pattern is that in all-boy pairs or groups, at least in the United States, physical aggression seems to remain both relatively high and constant over the childhood years. Indeed, at every age, boys show more physical aggression and more assertiveness than girls do, both within friendship pairs and in general (Fabes, Knight, & Higgins, 1995). Furthermore, school-aged boys often express approval for the aggressive behavior of peers (Rodkin, Farmer, Pearl, & Van Acker, 2000). Table 10.2 gives some highly representative data from a very large, careful survey in Canada, in which teachers completed checklists describing each child's behavior (Offord, Boyle, & Racine, 1991). It is clear that boys are described as far more aggressive on all of this study's measures of physical aggressiveness.

Results like these have been so clear and so consistent that most psychologists have concluded that boys are simply "more aggressive." But that conclusion may turn out to be wrong. Instead, it begins to look as if girls simply express their aggressiveness in a different way, using what has recently been labeled *relational aggression*, instead of physical aggression. Physical aggression hurts others physically or poses a threat of such damage; **relational aggression** is aimed at damaging the other person's self-esteem or peer relationships, such as by ostracism or threats of ostracism ("I won't invite you to my birthday party if you do that"), cruel gossip, or facial expressions of disdain. Children are genuinely hurt by such indirect aggression, and they are likely to express dislike for others who use this form of aggression a lot (Casas & Mosher, 1995; Cillessen & Mayeux, 2004; Cowan & Underwood, 1995; Crick & Grotpeter, 1995; Rys & Bear, 1997).

relational aggression aggression aimed at damaging another person's self-esteem or peer relationships, such as by ostracism or threats of ostracism, cruel gossiping, or facial expressions of disdain

Girls are more likely than boys to use relational aggression, especially toward other girls, a difference that begins as early as the preschool years and becomes very marked by the fourth or fifth grade. For example, in one study of nearly 500 children in the third through sixth grades, researchers found that 17.4% of the girls but only 2% of the boys were rated high in

Table 10.2 Aggressive Behavior in Boys and Girls Aged 4 to 11

	Percentages as Rated by Teachers	
Behavior	**Boys**	**Girls**
Mean to others	21.8	9.6
Physically attacks people	18.1	4.4
Gets in many fights	30.9	9.8
Destroys own things	10.7	2.1
Destroys others' things	10.6	4.4
Threatens to hurt people	13.1	4.0

(*Source*: Offord, Boyle, & Racine, 1991, from Table 2.3, p. 39.)

relational aggression—almost precisely the reverse of what is observed for physical aggression (Crick & Grotpeter, 1995). Researchers do not yet know whether this difference in form of aggression has some hormonal/biological basis or is learned at an early age or both. They do know that higher rates of physical aggression in males have been observed in every human society and in all varieties of primates. And scientists know that some link exists between rates of physical aggression and testosterone levels (e.g., Susman et al., 1987). But the origin of girls' apparent propensity toward relational aggression is still an open question.

Retaliatory aggression—aggression to get back at someone who has hurt you—increases among both boys and girls during the 6- to 12-year-old period (Astor, 1994). Its development is related to children's growing understanding of the difference between intentional and accidental actions. For example, if a child drops his pencil in the path of another child who is walking by and that child happens to kick the pencil across the floor, most 8-year-olds can identify this as an accident. Consequently, the child whose pencil was kicked feels no need to get back at the child who did the kicking. However, children over 8 view intentional harm differently. For example, let's say that one child intentionally takes another's pencil off her desk and throws it across the room. Most children over 8 will try to find a way to get back at a child who does something like this. In fact, children who don't try to retaliate in such situations are more likely to be seen as socially incompetent and to be bullied by their peers in the future (Astor, 1994), as discussed in the No Easy Answers feature.

Peers may approve of retaliatory aggression, but most parents and teachers strive to teach children that, like other forms of intentional harm, such behavior is unacceptable. Research suggests that children can learn nonaggressive techniques for managing the kinds of situations that lead to retaliatory aggression. In one program, called PeaceBuilders, psychologists have attempted to change individual behavior by changing a school's overall emotional climate. In this approach, both children and teachers learn to use positive social strategies (Flannery et al., 2000). For example, both are urged to try to praise others more often than they criticize them. Research suggests that when such programs are integrated into students'

retaliatory aggression aggression to get back at someone who has hurt you

NO EASY ANSWERS

Bullies and Victims

Research shows that, across the middle childhood years, aggressive interactions become increasingly complex (Hay, Payne, & Chadwick, 2004). As children get older, they tend to take on consistent roles—perpetrator, victim, assistant to the perpetrator, reinforcing onlooker, nonparticipant onlooker, defender of the victim, and so on (Andreou & Metallidou, 2004). The occupant of each of these roles plays a part in maintaining a particular aggressive incident and in determining whether another aggressive interaction involving the same perpetrator and victim will occur in the future.

Until fairly recently, both research on and interventions aimed at reducing aggression focused on the habitual perpetrators, or bullies. However, most developmentalists now believe that changing the behavior of children who occupy other roles in aggressive interactions, especially those who are habitual victims of aggression, may be just as important as intervening with aggressive children themselves (Green, 2001). Victims have certain characteristics in common, including anxiety, passivity, sensitivity, low self-esteem or self-confidence, lack of humor, and comparative lack of friends (Egan & Perry, 1998; Hodges, Malone, & Perry, 1997; Olweus, 1995). Cross cultural studies show that these characteristics are found among habitual victims across a wide variety of cultural settings (Eslea et al., 2004). Among boys, victims are also often physically smaller or weaker than their peers.

Teaching victims to be more assertive might seem to be a good way to reduce the prevalence of bullying among school-aged children. However, critics of such programs argue that they send the message that the victim deserves to be bullied. Moreover, by identifying habitual victims and including them in counseling sessions and the like, the adults who are responsible for victim-training programs subject these children to further stigmatization. Thus, critics argue that programs aimed at reducing bullying should focus primarily on the bullies' behavior and should include the clear message that bullying is wrong, regardless of their victims' behavior (Temko, 2005).

Take a Stand

Decide which of these two statements you most agree with and think about how you would defend your position:

1. Programs that seek to reduce bullying among school-aged children should include a component that teaches victims to be more assertive because the skills that children will learn are more important than the risk of stigmatizing or of appearing to justify bullying.
2. Programs that seek to reduce bullying among school-aged children should focus on changing the bully's behavior and helping him or her to understand how hurtful bullying is to its victims and to the emotional climate of the social setting in which it occurs.

classes every day for an entire school year or longer, aggression decreases and prosocial behavior increases. Thus, aggressive interactions between elementary school children may be common, but they do not appear to be an inevitable aspect of development.

Learning Objective 10.11

How do popular, rejected, and neglected children differ?

Social Status

Developmentalists measure popularity and rejection by asking children to list peers they would not like to play with or by observing which children are sought out or avoided on the playground. These techniques allow researchers to group children according to the degree to which they are accepted by peers—a variable often called **social status**. Typically, researchers find three groups: *popular*, *rejected*, and *neglected*.

Adults' goals for children's socialization usually include teaching them how to manage conflicts without resorting to aggression.

Some of the characteristics that differentiate popular children from those in the other two groups are things outside a child's control. In particular, attractive children and physically larger children are more likely to be popular. Conversely, being very different from her peers may cause a child to be neglected or rejected. For example, shy children usually have few friends (Fordham & Stevenson-Hinde, 1999). Similarly, highly creative children are often rejected, as are those who have difficulty controlling their emotions (Aranha, 1997; Maszk, Eisenberg, & Guthrie, 1999).

However, children's social behavior seems to be more important than looks or temperament. Most studies show that popular children behave in positive, supporting, nonpunitive, and nonaggressive ways toward most other children. They explain things, take their playmates' wishes into consideration, take turns in conversation, and are able to regulate the expression of their strong emotions. In addition, popular children are usually good at accurately assessing others' feelings (Underwood, 1997). Most are good at looking at situations from others' perspectives as well (Fitzgerald & White, 2003).

There are two types of rejected children. *Withdrawn/rejected* children realize that they are disliked by peers (Harrist, Zaia, Bates, Dodge, & Pettit, 1997). After repeated attempts to gain peer acceptance, these children eventually give up and become socially withdrawn. As a result, they often experience feelings of loneliness. *Aggressive/rejected* children are often disruptive and uncooperative and usually believe that their peers like them (Zakriski & Coie, 1996). Many appear to be unable to control the expression of strong feelings (Eisenberg et al., 1995; Pettit, Clawson, Dodge, & Bates, 1996). They interrupt their play partners more often and fail to take turns in a systematic way.

Aggression and disruptive behavior are often linked to rejection and unpopularity among Chinese children, just as they are among American children (Chen, Rubin, & Li, 1995; Chen, Rubin, & Sun, 1992). As you learned in Chapter 8, aggressive behavior persists into adulthood in some individuals. However, research suggests that aggression is most likely to become a stable characteristic among children who are *both* aggressive and rejected by peers.

Of course, not all aggressive children are rejected. Among girls, aggression, whether physical or relational, seems to lead to peer rejection consistently. Among boys, however, aggression may result in either popularity or rejection (Rodkin et al., 2000; Xie, Cairns, & Cairns, 1999). In fact, aggressiveness seems to be a fairly typical characteristic of popular African American boys.

Interestingly, too, aggressive boys and girls, although they are typically disliked by peers, are often perceived by them as having high social status, perhaps because of their ability to manipulate others and to control social situations (Cillessen & Mayeux, 2004). This association holds for both physical and relational aggression. However, as children enter adolescence, the link between physical aggression and social status becomes weaker, while the association between relational aggression and perceived status increases in strength. This may

social status an individual child's classification as popular, rejected, or neglected

happen because, by age 11 or 12, children regard relational aggression as a more mature form of social manipulation than physical aggression. Consequently, they may admire peers who are skilled in the use of relational aggression, even though they don't like them and prefer not to associate with them.

In addition, irrespective of aggressive boys' general popularity, their close friends tend to be aggressive as well. Furthermore, aggressiveness seems to precede these relationships. In other words, boys who are aggressive seek out boys like themselves as friends, and being friends doesn't seem to make either member of the pair more aggressive (Poulin & Boivin, 2000). Research also suggests that children have more positive attitudes toward aggressive peers whose aggressive acts are seen as mostly retaliatory and toward those who engage in both prosocial and aggressive behavior (Coie & Cillessen, 1993; Newcomb, Bukowski, & Pattee, 1993; Poulin & Boivin, 1999). Social approval may not increase aggressiveness, but it does seem to help maintain it; interventions to reduce aggressive behavior typically have little effect on aggressive boys who are popular (Phillips, Schwean, & Saklofske, 1997).

Neglect seems to be much less stable over time than rejection; neglected children sometimes move to the popular category when they become part of a new peer group. However, children who experience prolonged neglect are more prone to depression and loneliness than are popular children (Cillessen, van IJzendoorn, van Lieshout, & Hartup, 1992; Rubin, Hymel, Mills, & Rose-Krasnor, 1991; Wentzel & Asher, 1995). The association between peer neglect and depression may be explained by recent brain-imaging studies showing that, among school-aged children, social exclusion stimulates the same area of the brain as physical pain does (Eisenberger, 2003). In addition, this tendency toward depression among neglected children may be fostered by unrealistic expectations about adults' ability to "fix" the social situation—"Why doesn't the teacher make them be my friends?" (Galanaki, 2004).

Critical Thinking

1. If you had to explain an important developmental outcome, such as variations in optimism among adults, as a function of childhood social experiences, what percentage of influence would you assign to each of these factors: relationships with parents, friendships, experiences with gender segregation, experiences with aggression, and social status?

Influences beyond Family and Peers

The daily life of the school-aged child is shaped by more than the hours he spends with his family and peers. The circumstances in which a child lives also affect him. For example, some parents are at home when children come home from school; others are still at work. A child is also affected by his family's economic circumstances, by the neighborhood he lives in, and by the media to which he is exposed.

After-School Care

Learning Objective 10.12
How does self-care affect girls' and boys' development?

In the United States, 7.5 million children are at home by themselves after school for an hour or more each weekday (Crockett, 2003). They are often referred to as **self-care children**. Self-care arrangements differ so much from child to child that it is impossible to say whether, as a group, self-care children differ from others. For example, some self-care children are home alone but are closely monitored by neighbors or relatives, while others are completely without supervision of any kind (Brandon, 1999). Developmentalists have learned that the effects of self-care on a child's development depend on behavioral history, age, gender, the kind of neighborhood the child lives in, and how well parents monitor the child during self-care periods (Casper & Smith, 2002; NICHD, 2004b; Posner & Vandell, 1994; Steinberg, 1986).

Research consistently demonstrates that self-care children are more poorly adjusted in terms of both peer relationships and school performance. They tend to be less socially skilled and to have a greater number of behavior problems. However, some of these differences between self-care children and others arise from the effect of self-care on children who already have social and behavioral difficulties before self-care begins. Investigators have found that children who have such problems in the preschool years, before they experience any self-care,

self-care children children who are at home by themselves after school for an hour or more each day

The effects of after-school care depend on several factors. This child appears to be following his parents' instructions about what to do after school, a factor that helps children cope with the stress associated with caring for themselves.

are the most negatively affected by the self-care experience (Pettit, Laird, Bates, & Dodge, 1997).

With respect to age, most developmentalists agree that children under the age of 9 or 10 should not care for themselves. From a developmental perspective, children younger than 9 do not have the cognitive abilities necessary to evaluate risks and deal with emergencies. In fact, most cities and/or states have laws specifying the age at which a child may be legally left at home alone for long periods of time. Children who start self-care in the early elementary years are vulnerable to older self-care children in their neighborhoods who may hurt or even sexually abuse them and are more likely to have adjustment difficulties in school (Pettit et al., 1997). High-quality after-school programs can help these younger children attain a higher level of achievement (Peterson, Ewigman, & Kivlahan, 1993; Zigler & Finn-Stevenson, 1993).

Children older than 9 may be cognitively able to manage self-care, but they, too, benefit from participation in well-supervised after-school programs. Even part-time participation in supervised activities after school seems to make a difference in the adjustment of self-care children (Pettit et al., 1997). Good programs provide children with opportunities to play, do homework, and get help from adults (Posner & Vandell, 1994).

Self-care has the most negative effects for children in low-income neighborhoods with high crime rates (Marshall et al., 1997). Self-care children in such areas may use after-school time to "hang out" with socially deviant peers who are involved in criminal activity or who have negative attitudes about school. Predictably, then, the positive effects of organized after-school programs on academic achievement are greater for children in low-income neighborhoods (Mason & Chuang, 2001; Posner & Vandell, 1994).

When everything is taken into consideration, the most important factor in self-care seems to be parental monitoring. Many parents, particularly single mothers, enlist the help of neighbors and relatives to keep an eye on their self-care children (Brandon & Hofferth, 2003). Most require children to call them at work when they get home from school to talk about their school day and get instructions about homework and chores. For example, a working mother might tell a fifth-grader, "By the time I get home at 5:00, you should be finished with your math and spelling. Don't work on your history project until I get home and can help you with it. As soon as you finish your math and spelling, start the dishwasher." Research suggests that children whose periods of self-care are monitored in this way are less likely to experience the potential negative effects of self-care (Galambos & Maggs, 1991).

Learning Objective 10.13

What factors contribute to resilience and vulnerability among poor children?

Poverty

As you can see in Figure 10.5, the child poverty rate in the United States declined from 22% in 1993 to 17% in 2005 (DeNavas-Walt, Proctor, & Lee, 2006; U.S. Bureau of the Census, 1999). However, the child poverty rate continues to be higher in the United States than in many other industrialized countries in the world. By way of contrast, the poverty rate for children is roughly 5% in Denmark and is less than 15% in Sweden (House of Commons Work and Pensions Committee, 2006). Child poverty is also unequally distributed across ages, races, and family structures. With respect to age, children under 6 are more likely to live in poverty than those who are older (McLoyd, 1998). In addition, the proportions of African American, Native American, and Hispanic American children living in poverty are two to three times the overall child poverty rate (Nichols, 2006). Likewise, children reared by single mothers are far more likely to be living in poverty (Evans, 2004).

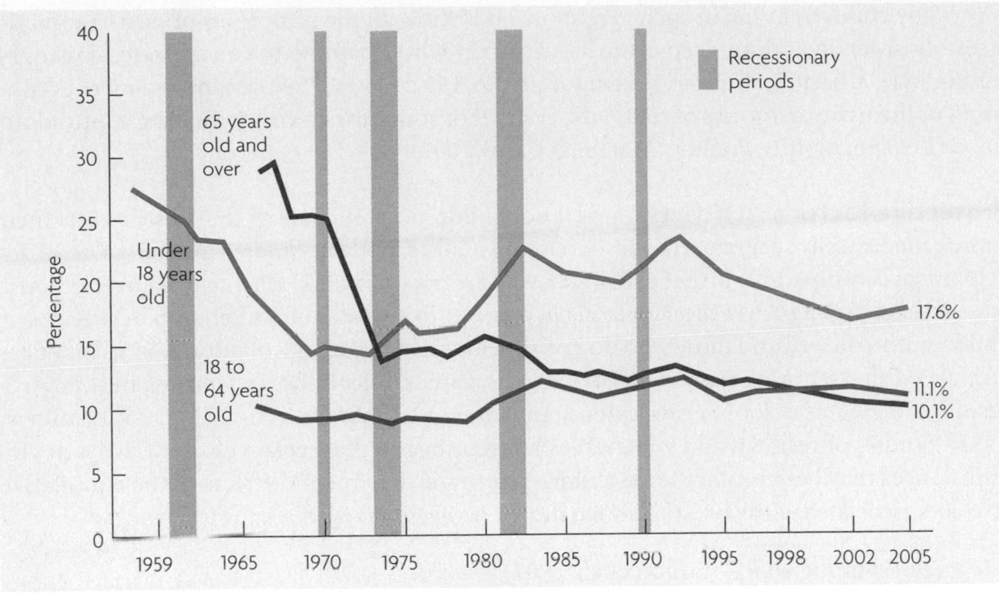

Figure 10.5
Poverty and Age

The graph shows the percentage of people in the United States living in poverty from 1959 to 2005, including children under 18. For families with at least one child, poverty is defined as annual income of less than $13,461 (in 2005 dollars).

(*Source:* DeNavas-Walt, Proctor, & Lee, 2006.)

The Effects of Poverty on Families and Children Overall, poor families live in more chaotic environments, are more highly stressed, and have fewer psychological and social resources than those who are more economically secure (Ackerman, Brown, & Izard, 2004; Brooks-Gunn, 1995; McLoyd & Wilson, 1991). As a result, parents living in poverty tend to treat their children differently than do working class or middle-class parents. They talk to them less, provide fewer age-appropriate toys, spend less time with them in intellectually stimulating activities, explain things less often and less fully, are less warm, and are stricter and more physical in their discipline (Dodge et al., 1994; Evans, 2004; Sampson & Laub, 1994). Some of this pattern of parental behavior is undoubtedly a response to the extraordinary stresses and special demands of living in poverty. To some extent, the stricter discipline and emphasis on obedience of poor parents may be thought of as a logical response to the realities of life in the neighborhoods in which they live.

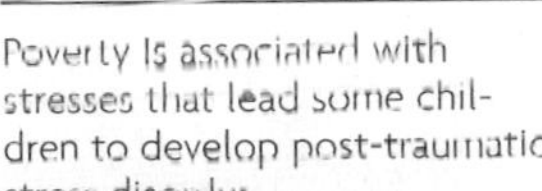
Poverty is associated with stresses that lead some children to develop post-traumatic stress disorder.

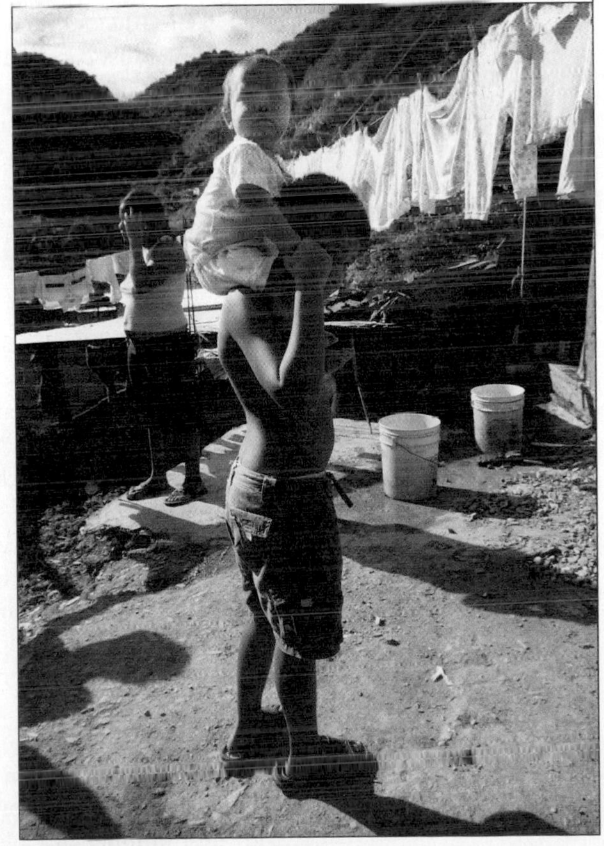

Not surprisingly, children in low-income families differ from their better-off peers across all developmental domains. The physical effects of poverty are evident very early in life. Infants born into low-income homes have higher rates of birth defects and early disabilities. As they grow older, poor children are also more often ill and more likely to be undernourished. With regard to intellectual development, low-income children have lower average IQ scores, move through Piaget's stages of cognitive development more slowly, and perform more poorly in school (Brooks-Gunn, 1995). Social development varies with income as well. Children from low-income homes exhibit more behavior problems in school than do peers whose families have more economic resources (Qi & Kaiser, 2003).

The negative effects of poverty are exacerbated for children growing up in neighborhoods where they are exposed to street gangs and street violence, to drug pushers, to overcrowded homes, and to abuse. Surveys indicate that nearly half of inner-city elementary and high school students have witnessed at least one violent crime in the past year (Osofsky, 1995). Predictably, children who are victimized by or who witness such crimes are more likely to suffer from emotional problems than are peers who are spared these experiences (Purugganan, Stein, Johnson Silver, & Benenson, 2003).

Many children living in such neighborhoods show all the symptoms of post-traumatic stress disorder, including sleep disturbances, irritability, inability to concentrate, and angry outbursts (Garbarino, Dubrow, Kostelny, & Pardo, 1992; Owen, 1998). Many experience flashbacks or intrusive memories of traumatic events. For some, these symptoms persist into adulthood (Koenen, Moffitt, Poulton, Martin, & Caspi, 2007).

Protective Factors Of course, most poor children develop along the same lines as their more economically secure peers. For developmentalists, *resilient children* are those whose development is comparable to that of children who are not poor, and *vulnerable children* are those who develop problems as a result of living in poverty. To help sort out differences between poor children who do well and those who do not, developmentalists think of poverty in terms of accumulated stresses (McLoyd, 1998). For example, parental alcoholism added to family poverty results in a greater risk of negative developmental outcomes for a child (Malo & Tramblay, 1997). Studies of resilient and vulnerable children suggest that certain characteristics or circumstances may help protect some children from the detrimental effects of the cumulative stressors associated with poverty. Among the key protective factors are the following:

- High IQ of the child (Koenon et al., 2007)
- Competent adult parenting, such as an authoritative style (good supervision or monitoring of the child seems especially important) (Eamon & Mulder, 2005)
- Parental knowledge about child development (Seo, 2006)
- An optimistic outlook (Lam et al., 2004)
- Effective schools (Woolley & Grogan-Kaylor, 2006)
- A secure initial attachment of the child to the parent (Li-Grining, 2007)
- A strong community helping network, including friends, family, or neighbors (Barrow et al., 2007)
- Stable parental employment (Terrisse, 2000)
- Strong sense of ethnic identity (Thomas, Townsend, & Belgrave, 2003)
- Participation in early childhood programs (Smokowski et al., 2004)

Thus, the effects of poverty depend on the combined effects of the number of stressors the child must cope with and the range of competencies or advantages the child brings to the situation. Poverty does not guarantee bad outcomes, but it stacks the deck against many children. Moreover, the same kinds of factors interact to affect development in other stressful contexts, such as neighborhoods in countries torn by war.

Learning Objective 10.14

How do television, computers, and video games affect children's development?

Media Influences

Another important feature of children's environment is the wide array of informational and entertainment media that are available nowadays. Televisions, computers, and video games are found in the great majority of homes in the industrialized world. How do these media affect children's development?

Television "But the kids on TV look so happy when they eat it! Don't you want me to be happy?" the 7-year-old son of one of the authors sobbed when his request for a sugary cereal was denied. The effect of advertising on children's food preferences is well documented (Chapman, Nicholas, & Supramaniam, 2006; Livingstone & Helsper, 2006). However, this is just one of several hazards that are associated with allowing children to watch too much TV. The association between viewing and aggressive behavior is perhaps of greatest concern.

Albert Bandura demonstrated the effects of televised violence on children's behavior in his classic "Bobo doll" studies (Bandura, Ross, & Ross, 1961, 1963). In these experiments, children were found to imitate adults' violent treatment of an inflatable clown that was depicted on film. Recent research suggests that such effects persist into the adult years. Psychologist L. Rowell Huesmann and his colleagues (2003) found that individuals who watched the greatest number of violent television programs in childhood were the most likely to engage in actual acts of violence as young adults. Brain-imaging studies suggest that these long-term effects may be the result of patterns of neural activation that underlie emotionally laden behavioral scripts that children learn while watching violent programming (Murray et al., 2006). These patterns of neural activation may also explain the finding that repeated viewing of TV violence leads to emotional desensitization regarding violence and to the belief that aggression is a good way to solve problems (Donnerstein, Slaby, & Eron, 1994; Funk, Baldacci, Pasold, & Baumgardner, 2004; Van Mierlo & Van den Bulck, 2004).

In the United States, children between 6 and 12 spend more time watching television than they do playing.

Of course, television isn't all bad. Researchers have found that science-oriented programs such as *Bill Nye the Science Guy* and *The Magic School Bus* are effective teaching tools (Calvert & Kotler, 2003). Likewise, programs designed to teach racial tolerance to school-aged children have consistently shown positive effects on children's attitudes and behavior (Persson & Musher-Eizenman, 2003: Shochat, 2003). However, such programs are far less popular among boys than they are among girls (Calvert & Kotler, 2003). Moreover, even among girls, their popularity declines as children progress through middle childhood years. Perhaps these findings are best summed up by adapting an old cliché: "You can lead a child to quality TV programming, but you can't make him watch it." Thus parental regulation of television viewing is the key to ensuring that exposure to TV will have more positive than negative effects on a child's development.

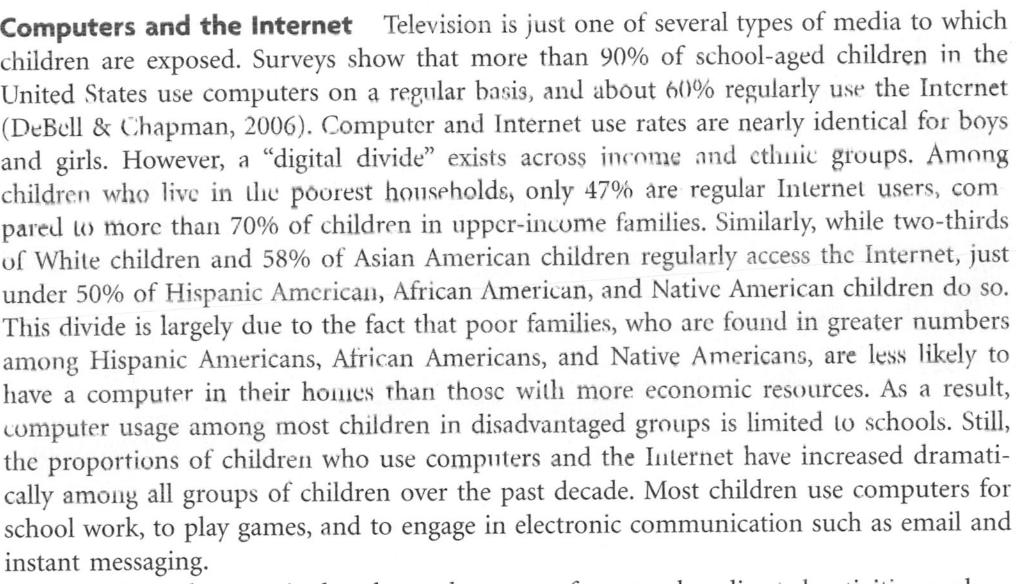

Computers and the Internet Television is just one of several types of media to which children are exposed. Surveys show that more than 90% of school-aged children in the United States use computers on a regular basis, and about 60% regularly use the Internet (DeBell & Chapman, 2006). Computer and Internet use rates are nearly identical for boys and girls. However, a "digital divide" exists across income and ethnic groups. Among children who live in the poorest households, only 47% are regular Internet users, compared to more than 70% of children in upper-income families. Similarly, while two-thirds of White children and 58% of Asian American children regularly access the Internet, just under 50% of Hispanic American, African American, and Native American children do so. This divide is largely due to the fact that poor families, who are found in greater numbers among Hispanic Americans, African Americans, and Native Americans, are less likely to have a computer in their homes than those with more economic resources. As a result, computer usage among most children in disadvantaged groups is limited to schools. Still, the proportions of children who use computers and the Internet have increased dramatically among all groups of children over the past decade. Most children use computers for school work, to play games, and to engage in electronic communication such as email and instant messaging.

Would you be surprised to learn that, apart from teacher-directed activities such as homework, children use computers in much the same ways as they use other environments? For the most part, children play when they are on a computer. Consequently, educators and parents need to keep an eye on children who are supposed to be doing school work on their computers and to be aware of the tendency of children to test digital boundaries, such as prohibitions against visiting chat rooms, just as they do physical boundaries. Nevertheless, many developmental psychologists see children's propensity for digital play as an opportunity to learn more about the natural course of child development (Sandvig, 2006). Here's a brief overview of one such study.

Researchers at Georgetown University provided 5th- and 6th-graders with an online, instant messaging environment in which the children created animated representations of themselves (Calvert et al., 2003). Each messaging session resembled a real-time, interactive cartoon in which the children's messages appeared in their characters' speech balloons.

Some of the sessions involved children of the same gender, while others were mixed-gender sessions. Interestingly, the researchers found that, just as they do in face-to-face interactions, female pairs engaged in more verbal than physical interactions, and male pairs spent more time engaged in role play and physical interactions than they did in verbal interactions. However, the interactions of mixed-gender pairs resembled those of female pairs; in other words, boys tended to adopt girls' interaction styles in mixed-gender sessions. These findings invite the speculation that the anonymity that is offered by virtual communication frees boys from the need to behave in gender-stereotypical ways. They also show that studying children's virtual communications can help developmentalists better understand their face-to-face interactions.

Video Games Some sources claim that families spend more money on video game systems and on the games themselves than they do on any other form of entertainment ("Children spend more time . . . ," 2004). Thus, developmentalists have looked at how these games affect children's cognitive and social/emotional development. Some studies suggest that video game playing enhances children's spatial-cognitive skills and may even eliminate the well-documented gender difference in this domain (Feng, Spence, & Pratt, 2007; Greenfield, Brannon, & Lohr, 1994).

Nevertheless, research suggests even short-term exposure to violent video games in laboratory settings increases research participants' general level of emotional hostility (Anderson & Dill, 2000; Bushman & Huesmann, 2006). Apparently, increases in emotional hostility and decreases in the capacity to empathize with others, which are engendered by violent video games, are the motivating forces behind the increases in aggressive behavior that often result from playing such games for extended periods of time (Funk, Buchman, Jenks, & Bechtoldt, 2003; Gentile, Lynch, Linder, & Walsh, 2004).

Violent video games also appear to be part of an overall pattern linking preferences for violent stimuli to aggressive behavior. The more violent television programs children watch, the more violent video games they prefer, and the more aggressively they behave toward peers (Mediascope, 1999b). This finding holds for both boys and girls; most girls aren't interested in violent games, but those who are tend to be more physically aggressive than average. Consequently, parents who notice that aggressive and violent themes characterize most of their children's leisure-time interests as well as their interactions with peers should worry about their children playing video games (Funk, Buchman, Myers, & Jenks, 2000).

Critical Thinking

1. You learned about some of the factors that determine a child's vulnerability or resilience to poverty. How do you think after-school care arrangements and media influences contribute to vulnerability and resilience among children from low-income families?

SUMMARY

Theories of Social and Personality Development

Learning Objective 10.1 How did the psychoanalytic theorists characterize the middle childhood years?

- Freud claimed that the libido is dormant between ages 6 and 12, a period he called the *latency* stage. Erikson theorized that 6- to 12-year-olds acquire a sense of industry by achieving educational goals determined by their cultures.

Learning Objective 10.2 What are the main ideas of the trait and social-cognitive theorists?

- Trait theorists propose that people possess stable characteristics that emerge during middle childhood as experiences modify the dimensions of temperament. Social-cognitive theories, such as Bandura's reciprocal determinism, argue that traits, and the emotional aspects of personality that were emphasized by psychoanalytic theories, represent one of three interaction sets of factors that shape personality: person factors, environmental factors, and behavioral factors.

Self-Concept

Learning Objective 10.3 What are the features of the psychological self?

- Between 6 and 12, children construct a psychological self. As a result, their self-descriptions begin to include personality traits, such as intelligence and friendliness, along with physical characteristics.

Learning Objective 10.4 How does self-esteem develop?

- Self-esteem appears to be shaped by two factors: the degree of discrepancy a child experiences between goals and achievements and the degree of perceived social support from peers and parents.

Advances in Social Cognition

Learning Objective 10.5 How does children's understanding of others change in middle childhood?

- Between 6 and 12, children's understanding of others' stable, internal traits improves.

Learning Objective 10.6 How do children in Piaget's moral realism and moral relativism stages reason about right and wrong?

- Piaget claimed that moral reasoning develops in sequential stages that are correlated with his cognitive-developmental stages.

The Social World of the School-Aged Child

Learning Objective 10.7 How does self-regulation affect school-aged children's relationships with their parents?

- Relationships with parents become less overtly affectionate, with fewer attachment behaviors, in middle childhood. The strength of the attachment, however, appears to persist.

Learning Objective 10.8 What changes occur in children's understanding of friendships during this period?

- Friendships become stable in middle childhood. Children's selection of friends depends on variables such as trustworthiness as well as overt characteristics such as play preferences and gender.

Learning Objective 10.9 In what ways do boys and girls interact during the middle childhood years?

- Gender segregation of peer groups is at its peak in middle childhood and appears in every culture. Individual friendships also become more common and more enduring; boys' and girls' friendships appear to differ in specific ways.

Learning Objective 10.10 What types of aggression are most common among school-aged children?

- Physical aggression declines during middle childhood, although verbal aggression increases. Boys show markedly higher levels of physical and direct verbal aggression, and higher rates of conduct disorders, than girls do. Girls show higher rates of relational aggression.

Learning Objective 10.11 How do popular, rejected, and neglected children differ?

- Rejected children are most strongly characterized by high levels of aggression or bullying and low levels of agreeableness and helpfulness, but some aggressive children are very popular. Neglected children may suffer depression.

Influences beyond Family and Peers

Learning Objective 10.12 How does self-care affect girls' and boys' development?

- Self-care is associated with several negative effects. Girls, children who live in safe neighborhoods, and children whose parents closely monitor their activities after school are the least likely to be negatively affected by self-care.

Learning Objective 10.13 What factors contribute to resilience and vulnerability among poor children?

- Children in low-income families are markedly disadvantaged in many ways. They do worse in school and move through the stages of cognitive development more slowly. Protective factors, including a secure attachment, relatively high IQ, authoritative parenting, and effective schools, can counterbalance poverty effects for some children.

Learning Objective 10.14 How do television, computers, and video games affect children's development?

- Experts agree that watching violence on television and playing violent video games increases the level of personal aggression or violence shown by a child.

KEY TERMS

moral realism stage *(p. 284)*
moral relativism stage *(p. 285)*
psychological self *(p. 280)*
reciprocal determinism *(p. 279)*
relational aggression *(p. 290)*
retaliatory aggression *(p. 291)*
self-care children *(p. 293)*
self-efficacy *(p. 281)*
self-esteem *(p. 281)*
self-regulation *(p. 286)*
social status *(p. 292)*
trait *(p. 278)*

TEST YOURSELF

Theories of Social and Personality Development

10.1 According to Erikson's view of children's psychosocial development in middle childhood, what factor is instrumental in children's development of a sense of industry or inferiority?

a. their developing relationships with cross-gender friends and peers
b. their growing independence from their parents
c. their success or failure at academic tasks
d. their developing motor skills and athletic accomplishments

10.2 Trait theorists argue that

a. emotions are the primary influence on personality development.
b. temperament evolves into five dimensions of personality by middle childhood.
c. traits exert less influence on development than other factors do.
d. emotions play no role in personality development.

10.3 Bandura's reciprocal determinism model proposes that children's personalities are influenced by

a. reinforcement.
b. internal traits.
c. their own behavior.
d. interactions of a, b, and c.

Self-Concept

10.4 Which of the following is more likely to be the self-description of a 10-year-old than of a 6-year-old?

a. "I am smart."
b. "I am better at math than my friend Paul."
c. "I'm bad."
d. "My brown hair is curly."

10.5 What are the key influences on a child's self-esteem in middle childhood?

a. her skills and abilities in key developmental areas such as academics, sports, and hobbies
b. the amount of support she receives from important people around her and the discrepancy between what she has achieved and what she desires to achieve
c. her perceptions about what children of her age should be able to accomplish or achieve
d. her popularity with other children and her popularity with the adults she knows

10.6 Where do differences in self-esteem originate?

a. from parents' and peers' values and attitudes about what skills, characteristics, or qualities are important
b. from a child's success or failure in a variety of endeavors and the comparison that can be made with others
c. from the labels and judgments of others
d. from all of the above

10.7 Which of the following best represents Bandura's concept of self-efficacy?

a. a child's sense of self-value
b. a child's understanding of her personality
c. a child's belief that she can accomplish goals
d. a child's understanding of others' opinions of her

10.8 Beginning about age 7 or 8, children begin to focus on ______ characteristics in their descriptions of others.

a. observable physical
b. concrete
c. apparent behavioral
d. inner personality

10.9 Which of the following best represents the way a school-aged child might describe a friend, in comparison to the way a preschool child would be likely to describe a friend?

a. "Miguel is the fastest runner in our class."
b. "Hoshi is always kind and helpful."
c. "DeShawna has pigtails in her hair."
d. "Darryl always sits next to Ms. Jones."

10.10 According to Piaget, children who are at the beginning of middle childhood are in which stage of moral development?

a. moral emotional
b. moral realism
c. moral judgmental
d. moral relativism

Advances in Social Cognition

10.11 As a result of the development of moral reasoning in middle childhood, children are capable of understanding all except which of the following?

a. You can change the rules of a game you are playing as long as all the other players agree to play by the different rules.
b. Accidents are not caused by deliberately "naughty" behavior.
c. Intentions are more important than consequences when the behaviors of others are being judged.
d. Standards of universal fairness dictate that no child should get a treat unless all the children get a treat.

The Social World of the School-Aged Child

10.12 Which of the following would be least helpful to parents who want to facilitate their child's development of self-regulation?

a. Provide discipline through authoritarian parenting.
b. Provide the child with models of good self-regulation.
c. Monitor the child's behavior.
d. Expect the child to demonstrate self-regulatory behavior.

10.13 What is the key feature that differentiates the friendships of middle childhood from those of preschoolers?

a. having fun

b. living close to each other

c. reciprocal trust

d. practice of communication skills

10.14 Which of the following is *not* an accurate statement about the peer group interactions of middle childhood?

a. During middle childhood, gender is the most important factor in children's selection of friends.

b. Both girls and boys enjoy rough-and-tumble play in same-sex groups.

c. Boys' friendships are more focused on competition and dominance than girls' friendships.

d. Collaborative and cooperative exchanges are the most common form of communication in girls' and boys' friendships in middle childhood.

10.15 Physical aggression _____ across middle childhood.

a. becomes increasingly more common among girls

b. goes up dramatically among boys but down among girls

c. is directed more toward inanimate objects

d. becomes progressively less common

10.16 Which of the following is *not* a true statement about relational aggression?

a. Girls are especially likely to use relational aggression against other girls.

b. Children who use relational aggression are apt to be shunned by their peers.

c. Children typically are not hurt by relational aggression because it is an indirect form of aggression.

d. Relational aggression can take the form of expressions of disdain or threats of ostracism.

10.17 In middle childhood, a popular child most likely

a. would have a feature or characteristic that made her unusual, in comparison to her peers.

b. would be highly creative.

c. would be shy.

d. would be physically attractive and larger than her peers.

10.18 Which of the following is *not* generally true of children who are bullies?

a. They have experienced excessive attention from their parents.

b. They have been subjected to physical punishment.

c. They have a difficult temperament.

d. They have experienced a lack of parental limits on aggressive behavior.

Influences beyond Family and Peers

10.19 Self-care children who are monitored closely are

a. more likely to be involved in criminal behavior.

b. more likely to make poor grades.

c. less likely to experience the negative effects of self-care.

d. less likely to complete their homework.

10.20 Many children living in inner-city poverty show all the symptoms of

a. self-regulatory behavior.

b. high self-esteem.

c. conscientiousness.

d. posttraumatic stress disorder.

10.21 Which of the following is *not* a factor that seems to help protect some children from the detrimental effects of poverty?

a. high IQ

b. a large network of peers who also are poor

c. a secure initial attachment to the mother

d. stable parental employment

10.22 What effect does television viewing have on children?

a. Television has nothing but harmful effects.

b. Television can have both positive and negative effects.

c. There is no consistent evidence of television's effects.

d. The evidence suggests the effects of television are mostly positive.

10.23 Which of the following has been associated with playing violent video games?

a. greater intelligence

b. greater self-reliance

c. reduction in aggressive behavior

d. increase in social skills

PEARSON

mydevelopmentlab Study Plan

Are You Ready for the Test?

Students who use the study materials on MyDevelopmentLab report higher grades in the course than those who use the text alone. Here are three easy steps to mastering this chapter and improving your grade...

Step 1

Take the chapter pre-test in MyDevelopmentLab and review your customized Study Plan.

Children who play violent video games for 90 minutes or more per day

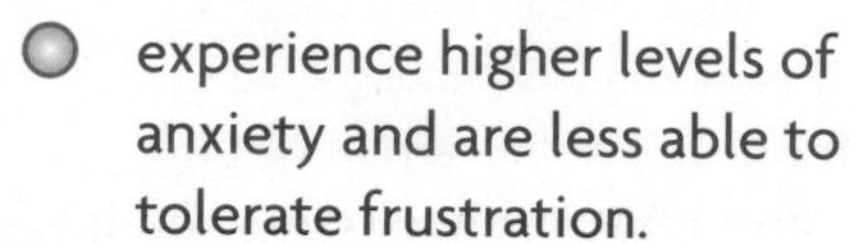

- experience higher levels of anxiety and are less able to tolerate frustration.
- have a greater sympathy for the suffering of others.
- have reduced visual acuity and reaction time.
- are more fearless and assertive than other children.

Step 2

Use MyDevelopmentLab's Multimedia Library to help strengthen your knowledge of the chapter.

Learning Objective 10.2

What are the main ideas of the trait and social-cognitive theorists?

Explore: The Five Factor Model

The Five Factor Model

Drag and drop the term from the left-hand column to the corresponding place in the right-hand column.

Agreeableness-antagonism

Conscientiousness-undirectedness

Extraversion-introversion

Openness to experience

Neuroticism-stability

The extent to which people are social or unsocial, talkative or quiet, affectionate or reserved

The extent to which people are good-natured or irritable, courteous or rude, flexible or stubborn, lenient or critical

The extent to which people are reliable or undependable, careful or careless, punctual or late, well organized or disorganized

The extent to which people are worried or calm, nervous or at ease, insecure or secure

The extent to which people are open to experience or closed, independent or conforming, creative or uncreative, daring or timid

Reset

"I liked how the book was in MyDevelopmentLab . . . the actual chapters. I could still study without the book and utilize my time better."

—Stephanie (student), University of Missouri—Columbia

Watch: Bullying

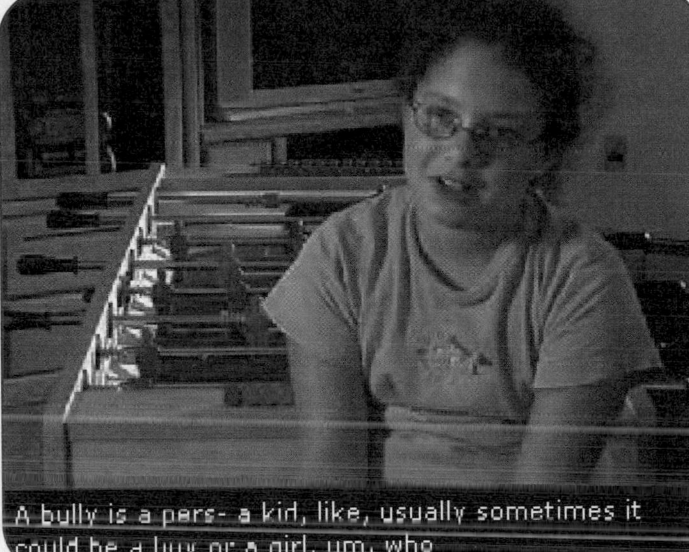

A bully is a pers- a kid, like, usually sometimes it could be a buy or a girl, um, who

Learning Objective 10.10

What types of aggression are most common among school-aged children?

Watch: Violence and Video Games: Douglas Gentile

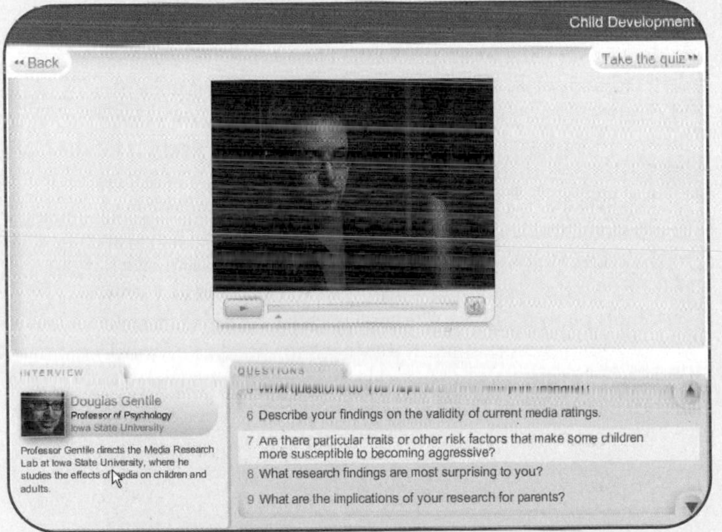

Child Development
Back
Take the quiz
INTERVIEW
Douglas Gentile
Professor of Psychology
Iowa State University
Professor Gentile directs the Media Research Lab at Iowa State University, where he studies the effects of media on children and adults.
QUESTIONS
6 Describe your findings on the validity of current media ratings.
7 Are there particular traits or other risk factors that make some children more susceptible to becoming aggressive?
8 What research findings are most surprising to you?
9 What are the implications of your research for parents?

Learning Objective 10.14

How do television, computers, and video games affect children's development?

Step 3

Take the chapter post-test and compare your results against the pre-test.

The major personality dimensions that are known as the "Big Five"

- fail to capture many essential aspects of personality.
- have little similarity to infant temperament.
- are stable across time.
- are unique to Western cultures.

POLICY QUESTION

Has Test-Based Reform Improved Schools in the United States?

In 2001, a comprehensive set of educational reforms known collectively as *No Child Left Behind (NCLB)* became law. These reforms addressed many aspects of public education, but one overriding theme of the new legislation was that standardized testing should play an important role in school improvement (U.S. Department of Education, 2004). Though widely touted as an innovation, the kind of testing associated with NCLB is the most recent manifestation of the *test-based school reform* movement, a series of changes in educational policy that have taken place over the past 4 decades in the United States.

High-Stakes Testing

Most historians of education say that the development of the National Assessment of Educational Progress in the 1960s marked the beginning of the test-based school reform movement (Bond, Braskamp, & Roeber, 1996). The NAEP, nicknamed the "Nation's Report Card," is designed to compare what American school children know with what the experts think they should know. At first, NAEP results were reported nationally. American students were described as performing at the advanced, proficient, basic, or below basic level (see the table).

The concept behind the NAEP, that of comparing student achievement to an "ideal" level of achievement, appealed to the public and to many educational policy analysts. Consequently, in the 1970s, many states began developing tests similar to the NAEP. By the 1980s, more than half were using them to assess both student learning and school quality.

In 1990, the federal government asked states to voluntarily participate in state-by-state NAEP score reporting. Thirty-seven states agreed to take part. This kind of reporting allowed taxpayers in each state to compare their schools to those in other states. Results were reported in local papers and on TV news programs. The public became accustomed to statements like "The Nation's Report Card shows that fourth-graders in California are scoring lower than children in most other states on math achievement tests."

NCLB requires that similar comparative testing programs be developed within local school districts (U.S. Department of Education, 2004). The idea behind this requirement is that parents should be able to compare scores obtained by students in their own children's schools to those achieved by children in other district schools. Moreover, NCLB requires that local school districts allow parents to move their children out of low-scoring schools if they choose to.

However, designing tests that can be used to compare one school to another isn't as simple as it might seem. In order to develop tests of this type, standards must be stated in measurable terms. Standards are statements about what knowledge and skills should be taught in schools. For example, a standard might be "All fourth-graders should learn the multiplication tables." A measurable standard would be "Fourth-graders will be able to multiply single-digit numbers with 80% proficiency." Long before NCLB became law, federal law in the United States required that all states develop such standards (Education Commission of the States [ECS], 2004). However, as you might imagine, the process of developing standards of this kind can be very costly. Thus, one argument that critics of legislation such as NCLB often make is that the federal government has a long history of failing to provide states with the necessary funding to implement its mandates (Fair Test, 2004). This lack of funding, critics say, explains why, as of 2006, only 27 of the 50 states had complied with the federal mandate to develop standards for reading, writing, mathematics, and science achievement, even though these mandates had been in place since 1994 (ECS, 2006). Critics further point out that new mandates, such as NCLB, that fail to address the funding issue are unlikely to lead to school improvement.

Criticisms of Test-Based School Reform

Test-based school reform has many critics. Educators claim that state-mandated tests encourage teachers to restrict what they teach to the content of the test (Neill, 2000). Studies showing that teachers are spending more time teaching test-taking skills than they used to lend weight to this criticism (Viadero, 2007). This problem is made worse, they say, when penalties are attached to low scores. A school in danger of losing money or being closed may force students to memorize things they really don't understand just to improve their test scores. Worse yet, in at least one state, local school officials have been caught deliberately reporting false scores to avoid penalties (Benton, 2007).

Teachers also claim that test-based reform has caused a decline in textbook quality (Neil, 1998). State agencies, educators say; force publishers to skimp on quality by demanding that they publish revisions of textbooks to fit state tests within very short periods of time. Despite textbook revisions, many school administrators still feel they need to spend thousands of dollars on materials published by test-preparation entrepreneurs (Associated Press, 1998).

NAEP Proficiency Levels

Level	Description
Basic	This level denotes partial mastery of prerequisite knowledge and skills that are fundamental for proficient work at each grade.
Proficient	This level represents solid academic performance for each grade assessed. Students reaching this level have demonstrated mastery of challenging subject matter, subject-matter knowledge, application of such knowledge to real-world situations, and analytical skills appropriate to the subject matter.
Advanced	This level signifies superior performance.

(*Source:* National Center for Educational Statistics, 1999.)

Claims of cultural bias have also been made against test-based reform (Tippeconnic, 2003). Civil rights organizations say that the knowledge that is tested in most American schools reflects the values and experiences of members of the White, middle-class culture. Further, many states require non-English-speaking children to take tests in English. To date, civil rights groups are unsatisfied with the efforts states have made to reduce bias. Thus, many have undertaken lawsuits against state education agencies and local schools, and these have yet to be decided.

The Impact of Test-Based Reform

Analyses of standards that have been developed show that, because of test-based reform, states are moving toward more emphasis on fundamental reading, writing, and mathematics skills (Bausell, 2007). Moreover, experimental evidence suggests that students try harder (as evidenced by longer and more complex answers to essay questions) and get higher scores on tests when passing tests is tied to outcomes such as high school graduation (DeMars, 2000).

With regard to younger students, testing advocates point out that as the number of statewide testing programs grew in the 1990s, NAEP mathematics scores among fourth- and eighth-graders increased accordingly (see the figure below; NCES, 2003a). Critics counter that NAEP reading scores have remained virtually unchanged since the early 1990s (NCES, 2003b). Thus, they say, systematic testing programs tied to specific curriculum standards may be beneficial in mathematics instruction but be of little value in helping students learn to be better readers. However, reading researchers argue that NCLB has motivated educators to turn to more empirically based approaches to teaching than were used in the past. As a result, these researchers say, NCLB has substantially raised minority children's reading skills and reduced the prevalence of reading disabilities in many school districts (Foorman & Nixon, 2006).

Other critics suggest that test-based reform has been most beneficial to students who would have done just as well without it. Research has demonstrated that average and above-average students perform at higher levels on such tests when they are exposed to intensive instruction in test content and test-taking strategies (Fuchs et al., 2000). Low-achieving students, however, seem to benefit very little from such approaches. Furthermore, say critics, despite decades of test-based reform, American public schools continue to turn out thousands of graduates who lack the skills to do college work (Schmidt, 2000).

Your Turn

- Talk to public school teachers and administrators about your state's testing program. How has No Child Left Behind affected their schools?
- Check your state education agency's Web site for information on standards and testing.
- Locate newspaper articles that report on what your governor and state legislators think about test-based reform. Do they support a national test?
- Find links to parent organizations in your state that oppose test-based reform at http://www.fairtest.org/parents.html.
- Visit http://nces.ed.gov/nationsreportcard/about/statehistorypublic.asp to learn about your state's history of participation in the NAEP.

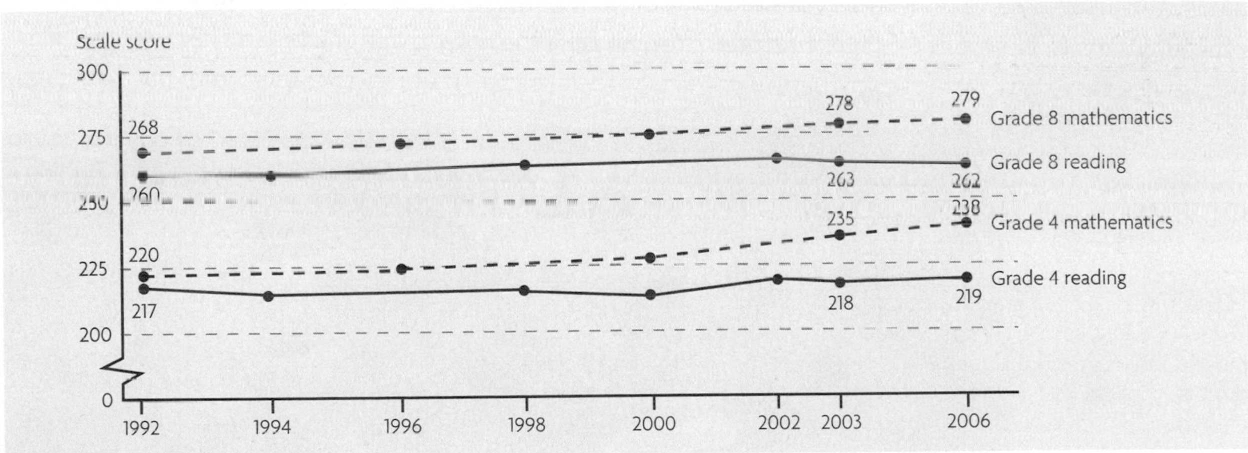

NAEP Average Scores

(*Sources:* NCES, 2004a; NCES, 2004b, 2006a, 2006b)

PART FIVE
Adolescence

11 Physical and Cognitive Development in Adolescence

Eighth-graders Aisha and Michelle had been best friends since second grade. Now that they were on the verge of going to high school, the girls felt that they needed a lot more independence than their parents were willing to give them. Both had their own computers and cell phones that their parents allowed them to use as they pleased. But when their parents denied the girls' request to attend a concert, Aisha and Michelle concluded that their parents lacked respect for their emerging maturity. "They just don't want us to grow up," the girls agreed, and they made a mutual promise that each would beg, bargain, and nag until their parents finally agreed to let them go to the concert. "All our friends will be there," pleaded Aisha to her unyielding parents. "Even Sally is going," Michelle told her father, "and she's just a seventh-grader." But all their pleading was to no avail, and both concluded their failed negotiation sessions with the tragic adolescent refrain, "You never let me do anything!"

"Time for Plan B," Aisha told Michelle one night as the pair lamented the severe state of deprivation that their parents had imposed upon them. "I looked up the bus schedule online, and the 7:30 bus goes to the arena. We can sneak out and ride the bus to the concert." Michelle had her doubts, though. "How can we get out early enough without anyone knowing about it?" she asked. Aisha smiled, "That's the best part of my plan. You tell your parents that you're spending the night at my house, and I'll tell mine that I'm sleeping over at your house." Michelle grinned broadly, "What a great idea! But how do we get the tickets?" Aisha responded with the confidence of an accomplished petty larcenist, "I'll use my mom's credit card to buy the tickets online. I'll print out the receipt, and we can exchange it for the tickets when we get there." The girls could hardly contain their excitement as they contemplated what seemed to be a perfect plan. "Okay," said Michelle, moving on, "so, what are we gonna wear?"

On the night of the concert, Aisha and Michelle executed their plan flawlessly and were riding high on an exhilarating wave of self-congratulation. As it turned out, there was just one flaw in Aisha's and Michelle's plan: The bus route that they had planned to take from the arena back to their neighborhood stopped running at 10:00 p.m. As the girls stood at the bus stop in front of the arena, shivering in the cold night air and growing increasingly anxious as the street became utterly deserted, Aisha had to admit that she had forgotten to check the return route schedule. They finally reached the conclusion that they had no choice but to call their parents, who, as you might imagine, were furious. Aisha's and Michelle's parents confiscated the girls' computers, cell phones, and other possessions that they regarded as luxuries, and it was quite a long time before the girls were allowed to go anywhere but to school again.

Are Aisha and Michelle budding criminals? Not likely, but their actions arose from a new form of thinking that is characteristic of **adolescence**, the transitional period between childhood and adulthood. The powerful intellectual tools that emerge in the early teens allow adolescents to make plans and to mentally project themselves into those plans as a way of testing them. The process is somewhat akin to that of a scientist who formulates a hypothesis and devises an experiment to test it. Armed with this new way of thinking, young adolescents embark upon a period of development that is characterized by risks and opportunities that compete for their attention. Some of their choices are good ones, but others, like those made by Aisha and Michelle, reflect poor judgment. Most of teenagers' poor choices turn out to have little effect on the rest of their lives, but others can significantly alter the developmental trajectory of an adolescent's life. How these risks and opportunities are manifested in the physical and cognitive domains is the topic of this chapter.

adolescence the transitional period between childhood and adulthood

Physical Changes

When we think of the physical changes of adolescence, we usually give the greatest amount of attention to the reproductive system. Reproductive changes are important, as the text will point out. But momentous changes occur in other systems, and we will discuss those as well.

Learning Objective 11.1
How do the brains and other body systems of adolescents differ from those of younger children?

Brain Development and Physical Growth

Have you noticed that you are much better able to make realistic plans now than you could when you were 13 or 14? If so, then you have first-hand knowledge of the changes in the brain that facilitate planning and logic that occur during adolescence. Likewise, you were probably better coordinated and had more physical endurance at 18 than you did at 13, thanks to changes in the body's other organ systems that happen during the teen years.

The Brain There are two major brain growth spurts in the teenaged years. The first occurs between 13 and 15 (Spreen et al., 1995). During this spurt, the cerebral cortex becomes thicker, and the neuronal pathways become more efficient. In addition, more energy is produced and consumed by the brain during this spurt than in the years that precede and follow it (Fischer & Rose, 1994). For the most part, these growth and energy spurts take place in parts of the brain that control spatial perception and motor functions. Consequently, by the mid-teens, adolescents' abilities in these areas far exceed those of school-aged children.

Neuropsychologists Kurt Fischer and Samuel Rose believe that a qualitatively different neural network emerges during the brain growth spurt that occurs between ages 13 and 15, which enables teens to think abstractly and to reflect on their cognitive processes (Fischer & Rose, 1994). As evidence, these researchers cite numerous neurological and psychological studies revealing that major changes in brain organization show up between ages 13 and 15 and that qualitative shifts in cognitive functioning appear after age 15. They claim that the consistency of these research findings is too compelling to ignore.

The second brain growth spurt begins around age 17 and continues into early adulthood (van der Molen & Molenaar, 1994). This time, the frontal lobes of the cerebral cortex are the focus of development (Davies & Rose, 1999). You may recall that this area of the brain controls logic and planning. Thus, it is not surprising that older teens differ from younger teens in terms of how they deal with problems that require these cognitive functions.

Other Body Systems An adolescent may grow 3 to 6 inches a year for several years. After the growth spurt, teenagers add height and weight slowly until they reach their adult size. Girls attain most of their height by age 16, while boys continue to grow until they are 18–20 years old (Tanner, 1990).

The shape and proportions of the adolescent's body also go through a series of changes. During the growth spurt, the normal cephalocaudal and proximodistal patterns are reversed. Thus, a teenager's hands and feet are the first body parts to grow to full adult size, followed by the arms and legs; the trunk is usually the slowest-growing part. In fact, a good signal for a parent that a child is entering puberty is a rapid increase in the child's shoe size. Because of this asymmetry in the body parts, adolescents are often stereotyped as awkward or uncoordinated. However, adolescents may look awkward, but they are better coordinated than school-aged children (Malina, 1990).

Adolescent girls reach adult height sooner than boys do because their bones grow and their joints develop more rapidly.

Joint development enables adolescents to achieve levels of coordination that are close to those of adults. As they do at younger ages, boys continue to lag behind girls. You may remember from earlier chapters that boys' fine-motor skills are poorer than girls' because their wrists develop more slowly. In early adolescence, this sex difference is very large; girls achieve complete development of the wrist by their mid-teens (Tanner, 1990). A similar pattern of sex differences is evident in other joints as well, enabling early-adolescent girls to outperform boys of the same age on a variety of athletic skills that require coordination, such as pitching a softball. However, by the late teens, at age 17 or 18, boys finally catch up with girls in joint development and, on average, gain superiority over them in coordinated movement.

Muscle fibers become thicker and denser, and adolescents become quite a lot stronger in just a few years. Both boys and girls show this increase in strength, but it is much greater in boys (Buchanan & Vardaxis, 2003). This difference in strength reflects the underlying sex difference in muscle tissue that is accentuated at adolescence: Among adult men, about 40% of total body mass is muscle, compared to only about 24% in adult women. This sex difference in muscle mass (and accompanying strength) seems to be largely a result of hormone differences. But sex differences in exercise patterns or activities may also be involved.

During the teenaged years, the heart and lungs increase considerably in size, and the heart rate drops. Both of these changes are more marked in boys than in girls—another of the factors that make boys' capacity for sustained physical effort greater than that of girls. Before about age 12, boys and girls have similar endurance limits, although even at these earlier ages, when there is a difference, it is usually boys who have greater endurance, because of their lower levels of body fat. After puberty, boys have a clear advantage in endurance, as well as in size, strength, and speed (Klomsten, Skaalvik, & Espnes, 2004).

Milestones of Puberty

Learning Objective 11.2
What are the major milestones of puberty?

The growth and development of teenagers' brains and bodies is remarkable. However, the physical change that most people associate with adolescence is the attainment of sexual maturity. **Puberty** is a collective term that encompasses all of the changes, both seen and unseen, that are needed for reproductive maturity. It begins when the **pituitary gland**, the gland that controls all of the body's other glands, signals a child's adrenal gland to step up its production of androgen (See Table 11.1). This milestone is called *adrenarche* and occurs around age 7 or 8. Next, the pituitary begins secreting hormones that stimulate the growth of the ovaries in girls and the testes in boys. As they grow, these glands secrete hormones that cause the sex organs to develop, testosterone in boys and a form of estrogen called *estradiol* in girls.

puberty collective term for the physical changes which culminate in sexual maturity

pituitary gland gland that triggers other glands to release hormones

The pituitary also secretes two other hormones, *thyroid stimulating hormone* and *general growth hormone*; these, along with adrenal androgen, interact with the specific sex hormones

Table 11.1 Major Hormones That Contribute to Physical Growth and Development

Gland	Hormone(s)	Aspects of Growth Influenced
Thyroid gland	Thyroxine	Normal brain development and overall rate of growth
Adrenal gland	Adrenal androgen	Some changes at puberty, particularly the development of secondary sex characteristics in girls
Testes (boys)	Testosterone	Crucial in the formation of male genitals prenatally; also triggers the sequence of changes in primary and secondary sex characteristics at puberty in the male
Ovaries (girls)	Estrogen (estradiol)	Development of the menstrual cycle and breasts in girls; has less to do with other secondary sex characteristics than testosterone does for boys
Pituitary gland	General growth hormone, thyroid stimulating hormone, and other activating hormones	Rate of physical maturation; signals other glands to secrete

and affect growth. Adrenal androgen, which is chemically very similar to testosterone, plays a particularly important role for girls, triggering the growth spurt and affecting development of pubic hair. For boys, adrenal androgen is less significant, presumably because boys already have so much male hormone in the form of testosterone in their bloodstreams. These hormonal changes trigger two sets of body changes: development of the sex organs and a much broader set of changes in the brain, bones, muscles, and other body organs.

The most obvious changes of puberty are those associated with sexual maturity. Changes in **primary sex characteristics** include growth of the testes and penis in the male and of the ovaries, uterus, and vagina in the female. Changes in **secondary sex characteristics** include breast development in girls, changing voice pitch and beard growth in boys, and the growth of body hair in both sexes. These physical developments occur in a defined sequence that is customarily divided into five stages, following a system originally suggested by J. M. Tanner (Tanner, 1990), examples from which are shown in Table 11.2.

Sexual Development in Girls Studies of preteens and teens in both Europe and North America show that the various sequential changes are interlocked in a particular pattern in girls. The first steps are the early changes in breasts and pubic hair, closely followed by the peak of the growth spurt and by the development of breasts and pubic hair. First menstruation, an event called **menarche** (pronounced men-ARE-kee), typically occurs 2 years after the beginning of other visible changes and is succeeded only by the final stages of breast and pubic hair development. Among girls in industrialized countries today, menarche occurs, on average, between 12 and 13; 99% of all girls experience this event between the ages of 9 and 12 (Adelman & Ellen, 2002).

primary sex characteristics the sex organs: ovaries, uterus, and vagina in the female; testes and penis in the male

secondary sex characteristics body parts such as breasts in females and pubic hair in both sexes

menarche the beginning of menstrual cycles

It is possible to become pregnant shortly after menarche, but irregular menstrual cycles are the norm for some time. In as many as three-quarters of the cycles in the first year and half of the cycles in the second and third years after menarche, the girl's body produces no ovum (Adelman & Ellen, 2002). Full adult fertility thus develops over a period of years. Such irregularity no doubt contributes to the widespread (but false) assumption among younger teenaged girls that they cannot get pregnant.

The Secular Trend Interestingly, the timing of menarche changed rather dramatically between the mid-19th and the mid-20th centuries. In 1840, the average age of menarche in Western industrialized countries was roughly 17; the average dropped steadily from that time

Table 11.2 Examples of Tanner's Stages of Pubertal Development

Stage	Female Breast Development	Male Genital Development
1	No change except for some elevation of the nipple.	Testes, scrotum, and penis are all about the same size and shape as in early childhood.
2	Breast bud stage: elevation of breast and the nipple as a small mound. Areolar diameter increases compared to stage 1.	Scrotum and testes are slightly enlarged. Skin of the scrotum reddens and changes texture, but little or no enlargement of the penis.
3	Breast and areola both enlarged and elevated more than in stage 2, but no separation of their contours.	Penis slightly enlarged, at first mainly in length. Testes and scrotum are further enlarged. First ejaculation.
4	Areola and nipple form a secondary mound projecting above the contour of the breast.	Penis further enlarged, with growth in breadth and development of glans. Testes and scrotum further enlarged, and scrotum skin still darker.
5	Mature stage. Only the nipple projects, with the areola recessed to the general contour of the breast.	Genitalia achieve adult size and shape.

(*Source:* Petersen & Taylor, 1980, p. 127)

until the 1950s at a rate of about 4 months per decade among European populations, an example of what psychologists call a **secular trend** (Roche, 1979). The change was most likely caused by significant changes in lifestyle and diet, particularly increases in protein and fat intake, that resulted in an increase in the proportion of body fat in females.

Data collected over much shorter periods of time in developing countries support the nutritional explanation of the secular trend. In one study, researchers found that the average age of menarche was 16 among North Korean girls who lived in squalid refugee camps (Ku et al., 2006). By contrast, studies involving impoverished groups in which food supplies suddenly increase reveal that the age of menarche can plummet from 16 to 13 within just a few years after improvements in nutrition are experienced (Khanna & Kapoor, 2004). Consequently, any change in eating patterns that affects girls' body fat, which must reach a critical value of 17% before menarche can occur, is likely to lead to a change in the age of menarche (Adelman & Ellen, 2002). But is there a lower limit on how early menarche can occur?

Exaggerated media accounts of the secular trend would have us believe that girls may some day attain sexual maturity during infancy (Viner, 2002). However, there is strong evidence for a genetic limit on the age range within which menarche may occur. For one thing, studies involving thousands of girls indicate that the average age of menarche for White girls in the United States is currently about 12.8 years and that it has not changed since the mid 1940s (Kaplowitz & Oberfield, 1999; Viner, 2002). Moreover, the average age at menarche stands at 12.1 among African American girls and 12.2 among Hispanic American girls, both of which represent a drop of about 2 months since the mid-1960s (Kaplowitz & Oberfield, 1999; Wu, Mendola, & Buck, 2002). Thus, the average age at menarche for the whole population of girls in the United States was stable from 1945 to 1965 and declined about 2.5 months between 1965 and 1995 (Kaplowitz & Oberfield, 1999).

In contrast to the stability of menarche, the average ages at which girls show secondary sex characteristics, such as the appearance of breast buds and pubic hair, have dropped significantly in recent decades (Anderson, Dallal, & Must, 2003). On average, girls nowadays show these signs 1 to 2 years earlier than their mothers and grandmothers did, resulting in a lengthening of the average time between the appearance of secondary sex characteristics and menarche (Parent et al., 2003). Researchers have found that this trend is attributable to the increased prevalence of overweight among children that you read about in Chapter 9 (Wang, 2002).

Overweight is both a cause and a consequence of early secondary sex characteristic development, because the hormonal changes that trigger the appearance of these characteristics also signal the body's weight regulation mechanisms to increase fat stores (Pierce & Leon, 2005; Remsberg et al., 2004). Little is known about how these early hormonal shifts affect girls' later health. Several studies are underway to determine whether overweight girls who exhibit early secondary sex characteristic development are at increased risk for breast cancer, adult obesity, and heart disease (National Cancer Institute, 2006; Pierce & Leon, 2005). Interestingly, too, researchers are also investigating why overweight delays pubertal development in boys and whether such delays affect boys' health later in life (Wang, 2002).

Sexual Development in Boys In boys, as in girls, the peak of the growth spurt typically comes fairly late in the sequence of physical development. Studies suggest that, on average, a boy completes stages 2, 3, and 4 of genital development and stages 2 and 3 of pubic hair development before reaching the peak of the growth spurt (Adelman & Ellen, 2002). His first ejaculation, or *spermarche*, occurs between 13 and 14 years of age, but the production of viable sperm production does not happen until a few months after the first ejaculation. Most boys do not attain adult levels of sperm production until stage 5 of genital development. The development of a beard and the lowering of the voice occur near the end of the sequence. Precisely when in this sequence the boy begins to produce viable sperm is very difficult to determine, although current evidence places this event some time between ages 12 and 14, usually before the boy has reached the peak of the growth spurt (Adelman & Ellen, 2002).

secular trend a change that occurs in developing nations when nutrition and health improve—for example, the decline in average age of menarche and the increase in average height for both children and adults that happened between the mid-18th and mid-19th centuries in Western countries

Learning Objective 11.3

What are the consequences of early, "on time," and late puberty for boys and girls?

Timing of Puberty

Although the order of physical developments in adolescence seems to be highly consistent, there is quite a lot of individual variability. In any random sample of 12- and 13-year-olds, you will find some who are already at stage 5 and others still at stage 1 in the steps of sexual maturation. We have already discussed the contribution of diet, exercise, and body fat to the timing of puberty. Researchers think that hereditary and behavioral factors also contribute to hormonal secretions in the bodies of individual teenagers, thereby controlling the timing of puberty (Dorn et al., 2003). Discrepancies between an adolescent's expectation and what actually happens determine the psychological effect of puberty. Those whose development occurs outside the desired or expected range are likely to think less well of themselves, to be less happy with their bodies and with the process of puberty. They may also display other signs of psychological distress.

Research in the United States indicates that girls who are early developers (who experience major body changes before age 10 or 11) show consistently more negative body images, such as thinking of themselves as too fat (Sweeting & West, 2002). Such girls are also more likely to get into trouble in school and at home, more likely to become sexually active and to be depressed than are girls who are average or late developers (Kaltiala-Heino, Kosunen, Rimpela, 2003). Among boys, both very early and very late puberty are associated with depression (Kaltiala-Heino, Kosunen, Rimpela, 2003). However, researchers have also consistently found that boys who are slightly ahead of their peers in pubertal development often occupy leadership roles and are more academically and economically successful in adulthood (Taga, Markey, & Friedman, 2006). In addition, substance use is associated with early puberty in both girls and boys, because, based on their appearance, early maturers are often invited to join groups of older teens among whom substance use is an important social activity (Costello, Sun, Worthman, & Angold, 2007).

Girls who develop early report much less positive adolescent experiences and more depression than girls who develop "on time" or later.

Research also indicates that pubertal timing interacts with a number of other variables to produce both positive and negative effects on adolescents' development. For instance, personality traits contribute to the effects of pubertal timing (Markey, Markey, & Tinsley, 2003). It appears that girls who experience early puberty and who are high in the Big Five trait of openness to experience are more likely to be sexually active at an early age than are girls who are early but who do not possess this trait. Moreover, parenting moderates the effects of pubertal timing such that both early-maturing boys and girls who are more likely to become involved in sexual activity and substance abuse if their parents are permissive (Costello, Sun, Worthman, & Angold, 2007).

Perhaps the most important variable that moderates the effects of pubertal timing, however, is the social context in which an adolescent experiences the physical changes associated with puberty. Consider the case of girls who are involved in activities that, by their nature, inhibit development of the proportion of body fat required to initiate puberty, such as ballet and gymnastics. In these contexts, girls who are late by general cultural standards are on time for the reference group with which they spend most of their time. Thus, early puberty may cause them to believe they can no longer be successful in their chosen pursuit and may devastate their self-esteem, whereas late puberty may enhance their self-confidence and self-esteem (Brooks-Gunn, 1987; Brooks-Gunn & Warren, 1985).

Critical Thinking

1. Suppose you were asked to give a talk to parents about young teenagers' need for sex education and for adult guidance with regard to romantic relationships. How would you integrate the information on brain development with the discussion of the stages of puberty in your presentation?

Adolescent Sexuality

Puberty brings with it the hormonal changes that underlie both sexual attraction and sexual behavior. Still, these important domains of experience are not entirely controlled by hormones. Each has psychological and social components, as you will see.

Sexual Behavior

Learning Objective 11.4

What are the patterns of adolescent sexual behavior in the United States?

Do you remember your first sexual experience? Nowadays, most people have their first sexual encounter in the mid- to late teens (Fryar et al., 2007). However, teens vary widely in how often they have sex and in how many partners they have.

Prevalence of Sexual Behavior Figure 11.1 graphs findings from a 2005 national survey of high school students in the United States (CDC, 2006). As you can see, boys were found to be more sexually active than girls. Furthermore, the proportion of sexually experienced teens increased across grades 9 to 12.

Consistent with earlier surveys, sexual experience was found to vary across racial and ethnic groups. About 67% of African American high school students reported having had sexual intercourse at least once in their lives. The rates among Hispanic American and White students were 51% and 44%, respectively. African American students were also more likely than Hispanic American and White teens to have had their first sexual encounter before age 13 (17% versus 7% and 4%, respectively).

There were also age and ethnic differences among students who were currently sexually active—defined as having had sex at least once within 3 months of responding to the survey. For example, roughly 41% of eleventh-grade females reported recent sexual activity, while only 20% of ninth-grade females did so. Researchers also found ethnic differences: 49% of African American students reported being currently sexually active, compared to 35% of Hispanic Americans and 32% of Whites.

Although sexual activity among boys is somewhat correlated with the amount of testosterone in the blood, social factors are much better predictors than hormones

Television programs aimed at adolescent audiences often portray teens in sexual situations, such as these two from the popular show Hannah Montana.

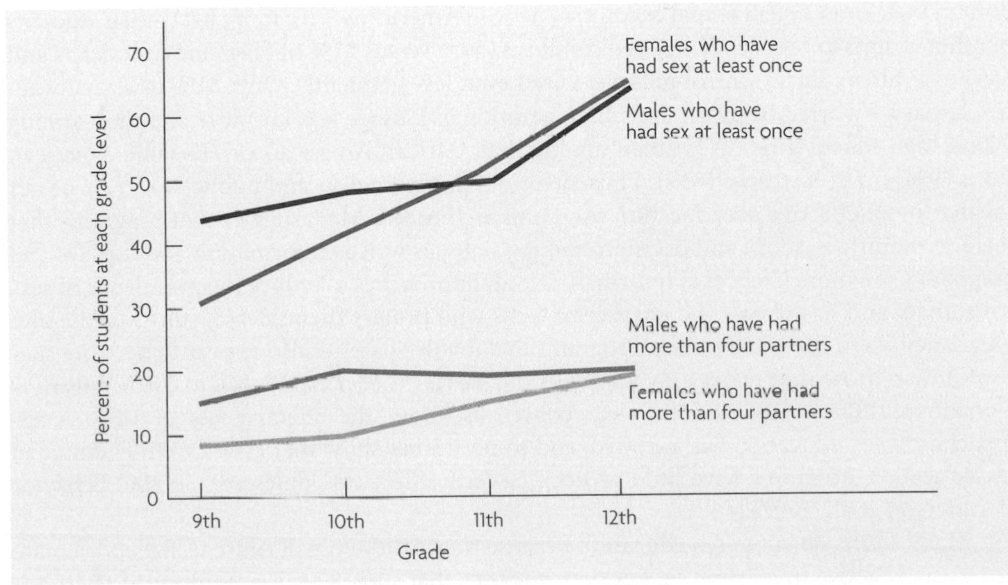

Figure 11.1
Sexual Activity among High School Students

The graph illustrates the data from a representative sample of more than 15,000 high school students interviewed in 2005.

(*Source*: CDC, 2006.)

Teens who date in early adolescence, as these middle-schoolers may be doing, are more likely to become sexually active while still in school than peers who begin dating later.

of teenagers' sexual activity (Halpern, Udry, Campbell, & Suchindran, 1993; Udry & Campbell, 1994). In fact, cross-cultural evidence suggests that the same factors are related to sexual behavior even in societies with very low rates of teenaged sexual activity, such as Taiwan (Wang & Chou, 1999). Those who begin sexual activity early are more likely to live in poor neighborhoods in which young people are not well monitored by adults. They come from poorer families or from families in which sexual activity is condoned and dating rules are lax. They are more likely to use alcohol. Many were abused and/or neglected in early childhood (Herrenkohl, Herrenkohl, Egolf, & Russo, 1998).

Among girls, those who are sexually active are also more likely to have experienced early menarche, to have problems in school, to have had their first date at a relatively early age, and to have a history of sexual abuse (Buzi, Roberts, Ross, Addy, & Markham, 2003; Ompad et al., 2006). The greater the number of risk factors present in the life of an individual teenager, the greater the likelihood that he or she will be sexually active. However, adolescents' moral beliefs and the activities in which they participate also predict their sexual activity. For example, teenagers who believe that premarital sex is morally wrong and who attend religious services frequently are less likely than their peers to become sexually active before reaching adulthood (Miller et al., 1998). Rates of sexual activity are also lower among teens who are involved in sports or other after-school pursuits than among their peers who do not participate in such activities (Savage & Holcomb, 1999). Moreover, alcohol use is associated with 25–30% of adolescent sexual encounters; thus, teens who do not use alcohol are less likely to be sexually active than are their peers who drink (CDC, 2000c).

Contraceptive Use Despite their high levels of sexual activity, teenagers know remarkably little about physiology and reproduction (Carrera et al., 2000). At best, only about half of teenagers can identify the time of greatest fertility in the menstrual cycle (Freeman & Rickels, 1993). Many teens are also woefully ignorant of sexually transmitted diseases and their potential consequences, although about 90% of high school students report having learned about sexually transmitted diseases in school (CDC, 2000c; Rosenthal, Lewis, Succop, & Burklow, 1997; Sharma & Sharma, 1997). Even when they are knowledgeable about STDs, many teens lack the assertiveness necessary to resist sexual pressure from a romantic partner or to discuss condom use.

Among students who reported recent sexual activity, only 63% said they had used a condom in their most recent sexual encounter. African Americans were more likely than students in other groups to report having used condoms (69% versus 57% of Hispanic Americans and 63% of Whites). Birth control pills were used even less frequently. Only 21% of sexually active females reported being on the pill. In addition, pill usage was far more common among White high school girls (27%) than among their African American or Hispanic American peers (9% and 11%, respectively). Thus, many developmentalists and public health advocates say that more effective sex education programs are needed. Most suggest that programs that include training in social and decision-making skills, as well as information about STDs and pregnancy, are more likely than information-only approaches to reduce the prevalence of sexual activity and to increase the number of teens who protect themselves against disease and pregnancy when they do have sex. Programs that involve parents also appear to be more successful than those that target only teenagers themselves (Lederman & Mian, 2003; Wilson & Donenberg, 2004). However, no clear consensus about the effectiveness of various approaches to sex education has emerged, and some studies show that even carefully designed sex education programs have little or no long-term effect on adolescents' sexual behavior (Henderson et al., 2007).

Many adults object to sex education because they believe it will cause teenagers who are not sexually active to become so. Research suggests that such fears are unfounded (Berne &

Huberman, 1996). There are also debates over the degree to which sex education programs should emphasize abstaining from sex or using contraceptives (Santelli et al., 2006). Studies examining several types of programs indicate that abstinence-based sex education is most likely to result in delay of first sexual intercourse when it is initiated with younger students—seventh- or eighth-graders—who are not yet sexually active (Borawski et al., 2005). Moreover, students who participate in multi-session programs are more likely to remain abstinent than those who are exposed to single-session presentations about abstinence (Postrado & Nicholson, 1992).

Sex education advocates suggest that abstinence and contraceptive education should not be thought of in either/or terms (Borawski et al., 2005). They point to research suggesting that programs that both encourage abstinence *and* provide basic information about reproduction and contraception appear to influence teen participants both to delay sexual intercourse and to use contraception when they do decide to become sexually active (St. Pierre, Mark, Kaltreider, & Aiken, 1995). Indeed, finding a way to encourage teens to avoid becoming sexually active too early may be critical to influencing contraceptive use. The older teenagers are when they become sexually active, the more likely it is that they will be cognitively capable of weighing the various options and consequences associated with intercourse.

Adolescent Pregnancy

Learning Objective 11.5

Which teenaged girls are most likely to get pregnant?

The rate of pregnancy among adolescents is higher in the United States than many other industrialized countries (Ambuel, 1995; Singh & Darroch, 2000). For example, the overall annual rate is about 40 pregnancies per 1,000 teens in the United States; it is only 17 pregnancies per 1,000 in Israel and 4 per 1,000 in Japan (Martin et al., 2006; Merrick & Morad, 2002). Ethnic differences exist within the United States as well (U.S. Bureau of the Census, 1998). Births to teenagers represent about a quarter of all births to African American women. Among Whites, only 11% of births involve teenaged mothers; among Hispanic women, about 17% of all births are to teenagers.

However, teen pregnancy statistics can be confusing, because they usually refer to all pregnancies among women under age 20. To clarify the extent of the teen pregnancy problem, it is useful to break down the statistics by adolescent subgroups. For example, in the United States, the annual pregnancy rate is less than 1 pregnancy per 1,000 for girls younger than 15; 22 per 1,000 among girls aged 15 to 17; and 70 per 1,000 among 18- to 19-year-olds (Martin et al., 2006). Looking at the numbers this way shows that teen pregnancy is far more frequent among older adolescents and, in fact, is most likely to happen after a girl leaves high school.

The age at which an adolescent becomes a parent is only one aspect of the teen pregnancy issue. Birth rates among teenagers have actually dropped in the entire U.S. population since the 1960s, including among 15- to 19-year-olds. What has increased is the rate of births to unmarried teens. During the 1960s, more than 80% of teens who gave birth were married. By contrast, in 2003, only 20% of teenaged mothers were married (CDC, 2004).

The proportion of teenaged mothers who eventually marry the baby's father has also declined in recent years, and, again, there are ethnic differences. Less than 5% of African American teen mothers marry the baby's father, compared to 26% of Hispanics and 41% of whites (Population Resource Center, 2004). Moreover, across ethnic groups, only 17% of teen mothers maintain romantic relationships with their babies' fathers beyond the first few months after birth (Gee & Rhodes, 1999, 2003).

Whether a girl becomes pregnant during her teenaged years depends on many of the same factors that predict sexual activity in general (Miller, Benson, & Galbraith, 2001). The younger a girl is when she becomes sexually active, the more likely she is to become pregnant. Among teenaged girls from poor families, from single-parent families, or from families with relatively uneducated parents, pregnancy rates are higher (Vikat, Rimpela, Kosunen, & Rimpela, 2002). Likewise, girls whose mothers became sexually active at an early age and bore their first child early are likely to follow a similar path.

In contrast, the likelihood of pregnancy is lower among teenaged girls who do well in school and have strong educational aspirations. Such girls are both less likely to be sexually active at an early age and more likely to use contraception if they are sexually active. Girls who have good communication about sex and contraception with their mothers are also less likely to get pregnant.

When teenaged girls become pregnant, in most cases, they face the most momentous set of decisions they have encountered in their young lives (see the Real World). About one-third of teen pregnancies across all ethnic groups end in abortion, and about 14% result in miscarriages (Alan Guttmacher Institute, 2004). Among Whites, 7% of teens carry the baby to term and place it for adoption, but only 1% of African American teens relinquish their babies to adoptive families.

The children of teenaged mothers are more likely than children born to older mothers to grow up in poverty, with all the accompanying negative consequences for the child's optimum development (Burgess, 2005). For instance, they tend to achieve developmental milestones more slowly than infants of older mothers (Pomerleau, Scuccimarri, & Malcuit, 2003). However, the children of teenaged mothers whose own parents help with child care, finances, and parenting skills are less likely to suffer such negative effects (Birch, 1998; Uno, Florsheim, & Uchino, 1998). Moreover, social programs that provide teenaged mothers with child care and the support they need to remain in school positively affect both these mothers and their babies. Such programs also improve outcomes for teenaged fathers (Kost, 1997).

THE REAL WORLD

Crisis Intervention for the Pregnant Teen

Brianna is a high school junior who has recently become sexually active. She fears that she is pregnant, but she doesn't know where to turn for help. Finally, after a great deal of agonizing over her situation, Brianna visited the clinic at her school, pretending to be suffering from a stomach ache. In her conversation with the nurse, Brianna casually asked about whether a girl who thought she was pregnant could talk to the school nurse about it without fearing that the nurse would tell her parents. The nurse recognized that Brianna was actually talking about herself. After some initial awkwardness, the nurse succeeded in establishing a trusting relationship with the girl through which she was able to use her crisis intervention skills to help Brianna deal with her situation.

A crisis intervention model proposed more than four decades ago continues to be helpful to health professionals, teachers, and parents in understanding and helping teens in crisis (Caplan, 1964). The first stage in a crisis, called the *initial phase*, is characterized by anxiety and confusion. Thus, the first step in crisis intervention in many teenaged pregnancies often happens when a significant adult in the teenager's life recognizes a change in behavior and questions the girl about it. However, mental health professionals recommend gentle confrontation during this phase (Blau, 1996). For example, a pregnant teenager might be reminded that it isn't possible to keep a pregnancy secret for very long, but this is clearly not the time to bombard them with questions such as "How are you going to support a baby? What about school? Are you going to go to college?"

The second stage of a crisis, the *escalation phase*, happens as the teenager begins to try to confront the crisis. In many cases, adolescents in this phase feel too overwhelmed to maintain daily functions such as getting to school and keeping track of homework. Teens in this phase may be responsive to helpers who simplify their decision-making by directly telling them what to do. For example, a pregnant teen's mother may make a doctor's appointment for her and see that she keeps it instead of nagging her to do it herself.

The third stage of a crisis is called the *redefinition phase*. Those who are providing emotional support for the pregnant teen in this stage can help by guiding her through the process of breaking the problem down into small pieces. For the teen who wants to raise her baby, counselors or parents can divide the decisions to be made into financial and educational categories. They can help the teen identify short-term and long-term goals in each category and assist her in finding the answers to important questions. For example, in the financial category, the girl must find out how much financial support she can expect to receive from the baby's father. With respect to continuing her education, she must determine the available day-care options.

Teens who leave the redefinition phase with a realistic plan of action are typically no longer in a crisis mode. However, teens who fail to redefine their problem appropriately enter the fourth crisis stage, the *dysfunctional phase*. In this stage, either the pregnant adolescent gives up hope or she goes into denial. The goal of crisis intervention is to prevent either of the stage-four outcomes. Yet the entire process probably depends on whether a pregnant teen has a sensitive adult in her life who will recognize the signs of the initial phase—just one more reason why teenagers, who may seem very grown up, still need warm, authoritative parenting.

Questions for Reflection

1. In which crisis phase was Brianna when she visited the school clinic?
2. Think about how the crisis phases might be manifested in a different kind of crisis. For instance, what phase-related behaviors might be shown by a teenager who has been arrested for under-age drinking?

Sexual Minority Youth

Learning Objective 11.6

What are some of the causes that have been proposed to explain homosexuality?

The emergence of a physical attraction to members of the opposite sex, or *heterosexuality*, is one of the defining features of adolescence for the great majority of teenagers. For some, though, adolescence is the time when they discover, or confirm a long-standing suspicion, that they are attracted to people of the same sex (*homosexuality*) or to both sexes (*bisexuality*). Still others become increasingly convinced that their psychological gender is inconsistent with their biological sex (*transgenderism*).

Gay, Lesbian, and Bisexual Adolescents Surveys involving thousands of teens have found that about 92% identify themselves as exclusively heterosexual in *sexual orientation*, a person's preference for same- or opposite-sex partners (Austin et al., 2004; Remafedi, Resnick, Blum, & Harris, 1998). About 7% of teens report that they are still unsure of their sexual orientation, and 1% say that they classify themselves as exclusively gay, exclusively lesbian, or bisexual. By adulthood, 94% report being exclusively heterosexual, and just over 5% describe themselves as gay, lesbian, or bisexual, leaving only a very small proportion who are still undecided as to their sexual orientation (Langer, Arnedt, & Sussman, 2004).

Lay people and researchers alike have wondered what causes some people to develop a gay, lesbian, or bisexual orientation. Several twin studies show that when one identical twin is homosexual, the probability that the other twin will also be homosexual is 50–60%, whereas the concordance rate is only about 20% for fraternal twins and only about 11% for pairs of biologically unrelated boys adopted into the same family (Dawood et al., 2000; Kendler et al., 2000). Family studies also suggest that male homosexuality runs in families—that is, the families of most gay men have a higher proportion of homosexual males than do the families of heterosexual men (Bailey et al., 1999). Such findings strengthen the hypothesis that homosexuality has a biological basis (Dawood et al., 2000). Such evidence does not mean that environment plays no role in homosexuality. For example, when one of a pair of identical twins is homosexual, the other twin does *not* share that sexual orientation 40–50% of the time. Something beyond biology must be at work, although developmentalists do not yet know what environmental factors may be involved.

Prenatal hormone patterns may be one factor in homosexuality (Rahman & Wilson, 2003). For example, women whose mothers took the drug diethylstilbestrol (DES, a synthetic estrogen) during pregnancy are more likely to be homosexual as adults than are women who were not exposed to DES in the womb (Meyer-Bahlburg et al., 1995). These studies are consistent with the hypothesis that homosexuality is programmed in at birth.

Whatever the cause of variations in sexual orientation, the process through which an individual comes to realize that he or she is homosexual appears to be a gradual one. Some researchers think that the process begins in middle childhood as a feeling of doubt about one's heterosexuality (Carver, Egan, & Perry, 2004). Retrospective studies have found that many gay men and lesbians recall having had homosexual fantasies during their teen years, but few fully accepted their homosexuality while still in adolescence (Wong & Tang, 2004). Instead, the final steps toward full self-awareness and acceptance of one's homosexuality appear to take place in early adulthood.

As homosexual teens grapple with questions about their sexual orientation, many report feeling isolated from and unaccepted by their peers (Martin & D'Augelli, 2003). This may help explain why a higher proportion of homosexual than heterosexual teens suffer from depression and attempt suicide (Cato & Canetto, 2003; Remafedi, French, Story, Resnick, & Blum, 1998; Safren & Heimberg, 1999; Savin-Williams & Ream, 2003). Many mental health professionals suggest that, to respond to these adolescents' needs, school officials provide emotional and social support for homosexual teens (Rostosky, Owens, Zimmerman, & Riggle, 2003; van Wormer & McKinney, 2003).

transgendered a person whose psychological gender is the opposite of his or her biological sex

Transgendered Teens **Transgendered** teens and adults are those whose psychological gender is the opposite of their biological sex. Some studies suggest that transgendered individuals may have been exposed to atypical amounts of androgens in the womb (Lippa, 2005). However, most do not have such histories, so the cause of transgenderism remains a mystery. Nevertheless, transgendered adolescents usually report that, since early childhood, they have been more interested in activities that are associated with the opposite sex than in those that are typical for their own (Lippa, 2005). However, most children who are attracted to cross-gender activities, and even those who express a desire to be the opposite gender, do not exhibit transgenderism after puberty (Cohen-Kettenis & van Goozen, 1997). Thus, such behaviors on the part of children are not considered to be predictive of the development of transgenderism in adolescence.

Out of fear of being stigmatized, most teens who suspect that they are transgendered keep their feelings to themselves. The denial and anger that is often expressed by family members when transgendered adolescents do venture to "come out" amplifies these teens' distress (Zamboni, 2006). As a result, like gay, lesbian, and bisexual teens, transgendered teens are more likely to suffer from depression and are at higher risk of suicide than heterosexual adolescents are (Rosenberg, 2003).

Once individuals accept their transgendered status, some choose to live as the opposite gender on a full-time basis, a pattern called *transsexualism.* Most transsexuals are content with their lives, but others are so anguished by the conflict between their sex and their psychological gender that they seek *sex reassignment*—a process involving hormonal treatment, reconstructive surgery, and psychological counseling—in order to achieve a match between the two. Typically, sex reassignment is reserved for adults, but some sex reassignment specialists accept teenaged patients (Smith et al., 2005). Regardless of the age at which sex reassignment is sought, at least half of those who explore this option, with the help of skilled counselors, ultimately reject it in favor of less drastic ways of coping with their dilemma. Among those who do actually go through the procedure, most are happy with the results and experience relief from their preoperative emotional distress.

Critical Thinking

1. Look back at Bronfenbrenner's ecological model of development in Chapter 2 (pages 43–44). Think of sexually developing adolescents as being in the innermost circle, or the biological context, and explain how the microsystem, exosystem, and macrosystem affect sexually active teens, pregnant adolescents, and sexual minority youth.

Adolescent Health

For most individuals, adolescence is one of the healthiest periods of life. However, as adolescents gain independence, they encounter numerous health risks.

Learning Objective 11.7

How does sensation-seeking affect risky behavior in adolescents?

Sensation-Seeking

Teenagers appear to have what many developmentalists describe as a heightened level of *sensation-seeking,* or a desire to experience increased levels of arousal such as those that accompany fast driving or the "highs" associated with drugs. Sensation-seeking leads to recklessness, which, in turn, leads to markedly increased rates of accidents and injuries in this age range. For example, adolescents drive faster and use seat belts less often than adults do (Centers for Disease Control [CDC], 2000c). To reduce the number of accidents among teenaged drivers, many states in the United States have enacted laws establishing "graduated" driver's licenses (Cobb, 2000). Sixteen-year-olds can drive in most such states, but they must remain accident- and ticket-free for a certain period of time before they can have privileges such as driving at night.

Risky behaviors may be more common in adolescence than other periods because they help teenagers gain peer acceptance and establish autonomy with respect to parents and other authority figures (Donnenberg, Emerson, Bryant & King, 2006; Letkato, 2006). Permissive parenting contributes as well, as does alcohol use (Donnenberg, Emerson, Bryant, & King, 2006). In addition, adolescents who are not involved in extracurricular activities at school or to whom popularity is important are more likely than their peers who value popularity less to engage in risky behavior (Carpenter, 2001; Stein, Roeser, & Markus, 1998).

The messages conveyed in the popular media about sex, violence, and drug and alcohol use may influence teens' risky behavior. In the United States, 13- to 17-year-olds spend more time watching television, listening to music, and playing video games than they do in school (Collins et al., 2004). Surprisingly, most teenagers report that their parents have few, if any, rules regarding media use (Mediascope Press, 2000). However, research indicates that media messages interact with individual differences in sensation-seeking (Greene, Krcmar, Rubin, Walters, & Hale, 2002). Thus, teens who are highest in sensation-seeking are those who are most strongly influenced by media portrayals of risky behavior.

Prime-time television programs contain about five sexual incidents per hour, and only 4% of these impart information about the potential consequences of sex (Henry J. Kaiser Family Foundation, 2005). Drugs and alcohol are even more prevalent than sex in the popular media. One survey found that 98% of 200 movies surveyed portrayed characters using some kind of substance, and in most cases characters used more than one substance (Mediascope Press, 1999c). Another group of researchers found that 51% of films they surveyed depicted teenagers smoking (Mediascope Press, 1999c). In another 46%, teenagers were shown consuming alcohol, and 3% contained images of teens using illegal drugs. Again, references to the consequences of drug or alcohol use were rare; they occurred in only 13% of films surveyed.

Drugs, Alcohol, and Tobacco

Learning Objective 11.8
What patterns of drug, alcohol, and tobacco use have been found among adolescents in the United States?

The story about Aisha and Michelle at the beginning of the chapter may have reminded you of some of the poor decisions that you made when you were younger. As we noted, most such decisions turn out to have little impact on teens' later lives. However, the choices that teenagers make about substance use can have life-long consequences.

As you can see in Figure 11.2, illicit drug use is far less common among recent than in past cohorts of teenagers (Johnston, O'Malley, Bachman, & Schulenberg, 2007). Researchers attribute this trend to declining approval of drug use among adolescents and to contemporary teens' better understanding of the negative consequences of taking drugs. Still, experts agree that drug use among teens continues to be a significant problem because of the risks to which teens expose themselves, such as drunk driving and the possibility of life-long addiction, when they use these substances.

Table 11.3 on page 320 lists the percentages of 8th-, 10th-, and 12th-grade students who reported using each drug listed in the 12 months preceding the survey. Clearly, as was true in earlier cohorts, marijuana is the illicit substance that teens use most often, but a surprising number of teenagers are using prescription drugs such as Ritalin, OxyContin, and Vicodin. Similar percentages of teens use over-the-counter drugs such as cough medicines.

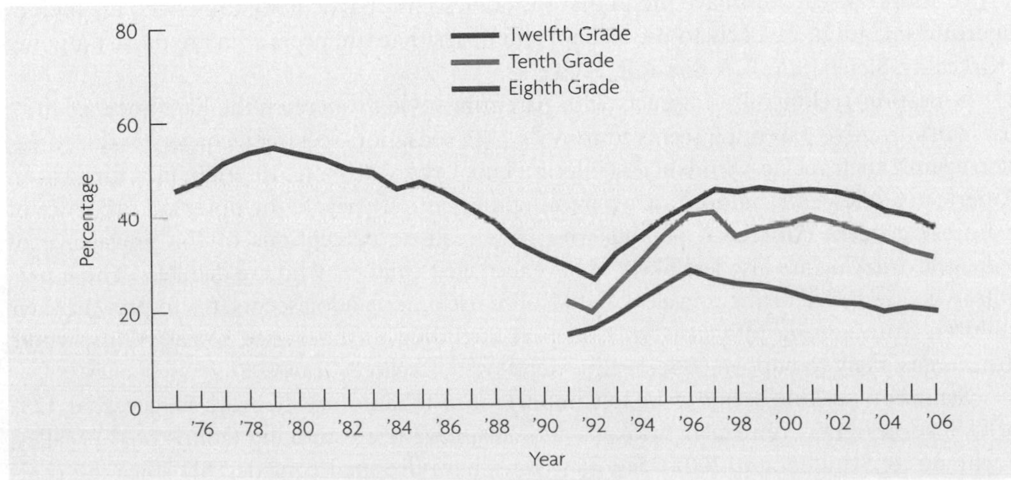

Figure 11.2
Illicit Drug Use Trends among Teenagers

This figure shows the percentage of teens who admitted to using illicit drugs in the previous 12 months. As you can see, drug use rates have declined since the 1970s.

Table 11.3 Percentages of Teens Who Have Used Illicit Drugs in the Past 12 Months

Drug	8th-graders	10th-graders	12th-graders
Alcohol	34%	56%	67%
Marijuana	12%	25%	32%
Vicodin*	3%	7%	10%
Diet pills*	5%	8%	8%
Tranquilizers*	3%	5%	7%
Over-the-counter cold medicines*	4%	5%	7%
Cocaine	2%	3%	5%
OxyContin*	3%	4%	4%
MDMA (Ecstasy)	1%	3%	4%
Crack cocaine	1%	1%	2%
Ritalin*	3%	4%	4%
Methamphetamine	2%	2%	3%
LSD	<1%	2%	2%
Heroin	1%	1%	1%

*Recreational usage outside the scope of the purpose for which drug is medically approved.

Source: Johnston et al., 2007.

(Note: Inclusion of such drugs in this discussion refers only to their use for purposes other than those for which they have been medically approved.) Nevertheless, illicit drug use is far less prevalent than alcohol use among teenagers. Moreover, nearly one-third of 12th-graders reported having been drunk in the month prior to the survey.

What makes a teenager want to use alcohol or drugs? Those who express the most interest in sensation-seeking are those who are most likely to use drugs and consume alcohol (Donohew et al., 1999). Indeed, researchers have found that individual levels of sensation-seeking predict peer associations—that is, teens who are high sensation-seekers choose friends who are similar. Once such groups are formed, sensation-seeking becomes a central feature of their activities. So, for example, if one member tries marijuana or alcohol, others do so as well. However, teens who spend a lot of time alone may also be vulnerable to substance abuse. Researchers have found that shy adolescents, particularly those who are high in neuroticism, are more likely to use alcohol and drugs than are peers who are more outgoing (Kirkcaldy, Siefen, Surall, & Bischoff, 2004).

Sensation-seeking also interacts with parenting style to increase the likelihood of drug use. Authoritative parenting seems to provide high sensation-seeking teenagers with protection against their reckless tendencies (Pilgrim, Luo, Urberg, & Fang, 1999). In fact, for African American adolescents, authoritative parenting may entirely negate the potential influence of drug-using peers. Moreover, parents who have realistic perceptions of the prevalence of teenaged drinking are also less likely to have teenaged children who are drinkers. These parents, who are aware of the prevalence of alcohol use among adolescents, try to prevent their children from getting into situations, such as attending unsupervised social events, where drinking is likely to happen (Bogenschneider, Wu, Raffaelli, & Tsay, 1998).

Sensation-seeking seems to be less important in tobacco use. Surveys suggest that 12% of U.S. adolescents are regular smokers, and 30% have tried smoking (Johnston, O'Malley, Bachman, & Schulenberg, 2007). Smoking rates have dropped considerably since the mid-

1970s when about 30% of older teenagers were regular smokers. Researchers argue that, thanks to public education campaigns and the inclusion of anti-smoking information in school curricula, more teenagers are aware of the health consequences of smoking than earlier cohorts. Moreover, many teens report that they oppose smoking because of its potential effect on their attractiveness to potential romantic partners.

Peer influence plays an important role in teen smoking. A non-smoking teenager who begins associating with a cohesive group of adolescents among whom smoking is a prominent behavior and a sign of group membership is likely to take up the habit, too. In fact, some developmentalists advise parents that if their teenaged child's friends smoke, especially close friends with whom the child spends a lot of time, parents should probably assume that their child smokes as well (Urberg, Degirmencioglu, & Pilgrim, 1997). Moreover, the period between ages 15 and 17 seems to be the time during which a teenager is most susceptible to peer influences with regard to smoking (West et al., 1999). Clearly, then, by monitoring the friends of their 15- to 17-year-olds and discouraging them from associating with smokers, parents may help prevent their teens from smoking (Mott, Crowe, Richardson, & Flay, 1999).

Eating Disorders

Learning Objective 11.9

What are the characteristics and causes of eating disorders?

Have you ever tried to lose weight? Surveys show that, at any given time, about half of women and a third of men in the United States are on some kind of weight-loss diet (Bish et al., 2005). Thus, it isn't surprising that 40% of teenagers diet regularly, and 20% of them use extreme measures such as taking diet pills (CDC, 2006; Neumark-Sztainer et al., 2006). However, dieting is quite different from an *eating disorder*, which is a category of mental disorders in which eating behaviors go far beyond most people's everyday experience with trying to lose weight (American Psychiatric Association, 2000). Most importantly, individuals with an eating disorder have a distorted body image that, in extreme cases, causes them to believe that they are overweight when they are actually on the verge of starvation. These disorders, which can be fatal, tend to make their first appearance in individuals' lives during the mid- to late teens. They are more common among girls than boys, but gay and lesbian youth, as well as teens who are unsure about their sexual orientation are also at higher risk than their heterosexual peers of developing eating disorders (Austin et al., 2004).

When this 15-year-old with anorexia looks at herself in the mirror, chances are she sees herself as "too fat," despite being obviously emaciated.

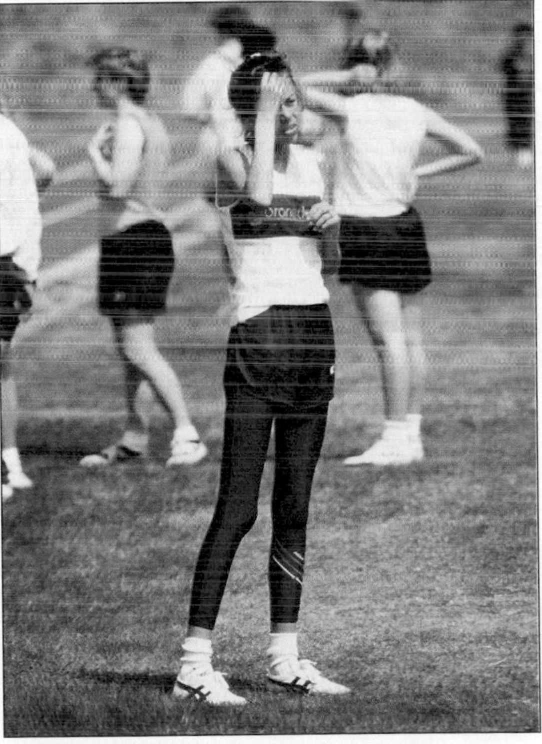

Anorexia Nervosa Teenagers who suffer from **anorexia nervosa** usually have a more distorted body image than those who have bulimia. This eating disorder is characterized by extreme dieting, intense fear of gaining weight, and obsessive exercising. In girls or women (who are by far the most common sufferers), the weight loss eventually produces a variety of physical symptoms associated with starvation: sleep disturbance, cessation of menstruation, insensitivity to pain, loss of hair on the head, low blood pressure, a variety of cardiovascular problems, and reduced body temperature. Between 10% and 15% of those with anorexia literally starve themselves to death; others die because of some type of cardiovascular dysfunction (Deter & Herzog, 1994).

Bulimia Nervosa **Bulimia nervosa** involves an intense concern about weight combined with twice-weekly or more frequent cycles of binge eating followed by purging, through self-induced vomiting, excessive use of laxatives, or excessive exercising (Attie, Brooks-Gunn, & Petersen, 1990). Teens with bulimia are ordinarily not exceptionally thin, but they are obsessed with their weight, feel intense shame about their abnormal behavior, and often experience significant depression. The physical consequences of bulimia include marked tooth

anorexia nervosa an eating disorder characterized by self-starvation

bulimia nervosa an eating disorder characterized by binge eating and purging

decay (from repeated vomiting), stomach irritation, lowered body temperature, disturbances of body chemistry, and loss of hair (Palla & Litt, 1988).

The incidence of bulimia appears to have been increasing in recent decades in many Western countries, particularly among adolescent girls, but firm numbers have been hard to establish. Current estimates are that from 1.0% to 2.8% of adolescent girls and young adult women show the full syndrome of bulimia; as many as 20% of girls in industrialized Western countries show at least some bulimic behaviors, such as occasional purging (Attie & Brooks-Gunn, 1995; Graber, Brooks-Gunn, Paikoff, & Warren, 1994). In contrast, bulimia is unheard of in countries where food is scarce.

Risk Factors Some theorists have proposed biological causes for eating disorders such as some kind of brain dysfunction. Researchers have also recently identified a gene that may play a causal role in the development of anorexia nervosa (Frisch et al., 2001). Others, however, argue for a psychoanalytic explanation, such as a fear of growing up. But the most promising explanation may lie in the discrepancy between the young person's internal image of a desirable body and her (or his) perception of her (or his) own body.

Some developmentalists suggest that an emphasis on thinness as a characteristic of attractive women, which is common in Western cultures, contributes to the prevalence of eating disorders (Pelletier, Dion, & Levesque, 2004). In one approach to testing this hypothesis, 6- to 12-year-old girls' responses to images of thin, sexy women were compared to boys' reactions to images of muscular, hyper-masculine men in order to find out how early children become aware of cultural stereotypes about ideal male and female body types (Murnen, Smolak, Mills, & Good, 2003). Researchers found that even the youngest children in this age group express admiration for the appearance of the models depicted in such images and that children are most interested in idealized images of adults of their own gender. However, girls are more likely than boys to compare their own appearance to that of the models. Moreover, among girls, those who are happiest with their own physical appearance are the least likely to compare their own bodies to media images of attractive women (Murnen et al., 2003; Rabasca, 1999).

These findings support the assertion of many developmentalists that girls internalize images representing what might be called the "thin ideal" during the middle childhood years and use them as standards against which to compare the changes in their bodies that happen during puberty (Hermes & Keel, 2003). In fact, research shows that, by age 11, girls are significantly more dissatisfied with their bodies than boys are with theirs, and the gender gap in body satisfaction increases across the teen years (Sweeting & West, 2002). As you might expect, given these results, researchers have also found that the tendency of girls to compare themselves to the thin ideal increases as they advance through puberty (Hermes & Keel, 2003).

Recent thinking, however, has placed more emphasis on the pre-existing psychological health of people who develop eating disorders than on cultural influences. Some researchers assert that the body images of individuals who suffer from eating disorders are the result of a general tendency toward distorted thinking (Dyl et al., 2006). In other words, these researchers say that people who have eating disorders tend to think in distorted ways about many things, not just their bodies. From this perspective, internalized images of the "perfect" body fuel the sales of diet products among psychologically healthy people, but they trigger a far more serious outcome, a true eating disorder, in individuals who have a mentally unhealthy tendency toward thought distortion. Longitudinal evidence seems to support this view. In one such study, young women who had anorexia in adolescence (94% of whom had recovered from their eating disorders) were found to be far more likely than the general population to suffer from a variety of mental disorders (Nilsson, Gillberg, Gillberg, & Rastam, 1999). *Obsessive-compulsive personality disorder*, a condition characterized by an excessive need for control of the environment, seemed to be especially prevalent in this group. The study's authors further stated that the young women's mental difficulties did not appear to be the result of having previously suffered from an eating disorder. Instead, both the adolescent eating disorders and the women's problems in adulthood seem to have been produced by a consistent tendency toward distorted perceptions.

Depression and Suicide

Learning Objective 11.10

Which adolescents are at greatest risk of depression and suicide?

Epidemiological studies reveal that, at any given time, 18–30% of adolescents are in the midst of an enduring depression (CDC, 2006; Saluja et al., 2004). Teenaged girls are twice as likely as boys to report feelings of depression, a sex difference that persists throughout adolescence and into adulthood. This sex difference has been found in a number of industrialized countries and across ethnic groups in the United States (Nolen-Hoeksema & Girgus, 1994; Petersen et al., 1993; Roberts & Sobhan, 1992).

Neuroimaging studies show that adolescent depression is associated with some kind of dysfunction in the pituitary gland (MacMaster & Kusumakar, 2004). But what causes the pituitary to function inappropriately in the first place? Genetic factors may be involved, as children growing up with depressed parents are much more likely to develop depression than are those growing up with nondepressed parents (Eley et al., 2004; Merikangas & Angst, 1995). The genetic hypothesis has also received support from at least a few studies of twins and adopted children (Petersen et al., 1993). However, the link between parental and child depression may also be explained in terms of the parenting behaviors of depressed parents, which you read about in earlier chapters. Furthermore, the contributions of a variety of family stressors to adolescent depression are just as clear among children whose parents are not depressed. Any combination of stresses—such as the parents' divorce, the death of a parent or another loved person, the father's loss of job, a move, a change of schools, or lack of sleep—increases the likelihood of depression or other kinds of emotional distress in the adolescent (Compas et al., 1993; D'Imperio, Dubow, & Ippolito, 2000; Fredriksen, Rhodes, Reddy, & Way, 2004).

Depression can hinder academic achievement, because it interferes with memory. For example, depressed adolescents are more likely to remember negative information than positive information (Neshat-Doost, Taghavi, Moradi, Yule, & Dalgleish, 1998). If a teacher says to a depressed adolescent, "You're going to fail algebra unless you start handing in your homework on time," the teenager is likely to remember the part about failing algebra and forget that the teacher also provided a remedy—getting homework done on time. Further, depressed adolescents seem to be less able than their nondepressed peers to store and retrieve verbal information (Horan, Pogge, Borgaro, & Stokes, 1997). Consequently, therapeutic interventions, such as antidepressant medications, may improve a depressed teenager's academic performance along with her emotional state. Most such treatments have been shown to be as effective for adolescents as they are for depressed adults (Findling, Feeny, Stansbrey, Delporto-Bedoya, & Demeter, 2004).

In some teenagers, sadly, the suicidal thoughts that often accompany depression lead to action. Surveys suggest that 17% of high school students in the United States have thought seriously about taking their own lives, and 2–8% have actually attempted suicide (CDC, 2006). A very small number of teens, about 1 in 10,000, actually succeed in killing themselves (CDC, 2007). However, public health experts point out that many teenaged deaths, such as those that result from single-car crashes, may be counted as accidents when they are actually suicides (NCIPC, 2000).

Although depression is more common among girls, the likelihood of actually completing a suicide attempt is almost four times as high for adolescent boys as for adolescent girls. In contrast, suicide attempts are estimated to be three times more common among girls than among boys (CDC, 2007). Girls, more often than boys, use methods that are less likely to succeed, such as self-poisoning. Contributing factors to completed suicides include:

- *Some triggering stressful event.* Studies of suicides suggest that this triggering event is often a disciplinary crisis with the parents or some rejection or humiliation, such as breaking up with a girlfriend or boyfriend or failing in a valued activity.
- *An altered mental state.* Such a state might be a sense of hopelessness, reduced inhibitions from alcohol consumption, or rage.
- *An opportunity.* A loaded gun in the house or a bottle of sleeping pills in the parents' medicine cabinet creates an opportunity for a teenager to carry out suicidal plans.

Critical Thinking

1. If you had the power to change U.S. culture in ways that you think would reduce the prevalence of the problems that were discussed in this section, what changes would you make?

Changes in Thinking and Memory

At the outset of the chapter, you read about two eighth-graders who succeeded in going to a concert without their parents' knowing about it. The kind of thinking that they used to plan their escapade was discovered by Piaget near the beginning of the 20th century. Such thinking enables adolescents to create an imaginary reality in their minds and project themselves into it. As Aisha and Michelle found out, however, the imagined world of the teenaged mind often excludes important details that help to ground such thinking in reality (see the Research Report on page 325). By the end of adolescence, though, teenagers' capacity to engage in this kind of thinking, which is similar to that of scientists, has dramatically improved.

Learning Objective 11.11

What are the characteristics of thought in Piaget's formal operational stage?

Piaget's Formal Operational Stage

Piaget carried out a number of studies suggesting that an entirely new form of thought emerges between about age 12 and age 16. He called the stage associated with this kind of thought the **formal operational stage**. Typically, this stage is defined as the period during which adolescents learn to reason logically about abstract concepts. Formal operational thinking has a number of key elements.

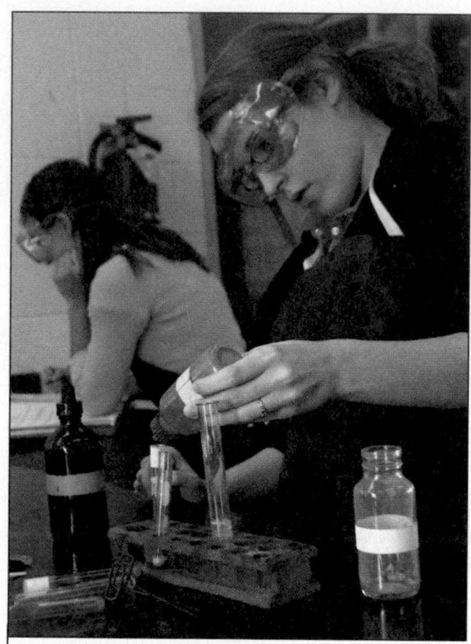

High school science classes may be one of the first places where adolescents are required to use deductive logic—a skill Piaget did not think was developed until the period of formal operations.

Systematic Problem Solving One important feature of formal operations is **systematic problem-solving**, the ability to search methodically for the answer to a problem. To study this, Piaget and his colleague Barbel Inhelder (Inhelder & Piaget, 1958) presented adolescents with complex tasks, mostly drawn from the physical sciences. In one of these tasks, subjects were given varying lengths of string and a set of objects of various weights that could be tied to the strings to make a swinging pendulum. They were shown how to start the pendulum different ways—by pushing the weight with differing amounts of force and by holding the weight at different heights. The subject's task was to figure out which factor or combination of factors—length of string, weight of object, force of push, or height of push—determines the "period" of the pendulum (that is, the amount of time for one swing). (In case you have forgotten your high school physics, the answer is that only the length of the string affects the period of the pendulum.)

If you give this task to a concrete operational child, she will usually try out many different combinations of length, weight, force, and height in an inefficient way. She might try a heavy weight on a long string and then a light weight on a short string. Because she has changed both string length and weight in these two trials, there is no way she can draw a clear conclusion about either factor. In contrast, an adolescent using formal operations is likely to be more organized, attempting to vary just one of the four factors at a time. She may try a heavy object with a short string, then with a medium string, then with a long one. After that, she might try a light object with the three lengths of string. Of course not all adolescents (or all adults, for that matter) are quite this methodical in their approach. Still, there is a very dramatic difference in the overall strategies used by 10-year-olds and 15-year-olds that marks the shift from concrete to formal operations.

Logic Another facet of this shift is the appearance in the adolescent's repertoire of skills of what Piaget called **hypothetico-deductive reasoning**, or the ability to derive conclusions from hypothetical premises. You may remember from Chapter 9 that Piaget suggested that the concrete operational child can use inductive reasoning, which involves arriving at a conclusion or a rule based on a lot of individual experiences, but performs poorly when asked to reason deductively. Recall that deductive reasoning involves considering hypotheses or hypothetical premises and then deriving logical outcomes. For example, the statement "If all people are equal, then you and I must be equal" involves logic of this type. Although children as young as 4 or 5 can understand some deductive relationships if the premises given are factually true, both cross-sectional and longitudinal studies support Piaget's assertion that only at

formal operational stage the fourth of Piaget's stages, during which adolescents learn to reason logically about abstract concepts

systematic problem-solving the process of finding a solution to a problem by testing single factors

hypothetico-deductive reasoning the ability to derive conclusions from hypothetical premises

adolescence are young people able to understand and use the basic logical relationships (Ward & Overton, 1990; Mueller, Overton, & Reene, 2001).

Piaget suggested that hypothetico-deductive thinking underlies many ideas and behaviors that are common to adolescents. For instance, hypothetico-deductive thinking leads to an outlook he called *naive idealism* in many adolescents (Piaget & Inhelder, 1969). Naive idealism is manifested when adolescents use formal operational thinking to mentally construct an ideal world and then compare the real world to it. Not surprisingly, the real world often falls short. As a result, some teenagers become so dissatisfied with the world that they resolve to change it. For many, the changes they propose are personal. So a teen whose parents have been divorced for years may suddenly decide she wants to live with the noncustodial parent because she expects that her life will be better. Another may express naive idealism by becoming involved in a political or religious organization.

Adolescent Egocentrism Psychologist David Elkind hypothesized that another common manifestation of hypothetico-deductive reasoning is a type of thought he called *adolescent egocentrism*, the belief that one's thoughts, beliefs, and feelings are unique. One component of adolescent egocentrism, Elkind said, is the **personal fable**, the belief that the events of one's life are controlled by a mentally constructed autobiography (Elkind, 1967). For example, a sexually active teenage girl might be drawing upon such a personal fable when she says "I just don't see myself getting pregnant" in response to suggestions that she use contraception. In contrast to this inappropriately rosy view of the future, a teen who is involved in a violent

personal fable the belief that the events of one's life are controlled by a mentally constructed autobiography

RESEARCH REPORT

Formal Operational Thinking and Everyday Problem Solving

Like those of Aisha and Michelle, the covert concert-goers at the beginning of the chapter, the plans of young adolescents often go awry due to their failure to include some important factor in them. In her classic study, Catherine Lewis (1981) found that younger teenagers were more likely than those who were older to base solutions on incomplete formulations of problems. For instance, Lewis asked eighth-, tenth-, and twelfth-grade students to respond to a set of dilemmas that involved a person facing a difficult decision, such as whether to have an operation to repair a facial disfigurement (Lewis, 1981). Forty-two percent of the twelfth-graders, but only 11% of the eighth-graders, mentioned future possibilities in their comments on these dilemmas. For example, in answer to the cosmetic surgery dilemma, a twelfth-grader said,

> Well, you have to look into the different things . . . that might be more important later on in your life. You should think about, will it have any effect on your future and with, maybe, the people you meet. (Lewis, 1981, p. 541)

An eighth-grader, in response to the same dilemma, said,

> The different things I would think about in getting the operation is like if the girls turn you down on a date, or the money, or the kids teasing you at school. (Lewis, 1981, p. 542)

The eighth-grader's answer focused on the here and now, on concrete things. By contrast, the twelfth-grader considered things that might happen in the future. Thus, when faced with a practical dilemma, young adolescents, most of whom can solve laboratory tasks that measure formal operational thinking, seem to use concrete rather than formal operational reasoning.

What accounts for this pattern of findings? Perhaps younger teens fail to use formal operational thinking effectively because the parts of the brain needed to connect it to everyday problems may not be sufficiently developed until the late teens. Neuroimaging studies comparing the brain activity of children, teens, and adults while they were engaged in a gambling task provide support for this hypothesis (Crone & van der Molen, 2004). However, Piaget would probably argue that young teens aren't good at applying their formal operational schemes to everyday problems because they haven't had much practice using them, a hypothesis that might also explain these neuroimaging results.

Recall that Piaget hypothesized that, when we apply a scheme to a problem, we are engaging in assimilation. According to his view, when teens assimilate problems to immature formal operational schemes, their failures trigger equilibration, the process that kicks in when our schemes don't faithfully represent reality. Equilibration leads to accommodations, or changes in the schemes, that are put to work on the next time an appropriate problem comes around. Applying the accommodated scheme to a new problem initiates a new cycle of assimilation, equilibration, and accommodation. Through this back and forth process, teenagers' formal operational schemes become more reliable. Thus, young teens have to experiment with their formal operational schemes in the real world, just as Aisha and Michelle did, before they can be expected to be able to be proficient at using them.

Questions for Critical Analysis

1. How do these aspects of adolescent thinking come into play when teenagers have to come up with ways of coping with teachers whom they don't like or of raising a failing grade?
2. To what extent does teens' limited ability to use formal operational thinking in everyday contexts explain findings about the ineffectiveness of sex education programs that you read about earlier in the chapter?

street gang may say "I'll probably get shot before I make 18" when advised to leave the gang and focus on acquiring the academic skills needed to graduate from high school.

Elkind also proposed that adolescent egocentrism drives teenagers to try out various attitudes, behaviors, and even clothing choices in front of an **imaginary audience** an internalized set of behavioral standards usually derived from a teenager's peer group. Think about the example of a teenaged girl who is habitually late for school because she changes clothes two or three times every day before leaving home. Each time the girl puts on a different outfit, she imagines how her peers at school will respond to it. If the imaginary audience criticizes the outfit, the girl feels she must change clothes in order to elicit a more favorable response. Similarly, a boy may spend hours in front of the mirror trimming his sideburns in an effort to achieve a look he thinks his peers will approve of.

Many developmentalists have found Elkind's personal fable and imaginary audience to be helpful in explaining a variety of adolescents' everyday behaviors. However, research examining these constructs has produced mixed results (Bell & Bromnick, 2003; Vartanian, 2000). While it is true that adolescents use idealized mental models to make all kinds of decisions about their own and others' behavior, researchers have found that school-aged children sometimes exhibit similar forms of thought (Vartanian, 2001). Nevertheless, developmentalists agree that the tendency to exaggerate others' reactions to one's own behavior and to base decisions on unrealistic ideas about the future are two characteristics that distinguish adolescents from younger children.

Learning Objective 11.12

What are some major research findings regarding the formal operational stage?

Direct Tests of Piaget's View

In an early cross-sectional study, researchers tested 20 girls in each of four grades (sixth, eighth, tenth, and twelfth) on ten different tasks that required one or more of what Piaget called formal operational skills (Martorano, 1977). Indeed, many of the tasks the researchers used were those Piaget himself had devised. Results of performance on two of these tasks are graphed in Figure 11.3 on page 326. The pendulum problem is the one described earlier in this section; the balance problem requires a youngster to predict whether two different weights, hung at varying distances on each side of a scale, will balance—a task similar to the balance scale problem Siegler used (recall Figure 9.4). To solve this problem using formal operations, the teenager must consider both weight and distance simultaneously. You can see from Figure 11.3 that older students generally did better, with the biggest improvement in scores between eighth and tenth grades (between ages 13 and 15).

imaginary audience an internalized set of behavioral standards usually derived from a teenager's peer group

Formal operational reasoning also seems to enable adolescents to understand figurative language, such as metaphors, to a greater degree. For example, one early study found that teenagers were much better than younger children at interpreting proverbs (Saltz, 1979). Statements such as "People who live in glass houses shouldn't throw stones" are usually interpreted literally by 6- to 11-year-olds. By 12 or 13, most adolescents can easily understand them, even though it isn't until much later that teenagers actually use such expressions in their everyday speech (Gibbs & Beitel, 1995). See the Research Report

Figure 11.3 Within Stage Development in Formal Operations

These are the results from two of the ten different formal operational tasks used in Martorano's cross-sectional study.

(*Source:* Martorano, 1977, p. 670. Copyright by the American Psychological Association.)

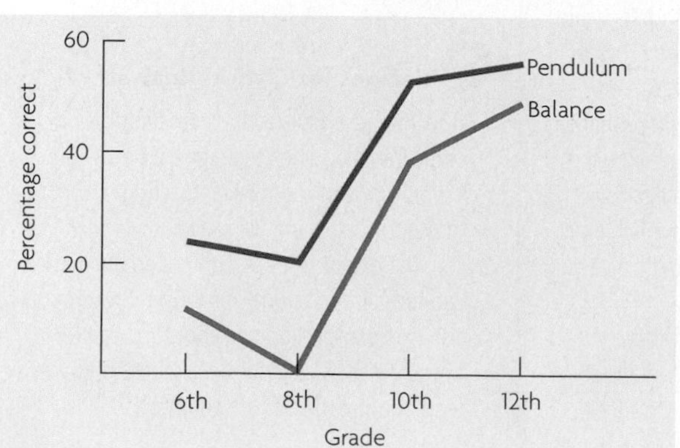

Take another look at Figure 11.3: Only about 50–60% of twelfth-graders solved the two formal operations problems, and only 2 of the 20 twelfth-grade participants used formal operational logic on all ten problems. Further, recent studies have found rates of formal operational thinking in high school students that are very similar to those found in studies conducted in the 1960s, 1970s, and 1980s (Bradmetz, 1999). The consistency of such findings over several cohorts of adolescents suggests that Piaget's predictions about adolescents' thinking abilities were overly optimistic—in contrast to his overly pessimistic estimates of young children's abilities, which you read about in earlier chapters.

In adulthood, rates of formal operational thinking increase with education. Generally, the better educated the adult participants in a study of formal operational thinking, the greater the percentage who display this kind of reasoning (Mwamwenda, 1999).

Piaget's belief in the universality of formal operations may have resulted from his failure to appreciate the role of education in the development of advanced forms of thought. The current consensus among developmentalists is that all teenagers and adults without mental retardation have the capacity for formal operational thinking, but they actually acquire it in response to specific demands, such as those imposed by higher levels of education. Thus, people whose life situations or cultures do not require formal operational thinking do not develop it.

Advances in Information Processing

Learning Objective 11.13
What kinds of advances in information processing capabilities occur during adolescence?

Adolescents process information faster, use processing resources more efficiently, understand their own memory processes better, and have more knowledge than do elementary school children (Kail, 1990, 1997). As a result, their working memories function more efficiently and they outperform school-aged children even on such simple memory tasks as recognizing faces (Gathercole, Pickering, Ambridge, & Wearing, 2004; Itier & Taylor, 2004). Moreover, they are much better at using strategies to help themselves remember things and can more easily understand and remember complex information, such as that presented in a textbook.

Metacognition, Metamemory, and Strategy Use By age 14 or 15, the metacognitive and metamemory skills of adolescents far exceed those of younger children. For example, in one classic study, 10- and 14-year-olds were instructed to do a particular activity for exactly 30 minutes (Ceci & Bronfenbrenner, 1985). Experimenters provided them with a clock and instructed them to use it to determine when they should stop. Few of the 10-year-olds periodically checked the time to see if 30 minutes had elapsed, but most of the 14-year-olds did. As a result, less than half of the younger participants succeeded in stopping on time, but more than three-quarters of the teenagers did so.

Another early study of metamemory involved offering fifth-graders, eighth-graders, and college students the opportunity to earn money for remembering words (Cuvo, 1974). Researchers designated the words to be recalled as being worth either 1 cent or 10 cents. Fifth graders rehearsed 1-cent and 10-cent words equally. In contrast, eighth-graders and college students put more effort into rehearsing the 10-cent words. At the end of the rehearsal period, fifth-graders recalled equal numbers of 1- and 10-cent words, while older participants remembered more 10-cent words. Further, college students outperformed eighth-graders in both rehearsal and recall. This finding suggests that the capacity to apply memory strategies selectively, based on the characteristics of a memory task, appears early in the teenaged years and continues to improve throughout adolescence.

Training studies, in which children and adolescents are taught to use a particular memory strategy, also suggest that metacognitive abilities enable teenagers to benefit more from training than younger children do. For example, researchers taught elementary school students and high school students a strategy for memorizing the manufacturing products associated with different cities (for example, Detroit-automobiles) (Pressley & Dennis-Rounds, 1980). Once participants had learned the strategy and were convinced of its effectiveness, researchers presented them with a similar task, memorizing Latin words and their English translations. Experimenters found that only the high school students made an effort to use the strategy they had just learned to accomplish the new memory task. The elementary school children used the new strategy only when researchers told them to and demonstrated how it could be applied to the new task. High school students' success seemed to be due to their superior ability to recognize the similarity between the two tasks—an aspect of metamemory.

Text Learning Differences between younger children's and adolescents' processing of and memory for text are even more dramatic. In a classic study of text processing, experimenters asked 10-, 13-, 15-, and 18-year-olds to read and summarize a 500-word passage. The researchers hypothesized that participants would use four rules in writing summaries (Brown & Day, 1983). First, they would delete trivial information. Second, their summaries would show categorical organization—that is, they would use terms such as "animals" rather than specific names of animals mentioned in the text. Third, the summaries would use topic sentences from the text. Finally, the participants would invent topic sentences for paragraphs that didn't have them.

The results of the study suggested that participants of all ages used the first rule, because all of the summaries included more general than detailed or trivial information about the passage. However, the 10-year-olds and 13-year-olds used the other rules far less frequently than did the 15- and 18-year-olds. There were also interesting differences between the two older groups. Fifteen-year-olds used categories about as frequently as 18-year-olds did, but the oldest group used topic sentences far more effectively. This pattern of age differences suggests that the ability to summarize a text improves gradually during the second half of adolescence.

Studies of text outlining reveal a similar pattern (Drum, 1985). Both elementary and high school students know that an outline should include the main ideas of a passage along with supporting details. However, research suggests that 17-year-olds generate much more complete outlines than 14-year-olds do. Moreover, 11-year-olds' outlines usually include only a few of the main ideas of a passage and provide little or no supporting details for those main ideas.

Critical Thinking

1. How could some of the cognitive advances that emerge during adolescence be used in an essay countering negative stereotypes of teenagers in the media?

Schooling

Do you remember your first day of secondary school? How many times did you get lost looking for a classroom? Did you carry all your books with you to avoid having to go to your locker between periods? Perhaps you forgot the combination to your locker. Such are the experiences of children who must transition from the relative simplicity of elementary school to the intimidating complexity of secondary school. Eventually, most students adjust to the new setting. Yet, as you will see, there are both benefits and costs that are associated with such transitions.

Learning Objective 11.14

How do changes in students' goals contribute to the transition to secondary school?

Transition to Secondary School

There are many places in the world, including some in North America, where children attend a lower school for 8 years before moving on to a high school for 4 years. Such an arrangement is known as an *8-4 system*. Because students typically show achievement declines after entering high school, educators have developed two models that include a transitional school—a junior high school, middle school, or intermediate school—between elementary and high school. The junior high system typically includes 6 years of elementary school followed by 3 years of junior high and 3 years of high school. The middle school model includes 5 years of elementary school, 3 years of middle school, and 4 years of high school.

Neither the junior high nor the middle school approach seems to have solved the transition problem. Students show losses in achievement and in self-esteem across both transition points in the 6-3-3 and 5-3-4 systems. Further, students in both of these systems show greater losses during the transition to high school than do those in 8-4 systems (Alspaugh, 1998; Anderman, 1998). Consequently, educators and developmentalists are currently searching for explanations and practical remedies.

Middle School One potential explanation for transition-related achievement declines associated with the transition to middle school is that students' academic goals change once they leave elementary school. Researchers classify such goals into two very broad categories: *task goals* and *ability goals*. **Task goals** are goals based on personal standards and a desire to become more competent at something. For example, a runner who wants to improve her time in the 100-meter dash has a task goal. An **ability goal** is one that defines success in competitive terms, being better than another person at something. For example, a runner who wants to be the fastest person on her team has an ability goal. Longitudinal research shows that most fifth-graders have task goals, but by the time they have been in

task goals goals based on a desire for self-improvement

ability goals goals based on a desire to be superior to others sixth grade a few months, most children have shifted to ability goals (Anderman & Anderman, 1999; Anderman & Midgley, 1997).

A student's goal influences his behavior in important ways. Task goals are associated with a greater sense of personal control and more positive attitudes about school (Anderman, 1999; Gutman, 2006). A student who takes a task-goal approach to school work tends to set increasingly higher standards for his performance and attributes success and failure to his own efforts. For example, a task goal–oriented student is likely to say he received an A in a class because he worked hard or because he wanted to improve his performance.

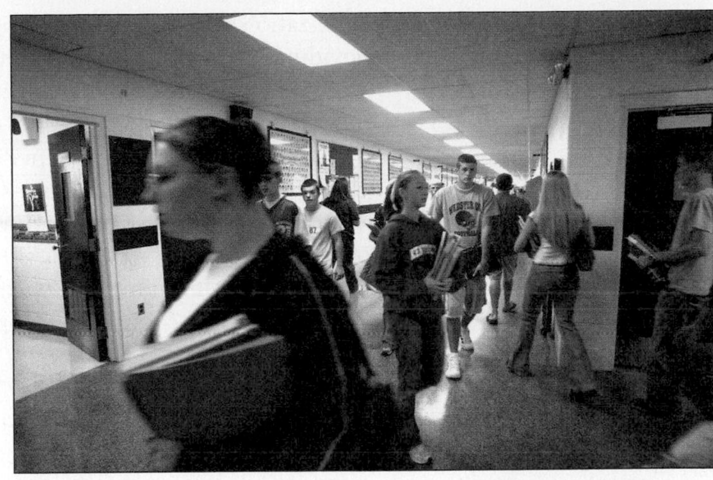

Some developmentalists argue that the transition to middle school or junior high school is difficult for many young adolescents because they are not developmentally ready for the secondary-school model. Children who attend middle and junior high schools where close relationships between teachers and students are encouraged, as they are in elementary school, show smaller declines in achievement and self-esteem.

In contrast, students with ability goals adopt relative standards—that is, they view performance on a given academic task as good as long as it is better than someone else's. Consequently, such students are more strongly influenced by the group with which they identify than by internal standards that define good and bad academic performance. Ability goal–oriented students are also more likely than others to attribute success and failure to forces outside themselves. For example, such a student might say he got an A in a class because it was easy or because the teacher liked him. Moreover, such students are likely to have a negative view of school (Anderman, 1999).

Because middle schools emphasize ability grouping more than elementary schools, it is likely that many middle school students change their beliefs about their own abilities during these years (Anderman, Maehr, & Midgley, 1999; Roeser & Eccles, 1998). Thus, high-achieving elementary students who maintain their levels of achievement across the sixth-grade transition gain confidence in their abilities (Pajares & Graham, 1999). In contrast, the changes in self-concept experienced by high achievers who fail to meet expectations in middle school as well as average and low-achieving students do probably lead to self-esteem losses for many of them. Once an ability goal–oriented student adopts the belief that her academic ability is less than adequate, she is likely to stop putting effort into school work. In addition, such students are likely to use ineffective cognitive strategies when attempting to learn academic material (Young, 1997). Consequently, achievement suffers along with self-esteem.

Another factor that influences young adolescents' adjustment to secondary school is their perception of the school's climate. Researchers have found that many middle school students perceive their schools to be impersonal and unsupportive (Barber & Olsen, 2004). To address this perception, some schools provide students with an adult mentor, either a teacher or a volunteer from the community, to whom they are assigned for a transitional period or throughout the middle school years. In practice, the characteristics of mentoring programs vary widely (Galassi, Gulledge, & Cox, 1997). Some consist simply of giving sixth-graders the name of a teacher they can consult if they encounter any problems. At the other end of the spectrum, some mentoring programs assign each student to a teacher, who is supposed to monitor several students' daily assignment sheets, homework completion, grades, and even school supplies. The homeroom teacher also maintains communication with each child's parents regarding these factors. If a student isn't doing his math homework or doesn't have any pencils, it is the homeroom teacher's responsibility to tell his parents about the problem. The parents are then responsible for follow-up.

Research suggests that programs of this level of intensity are highly successful in improving middle school students' grades (Callahan, Rademacher, & Hildreth, 1998). Their success probably lies in the fact that the homeroom teacher functions very much like an elementary school teacher. This is significant because, despite cultural expectations to the contrary, a sixth-grader is developmentally a child, whether she is in an elementary school or a middle school. Consequently, it isn't surprising that a strategy that makes a middle school more like an elementary school—a school designed for children, not adolescents—is successful. In fact, some observers think that middle schools have failed to meet their goal of easing the transition to high school because they have simply duplicated high school organization and imposed it on students who are not developmentally ready, rather than providing them with a real transition.

One approach aimed at making middle schools truly transitional involves organizing students and teachers into teams. For example, in some schools, sixth, seventh, and eighth grades are physically separated in different wings of the school building. In such schools, each grade is a sort of school-within-a-school. Teachers in each grade-level team work together to balance the demands of different subject-area classes, assess problems of individual students, and devise parent involvement strategies. Preliminary research suggests that the team approach helps to minimize the negative effects of the middle school transition. As a result, it has become the recommended approach of the National Middle School Association in the United States (NMSA, 2004).

High School Regardless of the type of school they attended previously, the early days of high school set a general pattern of success or failure for teenagers that continues into their adult years. For example, teenagers who fail one or more courses in the first year of high school are far less likely than their peers to graduate (Neild & Balfanz, 2006; Roderick & Camburn, 1999). It appears that minority students have a particularly difficult time recovering from early failure.

However, some psychologists emphasize the positive aspects of transition to high school, claiming that participation in activities that are usually offered only in high school allows students opportunities to develop psychological attributes that can't be acquired elsewhere. To demonstrate the point, a number of research studies had high school students use pagers to signal researchers whenever they were experiencing high levels of intrinsic motivation along with intense mental effort (Larson, 2000). The results showed that students experienced both states in elective classes and during extracurricular activities far more often than in academic classes (Larson, 2000). In other words, a student engaged in an art project or sports practice is more likely to experience this particular combination of states than one who is in a history class. Consequently, educators may be able to ease the transition to high school for many students by offering a wide variety of elective and extracurricular activities and encouraging students to participate.

Learning Objective 11.15

What gender and ethnic differences in science and math achievement have been found by researchers?

Gender, Ethnicity, and Achievement in Science and Math

Girls seem to be at particular risk for achievement losses after the transition to high school. For example, eighth-grade boys outscore girls in science achievement, and the gap widens substantially by the time adolescents reach tenth grade (Burkham, Lee, & Smerdon, 1997). Moreover, research suggests that the gender gap is widest among the most intellectually talented students. Nevertheless, girls possess characteristics that educators can build upon to improve their achievement in science classes. For one thing, associating with same-sex peers who are interested in and perform well in science classes influences girls' achievement in this domain (Riegle-Crumb, Farkas, & Muller, 2006). Thus, offering girls the opportunity to participate in science clubs and *learning communities*, small groups of students who take courses together, may be an effective means of increasing their science achievement (Reid & Roberts, 2006). Furthermore, girls' choices in course-taking during middle school are more influenced by parental encouragement than are those of boys (Simpkins, Davis-Kean, & Eccles, 2006). Thus, parental involvement may be the key to enhancing middle-school girls' interest in science and motivating them to take more advanced science courses in high school.

Clearly, cultural attitudes also influence girls' science achievement. For example, girls' and their parents' perceptions of science as a suitable career for females strongly predict girls' success in science courses (Jacobs, Finken, Griffin, & Wright, 1998). Even girls who are very high achievers in high school science have less confidence in their ability to succeed in college science courses and are, thus, less likely to pursue science majors in college (Catsambis, 1995; Guzzetti & Williams, 1996).

The gender gap in mathematics achievement widens in high school as well, although sex differences are smaller today than they were in the 1960s (Hyde, Fennema, & Lamon, 1990). Research suggests that variations in boys' and girls' approaches to problem-solving may be responsible for sex differences in high school. Boys seem to be better at identifying effective strategies for solving the types of problems found on standardized math tests (Gallagher et al., 2000). However, developmentalists still don't know how boys acquire this advantage.

Family interactive style predicts academic achievement in high school. Adolescents whose parents display authoritative parenting are more likely than those with authoritarian or permissive parents to achieve academic success in high school.

Like their scientifically talented peers, mathematically gifted high school girls have considerably less confidence in their abilities than their male counterparts do, even though the girls typically get better grades (Guzzetti & Williams, 1996; Marsh & Yeung, 1998). Research demonstrates that it is girls' beliefs about their abilities that shape their interest in taking higher-level high school and college math courses (Simpkins, Davis-Kean, & Eccles, 2006). Consequently, even though girls get better grades in math than boys do, they are still less likely to take advanced courses such as calculus or to choose careers in math (Davenport et al., 1998). However, as we noted with regard to science, girls whose same-sex friends are interested in math have more confidence in their math ability and are more open to taking advanced coursework in mathematics. Studies have shown that enrolling mathematically talented middle-school girls in single-sex, math-focused extracurricular activities increases their interest in the subject and their math-related confidence (Reid & Roberts, 2006).

As striking as the gender differences in math are, they pale in comparison to ethnic variations (Davenport et al., 1998). For example, by the last year of high school, only a third of African American and Hispanic American students have completed 2 years of algebra. In contrast, slightly more than half of White students and two-thirds of Asian American students have taken 2 years of algebra. Further, Asian American high school students earn twice as many credits in advanced courses as White students, and three to four times as many as African American and Hispanic American students.

One reason for the ethnic differences is that Asian American and White students are more likely to enter ninth grade with the skills they need to take their first algebra class. More than half of African American and Hispanic American teens are required to take remedial courses before beginning algebra, compared to about one-third of Asian American and White students (Davenport et al., 1998). Observers point out that about the same proportion of high school students across all ethnicities expect to go to college. However, it appears that Asian American and White students are much more likely to enter high school prepared to pursue college-preparatory courses (Thompson & Joshua-Shearer, 2002). Many researchers conclude that rigorous transitional classes in eighth and ninth grade might enable greater numbers of African American and Hispanic American students to complete college-preparatory math classes in high school (Gamoran, Porter, Smithson, & White, 1997).

Evidence for this position is drawn from studies involving mathematically talented students. There are large ethnic differences in high school course choices among highly able students—those who score in the top 25% of standardized math achievement tests. One study found that 100% of Asian American and 88% of White high school students scoring at this level were enrolled in advanced mathematics courses. In contrast, only 40% of mathematically talented African American and Hispanic American students were enrolled in such classes (Education Trust, 1996). It may be that high school counselors more often encourage Asian American and White students to take advanced math classes (Davenport, 1992).

Dropping Out of High School

Learning Objective 11.16

What variables predict the likelihood of dropping out of high school?

Dropping out of high school, like academic success, results from a complex interaction of academic and social variables (Garnier, Stein, & Jacobs, 1997). The proportion of U.S. students who drop out has steadily declined over the past few decades. Almost 90% of high school students in the United States receive a diploma (FIFCFS, 2000). Hispanic Americans have the highest drop-out rate at 24%, compared with 12% for African Americans and 7% for Whites (NCES, 2006).

Despite ethnic differences in drop-out rates, social class is a better predictor of school completion than is ethnicity. Children growing up in low-income families are considerably more likely to drop out of high school than are those from more economically advantaged families. For instance, in 2004, the drop-out rate for students whose families were in the lowest income quartile in the United States was 18%, while that of students whose household income placed them in the top quartile was only 3% (NCES, 2006). Because minority teenagers in the United States are so much more likely to come from poor families they are also more likely to drop out of school (see No Easy Answers).

It is important to remember, however, that the majority of students across all ethnic and income groups stay in school. Those who don't, again regardless of group, share several risk factors. Longitudinal studies show that students who have a history of academic failure, a pattern of aggressive behavior, and poor decisions about risky behavior are most likely to drop out (Cairns & Cairns, 1994; Farmer et al., 2003; Garnier et al., 1997; Jimerson, 1999). With respect to risky behavior, decisions about sexual intercourse seem to be especially critical. For girls, giving birth and getting married are strongly linked to dropping out. Another risky behavior, adolescent drug use, is also a strong predictor of dropping out (Garnier et al., 1997). In fact, alcohol and drug use better predict a high school student's grades than do the student's grades in elementary or middle school. Consequently, decisions about such risky behaviors seem to be one factor that can cause a teen to deviate from a previously positive developmental pathway.

Peer influence may also be a factor in dropping out. Teens who quit school are likely to have friends who have dropped out or who are contemplating leaving school (Ellenbogen & Chamberland, 1997). Family variables are also linked to dropping out. For example, children whose families move a lot when they are in elementary or middle school are at increased risk for dropping out of high school (Worrell, 1997).

NO EASY ANSWERS

Reaching the High School Drop-Out

One of the greatest challenges facing educators is how to motivate teenagers who have dropped out of high school to return. To address the problem, educators have developed programs for teenagers who have left school. Most such programs seek to improve participants' self-esteem and to enhance their belief in their ability to fashion a productive future for themselves (Gonzales, Dumka, Deardorff, Carter, & McCray, 2004; Romi & Kohan, 2004). One recent educational innovation, the *charter school*, seems to be especially promising with regard to meeting the educational needs of drop-outs. These schools are funded either by states or by local school districts, based on the number of students they attract. Recent surveys of charter schools reveal that about 5% are aimed at drop-outs (Consoletti & Allen, 2007).

YouthBuild/Boston is a good example. Part of a national network of programs, YouthBuild/Boston offers low-income dropouts an opportunity to achieve three goals. First, students learn marketable construction-related job skills such as carpentry, safety management, and computer-aided drafting. Second, they work toward either a GED or a high school diploma. Third, students work on construction projects that help provide poor families in their neighborhoods with affordable housing.

The 18- to 24-year-olds who attend YouthBuild/Boston spend half their time in academic classes and the other half working at construction sites. Each student has an individualized academic plan, and about a third plan to go on to college. To address students' motivational needs, the program includes counseling, help with goal-setting, and leadership skill development. Students also get help with material needs such as child care and income assistance through a network of social service providers, to which they are referred by school counselors.

Programs such as YouthBuild/Boston attract large numbers of students and have good attendance rates (Massachusetts Department of Education, 2000). About 30% of enrollees eventually obtain a GED or a high school diploma. Yet a high proportion of these charter school students drop out. (YouthBuild/Boston, 2000). Presumably, the same factors that led these youths to drop out of school in the first place continue to be problematic. For this reason, charter schools are continuing to strive to modify their programs to foster higher retention and graduation rates.

Take a Stand

Decide which of these two statements you most agree with and think about how you would defend your position:

1. Since a large proportion of students drop out of them, charter schools for high school drop-outs appear to be a waste of taxpayers' money.
2. The public should support charter schools, because they may save money in the long run by preventing high school drop-outs from ending up on the welfare rolls.

One group of researchers has explored the possibility that, by taking into consideration several relevant factors, a general profile of high school students who are potential drop-outs can be identified. Their research has led to identification of the type of high school student who is likely to drop out: one who is quiet, disengaged, low-achieving, and poorly adjusted (Janosz, Le Blanc, Boulerice, & Tremblay, 2000). Many such students display a pattern of chronic class-cutting prior to dropping out (Fallis & Opotow, 2003). Thus, students who exhibit this pattern may be targeted for drop-out prevention programs.

Whatever its cause, dropping out of high school is associated with a number of long-term consequences. For instance, unemployment is higher among adults who dropped out of high school than among those who graduated, and drop-outs who do manage to find jobs earn lower wages than peers who graduate (Crystal, Shae, & Krishnaswami, 1992). Adults who dropped out of high school are also more likely to experience depression (Hagan, 1997). Furthermore, research suggests that staying in school may be an important protective factor for boys who have poor self-regulation skills. When boys who are poor self-regulators stay in school, they appear to be less likely than poor self-regulators who drop out to become involved in criminal activity in early adulthood (Henry et al., 1999).

Critical Thinking

1. What kind of mentoring programs would you propose for helping children transition to secondary school, increasing math and science achievement among girls and minorities, and preventing high school students from dropping out?

SUMMARY

Physical Changes

Learning Objective 11.1 How do the brains and other body systems of adolescents differ from those of younger children?

- The brain continues to develop in adolescence. There are two major brain growth spurts: the first between ages 13 and 15 and the second between ages 17 and 19. Puberty is accompanied by a rapid growth spurt in height and an increase in muscle mass and in fat. Boys add more muscle, and girls more fat.

Learning Objective 11.2 What are the major milestones of puberty?

- Puberty is triggered by a complex set of hormonal changes, beginning at about age 7 or 8. Very large increases in gonadotrophic hormones are central to the process. In girls, mature sexuality is achieved as early as 12 or 13. Sexual maturity is achieved later in boys, with the growth spurt occurring a year or more after the start of genital changes.

Learning Objective 11.3 What are the consequences of early, "on time," and late puberty for boys and girls?

- Variations in the rate of pubertal development have some psychological effects. In general, children whose physical development occurs markedly earlier or later than they expect or desire show more negative effects than do those whose development is "on time."

Adolescent Sexuality

Learning Objective 11.4 What are the patterns of adolescent sexual behavior in the United States?

- Sexual activity among teenagers has increased in recent decades in the United States. Roughly half of all U.S. teens have had sexual intercourse by the time they reach their last year of high school.

Learning Objective 11.5 Which teenaged girls are most likely to get pregnant?

- Long-term consequences for adolescent girls who bear children are generally negative, although a minority of such girls are able to overcome the disadvantages.

Learning Objective 11.6 What are some of the causes that have been proposed to explain homosexuality?

- Hormonal, genetic, and environmental factors have been proposed to explain homosexuality. The process of realizing one's sexual orientation is a gradual one that often isn't completed until early adulthood. Transgendered teens are those whose psychological gender differs from their biological sex. Gay, lesbian, bisexual, and transgendered adolescents must cope with peer rejection and parental anger; they have higher rates of depression and other emotional difficulties as a result.

Adolescent Health

Learning Objective 11.7 How does sensation-seeking affect risky behavior in adolescents?

- Adolescents have fewer acute illnesses than younger children but, because of their heightened level of sensation-seeking, more injuries. In general, they show higher rates of various kinds of risky behavior, including unprotected sex, drug use, and fast driving.

Learning Objective 11.8 What patterns of drug, alcohol, and tobacco use have been found among adolescents in the United States?

- Alcohol and drug use among U.S. teenagers, after declining for several decades, is now on the rise. Those most likely to use or abuse drugs are those who also show other forms of deviant or problem behavior, including poor school achievement.

Learning Objective 11.9 What are the characteristics and causes of eating disorders?

- Eating disorders such as bulimia nervosa and anorexia nervosa are more common among teenaged girls than among boys.

Learning Objective 11.10 Which adolescents are at greatest risk of depression and suicide?

- Depression and suicide are mental health problems that are common during adolescence. Both are more common among girls, although boys are more likely to succeed with a suicide attempt.

Changes in Thinking and Memory

Learning Objective 11.11 What are the characteristics of thought in Piaget's formal operational stage?

- Piaget proposed a fourth stage of cognitive development in adolescence. The formal operational stage is characterized by the ability to apply basic cognitive operations to ideas and possibilities, in addition to actual objects.

Learning Objective 11.12 What are some major research findings regarding the formal operational stage?

- Researchers have found clear evidence of such advanced forms of thinking in at least some adolescents. But formal operational thinking is not universal, nor is it consistently used by those who are able to do it.

Learning Objective 11.13 What kinds of advances in information processing capabilities occur during adolescence?

- Memory function improves in adolescence as teens become more proficient in metacognition, metamemory, and strategy use.

Schooling

Learning Objective 11.14 How do changes in students' goals contribute to the transition to secondary school?

- The transition to middle school may be accompanied by changes in children's goal orientation that result in declines in achievement and self-esteem. The high school transition offers many teens more opportunities to pursue special interests and extracurricular activities.

Learning Objective 11.15 What gender and ethnic differences in science and math achievement have been found by researchers?

- Female, African American, and Hispanic American high school students score lower on science and math achievement tests and choose to take courses in these disciplines less often than do White and Asian American males. Girls may view success in science and math as unacceptable for women. African American and Hispanic American students may not be getting the preparation they need in middle school for advanced high school math courses.

Learning Objective 11.16 What variables predict the likelihood of dropping out of high school?

- Those who succeed academically in high school are typically from authoritative families. Those who drop out are more likely to be from low-income families or to be doing poorly in school.

KEY TERMS

ability goals *(p. 325)*
adolescence *(p. 307)*
anorexia nervosa *(p. 321)*
bulimia nervosa *(p. 321)*
formal operational stage *(p. 324)*
hypothetico-deductive reasoning *(p. 324)*
imaginary audience *(p. 326)*
menarche *(p. 310)*
personal fable *(p. 325)*
pituitary gland *(p. 309)*
primary sex characteristics *(p. 310)*
puberty *(p. 309)*
secondary sex characteristics *(p. 310)*
secular trend *(p. 311)*
systematic problem-solving *(p. 324)*
task goals *(p. 328)*
transgendered *(p. 317)*

TEST YOURSELF

Physical Changes

11.1 Which of the following brain changes is typical during adolescence?

a. The brain stem becomes thicker.
b. The corpus callosum becomes thicker.
c. The hypothalamus becomes larger.
d. The amygdala shrinks.

11.2 During adolescence, the average percentage of body weight made up of fat

a. increases for girls and decreases for boys.
b. decreases for both boys and girls.
c. decreases for girls and increases for boys.
d. increases for both boys and girls.

11.3 Which of the following endocrine glands is most important in the regulation of the hormonal processes of puberty?

a. the ovaries

b. the testes

c. thyroid

d. pituitary gland

11.4 Of the following hormones, which one is responsible for the prenatal formation of genitalia and triggers development of primary and secondary sex characteristics in males?

a. estrogen

b. testosterone

c. thyroxine

d. gonadotrophic hormone

11.5 Which of the following events could be attributed to the secular trend?

a. Girls begin to date earlier than they did at the beginning of the 20th century.

b. More sexualized images are available in programming for television, films, and video games.

c. Cultural values lead people to prefer a thin, angular body type.

d. The age of menarche has declined.

11.6 Among boys, the peak of the growth spurt occurs

a. at approximately the same time viable sperm are produced.

b. after growth of a beard and lowering of the voice.

c. to signal that puberty has begun.

d. after growth of the genitals and of pubic hair.

Adolescent Sexuality

11.7 Which of the following statements about the sexual behavior of teens is true?

a. The proportion of sexually experienced teens decreases across grades 9 to 12.

b. Sexual experience is consistent across racial and ethnic groups.

c. Boys are more sexually active than girls.

d. Teens consistently use effective contraceptive methods.

11.8 Which of the following adolescents are most likely to be sexually active?

a. teens who are well-monitored by adults

b. teens who live in poor neighborhoods

c. girls who have their first date at a relatively late age

d. boys who do not use alcohol

11.9 Which of the following is most likely to describe a teenaged girl who is pregnant?

a. She is 15 to 17 years old.

b. She has left high school.

c. She is married.

d. She is White.

11.10 Which of the following is associated with reduced likelihood that a teenaged girl will become pregnant?

a. Her mother is opposed to contraception and refuses to discuss it with her.

b. She has a number of different sexual partners rather than one regular sexual partner.

c. Her mother was sexually active and pregnant at a young age.

d. She does well in school and desires to go to college.

11.11 According to the crisis intervention model for understanding and helping teens in crisis, a teenager who has given up hope or who is in denial about a problem is in the ____________ stage.

a. initial

b. escalation

c. redefinition

d. dysfunctional

11.12 The concordance rate for homosexuality in identical twins suggests that homosexuality

a. is fully determined by genes.

b. is still completely unexplainable.

c. has an environmental component.

d. is on the rise.

11.13 Which statement best describes the process through which most people identify with a homosexual orientation?

a. They know it as soon as the hormones of puberty begin to flow.

b. Most people realize it gradually across the adolescent and early adulthood years.

c. Peers inform them that they are probably gay or lesbian.

d. There is no consistent pattern.

11.14 Most transgendered teens

a. are attracted to the opposite sex.

b. were exposed to high levels of male sex hormones before birth.

c. are warmly accepted by their peers.

d. have been interested in cross-gender activities since early childhood.

Adolescent Health

11.15 A desire to experience increased levels of arousal, such as those that accompany fast driving or the "highs" associated with drugs, is called

a. an extracurricular activity.

b. socializing.

c. independence.

d. sensation-seeking.

11.16 Of the following influences on teenagers' decisions about smoking, which seems to have the least impact?

a. factual knowledge about health risks
b. peer influences
c. parental influence
d. family rules about substance use

11.17 Which of the following best characterizes the eating disorder bulimia nervosa?

a. disturbed body image, extreme dieting, and excessive weight loss
b. an aversive, phobic reaction to food that triggers vomiting
c. obsessive and excessive eating that results in a weight gain in excess of 25% of base body weight
d. intense concern about weight combined with cycles of binge eating and purging

11.18 Which of the following health conditions is *not* an effect of anorexia nervosa?

a. sleep disturbance
b. prolonged menstrual flow
c. obsessive exercising
d. cardiovascular problems

11.19 Which of the following has *not* been proposed as a possible cause for eating disorders?

a. fear of growing up
b. biological causes, such as a form of brain dysfunction
c. history of abuse or abandonment
d. mental illness

11.20 Which of the following is *not* an accurate statement about depression among adolescents?

a. At any given time, 5–8% of adolescents are experiencing an enduring depression.
b. Teenaged boys are twice as likely as girls to report having experienced depression.
c. Depression can hinder academic achievement because it interferes with memory.
d. Depression may contribute to suicide by adolescents.

Changes in Thinking and Memory

11.21 A teenager who can derive conclusions from hypothetical premises, such as what his mother might say if she finds out that he failed a French test, is engaged in

a. hypothetico-deductive reasoning.
b. information processing.
c. metacognition.
d. logico-conditional thinking.

11.22 A teenager who knows the risks of driving under the influence but still insists on doing it because she would never have an accident is engaging in

a. an imaginary audience.
b. a personal fable.
c. projection.
d. naïve idealism.

11.23 Which of the following is the best example of a child who has task goals for her athletic activities?

a. Mia hopes to become the best goalie in her high school soccer league.
b. Tovah wants to improve her personal best time in the 100-meter freestyle swimming event.
c. Sharinda works hard at free-throw practice because she wants to have the best free-throw percentage on her basketball team.
d. Robin hopes that her fitness training program will help her become the best tennis player her school has ever had.

Schooling

11.24 Which of the following systems seems to provide the best transition to high school for students?

a. 6-3-3 system
b. 5-3-4 system
c. 8-4 system
d. 6-2-4 system

11.25 Which of the following statements is true about the transition from elementary school to high school?

a. Teenagers who fail one or more courses in the first year of high school are far less likely than their peers to graduate.
b. Mentoring programs are unsuccessful in improving middle school students' grades.
c. The grade-level team approach is useful only in elementary school.
d. An emphasis on ability grouping in middle school is essential in assisting young teenagers in making the transition to high school.

11.26 Which of the following statements about gender, ethnicity, and achievement in science and math is true?

a. Gender differences in achievement in math are greater than ethnic differences.
b. Ethnic differences in achievement in math are greater than gender differences.
c. Girls excel in math but not science.
d. Intellectually talented girls are encouraged to take courses in sciences such as chemistry and physics rather than zoology or botany.

11.27 Which of the following factors has *not* been found to be related to dropping out of high school?

a. low socioeconomic status
b. having a peer group that does not value academic achievement
c. drug use
d. authoritarian parenting

PEARSON
mydevelopmentlab Study Plan

Are You Ready for the Test?

Students who use the study materials on MyDevelopmentLab report higher grades in the course than those who use the text alone. Here are three easy steps to mastering this chapter and improving your grade...

Step 1

Take the chapter pre-test in MyDevelopmentLab and review your customized Study Plan.

To increase the effectiveness of sex education programs in the schools, public health advocates recommend that the programs

- place more emphasis on the reproductive functions of pregnancy.
- tell students that they can choose "secondary virginity" and stop being sexually active.
- involve both parents and adolescents, rather than just the adolescents themselves.
- report to public health agencies any suspicions they have about teens who may have a STD.

Step 2

Use MyDevelopmentLab's Multimedia Library to help strengthen your knowledge of the chapter.

Watch: Secular Trend

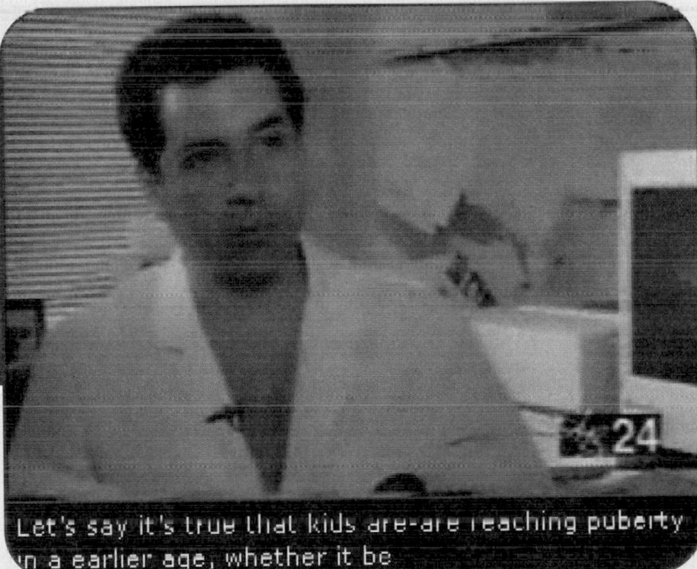

24
Let's say it's true that kids are-are reaching puberty
in a earlier age, whether it be

Learning Objective 11.2

What are the major milestones of puberty?

www.mydevelopmentlab.com

continued on the next page

84% of students responding to a national user survey believe MyDevelopmentLab helped them understand more of the material presented in class.

Watch: Sexuality in Adolescence: Pregnant Teen

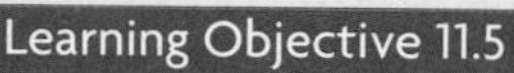

Learning Objective 11.5

Which teenaged girls are most likely to get pregnant?

I wouldn't – I wouldn't recommend this teen mom stuff just to anybody because it's-it's

Watch: Teen Drinking

Some parents think that a couple of drinks won't harm their kids. But often teens don't

Learning Objective 11.8

What patterns of drug, alcohol, and tobacco use have been found among adolescents in the United States?

Step 3

Take the chapter post-test and compare your results against the pre-test.

POST-TEST

The second brain growth spurt that occurs late in adolescence affects the

- parietal lobes, which improves processing of sensory inputs.
- cerebral cortex, which controls spatial perception and motor functions.
- corpus callosum, which improves the efficiency of memory processing.
- frontal lobes of the cerebral cortex, which control logic and planning.

www.mydevelopmentlab.com

Social and Personality Development in Adolescence

An expression of intense concentration appeared on 13-year-old Tanya's face as she stood before a mirror wrapping a brightly colored cloth around her head. She had learned the art of Gele headwrapping just a few hours earlier and wanted to demonstrate it for her mother and younger sister. Headwrapping was just one of many traditional African skills Tanya had learned in the rites of passage program she was attending at a local community college. The purpose of the program, one of hundreds like it across the United States, was to help Tanya and other African American teens develop a sense of ethnic heritage and to provide them with critical social support as they enter the teen years. Programs such as the one Tanya attends have arisen out of concern about the lack of formal rites of passage in Western society. How important are such rites?

In traditional cultures, rites of passage mark the transition of an individual from childhood to adulthood. For example, among the !Kung

In rites of passage programs, African American girls learn about the traditional styles of dress among African women.

people who inhabit the Kalahari desert in southern Africa, boys and girls are wed in arranged marriages in early childhood. However, these young couples are not allowed to live together until they reach puberty and are formally initiated into the adult community. These initiation rites require boys to learn hunting skills and, at 13, to kill an antelope. Girls must have had two menstrual periods before they are welcomed into the adult community. During each of these periods, they are sent to a menarcheal hut while the women of the group perform ritual dances to celebrate their coming of age.

Taking their cue from the pioneering work of psychoanalytic theorist Erik Erikson (1969), some developmentalists believe that the absence of formal rites of passage in industrialized societies makes adolescents more vulnerable to risky behaviors such as alcohol use, unprotected sex, and aggression. Teens who become involved in these activities, say some observers, are attempting to invent their own rites of passage. How adolescents accomplish this goal depends on the peer group with which they identify. For one teenager, the rite may involve preparing for a standardized test such as the PSAT that may win her a college scholarship. For another adolescent, it may involve joining a street gang.

Some developmentalists say that the fuzziness of the adolescent-to-adult transition in U.S. culture is more problematic for African American teens than for members of other minority groups who continue to practice the ancient rites of passage that are specific to their culture, such as the Jewish *bar mitzvah* and *bat mitzvah* and the Hispanic *quinceanera*. These rites help adolescents in these groups maintain a sense of pride in their cultural heritage that insulates them against the sometimes prejudicial attitudes of the dominant majority group. African Americans, argue some developmentalists, lost touch with these rites when the institution of slavery separated them from the traditions of their ancestors.

To fill the perceived need for a formal rite of passage for African American teenagers, many churches and other institutions have developed programs such as the one that Tanya attends. The goal of these programs is to enhance African American teens' sense of connection to the cultures from which their ancestors were taken through instruction in African history, values, and traditional practices such as Gele headwrapping. Research shows that passage programs help to promote resilience among African American teens that help them resist negative peer pressure and prevent them from internalizing negative stereotypes about their ethnic group (Harvey & Hill, 2004).

Consideration of rites of passage brings to mind Vygotsky's concept of scaffolding. Adolescents are conscious of the need to transition to adulthood, and they take many steps toward this goal on their own. But they need adults to lead the way and to support them when their steps toward maturity turn out to be missteps, whether that support occurs in the context of formal rites of passage or in more informal ways. This chapter begins with an examination of the aspects of the transition to adulthood that occur within adolescents themselves followed by a discussion of how the social world supports them.

Theories of Social and Personality Development

Thirteen-year-old Brendon took a deep breath to steady his nerves and punched in Melissa's cell phone number. He continued to breathe deeply as he waited for her to answer. Over the past few minutes, he had attempted to call her three times. However, the fear of rejection overcame him each time, and he punched the "hang-up" button before she could answer. This time he was determined to at least say "Hi."

Such dramas are played out every day in the world of young adolescents, and there is no denying the fact that the emergence of romantic interests is a prominent feature of this period of development. For Freud, these interests were the central theme of adolescence. Erikson and other theorists proposed models of adolescent development that were much broader in scope.

Psychoanalytic Perspectives

Learning Objective 12.1
What happens during Erikson's identity versus role confusion stage?

According to Freud, the post-pubertal years constitute the last stage of personality development; so both adolescents and adults are in what Freud called the *genital stage*, the period during which psychosexual maturity is reached. Freud believed that puberty awakens the sexual drive that has lain dormant during the latency stage. Thus, for Freud, the primary developmental task of adolescence is to channel the libido into a healthy sexual relationship.

Erikson, though not denying the importance of achieving sexual maturity, proposed that achievement of a sense of personal *identity* is a far more important developmental task faced by adolescents. He described *identity* as a sense of self-continuity (Erikson, 1969). More recent theorists, elaborating on his idea, define **identity** as an understanding of one's unique characteristics and how they are manifested across ages, situations, and social roles. Thus, in Erikson's model, the central crisis of adolescence is **identity versus role confusion**.

Erikson argued that the child's early sense of identity comes partly "unglued" in early adolescence because of the combination of rapid body growth and the sexual changes of puberty. Erikson claimed that during this period the adolescent's mind is in a kind of moratorium between childhood and adulthood. The old identity will no longer suffice; a new identity must be forged, one that will equip the young person for the myriad roles of adult life—occupational roles, sexual roles, religious roles, and others.

Confusion about all these role choices is inevitable and leads to a pivotal transition Erikson called the *identity crisis*. The **identity crisis** is a period during which an adolescent is troubled by his lack of an identity. Erikson believed that adolescents' tendency to identify with peer groups was a defense against the emotional turmoil engendered by the identity crisis. In a sense, he claimed, teens protect themselves against the unpleasant

identity an understanding of one's unique characteristics and how they have been, are, and will be manifested across ages, situations, and social roles

identity versus role confusion in Erikson's theory, the stage during which adolescents attain a sense of who they are

identity crisis Erikson's term for the psychological state of emotional turmoil that arises when an adolescent's sense of self becomes "unglued" so that a new, more mature sense of self can be achieved

emotions of the identity crisis by merging their individual identities with that of a group (Erikson, 1980a). The teenaged group thus forms a base of security from which the young person can move toward a unique solution of the identity crisis. Ultimately, however, each teenager must achieve an integrated view of himself, including his own pattern of beliefs, occupational goals, and relationships.

Learning Objective 12.2

How does Marcia explain identity development?

Marcia's Theory of Identity Achievement

Nearly all the current work on the formation of adolescent identity has been based on James Marcia's descriptions of *identity statuses*, which are rooted in Erikson's general conceptions of the adolescent identity process (Marcia, 1966, 1980). Following one of Erikson's ideas, Marcia argues that adolescent identity formation has two key parts: a crisis and a commitment. By a *crisis*, Marcia means a period of decision-making when old values and old choices are reexamined. This may occur as a sort of upheaval—the classic notion of a crisis—or it may occur gradually. The outcome of the reevaluation is a *commitment* to some specific role, value, goal, or ideology.

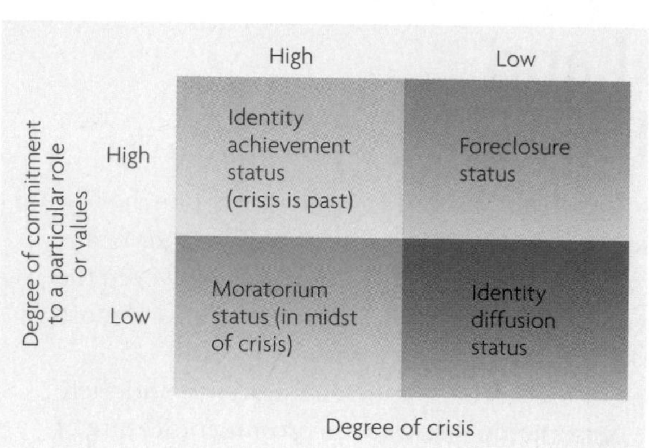

Figure 12.1
Marcia's Identity Statuses

The four identity statuses proposed by Marcia, based on Erikson's theory. For a fully achieved identity, the young person must have both examined her values or goals and reached a firm commitment.

(*Source:* Marcia, 1980.)

If you put these two elements together, as shown in Figure 12.1, you can see that four different *identity statuses* are possible.

- **Identity achievement:** The person has been through a crisis and has reached a commitment to ideological, occupational, or other goals.
- **Moratorium:** A crisis is in progress, but no commitment has yet been made.
- **Foreclosure:** The person has made a commitment without having gone through a crisis. No reassessment of old positions has been made. Instead, the young person has simply accepted a parentally or culturally defined commitment.
- **Identity diffusion:** The young person is not in the midst of a crisis (although there may have been one in the past) and has not made a commitment. Diffusion may thus represent either an early stage in the process (before a crisis) or a failure to reach a commitment after a crisis.

identity achievement in Marcia's theory, the identity status achieved by a person who has been through a crisis and reached a commitment to ideological or occupational goals

moratorium in Marcia's theory, the identity status of a person who is in a crisis but who has made no commitment

foreclosure in Marcia's theory, the identity status of a person who has made a commitment without having gone through a crisis; the person has simply accepted a parentally or culturally defined commitment

identity diffusion in Marcia's theory, the identity status of a person who is not in the midst of a crisis and who has made no commitment

The whole process of identity formation may occur later than Erikson and Marcia thought, perhaps because cognitive development is more strongly related to identity formation than either believed. Research suggests that teens who are most advanced in the development of logical thinking and other information-processing skills are also the most likely to have attained Marcia's status of identity achievement (Klaczynski, Fauth, & Swanger, 1998).

There is also evidence that the quest for personal identity continues throughout the lifespan, with alternating periods of instability and stability (Marcia, 2002). For example, a person's sense of being "young" or "old" and her integration of that idea into a sense of belonging to a particular generation appear to change several times over the course of the adolescent and adult years (Sato, Shimonska, Nakazato, & Kawaai, 1997). Consequently, adolescence may be only one period of identity formation among several.

Some research suggests that individuals who have attained Marcia's identity achievement status sometimes regress to other categories (Berzonsky, 2003). This may happen because the achievement status may not be the most adaptive one in every situation. For example, teenagers facing extreme stressors, such as life-threatening illnesses, seem to be most optimally adjusted when they adopt the status of foreclosure (Madan-Swain et al., 2000). Accept-

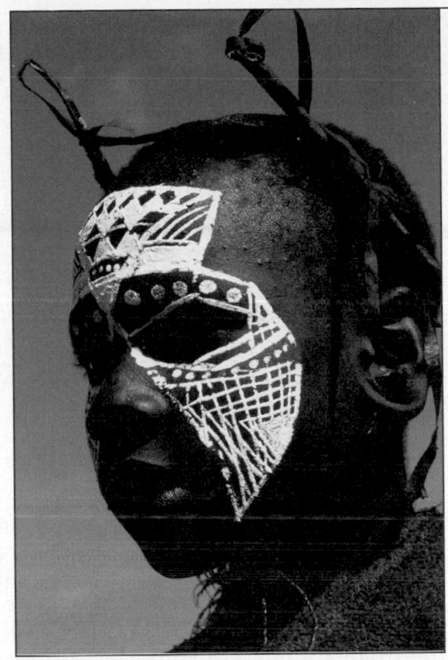

In the Jewish ceremony called bar mitzvah (for boys) or bat mitzvah (for girls), 13-year-olds read from the Torah in Hebrew and are admitted to full adult status in the congregation. The Tanzanian boy has had his face painted with white clay as part of an adolescent rite of passage.

ing others' goals for them, at least temporarily, seems to protect these teens against some of the negative emotional effects of the difficulties they must face. Thus, the idea that progression to identity achievement is the most psychologically healthy response to the identity crisis clearly doesn't apply to some adolescents.

As you might suspect, ideas about adolescent identity development and the kinds of experiences that drive it are firmly rooted in cultural assumptions. For example, in the United States, both parents and teenagers tend to believe that paid employment during adolescence helps adolescents sort out the career-selection aspects of identity development (Greenberger & Steinberg, 1986). Predictably, cross-cultural studies show that teens in the United States spend a great deal more time working than do their peers in other industrialized nations (Larson & Verma, 1999) (see the Research Report on page 345). Such cultural beliefs and the experiences that flow from them are likely to affect the process of identity development.

Clearly, too, the whole concept of an adolescent identity crisis has been strongly influenced by current cultural assumptions in Western societies, in which full adult status is postponed for almost a decade after puberty. In such cultures, young people do not normally or necessarily adopt the same roles or occupations as their parents. Indeed, they are encouraged to choose for themselves. These adolescents are faced with what may be a bewildering array of options, a pattern that might well foster the sort of identity crisis Erikson described. In less industrialized cultures, there may well be a shift in identity from that of child to that of adult, but without a crisis of any kind. Further, adolescents' search for identity in other cultures may be better supported by cultural initiation rites that clearly, at least in a symbolic sense, separate childhood from adulthood.

Critical Thinking

1. The implication in Marcia's formulation is that foreclosure is a less developmentally mature status—that one must go through a crisis in order to achieve a mature identity. Does this make sense to you? What is your current identity status? Has it changed much over the past few years?

Self-Concept

In Chapter 11, you read that thinking becomes more abstract in adolescence. Thus, you shouldn't be surprised to find that teenagers' self-concepts are a lot more complex than those of younger children.

Learning Objective 12.3

In what way does self-understanding in adolescence differ from that in childhood?

Self-Understanding

You should remember that, through the elementary school years, the child's self-concept becomes more focused on enduring internal characteristics—the psychological self. This trend continues in adolescence, with self-definition becoming more abstract. Advances in self-understanding among adolescents are both facilitated by and contribute to the increasing stability of the Big Five personality traits during this period. As a result, enduring traits such as shyness, or *introversion* in Big Five terminology, show up in adolescents' self-descriptions far more often than they do in those of younger children. This change was evident in the replies of a 9-year-old and an 11-year-old to the question "Who am I?" that you may recall from Chapter 10. Internal traits are even more pronounced in this 17-year-old's answer to the same question:

> I am a human being. I am a girl. I am an individual. I don't know who I am. I am a Pisces. I am a moody person. I am an indecisive person. I am an ambitious person. I am a very curious person. I am not an individual. I am a loner. I am an American (God help me). I am a Democrat. I am a liberal person. I am a radical. I am a conservative. I am a pseudoliberal. I am an atheist. I am not a classifiable person (i.e., I don't want to be). (Montemayor & Eisen, 1977, p. 318)

Clearly, this girl's self-concept is even less tied to her physical characteristics or even her abilities than are those of younger children. She is describing abstract traits or ideology.

You can see the change very graphically in Figure 12.2, which is based on the answers of all 262 participants in Montemayor and Eisen's study. Each of the answers to the "Who am I?" question was categorized as a reference either to physical properties ("I am tall," "I have blue eyes") or to ideology ("I am a Democrat," "I believe in God"). As you can see, appearance was a highly prominent dimension in the preteen and early teen years but became less dominant in late adolescence, a time when ideology and belief became more important. By late adolescence, most teenagers think of themselves in terms of enduring traits, beliefs, personal philosophy, and moral standards (Damon & Hart, 1988).

At the same time, the adolescent's self-concept becomes more differentiated, as she comes to see herself somewhat differently in each of several roles: as a student, with friends, with parents, and in romantic relationships (Harter & Monsour, 1992). Once these self-concepts are formed, they begin to influence adolescents' behavior. For example, teens whose academic self-concepts are strong take more difficult courses in high school than do teens who believe themselves to be less academically able. Further, they tend to select courses in disciplines in which they believe they have the greatest ability and to avoid courses in perceived areas of weakness (Marsh & Yeung, 1997).

Adolescents' academic self-concepts seem to come both from internal comparisons of their performance to a self-generated ideal and from external comparisons to peer performance (Bong, 1998). It also appears that perceived competency in one domain affects how a teenager feels about his ability in other areas. For example, if a high school student fails a math course, it is likely to affect his self-concept in other disciplines as well as in math. This suggests that teens' self-concepts are hierarchical in nature: Perceived competencies in various domains serve as building blocks for creating a global academic self-concept (Cheng, Xiaoyan, Dajun, 2006; Yeung, Chui, & Lau, 1999).

Social self-concepts also predict behavior. For example, a teenager's family self-concept reflects his beliefs about the likelihood of attaining and/or maintaining satisfactory rela-

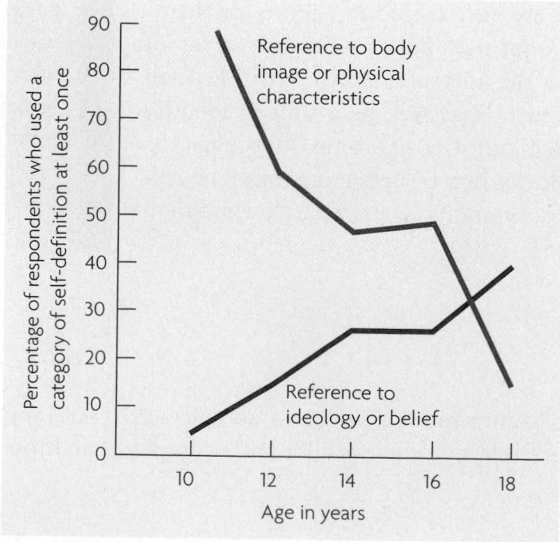

Figure 12.2
Changes in Teens' Self-Descriptions

As they get older, children and adolescents define themselves less and less by what they look like and more and more by what they believe or feel.

(*Source:* Montemayor & Eisen, 1977, from Table 1, p. 316.)

RESEARCH REPORT

The Effects of Teenaged Employment

In the United States, surveys of teenagers suggest that deciding on a career is one of the central themes of adolescent identity development (Mortimer, Zimmer-Gembeck, Holmes, & Shanahan, 2002). Moreover, many teens believe that engaging in part-time work during high school will help them with this aspect of identity achievement. Parents, too, often encourage their adolescent children to obtain part-time employment on the grounds that it "builds character" and teaches young people about "real life."

Are American teens and parents right about such beneficial effects of work? Research involving individuals who graduated from high school in the late 1980s and 1990s revealed that the more hours participants worked during high school, the more likely they were to use drugs (alcohol, cigarettes, marijuana, cocaine), to display aggression toward peers, to argue with parents, to get inadequate sleep, and to be dissatisfied with life. (Bachman & Schulenberg, 1993; Bachman, Safron, Sy, & Schulenberg, 2003). Moreover, as adults, individuals who worked while in high school were less likely than peers who did not work to go to college. Thus working may actually decrease teens' chances for successful careers during adulthood, precisely the opposite of what many adolescents and parents believe.

A quite different answer to the question of the impact of teenaged employment comes from studies that take into consideration the kind of work teenagers do, as well as how many hours they spend on the job (Mortimer & Finch, 1996; Mortimer, Finch, Dennehy, Lee, & Beebe, 1995; Mortimer & Harley, 2002). These findings indicate that unskilled work is much more likely to be associated with poor outcomes than is complex, skilled work. They also suggest that adolescents who have skill-based work experiences develop increased feelings of competence. In addition, those students who see themselves as gaining useful skills through their work also seem to develop confidence in their ability to achieve economic success in adulthood (Grabowski, Call, & Mortimer, 2001).

It is not clear how we should add up the results of these several studies. At the very least, this mixture of results should make parents think twice before encouraging teenagers to work. However, parents need to consider the quality of work a teen will do before assuming that a job will negatively affective his or her development.

Questions for Critical Analysis

1. Teen employment may be correlated with developmental outcomes because teens who work differ from those who do not in ways that are also related to such outcomes. What variables do you think might distinguish teens who choose to work from their peers who don't have jobs?
2. Are there developmental outcomes that have not been addressed by the research described in this discussion that you think might be positively affected by teen employment?

tionships with family members. Developmentalists have found that adolescents who are estranged from their families, such as runaways, perceive themselves to be less competent in the give-and-take of family relations than teens who are close to parents and siblings (Swaim & Bracken, 1997). Indeed, the perceived lack of competency in family relations appears to be distinct from other components of self-concept.

Girls and boys also appear to construct the various components of self-concept somewhat differently. For example, a study of teens' evaluations of their own writing abilities found that boys and girls rated themselves as equally capable writers (Pajares & Valiante, 1999). However, the girls scored higher on objective tests of writing ability. In addition, the girls were more likely to describe themselves as being better writers than their peers of both genders. The boys, by contrast, seemed to perceive few ability differences in their peers. In other words, the boys believed they were good writers, but they also thought that their classmates were as good as they were.

Such findings are predictable, given the information in the previous section about girls being influenced by both internal and external comparisons while boys attend more to internal, self-defined standards. The findings also raise interesting questions about the degree to which self-concept development is influenced by cultural ideas about sex roles. Perhaps girls pay more attention to their own and others' writing skills because they know that girls are supposed to be better at language skills than boys.

Self-Esteem

Learning Objective 12.4
How does self-esteem change across the teenage years?

Self-esteem shows some interesting shifts during the teenaged years. The overall trend is a steady rise in self-esteem through the years of adolescence. The average 19- or 20-year-old has a considerably more positive sense of her global self-worth than she did at age 8 or 11 (Diehl, Vicary, & Deike, 1997; Harter, 1990; Wigfield, Eccles, MacIver,

Reuman, & Midgley, 1991). However, the rise to higher self-esteem during adolescence is not continuous. At the beginning of adolescence, self-esteem very often drops rather abruptly. In one study, developmentalists followed a group of nearly 600 Hispanic American, African American, and white youngsters over the 2 years from sixth grade to junior high (Seidman, Allen, Aber, Mitchell, & Feinman, 1994). Researchers found a significant average drop in self-esteem over that period, a decline that occurred in each of the three ethnic groups.

To study the relationship of self-esteem to important developmental outcomes, such as school achievement, researchers often divide teens into four groups based on the stability of their self-esteem ratings across adolescence (Diehl et al., 1997; Zimmerman, Copeland, Shope, & Dielman, 1997). The largest group, about half in most studies, displays consistently high self-esteem throughout adolescence. The self-esteem of those in the second group steadily increases, and the self-esteem ratings of those in the third group are consistently low. Teens in the fourth group enjoy moderate to high self-esteem at the beginning of the period, but it declines steadily as adolescence progresses. One finding of concern is that girls outnumber boys in the third and fourth groups (Zimmerman et al., 1997). In addition, several studies have found that high self-esteem is correlated with positive developmental outcomes. For example, teens with high self-esteem are better able to resist peer pressure, get higher grades in school, and are less likely to be depressed (Repetto et al., 2004). You may also remember from Chapter 11 that such teens are less likely to become involved in substance abuse or early sexual intercourse.

Learning Objective 12.5

What are the gender role concepts of adolescents?

Gender Roles

Developmentalists use the term **gender role identity** to refer to gender-related aspects of the psychological self. In contrast to younger children, adolescents understand that gender roles are social conventions, so their attitudes toward them are more flexible (Katz & Ksansnak, 1994). Parental attitudes and parental behavior become increasingly important in shaping teens' ideas about gender and sex roles (Castellino, Lerner, Lerner, & von Eye, 1998; Ex & Janssens, 1998; Jackson & Tein, 1998; Raffaelli & Ontai, 2004). In addition, concepts that were largely separate earlier in development, such as beliefs about gender roles and sexuality, seem to become integrated into a conceptual framework that teens use to formulate ideas about the significance of gender in personal identity and social relationships (Mallet, Apostolidis, & Paty, 1997).

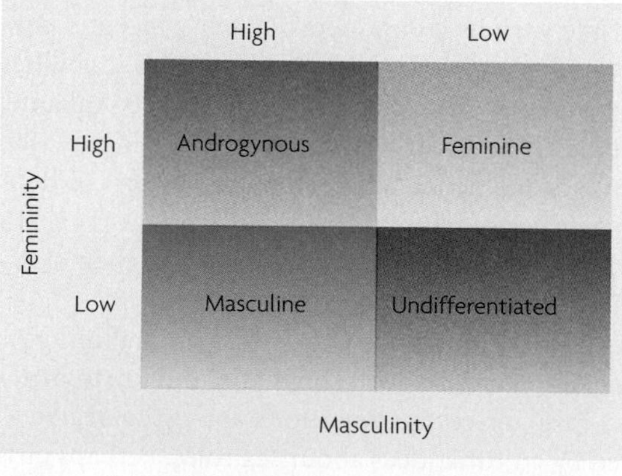

Figure 12.3 Bem's Gender Role Categories

This diagram illustrates how the dimensions of masculinity and femininity interact to produce four types of sex-role orientation.

In the early days of research on gender role identity, psychologists conceived of masculinity and femininity as polar opposites. A person could be masculine or feminine, but couldn't be both. However, theories first advanced in the 1970s by Sandra Bem and others have resulted in a large body of research in support of the notion that masculinity and femininity are separate dimensions and each may be found in varying quantities in the personalities of both men and women (Bem, 1974; Spence & Helmreich, 1978). A male or a female can be high or low on masculinity, femininity, or both. Indeed, if people are categorized as high or low on each of these two dimensions, based on their self-descriptions, four basic gender role types emerge: *masculine*, *feminine*, *androgynous*, and *undifferentiated* (see Figure 12.3).

The masculine and feminine types are the traditional categories; a person in either of these categories sees himself or herself as high in one and low in the other. A "masculine" teenager or adult, according to this view, is thus one who perceives himself (or herself) as having many traditional masculine qualities and few traditional feminine qualities. A feminine teenager or adult shows the reverse pattern. In contrast, androgynous individuals see themselves as having

gender role identity the gender-related aspects of the psychological self

both masculine and feminine traits; undifferentiated individuals describe themselves as lacking both.

Interestingly, research suggests that either an androgynous or a masculine gender role identity is associated with higher self-esteem among both boys and girls (Gurnáková & Kusá, 2004; Woo & Dei, 2006). This finding makes sense in light of the existence of a "masculine bias" in American and other Western societies, which causes both men and women to value traditionally masculine qualities such as independence and competitiveness more than many traditionally female qualities.

Teenaged boys like these may have an easier time achieving high self-esteem than girls of the same age, because both boys and girls seem to place a higher value on certain traditionally "masculine" qualities than on traditionally "feminine" qualities.

However, cross-cultural research suggests that adoption of an androgynous or masculine orientation by a girl can lead to lower self-esteem. For example, one study of Israeli girls found that pre-teens who were tomboys and who rated themselves high on masculine personality traits were less popular and had lower self-esteem than their more feminine peers (Lobel, Slone, & Winch, 1997). Consequently, when considering gender roles and gender role identity, it is important to remember that both are very strongly tied to culture. A particular society may value the masculine role more highly but also actively discourage girls from adopting it. Thus, it may not be universally true that teens who adopt the more highly valued gender role identity gain self-esteem.

Ethnic Identity

Learning Objective 12.6

How do minority, biracial, and immigrant teens develop a sense of ethnic identity?

Minority teenagers, especially those of color in a predominantly White culture, face the task of creating two identities in adolescence. Like other teens, they must develop a sense of individual identity that they believe sets them apart from others. In addition, they must develop an **ethnic identity** that includes self-identification as a member of their specific group, commitment to that group and its values and attitudes, and some attitudes (positive or negative) about the group to which they belong. Many minority families support children's ethnic identity development by providing them with specific teaching about how their group differs from the dominant one. Similarly, some families who speak a language different from that of the dominant group support children's ethnic identity development by teaching them the language of their home country. Researchers have found that minority teenagers whose families engage in such practices are likely to develop a strong sense of ethnic identity (Davey, Fish, Askew, & Robila, 2003; Phinney, Romero, Nava, & Huang, 2001).

Psychologist Jean Phinney has proposed that, in adolescence, the development of a complete ethnic identity moves through three stages (Phinney, 1990; Phinney & Rosenthal, 1992). The first stage is an *unexamined ethnic identity*. For some subgroups in U.S. society, such as African Americans and Native Americans, this unexamined identity typically includes the negative images and stereotypes common in the wider culture (see The Real World on page 349). Indeed, it may be especially at adolescence, with the advent of the cognitive ability to reflect and interpret, that the young person becomes keenly aware of how his own group is perceived by the majority.

Phinney's second stage is the *ethnic identity search*. This search is typically triggered by some experience that makes ethnicity relevant—perhaps an example of blatant prejudice or merely the widening experience of high school. At this point, the young person begins to compare his own ethnic group with others, to try to arrive at his own judgments.

This exploration stage is eventually followed by the *ethnic identity achievement* stage in which adolescents develop strategies for solving conflicts between the competing demands of the dominant culture and those of the ethnic group with which they identify. Most deal with such conflicts by creating two identities, one that they display when they are in the presence of members of the dominant group and another that they exhibit when they are with members of their own group.

ethnic identity a sense of belonging to an ethnic group

Young people of color often develop two identities: a psychological sense of self and an ethnic identity. Those who succeed at both tasks often think of themselves as "bicultural" and have an easier time relating to peers of the same and other ethnicities.

In both cross-sectional and longitudinal studies, Phinney has found that African American teens and young adults do indeed move through these steps or stages toward a clear ethnic identity. The "bicultural" orientation of the last stage has been found to be a consistent characteristic of adolescents and adults who have high self-esteem and enjoy good relations with members of both the dominant culture and their own ethnic group (Yamada & Singelis, 1999).

Biracial Adolescents Biracial adolescents experience a different pathway to ethnic identity, one that highlights the difference between the biological aspects of race and the psychosocial nature of ethnic identity. Studies showing that biracial siblings often develop different ethnic identities highlight this distinction. To explain these surprising findings, psychologist Maria Root, who has studied identity development in biracial teens for two decades, has proposed a theoretical model that includes four sets of factors that interact with a biracial adolescent's personality to shape the development of her ethnic identity.

Hazing and the emotional trauma that it engenders represent one factor. Often, Root says, biracial teens are challenged to prove their "authenticity" by the racial group of one parent. Such challenges force them to adopt new music and clothing preferences, change their speech patterns, and reject peers who represent their other parent's group. This kind of hazing, says Root, leads biracial teens to reject the group by whom they are hazed, even if, for the sake of social survival, they outwardly appear to have conformed to it.

Family and neighborhood variables constitute the second and third factors. If a biracial teen is abused or rejected by a parent, she tends to reject the ethnicity of that parent. Moreover, if a biracial adolescent grows up in a neighborhood in which the ethnic group of one of her parents is highly dominant, she is likely to adopt the ethnicity of that dominant group. The fourth factor that influences ethnic identity development in biracial teens is the presence of other salient identities. For example, for teens growing up in military families, the identity of "Army brat" or "Air Force brat" supersedes ethnic identity.

Immigrant Teens Adolescents in immigrant families often feel caught between the culture of their parents and that of their new homes. For example, cultures that emphasize the community rather than the individual view teens' acceptance of family responsibilities as a sign of maturity. A question such as whether a teen should get a job is decided in terms of family needs. If the family needs money, the adolescent might be encouraged to work. However, if the family needs the teenager to care for younger siblings while the parents work, then a part-time job is likely to be forbidden. By contrast, most American parents think that part-time jobs help teens mature and allow their children to work even if their doing so inconveniences the parents in some way. As a result, the immigrant teen feels that his parents are preventing him from fitting in with his American peers.

Research involving Asian American teenagers helps to illustrate this point. Psychologists have found that first-generation Asian American teens often feel guilty about responding to the individualistic pressures of North American culture. Their feelings of guilt appear to be based on their parents' cultural norms, which hold that the most mature adolescents are those who take a greater role in the family rather than trying to separate from it (Chen, 1999). Thus, for many Asian American adolescents, achievement of personal and ethnic identity involves balancing the individualistic demands of North American culture against the familial obligations

THE REAL WORLD

Role Models in Life and in the Media

Like many youngsters, Chérie idolizes professional athletes. Her current heroine is professional tennis star Serena Williams. Like her idol, Chérie is African American, and she is inspired not only by Williams's dynamic style of play, but also by the fact that Williams has become a star in what was once an all-White sport. Interestingly, Chérie's uncle is a professor of English literature at an ethnically diverse private college. He, too, has achieved success in a profession that was at one time closed to minorities. So, why does Chérie idolize Serena Williams and other professional athletes rather than her own uncle and others like him? This question has been examined by researchers who are concerned about the ways in which media portrayals of African Americans in various occupational roles influence children's career aspirations.

A good illustration of the complex nature of the influence of models comes from research examining African American children's ideas about which adults they consider to be their role models. Researchers conducted a survey in which 4,500 African American boys aged 10 to 18 were asked to name an important role model outside their own families (Assibey-Mensah, 1997). Investigators thought that these boys would name teachers as important role models because of their frequent interactions with them. However, a large majority of the boys named a professional athlete, and not a single boy named a teacher as an important personal role model (which is astounding when you think of the number of boys who participated in the study). These findings suggest that entertainment media are a more important source of role models for these youths than their real-life experiences with adults. Clearly, neither frequency of interaction with a model nor similarity between the observer and the model explain these findings. However, comparisons of portrayals of teachers to those of athletes in media may help explain why these boys responded as they did.

News reports about public education often characterize schools with large proportions of minority students as failures. The implication is that teachers in such schools are ineffective. Fictional teachers are often portrayed as inept, and many popular TV programs geared to young audiences (for example, "South Park" and "The Simpsons") depict teachers and other school officials as buffoons who are not respected by their students. In contrast, stories about both real and fictional athletes are dominated by themes of fame, wealth, popularity, and achievements such as league championships and record-breaking statistics. Considering the contrast between the two, it isn't surprising that African American boys prefer athletes as role models rather than teachers, even though they know many teachers and most likely have themselves no personal interactions with professional athletes.

Questions for Reflection

1. How might frequent interaction make it less likely that someone would be viewed by a child as a role model?
2. In your opinion, to what extent are the concerns highlighted by these researchers equally true for children of other ethnicities?

of their parents' cultures. Consequently, many teens in immigrant families develop a bicultural identity (Farver, Bradha, & Narang, 2002; Phinney, Horenczyk, Liebkind, & Vedder, 2001).

Moral Development

As you read in Chapter 10, theorists representing various orientations think differently about moral development. However, the theorist whose work has had the most powerful impact has been psychologist Lawrence Kohlberg (Bergman, 2002; Colby et al., 1983; Kohlberg, 1976, 1981). Moreover, theories of moral reasoning have been important in explanations of adolescent antisocial behavior.

Kohlberg's Theory of Moral Reasoning

Learning Objective 12.7

What are the features of moral reasoning at each of Kohlberg's stages?

You may recall from Chapter 10 that Piaget proposed two stages in the development of moral reasoning. Working from Piaget's basic assumptions, Kohlberg devised a way of measuring moral reasoning based on research participants' responses to moral dilemmas such as the following:

> In Europe, a woman was near death from a special kind of cancer. There was one drug that the doctors thought might save her. It was a form of radium that a druggist in the same town had recently discovered. The drug was expensive to make, but the druggist was charging ten times what the drug cost him to make. He paid $200 for the radium and charged $2000 for a small dose of the drug. The sick woman's husband, Heinz, went to everyone he knew to borrow the money, but he could only get together about $1000. . . . He told the druggist that his wife was dying, and asked him to sell it cheaper or let him pay later. But the druggist said, "No, I discovered the drug and I'm going to make money from it." So Heinz got desperate and broke into the man's store to steal the drug for his wife. (Kohlberg & Elfenbein, 1975, p. 621)

Table 12.1 Kohlberg's Stages of Moral Development

Level	Stages	Description
Level I: Preconventional	Stage 1: Punishment and Obedience Orientation	The child or teenager decides what is wrong on the basis of what is punished. Obedience is valued for its own sake, but the child obeys because the adults have superior power.
	Stage 2: Individualism, Instrumental Purpose, and Exchange	Children and teens follow rules when it is in their immediate interest. What is good is what brings pleasant results.
Level II: Conventional	Stage 3: Mutual Interpersonal Expectations, Relationships, and Interpersonal Conformity	Moral actions are those that live up to the expectations of the family or other significant group. "Being good" becomes important for its own sake.
	Stage 4: Social System and Conscience (Law and Order)	Moral actions are those so defined by larger social groups or the society as a whole. One should fulfill duties one has agreed to and uphold laws, except in extreme cases.
Level III: Postconventional	Stage 5: Social Contract or Utility and Individual Rights	This stage involves acting so as to achieve the "greatest good for the greatest number." The teenager or adult is aware that most values are relative and laws are changeable, although rules should be upheld in order to preserve the social order. Still, there are some basic absolute values, such as the importance of each person's life and liberty.
	Stage 6: Universal Ethical Principles	The small number of adults who reason at stage 6 develop and follow self-chosen ethical principles in determining what is right. These ethical principles are part of an articulated, integrated, carefully thought-out, and consistently followed system of values and principles.

(*Sources:* Kohlberg, 1976; Lickona, 1978.)

Kohlberg analyzed participants' answers to questions about such dilemmas (for example, "Should Heinz have stolen the drug? Why?") and concluded that there were three levels of moral development, each made up of two substages, as summarized in Table 12.1. It is important to understand that what determines the stage or level of a person's moral judgment is not any specific moral choice but the form of reasoning used to justify that choice. For example, either response to Kohlberg's dilemma—that Heinz should steal the drug or that he should not—could be justified with logic at any given stage.

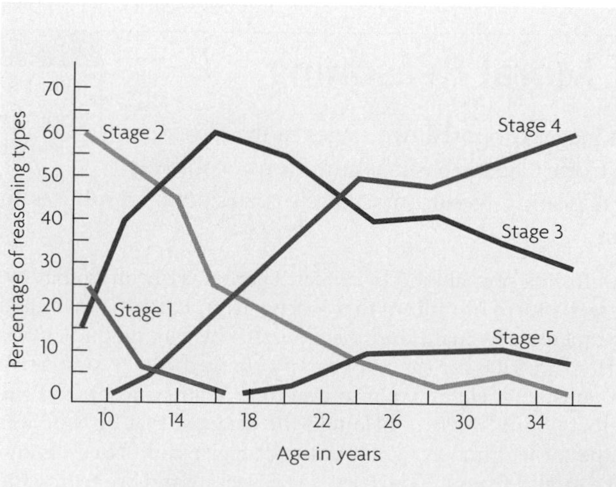

Figure 12.4 Colby and Kohlberg's Longitudinal Study of Moral Reasoning

These findings are from Colby and Kohlberg's long-term longitudinal study of a group of boys who were asked about Kohlberg's moral dilemmas every few years from age 10 through early adulthood. As they got older, the stage or level of their answers changed, with conventional reasoning appearing fairly widely at high school age. Postconventional, or principled, reasoning was not very common at any age.

(*Source*: Figure of "longitudinal study of moral judgement" by A. Colby et al, Figure 1, p. 46, © The Society for Research in Child Development. Reprinted by permission)

Age and Moral Reasoning

The stages are correlated somewhat loosely with age. Very few children reason beyond stage 1 or 2, and stage 2 and stage 3 reasoning are the types most commonly found among adolescents (Walker, de Vries, & Trevethan, 1987). Among adults, stages 3 and 4 are the most common (Gibson, 1990). Two research examples illustrate these overall age trends. The first, shown in Figure 12.4, comes from Kohlberg's own longitudinal study of 58 boys, first interviewed when they were

10 and then followed for more than 20 years (Colby et al., 1983). Figure 12.5 shows cross-sectional data from a study by Lawrence Walker and his colleagues (1987). They studied 10 boys and 10 girls at each of four ages, interviewing the parents of each child as well. The results of these two studies, although not identical, point to remarkably similar conclusions about the order of emergence of the various stages and about the approximate ages at which they predominate. In both studies, stage 2 reasoning dominates at around age 10, and stage 3 reasoning is most common at about age 16.

Preconventional Reasoning At level I, **preconventional morality**, the child's judgments are based on sources of authority who are close by and physically superior—usually the parents. Just as descriptions of others are largely external at this level, so the standards the child uses to judge rightness or wrongness are external rather than internal. In particular, it is the outcome or consequence of an action that determines the rightness or wrongness of the action.

In stage 1 of this level—*punishment and obedience orientation*—the child relies on the physical consequences of some action to decide whether it is right or wrong. If he is punished, the behavior was wrong; if he is not punished, it was right. He is obedient to adults because they are bigger and stronger.

In stage 2—*individualism, instrumental purpose, and exchange*—the child or adolescent operates on the principle that you should do things that are rewarded and avoid things that are punished. For this reason, the stage is sometimes called *naive hedonism*. If it feels good or brings pleasant results, it is good. Some beginning of concern for other people is apparent during this stage, but only if that concern can be expressed as something that benefits the child or teenager himself as well. So he can enter into agreements such as "If you help me, I'll help you."

To illustrate, here are some responses to variations of the Heinz dilemma, drawn from studies of children and teenagers in a number of different cultures, all of whom were at stage 2:

> He should steal the [drug] for his wife because if she dies he'll have to pay for the funeral, and that costs a lot. [Taiwan]
>
> [He should steal the drug because] he should protect the life of his wife so he doesn't have to stay alone in life. [Puerto Rico] (Snarey, 1985, p. 221)

preconventional morality in Kohlberg's theory, the level of moral reasoning in which judgments are based on authorities outside the self

Conventional Reasoning At the next major level, the level of **conventional morality**, rules or norms of a group to which the individual belongs become the basis of moral judgments, whether that group is the family, the peer group, a church, or the nation. What the chosen reference group defines as right or good is right or good in the individual's view. Again, very few children exhibit conventional thinking, but many adolescents are capable of this kind of moral reasoning.

conventional morality in Kohlberg's theory, the level of moral reasoning in which judgments are based on rules or norms of a group to which the person belongs

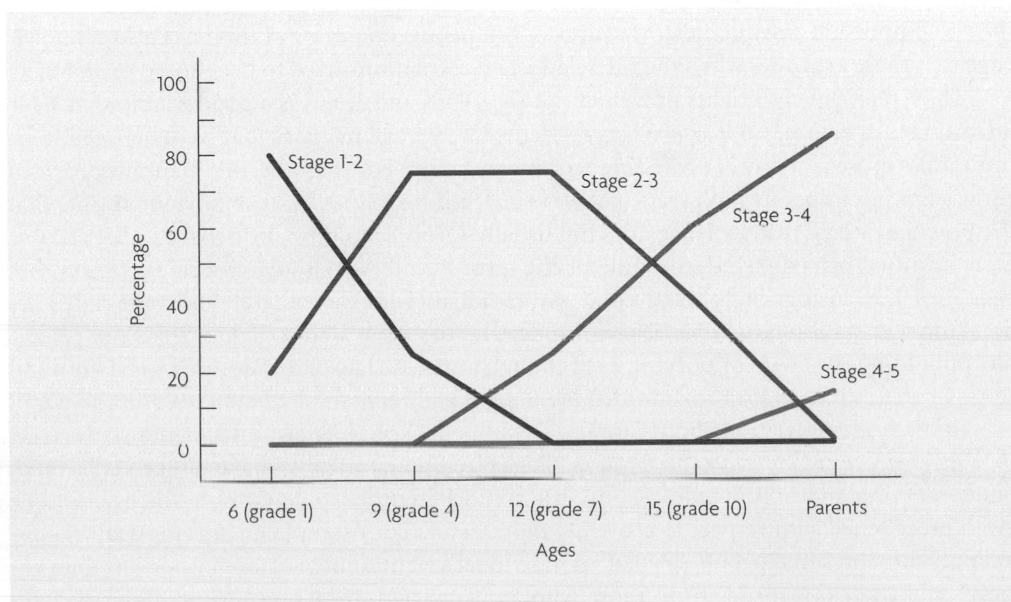

Figure 12.5 Percentages of Children and Parents Who Show Moral Reasoning at Each of Kohlberg's Stages

(*Source*: Walker et al., from Table 1, p. 849, "Moral stages and moral orientations in real-life and hypothetical dilemmas," Child Development, 60 [1987], 842–858. By permission of the Society for Research in Child Development.)

Civil disobedience involves intentionally breaking laws one believes to be immoral. For example, in the early years of the U.S. civil rights movement, African Americans broke laws that excluded them from certain sections of restaurants by "sitting in" at Whites-only lunch counters. Practitioners of civil disobedience do not try to evade the consequences of their actions, because they believe in upholding the law as a general principle even though they may view some specific laws as immoral. Thus, the thinking that underlies acts of civil disobedience represents Kohlberg's postconventional level of moral reasoning.

Stage 3 (the first stage of level II) is the stage of *mutual interpersonal expectations, relationships, and interpersonal conformity* (sometimes also called the *good boy/nice girl stage*). Regardless of age, individuals who reason at this stage believe that good behavior is what pleases other people. They value trust, loyalty, respect, gratitude, and maintenance of mutual relationships. Andy, a boy Kohlberg interviewed who was at stage 3, said:

> I try to do things for my parents, they've always done things for you. I try to do everything my mother says, I try to please her. Like she wants me to be a doctor and I want to, too, and she's helping me get up there. (Kohlberg, 1964, p. 401)

Another mark of this third stage is that the individual makes judgments based on intentions as well as on outward behavior. If someone "didn't mean to do it," the wrongdoing is seen as less serious than if the person did it "on purpose."

Stage 4, the second stage of the conventional morality level, incorporates the norms of a larger reference group into moral judgments. Kohlberg labeled this the stage of social system and conscience. It is also sometimes called the *law-and-order orientation*. People reasoning at this stage focus on doing their duty, respecting authority, following rules and laws. The emphasis is less on what is pleasing to particular people (as in stage 3) and more on adhering to a complex set of regulations. However, the regulations themselves are not questioned, and morality and legality are assumed to be equivalent. Therefore, for a person at stage 4, something that is legal is right, whereas something that is illegal is wrong. Consequently, changes in law can effect changes in the moral views of individuals who reason at stage 4.

Postconventional Reasoning The transition to level III, **postconventional morality**, is marked by several changes, the most important of which is a shift in the source of authority. Individuals who reason at level I see authority as totally outside of themselves; at level II, the judgments or rules of external authorities are internalized, but they are not questioned or analyzed; at level III, a new kind of personal authority emerges, in which an individual makes choices and judgments based on self-chosen principles or on principles that are assumed to transcend the needs and concerns of any individual or group. Postconventional thinkers represent only a minority of adults and an even smaller minority of adolescents.

In stage 5 at this level, which Kohlberg called the *social contract orientation*, such self-chosen principles begin to be evident. Rules, laws, and regulations are not seen as irrelevant; they are important ways of ensuring fairness. But people operating at this level also acknowledge that there are times when the rules, laws, and regulations need to be ignored or changed.

The American civil rights movement of the 1950s and 1960s is a good example of stage 5 reasoning in action. *Civil disobedience*—deliberately breaking laws that were believed to be immoral—arose as a way of protesting racial segregation. For example, in restaurants, African Americans intentionally took seats that were reserved for Whites. It is important to note that the practice of civil disobedience does not usually involve avoiding the penalties that accompany criminal behavior. Indeed, some of the most effective and poignant images from that period of U.S. history are photographs of individuals who surrendered and were jailed for breaking segregation laws. This behavior illustrates the stage 5 view that, as a general principle, upholding the law is important, even though a specific law that is deemed to be immoral can—or even should—be broken when breaking it will serve to promote the common good.

In his original writing about moral development, Kohlberg also included a sixth stage, *the universal ethical principles orientation*. Stage 6 reasoning involves balancing equally valid, but conflicting, moral principles against one another in order to determine which should be given precedence with respect to a specific moral issue. For example, in arguing against capital punishment, some people say that an individual's right to life is more important than society's right to exact justice from those who are convicted of heinous crimes. Such a claim

postconventional morality in Kohlberg's theory, the level of moral reasoning in which judgments are based on an integration of individual rights and the needs of society

might or might not be an example of stage 6 reasoning. Remember, the key to assessing an individual's stage of moral development is to fully probe the reasoning behind his or her answer to a question about a moral dilemma. Sometimes this kind of probing reveals that arguments that, on first glance, appear to represent stage 6 thinking are actually based on the authority of a religious tradition or a highly respected individual, in which case the reasoning is conventional rather than postconventional. Occasionally, though, the individual making such an argument is able to explain it in terms of a universal ethical principle that must always be adhered to regardless of any other considerations. In the case of opposition to the death penalty, the universal ethical principle would be the idea that the maintenance of human life is the highest of all moral principles. Note, however, that a person reasoning at stage 6 would not argue that society has no right to punish criminals. Instead, he or she would say that, in situations where upholding such rights involves termination of a human life, the right to life of the person whose life would be ended takes precedence.

Kohlberg argued that this sequence of reasoning is both universal and hierarchically organized. That is, each stage grows out of the preceding one. Kohlberg did not suggest that all individuals eventually progress through all six stages—or even that each stage is tied to specific ages. But he insisted that the order is invariant and universal. He also believed that the social environment determines how slowly or rapidly individuals move through the stages.

The evidence seems fairly strong that the stages follow one another in the sequence Kohlberg proposed. Long-term longitudinal studies of teenagers and young adults in the United States, Israel, and Turkey show that changes in participants' reasoning nearly always occur in the hypothesized order (Colby et al., 1983; Nisan & Kohlberg, 1982; Snarey et al., 1985; Walker, 1989). People do not skip stages, and movement down the sequence rather than up occurs only about 5–7% of the time.

Variations of Kohlberg's dilemmas have been used with children in a wide range of countries, including both Western and non-Western, industrialized and non-industrialized (Snarey, 1985). In every culture, researchers find higher stages of reasoning among older children, but cultures differ in the highest level of reasoning observed. In urban cultures (both Western and non-Western), stage 5 is typically the highest stage observed; in agricultural societies and those in which there is little opportunity for formal education, stage 4 is typically the highest. Collectively, this evidence seems to provide quite strong support for the universality of Kohlberg's stage sequence.

Causes and Consequences of Moral Development

Learning Objective 12.8

What are some important causes and effects in the development of moral reasoning?

The most obvious reason for the general correlations between Kohlberg's stages and chronological age is cognitive development. Specifically, it appears that children must have a firm grasp of concrete operational thinking before they can develop or use conventional moral reasoning. Likewise, formal operational thinking appears to be necessary for advancement to the postconventional level.

To be more specific, Kohlberg and many other theorists suggest that the decline of egocentrism that occurs as an individual moves through Piaget's concrete and formal operational stages is the cognitive-developmental variable that matters most in moral reasoning. The idea is that the greater a child's or adolescent's ability to look at a situation from another person's perspective, the more advanced she is likely to be in moral reasoning. Psychologists use the term **role-taking** to refer to this ability (Selman, 1980). Research has provided strong support for the hypothesized link between role-taking and moral development (Kuhn, Kohlberg, Languer, & Haan, 1977; Walker, 1980).

Nevertheless, cognitive development isn't enough. Kohlberg thought that the development of moral reasoning also required support from the social environment. Specifically, he claimed that in order to foster mature moral reasoning, a child's or teenager's social environment must provide him with opportunities for meaningful, reciprocal dialogue about moral issues.

role-taking the ability to look at a situation from another person's perspective

Longitudinal research relating parenting styles and family climate to levels of moral reasoning suggests that Kohlberg was right (Pratt, Arnold, & Pratt, 1999). Parents' ability to identify, understand, and respond to children's and adolescents' less mature forms of moral reasoning seems to be particularly important to the development of moral reasoning. This ability on the part of parents is important because people of all ages have difficulty understanding and remembering moral arguments that are more advanced than their own level (Narvaez, 1998). Thus, a parent who can express her own moral views in words that reflect her child's level of understanding is more likely to be able to influence the child's moral development.

As an individual's capacity for moral reasoning grows, so does her ability to think logically about issues in other domains. For example, the complexity of an individual's political reasoning is very similar to the complexity of her moral reasoning (Raaijmakers, Verbogt, & Vollebergh, 1998). Further, attitudes toward the acceptability of violence also vary with levels of moral reasoning. Individuals at lower levels are more tolerant of violence (Sotelo & Sangrador, 1999).

Perhaps most importantly, teenagers' level of moral reasoning appears to be positively correlated with prosocial behavior and negatively related to antisocial behavior (Schonert-Reichl, 1999). In other words, the highest levels of prosocial behavior are found among teens at the highest levels of moral reasoning (compared to their peers). Alternatively, the highest levels of antisocial behavior are found among adolescents at the lowest levels of moral reasoning.

Learning Objective 12.9

How has Kohlberg's theory been criticized?

Criticisms of Kohlberg's Theory

Criticisms of Kohlberg's theory have come from theorists representing different perspectives.

Culture and Moral Reasoning Cross-cultural research provides strong support for the universality of Kohlberg's stage sequence (Snarey, 1985, 1995). Nevertheless, cross-cultural researchers have argued that his approach is too narrow to be considered truly universal. These critics point out that there are many aspects of moral reasoning found in non-Western cultures that do not fit in well with Kohlberg's approach (Eckensberger & Zimba, 1997). The root of the problem, they say, is that Kohlberg's theory is strongly tied to the idea that justice is an overriding moral principle. To be sure, say critics, justice is an important moral concept throughout the world, and thus it isn't surprising that Kohlberg's stage sequence has been so strongly supported in cross-cultural research. However, these critics argue that the notion that justice supercedes all other moral considerations is what distinguishes Western from non-Western cultures. As these criticisms would predict, research has shown that the responses of individuals in non-Western cultures to Kohlberg's classic dilemmas often include ideas that are not found in his scoring system (Baek, 2002).

For example, in many cultures, respect for one's elders is an important moral principle that often overrides other concerns (Eckensberger & Zimba, 1997). Thus, if researchers alter the Heinz dilemma such that the sick woman is Heinz's mother rather than his wife, Western and non-Western research participants are likely to respond quite differently. Such differences are difficult to explain from the justice-based, stage-oriented perspective of Kohlberg's theory. Advocates for the theory have argued that respect for elders as the basis of moral reasoning represents Kohlberg's conventional level. Critics, by contrast, say that this classification underestimates the true moral reasoning level of individuals from non-Western cultures.

Moral Reasoning and Emotions Researchers studying the link between moral emotions and moral reasoning have also criticized the narrowness of Kohlberg's justice-based approach. Psychologist Nancy Eisenberg, for example, suggests that *empathy*, the ability to identify with others' emotions, is both a cause and a consequence of moral development (Eisenberg, 2000). Similarly, Eisenberg suggests that a complete explanation of moral development should include age-related and individual variations in the ability to regulate emotions (such as anger) that can motivate antisocial behavior.

Likewise, Carol Gilligan claims that an ethic based on caring for others and on maintaining social relationships may be as important to moral reasoning as are ideas about justice. Gilligan's theory argues that there are at least two distinct "moral orientations": justice and care (Gilligan, 1982; Gilligan & Wiggins, 1987). Each has its own central injunction—not to treat others unfairly (justice) and not to turn away from someone in need (caring). Research suggests that adolescents do exhibit a moral orientation based on care and that care-based reasoning about hypothetical moral dilemmas is related to reasoning about real-life dilemmas (Skoe et al., 1999). In response, Kohlberg acknowledged in his later writings that his theory deals specifically with development of reasoning about justice and does not claim to be a comprehensive account of moral development (Kohlberg, Levine, & Hewer, 1983). Thus, some developmentalists view Gilligan's ideas about moral development as an expansion of Kohlberg's theory rather than a rejection of it (Jorgensen, 2006).

Possible sex differences in moral reasoning are another focus of Gilligan's theory. According to Gilligan, boys and girls learn both justice and care orientations, but girls are more likely to operate from the care orientation whereas boys are more likely to operate from a justice orientation. Because of these differences, girls and boys tend to perceive moral dilemmas quite differently.

Given the emerging evidence on sex differences in styles of interaction and in friendship patterns, Gilligan's hypothesis makes some sense. Perhaps girls, focused more on intimacy in their relationships, judge moral dilemmas by different criteria. But, in fact, research on moral dilemmas has not consistently shown that boys are more likely to use justice reasoning or that girls more often use care reasoning. Several studies of adults do show such a pattern (e.g., Lyons, 1983; Wark & Krebs, 1996). However, studies of children and teenagers generally have not (Jadack, Hyde, Moore, & Keller, 1995; Smetana, Killen, & Turiel, 1991; Walker et al., 1987). Further, recent evidence suggests that such sex differences, if they exist, may be restricted to North American culture (Skoe et al., 1999).

Moral Reasoning and Behavior Finally, critics have questioned the degree to which moral reasoning predicts moral behavior (Krebs & Dexter, 2006). Researchers have found that moral reasoning and moral behavior are correlated, but the relationship is far from perfect. To explain inconsistencies between reasoning and behavior, learning theorists suggest that moral reasoning is situational rather than developmental. They point to a variety of studies to support this assertion.

First, neither adolescents nor adults reason at the same level in response to every hypothetical dilemma (Rique & Camino, 1997). An individual research participant might reason at the conventional level in response to one dilemma and at the postconventional level with respect to another. Second, the types of characters in moral dilemmas strongly influence research participants' responses to them, especially when the participants are adolescents. For example, hypothetical dilemmas involving celebrities as characters elicit much lower levels of moral reasoning from teenagers than those involving fictional characters such as Heinz (Einerson, 1998).

In addition, research participants show disparities in levels of moral reasoning invoked in response to hypothetical dilemmas and real-life moral issues. For example, Israeli Jewish, Israeli Bedouin, and Palestinian youths living in Israel demonstrate different levels of moral reasoning when responding to hypothetical stories such as the Heinz dilemma than they exhibit in discussing the moral dimensions of the long-standing conflicts among their ethnic groups (Elbedour, Baker, & Charlesworth, 1997). Thus, as learning theorists predict, it appears that situational factors may be more important variables for decisions about actual moral behavior than the level of moral reasoning exhibited in response to hypothetical dilemmas.

Moral Development and Antisocial Behavior

Learning Objective 12.10
What are the moral reasoning abilities and other characteristics of delinquents?

The consistent finding of low levels of moral reasoning among adolescents who engage in serious forms of antisocial behavior has been of particular interest to developmentalists (Aleixo & Norris, 2000; Ashkar & Kenny, 2007; Cheung, Chan, Lee, Liu, & Leung, 2001; Ma, 2003). Delinquency is distinguished from other forms

Adolescents who commit crimes are less advanced than their peers in moral reasoning because they lack the ability to look at situations from others' points of view.

of antisocial behavior, such as bullying, on the basis of actual law-breaking. Thus, the term **delinquency** applies specifically to adolescent behavior that violates the law. Serious forms of delinquency, such as rape and murder, have increased dramatically in the United States in recent years. Attempts to explain this phenomenon have resulted in research that has led to a more comprehensive understanding of youth violence.

Delinquents appear to be behind their peers in moral reasoning because of deficits in role-taking skills. For example, researchers have found that teenagers who can look at actions they are contemplating from their parents' perspective are less likely to engage in delinquent behavior than adolescents who cannot do so (Wyatt & Carlo, 2002). Most delinquent teens also seem to be unable to look at their crimes from their victims' perspectives or to assess hypothetical crimes from the victims' perspectives. Thus, programs aimed at helping delinquents develop more mature levels of moral reasoning usually focus on heightening their awareness of the victim's point of view. However, few such programs have been successful (Armstrong, 2003; Moody, 1997; Putnins, 1997). Consequently, psychologists believe that there is far more to delinquency than just a lack of role-taking and moral reasoning skills.

First, it appears that there are at least two important subvarieties of delinquents, distinguished by the age at which the delinquent behavior begins. Childhood-onset problems are more serious and are more likely to persist into adulthood. Adolescent-onset problems are typically milder and more transitory, apparently more a reflection of peer-group processes or a testing of the limits of authority than a deeply ingrained behavior problem.

The developmental pathway for early-onset delinquency seems to be directed by factors inside the child, such as temperament and personality. In early life, these children throw tantrums and defy parents; they may also develop insecure attachments (Greenberg, Speltz, & DeKlyen, 1993). Once the defiance appears, if the parents are not up to the task of controlling the child, the child's behavior worsens. He may begin to display overt aggression toward others, who then reject him, which aggravates the problem. The seriously aggressive child is pushed in the direction of other children with similar problems, who then become the child's only supportive peer group (Shaw, Kennan, & Vondra, 1994).

By adolescence, these youngsters may exhibit serious disturbances in thinking (Aleixo & Norris, 2000). Most have friends drawn almost exclusively from among other delinquent teens (Tremblay, Masse, Vitaro, & Dobkin, 1995). Of course, this situation is reinforced by frequent rejection by nondelinquent peers (Brendgen, Vitaro, & Bukowski, 1998). Many of these adolescents have parents with histories of antisocial behavior as well (Gainey, Catalano, Haggerty, & Hoppe, 1997). Early-onset delinquents are also highly likely to display a whole cluster of other problem behaviors, including drug and alcohol use, truancy or dropping out of school, and early and risky sexual behavior, including having multiple sexual partners (Dishion, French, & Patterson, 1995) (see No Easy Answers).

For young people whose delinquency appears first in adolescence, the pathway is different. They, too, have friends who are delinquents. However, associating with delinquent peers worsens their behavior, while the behavior of early-onset delinquents remains essentially the same, whether they have antisocial friends or are "loners" (Vitaro, Tremblay, Kerr, Pagani, & Bukowski, 1997). Moreover, the antisocial behavior patterns of adolescent-onset delinquents often change as their relationships change (Laird, Pettit, Dodge, & Bates, 1999). Consequently, peer influence seems to be the most important factor in the development of adolescent-onset delinquency.

Parenting style and other relationship variables seem to be additional factors in this type of antisocial behavior. Most of these teens have parents who do not monitor them sufficiently; their individual friendships are not very supportive or intimate; and they are drawn to a clique or crowd that includes some teens who are experimenting with drugs or mild law-breaking. After a period of months of hanging out with such a group of peers, previously

delinquency antisocial behavior that includes law-breaking

NO EASY ANSWERS

Preventing Youth Violence

Surveys showing that 20% of all violent crimes in the United States are committed by individuals under age 18 have increased public awareness of the growing problem of youth violence (National Center for Injury Prevention and Control [NCIPC], 2000). Public officials have turned to psychologists in the hopes of finding ways to reduce the incidence of youth violence. However, few programs designed to change aggressive and violent behavior in adolescents have been successful (Armstrong, 2003).

A number of psychologists have contributed to the development and evaluation of a promising program called the Fast Track Project, which involves several hundred aggressive elementary school children in four different U.S. cities (Conduct Problems Research Group, 2004). The children are divided into experimental and control groups. In special class sessions, children in the experimental group learn how to recognize others' emotions. They also learn strategies for controlling their own feelings, managing aggressive impulses, and resolving conflicts with peers.

Teachers in the program use a series of signals to help children maintain control. For example, a red card or a picture of a red traffic light might be used to indicate unacceptable behavior. A yellow card would mean something like "Calm down. You're about to lose control." Parenting classes and support groups help parents learn effective ways of teaching children acceptable behavior, rather than just punishing unacceptable behavior. In addition, parents are encouraged to maintain communication with their children's teachers. These strategies decrease the frequency of aggressive behavior among participants and enable them to manage their emotions more effectively and to get along better with their peers (Conduct Problems Research Group, 2004).

Clearly, such interventions require a considerable commitment of time and resources. Furthermore, they aren't effective for every child. However, they represent the best options developmentalists have to offer at this point. When balanced against the suffering of the half million or so victims of youth violence each year in the United States or against the personal consequences of violent behavior for the young perpetrators of these crimes, the costs don't seem quite so extreme.

Take a Stand

Decide which of these two statements you most agree with and think about how you would defend your position:

1. When adolescents behave aggressively, they should be referred to programs such as the Fast Track Project rather than punished.
2. Programs such as the Fast Track Project should not take the place of punishment; both punishment and emotional management skills are important in helping violent teenagers learn to behave less aggressively.

nondelinquent adolescents show some increase in risky or antisocial behaviors, such as increased drug-taking (Berndt & Keefe, 1995a; Dishion et al., 1995; Steinberg, Fletcher, & Darling, 1994). However, when parents do provide good monitoring and emotional support, their adolescent child is unlikely to get involved in delinquent acts or drug use even if she hangs around with a tough crowd or has a close friend who engages in such behavior (Brown & Huang, 1995; Mounts & Steinberg, 1995).

Critical Thinking

1. How might Kohlberg's views and those of his critics be integrated to explain variations in moral behavior among adolescents?

Social Relationships

Fifteen-year-old Sheronnah's mother told her long ago that she would not be able to go out on a date until she was 16. Recently, however, a boy at school has begun to pursue the girl, and she has spent untold hours debating the issue with her mother. However, the mother has refused to relent and, as a result, Sheronnah is giving her mother the "silent treatment." According to the progression in children's and adolescents' understanding of social conflicts that is described in Table 12.2 on page 358, Sheronnah is likely to expect that the division that has developed between her mother and herself over the dating issue is a temporary one. Nevertheless, Sheronnah's predicament illustrates the growing importance of peer relationships in adolescence, a trend that is shown in Figure 12.6 on page 358.

Relationships with Parents

Learning Objective 12.11
What are the features of adolescents' relationships with their parents?

Teenagers have two, apparently contradictory, tasks in their relationships with their parents: to establish autonomy from them and to maintain a sense of relatedness with them. As a result, the frequency of parent-child conflicts increases. This trend has been documented by a number of researchers (e.g., Flannery, Montemayor, & Eberly, 1994;

Age	Comments
5-Year-Olds	■ Go away from her and come back later when you're not fighting.
8-Year-Olds	■ Well, if you say something and don't really mean it, then you have to mean it when you take it back.
14-Year-Olds	■ Sometimes you got to get away for a while. Calm down a bit so you won't be so angry. Then get back and try to talk it out.
16-Year-Old	■ Well, you could talk it out, but it usually fades itself out. It usually takes care of itself. You don't have to explain everything. You do certain things and each of you knows what it means. But if not, then talk it out.

Table 12.2 Children's and Adolescents' Comments about How to Solve Disagreements Between Friends

(*Source:* Selman, 1980, pp. 107–113.)

Laursen, 1995; Steinberg, 1988). In the great majority of families, these conflicts center around everyday issues such as chores or personal rights—for example, whether the adolescent should be allowed to wear a bizarre hairstyle or whether and when the teen should be required to do chores. Teenagers and their parents also often disagree about the age at which certain privileges—such as dating—ought to be granted and about the amount of parental supervision teenagers need (Cunningham, Swanson, Spencer, & Dupree, 2003; Dekovic, Noom, & Meeus, 1997).

Individual traits of teenagers themselves may contribute to conflicts with parents. The adolescent's temperament, for example, contributes to the amount of conflict. Those who have been difficult from early childhood are the most likely to experience high degrees of conflict with parents in adolescence (Dekovic, 1999). Teens' pubertal status may be a factor as well. Among girls, conflict seems to rise after menarche (Holmbeck & Hill, 1991). Moreover, as noted earlier, cultural factors affect both the degree of parent-teen conflict and perceptions of its meaning.

Despite these conflicts, teenagers' underlying emotional attachment to their parents remains strong on average (see Figure 12.6). A study in the Netherlands suggests that the teenager's bond with her parents may weaken somewhat in the middle of adolescence (ages 15 and 16) and then return to former levels (van Wel, 1994). But virtually all the researchers who have explored this question find that a teenager's sense of well-being or happiness is

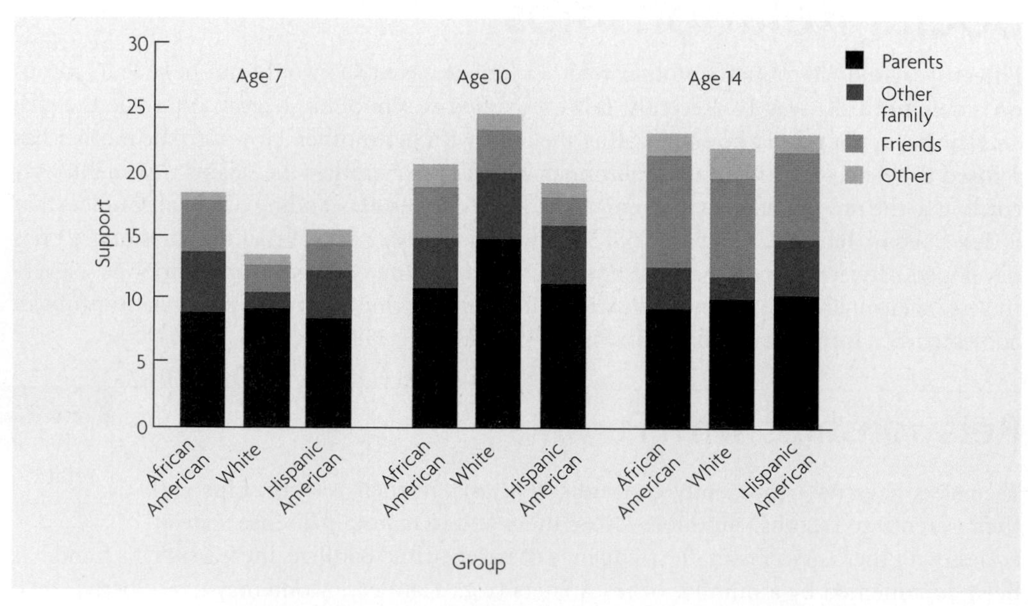

Figure 12.6
Sources of Support for Adolescents

Children and teens from different ethnic groups were asked about the amount and type of support they received from various sources. Note that for teens, friends become more significant sources of support, but parents do not become less important.

(*Source*: Adapted from Figure 2, p. 815, "Convoys of Social Support and Early Adolescence: Structure and Function" by M. Levitt, N. Guacci-Franco, and J. Levitt, from *Developmental Psychology*, 29. Copyright © 1993, by the American Psychological Association. Adapted with permission.)

more strongly correlated with the quality of her attachment to her parents than with the quality of her relationships with peers (e.g., Greenberg, Siegel, & Leitch, 1983; Raja, McGee, & Stanton, 1992). Moreover, research findings regarding the centrality of parent-teen relationships have been consistent across a variety of cultures (Claes, 1998; Okamoto & Uechi, 1999).

While it is true that the physical changes of puberty are often followed by an increase in the number of conflicts, it is a myth that conflict is the main feature of the parent-adolescent relationship.

Research in several countries has also found that teens who remain closely attached to their parents are the most likely to be academically successful and to enjoy good peer relations (Mayseless & Scharf, 2007; Turnage, 2004; Weimer, Kerns, & Oldenburg, 2004; Zimmermann, 2004). They are also less likely than less securely attached teens to engage in antisocial behavior (Ma, Shek, Cheung, & Oi Bun Lam, 2000). Further, the quality of attachment in early adolescence predicts drug use in later adolescence and early adulthood (Brook, Whiteman, Finch, & Cohen, 2000). Teens who are close to their parents are less likely to use drugs than peers whose bonds with parents are weaker. Thus, even while teenagers are becoming more autonomous, they need their parents to provide a psychological safe base.

Friendships

Learning Objective 12.12
What are the characteristics of adolescents' friendships?

Despite the importance of family relationships to adolescents, it is clear that peer relationships become far more significant in adolescence than they have been at any earlier period. For many, electronic communication devices that are available today serve as hubs around which their social networks revolve. Many teenagers have one group of friends with whom they communicate by phone, another with whom they exchange online instant messages and e-mail, and yet another with which they associate through online communities such as myspace.com (Foehr, 2006). As a result, teenagers have a wider range of acquaintances than their parents did in adolescence. However, they do not necessarily have more close friends.

Teens' friendships are increasingly intimate, in the sense that adolescent friends share more and more of their inner feelings and secrets and are more knowledgeable about each other's feelings. Loyalty and faithfulness become more valued characteristics of friendship. However, the ability to display intimacy, loyalty, and faithfulness in the context of a friendship doesn't come automatically with age. In fact, teens vary considerably in these interpersonal skills. The variation may be the result of individual differences in temperament and personality or of teens' experiences with family relationships (Updegraff & Obeidallah, 1999).

Adolescent friendships are also more stable than those of younger children (Bowker, 2004; Degirmencioglu, Urberg, & Tolson, 1998). In one longitudinal study, researchers found that only about 20% of friendships among fourth-graders lasted as long as a year, whereas about 40% of friendships formed by these same youngsters when they were tenth-graders were long-lasting (Cairns & Cairns, 1994). Friendship stability probably increases in adolescence because older teens work harder than younger teens and elementary school children at maintaining positive relationships with friends through negotiation of conflicts (Nagamine, 1999).

In addition, teens often choose friends who are committed to the same activities they are. For example, many teens, especially boys, report that peer companionship is their primary motive for playing computer and video games (Chou & Tsai, 2007; Colwell & Kato, 2005). Some studies suggest that shared video game-playing experiences promote the development of a masculine gender role among male teens (Sanford & Madill, 2006). Some developmentalists also argue that playing these games in group settings helps male adolescents learn to channel aggressive and competitive impulses into socially acceptable ways of expressing them (Jansz & Martens, 2005).

Finally, adolescents' reasons for ending friendships reflect the influence of individual differences in rate of development of social skills. For example, a change in identity status from a less mature to a more mature level often leads to acquisition of new friends (Akers, Jones, & Coyl, 1998). Likewise, girls seem to prefer friendships with other girls whose romantic status is the same as their own—that is, girls who have boyfriends prefer female friends who also have boyfriends. In fact, a girl who gets a boyfriend is likely to spend less time with female peers and to end long-standing friendships with girls who haven't yet acquired a romantic partner (Benenson & Benarroch, 1998; Zimmer-Gembeck, 1999). For boys, differences in athletic achievements can lead to the end of previously important friendships.

Learning Objective 12.13

How do peer groups change over the teen years?

Peer Groups

Like friendships, peer groups become relatively stable in adolescence (Degirmencioglu et al., 1998). Adolescents typically choose to associate with a group that shares their values, attitudes, behaviors, and identity status (Akers et al., 1998; Mackey & La Greca, 2007; Urberg, Degirmencioglu, & Tolson, 1998). If the discrepancy between their own ideas and those of their friends becomes too great, teens are more likely to switch to a more compatible group of friends than to be persuaded to adopt the first group's values or behaviors (Verkooijen, de Vries, & Nielsen, 2007). Furthermore, teenagers report that when explicit peer pressure is exerted, it is likely to be pressure toward positive activities, such as school involvement, and away from misconduct.

The structure of the peer group also changes over the years of adolescence. The classic, widely quoted early study is that of Dunphy (1963) on the formation, dissolution, and interaction of teenaged groups in a high school in Sydney, Australia, between 1958 and 1960. Dunphy identified two important subvarieties of groups. The first type, which he called a **clique**, is made up of four to six young people who appear to be strongly attached to one another. Cliques have strong cohesiveness and high levels of intimate sharing.

clique four to six young people who appear to be strongly attached to one another

crowd a combination of cliques, which includes both males and females

In the early years of adolescence, cliques are almost entirely same-sex groups—a holdover from the preadolescent pattern. Gradually, however, the cliques combine into larger sets that Dunphy called **crowds**, which include both males and females. Finally, the crowd breaks down again into mixed-gender cliques and then into loose associations of couples. In Dunphy's study, the period during which adolescents socialized in crowds was roughly between 13 and 15—the very years when they display the greatest conformity to peer pressure.

More recent researchers on adolescence have changed Dunphy's labels somewhat (Brown, 1990; Brown, Mory, & Kinney, 1994). They use the word *crowd* to refer to the *reputation-based group* with which a young person is identified, either by choice or by peer designation. In U.S. schools, these groups have labels such as "jocks," "brains," "nerds," "dweebs," "punks," "druggies," "toughs," "normals," "populars," "preppies," and "loners." Studies in American junior high and high schools make it clear that teenagers can readily identify each of the major crowds in their school and have quite stereotypical—even caricatured—descriptions of them (e.g., "The partyers goof off a lot more than the jocks do, but they don't come to school stoned like the burnouts do") (Brown et al., 1994, p. 133). Each of these descriptions serves as what Brown calls an *identity prototype*: Labeling others and oneself as belonging to one or more of these groups helps to create or reinforce the adolescent's own iden-

In the early teen years, same-sex peer groups predominate.

tity (Brown et al., 1994). Such labeling also helps the adolescent identify potential friends or foes.

Through the years of junior high and high school, the social system of crowds becomes increasingly differentiated, with more and more distinct groups. For example, in one midwestern school system, researchers found that junior high students labeled only two major crowds: one small high-status group, called "trendies" in this school, and the great mass of lower-status students, called "dweebs" (Kinney, 1993). A few years later, the same students named five distinct crowds: three with comparatively high social status and two low-status groups ("grits" and "punkers"). By late high school, these students identified seven or eight crowds, but the crowds now appeared to be less significant in the social organization of the peer group. These observations support other research that finds that mutual friendships and dating pairs are more central to social interactions in later adolescence than are cliques or crowds (Urberg, Degirmencioglu, Tolson, & Halliday-Scher, 1995).

Romantic Relationships

Learning Objective 12.14

How does interest in romantic relationships emerge among heterosexual and homosexual teens?

Heterosexual and homosexual teens follow somewhat different pathways. For both, the ups and downs that are associated with early romances are an important theme of development during adolescence.

Heterosexual Teens Most teens display a gradual progression from same-sex friendships to heterosexual relationships. The change happens gradually, but it seems to proceed at a somewhat more rapid pace in girls than in boys. At the beginning of adolescence, teens are still fairly rigid about their preferences for same-sex friends (Bukowski, Sippola, & Hoza, 1999). Over the next year or two, they become more open to opposite-sex friendships (Harton & Latane, 1997; Kuttler, LaGreca, & Prinstein, 1999). The skills they gain in relating to opposite-sex peers in such friendships and in mixed-gender groups prepare them for romantic relationships (Feiring, 1999). Thus, although adults often assume that sexual desires are the basis of emergent romantic relationships, it appears that social factors are just as important. In fact, research suggests that social competence in a variety of relationships—with parents, peers, and friends—predicts the ease with which teens move from exclusive same-sex relationships to opposite-sex friendships and romantic relationships (Theriault, 1998).

By 12 or 13, most adolescents have a basic conception of what it means to be "in love," and the sense of being in love is an important factor in adolescent dating patterns (Montgomery & Sorel, 1998). In other words, teenagers prefer to date those with whom they believe they are in love, and they view falling out of love as a reason for ending a dating relationship. In addition, for girls (but not for boys), romantic relationships are seen as a context for self-disclosure. Put another way, girls seem to want more psychological intimacy from these early relationships than their partners do (Feiring, 1999).

Early dating and early sexual activity are more common among the poor of every ethnic group and among those who experience relatively early puberty. Religious teachings and individual attitudes about the appropriate age for dating and sexual behavior also make a difference, as does family structure. Girls with parents who are divorced or remarried, for example, report earlier dating and higher levels of sexual experience than do girls from intact families, and those with a strong religious identity report later dating and lower levels of sexuality (Bingham, Miller, & Adams, 1990; Miller & Moore, 1990). But for every group, these are years of experimentation with romantic relationships.

Homosexual Teens Romantic relationships emerge somewhat differently in the lives of homosexual teens. Researchers have found that homosexual teenagers are more comfortable about revealing their sexual orientation to their parents and to their peers than was true in past cohorts (Floyd & Bakeman, 2006). Consequently, developmentalists have learned a great deal more about the development of a homosexual orientation in the past couple of decades.

One thing that researchers have learned is that homosexual teenagers become aware of same-sex attraction at around age 11 or 12, roughly the same age when their heterosexual peers begin to notice their attraction to the opposite sex (Rosario, Scrimshaw, & Hunter, 2004). In contrast to heterosexual teens, boys notice and act on same-sex attraction at somewhat earlier ages than girls do (Grov, Bimbi, Nanin, & Parsons, 2006). However, girls who ultimately commit to a homosexual orientation express more certainty about their sexual identity than boys do (Rosario, Scrimshaw, Hunter, & Braun, 2006).

There are many boys and girls, however, who experience some degree of attraction to both sexes prior to self-identifying as gay or lesbian. Thus, many homosexual teens go through a period of sexual discovery that begins with experimentation with heterosexual relationships. Shortly thereafter, these teenagers begin to experiment with same-sex relationships. By age 15 or so, most have classified themselves as primarily heterosexual or committed to a gay, lesbian, or bisexual orientation (Rosario, Scrimshaw, & Hunter, 2004). Many of those who are gay, lesbian, or bisexual participate in clubs and extracurricular activities that are designed to help sexual minority youth form social connections. In the company of these like-minded peers, gay, lesbian, and bisexual teens meet potential romantic partners and find important sources of social support (Rosario, Scrimshaw, & Hunter, 2004).

Critical Thinking

1. Think back to your own high school years and draw a diagram or map to describe the organization of crowds and cliques. Were those crowds or cliques more or less important in the last few years of high school than they had been earlier? In what ways did the formation of romantic relationships disrupt or reinforce crowds and cliques?

SUMMARY

Theories of Social and Personality Development

Learning Objective 12.1 What happens during Erikson's identity versus role confusion stage?

- According to Freud, adolescents are in the genital stage, a period during which sexual maturity is reached. Erikson viewed adolescence as a period when a person faces a crisis of identity versus role confusion, out of which the teenager must develop a sense of who he is and where he belongs in his culture.

Learning Objective 12.2 How does Marcia explain identity development?

- Building on Erikson's notion of an adolescent identity crisis, Marcia identified four identity statuses. Research suggests that the process of identity formation may take place somewhat later than either Erikson or Marcia believed.

Self-Concept

Learning Objective 12.3 In what way does self-understanding in adolescence differ from that in childhood?

- Self-definitions become increasingly abstract at adolescence, with more emphasis on enduring, internal qualities and ideology.

Learning Objective 12.4 How does self-esteem change across the teenage years?

- Self-esteem drops somewhat at the beginning of adolescence and then rises steadily throughout the teenaged years.

Learning Objective 12.5 What are the gender role concepts of adolescents?

- Teenagers also increasingly define themselves in terms that include both masculine and feminine traits. When high levels of both masculinity and femininity are present, the individual is described as androgynous. Androgyny is associated with higher self-esteem in both male and female adolescents.

Learning Objective 12.6 How do minority, biracial, and immigrant teens develop a sense of ethnic identity?

- Young people in clearly identifiable minority groups, biracial teens, and teens in immigrant families have the additional task in adolescence of forming an ethnic identity, a process that appears to have several steps analogous to those in Marcia's model of identity formation.

Moral Development

Learning Objective 12.7 What are the features of moral reasoning at each of Kohlberg's stages?

- Kohlberg proposed six stages of moral reasoning, organized into three levels. Preconventional moral reasoning includes reliance on external authority: What is punished is bad, and what feels good is good. Conventional morality is based on rules and norms provided by outside groups, such as the family, church, or society. Postconventional morality is based on self-chosen principles. Research evidence suggests that these levels and stages are loosely correlated with age, develop in a specified order, and appear in this same sequence in all cultures studied so far.

Learning Objective 12.8 What are some important causes and effects in the development of moral reasoning?

- The acquisition of cognitive role-taking skills is important to moral development, but the social environment is important as well. Specifically, to foster moral reasoning, adults must provide children with opportunities for discussion of moral issues. Moral reasoning and moral behavior are correlated, though the relationship is far from perfect.

Learning Objective 12.9 How has Kohlberg's theory been criticized?

- Kohlberg's theory has been criticized by theorists who place more emphasis on learning moral behavior and others who believe that moral reasoning may be based more on emotional factors than on ideas about justice and fairness.

Learning Objective 12.10 What are the moral reasoning abilities and other characteristics of delinquents?

- Delinquent teens are usually found to be far behind their peers in both role-taking and moral reasoning. However, other factors, such as parenting style, may be equally important in delinquency.

Social Relationships

Learning Objective 12.11 What are the features of adolescents' relationships with their parents?

- Adolescent-parent interactions typically become somewhat more conflicted in early adolescence, an effect possibly linked to the physical changes of puberty. Strong attachments to parents remain so and are predictive of good peer relations. Authoritative parenting continues to be the optimal style to use with adolescents.

Learning Objective 12.12 What are the characteristics of adolescents' friendships?

- Susceptibility to peer-group pressure appears to be at its peak at about age 13 or 14.

Learning Objective 12.13 How do peer groups change over the teen years?

- Reputation-based groups, or *crowds*, as well as smaller groups, called *cliques*, are important parts of adolescent social relationships.

Learning Objective 12.14 How does interest in romantic relationships emerge among heterosexual and homosexual teens?

- Heterosexual teens gradually move from same-sex peer groups to heterosexual couples. The feeling of being "in love" is important to the formation of couple relationships. Many homosexual teens experiment with heterosexual and homosexual relationships before committing to a gay, lesbian, or bisexual orientation in mid-adolescence.

KEY TERMS

clique *(p. 360)*
conventional morality *(p. 351)*
crowd *(p. 360)*
delinquency *(p. 356)*
ethnic identity *(p. 347)*
foreclosure *(p. 342)*
gender role identity *(p. 346)*
identity *(p. 341)*
identity achievement *(p. 342)*
identity crisis *(p. 341)*
identity diffusion *(p. 342)*
identity versus role confusion *(p. 341)*
moratorium *(p. 342)*
postconventional morality *(p. 352)*
preconventional morality *(p. 351)*
role taking *(p. 353)*

TEST YOURSELF

Theories of Social and Personality Development

12.1 According to Freud, what is the stage during which psychosexual maturity is reached?

a. anal
b. phallic
c. latency
d. genital

12.2 What is the pivotal transition of adolescence, according to Erikson?

a. the development of a libido
b. the development of sexual fixations
c. an identity crisis
d. commitment to ideological, occupational, or personal goals

12.3 According to James Marcia, adolescent identity formation has two parts, __________ and __________.

a. puberty; sexual maturation
b. intimacy; industry
c. crisis; commitment
d. autonomy; conformity

12.4 Bob has thought about numerous career options. He has had internships in some of the fields he was considering. After all his exploration, he decides to commit himself to a career in sales. James Marcia would describe Bob's status as

a. identity achievement.
b. moratorium.
c. foreclosure.
d. identity diffusion.

Self-Concept

12.5 When asked "Who are you?", which of the following individuals would be most likely to say "I am a liberal Democrat who opposes the death penalty"?
a. Chris, age 9
b. Pat, age 12
c. Lou, age 15
d. Hillary, age 18

12.6 Which of the following is an accurate statement about self-esteem during adolescence?
a. Across the teenaged years, girls consistently have higher self-esteem than boys.
b. Most teens have high self-esteem at the beginning of adolescence but experience a steady decline in self-esteem during the teenaged years.
c. Self-esteem typically drops at the beginning of adolescence, but then rises throughout the teenaged years.
d. Cross-cultural research shows that in all societies, girls who adopt masculine or androgynous characteristics are more popular and have higher self-esteem.

12.7 According to conceptualizations of gender role identity, an individual who has developed high dimensions of masculinity and high dimensions of femininity would be described as having a/an __________ sex-role orientation.
a. androgynous
b. ambivalent
c. undifferentiated
d. transgender

12.8 Which of the following is *not* an aspect of the development of an ethnic identity, as identified by Jean Phinney?
a. an unexamined ethnic identity
b. an ethnic identity search
c. an ethnic identity rejection
d. achievement of an ethnic identity

Moral Development

12.9 Which of the following is *not* a level in the stages of moral development proposed by Lawrence Kohlberg?
a. preconventional morality
b. formal operational morality
c. conventional morality
d. postconventional morality

12.10 The civil disobedience carried out by the American civil rights movement in the 1950s and 1960s is an example of which stage of moral reasoning?
a. naïve hedonism
b. interpersonal conformity
c. social contract orientation
d. universal ethical principles

12.11 Kohlberg would say that persons who assume personal responsibility for their actions based on fundamental universal principles, such as justice and basic respect for all people, are using __________ as the basis for their moral reasoning.
a. interpersonal conformity
b. social contract
c. instrumental purpose and exchange
d. universal ethical principles

12.12 Which of the following is least important in the development of moral reasoning?
a. increased ability to see the perspective of others
b. a social environment that provides opportunities for meaningful, reciprocal dialogue about moral issues
c. parents' ability to express moral views in words that reflect a child's level of understanding
d. a foreclosure identity

12.13 Which of the following statements best describes the relationship between moral reasoning and moral behavior?
a. There is no correlation.
b. There is a perfect negative correlation.
c. There is a perfect positive correlation.
d. They are correlated, but the relationship is far from perfect.

12.14 According to Gilligan, the two distinct moral orientations involved in moral reasoning are
a. justice and empathy.
b. justice and care.
c. honesty and sincerity.
d. right and wrong.

12.15 According to researchers, what are the two forms of delinquency among adolescents?
a. vandalism and law-breaking
b. male peer-directed and female peer-directed
c. childhood-onset and adolescent-onset
d. internal and external

12.16 Which of the following is *not* a factor in the developmental pathway for childhood-onset delinquency?
a. child-specific influences, such as personality and temperament
b. parents' lack of ability to control the child
c. rejection by nonaggressive peers and gravitation toward peers with similar behavior
d. peer influence

12.17 The Fast Track Project with aggressive elementary school children has resulted in all of the following except
a. better recognition of emotions.
b. lower ratings of aggressiveness.
c. better academic performance.
d. more competence in social relationships.

Social Relationships

12.18 Which of the following is *not* an accurate statement about the role and influence of parents during adolescence?

a. If teens are to successfully achieve autonomy, parents must be eliminated as the teens' primary source of emotional and psychological support.

b. Researchers have found that teens' sense of well-being or happiness is more strongly correlated with the quality of attachment to parents than with the quality of relationships with peers.

c. Teens who remain closely attached to their parents are more likely to be academically successful and less likely to engage in antisocial behavior.

d. Lack of parental involvement in school and extracurricular activities is associated with conduct or behavior problems on the part of teens.

12.19 A teenager's sense of well-being is most positively correlated with

a. the quality of her relationships with peers.

b. the quality of her attachment to her parents.

c. her academic success.

d. the quality of her relationships with siblings.

12.20 Among adolescents, membership in a/an _______ means identification with a reputation-based group of peers with a label such as "jocks," "brains," or "toughs."

a. clique

b. crowd

c. prototypical identity

d. achievement identity

12.21 Which of the following does *not* predict the ease with which heterosexual teens move from same-sex friendships to romantic relationships?

a. social competence with parents

b. sexual desires

c. skills in friendships with the opposite sex

d. whether the teen has opposite-sex siblings

12.22 Jeri is a 12-year-old girl who is sexually attracted to both males and females. Which of the following statements best corresponds to what research would predict about the development of romantic relationships in Jeri's life?

a. Her romantic relationships will be influenced by the fact that attraction to others of the same sex and self-identification as a homosexual occur simultaneously.

b. Jeri will probably experiment with both heterosexual and homosexual relationships before committing to a sexual orientation.

c. She is more likely to hide her attraction to same-sex peers than teenagers in earlier cohorts did.

d. Jerry will avoid associating with gay and lesbian teens, because they might try to persuade her to commit to a homosexual orientation.

PEARSON

mydevelopmentlab Study Plan

Are You Ready for the Test?

Students who use the study materials on MyDevelopmentLab report higher grades in the course than those who use the text alone. Here are three easy steps to mastering this chapter and improving your grade…

Step 1

Take the chapter pre-test in MyDevelopmentLab and review your customized Study Plan.

One of the ways in which friendships change from childhood to adolescence is that friendships

- in adolescence are more temporary and fleeting.
- become more stable and long-lasting in adolescence.
- in childhood are more loyal and intimate.
- in adolescence emphasize complementarity, not similarity.

Step 2

Use MyDevelopmentLab's Multimedia Library to help strengthen your knowledge of the chapter.

Learning Objective 12.2

How does Marcia explain identity development?

Simulate: Identity Status

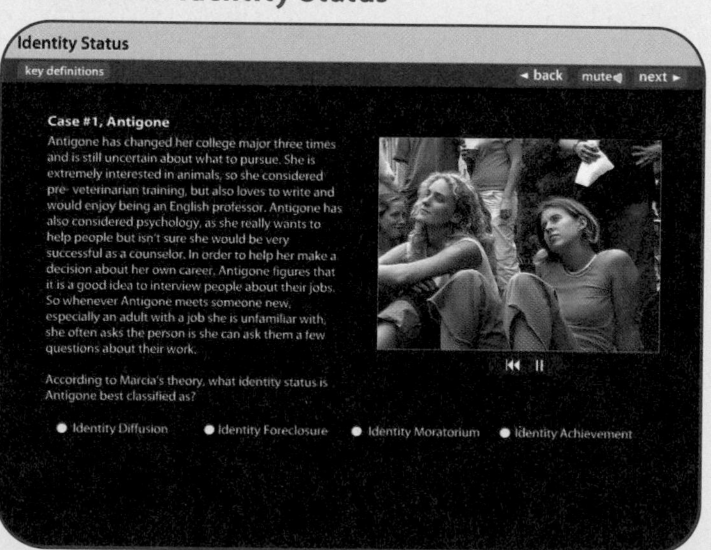

Identity Status
key definitions
◂ back
mute
next ▸
Case #1, Antigone
Antigone has changed her college major three times and is still uncertain about what to pursue. She is extremely interested in animals, so she considered pre- veterinarian training, but also loves to write and would enjoy being an English professor. Antigone has also considered psychology, as she really wants to help people but isn't sure she would be very successful as a counselor. In order to help her make a decision about her own career, Antigone figures that it is a good idea to interview people about their jobs. So whenever Antigone meets someone new, especially an adult with a job she is unfamiliar with, she often asks the person is she can ask them a few questions about their work.
According to Marcia's theory, what identity status is Antigone best classified as?
Identity Diffusion
Identity Foreclosure
Identity Moratorium
Identity Achievement

Did you know? MyDevelopmentLab comes with access to Research Navigator, which helps you with every step in the research paper writing process, from gathering sources to final paper formatting.

Watch: Adolescence: Identity and Role Development and Ethnicity

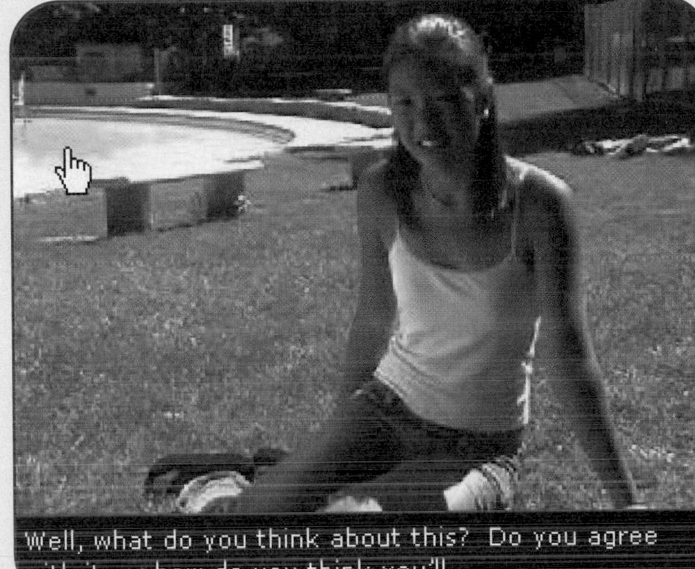

Well, what do you think about this? Do you agree with it, or how do you think you'll

Learning Objective 12.6

How do minority, biracial, and immigrant teens develop a sense of ethnic identity?

Watch: Lipstick: Emily's Story of Coming Out

Why wouldn't I be? She's a friend.

Learning Objective 12.14

How does interest in romantic relationships emerge among heterosexual and homosexual teens?

Step 3

Take the chapter post-test and compare your results against the pre-test.

Eileen has several people in her family who are teachers, so she is going to be a teacher also. She never really thought about doing anything else, so she is in Marcia's identify status of

- identify diffusion.
- foreclosure.
- moratorium.
- identity achievement.

Should Video Games Be Regulated by the Government?

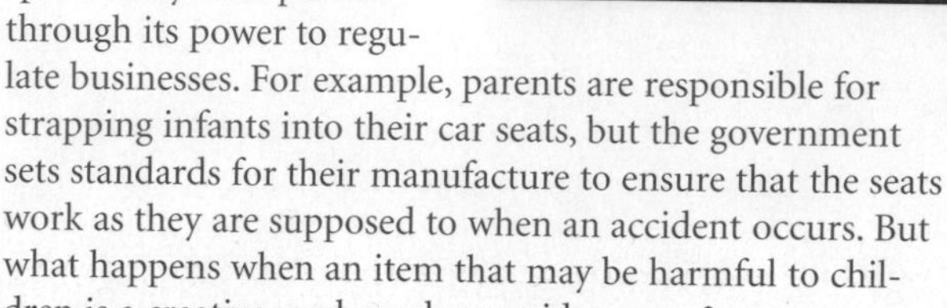

Most people agree that children and adolescents should be protected from potentially harmful experiences. Disagreements arise, however, in the context of discussions about who should be responsible for protecting them. Generally, parents are responsible for protecting their children, and legal authorities step in when they fail to do so. In some cases, though, the government shares this responsibility with parents through its power to regulate businesses. For example, parents are responsible for strapping infants into their car seats, but the government sets standards for their manufacture to ensure that the seats work as they are supposed to when an accident occurs. But what happens when an item that may be harmful to children is a creative work, such as a video game?

Regulation of Creative Works

In the United States, the production of creative works and consumers' right to have access to them are protected by the First Amendment to the Constitution. However, children do not have the same right to access creative works that adults do. Numerous court rulings have established the government's authority to set age limits on children's access to works that are of an obscene nature. A work meets the legal test for obscenity if it has no purpose other than to produce sexual arousal (Silver, 2003). Can a similar standard be applied to works that have no other purpose but to evoke visceral reactions to graphic depictions of violence?

Advocates of video game regulation answer this question affirmatively. They cite the gory scenes and callous characters that are found in many violent video games in support of their argument that the purpose of these games is to elicit hostility in players, just as the aim of obscene material is to cause sexual arousal. In support of their argument, advocates cite studies showing that playing violent video games produces feelings of hostility, increases the incidence of aggressive behavior, and desensitizes players to both real-world and fictional acts of violence (Bartholow, Bushman, & Sestire, 2006; Bushman, 2006; Bushman & Huesmann, 2006).

Those who support regulation of video games further argue that, like viewing obscene material, playing violent video games can develop into an obsession, or even an addiction (Ng & Wiemer-Hastings, 2005). They point to studies showing that teens who become involved in obsessive gaming sometimes skip school in order to continue playing (Khan, 2007). Moreover, these teens' game-playing habits are a frequent source of conflict with their parents and siblings. Some have even suggested that obsessive gaming is a prelude to horrific crimes such as the shooting spree that occurred on the campus of Virginia Tech in 2007 (Benedetti, 2007). Thus, proponents say, society has an obligation to protect its youngest members from being unwittingly drawn into an activity that may permanently alter the developmental trajectory of their lives.

These arguments have been the basis upon which regulation proponents have lobbied legislative bodies throughout the industrialized world over the past two decades. Their goal is to convince governments to develop standards and regulatory strategies for violent video games that are similar to those that exist for obscene material. How successful have these campaigns been?

Video Game Regulation Around the World

Thanks to the efforts of regulation advocates, most nations have passed laws that limit access to violent video games, but the strictness of these laws varies greatly from one country to another. In Greece, for example, electronic games of all kinds were banned in 2002 (Smith, 2004). The government eventually reversed the ban with regard to in-home gaming but left its prohibition against playing games in public places, such as internet cafés, intact. In the People's Republic of China (PRC), violent video games must include programming that limits players' access to weapons after three consecutive hours of play and forces them to quit the game for several hours after playing for five hours ("China imposes online gaming curbs," August 25, 2005).

Regulations are far less restrictive in Japan, Canada, New Zealand, Australia, and in most European countries (Electronic Frontiers Australia, 2002). In these nations, review boards are authorized to rate games on the basis of sexual and/or violent content and to limit minors' access to those that they deem inappropriate. These boards may also ban extremely violent games, but they seldom do so. Instead, review boards use their power to ban games as a means of forcing game manufacturers to reduce the amount of sexual or violent content. For instance, in 1997 regulators in the United Kingdom refused to allow *Carmageddon*, a game in which players intentionally run down pedestrians, to be sold in their country until the game's publisher substituted zombies for human pedestrians (Malvern & Robertson, 2007).

In the United States, the efforts of regulation advocates have led to the passage of several local and state laws (Thierer, 2003). In the 1980s, these laws limited minors' access to video game arcades. In the early 1990s, legislators focused on in-home game systems. As Internet access grew in the late 1990s, regulations on computer usage in public libraries and other venues where children might be in attendance were aimed at restricting patrons' access to violent online games. However, all of these laws have been overturned by U.S. courts that have consistently held that such restrictions violate the First Amendment (Thierer, 2003). Thus, say regulation advocates, children and teenagers in the United States, in contrast to their counterparts in most of the rest of the world, are not protected from the potentially detrimental effects of violent video games. Are they right?

Self-Regulation of the Video Game Industry

While continuing to argue that the First Amendment protects their products, video game industry officials state that they share parents' and public officials' concern about the potentially damaging effects of violent video games on young players. In 1994, industry representatives created a system of self-regulation in which the Entertainment Software Rating Board, an independent organization, reviews video games with regard to their appropriateness for players of various ages and makes recommendations about how they should be labeled (see esrb.org). Manufacturers voluntarily include the board's recommended ratings (e.g., "T" for teens; "AO" for adults only) and content advisories (e.g., Warning: Graphic violence) on video game packaging materials. Self-regulation, regulation opponents say, empowers parents to make informed choices about the games that their children are allowed to play (Thierer, 2003). Moreover, video game labels are regulated just as those on all products in the United States are, and manufacturers have had to pay stiff fines for inappropriately labeling games.

Critics of self regulation are skeptical. They argue that the financial motives of the multi-billion-dollar gaming industry render industry representatives incapable of self-regulation and point out that manufacturers apply the ESRB ratings so inconsistently that parents cannot rely on them (Glaubke, Miller, Parker, & Espejo, 2001). Thus, regulation advocates continue to press for government intervention and to try to persuade judges that violent video games, like obscene material, should be viewed as a special category of creative work to which youngsters' access can be limited without fear of violating the First Amendment.

Your Turn

- Research the history of video game regulation in your city and state.
- What do your classmates think about this issue?
- Compile a list of websites such as commonsensemedia.org where parents can find detailed information about the content of all kinds of media, including video games.
- Several lawsuits have been filed in the United States and in other countries against video game publishers in which it has been alleged that a game caused a player to commit a crime. Use your Internet skills to find out how most such suits have turned out. Note any differences in outcomes in different countries.

PART SIX
Early Adulthood

13

Physical and Cognitive Development in Early Adulthood

Sheila was happy in her work as a third-grade teacher, but a job posting for an open librarian position in her school district prompted the 26-year-old to think about changing her career goals. Sheila was intrigued by the job, but lacked a certificate in library science, one of the job's minimum requirements.

As Sheila began exploring library science certificate programs, she discovered that one of the universities in her state offered a master's degree in library science that was entirely online. The flexibility of being able to "attend" class and do her coursework whenever it best suited her schedule appealed to Sheila. Two years later, she received her graduate degree and a certificate in library science that qualified her to work in school libraries.

Sheila's story represents one of the most important contemporary trends in post-secondary education. In only five years, from 2002 to

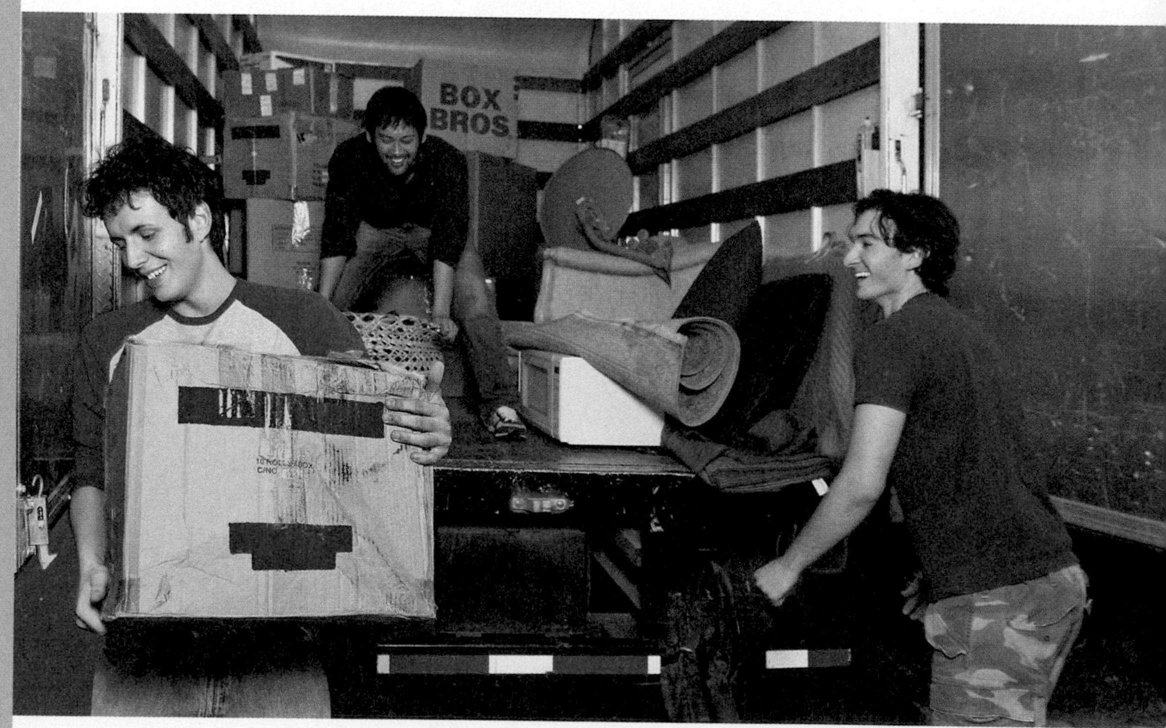

2007, the number of students enrolled in distance learning programs grew from just under 500,000 to more than 2 million (Romano, 2006). Moreover, in 2006, the federal government began allowing schools that participate in its financial aid programs to offer degrees entirely online. As a result, by 2007, 7% of all degree-seeking students in the United States were enrolled in online-only programs.

Students are attracted to the flexibility of distance learning, but what are its disadvantages? One factor involves student interaction. During face-to-face sessions, students hear each other's questions, an experience that sometimes tells a student that she has failed to understand a concept. Professors can create similar experiences for online students, such as requiring that they post questions on a message board that is available to all students. However, research suggests that increasing the amount of interaction between instructors and students is a more effective way of meeting online learners' needs (Arbaugh & Benbunan-Fich, 2007). Thus, the quality of an online course and how much a student learns from it often depend on the professor's willingness and ability to spend more time with individual students than she typically does in a traditional class.

Students must also be prepared to adjust their behavior to the demands of online courses in order to succeed in them. Distance learning students who exhibit high degrees of self-discipline are the ones who are most successful (Tyler-Smith, 2006). This finding makes sense if you think about the frequent verbal reminders that students in on-campus classes receive about upcoming exams, term paper requirements, group projects, and the like. Successful distance learning students are those who thoroughly familiarize themselves with course requirements so that they can stay on track without the verbal cues that are common in face-to-face classes.

Finally, distance learning raises questions about fraud and cheating (Grijalva, Nowell, & Kerkvliet, 2006). How can a professor know whether an online student has used forbidden materials during an exam or whether students are collaborating on tests or, worse yet, if students are getting others to take their exams for them? Institutions are working to develop technological solutions to such problems, but the vulnerability of online courses to cheating is an obstacle to widespread acceptance of distance learning as equivalent to on-campus learning.

Of course, not all young adults pursue post-secondary education. Some enter the military or the workforce immediately after high school graduation. Regardless of the pathway that a young adult's life follows, though, the years between 18 and 40 are a time of optimum physical and cognitive functioning. In this chapter, you will read about the improvements and the declines in these domains that take place across these years.

Physical Functioning

Do you see yourself continuing to play your favorite recreational sport—basketball, skiing, tennis, golf, softball, or flag football—through your 20s and into your 30s? If so, then you should be prepared for the fact that "weekend" athletes suffer more injuries and take longer to heal than their professional counterparts do (Stroud, 2004). Sports-related injuries trend upward in the 20s and 30s because most people reach their physical peak in their late teens or very early 20s and begin declining almost immediately. Of course, factors such as diet and exercise slow down these declines, but many of them are inevitable.

Learning Objective 13.1

What is the difference between primary and secondary aging?

Primary and Secondary Aging

Researchers distinguish between two types of aging. The basic, underlying, inevitable aging process is called **primary aging**, sometimes called **senescence**, by most developmentalists. Gray hair, wrinkles, and changes in visual acuity, for example, are attributable to primary aging.

Secondary aging, in contrast, is the product of environmental influences, health habits, or disease, and it is neither inevitable nor experienced by all adults. Research on age differences in health and death rates reveals the expected pattern. For example, 18- to 40-year-olds rarely die from disease (Hoyert et al., 2006). However, researchers have found that age interacts with other variables to influence health, a pattern suggesting the influence of secondary aging.

For example, age interacts with social class such that differences among young adults across social class groups are fairly small. However, with increasing age, the differences become much larger. Such social class differences in adult health have been found in Sweden, Ireland, and England, and they occur within ethnic groups in the United States as well as in the overall population (Eames, Ben-Schlomo, & Marmot, 1993; Kelleher, Friel, Gabhainn, & Tay, 2003; Thorslund & Lundberg, 1994).

Social class differences in health may be due to group variations in patterns of primary aging. However, most developmentalists believe they represent secondary aging (Koster et al., 2006). In other words, the health differences result from income-related variations in both social environments and individual behavior. Consider the findings that people who live in low-income neighborhoods have higher rates of cardiovascular disease than those who live in more affluent areas and that social class differences in rates of such diseases are the most likely cause of income-related differences in mortality rates (Roux et al., 2001; Wong, Shapiro, Boscardin, & Ettner, 2002). One reason for these findings may be that doctors who practice in low-income neighborhoods tend to have less training than those who serve higher-income areas (Bach, Pham, Schrag, Tate, & Hargraves, 2004). These doctors are also less likely than their peers in higher-income neighborhoods to have access to hospitals equipped with advanced diagnostic and treatment facilities. Such findings suggest that even if residents in low-income areas have adequate health insurance, the care they receive—if they obtain that care in neighborhood clinics and physicians' offices—may be inferior to that available to people who live in other areas.

Nevertheless, quality of health care is only part of the explanation for social class differences in secondary aging. Perhaps equally important is the finding that many of the same factors that contribute to economic differences are also related to health habits. Longitudinal studies show that, among individuals who drop out of high school, physical activity rates decline significantly during the late teens and remain low in adulthood (Kimm et al., 2002). Physical activity is a predictor of cardiovascular health, and educational level is associated with income. Moreover, the emotions underlying individuals' perceptions of their social class may be more important than their actual economic status. Some researchers have found that people who are unhappy with their economic situation are more likely to be sick than those who are relatively satisfied, regardless of income level (Operario, Adler, & Williams, 2004). Thus, as you can see, the link between social class and secondary aging is fairly complex. Research also suggests that, regardless of income level, changes in behavior such as those listed in Table 13.1 may prevent or even reverse the effects of aging.

primary aging (senescence) age-related physical changes that have a biological basis and are universally shared and inevitable

secondary aging age-related changes that are due to environmental influences, poor health habits, or disease

Table 13.1 Benefits of Lifestyle Changes

Lifestyle Change	Benefits
If overweight, lose just 10% of your body weight.	Reduction in triglyceride levels; decrease in total cholesterol; increase in HDL ("good" cholesterol); significant reduction in blood pressure; decreased risk of diabetes, sleep apnea, and osteoarthritis (Fransen, 2004; Wee, Hamel, Dans, & Phillips, 2004).
Add 20 to 30 grams of fiber to your diet each day.	Improved bowel function; reduced risk of colon cancer and other digestive-system diseases; decrease in total cholesterol; reduced blood pressure; improved insulin function in both diabetics and nondiabetics (Mayo Clinic, 2005).
Engage in moderate physical activity every day (e.g., walk up and down stairs for 15 minutes; spend 30 minutes washing a car).	Reduced feelings of anxiety and sadness; increased bone density; reduced risk of diabetes, heart disease, high blood pressure, and many other life-shortening diseases (CDC, 2007).
Stop smoking at any age, after any number of years of smoking.	*Immediate:* improved circulation; reduced blood level of carbon monoxide; stabilization of pulse rate and blood pressure; improved sense of smell and taste; improved lung function and endurance; reduced risk of lung infections such as pneumonia and bronchitis. *Long-term:* reduced risk of lung cancer (declines substantially with each year of abstinence); decreased risk of other smoking-related illnesses such as emphysema and heart disease; decreased risk of cancer recurrence in those who have been treated for some form of cancer (National Cancer Institute, 2000).
Get recommended annual or 5-year screenings beginning at these ages	*Women:* (21) Chlamydia, cervical cancer, screenings if sexually active; (35), cholesterol test; (50) mammogram, colorectal exam; (65) vision, hearing tests *Men:* (30) EKG, cholesterol test; (40) PSA test for prostate cancer; (50) colorectal exam; (65) vision, hearing tests

The Brain and Nervous System

Learning Objective 13.2

What changes in the brain take place in early adulthood?

No matter what age or gender an individual is, new synapses are forming, myelinization is occurring, and old connections are dying off. (See the Research Report on page 374). Further, there is recent evidence that, contrary to what neurologists have believed for a long time, some parts of the brain produce new neurons to replace those that die, even in the brains of older adults (Gould, Reeves, Graziano, & Gross, 1999). Interestingly, too, animal research suggests that production of these new neurons is stimulated by an enriched environment, as well as by physical exercise (Cao et al., 2004; Rhodes et al., 2003). Thus, just as is true in childhood and adolescence, a challenging environment probably supports brain development. At some point in development, though, usually in the late teens, developmental processes reach a balance and the brain attains a stable size and weight. Similarly, by early adulthood, most functions have become localized in specific areas of the brain (Gaillard et al., 2000).

Neurologists have found two spurts in brain growth in early adulthood, like those you have read about in earlier chapters. As you may remember from Chapter 11, a major spurt in the growth of the frontal lobes—the area of the brain devoted to logic, planning, and emotional control—begins around age 17. This spurt continues until age 21 or 22 (Crone et al., 2006; Gotay et al., 2004). Many neuropsychologists believe that this spurt is strongly connected to the increases in the capacity for formal operational thinking and other kinds of abstract reasoning that occur in late adolescence.

In addition to this brain growth spurt between 17 and 21, some neuropsychologists hypothesize that another peak in brain development happens in the mid- to late 20s (Fischer & Rose, 1994). They claim that the cognitive skills that emerge in the middle of the

RESEARCH REPORT

Gender Differences in the Brain

As you should remember from earlier chapters, the brains of males and females differ to some extent at every age. However, sex differences are even more striking in the adult brain. For example, the brain contains two types of tissue: *gray matter* and *white matter*. Gray matter is made up of cell bodies and axon terminals (look back at Figure 3.3); white matter contains myelinated axons that connect one neuron to another. Men have a higher proportion of white matter than women do (Gur et al., 1999). In addition, the distributions of gray and white matter differ in the brains of men and women. Men have a lower proportion of white matter in the left brain than in the right brain. In contrast, the proportions of gray matter and white matter in the two hemispheres are equal in women's brains. Such findings have led some neuropsychologists to speculate that men's overall superior spatial perception is associated with sex differences in the distribution of gray and white matter.

Researchers also speculate that gender differences in emotional behavior may be explained by the finding that women have more gray matter in the area of the brain that controls emotions (Gur, Gunning-Dixon, Bilker, & Gur, 2002). However, studies have also shown differences between males and females in the role played by the ratio of gray matter to white matter. In one study, researchers found that the ratio was associated with individual differences in performance on verbal learning tasks among male participants but was not associated with differences in such performance among female participants (Yurgelun-Todd, Killgore, & Young, 2002).

There are other sex differences in adult brains. Some listening tasks activate the left hemisphere in men, whereas women respond to them with the right hemisphere (Spreen et al., 1995). Similarly, men and women appear to use different areas of the brain when determining the location of a sound (Lewald, 2004). However, there isn't yet enough consistency across studies to allow neuroscientists to draw definitive conclusions about sex differences in brain function. Moreover, these scientists are still a long way from finding direct links between neurological and behavioral sex differences.

Questions for Critical Analysis

1. In what ways might the experiences of men and women contribute to gender differences in the brain?
2. How might the research on gender differences in the brain be distorted and misused to justify discrimination against women?

early adulthood period seem to depend on changes in the brain. For example, when you take a multiple-choice test, you need to be able to keep yourself from responding too quickly to the options in order to carefully weigh them all. Neuropsychologists suggest that this kind of *response inhibition* may depend on the ability of the frontal lobes of the brain to regulate the **limbic system**, or the emotional part of the brain. Many scientists believe that the capacity to integrate various brain functions in this way does not become fully developed until early adulthood (Spreen et al., 1995).

Still, the brain begins to lose volume in the early adulthood period (Raz et al., 2006). Moreover, the gradual loss of speed in virtually every aspect of bodily function appears to be the result of very gradual changes at the neuronal level, particularly the loss of dendrites and a slowing of the "firing rate" of nerves (Birren & Fisher, 1995; Earles & Salthouse, 1995; Salthouse, 1993). As you get older, it takes longer to warm up after you have been very cold or to cool off after you have been hot. Your reaction time to sudden events slows; you don't respond quite as quickly to a swerving car, for example.

Learning Objective 13.3

How do other body systems change during these years?

Other Body Systems

Young adults perform better than do the middle-aged or old on virtually every physical measure. Compared to older adults, adults in their 20s and 30s have more muscle tissue; maximum bone calcium; more brain mass; better eyesight, hearing, and sense of smell; greater oxygen capacity; and a more efficient immune system. The young adult is stronger, faster, and better able to recover from exercise or to adapt to changing conditions, such as alterations in temperature or light levels.

Declines in Physical Functioning There is a gradual decline on almost every measure of physical functioning through the years of adulthood. Table 13.2 summarizes these changes. Most of the summary statements in the table are based on both longitudinal and cross-sectional data; many are based on studies in which both experimental and control groups consisted of participants in good health. So developmentalists can be reasonably confident

limbic system the part of the brain that regulates emotional responses

Table 13.2 A Summary of Age Changes in Physical Functioning

Body Function	Age at Which Change Begins to Be Clear or Measurable	Nature of Change
Vision	Mid-40s	Lens of eye thickens and loses accommodative power, resulting in poorer near vision and more sensitivity to glare
Hearing	50 or 60	Loss of ability to hear very high and very low tones
Smell	About 40	Decline in ability to detect and discriminate among different smells
Taste	None	No apparent loss in taste discrimination ability
Muscles	About 50	Loss of muscle tissue, particularly in "fast twitch" fibers used for bursts of strength or speed
Bones	Mid-30s (women)	Loss of calcium in the bones, called osteoporosis; also wear and tear on bone in joints, called osteoarthritis, more marked after about 60
Heart and lungs	35 or 40	Most functions (such as aerobic capacity or cardiac output) do not show age changes at rest, but do show age changes during work or exercise
Nervous system	Probably gradual throughout adulthood	Some loss (but not clear how much) of neurons in the brain; gradual reduction in density of dendrites; gradual decline in total brain volume and weight
Immune system	Adolescence	Loss in size of thymus; reduction in number and maturity of T cells; not clear how much of this change is due to stress and how much is primary aging
Reproductive system	Mid-30s (women)	Increased reproductive risk and lowered fertility
	Early 40s (men)	Gradual decline in viable sperm beginning at about age 40; very gradual decline in testosterone from early adulthood
Cellular elasticity	Gradual	Gradual loss of elasticity in most cells, including skin, muscle, tendon, and blood vessel cells; faster deterioration in cells exposed to sunlight
Height	40	Compression of disks in the spine, with resulting loss of height of 1 to 2 inches by age 80
Weight	Nonlinear	In U.S. studies, weight reaches a maximum in middle adulthood and then gradually declines in old age
Skin	40	Increase in wrinkles, as a result of loss of elasticity; oil-secreting glands become less efficient.
Hair	Variable	Hair becomes thinner and may gray

(*Sources*: Bartoshuk & Weiffenbach, 1990; Blatter et al., 1995; Braveman, 1987; Briggs, 1990; Brock, Guralnik, & Brody, 1990; Doty et al., 1984; Fiatarone & Evans, 1993; Fozard, 1990; Fozard, Metter, & Brant, 1990; Gray, Berlin, McKinlay, & Longcope, 1991; Hallfrisch, Muller, Drinkwater, Tobin, & Adres, 1990; Hayflick, 1994; Ivy, MacLeod, Petit, & Marcus, 1992; Kallman, Plato, & Tobin, 1990; Kline & Scialfa, 1996; Kozma, Stones, & Hannah, 1991; Lakatta, 1990; Lim, Zipursky, Watts, & Pfefferbaum, 1992; McFalls, 1990; Miller, 1990; Mundy, 1994; Scheibel, 1992, 1996; Shock et al., 1984; Weisse, 1992.)

that most of the age changes listed reflect primary aging and not secondary aging. The center column of the table lists the approximate age at which the loss or decline reaches the point where it becomes fairly readily apparent. Virtually all these changes begin in early adulthood. But the early losses or declines are not typically noticeable in everyday physical functioning during these years.

Another way to think of these changes is in terms of a balance between physical demand and physical capacity (Welford, 1993). In early adulthood, almost all of us have ample physical capacity to meet the physical demands we encounter in everyday life. We can read

It's hard to draw a clear line between "early adulthood" and "middle adulthood" because the physical and mental changes are so gradual; even at 30, adults may find that it takes a bit more work to get into or stay in shape than it did at 20.

the fine print in the telephone book without bifocals; we can carry heavy boxes or furniture when we move; our immune systems are strong enough to fight off most illnesses, and we recover quickly from sickness. As we move into middle adulthood, the balance sheet changes: We find more and more arenas in which our physical capacities no longer quite meet the demands.

Heart and Lungs The most common measure of overall aerobic fitness is **maximum oxygen uptake (VO_2 max)**, which reflects the ability of the body to take in and transport oxygen to various body organs. When VO_2 max is measured in a person at rest, scientists find only minimal decrements associated with age. But when they measure VO_2 max during exercise (such as during a treadmill test), it shows a systematic decline with age of about 1% per year, beginning between ages 35 and 40 (Goldberg, Dengel, & Hagberg, 1996).

VO_2 max during exercise declines more with age than does VO_2 max at rest for a variety of reasons. Primary aging effects have been demonstrated in studies showing that, even in healthy individuals who exercise regularly, age is associated with a loss of arterial elasticity and with calcification of the valves that regulate the flow of blood to and from the heart (Cheitlin, 2003). As a result, the older adult's heart responds less efficiently to the demands of exercise than the younger adult's. Research has also revealed, however, that aerobic exercise can improve VO_2 max in both younger and older adults (Wilmore et al., 2001). Thus, age-related declines in this variable may reflect the cumulative effects of a sedentary lifestyle.

Figure 13.1
Changes in Grip Strength

These data, from the Baltimore Longitudinal Study of Aging, show both cross-sectional data (the dots) and longitudinal data (the lines) for grip strength among men. Once again, there is striking agreement between the two sets of information.

(*Source:* Kallman et al., 1990, Figure 2, p. M84.)

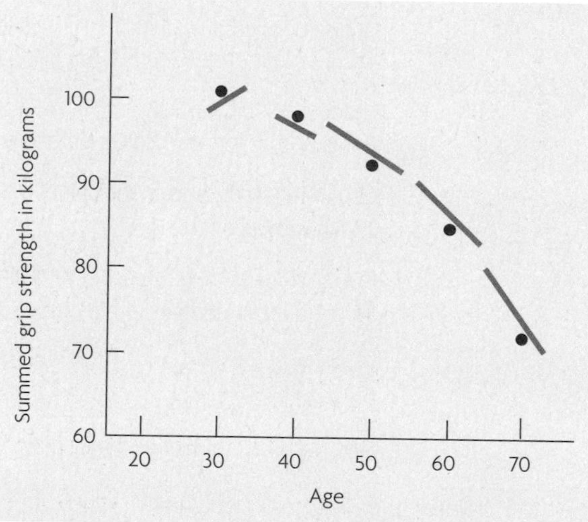

Strength and Speed The collective effect of changes in muscles and cardiovascular fitness is a general loss of strength and speed with age—not just in top athletes, but in all of us. Figure 13.1 shows both cross-sectional and 9-year longitudinal changes in grip strength in a group of men who participated in the Baltimore Longitudinal Studies of Aging (Kallman et al., 1990). Clearly, strength was at its peak in the men's 20s and early 30s and then declined steadily. Once again, though, such a difference might be the result of the fact that younger adults are more physically active or more likely to be engaged in activities or jobs that demand strength. Arguing against this conclusion, however, are studies of physically active older adults, who also show loss of muscle strength (e.g., Phillips, Bruce, Newton, & Woledge, 1992).

Reproductive Capacity In Chapter 3, you read that the risk of miscarriage and other complications of pregnancy is higher in a woman's 30s than in her 20s. An equivalent change occurs in fertility—the ability to conceive—which is at its highest in the late teens and early 20s and drops steadily thereafter (McFalls, 1990; Mosher, 1987; Mosher & Pratt, 1987). Men's reproductive capacity declines as well, but far more slowly than is common among women. Moreover, older men have a diminished sperm count, but, as long as their reproductive organs remain disease free, men retain the ability to father children throughout their lives. Why does this pattern of reproductive aging exist?

Genetic studies in mice suggest that a single protein is responsible for the regulation of reproductive aging in both sexes (Baker et al., 2004). However, the end point of the reproduc-

maximum oxygen uptake (VO_2 max) a measure of the body's ability to take in and transport oxygen to various body organs

tive aging process is different for men and women. Men's capacity diminishes, as stated earlier, but remains intact. By contrast, the end point of reproductive aging for women involves a total loss of the capacity for reproduction. Because of this difference, fertility problems in men (e.g., low sperm count) are almost always the result of some kind of disease or abnormal developmental process. By contrast, fertility problems in women are more often a by-product of the normal aging process.

As you will learn in Chapter 15, in preparation for menopause, ovulation becomes sporadic and unpredictable in many women, sometimes as soon as the early 30s. Consequently, the natural process of reproductive aging leads many women to experience periods of time during which conception is impossible. However, because menstrual cycles continue to occur, many women who are ovulating intermittently are unaware of the problem. Thus, to achieve conception, many women in their 30s turn to specialists in reproductive medicine who can help them identify the times when they are fertile or can prescribe drugs that stimulate the ovaries to produce more eggs, as discussed in the No Easy Answers discussion below.

Immune System Functioning The two key organs in the immune system are the thymus gland and the bone marrow. Between them, they create two types of cells, B cells and T cells, each of which plays a distinct role. B cells fight against external threats by producing antibodies against such disease organisms as viruses or bacteria; T cells defend against essentially internal threats, such as transplanted tissue, cancer cells, and viruses that live within the body's

NO EASY ANSWERS

Assisted Reproductive Technology

Researchers are making amazing advances in developmentalists' understanding of the earliest hours of life almost every day. These advances have led to the development of *assisted reproductive techniques (ART)* for helping couples who have difficulty conceiving. For example, the use of *fertility drugs* to stimulate the ovaries to produce eggs is the most common approach to treating infertility. Increasing the number of eggs a woman produces increases the chances of a natural conception. Moreover, fertility drugs play an important role in other assisted reproductive techniques. They are often used along with *artificial insemination*, the process of injecting sperm into a woman's uterus at times when eggs are known to be present.

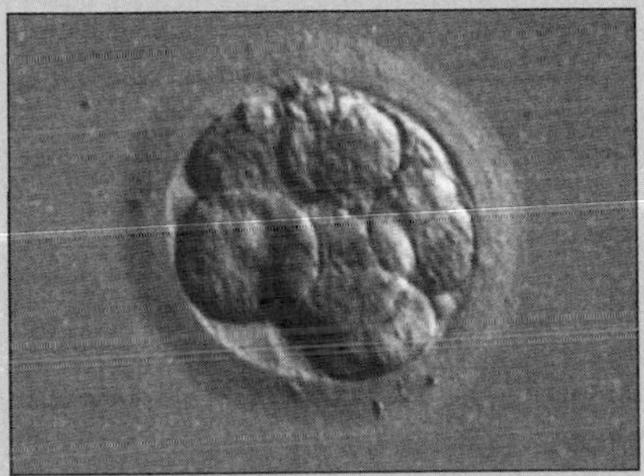

An eight-celled embryo is ideal for an IVF transfer. Pictured here is an embryo on the day of transfer into a woman's uterus.

Fertility drugs are also employed in *in vitro fertilization* (IVF; *in vitro* is Latin for *glass*), popularly known as the "test-tube baby" method. Eggs are extracted from a woman's ovaries and combined with sperm in a laboratory dish. If conception takes place, one or more embryos—ideally at the six to eight-cell stage of development—are transferred to the woman's uterus. The eggs used in IVF can come from the woman who will carry the child or from a donor. Likewise, the sperm can be from the woman's partner or a donor.

However, the older a woman is, the lower the probability that she will be able to have a successful IVF pregnancy. Roughly 35% of 20- to 29-year-old IVF patients achieve a live birth, but only 13% or so of IVF procedures involving women over age 40 are successful (Schieve et al., 1999). It's important to note here, though, that these are aggregate statistics; each reproductive clinic keeps track of its own success rate, and these can vary considerably from one facility to another (Society for Assisted Reproductive Technology, 2004). Still, in even the most successful clinics, failure rates are high.

Successful IVF carries a different set of risks. Multiple birth is more frequent among IVF patients, primarily because doctors typically transfer several zygotes at once in order to increase the likelihood of at least one live birth (Society for Assisted Reproductive Technology, 2004). Consequently, 20–25% of IVF patients deliver twins, and another 2–5% give birth to triplets (Schieve et al., 1999). As you learned in Chapter 3, multiple pregnancies are associated with premature birth, low birth weight, and birth defects.

Researchers have also found that, even when only one embryo is transferred, IVF is still associated with a higher rate of multiple births than is natural conception. For reasons that are not yet understood, implanted zygotes conceived through IVF are more likely to spontaneously divide into two embryos than are naturally conceived zygotes (Blickstine, Jones, & Keith, 2003). This finding suggests that multiple pregnancy must always be considered as a possible outcome when infertile couples are advised of the risks associated with IVF.

Take a Stand

Decide which of these two statements you most agree with and think about how you would defend your position:

1. The benefits of ART outweigh its risks. If I were faced with fertility problems, I would look into ART.
2. The risks of ART outweigh its benefits. If I were faced with fertility problems, I would prefer to adopt a child rather than to seek help from an ART specialist.

cells (Kiecolt-Glaser & Glaser, 1995). It is T cells that decline most in number and efficiency with age (Garcia & Miller, 2001).

Changes in the thymus gland appear to be central to the aging process (Cohen, 2006). This gland is largest in adolescence and declines dramatically thereafter in both size and mass. By age 45 or 50, the thymus has only about 5–10% of the cellular mass it had at puberty (Braveman, 1987; Hausman & Weksler, 1985). This smaller, less functional thymus is less able to turn the immature T cells produced by the bone marrow into fully "adult" cells. As a result, both of the basic protective mechanisms work less efficiently. Adults produce fewer antibodies than do children or teenagers. And T cells partially lose the ability to "recognize" a foreign cell, so that the body may fail to fight off some disease cells (cancer cells, for example). Thus, one of the key physical changes over the years of adulthood is an increasing susceptibility to disease.

But it is not entirely clear whether this susceptibility is due to primary or secondary aging. These changes in the immune system are found in healthy adults, which makes them look like part of primary aging. But there also is growing evidence that the functioning of the immune system is highly responsive to psychological stress and depression (Hawkley & Cacioppo, 2004). College students, for example, show lower levels of one variety of T cells ("natural killer" T cells) during exam periods than at other times (Glaser et al., 1992). And adults who have recently been widowed show a sharp drop in immune system functioning (Irwin & Pike, 1993). Chronic stress, too, has an effect on the immune system, stimulating an initial increase in immune efficiency, followed by a drop (Hawkley & Cacioppo, 2004).

Collectively, this research points to the possibility that life experiences that demand high levels of change or adaptation will affect immune system functioning. Over a period of years and many stresses, the immune system may become less and less efficient. It may well be that the immune system changes with age in basic ways regardless of the level of stress. But it is also possible that what is thought of as normal aging of the immune system is a response to cumulative stress.

Critical Thinking

1. Elite swimmers reach their peak in their early 20s, while the best amateur and professional golfers are at their best in their 30s. How do the physical changes that you have learned about in this section explain this difference?

Health and Wellness

Early adulthood is a relatively healthy period of life, but risky behaviors—having multiple sex partners or engaging in substance use, for example—along with generally poor health habits can be problematic.

Learning Objective 13.4
What habits and personal factors are associated with good health?

Health Habits and Personal Factors

Do you remember Ponce de Leon, the 16th-century Spanish explorer who traveled to the New World in search of the "fountain of youth"? Although de Leon was responsible for providing his fellow European mariners with their first chart of the Gulf Stream, he never succeeded in finding a source of everlasting youth. Like de Leon, many adults today are searching for a vitamin or a special diet that can keep them young forever. The truth is, though, that maintaining optimum health results from the development of health-enhancing habits and the cultivation of personal factors that can stave off some of the effects of primary aging.

Health Habits The best evidence for the long-term effects of various health habits comes from the Alameda County Study, a major longitudinal epidemiological study conducted in one county in California (Berkman & Breslow, 1983; Breslow & Breslow, 1993; Kaplan, 1992; Stallworth & Lennon, 2003). The study began in 1965, when a random sample of all residents of the county, a total of 6,928 people, completed an extensive questionnaire about many aspects of their lives, including their health habits and their health and disability. These participants were contacted again in 1974 and in 1983, when they again described their health and disability. The researchers also monitored death records and were able to specify the date of death of each of the participants who died between 1965 and 1983. They could then link health practices reported in 1965 to later death, disease, or disability. The researchers initially identified seven good health habits that they thought might be critical: getting physical exercise; not smoking, drinking, over- or undereating, or snacking; eating breakfast; and getting regular sleep.

Sexually transmitted diseases are one of the most significant health risks of young adulthood. Casual sexual encounters with multiple partners carry with them a higher risk of contracting such diseases than do more careful relationship choices.

Data from the first 9 years of the Alameda study show that five of these seven practices were independently related to the risk of death. Only snacking and eating breakfast were unrelated to mortality. When the five strong predictors were combined in the 1974 data, researchers found that, in every age group, those with poorer health habits had a higher risk of mortality. Not surprisingly, poor health habits were also related to disease and disability rates over the 18 years of the study. Those who described poorer health habits in 1965 were more likely to report disability or disease symptoms in 1974 and in 1983 (Breslow & Breslow, 1993; Guralnik & Kaplan, 1989; Strawbridge, Camacho, Cohen, & Kaplan, 1993). Moreover, the study showed that a sendentary lifestyle in early adulthood predisposes people to develop life-threatening illnesses such as diabetes in later years (Hu, Li, Colditz, Willet, & Manson, 2003).

The Alameda study is not the only one to show these connections between health habits and mortality. For example, a 20-year longitudinal study in Sweden confirms the link between physical exercise and lower risk of death (Lissner, Bengtsson, Bjorkelund, & Wedel, 1996). In addition, the Nurses' Health Study, a longitudinal investigation that examined the health behaviors of more than 115,000 nurses in the United States for almost 2 decades, found that the lower a woman's initial body-mass index (a measure of weight relative to height), the lower her likelihood of death (Manson et al., 1995).

These longitudinal studies suggest that the lifestyle choices of early adulthood have cumulative effects. For example, the effect of a high cholesterol diet appears to add up over time. However, a radical lowering of fat levels in the diet may reverse the process of cholesterol build-up in the blood vessels (Ornish, 1990). Similarly, the effects of smoking begin to reverse themselves shortly after a person quits (see The Real World on page 380). Thus, the long-term effects of lifestyle choices made in early adulthood may be either negative or positive. So there is likely to be a payoff for changing your health habits.

Social Support Abundant research shows that adults with adequate *social support* have lower risk of disease, death, and depression than do adults with weaker social networks or less supportive relationships (e.g., Berkman, 1985; Berkman & Breslow, 1983; Cohen, 1991). The link between social support and health was revealed in some of the findings from the Alameda study. In this study, the *social network index* reflected an objective measurement: number of contacts with friends and relatives, marital status, church and group membership. Even using this less than-perfect measure of support, the relationship is vividly clear: Among both men and women in three different age groups (30–49, 50–59, and 60–69), those with the fewest social connections had higher death rates than those with more social connections. Since similar patterns have been found in other countries, including Sweden and Japan, this link between social contact and physical hardiness is not restricted

Research shows that social support, as exhibited between these two women, lowers the risk of disease, death, and depression in adults.

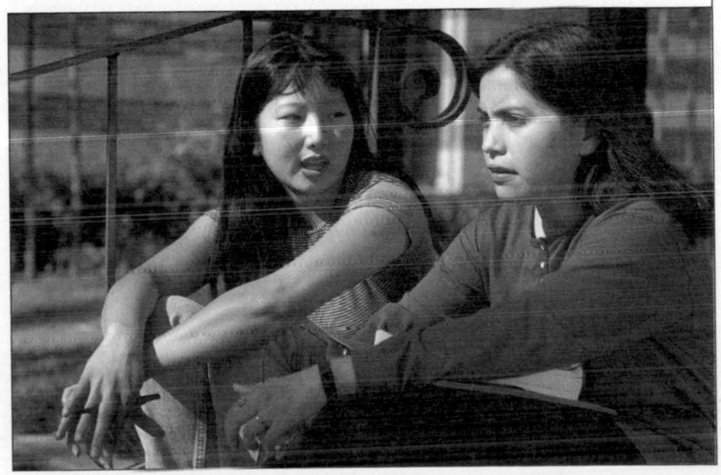

THE REAL WORLD

Smoking Cessation

Ever since Lana started college, she has been trying to quit smoking. Her first attempt at quitting failed, she thought, because she had tried to do it during finals week of her first semester. Lana also blamed her failure on her use of the "cold turkey" method. The next time, she tried nicotine gum, but she didn't like the taste of it and soon found herself smoking again. An advertisement for a hypnotherapist prompted her to call about hypnosis sessions, but she couldn't afford the therapist's fees. At this point, Lana doesn't know what to do.

Surveys of smokers show that, like Lana, 70% of current smokers want to quit (Trosclair, Husten, Pederson, & Dhillon, 2002). The problem they face is that nicotine is a highly addictive drug and is associated with withdrawal symptoms that many smokers find to be unbearable. Within an hour of denying themselves the first cigarette in their quest for non-smoker status, smokers experience cravings and become irritable (Hendricks, Ditre, Drobes, & Brandon, 2006). Because these withdrawal symptoms arise from the effects of nicotine on the brain, the longer a person has smoked, and the more cigarettes she smokes each day, the more severe her withdrawal symptoms. However, even in long-term heavy smokers, withdrawal symptoms are temporary. They subside when the brain adjusts to the lack of nicotine, a process that begins, like withdrawal symptoms, as soon as a smoker skips her first cigarette. Thus, if a smoker can get through two weeks or so without smoking, she is very likely to succeed at quitting.

There are many nicotine replacement products—patches, gum, lozenges—that are available to help smokers dampen the cravings they will inevitably experience during their first few days without cigarettes. All such products have been found to be effective for some smokers (Prepavessis et al., 2007). However, there is some evidence that using a nicotine replacement product makes a smoker more likely to relapse than either tapering down gradually or going "cold turkey" (Alberg et al., 2005). In addition, both psychotherapy and exercise can help a smoker stay on track toward her goal of becoming a non-smoker (Prapvessis et al., 2007). Additional tips and live, on-line counselors are available to smokers who want to quit at https://cissecure.nci.nih.gov/livehelp/welcome.asp.

The timing of a smoker's efforts to quit may be more important than the method she chooses. In one study involving more than 600 college students, participants' overall success rate over the 18-month-long study was only 18%, but students who were under the least amount of stress in their academic and personal lives when they tried to quit achieved a success rate of 52% (Norman et al., 2006). The implication of these findings for those who want to quit smoking is that the often-heard recommendation that they choose a "quit date" is probably good advice. Planning a quit date to coincide with times of reduced stress, such as immediately after final exams, might be better than trying to quit at time when a smoker is most stressed.

Questions for Reflection

1. Why do you think Lana has been unsuccessful so far in her attempts to quit smoking?
2. What advice would you give her to improve her chances of quitting?

to the United States or to Western cultures (Orth-Gomer, Rosengren, & Wilhelmsen, 1993; Sugisawa, Liang, & Liu, 1994).

How does social support contribute to health? One reason may be that the size and perceived adequacy of a person's social network is correlated with the functioning of her immune system (Bouhuys et al., 2004). Likewise, adults who have adequate social support are less likely than their peers to be depressed, a factor that indirectly affects the immune system (Symister & Friend, 2003).

A Sense of Control Another personal characteristic that affects health is an individual's level of *self-efficacy*, the belief in one's ability to perform some action or to control one's behavior or environment, to reach some goal or to make something happen (Bandura, 1977b, 1982b, 1986). As you learned in Chapter 10, this aspect of the psychological self first appears in middle childhood. In adulthood, it is linked to many health outcomes. For instance, individuals who are high in self-efficacy are more likely than those who are low to follow medical advice with regard to health problems such as chronic headaches (Nicholson, Houle, Rhudy, & Norton, 2007).

A similar variable, **locus of control**, which is an individual's set of beliefs about the causes of events, also contributes to health. A person who has an *internal* locus of control sees herself as capable of exerting some control over what happens to her (Rotter, 1990). One who has an *external* locus of control believes that other people or uncontrollable forces such as luck determine the future.

locus of control a set of beliefs about the causes of events

To understand how locus of control influences health, think about what would happen if you had an ear infection for which a doctor prescribed an antibiotic that you took for only half as long as directed. If your ear infection failed to go away, how would you explain it? If you have an internal locus of control, you would have no difficulty acknowledging the fact that your failure to take the medicine as directed was responsible for your still aching ear. However, if you have an external locus of control, you might respond to the pain in your ear with a remark such as, "Just my luck! Nothing ever goes my way."

Research suggests that the tendency to make realistic attributions is what counts when it comes to health (Frick et al., 2007). The best outcomes for patients happen when they are able to accurately determine which aspects of their conditions are controllable and which are not. For instance, with regard to our ear infection example, a person who is able to balance attributions in this way would realize that taking medicine is under her control and would take responsibility for that aspect of her treatment. However, she would understand that the physician is responsible for determining which antibiotic to prescribe. Balancing her thinking about the reasons for her recovery or her failure to recover helps her cope with the stress of being ill.

Both self-efficacy and locus of control are related to yet another control-related psychological characteristic, the continuum that ranges from *optimism* to *pessimism* (Seligman, 1991). The pessimist, who feels helpless, believes that misfortune will last a long time, will undermine everything, and is his own fault. The optimist believes that setbacks are temporary and usually caused by circumstances. He is convinced that there is always some solution and that he will be able to work things out. Confronted by defeat, the optimist sees it as a challenge and tries harder, whereas the pessimist gives up. Not surprisingly, optimism affects health in many ways, including enhancing the effects of medication (Geers et al., 2007). That is, optimists show larger benefits from medication than pessimists do. These results are in line with other studies showing that optimism has positive effects on the immune system (Segerstrom, Taylor, Kemeny, & Fahey, 1998). In addition, it fits with the results of a classic longitudinal study which found that pessimism at age 25 was correlated with poor health in middle and late adulthood (Peterson, Seligman, & Vaillant, 1988).

Sexually Transmitted Diseases

Learning Objective 13.5
What are some of the viral and bacterial STDs that afflict young adults?

In contrast to other types of disease, most sexually transmitted diseases (STD)—including gonorrhea, syphilis, genital herpes, and HIV—are more common among 15- to 24-year-olds than any other age group (CDC, 2006). In Chapter 3, you learned about how these diseases affect prenatal development in pregnant women. Now, we will consider how a few such diseases affect those who carry them.

Bacterial STDs Bacterial STDs are STDs caused by microorganisms that can be eradicated through the use of antibiotic medications. The most prevalent of the bacterial STDs is *chlamydia*, a bacterial infection that can be transmitted through many kinds of physical contact involving the genitals, as well as actual intercourse (CDC, 2006). Women are about three times as likely as men to suffer from chlamydia. Community studies show that as many as one-third of young women who are screened at family planning clinics are infected with chlamydia. Many of these women are symptom-free because the disease can remain hidden for several years. Unfortunately, undiagnosed chlamydia can lead to **pelvic inflammatory disease**, an infection of the female reproductive tract that can cause infertility.

Another bacterial STD is *gonorrhea*. Because of educational programs about the disease and increased use of condoms, the prevalence of gonorrhea has declined considerably in recent years (CDC, 2006). However, the strains that infect today's gonorrhea sufferers are far more resistant to antibiotics than those that existed decades ago (CDC, 2006). As a result, in some cases the disease is extremely difficult to cure and causes long-term damage to the reproductive systems of those who suffer from it. Men and women experience roughly equivalent rates of gonorrhea, but women's bodies are more susceptible to long-term damage from this infection.

pelvic inflammatory disease an infection of the female reproductive tract that may result from a sexually transmitted disease and can lead to infertility

Another bacterial STD is *syphilis*, a disease that can lead to serious mental disorders and death if not treated in the early stages of infection. Fortunately, widespread screening for the disease has led to significant declines in its prevalence. Only about 7,000 cases were reported to the Centers for Disease Control in 2002 (CDC, 2003b). However, syphilis continues to be a much more extensive health problem in some groups. For example, during the late 1990s, the infection rate among African Americans was 34 times that of Whites (CDC, 2003b). Thanks to intensive educational campaigns geared toward African Americans, the cross-racial difference in syphilis rates decreased substantially in the first years of the 21st century. However, public health officials note that the decrease in the disparity across races is due both to declining numbers among African Americans and to increasing numbers among Whites. The increase in syphilis infection in the White population is confined to men, largely because the number of cases among homosexual males who live in highly populated urban areas continues to rise each year at an alarming rate (CDC, 2006).

Viral STDs Unlike STDs caused by bacteria, STDs caused by viruses cannot be treated with antibiotics. In fact, these diseases are considered to be incurable. One such disease is *genital herpes*. This disease can be acquired through either intercourse or oral sex. The Centers for Disease Control report that 20 to 30% of the adult population in the United States is infected with herpes (CDC, 2006). Attacks of the disease, which include the development of painful blisters on the genitals, occur periodically in most people who carry the virus.

A more serious viral STD is *genital warts* caused by the *human papillomavirus (HPV)*. The primary symptom of the disease, the presence of growths on the genitals, is not its most serious effect. The virus is strongly associated with cervical cancer, accounting for more than 80% of all cases (CDC, 2006). Studies indicate that, in the United States, 22% of women in their 20s, and 10% of women over 30 are infected with HPV (CDC, 2006).

In 2006, the Food and Drug Administration approved a vaccine that officials believe will protect young women against four types of HPV (CDC, 2006). However, the vaccine is only licensed for use in females between the ages of 9 and 26, and researchers do not yet know how long the vaccine's protective effects will last. Moreover, officials point out that there are other forms of HPV against which the vaccine offers no protection. For these reasons, public health officials state that women who get the vaccine should continue to be vigilant about safe sex practices and routine medical screening.

HIV/AIDS The most feared STD is the *human immunodeficiency virus (HIV)*, the virus that causes *acquired immune deficiency syndrome (AIDS)*. Since HIV was discovered in the early 1980s, more than 1 million cases have been documented in the United States (Merson, 2006). By contrast, more than 30 million people in sub-Saharan Africa are HIV-positive. HIV is transmitted through an exchange of bodily fluids. Such exchanges can happen during sexual intercourse, when intravenous drug users share needles, or as a result of a blood transfusion or other kinds of invasive medical treatment. Male homosexuals have higher rates of HIV than other groups primarily because of the tendency to engage in anal intercourse, during which bodily fluids are more likely to be exchanged than in other kinds of sexual encounters.

Prevention How much do you know about STD prevention? Your score on the quiz in Table 13.3 might surprise you. Knowledge notwithstanding, older teens and young adults have higher rates of these diseases than older people primarily because they engage in more sexually risky behavior. In particular, many young adults engage in casual, unprotected sex with multiple partners. To compound the problem, young adults seldom discuss STD prevention with potential sex partners. Further, most do not insist that their partners use condoms, and they delay seeking treatment for STD symptoms (Lewis, Malow, & Ireland, 1997; Schuster, 1997). Thus, reducing the rates of such risky behaviors could reduce the rates of STDs and prevent many young adults from experiencing the adverse health consequences associated with them.

intimate partner abuse physical acts or other behavior intended to intimidate or harm an intimate partner

Learning Objective 13.6

What are the causes and effects of intimate partner abuse?

Intimate Partner Abuse

Researchers define **intimate partner abuse** as physical acts or other behavior intended to intimidate or harm an intimate partner. Intimate partners are couples who are dating, cohabiting, engaged, or married or who were formerly partners. The more

Table 13.3 Mayo Clinics STD Quiz: What You Don't Know Can Hurt You

Answer these questions True or False. (Note: full explanations of the answers to these questions can be found at http://mayoclinic.com/health/stds/QZ00037)

1. The rate of STDs in the United States is on the rise.
2. Condoms—so long as they're still wrapped—will stay effective even if carried around for months at a time in your wallet.
3. Animal skin (lambskin) condoms protect against pregnancy, but don't protect you from STDs, such as HIV/AIDS.
4. You should lubricate condoms with petroleum jelly or baby oil to reduce their risk of tearing.
5. When condoms fail, it's usually because of incorrect use.
6. If you have a history of genital herpes, you can infect your partner even when you don't have symptoms of the disease.
7. Having regular Pap tests will prevent cervical cancer.
8. You can't get an STD from Oral sex.
9. Taking birth control pills eliminates your need for a condom.
10. STDs aren't life-threatening.

Answers: 1. T; 2. F; 3. T; 4. F; 5. T; 6. T; 7. F; 8. F; 9. F; 10. F

common term, *domestic abuse*, refers only to incidents involving individuals who live in the same household.

Prevalence When intimate partners get into a physical altercation, men and women are about equally likely to push, slap, or kick their partners. However, analyses of medical records show that, throughout the world, women are more likely than men to be injured during physical confrontations between intimate partners (McHugh, 2005). In the United States, surveys suggest that about 25% of women have been injured by a partner, compared to only 8% of

Criminologists point out that intimate partner abuse happens most often in the context of arguments over long-standing disagreements that take place when partners are home from work in the evening, on holidays, or on weekends, and/or have been drinking or using drugs.

men (NCIPC, 2000). However, rates of abuse among women vary significantly around the world, as Figure 13.2 reveals (World Health Organization [WHO], 2000).

Rates vary across ethnic groups within the United States as well. As many as half of all African American women in the United States have been physically abused by an intimate partner at some time in their adult lives (Raj & Silverman, 2002; Wyatt, Axelrod, Chin, Carmona, & Loeb, 2000). Similarly, some studies suggest that Hispanic American and Asian American women experience partner abuse more frequently than their White counterparts (Duncan, Stayton, & Hall, 1999; Raj & Silverman, 2002). However, careful analyses of these findings show that the critical factor is socioeconomic status rather than race (Rennison & Planty, 2003). In other words, low-income women are more likely to be abused than those with higher incomes, and African American and Hispanic American households have lower average income levels than those of other ethnic groups.

Researchers estimate that gay men and lesbians are about as likely to be abused by a partner as are women in heterosexual relationships (Freedberg, 2006). However, the exact prevalence rate of abuse in same-sex relationships is difficult to ascertain, because homosexuals are less likely than heterosexuals to seek medical attention for their injuries due to fear of discrimination. When gays and lesbians do seek help, researchers have found that health care professionals tend to overlook intimate partner abuse as a possible source of their injuries. As a result, emergency medical personnel may fail to question gays and lesbians about intimate partner abuse as they would heterosexuals.

Causes of Partner Abuse Cultural attitudes contribute to rates of abuse (McHugh, 2005). Specifically, in many societies, women are regarded as property, and a man's "right" to beat his partner may be protected by law. In fact, there was a time when, based on English common law traditions, this was true in the United States.

Gender-role prescriptions may also contribute to abuse. For example, rates of abuse are particularly high among Japanese women, over 50% of whom claim to have been victimized (Kozu, 1999). Researchers attribute the prevalence of abuse to the cultural belief that Japanese husbands are absolute authorities over their wives and children. Further, to avoid bringing dishonor on her husband, the Japanese wife is obligated to conceal abusive incidents from those outside the family.

Figure 13.2
Rates of Physical Abuse among Women around the World

These data on physical abuse are based on a World Health Organization international survey of medical records.

(*Source*: WHO, 2000.)

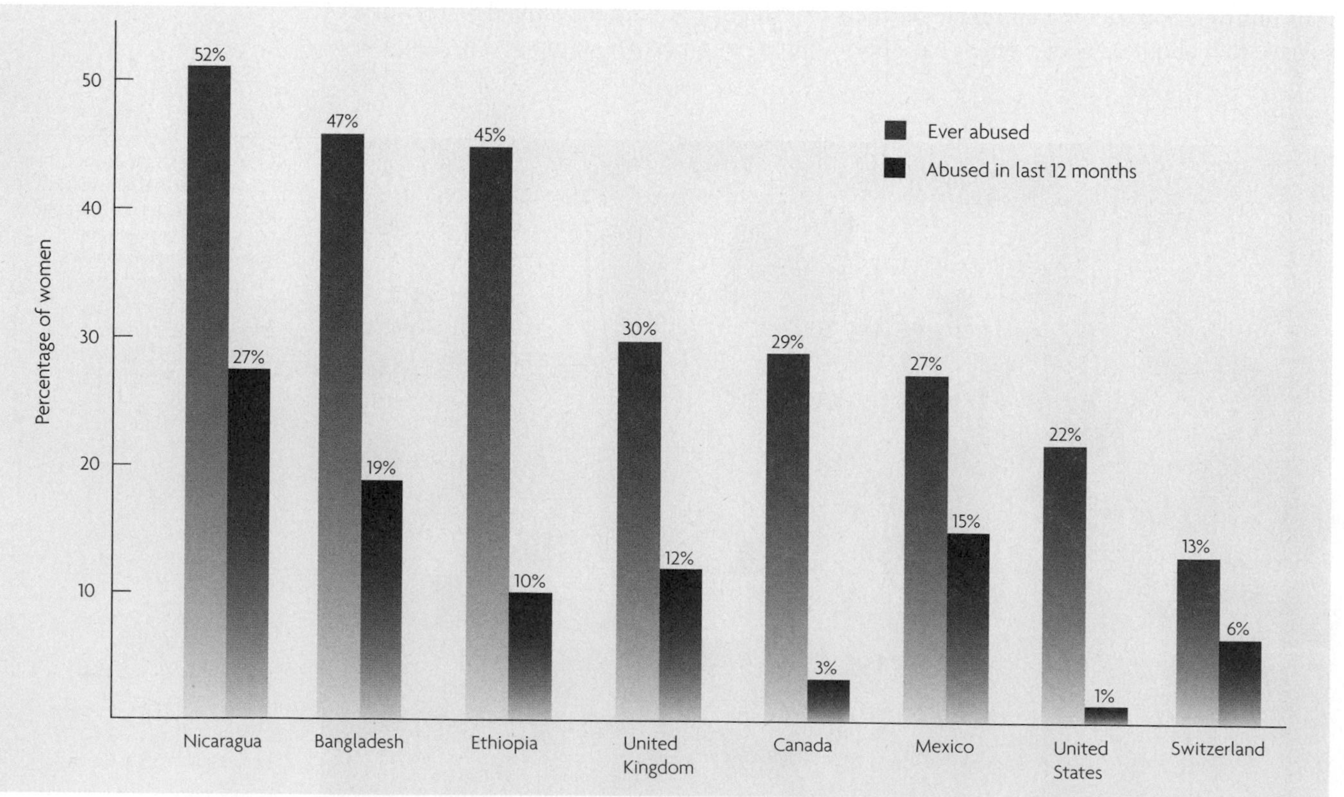

In addition to cultural beliefs, a number of characteristics of abusers and their victims are associated with intimate partner abuse. For example, the same cluster of personality traits in abusers contributes to abuse in both heterosexual and homosexual couples (Burke & Follingstad, 1999). The cluster includes a tendency toward irrational jealousy, a need for the partner's dependency and for control in a relationship, sudden mood swings, and a quick temper (Landolt & Dutton, 1997). Men who are generally aggressive are also more likely than less aggressive men to abuse their partners (Kane, Staiger, & Ricciardelli, 2000). In addition, men who are high school dropouts or who are frequently unemployed abuse their partners more often than other men (Kyriacou et al., 1999).

Abuse victims are more likely to have been abused as children than are their peers who are not involved in abusive relationships (Smith, White, & Holland, 2003; Wyatt et al., 2000). Age is also a factor. Young women between the ages of 16 and 24 are more likely to be abused than those who are older (NCIPC, 2006). This pattern of age differences may result from younger women's lesser ability to function independently from abusive partners. They may lack the education and/or work experience necessary to gain employment. Finally, younger women are more likely to be caring for infants and young children for whom they cannot obtain childcare. As a result, many such women remain in abusive relationships, believing they have no other choice (Kaplan & Sadock, 1991).

Alcohol and drug problems are more common among both abusers and victims than among nonabusive partners (NCIPC, 2006). One extensive study of more than 8,000 intrafamily killings found that, in about half of spousal homicides, the perpetrator had been drinking alcohol or using drugs (Dawson & Langan, 1994). Similarly, in 50% of cases, the victim had been using alcohol or drugs.

Effects of Abuse on Individuals Women who are abused may develop feelings of anxiety, depression, shame, and low self-esteem (Buchbinder & Eisikovits, 2003; NCIPC, 2006). Such feelings are intensified when victims believe they cannot escape from the abusive relationship. Some become so despondent that they consider or attempt suicide as an escape (NCIPC, 2000).

Witnessing abuse influences children's development. One study involving 420 adults who had witnessed physical violence between their parents as children suggested that there are strong relationships between parental violence and a variety of negative developmental outcomes (McNeal & Amato, 1998). For one thing, many of these adults were found to have poor relationships with their own partners and children. Moreover, many had become perpetrators or victims of partner abuse themselves.

Prevention Vigorous law enforcement is one approach to prevention (Dugan, Nagin, & Rosenfeld, 2003). Advocates of this approach suggest that the stigma of arrest may force abusers to face the reality that they have a serious problem. Training programs for law enforcement officials and hospital emergency room personnel that teach them to recognize signs of abuse are also essential (Hamberger & Minsky, 2000). Many experts also recommend training physicians and nurses to recognize and question patients about signs of abuse during routine medical exams (Scholle et al., 2003). As a result of such training, advocates claim, perpetrators may be identified and prosecuted even when victims do not voluntarily report abusive incidents.

A different approach is to provide victims with problem-solving skills and temporary shelters that may prevent their revictimization (NCIPC, 2000). Further, community-wide and school-based approaches to prevention seek to educate the public about intimate partner abuse and to change attitudes about the acceptability of violence in intimate relationships, so that abuse will not happen in the first place.

Sexual Violence **Sexual violence** is the term applied to episodes of partner abuse in which one individual uses force to coerce the other into engaging in sexual acts. Many such episodes involve strangers; however, more than three-quarters of sexually violent incidents in the United States occur in the context of some kind of relationship (Taylor & Gaskin-Laniyan, 2007). Surveys indicate that 14 to 25% of women have been victims of sexual

sexual violence the use of physical coercion to force a person to engage in a sexual act against his or her will

violence, while only 3% of men report such experiences (Elliott, Mok, & Briere, 2004; McFarlane & Malecha, 2005; NCIPC, 2000).

The psychological effects of being a victim of sexual violence include the development of sexual dysfunctions and posttraumatic stress disorder, as well as the possibility of physical trauma and pregnancy (Elliott et al., 2004). Men who are raped by other men also sometimes experience doubts about their sexual orientation (Kaplan & Sadock, 1991). Moreover, the psychological effects of sexual violence have been found to persist more than a decade in many victims (Elliott et al., 2004). Thus, being victimized by sexual violence can, overall, be one of the most traumatic episodes in a young adult's life.

One particularly troubling type of sexual violence among young adults is *date rape*, or rape that occurs in the context of a date. Men's belief that women say no when they mean yes is believed to contribute to such incidents. However, many cases of date rape are premeditated and involve the use of alcohol and drugs to loosen the inhibitions of the victim. Research indicates that such episodes may be more traumatic than rapes perpetrated by strangers because victims of date rape believe they should have been able to prevent the assault. Victims who were coerced with drugs and/or alcohol also frequently have incomplete memories of the event, a factor that increases their vulnerability to long-term negative emotional consequences (Gauntlett-Gilbert, Keegan, & Petrak, 2004).

Prevention of sexual violence often involves training potential victims to avoid situations in which such episodes are likely to occur (Kalmuss, 2004). Training in self-defense techniques, both verbal and physical, can also help women learn how to deal effectively with the initial phases of a threatened sexual assault (Hollander, 2004).

Learning Objective 13.7

Which mental disorders occur most frequently in young adulthood?

Mental Health Problems

Studies in a number of developed countries show that the risk of virtually every kind of emotional disturbance is higher in early adulthood than in middle age (Kessler et al., 2005). In fact, survey research suggests that as many as 10% of younger adults, those aged 18 to 24, have seriously considered committing suicide (Brener, Hassan, & Barrios, 1999).

Causes and Consequences of Mental Disorders The most plausible explanation for the differing rates of mental illness between young adults and middle-aged adults is that early adulthood is the period in which adults have both the highest expectations and the highest levels of role conflict and role strain. These are the years when each of us must learn a series of major new roles (spouse, parent, worker). If we fall short of our expectations, emotional difficulties such as anxiety and depression become more likely.

Some people respond very effectively to the challenges of young adulthood, while others do not. For example, the personal factors you read about in an earlier section are important to mental health as well as physical health. However, with respect to mental illness, researchers' attention is becoming more focused on biological causes.

First, mental illnesses tend to run in families, suggesting a genetic factor. In fact, the number of close relatives a person has who suffer from depression or other mood disorders is the best predictor of the likelihood that the individual will develop a mood disorder (Kendler et al., 1995). In addition, an increasing number of studies demonstrate links between mental illnesses and disturbances in specific brain functions (Drevets et al., 1997; Monarch, Saykin, & Flashman, 2004). Consequently, the current view of most psychologists is that mental disorders result from an interaction of biological and environmental factors.

When a young adult develops a mental health problem, the long-term impact of the problem depends on the degree to which it diverts her from an adaptive developmental pathway. For instance, if a college student develops one of these problems, she may have to leave school. Thus, many mental health professionals believe that once an effective treatment has been identified, educational and vocational rehabilitation services are critical to the young adult's full recovery. Longitudinal studies involving young adults with mental illnesses who have participated in educational/vocational rehabilitation programs support this view (Ellison, Danley, Bromberg, & Palmer-Erbs, 1999; Gralinski-Bakker et al., 2005).

Anxiety and Mood Disorders The most common mental disorders are those that are associated with fear and anxiety (Kessler et al., 1994). For example, *phobias* are fairly common. A **phobia** is an irrational fear of an object, a person, a place, or a situation. Most phobias are learned through association of the experience of being in a state of fear with a specific stimulus. For example, a college student who was injured in a car crash may avoid the intersection where the crash occurred, even though doing so adds time and distance to his daily trip from home to campus.

Since phobias are usually learned, therapeutic interventions usually involve some process of *un*learning the association. The most common way of accomplishing this is to expose a person to the stimulus that she is afraid of in some systematic way (Choy, Fyer, & Lipsitz, 2007). In fact many people "cure" their own phobias simply by exposing themselves to the fear-producing stimulus until it no longer induces anxiety. Thus, the student who is phobic about a particular intersection may tell himself that he is being silly and force himself to drive through it repeatedly until the phobic reaction no longer occurs.

After anxiety disorders, problems associated with moods are the most common type of mental difficulty (Kessler et al., 2005). Depression is the most frequent of these disorders. Rates of depression are higher in early adulthood than in either adolescence or middle age. Thus, paradoxically, the time of life in which people experience their peak of physical and intellectual functioning is also the time when they may be most prone to feelings of sadness. Depression rates may be higher in early adulthood because these are the years when people must create new attachment relationships while at the same time separating from parents (Erikson's task of *intimacy*). Consequently, feelings of loneliness and social failure may lead to depression (Comninos & Grenyer, 2007).

Researchers have found that about 40% of those who are diagnosed with depression display no signs of the disorder one year later (American Psychiatric Association, 2000). Another 20% are slightly depressed, but not sufficiently so to warrant a formal diagnosis of depression. Despite this rosy outlook, depression is a recurrent problem for many young adults and is linked to suicide (NCIPC, 2007). Antidepressant drugs help some sufferers recover, but some studies suggest that psychotherapy can be just as effective (Hollon, Thaw, & Markowitz, 2002).

Personality Disorders In a few cases, the stresses of young adulthood, presumably in combination with some biological factor, lead to serious disturbances in cognitive, emotional, and social functioning that are not easily treated. For example, a **personality disorder** is an inflexible pattern of behavior that leads to difficulties in social, educational, and occupational functioning. In many cases, the problems associated with these disorders appear early in life. However, the behavior pattern is usually not diagnosed as a mental disorder until late adolescence or early adulthood (APA, 2000). The five most common types of personality disorders are listed in Table 13.4 on page 388.

Some young adults may exhibit behavior that suggests a personality disorder because of stressors such as the break-up of a long-term relationship. For this reason, mental health professionals have to assess an individual's long-term and current levels of functioning in order to diagnose personality disorders. Ethnic and cultural standards of behavior also have to be taken into account, and physical illnesses that can cause abnormal behavior, such as disturbances in the endocrine system, have to be ruled out. Clinicians also have to keep in mind that some of these disorders are closely related, such as the narcissistic and histrionic disorders, and that some individuals suffer from more than one.

Generally, to be diagnosed with any of the disorders in Table 13.4, a young adult has to have been exhibiting the associated behavior since mid or late adolescence. In addition, the person should demonstrate the behavior consistently, across all kinds of situations. For example, a person who steals from an employer but generally respects the property rights of

phobia an irrational fear of an object, a person, a place, or a situation

personality disorder an inflexible pattern of behavior that leads to difficulty in social, educational, and occupational functioning

Table 13.4 Personality Disorders

Type	Characteristics
Antisocial	Difficulty forming emotional attachments; lack of empathy; little regard for the rights of others; self-centered; willing to violate the law or social rules to achieve a desired objective
Paranoid	Suspicious of others' behavior and motives; emotionally guarded and highly sensitive to minor violations of personal space or perceived rights
Histrionic	Irrational, attention-seeking behavior; inappropriate emotional responses; sexually seductive behavior and clothing
Narcissistic	Exaggerated sense of self-importance; craves attention and approval; exploits others; lack of empathy
Borderline	Unstable moods, relationships; fear of abandonment; tendency to self-injury; highly dependent on others; impulsive and reckless behavior

(*Source*: APA, 2000.)

others outside the work environment would probably not be diagnosed with antisocial personality disorder. The individual's functioning at work, at school, or in social relationships also must be impaired to some degree. Psychological tests can be helpful in distinguishing whether an individual simply has a troublesome personality trait, such as suspiciousness, or a genuine mental illness, such as paranoid personality disorder.

Some personality disorders, such as antisocial and borderline disorders, get better on their own as adults gain maturity (APA, 2000). However, most of these disorders remain problematic throughout adult life. In addition, they are not easily treated. In most cases, they do not respond to psychotherapy, because those who suffer from them seem to believe their problems result from others' behavior rather than their own.

Schizophrenia Another type of serious mental illness that is often first diagnosed in early adulthood is **schizophrenia**, a mental disorder characterized by false beliefs known as delusions and false sensory experiences called *hallucinations*. For example, a first-year biology student who breaks into a laboratory on his college campus to work on a cure for cancer he has just thought of may suffer from a *delusion of grandeur*. Likewise, a young woman who hears voices that guide her behavior is likely to be experiencing hallucinations.

For most people with schizophrenia, these disturbances of thought become so severe that they can no longer function at work, at school, or in social relationships. In fact, many engage in behavior that endangers themselves or others. For example, a person with schizophrenia may believe that he can fly and jump out of an upper-story window. Consequently, people with schizophrenia are frequently hospitalized. Fortunately, powerful antipsychotic medications can help most people with schizophrenia regain some degree of normal functioning (Lauriello et al., 2005). Yet many continue to experience recurring episodes of disturbed thinking even when medication helps them to gain control over their behavior.

schizophrenia a serious mental disorder characterized by disturbances of thought such as delusions and hallucinations

Learning Objective 13.8

What is the difference between physical and psychological substance dependence?

Substance Use and Abuse

Alcoholism and significant drug addiction also peak between ages 18 and 40, after which they decline gradually. The rates of addiction are higher for men than for women, but the age pattern is very similar in both genders (Thompson & Lande, 2007). Binge drinking (usually defined as consuming five or more drinks on one occasion) is also particularly common among 18- to 25-year-olds in the United States. Although most binge drinkers do not think of themselves as having a problem with alcohol, they clearly display a variety of problem behaviors, including substantially higher rates of unprotected sex, physical injury, driving while intoxicated, and trouble with the police (Wechsler, Davenport, Dowdall, Moeykens, & Castillo, 1994; Wechsler, Dowdall, Maenner, Gledhill-Hoyt, & Lee, 1998). Thus, alarmed by surveys showing that as many as 60% of 18- to 25-year-olds engage in binge drinking, a growing number of colleges and universities are strictly enforcing rules against on-campus substance use (Wechsler et al., 1998). Many also provide students with treatment for alcohol and substance abuse problems. Binge drinking is one of several substance use behaviors that can lead to **substance abuse**, a pattern of behavior in which a person continues to use a substance even though it interferes with psychological, occupational, educational, and social functioning. The journey from first use of a drug to abuse may be long or short. Four factors influence the addictive potential of a drug:

- how fast the effects of the drug are felt
- how pleasurable the drug's effects are in producing euphoria or in extinguishing pain
- how long the pleasurable effects last
- how much discomfort is experienced when the drug is discontinued

Some drugs create a physical or chemical dependence; others create a psychological dependence. *Physical drug dependence* comes about as a result of the body's natural ability to protect itself against harmful substances by developing a *drug tolerance*. This means that the user becomes progressively less affected by the drug and must take larger and larger doses to get the same effect or high (Ramsay & Woods, 1997). Tolerance occurs because the brain adapts to the presence of the drug by responding less intensely to it. In addition, the liver produces more enzymes to break down the drug. The various bodily processes adjust in order to continue to function with the drug present in the system.

Once drug tolerance is established, a person cannot function normally without the drug. If the drug is taken away, the user begins to suffer withdrawal symptoms. The *withdrawal symptoms*, both physical and psychological, are usually the exact opposite of the effects produced by the drug. For example, withdrawal from stimulants leaves a person exhausted and depressed; withdrawal from tranquilizers leaves a person nervous and agitated. Since taking the drug is the only way to escape these unpleasant symptoms, withdrawal can lead to relapse into addiction.

Psychological drug dependence is a craving or irresistible urge for the drug's pleasurable effects, and it is more difficult to combat than physical dependence (O'Brien, 1996). Some experts believe that drug cravings are controlled by a neural network that operates independently from and competes with a different network that controls deliberative decision making (Bechara, 2005). The drug-craving network acts on impulse that is largely influenced by the desire for immediate gratification. By contrast, the decision-making network identifies the consequences of potential actions and makes conscious decisions to engage in constructive behaviors and to avoid those that are destructive. This model of competing neural networks may explain why individuals who suffer from addiction often relapse despite their knowledge of the painful consequences that may occur as a result of doing so. Continued use of drugs to which an individual is physically addicted is influenced by the psychological component of the habit. There are also drugs that are probably not physically addictive but may create psychological dependence. Learning processes are important in the development and maintenance of psychological dependence. For example, drug-taking cues—the people, places, and things associated with using—can produce a strong craving for the abused substance (Hillebrand, 2000).

substance abuse a pattern of behavior in which a person continues to use a substance even though it interferes with psychological, occupational, educational, and social functioning

Alcohol is but one of many potentially addictive substances. However, it is the most commonly used of all of those that are listed in Table 13.5 on page 390. As a result of the widespread availability of alcohol, and the social acceptability of drinking, rates of abuse are much higher for alcohol than they are for other substances. Experts estimate more than 30% of adults in the United States have abused alcohol at some time in their lives (Hasin, Stinson, Ogburn, & Grant, 2007). Moreover, many individuals who abuse alcohol use other substances as well, and only 1 in 4 ever seek treatment for their drinking problems.

Critical Thinking

1. How would you rate your own health habits and personal factors, and how vulnerable do you think you are to sexually transmitted diseases, intimate partner abuse, mental health problems, and substance abuse? What behavioral changes might you make to reduce your risk?

Table 13.5 Substances of Abuse

Drug	Effects	Withdrawal Symptoms
Stimulants		
Caffeine	Produces wakefulness and alertness; increases metabolism but slows reaction time	Headache, depression, fatigue
Nicotine (tobacco)	Effects range from alertness to calmness; lowers appetite for carbohydrates; increases pulse rate and other metabolic processes	Irritability, anxiety, restlessness, increased appetite
Amphetamines	Increase metabolism and alertness; elevate mood, cause wakefulness, suppress appetite	Fatigue, increased appetite, depression, long periods of sleep, irritability, anxiety
Cocaine	Brings on euphoric mood, energy boost, feeling of excitement, suppresses appetite	Depression, fatigue, increased appetite, long periods of sleep, irritability
Depressants		
Alcohol	First few drinks stimulate and enliven while lowering anxiety and inhibitions; higher doses have a sedative effect, slowing reaction time; impairing motor control and perceptual ability	Tremors, nausea, sweating, depression, weakness, irritability, and in some cases hallucinations
Barbiturates	Promote sleep, have calming and sedative effect, decrease muscular tension, impair coordination and reflexes	Sleeplessness, anxiety, sudden withdrawal can cause seizures, cardiovascular collapse, and death
Tranquilizers (e.g., Valium, Xanax)	Lower anxiety, have calming and sedative effect, decrease muscular tension	Restlessness, anxiety, irritability, muscle tension, difficulty sleeping
Narcotics	Relieve pain; produce paralysis of intestines	Nausea, diarrhea, cramps, insomnia
Hallucinogens		
Marijuana	Generally produces euphoria, relaxation, affects ability to store new memories	Anxiety, difficulty sleeping, decreased appetite, hyperactivity
LSD	Produces excited exhilaration, hallucinations, experiences perceived as insightful and profound	None Known
MDMA (Ecstasy)	Typically produces euphoria and feelings of understanding others and accepting them; lowers inhibitions; often causes overheating, dehydration, nausea; can cause jaw clenching, eye twitching, and dizziness	Depression, fatigue, and in some cases a "crash," during which the person may be sad, scared, or annoyed

Cognitive Changes

Like most aspects of physical functioning, intellectual processes are at their peak in early adulthood. Indeed, it now seems clear that the intellectual peak lasts longer than many early researchers had thought and that the rate of decline is quite slow. Current research also makes clear that the rate and pattern of cognitive decline vary widely—differences that appear to be caused by a variety of environmental and lifestyle factors, as well as by heredity.

Learning Objective 13.9

What types of postformal thought have developmentalists proposed?

Formal Operations and Beyond

As you should recall from Chapter 11, Piaget's formal operational stage emerges in mid- to late adolescence, but some theorists dispute Piaget's hypothesis that the formal operations stage is the last stage of cognitive development (Labouvie-Vief, 2006). These theorists hypothesize that a fifth stage emerges in early adulthood, typically in the early 20s, in response to the kinds of problems that are unique to adult life.

The term **postformal thought** is collectively applied to the types of thinking that these theorists propose to be characteristic of the fifth stage of cognitive development.

What kind of thinking might this young couple be using to make a budget decision?

The work of postformal theorists owes its origins to the ideas of Lawrence Kohlberg, whose theory of moral development you read about in Chapter 12, and William Perry (Labouvie-Vief, 2006). Kohlberg and Perry emphasized the shift toward **relativism**, the idea that some propositions cannot be adequately described as either true or false, that occurs in early adulthood (Kohlberg, 1969; Perry, 1968). Perry studied undergraduates at Harvard University in the 1960s and concluded that they began their studies with the view that knowledge is comprised of truthful statements and that the purpose of education is to accumulate an increasing number of such propositions. As young adults progress through college, Perry's work suggested, conflicts among the many ideas to which they are exposed push them toward a relativistic approach that enables them to evaluate propositions in terms of their underlying assumptions and the contexts in which they occur.

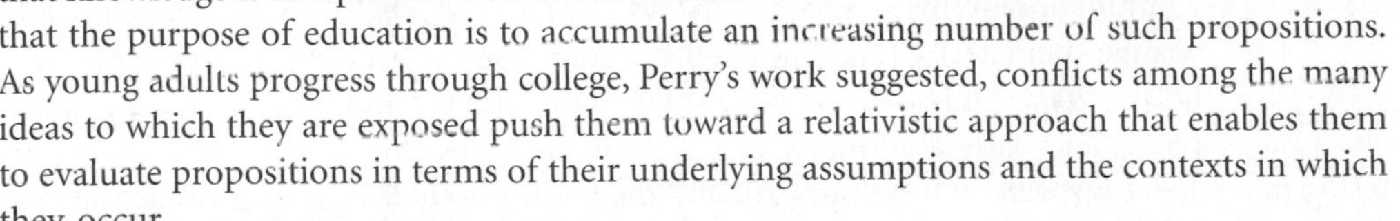

For example, in the United States, most high school history students learn that slavery was the main cause of the Civil War (1861–1865). According to Perry's view, a student who is presented with a different idea about the main cause of the war is likely to dismiss it as "false" rather than to analyze it with regard to the supporting evidence that is cited by the person who advocates it. Perry argued that college classes reframe the "facts" that students acquired in earlier years in just this way and, in the process, help students develop a postformal approach to such complex issues.

Other theorists place more emphasis on everyday thought processes than they do on thinking that occurs in academic contexts. One such theorist, Gisela Labouvie-Vief argues that adults learn how to solve the problems associated with the particular social roles they occupy or the particular jobs they hold (Labouvie-Vief, 1980, 1990). In the process, they trade the deductive thoroughness of formal operations for what Labouvie-Vief calls *contextual validity*. In her view, this trade-off does not reflect a regression or a loss, but rather a necessary structural change.

Another theorist, Michael Basseches, points out that many young adults turn away from a purely logical, analytic approach, toward a more open, perhaps deeper, mode of understanding that accepts paradox and uncertainty. He calls this new adult type of thinking **dialectical thought** (Basseches, 1984, 1989). According to this view, adults do not give up their ability to use formal reasoning. Instead, they acquire a new ability to deal with the fuzzier problems that make up the majority of the problems of adulthood—problems that do not have a single solution or in which some critical pieces of information may be missing. Choosing what type of refrigerator to buy might be a decision aided by formal operational thought. But such forms of logical thought may not be helpful in making a decision about whether to adopt a child or whether to place an aging parent in a nursing home. Basseches argues that such problems demand a different kind of thinking—not a "higher" kind of thinking, but a different one.

Psychologists Patricia King and Karen Kitchener (2004) have proposed that **reflective judgment**, the capacity to identify the underlying assumptions of differing perspectives on controversial issues, is an important feature of postformal thought. For example, reflective thinkers are capable of ascertaining that a person argues that the key to reducing drug use is to educate people about the adverse effects of drugs is assuming that those who use drugs do so because they lack such knowledge. According to the studies that King and Kitchener have carried out, the capacity to analyze arguments in this way develops in a series of seven stages across childhood, adolescence, and adulthood (King & Kitchener, 2004). Like Kohlberg's stages of moral judgment, these stages are loosely tied to age and are influenced by an individual's level of education.

postformal thought types of thinking that are associated with a hypothesized fifth stage of cognitive development

relativism the idea that some propositions cannot be adequately described as either true or false

dialectical thought a form of thought involving recognition and acceptance of paradox and uncertainty

reflective judgment the ability to identify the underlying assumptions of differing perspective on controversial issues

Many of these new theories of adult cognition are intriguing, but they remain highly speculative, with little empirical evidence to back them up. More generally, psychologists do not yet agree on whether these new types of thinking represent "higher" forms of thought, built on the stages Piaget described, or whether it is more appropriate simply to describe them as different forms of thinking that may or may not emerge in adulthood. What may be most important about such theories is the emphasis on the fact that the normal problems of adult life, with their inconsistencies and complexities, cannot always be addressed fruitfully using formal operational logic. It seems entirely plausible that adults are pushed toward more pragmatic, relativistic forms of thinking and use formal operational thinking only occasionally, if at all. Postformal theorists agree that this change should not be thought of as a loss or a deterioration, but rather as a reasonable adaptation to a different set of cognitive tasks.

Learning Objective 13.10

How do the concepts of crystallized and fluid intelligence help to explain age-related changes in IQ scores?

Intelligence

Examination of intelligence in early adulthood suggests that both continuity and change characterize this component of cognitive functioning (Schroeder & Salthouse, 2004). IQ scores remain quite stable across middle childhood, adolescence, and early adulthood. For example, a study of Canadian army veterans, tested first when they were in their early 20s and then again in their early 60s, yielded similar results; there was a correlation of .78 between verbal IQ scores achieved at the two ages (Gold et al., 1995). Over shorter intervals, the correlations were even higher.

The best single source of evidence on the stability of IQ in adulthood is a remarkable 50-year study by Werner Schaie, referred to as the Seattle Longitudinal Study (Schaie & Willis, 2005). Schaie's study has provided developmentalists with a number of important insights into how intellectual functioning changes across adulthood. One is the finding that longitudinal and cross-sectional data yield somewhat different pictures of these changes, a phenomenon first reported by Schaie in 1983 (Schaie & Hertzog, 1983). He began in 1956 with a set of cross-sectional samples; the participants in different samples were 7 years apart in age and ranged in age from 25 to 67. All participants took an IQ test at the outset of the study; a subset of the participants in each age group was then followed over 35 years and retested every 7 years. In 1963, another set of cross-sectional samples, covering the same age ranges, was tested, and a subset of these was retested 7, 14, 21, and 28 years later. Further samples were added in 1970, 1977, 1984, and 1991. This remarkable data-collection process enabled Schaie to look at IQ changes over 7-, 14-, 21-, and 28-year intervals for several sets of participants, each from a slightly different cohort. Figure 13.3 graphs one set of cross-sectional comparisons made in 1977, as well as 14-year longitudinal results smoothed over the whole age range. The test involved in this case is a measure of global intelligence on which the average score is set at 50 points (equivalent to an IQ of 100 on most other tests).

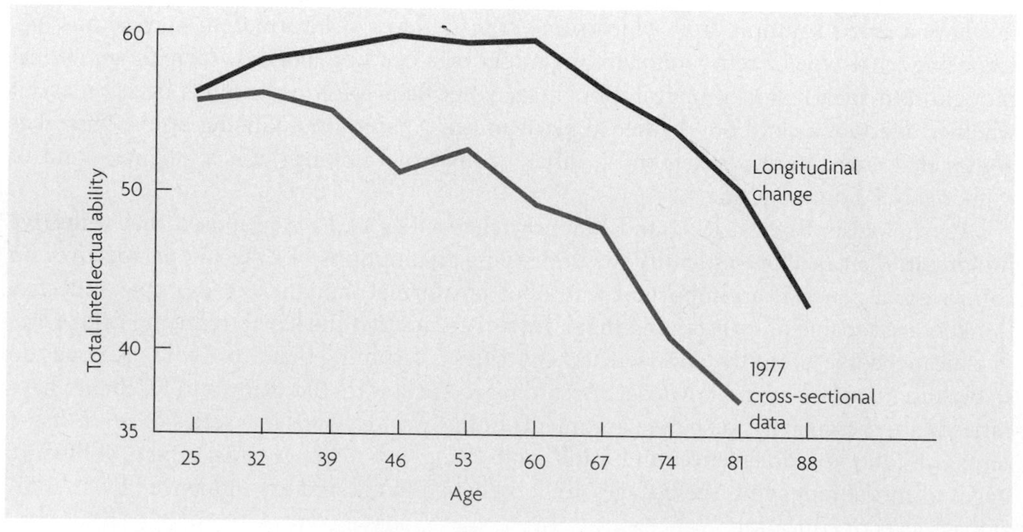

Figure 13.3 Cross-Sectional and Longitudinal Data on IQ Scores

These results from the Seattle Longitudinal Study show both cross-sectional and longitudinal data for a measure of overall intellectual skill (average score = 50).

(*Source*: Schaie, 1983, Tables 4.5 and 4.9, pp. 89 and 100.)

You can see that the cross-sectional comparisons show a steady drop in IQ. But the longitudinal evidence suggests that overall intelligence test scores actually rise in early adulthood and then remain quite constant until perhaps age 60, when they begin to decline. Since this pattern has also been found by other researchers (e.g., Sands, Terry, & Meredith, 1989; Siegler, 1983), there is good support for the temptingly optimistic view that intellectual ability remains essentially stable through most of adulthood.

Looking at different components of intellectual ability gives a clearer picture of change and stability across the adult years. **Crystallized intelligence** depends heavily on education and experience (Horn, 1982). It consists of the set of skills and bits of knowledge that every adult learns as part of growing up in any given culture, such as vocabulary, the ability to read and understand the newspaper, and the ability to evaluate experience. Technical skills you may learn for your job or your life—balancing a checkbook, using a computer, making change, finding the mayonnaise in the grocery store—also represent crystallized intelligence.

Fluid intelligence, in contrast, involves more "basic" abilities—it is the aspect of intelligence that depends more on the efficient functioning of the central nervous system and less on specific experience (Horn, 1982). A common measure of fluid intelligence is a "letter series test," in which a participant is given a series of letters (for example, A C F J O) and must figure out what letter should go next. This problem demands abstract reasoning rather than reasoning about known or everyday events. Most tests of memory also measure fluid intelligence, as do many tests measuring response speed and those measuring higher-level or abstract mathematical skills. Schaie's results, and the results of many other investigators, suggest that adults maintain crystallized intelligence throughout early and middle adulthood, but that fluid intelligence declines fairly steadily over adulthood, beginning at perhaps age 35 or 40 (Harvey, 2005; Schaie & Willis, 2005).

So where does this leave us in answering the question about intellectual maintenance or decline over adulthood? It seems safe to conclude, at least tentatively, that intellectual abilities show essentially no decline in early adulthood except at the very top levels of intellectual demand. In middle adulthood, though, declines on fluid intelligence abilities those tasks that are thought to represent the efficiency of the basic physiological process become evident (Harvey, 2005).

Critical Thinking

1. Earlier in the chapter you learned that most people reach their physical peak during early adulthood. What would you conclude about the development of a cognitive peak? When is it likely to occur, and in what ways is the process similar to and different from the development of one's physical peak?

Post-Secondary Education

In today's high-tech, global economy, **post-secondary education**—any kind of formal educational experience that follows high school—has become a necessity for virtually everyone. For some, post-secondary education may be a 1-year course of study that culminates in a certificate attesting to a marketable set of job skills, such as training in medical office management. For others, post-secondary education takes the form of enrollment in a 2- or 4-year college. At some point in their academic careers, most college students wonder whether all the hassles they experience are really worth the effort, as perhaps you may have. It should be somewhat heartening, then, to learn that college attendance is associated with a number of positive developmental outcomes.

crystallized intelligence knowledge and judgment acquired through education and experience

fluid intelligence the aspect of intelligence that reflects fundamental biological processes and does not depend on specific experiences

Developmental Impact

Learning Objective 13.11
What are some of the ways in which college attendance affects individual development?

There is no doubt about the economic value of post-secondary education. College graduates earn more than nongraduates for a variety of reasons (Pascarella & Terenzi, 1991). First, graduates get more promotions and are far less likely than nongraduates to be unemployed for prolonged periods of time. In fact, for minorities, a college education seems to outweigh the potential effects of racial prejudice in hiring decisions. Supervisors prefer minority college graduates to White nongraduates. In addition, college graduates have higher real and perceived status. This means that they are more likely

post-secondary education any kind of formal educational experience that follows high school

than nongraduates to get high-status managerial, technical, and professional positions, and they are viewed by those who make hiring decisions as more desirable employees than are nongraduates. This finding raises the question of whether college graduates are really different from nongraduates or are simply perceived to be. However, longitudinal evidence suggests that the longer a person remains in college, the better her performance on Piaget's formal operational tasks and other measures of abstract reasoning (Lehman & Nisbett, 1990; Pascarella, 1999).

There is also evidence that, during their years of college enrollment, students' academic and vocational aspirations rise (Sax & Bryant, 2006). For example, a young woman may enter college with the goal of becoming a biology teacher but graduate with the intention of going on to medical school. What seems critical to such decisions is that college-level classes allow students to make realistic assessments—for better or worse—of their academic abilities. Thus, another student may intend to be a doctor when he is a freshman but soon conclude that becoming a biology teacher is a more realistic, attainable goal, given his performance in college-level classes. Further, college attendance enhances students' internal locus of control and, as a result, helps them to understand how the daily behavioral choices they make shape their future lives (Wolfle & List, 2004).

In addition to cognitive and motivational benefits, going to college provides students with new socialization opportunities. Many students encounter people from racial or ethnic groups other than their own for the first time in college. Advances in moral and social reasoning, as well as increases in the capacity to empathize with others' feelings, are also linked to college attendance (Chickering & Reisser, 1993; Pascarella & Terenzi, 1991). However, the relationships among authoritative parenting, academic performance, and social adjustment you have read about so often in earlier chapters hold true for college students as well (Wintre & Yaffe, 2000). Thus, students' social experiences prior to entering post-secondary education seem to be critical to their ability to benefit fully from the college experience.

Learning Objective 13.12

How do traditional and nontraditional post-secondary students differ?

Traditional and Nontraditional Students

Due to the economic advantages of a college degree, more people than ever are enrolled in post-secondary education. However, only 27% of those who are enrolled are **traditional post-secondary students** who enrolled in college full-time directly after high school graduation (NCES, 2002). Just over 50% of traditional students manage to obtain a degree within six years of their first enrollment.

More than 70% of college students are **nontraditional post-secondary students** (NCES, 2006). Researchers classify students as nontraditional if they (1) delay entering college more than 1 year after high school graduation, (2) are independent from parents, (3) are employed full-time while enrolled, (4) are enrolled part-time, (5) have one or more children, (6) possess a GED rather than a high school diploma, or (7) are single parents.

Clearly, many of these variables apply to traditional students as well. To clarify traditional and nontraditional status, researchers classify students as *minimally*, *moderately*, or *highly* nontraditional, based on the number of these factors present in their lives. There is a clear association between traditional or nontraditional status and college graduation. As a result, only 30% of nontraditional students succeed in obtaining a degree within five years of their first enrollment. The more nontraditional factors a student possesses, the less likely he is to graduate from college.

Surveys of nontraditional students suggest that the supportiveness of an educational institution can be critical to helping then manage the conflicting demands of school, family, and work (Kirby, Biever, Martinez, & Gomez, 2004). These findings point to another important difference between traditional and nontraditional post-secondary students. Those who go directly from high school to college are concentrated in 4-year institutions, while the majority of nontraditional students attend 2-year colleges (NCES, 1997). Thus, graduation rates may vary across the two groups not only because of variables on which the students themselves differ but also because there are important differences between 2- and 4-year colleges. For example, 4-year institutions are more likely to have counseling centers where students can obtain career

traditional post-secondary student a student who attends college full-time immediately after graduating from high school

nontraditional post-secondary student a student who either attends college part-time or delays enrollment after high school graduation

guidance and help with personal problems. Likewise, students at 4-year schools, especially those who live on campus, spend more time socializing with one another. Thus, they have a greater opportunity to establish social networks on which they can rely for support in times of difficulty. In contrast, students at 2-year colleges typically do not socialize with or even see one another outside of class. Thus, students in 4-year college settings may be better supported both formally and informally by the institutions they attend.

Fortunately, officials at 2-year colleges have begun to recognize the need for greater student support. Many are therefore developing innovative programs—such as on-campus child care—based on students' needs. Likewise, officials are attempting to provide greater financial and facility support for student organizations so that students will have more opportunities for social interaction.

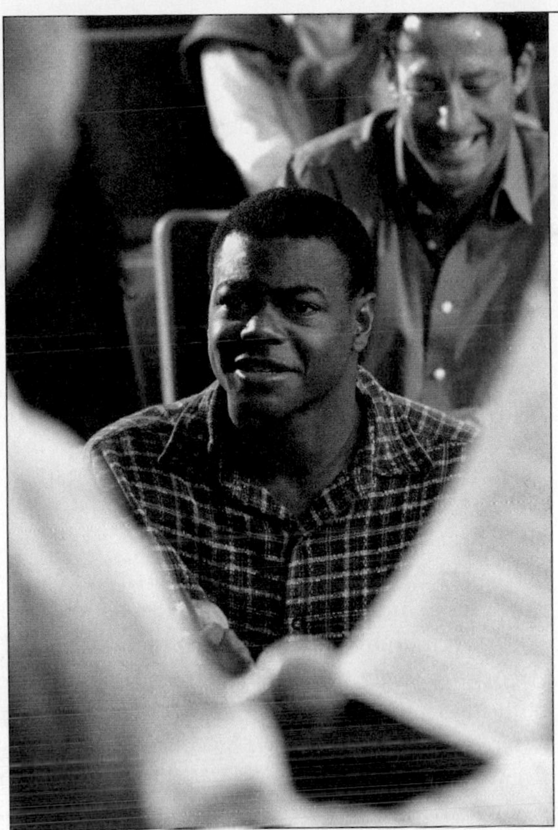

College attendance is associated with developmental advances in both the cognitive and social domains.

Students with Disabilities

Learning Objective 13.13

What does research suggest about the experiences of college students with disabilities?

Thanks to a federal law passed by the U.S. Congress in 1990, the Americans with Disabilities Act, many students with disabilities have access to post-secondary education. Colleges are now required to provide them with the same kinds of modifications provided by special education services in the public school system. Thus, blind students are provided with readers and Braille textbooks, hearing impaired students are accompanied by sign language interpreters when they attend class, and students in wheelchairs are guaranteed that classroom doors will be wide enough to allow them to enter. Moreover, many high schools have created partnerships with community colleges to provide transitional programs for students with disabilities that help them acquire the study techniques and life management skills essential for success in college (Hart, Mele-McCarthy, Pasternack, Zimbrick, & Parker, 2004; Pearman, Elliot, & Aborn, 2004). Consequently, students with disabilities now make up about 9% of the college population in the United States (NCES, 2003).

Although it is still too early to draw firm conclusions from research on college students with disabilities, recent studies contain some hints about how such students fare. For example, one reason for recent increases in college enrollment among students with disabilities is their belief that the required instructional modifications make it possible for them to compete academically with other students. The most common modification for such students is extended time for taking tests (Ofiesh, Hughes, & Scott, 2004). Research suggests that, with extended time, students with disabilities are able to approach or meet the same standards of academic performance required of other students in college classes (Alster, 1997). In addition, tutoring that helps students with learning disabilities learn reading strategies that are particularly helpful for reading college-level textbooks increase these students' chances for success (Gajria, Jitendra, Sood, & Sacks, 2007). Still, students with disabilities usually receive lower course grades than their non-disabled peers (Cosden & McNamara, 1997).

Research also suggests that students with disabilities perceive the college environment to be somewhat inhospitable to them. Although they perceive their peers to be accepting and supportive, many students with disabilities believe that college faculty do not fully accept them (Beilke & Yssel, 1999; Cosden & McNamara, 1997). They say that most professors are willing to comply with classroom modifications but have negative attitudes toward the required modifications and the students themselves.

Learning Objective 13.14

How is the college experience different for men and women?

Gender and the College Experience

Nearly 60% of college students are female, and women have slightly higher graduation rates than men at all degree levels and in both traditional and nontraditional post-secondary groups (NCES, 2005, 2007). Paradoxically, women's college entrance examination scores, especially in math, tend to be lower than men's. As a result, more males are admitted to selective universities. In addition, more men are accepted into honors programs. Thus, the different graduation rates of males and females are unlikely to be attributable to sex differences in intellectual ability. Rather, college men and women differ in attitudes and behavior in ways that significantly affect the likelihood of graduation (Noldon & Sedlacek, 1998).

Women's higher graduation rates may be due to their tendency to spend almost twice as much time studying as men do, while men spend about 50% more time partying than women do (Sax, Lindholm, Astin, Korn, & Mahoney, 2002). Moreover, when research reveals sex differences in study strategies, they usually favor the females. For example, college women in both the United States and Europe use a greater number of study techniques than do men (Braten & Olaussen, 1998). By contrast, college men are more likely to cheat (Szabo & Underwood, 2004; Thorpe, Pittenger, & Reed, 1999). Moreover, the kinds of study strategies women use are those that are most likely to lead to long-term retention of information (Pearsall, Skipper, & Mintzes, 1997).

Women also appear to adapt easily to the demands of new educational experiences. For example, women outperform men in distance learning classes. They also usually begin with lower levels of computer skills than men. However, when they enroll in classes that require such skills, they learn them very quickly and exhibit levels of performance equal to those of men whose initial skill levels were higher (Clawson & Choate, 1999).

Behaviors outside the classroom may matter as well. For example, binge drinking is more prevalent among college men than women (Keller et al., 2007). Similarly, men seem to be more influenced by peer behavior than women do. If a man is with a group of men who are drinking, he is likely to do so as well. Women are more likely to make individual decisions about behaviors such as alcohol use (Senchak, Leonard, & Greene, 1998).

Learning Objective 13.15

How does ethnicity affect the college experiences of minority students?

Race and the College Experience

As you can see in Figure 13.4, graduation rates vary across ethnic groups in the United States. Note, however, that these data refer to degree completion within a six-year time frame. Economic pressures often force students from disadvantaged groups to leave college temporarily or to reduce the number of credit hours they take each semester. As a result, these students may be less likely to finish college in six years than more economically advantaged Asian and White students (Seidman, 2005).

Of course, economic reasons alone cannot fully explain race differences in college completion. As we discussed in Chapter 11, many minority high school graduates lack the necessary academic preparation for college. Moreover, minority students who attend colleges that offer supportive programs whose aim is to prevent them from dropping out have higher graduation rates than their peers who do not attend such institutions (Gary, Kling, & Dodds, 2004; Hesser, Cregler, & Lewis, 1998).

The success of supportive programs for minority students may derive from their capacity for helping such students develop a sense of belonging to the college community. Research examining the relationship between student success and the ethnic composition of a college's student population support this view (Seidman, 2005). Studies have shown that Hispanic

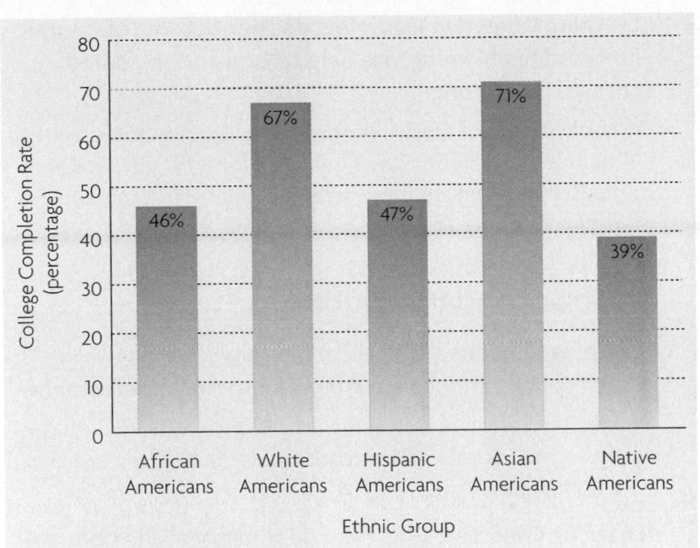

Figure 13.4
Degree Completion Rates in the United States

College completion rates vary considerably from one racial group to another. These figures represent the percentage of students who complete a degree within six years of taking their first course as a degree-seeking student.

(*Source*: NCES (2004), NEA (2004), Education Trust (2004)).

Americans, for example, exhibit higher levels of academic success when they attend colleges at which their ethnic group is in the majority and is also well represented among the faculty (Hagedorn et al., 2007). Researchers hypothesize that the levels of comfort and sense of belonging that such students feel on Hispanic-majority campuses make them more likely to seek help when they have academic problems.

Similarly, studies indicate that African American students who attend historically Black institutions show more gains in both cognitive and social competence than their peers who attend predominantly White colleges (Flowers, 2002; Flowers & Pascarella, 1999). In addition, attending historically Black colleges may help African American students achieve a stronger sense of ethnic identity, a factor which is correlated with persistence in college (Rowley, 2000).

The tribal college movement led by Native American educators has sought to provide the same type of culturally sensitive learning environment for reservation-dwelling Native Americans that historically Black colleges provide for African American students (American Indian Higher Education Council, 1999). By higher education standards, however, tribal colleges are newborns. Many European universities have existed for 800 years or more, and several universities in the United States have been in existence for more than 300 years. Moreover, the oldest historically Black colleges were founded in the first half of the nineteenth century. Thus, it is far too soon to determine whether the tribal college movement has been successful.

Critical Thinking

1. Review Erikson's stage of industry versus inferiority, discussed in Chapter 10. What would his theory predict about the link between experiences in elementary school and obtaining a college degree?

SUMMARY

Physical Functioning

Learning Objective 13.1 What is the difference between primary and secondary aging?

- It is important to distinguish between the unavoidable effects of primary aging and the preventable consequences of secondary aging.

Learning Objective 13.2 What changes in the brain take place in early adulthood?

- The brain reaches a stable size and weight in early adulthood. There is strong evidence that at least one spurt in brain development occurs between ages 17 and 21. Neuropsychologists hypothesize that a second spurt occurs in the mid- to late 20s. Sex differences are apparent in the adult brain, although their significance has yet to be established.

Learning Objective 13.3 How do other body systems change during these years?

- It is clear that adults are at their peak both physically and cognitively between ages 20 and 40. In these years, a person has more muscle tissue, more calcium in the bones, better sensory acuity, greater aerobic capacity, and a more efficient immune system.

Health and Wellness

Learning Objective 13.4 What habits and personal factors are associated with good health?

- The rate of loss of physical and cognitive abilities varies widely across individuals. Some of this difference seems to be explained by varying health habits. Social support and a sense of personal control also affect rates of disease and death, especially in the face of stress.

Learning Objective 13.5 What are some of the viral and bacterial STDs that afflict young adults?

- In contrast to other diseases, sexually transmitted diseases are more common among young adults than among older adults.

Learning Objective 13.6 What are the causes and effects of intimate partner abuse?

- Intimate partner abuse is a significant global health problem. Causal factors include cultural beliefs about gender roles, as well as personal variables such as alcohol and drug use.

Learning Objective 13.7 Which mental disorders occur most frequently in young adulthood?

- Rates of mental illness are higher in early adulthood than in middle adulthood; young adults are more likely to be depressed, anxious, or lonely than are the middle-aged. Early adulthood is the period during which personality disorders and schizophrenia are usually diagnosed.

Learning Objective 13.8 What is the difference between physical and psychological substance dependence?

- Physical dependence occurs when changes in the brain make it necessary to take a drug in order to avoid withdrawal symptoms. Psychological dependence is the craving that some substance abusers have for the effects of the drugs on which they are dependent.

Cognitive Changes

Learning Objective 13.9 What types of postformal thought have developmentalists proposed?

- There may be a change in cognitive structure in adult life, and theorists have suggested that cognitive development goes beyond Piaget's formal operational stage.

Learning Objective 13.10 How do the concepts of crystallized and fluid intelligence help to explain age-related changes in IQ scores?

- Some studies of measures of intelligence show a decline with age, but the decline occurs quite late for well-exercised abilities (crystallized abilities) such as vocabulary. A measurable decline occurs earlier for so-called fluid abilities.

Post-Secondary Education

Learning Objective 13.11 What are some of the ways in which college attendance affects individual development?

- Post-secondary education has beneficial effects on both cognitive and social development in addition to being associated with higher income.

Learning Objective 13.12 How do traditional and nontraditional post-secondary students differ?

- Nontraditional post-secondary students are more likely to obtain vocational certificates than bachelor's or associate's degrees.

Learning Objective 13.13 What does research suggest about the experiences of college students with disabilities?

- There is not yet enough research on students with disabilities to draw firm conclusions about their college experiences, but studies suggest that, with certain accommodations, they can be just as successful in college as students who do not have disabilities.

Learning Objective 13.14 How is the college experience different for men and women?

- Female students seem to have a number of important advantages over male students, including a higher graduation rate. However, many women lack confidence in their academic abilities and are reluctant to enter traditionally male occupations.

Learning Objective 13.15 How does ethnicity affect the college experiences of minority students?

- African American students are less likely to complete post-secondary programs than other groups, perhaps because they perceive White-dominated educational environments as hostile.

KEY TERMS

crystallized intelligence *(p. 393)*
dialectical thought *(p. 391)*
fluid intelligence *(p. 393)*
intimate partner abuse *(p. 382)*
limbic system *(p. 374)*
locus of control *(p. 380)*
maximum oxygen uptake (VO_2 max) *(p. 376)*
nontraditional post-secondary student *(p. 394)*
pelvic inflammatory disease *(p. 381)*
personality disorder *(p. 387)*
phobia *(p. 387)*
postformal thought *(p. 391)*
post-secondary education *(p. 393)*
primary aging (senescence) *(p. 372)*
reflective judgment *(p. 391)*
relativism *(p. 391)*
schizophrenia *(p. 388)*
secondary aging *(p. 372)*
sexual violence *(p. 385)*
substance abuse *(p. 389)*
traditional post-secondary student *(p. 394)*

TEST YOURSELF

Physical Functioning

13.1 Researchers have determined that, among adults, _________ has a very powerful influence on life expectancy and quality of health.

a. social class
b. IQ
c. number of children
d. marital status

13.2 Age-related, inevitable physical changes that have a biological basis and that are shared by all human beings are known as _________ aging.

a. normative
b. primary
c. secondary
d. tertiary

13.3 Which of the following is *not* an example of primary aging?

a. decline in ability to detect and discriminate among various smells
b. reduction in the density of dendrites
c. lowered fertility of women
d. obesity

13.4 Which of the following is *not* one of the recommendations for slowing the effects of secondary aging?

a. Get enough calcium.
b. Stop smoking.
c. Eat a lower-fat diet.
d. Exercise moderately once a week.

13.5 The part of the brain that regulates emotional responses is the

a. pituitary gland.
b. thymus.
c. limbic system.
d. gray matter.

13.6 Measured in a person at rest, VO_2

a. begins to decline gradually at about age 35.
b. shows no change with age.
c. increases gradually starting at age 40.
d. declines for women and goes up for men as a function of aging.

13.7 Ovulation becomes sporadic and unpredictable in some women as early as

a. the late 20s.
b. the early 30s.
c. the late 30s.
d. the early 40s.

Health and Wellness

13.8 According to the longitudinal Alameda County Study of health habits, the habit of _________ is not related to mortality.

a. eating breakfast
b. getting physical exercise
c. smoking
d. getting regular sleep

13.9 Which of the following is not linked with adequate social support?

a. lower risk of depression
b. increased stress
c. lower risk of disease
d. lower risk of death

13.10 Which of the following terms represents the belief that luck determines what happens to a person?

a. dialectical thought
b. external locus of control
c. post-formal thinking
d. self-efficacy

13.11 Viral STDs

a. can be treated with antibiotics.
b. are very rare.
c. afflict only women.
d. are incurable.

13.12 A vaccine was recently developed to protect women against some forms of

a. human immunodeficiency virus.
b. human papilloma virus.
c. herpes simplex virus.
d. hepatitis D virus.

13.13 Which of the following is *not* a characteristic associated with abusiveness in an intimate relationship?

a. alcohol and drug problems
b. mental illness
c. need for control in the relationship
d. frequent unemployment

13.14 Intimate partner abuse may have all of the following effects on women except

a. low self-esteem.
b. depression.
c. increased risk of heart disease.
d. suicidality.

13.15 All but which one of the following might result from being a victim of sexual violence?

a. posttraumatic stress disorder
b. decreased intelligence
c. physical trauma
d. sexual dysfunction

13.16 The risk of mental health problems, such as depression or anxiety, is higher

a. for men than for women.
b. in early adulthood.
c. for the elderly than for young adults.
d. for middle-aged adults than for young adults.

13.17 Which of the following is *not* a mental disorder that is more common in young adulthood than in middle adulthood?

a. substance abuse disorder
b. depression
c. alcoholism
d. dementia

13.18 In the United States, binge drinking is particularly common among

a. 18- to 24-year-olds.
b. those who dropped out of high school.
c. those who have been unable to find employment.
d. individuals who are professionally employed.

Cognitive Changes

13.19 Many researchers propose that new cognitive structures, or stages of thinking, develop in adulthood. Which of the following is *not* a structure, or stage, of thinking that develops in adulthood?

a. contextual validity
b. crystallized intelligence
c. dialectical thought
d. problem finding

13.20 Research evidence indicates that the term that best describes intellectual ability across adulthood is

a. crystallized.
b. declining.
c. increasing.
d. stable.

13.21 Which form of intelligence depends heavily on education and experience, such as the skills and knowledge learned as part of growing up in a culture?

a. contextual
b. crystallized
c. dialectical
d. fluid

Post-Secondary Education

13.22 What is the approximate percentage of U.S. college students who enrolled in college as full-time students immediately after high school graduation?

a. 27%
b. 34%
c. 54%
d. 73%

13.23 Which of the following statements about traditional and nontraditional students is true?

a. Nontraditional students are less likely to obtain a degree within six years.
b. Traditional students are less likely to obtain a degree within six years.
c. Nontraditional students are less likely to enroll in 2-year institutions.
d. Traditional students are less likely to enroll in 2-year institutions

13.24 Which of the following is a true statement about gender differences in college?

a. Women are more likely than men to cheat.
b. Women have higher graduation rates than men.
c. Women score higher than men on college entrance examinations.
d. Women are more likely than men to be admitted into honors programs.

13.25 Which of the following is *not* a true statement about the effect of race on the college experience?

a. Native Americans have the highest drop-out rate of all the ethnic groups.
b. African American students are more likely than students of other races or ethnicities to perceive themselves as not fitting into the college community.
c. A strong sense of racial identity is associated with persistence and academic performance for African American students.
d. African Americans who attend historically black colleges show more improvement in cognitive development than African Americans who attend predominantly white schools.

PEARSON mydevelopmentlab™ Study Plan

Are You Ready for the Test?

Students who use the study materials on MyDevelopmentLab report higher grades in the course than those who use the text alone. Here are three easy steps to mastering this chapter and improving your grade…

Step 1

Take the chapter pre-test in MyDevelopmentLab and review your customized Study Plan.

Between age 50 and 60, hearing changes so that

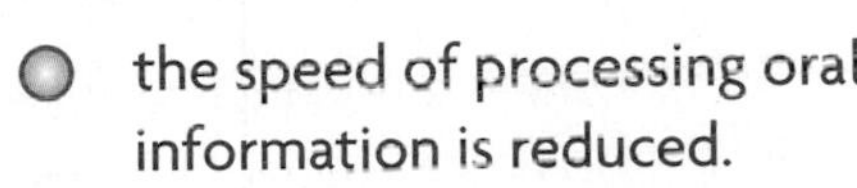

- the speed of processing oral information is reduced.
- there is a loss of ability to hear very high and very low tones.
- people have trouble distinguishing the sounds of language.
- people hear best at high frequencies.

Step 2

Use MyDevelopmentLab's Multimedia Library to help strengthen your knowledge of the chapter.

Simulate: Aging and Changes in Physical Appearance

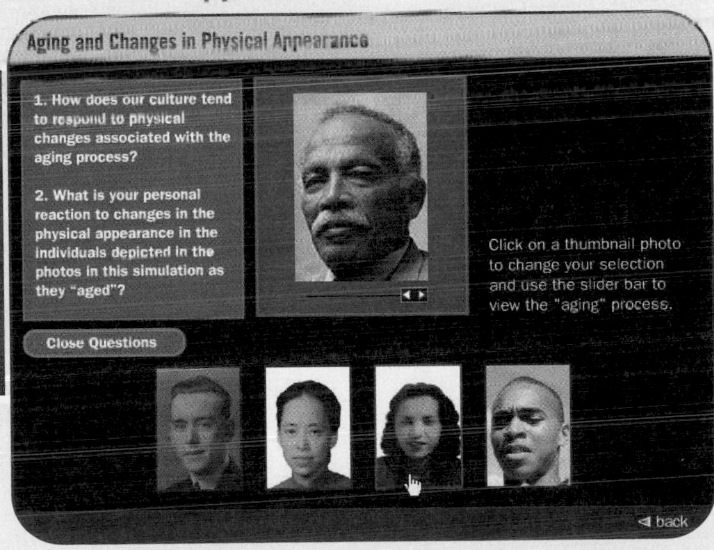

Aging and Changes in Physical Appearance
1. How does our culture tend to respond to physical changes associated with the aging process?
2. What is your personal reaction to changes in the physical appearance in the individuals depicted in the photos in this simulation as they "aged"?
Click on a thumbnail photo to change your selection and use the slider bar to view the "aging" process.
Close Questions
back

Learning Objective 13.1
What is the difference between primary and secondary aging?

www.mydevelopmentlab.com

continued on the next page

"MyDevelopmentLab is worth every cent! MyDevelopmentLab really furthered my understanding of course material and assisted me in areas I struggled with. The interactive format was much more enjoyable than simply memorizing a textbook."

—Sarah (Student), University of Wisconsin—Whitewater

Explore: Sources of HIV Infection in Adults

Learning Objective 13.5

What are some of the viral and bacterial STDs that afflict young adults?

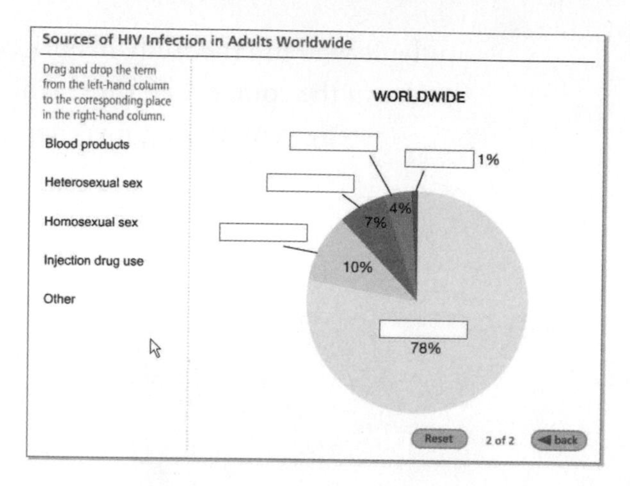

Sources of HIV Infection in Adults Worldwide
Drag and drop the term from the left-hand column to the corresponding place in the right-hand column.
Blood products
Heterosexual sex
Homosexual sex
Injection drug use
Other
WORLDWIDE
1%
4%
7%
10%
78%
Reset
2 of 2
back

Explore: Post-Secondary Education in Early Adulthood

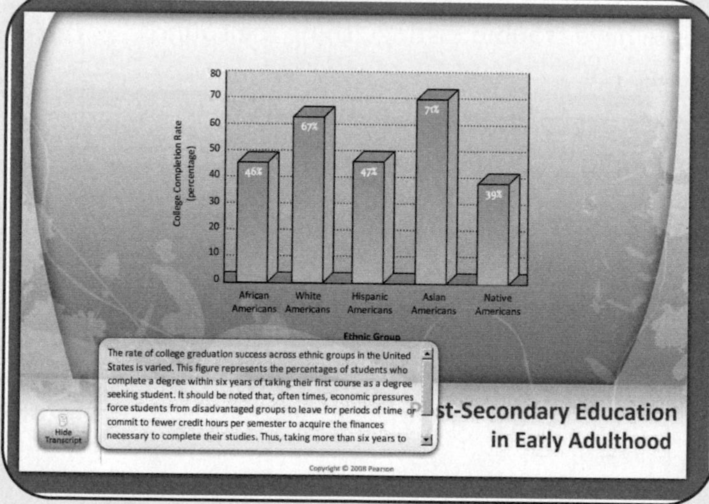

College Completion Rate (percentage)
80
70
60
50
40
30
20
10
0
46%
67%
47%
71%
39%
African Americans
White Americans
Hispanic Americans
Asian Americans
Native Americans
Ethnic Group
The rate of college graduation success across ethnic groups in the United States is varied. This figure represents the percentages of students who complete a degree within six years of taking their first course as a degree seeking student. It should be noted that, often times, economic pressures force students from disadvantaged groups to leave for periods of time or commit to fewer credit hours per semester to acquire the finances necessary to complete their studies. Thus, taking more than six years to
Hide Transcript
st-Secondary Education in Early Adulthood
Copyright © 2008 Pearson

Learning Objective 13.15

How does ethnicity affect the college experience of minority students?

Step 3

Take the chapter post-test and compare your results against the pre-test.

POST-TEST

The slightly higher graduation rates of female college students may be attributable to

- their use of study strategies which lead to long-term retention of information.
- the fact that college professors are more accepting of their answers.
- their overall superiority in intellectual abilities.
- their confidence in their ability to succees in even the most difficult professions.

Social and Personality Development in Early Adulthood

At what age is a person ready to get married? If you are from a Western culture, your answer to this question will probably begin with "it depends." In such cultures, the standards of the *social clock*, the ages at which adults are expected to achieve specific milestones, depend more on a person's educational, economic, and social status than on chronological age.

By contrast, there are many cultures in the world in which the social clock is far more rigidly tied to chronological age or to physical milestones such as puberty. Consider the case of Ferzana Riley whose family immigrated to the United Kingdom from Pakistan when she was just three years old. Ferzana's father insisted that his children be raised with the values of their host country, because he felt that embracing Western European culture would be best for their futures. Consequently, most of Ferzana's childhood friends were British, and

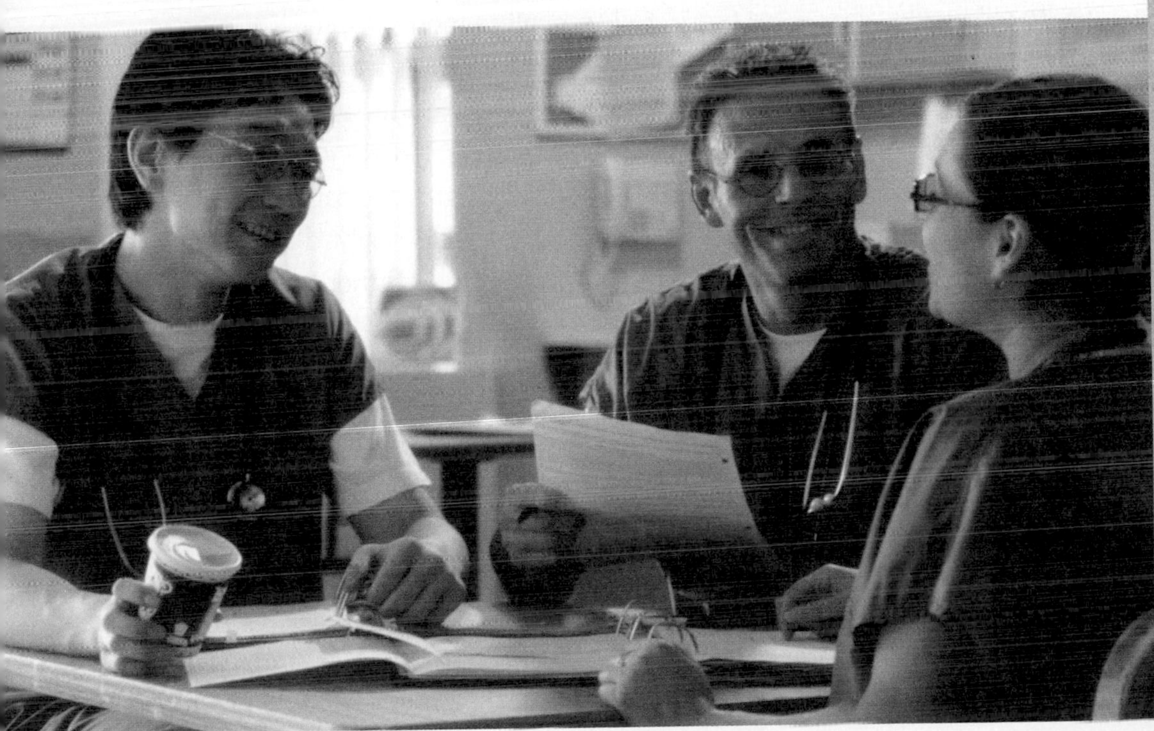

she acquired the beliefs about individual liberty that are common to all Western societies.

When Ferzana and her younger sister, Farah, reached adolescence, however, their mother began complaining of the shame she felt over their being unmarried and began exerting pressure on them to return to Pakistan to find suitable mates. This option was unthinkable to Ferzana and Farah, who thought of themselves as British and felt no special ties to the culture from which their parents had emigrated. As the years passed, Ferzana concluded that the only way to escape from her mother's harangues was to go away to college, an option that she knew her Western-minded father would endorse.

At college, Ferzana felt relieved to no longer be under the constant pressure to marry. She enjoyed her freedom so much that she dropped out of college, got a job, and began to live on her own. Shortly afterward, Farah left home and joined her. The young women's parents were furious but, after a while, family interactions returned to what Ferzana and Farah thought was an amicable state. When their mother asked them to accompany her on a two-week trip to visit family in Pakistan, they readily agreed.

Soon after they arrived in Pakistan, Ferzana and Farah realized that their mother had conspired with her extended family to keep them in Pakistan until they agreed to marry two local men of their family's choosing. The sisters' passports were confiscated so that they couldn't leave the country, and they were confined to a single room in their uncle's home. Day after day for 14 weeks, they were presented to eligible men. Despite these oppressive circumstances, the two young women made it clear that they would rather die than marry a stranger and demanded to return to Britain. In their darkest moments, Ferzana and Farah feared that they would become the victims of an *honor killing*, a form of homicide that some cultures practice to rid families of daughters who have brought disgrace upon them. The sisters' lowest point came when their father beat Ferzana to unconsciousness one night in hopes of forcing her into submission. Stunned by the ferocity of Ferzana's beating, a cousin intervened on behalf of the sisters. He persuaded their parents that the marriage mission had failed and that they had to go back to the United Kingdom. Today, Ferzana is happily married to a man whom she chose for herself, and she has told her story in a book called *Unbroken Spirit* (Riley, 2007).

Fortunately, Ferzana's experience is not typical. Most Middle Eastern immigrants to the United Kingdom find ways of integrating their customs with those of the British. For instance, arranged marriages are common in their communities, but the vast majority of parents recognize their children's right to accept or reject proposed matches. Nevertheless, British officials estimate that nearly 300 immigrant children, teenagers, and young adults are taken back to their countries of origin and forced to marry every year (Home Office Press Office, 2004). This practice is condemned by these countries' governments as well as by that of the United Kingdom (Associated Press, 2007). Thus, in Pakistan, India, and other countries, British and local officials are working together to end the practice of forced marriage.

As you will learn in this chapter, even under the best of circumstances, the role transitions of early adulthood can be stressful. Part of the stress comes from the fact that so many transitions occur in such a relatively short period of time. Still, each of these transitions brings with it new opportunities for personal growth.

Social scientists have not done very well at devising theories to explain lovely romantic moments like these.

Theories of Social and Personality Development

Psychoanalytic theories view adult development, like development at younger ages, as a result of a struggle between a person's inner thoughts, feelings, and motives and society's demands. Other perspectives provide different views of this period. Integrating ideas from all of them allows us to better understand early adult development.

Erikson's Stage of Intimacy versus Isolation

Learning Objective 14.1
What did Erikson mean when he described early adulthood as a crisis of intimacy versus isolation?

For Erikson, the central crisis of early adulthood is **intimacy versus isolation**. The young adult must find a life partner, someone outside her own family with whom she can share her life, or face the prospect of being isolated from society. More specifically, **intimacy** is the capacity to engage in a supportive, affectionate relationship without losing one's own sense of self. Intimate partners can share their views and feelings with each other without fearing that the relationship will end. They can also allow each other some degree of independence without feeling threatened.

As you might suspect, successful resolution of the intimacy versus isolation stage depends on a good resolution of the identity versus role confusion crisis you read about in Chapter 12. Erikson predicted that individuals who reached early adulthood without having established a sense of identity would be incapable of intimacy. That is, such young adults would be, in a sense, predestined to social isolation.

Still, a poor sense of identity is only one barrier to intimacy. Misunderstandings stemming from sex differences in styles of interaction can also get in the way. To women, intimacy is bound up with self-disclosure. Thus, women who are involved with a partner who does not reveal much that is personal perceive the relationship as lacking in intimacy. However, most men don't see self-disclosure as essential to intimacy. Consequently, many men are satisfied with relationships that their female partners see as inadequate.

Though many people involved in intimate relationships wish their relationships were better, most adults succeed in establishing some kind of close relationship. Not everyone marries, of course, but many adults develop affectionate, long-lasting friendships that are significant

intimacy versus isolation Erikson's early adulthood stage, in which an individual must find a life partner or supportive friends in order to avoid social isolation

intimacy the capacity to engage in a supportive, affectionate relationship without losing one's own sense of self

sources of support for them and may, in some cases, serve the same functions as having an intimate life partner.

Learning Objective 14.2

What is a life structure, and how does it change?

Levinson's Life Structures

Daniel Levinson's concept of *life structure* represents a different approach to adult development (Levinson, 1978, 1990). A **life structure** includes all the roles an individual occupies, all of his or her relationships, and the conflicts and balance that exist among them. Figure 14.1 illustrates how life structures change over the course of adulthood.

life structure in Levinson's theory, the underlying pattern or design of a person's life at a given time, which includes roles, relationships, and behavior patterns

Like Erikson, Levinson theorized that each of these periods presents adults with new developmental tasks and conflicts. He believed that individuals respond psychologically to these tasks and conflicts by creating new life structures. Consequently, adults cycle through periods of stability and instability.

As adults enter a period in which a new life structure is required, there is a period of adjustment, which Levinson called the *novice* phase. In the *mid-era* phase, adults become more competent at meeting the new challenges through reassessment and reorganization of the life structure they created during the novice phase. Stability returns in the *culmination* phase, when adults have succeeded in creating a life structure that allows them to manage the demands of the new developmental challenges with more confidence and less distress.

For example, marriage requires a new life structure. Even if the newlyweds have known each other for a very long time or have been living together, they have not known each other in the roles of husband and wife. Moreover, they have never had in-laws. So, young adults who marry acquire a whole new set of relationships. At the same time, they face many new day-to-day, practical issues such as how finances will be managed, how housekeeping chores will be done, and whose family they will visit on which holidays. As Levinson's theory predicts, newlyweds usually go through a period of adjustment, during which they experience more conflict than before the wedding, and after which things are much calmer. The calm comes, as Levinson would put it, when each spouse has achieved a new life structure that is adapted to the demands of marriage.

Figure 14.1
Levinson's Model of Adult Development

Levinson's model of adult development. Each stable life structure is followed by a period of transition in which that structure is re-examined.

(*Source*: From *The Seasons of A Man's Life* by Daniel Levinson, copyright © 1975, 1978 by Daniel J. Levinson. Used by permission of Alfred A. Knopf, a division of Random House, Inc., and SII/Sterling Lord Literistic, Inc.)

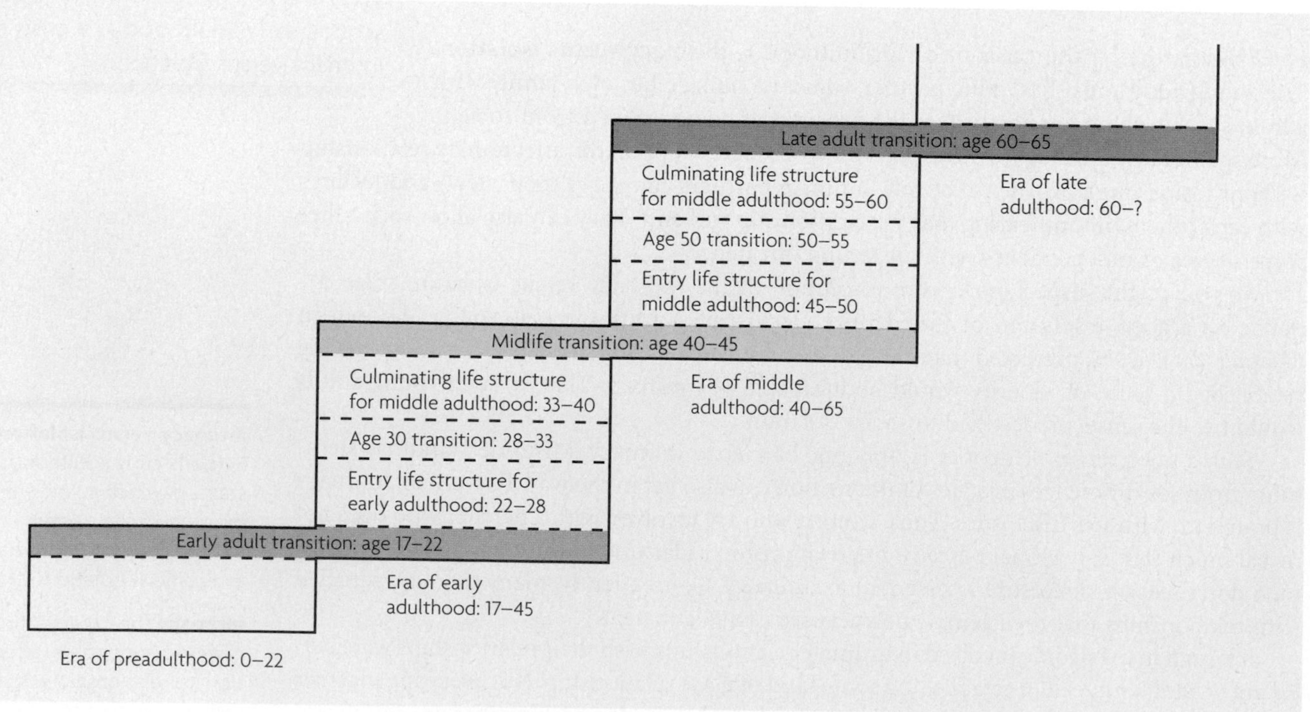

Emerging Adulthood

Learning Objective 14.3

What are the characteristics of emerging adulthood?

Like Levinson, a growing number of developmentalists view the period between 17 and 22 as a transitional one. Psychologist Jeffrey Arnett has proposed that the educational, social, and economic demands that modern cultures make in individuals in this age range have given rise to a new developmental period he calls **emerging adulthood**. Arnett defines this phase as the period from the late teens to the early twenties when individuals experiment with options prior to taking on adult roles (Arnett, 2000). Research examining the self-concepts of men and women in this age group support Arnett's view. His own studies and those of other researchers indicate that, at least in the United States, young people do not tend to think of themselves as having fully attained adulthood until the age of 25 or so (Galambos, Turner, & Tilton-Weaver, 2005).

Neuroimaging studies have provided some support for the notion that emerging adulthood is a unique period of life. These studies suggest that the parts of the brain that underlie rational decision making, impulse control, and self-regulation mature during these years (Crone et al., 2006; Gotay et al., 2004). As a result, early on in this phase of life, individuals make poorer decisions about matters such as risky behaviors (e.g., unprotected sex) than they do when these brain areas reach full maturity in the early to mid-twenties.

The neurological changes of the emerging adult period combine with cultural demands to shape the psychosocial features of this period of development. Researcher Glenn Roisman and his colleagues have hypothesized that emerging adults must address developmental tasks in five domains: academic, friendship, conduct, work, and romantic (Roisman et al., 2004). Roisman's research suggests that skills within the first three of these domains transfer easily from adolescence to adulthood. Useful study skills (academic) acquired in high school, for instance, are just as helpful in college. Likewise, the skills needed to make and keep friends (friendship) are the same in both periods, and the process of adapting to rules (conduct) is highly similar as well.

By contrast, emerging adults must approach the work and romantic domains differently than they did as adolescents, according to Roisman. Certainly, many teenagers have jobs and are involved in romances. However, the cultural expectations associated with emerging adulthood require them to commit to a career path that will enable them to achieve full economic independence from their families. Likewise, emerging adults must make decisions about the place of long-term romantic relationships in their present and future lives as well as participate in such relationships. As predicted by his hypothesis, Roisman's findings and those of other researchers suggest that emerging adults experience more adjustment difficulties related to these two domains than they do in the academic, friendship, and conduct domains (Korobov & Thorne, 2006).

Finally, psychologists speculate that the tendency of emerging adults to push the limits of the independence from their families that most acquire in the late teens contributes to the remarkable neurological changes that occur during this phase. Thus, the road that leads to fulfillment of the developmental tasks outlined by Roisman is often a bumpy one. The hope of most parents and teachers of emerging adults is that each of these bumps further opens, rather than closes, the doors of opportunity to emerging adults.

Critical Thinking

1. What are the similarities and differences among Erikson's, Levinson's, and Arnett's approach to early adulthood?

Intimate Relationships

Was Erikson correct about the importance of intimate relationships in early adulthood? Statistics on household composition in the United States (see Figure 14.2 on page 408) suggest that he was if you examine them closely. Households are about evenly divided between those that are headed by a married couple and living arrangements that involve other kinds of relationships. However, a broader interpretation of the data below suggests that "coupled" households continue to be more common among adults than those that are headed by singles (54%

emerging adulthood the period from the late teens to early twenties when individuals explore options prior to committing to adult roles

Figure 14.2
Household Composition in the United States

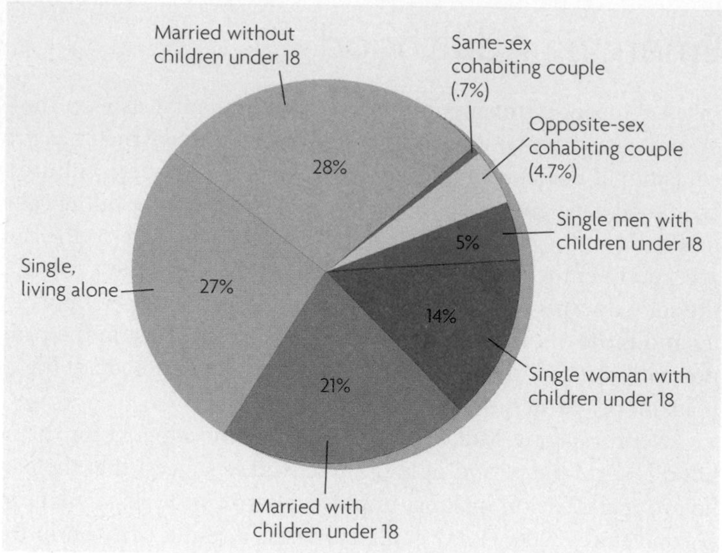

versus 46%). Furthermore, many individuals in the single-person-household and single-parent-household groups were previously married or partnered, and many of them have partners who also live in single-person households. Thus, partnering, or as Erikson would put it, the search for intimacy, continues to be an important facet of adult life in the United States.

Learning Objective 14.4
What types of research do evolutionary and social role theorists cite to support their theories of mate selection?

Theories of Mate Selection

What are the characteristics that men and women look for in an intimate partner? Some theorists claim that males and females answer this question differently because of evolutionary pressures. Others argue that the roles that men and women occupy in the cultures in which they live shape their ideas about what kind of person would be an ideal mate.

Evolutionary Theories As you should remember from Chapter 2, evolutionary explanations of behavior focus on survival value. Heterosexual relationships ensure the survival of the species, of course, because they are the context in which conception takes place. However, when choosing a mate, heterosexuals don't simply look for someone of the opposite sex. Instead, mating is a selective process, and evolutionary theorists often cite research on sex differences in mate preferences and mating behavior in support of their views. Cross-cultural studies conducted over a period of several decades suggest that men prefer physically attractive, younger women, while women look for men whose socio-economic status is higher than their own, who offer earning potential and stability (Buss, 1999; Schmidt, Shackelford, & Buss, 2001).

The reasons behind men's and women's divergent mating goals are explained by **parental investment theory** (Trivers, 1972). This theory proposes that men value health and availability in their mates and are less selective because their minimum investment in parenting offspring—a single act of sexual intercourse—requires only a few minutes. In contrast, women's minimum investment in childbearing involves nurturing an unborn child in their own body for 9 months as well as enduring the potentially physically traumatic experience of giving birth. Given their minimum investments, men seek to maximize the likelihood of survival of the species by maximizing the number of their offspring; women seek to minimize the number of their offspring because their investment is so much greater.

parental investment theory the theory that sex differences in mate preferences and mating behavior are based on the different amounts of time and effort men and women must invest in child-rearing

Further, evolutionary theorists argue that both men and women realize that a truly adaptive approach to child-rearing requires much more than a minimum investment (Buss, 1999). Human offspring cannot raise themselves. Therefore, men value health and youth in their mates not only because these traits suggest fertility but also because a young, healthy woman is likely to live long enough to raise the children. Similarly, women realize that to be able to nurture children to adulthood, they must have an economic provider so that they will be able to invest the time needed to raise offspring. Consequently, they look for men who seem to be capable of fulfilling these requirements.

As mentioned above, consistent sex differences in mate preferences and mating behavior have been found across many cultures, and evolutionary theorists suggest that this cross-cultural consistency is strong evidence for a genetic basis for the behavior. However, these claims take us back to the basic nature-versus-nurture arguments we have examined so many times before. Certainly, these sex differences are consistent, but they could be the result of variations in gender roles that are passed on within cultures.

Social Role Theory **Social role theory** provides a different perspective on sex differences in mating (Eagly & Wood, 1999). According to this view, such sex differences are adaptations to gender roles that result from present-day social realities rather than from natural selection pressures that arose in a bygone evolutionary era. To test this hypothesis, social role theorists reanalyzed a very large set of cross-cultural data, a data set produced and interpreted by evolutionary psychologist David Buss in support of parental investment theory (Buss et al., 1990). In their reanalysis, advocates of social role theory found that both men's and women's mate preferences changed as women gained economic power (Eagly & Wood, 1999): Women's emphasis on potential mates' earning power declined, and men's focus on potential mates' domestics skills decreased.

Researchers have also found that college-educated women with high earning potential prefer to date and marry men whose income potential is higher than their own (Wiederman & Allgeier, 1992). In fact, the more a woman expects to earn herself, the higher are her income requirements in a prospective mate. This study was widely cited by evolutionary theorists as supporting their view that such preferences are genetic and are not influenced by cultural conditions. However, a different perspective on the same study, proposed by social role theorists, led to a different conclusion (Eagly & Wood, 1999). These theorists suggest that many of today's high income women desire to take time off to have and raise children. To be able to do so without lowering their standard of living substantially, these women require a mate who can earn a lot of money. Thus, social role theorists say, such research findings can be explained by social role theory just as well as by evolutionary theory.

In addition, social role theorists point out that high-income women desire high-income husbands because members of both sexes prefer mates who are like themselves. People are drawn to those who are similar in age, education, social class, ethnic group membership, religion, attitudes, interests, and temperament. Sociologists refer to this tendency as **assortative mating**, or **homogamy**. Further, partnerships based on homogamy are much more likely to endure than are those in which the partners differ markedly (Murstein, 1986).

Marriage

Learning Objective 14.5

How do marriage and divorce affect the lives of young adults?

News reports about the trend toward later marriage in the United States today might make you think that the popularity of this ancient institution is on the wane. Indeed, the average age at first marriage in the United States rose from about 21 for both men and women in 1970 to 27 for men and 25 for women in the early years of the 21st century (Johnson & Dye, 2005). Still, nearly 300,000 couples get married every month and there are 2.4 million formal weddings every year (Hallmark Corporation, 2004; Sutton & Munson, 2004). Clearly, the institution of marriage is alive and well (see No Easy Answers on page 410). Moreover, most marriages endure. The often-quoted statistic of a 50% divorce rate is derived from dividing the number of marriages each year by the number of divorces. For instance, in 2002, 8 in every 1,000 adults in the United States married, while 4 in every 1,000 divorced (U.S. Bureau of the Census, 2003a). Like cross-sectional studies, though, such statistics often reflect cohort differences. Longitudinal studies of marital duration suggest that only about 20% of marriages end in divorce (U.S. Bureau of the Census, 1997). Moreover, after a couple have been married for 8 years, the probability that they will divorce declines to nearly zero.

social role theory the idea that sex differences in mate preferences and mating behavior are adaptations to gender roles

assortative mating (homogamy) sociologists' term for the tendency to mate with someone who has traits similar to one's own

NO EASY ANSWERS

Avoiding Bridal Stress Disorder

Imagine that you just got engaged to be married and shared the news with your best friend. What kinds of questions do you think your friend would ask about your future plans? If you are female (and so is your best friend), the questions are likely to focus on the characteristics of your wedding ceremony. Studies show that weddings continue to be a feminine domain, with future brides far more concerned about the particulars of the event than future grooms are (Knox, Zusman, McGinty, & Abowitz, 2003).

Marriage rituals, of course, have been an integral part of societies all over the world for thousands of years. The difference between the modern-day version and those that were common in earlier days is one of degree. The *average* formal wedding in the United States now costs more than $27,000, but the price tag varies widely from one part of the country to another. In some regions, the average wedding costs almost $40,000. At www.costofwedding.com, you can enter your zip code and find out the average for your area.

With so much money at stake and with the potential for hurt feelings on the part of acquaintances who aren't invited to the reception or cousins who aren't asked to be bridesmaids, not to mention concerns about how she will look in a wedding gown, wedding planning can be a stressful experience for the bride-to-be. Consequently, there are now dozens of books and several Internet sites devoted to advice on how to reduce wedding-related stress. One such site even purports to address prevention of "bridal stress disorder" (see http://www.uniquethemeweddings.com).

It's doubtful that the stresses associated with wedding planning constitute an actual psychological disorder, but these stresses, like many others in life, can significantly diminish an individual's quality of life. Psychological research says that the best approach to managing wedding-related stress is one that balances *problem-focused coping* and *emotion-focused coping* (Folkman & Lazarus, 1980). Problem-focused coping involves managing the actual source of stress. When brides-to-be set firm budget guidelines for themselves and research ways to limit spending in order to conform to them, they are engaging in this kind of coping. Emotion-focused coping has to do with managing emotional responses to current or potential stressors. A bride-to-be who treats herself to a massage in the midst of the wedding-planning frenzy is using emotion-focused coping.

Finally, most engaged couples nowadays enroll in wedding gift registries so that those who want to give them gifts will know what kinds of dishes, sheets, and other household items they want. However, the best gift for a couple to request might be a new service, called *marriage insurance*—a series of post-wedding counseling sessions that help couples cope with the transition to marriage (Thomas, 2003). Such a gift may help future brides remember that a beautiful wedding doesn't ensure a happy marriage.

Take a Stand

Decide which of these two statements you most agree with and think about how you would defend your position:

1. A wedding marks one of the most important events in a person's life; thus it is worth whatever it costs both financially and psychologically.
2. It is foolish to spend thousands of dollars on an event that usually lasts only a few hours, and such spending takes funds away from the couple's financial goals such as buying their first home.

On average, married adults are happier and healthier, live longer, and have lower rates of a variety of psychiatric problems than do adults without committed partners, findings that are discussed further in the Research Report on page 412 (Coombs, 1991; Glenn & Weaver, 1988; Lee, Seccombe, & Shehan, 1991; Ross, 1995; Sorlie, Backlund, & Keller, 1995). Clearly, though, not all marriages are happy ones. What are the factors that contribute to marital satisfaction?

Relationship Quality While we often discuss differences across ethnic groups, you can see in Figure 14.3 that there is a remarkable amount of agreement across groups about what makes a marriage work (Taylor, Funk, & Clark, 2007). Importantly, a large majority of adults

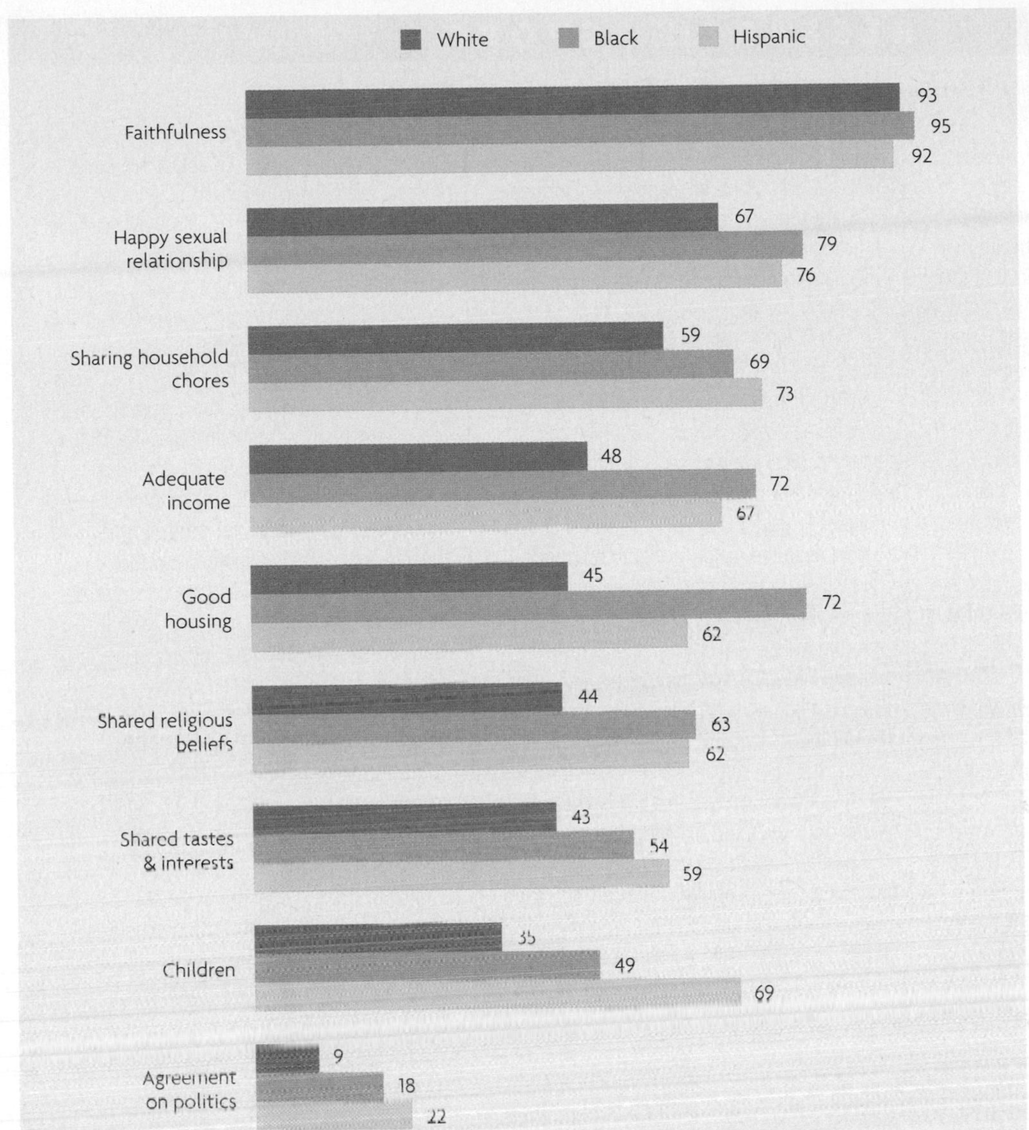

Figure 14.3
Rating Components of Marital Success, by Race and Ethnicity

Percent saying each is very important for a successful marriage

Note: Whites include only non-Hispanic Whites. Blacks include only non-Hispanic Blacks. Hispanics are of any race.

(*Source*: From *Generation Gap in Values, Behaviors As Marriage and Parenthood Drift Apart, Public Is Concerned about Social Impact*, July 2007. By permission of PewResearch Center, 2007.)

in all groups believe that intimacy issues, that is, faithfulness and a satisfactory sexual relationship, are more important than the material aspects of marriage, such as how labor is divided and having an adequate income. Thus, relationship quality appears to be what most people look for to judge whether their marriages are satisfactory.

Many powerful influences on marital success are in place long before a marriage even begins. Each partner brings to the relationship certain skills, resources, and traits that affect the emerging partnership system. The personality characteristics of the partners seem to be especially important (Arrindell & Luteijn, 2000; Haring, Hewitt, & Flett, 2003). For example, a high degree of neuroticism in one or both partners usually leads to dissatisfaction and instability in the relationship (Robins, Caspi, & Moffitt, 2000). Likewise, attitudes toward divorce affect marital stability. Couples who have favorable attitudes are less likely to be satisfied with their marriages than those who view divorce as highly undesirable (Amato & Rogers, 1999).

Another important factor appears to be the security of each partner's attachment to his or her family of origin. Theorists speculate that the parental attachment relationship contributes to the construction of an internal model of intimate relationships that children bring with them into adulthood and into their marriages (e.g., Crowell & Waters, 1995; Feeney, 1994; Fuller & Fincham, 1995; Hazan & Shaver, 1987; Owens et al., 1995; Rothbard & Shaver, 1994). Research supports this hypothesis. For example, one study found that

RESEARCH REPORT

Sex Differences in the Impact of Marriage

As you have learned, married adults appear to be healthier and happier than their single counterparts. Why? One possible explanation is that married adults follow better health practices. For example, Dutch researchers find that married adults are less likely to smoke or drink to excess and more likely to exercise than are unmarried adults (Joung, Stronks, van de Mheen, & Mackenbach, 1995).

However, an important finding in this body of research is that, at least in the United States, men generally benefit more from marriage than do women on measures of physical and mental health. That is, married men are generally the healthiest and live the longest, while unmarried men are collectively the worst off. The two groups of women fall in between, with married women at a slight advantage over unmarried women. But unmarried women are considerably healthier and happier than are unmarried men. Why should this difference exist?

An interesting two-phase study of marital quality and health looked for a possible correlation between levels of a stress-related hormone called *cortisol* and marriage quality (Kiecolt-Glaser, 2000). Researchers focused on cortisol because it is known to increase when individuals experience negative emotions, and it is one of many stress hormones that are thought to impair immune system functioning. Thus, it may be an important mechanism through which relationship quality affects health.

Investigators measured newlyweds' cortisol levels after they had discussed issues involving conflict, such as in-law relationships and finances. As expected, both husbands' and wives' cortisol levels were somewhat elevated after these discussions. Next, researchers asked couples to tell the story of how they met. As expected, in the majority of both husbands and wives, cortisol levels dropped as they discussed the emotionally neutral topic of relationship history. However, cortisol levels dropped least in those participants who were the most emotionally negative (as measured by number of negative words used) in describing their relationships. This component of the study demonstrated a direct link between stress hormones and marital negativity.

In addition, an important sex difference emerged. When couples described negative events in their relationships, wives' cortisol levels increased while husbands' levels remained constant. This finding suggests that women may be more physiologically sensitive to relationship negativity than men. These results may help explain why marriage is a more consistent protective factor for men than for women.

Sex differences were also apparent in the study's second phase, during which researchers surveyed participants 8 to 12 years later to find out whether they were still married. Remarkably, they found that the higher the wife's cortisol response to emotional negativity in the first phase, the more likely the couple were to be divorced. Consequently, researchers hypothesized that women's physiological responses to marital quality are an important determinant of relationship stability.

Questions for Critical Analysis

1. In your view, what is it about marriage that causes spouses to follow better health practices than their single counterparts?
2. Aside from women's sensitivity to relationship negativity, what are some possible reasons for the finding that the psychological benefits of marriage are greater among men than they are among women?

nearly two-thirds of a sample of about-to-be-married young people showed the same attachment category (secure, dismissing, or preoccupied) when they described their love relationship as when they described their relationship with their parents (Owens et al., 1995). However, once the marriage takes place, spouses must know when and how to let go of their families of origin in favor of the new family they are in the process of establishing. Research shows that, among newlyweds, the frequency of arguments about in-laws is exceeded only by the frequency of disagreements about financial matters (Oggins, 2003).

Emotional affection contributes to relationship quality as well. The most compelling theory of romantic love comes from Robert Sternberg, who argues that love has three key components: (1) *intimacy*, which includes feelings that promote closeness and connectedness; (2) *passion*, which includes a feeling of intense longing for union with the other person, including sexual union; and (3) *commitment to a particular other*, often over a long period of time (Sternberg, 1987). When these three components are combined in all possible ways, you end up with the seven subvarieties of love listed in Figure 14.4. Sternberg's theory suggests that the characteristics of the emotional bond that holds a couple together influence the unique pattern of interaction that develops in each intimate relationship.

validating couples partners who express mutual respect, even in disagreements, and are good listeners

volatile couples partners who argue a lot and don't listen well, but still have more positive than negative interactions

How a couple manage conflict is also an important predictor of relationship quality. Drawing on a large body of research, psychologists have identified three quite different types of stable, or enduring, marriages (Gottman, 1994b). **Validating couples** have disagreements, but the disagreements rarely escalate. Partners express mutual respect, even when they disagree, and listen well to each other. **Volatile couples** squabble a lot, disagree, and don't listen

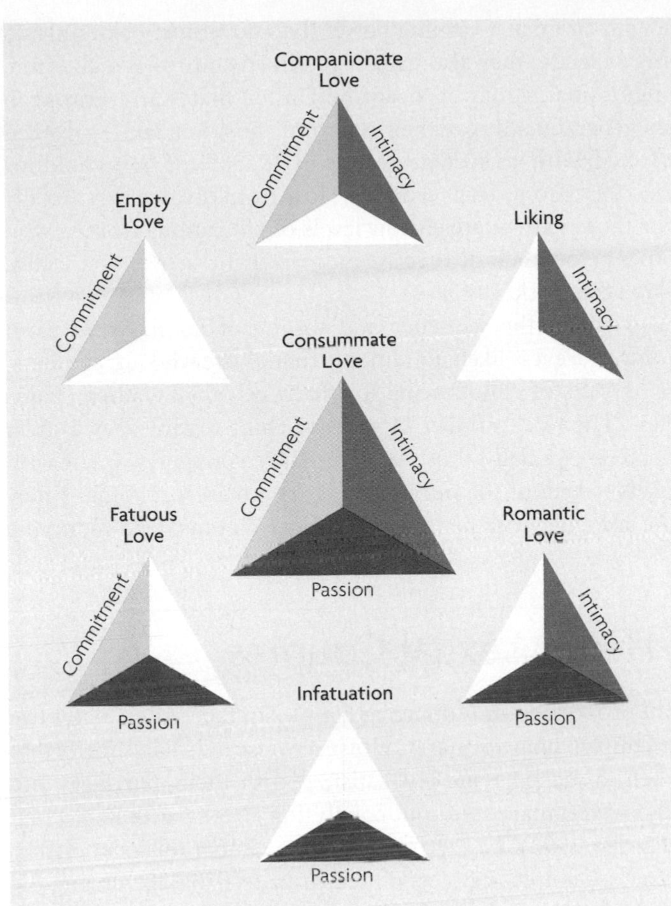

Figure 14.4
Sternberg's Theory of Love

Sternberg's theory postulates three components of love: passion, intimacy, and commitment. Relationships can be classified according to which of the three components is present.

to each other very well when they argue. But they still have more positive than negative encounters, showing high levels of laughter and affection. **Avoidant couples**, called "conflict minimizers," don't try to persuade each other; they simply agree to disagree, without apparent rancor, a pattern sometimes described as "devitalized."

Similarly, psychologists find two types of unsuccessful marriages. Like volatile couples, **hostile/engaged couples**, have frequent hot arguments, but they lack the balancing effect of humor and affection. **Hostile/detached couples** fight regularly (although the arguments tend to be brief), rarely look at each other, and lack affection and support. In both unsuccessful types, the ratio of negative to positive encounters gets out of balance, and the marriage spirals downward toward dissolution.

Divorce For couples whose marriages end in divorce, the experience is often one of the most stressful of their entire lives. Not surprisingly, divorce is associated with increases in both physical and emotional illness. Recently separated or divorced adults have more automobile accidents, are more likely to commit suicide, lose more days at work because of illness, and are more likely to become depressed (Bloom, White, & Asher, 1979; Menaghan & Lieberman, 1986; Stack, 1992a, 1992b; Stack & Wasserman, 1993). They also report strong feelings of failure and a loss of self-esteem, as well as loneliness (Chase-Lansdale & Hetherington, 1990). These negative effects are strongest in the first months after the separation or divorce, much as we see the most substantial effects for children during the first 12 to 24 months (Chase-Lansdale & Hetherington, 1990; Kitson, 1992). However, social networks and close relationships with friends provide some degree of protection against these negative outcomes for recently divorced adults (Kumrei et al., 2007).

The psychological effects of divorce are often significantly exacerbated by serious economic effects, particularly for women. Because most men have had continuous work histories,

avoidant couples partners who agree to disagree and who minimize conflict by avoiding each other

hostile/engaged couples partners who have frequent arguments and lack the balancing effect of humor and affection

hostile/detached couples partners who fight regularly, rarely look at each other and lack affection and support

they commonly leave a marriage with far greater earning power than do women. Not only do women typically lack high earning capacity; they also usually retain custody of any children, with attendant costs. Several longitudinal studies in both the United States and European countries show that divorced men generally improve their economic position, while divorced women are strongly adversely affected, with an average decline of 40–50% of household income (e.g., Morgan, 1991; Smock, 1993). Long-term economic loss from divorce is especially likely for working-class women or those with relatively low levels of education. Women who were earning above-average incomes before their divorce are more likely to recover financially, even if they do not remarry (Holden & Smock, 1991).

For many adults, divorce also affects the sequence and timing of family roles. Even though divorced women with children are less likely to remarry than those who are childless, remarriage expands the number of years of childbearing for many divorced women (Lampard & Peggs, 1999; Norton, 1983). The total number of years of child-rearing may also be significantly larger for divorced men, especially those who remarry younger women with young children. One effect of this is to reduce the number of years a man (or woman) may have between the departure of the last child and the time when elder parents need economic or physical assistance.

Learning Objective 14.6
What factors contribute to the relationship between premarital cohabitation and divorce?

Cohabiting Heterosexual Couples

As noted, a significant proportion of unmarried couples in the United States live together. Most such couples plan to marry. However, research has shown that those who cohabit before marriage are less satisfied with their marriages and more likely to divorce than are those who marry without cohabiting (DeMaris & Rao, 1992; Hall & Zhao, 1995; Thomson & Colella, 1992). Research has also shown that this relationship exists across historical cohorts. That is, couples who cohabited prior to marriage during the 1980s and 1990s display the same rates of marital dissatisfaction and divorce as those who cohabited in the 1960s and 1970s (Dush, Cohan, & Amato, 2003).

Several theories have been proposed to explain the relationship between premarital cohabitation and divorce. First, couples who cohabit are less *homogamous* (similar) than those who do not (Blackwell & Lichter, 2000). For instance, in about 12% of cohabiting couples in the United States partners are of different races, compared to only 6% of marriages (U.S. Bureau of the Census, 2003b). Cohabiting couples also differ more often in religious beliefs, educational levels, and socioeconomic status (Blackwell & Lichter, 2000). Homogamy contributes to relationship stability. Thus, the difference in marital stability between premarital cohabitants and noncohabitants may be a matter of self-selection, not the result of some causal process attributable to cohabitation itself.

Other developmentalists believe that these findings result from the tendency of researchers to lump all kinds of cohabiting couples into a single category. This kind of aggregation, they say, may distort a study's findings because it ignores that there are two rather distinct types of heterosexual cohabitation (Kline, Stanley, Markman, & Olmos-Gallo, 2004). One type involves couples who are fully committed to a future marriage. In most cases, these couples have firm wedding plans and choose to live together for convenience or for economic reasons. In the second type of cohabitation, the relationship between the two partners is more ambiguous. Many such couples regard future marriage as a possibility but also believe that the relationship may be temporary.

Sociologist Jay Teachman points out that one important difference between these two types of couples is previous cohabitation and premarital sexual experience (Teachman, 2003). His findings are derived from the National Survey of Family Growth, a longitudinal study that focuses on women's family transitions. Teachman's analyses of these data show that married women whose premarital cohabitation and sexual experience was limited to their future husband are no more likely to divorce than women who did not cohabit prior to marriage. Thus, says Teachman, the critical variable at work in the cohabitation-divorce relationship is the fact that a large proportion of cohabitants have been in prior cohabiting or sexual relationships.

Researchers have also identified interaction differences between cohabitants with firm intentions to marry and those whose future plans are less clear. For instance, cohabiting men who intend to marry their partner do more housework than men who are not so committed (Ciabittari, 2004). This difference may be the result of communication patterns that distinguish cohabiting women of the two types. In other words, cohabiting women who intend to marry their partner may do a better job of communicating their expectations about a fair division of labor. Another important finding is that cohabiting couples who are clear about their intentions to marry are happier during the period of cohabitation than couples whose future plans are more ambiguous (Brown, 2003). Thus, looking at the kinds of interaction patterns that exist among cohabitants who intend to marry helps us understand why, after marriage, they differ little in satisfaction and stability from those who do not cohabit until after marriage (Brown, 2003; Brown & Booth, 1996; Kline et al., 2004; Teachman, 2003).

Gay and Lesbian Couples

Learning Objective 14.7

In what ways are gay and lesbian couples similar to and different from heterosexual couples?

As noted earlier, about 1% of households in the United States are headed by partners of the same sex. Further, as you will learn in the Policy Question that follows Chapter 16, there is a growing international movement to legalize same-sex marriage. As a result, in recent years, developmentalists have become interested in whether the same factors that predict satisfaction and stability in heterosexual partnerships also relate to these variables in same-sex partnerships (Kurdek, 1998).

One factor that appears to be just as important to same-sex unions as it is to opposite-sex relationships is attachment security (Elizur & Mintzer, 2003). Moreover, as is true for heterosexual couples, neuroticism in one or both partners is related to relationship quality and length (Kurdek, 1997, 2000). Homosexual couples argue about the same things as heterosexual couples, and, like marriages, gay and lesbian relationships are of higher quality if the two partners share similar backgrounds and are equally committed to the relationship (Krueger-Lebus & Rauchfleisch, 1999; Kurdek, 1997; Peplau, 1991; Solomon, Rothblum, & Balsam, 2004).

For the most part, the same factors contribute to relationship satisfaction among heterosexual and homosexual couples.

Despite these similarities, there are important differences between the two kinds of relationships. For one, gay and lesbian partners are often more dependent on each other for social support than men and women in heterosexual partnerships are. This happens because many homosexuals are isolated from their families, primarily because of their families' disapproval of their sexual orientation (Hill, 1999). Thus, many gays and lesbians build *families of choice* for themselves. These social networks typically consist of a stable partner and a circle of close friends. They provide for gay and lesbian couples the kind of social support that most heterosexual adults receive from their families of origin (Kurdek, 2003; Weeks, 2004).

Another difference is in the nature of the power relation between the partners. Homosexual couples seem to be more egalitarian than heterosexual couples, with less specific role prescriptions. It is quite uncommon in homosexual couples for one partner to occupy a "male" role and the other a "female" role. Instead, power and tasks are more equally divided. However, some research indicates that this is more true of lesbian couples, among whom equality of roles is frequently a strong philosophical ideal, than of gay couples (Kurdek, 1995a).

Finally, homosexual and heterosexual partners appear to differ with regard to expectations for monogamy. Both men and women in heterosexual relationships overwhelmingly state that they expect their partners to be sexually faithful to them. Similarly, lesbian partners often insist on sexual exclusivity. However, gay men, even those in long-term partnerships, do not necessarily regard sexual fidelity as essential to their relationships. Couples therapists report that monogamy is important to gay men, but it is an issue that is considered to be negotiable by most (LaSala, 2001).

Learning Objective 14.8

How do singles accomplish Erikson's psycho-social developmental task of intimacy?

Singlehood

In the United States, about 56% of adults between the ages of 20 and 34 have never been married (U.S. Census Bureau, 2006). Surveys show that about two-thirds of them will have married at least once by the time they reach their mid-40s. For those who remain single, the impact of singlehood on their lives depends on the reason for their relationship status. For instance, continuous singlehood is associated with greater individual autonomy and capacity for personal growth than is a life path that has included divorce or loss of a spouse (Marks & Lamberg, 1998). Another important point to keep in mind is that many single adults participate in intimate relationships that do not involve either cohabitation or marriage. These people show up in surveys and census reports as "single" but might be better described as "partnered." Even among singles who have an intimate partner, though, close relationships with their families of origin are more likely to be an important source of psychological and emotional intimacy than they are for individuals who are married or cohabiting (Allen & Pickett, 1987; Campbell, Connidis, & Davies, 1999). Further, close friends are likely to play a more prominent role in the social networks of singles than among marrieds or cohabitants.

Close friends play an important role in the social networks of singles.

The number of years an individual has been single appears to be an important factor in the influence of singlehood on his or her development. Developmentalists have found that there is a transition during which long-term singles move from thinking of themselves as people who will be married or partnered in the future to viewing themselves as single by choice (Davies, 2003). Afterward, singlehood becomes an important, positive component of the individual's identity. This kind of self-affirmation may protect singles from some of the negative health consequences associated with singlehood that you read about earlier.

Critical Thinking

1. A statement that is widely attributed to anthropologist Margaret Mead is, "One of the oldest human needs is having someone to wonder where you are when you don't come home at night." In what way does the research in this section suggest that Mead made a profoundly accurate statement about human nature?

Parenthood and Other Relationships

Referring to couples who do not have children, comedian Bill Cosby once said, "Why shouldn't you be miserable like the rest of us?" Yet, despite all the trials and tribulations of parenting, 85% of parents cite relationships with their children as the most fulfilling aspect of their lives (Taylor, Funk, & Clark, 2007). However, the transition to parenthood is stressful, and to make matters more complicated, it usually happens at a time when most other social relationships are in transition as well.

Learning Objective 14.9

What happens during the transition to parenthood?

Parenthood

Most parents would agree that parenthood is a remarkably mixed emotional experience. On one hand, the desire to become a parent is, for many adults, extremely strong. Thus, fulfilling that desire is an emotional high point for most. On the other hand, parenthood results in a number of stressful changes.

Becoming a Parent In the United States, nine out of every ten women aged 18 to 34 have had or expect to have a child (U.S. Bureau of the Census, 1997). Despite the opportunistic attitude toward mating that evolutionary theory ascribes to men, the percentage of men who feel strongly that they want to become parents and who view parenting as a life-enriching experience is actually greater than the percentage of women who feel this way (Horowitz, McLaughlin, & White, 1998; Muzi, 2000). Furthermore, most expectant fathers become emotionally attached to their unborn children during the third trimester of pregnancy and eagerly anticipate the birth (White, Wilson, Elander, & Persson, 1999).

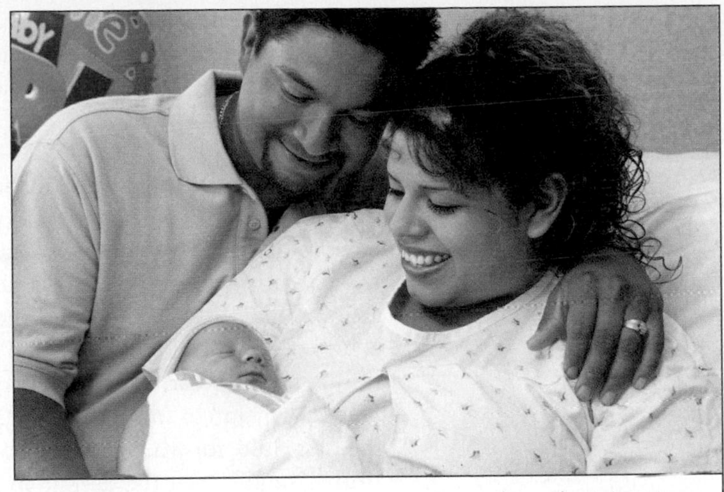

For most couples in long-term relationships, especially those who are married, having a child is an important goal.

As we noted in Chapter 3, in 1970, the average age at which a woman delivered her first child was 21.4 years in the United States. By the early years of the 21st century, the average age of first birth had climbed to 25.2 years (Martin et al., 2005). One reason that contemporary cohorts delay parenthood is that more of them are enrolled in post-secondary education than was true in their parents' and grandparents' early adulthood years. Moreover, the majority of young adults in the United States believe that the best environment for raising a child is a household that is headed by a married couple (Taylor, Funk, & Clark, 2007). Thus, the social clock that we talked about at the beginning of the chapter underlies all of these trends. Although it doesn't include specific ages for the milestones of adulthood, the social clock in the United States nowadays does include the idea that people ought to become socially and economically established before they bring children into the world.

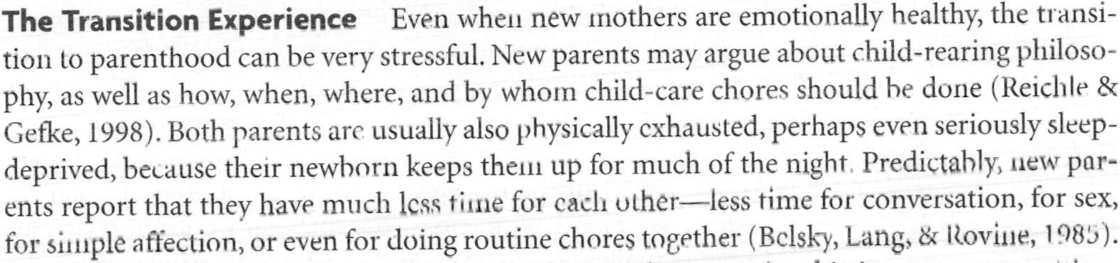

The Transition Experience Even when new mothers are emotionally healthy, the transition to parenthood can be very stressful. New parents may argue about child-rearing philosophy, as well as how, when, where, and by whom child-care chores should be done (Reichle & Gefke, 1998). Both parents are usually also physically exhausted, perhaps even seriously sleep-deprived, because their newborn keeps them up for much of the night. Predictably, new parents report that they have much less time for each other—less time for conversation, for sex, for simple affection, or even for doing routine chores together (Belsky, Lang, & Rovine, 1985).

Some cultures have developed ritualized rites of passage for this important transition, which can help new parents manage stress. For example, in Hispanic cultures, *la cuarenta* is a period of 40 days following the birth of a child, during which fathers are expected to take on typically feminine tasks such as housework. Extended family members are also expected to help out. Researchers have found that Hispanic couples who observe *la cuarenta* adjust to parenthood more easily than those who do not (Niska, Snyder, & Lia-Hoagberg, 1998).

Postpartum Depression Between 10% and 25% of new mothers experience a severe mood disturbance called *postpartum depression (PPD)*—a disorder found among mothers in Australia, China, Sweden, and Scotland as well as in the United States (Campbell, Cohn, Flanagan, Popper, & Meyers, 1992; Guo, 1993; Lundh & Gyllang, 1993; Oates et al., 2004; Webster, Thompson, Mitchell, & Werry, 1994). Women who develop PPD suffer from feelings of sadness for several weeks after the baby's birth. Most cases of PPD persist only a few weeks, but 1–2% of women suffer for a year or more. Moreover, more than 80% of women who suffer from PPD after their first pregnancy experience the disorder again following subsequent deliveries (Garfield, Kent, Paykel, Creighton, & Jacobson, 2004).

Women whose bodies produce unusually high levels of steroid hormones toward the end of pregnancy are more likely to develop postpartum depression (Harris et al., 1994). The disorder is also more common in women whose pregnancies were unplanned, who were anxious about the pregnancy, or whose partner was unsupportive (Campbell et al., 1992; O'Hara, Schlechte, Lewis, & Varner, 1992). The presence of major life stressors during pregnancy or immediately after the baby's birth—such as a move to a new home, the death of someone close, or job loss—increases the risk of PPD (Swendsen & Mazure, 2000). Fatigue and difficult temperament in the infant can also contribute to PPD (Fisher, Feekery, & Rowe-Murray, 2002).

However, the best predictor of postpartum depression is depression during pregnancy (Da Costa, Larouche, Dritsa, & Brender, 2000; Martinez-Schallmoser, Telleen, & MacMullen,

2003). Thus, many cases of PPD can probably be prevented by training health professionals to recognize depression in pregnant women. Similarly, family members of women with absent or unsupportive partners can help them locate agencies that provide material and social support.

Developmental Impact of Parenthood Despite its inherent stressfulness, the transition to parenthood is associated with positive behavior change: Sensation-seeking and risky behaviors decline considerably when young adults become parents (Arnett, 1998). However, marital satisfaction tends to decline after the birth of a child. The general pattern is that such satisfaction is at its peak before the birth of the first child, after which it drops and remains at a lower level until the last child leaves home. Figure 14.5 illustrates the pattern, based on results from an early and widely quoted study (Rollins & Feldman, 1970). The best-documented portion of this curvilinear pattern is the drop in marital satisfaction after the birth of the first child, for which there is both longitudinal and cross-sectional evidence. More recent studies suggest that the decline in marital satisfaction is characteristic of contemporary cohorts of new parents as well, and researchers have found a pattern of marital satisfaction similar to that reported by Rollins and Feldman across a variety of cultures (Ahmad & Najam, 1998; Gloger-Tippelt & Huerkamp, 1998; Twenge, Campbell, & Foster, 2003). Nevertheless, studies that examine the relationship between marital satisfaction and parenthood in a more complex fashion suggest that it is neither universal nor inevitable. Longitudinal studies show that the length of time that a couple has been together before having their first child, the amount of education they have, and the number of children that they have are all positively related to marital satisfaction (Jose & Alfons, 2007).

The link between marital satisfaction and parenthood probably results from one or more underlying factors. One such factor is the division of labor. The more a partner feels that he or she is carrying an unfair proportion of the economic, household, or child-care workload, the greater his or her loss of satisfaction (Wicki, 1999). Support from extended family members is another variable that predicts maintenance or loss of satisfaction (Lee & Keith, 1999). Moreover, couples who have established effective conflict-resolution strategies before the birth of a child experience less loss of satisfaction (Cox, Paley, Burchinal, & Payne, 1999; Lindahl, Clements, & Markman, 1997).

It's important to keep in mind, too, that new parents who are married or cohabiting experience a much smaller decline in overall life satisfaction than new single parents, whose lives are far more complicated and stressful (Lee, Law, & Tam, 1999). Likewise, single par-

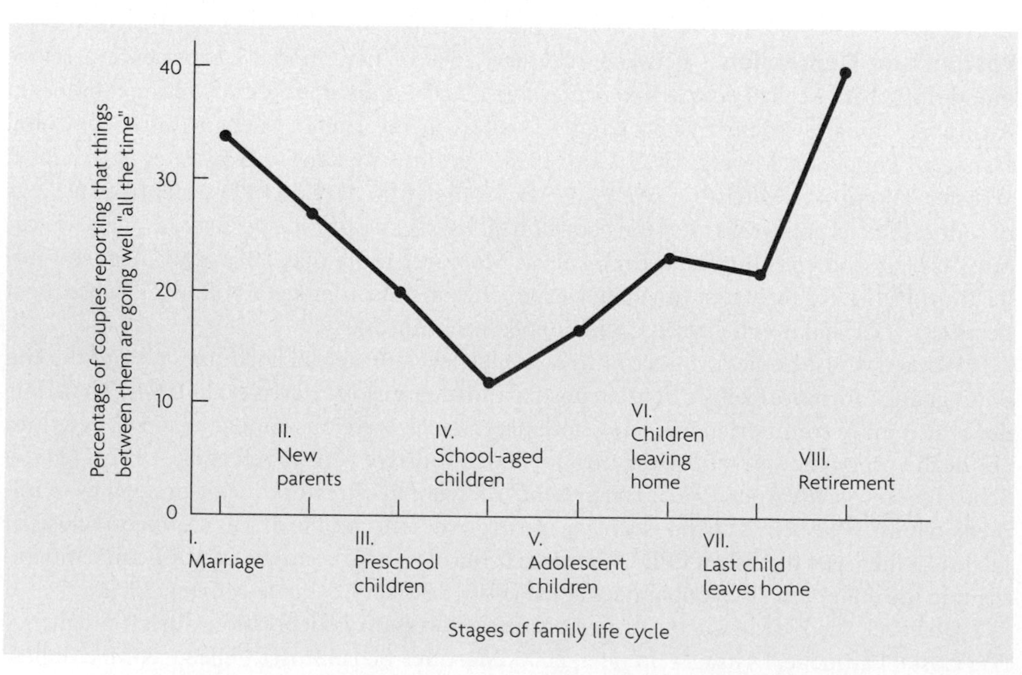

Figure 14.5 Changes in Marital Satisfaction through the Family Life Cycle

This pattern of change in marital satisfaction over the stages of the family life cycle is one of the best-documented findings in family sociology research.

(*Source*: From "Marital Satisfaction over the Family Life Cycle" Boyd C. Rollins and Harold Feldman, from *Journal of Marriage and the Family*, Vol. 32, 1970. (National Council of Family Relations) Reprinted by permission.)

ents are more likely to suffer from health problems and are less likely to advance to management positions at work (Khlat, Sermet, & Le Pape, 2000; Tharenou, 1999). Instead of focusing on declines in relationship satisfaction, some developmentalists suggest that more attention be paid to the consistent finding that having a parenting partner—especially one to whom one is married—is a significant protective factor in managing the stressful transition to parenthood.

Childlessness Like parenthood, childlessness affects the shape of an adult's life, both within marriages and in work patterns. Without the presence of children, marital satisfaction fluctuates less over time. Like all couples, those who do not have children are likely to experience some drop in satisfaction in the first months and years of marriage. But over the range of adult life, their curve of marital satisfaction is much flatter than the one shown in Figure 14.5 (Houseknecht, 1987; Somers, 1993). Childless couples in their 20s and 30s consistently report higher cohesion in their marriages than do couples with children.

Childlessness also affects the role of worker, especially for women. Childless married women, like unmarried women, are much more likely to have full-time continuous careers (Abma & Martinez, 2006). However, a survey involving more than 2,000 participants found that single, childless women had no higher rates of managerial advancement than mothers (Tharenou, 1999). Thus, one of the disadvantages associated with childlessness may be that it is always socially a bit risky to be seen as "different" from others in any important way (Mueller & Yoder, 1999). Tharenou's survey's finding that married fathers whose wives were not employed were more likely to advance than workers of any other marital or parental status supports this conclusion.

Social Networks

Learning Objective 14.10
How are family and friends important to young adults?

Creating a partnership may be the most central task of the process of achieving intimacy, but it is certainly not the only reflection of that basic process. In early adult life, each of us creates a social network made up of family and friends as well as our life partner.

Family If you ask children and adults "Who is the person you don't like to be away from?" or "Who is the person you know will always be there for you?" children and teenagers most often list their parents, while adults most often name their spouse or partner and almost never mention their parents (Hazan, Hutt, Sturgeon, & Bricker, 1991). However, most adults feel emotionally close to their parents and see or talk to them regularly (Belsky, Jaffee, Caspi, Moffitt, & Silva, 2003; Campbell et al., 1999; Lawton, Silverstein, & Bengtson, 1994).

Not surprisingly, the amount and kind of contact an adult has with kin are strongly influenced by proximity. Adults who live within 2 hours of their parents and siblings see them far more often than those who live farther away. But distance does not prevent a parent or sibling from being part of an individual adult's social network. These relationships can provide support in times of need, even if physical contact is infrequent.

There are also important cultural differences in young adults' involvement with their families. For example, one study compared the development of social independence among Australian, Canadian, and Japanese children and adults (Takata, 1999). In all three cultures, the sense of being independent from parents and family increased with age. However, Australian and Canadian participants appeared to develop self-perceptions of independence earlier in life. Consequently, Japanese young adults reported a greater sense of connectedness to their families of origin than either Australian or Canadian young adults.

Although patterns of interaction with family members are similar across U.S. ethnic groups, Hispanic Americans perceive family ties to be more important than young adults of other races or ethnicities (Schweizer, Schnegg, & Berzborn, 1998). Given a choice, many non-Hispanics de-emphasize kin networks in early adulthood, whereas Hispanic Americans embrace them enthusiastically (Vega, 1990). In the Hispanic American culture, extensive kin networks are the rule rather than the exception, with frequent visiting and exchanges not only between parents, children, and siblings, but with grandparents, cousins, aunts, and uncles (Keefe, 1984). These frequent contacts facilitate the development of mentoring relationships between young adults and the older members of their extended families (Sánchez, Reyes, & Singh, 2006).

African American young adults also tend to value family connections highly, although the reasons are somewhat different. For one thing, African American young adults are less likely to marry than are young adults in other groups (Johnson & Dye, 2005). Consequently, more African American young adults live in multigenerational households and report higher levels of intimacy and warmth in relationships with parents than do Whites (Brent, 2006; Kane, 1998). Frequent kin contact is also a significant part of the daily life of most African American adults who do not live in extended family households (Hatchett & Jackson, 1993).

Friends Friends, too, are important members of a social network, even those with whom young adults interact exclusively online (Sherman, Lansford, & Volling, 2006). We choose our friends as we choose our partners, from among those who are similar to us in education, social class, interests, family background, or family life cycle stage. Cross-sex friendships are more common among adults than they are among 10-year-olds, but they are still outnumbered by same-sex friendships. Young adults' friends are also overwhelmingly drawn from their own age group. Beyond this basic requirement of similarity, close friendship seems to rest on mutual openness and personal disclosure.

Because of the centrality of the task of intimacy in early adulthood, most researchers and theorists assume that young adults have more friends than do middle-aged or older adults. Research has offered some hints of support for this idea, but it has been a difficult assumption to test properly. Developmentalists lack longitudinal data and do not agree on definitions of friendship, which makes combining data across studies very difficult.

Sex Differences in Relationship Styles As in childhood, there are very striking sex differences in both the number and the quality of friendships in the social network of young adults (Radmacher & Azmitia, 2006). Women have more close friends, and their friendships are more intimate, with more self-disclosure and more exchange of emotional support. Young men's friendships, like those of boys and older men, are more competitive. Male friends are less likely to agree with each other or to ask for or provide emotional support to one another (Dindia & Allen, 1992; Maccoby, 1990). Adult women friends talk to one another; adult men friends do things together.

Another facet of this difference is that women most often fill the role of **kin-keeper** (Moen, 1996; Salari; & Zhang, 2006). They write the letters, make the phone calls, arrange the gatherings of family and friends. (In later stages of adult life, it is also the women who are likely to take on the role of caring for aging parents—a pattern you'll learn more about in Chapter 16.)

Taken together, all this means that women have a much larger "relationship role" than men do. In virtually all cultures, it is part of the female role to be responsible for maintaining the emotional aspects of relationships—with a spouse, with friends, with family, and, of course, with children.

Critical Thinking

1. Having children often means that a couple's social networks change such that the parents of their children's playmates take the place of other adults with whom they have associated in the past. What are the long-term advantages and disadvantages of this trend for parents' future post-child-rearing lives?

The Role of Worker

In addition to the roles of spouse or partner and parent, a large percentage of young adults are simultaneously filling yet another major and relatively new role: that of worker. Most young people need to take on this role to support themselves economically. But that is not the only reason for the centrality of this role. Satisfying work also seems to be an important ingredient in mental health and life satisfaction, for both men and women (Meeus, Dekovic & Iedema, 1997; Tait, Padgett, & Baldwin, 1989). However, before looking at what developmentalists know about career steps and sequences in early adulthood, let's examine how young people choose an occupation.

kin-keeper a family role, usually occupied by a woman, which includes responsibility for maintaining family and friendship relationships

Choosing an Occupation

Learning Objective 14.11

What factors influence an individual's occupational choices?

As you might imagine, a multitude of factors influence a young person's choice of job or career: family background and values; intelligence and education; gender; and personality (in addition to other factors such as ethnic group, self-concept, and school performance).

Family and Educational Influences Typically, young people choose occupations at the same general social class level as those of their parents—although this is less true today than it was a decade or two ago (Biblarz, Bengtson, & Bucur, 1996). In part, this effect operates through the medium of education. For example, researchers have found that young adults whose parents are college graduates are less likely to enlist in the military than those whose parents have less education (Bachman, Segal, Freedman-Doan, & O'Malley, 2000). Such findings suggest that parents who have higher-than-average levels of education themselves are more likely to encourage their children to go on to postsecondary education. Such added education, in turn, makes it more likely that the young person will qualify for middle-class jobs, for which a college education is frequently a required credential.

Young adults who enter military service differ from peers who go to college or into civilian careers. Their parents are less likely to have gone to college and more likely to be poor than parents of young adults who do not go into military service. However, some families encourage their young adult children to join the military in order to have access to educational opportunities that they cannot afford to provide for them but that often accompany military service.

Families also influence job choices through their value systems (Jacobs, Chhin, & Bleeker, 2006). In particular, parents who value academic and professional achievement are far more likely to have children who attend college and choose professional-level jobs. This effect is not just social-class difference in disguise. Among working-class families, it is the children of those who place the strongest emphasis on achievement who are most likely to move up into middle-class jobs (Gustafson & Magnusson, 1991). Further, families whose career aspirations for their children are high tend to produce young adults who are more intrinsically motivated as employees (Cotton, Bynum, & Madhere, 1997).

Another way in which parents influence young adults' career choice is by urging them to go to college. In one survey of traditional college students, 40% of freshmen indicated that the main reason that they entered college immediately after high school graduation was that their parents wanted them to (*Chronicle of Higher Education*, 1997). After a few years on campus, however, most students have developed their own reasons for pursuing a degree, and, in some cases, students' majors strongly influence the types of jobs they seek after graduation. For example, an engineering graduate is most likely to look for a job in the field for which he is academically prepared. By contrast, students who major in a field such as psychology may consider a variety of career options before settling on one. Moreover, many graduates take advantage of networking opportunities that are available to them because of their college affiliation.

Gender Specific job choice is also strongly affected by gender. Despite the women's movement and despite the vast increase in the proportion of women working, it is still true that sex-role definitions designate some jobs as "women's jobs" and some as "men's jobs" (Reskin, 1993; Zhou, Dawson, Herr, & Stukas, 2004). Stereotypically male jobs are more varied, more technical, and higher in both status and income (e.g., business executive, carpenter). Stereotypically female jobs are concentrated in service occupations and are typically lower in status and lower paid (e.g., teacher, nurse, secretary). One-third of all working women hold clerical jobs; another quarter are in health care, teaching, or domestic service.

Children learn these cultural definitions of "appropriate" jobs for men and women in their early years, just as they learn all the other aspects of sex roles. So it is not surprising

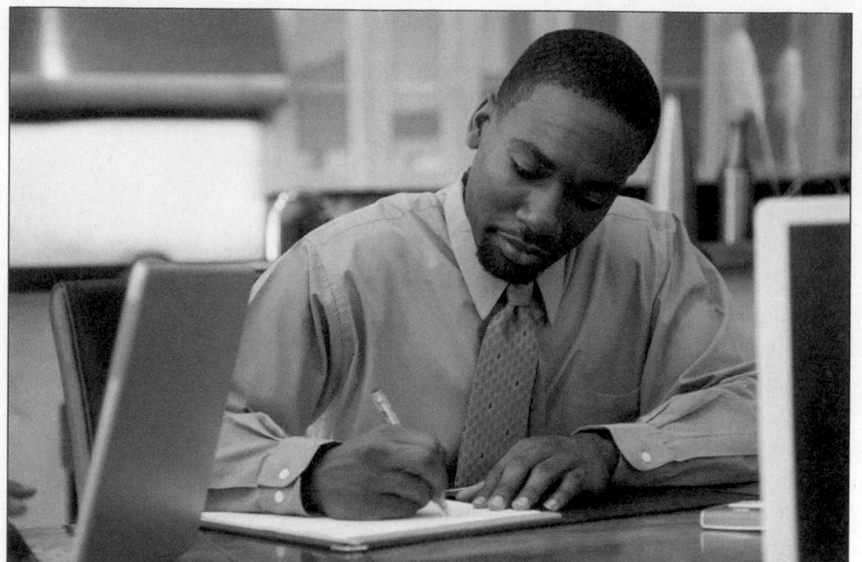

Which of Holland's personality traits best suit a young adult for working in a setting such as this?

that most young women and men choose jobs that fit these sex-role designations. Nonstereotypical job choices are much more common among young people who see themselves as androgynous or whose parents have unconventional occupations. For instance, young women who choose traditionally masculine careers are more likely to have a mother who has had a long-term career and are more likely to define themselves either as androgynous or as masculine (Betz & Fitzgerald, 1987; Fitzpatrick & Silverman, 1989).

Personality Another influence on job choice is the young adult's personality. John Holland, whose work has been the most influential in this area, proposes six basic personality types, summarized in Table 14.1 (Holland, 1973, 1992). Holland's basic hypothesis is that each of us tends to choose, and be most successful at, an occupation that matches our personality.

Research in non-Western as well as Western cultures, and with African Americans, Hispanic Americans, and Native Americans as well as Whites in the United States, has generally supported Holland's proposal (Spokane & Cruza-Guet, 2005). Ministers, for example, generally score highest on Holland's social scale, engineers highest on the investigative scale, car salespeople on the enterprising scale, and career army officers on the realistic scale.

People whose personalities match their jobs are also more likely to be satisfied with their work. Moreover, obtaining a personality assessment prior to making an occupational choice is associated with greater feelings of confidence about the decision (Francis-Smythe & Smith, 1997).

TABLE 14.1 Holland's Personality Types and Work Preferences

Type	Personality and Work Preferences
Realistic	Aggressive, masculine, physically strong, often with low verbal or interpersonal skills; prefer mechanical activities and tool use, choosing jobs such as mechanic, electrician, or surveyor
Investigative	Oriented toward thinking (particularly abstract thinking), organizing, and planning; prefer ambiguous, challenging tasks, but are low in social skills; are often scientists or engineers
Artistic	Asocial; prefer unstructured, highly individual activity; are often artists
Social	Extraverts; people-oriented and sociable and need attention; avoid intellectual activity and dislike highly ordered activity; prefer to work with people and choose service jobs like nursing and education
Enterprising	Highly verbal and dominating; enjoy organizing and directing others; are persuasive and strong leaders, often choosing careers in sales
Conventional	Prefer structured activities and subordinate roles; like clear guidelines and see themselves as accurate and precise; may choose occupations such as bookkeeping or filing

(*Source:* Holland, 1973, 1992.)

Career Development

Learning Objective 14.12

How do career goals and job satisfaction change over time?

Once the job or career has been chosen, what kinds of experiences do young adults have in their work life? **Career development** is the process of adapting to the workplace, managing career transitions, and pursuing personal goals through employment. Psychologists who study career development focus on issues such as the phases of workplace adaptation, job satisfaction, and the ways in which individuals integrate work with other aspects of their lives.

Super's Stage of Career Development Psychologist Donald Super claims that the roots of the career development process are found in infancy. Between birth and age 14, Super says, we are in the *growth stage*, a period during which we learn about our abilities and interests. Next comes the *exploratory stage*, roughly from 15 to 24. In this stage, the young person must decide on a job or career, and he searches for a fit between his interests and personality and the jobs available. The whole process involves a good deal of trial and error as well as luck or chance. Perhaps because many of the jobs available to those in this age range are not terribly challenging and because many young adults have not yet found the right fit, job changes are at their peak during this period.

Next comes the *establishment stage* (also called the *stabilization stage*), roughly from age 25 to age 45. Having chosen an occupation, the young person must learn the ropes and begin to move through the early steps in some career ladder as he masters the needed skills, perhaps with a mentor's help. In this period, the worker also focuses on fulfilling whatever aspirations or goals he may have set for himself. In Levinson's terms, he tries to fulfill his dream. The young scientist pushes himself to make an important discovery; the young attorney strives to become a partner; the young business executive tries to move as far up the ladder as he can; the young blue-collar worker may aim for job stability or promotion to foreman. It is in these years that most promotions do occur.

The final phase of career development in Super's model is the *maintenance stage*. It begins around age 45 and ends at retirement. The primary goals of the maintenance stage are to protect and maintain the gains that were made during the establishment stage. To accomplish these goals, older workers must keep up with new developments in their fields. They must also acquire new skills in order to avoid becoming obsolete. Moreover, individuals in the maintenance phase must make preparations for retirement.

Super's model is useful for describing the challenges that individuals face in the various phases of their careers. However, to be validly applied in today's rapidly changing economy, Super's stages must be thought of independently from the ages to which he originally linked them (Super, 1990). This is necessary because of the frequency with which adults change careers or move from one workplace to another. Thus, regardless of age, a person who makes a major career change probably exhibits the characteristics of Super's exploratory stage prior to doing so and experiences some of the features of his establishment and maintenance phases in the years following the change.

Job Satisfaction Early studies of job satisfaction found that job satisfaction was at its lowest in early adulthood and rose steadily until retirement (Glenn & Weaver, 1985). More recently, however, researchers have found that satisfaction is lowest at mid-career, usually toward the end of the early adulthood period (Fullerton & Wallace, 2007). This trend is attributable to changes in workers' perceptions of job security. In the past, security increased with time on the job. Nowadays, job security is elusive because of the speed with which job requirements and employers' priorities shift. Thus, workers who have been on the job for some time are no longer assured of having greater security, higher incomes, or higher status positions than beginning workers do.

Research also suggests that there are a number of important variables that contribute to job satisfaction in young adults. As with almost every life situation, individual personality traits such as neuroticism affect job satisfaction (Judge, Bono, & Locke, 2000; Wright &

career development the process of adapting to the workplace, managing career transitions, and pursuing goals through employment

Bonett, 2007). In addition, young adults engaged in careers for which they prepared in high school or college have higher levels of satisfaction (Blustein et al., 1997).

Learning Objective 14.13

What are some of the innovations that are associated with the quality of work-life movement?

The Quality of Work Life Movement

Workers who are happy have lower turnover rates, meaning that companies are spared the expense of searching for and training replacements for them (Castle, Engberg, & Anderson, 2007; Wright & Bonett, 2007). This factor influences an organization's efficiency and profitability. Therefore, job satisfaction can be just as important to employers as it is to their employees.

Assistance with child care is one of many quality of work-life (QWL) policies that have been implemented by some organizations in recent years.

In an effort to enhance job satisfaction among employees, employers have developed new policies that focus on a variable called **work-life balance**, the interactions among workers' work and non-work roles. Research has shown that work-life balance issues affect not only workers' mental and physical health, but also their job performance (Thompson, Brough, & Schmidt, 2006). Moreover, workers are more satisfied with their jobs when they believe that their supervisors share their views on work-life balance. Thus, to address the work-life balance needs of today's employees, psychologists have developed the **quality of work-life (QWL) movement**. Advocates of the QWL movement emphasize job and workplace designs based on analyses of the quality of employees' experiences in an organization. The idea is that when people are happier at work, they will be more productive. For example, the on-site child-care center is one innovation that has come about because of concern for the quality of work life. Even though providing on-site child-care can be expensive, QWL advocates argue that it will pay for itself in terms of reduced absences and lower stress levels among employees who are parents.

Another QWL innovation is *telecommuting*. Telecommuters work in their homes and are connected to their workplaces by computer, fax machine, and telephone. Some telecommuters work at home every day; others do so only one or two days each week. Such flexibility can increase job satisfaction (Wilde, 2000). Moreover, telecommuting helps employees balance work and family responsibilities. It can also be helpful to employees with disabilities that make it difficult for them to get around. Government statistics in the United States show that 17% of employees now work at home (U.S. Bureau of Labor Statistics, 2005).

Two other innovations associated with the QWL movement are flextime and job sharing. *Flextime* involves allowing employees to create their own work schedules. Most organizations that use flextime have certain times (usually called "core hours") when all employees must be present. At other times, though, employees are free to come and go as long as their work is done and they put in the required number of hours. Many employees take advantage of the flextime option to reduce work-family conflicts (Sharpe et al., 2002). Others use this option to enhance their job performance by coming to the workplace at times when they believe they can be most productive. Further, flextime workers report that they experience less transportation-related stress—that is, they don't worry as much about rush-hour traffic jams and late trains or buses as they would if working a conventional schedule (Lucas & Heady, 2002). Researchers have found that flextime helps to build employee loyalty, thereby reducing turnover (Roehling et al., 2001).

Job sharing is a QWL innovation in which a full-time job is shared by two or more employees. For example, a receptionist's position might be filled by one person on Monday, Wednesday, and Friday and by another on Tuesday and Thursday. In fact, it's theoret-

work-life balance the interactive influences among employees' work and non-work roles

quality of work-life (QWL) movement an approach to reducing work-related stress by basing job and workplace design on analyses of the quality of employee experiences in an organization

ically possible that the job could be filled by a different individual each day of the week. Employers have found job sharing to be a particularly effective way to help employees gradually return to full-time work after a leave of absence for reasons such as illness or pregnancy (Krumm, 2001).

Women's Work Patterns

Learning Objective 14.14

In what way do women's work patterns differ from those of men?

Some findings about work patterns hold true for both women and men. For example, women's work satisfaction goes up with age (and with job tenure), just as men's does. But women's work experience in early adulthood differs from men's in one strikingly important respect: The great majority of women move in and out of the work force at least once, usually to have and raise children (Drobnic, Blossfield, & Rhwer, 1999; Hofferth & Curtin, 2006). Most such women return to work and, as a result, the representation of mothers in the workplace has increased dramatically over the past three decades. In 1975, only 34% of women with children under the age of 3 were employed. By 2004, the proportion had increased to 57% (U.S. Bureau of Labor Statistics, 2005). Although there was a slight decline in the percentage of mothers who worked outside the home in the early years of the 21st century, more than 70% of mothers of children under age 18 are employed at least part-time.

Prior to actually having children, many women tell researchers that they intend to return to full-time work shortly after the birth of their first child. However, longitudinal research shows that many women change their plans after giving birth. In one study, researchers found that only 44% of female professionals followed through on their pre-pregnancy intention to return to full-time work shortly after giving birth (Abele, 2005). By contrast, very few of the male professionals that these researchers followed over the same period made any kind of change to their working conditions after becoming fathers.

Such findings often lead researchers to conclude that work-family conflict more strongly influences women's career decisions than those of men (see The Real World on page 426). Research showing that women are both more concerned about and more adept at integrating work and family roles than men are provides support for this view (Hoff et al., 2005; Kafetsios, 2007; Wharton & Blair-Loy, 2006). However, some researchers point out that it may be more useful to think of work-family conflict as qualitatively different for mothers and fathers rather than important to one but not the other (McElwain, Korabik, & Rosin, 2005). Because of the traditional division of labor, they say, most of women's concerns about work-family conflicts involve situations in which family demands override those of work. For instance, a woman may worry that her decision to take time off from work for teacher-parent conferences will reduce her chances of advancing to a higher position. Among men, the pattern is the opposite; their work-family stress is more likely to involve prioritizing work over family than vice versa. For example, a father may regret that a business trip caused him to miss his daughter's dance recital.

Women are working in larger and larger numbers, but fewer than a third work continuously during the early adult years.

Surveys showing that the division of work and family responsibilities among couples has changed very little in the last 30 years, despite the growing participation of mothers in the work force, support this view as well (Crompton, Brockman, & Lyonnette, 2005). For instance, fathers are seldom thought of as having a choice between working and staying home to rear children (Daly & Palkovitz, 2004). Like their fathers and grandfathers before them, they are expected to provide material support to their families even when their wives are pursuing their own lucrative careers. At the same time, although there is no

THE REAL WORLD

Strategies for Coping with Conflict between Work and Family Life

Ramona had just settled in at her office, ready for a full day's work, when her cell phone rang. Recognizing the number on the screen as that of her son's babysitter, she reluctantly answered. When the woman who cared for her 3-year-old told Ramona that the child had a fever, the young mother knew that she would have to miss yet another day of work. During her last evaluation, Ramona's supervisor had noted that she was an excellent employee, but her frequent absences were standing in the way of her advancement in the organization. Moreover, tensions were rising between Ramona and her husband, because she resented his failure to volunteer to miss part or all of a workday to take their son to the doctor.

The need to balance work and family roles is one of the major themes of young adults' lives these days. But can a person really balance the demands of these roles? While there is no magic formula for creating such a balance and eliminating conflict and distress, there are some strategies that can help.

The most helpful strategy overall is something psychologists call *cognitive restructuring*—recasting or reframing the situation for yourself in a way that identifies the positive elements. Cognitive restructuring might include reminding yourself that you had good reasons for choosing to have both a job and a family and recalling other times when you have coped successfully with similar problems (Paden & Buehler, 1995).

A related kind of restructuring involves redefining family roles. A couple could begin the process by making a list of household chores, child care responsibilities, and other tasks noting which person does each chore. If the responsibilities are unbalanced, then the couple could work toward finding a more equitable distribution of labor. If economic resources are sufficient, help can also be hired.

Finally, a stressed-out Supermom or Superdad might find it helpful to take a class in time management. Research reveals that good planning can, in fact, reduce the sense of strain you feel (Paden & Buehler, 1995). You have probably already heard lots of advice about how to organize things better. Easier said than done! But there are techniques that can help, and many of these are taught in workshops and classes in most cities. What does not help is simply trying harder to do it all yourself.

Questions for Reflection

1. How do you think Ramona should approach her husband about sharing the responsibility for taking care of their son when he is ill?
2. What are some ways that young adults can cope with the pressure to "do it all"?

Critical Thinking

1. What are your own plans for achieving a satisfactory work-life balance after graduating from college? Based on the research in this section, how realistic do you think your goals are?

denying the fact that women have many more life choices today than they did in the past, it is nonetheless true that mothers are the ones whose poor parenting skills or work-family priorities are likely to be blamed when children develop problems such as ADHD or substance abuse (Barnett, 2004; Jackson & Mannix, 2004; Singh, 2004). The prevalence of such views may influence women in the direction of prioritizing family over work. However, it is also important to note that many women willingly adapt their work lives to the demands of raising children simply because that is what they believe is best for their families rather than out of a sense of duty to culturally prescribed roles or the fear that they will be blamed if their children develop problems.

SUMMARY

Theories of Social and Personality Development

Learning Objective 14.1 What did Erikson mean when he described early adulthood as a crisis of intimacy versus isolation?

- Erikson proposed that young adults face the crisis of intimacy versus isolation. Those who fail to establish a stable relationship with an intimate partner or a network of friends become socially isolated.

Learning Objective 14.2 What is a life structure, and how does it change?

- Levinson hypothesized that adult development involves alternating periods of stability and instability, through which adults construct and refine life structures.

Learning Objective 14.3 What are the characteristics of emerging adulthood?

- The parts of the brain that are involved in decision making and self-control mature between the late teens and early twenties. Emerging adults use skills they acquired earlier in life to accomplish developmental tasks in the academic, conduct, and friendship domains. New skills are required for tasks in the work and romantic domains.

Intimate Relationships

Learning Objective 14.4 What types of research do evolutionary and social role theorists cite to support their theories of mate selection?

- Evolutionary theories of mate selection suggest that sex differences in mate preferences and mating behavior are the result of natural selection. Social role theory emphasizes factors such as gender roles, similarity, and economic exchange in explaining sex differences in mating.

Learning Objective 14.5 How do marriage and divorce affect the lives of young adults?

- Personality characteristics, as well as attachment and love, contribute to marital success. Marriage is associated with a number of health benefits, while divorce tends to increase young adults' risk of depression.

Learning Objective 14.6 What factors contribute to the relationship between premarital cohabitation and divorce?

- People who cohabit prior to marriage are more likely to divorce. However, research has shown that among cohabiting couples in which the intention to marry is firm and the woman has had no prior cohabitation experience, divorce or dissatisfaction with the relationship is no more likely than among couples who do not live together before marriage.

Learning Objective 14.7 In what ways are gay and lesbian couples similar to and different from heterosexual couples?

- The factors that contribute to relationship satisfaction are similar across homosexual and heterosexual couples. However, the two types of couples often differ in the power relation within the partnership. Further, monogamy is not as important to gay male couples as it is to lesbian or heterosexual partners.

Learning Objective 14.8 How do singles accomplish Erikson's psycho-social developmental task of intimacy?

- Singles who do not have intimate partners rely on family and friends for intimacy. After many years of singlehood, unpartnered adults tend to incorporate "singleness" into their sense of personal identity.

Parenthood and Other Relationships

Learning Objective 14.9 What happens during the transition to parenthood?

- Most men and women want to become parents, because they view raising children as a life-enriching experience. The transition to parenthood is stressful and leads to a decline in relationship satisfaction. Factors such as the division of labor between mother and father, individual personality traits, and the availability of help from extended family members contribute to relationship satisfaction.

Learning Objective 14.10 How are family and friends important to young adults?

- Young adults' relationships with their parents tend to be steady and supportive, even if less central than they were at earlier ages. The quality of attachment to parents continues to predict a number of important variables in early adulthood. Each young adult creates a network of relationships with friends as well as with a partner and family members.

The Role of Worker

Learning Objective 14.11 What factors influence an individual's occupational choices?

- The specific job or career a young adult chooses is affected by his or her education, intelligence, family background and resources, family values, personality, and gender. The majority of adults choose jobs that fit the cultural norms for their social class and gender. More intelligent young people, and those with more education, are more upwardly mobile. Super's stage theory proposes that career development involves the growth (birth to 14), exploratory (15–24), establishment (25–44), and maintenance stages (45 to retirement).

Learning Objective 14.12 How do career goals and job satisfaction change over time?

- Job satisfaction rises steadily throughout early adulthood, in part because the jobs typically available to young adults are less well paid, more repetitive, and less creative and allow the worker very little power or influence.

Learning Objective 14.13 What are some of the innovations that are associated with the quality of work-life movement?

- The QWL movement includes on-site child care, telecommuting, flextime, and job sharing. These innovations help employees achieve a balance between work and non-work roles.

Learning Objective 14.14 In what way do women's work patterns differ from those of men?

- For most women, the work role includes an additional in-and-out stage, in which periods of focusing on family responsibilities alternate with periods of employment. The more continuous a woman's work history, the more successful she is likely to be at her job.

KEY TERMS

assortative mating (homogamy) *(p. 409)*
avoidant couples *(p. 413)*
career development *(p. 423)*
emerging adulthood *(p. 407)*
hostile/detached couples *(p. 413)*
hostile/engaged couples *(p. 413)*
intimacy *(p. 405)*
intimacy versus isolation *(p. 405)*
kin-keeper *(p. 420)*
life structure *(p. 406)*
parental investment theory *(p. 408)*
quality of work life (QWL) movement *(p. 424)*
social role theory *(p. 409)*
validating couples *(p. 412)*
volatile couples *(p. 412)*
work-life balance *(p. 424)*

TEST YOURSELF

Theories of Social and Personality Development

14.1 According to Erikson, which of the following is an essential prerequisite to the successful resolution of the crisis of intimacy versus isolation?

a. an identity
b. maturity
c. a life structure
d. dialectical thought

14.2 According to Levinson, the first phase of a period of adjustment is called the

a. culmination phase.
b. beginning phase.
c. mid-era phase.
d. novice phase.

14.3 Changes in the brain during the late teens and early twenties enable emerging adults to develop better ________________ skills than they could when they were younger.

a. empathic understanding
b. planning and self-control
c. abstract thinking
d. verbal

Intimate Relationships

14.4 A woman who chose her marital partner according to the basic premises of evolutionary theory would choose

a. another woman.
b. a man who provided financial resources and stability.
c. a sexually proficient partner.
d. a healthy younger man.

14.5 Which of the following is *not* an element of social role theory explanations of mate selection?

a. women's and men's different investments in childbearing and parenting
b. women's and men's different gender roles
c. choosing mates on the basis of similarity of key traits or characteristics
d. acquiring a mate by offering one's assets, such as earning power

14.6 After eight years, the probability that a couple will divorce is approximately

a. 50%.
b. 20%.
c. 10%.
d. 0%.

14.7 Which of the following factors does *not* contribute to marital satisfaction?

a. personality characteristics of the partners
b. sexual compatibility
c. negative attitudes toward divorce
d. emotional affection

14.8 Which of the following types of conflict management is associated with divorce?

a. avoiding conflict and agreeing to disagree without rancor
b. having disagreements that don't escalate
c. having frequent hot arguments and little humor and affection in the relationship
d. having frequent hot arguments but high levels of laughter and affection in the relationship

14.9 Which of the following would *not* be typical following a divorce?

a. increase in physical illness
b. decrease in automobile accidents
c. higher risk of suicide
d. increased feelings of failure

14.10 How do lesbian couples differ from heterosexual couples?

a. Attachment is not important in predicting satisfaction in a lesbian relationship, whereas it is for heterosexual couples.
b. Lesbian couples do not argue as much as heterosexual couples.
c. Lesbian couples are more egalitarian than heterosexual couples.
d. Lesbian couples do not usually expect monogamy, whereas heterosexual couples do.

14.11 Which of the following statements about the impact of marriage is true?

a. Men appear to benefit more from marriage than women do.
b. Married adults are more likely to smoke or drink to excess than singles are.
c. Men are more sensitive to negativity in their relationships than women are.
d. Married adults are less likely to exercise than single women are.

Parenthood and Other Relationships

14.12 What is the best predictor of postpartum depression?

a. being depressed during the pregnancy
b. giving birth to twins
c. having an unplanned and unwanted pregnancy
d. having a premature delivery

14.13 Of the following couples, which would most likely report the lowest level of marital satisfaction?

a. a recently married couple who do not have children
b. a couple who have three children in elementary school
c. a couple whose children are in college or employed
d. a retired couple who frequently take care of their grandchildren

14.14 Which of the following variables does *not* contribute to a couple's satisfaction or dissatisfaction following the birth of a child?

a. the division of labor
b. support from extended family members
c. the couple's coping strategies
d. the couple's intelligence

14.15 Which of the following statements about adult friendships appears to be true?

a. Men are generally less satisfied with their friendships than women are.
b. Men's friendships involve a lot more social support than women's friendships.
c. Women have fewer friends, but they are very close to them.
d. There tend to be no real significant differences between men's and women's friendships.

14.16 If a young man described his friendships, he would mostly speak of

a. self-disclosure and emotional support.
b. lengthy conversations.
c. shared activities.
d. the close, intimate quality of the relationships.

The Role of Worker

14.17 A young adult's choice of an occupation or a career is least likely to be influenced by

a. the social class of her/his family.
b. the family's value system and moral beliefs.
c. lifestyle habits.
d. gender.

14.18 As a scientist with a national research institute, Maria has conceived, planned, and organized a number of national research initiatives that have examined influences on the physical and mental health of adolescents. According to Holland's personality and work typology, Maria is most likely of which personality type?

a. conventional
b. enterprising
c. investigative
d. social

14.19 Donald Super proposes that the work sequence of young adulthood has two stages, the ____ stage and the _____ stage.

a. familial; external
b. investigative; realistic
c. interrupted; continuous
d. trial; establishment

14.20 Which of the following statements about job satisfaction is true?

a. It stays high for men until retirement.
b. It is lowest in early adulthood.
c. It is highest in young adulthood.
d. It stays high for women until retirement.

14.21 Which of the following is not one of the innovations associated with the quality of work life movement?

a. telecommuting
b. job sharing
c. on-site childcare
d. car pooling

14.22 Which of the following is the best example of role conflict?

a. Sandra is seeking another job because she is uncomfortable with her supervisor's sexual advances.
b. When her daughter had a high fever, Carmen had to miss an important meeting with a client.
c. When another accountant left, Lauren agreed to take on additional clients on a temporary basis.
d. Larry feels overwhelmed with the multiple responsibilities of his new job as a systems engineer.

14.23 Recasting or reframing a situation in a way that identifies the positive elements is called

a. conflict management.
b. depression.
c. homogamy.
d. cognitive restructuring.

PEARSON

mydevelopmentlab™ Study Plan

Are You Ready for the Test?

Students who use the study materials on MyDevelopmentLab report higher grades in the course than those who use the text alone. Here are three easy steps to mastering this chapter and improving your grade…

Step 1

Take the chapter pre-test in MyDevelopmentLab and review your customized Study Plan.

The quality of an individual's early attachment relationship to his or her family of origin is important because

- marriages are stronger if each partner has a different attachment style.
- these relationships contribute to an internal model of intimate relationships that children bring with them to adulthood.
- most people use their parents' marriage as a model for their own marriage.
- people tend to seek partners who are different from their parents.

Step 2

Use MyDevelopmentLab's Multimedia Library to help strengthen your knowledge of the chapter.

Explore: Erikson's Last Four Stages of Psychosocial Development

Erikson's Last Four Stages of Psychosocial Development

Drag and drop the term from the left-hand column to the corresponding place in the right-hand column.

Ego Integrity versus despair

Generativity versus stagnation

Identity versus role confusion

Intimacy versus isolation

Love Relationships

Parenting and Work

Peer Relationships

Reflection on and acceptance of one's life

Stage

Approximate Age Young Adulthood

Important Event

Description The young adult must develop intimate relationships or suffer feelings of isolation.

Reset 2 of 4 back next

Learning Objective 14.1

What did Erikson mean when he described early adulthood as a crisis of intimacy versus isolation?

83% of students responding to a national user survey report that the variety of activities available in MyDevelopmentLab made the material more interesting.

Explore: Strategies in Mate Selection

Strategies in Mate Selection

Based on evolutionary explanations of mate selection, actors Michael Douglas and Catherine Zeta-Jones have the qualities men and women seek in prospective mates in order to be sure that their genes are passed on to future generations. Michael Douglas has attained success in his field, meaning that he can provide material support to his wife and their children. Catherine Zeta-Jones' youth and beauty are likely to secure her husband's emotional commitment.

STOP

Learning Objective 14.4
What types of research do evolutionary and social role theorists cite to support their theories of mate selection?

Watch: Flow, Strength, and Work

And we talk them through it.

Learning Objective 14.12
How do career goals and job satisfaction change over time?

Step 3

Take the chapter post-test and compare your results against the pre-test.

POST-TEST

Many studies show that job satisfaction

- starts low and then rises for males, but maintains a uniformly high level for females.
- is lowest in early adulthood and rises steadily until retirement for both males and females.
- starts high and then declines for men, but is initially low and then rises for women.
- is high in early adulthood and then declines throughout adulthood until the low point before retirement.

What Reforms Are Needed in the Student Loan System?

Would you be surprised to learn that there is at least one issue on which there is near unanimous agreement among Americans? Surveys show that 94% of Americans support universal access to higher education (American Association of Colleges and Universities, 2005). Virtually everyone believes that high school graduates who want to pursue a college degree should be able to do so and that cost should not be a determining factor in who goes to college. Thus, there is broad support for a continued government role in funding the education of individual students. Still, questions remain about the best way to accomplish this goal.

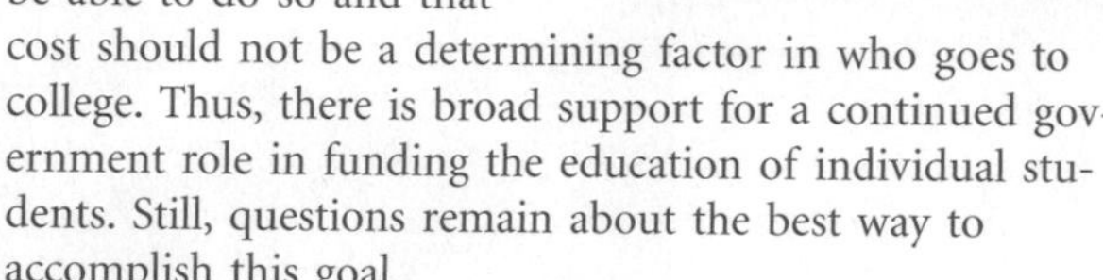

Student Loans

Since the early 1970s, the federal government has maintained a financial aid program with which you are probably familiar. The system includes grants for low-income students, but most students do not qualify for these grants. Moreover, they are too small to pay all of a student's expenses. Consequently, two-thirds of students borrow money to pay for college. Some of these loans are insured by the federal government and are available through the same application process as are government grants. However, like grants, the amounts of these loans are limited. As a result, many students, especially those who attend private institutions, also borrow from private lenders to meet their college expenses.

Thanks to the popularity of student loans, they now constitute a multi-billion dollar industry in the United States. As a result of the fierce competition among lenders, corruption has become a major problem (Paley, April 20, 2007). For instance, some college administrators have steered students to specific lenders in exchange for cash payments and other inducements from those lenders.

Additional concerns about the student loan system involve its economic effects. Some economists argue that the easy availability of these loans cause students and their families to be less concerned about college costs than they would be if loans were either unavailable or more difficult to obtain (Wolfram, 2005). More importantly, lack of concern about costs may lead students to choose educational options that are not the best ones for them (Vedder, 2004). For one thing, they may fail to consider career options that do not require a college degree. Professionals in some of these fields, such as self-employed plumbers and auto mechanics, make more money than many college graduates do. Furthermore, there are many well-paying careers, especially in health care, for which a two-year degree is sufficient, an option that is far less costly than a four-year degree.

The Impact of Indebtedness on College Graduates

Perhaps the most important consequence of the popularity of student loans, and one that many people believe policymakers should address, is the impact of student loan indebtedness on the lives of students and their families. As of 2006, the average total indebtedness of college graduates in the United States was nearly $18,000 (American Association of Colleges and Universities, 2006). Some students at private universities incur indebtedness of $100,000 or more before getting their

TABLE PQVI.1 Tips for Graduating with a Minimal Amount of Debt

1. If you can qualify for scholarships, great, but don't count on them to fully fund your college education.
2. If you must borrow, do so only to pay for your school expenses; get a part-time job to pay for other items and for luxuries.
3. Take a full course load every semester to shorten the amount of time that you are in school. This will reduce your fees and living expenses.
4. Complete every course in which you enroll. Unless you drop within a few days of the beginning of a term, a "withdrawal" costs just as much as a completed course does.
5. Transfer as many credits as you can from low-cost institutions such as community colleges that you can afford to pay for out-of-pocket.
6. Start making interest payments before you graduate to prevent a relatively small loan from turning into a large debt.
7. Use credit cards as little as possible or, better yet, not at all.
8. If you purchase an on-campus meal plan, use it.
9. Read books on personal finance to learn how to live on a budget and manage credit wisely.
10. Explore careers that feature student loan repayment as a benefit (e.g., teaching).

diplomas. As a result, some students delay graduating by enrolling part-time when they are near the end of their course of study, because student loan payments are deferred until a student has actually graduated. However, this strategy serves only to increase their indebtedness because, on most student loans, interest accrues even though the student is not making payments.

Another consequence of student loan indebtedness is that a large proportion of today's college graduates have to delay financial milestones such as purchasing their first homes because of the adverse impact of large student loans on their credit ratings. Some are forced to live with their parents until their incomes catch up with their student loan payments. Moreover, the reluctance of new graduates to participate in employer-sponsored retirement programs in favor of retiring their student debts has led to concern among public officials about the financial crisis that young workers may face thirty or forty years from now when they reach retirement age (Block, 2006).

Reform Proposals

A number of reforms have been enacted to address corruption in the financial aid system. In the early 1990s, for example, legislation authorized colleges to make direct loans to students (Kunin, June 13, 2007). However, most colleges lack the funds necessary to fully cover the demand for student loans, so private lenders remain an essential part of the financial aid system. Thus, the government has strengthened oversight strategies and enacted stiffer penalties to prevent college officials from being influenced by gifts and bribes from lenders (Carbone, June 19, 2007).

Reductions in the interest rates and fees that lenders are allowed to charge for student loans have been proposed to lessen the impact of student loan debt on graduates (Palmer, June 22, 2007). Moreover, the criteria for awarding grants have been expanded to include more students. In addition, many states pay off the student loans of graduates who enter public service careers such as teaching and law enforcement.

New Strategies for Helping Students Pay for College

Some policy experts argue that the time has come to completely overhaul the financial aid system. One proposal for such sweeping reform is a new twist on an old idea. After World War II, the "GI Bill" enabled millions of veterans to attend college. The program was so successful, that it was extended to include all of those who serve in the armed forces, and it continues to be an important source of college funding for students who have served in the military today. Some policymakers have argued that a similar system should be developed to provide college funding to students who are willing to commit to other kinds of service. To that end, legislation that created the AmeriCorps program was enacted in 1993 (AmeriCorps.org, 2007). AmeriCorps participants serve in volunteer positions for two years after which they are rewarded with money for college.

Although AmeriCorps has been quite successful, there are obviously many students who cannot commit to spending two years of their lives in low-paying or unpaid volunteer positions. Consequently, some advocates of a service-based approach to college funding argue that there should be a mandatory national service program for all high school graduates on which college funding is dependent (Alter, 2007). Such a program would allow young adults to fulfill their service requirement either by joining the military or by filling other socially necessary positions such as serving as tutors to elementary school students. The program would include provisions for volunteers' living expenses, just as military service does.

By contrast, what if you looked to Wall Street to fund your college education? A financial instrument called a *human capital contract* would allow you to do just that (Palacios, 2004). In a human capital contract, a student and a mutual fund specifically created for the purpose of funding student's college expenses enter into a legally binding agreement. The mutual fund pledges to pay all or some of the student's expenses. The student promises to pay a small percentage of her post-graduation earnings to the mutual fund for a specified amount of time, such as 10 years. A student's ability to obtain a human capital contract would depend on her academic qualifications. Theoretically, the better a student's grades in high school, the more likely she would be to garner enough money from investors to fully fund her education.

Advocates of human capital contracts argue that they are more equitable than the current student loan system (Palacios, 2004). Under the present system, for instance, accounting and social work majors are subject to the same loan payments even though a beginning accountant's salary may be twice that of a social worker. Because human capital contract payments would be based on income, the accountant would pay more than the social worker, although both would pay the same percentage of their salaries. Moreover, armed with a human capital contract, a student who has a strong sense of calling to a field such as social work would feel free to follow her heart without worrying about how she would make her student loan payments after graduation.

Financial aid experts doubt that either national service or human capital contracts will ever fully replace the current financial aid system. However, they do regard these options as possible sources of additional funding that will help students bridge the gap between grants and the actual costs of college. Moreover, everyone agrees that new and more flexible approaches to funding are vital to meeting the goal of universal access to higher education.

Your Turn

- Are you concerned about your own student loans? Look over the tips in Table PQV1.1 to see how you can minimize the amount of debt you will have when you graduate.
- Find out how your representatives in the U.S. Congress and in the U.S. Senate have voted on recent financial aid reform measures.
- What efforts are being made in your state to make college more affordable?
- Based on your own experiences, create a presentation for high school students titled "Going to College without Going Broke."
- Use your internet skills to learn more about national service and human capital contracts. Make a list of the pros and cons associated with these approaches to college funding.

PART SEVEN Middle Adulthood

15

Physical and Cognitive Development in Middle Adulthood

The ring of his cell phone woke Sonny up from a sound night's sleep. Sonny looked at the clock and blinked several times before his brain registered that the time was 6:15 a.m. "It's Saturday," he thought, "Why would anyone be calling me at this hour?" Sonny looked at the caller ID screen and saw that the caller was Joe, his old college roommate. Sonny and Joe weren't close, but they kept in touch and regularly filled each other in on what was happening in the lives of the other people that they had hung out with in their college days that were now 25 years behind them. He answered the phone, puzzled as to why Joe would need to talk to him so early on a Saturday morning.

Joe was calling to give Sonny the news that a mutual acquaintance, Ben, had unexpectedly and suddenly died of a heart attack. Ben's wife had become concerned when he didn't come home from work

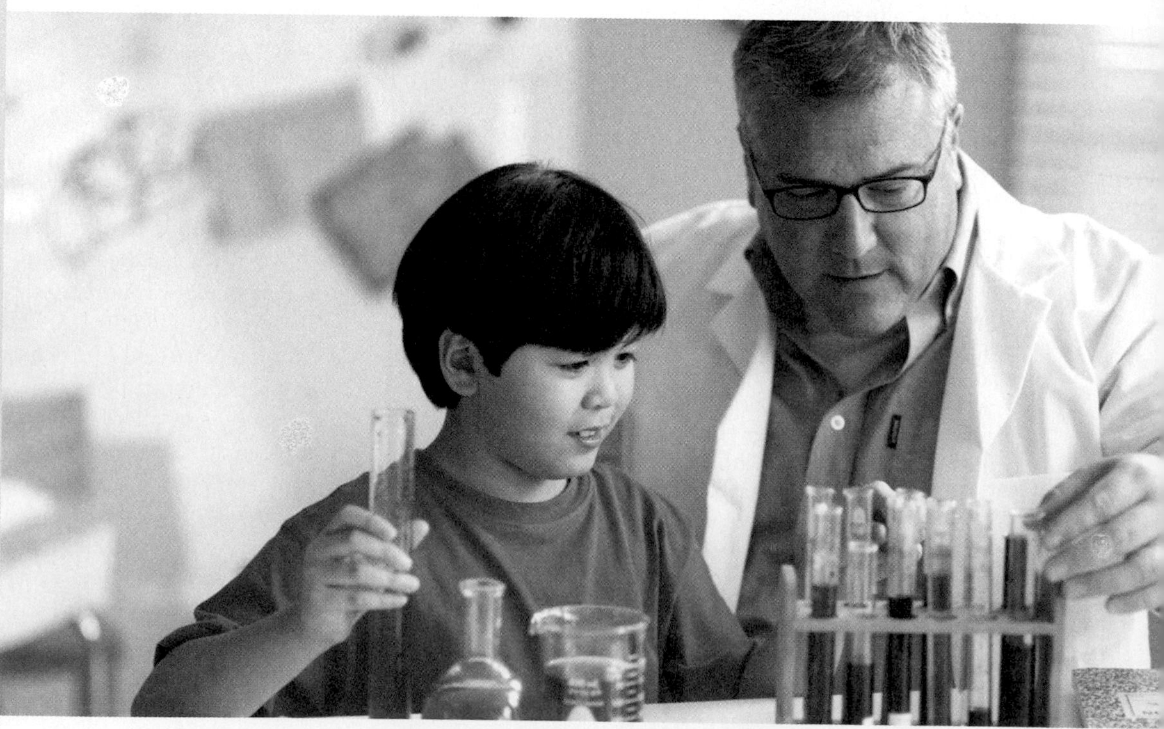

Friday night and went to his office. She found him slumped over the steering wheel of his car and called 911, but it was too late. Shocked and feeling numb, Sonny ended the call after Joe promised to update him about the pending funeral plans. He sat on the edge of his bed staring at the floor and wondering how it was possible for someone who had appeared to be perfectly healthy to suddenly drop dead at the age of 47.

Doctors often refer to heart disease as a "silent killer" because of its capacity for producing a great deal of damage without causing any symptoms. In fact, cardiologists estimate that 30% of adults in the United States who have heart disease have no symptoms (American College of Cardiology, 2002). The most common form of the disease occurs when arteries that supply the heart with oxygen become increasingly constricted as a result of fatty deposits called *plaque*. As blockage in the vessels become progressively worse, the amount of oxygen that reaches the heart muscle decreases. Without vital oxygen, the muscles begin to weaken and die. Once the arteries are sufficiently narrowed, a tiny blood clot can cut off all of the heart's oxygen supply, causing sudden cardiac death like that of Sonny's and Joe's college friend, Ben. More than 250,000 such deaths occur every year in the United States (American College of Cardiology, 2002).

Sonny's experience is not an uncommon one. Nearly every middle-aged person has a similar story about a peer who has died unexpectedly from an undiagnosed disease. The rates of such deaths remain fairly stable through the 20s and early 30s when there is about 1 disease-related death for every 1,000 people between the ages of 20 to 35. Then the rates begin to double every 10 years, reaching 1 per 100 people by age 65 (National Vital Statistics System, 2006). This increase in mortality from disease is largely caused by the effects of secondary rather than primary aging (American College of Cardiology, 2002). Clearly, middle age is the period when poor health habits begin to catch up with us, but physicians note that the advent of emergency treatments that can literally stop a heart attack in its tracks have made middle-aged adults complacent about their health-related behaviors (Eckel, 2006). While noting the value of these treatments, cardiologists point out that by changing their health habits, middle-aged adults can slow the progress of diseases that have already begun, prevent others from ever developing at all, and avoid ever having to rely on emergency treatment techniques (Eckel, 2006).

In this chapter you will learn that, with advancing age, the story of human development seems to become more an account of differences than a description of universals. This happens because there are so many factors—behavioral choices, poor health, and so on—that determine the specific developmental pathway an adult follows. Most middle-aged adults are healthy, energetic, and intellectually productive, but others are in decline. Moreover, because developmental psychology has focused more on younger individuals, there simply isn't as much knowledge about universal changes in adulthood.

Physical Changes

What comes to mind when you think about middle age—graying hair, reading glasses, an expanding waistline? As you learned in Chapter 13, some of these characteristics are the result of primary aging, such as graying hair and the need for reading glasses (look back at Table 13.1 on page 373 for a review). Others, such as an expanding waistline, are usually due to secondary aging. Nevertheless, the effects of primary aging, though subtle during the early adult years, become far more obvious after age 40.

Learning Objective 15.1
What do researchers know about brain function in middle age?

The Brain and Nervous System

Relatively little is known about the normal, undamaged brains of middle-aged adults. This is because research has focused on changes associated with trauma and disease rather than changes due to primary aging. However, in recent years, neuropsychologists have learned a great deal about the extent to which changes in cognitive functioning are attributable to age-related changes in the brain. To examine this question, researchers examine how the brains of young and middle-aged people respond to cognitive tasks. Such studies have produced a rather complex set of findings.

One fairly consistent finding is that middle-aged adults' brains respond more slowly to cognitive tasks than those of younger adults (Zysset, Schroeder, Neumann, & von Cramon, 2007). Another is that such tasks activate a larger area of brain tissue in middle-aged adults than they do in younger adults (Gunter, Jackson, & Mulder, 1998). Of course, neuropsychologists don't know why, but they speculate that cognitive processing is less selective in middle-aged adults than it is in younger adults. It's as if the middle-aged brain has a more difficult time finding just the right neurological tool to carry out a particular function, and so it activates more tools than are necessary. This lack of selectivity could account for differences between age groups in the speed at which cognitive tasks are carried out.

The brains of middle-aged and younger adults also respond differently to sensory stimuli. For example, when participants are presented with a simple auditory stimulus such as a musical tone, patterns of brain waves in different areas vary across age groups (Yordanova, Kolev, & Basar, 1998). Research along this line has suggested that middle-aged adults may have less ability to control attention processes by inhibiting brain responses to irrelevant stimuli (Amenedo & Diaz, 1998, 1999). Their difficulty with attentional control could be another reason for the average difference in processing speed between young and middle-aged adults.

Such findings might lead you to conclude that, in everyday situations requiring intense concentration and rapid judgments, middle-aged adults would perform more poorly than their younger counterparts. Interestingly, though, recent research on lapses of concentration and poor decision-making among drivers shows just the opposite (Dobson, Brown, Ball, Powers, & McFadden, 1999). Younger drivers exhibit more lapses in attention and driving errors than middle-aged drivers. These lapses and errors, combined with younger drivers' greater likelihood of driving after drinking alcohol, help account for the different accident rates of young and middle-aged adults. Such findings, when considered with those on age differences in brain function, illustrate the difficulty researchers face in finding direct relationships between age-related brain differences and cross-age variations in behavior.

Another point to keep in mind about studies of the middle-aged brain is that the results of these studies are likely due to both primary and secondary aging. That is, part of the difference in brain function between young and middle-aged adults is due to natural aging processes. The remainder is attributable to the effects of health. Studies show, for example, that health-related changes in the circulatory system cause damage in the parts of the brain that are critical to processing speed, planning, and memory in middle age (Raz & Rodrigue, 2006; Raz, Rodrigue, Kennedy, & Acker, 2007). Consequently, healthy middle-aged adults exhibit both neurological and cognitive functioning that is more similar to that of young adults than their peers who suffer from health conditions that affect the circulatory system.

The Reproductive System

Learning Objective 15.2

How does reproductive function change in men and women in middle age?

If you were asked to name a single significant physical change occurring in the years of middle adulthood, chances are you'd say *menopause*—especially if you're a woman. The more general term is the **climacteric**, which refers to the years of middle or late adulthood in both men and women during which reproductive capacity declines or is lost.

Male Climacteric In men, the climacteric is extremely gradual, with a slow loss of reproductive capacity, although the rate of change varies widely from one man to the next, and there are documented cases of men in their 90s fathering children. On average, the quantity of viable sperm produced declines slightly, beginning perhaps at about age 40. The testes also shrink very gradually, and the volume of seminal fluid declines after about age 60.

The causal factor is most likely a very slow drop in testosterone levels, beginning in early adulthood and continuing well into old age. This decline in testosterone is implicated in the gradual loss of muscle tissue (and hence strength) that becomes evident in the middle and later years, as well as in the increased risk of heart disease in middle and old age. It also appears to affect sexual function. In particular, in the middle years, the incidence of erectile dysfunction begins to increase—although many things other than the slight decline in testosterone contribute to this change, including an increased incidence of poor health (especially heart disease), obesity, use of blood pressure medication (and other medications), alcohol abuse, and smoking. *Erectile dysfunction*, sometimes called *impotence*, is the inability to achieve or maintain an erection.

Lifestyle changes can sometimes restore sexual function. In one study, researchers enrolled 35- to 55-year-old obese men with erectile dysfunction in a 2-year weight loss program that required participants to make changes in their diets and exercise habits (Esposito et al., 2004). About one-third of the men experienced improvements in erectile dysfunction along with reductions in body fat.

Among healthy middle-aged men, performance anxiety is a frequent cause of erectile dysfunction. The drugs *sildenafil* (Viagra), *tadalafil* (Cialis), and *vardenafil* (Levitra) have been found to be effective in treating this problem (Chen, Paik, & Ishii, 2007; Rosen, 1996; Skoumal et al., 2004). However, physicians warn that men with erectile dysfunction should avoid so-called natural treatments such as food supplements because most of them have not been studied in placebo-controlled experiments (Rowland & Tai, 2003). Moreover, men who turn to supplements for symptom relief may delay seeking medical attention and, as a result, may continue to suffer from a serious underlying condition without realizing it.

climacteric the term used to describe the adult period during which reproductive capacity declines or is lost

menopause the cessation of monthly menstrual cycles in middle-aged women

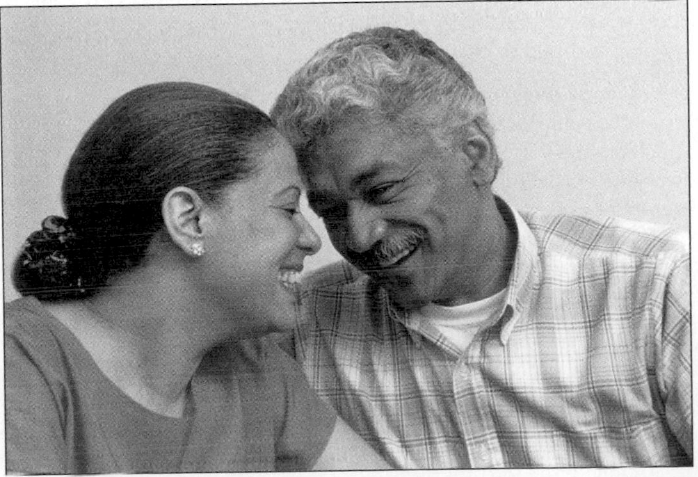

During middle age, supportive partners help each other cope with the changes in sexual function that are brought about by the natural aging of the reproductive system.

Menopause Declines in key sex hormones are also clearly implicated in the set of changes in women called **menopause**, which means literally the cessation of the menses. You'll remember from Chapter 11 that secretion of several forms of estrogen by the ovaries increases rapidly during puberty, triggering the onset of menstruation as well as stimulating the development of breasts and secondary sex characteristics. In the adult woman, estrogen levels are high during the first 14 days of the menstrual cycle, stimulating the release of an ovum and the preparation of the uterus for possible implantation. *Progesterone*, which is secreted by the ruptured ovarian follicle from which the ovum emerges, rises during the second half of the menstrual cycle and stimulates the sloughing off of accumulated material in the uterus each month if conception has not occurred.

The average age of menopause for both African American and White American women, and for women in other countries for which data are available, is roughly age 50; anything between ages 40 and 60 is considered within the normal range (Bellantoni & Blackman, 1996). However, there are some indications that there has been a secular trend in the age of menopause that is similar to the one you read about for menarche in Chapter 11, that is, menopause may be occurring at later ages today than it did in past cohorts of women (Rodstrom et al., 2003; Varea et al., 2000). At present, researchers are trying to identify the contributing factors to individual differences in the age of menopause in order to learn more about this trend and to determine whether menopause will occur at even later ages in future cohorts. Moreover, like puberty, menopause is not a single event but a series of changes that are strongly influenced by hormones.

Menopausal Phases Menopause, like puberty, is often thought of as a single event. However, it actually occurs over several years, and researchers generally agree that it consists of three phases. First, during the **premenopausal phase**, estrogen levels begin to fluctuate and decline, typically in the late 30s or early 40s, producing irregular menstrual periods in many women. The ovaries are less sensitive to cyclical hormonal signals, and many women experience *anovulatory cycles*, or cycles in which no ovum is released. Even though no ovum is produced, estrogen levels are high enough in premenopausal women to produce periodic bleeding. However, the lack of ovulation results in a dramatic drop in progesterone. Thus, many experts believe that the menstrual irregularity associated with the premenopausal period is due to progesterone loss rather than estrogen loss (Lee, 1996).

During the **perimenopausal phase**, estrogen levels decrease and women experience more extreme variations in the timing of their menstrual cycles. In addition, about 75% of perimenopausal women experience *hot flashes*, sudden sensations of feeling hot. Of those who have hot flashes, 85% will have them for more than a year; a third or more will have them for 5 years or more (Kletzky & Borenstein, 1987). It is hypothesized that fluctuating levels of estrogen and other hormones cause a woman's blood vessels to expand and contract erratically, thus producing hot flashes (see No Easy Answers).

During a hot flash, the temperature of the skin can rise as much as 1–7 degrees in some parts of the body, although the core body temperature actually drops (Kronenberg, 1994). Hot flashes last, on average, about 3 minutes and may recur as seldom as daily or as often as three times per hour (Bellantoni & Blackman, 1996). Most women learn to manage these brief periods of discomfort if they occur during the day. However, hot flashes frequently disrupt women's sleep. When this happens, it sets in motion a series of changes that are actually due to sleep deprivation rather than menopause. For example, lack of sleep can lead to mental confusion, difficulty with everyday memory tasks, and emotional instability. Thus, perimenopausal women may have the subjective feeling that they are "going crazy" when the real problem is that hot flashes are preventing them from getting enough sleep. The general light-headedness and shakiness that accompany some women's hot flashes can add to this sensation.

Eventually, estrogen and progesterone drop to consistently low levels and menstruation ceases altogether. Once a women has ceased to menstruate for a year, she is in the **postmenopausal phase**. In postmenopausal women, estradiol and estrone, both types of estrogen, drop to about a quarter or less of their premenopausal levels. Progesterone decreases even more, as a result of the cessation of ovulation, although the adrenal glands continue to provide postmenopausal women with some progesterone.

The reduction in estrogen during the perimenopausal and postmenopausal phases also has effects on genital and other tissue. The breasts become less firm, the genitals and the uterus shrink somewhat, and the vagina becomes both shorter and smaller in diameter. The walls of the vagina also become somewhat thinner and less elastic and produce less lubrication during intercourse (McCoy, 1998; Wich & Carnes, 1995).

premenopausal phase the stage of menopause during which estrogen levels fall somewhat, menstrual periods are less regular, and anovulatory cycles begin to occur

perimenopausal phase the stage of menopause during which estrogen and progesterone levels are erratic, menstrual cycles may be very irregular, and women begin to experience symptoms such as hot flashes

postmenopausal phase the last stage of menopause beginning when a woman has had no menstrual periods for a year or more

NO EASY ANSWERS

The Pros and Cons of Hormone Therapy

Most of the physical symptoms and effects of menopause—including hot flashes, thinning of the vaginal wall, and loss of vaginal lubrication—can be reduced by taking estrogen and progesterone (*hormone therapy*, or *HT*). Moreover, in the 1990s, physicians thought that HT would protect women against heart disease and dementia. Thus, they commonly prescribed HT for women who complained of menopausal symptoms such as hot flashes.

Everything changed in 2002 with the publication of the results of the Women's Health Initiative (WHI), a longitudinal placebo-controlled study of HT (Writing Group for the Women's Health Initiative Investigators, 2002). These results included alarming evidence showing that long-term use of either estrogen alone or combined estrogen-progesterone hormone replacement therapy significantly increased the risk of both breast and ovarian cancers (Chlebowski et al., 2003; Lacey et al., 2002). Data from the Heart and Estrogen Replacement Study (HERS) also showed that HT provided women with no protection against cardiovascular disease and may even have increased the severity of the disease among study participants who already had it (Grady et al., 2002; Hulley et al., 2002). The evidence suggesting that HT might seriously harm women's health was so strong that the WHI was immediately terminated; all of the study's participants who had been given HT were advised to stop taking it (Writing Group for the Women's Health Initiative Investigators, 2002). Further, research failed to support the hypothesized link between estrogen and Alzheimer's disease, and some studies showed that estrogen treatment might actually increase the incidence of the disorder (Nelson, Humphrey, Nygren, Teutsch, & Allan, 2002; Shumaker et al., 2003). Consequently, the number of women who take HT declined dramatically soon after these results were published (Udell, Fischer, Brookhart, Solomon, & Choudhry, 2006).

To date, the accumulated evidence indicates that the only consistent benefits associated with hormone replacement therapy are the reduction of hot flashes and protection against osteoporosis (Nelson, 2004; Nelson et al., 2002; Torgerson & Bell-Syer, 2001). However, there may be ways of achieving these results without the risks associated with HT. Some modes of hormone delivery may be less harmful than others as well. Studies have shown that hormones can be readily absorbed from creams applied either to the skin or directly to the vagina and from patches worn on any area of the body (Nelson, 2004). Doctors believe that creams and patches may be less risky than pills that must be metabolized through the digestive system (American College of Obstetricians and Gynecologists [ACOG], 2004b).

As a result of the most recent findings, the American College of Obstetricians and Gynecologists recommends that women be extremely cautious about entering into any regimen involving HT (ACOG, 2004b). First, they say that women should aim for the lowest dosage that provides symptom relief and avoid taking hormones for more than a year or two. Second, they suggest that hormone treatment be symptom-specific. For example, if a woman's main complaint is vaginal dryness, then the best treatment for her is a vaginal cream. Finally, ACOG recommends that women undergoing any kind of treatment for menopausal symptoms see their doctors regularly and follow their instructions with regard to cancer screenings (e.g., mammograms).

Take a Stand

Decide which of these two statements you most agree with and think about how you would defend your position:

1. Due to the risks involved, hormone therapy should be a last resort for menopausal women who have hot flashes and other symptoms.
2. No medical treatment is entirely free of risk, so women who want to take hormone therapy to relieve symptoms of menopause should do so.

Psychological Effects of Menopause One other aspect of the climacteric in women deserves some mention. It has been part of folklore for a very long time that menopause involves major emotional upheaval as well as clear physical changes. However, research findings are mixed. Longitudinal studies show that depressive symptoms increase during menopause (Freeman et al., 2004). Nevertheless, experts note that serious depression, as defined by the DSM-IV-TR criteria for major depressive disorder, is no more frequent among menopausal women than among those who are nonmenopausal (Bromberger, 2007).

A woman's overall negativity and number of life stressors before entering menopause contributes to her emotional state (Dennerstein, Lehert, & Guthrie, 2002). In other words, a woman's negativity may be attributed to menopause when, in reality, it may be a longstanding component of her personality. Alternatively, she may have a particularly stressful life, and menopausal symptoms are just one more source of difficulty.

In addition, the actual level of symptoms women experience makes a difference. It isn't surprising that women who are most uncomfortable because of hot flashes and other physical changes, and whose symptoms last the longest, experience the most depression and negative mood. Researchers have also found that menopausal women who suffer from sleep deprivation due to hot flashes at night, or night sweats, may be misdiagnosed with generalized anxiety disorder. Not only are the symptoms of the two conditions similar, but electroencephalographic studies reveal that the patterns of brain activity across the two conditions are quite similar, too (Terashima et al., 2004).

Figure 15.1
Ethnic Group Differences in Women's Attitudes about Aging and Menopause

The more positively women feel about aging, the less negatively they view menopause. African American women appear to have the most positive view of aging and the least negative view of menopause.

(*Source*: Sommer, B., et al., "Attitudes toward menopause and aging across ethnic/racial groups", *Psychosomatic Medicine*, 61, 868–875, 1999. Reprinted by permission.)

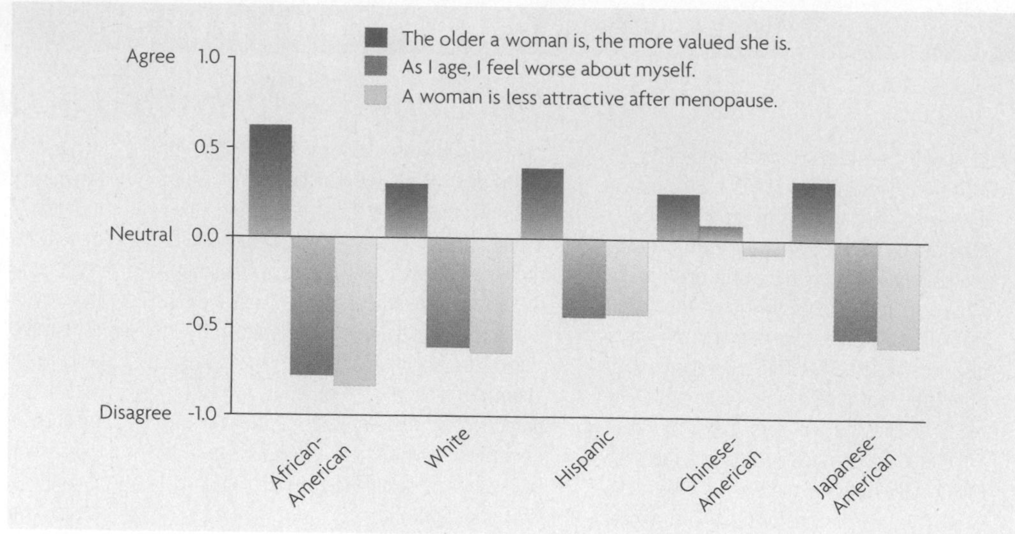

Any weight-bearing exercise—even walking—will help prevent osteoporosis.

Women's attitudes toward menopause vary somewhat across ethnic groups. Interestingly, one study suggested that these views are linked to women's general feelings about getting older (Sommer et al., 1999). Figure 15.1 shows that the researchers found that women who agreed with the statement "the older a woman is, the more valued she is" were likely to disagree with the statement "a woman is less attractive after menopause." As you can see, African American participants expressed a more positive view of aging and a less negative view of menopause than did women in the other groups. Interestingly, however, African American women, on average, experience more menopause symptoms such as hot flashes than women in other groups do (Gold, 2006). Thus, having a positive outlook on aging and menopause does not appear to protect women against its symptoms. Moreover, across all groups, menopausal status is only one of many aspects of midlife that women consider when they are asked to evaluate the quality of their lives (Beyene, Gillis, & Lee, 2007). Thus, some researchers argue that menopause should be studied within the whole context of a middle-aged woman's life rather than as the universal defining feature of this period of life.

Sexual Activity Despite changes in the reproductive system, the great majority of middle-aged adults remain sexually active, although the frequency of sex declines somewhat during these years (Association of Reproductive Health Professionals, 2000; Laumann, Gagnon, Michael, & Michaels, 1994; Michael, Gagnon, Laumann, & Kolata, 1994). It is unlikely that this decline during midlife is due wholly or even largely to drops in sex hormone levels; women do not experience major estrogen declines until their late 40s, but the decline in sexual activity begins much sooner. And the drop in testosterone among men is so gradual and slight during these years that it cannot be the full explanation. An alternative explanation is that the demands of other roles are simply so pressing that middle-aged adults find it hard to find time for sex. Increasing rates of chronic diseases such as diabetes and arthritis may also explain the declines in the frequency of sexual activity among people in their 50s (Association of Reproductive Health Professionals, 2000).

osteoporosis loss of bone mass with age, resulting in more brittle and porous bones

Learning Objective 15.3

What is osteoporosis, and what factors are associated with it?

The Skeletal System

Another change that begins to be quite significant in middle adulthood is a loss of calcium from the bones, resulting in reduced bone mass and more brittle and porous bones. This process is called **osteoporosis.** Bone loss begins at about age 30 for both men and women, but in women the process is accelerated by menopause. The major conse-

Table 15.1 Risk Factors for Osteoporosis

Risk Factor	Explanation
Race	Whites are at higher risk than other races.
Gender	Women have considerably higher risk than men.
Weight	Those who are underweight are at higher risk.
Timing of climacteric	Women who experience early menopause and those who have had their ovaries removed are at higher risk, presumably because their estrogen levels decline at earlier ages.
Family history	Those with a family history of osteoporosis are at higher risk.
Diet	A diet low in calcium during adolescence and early adulthood results in lower peak levels of bone mass, and hence greater risk of falling below critical levels later. Whether there is any benefit in increasing intake of calcium postmenopausally remains in debate. Diets high in either caffeine (especially black coffee) or alcohol are also linked to higher risk.
Exercise	Those with a sedentary lifestyle are at higher risk. Prolonged immobility, such as bed rest, also increases the rate of bone loss. Exercise reduces the rate of bone loss.

(*Sources*: Duursma et al., 1991; Gambert, Schultz, & Hamdy, 1995; Goldberg & Hagberg, 1990; Gordon & Vaughan, 1986; Lindsay, 1985; Morrison et al., 1994; Smith, 1982.)

quence of this loss of bone density is a significantly increased risk of fractures, beginning as early as age 50 for women, much later for men. Among older women (and men), such fractures can be a major cause of disability and reduced activity, so osteoporosis is not a trivial change.

In women, it is clear that bone loss is linked quite directly to estrogen and progesterone levels. Researchers know that these hormones fall dramatically after menopause, and it is the timing of menopause rather than age that signals the increase in rate of bone loss (Recker, Lappe, Davies, & Heaney, 2000). Researchers also know that the rate of bone loss drops to premenopausal levels among women who take hormones, all of which makes the link quite clear (Rossouw et al., 2003). While the overall pattern of bone loss seems to be a part of primary aging, the amount of such loss nonetheless varies quite a lot from one individual to another. Table 15.1 lists the known risk factors for osteoporosis.

Aside from taking hormones, women can help prevent osteoporosis with one or both of the following strategies. First, they can get enough calcium during early adulthood so that peak levels of bone mass are as robust as possible. Second, throughout adult life women can get regular exercise, particularly weight-bearing exercise such as walking or strength training. In one study, a group of middle-aged or older women were randomly assigned to a strength-training program consisting of twice-weekly sessions for a year. They showed a gain in bone density over the year, whereas women in a control group without such weight training showed a loss (Nelson et al., 1994). Third, *bone mineral density (BMD)* tests can identify osteoporosis long before it causes serious damage to bones. Once it is diagnosed, women can take bone-building medications such as *alendronate sodium* (Fosamax). Studies show that the combination of BMD testing and medication dramatically reduces the risk of fractures among women over the age of 50 (Jaglal et al., 2005).

presbyopia normal loss of visual acuity with aging, especially the ability to focus the eyes on near objects

Vision and Hearing

Learning Objective 15.4

How do vision and hearing change in middle age?

One of the most noticeable physical changes occurring in the middle years is a loss of visual acuity. Two changes in the eyes, collectively called **presbyopia**, are involved. First, the lens of the eye thickens. In a process that begins in childhood but produces

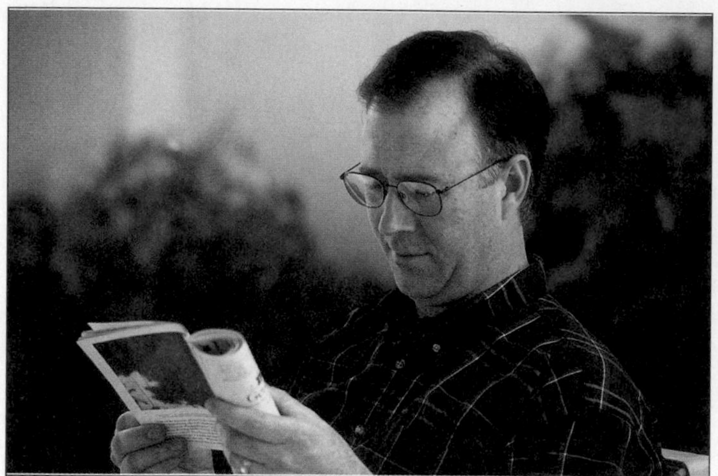

By age 45 or 50, nearly everyone needs glasses, especially for reading.

noticeable effects only in middle adulthood, layer after layer of slightly pigmented material accumulates on the lens. Because light coming into the eye must pass through this thickened, slightly yellowed material, the total amount of light reaching the retina decreases, which reduces a person's overall sensitivity to light waves, particularly short wavelengths that are perceived as blue, blue-green, and violet (Fozard, 1990).

Because of this thickening of the lens, it is also harder and harder for the muscles surrounding the eye to change the shape of the lens to adjust the focus. In a young eye, the shape of the lens readily adjusts for distance, so no matter how near or far away some object may be, the light rays passing through the eye converge where they should, on the retina in the back of the eye, giving a sharp image. But as the thickening increases, the elasticity of the lens declines and it can no longer make these fine adjustments. Many images become blurry. In particular, the ability to focus clearly on near objects deteriorates rapidly in the 40s and early 50s. As a result, middle-aged adults often hold books and other items farther and farther away, because only in that way can they get a clear image. Finally, of course, they cannot read print at the distance at which they can focus, and they are forced to wear reading glasses or bifocals. These same changes also affect the ability to adapt quickly to variations in levels of light or glare, such as from passing headlights when driving at night or in the rain. So driving may become more stressful. All in all, these changes in the eyes, which appear to be a genuine part of primary aging, require both physical and psychological adjustment.

The equivalent process in hearing is called **presbycusis**. The auditory nerves and the structures of the inner ear gradually degenerate as a result of basic wear and tear, resulting primarily in losses in the ability to hear sounds of high and very low frequencies. But these changes do not accumulate to the level of significant hearing loss until somewhat later in life than is typical for presbyopia. Hearing loss is quite slow until about age 50. After age 50 or 55, however, the rate of hearing loss accelerates. Some of this loss is due to conditions that are more common among older adults than among younger individuals, such as excessive ear wax, chronic fluid in the ear, or abnormal growth of the bones of the inner ear (Public Health Agency of Canada, 2006). Most commonly, however, hearing loss in adulthood appears to be the result of lifelong exposure to excessive noise (Rabinowitz, 2000).

Critical Thinking

1. Given the changes in the brain, reproductive system, bones, and sensory abilities that you have learned about in this section, how would you evaluate a statement such as "age is just a state of mind"?

Health and Wellness

How long do you expect to live? Most young and middle-aged people these days expect to live into their 80s. The reason for this optimistic prediction is that most adults are aware of the trend toward increased life expectancy that is shown in Figure 15.2. Still, many are concerned about the quality of their lives, and no single variable affects the quality of life in middle and late adulthood as much as health. A middle-aged person in good health often functions as well and has as much energy as much younger adults.

presbycusis normal loss of hearing with aging, especially of high-frequency tones

Learning Objective 15.5

How does cardiovascular disease develop?

Cardiovascular Disease

At the beginning of the chapter you read about a middle-aged man who learned that a friend who had shown no signs of disease suddenly died of a heart attack. As we noted, deaths of this sort are often caused by the build-up of *plaque* in the arteries that

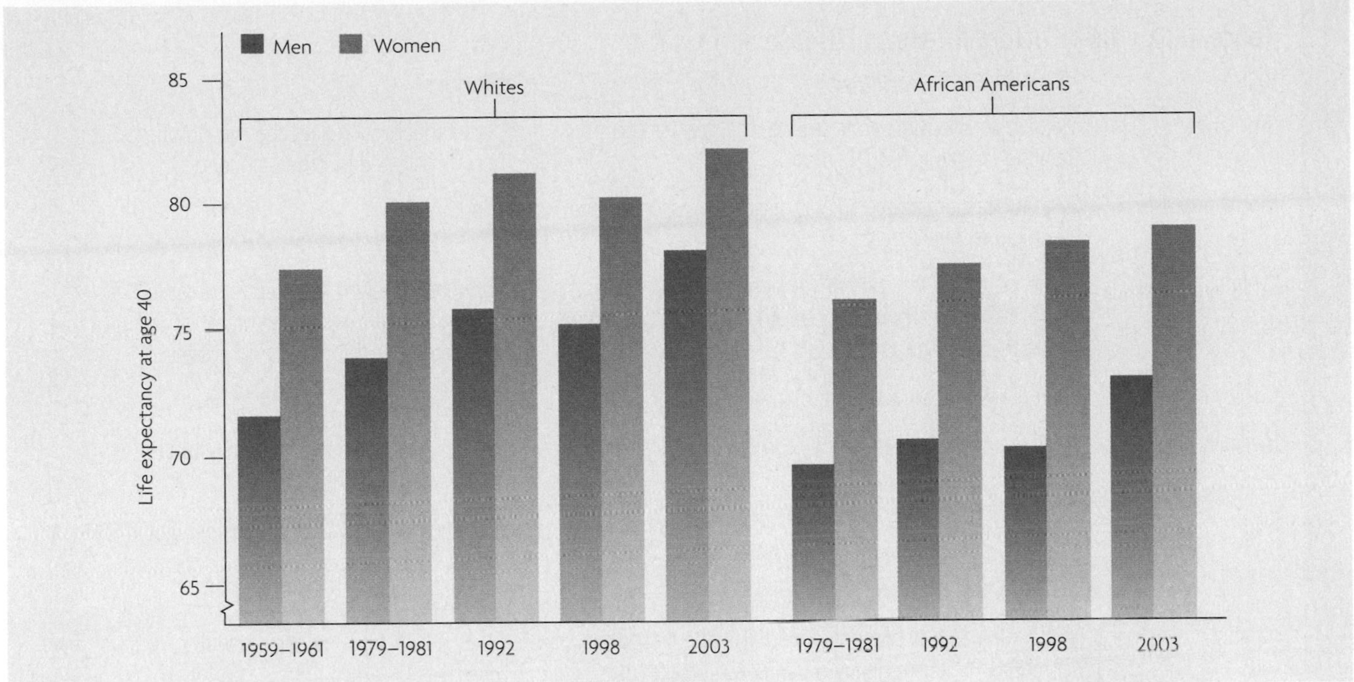

Figure 15.2
Trends in Life Expectancy for White and African American Men and Women in the United States

Life expectancy at age 40 in the United States from 1959 through 1998 for women and men, blacks and whites.

(*Sources:* Arias, 2006; CDC, 1998c; U.S. Bureau of the Census, 1990, Table 104, p. 73; U.S. Bureau of the Census, 1995a, Table 115, p. 86.)

supply the muscles of the heart with oxygen, one of many conditions that are covered by the term **cardiovascular disease (CVD)**. The process that causes plaque to accumulate in the arteries is **atherosclerosis**. It is not a normal part of aging. It is a disease, increasingly common with age, but not inevitable.

The rate of CVD has been dropping rapidly in the United States and in most other industrialized countries in recent years. Between 1973 and 1987, for example, it decreased 42% among those under age 55 and dropped by a third for those aged 55 to 84—fairly startling declines that have contributed greatly to the increased life expectancy among today's adults (Davis, Dinse, & Hoel, 1994). During the 1990s, CVD declined another 20% among adults of all ages (U.S. Department of Health and Human Services, 1998b). Yet CVD remains the leading cause of death among adults in the United States and throughout the developed world (NCHS, 2006; WHO, 2006).

General Risk Factors The best information about who is at risk for CVD comes from a number of long-term epidemiological studies, such as the Framingham study and the Nurses' Health Study, in which the health and habits of large numbers of individuals have been tracked over time. In the Framingham study, 5,209 adults were first studied in 1948, when they were aged 30 to 59. Their health (and mortality) has since been assessed repeatedly, which makes it possible to identify characteristics that predict CVD (Anderson, Castelli, & Levy, 1987; Dawber, Kannel, & Lyell, 1963; Garrison, Gold, Wilson, & Kannel, 1993; Kannel & Gordon, 1980). More recent studies continue to suggest the same risk factors (Dwyer et al., 2004; U.S. Department of Health and Human Services, 1998b). The left side of Table 15.2 on page 444 lists the well-established risk factors that emerged from the Framingham study and similar studies, along with a few other risk factors that are more speculative.

First, the great majority of Americans have at least one of these risk factors (NCHS, 2006). Second, it is important to understand that these risks are cumulative in the same way that the health habits investigated in the Alameda County study seem to be cumulative: The more high-risk behaviors or characteristics you have, the higher your risk of heart disease; the effect is not just additive. For example, high cholesterol is more serious for a person who has diabetes and high blood pressure than it is for adults who do not suffer from these conditions (Cohen, Hailpern, & Alderman, 2004).

cardiovascular disease (CVD) a set of disease processes in the heart and circulatory system

atherosclerosis narrowing of the arteries caused by deposits of a fatty substance called plaque

Table 15.2 Risk Factors for Heart Disease and Cancer

Risk	Heart Disease	Cancer
Smoking	Major risk; the more you smoke, the greater the risk. Quitting smoking reduces risk.	Substantially increases the risk of lung cancer; also implicated in other cancers.
Blood pressure	Systolic pressure above 140 or diastolic pressure above 90 linked to higher risk.	No known risk.
Weight	Some increased risk with any weight above the normal range; risk is greater for those with weight 20% or more above recommended amount.	Being overweight is linked to increased risk of several cancers, including breast cancer, but the risk is smaller than for heart disease.
Cholesterol	Clear risk with elevated levels of low-density lipoproteins.	No known risk.
Inactivity	Inactive adults have about twice the risk of those who exercise.	Inactivity is associated in some studies with higher rates of colon cancer.
Diet	High-fat, low-fiber diet increases risk; antioxidants such as Vitamin E, Vitamin C, or beta-carotene may decrease risk.	Results are still unclear; a high-fat diet is linked to risk of some cancers; high-fiber diets appear to be protective for some cancers.
Alcohol	Moderate intake of alcohol, especially wine, linked to decreased CVD risk. Heavy drinking can weaken the heart muscle.	Heavy drinking is associated with cancers of the digestive system.
Heredity	Those with first-degree relatives with CVD have seven to ten times the risk; those who inherit a gene for a particular protein are up to twice as likely to have CVD.	Some genetic component with nearly every cancer.

(*Sources:* Centers for Disease Control, 1994; Dwyer et al., 2004; Gaziano & Hennekens, 1995; Hunter et al., 1996; Lee, Manson, Hennekens, & Paffenbarger, 1993; Manson et al., 1995; Manson et al., 2002; Morris, Kritchevsky, & Davis, 1994; Rich-Edwards, Manson, Hennekens, & Buring, 1995; Risch, Jain, Marrett, & Howe, 1994; Rose, 1993; Stampfer et al., 1993; Trichopoulou, Costacou, Bamia, & Trichopoulou, 2003; Willett et al., 1992, 1995; Woodward & Tunstall-Pedoe, 1995.)

Personality and Health Personality may also contribute to heart disease. The *type A personality* was first described by two cardiologists, Meyer Friedman and Ray Rosenman (1974; Rosenman & Friedman, 1983). They were struck by the apparently consistent presence among patients who suffered from heart disease of several other characteristics, including competitive striving for achievement, a sense of time urgency, and hostility or aggressiveness. These people, whom Friedman and Rosenman named type A personalities, were perpetually comparing themselves to others, always wanting to win. They scheduled their lives tightly, timed themselves in routine activities, and often tried to do such tasks faster each time. They had frequent conflicts with their co-workers and family. *Type B personality* people, in contrast, were thought to be less hurried, more laid back, less competitive, and less hostile.

Early research by Friedman and Rosenman suggested that type A behavior was linked to higher levels of cholesterol, and hence to increased risk of CVD, even among people who did not suffer from observable heart disease. Contradictory results from more extensive studies since then, however, have forced some modifications in the original hypothesis (e.g., Miller, Turner, Tindale, Posavac, & Dugoni, 1991; O'Connor, Manson, O'Connor, & Buring, 1995). However, not all facets of the type A personality, as originally described, seem to be equally significant for CVD. The most consistent link has been found between CVD and hostility (Mohan, 2006; Olson et al., 2005). Moreover, careful studies have shown that anger and hostility may be part of a larger complex of variables that includes anger, anxiety, cynicism, and other negative emotions (Kubzansky et al., 2006; Olson et al., 2005).

The finding that negative emotions are correlated with CVD has led some researchers to propose a new classification, *Type D personality* ("D" for distress; Denollet, 1997). People with this profile exhibit a chronic pattern of emotional distress combined with a tendency to suppress negative emotions. In one study of men who were enrolled in a rehabilitative therapy program after having had a heart attack, those with the Type D profile were found to have four times the risk of death as other patients in the program (Sher, 2004).

Most people who have analyzed this research would now agree that there is some kind of connection between personality and CVD. What is less clear is just which aspects of personality are most strongly predictive. Some research suggests that measures of neuroticism or depression may be even better risk predictors than measures of hostility (e.g., Cramer, 1991).

Cancer

Learning Objective 15.6
What factors contribute to cancer?

The second leading cause of death among adults over the age of 45 is cancer (NCHS, 2006). In middle-aged men, the likelihood of dying of heart disease or cancer is about equal. Among middle-aged women, though, cancer is considerably more likely than heart disease to cause death.

Like heart disease, cancer does not strike in a totally random fashion. Indeed, as you can see in the right-hand column of Table 15.2, some of the same risk factors are implicated in both diseases. Most of these risk factors are at least partially under your own control. It helps to have established good health habits in early adulthood, but it is also clear from the research that improving your health habits in middle age can reduce your risks of both cancer and heart disease.

The most controversial item listed in Table 15.2 is diet; in particular, scientists debate the role of dietary fat as a potential risk factor. However, there is some evidence that reducing consumption of red meat may decrease the risk of colorectal cancer (Kuchi & Giovannucci, 2002).

While the debate over the role of diet continues, there is now little doubt that several types of cancers are caused by infectious agents (Ewald, 2000). For example, in Chapter 13 you learned about the link between the human papilloma virus (HPV) and cervical cancer (Castellsagué et al., 2002). This sexually transmitted disease is apparently also responsible for many cancers of the mouth, nose, and throat, presumably because of oral sex, and for some cases of anal cancer in gay men (Frisch et al., 1997; Mork et al., 2001).

Studies have shown that Epstein-Barr virus is also associated with cancers of the nose and throat, as well as one type of non-Hodgkin's lymphoma (Chien et al., 2001). Another virus, hepatitis B, is linked to liver cancer (Yang et al., 2002). Thus, screening people who do not yet have symptoms of these viral infections may help to identify cancers at very early stages of development, when they are most curable.

Correlations between bacterial infections and cancer have also been identified. For example, *Helicobacter pylori* has been implicated in many studies of stomach cancer and one type of non-Hodgkin's lymphoma (Uemura et al., 2001). This microorganism also causes stomach ulcers. Typically, antibiotic treatment clears up both the infection and the ulcers and, coincidentally, reduces the risk of stomach cancer. However, most people who carry *H. pylori* do not have ulcers or any other symptoms. Moreover, a fairly high proportion of people, especially those in developing nations with poor water purification systems, carry the infection (Brown, 2000). Consequently, researchers are currently trying to determine whether treating carriers who are asymptomatic will reduce rates of stomach cancer. Others are examining whether improvements in sanitary conditions in developing nations will lead to lower rates of *H. pylori* infection and stomach cancer.

Television personality Katie Couric became an advocate for routine cancer screening after losing her husband to colon cancer in 1998 and her sister to pancreatic cancer in 2001.

Studies of the role of infection in the development of cancer provide yet another example of the importance of health-related choices. Specifically, safe sex practices can limit an individual's risk of contracting sexually transmitted diseases and the cancers in which they have been implicated. Moreover, vaccines against many viruses, including HPV and hepatitis B, are widely available.

Learning Objective 15.7

What are some important differences in the health of middle-aged men and women?

Gender and Health

Figure 15.2 makes clear that women's life expectancy is greater than men's. But what is not evident is an interesting paradox: Women live longer, but they have more diseases and disabilities. Women are more likely to describe their health as poor, to have chronic conditions such as arthritis, and to be limited in their daily activities. Such differences have been found in every country in which the pattern has been studied, including nonindustrialized countries (Rahman, Strauss, Gertler, Ashley, & Fox, 1994).

This difference is already present in early adulthood and grows larger with age. By old age, women are substantially more likely than men to be chronically ill (Guralnik et al., 1993; Kunkel & Applebaum, 1992). In early adulthood, this gender difference in disease rate can be largely attributed to health problems associated with childbearing. At later ages, the difference cannot be explained in this same way.

How is it possible that men die younger but are healthier while they are alive? Researchers suggest that the apparent paradox can be resolved by considering sex differences in potentially fatal conditions such as cardiovascular disease (Verbrugge, 1989). In the United States, 143 of every 100,000 men between the ages of 45 and 54 die of heart disease annually, compared with only 50 of every 100,000 women (U.S. Bureau of the Census, 2003a). This difference in rates of heart disease diminishes once women are past menopause, although it does not disappear totally even in late old age.

It isn't just that men have higher rates of CVD; they also are more likely to die from the disease once it has been acquired. One reason may be that the heart muscles of women who have CVD seem to be better able to adapt to stresses such as physical exertion (van Doornen, Snieder, & Boomsma, 1998). In addition, once they suffer a heart attack, women recover to a higher level of physical functioning than men do (Bosworth et al., 2000). Sex differences in health habits also seem to contribute to women's greater ability to recover from CVD. For example, women are more likely to get regular checkups and to seek help early in an illness than men are (Addis & Mahalik, 2003; Verbrugge & Wingard, 1987).

By contrast, women are more likely than men to suffer from nonfatal chronic ailments such as arthritis. Because chronic pain is characteristic of arthritis, the activities of women who suffer from it are often limited. Understandably, too, living with chronic pain affects their general sense of well-being.

Learning Objective 15.8

How are socioeconomic status and ethnicity related to health in middle adulthood?

Socioeconomic Class, Ethnicity, and Health

While emphasizing preventive actions such as exercise, developmentalists cannot ignore the importance for health and mental ability in middle adulthood of those familiar demographic variables social class and race. If you look again at Figure 13.1 (page 376), you'll see that social class is a more significant predictor of variations in health in middle age than at any other time of adult life. In middle adulthood, occupational level and education (both of which correlate strongly with socioeconomic class) are most predictive of health. Figure 13.1 does not break this pattern down by ethnic group, but research suggests that the same link between social class and health is found among Hispanic Americans and African Americans (Chatters, 1991; James, Keenan, & Browning, 1992; Markides & Lee, 1991).

Ethnicity is also linked to overall health. For example, African Americans have shorter life expectancies than White Americans, as Figure 15.2 shows. There are also ethnic group differences in incidence of specific diseases (CDC, 2003a). In recent years, public health officials in the United States have begun to study and address these disparities. These efforts have focused on three diseases: cardiovascular disease, diabetes, and cancer.

Cardiovascular Disease Although cardiovascular disease (heart attack and stroke) is the leading cause of death in all ethnic groups, it disables and/or kills a higher proportion of African Americans, Mexican Americans, and Native Americans than of either White or Asian Americans (U.S. Department of Health and Human Services, 1998b; Wong et al., 2002). Rates of disease are higher in these groups because they are more likely to possess every risk factor listed in Table 15.2.

Among minority women, the major factor seems to be obesity. Three-quarters of African American and Mexican American women are overweight, compared to 57% of White women (NCHS, 2006). Among men, the key risk factor is high blood pressure, or **hypertension** (NCHS, 2006). About 15% of White and Mexican American men have elevated blood pressure, compared to 27% of African American men.

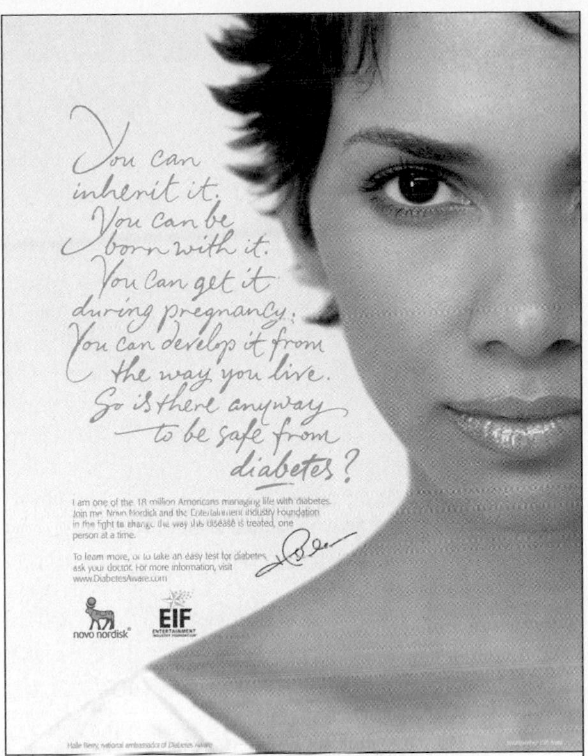

Public health officials in the United States believe that public awareness of the risks associated with diabetes will encourage people to seek treatment for the disease earlier, thereby avoiding some of its more serious complications.
WWW.DIABETESAWARE.COM

Diabetes The proportion of adults in the United States who suffer from diabetes is growing in all ethnic groups, but minorities have significantly higher rates of the condition than Whites (NCHS, 2006). Thus, public education about diabetes has become a major health goal in the United States, because the disease can lead to severe complications such as cardiovascular disease, kidney failure, and blindness (CDC, 1998a). Just as they are more likely than Whites to have the disease in the first place, minority adults who have been diagnosed with diabetes are more likely than their White counterparts to develop complications (U.S. Department of Health and Human Services, 1998c). Although diabetes itself kills few people, it is the underlying cause of so many other potentially deadly diseases and conditions that death rates among adults who have diabetes are about twice as high at every age as those among individuals who do not have this disease (CDC, 1998a).

Public health officials don't yet have an explanation for ethnic group differences in diabetes rates. However, they hypothesize that complication rates vary because minorities tend to develop the disease earlier in life than Whites do (U.S. Department of Health and Human Services, 1998c). Therefore, it affects all of their body systems for a longer period of time. Once diagnosed, minority adults often have less access to regular medical care than Whites. However, researchers have found that, even among diabetic Whites and African Americans who have the same health insurance benefits and equal access to diabetes care services, African Americans are less likely to seek care for complications at a point when medical intervention can be most effective (U.S. Department of Health and Human Services, 1998c).

Cancer African Americans have higher incidences of some types of cancer (Ries et al., 2007). For example, African Americans have the highest rates of prostate, colon, and lung cancer in the United States (Ries et al., 2007). In addition, African American women have higher rates of breast cancer than their peers in other groups. Asian Americans have the highest rate of liver cancer, and Native Americans are more often diagnosed with cancer of the kidney than those in other groups.

The main cause for ethnic group variations in cancer rates, according to public health officials, is failure to receive routine cancer screenings. Minority men and women are less likely than Whites to obtain mammograms, Pap smears, and colorectal examinations. Thanks to recent improvements in public knowledge about and access to such screenings, the five-year survival rates of adults who are diagnosed with cancer are highly similar across ethnic groups (Ries et al., 2007). Still, ensuring that screened adults have access to follow-up care is another public health goal.

hypertension elevated blood pressure

Alcoholism

Learning Objective 15.9
What are some of the consequences of alcoholism for middle-aged adults?

There is a tendency nowadays to use the term "addiction" to label any form of behavior that people engage in to excess (see the Research Report on page 448). However, addiction, or substance abuse as psychologists call it, involves both psychological and physical dependence on a stimulus, so simply spending a lot of time doing something doesn't mean that you are addicted to it. Moreover, substance abuse, especially

RESEARCH REPORT

Is the Internet Addictive?

Recently, some mental health professionals have raised concerns about the amount of time some individuals spend online. Some claim to have discovered a new disorder they call *Internet addictive disorder*, or IAD (Griffiths, 1999). The criteria for the disorder are the same as for other addictions. Specifically, to be diagnosed with IAD, a person must demonstrate a pattern of Internet use that interferes with normal educational, occupational, and social functioning.

To be sure, there are individuals who spend a great deal of time online and who admit that Internet use often interferes with other activities (Brenner, 1997). However, to justify the use of the term *addiction* in relation to a specific activity, the activity itself must have some addictive power. For example, alcohol induces an altered state of consciousness that users find desirable. The altered state reinforces the behavior of consuming alcohol. Thus, those who propose that IAD exists are, by implication, saying that the experience of being online has the capacity to induce some kind of reinforcing state in users.

Some Internet users report that online communication is more pleasurable than face-to-face social encounters (Chou et al., 1999). But is this sense of pleasure enough to bring about an addiction, or is socializing on the Internet nothing more than an easy way to escape the usual pressures of social interaction? Similarly, use of online pornography for sexual gratification is clearly a problem for some people (Cooper, Putnam, Planchon, & Boies, 1999). However, is it any different from use of conventional sources of pornography such as adult magazines and videos?

Research has suggested that rather than a true addiction, excessive Internet use may be part of a behavior pattern that is consistent across several media (Greenberg, Lewis, & Dodd, 1999). Those who are "addicted" to the Internet also spend inordinate amounts of time watching television and playing video games. They are also more likely to be addicted to alcohol and other substances (Yellowlees & Marks, 2007).

Thus, the Net is no different from books, television, movies, or even drugs. It may simply provide people who have some kind of tendency toward addiction with an additional avenue through which to express this tendency (Fabi, 2004; Griffiths, 2003). Thus, mental health professionals who oppose the idea of Internet addiction suggest that excessive time online either is a symptom of another disorder or simply reflects fascination with a new medium (Griffiths, 1999; Grohol, 1999).

Questions for Critical Analysis

1. In your view, why is the Internet a more attractive means of "escaping" from the stresses of everyday life than books, movies, and other forms of entertainment?
2. How might neuropsychological research approach the hypothesis that Internet use produces an altered state of consciousness?

when it occurs over a long period of time, causes a significant amount of damage to the body's organs.

As you learned in Chapter 13, alcohol is the most frequently abused substance in the United States. More than 40% of men and about 20% of women report having had a problem with alcohol abuse at some time in their lives. And, as you probably know, **alcoholism**, defined as psychological and physical dependence on alcohol, can develop at any age. However, during the middle adulthood years, as the toxic effects of heavy drinking combine with those of primary aging and other sources of secondary aging, alcoholism begins to take a heavy toll on the body (Thun et al., 1997).

Long-term heavy drinking damages every organ in the body. It is especially harmful to the liver, and it weakens the heart muscle and the valves and walls of the blood vessels. Thus, rates of liver disease, cardiovascular disease, and cancers of the digestive and urinary systems are higher among alcoholics than they are among non-alcoholics (Thun et al., 1997). Moreover, heavy alcohol use damages the brain causing impairments in memory and language functions (Daurignac et al., 2005).

alcoholism physical and psychological dependence on alcohol

The result of this interaction between aging and alcohol abuse is that alcoholics face an increased risk of death (Dawson, 2000). A longitudinal study involving more than 40,000 males in Norway found that the rate of death prior to age 60 was significantly higher among alcoholics than among nonalcoholics (Rossow & Amundsen, 1997). Studies further indicate that the death rates of men with alcoholism who are in their 50s and early 60s are 5 to 6 times higher than those of nonalcoholics in the same age group (Kristenson, Österling, Nilsson, & Lindgärde, 2002).

Thankfully, the effects of alcohol on the brain may be reversible if an alcoholic quits drinking (Kensinger, Clarke, & Corkin, 2003). Likewise, giving up alcohol is essential to stopping the progression of alcohol-induced liver damage. A drug called *acamprosate* can be prescribed to help recovering alcoholics deal with withdrawal symptoms and maintain abstinence from alcohol (Mason et al., 2006).

Critical Thinking

1. Considering all the risk factors for the various health problems that were described in this section, what can you predict about your own health in middle age? Which factors can you change?

Cognitive Functioning

In the middle adult years, some cognitive abilities improve, while others slow down a bit. Still, many adults have acquired large bodies of knowledge and skill that help them compensate for losses and solve problems within their areas of expertise more efficiently than younger adults do.

Models of Physical and Cognitive Aging

> **Learning Objective 15.10**
> How do Denney's and the Balteses' models explain the relationship between health and cognitive functioning in middle age?

Many of the various bits and pieces of information you've encountered so far about physical and cognitive changes in adulthood can be combined in a single model, suggested by Nancy Denney and illustrated in Figure 15.3 (Denney 1982, 1984). Denney proposed that on nearly any measure of physical or cognitive functioning, age-related changes follow a typical curve, like those shown in the figure. But she also argued that the height of this curve varies, depending on the amount an individual exercises some ability or skill. Denney used the word *exercise* very broadly, to refer not only to physical exercise but also to mental exercise and to the extent to which some specific task has been performed before. Unexercised abilities generally have a lower peak level of performance; exercised abilities generally have a higher peak.

Many laboratory tests of memory, for example, such as memorizing lists of names, tap unexercised abilities. Everyday memory tasks, such as recalling details from a newspaper column, tap much more exercised abilities. The distinction is somewhat similar to the distinction between crystallized and fluid abilities (see Chapter 13). Most crystallized abilities are at least moderately exercised, whereas many fluid abilities are relatively unexercised. But Denney was making a more general point: Whether abilities are crystallized or fluid, those that are more fully exercised will have a higher peak.

The gap between the curve for unexercised abilities and the curve for maximally exercised abilities represents the degree of improvement that would be possible for any given skill. Any skill that is not fully exercised can be improved if the individual begins to exercise that ability. There is clear evidence, for example, that aerobic capacity (VO_2 max) can be increased at any age if a person begins a program of physical exercise (e.g., Blumenthal et al., 1991; Buchner, Beresford, Larson, LaCroix, & Wagner, 1992; Cheitlin, 2003). Nonetheless, in Denney's model, the maximum level an adult will be able to achieve, even with optimum exercise, will decline with age, just as performance of top athletes declines, even with optimum training regimens. One implication of this is that young adults are more likely to be able to get away with laziness or poor study habits and still perform well; as they age, this becomes less and less true, because they are fighting against the basic decay curve of aging.

A somewhat different approach was taken by researchers Paul Baltes (1939–2006) and Margaret Baltes (1939–2000). In their view, the physical declines of middle age give rise to a

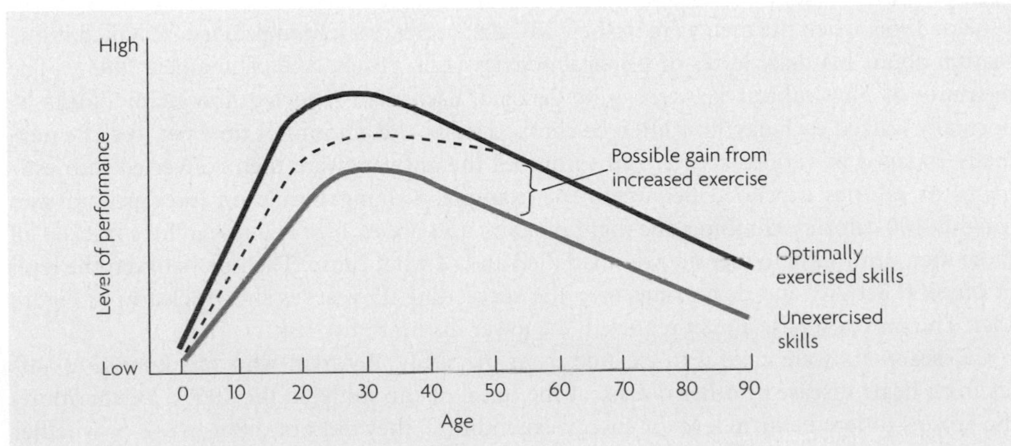

Figure 15.3 Denney's Model of Physical and Cognitive Aging

Denney's model suggests both a basic decay curve and a fairly large gap between actual level of performance on exercised and unexercised abilities.

(*Source:* Denney, 1982, 1984.)

strategy they call **selective optimization with compensation**, the process of balancing the gains and losses associated with aging (Baltes & Baltes, 1990). The idea is that, as the body ages resources such as physical agility and working memory capacity decrease. In order to manage the demands of competing tasks, aging adults select one to which they devote most or all of these resources. Moreover, adults optimize the skills that they believe can be improved by exercising them as much as possible. At the same time, they use compensatory strategies to offset the effects of aging.

Selection occurs when a middle-aged adult reduces distractions in order to more efficiently carry out a cognitive task. For example, a middle-aged college student might be more likely than a younger student to turn off the television when she studies. Optimization is involved when middle-aged adults work to improve their physical fitness or to expand their knowledge. Compensation takes many forms, including the use of reading glasses to correct for presbyopia and the development of organizational strategies, such as being diligent about recording important events on a calendar, to offset declines in memory.

Learning Objective 15.11

What has research revealed about the link between health and cognitive functioning?

Health and Cognitive Functioning

You should remember from Chapter 13 that it is often difficult to separate the effects of primary and secondary aging, because they happen at the same time. Research examining correlations between health and cognition helps developmentalists understand the effects of secondary aging. Specifically, many of the same characteristics that are linked to increased or decreased risk of heart disease and cancer are also linked to the rate of change or the maintenance of intellectual skill in the middle years.

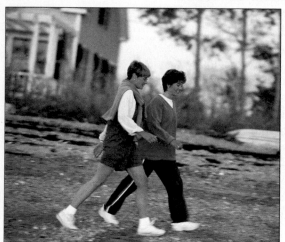

Research shows that middle-aged adults who are physically active have lower mortality rates over the next 20–30 years than their peers who are less active. Physical exercise during middle age is also positively correlated with scores on tests of intellectual functioning.

One illustration of this relationship comes from Warner Schaie's analysis of data from the Seattle Longitudinal Study (Schaie & Willis, 2005). He found that those research participants who had some kind of cardiovascular disease (either coronary heart disease or high blood pressure) showed earlier and larger declines on intellectual tests than did those who were disease-free. Other researchers have found similar linkages. Even adults whose blood pressure is controlled by medication seem to show earlier declines (Sands & Meredith, 1992; Schultz, Elias, Robbins, Streeten, & Blakeman, 1986). Schaie cautions against taking these findings too far. The size of the effect is quite small, and it may operate indirectly rather than directly. For example, adults with cardiovascular disease may become physically less active as a response to their disease. The lower level of activity, in turn, may affect the rate of intellectual decline. This raises the possibility that exercise may be one of the critical factors in determining an individual person's overall physical health and cognitive performance during middle adulthood. A growing amount of information confirms such an effect.

One particularly large and well-designed study of the effects of exercise on physical health involved 17,321 Harvard alumni who had been students between 1916 and 1950. In 1962 or 1966, when the men were in their 30s, 40s, or 50s, each man provided detailed information about his daily levels of physical activity (Lee, Hsieh, & Paffenbarger, 1995). (The measures of physical activity were quite detailed. Each man reported how many blocks he normally walked each day, how often he climbed stairs, the amount of time per week he normally engaged in various sports, and so on. All the answers were then converted into estimates of calories expended per week. For example, walking 1 mile on level ground uses roughly 100 calories; climbing one flight of stairs uses about 17.) The researchers tracked all these men until 1988 to identify who had died and of what cause. The link between the level of physical activity and death rates over the succeeding 25 years is shown clearly in Figure 15.4: The more exercise a man reported, the lower his mortality risk.

Researchers were careful to exclude from the study any man who was known to suffer from heart disease or other disease at the onset of the study, in the 1960s. Furthermore, the groups differed *only* in level of energy expenditure; they did not differ in age or whether

selective optimization with compensation the process of balancing the gains and losses associated with aging

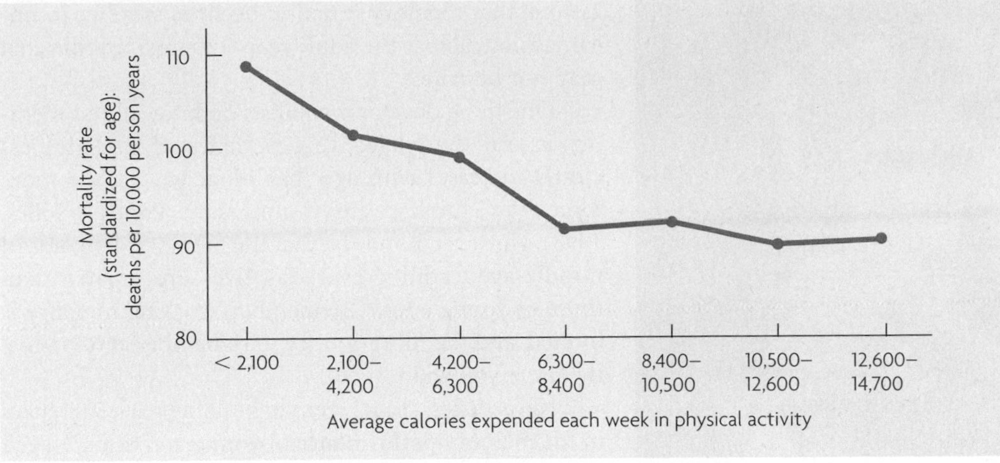

Figure 15.4
Exercise and Mortality

Results from the Harvard Alumni Study show clearly that those who are more physically active in middle adulthood have lower risk of mortality over the next decades.

(*Source:* Lee et al., 1995, adapted from data from Table 2, p. 1181.)

they smoked, had high blood pressure, were overweight, or had a family history of early death—which makes the effect of exercise even clearer. To be sure, because the level of exercise was each man's own choice, there may have been other differences separating the various exercise groups that could account for the different death rates. But the pattern, which has been replicated in other groups of both men and women, is so substantial and striking that alternative explanations are hard to come by (e.g., Blair et al., 1995; Lissner et al., 1996). By far the most likely explanation is that there is a causal connection between longevity and level of physical activity.

Physical exercise also seems to help maintain cognitive abilities in the middle adult years, very likely because it helps to maintain cardiovascular fitness (Rogers, Meyer, & Mortel, 1990). Among physically healthy middle-aged and older adults, those who are more physically active—doing gardening, heavy housework, or aerobic exercise such as walking, running, or swimming—score higher on tests of reasoning, reaction time, and short-term memory (Van Boxtel et al., 1997).

A different approach to studying exercise and cognitive functioning would involve randomly assigning some people to an exercise program and some to a nonexercise control group, and then seeing whether the two groups differed in their cognitive functioning after a period of exercise. The results of the small number of studies of this type have been quite mixed. Every study finds that exercise increases measures of physical functioning, such as VO_2 max, even in very elderly adults. Some—but not all—such studies also show that exercise improves thinking (Hawkins, Kramer, & Capaldi, 1992; Hill, Storandt, & Malley, 1993; Winter et al., 2007). Other studies do not come to that conclusion (e.g., Buchner et al., 1992; Emery & Gatz, 1990). In most cases, the experimental exercise program lasts only a few months, and that may not be sufficient to make any difference in mental functioning. Still, because researchers already know that exercise is linked to lower levels of disease and greater longevity, prudence alone would argue for including it in your life.

Changes in Memory and Cognition

Learning Objective 15.12
How do young and middle-aged adults differ in performance on memory tests?

When developmentalists study changes in cognitive functioning in middle age, they find almost precisely what Denney's model and Schaie's longitudinal study suggest. That is, lack of mental exercise tends to be correlated with declines in memory and cognitive skills, but major deficits are not found until after age 60 to 65.

Memory Function Drawing conclusions about memory function in middle age is difficult because studies of age differences in adult memory rarely include middle-aged people. Typically, researchers compare very young adults, such as college students, to adults in their 60s and 70s. When the two groups are found to differ, psychologists often infer that middle-aged adults' performance falls somewhere between the two. In other words, they

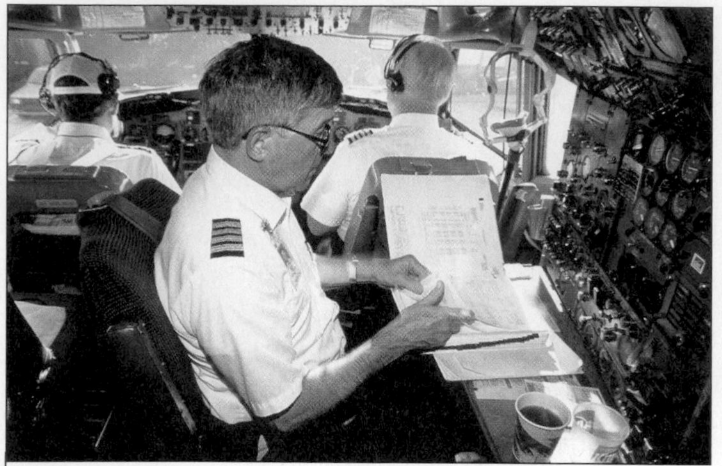

Some declines in cognitive performance, such as increased reaction times, are evident even when middle-aged individuals are engaged in activities with which they have had many years of relevant experience. However, expertise is associated with the development of cognitive strategies that help to buffer the effects of aging (Morrow et al., 2003). Consequently, middle-aged adults are able to maintain high levels of performance on cognitively demanding tasks, such as flying a commercial airliner.

assume that memory function declines steadily, in linear fashion, across the adult years—an assumption that may not be true.

One thing developmentalists do know about memory is that the subjective experience of forgetfulness clearly increases with age. The older we get, the more forgetful we think we are (Commissaris, Ponds, & Jolles, 1998). However, it may be that the memory demands of middle-aged adults' everyday lives are greater than those of young adults'. Remember, working memory is limited, and the more you try to remember at one time, the more you will forget.

Nevertheless, there seem to be some real differences in the memory performance of young and middle-aged adults. For example, visual memory, the ability to remember an object you have seen for just a few seconds, declines in middle age (Fahle & Daum, 1997; Giambra, Arenberg, Zonderman, Kawas, & Costa, 1995). Further, the more complex the visual stimulus and the longer the interval between presentation and recall, the greater the difference. By contrast, memory for auditory stimuli seems to remain stable throughout adulthood.

Performance on more complex memory tasks, such as remembering lists of words and passages of text, also declines with age, but usually not until after about age 55. In contrast, recognition of words and texts appears to remain stable throughout adulthood (Zelinski & Burnight, 1997). Such findings suggest that there are age differences in working memory. Research examining short-term memory capacity at various ages shows that it remains very stable throughout early, middle, and late adulthood. What changes, apparently, is the ability to make efficient use of available capacity (Lincourt, Rybash, & Hoyer, 1998).

Semantic and Episodic Memories Researchers can gain additional insight into age-related memory changes by studying how well young and middle-aged adults encode different kinds of memories. **Episodic memories** are recollections of personal events or episodes. **Semantic memories** represent general knowledge. For example, a person's memories of a vacation in Hawaii are episodic, and her knowledge that Hawaii was the 50th state is semantic.

Researchers find that young and middle-aged adults differ more with respect to new episodic memories than they do with respect to semantic memories (Maylor, 1998; Nilsson, Baeckman, Erngrund, & Nyberg, 1997). For example, a middle-aged person attending a baseball game may forget where he parked his car (episodic memory). However, he is unlikely to forget the basic rules of the game (semantic memory).

Middle-aged adults are very proficient at overcoming episodic memory limitations by using reminders, or *cues*, to help themselves remember information. Thus, the middle-aged person who knows that she may forget where her car is parked makes a point of noting nearby landmarks that will help her remember its location. This may be because middle-aged adults, in contrast to those who are older, continue to have a high sense of self-efficacy with respect to memory (Lineweaver & Hertzog, 1998). In other words, they believe their efforts will make a difference, so they actively work to improve their memories.

Use It or Lose It? In general, adults maintain or even gain in skill on any task that they use often or that is based on specific learning. For example, verbal abilities increase in middle age (Giambra et al., 1995; Salthouse, 2004). It appears that vocabulary—or, more precisely, performance on vocabulary tests—doesn't begin to decline until about age 65. And the "use it or lose it" dictum seems to hold true for cognitive abilities. That is, adults who engage in intellectually challenging activities show fewer losses in cognitive skills than those who do not (Salthouse, 2004; Schaie, Nguyen, Willis, Dutta, & Yue, 2001).

episodic memories recollections of personal events

semantic memories general knowledge

Similarly, expertise in a particular field helps to compensate for age-related deficits in cognitive functioning (Colonia-Willner, 1999; Morrow et al., 2003; Tsang, 1998). For example, in one study, researchers examined 17- to 79-year-old participants' ability to recognize melodies performed at varying tempos (Andrews, Dowling, Bartlett, & Halpern, 1998). Some tunes were played very rapidly and then slowed until participants could recognize them. Both age and years of musical training predicted participants' ability to recognize melodies presented in this way, but the relationship between age and recognition was much weaker than the relationship between recognition and musical training. Other melodies were played too slowly to be recognized at the beginning and then speeded up. Interestingly, only musical training correlated with recognition of tunes played this way; there was no association with age whatsoever.

Due to the accumulated effects of many years of using some cognitive skills and the development of a large body of relevant information in long-term memory, middle-aged adults outperform those who are younger on tasks that involve comprehending and remembering reading material. For instance, researchers have found that middle-aged and younger adults take different approaches to learning from expository text (the kind of text you're reading right now!) (Noh et al., 2007). Younger adults focus on creating a word-for-word representation of the text in their memories. By contrast, middle-aged adults pay more attention to overarching themes than to details. In memory, this difference might be reflected in a decline in memory for surface detail, accompanied by an increase in memory for themes and meanings.

A study in which researchers asked adults of various ages to read a story and then to recall it immediately afterward, in writing, yielded support for this hypothesis (Adams, 1991). Younger adults were more likely to report specific events or actions in the story, while middle-aged adults recalled more of the psychological motivations of the characters and offered more interpretations of the story in their recall. What this may mean is that, along with a shift in schematic processing, the encoding process changes as we get older. We may not attempt to encode as much detail, but may store more summarizing information.

Creativity

Learning Objective 15.13
What does research suggest about age-related changes in creativity?

A somewhat different question about cognitive functioning in the middle years of adulthood has to do with **creativity**, the ability to produce original, appropriate, and valuable ideas and/or solutions to problems. One psychologist looked at the lifetime creativity of thousands of notable scientists from the 19th century and earlier (Simonton, 1991, 2000). Simonton identified the age at which these individuals (nearly all men) published their first significant work, their best work, and their last work. In every scientific discipline represented, the thinkers produced their best work at about age 40, on average. But most of them were publishing significant, even outstanding, research through their 40s and into their 50s.

You might be wondering how the creative process actually works (see The Real World on page 454). Psychologists have been studying it for some time and still have much to learn. However, one useful approach describes creativity as a type of thought process called *divergent thinking* (Guilford, 1967). A person who uses divergent thinking can provide multiple solutions to problems that have no clear answer. Thus, divergent thinking is as vital to science as it is to art. For instance, when scientists were faced with the problem of identifying the cause of AIDS, they proposed and tested many hypotheses before it became clear that the disease was caused by a virus. Likewise, a novelist who wants to provide readers with insight into a character's motivations tries out several ways of communicating the information before she settles on the one that works best.

Creative solutions sometimes pop into the mind of a creative person fully formed, but, most of the time, they arise from bits and pieces of several solutions that she has been mulling over for a while. Psychologist Daniel Goleman describes this mulling over

creativity the ability to produce original, appropriate, and valuable ideas and/or solutions to problems

THE REAL WORLD

Maintaining the Creative "Edge" at Mid-Life and Beyond

The songwriting career of music legend Willie Nelson began when he started writing poetry at the age of 5. When his grandparents gave him a guitar, he figured out how to set his poems to music. Nearly three thousand songs later, Nelson continues to be inspired more by lyrics than he is by melodies. And even though Nelson is in his mid-70s, he doesn't seem to have lost his creative edge. What is the secret to maintaining one's creativity and productivity through middle age and into the later years?

In a fascinating set of interviews, a number of highly successful and creative older adults described how they viewed creativity ("The creators," 2000). Interestingly, all reported that they viewed themselves as more creative than they had been when they were younger. Their comments suggested that the creative process is a highly individualized intellectual activity. However, what was remarkable was that, by middle age, all had arrived at firm conclusions about what did and did not work for them. So, some part of the maintenance of creativity included acceptance of their own creative idiosyncrasies. Some, for example, expressed the need for external motivation, such as a deadline. Guitarist B. B. King, 74, said, "If you want me to be creative, give me the line to cross and when I have to cross it" (p. 44). Others were more motivated by self-imposed standards than by externals. For example, writer Isabel Allende, 57, reported that she always begins a new work on January 8, because the date is a personally meaningful anniversary for her. Advertising writer Stan Freberg, 73, claimed that when he needs an idea, he takes a shower, because he often gets inspiration while in the shower.

A second theme pervaded these reports. Each creative person, in one way or another, recognized the value of accumulated knowledge and experience. They also tended to acknowledge important sources of this knowledge, such as parents, spouses, and friends. Consequently, these people saw their creative work not only as the product of their own abilities but also as the result of a complex network of influential individuals, life experiences, and their own capacity to reflect on their lives.

From these extraordinary individuals we can learn two important things about maintaining creativity and productivity in the middle and late adult years: First, being consciously aware of one's own creative process—and accepting its boundaries—seems to be critical. Second, some degree of humility, a sense of indebtedness to those who have contributed to and supported one's creative development, appears to be associated with continuing productivity in the middle and late adult years.

Questions for Reflection

1. To what extent can a young adult improve his or her own creativity and productivity by following the example of a successful middle-aged or older adult?
2. Why is humility important to maintaining creativity?

Critical Thinking

1. Given what you have learned in this section, where would you place cognitive functioning in middle age on a 10-point scale ranging from "age and health have no effect on cognitive functioning" at the low end to "age and health cause inevitable declines in cognitive functioning" at the high end? What reasons would you give if you were asked to explain your assessment?

process as involving four stages when it is used to solve problems (Goleman et al., 1992). During *preparation*, relevant information is gathered. The next phase, *incubation*, involves digesting the information without actually trying to work on the problem. *Illumination* occurs when this digestive process produces an aha! moment in which the solution to the problem becomes clear. Finally, during *translation*, the solution is applied to the problem and adjustments are made as needed. As you probably know from experience, it is the last step that is the most difficult and time-consuming, because, in the real world, things don't often go as we imagine they will. As Thomas Edison put it, "genius is 1% inspiration and 99% perspiration." Edison should know; after theoretically working out how to design a commercially viable electric light bulb, he spent over a year making prototypes before he finally found the design that worked. Thus, Edison believed that failure was essential to the creative process.

SUMMARY

Physical Changes

Learning Objective 15.1 What do researchers know about brain function in middle age?

- Brain size diminishes a bit in the middle adult years. Some changes in brain function suggest that middle-aged adults are more subject to distraction. However, middle-aged adults often outperform younger adults on everyday tasks that require concentration and rapid judgments, such as driving.

Learning Objective 15.2 How does reproductive function change in men and women in middle age?

- The loss of reproductive capacity, called the climacteric in both men and women, occurs very gradually in men, but more rapidly in women. Menopause is a three-phase process that results from a series of hormonal changes.

Learning Objective 15.3 What is osteoporosis, and what factors are associated with it?

- Bone mass declines significantly beginning at about age 30; accelerated declines in women at menopause are linked to decreased levels of estrogen and progesterone. Faster bone loss occurs in women who experience early menopause, who are underweight, who exercise little, or who have low-calcium diets.

Learning Objective 15.4 How do vision and hearing change in middle age?

- Thickening of the lens of the eye, with accompanying loss of elasticity, reduces visual acuity noticeably in the 40s or 50s. Hearing loss is more gradual.

Health and Wellness

Learning Objective 15.5 How does cardiovascular disease develop?

- Cardiovascular disease is not a normal part of aging; it is a disease for which there are known risk factors, including smoking, high blood pressure, high blood cholesterol, obesity, and a high-fat diet.

Learning Objective 15.6 What factors contribute to cancer?

- Cancer, too, has known risk factors, including smoking, obesity, and an inactive lifestyle. The role of a high-fat diet has been debated, but most evidence supports the hypothesis that such a diet contributes to the risk. Recent research shows that several cancers are caused by infectious agents (viral and bacterial).

Learning Objective 15.7 What are some important differences in the health of middle-aged men and women?

- Women tend to live longer than men but are more likely to suffer from chronic illnesses.

Learning Objective 15.8 How are socioeconomic status and ethnicity related to health in middle adulthood?

- Low-income adults have more chronic illnesses and a higher rate of death than those who are better off economically. African Americans, Hispanic Americans, and Native Americans are more likely to suffer from cardiovascular disease, cancer, and diabetes than Whites.

Learning Objective 15.9 What are some of the consequences of alcoholism for middle-aged adults?

- Alcoholism can develop at any age, but its effects become evident in middle age when it is associated with increased mortality.

Cognitive Functioning

Learning Objective 15.10 How do Denney's and the Balteses' models explain the relationship between health and cognitive functioning in middle age?

- Denney's model of aging suggests that exercising either physical or cognitive abilities can improve performance at any age, but the upper limit on improvement declines with increasing age. Paul and Margaret Baltes assert that middle-aged adults balance the gains and losses associated with aging by selecting tasks on which to focus limited resources, optimizing some skills through practice, and compensating for declines.

Learning Objective 15.11 What has research revealed about the link between health and cognitive functioning?

- Some studies suggest that differences in health contribute to variations in cognitive functioning among middle-aged adults. Exercise clearly affects the physical health of middle-aged adults, but research is less conclusive with regard to its effects on cognitive functioning.

Learning Objective 15.12 How do young and middle-aged adults differ in performance on memory tests?

- Verbal abilities continue to grow in middle age. Some loss of memory speed and skill occurs, but by most measures the loss is quite small until fairly late in the middle adult years. Expertise helps middle-aged adults compensate for losses in processing speed.

Learning Objective 15.13 What does research suggest about age-related changes in creativity?

- Creative productivity also appears to remain high during middle adulthood, at least for adults in challenging jobs (the category of adults on whom most of this research has focused).

KEY TERMS

alcoholism *(p. 448)*
atherosclerosis *(p. 443)*
cardiovascular disease (CVD) *(p. 443)*
climacteric *(p. 437)*
creativity *(p. 453)*
episodic memories *(p. 452)*
hypertension *(p. 447)*
menopause *(p. 437)*
osteoporosis *(p. 440)*
perimenopausal phase *(p. 438)*
postmenopausal phase *(p. 438)*
premenopausal phase *(p. 438)*
presbycusis *(p. 442)*
presbyopia *(p. 441)*
selective optimization with compensation *(p. 450)*
semantic memories *(p. 452)*

TEST YOURSELF

Physical Changes

15.1 Which of the following statements is true about the brain at mid-life?

a. The distribution of electrical activity is the same in the brains of alcoholics and those of nonalcoholics.
b. Cognitive tasks activate a larger area of brain tissue in middle-aged adults than in younger adults.
c. In middle age, more new synapses are formed than are lost.
d. Synaptic density continues to increase across adulthood.

15.2 What is the most consistent finding when neuropsychologists study how the aging brain affects cognitive functioning?

a. Dementia is the primary form of change in the aging brain.
b. Middle-aged adults have more lapses of attention and make poorer decisions than young adults.
c. Cognitive tasks activate a larger area of brain tissue in middle-aged adults than in younger adults.
d. Difficult tasks activate less brain tissue than easy tasks.

15.3 Which of the following terms refers to the time in middle or late adulthood when the reproductive capacity declines or is lost?

a. climacteric
b. genital senility
c. menopause
d. presbyopia

15.4 The term __________ means cessation of the menses.

a. menopause
b. osteoporosis
c. presbycusis
d. perimenopause

15.5 Which of the following is *not* a change typically associated with menopausal phases?

a. irregular menstrual periods
b. fluctuating hormone levels
c. thinner and less elastic vaginal tissue
d. major depression

15.6 The primary cause of menopause is

a. increasing testosterone levels.
b. decreasing estrogen levels.
c. shrinking of the uterus.
d. increased estrogen levels and decreased estradiol levels.

15.7 Which of the following is the best summary of the current research on hormone therapy?

a. Hormone therapy has no positive effects.
b. Hormone therapy reduces the incidence of heart disease and Alzheimer's disease.
c. Hormone therapy has some positive effects, but there are ways of achieving these results without the risks associated with hormone therapy.
d. Hormone therapy has many benefits and no known risks.

15.8 In the condition known as ____________, bone mass is reduced and bones become more brittle and porous when calcium is lost from the bones.

a. atherosclerosis
b. osteoporosis
c. presbycusis
d. Perthes' disease

15.9 Which of the following statements about the incidence of osteoporosis in middle adulthood is accurate?

a. It occurs only in women.
b. The process for women is accelerated by menopause.
c. The process for men is linked to impotence.
d. It is unavoidable.

15.10 Which of the following conditions makes it necessary to use reading glasses or bifocals in order to focus on near objects?

a. cataracts
b. glaucoma
c. presbycusis
d. presbyopia

15.11 What is the central physiological process of cardiovascular disease?

a. atherosclerosis
b. an autoimmune reaction
c. hypertension
d. osteoarthritis

Health and Wellness

15.12 Which of the following statements about risk factors for heart disease is true?

a. The risk factors are cumulative.
b. The risk factors are completely controllable with the right effort.
c. The only consistent controllable cause is smoking.
d. Men are at a higher risk because they strain their hearts more than women do.

15.13 What is the type A personality characteristic that is most consistently linked to cardiovascular disease?

a. extraversion
b. hostility
c. neuroticism
d. urgency

15.14 Which of the following is *not* a known risk factor for cancer?

a. alcohol consumption
b. high blood pressure
c. smoking
d. fat consumption

15.15 Which of the following groups has the highest rates of prostate and breast cancer?

a. Whites
b. Native Americans
c. Hispanic Americans
d. African Americans

15.16 Alcoholism increases the risk of death in middle age because

a. it damages all of the body's organ systems.
b. no effective treatments are available for it.
c. alcoholics often die in car crashes.
d. it shuts down the brain's ability to regulate vital functions.

Cognitive Functioning

15.17 According to Nancy Denney's model of physical and cognitive aging, the positive effects of exercise on an individual's physical or cognitive abilities will be limited by the person's

a. age.
b. level of life satisfaction.
c. level of motivation.
d. temperament.

15.18 The "selective" component of the selective compensation with optimization model involves

a. relying on physical abilities that have not yet become impaired.
b. practicing skills that can be improved.
c. focusing limited resources on some tasks more than others.
d. finding ways to adjust to declining physical abilities.

15.19 According to the Seattle Longitudinal Study, __________ has been linked to intellectual decline.

a. cardiovascular disease
b. menopause
c. obesity
d. prostate cancer

15.20 A review of the research findings on cognitive change in middle adulthood reveals that

a. vocabularies decline.
b. problem-solving ability is significantly impaired.
c. mental processes get slower, but actual losses are small.
d. performance is maintained or even slightly improved on tasks of fluid intelligence.

15.21 What aspect of memory do we utilize when we try to recall the words of a song or a poem?

a. dialectic
b. episodic
c. mnemonic
d. semantic

15.22 When learning from text, middle-aged adults are more likely than young adults to remember

a. material that is visually scanned better than material that is heard.
b. episodic memories better than semantic memories
c. broad themes or summary information better than specific words.
d. problem-solving strategies better than verbal skills.

15.23 According to Simonton's review of the lifetime creativity and productivity of thousands of notable scientists, people are most creative

a. in their adolescent years.
b. in their 20s.
c. at about age 40.
d. in their 60s.

PEARSON **mydevelopmentlab™ Study Plan**

Are You Ready for the Test?

Students who use the study materials on MyDevelopmentLab report higher grades in the course than those who use the text alone. Here are three easy steps to mastering this chapter and improving your grade...

Step 1

Take the chapter pre-test in MyDevelopmentLab and review your customized Study Plan.

Middle-aged adults may be more proficient than older adults at overcoming perceived memory limitations through strategies such as using cues as reminders because

- they have a larger collection of episodic memories.
- their neurons transmit information at a higher rate.
- there is a richer network of interneural connections.
- they have a high sense of self-efficacy with respect to memory.

Step 2

Use MyDevelopmentLab's Multimedia Library to help strengthen your knowledge of the chapter.

Watch: Menopause

Learning Objective 15.2

How does reproductive function change in men and women in middle age?

Did you know? MyDevelopmentLab offers the complete Grade Aid Study Guide online, accessible from within each chapter. "The Grade Aid is a good way to study because you have to read and look for the answers to the questions, and so in some ways you are studying while you are reading. That was very helpful for me."

—Richard (student), Syracuse University

Watch: Health Disparities and Latinos

Learning Objective 15.8

How are socioeconomic status and ethnicity related to health in middle adulthood?

Watch: Memory Hazards

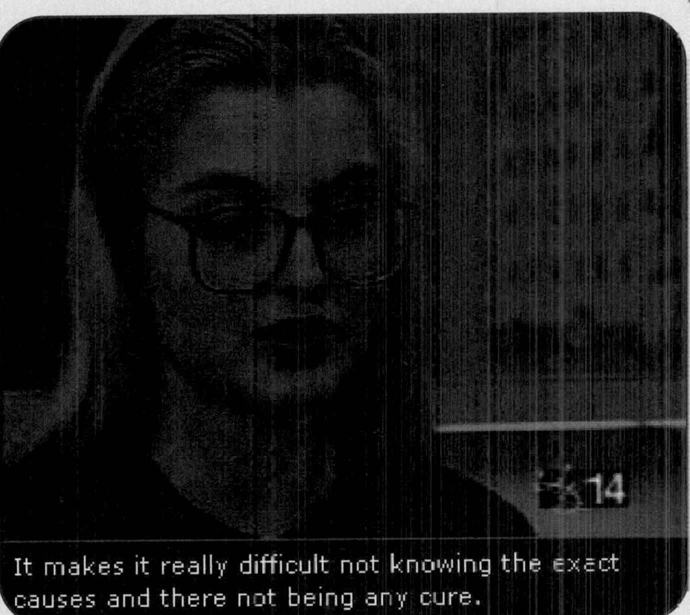

14
It makes it really difficult not knowing the exact causes and there not being any cure.

Learning Objective 15.12

How do young and middle-aged adults differ in performance on memory tests?

Step 3

Take the chapter post-test and compare your results against the pre-test.

The main cause for cross-racial variations in cancer incidence and death rates is

- dietary differences.
- failure to receive routine cancer screenings.
- differences in attitudes toward health care.
- failure to get a full set of immunizations.

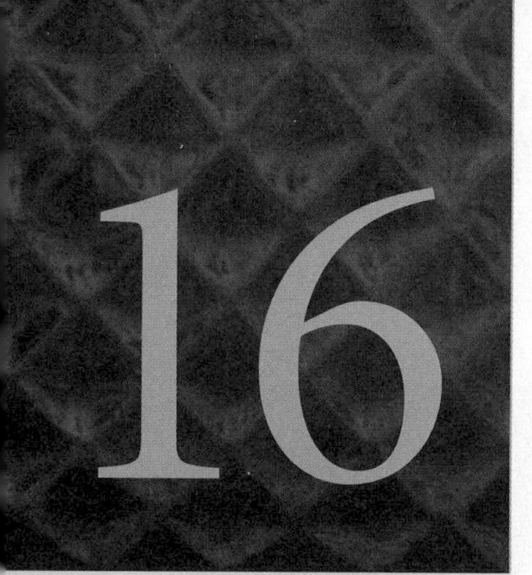

16 Social and Personality Development in Middle Adulthood

According to an ancient proverb, "a gray head is a crown of glory." Apparently, few middle-aged adults agree, because sales of hair coloring began to soar in the United States and other industrialized nations as the first wave of the massive Baby Boom generation hit their 40s in the early 1990s (Grossman, 1998). And the older the boomers get, the more they look to youth-preserving strategies such as hair transplants, liposuction, facelifts, tummy tucks, and "minimally invasive" techniques such as Botox injections (Carne & Burke, 2007). What are the psychosocial factors that have spurred this trend?

As you learned in Chapter 1, *ageism* is a form of prejudice that is based on the idea that older people are less competent than those who are younger. Among middle-aged job seekers, ageism is

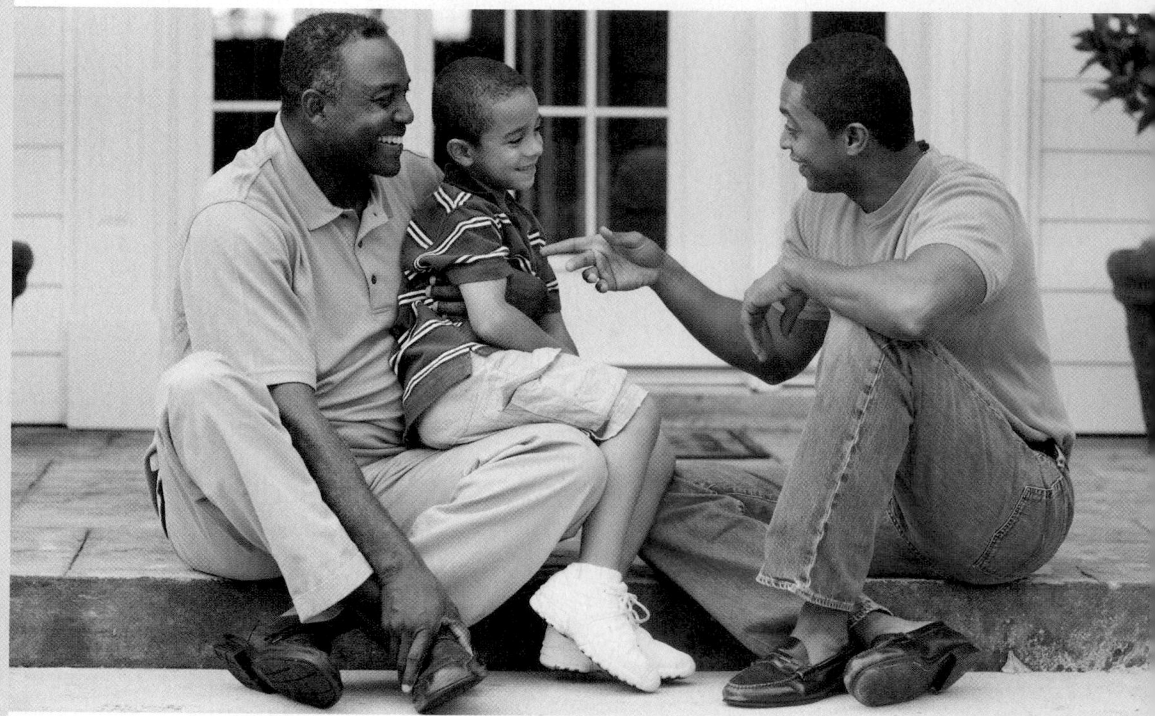

a significant barrier to obtaining work. Employers' reluctance to hire older workers appears to stem from concerns about the degree to which they can fit in with younger co-workers, a worry that is not substantiated by research, by the way (Handy & Davy, 2007). Moreover, studies show that age-related appearance cues, such as gray hair, often trigger such perceptions in interviewers, especially when the interviewee is a middle-aged woman (Duncan & Loretto, 2004). Consequently, the increased focus on body image among women in the middle adulthood years that researchers have often found are based on subtle real-world experiences and are not simply the product of vanity or a desire to stay young forever (Saucier, 2004).

Remember, too, that beginning in middle childhood, people form ideas about self-worth based on comparisons of their actual selves to an ideal self (see Chapter 10). Even young adults report that, subjectively speaking, they feel much younger than their chronological age would indicate (Öberg & Tornstam, 2001). Among younger adults, this sense of subjective age has led to an upsurge in sales of products that take them back to their childhood days (Furedi, 2003). For instance, sales of "Hello Kitty" products rose dramatically in the early years of the 21st century thanks to women in their 20s who had also been the driving force behind the initial popularity of these products two decades earlier. Thus the popularity of anti-aging products and surgical procedures among Baby Boomers may represent a theme that is common to all adults, that of reconciling physical age with psychological age. Today's middle-aged adults may simply be the first cohort that has had the economic resources needed to bring aging bodies into line with youthful minds.

Worries about the physical signs of aging aside, what seems most striking about everyday life in middle age is how much less constricting social roles feel. Most middle-aged adults are spouses, parents, and workers, but by age 40 or 50, these roles have changed in important ways. Children have begun to leave home, which dramatically alters and reduces the intensity of the parental role; job promotions have usually reached their limit, so workers have less need to learn new work skills. And when both parenting and work are less demanding, partners can find more time for themselves and for each other. Such changes are the topics that we address in this chapter.

Theories of Social and Personality Development

You should remember from Chapter 2 that Erik Erikson viewed middle age as a period when attention turns to creation of a legacy. Adults do this by influencing the lives of those in younger generations. Yet many have characterized middle age less positively, suggesting that it is a period of intense crisis.

Learning Objective 16.1

How do the views of Erikson and Vaillant differ with regard to generativity?

Erikson's Generativity versus Stagnation Stage

Middle-aged adults are in Erikson's *generativity versus stagnation stage*. Their developmental task is to acquire a sense of **generativity**, which involves an interest in establishing and guiding the next generation. Generativity is expressed not only in bearing or rearing one's own children, but through teaching, serving as mentor, or taking on leadership roles in various civic, religious, or charitable organizations. The optimum expression of generativity requires turning outward from a preoccupation with self, a kind of psychological expansion toward caring for others. Those who fail to develop generativity often suffer from a "pervading sense of stagnation and personal impoverishment [and indulge themselves] as if they were their own one and only child" (Erikson, 1963, p. 267).

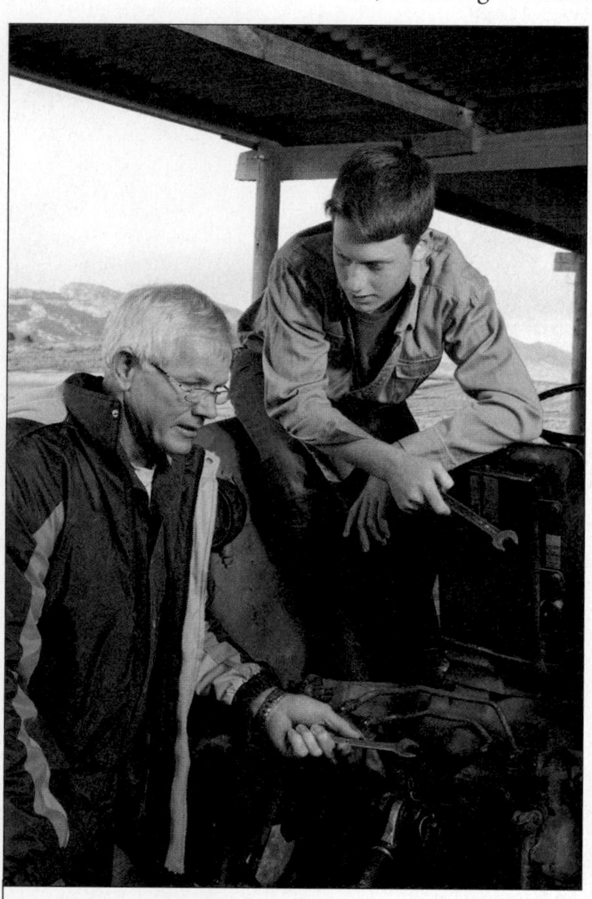

Erikson proposed that passing on one's knowledge to younger individuals is the primary theme of psychosocial development in middle adulthood.

Research on Generativity Research has produced hints of such a developmental stage, but the findings are much less clear than data on changes in earlier years. One cross-sectional study of young, mid-life, and older women found that generativity increased in middle age, as Erikson's theory suggests (Zucker, Ostrove, & Stewart, 2002). Contrary to what his theory would predict, however, the oldest group of participants, whose average age was 66, cited generative concerns as being important to them just as frequently as the middle-aged group did. These findings support Erikson's claim that generativity is more common in middle than in early adulthood, but they also indicate that generativity continues to be important in old age. Other research suggests that generativity is a more prominent theme in the lives of middle-aged women than in the lives of middle-aged men (Morfei, Hooker, Carpenter, Mix, & Blakeley, 2004).

Despite these inconsistencies, studies support Erikson's belief that generativity is related to mental health among middle-aged adults. For instance, researchers have found that generativity is positively related to satisfaction in life and work and to emotional well-being (Ackerman, Zuroff, & Moskowitz, 2000). Further, in a study that measured middle-aged women's sense of being burdened by caring for elderly parents, those who exhibited the highest levels of generativity felt the least burdened by elder care (Peterson, 2002).

Erikson's theory also raises questions about the impact of childlessness on adult development. One very interesting analysis comes from a 40-year longitudinal study of a group of inner-city, nondelinquent boys who had originally served as a comparison group in a study of delinquent boys (Snarey, Son, Kuehne, Hauser, & Vaillant, 1987). Of the 343 married men who were still part of this sample in their late 40s, 29 had fathered no children. Researchers found that the way a man had responded earlier to his childlessness was predictive of his psychological health at age 47. At that age, each man was rated on his degree of generativity. A man was considered to be "generative" if he had participated in some kind of mentoring or

generativity a sense that one is making a valuable contribution to society by bringing up children or mentoring younger people in some way

other teaching or supervising of children or younger adults. Among those with no children, those who were rated as most generative were likely to have responded to their childlessness by finding another child to nurture. They adopted a child, became Big Brothers, or helped with the rearing of someone else's child, such as a niece or nephew. Those childless men rated as nongenerative were more likely to have chosen a pet as a child substitute.

When civil rights icon Rosa Parks passed away in 2005, Oprah Winfrey spoke at her funeral and explained how Ms. Parks's defiance of an Alabama law that required African Americans to give up their seats to Whites on buses inspired her as a young girl growing up in the segregated South. According to Vaillant, such actions represent middle-aged adults' function as "keepers of meaning" who serve as bridges between past and future generations.

Vaillant's Revision of Erikson's Theory Psychiatrist George Vaillant has spent the past three decades chronicling the development of several hundred adults through early, middle, and late adulthood. His research has included measures of change in the physical, cognitive, personality, and social domains. His findings for the middle adulthood period prompted him to propose a modification of Erikson's theory of lifespan development (Vaillant, 2002).

Vaillant argued that there is a stage between intimacy and generativity called *career consolidation*. Like Erikson, Vaillant tended to define the domains of life fairly broadly, so "career" may mean a paid vocation or it could involve a decision to be a stay-at-home mother or father. The outcome of this phase is the creation of a new social network for which the middle-aged adult's primary work serves as a hub. Involvement with this social network helps the individual meet the psychosocial needs of this substage. Such needs include contentment, compensation, competence, and commitment (Vaillant, 2002). Individuals need to be happy with the work-related choices they have made, to feel that they are adequately compensated, to view themselves as competent in their chosen field, and to be able to maintain a sense of commitment to their work.

Following generativity versus stagnation, Vaillant argued, is another stage called *keeper of the meaning*. In this phase, middle-aged adults focus on preserving the institutions and values of their culture that they believe will benefit future generations. For some, religious organizations become paramount. Others focus on the arts, educational institutions, historical preservation societies, or political organizations. The key is that participation in these institutions is motivated by the desire to ensure their survival rather than by a concern for how the institution can benefit the individual middle-aged adult. In other words, the well adjusted adult in the *keeper of meaning* stage wants to give something to the institution rather than to get something from it. Moreover, the social networks that are created through middle-aged adults' associations with institutions support their need to feel that the work they are doing will make a difference for future generations.

Mid-Life Crisis: Fact or Fiction?

Learning Objective 16.2

How do proponents of the midlife crisis and the life events perspective approach middle age differently?

You may recall that the crisis concept is central to Erikson's theory, and a specific mid-life crisis has been part of several other theories as well, including Levinson's (see Chapter 14). Levinson argued that each person must confront a constellation of difficult tasks at mid-life: accepting one's own mortality, recognizing new physical limitations and health risks, and adapting to major changes in most roles. Dealing with all these tasks, according to Levinson, is highly likely to exceed an adult's ability to cope, thus creating a crisis.

When developmentalists look at the relevant research evidence, however, they often question this conclusion. Just over a quarter of middle-aged and older adults report having had a crisis such as the one that Levinson's theory predicts (Lachman, 2004). However, these crises appear to have been triggered by specific events such as the loss of a job or the death of a close friend or relative. Thus, some developmentalists argue that a **life events approach** to explaining the unique stresses of the middle adulthood period is preferable to a theoretical perspective that proposes a universal crisis. The life events approach focuses on normative and non-normative events and middle-aged adults' responses to them.

life events approach a theoretical perspective on middle adulthood that focuses on normative and non-normative events and how adults in this age group respond to them

The physical changes of middle age that you learned about in Chapter 15 are the backdrop against which the major life events of this period are played out. Consequently, all middle-aged adults are dealing with new stressors for which they must develop new ways of coping, and research shows that concerns about the limitations imposed by these physical changes increases across the middle adulthood years (Cate & John, 2007). In addition, most middle-aged adults experience the loss of a parent or must cope with major declines in their parents' ability to care for themselves. Most are also dealing with work-related issues. At the same time, for those who have children, major shifts are occurring in the nature of parent-child relationships. Another important factor, one that adds another layer of complexity, is that many of these stressors last for some time. A middle-aged person can spend years, for example, caring for an incapacitated parent. With all of these changes going on at the same time, it isn't surprising that middle-aged adults often feel stressed.

Some developmentalists argue that the best way to understand middle adulthood is to study how people in this age group manage to integrate all of these changes and their interpretations of them into the coherent stories of their own middle adulthood experiences (Glück, Bluck, Baron, & McAdams, 2005; Ville & Khlat, 2007). It is particularly important to understand how each middle-aged person's understanding of her experiences is influenced by characteristics that she brings to the developmental tasks of middle age. For example, men and women with histories of depression are likely to integrate the life events of middle age differently from those who do not have such histories (Kikhavani & Kunar, 2005). Variations in general optimism and in personality are likely to contribute to the integration process (Clarke & Singh, 2005; McAdams & Pals, 2006). Likewise, adults who face a major health crisis such as breast cancer along with the more normative events of middle age are likely to think differently about this period than their peers who are blessed with good health during these years do (Low et al., 2006).

Finally, the stresses associated with the events of middle age are often complicated by **role conflict**, any situation in which two or more roles are at least partially incompatible, either because they call for different behaviors or because their separate demands add up to more hours than there are in the day. Role conflict happens, for example, when a middle-aged father must choose between helping his aging parents with financial or health problems and attending his teenaged son's football games. A person experiences *role strain* when her own qualities or skills do not measure up to the demands of some role. For example, a 40-year-old worker who is forced to return to college to acquire new skills after a job layoff and who feels anxious about her ability to succeed is experiencing role strain.

Critical Thinking

1. How could the stage models of Erikson and Vaillant be integrated with the life events approach to provide a more comprehensive description of middle adulthood than any of them could alone?

role conflict any situation in which two or more roles are at least partially incompatible, either because they call for different behaviors or because their separate demands add up to more hours than there are in the day

Changes in Relationships and Personality

As suggested previously, family roles are still an important part of life in middle age. However, these roles change significantly during this period of life.

Learning Objective 16.3

What contributes to the "mellowing" of partnerships in middle adulthood?

Partnerships

Several lines of evidence suggest that, on average, marital stability and satisfaction increase in mid-life as conflicts over child-rearing and other matters decline (Swensen, Eskew, & Kohlhepp, 1981; Veroff, Douvan, & Kulka, 1981; Wu & Penning, 1997). In addition, as couples get older, the number of shared friends they have increases and the number of non-shared friends decreases (Kalmijn, 2003). As a result, the social network tends to get a bit tighter—and probably more supportive—in middle age. This may be one reason for age-related improvements in relationship satisfaction. So, despite considerable diversity among mid-life marriages and partnerships, overall they are less conflicted than those of young adults.

Improvements in marital satisfaction may also derive from middle-aged adults' increased sense of control—a kind of marital self-efficacy (Lachman & Weaver, 1998). It is likely that middle-aged partners' identification of successful problem-solving strategies contributes to the sense that they have control over their relationship. Research has provided useful illustrations of this point. For example, researchers typically find that marital problem themes among middle-aged couples are remarkably similar to those of younger adults. Wives complain of an unjust division of labor; husbands express dissatisfaction with limits on their freedom. Yet relationship stability among middle-aged couples is maintained through the practice of what one researcher called "skilled diplomacy," an approach to solving problems that involves confrontation of the spouse about an issue, followed by a period during which the confronting spouse works to restore harmony (Perho & Korhonen, 1999). Skilled diplomacy is practiced more often by wives than by husbands, but it appears to be an effective technique for marital problem-solving no matter which spouse uses it.

Once the children are grown and gone, many couples find it easier to spend time together—perhaps one of the reasons that marital satisfaction generally rises in middle age.

As age-related increases in marital satisfaction would predict, middle-aged couples are far less likely to divorce than those who are younger (Uhlenberg, Cooney, & Boyd, 1990). Moreover, research suggests that middle-aged women are better able to cope with divorce then younger women (Marks & Lambert, 1998). Perhaps a "mellowing" of personality (which you will read about later in this chapter) renders the middle-aged woman more resilient in the face of such traumatic events. Moreover, some women remain in unsatisfactory marriages through their 20s and 30s because they think that divorce will be harmful to their children. Once the children are grown, such women feel free to move out of these relationships and report that the stress associated with divorce was less problematic than the emotional turmoil they experienced in the years prior to splitting from their husbands (Enright, 2004).

Research suggests that middle-aged women are more resilient than younger women in managing transitions such as divorce.

Children and Parents

Learning Objective 16.4

What is the family role of middle-aged adults with respect to older and younger generations?

The discussion of the relationship between young adults and their families in Chapter 14 focused almost entirely on connections *up* the chain of family generations—that is, relationships between the young adults and their own middle-aged parents. When looking at family relationships from the perspective of middle age, we have to look in both directions: down the generational chain to relationships with grown children (see the Research Report on page 466) and up the chain to relationships with aging parents.

Each of the positions in a family's generational chain has certain role prescriptions (Hagestad, 1986, 1990). In middle adulthood, the family role involves not only giving assistance in both directions in the generational chain but also shouldering the primary responsibility for maintaining affectional bonds. These responsibilities produce what is sometimes called the mid-life "squeeze," and those being squeezed form the *sandwich generation.*

RESEARCH REPORT

The Empty Nest and the Revolving Door

Folklore in Western cultures argues that the role of mother is so central to women's lives that they suffer from "empty nest" syndrome, a pattern of symptoms characterized by anxiety and depression, when their grown children leave home. However, research suggests that most women are happy when they reach this milestone (Segatto & Di Filippo, 2003). But what happens when the children don't leave home?

In 1970 only 8% of 25-year-olds lived with their parents. By the early years of the 21st century, estimates of the proportion of young adults who were still living with their parents ranged from 38% in the United States to 46% in the United Kingdom to 70% in Japan (Furedi, 2003). Further, a survey in the United Kingdom found that even when these young adults, or "adultescents" as they are sometimes called, do leave home, more than half return home for a meal or other social activity at least once a week, about 1 in 5 still receive mail at their parents' home, and, remarkably, 13% at least occasionally drop off their laundry for Mom to do (Bristow, 2002). Such findings have been described as the "revolving door" pattern in which children leave home at the end of high school and return one or more times before becoming fully independent. What's behind this trend?

One explanation for the trend that some writers have called "Peter-Pandemonium" is that many of today's young adults simply do not want to grow up (Furendi, 2002). Marketing studies which show that stay-at-home adult children spend a great deal of money on luxuries while their parents are footing the bill for their living expenses support this view. However, a psychosocial explanation would hypothesize that single young adults, like all human beings, enjoy and are nurtured by family life (Robbins, 2001). With today's singles marrying and having their own children at later ages, some observers argue that it is natural for unattached young adults to turn to the most reliable source of nurturance and social connectedness that they know, that is, to their family of origin.

How do these "boomerang kids" affect the lives of their middle-aged parents? There is little doubt that dealing with an adult child who appears to be unwilling to leave home is a stressful experience, perhaps because it happens at the same time as other stress-inducing events such as the need to care for aging parents and to prepare for retirement (Lachman, 2004). It should be noted, however, that there are many middle-aged parents who welcome the opportunity to maintain warm relationships with their adult children that is afforded by having them remain at home. Thus, like so many other trends which involve changing family structures in today's world, this one should be viewed as a function of personal choice and, in most cases, representative of a living situation that is viewed as mutually beneficial by those who are involved in it.

Questions for Critical Analysis

1. Aside from that which was cited in this discussion, what evidence would suggest that the economic explanation of the "revolving door" is the best one? What kinds of data would favor the psychosocial explanation?
2. The discussion mentioned some of the advantages that are enjoyed by single young adults who live with their parents. What are some of the disadvantages of such a living arrangement?

Such a squeeze was illustrated in the results of interviews with over 13,000 adults in one frequently cited national survey. Among many other things, respondents were asked about the amount of help of various kinds—financial, child care, household assistance, and so forth—they gave to and received from both adult children and aging parents (Bumpass & Aquilino, 1995). The results, graphed in Figure 16.1, make clear that those between ages 40 and 65 give more help than they receive in both directions within the family—to adult chil-

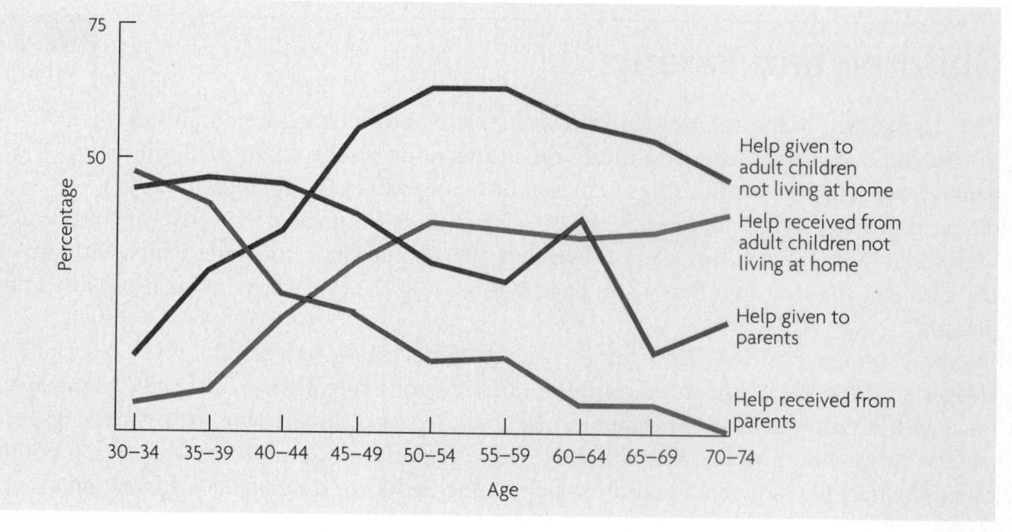

Figure 16.1 The Middle Age "Squeeze"

The mid-life "squeeze," or "sandwich generation," is illustrated in this graph of data from a national survey of adults. Middle-aged adults give more help to both their adult children and their own parents than they receive. (*Source:* Bumpass & Aquilino, 1995, data from Tables 11, 12, 25, and 26.)

dren and to aging parents—a pattern confirmed in a variety of other studies, in Canada as well as the United States (e.g., Gallagher, 1994; Hirdes & Strain, 1995).

Whether most middle-aged adults experience this combination of responsibilities as a burden is not clear from the available information (Bengtson, Rosenthal, & Burton, 1996). Doubtless some do and some do not, depending on the degree of infirmity of the aging parents, the nature of the relationship the middle-aged adult has with those aging parents, and the degree of help required by the young adult children. The adult child caregiver's own situation contributes to the sense of feeling burdened as well (Andrén & Elmståhl, 2007). Those who lack sufficient income to care for their elders and whose own health is less than optimal feel more burdened by the responsibility of caring for an elderly parent. The social clock is also relevant, because adult children who feel that their parents need for care is "on time" feel less burdened than those whose parents' incapacity is perceived as "early."

Contrary to popular belief, when this woman's daughter leaves the nest in a few years, it will be a joyful experience.

Grandparenting

Learning Objective 16.5

How does the grandparent role affect middle-aged adults?

Middle-aged adults typically move into several new roles—for example, becoming in-laws as their children marry (see the Real World feature on page 468). In addition, in the United States, about a third of adults become grandparents by their late 40s, and half of women become grandmothers by their early 50s (Bumpass & Aquilino, 1995). As the average age of childbearing has risen in recent cohorts, the timing of grandparenthood may shift to a slightly later age, but such a shift would not change the basic fact that this role is normally acquired in middle adulthood.

Most grandparents—92% in one study—express high levels of satisfaction with this role (Kaufman & Elder, 2003; Peterson, 1999; Segatto & Di Filippo, 2003). A majority see or talk to their grandchildren regularly. They may write, call, or visit as often as every couple of weeks, and most describe their relationships as warm and loving. Likewise, many studies have demonstrated the positive impact of warm relationships with grandparents on children's development (Adkins, 1999).

Grandparents seem to be an especially important source of stability in the lives of children of divorced parents. However, court rulings in the United States make clear that the rights of grandparents are limited by the rights of parents (Jacoby, 2000). In extreme cases, such as when a grandparent is dying or has never been allowed to visit a grandchild, grandparents may sue parents, whether divorced or married, for the right to see their grandchildren. However, courts have ruled that, under most circumstances, denying visitation to a grandparent is within a parent's constitutionally protected right to make decisions about a child's upbringing.

This girl seems delighted with her grandmother, with whom she seems to have what Cherlin and Furstenberg would call a "companionate" relationship.

Fortunately, most parents welcome the involvement of their own parents in their children's lives, and surveys suggest that grandparents and grandchildren engage in many of the same activities—watching television, shopping, attending religious services—that parents and children share (Waggoner, 2000). However, while parenthood clearly involves full-time responsibility, there are many degrees of being a grandparent.

Most behavioral scientists place grandparents in one of several categories derived from a study in which researchers interviewed a nationally representative sample of over 500 grandparents (Cherlin & Furstenberg, 1986). Twenty-nine percent of grandparents in the study had **remote relationships**; they saw their grandchildren relatively infrequently and had little direct influence over their grandchildren's lives. The most common reason for this remoteness was physical distance.

By contrast, this statement by one of the grandmothers in the study illustrates a different kind of relationship, for which researchers used the term **companionate relationship**:

remote relationships relationships in which grandparents do not see their grandchildren often

companionate relationships relationships in which grandparents have frequent contact and warm interactions with grandchildren

involved relationships relationships in which grandparents are directly involved in the everyday care of grandchildren or have close emotional ties with them

> When you have grandchildren, you have more love to spare. Because the discipline goes to the parents and whoever's in charge. But you just have extra love and you will tend to spoil them a little bit. And you know, you give. (Cherlin & Furstenberg, 1986, p. 55)

Just over half of the survey's participants exhibited such attitudes toward their grandchildren and responded that they had very warm, pleasurable relationships with them. Yet these grandparents also said that they were glad they no longer had the day-to-day responsibility. They could love the grandchildren and then send them home.

The third and least common (16%) type of relationship was exhibited by grandparents who had **involved relationships** with their grandchildren. These grandparents were everyday participants in the rearing of their grandchildren. Some of them lived in three-generation households with one or more children and grandchildren; some had nearly full-time care of the grandchildren. But involved relationships also occurred in some cases in which the grandparent had no daily responsibility for the grandchildren's care but created an unusually close link.

THE REAL WORLD

Me, a Mother-in-Law?

Sophia was thrilled when her son announced that he was engaged to be married and that the couple planned to have the kind of traditional wedding that Sophia knew her large Italian American family would enjoy. But as she sat watching her future daughter-in-law open gifts at yet another bridal shower, she was suddenly struck by the realization that she was about to acquire one of the most maligned social roles there is: that of mother-in-law. Mother-in-law jokes abound in films and TV shows, and relationships between mothers-in-law and their children's spouses are regularly characterized as full of tension and conflict. Typically, it is the relationship between the mother-in-law and the daughter-in-law that is depicted most negatively. Thus, it isn't surprising that most middle-aged women don't look forward to becoming mothers-in-law. But is the negative stereotyping of mothers-in-law justified?

Research in some societies (e.g., rural communities in Latin America, India, and Korea) suggests that the stereotype is somewhat accurate. In these societies, newlyweds usually reside with the husband's parents, and the mother-in-law is responsible for socializing her daughter-in-law into the family. In such cultures, wives remain under the authority of their mothers-in-law for many years, usually until the older woman is no longer physically able to fulfill her role's requirements.

Despite the cultural reinforcement of the relationship between mother-in-law and daughter-in-law in traditional societies, these relationships are often high in conflict (Chiapin, DeAraujo, & Wagner, 1998). Most such conflicts involve the husband: The daughter-in-law thinks her husband is too loyal to his mother, or the mother-in-law thinks her son's wife is trying to undermine her relationship with him. Some mothers-in-law go so far as to physically abuse daughters-in-law, and abusive husbands sometimes receive praise from their mothers for keeping young wives in line (Fernandez, 1997).

Parallels exist in more industrialized societies like the United States. Mothers-in-law are perceived as interfering in the marital relationship; daughters-in-law are accused of trying to turn their husbands against their mothers. Consequently, family therapists have devised recommendations to help middle-aged women such as Sophia adjust to the mother-in-law role and to forestall conflict (Greider, 2000). Here are a few such recommendations:

- Don't give unsolicited advice or make unannounced visits.
- When asked for your advice, share your experience in a nonjudgmental way.
- Don't criticize your daughters- or sons-in-law behind their backs.
- Don't insist on being visited every weekend or holiday.
- Respect your children's wishes regarding how grandchildren are to be cared for.

Questions for Reflection

1. How much of the conflict between mothers-in-law and their children's spouses is brought about by expectations that are based on cultural stereotypes?
2. What items would you include in a list of tips that might help spouses avoid conflicts with their in-laws?

About 20% of low-income grandparents have full-time responsibility for a grandchild (Pearson, Hunter, & Cook, 1997). However, the incidence of custodial grandparenting has increased in all ethnic and socioeconomic groups in recent years (Goodman & Silverstein, 2002). Across groups, about 10% of grandparents have had full-time responsibility for a grandchild for 6 months or longer, and no matter what the family's socioeconomic status, full-time grandparent care is especially likely when the grandchild's mother is unmarried. In such cases, the grandmother frequently takes on child-care responsibilities so that her daughter can continue in school or hold down a job.

Gender is related to grandparenting as well. Among all ethnic groups, the role of grandmother is likely to be both broader and more intimate than that of grandfather (Hagestad, 1985). In addition, young grandparents, those in their 40s, have less day-to-day contact with grandchildren than those who are older, perhaps because they often are still working (Watson, 1997). As a result, they know less about and are less involved in their grandchildren's everyday lives than older grandparents are.

The role of grandparent obviously brings many middle-aged and older adults a good deal of pleasure and satisfaction. However, grandparents who see their grandchildren more often do not describe themselves as happier than those who see theirs less often (Palmore, 1981). Thus, for most adults in middle age, grandparenthood is not central to their lives, to their sense of self, or to their overall morale.

Caring for Aging Parents

Learning Objective 16.6

How might caregiver burden affect a middle-aged adult's life?

Another role that may be added at mid-life and that *does* have a powerful effect on overall life satisfaction, is the role of major caregiver for aging parents (see No Easy Answers on page 470). The great majority of adults, in virtually every

NO EASY ANSWERS

Who Cares for Aging Parents?

One of the most difficult dilemmas of mid-life arises when elderly parents become incapable of caring for themselves. Inevitably, the issue of who will care for them creates conflicts. Families typically negotiate the caregiving task along a number of dimensions, including each family member's competing demands and availability of resources (Ingersoll-Dayton, Neal, Ha, & Hammer, 2003). Within a group of siblings, the one most likely to take on the task of caregiving is the one who has no children still at home, is not working, is not married, and lives closest to the aging parent (Brody, Litvin, Albert, & Hoffman, 1994; Stoller, Forster, & Duniho, 1992).

Most of these factors combine to make a daughter or daughter-in-law the most likely candidate for the role of caregiver. Some studies have found that as many as 90% of the primary caregivers for elders with Alzheimer's are either daughters or daughters-in-law (Daire, 2004). One factor that increases daughters' involvement in parental care is simple proximity. Perhaps because of greater emotional closeness to their parents or their socialization for the role of kin-keeping, daughters are more likely to live near their parents. And parents, when they approach their later years, are more likely to move to be close to a daughter than to a son.

Even when sons are involved in the care of an elder, research indicates that they experience far less caregiver burden than daughters do (Pincuart & Sorensen, 2006a). This difference results from the tendency of daughters to provide more hours of care, more personal types of care such as bathing, and to view the recipient of care as more difficult to deal with than sons do. The psychological and physical aspects of the types of care that daughters give and their attitudes toward their role of caregiver result in increases in depressive symptoms and decreases in health.

Researchers have found that multidimensional interventions can ease the strain of the caregiver burden (Pinquart & Sorensen, 2006b). These interventions should include education for the caregiver about the care recipient's condition or illness. The educational component should include information on the availability of resources such as daycare and home health aides, both of which can provide the caregiver with a much needed respite from the physical aspects of caring for an elderly parent. Similarly, counseling sessions and support groups can help with the emotional aspects of caregiving.

Take a Stand

Decide which of these two statements you most agree with and think about how you would defend your position:

1. Caring for aging parents is a moral duty even if doing so interferes with a middle-aged adult's other family and professional responsibilities.
2. Caring for aging parents is a moral duty, but it must be balanced with a middle-aged adult's other family and professional responsibilities that sometimes must take precedence over caring for an elder.

Daughters, far more than sons, are likely to take on the role of significant caregiver for a disabled parent or a parent with dementia, as this daughter has done now that her mother is suffering from Alzheimer's disease.

culture, feel a strong sense of filial responsibility. When their parents need assistance, they endeavor to provide it (Lachman, 2004).

Just what impact does caregiving have on the middle-aged adult? Not surprisingly, such a demanding role takes its toll. The cumulative evidence indicates that caregivers are more depressed and have lower marital satisfaction than those in comparison groups of similar age and social class (Hoyert & Seltzer, 1992; Jutras & Lavoie, 1995; Li & Seltzer, 2003; Schulz, Visintainer, & Williamson, 1990). Some research also suggests that those who care for frail elders are more often ill themselves or have some reduced efficiency of immune system function (Dura & Kiecolt-Glaser, 1991; Hoyert & Seltzer, 1992; Kiecolt-Glaser et al., 1987). Collectively, these effects are often termed **caregiver burden**.

Still, for the majority of mid-life adults, the relationship with aging parents is mostly positive. Most give more assistance to their parents than they did before, but they also continue to see them regularly for ceremonial and celebratory occasions and to feel affection as well as filial responsibility (Stein et al., 1998). Parents are also symbolically important to middle-aged adults, because as long as they are alive, they occupy the role of elder in the family lineage. When they are gone, each generation moves up a notch in the sequence: Those in the middle generation must come to terms with the fact that they have now become the elders and are confronted directly with their own mortality.

Learning Objective 16.7

How do social networks change during middle adulthood?

Friends

The scant research on friendships in middle adulthood suggests that the total number of friendships is lower in these years than in young adulthood (Kalmijn, 2003). For example, in one small study, researchers interviewed three generations of women in each of 53 families, some White American and some Hispanic American (Levitt, Weber, & Guacci, 1993). Each woman was asked to describe her close relationships. Among both groups, the young adult women had more friends in their social networks than did their middle-aged mothers.

At the same time, there are other bits of research suggesting that mid-life friendships are as intimate and close as those at earlier ages. For example, researchers have analyzed information from the files of 50 participants in the now-familiar Berkeley/Oakland longitudinal study, who had been interviewed or tested repeatedly from adolescence through age 50 (Carstensen, 1992). These analyses revealed that the frequency of interaction with best friends dropped between age 17 and age 50, but that the best-friend relationships remained very close.

These studies suggest that the social network of middle-aged adults is relatively small, although relationships are just as intimate as they were at earlier ages. It may be that the social network shrinks as adults age because there is less need for it. Role conflict and role strain decline significantly in middle age, and the need for emotional support from a social network outside the family seems to decrease accordingly (Due, Holstein, Lund, Modvig, & Avlund, 1999). Yet, because the relationships that do endure are close, the social network is available when needed. Friendship depends less on frequent contact than on a sense that friends are there to provide support as needed. Thus, the nature of friendship itself may be different in middle age.

caregiver burden a term for the cumulative negative effects of caring for an elderly or disabled person

Learning Objective 16.8

What is the evidence for continuity and change in personality throughout adulthood?

Continuity and Change in Personality

Can developmentalists tell what kind of person someone will be in middle adulthood, based on what is known about his childhood, adolescence, or early adult life? As you learned in Chapter 10, a stable set of personality traits that psychologists call the *Big Five* emerge during middle childhood. Notice in this brief review of the traits that they can be easily remembered with the acronym *OCEAN*:

- *Openness:* willingness to try new things
- *Conscientiousness:* need for order in the environment
- *Extraversion:* sociability
- *Agreeableness:* ease with which a person gets along with others
- *Neuroticism:* emotional negativity, pessimism, and irritability

Many studies show that the Big Five are relatively stable from childhood to old age (Hampson & Goldberg, 2006). Such findings are consistent with the proposition that the five factors are determined very early in life and are stable throughout the lifespan (Caspi, 2000; McCrae & Costa, 1990). However, there are subtle age-related changes in the five factors across the years of adulthood (Terracciano et al., 2005). Longitudinal research indicates that openness, extraversion, and neuroticism decline as adults age. Agreeableness increases, as does conscientiousness up until around age 70 when it begins to show declines. Thus, the best statement that we can make about the stability of the Big Five is that these traits follow a general pattern of stability in most people but that they are also subject to some degree of modification (Branje, Van Lieshout, & Gerris, 2007).

Studies of negative and positive emotionality suggest a similar pattern. Even though negative emotionality in early adulthood is moderately to strongly correlated with negative emotionality in middle adulthood, longitudinal studies show that many individuals, particularly women, become *less* negative over time (Helson & Klohnen, 1998; Srivastava, John, Gosling, & Potter, 2003). Similarly, agreeableness appears to increase with age (Srivastava, John, Gosling, & Potter, 2003). At the same time, tolerance for risk-taking and impulsivity decline with age (Deakin, Aitken, Robbins, & Sahakian, 2004). Apparently, then, when researchers consider large groups—which they must do to correlate variables such as personality factors—they find that personality is fairly stable over time. However, the correlations can mask a number of individual cases in which there is a great deal of change. Consequently, the best conclusion to draw is that stability is the general pattern, but the increased individual variability in personality that is typically found among middle-aged and older adults suggests that change is clearly possible and may even be common (Nelson & Dannefer, 1992).

> **Critical Thinking**
>
> 1. In your view, how do the changes in social relationships that are described in this section contribute to maintaining some personality traits while modifying others in middle age?

Personality is an important contributor to middle-aged adults' capacity for managing stress. For example, in one study researchers found that adults who were higher in extraversion and conscientiousness were less likely to feel strained by work-related stressors (Grant & Langan-Fox, 2007). By contrast, those who were high in neuroticism were less able to cope with on-the-job problems. Likewise, personality moderates the effects of caregiver burden on the subjective sense of well-being among middle-aged adults who are caring for elderly parents (Koerner & Kenyon, 2007).

Mid-Life Career Issues

Work in mid-life is characterized by two paradoxes: First, work satisfaction is at its peak in these years, despite the fact that most adults receive few work promotions in middle age. Second, the quality of work performance remains high, despite declines in some cognitive and physical skills.

burnout lack of energy, exhaustion, and pessimism that results from chronic stress

Work Satisfaction

> Learning Objective 16.9
>
> What factors influence work satisfaction in middle adulthood?

As we have noted before, there are many aspects of life that improve with age. Interestingly, middle-aged workers are less likely than younger workers to experience work-related **burnout** (Freudenberger & Richelson, 1981). People with burnout lack energy and feel emotionally drained and are pessimistic about the possibility of changing

Studies show that men are more likely than women to use problem-focused strategies to cope with job stress. By contrast, women use emotion-focused coping more often than men. These differences help explain why middle-aged men and women differ in work satisfaction.

their situations. People who feel that their work is unappreciated are more subject to burnout than others. For example, one survey suggested that nearly half of the social workers in the United Kingdom suffer from burnout, and the sense of being unappreciated was the best predictor of the condition (Evans et al., 2006). Developmentalists suggest that middle-aged workers who have avoided burnout in high-stress professions are those who have learned to pace themselves and to rely less on external sources of job satisfaction (Randall, 2007).

In addition, despite the plateau in promotions that occurs for most adults in the middle years, job satisfaction is typically at its peak, as is a sense of power, or job clout. One reason for these increases may be that careers become more stable in middle age, with fewer interruptions caused by either voluntary or involuntary job changes (Boxall, Macky, & Rasmussen, 2003). Still, patterns of work and work satisfaction do vary between men and women in middle adulthood.

Some studies suggest that women and men use the same criteria to assess whether they are satisfied with their jobs. In one study, for example, researchers found that male and female workers across four different countries (China, Japan, Germany, and the United States) had similar preferences with regard to performance awards and management styles (Gunkel, Lusk, Wolff, & Li, 2007). However, research also suggests that men and women think differently about their work. For instance, one consistent finding is that women worry much more about the effects of having children on their career advancement (Hagan & Kay, 2007; Stewart & Ostrove, 1998).

Similarly, men and women may follow somewhat different pathways to job satisfaction (Perho & Korhonen, 1999). Men and women cite the same sources of work dissatisfaction in middle age: time pressure, difficult co-workers, boring tasks, and fear of losing one's job. However, they cope with these challenges differently. Men are more likely to negotiate with supervisors and co-workers directly to effect change. In contrast, women tend to withdraw and to engage in collective complaining with female co-workers. Still, women are better able than men to balance their dissatisfactions with areas of contentment. Consequently, a statement such as "I don't like the boss, but the hours fit my needs" is more likely to come from a woman than a man. Because of their different coping styles, men are more likely to improve their level of satisfaction in situations where change is possible. By contrast, women are probably better able to cope with work settings where they must adjust to dissatisfaction because the situation can't be changed.

Despite their differences, both men and women in mid-life have a greater sense of control over their work lives than younger adults do (Lachman & Weaver, 1998). One reason for the increased feeling of control may be that social-cognitive skills improve from early to middle adulthood (Blanchard-Fields, Chen, Schocke, & Hertzog, 1998; Hess, Bolstad, Woodburn, & Auman, 1999). Middle-aged adults are better than they were when younger at "sizing up" people, relationships, and situations. At the same time, by middle age, they have become proficient at directing their own behavior in ways that allow them to maintain levels of personal satisfaction even in unpleasant circumstances.

Learning Objective 16.10

What strategies do middle-aged workers use to maintain job performance at a satisfactory level?

Job Performance

Early studies suggested that job performance remained high throughout middle adulthood except in professions in which speed is a critical element (Sparrow & Davies, 1988). More recent cohorts of middle-aged adults in such professions, such as air traffic controllers, have been found to perform equally as well as their younger peers (Broach & Schroeder, 2006). Improvements in health that have led to increases in general life expectancy are also credited with producing this historical change. As a result, many governments around the world are examining regulations that force employees in these professions to retire at a certain age. Instead, research based reform proposals argue that older occupants of these jobs be tested individually to determine whether they can continue.

You should recall from Chapter 15 that researchers Paul Baltes and the late Margaret Baltes argue that maintaining high job productivity or performance is possible because adults, faced with small but noticeable erosions of cognitive or physical skill, engage in a process the Balteses call "selective optimization with compensation" (Baltes & Baltes, 1990). Three subprocesses are involved:

- *Selection.* Workers narrow their range of activities—for example, by focusing on only the most central tasks, delegating more responsibilities to others, or giving up or reducing peripheral job activities.
- *Optimization.* Workers deliberately "exercise" crucial abilities—such as by taking added training or polishing rusty skills—so as to remain as close to maximum skill levels as possible.
- *Compensation.* Workers adopt pragmatic strategies for overcoming specific obstacles—for example, getting stronger glasses or hearing aids, making lists to reduce memory loads, or even carefully emphasizing strengths and minimizing weaknesses when talking to co-workers or bosses.

A growing body of evidence supports the Balteses' view (Baltes & Heydens-Gahir, 2003). Researchers have tested this model in a study of 224 working adults aged 40 to 69 (Abraham & Hansson, 1995). Measuring each of the three aspects of the proposed compensatory process as well as job competence, they found that the link between the use of selection, optimization, and compensation on the one hand and the quality of work performance on the other got stronger with increasing age. That is, the older the worker, the more it mattered whether she used helpful compensatory practices. In the older groups (primarily those in their 50s and early 60s), those who used the most selection, optimization, and compensation had the highest work performance. But among the younger workers in this sample (those in their early 40s), the same relationship did not hold. This is obviously only one study, but the results provide some support for the idea that job performance remains high during middle age at least in part because adults take deliberate compensatory actions.

Unemployment and Career Transitions

Learning Objective 16.11
What are the factors that contribute to career transitions in mid-life?

In today's rapidly changing job market, it is not unusual for men and women to change occupations. However, career transitions can be more difficult in middle age than earlier in adulthood. For one thing, potential employers tend to believe that young adults are more capable of learning a new job than are middle-aged applicants, even though research suggests that this generalization is untrue (Forte & Hansvick, 1999). Employers give middle-aged applicants higher ratings on variables such as dependability, but they tend to think that younger applicants will be able to acquire new skills (especially computer skills) more rapidly. Thus, mid-life career changers must often overcome ageism in obtaining new employment.

Career counselors also point out that to understand mid-life career changes, it is useful to categorize workers on the basis of their reasons for changing occupations (Zunker, 1994). They suggest that people change careers for either external or internal reasons and can thus be classified as either *involuntary* or *voluntary* career changers.

Involuntary Career Changers Involuntary career changers are people who are in transition for external reasons: Their skills have become obsolete, their jobs have been eliminated through organizational restructuring, or they have been laid off because of shifting economic conditions. They experience heightened levels of anxiety and depression and higher risk of physical illness in the months after the job loss (Crowley, Hayslip, & Hobdy, 2003; He,

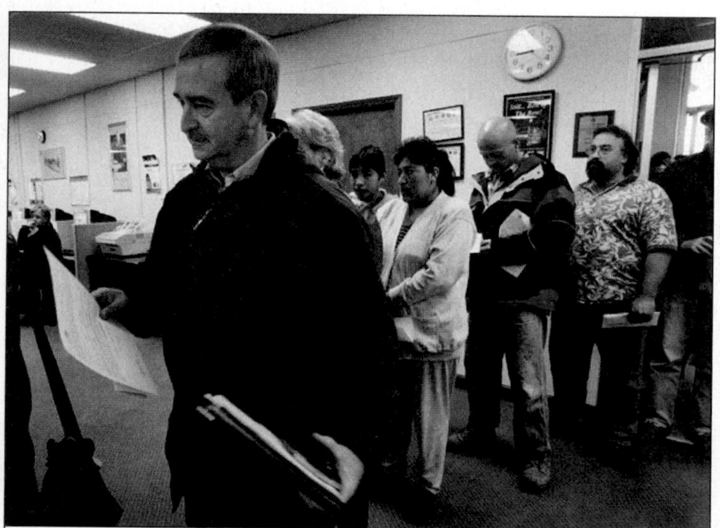

Involuntary career changers must confront a series of stressful situations, such as applying for unemployment benefits.

Colantonio, & Marshall, 2003; Isakson, Johansson, Bellaagh, & Sjöberg, 2004). Such effects are not unique to workers in the United States. Similar results have been found in studies in Australia, England, Denmark, and other Western developed countries (e.g., Broom et al., 2007; Iversen & Sabroe, 1988; Warr, Jackson, & Banks, 1988). Interestingly, just as remarriage alleviates many of the stresses associated with divorce, re-employment seems to restore health, emotional stability, and a sense of well-being quite rapidly.

The effects of job loss include changes in family relationships and loss of self-esteem. Most strikingly, marital relationships deteriorate rapidly after one or the other spouse has been laid off. The number of hostile or negative interactions increases, and the number of warm and supportive interactions declines—which means that the crucial ratio of positive to negative interactions spirals downward. Separation and divorce become much more common as a result (Ahituv & Lehman, 2004).

Predictably, the Big Five personality dimensions, especially neuroticism and openness to experience, contribute to mental health during involuntary career transitions across all racial and ethnic groups (Heppner, Fuller, & Multon, 1998). Nevertheless, mental health professionals suggest that the impact of an involuntary career change on an individual's life may be more directly affected by his or her coping skills (Zunker, 1994). For example, the person must be able to assess the situation realistically. If new work skills are needed, then the person must be able to formulate and carry out a plan for obtaining such skills. Researchers have found that mid-life career changers who have good coping skills and use them to manage involuntary transitions are less likely to become depressed (Cook & Heppner, 1997).

As with all types of stress, the effects of unemployment can be partially buffered by having adequate social support (Vinokur & van Ryn, 1993). Further, involuntary career changers benefit from career counseling that addresses both their occupational needs and their psychosocial development (Schadt, 1997). Counselors can help people who are forced to change jobs learn to think of the transition as an opportunity to re-examine goals and priorities—to treat the crisis as an opportunity (Zunker, 1994).

Voluntary Career Changers Voluntary career changers leave one career to pursue another for a variety of internal reasons (Allen, Dreves, & Ruhe, 1999). For example, they may believe that the new job will be more fulfilling. One pattern occurs when workers look at the next step on the career ladder and decide they don't want to pursue further advancement in their current occupation. For example, both male and female certified public accountants are more likely to leave their profession for this reason than for any other (Greenhaus, Collins, Singh, & Parasuraman, 1997). Others change careers in order to be able to express aspects of their personalities that they believe aren't utilized in their present jobs (Young & Rodgers, 1997).

Twin studies suggest that the tendency to change careers voluntarily in adulthood may have a genetic basis (McCall, Cavanaugh, Arvey, & Taubman, 1997). These findings further suggest that such transitions are a by-product of personality. Specifically, voluntary job changers appear to have a higher tolerance for risk-taking than do people who generally do not actively seek to change jobs (Roth, 2003). Most also appear to be people who do not regard either working or job-seeking as particularly stressful (Mao, 2003). Although voluntary career changers have a better sense of control over their situation than do people whose job changes are forced on them, the transition may still be stressful. Spouses and family members may not understand why the person wants to change careers. Moreover, changing careers can involve periods of unemployment and, often, a reduction in income. Thus, voluntary career changers manifest many of the same symptoms of anxiety and depression seen in involuntary career changers (Ahituv & Lehman, 2004). Consequently, they, too, benefit from social support and career counseling.

Preparing for Retirement

Learning Objective 16.12

How do Baby Boomers differ from previous cohorts with respect to preparation for retirement?

Studies that were done in the 1980s and 1990s suggested that many middle-aged adults begin to prepare for retirement as early as 15 years before their anticipated retirement date (e.g., Herzog, House, & Morgan, 1991).

However, the notion of retirement is relatively new and tends to be exclusive to industrialized cultures, and the retirement preparations of the Baby Boom cohort, who are all now middle-aged, are quite different from those of their parents (Monroy, 2000). For one thing, among their parents, retirement planning was primarily a male responsibility. In contrast, Baby Boom women are also doing retirement planning, sometimes together with their husbands, but sometimes independently (Dietz, Carrozza, & Ritchey, 2003; Glass & Kilpatrick, 1998). Further, retirement-minded Boomers are largely responsible for the growth of electronic financial services because of their enthusiastic response to the availability of such services on the Internet.

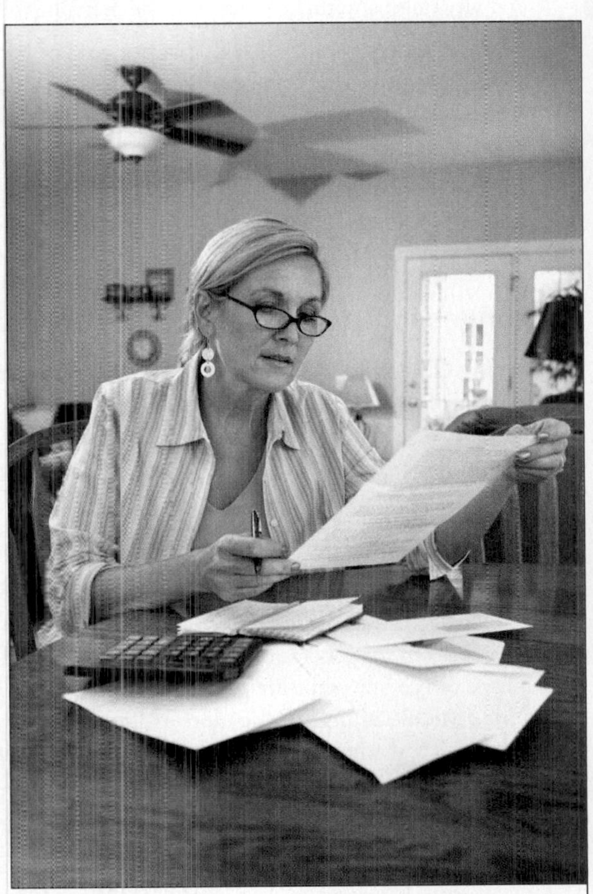

One difference between Baby Boomers and earlier cohorts is that among Baby Boomers, more women are involved in retirement planning.

Most Baby Boomers expect to die in their mid-80s or later but expect to retire fairly early, in their early 60s (Monroy, 2000). This means that their expected length of retirement is 20 years or more, far longer than that of earlier generations. What do boomers plan to do with all that time?

In a survey involving more than 3,000 boomers, gerontologist Ken Dychtwald found that virtually all of the respondents intended to continue working into retirement, but most intended to combine paid work with other pursuits (Mauldin, 2005). Dychtwald identified five distinct approaches to what those non-work pursuits should be (Mauldin, 2005). *Wealth Builders* (31%) intend to spend their spare time finding new ways to make money and building upon the wealth that they have already accumulated. Predictably, this group plans to devote more hours to paid work than their peers in other groups do. *Anxious Idealists* (20%) would like to do volunteer work and give money to charity after they retire but they recognize that their tendency toward impracticality has left them with insufficient economic resources to do either. *Empowered Trailblazers* (18%) expected to spend time traveling, taking classes, and doing volunteer work, and they believe that they are financially secure enough to meet these goals. *Stretched and Stressed* boomers (18%) are in deep trouble financially, and they are well aware of it. Most are worried about how they will be able to pay for basic necessities such as food and health care. *Leisure Lifers* (13%) intend to spend most of their time engaging in recreational pursuits and are geared toward very early retirement in their early to mid-50s.

Clearly, boomers have devoted a great deal of thought to what they would like to do during their retirement years. However, few have devoted as much energy to preparing for the financial aspects of retirement. Dychtwald's survey found that only 2% had actually saved enough money to be able to do what they said they wanted to do in retirement. Consequently, many boomers appear to be headed on a path toward disappointment when financial realities set in just a few years from now.

Nevertheless, economic analysts predict that as a group they are likely to enjoy levels of affluence in retirement that far exceed those of their parents. Further, Boomers are projected to be the healthiest, best-educated, and longest-living retirees in history. Thus, they are likely to substantially change ideas about both preparing for retirement and retirement itself.

Critical Thinking

1. How do the retirement plans of Baby Boomers fit in with the stage and life events approaches to middle age that you learned about at the beginning of the chapter?

SUMMARY

Theories of Social and Personality Development

Learning Objective 16.1 How do the views of Erikson and Vaillant differ with regard to generativity?

- Erikson proposed that the primary developmental task of middle adulthood is to acquire a sense of generativity through mentoring younger individuals. Vaillant proposed that the stage of career consolidation precedes Erikson's generativity stage, and that of keeper of the meaning follows it.

Learning Objective 16.2 How do proponents of the midlife crisis and the life events perspective approach middle age differently?

- Many different models of the "mid-life crisis" in middle adulthood have been proposed, but none has been strongly supported by research. A life events approach to understanding the unique stresses of middle age is more useful.

Changes in Relationships and Personality

Learning Objective 16.3 What contributes to the "mellowing" of partnerships in middle adulthood?

- Marital satisfaction is typically higher at mid-life than it is earlier. This higher level of satisfaction appears to be due primarily to a decline in problems and conflicts.

Learning Objective 16.4 What is the family role of middle-aged adults with respect to older and younger generations?

- Middle-aged adults have significant family interactions both up and down the generational chain. The two-way responsibilities can create a mid-life "squeeze," or a "sandwich generation." Middle adults provide more assistance in both directions and attempt to influence both preceding and succeeding generations.

Learning Objective 16.5 How does the grandparent role affect middle-aged adults?

- Most adults become grandparents in middle age. The majority have warm, affectionate relationships with their grandchildren, although there are also many remote relationships. A minority of grandparents are involved in day-to-day care of grandchildren.

Learning Objective 16.6 How might caregiver burden affect a middle-aged adult's life?

- Only a minority of middle-aged adults seem to take on the role of significant caregiver for an aging parent. Those who do report feeling a considerable burden and experience increased depression, particularly if the parent being cared for suffers from some form of dementia. Women are two to four times as likely as men to fulfill the role of caregiver to a frail elder.

Learning Objective 16.7 How do social networks change during middle adulthood?

- Friendships appear to be somewhat less numerous in middle adulthood, although they appear to be as intimate and central to the individual.

Learning Objective 16.8 What is the evidence for continuity and change in personality throughout adulthood?

- The Big Five personality traits and other aspects of personality are correlated across early and middle adulthood. There is evidence for personality change in middle age as well.

Mid-Life Career Issues

Learning Objective 16.9 What factors influence work satisfaction in middle adulthood?

- Job satisfaction is at its peak in middle adulthood, and productivity remains high. But the centrality of the work role appears to wane somewhat, and job satisfaction is less clearly linked to overall life satisfaction than at earlier ages. Research suggests that patterns of work and satisfaction are different for men and women in middle age.

Learning Objective 16.10 What strategies do middle-aged workers use to maintain job performance at a satisfactory level?

- Levels of job performance in middle adulthood are consistent with those at earlier ages, with the exception of work that involves physical strength or reaction time.

Learning Objective 16.11 What are the factors that contribute to career transitions in mid-life?

- Involuntary career changes are associated with anxiety and depression. Even many middle-aged adults who make voluntary career transitions experience negative emotions.

Learning Objective 16.12 How do Baby Boomers differ from previous cohorts with respect to preparation for retirement?

- Middle-aged adults prepare for retirement in several ways, not only by specific planning but also by reducing the number of hours they work.

KEY TERMS

burnout *(p. 471)*
caregiver burden *(p. 469)*
companionate relationships *(p. 468)*
generativity *(p. 462)*
involved relationships *(p. 468)*
life events approach *(p. 463)*
remote relationships *(p. 468)*
role conflict *(p. 464)*

TEST YOURSELF

Theories of Social and Personality Development

16.1 According to Erik Erikson, what is the developmental dilemma faced by middle-aged adults?

a. ego integrity versus despair
b. generativity versus stagnation
c. inferiority versus extraversion
d. role resolution versus identity ambivalence

16.2 Which of the following is *not* generative behavior, as described by Erikson?

a. indulging oneself with the purchase of luxury items
b. adopting a child
c. teaching at the neighborhood community center
d. serving as a leader in one's religious or faith organization

16.3 How does generativity affect later mental health?

a. Generative people are more likely to be satisfied with their lives
b. Generative people are less likely to have dementia.
c. Generative people are more likely to have attachment disorders.
d. Generative people are less likely to commit suicide.

16.4 According to Vaillant, after establishing intimacy, adults

a. look for ways to help others.
b. consolidate their careers.
c. engage in a prolonged period of self-examination.
d. experience a second identity crisis.

16.5 The research suggests that the idea of a mid-life crisis

a. is true for men but not women.
b. is true for women but not men.
c. is true for most American adults.
d. is not true.

16.6 Which of the following best represents the life events approach to middle age?

a. The death of a parent is a traumatic event for all middle-aged adults.
b. Because it fits with the social clock, the death of a parent is rarely stressful.
c. The death of a parent is more stressful for some middle-aged adults than it is for others.
d. The death of a parent precipitates a midlife crisis, because it focuses the middle-aged adult's attention on mortality.

Changes in Relationships and Personality

16.7 Professionals label the middle adulthood cohort the ________ generation, because their family role involves giving assistance and maintaining affectional bonds in both directions in the generational chain.

a. enabling
b. co-dependent
c. sandwich
d. pipeline

16.8 Which of the following is *not* a true statement regarding the "empty nest"?

a. Almost all women experience an identity crisis when their children leave home.
b. Women are more likely to describe the empty nest as a positive event than a negative event.
c. Marital satisfaction often rises among mid-life adults when their children leave home.
d. During the empty next stage, the parental role continues, but the nature of the role is different from what it was when the children were home.

16.9 According to research on grandparent-grandchildren relationships, ________ grandparents may be everyday participants in the rearing of their grandchildren or may create unusually close emotional bonds with them.

a. companionate
b. compassionate
c. enmeshed
d. involved

16.10 The Green children see their grandparents frequently and spend time with them participating in routine, everyday activities such as watching television, visiting relatives, or preparing meals. According to the categories developed by behavioral scientists, this situation most closely resembles which type of relationship?

a. approximal
b. companionate
c. congenial
d. involved

16.11 Which of the following suggestions would *not* help a mother-in-law avoid conflict with her daughter-in-law?

a. Frequently drop in to see your son unexpectedly.
b. Don't criticize your daughter-in-law behind her back.
c. Don't insist on being visited every weekend or holiday.
d. Respect your children's wishes regarding how grandchildren are to be cared for.

16.12 When families negotiate the task of providing care to elderly parents, who is most likely to assume the caregiving role?

a. either the youngest or the oldest child
b. young adult grandchildren who do not have full-time employment or educational roles
c. family members who have the greatest financial resources
d. daughters or daughters-in-law

16.13 Which of the following terms refers to the cumulative negative effects, such as more frequent illness, experienced by caregivers who provide care to frail or demented family members?

a. caregiver's lament
b. caregiver burden
c. filial burden
d. sandwich generation effect

16.14 Which of the following does *not* characterize social networks in middle age, according to research?

a. more friends
b. less frequent interaction among friends
c. relationships as intimate as they were at earlier ages
d. less need for emotional support from individuals outside the family

16.15 Which of the following statements is true about continuity and change in personality?

a. Masculinity and femininity are correlated with self-esteem in adults of all ages.
b. The Big Five personality traits are relatively stable across adolescence and adulthood.
c. Personality consistently changes with age.
d. Traits are gained across adulthood, but traits are not lost.

Mid-Life Career Issues

16.16 Which of the following is the most accurate statement about the way middle-aged women and men experience and deal with work satisfaction?

a. Women and men cite similar sources of job dissatisfaction in middle age: time pressure, boring work, and difficult co-workers.
b. Women who are dissatisfied at work tend to communicate and negotiate with their supervisors and co-workers in order to improve unsatisfactory conditions.
c. Men who are dissatisfied at work tend to complain and encourage discontent among co-workers.
d. Men's work satisfaction is linked to their perceptions about the value and meaning of their work and the quality of relationships they formed on the job.

16.17 Which of the following is the best example of optimization in the "selective optimization with compensation" model of compensatory strategies for job performance?

a. Eric believes that one of his most effective managerial skills is to delegate important tasks and responsibilities to the junior executives in his department.
b. In order to remain up to date in her clinical knowledge and therapeutic techniques, Dr. Smith completes approximately 50 hours of continuing education seminars and workshops each year.
c. When Mrs. Washington anticipates that her busy day will trouble her arthritic knee, she wears her knee brace and takes anti-inflammatory pain medication.
d. Carmen has managed to lose 50 pounds by eating a low-fat, vegetarian diet and following an exercise program recommended by her physician.

16.18 Which of the following is *not* a reason for an involuntary career change?

a. An employee wishes to pursue advancement to the next career level.
b. A departmental reorganization has eliminated certain jobs.
c. New technology means that job skills are out of date.
d. Economic problems have triggered job layoffs.

16.19 What do Baby Boomers expect from retirement?

a. They expect to work at least part-time.
b. They expect to enjoy their leisure time.
c. They expect an increase in income after retirement.
d. They expect to have only 5 years in retirement.

16.20 Many financial analysts claim that some individual Baby Boomers will be in precarious positions during retirement because of all except which one of the following?

a. They have invested in the stock market.
b. They have borrowed to achieve their financial objectives.
c. They expect to have more years in retirement.
d. They have inherited substantial wealth.

PEARSON

mydevelopmentlab Study Plan

Are You Ready for the Test?

Students who use the study materials on MyDevelopmentLab report higher grades in the course than those who use the text alone. Here are three easy steps to mastering this chapter and improving your grade…

Step 1

Take the chapter pre-test in MyDevelopmentLab and review your customized Study Plan.

For the majority of middle-aged women in the United States, having their children leave the family home

- is associated with a significant depression.
- threatens their identity because they lose a core identity role.
- is more likely to be described as a positive than a negative event.
- led to an increase in conflict between the husband and wife.

Step 2

Use MyDevelopmentLab's Multimedia Library to help strengthen your knowledge of the chapter.

Explore: Theories of Social and Personality Development

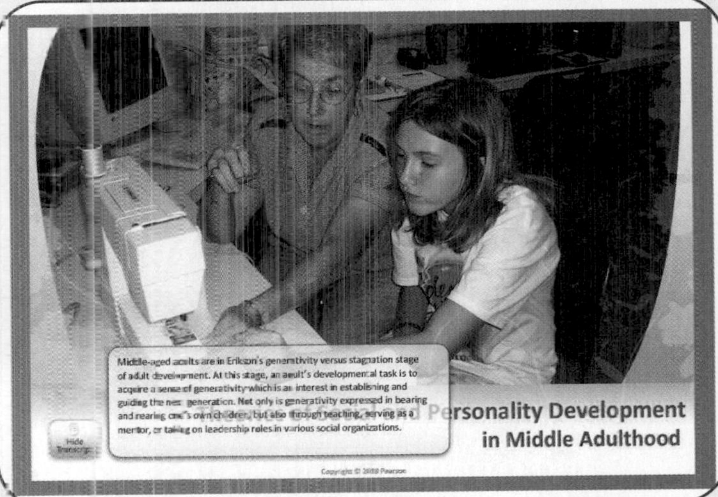

Middle-aged adults are in Erikson's generativity versus stagnation stage of adult development. At this stage, an adult's developmental task is to acquire a sense of generativity which is an interest in establishing and guiding the next generation. Not only is generativity expressed in bearing and rearing one's own children, but also through teaching, serving as a mentor, or taking on leadership roles in various social organizations.
Personality Development in Middle Adulthood
Hide Transcript

Learning Objective 16.1

How do the views of Erikson and Vaillant differ with regard to generativity?

www.mydevelopmentlab.com

continued on the next page

67% of instructors who have used MyDevelopmentLab believe the program has a positive impact on student success rates.

Watch: Changing Parent-Child Relationships

felt lonely a little bit without the children.

Learning Objective 16.4

What is the family role of middle-aged parents with respect to older and younger generations?

Watch: Rude Atmosphere in the Workplace

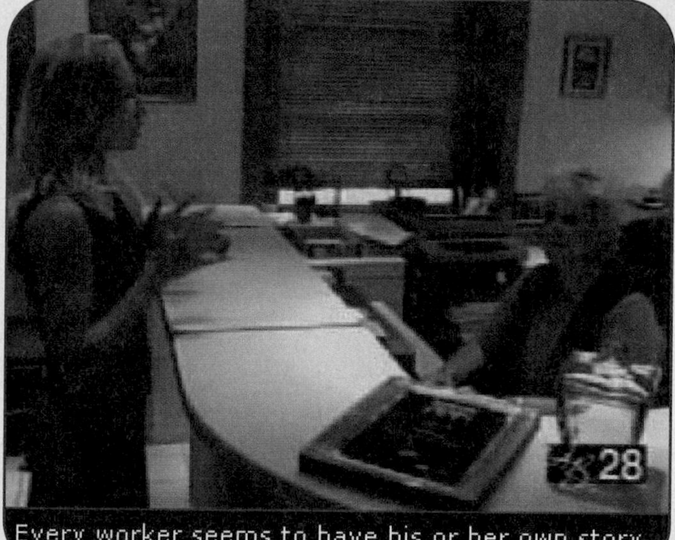
28
Every worker seems to have his or her own story.

Learning Objective 16.9

What factors influence work satisfaction in middle adulthood?

Step 3

Take the chapter post-test and compare your results against the pre-test.

POST-TEST

In order to achieve a sense of *generativity*, an individual

- must bear and raise children of their own.
- must turn outward from a preoccupation with self.
- must develop a strong sense of self and one's own importance.
- must rise to the top of his or her chosen profession.

What Types of Couples Should Be Sanctioned by Society?

During the sexual revolution of the 1960s and early 1970s, young adults often referred to marriage as "just a piece of paper." The real bond between intimate partners was psychological, many asserted, and need not be validated by a government license. This view became the driving force behind a movement away from marriage and toward cohabitation. At the same time, gay rights advocates began to suggest that, if being a couple is essentially a psychological union, then sexual orientation should be irrelevant. That is, they argued, homosexuals are capable of establishing the same kinds of interpersonal relationships as heterosexuals. Therefore, heterosexual unions should not be seen as superior in any way simply because they are legally sanctioned by society.

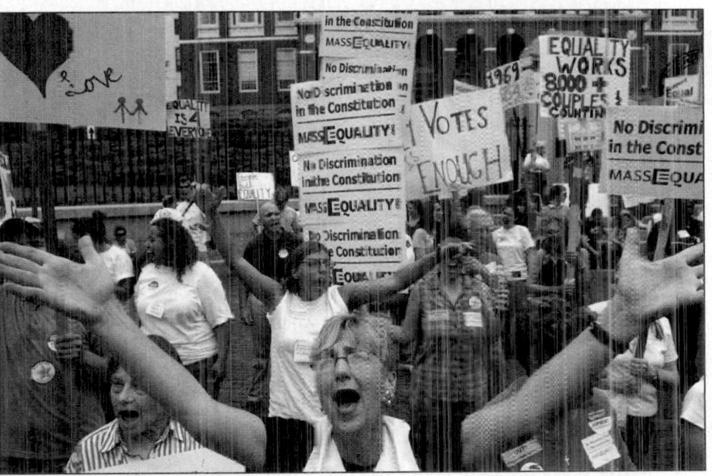

Legislators in the United States have responded to the demands of gay rights advocates to expand marriage to include homosexual couples by creating registered domestic partnerships and civil unions.

However, changing ideas about relationships, instead of causing marriage to disappear, have led to an increase in the number of legal options available to intimate partners. Thus, it seems that both heterosexual and homosexual couples, rather than regarding a license as "just a piece of paper," continue to want to have their relationships recognized by society in some official way. Currently, the notion that same-sex couples should have the same marital rights as opposite-sex couples is at the center of a heated public debate.

Domestic Partnerships and Civil Unions

For quite some time, homosexual rights activists have argued that same-sex couples need a legal means by which to make health insurance and other employee benefits available to their partners. In the absence of a legal relationship, they have pointed out, homosexuals have no right to authorize or terminate medical treatment for an ailing or injured partner. On a more personal level, many gay and lesbian couples, especially those in long-term relationships, want access to a public, socially recognized way to declare their affection for and commitment to each other (Solomon, Rothblum, & Balsam, 2004).

In the first wave of official responses to these concerns, numerous jurisdictions enacted laws that allow both opposite-sex and same-sex couples to enter into *registered domestic partnerships*. Some jurisdictions, including a number of cities in the United States, require employers to provide to domestic partners the same benefits that are available to married employees' spouses. In most cases, domestic partners have fewer rights, privileges, and legal obligations to each other (such as joint responsibility for debts) than do spouses. However, Hawaii and California have domestic partnership laws that grant many of the rights that married couples have, such as the right to file joint state income tax returns, to registered domestic partners.

The *civil union* is a newer type of relationship, created specifically to answer homosexual couples' demands for rights equivalent to those of married heterosexuals. In 2000, the first civil union legislation was passed in the state of Vermont. New Jersey, New Hampshire, and Connecticut have passed similar laws. Many European countries have also enacted civil union legislation. The only legal difference between a civil union and a marriage is that the latter is restricted to male-female couples. Civil unions differ from domestic partnerships in that couples in civil unions have the same rights and obligations as those who are married. Further, those who decide to end their relationships must do so in family court, adhering to the same set of rules that apply to divorce, although the term *dissolution* is used rather than divorce.

The Right-to-Marry Movement

Despite the increasing availability of domestic partnerships and civil unions, many homosexual rights activists say that homosexual couples will never have the same status as heterosexual couples until they are allowed to marry (Patterson, 2004). Advocates of same-sex marriage argue that, unlike domestic partnerships and civil unions, marriage is a legal relationship that is universally recognized. They point out, for instance, that the U.S. Constitution guarantees that marriages performed in one state must be recognized in all others. No such protections exist for domestic partnerships and civil unions. Moreover, many argue that marriage is a civil right and that laws restricting marriage to opposite-sex couples are discriminatory.

Same-sex marriage advocates also claim that allowing homosexual couples to marry may be beneficial to the larger society (Green, 2004). They point to studies showing that married heterosexuals enjoy better mental health than those who are not married. Advocates say that marriage may similarly enhance the mental health of gays and lesbians by providing them with protection against the stresses associated with exposure to homophobia.

The efforts of activists who support same-sex marriage have led to a number of policy changes. In Denmark, the Netherlands, Belgium, Spain, Canada, and South Africa, marital rights have been extended to same-sex couples (Associated Press, 2000). In the United States, judges in several states have ruled that laws restricting marriage to opposite-sex couples are unconstitutional (Peterson, 2004). The most significant of these rulings occurred in Massachusetts in 2003 when the Commonwealth's highest court declared its marriage laws unconstitutional and directed the legislature to pass a new marriage law that was free of gender-based language. As a result, Massachusetts became the only state in the United States in which same-sex marriage is legal. Moreover, efforts to pass an amendment to the state constitution that would have superseded the court's ruling failed by a very slim margin in the state legislature in 2007.

The prevalence of legal relationships among homosexuals may increase in the future, as societal views of homosexuality and the meaning of marriage continue to change.

Opposition to Same Sex Unions

Nevertheless, a clear majority of people in the United States oppose same-sex marriage (Gallup Poll, 2006). Moreover, proposals to legalize same-sex marriage through public referenda have been soundly defeated in several states; likewise, referenda in favor of limiting marriage to opposite-sex couples have passed by substantial majorities (Jones, 2004; O'Sullivan, 2006; Peterson, 2004). Many religious groups, such as the Roman Catholic church, continue to oppose any kind of legal status for homosexual couples because they believe that homosexuality is immoral (United States Conference of Catholic Bishops, 2003).

Other opponents of same-sex marriage have challenged the assumptions underlying the right-to-marry movement. The movement, they claim, inappropriately defines marriage as a public declaration of love between romantic partners. By contrast, these critics say, marriage is a cultural invention that was designed to provide children with a stable environment in which to grow up (Sprigg, 2004; Young & Nathanson, 2003). Therefore, marriage carries the same kinds of legal and familial obligations in societies where parents arrange marriages for their infant children as it does in cultures in which men and women marry because they fall in love. Consequently, these critics say, relationships between individuals who cannot naturally procreate, while they may be intensely loving and may even be legally recognized in some way, will never be true marriages. This argument also asserts that society has an obligation to promote heterosexual relationships by providing spouses with legal protections that are unavailable to others because marriage is the primary structure through which cultural knowledge is transmitted to children (Young & Nathanson, 2003). In other words, they say, marriage is essential to the survival of the culture; thus, experimentation with this critically important institution ought to be avoided.

The activities of groups and individuals who believe that the heterosexual nature of marriage should be preserved have resulted in a number of legislative actions aimed at countering the right-to-marry movement. In 1998, President Bill Clinton signed into law the *Defense of Marriage Act (DOMA)*, a law defining marriage as limited to one man and one woman. Immediately thereafter, 30 states passed similar laws. However, by 2007, the 2003 Massachusetts court ruling had prompted legislators and voters in more than half of the states to pass amendments to their state constitutions that define marriage as involving one man and one woman. Such amendments are pending in several other states as of this writing (stateline.org). In the future, advocates for maintaining traditional marriage hope to amend the U.S. Constitution so that policies regarding who can and cannot marry are uniform throughout the United States.

Your Turn

The influence of the right-to-marry movement has been felt throughout the industrialized world. What is the situation in your area? Use your research skills to find answers to these questions:

- How have policymakers in your area responded to the same-sex marriage movement? (Go to http://www.stateline.org and http://www.gay-civil-unions.com to find out.) How much support does the movement have in your state's legislature and among the citizens of your state?
- What do your classmates and friends think about the idea of same-sex marriage?
- Find out whether your city and/or state has a domestic partnership law. If so, does the law guarantee employer benefits such as health insurance coverage to domestic partners?
- Interview a marriage therapist. What does this professional think about the effects of legal status on partners' commitment to each other, the quality of their relationship, and their development as individuals?

Physical and Cognitive Development in Late Adulthood

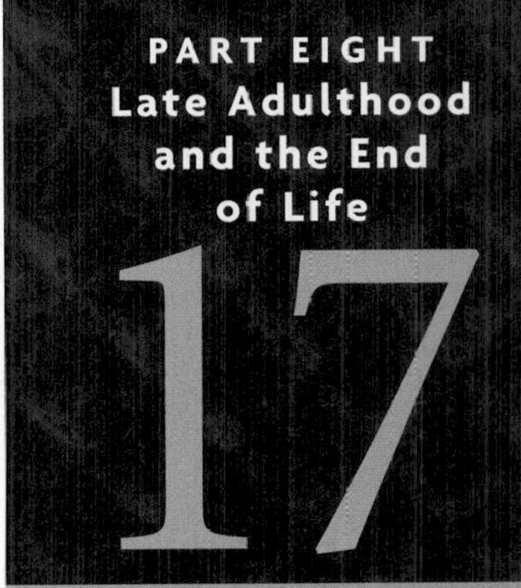

Do you fear growing old? Many people do because they associate old age with failing health, loneliness, decreased mobility, and impaired mental functioning. Certainly, some very real physical declines inevitably happen as we age. But for some people, even very old age is a time of continuing health and enthusiasm for life. Consider Tom Spear, who lived to be almost 104. It was reported that up until his death he played 18 holes of golf three times a week. And then there's Lily Hearst who lived to be 107.

She swam eight laps a day, did yoga, and even taught piano lessons. Spear and Hearst were just two of the more than 1,000 centenarians (people who have lived a century or more) whose longevity has been studied by Dr. Thomas Perls and his colleagues at the New England Centenarian Study, located at Boston University Medical School.

Perls and his colleagues are gathering data about all aspects of centenarians' lives. So far, they have made the following discoveries:

- Most centenarians have a long history of regular physical activity.
- The majority have remained mentally active by pursuing work or hobbies that they enjoy.
- Ninety percent of centenarians are able to live independently until the age of 90, and 75% do so until the age of 95.
- Many centenarians have experienced long periods of deprivation and hardship. Some were born as slaves; others survived the Holocaust.
- Worldwide, women centenarians outnumber men by a ratio of nine to one.
- Very few centenarians are obese, and most are lean, especially the men.
- A substantial history of smoking is rare.
- Centenarians tend to be optimistic and are able to shrug off worries.
- A good sense of humor seems to be a common trait.
- Most centenarians have one or more parents, siblings, or grandparents who also lived a very long time.
- Centenarians tend to enjoy close family relationships, and many of them live within daily visiting distance of family members.

Perls has developed an online quiz that can help you determine your own chances of living to 100 (www.livingto100.com/quiz.cfm). But the scientific study of old age has ramifications that go far beyond our individual concerns about aging. Centenarians are the fastest-growing segment of the population in developed countries. Approximately 60,000 centenarians now live in the United States, for example; if current trends continue, there will be more than 800,000 by the year 2050. In the rest of the world, the odds of reaching age 100 are considerably lower, but the United Nations predicts that improvements in public health will rapidly increase the proportion of centenarians who live in developing countries. The United Nations estimates that there will be more than 3 million centenarians in the world by 2050. Social scientist and politicians alike have raised concerns about the costs—both social and economic—of caring for this unprecedented number of extremely elderly individuals. For these reasons, understanding the aging process and those who seem to defy it is vital to our future.

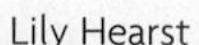
Lily Hearst

Variability in Late Adulthood

The scientific study of aging is known as **gerontology**. For many years, gerontologists thought about old age almost exclusively in terms of decline and loss. However, perspectives on the later years are rapidly changing, and late adulthood is now thought of as a period of tremendous individual variability rather than one of universal decline (Weaver, 1999).

Life Expectancy and Longevity

Learning Objective 17.1
What factors contribute to life expectancy and longevity?

Animal species vary widely in their expected lifespans. Fruit flies, for instance, live for only a few weeks, while giant Galapagos turtles often live to be more than 100 years old. Among humans, cases such as that of Jeanne Calmet, a French woman who lived to be 122 years old, suggest that the maximum lifespan is about 120 years, but this estimate may change as more individuals pass the centenarian mark. Yet there is no denying that death rates increase dramatically when humans reach their 60s, and scientists are learning more about the variables that distinguish individuals who die in their 60s from those who live for 100 years or more.

Trends in Life Expectancy You have probably heard that life expectancy in the industrialized world these days is far greater than in the past. The average male infant who was born in the United States in 1930 lived to be 58, and his female counterpart survived to age 62 (Federal Interagency Forum on Aging-Related Statistics [FIFARS], 2006). By contrast, the average male born in the early years of the 21st century is expected to live 75 years and the average female is expected to live to age 80. However, such predictions are strongly influenced by the fact that the highest death rates in the entire human lifespan are found in the first few years of life. Thus, the increases in average life expectancy that have occurred over the past 7 to 8 decades result from improvements in nutrition, health care, and general living conditions for pregnant women, infants, and young children.

Improvements in these variables among the elderly themselves over the past several decades are responsible for changes in the expected lifespans of adults in their 60s and beyond. For example, in the United States, the average 65-year-old man lives to about age 82, but once a man reaches 85, he is likely to live to be 91 (FIFARS, 2006). Life expectancy among women is even longer. The average 65-year-old woman lives to the age of 85, and the average 85-year-old woman can expect to live to over 92. Because of this sex difference in life expectancy, there are more elderly women than men. Life expectancy varies by racial group as well. In general, 65- to 74-year-old White Americans have longer life expectancies than African Americans in this age group, perhaps because of different rates of cancer and the other diseases you learned about in Chapter 15. However, by age 75, the life expectancies of White American and African American elders are essentially equivalent (NCHS, 2006).

Subgroups Gerontologists divide older adults into subgroups of *young old* (aged 60–75), the *old old* (aged 75–85), and the *oldest old* (aged 85 and over). The oldest old are the fastest-growing segment of the population in the United States, which means that terms such as *octogenarian* (a person in his or her 80s) and *centenarian* (a person over 100 years of age) will be used far more often than in the past. From 1960 to 1994, the over-65 population in the United States doubled, while the over-85 population tripled (FIFARS, 2000). By contrast, the overall U.S. population grew only 45% during the same period. Moreover, demographers project that the over-85 population in the United States will exceed 19 million by 2050. Furthermore, every industrialized country in the world is experiencing this same kind of growth in the elderly population (Century Foundation, 1998). (See No Easy Answers on page 486.)

gerontology the scientific study of aging

NO EASY ANSWERS

The Coming Demographic Crisis

Every industrialized nation in the world will face a demographic crisis in the near future. The reason for this crisis is that an extraordinarily large number of people were born in the years from 1946 until the early 1960s. (In the United States, this cohort is known as the Baby Boomers.) When the people born in this period reached maturity, however, they had many fewer children than their parents did. As a result, when the first wave reaches 65 in 2011, there will be fewer young and middle-aged adult workers for each of them than there are for each of the current cohort of elderly adults (Ball, 2006). Consequently, governments may lack sufficient tax revenues to pay for the many benefits they have guaranteed to senior citizens.

With respect to pension plans, such as the Social Security system in the United States, there are really only two options: decreasing benefits to recipients or increasing taxes on workers. Moreover, economic analysts report that neither option alone will solve the problem. Any workable solution must include both reducing the financial burden of elderly entitlements and generating additional revenues.

Unfortunately, polls suggest that the public is opposed to both options (Public Agenda, Inc., 2007). Voters in the United States overwhelmingly oppose reducing benefits for the current cohort of retired people and are only slightly less opposed to reducing benefits for future retirees. At the same time, most workers believe that their Social Security taxes are already too high but do not want the government to use other funds, such as those generated by income taxes, to pay for Social Security benefits. Moreover, U.S. workers blame the problem on government mismanagement rather than on the mathematical inevitabilities of the demographic crisis. Consequently, lawmakers face a dilemma: A solution must be found, or governments may go bankrupt trying to fulfill their obligations to future elderly citizens. However, any solution politicians impose on voters is likely to be unpopular.

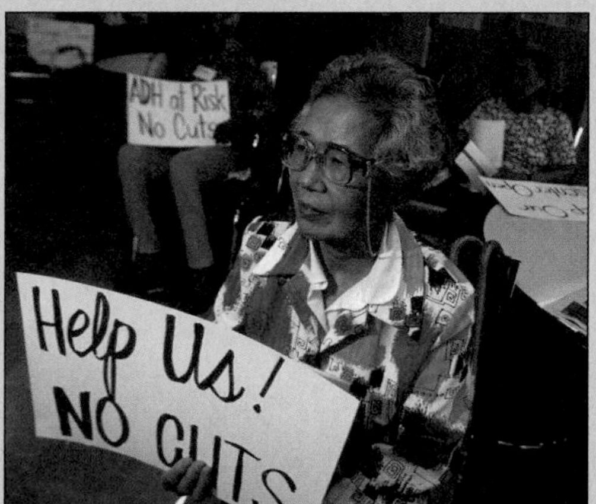

For these reasons, policy makers are looking for ways to make elderly entitlement reform more palatable to voters. For example, one proposal involves workers' taking responsibility for their own retirement income by directing how their Social Security taxes are to be invested. The appeal of this option is that it offers workers more autonomy. However, unlike the current system, it would not include a guaranteed retirement income. Those who invest wisely will enjoy a comfortable retirement; those who are less astute may be left with little or nothing.

Surveys suggest that the public wants both autonomy over retirement investments and a guaranteed income (Public Agenda, Inc., 2007). People would like to be able to invest their own Social Security taxes and retain the present system. Clearly, U.S. voters are reluctant to acknowledge that it is impossible to create a system that offers benefits without costs. As a result, workers in the United States are likely to end up with a solution that is imposed on them by legislators rather than one that represents a public consensus.

Take a Stand

Decide which of these two statements you most agree with and think about how you would defend your position:

1. Having autonomy over how my Social Security taxes are invested is more important to me than having a guaranteed income when I reach retirement age.
2. Having a guaranteed income when I reach retirement age is more important to me than having autonomy over how my Social Security taxes are invested.

Learning Objective 17.2

What variables contribute to individual differences in health among older adults?

Health

Stereotypes may lead you to think that most elders are in poor health. However, the majority of older adults do not suffer from ailments that seriously impair their day-to-day functioning (FIFARS, 2006). Moreover, the inevitable physical declines that are associated with aging do not seem to decrease older adults' satisfaction with their lives.

Self-Rated Health As Figure 17.1 indicates, a majority of older adults across all three age subgroups regard their health as good (FIFARS, 2006). These data contradict stereotypes of old age as a period of illness. However, the proportions of elderly with good health are a great deal lower than the equivalent proportions for young and middle-aged adults. Thus, as you might suspect, health is the single largest factor determining the trajectory of an adult's physical or mental status over the years beyond age 65. As you read more about the prevalence of disability and disease among older adults, keep Figure 17.1 in mind. You will see that these data are a testimony to the emotional resilience of older adults, a majority of whom are able to maintain an optimistic view of themselves and their lives in the face of growing physical challenges.

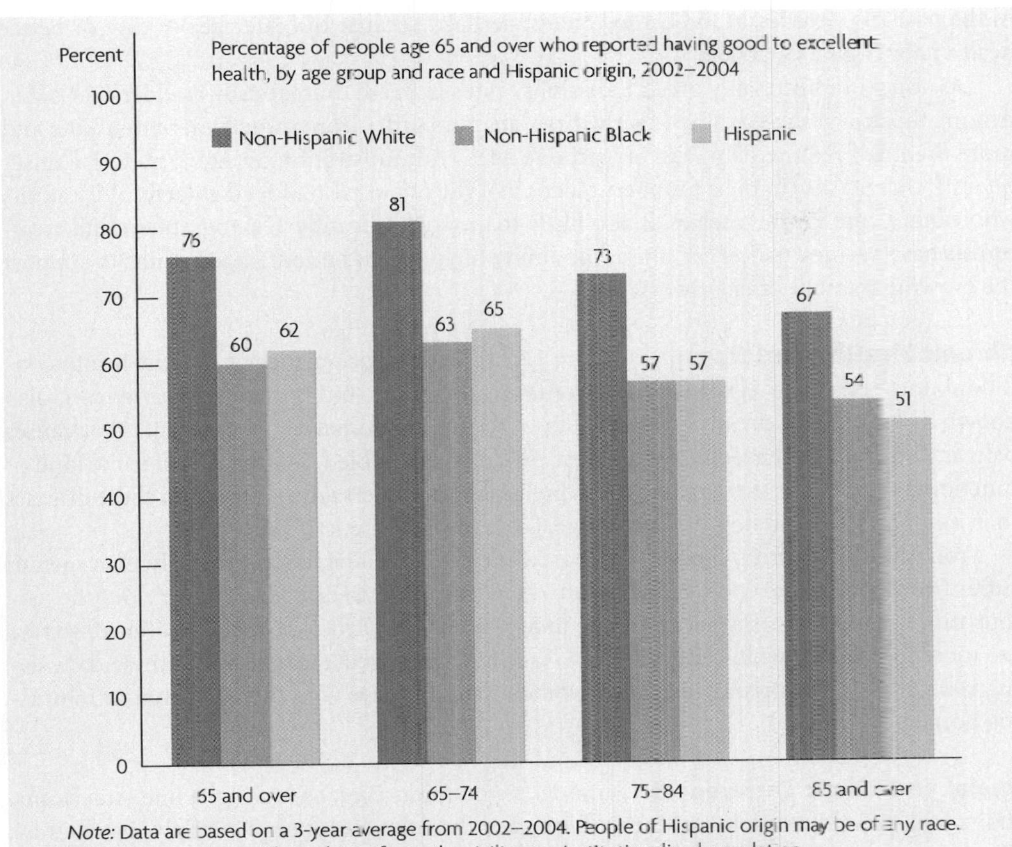

Figure 17.1
Self-Rated Health Status among Older Adults

Most elders rate their health positively.

(*Source*: FIFARS, 2006)

Further, their optimistic view seems to help protect older adults against the long-term effects of serious health threats such as strokes. Researchers have found that elders who rate their health as good, regardless of how an objective observer might rate it, recover more physical and cognitive functions after a stroke than their peers who rate their health more poorly (Hillen, Davies, Rudd, Kieselbach, & Wolfe, 2003). Older adults who are already suffering from one or more chronic diseases at 65 show far more rapid declines than do those who begin late adulthood with no disease symptoms. In part, of course, this is an effect of the disease processes themselves. Cardiovascular disease results, among other things, in restricted blood flow to many organs, including the brain, with predictable effects on an adult's ability to learn or remember. Longitudinal studies show that adults with this disease show earlier declines in all mental abilities (Schaie & Willis, 2005). And, of course, those suffering from the early stages of Alzheimer's disease or another disease that causes dementia will experience far more rapid declines in mental abilities than will those who do not have such diseases.

Limitations on Activities Gerontologists generally define a *disability* as a limitation in an individual's ability to perform certain roles and tasks, particularly self-help tasks and other chores of daily living (Jette, 1996). Daily living tasks are grouped into two categories: **Activities of daily living,** or **ADLs,** include bathing, dressing, and using the toilet. **Instrumental activities of daily living,** or **IADLs,** include activities that are more intellectually demanding, such as managing money.

As you might expect, proportions of older adults with disabilities rise with age. Nearly half of those over 75 report at least some level of difficulty performing some basic daily life activities (NCHS, 2006). But this means that half of these elders do *not* have such problems. To be sure, surveys generally exclude adults who are living in institutions, the vast majority of whom are severely disabled, according to the usual definition. Still, it is important to understand that among the oldest old who live outside of nursing homes, the proportion who have some disability is nowhere near 100%. Even more encouraging is the finding that the rate of disability among the old old and the oldest old has been declining slowly but steadily

activities of daily living (ADLs) self-help tasks such as bathing, dressing, and using the toilet

instrumental activities of daily living (IADLs) more intellectually demanding daily living tasks such as doing housework, cooking, and managing money

in the past few decades in the United States, perhaps because of better health care or better health habits (NCHS, 2006).

As you would probably predict, disability rates increase dramatically as elders get older. Among those over the age of 80, nearly three-quarters suffer from some kind of disability and more than half require help with at least one ADL (Administration on Aging, 2003). Consequently, the increase in their numbers means that the population of **frail elderly**, older adults who cannot care for themselves, is also likely to grow significantly. Demographers and economists have become concerned about the ability of young and middle-aged adults to support the growing number of elderly.

Chronic Health Conditions As Figure 17.2 shows, the prevalence of chronic health conditions increases with age. The most common of these conditions are *hypertension*, also known as high blood pressure, followed by *arthritis*, inflammation in the joints that causes pain and stiffness. Not everyone with these problems is disabled. But the risk of some kind of functional disability is two to three times higher among elders who suffer from these diseases than among those who do not (Verbrugge, Lepkowski, & Konkol, 1991).

You can also see from Figure 17.2 that women are considerably more likely than men to suffer from arthritis, so they are also more often limited in their ability to carry out the various movements and tasks necessary for independent life (Brock et al., 1990). Since women are more likely to be widowed and thus to lack a partner who can assist with these daily living tasks, it is not surprising that more women than men live with their children or in nursing homes.

Racial and Ethnic Differences Among ethnic minorities, as among White Americans, individual variability in old age is the rule rather than the exception. Certainly, averages for life expectancy and disabling conditions such as heart disease differ across groups. For example, the prevalence of arthritis among elderly White Americans is about 58%, whereas 50% of Hispanic Americans and 67% of African Americans have this potentially disabling condition (FIFARS, 2000). Nevertheless, as Figure 17.1 showed, a majority of elders across these three ethnic groups rate their health as good to excellent.

frail elderly older adults whose physical and/or mental impairments are so extensive that they cannot care for themselves

Moreover, everything you have learned so far about the correlations between health habits and health status in adulthood is just as applicable to minorities as to Whites. Thus,

Figure 17.2
Chronic Conditions among Older Adults

Chronic conditions such as these often interfere with older adults' daily lives.

(*Source*: FIFARS, 2006)

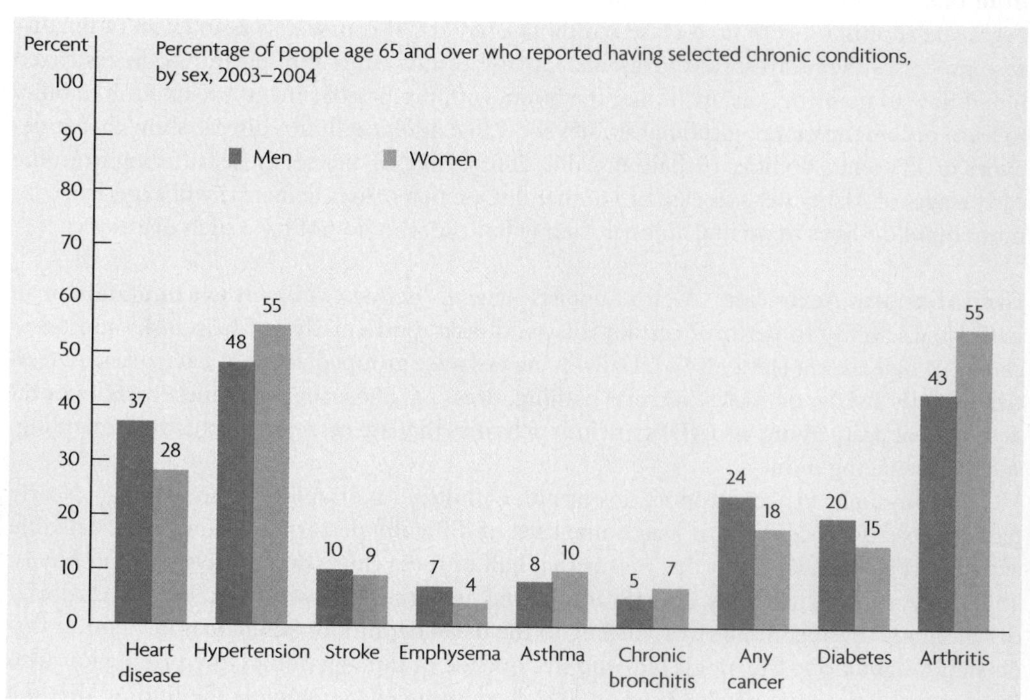

improved diet, increased physical activity, and participation in treatment programs for debilitating chronic ailments can potentially benefit elders of any race or ethnic group.

There are many ways to maintain physical fitness in old age. In China, elderly people often can be found practicing Tai Chi in the early morning.

Heredity Some general tendency to live a long life is clearly inherited (Heun & Bonsignore, 2004). Identical twins are more similar in length of life than are fraternal twins, and adults whose parents and grandparents were long-lived are also likely to live longer (Plomin & McClearn, 1990). Twin studies in Sweden showed that identical twins have more similar illness rates than do fraternal twins (Pedersen & Harris, 1990). Similarly, for the Harvard men in the Grant study sample discussed in Chapter 1, there was a small but significant correlation between health and the longevity of each man's parents and grandparents. Only about a quarter of those whose oldest grandparent had lived past 90 had any kind of chronic illness at age 65, compared with nearly 70% of those whose oldest grandparent had died at 78 or younger (Vaillant, 1991).

Health Habits The same health habits that are important predictors of longevity and health in early adulthood continue to be significant predictors in late adulthood. For example, a 17-year follow-up of participants in the Alameda County epidemiological study who were 60 or over at the start of the study showed that smoking, low levels of physical activity, and being significantly underweight or overweight were linked to increased risk of death over the succeeding 17 years (Kaplan, 1992). Many other large epidemiological studies confirm such connections (e.g., Brody, 1996; Paffenbarger, Hyde, Wing, & Hsieh, 1987).

Perhaps the most crucial variable is physical exercise, which has been clearly linked not only to greater longevity but also to lower rates of diseases such as heart disease, cancer, osteoporosis, diabetes, gastrointestinal problems, and arthritis (Brody, 1995; Deeg, Kardaun, & Fozard, 1996). Good evidence on this point comes from studies in which older adults were assigned randomly to exercise and nonexercise groups (e.g., Blumenthal et al., 1991; Tsang & Hui-Chan, 2003). In these studies, too, those who exercised had better scores on various measures of physical functioning. One such experiment, with a group of adults who were all over age 80, found that muscular strength increased and motor skills improved after only 12 weeks of exercise (Carmeli, Reznick, Coleman, & Carmeli, 2000).

If anything, physical exercise seems to be even more important in the later years than at earlier ages. For example, one investigation used medical records and self-reports of exercise to examine the degree to which physical activity influenced height loss in the elderly (Sagiv, Vogelaere, Soudry, & Shrsam, 2000). Investigators found that study participants who had exercised regularly lost significantly less height over a 30-year period than those who had not exercised. Further, exercise after age 40 seemed to be especially important in preventing height loss.

Finally, a person's eating pattern may turn out to be the most important health habit of all when it comes to aging. Recommendations about the contributions of a healthy diet to one's health are familiar, but recent findings suggest that *calorie restriction* may be equally important. Until recently, studies supporting this view were restricted to animals, but a study published in 2006 (Heilbronn et al., 2006) involved humans who were randomly assigned to follow different kinds of calorie-restricted diets and exercise regimens for 6 months. The study found that biological markers of aging such as fasting improved insulin levels among elders who consumed 25% fewer calories than they needed to maintain their body weight regardless of whether they exercised. A different form of calorie restriction called *alternate day fasting* also appears to moderate the effects of physical aging (Varady & Hellerstein, 2007). Calorie restriction and alternate day fasting are believed to influence aging and longevity by reducing an individual's overall metabolic rate.

Critical Thinking

1. How would you characterize your own chances for a long life based on the genes you have inherited and on your health habits?

Physical Changes

Despite variability in health among the elderly, there are several changes in physical functioning that characterize the late adult years for almost everyone.

Learning Objective 17.3

How does the brain change in late adulthood?

The Brain and Nervous System

If you look back at Table 13.1 (p. 376), you'll see four main changes in the brain during the adult years: a reduction of brain weight, a loss of gray matter, a decline in the density of dendrites, and slower synaptic speed. The most central of these changes is the loss of dendritic density. You'll remember from Chapter 4 that dendrites are "pruned" during the first few years after birth so that redundant or unused pathways are eliminated. The loss of dendrites in middle and late adulthood does not seem to be the same type of pruning. Rather, it appears to be a decrease in useful dendritic connections.

However, research suggests that experience as well as aging is involved in the loss of dendritic density. Neurologists have found that, across the years from 60 to 90, adults with higher levels of education show significantly less atrophy of the cerebral cortex than those who have fewer years of schooling (Coffey, Saxton, Ratcliff, Bryan, & Lucke, 1999). Moreover, the brains of well and poorly educated elderly adults do not differ in areas that are less involved in academic learning than the cerebral cortex is. This finding suggests that education itself is the cause of the reduced atrophying of the cerebral cortex rather than some general factor, such as socioeconomic status, that is coincidentally related to education.

Dendritic loss also results in a gradual slowing of synaptic speed, with a consequent increase in reaction time for many everyday tasks. Neural pathways are redundant enough that it is nearly always possible for a nerve impulse to move from neuron A to neuron B or from neuron A to some muscle cell. Neurologists usually refer to this redundancy as **synaptic plasticity**. But with the increasing loss of dendrites, the shortest route may be lost, so plasticity decreases and reaction time increases.

One final change in the nervous system, about which physiologists disagree, is the loss of neurons themselves. For many years, it was believed that an adult lost 100,000 neurons every day. It now appears that this conclusion, like many such conclusions about primary aging, was based on cross-sectional comparisons that included many older adults who had diseases known to affect brain composition and functioning. Researchers have not yet reached a consensus on just how much loss occurs among healthy aging adults, but most agree that 100,000 neurons per day is a considerable overestimation (e.g., Ivy et al., 1992; Scheibel, 1996).

synaptic plasticity the redundancy in the nervous system that ensures that it is nearly always possible for a nerve impulse to move from one neuron to another or from a neuron to another type of cell (e.g., a muscle cell)

Current estimates are that the brain has perhaps 1 trillion neurons (Morgan, 1992). A loss of 100,000 per day, even if it began at birth and lasted for a lifespan of 100 years, would be only about 4 billion neurons, leaving the vast majority (over 99%) still intact. It is only when the brain loses a significant amount of interconnectivity, which occurs as dendrites decrease in number, that "computational power" declines and symptoms of old age appear (Scheibel, 1992, p. 168). In addition, as you learned in Chapter 13, scientists have only recently discovered that new neurons are produced in some parts of the brain even in adulthood, although the effect of this neuron regeneration is not yet known (Gould et al., 1999).

Learning Objective 17.4

What changes happen in the sensory organ?

The Senses

In Chapter 15, you read about declines in sensory and other physical functions that occur in middle age. Such deficits become larger in late adulthood, and several more serious threats to the health of these systems arise.

Vision In addition to presbyopia (farsightedness), late adulthood can bring other vision defects due to body changes. For example, blood flow to the eye decreases (perhaps as a side effect of atherosclerosis), which results in an enlarged "blind spot" on the retina and thus a reduced field of vision. The pupil does not widen or narrow as much or as quickly as it previously did, which means that the older adult has more difficulty seeing at night and responding to rapid changes in brightness (Kline & Scialfa, 1996).

Hearing aids improve many older adults' quality of life.

In addition, a significant minority of older adults suffer from diseases of the eye that further diminish visual acuity and adaptability. Only about 2% of U.S. adults under age 65 suffer from *cataracts*, a condition in which the lens inside the eye becomes clouded and obscures vision. For those over 65, the rate is roughly twenty times that figure (NHIS, 2002). In addition, only 3% of adults between the ages of 55 and 64 have a limited range of vision, but more than 5 times as many, about 17%, do so after age 85. The leading causes of field restriction are *glaucoma*, a condition in which the pressure inside the eye is increased, and *macular degeneration*, a type of age-related deterioration of the retina. Thus, many older adults must adapt to significant impairments of vision, and the process of adaptation doesn't always go smoothly. Researchers have found that middle-aged adults adjust more easily to the difficulties associated with living with a serious vision impairment (Lindo & Nordholm, 1999). Moreover, vision loss has a greater negative effect on an elderly adult's sense of well-being. Fortunately, many age-related diseases of the eye can be effectively treated with medications and/or surgery.

Hearing You'll recall from Chapter 15 that wear and tear on the auditory system results in some hearing loss (*presbycusis*) beginning in middle adulthood, but these gradual losses don't typically add up to functionally significant loss until late adulthood. Auditory problems, unlike many other disabilities of old age, are more likely to be experienced by men than by women. This sex difference is normally attributed to differential exposure to noise: More men have worked in environments with high levels of noise (at least in current cohorts of older adults in developed countries).

Hearing difficulties in late adulthood have several components: First, there is the loss of ability to hear high-frequency sounds. Both cross-sectional and longitudinal studies suggest that, for the range of sounds used in normal human speech, the loss after age 60 is such that a given sound has to be about 1–2 decibels louder each year for the individual to report that he hears it (Fozard, 1990; Kline & Scialfa, 1996).

Second, most older adults develop difficulties with word discrimination. Even when the sound is loud enough, older adults have more difficulty identifying individual words they have just heard (Schieber, 1992). In addition, many adults over the age of 60 have problems hearing under noisy conditions. The loss of ability to discriminate individual words is even greater in such situations, so large gatherings become increasingly difficult for older adults.

Tinnitus, a persistent ringing in the ears, also increases in incidence with age, although this problem appears to be independent of the other changes just described. Between 12 and 14% of adults over 65 experience this problem (Asplund, 2003), which may be caused by exposure to noise, although that is not well established.

Even mild hearing loss can pose communication problems in some situations. Those with such problems may be perceived by others as disoriented or suffering from poor memory, especially if the person with the hearing loss is unwilling to admit the problem and ask for a comment or instruction to be repeated. Nonetheless, the older adult with a hearing impairment is *not* necessarily socially isolated or unhappy. Mild and moderate hearing losses, even if uncorrected with a hearing aid, are simply not correlated with measures of general social, emotional, or psychological health among elderly adults. It is only severe hearing loss that is associated with an increase in social or psychological problems, including heightened rates of depression (Corso, 1987; Schieber, 1992).

Presbycusis and the other changes in hearing seem to result from gradual degeneration of virtually every part of the auditory system. Older adults secrete more ear wax, which may block the ear canal; the bones of the middle ear become calcified and less elastic; the cochlear

tinnitus persistent ringing in the ears

Figure 17.3
Age-Related Decline in the Sense of Smell

Doty's classic data show a very rapid drop in late adulthood in the ability to identify smells.

(*Source*: Reprinted from "Smell Identification Ability: Changes with Age" by R. L. Doty et al, from *Science*, Vol. 226, p. 1441, 1984, with permission from American Association for the Advancement of Science and Richard L. Doty.)

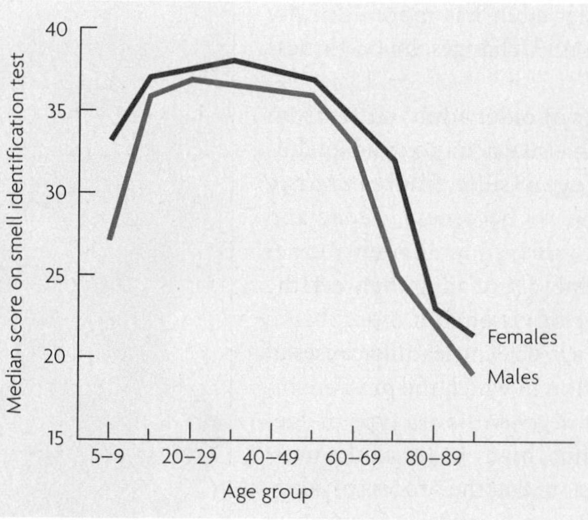

membranes of the inner ear become less flexible and less responsive; and the nerve pathways to the brain show some degeneration (Schieber, 1992).

Taste, Smell, and Touch The ability to taste the four basic flavors (salty, bitter, sweet, and sour) does not seem to decline over the years of adulthood. Taste receptor cells (taste buds) have short lives and are continually replaced (Bornstein, 1992). But other changes in the taste system affect older adults, such as the secretion of somewhat less saliva, producing a sensation of "wooly mouth" for some. Many elders also report that flavors seem blander than in earlier years, leading them to prefer more intense concentrations of flavors, particularly sweetness (de Graaf, Polet, & van Staveren, 1994). But it may well be that this perception of flavor blandness is due largely to a loss of the sense of smell.

The sense of smell clearly deteriorates in old age. The best information comes from a cross-sectional study in which researchers tested nearly 2,000 children and adults on their ability to identify 40 different smells—everything from pizza to gasoline (Doty et al., 1984). As Figure 17.3 reveals, young and middle-aged adults had equally good scores on this smell identification test, but scores declined rapidly after age 60. However, the loss of sensitivity to odors is far greater among elderly men than elderly women (Morgan, Covington, Geisler, Polich, & Murphy, 1997).

Interestingly, like hearing loss, the loss of the sense of smell seems to have an environmental component. Specifically, both men and women who worked in factories (where, presumably, they were exposed to more pollutants) show much greater losses of sense of smell in old age than do those who worked in offices (Corwin, Loury, & Gilbert, 1995).

The skin of elderly adults is also less responsive to cold and heat (Stevens & Choo, 1998). Research suggests that the loss of sensitivity occurs in a pattern that is a reversal of the proximodistal principle of growth you learned about in Chapter 3. In other words, the extremities, usually the feet, are the first body parts to decline in sensitivity. Consequently, elderly people are less able to benefit from the potential comforts associated with physical stimuli. For example, for an elderly person to be able to feel a warm bath, the water temperature may have to be so high that it will burn the skin.

Learning Objective 17.5
How do theories explain biological aging?

Theories of Biological Aging

What are the causes of physical aging? Current theorists agree that the most likely explanation lies in basic cellular processes, which appear to change with age in specific ways that reduce the efficiency of cellular functioning. A number of theoretical variations on this theme have been proposed.

The Hayflick Limit As we pointed out earlier, species vary widely in how long, on average, individuals live. For humans, the maximum lifespan seems to be about 110 or 120 years. These differences have persuaded some biologists that there may be a universal genetic process that triggers age-related declines and limits the lifespan (e.g., Hayflick, 1977, 1987). For turtles, the lifespan is far longer, and for chickens, far shorter.

Advocates of this view support their argument with research demonstrating that cells taken from the embryos of different species and placed in nutrient solution double only a fixed number of times, after which the cell colony degenerates. Human embryo cells double about 50 times; those from the Galapagos tortoise double roughly 100 times; chicken cells double only about 25 times. Furthermore, cells taken from human adults double only about 20 times, as if they had already "used up" some of their genetic capacity. The theoretical proposal that emerges from such observations is that each species is subject to a time limit, known as the **Hayflick limit** (because it was proposed by biologist Leonard Hayflick), beyond which cells simply lose their capacity to replicate themselves (Norwood, Smith, & Stein, 1990).

The genetic limits argument has been strengthened by the recent discovery that each chromosome in the human body (and presumably in other species, too) has, at its tip, a string of repetitive DNA called a **telomere** (Angier, 1992; Campisi, Dimri, & Hara, 1996). Among other functions, telomeres appear to serve as a kind of timekeeping mechanism for the organism. Researchers have found that the number of telomeres is reduced slightly each time a cell divides, so the number remaining in a 70-year-old is much lower than what is found in a child. This raises the possibility that there may be a crucial minimum number of telomeres; when the total falls below that number, disease or death comes fairly quickly.

Genetically Programmed Senescence *Senescence* is the gradual deterioration of body systems that happens as organisms age. **Programmed senescence theory** suggests that age-related physical declines result from species-specific genes for aging. Evolutionary theorists argue that programmed senescence prevents older, presumably less fit, individuals from becoming parents at an age when they are unlikely to be able to raise offspring to maturity (Buss, 1999). The idea is that these aging genes are equipped with some kind of built-in clock that prevents the genes from having an effect when humans are in their reproductive years but switches them on once the reproductive peak has passed.

Repair of Genetic Material and Cross-Linking Another theory of aging focuses on the cells' ability to repair breaks in DNA. Breaks in DNA strands are common events, resulting from unknown metabolic processes. Because the organism is apparently unable to repair all the damage, the theory proposes, the accumulation of unrepaired breaks results over time in a loss of cellular function, and the organism ages (Tice & Setlow, 1985).

A related theory focuses on another cellular process called cross-linking, which occurs more often in cell proteins of older adults than in those of younger adults. **Cross-linking** occurs when undesirable chemical bonds form between proteins or fats. In skin and connective tissue, for example, two proteins called *collagen* and *elastin* form cross-linkages, either between their molecules or within a given molecule. The resulting molecules cannot assume the correct shape for proper function, leading to effects such as wrinkling of the skin and arterial rigidity. (An equivalent process, by the way, occurs in old rubber, which explains why windshield wipers become stiffer over time.)

Free Radicals A third type of cellular process that may contribute to aging relates to the body's ability to deal with free radicals. **Free radicals,** which are molecules or atoms that possess an unpaired electron, are a normal by-product of body metabolism and also arise as a result of exposure to certain substances in foods, sunlight, X-rays, or air pollution. They may also occur more frequently in older than in younger people's bodies because of age-related deterioration of the mitochondria, the cell structures that convert food into energy (Nichols & Melov, 2004). These radicals, especially the subgroup called *oxygen free radicals*, enter into many potentially harmful chemical reactions, resulting in irreparable cellular damage that accumulates with age. For example, oxidation reactions caused by free radicals can damage cell membranes, thereby reducing the cell's protection against toxins and carcinogens.

Research on diet variations points to the possibility that some foods, especially those high in fat and/or food additives such as preservatives, promote the formation of oxygen free radicals, whereas others, referred to as *antioxidants*, inhibit the formation of these radicals or promote chemical processes that help the body defend against them. Foods high in vitamins C and E and beta carotene (vitamin A) all belong in the latter group (Ornish, 1993). Several large epidemiological studies show that people who eat diets high in antioxidants or who take

Hayflick limit the genetically programmed time limit to which each species is theoretically proposed to be subject, after which cells no longer have any capacity to replicate themselves accurately

telomere a string of repetitive DNA at the tip of each chromosome in the body that appears to serve as a kind of timekeeping mechanism

programmed senescence theory the view that age-related declines are the result of species-specific genes for aging

cross-linking the formation of undesirable bonds between proteins or fats

free radicals molecules or atoms that possess an unpaired electron

regular supplements of vitamin E or beta carotene live somewhat longer and have lower rates of heart disease (Blumberg, 1996).

Such findings do not mean that age-related problems such as heart disease and vision loss are *caused* by antioxidant deficiencies. Moreover, some studies suggest that free radicals may not contribute as much to physical aging as researchers once believed (Sanz, Pamplona, & Barja, 2006). Nevertheless, studies showing associations between antioxidants and improvements in health support the general notion that many of the effects of aging are modifiable and perhaps even preventable.

Terminal Drop Some theorists claim that physical and mental declines in old age are actually part of the dying process. For example, the **terminal drop hypothesis** asserts that all adults retain excellent physical and mental function until just a few years before death, at which time there are significant declines in all functions (Kleemeier, 1962). However, longitudinal research suggests that declines in most functions are gradual across late adulthood (Berg, 1996; Birren & Schroots, 1996). Only changes in cognitive functions seem to fit the terminal drop pattern (Johansson et al., 2004).

Learning Objective 17.6

What are the behavioral effects of changes in the various body systems of older adults?

Behavioral Effects of Physical Changes

The great majority of older adults cope effectively with most everyday tasks—buying groceries, managing their finances, reading bus schedules, planning their lives, and so on—despite changes in vision, hearing, and other physical functions (Willis, 1996). Thus, in addition to knowing what these changes are and how they might be explained, it's important to know just how they affect older adults' daily lives.

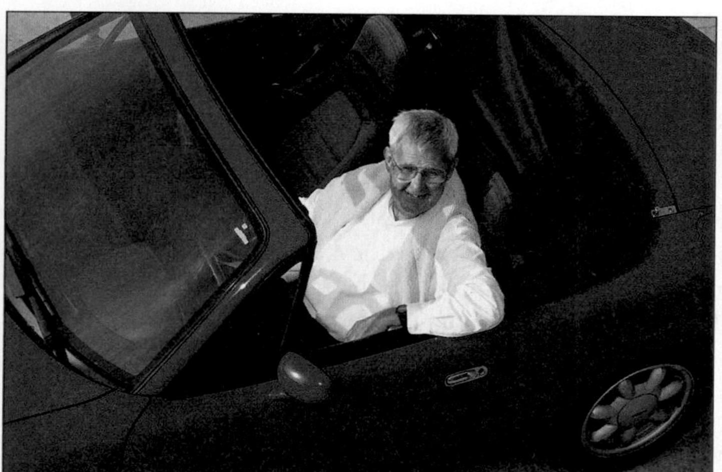

This older man has bought himself a very sporty car and doubtless thinks of himself as still a skillful driver. But it is nonetheless true that many of the physical changes associated with aging will make it harder for him to respond quickly, to see clearly in glare, and to adapt rapidly to changing driving conditions.

General Slowing The biggest single behavioral effect of age-related physical changes is a general slowing down. Dendritic loss at the neuronal level clearly contributes substantially to this general slowing, but other factors are also involved, including arthritic changes in the joints and loss of elasticity in the muscles. Everything takes longer—writing things down, tying one's shoes, and adapting to changes in temperature or changes in light conditions (Schaie & Willis, 2005). Even tasks that involve word skills, which tend to decline very little in accuracy with age, nonetheless are done more slowly (Spieler & Griffin, 2006).

Further, many developmentalists believe that the decline in the speed of nerve impulses is responsible for age-related difficulties in translating thoughts into action. For example, neurologists sometimes assess nervous system functioning by having patients demonstrate a physical action involving a tool, such as hammering. Demonstrating an appropriate hand posture and moving the arm in an appropriate way are taken as indicators of neurological health. Developmentalists have found that healthy individuals in late adulthood make more initial errors than younger adults in trying to carry out such activities (Peigneux & van der Linden, 1999). However, they correct their errors just as quickly as those who are younger. Consequently, neuropsychologists think that general slowing of brain activity interferes with older adults' retrieval of the knowledge they need to accomplish the task and that they use behavioral feedback to compensate for mistakes.

Age-related physical changes add up to really significant differences in functioning in a complex motor activity such as driving. Young adults have more auto accidents than any other age group, primarily because they drive too fast. But adults over the age of 80 have more accidents per miles driven (Market Wire, 2003). Of course, other physical changes beyond general slowing contribute to driving problems in old age. Changes in the eyes mean that older adults have more trouble reading signs at night and adjusting to the glare of oncoming

terminal drop hypothesis the hypothesis that mental and physical functioning decline drastically only in the few years immediately preceding death

headlights. In addition, reduced range of motion in the neck, which often accompanies arthritis, may contribute to automobile accidents involving elderly drivers. Older adults also say that they have more trouble judging their own speed and that the instrument panel is too dim to be seen (Kline et al., 1992). Similarly, they seem to be less able to judge the speed of oncoming traffic when trying to execute turns and carry out other driving maneuvers (Keskinen, Ota, & Katila, 1998). And the general increase in reaction time affects elders' ability to switch attention from one thing to the next or to react quickly and appropriately when a vehicle or obstacle appears unexpectedly.

Changes in temperature sensitivity, together with general slowing, lead to increases in accidental burns. For example, the elderly are more likely to burn themselves when they mistakenly pick up a hot pan while cooking. The neurological message "Put down this pan because it's going to burn your skin" moves from the hand to the brain almost instantaneously in a young or middle-aged adult. In older adults, however, a greater amount of heat is required to initiate the message, the message itself travels to the brain more slowly, and the response from the brain that signals the hand to let go of the pan travels more slowly as well. Consequently, burns are far more common in late adulthood than earlier.

Sleeping and Eating Patterns Another common effect of physical change is a shift in sleep patterns in old age, which occurs among both healthy and less healthy elders. Adults older than 65 typically wake up more frequently in the night and show decreases in rapid eye movement (REM) sleep, the lighter sleep state in which dreaming occurs. Older adults are also more likely to wake early in the morning and go to bed early at night. They become "morning people" instead of "night people" (Cataletto & Hertz, 2005). And because their night sleep is more often interrupted, older adults also nap more during the day in order to accumulate the needed amount of sleep. These changes in sleep and activity patterns are presumed to be related to changes in nervous system functioning.

The ability of the brain to regulate appetite also changes with advancing age. When you eat, your blood sugar rises, resulting in a chemical message to the brain that creates a sensation called **satiety**, the sense of being full. The feeling of satiety continues until your blood sugar drops, at which time another chemical message is sent to the brain that causes you to feel hunger. In older adults, the satiety part of the pattern seems to be impaired (Keene, Hope, Rogers, & Elliman, 1998). As a result, older adults may feel hungry all the time and may overeat. To compensate, they come to rely more on habits such as taking their meals at certain times and eating the same foods every day. Thus, they may seem to be unnecessarily rigid to those who are younger when, in reality, their adherence to a particular eating regime is simply a (perhaps unconscious) way of coping with a physiological change.

Motor Functions The various physical changes associated with aging also combine to produce a reduction in stamina, dexterity, and balance. The loss of stamina clearly arises in large part from changes in the cardiovascular system, as well as from changes in muscles. Dexterity is lost primarily as a result of arthritic changes in the joints.

Another significant change, one with particularly clear practical ramifications, is a gradual loss of the sense of balance (Guralnik et al., 1994; Simoneau & Liebowitz, 1996; Slobounov, Moss, Slobounova, & Newell, 1998). Older adults, who may be quite mobile in their home environments, are likely to have greater difficulty handling an uneven sidewalk or adapting their bodies to a swaying bus. Such situations require the ability to adjust rapidly to changing body cues and the muscular strength to maintain body position, both of which decline in old age. So older adults fall more often. About one-quarter of the young old and more than a third of the old old interviewed for one study reported having fallen in the previous year (Hornbrook, Stevens, & Wingfield, 1994). However, the kinds of activities in which older adults participate affect both the sense of balance and the frequency of falls. Those who practice Tai Chi or who play golf regularly are better able to maintain their balance than their peers who do not engage in these activities (Tsang & Hui-Chan, 2004).

Older adults also have more problems with fine-motor movements (Smith et al., 1999). Such losses are small and gradual with respect to well-practiced skills such as handwriting. However, research suggests that some fine-motor activities, especially those that require

satiety the feeling of fullness that follows a meal

learning a new pattern of movement, may be extremely difficult for elderly people. For example, older adults take far longer than young and middle-aged adults do to learn complex computer mouse skills such as clicking and dragging objects across the screen (Smith, Sharit, & Czaja, 1999).

Sexual Activity Another behavior that is affected by the cumulative physical changes of aging is sexual behavior. You read in Chapter 15 that the frequency of sexual activity declines gradually in middle adulthood. Both cross-sectional and longitudinal data suggest that this trend continues in late adulthood (Marsiglio & Donnelly, 1991; Palmore, 1981).

The decline in the frequency of sexual activity in late adulthood doubtless has many causes (National Institute on Aging [NIA], 2000b). The continuing decline in testosterone levels among men clearly plays some role. The state of one's overall health plays an increasingly larger role with advancing age. For example, blood pressure medication sometimes produces impotence as a side effect; chronic pain may also affect sexual desire. Stereotypes that portray old age as an essentially asexual period of life may also have some effect.

Despite declining frequency, though, more than 70% of adults continue to be sexually active in old age (Bartlik & Goldstein, 2000). Moreover, the physiological capacity to respond to sexual stimulation, unlike other aspects of functioning, appears not to diminish with age. Indeed, some studies suggest that older adults, especially women, are more sexually adventurous; that is, they appear to be more willing to engage in sexual experimentation than young and middle-aged adults (Purnine & Carey, 1998).

Critical Thinking

1. In what ways do you think the behavioral effects of aging influence stereotypes about older adults?

Mental Health

The best-known mental health problems of old age are the **dementias**, a group of neurological disorders involving problems with memory and thinking that affect an individual's emotional, social, and physical functioning. Dementia is the leading cause of institutionalization of the elderly in the United States (FIFARS, 2000). However, depression is also a concern in the late adult years.

Learning Objective 17.7

What is Alzheimer's disease, and how does it differ from other dementias?

Alzheimer's Disease and Other Dementias

Alzheimer's disease (technically known as *dementia of the Alzheimer's type*) is a very severe form of dementia. The early stages of Alzheimer's disease usually become evident very slowly, beginning with subtle memory difficulties, repetitive conversation, and disorientation in unfamiliar settings. Then, memory for recent events begins to go. Memory for long-ago events or for well-rehearsed cognitive procedures, such as simple calculations, is often retained until late in the illness, presumably because these memories can be accessed through many alternative neural pathways (Martin et al., 2003).

Eventually, however, an individual with Alzheimer's disease may fail to recognize family members and may be unable to remember the names of common objects or how to perform such routine activities as brushing her teeth or dressing. Those afflicted with Alzheimer's suffer declines in the ability to communicate, as well as the ability to carry out daily self-care routines. The changes in appetite regulation you read about earlier in this chapter are particularly problematic for those with Alzheimer's, because they can't rely on habit to regulate their eating behavior, as healthy older people do. Left to their own devices, Alzheimer's victims may consume as many as three or four complete meals at one sitting without realizing how much they have eaten. Consequently, their eating behavior must be closely supervised.

Alzheimer's patients also have difficulty processing information about others' emotions, such as facial expressions (Burnham & Hogervorst, 2004). Some have problems controlling their own emotions and display sudden bursts of anger or even rage. Others exhibit an in-

dementia a neurological disorder involving problems with memory and thinking that affect an individual's emotional, social, and physical functioning

Alzheimer's disease a very severe form of dementia, the cause of which is unknown

creased level of dependency and clinginess toward family or friends (Raskind & Peskind, 1992). Research suggests that the incidence of depression among elders with Alzheimer's disease may be as high as 40% (Harwood et al., 2000).

Diagnosing and Treating Alzheimer's Disease Alzheimer's disease can be definitively diagnosed only after a person has died. At autopsy, the brains of Alzheimer's victims are far more likely to contain extensive *neurofibrillary tangles* than are the brains of individuals with other kinds of dementia (Silver, Newell, Brady, Hedley-White, & Perls, 2002). Neurofibrillary tangles are stringy masses of tissue that appear to "clog" connections between neurons. They are typically surrounded by deposits of proteins and other substances called *plaques*.

The difficulty involved in diagnosing Alzheimer's disease is magnified by the fact that nearly 80% of elderly individuals complain of memory problems (Hanninen et al., 1996). As a result, researchers are currently looking for a set of predictors that may distinguish individuals who are in the process of developing Alzheimer's from those who are suffering from the effects of normal aging. A few indicators, such as the syndrome known as *mild cognitive impairment*, show promise (see the Research Report). At present, though, a diagnosis of Alzheimer's disease represents a health professional's best educated guess about the source of an individual's cognitive difficulties.

RESEARCH REPORT

Mild Cognitive Impairment and Alzheimer's Disease

When an elder seeks help for memory problems or difficulties with logical thinking but is clearly not suffering from any kind of dementia, health care professionals usually try to determine whether he should be diagnosed with *mild cognitive impairment (MCI)* or with *age-associated cognitive decline (AACD)*. Criteria for both diagnoses include a gradual decline in cognitive function along with low scores on standardized tests (compared to scores of others of the same age). Physicians must also rule out the possibility that the individual is suffering from a specific disorder that might account for his symptoms (e.g., brain tumor, stroke, depression). Of the two disorders, AACD is the more common, afflicting just under one-third of older adults (Hanninen et al., 1996). By contrast, MCI is found in about 9% of elders (Tervo et al., 2004).

The procedures involved in determining which diagnosis is appropriate can take several weeks to complete and must usually be repeated a few months later. Although this process can be frustrating for elderly adults and their caregivers, getting the correct diagnosis is important because MCI is believed to be a precursor to Alzheimer's disease, while AACD is not. Thus, the prognosis for individuals with MCI is quite different from that for elders with AACD. Moreover, many researchers think that the progression to dementia in patients with MCI can be slowed or even prevented through the use of drugs that have shown to be effective against fully developed Alzheimer's (Amieva et al., 2004; Maruyama et al., 2003).

However, the idea that MCI is an early stage in the development of Alzheimer's disease is somewhat controversial. Some of the strongest evidence in favor of the stage hypothesis has involved brain-imaging and DNA studies. Generally, imaging studies show similar patterns of brain degeneration in individuals with MCI and Alzheimer's disease (Johnson, Vogt, Kim, Cotman, & Head, 2004), and these patterns appear to be distinguishable from those associated with both normal aging and other kinds of dementia. Similarly, defects in the *apolipoprotein E* gene are strongly associated with both Alzheimer's disease and MCI (Tervo et al., 2004).

Additional support for the stage view comes from other kinds of physiological research. For example, individuals with either MCI or Alzheimer's disease differ from normal older adults in the degree to which free-radical-fighting substances such as vitamin C are present in their bloodstreams (Rinaldi et al., 2003). Further, studies examining substances in the cerebrospinal fluid of normal elderly adults, elders with MCI, and Alzheimer's sufferers indicate that both MCI and Alzheimer's are associated with rapid neuronal death (Maruyama et al., 2003).

Despite these compelling lines of evidence, it is abundantly clear that MCI does not inevitably lead to Alzheimer's disease. Longitudinal studies show that only one-third of adults aged 70 and over exhibit full-blown dementia within 2 years of receiving the diagnosis of MCI (Amieva et al., 2004). In addition, the cognitive functioning of many MCI sufferers remains entirely stable for many years.

Scientists on both sides of the debate about the nature of the MCI–Alzheimer's link agree that continued research into the correlation between the two is important to discovering the disease process that underlies the symptoms of Alzheimer's disease. Such research could lead to preventive measures that spare many MCI sufferers from this devastating disease.

Questions for Critical Analysis

1. In what way is research on the links among AACD, MCI, and Alzheimer's disease related to the issues discussed in the No Easy Answers box on p. 486?
2. In your opinion, to what degree might misdiagnosis of AACD as MCI contribute to the finding that only one-third of individuals who are diagnosed with MCI develop full-blown Alzheimer's disease?

A few drugs—such as *galantamine*, a drug that increases the amounts of some neurotransmitters in the brain—appear to slow down progress of Alzheimer's disease (Kurz, Erkinjuntti, Small, Lilienfeld, & Damaraju, 2003). Researchers are also studying the potential uses of anti-inflammatory drugs (e.g., aspirin) in the treatment and prevention of the disease (Nilsson et al., 2003). Experimental studies have shown that training Alzheimer's sufferers to use specific strategies (e.g., making notes in a journal) can to some degree improve their performance of everyday memory tasks such as associating names with faces and remembering to take medication (Lowenstein, Acevedo, Czaja, & Duara, 2004).

Heredity and Alzheimer's Disease Genetic factors seem to be important in some, but not all, cases of Alzheimer's (Heun & Bonsitnore, 2004). Researchers have found a gene on chromosome 19 (apoliprotein E or ApoE) that controls production of a protein that is linked to Alzheimer's disease (Rose, 1995). When errors in the production of this protein occur, the dendrites and axons of neurons in the brain become tangled and, as a result, do not function as efficiently. However, this gene does not act alone. Many other genes combine with ApoE in ways that researchers don't yet fully understand to trigger the onset of the disease (Bertram et al., 2007; Reiman et al., 2007).

Even in families with very high prevalences of Alzheimer's disease, ages of onset are highly variable. In one family study, age of onset ranged from 44 to 67 years, and in another, onset ranged from the early 60s to the mid-80s (Axelman, Basum, & Lannfelt, 1998; Silverman et al., 2005). Morever, there were wide variations in the severity of the disease's behavioral effects and in the length of time the victims lived once they developed Alzheimer's.

Other Types of Dementia Strictly speaking, dementia is a symptom and not a disease, and neurological research indicates that Alzheimer's and non-Alzheimer's dementias involve very different disease processes (Fokin, Ponomareva, Androsova, & Gavrilova, 1997). For example, signs of dementia frequently appear after a person suffers multiple small strokes; in this case, the condition is called **multi-infarct dementia**. The brain damage caused by such strokes is irreversible. However, in contrast to the situation with most cases of Alzheimer's disease, various forms of therapy—occupational, recreational, and physical—can improve victims' functioning (see The Real World on page 500).

In addition, dementia can be caused by depression, cardiovascular disease, metabolic disturbances, drug intoxication, Parkinson's disease, hypothyroidism, multiple blows to the head (frequent among boxers), a single head trauma, some kinds of tumors, vitamin B_{12} deficiency, anemia, or alcohol abuse (Anthony & Aboraya, 1992; Butters et al., 2004; Suryadevara, Storey, Aronow, & Ahn, 2003). Clearly, many of these causes are treatable; indeed, roughly 10% of all patients who are evaluated for dementia turn out to have some reversible problem. So, when an older person shows signs of dementia, it is critical to arrange for a careful diagnosis.

Group Differences in the Rates of Dementia Evidence from research in China, Sweden, France, Great Britain, Italy, the United States, Canada, and Japan, as well as studies involving several U.S. ethnic groups, shows that somewhere between 2% and 8% of all adults over age 65 exhibit significant symptoms of some kind of dementia, and about half of them have Alzheimer's disease (Corrada, Brookmeyer, & Kawas, 1995; Gurland et al., 1999; Rockwood & Stadnyk, 1994). Experts also agree that the rates of all kinds of dementias, including Alzheimer's disease, rise rapidly among people in their 70s and 80s. For instance, studies in the United States suggest that 19% of 75- to 84-year-olds suffer from Alzheimer's disease, while 42% of adults over the age of 85 have it (Alzheimer's Association, 2007).

Base rates of dementia vary despite the consistency of age trends across groups. For instance, Alzheimer's disease is less prevalent in Africa than it is in the United States. Yet, African Americans exhibit higher rates of the disease than White Americans do (Hendrie, 2006). Studies show that such variations are associated with group differences in the frequencies of the genes that contribute to Alzheimer's disease, experiential factors such as education, and in rates of vascular disease (Green et al., 2002).

multi-infarct dementia a form of dementia caused by one or more strokes

Depression

Learning Objective 17.8

What does research suggest about depression among older adults?

The earliest studies of age differences in depression suggested that older adults were at higher risk for this disorder than any other age group, which contributed to a widespread cultural stereotype of the inevitably depressed elder. Certainly, suicide statistics suggest that depression increases in old age (see Figure 17.4). However, the full story on depression in late adulthood is complex.

Prevalence and Risk Factors Estimates of the prevalence of depression depend on how it is defined. Studies by researchers who define depression as the presence of any kind of depressive symptom suggest that as many as a quarter of the old old and the oldest old suffer from depression, a higher proportion than in any other adult group (FIFARS, 2006).

The risk factors for depression among the elderly include inadequate social support, inadequate income, emotional loss (such as following the death of spouse, family, or friends) and nagging health problems. However, the strongest predictor appears to be health status. Across all ethnic and socioeconomic groups, the more disabling conditions older adults have, the more depressive symptoms they have (Black, Markides, & Miller, 1998; Curyto, Chapleski, & Lichtenberg, 1999; FIFARS, 2000; Lam, Pacala, & Smith, 1997; Okwumabua, Baker, Wong, & Pilgram, 1997). Determining the direction of causation in the association between health status and depression is difficult because depression impairs an older adult's ability to respond to therapeutic interventions that might be helpful (Mast, Azar, MacNeil, & Lichtenberg, 2004). To put it differently, elders who have chronic health conditions such as arthritis are more likely to be depressed than their peers who do not, but depression is a risk factor for a poor response to therapy. Thus, for many elderly adults, the link between health and depression becomes circular.

Gender is also a risk factor; depressed women outnumber depressed men two to one among the elderly, just as they do at younger ages (FIFARS, 2000; Forsell & Winblad, 1999). It's not easy, however, to sort out the causes of this difference. For one thing, women appear to be more resilient in response to many life stressors. The death of a spouse, for example, is more likely to lead to depression in a man than in a woman (Byrne & Raphael, 1999; Chen et al., 1999). Such findings suggest that depression in women may more often be the result of an accumulation of everyday stresses, whereas traumatic events are more likely to bring on feelings of depression in men. Another possible explanation is that women are more willing to seek help for depression and, as a result, are more often diagnosed.

There is a fair amount of consistency in findings that elders living in poverty are at higher risk for depression than others (Beekman et al., 1999). Education is also independently related to depression; that is, poorly educated older adults are more likely to be depressed (Gallagher-Thompson, Tazeau, & Basilio, 1997; Miech & Shanahan, 2000). The association between education and depression exists among elderly adults at all levels of income and in all racial and ethnic groups.

Ethnic and Cultural Differences Poverty and education account for only some of the ethnic differences in depression among older adults. Other differences are explained by health status. That is, on average, minorities have poorer health than Whites in the United States; so, on average, most minority groups have higher rates of depression.

For example, the prevalence of depressive symptoms in elderly Native Americans may be as high as 20% (Curyto et al., 1999). You may remember from Chapter 15 that Native Americans suffer from chronic illnesses

Figure 17.4 Gender Differences in Elder Suicide Rates

The data on which this figure is based indicate that suicide rates increase substantially in old age among men but remain fairly stable among women.

(*Sources*: NCHS, 1999a; U.S. Bureau of the Census, 1997.)

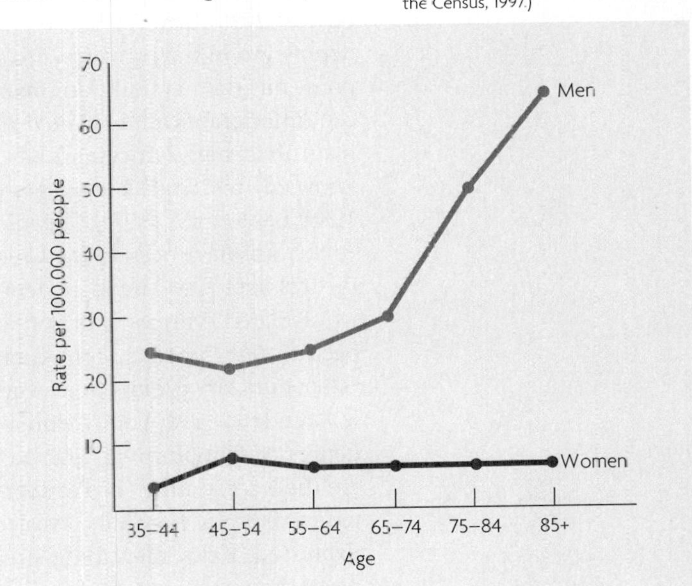

THE REAL WORLD

Computers in Rehabilitation Programs

Although her children and grandchildren had been urging her for a long time to get a computer, at 75, Leta believed that she had little need for one. Then, when she had a mild stroke, Leta learned that computers have uses far beyond the e-mail tools and online information sources that her family had encouraged her to learn how to use. The rehabilitation specialists who helped Leta recover showed her how to use them to overcome the language deficits that had resulted from her stroke. Leta enjoyed the computer training sessions so much that she decided that her family was right about her need for a computer and about their insistence that she join the millions of other senior citizens who have embraced the information age.

Computers are becoming increasingly important in the treatment of neurological disorders affecting the elderly. For example, many stroke victims have problems with comprehending speech and/or speaking themselves. Researchers have found that computerized speech rehabilitation programs are highly effective at improving the language skills of such people (Katz & Wertz, 1997; Waller, Dennis, Brodie, & Cairns, 1998).

Dementia sufferers benefit from computerized rehabilitation as well (Cipriani, Bianchetti, & Trabucchi, 2005). For example, one program trains those with Alzheimer's and other types of dementia to remember routes from one place to another by guiding them through a virtual apartment. Neuropsychologists report that practicing route-learning in the virtual environment improves these patients' ability to remember such routes in their own living environments (Schreiber, Lutz, Schweizer, Kalveram, & Jaencke, 1998; Schreiber, Schweizer, Lutz, Kalveram, & Jaencke, 1999).

Questions for Reflection

1. If you worked in a rehabilitation facility and had to convince a techno-phobic older adult to participate in a computer-based program, what strategies would you use to persuade the patient to give the new technology a try?
2. How do you think computers might be useful to older adults who complain of everyday memory problems?

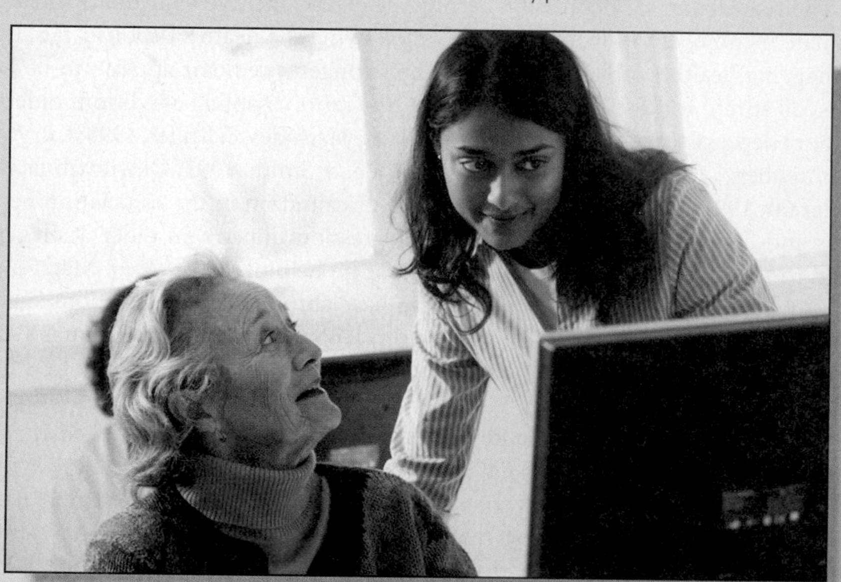

at higher rates than White Americans. Moreover, among depressed Native Americans, those with the greatest number of physical limitations are the most depressed (Curyto et al., 1999).

The rate of depression among Chinese American and Mexican American elders may also be near 20% (Black et al., 1998; Lam et al., 1997). There is an association between health and depression in these groups, just as there is in others (Schneider, 2004). However, researchers point out that, in addition, many older Chinese Americans and Mexican Americans are recent immigrants to the United States and have poor English skills. These factors may help explain their higher incidence of depression, because length of time in the United States and knowledge of English are negatively associated with depression in these groups (Black et al., 1999; Lam et al., 1997). This means that the longer older Chinese Americans and Mexican Americans have been in the United States, and the better integrated they are into the society, the less likely they are to be depressed.

Isolated symptoms of depression, such as insomnia and poor appetite, have sometimes been found to occur more often in elderly African Americans than in elderly members of other minority groups or in elderly White Americans (Blazer, Landerman, Hays, Simonsick, & Saunders, 1998; Foley, Monjan, Izmirlian, Hays, & Blazer, 1999). But the entire cluster of depressive symptoms appears to occur much less often in African Americans, even those who are the least healthy (Leo et al., 1997). For example, a study of several thousand men admitted to veterans' hospitals revealed that African Americans were half as likely as Whites to be depressed (Kales, Blow, Bingham, Copeland, & Mellow, 2000). Furthermore, a study in which researchers reviewed the medical records of several hundred African American and White American patients produced similar findings (Leo et al., 1997). However, in both studies, researchers found that elderly African Americans were more likely than elderly White Americans to suffer from schizophrenia. In addition, among those older African Americans who are depressed, the tendency toward suicidal thoughts may be greater than it is among depressed older White Americans (Leo et al, 1997).

Researchers often attribute low rates of depression in African Americans to underdiagnosis. They hypothesize that African Americans' lack of access to mental health services, reluctance to seek help, and unwillingness to take antidepressant medications contribute to underdiagnosis (Blazer, Hybels, Simonsick, & Hanlon, 2000; Steffens, Artigues, Ornstein, & Krishnan, 1997). However, some developmentalists take issue with this view. These critics point to cultural differences between African Americans and other groups. Specifically, African Americans are more likely to view feelings of sadness as a spiritual issue rather than a mental health problem. Research examining the association between depression and religious beliefs and activities has shown that the tendency to turn to faith and the church for support in times of emotional difficulty is much more prevalent among African Americans than among White Americans (Husaini, Blasi, & Miller, 1999; Steffens et al., 1997). In fact, research demonstrates that religious faith and practice are associated with lower incidences of long-term depression in most ethnic groups, no matter what religion is considered (Braam, Beekman, Deeg, Smit, & van Tilburg, 1997; Idler & Kasl, 1997a; Meisenhelder & Chandler, 2000; Musick, Koenig, Hays, & Cohen, 1998; Tapanya, Nicki, & Jarusawad, 1997). And, as you will learn in Chapter 18, these effects are a result of the way elders think about their lives in religious terms, rather than being due to self-selection or the social support provided to elders by religious institutions.

African American elders may be less likely to be depressed than their peers in other ethnic groups because they may treat sad feelings as a spiritual issue rather than a mental health problem.

Suicide Despite higher rates of depression among women and some minority groups in the United States, elderly White men are more likely to commit suicide than any other group (National Center for Health Statistics, 1999a). Thus, White males are largely responsible for the dramatic increase with age in male suicide illustrated in Figure 17.4. However, the overall age-related pattern of sex differences indicated by the figure exists among minority groups as well (U.S. Bureau of the Census, 1994).

The reasons for this dramatic sex difference are not entirely clear. The loss of economic status through retirement may be more troubling for men than for women in present cohorts of the elderly, because traditional socialization patterns may have led men to equate earnings with self-worth (Mooney, Knox, & Schacht, 2000). Similarly, declining health may cause an elderly man to view himself as a burden on others. The death of a spouse may also be a factor in many male suicides because, as you will learn in Chapter 19, men do not adjust as well as women do to the death of a spouse (Stroebe & Stroebe, 1993). Finally, as is true of younger people, older women attempt suicide more often than older men do, but the men complete the act more often, mostly because they are more likely than women to choose violent methods such as firearms.

Therapy, Medication, and Prevention Therapies for depression are the same for older adults as for those who are younger. Psychotherapy is often recommended, especially interventions that help sufferers develop optimistic thought patterns (NIA, 2000a). However, as with younger adults, therapy appears to be most effective when combined with antidepressant medications ("Depressed elderly," 1999).

Experts point out that appropriate use of antidepressant medications among the elderly is critical. For

Interacting with children may help prevent depression in late adulthood.

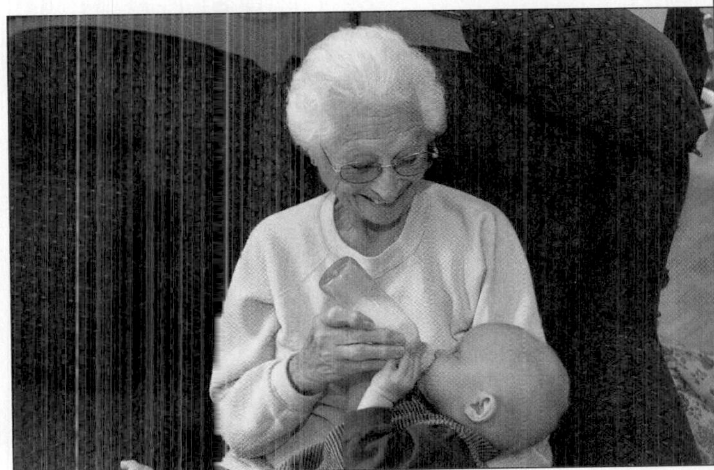

one thing, antidepressants may reduce the effectiveness of the life-sustaining drugs some older adults take (NIA, 2000a). In addition, antidepressants are linked to an increased incidence of falls among the institutionalized elderly. One study found a remarkable 80% increase in falls in a group of more than 2,000 nursing home residents who began taking antidepressants (Bender, 1999).

Social involvement may be important in preventing depression in the elderly. For example, in one study, researchers in Mexico examined how participation in activities with children, such as attending children's plays or helping plan children's parties, might affect nursing home residents' emotions (Saavedra, Ramirez, & Contreras, 1997). Researchers found that such activities significantly improved participants' emotional states. So periodic involvement with children might be an effective way to prevent depression in institutionalized elders.

In addition, research on the connection between religion and depression suggests that caretakers can help elders avoid depression by supporting their spiritual needs. Many older adults need help getting to religious services; those who live in institutions may need to have services brought to them. Declines in vision may mean that an elderly person can no longer read religious books and may deeply appreciate having someone read to him or provide him with recordings. Helping elders maintain religious faith and practice in these ways may be an important key to reducing depression rates.

Critical Thinking

1. Many of the techniques that mental health professionals use require them to empathize with and develop trusting relationships with the people whom they are trying to help. In what ways do the characteristics of Alzheimer's disease and depression interfere with mental health professionals' efforts to do so with those who suffer from them?

Cognitive Changes

Among the young old (aged 65–75), cognitive changes are still fairly small, and these older adults show little or no average decline on a few measures, such as vocabulary knowledge. But the old old and the oldest old show average declines on virtually all measures of intellectual skill, with the largest declines evident on any measures that involve speed or unexercised abilities (Cunningham & Haman, 1992; Giambra et al., 1995).

Learning Objective 17.9
What kinds of memory differences distinguish older and younger adults?

Memory

As you learned in Chapter 15 and as Figure 17.5 shows, forgetfulness becomes more frequent with age (Ponds, Commissaris, & Jolles, 1997). However, it's important to remember that the same basic rules seem to apply to memory processes among both older and younger adults. For both groups, for example, recognition is easier than recall, tasks that require speed are more difficult, and metamemory skills are important to memory function (Olin & Zelinski, 1997). Further, in many studies, older adults achieve scores very similar to those of younger adults on tests of memory accuracy, although they typically take longer to complete memory tasks and make more errors (Babiloni et al., 2004).

Older adults' memories function most proficiently when they are engaged in activities in which they have a great deal of prior experience, but they are still capable of learning new skills and strategies.

Short-Term Memory Function One area in which researchers see significant changes in late adulthood is in short-term, or working, memory capacity (Hester, Kinsella, & Ong, 2004; Jenkins, Myerson, Hale, & Fry, 1999). You should remember from earlier chapters that there is a limitation on the number of items a person can retain in her memory at once. The more pieces of information she has to handle, the more she forgets, and the poorer her performance on memory and other kinds of cognitive tasks. Thus, the more any given cognitive task makes demands on working memory, the larger the decline with age.

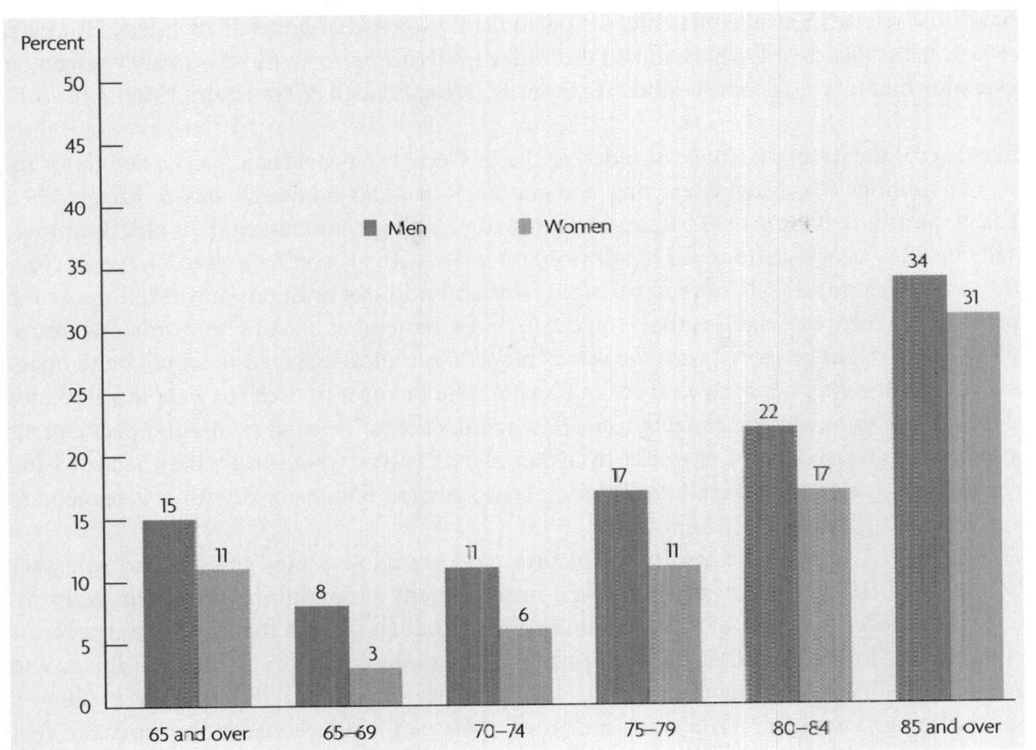

Figure 17.5 Percentage of Older Adults with Moderate to Severe Memory Impairment

The prevalence of memory problems increases as older adults age.

(*Source:* FIFARS, 2006)

A good illustration comes from a study involving a familiar, everyday task—remembering telephone numbers (West & Crook, 1990). Participants were shown a series of seven-digit or ten-digit telephone numbers on a computer screen, one at a time. The participant said each number as it appeared; then the number disappeared from the screen and the participant had to dial the number she had just seen on a push-button phone attached to the computer. On some trials, the participants got a busy signal when they first dialed and then had to dial the number over again. Figure 17.6 shows the relationship between age and the correct recall of the phone numbers under these four conditions.

Notice that there is essentially no decline with age in immediate recall of a normal seven-digit telephone number (the equivalent of what you do when you look a number up in the phone book, say it to yourself as you read it, and then dial it immediately). When the length of the number increases to the ten digits used for long-distance numbers, however, a decline with age becomes evident, beginning at about age 60. And with even a brief delay between saying the number and dialing it, the decline occurs earlier.

However, patterns of age differences are not identical for all memory tasks. For example, older adults typically perform more poorly than younger adults on tasks involving *retrospective memory*, or recalling something in the past (Henry, MacLeod, Phillips, & Crawford, 2004). By contrast, older adults' performance on *prospective memory tasks* (which require individuals to remember to do something in the future) depends on the type of task involved. On laboratory prospective memory tasks that

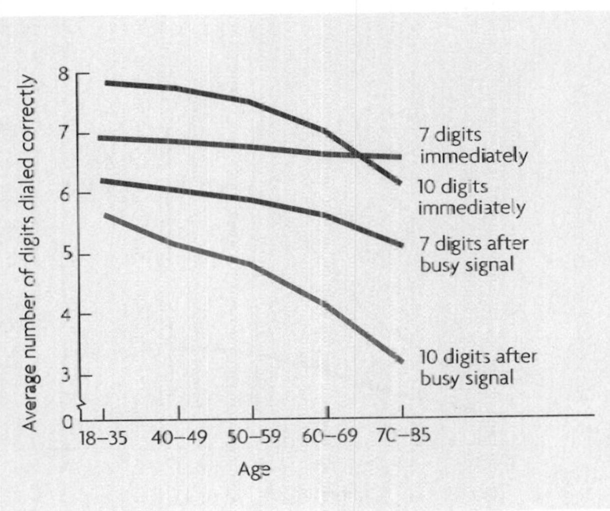

Figure 17.6 West and Crook's Classic Study of Memory across Adulthood

The graph shows the results from West and Crook's classic study of memory for telephone numbers. Notice that there is no loss of memory in middle adulthood for the most common condition: a seven-digit number dialed immediately. But if the number of digits increases or if you have to remember the number a bit longer, some decline in memory begins around age 50 or 60.

(*Source:* West & Crook, 1990, from Table 3, page 524.)

have little relevance to everyday life, young adults do somewhat better than elders. However, several naturalistic studies have shown that older adults outperform those who are younger on everyday memory tasks of this kind (Henry et al., 2004; Rendell & Thomson, 1999).

Strategy Learning A study of older adults in Germany provides a good example of research findings on strategy learning and memory in older adults (Baltes & Kliegl, 1992; Kliegl, Smith, & Baltes, 1990). Researchers tested 18 college students and 19 old, but physically healthy, adults who ranged in age from 65 to 80, with an average age of 71.7 years. Participants were shown sets of pictures of 30 familiar buildings in Berlin and asked to use the pictures to create associations that would help them remember a list of 30 words. For example, a castle might be paired with the word "bicycle." A typical association would be to imagine someone riding a bicycle in front of a castle. The pictures in each set were displayed for different amounts of time, ranging from 20 seconds each to 1 second each. After participants attempted to learn each list of words, the experimenters asked what images they had used and suggested possible improvements. Training sessions were interspersed with test sessions to check on the participants' progress.

Figure 17.7 shows the results for pictures and words presented at 5-second intervals. You can see that the older adults showed improvement after training, but their performance was poorer than that of younger adults. These findings suggest that the learning process simply takes longer for older adults—more time is needed to create the mental image and to link that image up with the word in the list. However, when older adults were allowed more time to associate each picture and word, their performance was more similar to that of younger participants.

Studies comparing younger and older adults' performance on arithmetic tasks involving the "five rule" show a somewhat different pattern, however. The "five rule" is researchers' term for the common finding that arithmetic problems involving multiples of five are easier to work with than problems that do not involve these multiples. For instance, people more quickly say that $5 \times 12 = 50$ is false than that $4 \times 12 = 50$ is false. Researchers have found that the five rule is used far less often by elderly than by younger research participants (Lemaire & Lecacheur, 2004). Such findings suggest that the tendency to apply some cognitive strategies automatically—that is, without giving them much thought—may decline with age.

Everyday Memory One common argument from those who take an optimistic view of the effects of aging on cognitive functioning is that older adults may be able to remember just as well as younger adults but may simply be less motivated to memorize lists of unrelated words given to them by researchers in a laboratory. However, on virtually all everyday tasks—remembering the main points of a story or a newspaper article; recalling movies, conversations, grocery lists, or recipes; recalling the information from a medicine label; remembering whether they did something ("Did I turn off the stove before I left the house?"); or remembering where they heard something (called *source memory*)—older adults perform less well than younger adults (Brown, Jones, & Davis, 1995; Light, 1991; Mäntylä, 1994; Maylor, 1993; Salthouse, 1991; Verhaeghen & Marcoen, 1993; Verhaeghen, Marcoen, & Goossens, 1993). These results have been found in longitudinal as well as cross-sectional studies, particularly after age 70 (Arenberg, 1983; Hultsch, Hertzog, Small, McDonald-Miszczak, & Dixon, 1992; Zelinski, Gilewski, & Schaie, 1993).

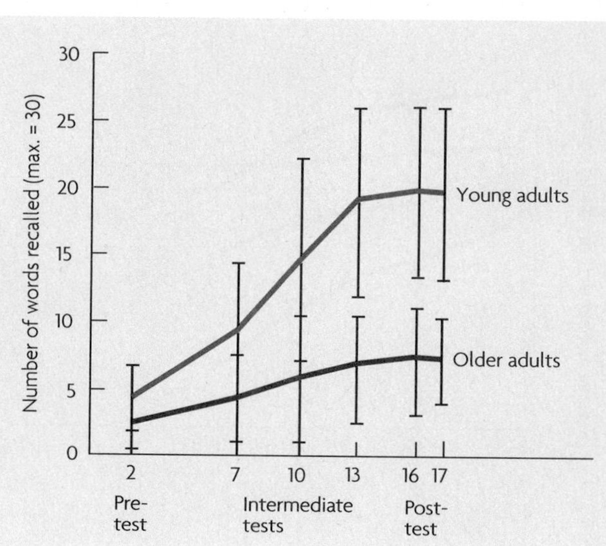

Figure 17.7
Strategic Learning in Later Adulthood

These results from Kliegl's classic study show that older adults can learn complex information-processing skills and improve their performance after training, but they don't gain as much as younger adults do. However, this study also suggests that, given enough time, older adults can learn new strategies.

(*Source*: Adapted from Fig. 2, p. 899, "On the Locus and Process of Magnification of Age Differences During Mneumonic Training" by R. Kliegel, J. Smith, and P.B. Baltes from *Developmental Psychology*, 26. Copyright © 1990 by the American Psychological Association. Adapted with permission.)

Still, task-specific knowledge seems to make a difference among the elderly. For example, older adults who have larger vocabularies outperform peers who know fewer words on tasks involving rapid recognition of words (Kitzan, Ferraro, Petros, & Ludorf, 1999). Researchers know that prior knowledge is the critical factor in such findings, because elders with large vocabularies perform just as poorly as their less knowledgeable peers on tasks involving nonsense words.

Preliminary Explanations How do researchers account for these changes in memory? Neuroimaging studies show that age-related memory decline is associated with changes in the ratio of gray to white matter in the brain (Kramer et al., 2007). In addition, a reduction in the volume of the hippocampus is associated with memory deficits among the elderly.

Functionally speaking, forgetfulness among the elderly may result from the kind of general slowing that you read about earlier in the chapter. Older adults take longer to register some new piece of information, encode it, and retrieve it. Some of the clearest evidence of the important role of speed in memory decline in old age comes from an extensive series of studies by Timothy Salthouse (e.g., Salthouse, 2004).

Salthouse has tested both basic reaction speed and memory or other cognitive skills in adults of various ages. According to Salthouse, a very large portion of the age decline in memory can be accounted for simply by slower reaction times in older adults. He is convinced that the loss of speed occurs at the level of the central nervous system and not in the peripheral nerves. So physiological changes in neurons and the accompanying loss of nerve conductance speed may be the root causes of these changes in memory.

Virtually all experts now agree with Salthouse that loss of speed is a key aspect of the process of memory decline, and studies have shown that quantitative losses in speed of information-processing very strongly predict qualitative changes in memory function (Byrne, 1998; Maylor, Vousden, & Brown, 1999). But most also believe that speed is not the entire explanation. There appear to be other factors as well, such as changes in attention strategies that lead to less effective processing of information (Gottlob & Madden, 1999).

Wisdom and Creativity

Learning Objective 17.10

What do theory and research on wisdom and creativity reveal about cognitive functioning in late adulthood?

Theorists who study cognition in older adults have recently begun to ask whether elders might have some advantages over the young because of their accumulation of knowledge and skills. In other words, older adults might be more wise. Researchers have not yet agreed on a common definition of wisdom, but most authors emphasize that it goes beyond mere accumulations of facts. **Wisdom** reflects understanding of "universal truths" or basic laws or patterns; it is knowledge that is blended with values and meaning systems; it is knowledge based on the understanding that clarity is not always possible, that unpredictability and uncertainty are part of life (Baltes & Kunzmann, 2004).

You may be wondering how researchers measure wisdom. The leading researcher in this field, the late Paul Baltes (1939–2006), devised one useful technique (Baltes & Staudinger, 2000). Baltes presents research participants with stories about fictional characters who are trying to make some major life decision. For example, one dilemma Baltes has used involves a 15-year-old girl who wants to get married. Participants' responses to the stories are judged according to five criteria Baltes hypothesizes to be central to wisdom as it relates to solving practical life problems:

- Factual knowledge
- Procedural knowledge
- Understanding relevance of context
- Understanding relevance of values
- Recognition that it is impossible to know in advance how any decision will ultimately affect one's life

wisdom a cognitive characteristic that includes accumulated knowledge and the ability to apply that knowledge to practical problems of living, popularly thought to be more commonly found in older adults

Seeking advice from an elder who is presumed to be wise is one way young adults act on the belief that those who are older have accumulated knowledge and information that can benefit them.

A person would be judged to be low in wisdom if her response to the 15-year-old's desire to marry were something like "A 15-year-old getting married? That's stupid. I would tell the girl to forget about it until she's older." The answer of a person judged to be high in wisdom would be more complex. A wise person might point out, "There are circumstances when marriage at such a young age might be a good decision. Is she motivated by a desire to make a home for a child she is expecting? Also, the girl might come from a culture where marriage at 15 is quite common. You have to consider people's motivations and their backgrounds to understand their decisions. You also have to know how the person involved views the situation to be able to give advice."

Virtually all theorists who have written about wisdom assume that it is more likely to be found in the middle-aged and the elderly. However, Baltes has found that younger adults perform as well as older adults in response to the fictional dilemma task. In fact, Baltes has found that, rather than age, intelligence and professional experience are correlated with responses to the dilemma task. So, Baltes's research seems to suggest that the popular notion that age and wisdom are associated is probably not true. Wisdom does not appear to be a characteristic of the elderly that distinguishes them from other subgroups of adults.

Critics have suggested that Baltes is simply measuring general cognitive ability rather than what is usually thought of as wisdom. Nevertheless, Baltes's research has produced an important finding about wisdom and old age: In contrast to performance on information-processing tasks such as memorizing nonsense words, performance on wisdom tasks does not decline with age (Baltes & Staudinger, 2000). Moreover, the speed of accessing wisdom-related knowledge remains constant across adulthood, unlike speed of information processing in other domains. In addition, other researchers (e.g., Orwoll & Perlmutter, 1990) have found that those older adults singled out by their peers as wise are more likely to rank high in what Erikson called ego integrity and are more likely to show concern for humanity as a whole.

Enhanced creativity may also be an element of cognition in older adults. As you learned in Chapter 15, some highly creative individuals, especially composers and artists, reach their peak in late adulthood. To describe the potential for creative work in the later years, a leading gerontologist, Gene Cohen, has developed a four-stage theory of mid- to late-life creativity (G. Cohen, 2000). Cohen believes that these phases apply to ordinary people who are more creative than others in their everyday lives as well as to "professional creators" such as composers and artists.

Cohen proposes that at around age 50, creative individuals enter a *reevaluation phase*, during which they reflect on past accomplishments and formulate new goals. The reevaluation process, along with an increasing sense of time limitations, leads to an intensification of the desire to create and produce. During the next stage, the *liberation phase*, individuals in their 60s become freer to create, because most have retired from everyday work. Most are also more tolerant of their own failures, and thus are willing to take risks that they would not have taken at earlier ages. In the *summing-up phase*, creative people in their 70s have a desire to knit their accomplishments together into a cohesive, meaningful story. They begin to view their early accomplishments in terms of how those accomplishments prefigured later achievements. Finally, in the *encore phase*, during the 80s and beyond, there is a desire to complete unfinished works or to fulfill desires that have been put aside in the past.

Critical Thinking

1. Make a list of the people you think of as wise. How old are they? Is old age necessary for wisdom? If not, how do you think wisdom is acquired?

SUMMARY

Variability in Late Adulthood

Learning Objective 17.1 What factors contribute to life expectancy and longevity?

- Developmentalists group the elderly into three subgroups: the young old (60–75), the old old (75–85), and the oldest old (85 and older). The oldest old are the fastest-growing group of the elderly in the United States. Heredity, overall health, current and prior health habits (particularly exercise), and availability of adequate social support influence longevity.

Learning Objective 17.2 What variables contribute to individual differences in health among older adults?

- Most elders view their health status positively. With increasing age, the proportion of elders whose health interferes with activities of living rises. Chronic diseases such as arthritis and hypertension afflict many older adults.

Physical Changes

Learning Objective 17.3 How does the brain change in late adulthood?

- Changes in the brain associated with aging include, most centrally, a loss of dendritic density of neurons, which has the effect of slowing reaction time for almost all tasks.

Learning Objective 17.4 What changes happen in the sensory organ?

- Older adults have more difficulty adapting to darkness and light. Loss of hearing is more common and more noticeable after 65 than at earlier ages. Taste discrimination remains largely unchanged with age, but ability to discriminate smells declines substantially in late adulthood.

Learning Objective 17.5 How do theories explain biological aging?

- Theories of biological aging emphasize the possible existence of genetic limiting mechanisms and/or the cumulative effects of malfunctions within cells.

Learning Objective 17.6 What are the behavioral effects of changes in the various body systems of older adults?

- General slowing alters behavior in old age and makes tasks such as driving more dangerous. Older adults also change their sleeping and eating patterns. Motor abilities decline, causing more accidents due to falls. Sexual activity also decreases in frequency, although most older adults continue to be sexually active.

Mental Health

Learning Objective 17.7 What is Alzheimer's disease, and how does it differ from other dementias?

- Dementia is rare before late adulthood, becoming steadily more common with advancing age. The most common cause of dementia is Alzheimer's disease. It's difficult to diagnose definitively, and its causes are not fully understood.

Learning Objective 17.8 What does research suggest about depression among older adults?

- Mild or moderate depression appears to rise in frequency after age 70 or 75. Serious clinical depression, however, appears not to become more common in old age. Ethnic groups vary in rates of depression, with older African Americans being the least likely to be depressed.

Cognitive Changes

Learning Objective 17.9 What kinds of memory differences distinguish older and younger adults?

- The elderly experience difficulties in a variety of mental processes, which appear to reflect a general slowing of the nervous system and perhaps a loss of working-memory capacity.

Learning Objective 17.10 What do theory and research on wisdom and creativity reveal about cognitive functioning in late adulthood?

- Wisdom and creativity may be important aspects of cognitive functioning in old age.

KEY TERMS

activities of daily living (ADLs) *(p. 487)*
Alzheimer's disease *(p. 496)*
cross-linking *(p. 493)*
dementia *(p. 496)*
frail elderly *(p. 488)*
free radicals *(p. 493)*
gerontology *(p. 485)*
Hayflick limit *(p. 493)*
instrumental activities of daily living (IADLs) *(p. 487)*
multi-infarct dementia *(p. 498)*
programmed senescence theory *(p. 493)*
satiety *(p. 495)*
synaptic plasticity *(p. 490)*
telomere *(p. 493)*
terminal drop hypothesis *(p. 494)*
tinnitus *(p. 491)*
wisdom *(p. 505)*

TEST YOURSELF

Variability in Late Adulthood

17.1 Which of the following is one of the reasons that the United States will face a demographic crisis in the near future?

a. There were many births between 1946 and the early 1960s.
b. Baby Boomers had more children than their parents did.
c. Most Baby Boomers are not astute enough to manage their own finances.
d. Americans value their autonomy.

17.2 Which of the following groups of individuals is growing most rapidly?

a. teenagers
b. the young old (aged 60–75)
c. the old old (aged 75–85)
d. the oldest old (aged 85 and over)

17.3 The most important determinant of the trajectory of an adult's mental health after age 65 is

a. his parents' health.
b. his parents' mental health.
c. his family life.
d. his health.

17.4 Which of the following is the term used by gerontologists to describe a limitation in an individual's ability to perform certain roles and tasks, such as self-care, cooking, or managing money?

a. functional capacity
b. independence boundary
c. disability
d. senility

17.5 Which of the following would *not* be considered an instrumental activity of daily living (or IADL)?

a. bathing
b. dressing
c. boarding an airplane
d. cooking

17.6 Which of the following is *not* one of the reasons that there are more women than men in nursing homes?

a. Women live longer than men.
b. More women than men have restricted movement because of arthritis.
c. Women are more sociable than men.
d. More women than men lack partners who can assist with daily living tasks.

17.7 According to scientists, what is the function of telomeres?

a. They accelerate the onset of dementia.
b. They cause Alzheimer's disease.
c. They facilitate synaptic plasticity.
d. They regulate the aging process.

17.8 If you could recommend one health habit to help older family members reduce their risk of mortality and lower their risk of diseases such as diabetes, arthritis, or cancer, which of the following would be the best recommendation?

a. Eat a diet high in antioxidants.
b. Reduce your amount of nightly sleep.
c. Develop and use a social support network.
d. Get regular physical exercise.

Physical Changes

17.9 Which of the following explains why nerve impulses continue to move from neuron to neuron even when some dendrites have been lost?

a. cross-linking
b. spontaneous generation
c. synaptic plasticity
d. telomeres

17.10 Which of the following is *not* an age-related change to the auditory system that affects older adults?

a. Excess ear wax is secreted.
b. The eardrum gradually collapses.
c. Bones of the middle ear calcify and become less elastic.
d. Nerve pathways to the brain show some degeneration.

17.11 Age-based deterioration in the sense of _________ is least likely to have negative implications for an older adult's health or well-being.

a. smell
b. taste
c. touch
d. vision

17.12 Which of the following theories suggests that aging occurs when atoms or molecules possessing an unpaired electron enter into harmful chemical reactions within the body's cells?

a. cross-linking
b. DNA reparation
c. free radicals
d. programmed senescence

17.13 Which of the following is *not* an effect that is hypothesized to occur as a result of eating a diet high in antioxidants?

a. enhanced sex drive
b. somewhat increased longevity
c. lower rates of heart disease
d. improved vision among patients who have retinal degeneration

17.14 How do sleep patterns change in old age?

a. Older adults go to bed later at night.
b. Older adults wake earlier in the morning.
c. Older adults enter "deep sleep" more easily.
d. Older adults wake up less frequently in the middle of the night.

17.15 How does the frequency of sexual activity change across the lifespan?

a. For men, the frequency of sexual activity increases, but for women, it decreases.

b. The frequency of sexual activity increases with age.

c. The frequency of sexual activity decreases with age.

d. The frequency of sexual activity remains stable.

Mental Health

17.16 How is Alzheimer's disease diagnosed?

a. from an autopsy

b. from a CAT scan when symptoms occur

c. based on behavioral observations at age 60

d. based on memory tests done when symptoms occur

17.17 According to current estimates, what percentage of adults over age 65 in the United States are in a form of institutional care?

a. 48%

b. 24%

c. 16%

d. 4%

17.18 Which of the following is *not* an accurate statement about institutionalization among the elderly?

a. More older men than older women are in nursing homes.

b. Approximately 25% of those over 65 can expect to spend as long as a year in a nursing home.

c. Approximately 40% of current older adults can expect to spend some amount of time in a nursing home before death.

d. Although it is not inevitably so, involuntary institutionalization may be a causal factor in the rapid decline and death of older persons.

17.19 What is the strongest predictor of depression among older adults?

a. family size

b. health status

c. marital status

d. degree of community involvement

Cognitive Changes

17.20 According to experts, which of the following is most responsible for age-based decline in older adults' memory?

a. disease processes, such as atherosclerosis or multi-infarct dementia

b. depression

c. physiological changes in neurons and loss of nerve conductance speed

d. insufficient practice of metamemory skills

17.21 Which of the following is *not* one of Paul Baltes' criteria of wisdom?

a. understanding relevance of context

b. semantic knowledge

c. factual knowledge

d. procedural knowledge

17.22 According to Gene Cohen, at what age are older adults in the encore phase of creativity?

a. 50s

b. 60s

c. 70s

d. 80s

PEARSON

mydevelopmentlab™ Study Plan

Are You Ready for the Test?

Students who use the study materials on MyDevelopmentLab report higher grades in the course than those who use the text alone. Here are three easy steps to mastering this chapter and improving your grade…

Step 1

Take the chapter pre-test in MyDevelopmentLab and review your customized Study Plan.

When people develop cataracts,

- they lose their peripheral vision.

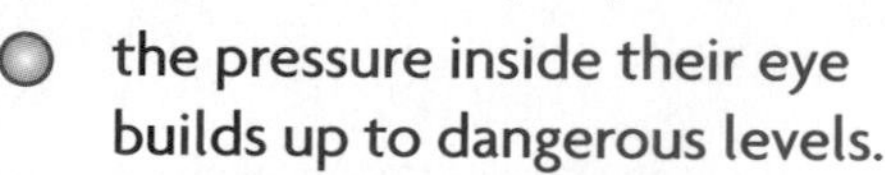

- the pressure inside their eye builds up to dangerous levels.

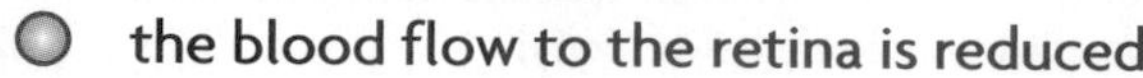

- the blood flow to the retina is reduced.

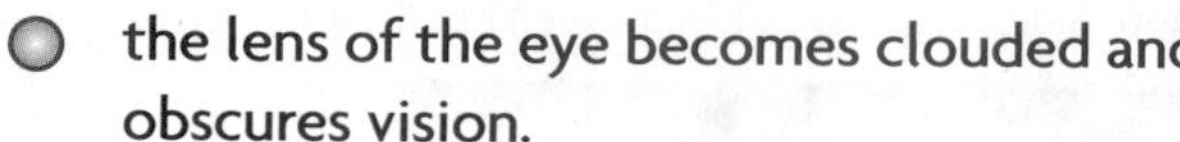

- the lens of the eye becomes clouded and obscures vision.

Step 2

Use MyDevelopmentLab's Multimedia Library to help strengthen your knowledge of the chapter.

Watch: Centenarian

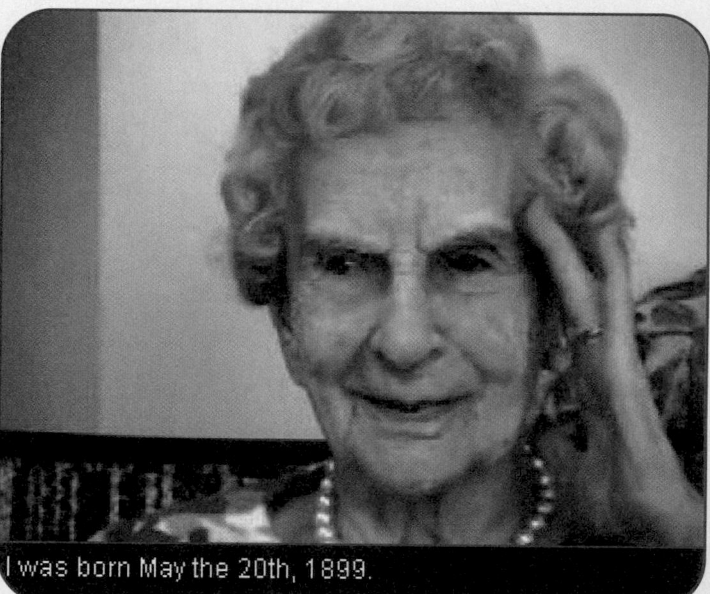

Learning Objective 17.1

What factors contribute to life expectancy and longevity?

www.mydevelopmentlab.com

continued on the next page

"It's good to know that there is a backup education program to help me understand something that I might not grasp completely just from reading the text."

—Bettina (Student), Western Iowa Technical Community College

Explore: Physical Changes in Late Adulthood

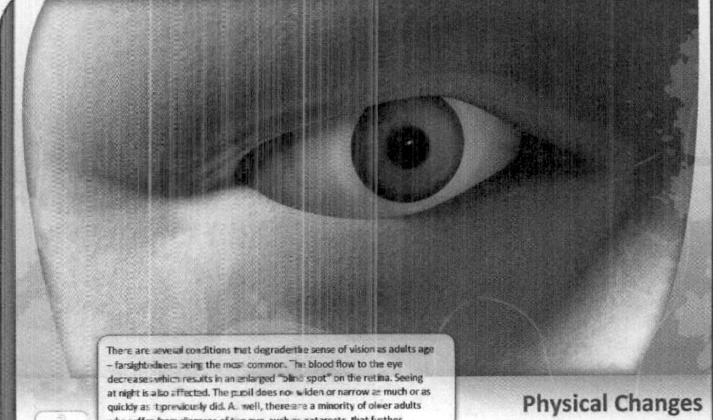

There are several conditions that degrade the sense of vision as adults age – farsightedness being the most common. The blood flow to the eye decreases which results in an enlarged "blind spot" on the retina. Seeing at night is also affected. The pupil does not widen or narrow as much or as quickly as it previously did. As well, there are a minority of older adults who suffer from diseases of the eye, such as cataracts, that further diminish vision.
Hide Transcript
Physical Changes in Late Adulthood

Learning Objective 17.4

What changes happen in the sensory organ?

Watch: Alzheimer's and Dementia

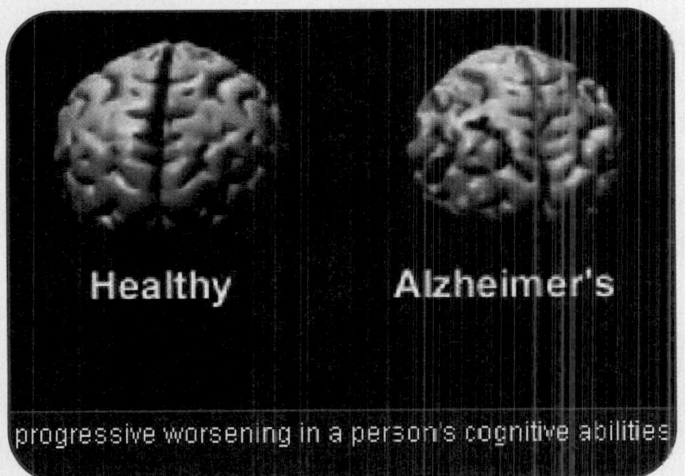

Learning Objective 17.7

What is Alzheimer's disease, and how does it differ from other dementias?

Step 3

Take the chapter post-test and compare your results against the pre-test.

POST-TEST

One characteristic that many centenarians have in common is that they

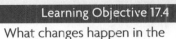

- tend to be optimistic and shrug off worries.
- are often the first-born child in the family.
- are the only ones in their family to have lived to 100 years of age.
- are more likely to be males than females.

18

Social and Personality Development in Late Adulthood

Can you imagine being married for 80 years? Thanks to increases in longevity and the relatively young ages at which couples married in times past, an increasing number of elderly couples are celebrating their 60th, 70th, and even 80th anniversaries. In fact, in the past few years, controversies have arisen regarding which couple should be awarded the marital longevity title.

In June, 2005, the BBC aired a report about a British couple, Percy and Florence Arrowsmith, who were just days away from their 80th anniversary. At the time, the Arrowsmiths had been recognized by the *Guinness Book of World Records* as having the longest marriage on record. Soon afterward, though, reporters affiliated with the French newspaper *Le Monde* challenged the Arrowsmiths' claim to the title. They cited a French couple, Andre and Marguerite Pingaud, who were due to celebrate their 81st anniversary in August of that year. How-

ever, further investigation led to the discovery of an American couple, John and Amelia Rocchio of Providence, Rhode Island, who had celebrated their 82nd anniversary in June, 2005.

The Rocchios were listed in the *Guinness Book of World Records* for a while as having the world's longest running marriage. However, in 2006 they lost the coveted Guinness title to Bill and Eluned Jones of the United Kingdom who attained their 83rd anniversary in January of that year. Subsequently, Guinness officials discovered a Chinese couple who were documented to have been married for 86 years at the time of the husband's death in 2003 and whom they now credit with having the longest marriage.

No doubt there are other such couples who have yet to come to public attention. When they are discovered, it is likely that, like the Rocchios and the Arrowsmiths, they will be more than willing to share their views on how to have a long and happy marriage. According to the Rocchios, compromise and patience are vital. Florence Arrowsmith told BBC reporters that the key is to never go to bed angry, but Percy argued that the secret is two words: "Yes, dear."

No matter how long an older couple has been together, the emotional support that most elders derive from an intimate partnership helps them cope with the loudly ticking biological clock that reminds them every day that they aren't as young as they used to be. As you will learn in this chapter, changes in roles and relationships are perhaps just as significant as physical ones. And for many older adults, these changes are perceived not as losses but as opportunities to create new roles and to make old age a time of personal and social gains.

Theories of Social and Personality Development

If the social and personality changes of young adulthood can be described as "individuation" and those of middle adulthood can be described (more tentatively) as "mellowing," how might the changes of late adulthood be described? Several theorists have hypothesized specific forms of change, but there is little agreement among them and very little information supporting any of their theories.

Erikson's Stage of Ego Integrity versus Despair

Learning Objective 18.1

What does research say about Erikson's stage of ego integrity versus despair?

Erikson termed the last of his eight life crises the *ego integrity versus despair stage*. He thought that the task of achieving **ego integrity**, the sense that one has lived a useful life, began in middle adulthood but was most central in late adulthood. To achieve ego integrity, the older adult must come to terms with who she is and has

ego integrity the feeling that one's life has been worthwhile

been, how her life has been lived, the choices that she has made, the opportunities gained and lost. The process also involves coming to terms with death and accepting its imminence. Erikson hypothesized that failure to achieve ego integrity in late adulthood would result in feelings of hopelessness and despair because there would be too little time to make changes before death.

Developmentalists have essentially no longitudinal or even cross-sectional data to suggest whether older adults are more likely than younger or middle-aged adults to achieve such self-acceptance. What they have instead are a few bits of information suggesting that adults become more reflective and somewhat more philosophical in orientation as they move through the late adulthood years (Prager, 1998). Moreover, those who use their growing capacity for philosophical reflection to achieve a degree of self-satisfaction are less fearful of death. There is also some evidence that older adults are more likely than young and middle-aged adults to respond to thwarted personal goals with feelings of sadness—a hint that the kind of despair Erikson talked about may be more common in old age than earlier in life (Levine & Bluck, 1997).

One aspect of Erikson's theory that has received a great deal of attention from researchers is the notion that the process of **reminiscence**, thinking about the past, is a necessary and healthy part of achieving ego integrity, and thus an important aspect of old age and preparation for death. However, few developmentalists today would say that the only—or even the most important—purpose of these processes is to help an individual prepare for death. Instead, recent research has examined the link between reminiscence and health.

First, it's important to note that adults of all ages engage in reminiscence. In fact, young adults reminisce more often than middle-aged or older adults (Parker, 1999). However, developmentalists hypothesize that young and older adults feel differently about reminiscence because they use it for different purposes (Webster & McCall, 1999). Young adults often use reminiscence to search for tried and true methods of solving problems ("How did I handle this the last time it happened?"). For older adults, reminiscence is more often seen as a way of communicating their experiences to younger individuals.

Among older adults, reminiscence is also the foundation for the process of **life review**, an evaluative process in which elders make judgments about their past behavior (Butler, 1963, 2002). Consistent with Erikson's view of the ego integrity/despair crisis, life review results in both positive and negative emotional outcomes, and the overall balance of positive and negative emotions that results from the life review process is correlated with elders' mental health. Researchers have found that elders whose life reviews produce more regrets over past mistakes and missed opportunities than satisfaction with how they handled problems earlier in life are more prone to depression than those who have generally positive feelings about their lives.

Learning Objective 18.2

What are the main ideas of activity, disengagement, and continuity theory?

Other Theories of Late-Life Psychosocial Functioning

As you learned in Chapter 16, the ideas of Paul Baltes and Margaret Baltes about selection, optimization, and compensation have been important in the study of middle-aged adults' psychosocial functioning. They are often applied to the study of older adults as well. Recall that the Balteses proposed that, as adults get older, they maintain high levels of performance by focusing on their strengths. In this way, they compensate for weaknesses.

Another theoretical perspective on old age focuses on the question of whether it is normal, necessary, or healthy for older adults to remain active as long as possible, or whether the more typical and healthy pattern is some kind of gradual turning inward. The perspective typically referred to as **activity theory** argues that the psychologically and physically healthiest response to old age is to maintain the greatest possible level of activity and involvement in the greatest possible number of roles.

Activity theorists often cite research demonstrating that the most active older adults report slightly greater satisfaction with themselves or their lives, are healthiest, and have the

reminiscence reflecting on past experience

life review evaluative process in which elders make judgments about past behavior

activity theory the idea that it is normal and healthy for older adults to try to remain as active as possible for as long as possible

highest morale (Adelmann, 1994; Bryant & Rakowski, 1992; McIntosh & Danigelis, 1995). The effect is not large, but its direction is consistently positive: More social involvement is linked to better outcomes, even among elders who suffer from disabilities such as arthritis, for whom active social participation may be physically painful (Zimmer, Hickey, & Searle, 1995). Yet it is also true that every in-depth study of lifestyles of older adults identifies at least a few who lead socially isolated lives but remain contented, sometimes because they are engaged in an all-consuming hobby (e.g., Maas & Kuypers, 1974; Rubinstein, 1986).

Some older adults are quite content with solitary lives, but disengagement from social contacts is neither a typical nor an optimal choice for most elders.

An alternative theory on social and personality development in old age is disengagement theory, first proposed as a formulation of the central psychological process for older adults (Cumming, 1975; Cumming & Henry, 1961). In its current form, **disengagement theory** proposes that aging has three aspects:

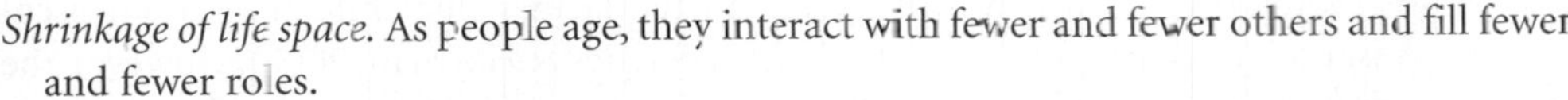

Shrinkage of life space. As people age, they interact with fewer and fewer others and fill fewer and fewer roles.

Increased individuality. In the roles and relationships that remain, the older individual is much less governed by strict rules or expectations.

Acceptance of these changes. The healthy older adult actively disengages from roles and relationships, turning increasingly inward and away from interactions with others.

The first two of these aspects seem largely beyond dispute. What has been controversial about disengagement theory is the third aspect. Advocates argue that the normal and healthy response to the shrinkage of roles and relationships is for the older adult to step back still further, to stop seeking new roles, to spend more time alone, to turn inward. In essence, they propose a kind of personality change, not just a decline in involvement.

disengagement theory the theory that it is normal and healthy for older adults to scale down their social lives and to separate themselves from others to a certain degree

Although it is possible to choose a highly disengaged lifestyle in late adulthood and to find satisfaction in it, such disengagement is neither normal for the majority of older adults nor necessary for overall mental health in the later years. For most elders, some level of social involvement is a sign—and probably a cause—of higher morale and lower levels of depression and other psychiatric symptoms (Zunzunegui, Alvarado, Del Ser, & Otero, 2003).

Finally, **continuity theory** argues that the primary means by which elders adjust to aging is by engaging in the same kinds of activities that interested and challenged them in their earlier years (Atchley, 1989). For instance, an older woman who was an avid gardener during early and middle adulthood, but whose physical condition renders continuation of this hobby impossible, may adjust to her body's decline by limiting her passion for gardening to a small selection of potted plants. Research supports continuity theorists' assertions that aging adults work to maintain consistency of this kind and that achieving such consistency is essential to older adults' maintenance of a positive outlook on the aging process (Agahi, Ahacic, & Parker, 2006; Greenfield & Marks, 2007). Therefore, they argue, providing ways in which elders can meet these continuity goals should be integral to their care.

Critical Thinking

1. Think about the oldest person you know. How are the themes of ego integrity, reminiscence, life review, activity, disengagement, and continuity manifested in their lives?

Individual Differences

Individual differences continue to make substantial contributions to the experiences of older men and women. In fact, research suggests that differences in a variety of behaviors are related to overall quality of life as well as to longevity. Similarly, individual differences in reliance on religious beliefs and institutions as sources of support are also correlated with well-being in late adulthood.

continuity theory the idea that older adults adapt lifelong interests and activities to the limitations imposed upon them by physical aging

Learning Objective 18.3

How is successful aging manifested in the lives of older adults?

The Successful Aging Paradigm

In recent years, one of the dominant themes in gerontology literature has been the concept of successful aging. As defined by authors John Rowe and Robert Kahn, **successful aging** has three components: good physical health, retention of cognitive abilities, and continuing engagement in social and productive activities (Rowe & Kahn, 1997, 1998). An additional aspect of successful aging is an individual's subjective sense of life satisfaction. (Table 18.1 describes these components.) The concept of successful aging is referred to as a *paradigm* because it presents patterns for or examples of such aging. Rather than stating a theory of development, the paradigm of successful aging offers a way of thinking about late adulthood and about how earlier decisions and patterns of behavior contribute to quality of life at later ages.

Staying Healthy and Able By now, you should be familiar with the factors that predict health and physical functioning across the lifespan: diet, exercise, avoidance of tobacco, and so on. In a sense, older people reap the consequences of the behavioral choices they made when younger. Thus, it isn't surprising that making wise choices in this domain during early and middle adulthood, especially with regard to the factors that influence cardiovascular health, is essential to successful aging later in life (Hughes & Hayman, 2007). However, there are also aspects to staying healthy and able that most of us never face until old age.

For example, when an older adult suffers a stroke or fractures a bone, his willingness to engage in the sometimes painful process of rehabilitation significantly affects his degree of recovery. Researchers have found that older adults vary considerably in their willingness to comply with physicians and therapists who supervise their rehabilitation after such events. In both the United States and Japan, an individual's willingness to adopt recovery goals suggested by rehabilitation professionals is related to recovery prospects (Ushikubo, 1998). Those who believe they can reach the suggested goals appear to be the most willing to do the work required for optimal recovery of functioning. Not surprisingly, these individuals gain the most from rehabilitation. So life-long health habits contribute to successful aging, but individuals' responses to the health crises of old age also matter.

Retaining Cognitive Abilities The degree to which elders maintain cognitive functioning seems to be linked to education. As you learned in Chapter 17, those who are the best educated show the least cognitive decline. Moreover, researchers who have examined correlations between cognitive functioning and the other two dimensions of successful aging—physical health and social engagement—have found that verbal intelligence and education are related to both (Jorm et al., 1998). Cross-cultural research has found relationships among cognitive functioning, health, and social involvement in Taiwanese and North American elders, as well as in both Mexican Americans and White Americans (Hazuda, Wood, Lichtenstein, & Espino, 1998; Ofstedal, Zimmer, & Lin, 1999).

Table 18.1 The Components of Successful Aging

Health	Good health must be maintained through middle and late adulthood.
Mental Activity	Engaging in cognitively stimulating activities and hobbies helps older adults retain mental abilities.
Social Engagement	Remaining socially active is critical; social contacts that involve helping others are especially important.
Productivity	Volunteer activities can help by engaging retired adults in productive pursuits.
Life Satisfaction	Older adults must learn how to adjust expectations such that life satisfaction remains high.

successful aging the term gerontologists use to describe maintaining one's physical health, mental abilities, social competence, and overall satisfaction with one's life as one ages

In addition to education, the complexity of the cognitive challenges older adults are willing to take on influences their cognitive functioning. For example, older adults are sometimes reluctant to use new technologies such as automatic teller machines (Echt, Morrell, & Park, 1998). Psychologists suggest that self-stereotyping contributes to this reluctance; older people may believe that they can't learn as well as younger people can, and so they stick to established routines. However, neuropsychologists suggest that such avoidance of learning may actually contribute to cognitive decline (Volz, 2000). New learning, these scientists hypothesize, helps to establish new connections between neurons, connections that may protect the aging brain against deterioration (Calero & Navarro, 2007). Thus, what might be called *cognitive adventurousness*, a willingness to learn new things, appears to be a key component of successful aging.

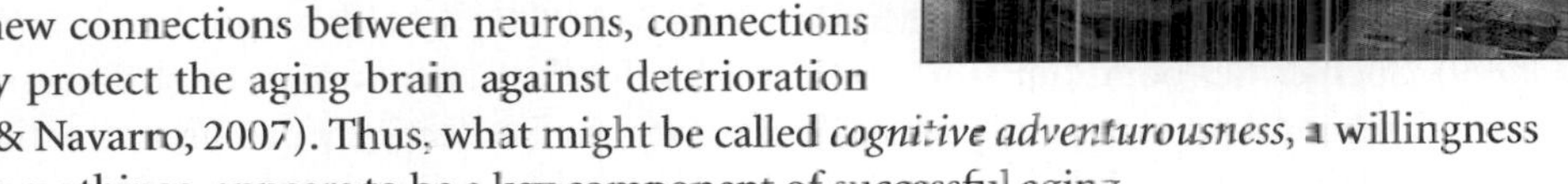

For some elders, remaining productive means venturing into new hobbies such as painting, sculpting, or other artistic pursuits.

Social Engagement Social connectedness and participation in productive activities are clearly important to successful aging. For example, nursing home residents report greater satisfaction with their lives when they have frequent contact with family and friends (Guse & Masesar, 1999). Similarly, among elders with disabilities, frequency of contact with family and friends is associated with reduced feelings of loneliness (Bondevik & Skogstad, 1998).

Social engagement contributes to successful aging because it provides opportunities for older adults to give support as well as to receive it. For example, researchers studying Japanese elders found that a majority of them say that helping others contributes to their own health and personal sense of well-being (Krause, Ingersoll-Dayton, Liang, & Sugisawa, 1999). In addition, researchers who have asked U.S. nursing home residents to rate various quality-of-life factors have found that they often give high ratings to "opportunities to help others" (Guse & Masesar, 1999). Thus, even when elderly adults have significant disabilities, many are still oriented toward helping others and feel more satisfied with their lives when they can do so.

Productivity Contributing to a social network may be one important way of remaining productive, especially for older adults who are retired. **Volunteerism**, or performing unpaid work for altruistic reasons, has been linked to successful aging. Remarkably, a California study involving nearly 2,000 older adults found that mortality rates were 60% lower among volunteers than among nonvolunteers (Oman, Thoresen, & McMahon, 1999) Surveys suggest that 10–30% of older adults are involved in volunteer activities (Chou, Chouw, & Chi, 2003; FIFARS, 2000; Oman et al., 1999).

Some older adults remain productive by venturing into new pursuits, such as taking music lessons, attending college classes, or learning to paint or sculpt. Researchers conducting a study of 36 artists over age 60 asked them to explain how artistic productivity contributed to their successful aging (Fisher & Specht, 1999). Their responses contained several themes: Producing art gave them a purpose in life, opportunities to interact with like-minded peers, and a sense of competence. The older artists also claimed that creating art helped them stay healthy. Thus, creative productivity may help older adults maintain an optimistic outlook, which, as you have learned, contributes to physical and mental health (Flood, 2007).

Life Satisfaction *Life satisfaction*, or a sense of personal well-being, is also an important component of successful aging. What is critical to life satisfaction in almost all cases is an individual's perception of her own situation, which seems to be more important than objective measures (Gana, Alphilippe, & Bailly, 2004). Perceived adequacy of social support and perceived adequacy of income are critical. Moreover, self-ratings of health, rather than objective measures of health, may be the most significant predictors of life satisfaction and morale (Draper, Gething, Fethney, & Winfield, 1999).

volunteerism performance of unpaid work for altruistic motives

Research also suggests that social comparisons—how well an older adult thinks he is doing compared to others his age—are just as important to these perceptions as the older adult's awareness of the changes he has undergone since his younger years (Robinson-Whelen & Kiecolt-Glaser, 1997). A majority of older adults, no matter what their personal circumstances, believe that most others their age are worse off than they are (Heckhausen & Brim, 1997). Developmentalists speculate that the tendency to see others as having more problems is an important self-protective psychological device employed by those who are aging successfully (Frieswijk, Buunk, Steverink, & Slaets, 2004).

Criticisms of the Successful Aging Paradigm Critics of the successful aging paradigm suggest that the concept can be misleading. For one thing, they say, the paradigm has the potential to become a new kind of ageist stereotype, one that portrays older adults who suffer from disabilities as incompetent (Minkler & Fadem, 2002; Scheidt, Humpherys, & Yorgason, 1999). Such critics point out that, for many elderly adults, no amount of optimism, willingness to rehabilitate, social support, or involvement in intellectually demanding activities can moderate their physical limitations. For example, studies comparing the performance of university professors over age 70 and graduate students on reading comprehension tests show that some degree of age-based cognitive decline can be expected, even among very bright, highly experienced, and productive adults (Christensen, Henderson, Griffiths, & Levings, 1997). Thus, these critics claim, the danger of the successful aging paradigm is that it can give the erroneous impression that all the effects of aging are under one's control (Holstein & Minkler, 2003).

Another danger in shifting the focus of gerontology research from disease and decline to quality of life, some critics say, is that medical research still has enormous potential for discovering cures for many of the diseases of old age (Portnoi, 1999). Critics fear that emphasis on successful aging may cause public and institutional support for disease-related research to decline. These critics point out that there is good reason to believe that many conditions now thought to be part of "normal" aging are actually disease processes for which medical science can find effective treatments (Portnoi, 1999).

Nevertheless, critics concede that the successful aging paradigm has broadened gerontologists' approaches to studying old age. Thus, they agree that its influence has been largely positive. Still, keeping their criticisms in mind can help balance the optimism of the successful aging paradigm against the realities of life in late adulthood and the need to continue to encourage researchers to search for treatments for age-related diseases such as Alzheimer's.

Learning Objective 18.4

How does religious coping influence physical and mental health in late adulthood?

Religious Coping

Religion appears to be one factor contributing to individual differences in life satisfaction. Psychologists use the term **religious coping** to refer to the tendency to turn to religious beliefs and institutions in times of stress or trouble. People of all ages use religious coping. However, many developmentalists suggest that religious coping may be particularly important in the later years because of the high number of life stressors—including deaths of loved ones, chronic illnesses, and declining sensory abilities. And elders themselves often cite religious coping as their primary means of managing stress (Barusch, 1999).

Racial and Sex Differences As you learned in Chapter 17, the tendency to turn to religion for comfort is stronger among African Americans than among other racial or ethnic groups. For example, research suggests that participation in church social activities is linked to high reported levels of well-being among older African Americans more than among older White Americans (Bryant & Rakowski, 1992; Husaini et al., 1999; Walls & Zarit, 1991). Further, the negative correlation between church involvement and depressive feelings is stronger for elderly African American cancer sufferers than for their White counterparts (Musick et al., 1998).

religious coping the tendency to turn to religious beliefs and institutions for support in times of difficulty

In addition, some studies suggest that women make more use of religious coping than men do (e.g., Coke, 1992). Most developmentalists attribute this finding to sex differences in social behavior that are observed across the lifespan. However, it's important to keep in mind that, even though the frequency with which religious coping is used may differ according to race and gender, its effects seem to be similar in all racial and ethnic groups and for both women and men. These effects can be best examined by separating the psychological and social components of religious coping.

Strong religious beliefs appear to be positively associated with elders' health and well-being.

Religious Beliefs The psychological component of religious coping involves people's beliefs and attitudes. A number of investigators have examined links between religious beliefs and various measures of well-being among the elderly. For example, elders who place a great deal of emphasis on religious faith worry much less than those who do not (Tapanya et al., 1997). Moreover, associations between religious faith and physical and mental health have been found among older adults of diverse faiths—Christians, Buddhists, Muslims, Hindus, Taoists, and Sikhs—and from a variety of cultures and ethnic groups (Krause et al., 1999; Meisenhelder & Chandler, 2000; Tapanya et al., 1997; Zhou, Yao, & Xu, 2002). Thus, the positive effects of religious faith may have more to do with a general attitude of *spirituality*, a tendency to focus on the aspects of life that transcend one's physical existence, than on any particular set of doctrines or teachings.

The positive effects of religious coping seem to arise from its influence on how elders think about their lives. For example, older adults who rate their religious beliefs as highly important to them are more likely than others to think that their lives serve an important purpose (Gerwood, LeBlanc, & Piazza, 1998). In addition, religious faith seems to provide older adults with a theme that integrates the various periods of their lives. As a result, religious elders are more likely than their nonreligious peers to view old age as a chapter in an ongoing story rather than as primarily a period of loss of capacities. Further, among low-income elders, divine power is viewed as a resource on which those who have little social power in the material world can rely (Barusch, 1999).

Attendance at Religious Services The social aspect of religious coping most often examined by researchers is attendance at religious services. Research suggests that adults who regularly attend such services are physically and emotionally healthier than their nonattending peers (Bosworth, Park, McQuoid, Hays, & Steffens, 2003; Koenig, 2007). Once again, selection effects are possible. However, longitudinal studies suggest that patterns of attendance, as well as the association between attendance and health, change little when elders become ill or disabled (Idler & Kasl, 1997b).

In addition, attendance at religious services is linked to health habits. For example, African American elders with hypertension who attend church regularly are more likely than those who attend intermittently to comply with medical advice regarding blood pressure medication; also, the average blood pressure readings of the regular attendees are lower (Koenig et al., 1998). Researchers don't know why, but one explanation might be that church attendance provides opportunities for interaction with peers who suffer from the same disorder. In the context of such interactions, African American elders may receive encouragement to persevere in dealing with such chronic ailments as hypertension by complying with medical advice.

Elders themselves cite a number of reasons for the benefits of religious involvement. For example, many say that religious institutions provide them with opportunities to help others (la Cour, Avlund, & Schultz-Larsen, 2006; Krause et al., 1999). Intergenerational involvement is another aspect of religious participation often mentioned by older adults. For many, religious institutions provide a structure within which they can pass on their knowledge and beliefs to younger individuals.

Alternative Explanations Researchers must always consider selection effects when examining links between variables such as religious coping and health. There are other possible confounding factors as well. For example, religious and nonreligious elders may differ in personality traits. It seems likely that those with higher levels of extraversion would be the most comfortable in religious social environments—and scientists know that extraversion is correlated with successful aging. Thus, the connection between religious coping and health in old age may be a manifestation of personality rather than an independent effect of religion.

In addition, research on the association between religious faith and health focuses on the personal relevance of spirituality rather than on intellectual acceptance of a set of doctrines. So it may be the intensity and the personal nature of these beliefs, rather than the fact that they have a religious focus, that are responsible for the correlations. In addition, in most research studies, the participants have had longstanding belief and attendance patterns. Thus, these elders may persist in religious faith and involvement, even when they are ill or disabled, because it helps them achieve a sense of continuity of identity. That is, religious involvement may allow an older adult to feel that, despite physical losses, she is still the same person. So it may be that the sense of personal integration that religion provides is responsible for the correlations. Whatever the reasons, the research evidence suggests that supporting the spiritual needs of the elderly may be just as important to maintaining their health and functioning as meeting their physical and material needs.

Critical Thinking

1. How do the concepts of successful aging and religious coping apply to people who have not yet reached late adulthood?

Social Relationships

The social roles older adults occupy are usually different from those they held at younger ages. Nevertheless, most elderly adults cite meaningful social roles as essential to life satisfaction (Bowling et al., 2003). Moreover, there is no doubt that social relationships contribute to older adults' sense of well-being. Both consistency and change characterize social relationships during this period.

Learning Objective 18.5

What are the living arrangements of most elderly people in the United States and in other industrialized countries?

Living Arrangements

Most older adults prefer to live in private homes. However, the physical changes associated with aging mean that some kind of change in living arrangements generally must be made at some point in an individual's later years.

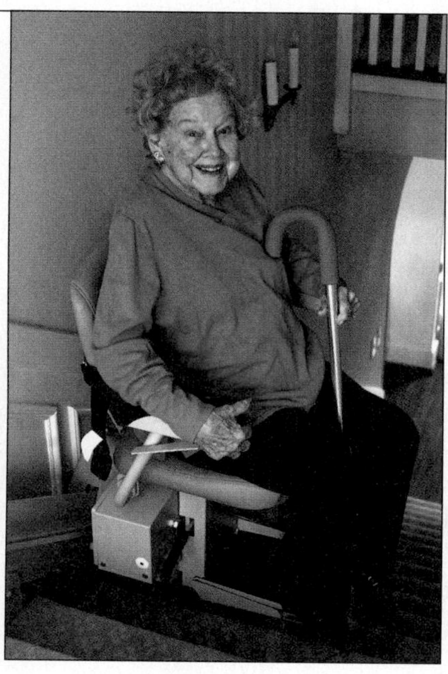

Adapting living spaces to the physical needs of elderly adults helps them achieve the goal of aging in place.

Aging in Place Elders' preference for living in a private home environment has led to a pattern known as **aging in place**. Aging in place involves making modifications to a private residence in response to the changing needs of older adults, such as making doorways wider to accommodate a wheelchair. It may also include hiring a *home health aide* to provide assistance with ADLs when necessary. At the core of the aging-in-place concept is the idea that, as much as possible, changing a normal living environment to meet an elder's needs is preferable to moving the elder to an institutional environment. Aging in place can involve the services of a wide range of health care professionals, including physical therapists and mental health counselors. Researchers have found that comprehensive home-based care of this kind has strong positive effects on elders' physical and mental health (Gill et al., 2002). Thus, compared to institutional

aging in place living in a non-institutional environment, to which modifications have been made to accommodate an older adult's needs

care, aging in place is believed by many to be both more supportive of elders' psychosocial needs and less costly.

For more than 70% of the adults over the age of 65 in the United States, aging in place means living in their own homes either alone or with a spouse, although, as you can see in Figure 18.1, the percentage who live alone varies across ethnic groups (see the Research Report on page 522). Another variation on the aging-in-place theme arises when an older adult moves into the home of a relative, usually one of his own children. In many such cases, modifications must be made to the caretaker's home in order to meet the elder's needs, and a home health aide may be hired to help with ADLs. In the United States, just over 20% of older adults live in the homes of relatives, usually their adult children. Four factors influence an older adult's decision to live with an adult child:

- *Health.* Elders who need help with ADLs because of health problems are more likely to live in the homes of family members than are those who can manage the physical demands of living independently (Choi, 2003).
- *Income.* Those with lower incomes are more likely to live with family members (Choi, 1991).
- *Adult children's characteristics.* Elders with several daughters are more likely than those with few daughters to live with grown children (Soldo, Wolf, & Agree, 1990). Married adults are more likely than those who are single to take in their aging parents (Choi, 2003).
- *Ethnicity.* Hispanic American, African American, and Asian American elders are more likely to live with relatives than are those in other groups (Choi, 2003; FIFARS, 2000).

Residential Options for Older Adults Older adults who are no longer able to live independently or who don't want to deal with the demands of caring for a home often turn to one of several residential options. An *independent living community* is an apartment complex or housing development in which all the residents are over a certain age, typically 55 or 60. In most such communities, residents join together for a variety of social activities and

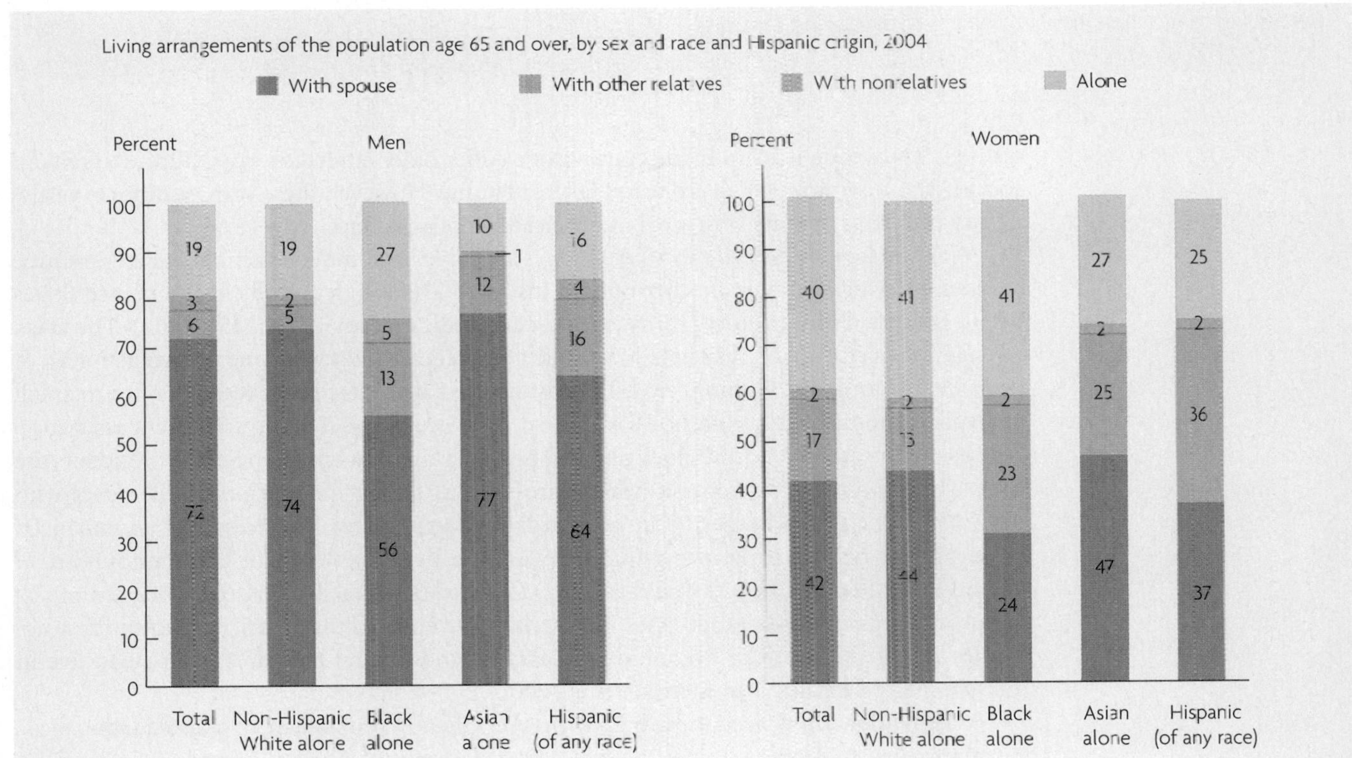

Figure 18.1
Older Adults' Living Arrangements

In the United States, most older adults live with a spouse or alone, but living arrangements vary to some degree across ethnic groups.

(*Source:* FIFARS, 2006)

RESEARCH REPORT

Filial Piety

In the United States and in other Western nations, most elderly people live on their own, but in Asian societies allowing one's elders to live alone has traditionally been viewed as a violation of a set of cultural beliefs called *filial piety*. Central to this set of beliefs is the notion that children have a duty to care for their elderly parents. As a result, few elders in such societies live on their own. In Japan, for example, only one-third of older adults live alone or with a spouse (Tsuya & Martin, 1992). Most of the remaining two-thirds live with their children. Asian elders who are dependent on their adult children are less likely to be depressed than those who live independently, and many Asian countries have no formal employer- or government-sponsored pension programs for the elderly (Chou, Chi, & Chow, 2004; McDonald, 2004; Min, 2004).

The concept of filial piety exists in Western cultures as well. However, among Westerners, filial piety is more often based on affection and attachment than on a sense of duty (Datta, Poortinga, & Marcoen, 2003). Spiritual and religious values also often motivate families to provide care for their elders (Pierce, 2001). Further, individualistic values motivate elderly adults in Western cultures to take into account their children's own financial and social resources, as well as their need for independence, when making judgments about whether their children have met their filial piety obligations (Iecovich & Lankri, 2002). Thus, unlike elders in Asian cultures, adults in Western societies who must depend on their children for financial help, especially men, often experience emotional distress (Nagumey, Reich, & Newsom, 2004).

The spread of Western ideas to non-Western societies via mass media and other means appears to be changing the concept of filial piety in Asian countries. Researchers have found that the concept of filial piety held by both middle-aged and elderly adults in highly Westernized areas, such as Hong Kong, is much more like that of North Americans and Europeans than that of traditional Asian culture (Ng, Ying, Phillips, & Lee, 2002). These changes have had a number of adverse consequences for elderly Asians. In some locales, older adults have been reduced to begging on the streets because their children aren't taking care of them and there are no government programs to help them. In response, many countries are enacting legislation that criminalizes a family's failure to provide for elders (Min, 2004). Others are recognizing that a shift toward Western values will necessitate adoption of Western-style government programs for the elderly (McDonald, 2004).

In Asian countries, most elderly adults live with their adult children.

Questions for Critical Analysis

1. In what ways do Western families display filial piety other than by having elders live in their homes?
2. Beyond the influence of Western media, what kinds of internal social changes in Asian societies might have contributed to declines in filial piety?

outings. Thus, independent living communities offer older adults the opportunity to remain socially active without having to travel far from home. However, these communities typically do not provide residents with any kind of health care assistance.

When older adults need more help than is available in an independent living community, an *assisted living facility* is another option. Just over 2% of older adults in the United States live in these facilities (Centers for Medicare and Medicaid Services [CMS], 2004). The average age of assisted living residents is 80, and most require help with one or two activities of daily living (toileting, bathing, etc.). In most assisted living facilities, residents live in small apartments and get help with housework and meal preparation along with ADL assistance. Nurses are on site around the clock and can be called upon in emergencies, but residents are generally responsible for routine health care such as taking medications. Still, elders who move from their own homes to an assisted living facility have less stress and an enhanced sense of well-being just knowing that help is close by if they need it (Cutchin, Owen, & Chang, 2003; Fonda, Clipp, & Maddox, 2002). Assisted living facilities also provide senior citizens with organized social activities. Researchers have found that participation in these activities is important to the overall life satisfaction and mental health of elders who live in assisted living facilities (Zimmerman et al., 2003).

When older adults need more help with ADLs than is available in an assisted living facility, many turn to nursing homes, or *skilled nursing facilities*. As you learned in Chapter 17, about 4% of the elderly adults in the United States live in nursing homes. The typical nursing home resident is a female in her late 70s or early 80s (CMS, 2004). Most require help with three to four ADLs. About half of nursing home residents have dementia. Of course, the decision to admit an elderly adult to a skilled nursing facility can be difficult (see No Easy Answers). However, for older adults who require 24-hour supervision, particularly those with dementia, nursing homes often represent the best residential option.

Finally, *continuing-care retirement communities (CCRCs)* offer a continuum of care ranging from independent living to skilled nursing care. Residents can move from one level of care to another on an as-needed basis while remaining within the same community. For example, an elder who lives in the independent living part of the facility can temporarily move to the skilled nursing sector for a few days or weeks while she recovers from surgery or an accident. Similarly, a resident who is in the process of developing dementia may start out in independent living and move to assisted living before finally being admitted to skilled nursing care.

Only a tiny fraction of older adults in the United States currently live in this new kind of community, but interest in CCRCs is growing. Like assisted living facilities, they are most popular with seniors who pay for their own care. The flexibility and social continuity provided by CCRCs are the keys to their appeal.

Partnerships

Learning Objective 18.6

How do intimate partnerships contribute to development in late adulthood?

Because men typically marry younger women and because women live longer than men, a man can normally expect to have a spouse or intimate partner until he dies. The normal expectation for a woman is that she will eventually

NO EASY ANSWERS

Deciding on Nursing Home Care

A relatively small number of elderly adults in the United States lives in nursing homes. Even among the oldest old, only 17% reside in such institutions (FIFARS, 2006). Furthermore, most people would prefer to take care of their older loved ones at home. However, when elders require assistance with several activities of daily living (e.g., bathing, cooking, taking medication) or when they require medical procedures that are difficult to manage at home (e.g., tube feeding), many families decide that moving the older adult into a long-term care facility is the best available option. How do families choose such a facility?

The pathway toward finding the best long-term placement for an older adult begins with an assessment of his or her needs and resources. Elders who are still able to function somewhat independently may be best served by an assisted living facility. However, assisted living facilities are not covered by government insurance programs such as Medicare and Medicaid. Moreover, skilled nursing care is not covered by either government or private insurance unless it is medically necessary. Thus, cost is often a barrier that prevents an older adult from receiving the kind of care that best suits his or her needs. For this reason, a growing number of young and middle-aged adults are opting to buy long-term care insurance. Long-term care insurance enables elders and their families to make decisions about their needs with less regard for cost than is required for those who do not have such coverage.

Beyond cost considerations, agencies that serve older adults have suggested several criteria for evaluating a long-term care facility (U.S. Department of Health and human Services, 2007). Here are a few.

- Be certain that the facility has the staff and equipment required to meet your elder's physical needs.
- Check with authorities to see whether any complaints have been filed and how they were resolved; avoid facilities with many outstanding complaints.
- Research the results of state and local inspections and the extent to which any deficiencies were corrected; do not admit your elder to a facility that has any current deficiencies.
- Visit at different times such as during meals, recreation periods, early morning, late evening, and so on to note how residents are cared for in different situations.
- Talk to family members of other residents if possible.
- Ask about the facility's policies regarding medical emergencies.

Of course, a facility can receive high marks on these criteria and still not be the best one for an older adult. Thus, once a facility has satisfied these basic criteria, families must determine whether it can meet their older loved one's cognitive, social, and spiritual needs. Moreover, once an elder has been admitted, family members should closely monitor their care and be prepared to make a change if needed.

Take a Stand

Decide which of these two statements you most agree with and think about how you would defend your position:

1. In some cases, an older adult is probably better off living in a long-term care facility than with a family member.
2. Living with a family member is always preferable to placement in a long-term care facility.

Affection between married partners and pleasure in each other's company clearly do not disappear in old age.

be without such a partner, often for many years. Clearly this helps explain why there are more women than men in nursing homes and among the victims of elder abuse (see the Real World). But what are the marital relationships of older adults like?

Cross-sectional comparisons show that marital satisfaction is higher in the late adult years than when children are still at home. But this high marital satisfaction may have a somewhat different basis than that of the early years of marriage. In late adulthood, marriages tend to be based less on passion and mutual disclosure and more on loyalty, familiarity, mutual investment in the relationship, and companionship (Bengtson et al., 1990; Fouquereau & Baudoin, 2002). In Sternberg's terms (look back at Figure 14.4, page 413), late adult marriages are more likely to reflect companionate love than romantic or even consummate love.

Of course, this does not mean that the marriages of older adults are necessarily passionless. That may well be true of some marriages, but there is evidence to the contrary for many. You'll recall from Chapter 17 that the majority of older adult couples are still sexually active and may be somewhat more sexually adventurous than younger adults. Collectively, older couples report higher levels of pleasure and lower levels of conflict in their relationships than do middle-aged couples. When older couples do have conflicts, they resolve them in more affectionate and less negative ways (Carstensen, Gottman, & Levenson, 1995; Levenson, Carstensen, & Gottman, 1993). Older couples also spend more time with each other than with family or friends, and although much of this time is spent in passive or basic maintenance activities—watching TV, doing housework, running errands—it is also true that those married elders who spend more time with their spouses report high levels of happiness (Larson, Mannell, & Zuzanek, 1986).

THE REAL WORLD

Elder Abuse

Fred is a 43-year-old unemployed cocaine addict. When Fred's father died, his mother received a $50,000 life insurance payment. Since she had almost no savings prior to her husband's death, Fred's mother put the money into a savings account and restricts her living expenses to the amount of her monthly Social Security check. Having the money has helped her worry less about the future. However, shortly after his father's death, Fred began nagging his mother about his new "life plan." His plan is to move in with her and to use her insurance money to finance his enrollment in a drug rehabilitation program. As soon as he is off cocaine and finds a job, Fred has vowed, he will pay her back. Fred's siblings say that he is "abusing" their mother by manipulating her emotions in order to get financial support from her.

The term "abuse" is often associated with physical aggression. However, only about 3% of U.S. elders are physically abused (Bengtson, Rosenthal, & Burton, 1996). Physical abuse is most likely to be directed at elders who have some type of dementia, and abuse by spouses is twice as likely as abuse by children (Pillemer & Finkelhor, 1988). However, many experts believe that elder abuse is underreported because health care providers do not get enough training in recognizing its effects (Thobaben & Duncan, 2003).

Psychological abuse may be far more subtle, including financial exploitation or failure to provide needed aid. The existence of such destructive forms of interaction is a clear reminder that older adults' relationships with their kin are not all sweetness and light. But it is also important to remember that these highly negative patterns are the exception rather than the rule. For most elders, relationships with children and other kin may be a mixture of positive and negative, but the scale most often tips toward the positive.

Researchers have identified several risk factors for elder abuse, including mental illness or alcoholism in the abuser, financial dependency of the abuser on the victim, social isolation, and external stresses (Pillemer & Suitor, 1990, 1992). A likely victim of abuse is an elderly widow sharing her household with a dependent son who has a mental disorder or a drug or alcohol problem; the mother is typically too dependent on her son to kick him out and too ashamed of the abuse to tell others about it (Bengtson et al., 1996). Abuse is also more likely when the elder with dementia is physically violent and when a husband has physically abused his wife throughout their adult lives and simply continues to do so in old age.

Questions for Reflection

1. What arguments could be made for and against the claim that Fred's behavior toward his mother is abusive?
2. If you were one of Fred's siblings, how would you handle the situation?

Further evidence of the deep bond that continues to exist in late-life marriages is the remarkable degree of care and assistance older spouses give each other when one or the other is disabled. For married elders with some kind of disability, by far the largest source of assistance is the spouse, not children or friends. Many husbands and wives care for spouses who are ill or who suffer from dementia for very long periods of time. And even when both spouses suffer from significant disabilities, they nonetheless continue to care for each other "until death do us part." Marriages may thus be less romantic or less emotionally intense in late adulthood than they were in earlier years, but they are typically satisfying and highly committed.

Researchers have found similar characteristics and effects in long-term gay and lesbian relationships (Grossman, Daugelli, & Hershberger, 2000). Like heterosexuals, elderly homosexuals who have a long-term partner typically identify the partner as their most important source of emotional support. In addition, those who live with a partner report less loneliness and better physical and mental health.

It is the loss of the marriage or partnership relationship through the death of the spouse or partner that alters this pattern for so many older adults. The gender difference in marital status among elders is further increased by a higher rate of remarriage for men than for women, a pattern found among both the widowed and the divorced at every age. Twenty percent of single men over 65 remarry, compared with only 2% of women. Older unmarried men are also more likely to date and more likely to live with someone (Bulcroft & Bulcroft, 1991). By contrast, research suggests that widows have little interest in dating or remarriage (Talbott, 1998). Despite older women's reluctance to remarry, studies of the emotional impact of remarriage in late adulthood suggest that both men and women benefit emotionally (Curran, McLanahan, & Knab, 2003; Winter, Lawton, Casten, & Sando, 2000). When researchers examine self-ratings of life satisfaction, elderly newlyweds rate their personal happiness higher than do either long-married or single peers.

Married older adults, like married adults of any age, have certain distinct advantages: They have higher life satisfaction, better health, and lower rates of institutionalization (Iwashyna & Christakis, 2003). Such differential advantages are generally greater for married older men than for married older women (again, this is also true among younger adults). This difference might be interpreted as indicating that marriage affords more benefits to men than to women or that men rely more on their marriage relationship for social support and are thus more affected by its loss. Whatever the explanation, it seems clear that, for older women, marital status is less strongly connected to health or life satisfaction, but still strongly connected to financial security.

The protective nature of marriage for older adults is supported by research showing that single adults over the age of 65 have higher mortality rates, even when factors such as poverty are controlled (Manzoli, Villari, Pironec, & Boccia, 2007). Moreover, these rates are consistent across gender and culture. Interestingly, though, elders whose single status is the result of divorce have higher mortality rates than either those who have been widowed or peers who have never married. In addition, divorced older adults have higher rates of alcohol abuse, depression, and suicide (Hahn et al., 2004; Lorant et al., 2005; Onen et al., 2005). This may be the case because divorced elders, especially men, are more likely to be disconnected from their families than their never-married or widowed peers are (Tomassini et al., 2004). However, participation in religious activities and other forms of social engagement appear to moderate the associations among single status, substance abuse, depression, poor health, and mortality risk (Hahn et al., 2004). Thus, the key advantage of intimate partnerships for older adults is that they provide them with readily available sources of support. For single elders, more effort is required to identify and connect with sources of support, and physical disabilities are more likely to interfere with maintaining them than is the case for partnered elders who share the same household.

Elderly newlyweds report higher levels of personal happiness than either long-married or single peers.

Learning Objective 18.7

What is the significance of family relationships and friendships for older adults?

Family Relationships and Friendships

Folklore and descriptions of late adulthood in the popular press suggest that family, particularly children and grandchildren, forms the core of the social life of older adults, perhaps especially those who are widowed. Older adults do describe intergenerational bonds as strong and important; most report a significant sense of family solidarity and support (Bengtson et al., 1996). These bonds are reflected in, among other things, regular contact between elders and family members. Moreover, researchers have found that family relationships become more harmonious as adults get older (Akiyama, Antonucci, Takahashi, & Langfahl, 2003). Thus, they represent an important component of most elders' overall life satisfaction.

Contacts with Adult Children In one national sample of over 3,000 adults aged 65 and older, 86% reported that they saw at least one of their children once a week or more often (Taylor, Funk, Craighill, & Kennedy, 2006). Regular contact is made easier by the fact that even in the highly mobile U.S. society, 65% of elders live within an hour's travel of at least one of their children. Very similar figures are reported by researchers in other developed countries such as those in the European Union, so this pattern is not unique to the United States (Hank, 2005).

Part of the regular contact between elders and their adult children, of course, involves giving aid to or receiving it from the elder person—a pattern you learned about in Chapter 16. Most of the time, when older adults need help that cannot be provided by a spouse, it is provided by other family members, principally children. However, relationships between older parents and their adult children cannot be reduced simply to the exchange of aid. A great deal of the interaction is social as well as functional, and the great majority of older adults describe their relationships with their adult children in positive terms. Most see their children not only out of a sense of obligation or duty but because they take pleasure in such contact, and a very large percentage describe at least one child as a confidant (Taylor et al., 2006).

Effects of Relationships with Adult Children Some studies indicate that when relationships between elders and adult children are warm and close, they are more important to elders' sense of well-being than any other kind of social relationship (Pinquart & Soerensen, 2000). By contrast, other researchers have found that elders who see their children more often or report more positive interactions with their children do not describe themselves as happier or healthier overall than do those who have less frequent contact or less positive relationships with their children (e.g., Mullins & Mushel, 1992). Moreover, such results have been obtained in very different cultural settings, such as in India and among Mexican Americans (Lawrence, Bennett, & Markides, 1992; Venkatraman, 1995). In all these studies, the older adults reported regular contact with their children and said that they enjoyed it, but these relationships did not seem to enhance happiness or health. Moreover, research has shown that childless elders are just as happy and well adjusted as those who have children (Taylor et al., 2006). Many developmentalists have concluded that good relationships and regular contact with adult children can add to an elderly adult's quality of life, but are not necessary for it.

Most elders enjoy maintaining relationships with younger family members. However, research suggests that such connections are not essential to life satisfaction in old age.

One possible explanation for this inconsistency in findings is that the relationship with one's children is still governed by role prescriptions, even in old age. It may be friendly, but it is not chosen in the same way that a relationship with a friend is. With your friend, you feel free to be yourself and feel accepted as who you are. With your children, you may feel the need to live up to their demands and expectations.

Grandchildren and Siblings As you learned in Chapter 16, interactions between grandchildren and middle-aged grandparents are beneficial to both. However, in late adulthood, contact between grandchildren and grandparents declines as the grandchildren become adults themselves (Barer, 2001; Silverstein & Long, 1998). Thus, grandchildren are rarely part of an elderly adult's close family network.

Interestingly, though, it appears that relationships with siblings may become more important in late adulthood (Taylor et al., 2006). Siblings seldom provide much practical assistance to one another in old age, but they can and often do serve two other important functions. First, siblings can provide a unique kind of emotional support for one another, based on shared reminiscences and companionship. Once parents are gone, no one else knows all the old stories, all the family jokes, the names and history of former friends and neighbors. Second, many elders see their siblings as a kind of "insurance policy" in old age, a source of support of last resort (Connidis, 1994).

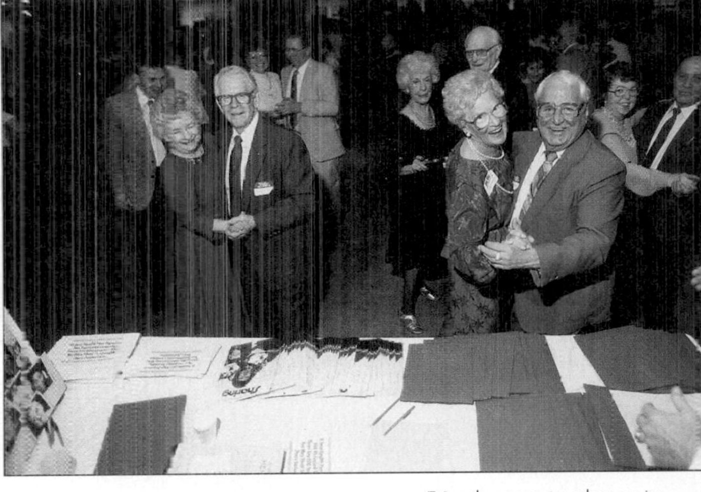

Friends seem to play an important role in late adulthood, perhaps because they share the same background and memories—like favorite old tunes and dances.

Friendships Mounting evidence suggests that contact with friends has a significant impact on overall life satisfaction, on self-esteem, and on the amount of loneliness reported by older adults (Antonucci, Lansford, & Akiyama, 2001; Antonucci, 1990; Jerrome, 1990). Moreover, for those elders whose families are unavailable, friendships seem to provide an equally effective support network (Takahashi, Tamura, & Tokoro, 1997). This is particularly true of unmarried elders, but is at least somewhat true of married ones as well.

Friends meet different kinds of needs for older adults than do family members. For one thing, relationships with friends are likely to be more reciprocal or equitable, and developmentalists know that equitable relationships are more valued and less stressful. Friends provide companionship, opportunities for laughter, and shared activities. In one Canadian study, for example, friends were second only to spouses as sources of companionship among those over 65 (Connidis & Davies, 1992). Friends may also provide assistance with daily tasks, such as shopping or housework, although they typically provide less help of this kind than do family members.

Gender and Ethnic Differences in Social Networks

Learning Objective 18.8

What are some gender and ethnic differences in older adults' social networks?

As at earlier ages, women and men in late adulthood appear to form different kinds of social networks, with men's friendships involving less disclosure and less intimacy than women's. In addition, older women's networks tend to be larger and closer than those of older men. Developmentalists attribute these findings to a continuation of a pattern evident across most of the lifespan (Taylor et al., 2005). If you think back on what you learned about sex differences in the chapters on childhood, adolescence, early adulthood, and middle adulthood, sex differences in late adulthood social networks should not be surprising.

However, it would be a mistake to assume that, because men have smaller social networks, their relationships are unimportant to them. Some developmentalists suggest that research on social networks may be biased in such a way that women will always be found to have stronger networks. This bias, critics say, originates in the fact that research emphasizes shared activities and frequency of contact more than the quality of the relationships. Indeed, when quality of relationships is considered, research shows that men's social networks are just as important to them and provide them with the same kinds of emotional support as women's networks, even though men's networks tend to be smaller (Riggs, 1997).

African Americans tend to have warmer relationships with their siblings and to live with their children more often than White Americans do. In addition, they show two other distinctive patterns in their social networks. They create strong relationships with "fictive kin," a type of relationship you first learned about in Chapter 14. In African American groups, friends often acquire the status of a close sibling, aunt, uncle, or grandparent. Such fictive kin may be important sources of both emotional and instrumental support among elders of all ethnic groups, but the pattern is particularly prevalent among African Americans (Johnson & Barer, 1990; MacRae, 1992).

Other ethnic groups, including Hispanic Americans and Asian Americans, are also often found to have more extensive social networks than White Americans. However, the correlations between social networks and various measures of well-being seem to be similar across these groups (Barker et al., 1998; Baxter et al., 1998; Takahashi et al., 1997). Moreover, most studies suggest that the quality of the social network, not just its size, is important. Thus, as the earlier discussion of successful aging suggested, the number of contacts with family and friends and the quality of interactions with them are important predictors of elders' well-being.

Critical Thinking

1. What kinds of physical and social barriers are there to creating new social relationships in late adulthood?

Career Issues in Late Life

A remarkable capacity for adaptation marks the transition from work to retirement. Although this transition certainly brings the loss of a major role, virtually all the folklore about the negative effects of this particular role loss turns out to be wrong, at least for current older cohorts in developed countries. Developmentalists' knowledge about the process of retirement has been greatly enhanced by a series of excellent longitudinal studies, each following a group of men or women from before retirement into the years past retirement. In one particularly helpful analysis, Erdman Palmore and his colleagues combined the results of seven such studies, yielding a sample of over 7,000 adults, each interviewed at least twice and often many more times (Palmore, Burchett, Fillenbaum, George, & Wallman, 1985). Although these data are not completely current, they comprise by far the most comprehensive set of longitudinal data available.

Learning Objective 18.9

What factors contribute to the decision to retire?

Timing of and Reasons for Retirement

One inaccurate bit of folklore is that 65 is the normal age of retirement. As recently as 1970, 65 was indeed the most common age of retirement for men in the United States. One reason for the uniformity was that many employers forced all workers to retire at 65. However, during the 1980s, age-discrimination legislation outlawed mandatory retirement in the United States (Mooney, Knox, & Schacht, 2000).

Knowing that there is a ban on mandatory retirement might lead you to believe that people are continuing to work to more advanced ages. However, the trend is quite the opposite. Although most older adults plan to continue working at least part-time during retirement (Lim, 2003; Mature Market Institute, 2004), the average age of retirement from full-time work has been declining in recent years throughout the industrialized world. However, determining an "average" age of retirement in the United States and other industrialized countries has become increasingly difficult because retirement has become more of a multi-phase process than a single life event. Many hold *bridge jobs* that allow them to transition from full-time work to full-time retirement, and they can do so for many years before withdrawing entirely from the workforce (Adams & Rau, 2004). Though such individuals may have left careers that they pursued for decades, government surveys continue to count them as "employed" though they may actually think of themselves as retired or on the pathway to retirement. As a result, while the percentage of older adults' income derived from employment was only 10% in 1967, nowadays it is about 25% (FIFARS, 2006). Moreover, 40% of the income of the top 20% of wage-earners over the age of 65 comes from work.

Presumably, many older adults continue to work because they need to, but financial needs represent only one factor in retirement trends. Poor health provides a particularly strong push toward early retirement (Schulz, 1995). Poor health lowers the average age of retirement by 1–3 years, an effect seen among Hispanic Americans and African Americans as well as among White Americans, and in countries other than the United States (Hayward, Friedman, & Chen, 1996; McDonald & Wanner, 1990; Sammartino, 1987; Stanford, Happersett, Morton, Molgaard, & Peddecord, 1991). However, among those who retire at 65 or later, health is a less powerful factor, presumably because most of these later retirees are in good health.

Family composition is important in the decision to retire. Those who are still supporting minor children retire later than do those in the postparental stage. Thus, men and women who bear their children very late, those who acquire a second and younger family in a second marriage, and those rearing grandchildren are likely to continue to work until these children have left home. Furthermore, a surprising 50% of adults in the United States who are in their 60s still have living parents, many of whom require financial assistance. Consequently, the concept of the generational sandwich that you read about in Chapter 16 is relevant to many older adults and influences their decisions about retirement.

Important, too, is the finding that many older adults continue to work because they want to. Those who like their work and are highly committed to it, including many self-employed adults, retire later—often quite a lot later—than do those who are less gratified by their work. Those in challenging and interesting jobs are likely to postpone retirement until they are pushed by ill health or attracted by some extra financial inducement. For them, availability of a normal pension is less of an influence (Hayward & Hardy, 1985).

A quite different kind of work influence occurred in the 1990s in occupations or industries in which the work force suffered major "downsizing." A great many workers, blue collar and white collar alike, were pushed to accept early retirement, as their employers offered them special incentives (Hardy & Quadagno, 1995).

Women retire at about the same age as men do, on average, but retirement benefits, health, or job characteristics do not predict just when they will retire. One factor that tends to keep women in the labor force is the lure of higher earnings that will augment future Social Security benefits—a factor that may be especially important for women who took several years off from full-time work in order to raise children. However, financial experts point out that even if retirement-aged women have as many years of full-time employment as men do, they are still likely to receive less money from pensions and Social Security because, on average, their earnings are lower (Powell, 2006).

By contrast, the factors that lead to positive views of retirement are very similar for men and women. For example, one study found that health was the most important predictor of quality of life in retirement for both sexes (Quick & Moen, 1998). However, extensive preretirement planning seemed to be more important for men. Almost all of the study's male participants had worked continuously until retirement. Although some of the retired women had worked continuously, others had spent a significant number of years in the home or in part-time employment. The researchers found that those who had worked continuously expressed more satisfaction with the quality of their retirement.

Effects of Retirement

Learning Objective 18.10

How does retirement affect income, health, attitudes, emotions, mobility, and social relationships?

There are a number of shifts that take place at retirement, some positive and some negative. But, overall, retirement seems to have positive effects on the lives of older adults.

Income One potentially significant change at retirement is a change in income. In the United States, retired adults have five potential sources of income: government pensions, such as Social Security; other pensions, such as those offered through an employer or the military; earnings from continued work; income from savings or other assets; and, for those living below the poverty line, public assistance, including food stamps and Supplemental Security Income. For most elderly in the United States, Social Security is the largest source of income (FIFARS, 2006).

Of course, statistics on income sources indicate nothing about changes in income level after retirement. Here again, Palmore's longitudinal data can be helpful. These data suggest that incomes decline roughly 25% after retirement. But this figure paints a misleadingly negative picture of the actual financial status of retired persons.

In the United States, as in many developed countries, many retired adults own their own homes and thus have no mortgage payments, and their children are self-reliant. Furthermore, retirees are eligible for Medicare as well as for many special senior citizen benefits. When these factors are taken into consideration, retired adults in the United States, Australia, and most European countries have, on average, incomes that are at 85–100% of pre-retirement levels (Smeeding, 1990).

Poverty It used to be that post-retirement income losses resulted in high poverty rates among the elderly. However, over the past several decades, poverty rates among the elderly have declined substantially. In 1959, 35% of adults over 65 in the United States were living below the poverty line. In 2004, slightly more than 10% were at that low economic level (FIFARS, 2006).

A variety of factors are responsible for declining poverty rates among the elderly. For one thing, significant improvements in Social Security benefits in the United States (and equivalent improvements in many other countries), including regular cost-of-living increases, have meant that the relative financial position of the elderly has improved more than that of any other age group in the population. Moreover, more elderly adults than ever before are high school or college graduates. In 1950, only 18% of adults over 65 were high school graduates, compared to three-quarters of the over-65 population in 2004 (FIFARS, 2006). Thus, most elderly adults today had better jobs and earned a great deal more money before retirement than did members of previous cohorts. As a result, today's elders have more savings and better retirement benefits.

However, low rates of poverty in the total elderly population obscure much higher rates in various subgroups. Figure 18.2 shows poverty rates of men and women in the major ethnic groups in the United States in 2002. Clearly, large disparities across groups remain (FIFARS, 2006). Moreover, poverty is strongly associated with disability among the elderly across all ethnic groups. Thus, low-income older adults are more highly represented among elders with disabilities than they are in the general population. Some studies show that even

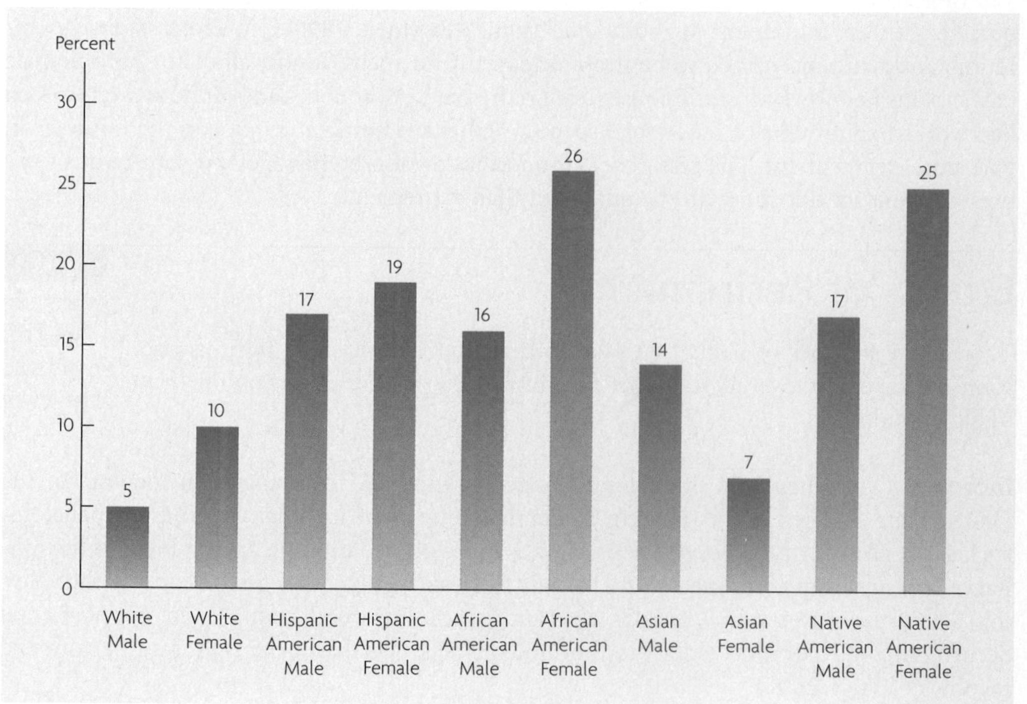

Figure 18.2
Gender, Ethnicity, and Poverty among the elderly in the United States

These data show the percentages of White, African American, and Hispanic American men and women who were classified as poor in 2002.

(*Source*: U.S. Census Bureau (2002))

relatively young elders, those between 55 and 65 years of age, who live below the poverty level, are six times as likely to need assistance with at least one activity of daily living as their peers who are better off (Minkler, Fuller-Thomson, & Guralnik, 2006). Such disparities diminish with age, but income-related differences in disability rates are found even among elders who are in their 80s.

Ethnic group differences in poverty are, no doubt, related to differences in educational attainment. Among older adults in the United States today, nearly three-quarters of Whites and about two-thirds of Asian Americans are high school graduates. So it is perhaps not surprising that these two groups have the lowest poverty rates. By contrast, less than half of the elders in other ethnic and racial groups graduated from high school. Consequently, the employment histories of these groups are different, leading to income disparities in retirement. However, in future cohorts of retirees, these disparities are likely to diminish because of greatly increased rates of high school graduation and college attendance among younger minorities (U.S. Bureau of the Census, 1995a).

Similarly, single older adults continue to be more likely to be poor than their married peers, and among older singles, women are more likely to be poor than men (16% versus 9%, respectively) (FIFARS, 2000). Different poverty rates for single men and women in old age arise from a number of differences in adult life experiences. Current cohorts of older women are much less likely than their male peers to have had paid employment, are less likely to have earned retirement benefits even if they did work, and generally worked for lower wages (Powell, 2006). As a result, many older widows rely entirely on Social Security income. Women in younger cohorts are more likely to have been employed and to have participated in a retirement plan, but, as you learned in earlier chapters, gender differences in work patterns still exist. Moreover, many more retirement-age women today are divorced than in past cohorts. The combination of income inequality and the increased prevalence of divorce are likely to lead to a dramatic rise in the number of women who live in poverty after retirement (Powell, 2006).

Health, Attitudes, and Emotions Longitudinal studies indicate quite clearly that health does not change, for better or worse, simply because of retirement (van Solinge, 2007). When ill health accompanies retirement, the causal sequence is nearly always that the individual retired because of poor health. Among those in good health at retirement age, retirement itself has little or no effect on health status over the succeeding years (Palmore et al., 1985). This clear set of research results is interesting because it suggests that retirement is not a highly stressful life change for the vast majority of adults.

Similarly, the bulk of the evidence suggests that retirement has essentially no impact on overall life satisfaction or subjective well-being. Longitudinal studies that have included measures of such attitudes show little difference in scores before and after retirement, and those recently retired show little sign of an increase in depression (Palmore et al., 1985). For most, retirement is not perceived as a stressor at all.

One set of data that makes this point particularly clearly comes from a study of a group of more than 1,500 men over a period of years (Bossé, Aldwin, Levenson, & Workman-Daniels, 1991). In the most recent interviews, participants were asked to indicate which of 31 possibly stressful life events they had experienced in the past year and to rate the overall stressfulness of each of these events. Retirement was ranked 30th out of 31 in overall stressfulness, below even such items as "move to a less desirable residence" and "decrease in responsibilities or hours at work or where you volunteer." Of those who had retired in the previous year, seven out of ten said that they found retirement either not stressful at all or only a little stressful. Among the 30% of retired men in this study who did list some problems with retirement, poor health and poor family finances were the most likely causes. Those with marital problems were also likely to report more daily hassles in their retired lives.

Other evidence suggests that those who respond least well to retirement are those who had the least control over the decision (Smith & Moen, 2004). For example, those who go into retirement because of a late-career job loss show declines in physical and mental health (Gallo, Bradley, Siegel, & Kasl, 2000). Similarly, those who are forced to retire by poor health typically adjust more poorly to retirement (Hardy & Quadagno, 1995). Even workers who accept special early retirement offers from their employers are likely to report lower satisfaction

Elders who have moved to resort communities specifically designed for retired people have made what social scientists call an amenity move.

and higher levels of stress than do those who feel they had more control over the retirement decision (Herzog et al., 1991). Retirement is also likely to be more stressful for those whose economic situation is poor or for those who must simultaneously cope with both retirement and other major life changes, such as widowhood (Stull & Hatch, 1984). But for those for whom retirement is anticipated and on time, this role loss is not stressful.

It appears that what predicts life satisfaction in late adulthood is not whether a person has retired but whether he was satisfied with life in earlier adulthood. We take ourselves with us through the years: Grumpy, negative young people tend to be grumpy, negative old people, and satisfied young adults find satisfaction in retirement as well. The consistency of this finding is quite striking and provides very good support for continuity theories of adulthood. Work does shape daily life for 40 years or more of adulthood, but a person's happiness or unhappiness with life, her growth or stagnation, seems less a function of the specifics of the work experience than a function of the attitudes and qualities she brings to the process.

Mobility For many adults, retirement brings an increase in choices about where to live. When your job or your spouse's job no longer ties you to a specific place, you can choose to move to sunnier climes or to live nearer one of your children. Surprisingly, however, most retirees stay fairly close to the place they have called home for many years (Brown, 2004).

Charles Longino, who has been one of the most diligent investigators of residential moves among the elderly, suggests that elderly adults make three types of moves (Longino, 2003). The first type, which he calls an amenity move, is the one most of us probably think of when we think of older adults changing residences. If an older adult makes such a move, it is almost always right around the time of retirement. Most typically, an **amenity move** is in a direction away from the older person's children, frequently to a warmer climate. Florida, California, and Arizona are the most popular destinations for amenity moves in the United States. In Canada, amenity moves are most often westward, particularly to British Columbia; in Britain, the equivalent move is to the seaside.

Those who make amenity moves are likely to be still married and relatively healthy and to have adequate or good retirement income (De Jong et al., 1995; Hazelrigg & Hardy, 1995). Often the relocating couple has vacationed in the new location; many have planned the move carefully over a number of years (Cuba & Longino, 1991). Most report higher levels of life satisfaction or morale after such a move, although some move back to where they came from because they find themselves too isolated from family and friends.

Another pattern of amenity move is to move seasonally rather than making a permanent move to a new location. Some elders, often called "snowbirds," spend the winter months in sunnier areas and the summer months at home, nearer their families. One survey of older retired residents of Minnesota found that 9% followed such a pattern (Hogan & Steinnes, 1994).

The second type of move, which Longino calls **compensatory (kinship) migration**, occurs when the older adult—most often, a widow living alone—develops such a level of chronic disability that she has serious difficulty managing an independent household. When a move of this type occurs, it is nearly always a shift to be closer to a daughter, son, or some other relative who can provide regular assistance. In some cases, this means moving in with that daughter or son, but often the move is to an apartment or house nearby or into a retirement community in which the individual can live independently but has supportive services available. The final type of move in late adulthood is what Longino calls **institutional migration**, to nursing home care.

Of course, very few older adults actually move three times. Longino's point is that these are three very different kinds of moves, made by quite different subsets of the population of

amenity move post-retirement move away from kin to a location that has some desirable feature, such as year-round warm weather

compensatory (kinship) migration a move to a location near family or friends that happens when an elder requires frequent help because of a disability or disease

institutional migration a move to an institution such as a nursing home that is necessitated by a disability

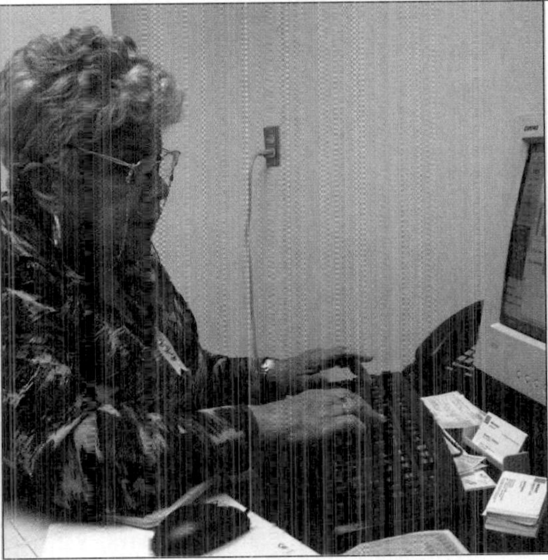

About 47% of older men and 37% of older women in the United States are employed at least part-time (FIFARS, 2000). Further, a fairly high proportion of middle-aged people say they plan to work at least part-time after retirement. Consequently, employers are eager to learn how to best train older workers.

elderly and at different times in the late adult years. Amenity moves usually occur early, kinship or compensatory migration is likely to occur in middle to late old age, and institutional migration clearly occurs late in life. Only the first of these types of moves reflects the increase in options that may result from retirement.

One of the most recent developments in connection with post-retirement mobility is the trend among universities and colleges to make their on-campus housing facilities available to alumni and senior citizens who want to attend college (Kressley & Huebschmann, 2002). This trend is in response to the significant portion of elders who want to spend their increased leisure time on intellectual pursuits (Trentin, 2004). Moreover, increased enrollment by older adults has helped some institutions overcome the financial difficulties associated with declining college attendance among young adults.

Choosing Not to Retire

Learning Objective 18.11

What does research suggest about the decision not to retire?

A significant number of adults plan to continue working past the typical retirement age (Mature Market Institute, 2004). Research has focused on men who shun retirement. Some are men with very limited education, poor retirement benefits, and thus very low incomes. Many of these men continue working out of economic necessity.

A larger fraction of those who shun retirement are highly educated, healthy, highly work-committed professionals, whose wives often are also still working (Parnes & Sommers, 1994). Many of them have been highly work-committed all their adult lives. For example, men in the National Longitudinal Surveys sample, a group that has been studied over a period of 25 years, were asked in their 50s whether they would continue working if they suddenly found themselves with enough money to live comfortably. Those who said they would continue working are much more likely to shun retirement and to be still working in their 70s and 80s (Parnes & Sommers, 1994). For these men, work continues to provide more satisfaction than they expect retirement to offer.

Perhaps the greatest obstacle to employment for older adults is that many potential employers express concerns about older adults' ability to learn new job skills (Forte & Hansvick, 1999). However, studies of age differences in learning demonstrate that the learning process itself does not change with age. The same factors—interest, anxiety, motivation, quality of instruction, self-efficacy, and so on—predict learning success in both older and younger adults (Chasseigne, Grau, Mullet, & Cama, 1999; Gardiner, Luszcz, & Bryan, 1997;

Research suggests that older adults respond to computer training very much the way younger adults do. Most get over their anxiety about computers after receiving training, and they can become just as proficient as younger adults, although they may require slower-paced training.

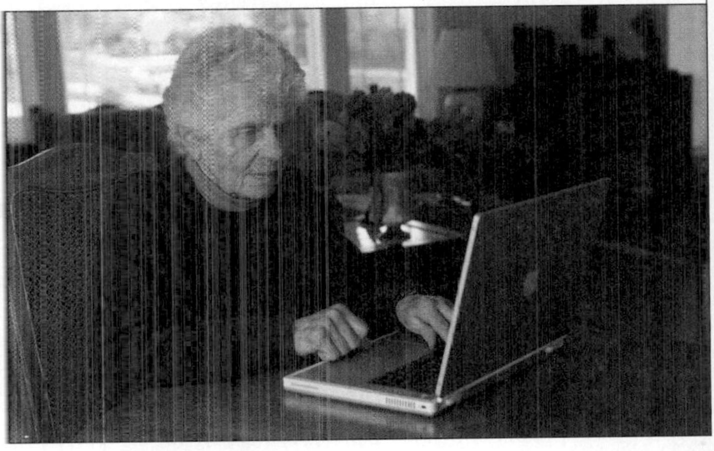

Mead & Fisk, 1998; Plaud, Plaud, & von Duvillard, 1999; Truluck & Courtenay, 1999). Thus, it seems reasonable that many aspects of effective training programs designed for younger workers, such as financial incentives for accomplishment of training goals, should also apply to older employees.

Moreover, an extensive body of research shows that, with appropriately paced training, older adults can significantly improve their performance on many cognitive tasks that are relevant to the workplace (Baltes & Kliegl, 1992; Dittmann-Kohli, Lachman, Kliegl, & Baltes, 1991; Kliegl, Smith, & Baltes, 1989, 1990; Verhaeghen, Marcoen, & Goossens, 1992). Pacing is important, because these studies do suggest that learning new skills sometimes takes longer for older adults. However, even training in the use of new technologies usually results in similar or identical skill levels among younger and older adults.

With respect to aspects of job functioning other than learning of new skills, supervisors typically give older adults higher ratings than younger adults (Forte & Hansvick, 1999). For example, they view older employees as more reliable. In addition, managers typically report that although younger workers produce a greater quantity of work, the quality of older employees' work is better (Rao & Rao, 1997). Consequently, many employers view older adults as desirable employees.

Critical Thinking

1. In what ways do the educational and career decisions that people make in their 20s and 30s shape the decisions they make about retirement in late adulthood?

SUMMARY

Theories of Social and Personality Development

Learning Objective 18.1 What does research say about Erikson's stage of ego integrity versus despair?

- Erikson's concept of ego integrity has been influential, but research does not indicate that the development of ego integrity is necessary to adjustment in old age. The notions of reminiscence and life review have been helpful in researchers' attempts to understand development in late adulthood.

Learning Objective 18.2 What are the main ideas of activity, disengagement, and continuity theory?

- Similarly, disengagement has been found not to be essential in old age; high life satisfaction and good mental health are found most often among elders who disengage the least and who maintain continuity with their earlier interests.

Individual Differences

Learning Objective 18.3 How is successful aging manifested in the lives of older adults?

- Successful aging is defined as maintenance of health along with cognitive and social functioning. Productivity and life satisfaction are also elements of successful aging.

Learning Objective 18.4 How does religious coping influence physical and mental health in late adulthood?

- Religious coping has psychological and social components. It is associated with a lower mortality rate as well as with better physical and mental health.

Social Relationships

Learning Objective 18.5 What are the living arrangements of most elderly people in the United States and in other industrialized countries?

- Among unmarried elders in the United States, living alone is the most common living arrangement. However, a number of residential options are available for seniors who do not want to care for a home or who have become physically disabled.

Learning Objective 18.6 How do intimate partnerships contribute to development in late adulthood?

- Marriages in late adulthood are, on average, highly satisfying for both spouses, who exhibit strong loyalty and mutual affection.

Learning Objective 18.7 What is the significance of family relationships and friendships for older adults?

- The majority of elders see their children regularly. There is some indication that relationships with siblings may become more significant in late adulthood than at earlier ages. Degree of contact with friends is correlated with overall life satisfaction among older adults.

Learning Objective 18.8 What are some gender and ethnic differences in older adults' social networks?

- Women in this age group continue to have larger social networks than men do, and African Americans tend to have larger social networks than White Americans.

Career Issues in Late Life

Learning Objective 18.9 What factors contribute to the decision to retire?

- The typical age of retirement is closer to 62 than 65 in the United States and in most Western developed countries. Time of retirement is affected by health, family responsibilities, adequacy of anticipated pension income, and satisfaction with one's job.

Learning Objective 18.10 How does retirement affect income, health, attitudes, emotions, mobility, and social relationships?

- Income typically decreases with retirement, but income adequacy does not decline very much. Among elders, women and minorities are most likely to live in poverty. The minority of older adults who find retirement stressful are likely to be those who feel they have least control over the decision to retire.

Learning Objective 18.11 What does research suggest about the decision not to retire?

- Those who choose not to retire do so for economic reasons or because of particularly strong commitments to work. Research indicates that older adults can learn new job skills but may do so at slower rates than younger workers.

KEY TERMS

activity theory *(p. 514)*
aging in place *(p. 520)*
amenity move *(p. 532)*
compensatory (kinship) migration *(p. 532)*
continuity theory *(p. 515)*
disengagement theory *(p. 515)*
ego integrity *(p. 513)*
institutional migration *(p. 532)*
life review *(p. 514)*
religious coping *(p. 518)*
reminiscence *(p. 514)*
successful aging *(p. 516)*
volunteerism *(p. 517)*

TEST YOURSELF

Theories of Social and Personality Development

18.1 A man who accepts the way he has lived his life has developed which of the following psychological dimensions, according to Erikson?

a. a psychological moratorium
b. dissonance
c. ego integrity
d. maturation

18.2 The notion that reminiscence is a necessary and healthy aspect of aging and preparation for death is a component of which of the following theories?

a. Erikson's stage of ego integrity versus despair
b. disengagement theory
c. Rowe and Kahn's successful aging paradigm
d. Loevinger's theory of adult development

18.3 Which of these statements best describes the process of life review?

a. Life review is an uncritical recounting of the events of one's life.
b. Life review is essential to healthy aging.
c. Life review can have both positive and negative effects on older adults' adjustment.
d. Life review is a process that mental health professionals discourage older adults from engaging in.

Individual Differences

18.4 The paradigm for successful aging proposed by Rowe and Kahn does *not* include which of the following dimensions?

a. staying healthy and able
b. retaining communication and problem-solving skills
c. retaining cognitive abilities
d. social engagement

18.5 Which of the following best predicts life satisfaction among older adults?

a. high intelligence
b. a sense of control over one's life
c. a past history that included diverse experiences and adventures
d. communication and problem-solving skills

18.6 Which of the following does *not* accurately describe how religious coping affects older adults?

a. Elders who place a great deal of emphasis on religious faith worry less than those who do not.
b. Elders who say their religious beliefs are important to them think that their lives serve an important purpose.
c. Elders who have strong religious beliefs are more likely to commit suicide to be with God.
d. Elders who regularly attend religious services are healthier, both physically and emotionally.

Social Relationships

18.7 Which of the following would *not* be included in the definition of aging in place?

a. making modifications to a home in response to the changing needs of an older adult
b. going to a nursing home
c. hiring a home-based physical therapist
d. living in one's home

18.8 Which of the following factors does *not* influence an older adult's decision to live with an adult child?

a. intelligence
b. health status
c. income
d. ethnicity

18.9 Who is most likely to abuse an elderly person?

a. the person's children
b. the person's spouse
c. nursing home personnel or other professional caregivers
d. strangers, such as muggers or thieves

18.10 Who is likely to provide most of the care and assistance needed by a married older adult who has a significant disability or dementia?

a. children or other relatives
b. professional health care providers
c. a community or volunteer service such as a hospice
d. the spouse

18.11 Which of the following is *not* a true statement about the family relationships of older adults?

a. Most older adults report regular contact with their adult children.
b. The interaction between older adults and their children occurs for both social and functional purposes.
c. Good relationships and regular contact with adult children are necessary for happiness and life satisfaction in old age.
d. According to research, childless elders are just as happy and well adjusted as those who have children.

18.12 Contact with friends has a significant impact on all of the following except

a. overall life satisfaction.
b. self-esteem.
c. likelihood that an individual will divorce.
d. amount of loneliness.

18.13 In comparison to men's, women's

a. friendships involve less disclosure.
b. friendships involve less intimacy.
c. social networks are smaller.
d. social networks are larger.

Career Issues in Late Life

18.14 Which of the following is *not* an accurate statement about the factors that influence the decision to retire?

a. Poor health lowers the average age of retirement by one to three years.
b. Retirement-age adults who have young children at home are likely to retire early in order to rear their children.
c. Poor health and social norms often cause working-class adults to retire earlier than individuals in the middle or upper socioeconomic groups.
d. The most reliable predictor of retirement for a woman is whether her spouse has retired.

18.15 Which of the following does *not* play a role in older adults' decisions to retire?

a. age
b. religion
c. financial support
d. health

18.16 What is the largest source of retirement income for most older adults in the United States?

a. financial support from children
b. investments such as stocks, bonds, or individual retirement accounts
c. public assistance such as food stamps
d. Social Security

18.17 Which of the following is *not* an accurate statement about income during retirement for older adults in the United States?

a. In 2004, only 10% of adults over age 65 were living below the poverty line.
b. Married older adults have a higher poverty rate than single older adults.
c. Improvements in Social Security benefits have benefited older adults more than any other age group.
d. Compared to previous cohorts of retired adults, the current cohort of older adults had better jobs and earned more money before retirement and therefore has more savings and better benefits after retirement.

18.18 According to Charles Longino's typology of residential moves among the elderly, a/an __________ migration occurs when an older person's health deteriorates and regular nursing care is necessary.

a. amenity
b. compensatory
c. familial
d. institutional

18.19 According to Charles Longino, those who make amenity moves are likely to be

a. in poor health.

b. experiencing a health crisis that necessitates nursing care.

c. married, healthy, and in possession of an adequate income.

d. women.

18.20 Which of Longino's migrations is most likely to occur latest in adulthood?

a. kinship

b. amenity

c. compensatory

d. institutional

18.21 What is the biggest obstacle to employment for older adults who choose not to retire?

a. poor health that interferes with job responsibilities

b. the concerns of potential employers about older adults' ability to learn new job skills

c. poor work habits, such as absenteeism or inability to get along with co-workers

d. an absence of jobs or work opportunities suitable for older adults

18.22 Which of the following is *not* a reason that some men choose to continue working instead of retiring?

a. They must continue working out of economic necessity.

b. They want to venture into new lines of work.

c. Their spouses do not want them at home all day.

d. They enjoy the satisfaction that work offers.

18.23 How does skill learning in the old old compare to skill learning in younger adults?

a. The old old take less time to learn new material than do younger adults.

b. The old old are not able to learn new skills, whereas younger adults are.

c. The old old take more time to learn new material than do younger adults.

d. There is no difference in the skill learning of the old old and younger adults.

Are You Ready for the Test?

Students who use the study materials on MyDevelopmentLab report higher grades in the course than those who use the text alone. Here are three easy steps to mastering this chapter and improving your grade…

Step 1

Take the chapter pre-test in MyDevelopmentLab and review your customized Study Plan.

In late adulthood,

- marital satisfaction declines for most couples and individuals drift apart.
- women are more likely to be married and living with a spouse than men are.
- most marriages are passionless and sexual activities are very infrequent.
- marriages are more likely to be based on compassionate love than romantic love.

Step 2

Use MyDevelopmentLab's Multimedia Library to help strengthen your knowledge of the chapter.

Learning Objective 18.1

What does research say about Erikson's stage of ego integrity versus despair?

Watch: **Looking Back**

92% of students responding to a user survey believe MyDevelopmentLab was a beneficial addition to their course.

Watch: Leroy and Geneva

I've been married a my life.

Learning Objective 18.6

How do intimate partnerships contribute to development in late adulthood?

Watch: Retirement and Adult Development

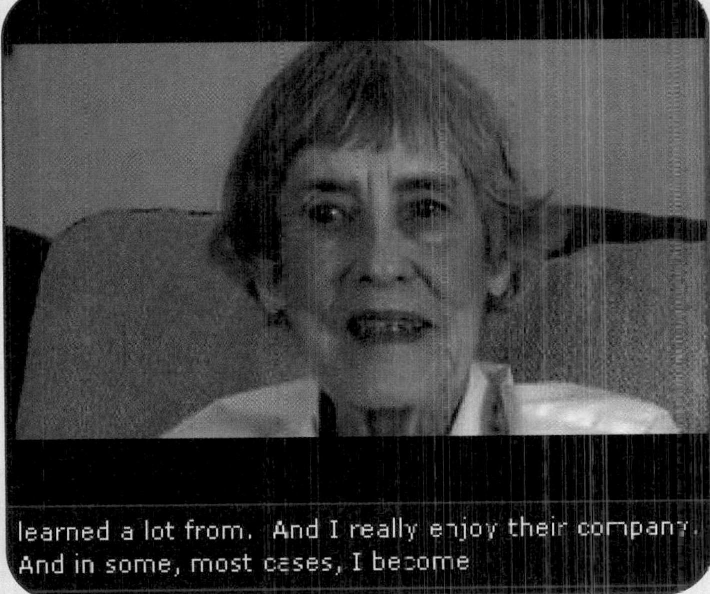

learned a lot from. And I really enjoy their company.
And in some, most cases, I become

Learning Objective 18.10

How does retirement affect income, health, attitudes, emotions, mobility, and social relationships?

Step 3

Take the chapter post-test and compare your results against the pre-test.

POST-TEST

One of the key components of successful aging is

- sticking to routines that are comfortable and familiar so you aren't overwhelmed.
- actively disengaging from roles and relationships and turning inward.
- to expect that other people will help with activities of daily living.
- cognitive adventurousness, or a willingness to learn new things.

19 Death, Dying, and Bereavement

With its soaring Alpine peaks, tranquil lakes, and bustling cities, Switzerland is one of Europe's top vacation destinations. But Switzerland is also the favored destination of travelers whose purpose is far more serious than that of the typical tourist. These visitors come to Switzerland to die.

Switzerland has the most liberal laws in the world regarding *assisted suicide*, a means of dying in which a physician prescribes a lethal dose of drugs to a patient who then administers those drugs to herself. The practice is also legal in the Netherlands, Belgium, and in the state of Oregon, but it is restricted to residents. Thus, individuals who want to end their lives in this manner but whose home countries or states do not allow the procedure have only one option, to travel to Switzerland. Nevertheless, in some cases, the process of going to Switzerland to die is more complicated than you might expect.

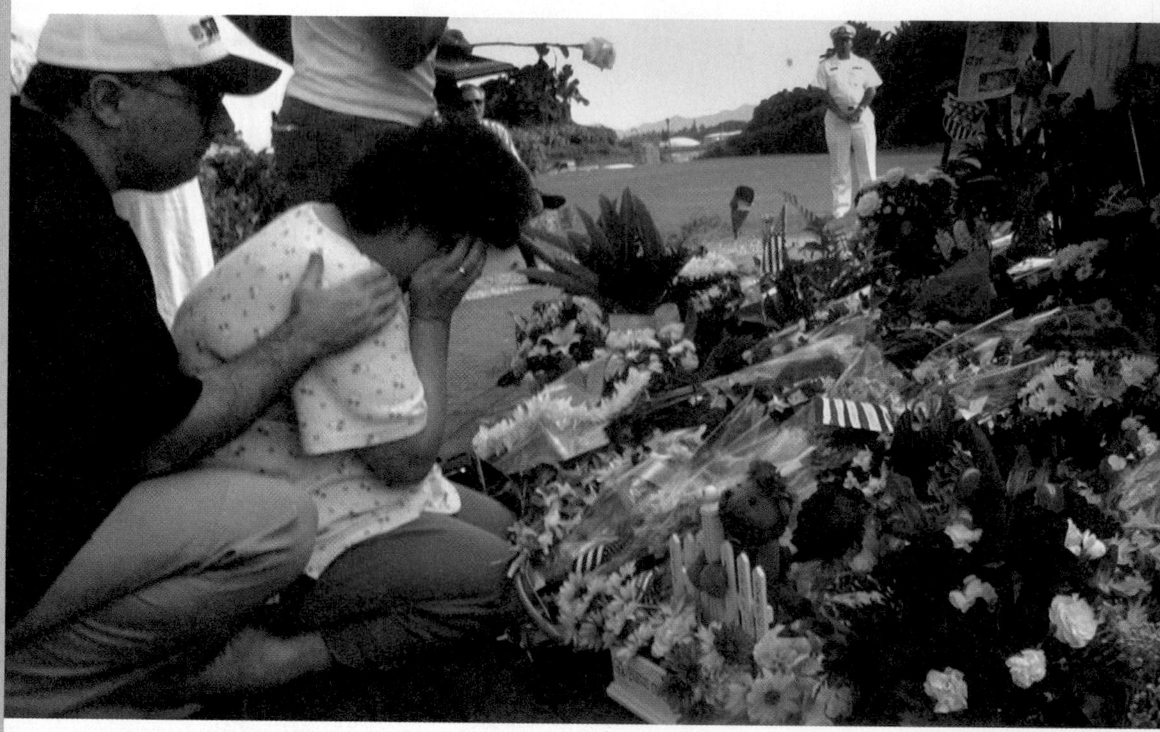

Consider the case of Fiona Cross, a British woman who, in her early 60s, was stricken by a rare neurological disorder that had left her bed-ridden and unable to speak within months of her initial diagnosis. Her cognitive functioning was spared by the disease, but Fiona's only means of communicating with her family and caregivers was to tap out messages on an alphabet board. The woman's family was shocked one day when Fiona used the board to tell them that she wanted to die. Her husband, Harry, and three grown children learned that she had seen a story on television about a clinic in Switzerland where assisted suicide services were available to anyone who sought the procedure as a means of relieving the symptoms of a devastating disease such as the one that had wreaked havoc on Fiona's body for more than six years.

Although her family diligently worked to persuade her to go on living, Fiona was determined to end her life and begged for their help. Reluctantly, Harry arranged to take her to the Swiss clinic in September of 2004. However, when local medical authorities learned of the Crosses' plans, they filed a motion in court to prevent them from leaving the country. The issue that was taken up by the British courts was whether an individual who is ill has the right to leave the country for the purpose of hastening death. Understandably, British officials worried that, if they ruled in favor of the Crosses, individuals with disabilities might be taken advantage of by family members who were no longer willing to care for them. Ultimately, though, the courts ruled that British medical authorities do not have the right to interfere with a patient's decision to leave the country for the purpose of obtaining assisted suicide services. Soon afterward, Fiona died peacefully in a Swiss assisted suicide facility surrounded by her family.

Fiona Cross's case and others like it have become central to a movement in the United Kingdom that seeks to legalize assisted suicide in that country. Similar movements can be found in every nation in the industrialized world. Unlike *euthanasia*, a procedure in which one person intentionally kills another for the purpose of relieving the person's suffering, assisted suicide is, of course, self-inflicted. As a result, debates about its moral acceptability involve elements of both individual rights and the thorny moral questions that surround all issues that involve life and death decisions. Thus, this is yet another of life's complex questions that does not have a simple answer.

The Experience of Death

Most of us use the word *death* as if it described a simple phenomenon. You are either alive or dead. But, in fact, death is a process as well as a state, and physicians have different labels for different aspects of this process. Moreover, for both the deceased and the bereaved, the experience of death is shaped by the circumstances surrounding the end of life.

Learning Objective 19.1

What are the characteristics of clinical death, brain death, and social death?

Death Itself

The term **clinical death** refers to the few minutes after the heart has stopped pumping, when breathing has stopped and there is no evident brain function, but during which resuscitation is still possible. Heart attack patients are sometimes brought back from clinical death; presumably those who report near-death experiences were in a state of clinical death.

Brain death describes a state in which the person no longer has reflexes or any response to vigorous external stimuli and no electrical activity in the brain. When the cortex, but not the brain stem, is affected, the person may still be able to breathe without assistance and may survive for long periods in a vegetative state or on life-support systems. When the brain stem is also dead, no body functioning can occur independently, and the individual is said to be legally dead (Detchant, 1995). Brain death most often occurs after a period of 8–10 minutes of clinical death, but there are cases in which brain death has occurred because of brain injury, as in an auto accident, and other body functions can still be maintained artificially. In such cases, other body organs, such as the heart and kidneys, can be used for organ donation, as long as they are removed without delay.

Social death occurs at the point when the deceased person is treated like a corpse by others; for instance, someone may close the eyes or sign a death certificate. Once social death has been acknowledged, family and friends must begin to deal with the loss.

Learning Objective 19.2

How do hospice and hospital care differ with respect to their effects on terminally ill patients?

Where Death Occurs

Until recently, the great majority of adults died in hospitals. As a result of rising health care costs and changing views about the process of dying, just under half of all deaths in the United States occur in hospitals these days (NCHS, 2007). About 24% take place in the decedent's home, and another 22% happen in nursing homes. The frequency of hospital, nursing home, and home deaths are similar in the United Kingdom and other European countries (Seagroatt & Goldacre, 2004).

The location of an individual's death depends on such factors as age and type of disease or injury. Among the old old, for example, death in a nursing home is quite common. Among younger adults, in contrast, hospital death is the norm. Similarly, adults with progressive diseases, such as cancer or AIDS, are typically in and out of the hospital for months or years before death; at the other end of the continuum are many who are hospitalized with an acute problem, such as a heart attack or pneumonia, and who die soon thereafter, having had no prior hospitalization. In between fall those who have experienced several different types of care in their final weeks or months, including hospitalization, home health care, and nursing home care.

In recent years, however, an alternative form of terminal care that has become common is **hospice care**, an approach to caring for the dying that emphasizes individual and family control of the process. The hospice movement was given a boost by the writings of the late Elisabeth Kübler-Ross, who emphasized the importance of a "good death," or a "death with dignity," in which the patient and the patient's family have more control over the entire process (Kübler-Ross, 1974). Many health care professionals, particularly in England and the United States, believe that such a good death is more likely if the dying person remains at home or in a homelike setting in which contact with family and other friends can be part of daily experience.

Hospice care emerged in England in the late 1960s and in the United States in the early 1970s (Mor, 1987). By 1982, the idea had gained so much support in the United States that Congress was persuaded to add hospice care to the list of benefits paid for by Medicare. There are now more than 1,500 hospice programs in the United States, serving thousands of terminally ill patients and their families. In the United States, roughly 22% of individuals with terminal illnesses receive some kind of hospice care (Stein, 2004).

clinical death a period during which vital signs are absent but resuscitation is still possible

brain death the point at which vital signs, including brain activity, are absent and resuscitation is no longer possible

social death the point at which family members and medical personnel treat the deceased person as a corpse

hospice care an approach to care for the terminally ill that emphasizes individual and family control of the process of dying

The philosophy that underlies this alternative approach to the dying patient has several aspects (Bass, 1985):

- Death should be viewed as normal, not to be avoided but to be faced and accepted.
- The patient and family should be encouraged to prepare for the death by examining their feelings, planning for after the death, and talking openly about the death.
- The family should be involved in the patient's care as much as is physically possible, not only because this gives the patient the emotional support of loved ones, but also because it allows each family member to come to some resolution of her or his relationship with the dying person.
- Control over the patient's care should be in the hands of the patient and the family. They decide what types of medical treatment they will ask for or accept; they decide whether the patient will remain at home or be hospitalized.
- Medical care should be primarily **palliative care** rather than curative treatment. The emphasis is on controlling pain and maximizing comfort, not on invasive or life-prolonging measures.

Three somewhat different types of hospice programs have been developed following these general guidelines (see Table 19.1). The most common hospice programs are home-based programs, in which one family caregiver—most frequently, the dying person's spouse—provides constant care for the dying person with the support and assistance of specially trained nurses or other staff who visit regularly, provide medication, and help the family deal psychologically with the impending death. A second type of program is the special hospice center, where a small number of patients in the last stages of a terminal disease are cared for in a homelike setting. Finally, hospital-based hospice programs provide palliative care according to the basic hospice philosophy, with daily involvement of family members in the patient's care. It is interesting that these three options parallel so closely the basic birth options now available: home delivery, birthing centers, and hospital-based birthing rooms. The fourth choice, both at birth and at death, is traditional hospital care.

The choice of traditional hospital care versus hospice care is most often made on philosophical rather than medical grounds. But it is still worth asking how the two types of care compare in terms of patients' and caregivers' experiences. Two large comparison studies suggest that the differences are small, although the results indicate that patients and caregivers may slightly prefer hospice care.

The National Hospice Study analyzed the experiences of 1,754 terminally ill cancer patients who were treated in 40 different hospices and 14 conventional hospitals (Greer et al., 1986; Mor, Greer, & Kastenbaum, 1988). Half of the hospice programs were home-based, half were hospital-based. The patients were not assigned randomly to hospice or conventional hospital care, but chose their own form of care.

In comparing the two forms of care, the researchers looked at the patient's reported pain and satisfaction with care and at the main caregiver's quality of life and satisfaction. What is remarkable is how similar the experiences of the hospital patients and those of the hospice

Table 19.1 Three Types of Hospice Care

Home-Based Programs	Family caregiver(s) supported by specially trained health care workers
Hospice Centers	A small number of patients cared for by specially trained health care workers in a homelike setting
Hospital-Based Programs	Palliative care provided by hospital personnel, with daily involvement of family members

palliative care a form of care for the terminally ill that focuses on relieving patients' pain, rather than curing their diseases

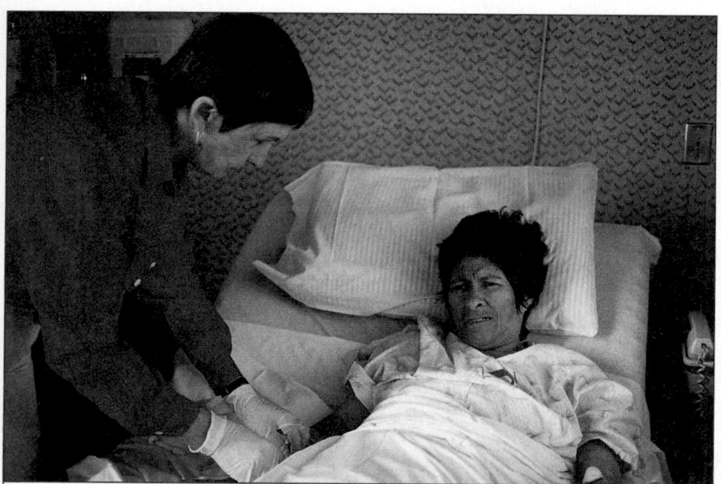

This woman, who is dying of cancer, has chosen to stay at home during her last months, supported by regular visits from hospice nurses.

patients were. There were no differences in patients' reported pain, length of survival, or satisfaction with care. The major finding of the study was that family members were most satisfied with hospital-based hospice care, while those whose loved one chose home-based hospice care reported feeling a greater sense of burden.

In a smaller study, researchers assigned participants randomly to either hospice care or normal hospital care (Kane, Klein, Bernstein, Rothenberg, & Wales, 1985; Kane, Wales, Bernstein, Leibowitz, & Kaplan, 1984). The hospice care in this case was a combination of home-based and hospital-based. Most hospice patients remained at home but spent brief periods in the hospital's hospice ward, either when the family needed a break or when the patient's care become too complex to be handled at home. As in the National Hospice Study, investigators found no differences between these two groups in reports of pain or in length of survival. But they did find that patients in the hospice group were more consistently satisfied with the quality of care they received and with their degree of control over their own care. Similarly, the family members in the hospice group in Kane's study were more satisfied with their own involvement with the patient's care and had lower levels of anxiety than did family members in the hospital-treatment group.

Taken together, these two studies, as well as more recent research, suggest that based on purely objective measures, such as control of pain or survival duration, these two types of terminal care do not differ in effectiveness (Bretscher et al., 1999). Where there is a difference, it is on measures of attitudes or feelings. On some—but not all—of such measures, those in hospice care and their families are slightly more satisfied. In addition, terminally ill patients who are cared for at home through hospice arrangements are admitted to the hospital less often in the last 6 months of life than those who do not receive home-based care (Gozalo & Miller, 2007; Stewart, Pearson, Luke, & Horowitz, 1998). Thus, the economic costs of death are reduced by hospice care. At the same time, both studies make clear that home-based hospice care is a considerable burden, especially on the central caregiver, who may spend as many as 19 hours a day in physical care.

However, both patients and caregivers express concerns about hospice care. For example, both sometimes have more faith in hospital personnel when it comes to providing pain relief. Consequently, patients and their caregivers want assurances that the medical care they will receive in a hospice arrangement will be equivalent in quality to that of a hospital (Vachon, 1998).

In addition, hospice care providers must recognize that caregivers have needs as well. In fact, caring for a dying loved one, particularly someone with dementia, induces a grief response (Lindgren, Connelly, & Gaspar, 1999; Rudd, Viney, & Preston, 1999). Consequently, another important element of hospice care is grief support for the primary caregiver, support that includes both psychosocial and educational components (Meredith & Rassa, 1999; Murphy, Hanrahan, & Luchins, 1997; Tadmor, 2004). Similarly, hospice care providers themselves also often require support services because of the emotional strain involved in caring for patients who are terminally ill.

Critical Thinking

1. What are the advantages and disadvantages of hospice care, and how would you balance them in making a decision about this option for yourself or a loved one?

The Meaning of Death across the Lifespan

As an adult, you understand that death is irreversible, that it comes to everyone, and that it means a cessation of all function. But do children and teenagers understand these aspects of death? And what does death mean to adults of different ages?

Children's and Adolescents' Understanding of Death

Learning Objective 19.3

What are the characteristics of children's and adolescents' ideas about death?

Results from a variety of studies suggest that preschool-aged children typically understand none of these aspects of death. They believe that death can be reversed, for instance, through prayer, magic, or wishful thinking; they believe that dead persons can still feel or breathe. Research shows that young children's ideas about death are rooted in their lack of understanding of life (Slaughter & Lyons, 2003). This link between understanding life and understanding death has been illustrated in a series of studies showing that teaching young children about the nature of biological life helps them understand what causes death and why it is irreversible.

By the time they start school, just about the time Piaget described as the beginning of concrete operations, most children seem to understand both the permanence and the universality of death. Children 6 to 7 years of age comprehend death as a biological event in which the heart ceases to beat, the lungs no longer take in air, and brain activity stops (Barrett & Behne, 2005; Slaughter, 2005). This understanding is clear from children's own comments. In one study, children were told a story about two children who used to go into a candy store kept by an old lady who had recently died (Lansdown & Benjamin, 1985). After they heard the story, the participants were asked some questions about the old lady and about what it meant that she was dead.

> A 5-year-old: "Someone came into the shop to kill her. She'll see them again and she'll die again. She can try to get up."
>
> A 7-year-old: "They never come alive again. You can't move because your heart has stopped. People wish you can come alive but you can't. Children can't die because they start at one and go to 100."
>
> A 9-year-old: "Their heart can't take it any longer and they die. Babies can die of cancer, kidney problems. Heaven is much nicer than down here." (Lansdown & Benjamin, 1985, p. 20)

The first of these children did not yet understand the permanence of death, and the second did not understand its universality, but the third seems to have grasped all three.

As is true of so many other milestones of this age range, the child's specific experience seems to make a good deal of difference. Four- and five-year-olds who have had direct experience with the death of a family member are more likely to understand the permanence of death than are those who have had no such personal experience (Stambrook & Parker, 1987). Experiences in which children discover a dead animal, lose a pet, or are exposed to a story in which a character dies (e.g., *Bambi*, *The Lion King*) can also speed up the process of developing an understanding of death somewhat (Cox, Garrett, & Graham, 2004–2005). Such experiences influence children's understanding of death because they serve as the catalyst for discussions of death with children's parents. Such discussions, when they focus on the concrete, biological aspects of death, provide children with the scaffolding they need to achieve a cognitive understanding of death. Linking death to broader values with which children are familiar helps them grasp the social aspects of death.

These children being comforted by an adult at a loved one's grave are likely to have far more mature concepts of death than others their age who have not encountered death firsthand.

Adolescents understand the finality of death better than children do. Moreover, in an abstract sense, they understand that death is inevitable. Unrealistic beliefs about personal death, however, appear to contribute to adolescent suicide. Typically, teens who attempt suicide claim to understand that death is final, but many tell researchers and counselors that the purpose of their suicidal behavior was to achieve a temporary escape from a stressful personal problem (Blau, 1996). Further, researchers have found that some teenagers who attempt suicide believe that death is a pleasurable experience for most people who die (Gothelf et al., 1998). Certainly, such distorted beliefs may be the result of the powerful emotions that lead teens to attempt suicide, rather than the product of adolescent thinking. However, suicidal adults typically think of death, even when it is desired, as painful and unpleasant. So there may be a developmental difference between suicidal adolescents' and suicidal adults' understanding of death.

Like those of children, adolescents' ideas about death are affected by their personal experiences. Experiencing the death of a family member or friend, especially someone who is near the teenager's own age, tends to shake an adolescent's confidence in her own immortality. In fact, research suggests that the loss of someone close, such as a sibling, may lead an adolescent to critically re-examine her ideas about death—both as a general concept and as something that is inevitable for herself (Batten & Oltjenbruns, 1999).

Learning Objective 19.4

How do young, middle-aged, and older adults think about death?

The Meaning of Death for Adults

Adults' ideas about death vary with age. Death seems remote to most young adults. The notion of personal mortality is a more common focus of thought in middle age, and by the later years, the idea of death becomes very personally relevant for most adults.

After the death of Steve Irwin, members of the public left thousands of flowers and gifts in front of the Australia Zoo, an institution that Irwin founded, in a spontaneous gesture of grief. Based on analyses of such responses to the deaths of public figures, some developmentalists believe that young adults idealize celebrities who die in early adulthood in order to avoid confronting their own mortality.

Early Adulthood In recent years, research examining young adults' views on death has been guided by a theoretical concept similar to the personal fable, discussed in Chapter 12. Psychologists point out that young adults have a sense of **unique invulnerability**—a belief that bad things, including death, happen to others but not to themselves. Although young adults are more realistic about personal mortality than adolescents are, researchers find that many believe they possess unique personal characteristics that somehow protect them against death. For example, researchers often ask participants of various ages to use life-expectancy statistics and risk-factor self-ratings to predict the age at which they will die. Such studies usually find that young adults overestimate their own life expectancy (Snyder, 1997). Moreover, young adults are more likely than those who are middle-aged or older to show increased fear of death following open discussions of the process of dying (Abengozar, Bueno, & Vega, 1999).

Here again, actual experience with death makes a difference. For example, nursing students display less fear of death than college students pursuing other careers, and their anxieties about death lessen with each additional year of training (Sharma, Monsen, & Gary, 1997). Moreover, the loss of a loved one appears to shake a young adult's belief in unique invulnerability and, as a result, is often more traumatic for younger than for older adults (Liu & Aaker, 2007). In fact, such losses frequently lead to suicidal thoughts in young adults. Young adults who have recently lost a loved one in an accident or to a homicide or suicide are about five times as likely to formulate a suicide plan as young adults who have not had such a loss, although most never follow through with their plans (Prigerson et al., 1999).

Analyses of public reactions to the deaths of relatively young celebrities, such as Princess Diana and crocodile hunter Steve Irwin, provide additional insight into young adults' ideas about death. As you may have noticed, perceptions of these public figures often change dramatically after their deaths, and they are given heroic status (Bourreille, 1999; Gibson, 2007). Moreover, public interest in the events surrounding their deaths, as evidenced by the frequency of tabloid headline stories devoted to them, continues for many years afterward (Brown, Basil, & Bocarnea, 2003). Psychologists hypothesize that such early deaths challenge young people's beliefs in unique invulnerability and, therefore, provoke defensive reactions that cause them to place those who die young in a special category. In other words, to maintain belief in their own unique invulnerability, young people must come up with reasons why death came early to Steve Irwin but will not happen to them. As a result, they elevate such figures to near-sainthood.

unique invulnerability the belief that bad things, including death, happen only to others

Middle and Late Adulthood In middle and late adulthood, an understanding of death goes well beyond the simple acceptance of finality, inevitability, and universality. A death changes the roles and relationships of everyone else in a family. For example, when an elder dies, everyone else in that particular lineage "moves up" in the generational system. As you learned in Chapter 16, the death of a parent can be particularly unsettling for a middle-aged adult if the adult does not yet consider himself ready to assume the elder role.

An individual's death also affects the roles of people beyond the family such as younger adults in a business organization, who then take on new and perhaps more significant roles. Retirement serves the same function, as an older adult steps aside for a younger one. But death brings many permanent changes in families and social systems.

At an individual level, the prospect of death may shape one's view of time (Kalish, 1985). In middle age, most people exhibit a shift in their thinking about time, thinking less about "time since birth" and being more aware of "time till death," a transition clearly reflected in the comment of this middle-aged adult:

> Before I was 35, the future just stretched forth. There would be time to do and see and carry out all the plans I had. . . Now I keep thinking, will I have time enough to finish off some of the things I want to do? (Neugarten, 1970, p. 78)

Such an "awareness of finitude" is not a part of every middle-aged or older adult's view of death (Marshall, 1975). One study of a group of adults aged 72 and older found that only about half thought in terms of "time remaining" (Keith, 1981/1982). Interestingly, those who did think of death in these terms had less fear of death than did those who thought of their lives as "time lived." Other research confirms this: Middle-aged and older adults who continue to be preoccupied with the past are more likely to be fearful and anxious about death (Pollack, 1979/1980).

Death as Loss The most pervasive meaning of death for adults of all ages is loss. Which of the many potential losses is feared or dreaded the most seems to change with age. Young adults are more concerned about loss of opportunity to experience things and about the loss of family relationships; older adults worry more about the loss of time to complete inner work. Such differences are evident in the results of a classic study in which researchers interviewed roughly 400 adults, equally divided into four ethnic groups: African American, Japanese American, Mexican American, and White American (Kalish & Reynolds, 1976). Among many other questions, researchers asked, "If you were told that you had a terminal disease and 6 months to live, how would you want to spend your time until you died?" Think about this question for a moment yourself. Then look at Table 19.2, which shows both the ethnic differences and the age differences in responses to this question.

Table 19.2 Responses to Hypothetical Impending Death (percentages)

	Ethnic Group				Age Group		
	African American	Japanese American	Mexican American	White American	20–39	40–59	60+
Make a marked change in lifestyle (e.g., travel, have new experiences)	16	24	11	17	24	15	9
Center on inner life (e.g., read, contemplate, pray)	26	20	24	12	14	14	37
Focus concern on others; be with loved ones	14	15	38	23	29	25	12
Attempt to complete projects, tie up loose ends	6	8	13	6	11	10	3
No change in lifestyle	31	25	12	36	17	29	31

(*Source*: Kalish & Reynolds, 1976, p. 205, Item 037.)

You can see that the only sizable ethnic difference was that Mexican Americans were the most likely to say that they would increase the time they spent with family or other loved ones. Age differences were more substantial. Younger adults were more likely to say that they would seek out new experiences; older adults were considerably more likely to say that they would turn inward—an interesting piece of support for disengagement theory.

Learning Objective 19.5

What factors are related to fear of death in adults?

Fear of Death

Surveys show that more than 80% of adults in the United States say that they do not fear death (Public Agenda, 2004b). However, survey questions such as "Do you fear death?" are far too simplistic to capture how people really feel about an issue as momentous as their own death. Thus, psychologists who study people's death-related fears have tried a number of ways to elicit more thoughtful responses than are typically generated by surveys.

One such approach is to ask participants to indicate, on a 5-point scale, how disturbed or anxious they feel when thinking about various aspects of death or dying, such as "the shortness of life" or "never thinking or experiencing anything again" or "your lack of control over the process of dying" (Lester, 1990). Another approach asks participants to respond to statements such as "I fear dying a painful death" or "Coffins make me anxious" or "I am worried about what happens to us after we die" (Thorson & Powell, 1992).

Fear of Death across Adulthood Although you might think that those closest to death would fear it the most, research suggests that middle-aged adults are most fearful of death (Kumabe, 2006). For young adults, the sense of unique invulnerability probably prevents intense fears of death. In middle-age, though, belief in one's own immortality begins to break down, resulting in increasing anxiety about the end of life. However, by late life, the inevitability of death has been accepted, and anxieties are focused on how death will actually come about.

The difference between the middle-aged and the aged is especially clear from a study in which researchers interviewed a sample of adults, aged 45 to 74, chosen to represent the population of Los Angeles (Bengtson, Cuellar, & Ragan, 1977). Figure 19.1 shows the percentage of people in each age group who said they were "very afraid" or "somewhat afraid" of death. The fact that the shape of the curve is so remarkably similar for all three ethnic groups makes the results even more persuasive. And although these are cross-sectional results, similar patterns have emerged from cross-sectional comparisons done in the 1960s and the 1980s, which makes the conclusion that much more credible (e.g., Gesser, Wong, & Reker, 1987/1988).

Figure 19.1
Age and Fear of Death

The remarkable similarity in the pattern of results for these three ethnic groups lends support to the generalization that older adults are less afraid of death than are the middle-aged.

(*Source*: Bengtson et al., 1977, Figure 1, p. 80.)

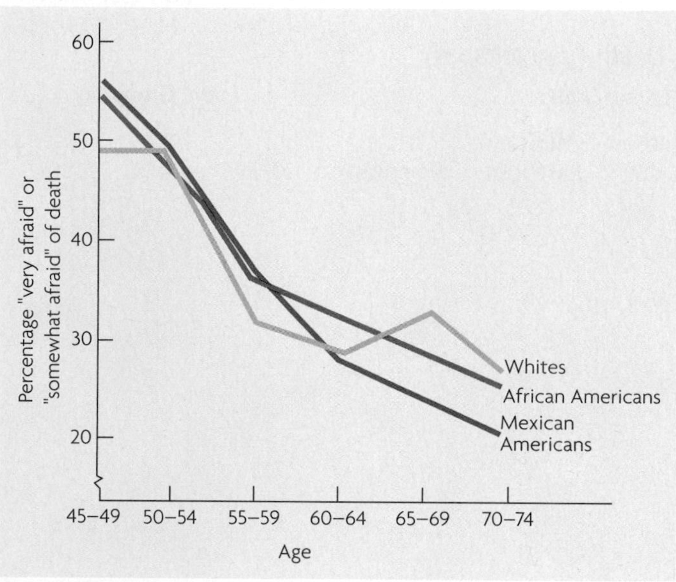

However, older adults do not become less preoccupied with death. On the contrary, the elderly think and talk more about death than do those at any other age. Predictably, these discussions lead to less fear and anxiety about death among older adults (Abengozar et al., 1999). Thus, to an older person, particularly one who has a strong sense of having lived for some higher purpose, death is highly important, but it is apparently not as frightening as it was at mid-life (Cicirelli, 2006). Older adults are more likely to fear the period of uncertainty before death than they are to fear death itself (Sullivan, Ormel, Kempen, & Tymstra, 1998). They are anxious about where they may die, who will care for them until they do, and whether they will be able to cope with the pain and loss of control and independence that may be part of the last months or years of life (Marshall & Levy, 1990).

Religious Beliefs Researchers typically find that adults who are religious are less afraid of death than are those who describe themselves as less religious (Ardelt, 2003; Kalish, 1985; Lin, 2003; Thorson & Powell, 1990). In some instances, however, researchers have found that both those who are deeply religious and those who are totally irreligious report less fear of death. Thus, the most fearful may be those who are uncertain about or uncommitted to any religious or philosophical tradition.

Religious beliefs may moderate fears of death because religious people tend to view death as a transition from one form of life to another, from physical life to some kind of immortality. In the United States, roughly 80% of the population believes in some kind of life after death (CBS News Polls, 2005). Such a belief is more common among women than among men, and more common among Catholics and Protestants than among Jews, but there is no age difference. Twenty-year-olds are just as likely to report such a belief as are those over 60.

In addition to framing death as a transition rather than an end, religious beliefs provide adults with death stories that help them cope with both their own deaths and those of loved ones (Winter, 1999). For example, Jewish scriptures, the Christian Bible, and the Muslim Quran all contain many stories that convey the idea that death comes when one's purpose in life has been fulfilled. Many such stories also teach that each individual life is part of a larger, multi-generational story. In this larger context, death is portrayed as a necessary part of the transfer of responsibility from one generation to another. This kind of philosophical approach to death leads believers to focus on the contributions to family and community that they have made during their lives rather than on the losses they will experience at their deaths.

Personal Worth Feelings about death are also linked to one's sense of personal worth or competence. Adults who feel that they have achieved the goals they set out to achieve or who believe that they have become the person they wanted to be are less anxious about death than are those who are disappointed in themselves (Ardelt & Koenig, 2006). Adults who believe that their lives have had some purpose or meaning also appear to be less fearful of death, as do those who have some sense of personal competence (Durlak, 1972; Pollack, 1979/1980).

Such findings suggest the possibility that adults who have successfully completed the major tasks of adult life, who have adequately fulfilled the demands of the roles they occupied, and who have developed inwardly are able to face death with greater equanimity. Adults who have not been able to resolve the various tasks and dilemmas of adulthood face their late adult years more anxiously, even with what Erikson described as despair. Fear of death may be merely one facet of such despair.

Preparation for Death

Learning Objective 19.6
How do adults prepare for death?

Preparation for death occurs on a number of levels (see No Easy Answers on page 550). At a practical level, regardless of age, most adults agree that it is important to make preparations for death (Steinhauser et al., 2001). According to most people, in addition to purchasing life insurance and making a will, such preparations should include issuing directives regarding end-of-life care, often called a *living will*. Individuals can use living wills to make clear to health care professionals and to their families that they either do or do not wish to have their lives prolonged with feeding tubes and other devices. Moreover, most people agree that advance funeral planning can help bereaved family members deal with the many decisions they must make in the hours and days following the death of a loved one. However, researchers have found that older adults are far more likely than younger adults to have actually made such preparations (Bravo, Dubois, & Paquet, 2003).

At a somewhat deeper level, adults may prepare for death through some process of reminiscence. Deeper still, there may be unconscious changes that occur in the years just before death, which might be thought of as a type of preparation. You read about the physical and mental changes associated with terminal drop in Chapter 17. Research has pointed to the possibility that there may be terminal psychological changes as well.

NO EASY ANSWERS

Saying Goodbye

The Kaliai, a small Melanesian society in Papua New Guinea, believe that all deaths are caused by a person or spirit whom the dying person has offended in some way (Counts, 1976/1977). Any person who feels that he is near death moves from his house into a temporary shelter, where he attempts to appease whichever person or spirit he thinks he may have offended. He also attempts to thwart death through the use of various medicines and cures. When death becomes imminent, family members and friends return items borrowed from the dying person and pay debts they owe him. Likewise, the dying person returns borrowed items and repays debts owed to family and friends. The Kaliai believe that this process of bringing relationships into balance prepares the dying person for an afterlife in which he will become a powerful superhuman being.

But how do you say goodbye to a dying loved one, or how does a dying person say goodbye to loved ones, in a culture where discussions of death are largely taboo? Research suggests that in the United States, even physicians who routinely treat terminally ill patients are reluctant to state directly that a patient is going to die (Lutfey & Maynard, 1998). Moreover, the sufferer and her loved ones may avoid discussions of death because admitting that death is approaching may be seen as rejection of the possibility of recovery. Family members may believe that discussing death will undermine the terminally ill patient's optimism and ability to fight the disease. Likewise, those who are dying may not want to make their loved ones feel bad. Still, most people in these situations feel that they must balance the need for closure against fears of fostering pessimism. Consequently, many terminally ill adults and their families create indirect methods of saying farewell.

A classic study in Australia gives a glimpse of the variety of such goodbyes devised by the dying (Kellehear & Lewin, 1988/1989). Researchers interviewed 90 terminally ill cancer patients, all of whom expected to die within a year. Most had known of their cancer diagnosis for at least a year prior to the interview but had only recently been given a short-term prognosis. As part of the interview, these 90 people were asked if they had already said farewell to anyone, and to describe any plans they had for future farewells. To whom did they want to say goodbye, and how would they say it?

About a fifth of these people planned no farewells. Another three-fifths thought it was important to say goodbye, but wanted to put it off until very near the end so as to distress family and friends as little as possible. They hoped that there would then be time for a few final words with spouses, children, and close friends. The remaining fifth began their farewells much earlier and used many different avenues. In a particularly touching farewell gesture, one woman who had two grown daughters but no grandchildren knitted a set of baby clothes for each daughter, for the grandchildren she would never see.

Kellehear and Lewin make the important point that such farewells are a kind of gift. They signal that the dying person feels that someone is worthy of a last goodbye. Such farewells may also represent a balancing of the relationship slate just as important as the balancing of material possessions is among the Kaliai.

Farewells also may allow the dying person to disengage more readily when death comes closer, and to warn others that death is indeed approaching. Hearing someone say farewell may thus help the living to begin a kind of anticipatory grieving, and in this way prepare better for the loss.

Take a Stand

Decide which of these two statements you most agree with and think about how you would defend your position:

1. Neither a person who is ill nor her loved ones should ever give up on life. They should always be thinking in terms of how to help the sick person survive rather than focusing on saying goodbye.
2. Acknowledging the reality of approaching death is the best way to help a person who is ill and those who are close to her cope with the stress of losing a loved one.

For example, in a still influential study, researchers studied a group of older adults longitudinally, interviewing and testing each participant regularly over a period of 3 years (Lieberman, 1965; Lieberman & Coplan, 1970). After the testing, investigators kept track of the participants and noted when they died. They were able to identify one group of 40 participants who had all died within 1 year of the end of the interviewing and to compare them with another group of 40, matched to the first group by age, sex, and marital status, who had survived at least 3 years after the end of the testing. By comparing the psychological test scores obtained by those in these two groups during the course of the 3 years of testing, researchers could detect changes that occurred near death.

The study's results revealed that those nearer death not only showed terminal drop on tests of memory and learning, but also became less emotional, introspective, and aggressive or assertive and more conventional, docile, dependent, and warm. In those near death, all these characteristics increased over the 3 years of interviewing, a pattern that did not occur among those of the same age who were further from death. Thus, conventional, docile, dependent, and nonintrospective adults did not die sooner; rather, these qualities became accentuated in those who were close to death.

This is only a single study. As always in such cases, it's important to be careful about drawing sweeping conclusions from limited evidence. But the results are intriguing and suggestive. They paint a picture of a kind of psychological preparation for death—conscious or unconscious—in which an individual "gives up the fight," becoming less active physically and psychologically. Thus, near death, individuals do not necessarily become less involved with other people, but they do seem to show some kind of disengagement.

> ### Critical Thinking
> **1.** What role do age and fear of death play in people's decisions about death preparations such as living wills and prepaid funeral arrangements?

The Process of Dying

The late Elisabeth Kübler-Ross (1926–2004) was a Swiss-American psychiatrist who studied the experiences of the dying and their loved ones. In the 1960s, Kübler-Ross formulated a model that asserted that those who are dying go through a series of psychological stages. These stages of dying, which were formulated on the basis of interviews with approximately 200 adults who were dying of cancer, continue to be highly influential, although Kübler-Ross's model has many critics. In addition, research suggests that individual differences affect the process of dying in important ways.

Kübler-Ross's Stages of Dying

> **Learning Objective 19.7**
> How did Kübler-Ross explain the process of dying?

In Kübler-Ross's early writings, she proposed that those who know they are dying move through a series of steps, or stages, arriving finally at the stage she called *acceptance* (see Table 19.3). Kübler-Ross's ideas and her terminology are still widely used. In fact, surveys of death education programs suggest that Kübler-Ross's model is the only systematic approach to the dying process to which health professionals-in-training are exposed (Downe-Wamboldt & Tamlyn, 1997). Thus, you should at least be familiar with the stages she proposed.

Kübler-Ross's model predicts that most people who are confronted with a terminal diagnosis react with some variant of "Not me!" "It must be a mistake," "I'll get another opinion," or "I don't feel sick." All of these are forms of *denial*, a psychological defense that may be highly useful in the early hours and days after such a diagnosis. Denial of this kind may be helpful in insulating a person's emotions from the trauma of hearing such news. Keeping emotions in check in this way may help an individual formulate a rational plan of action based on "what if it's true?" Having a plan of action may help moderate the effects of acknowledging the reality of the diagnosis. Kübler-Ross thought that these extreme forms of denial would fade within a few days, to be replaced by *anger*.

The model further suggests that anger among the dying expresses itself in thoughts like "It's not fair!" but a dying person may also express anger toward God, the doctor who made the diagnosis, nurses, or family members. The anger seems to be a response not only to the

Table 19.3 Stages of Dying Proposed by Kübler-Ross

Denial	People's first reaction to news of a terminal diagnosis is disbelief.
Anger	Once the diagnosis is accepted as real, individuals become angry.
Bargaining	Anger and stress are managed by thinking of the situation in terms of exchanges (e.g., If I take my medicine, I will live longer; if I pray hard enough, God will heal me).
Depression	Feelings of despair follow when the disease advances despite the individual's compliance with medical and other advice.
Acceptance	Grieving for the losses associated with one's death results in acceptance.

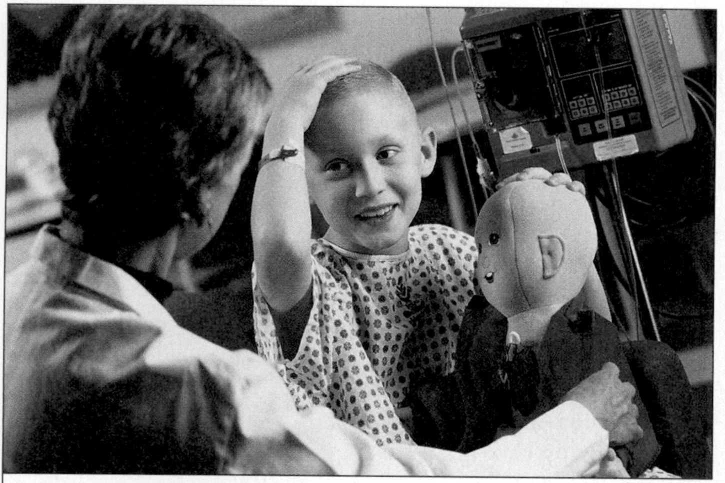

Children use some of the same defenses as adults to deal with impending death. Young cancer patients may deny or bargain—for instance, "If I take my medicine I'll be able to go back to school in the fall."

diagnosis itself but also to the sense of loss of control and helplessness that many patients feel in impersonal medical settings.

Bargaining follows anger in the Kübler-Ross model. This is a form of defense in which the patient tries to make "deals" with doctors, nurses, family, or God: "If I do everything you tell me, then I'll live till spring." Kübler-Ross gave a particularly compelling example of this defense reaction: A patient with terminal cancer wanted to live long enough to attend the wedding of her eldest son. The hospital staff, to help her try to reach this goal, taught her self-hypnosis to deal with her pain, and she was able to attend the wedding. Kübler-Ross reported, "I will never forget the moment when she returned to the hospital. She looked tired and somewhat exhausted and—before I could say hello—said, 'Now don't forget, I have another son!' " (1969, p. 83).

Bargaining may be successful as a defense for a while, but the model predicts that, eventually, bargaining breaks down in the face of signs of declining health. At this point, Kübler-Ross's theory predicts, the patient enters the stage of *depression*. According to Kübler-Ross, depression, or despair, is a necessary preparation for the final stage of *acceptance*. In order to reach acceptance, the dying person must grieve for all that will be lost with death.

Learning Objective 19.8

What are some other views of the process of dying?

Criticisms and Alternative Views

Kübler-Ross's model has provided a common language for those who work with dying patients, and her highly compassionate descriptions have, without doubt, sensitized health care workers and families to the complexities of the process of dying. At some moments, what the patient needs is cheering up; at other moments, he simply needs someone to listen to him. There are times to hold his hand quietly and times to provide encouragement or hope. Many new programs for terminally ill patients are clearly outgrowths of this greater sensitivity to the dying process.

These are all worthwhile changes. But Kübler-Ross's basic thesis—that the dying process necessarily involves these specific five stages, in this specific order—has been widely criticized. Kübler-Ross responded to critics by pointing out that she had not meant for the stages she proposed to be interpreted as rigidly as some researchers and practitioners suggested they should be. Nevertheless, criticisms of her model go beyond concerns about its stages.

Methodological Problems Kübler-Ross's hypothesized sequence was initially based on clinical observation of 200 patients, and she did not provide information about how frequently she talked to them or over how long a period she continued to assess them. She also did not report the ages of the patients she studied, although it is clear that many were middle-aged or young adults, for whom a terminal illness was obviously "off time." Nearly all were apparently cancer patients. Would the same processes be evident in those dying of other diseases, for which it is much less common to have a specific diagnosis or a short-term prognosis? In other words, Kübler-Ross's observations might be correct, but only for a small subset of dying individuals.

Cultural Specificity A related question has to do with whether reactions to dying are culture-specific or universal. Kübler-Ross wrote as if the five stages of dying were universal human processes. However, cross-cultural studies suggest that cultures vary considerably in what they believe to be a "good death" (Westerhof, Katzko, Dittman-Kohli, & Hayslip, 2001). For individuals in Western societies, such as the United States, maintenance of individual autonomy over the dying process is of paramount importance. The idea that a dying person should have the right to take his or her own life is more widely accepted in individualistic than in collectivist cultures (Kemmelmeier, Wieczorkowska, Erb, & Burnstein, 2002). Thus, certain aspects of Kübler-Ross's theory, such as the concepts associated with the bargaining stage, may be less important to people in collectivist cultures than they were to the people who participated in her initial studies.

Similarly, in some Native American cultures, death is to be faced and accepted with composure. Because it is part of nature's cycle, it is not to be feared or fought (DeSpelder & Strickland, 1983). And, in Mexican culture, death is seen as a mirror of the person's life. Thus, your way of dying tells much about what kind of person you have been. Furthermore, in Mexican culture, death is discussed frequently, even celebrated in a national feast day, the Day of the Dead (DeSpelder & Strickland, 1983). Would it be reasonable to expect denial, anger, bargaining, and so on, in the context of such cultural expectations?

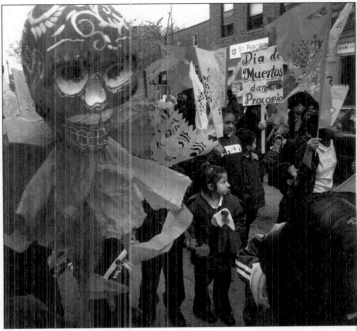

In Mexican culture, the Day of the Dead is an important feast day on which the lives of the dead are remembered and honored.

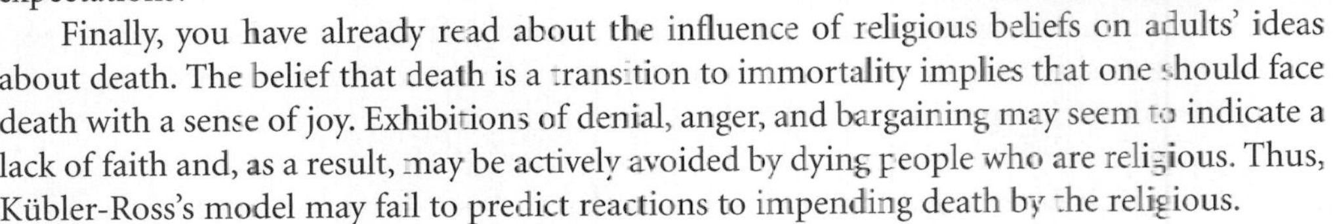

Finally, you have already read about the influence of religious beliefs on adults' ideas about death. The belief that death is a transition to immortality implies that one should face death with a sense of joy. Exhibitions of denial, anger, and bargaining may seem to indicate a lack of faith and, as a result, may be actively avoided by dying people who are religious. Thus, Kübler-Ross's model may fail to predict reactions to impending death by the religious.

The Stage Concept The most potent criticism of Kübler-Ross's model, however, centers on the issue of stages. Many clinicians and researchers who have attempted to study the process systematically have found that not all dying patients exhibit these five emotions, let alone in a specific order. Of the five, only depression seems to be common among Western patients. Further, neither Kübler-Ross's acceptance nor Cumming and Henry's disengagement (discussed in Chapter 18) appears to be a common end point of the dying process (Baugher, Burger, Smith, & Wallston, 1989/1990). Some patients display acceptance; others remain as active and engaged as possible right up to the end. Edwin Shneidman (1980, 1983), a major theorist and clinician in the field of **thanatology** (the scientific study of death and dying), puts it this way:

> I reject the notion that human beings, as they die, are somehow marched in lock step through a series of stages of the dying process. On the contrary, in working with dying persons, I see a wide [array] of human feelings and emotions, of various human needs, and a broad selection of psychological defenses and maneuvers—a few of these in some people, dozens in others—experienced in an impressive variety of ways. (1980, p. 110)

Instead of stages, Shneidman suggests that the dying process has many "themes" that can appear, disappear, and reappear in any one patient in the process of dealing with death. These themes include terror, pervasive uncertainty, fantasies of being rescued, incredulity, feelings of unfairness, a concern with reputation after death, and fear of pain.

Another alternative to Kübler-Ross's model is a "task-based" approach suggested by Charles Corr (1991/1992). In his view, coping with dying is like coping with any other problem or dilemma: You need to take care of certain specific tasks. He suggests four such tasks for the dying person:

- Satisfying bodily needs and minimizing physical stress
- Maximizing psychological security, autonomy, and richness of life
- Sustaining and enhancing significant interpersonal attachments
- Identifying, developing, or reaffirming sources of spiritual energy, and thereby fostering hope

thanatology the scientific study of death and dying

Corr does not deny the importance of the various emotional themes described by Shneidman. Rather, he argues that for health professionals who deal with dying individuals, it is more helpful to think in terms of the patient's tasks, because the dying person may need help in performing some or all of them.

Whichever model one uses, what is clear is that there are no common patterns that typify most or all reactions to impending death. Common themes exist, but they are blended together in quite different patterns by each person who faces this last task.

Learning Objective 19.9

How do people vary in the ways they adapt to impending death?

Responses to Impending Death

Individual variations in responding to imminent death have themselves been the subject of a good deal of research interest in the past few decades. In one study involving 26 terminally ill men, researchers found that many of the men believed that they could avoid entering into the process of actively dying by continuing to engage in their favorite hobbies (Vig & Pearlman, 2003). Such findings raise questions about whether attitudes and behavioral choices can influence the course of a terminal disease.

The most influential research along these lines has been the work of Steven Greer and his colleagues (Greer, 1991, 1999; Greer, Morris, & Pettingale, 1979; Pettingale, Morris, Greer, & Haybittle, 1985). They followed a group of 62 women diagnosed in the 1970s with early stages of breast cancer. Three months after the original diagnosis, each woman was interviewed at some length and her reaction to the diagnosis and to her treatment was classed in one of five groups:

- *Denial (positive avoidance).* Person rejects evidence about diagnosis; insists that surgery was just precautionary.
- *Fighting spirit.* Person maintains an optimistic attitude and searches for more information about the disease. These patients often see their disease as a challenge and plan to fight it with every method available.
- *Stoic acceptance (fatalism).* Person acknowledges the diagnosis but makes no effort to seek any further information, or person ignores the diagnosis and carries on normal life as much as possible.
- *Helplessness/hopelessness.* Person acts overwhelmed by diagnosis; sees herself as dying or gravely ill and as devoid of hope.
- *Anxious preoccupation.* Women in this category had originally been included in the helplessness group, but they were separated out later. The category includes those whose response to the diagnosis is strong and persistent anxiety. If they seek information, they interpret it pessimistically; they monitor their body sensations carefully, interpreting each ache or pain as a possible recurrence.

Greer then checked on the survival rates of these five groups after 5, 10, and 15 years. Table 19.4 shows the 15-year survival rates. Only 35% of those whose initial reaction had been either denial or fighting spirit had died of cancer 15 years later, compared with 76% of those whose initial reaction had been stoic acceptance, anxious preoccupation, or helplessness/hopelessness. Because those in the five groups did not differ initially in the stage of their disease or in their treatment, these results support the hypothesis that psychological responses contribute to disease progress—just as coping strategies more generally affect the likelihood of disease in the first place.

Similar results have emerged from studies of patients with melanoma (a form of skin cancer), as well as other cancers, and from several studies of AIDS patients (Juan et al., 2003; Penedo et al., 2005; Reed, Kemeny, Taylor, Wang, & Visscher, 1994; Solano et al., 1993; Temoshok, 1987). And at least one study of coronary bypass patients showed that men who had a more optimistic attitude before the surgery recovered more quickly in the 6 months after surgery and returned more fully to their presurgery pattern of life (Scheier et al., 1989). In general, individuals who report less hostility, who express more stoic acceptance and more

Table 19.4 15-Year Outcomes among Women Cancer Patients

Psychological Attitude 3 Months after Surgery	Alive and Well	Died from Cancer	Died from Other Causes	Total
	Outcome 15 Years Later			
Denial	5	5	0	10
Fighting spirit	4	2	4	10
Stoic acceptance	6	24	3	33
Anxious preoccupation	0	3	0	3
Helplessness/hopelessness	1	5	0	6
Total	16	39	7	62

(*Source*: Adaptation from "Psychological Response to Cancer and Survival", by S. Greer from *Psychological Medicine*, Vol 21, Table 1, p. 45, 1991. Reprinted with permission of Cambridge University Press.)

helplessness, and who fail to express negative feelings die sooner (O'Leary, 1990). Those who struggle the most, who fight the hardest, who express their anger and hostility openly, and who also find some sources of joy in their lives live longer. In some ways, the data suggest that "good patients"—those who are obedient and who do not question or fight with their doctors or make life difficult for those around them—are in fact likely to die sooner. Difficult patients, who question and challenge those around them, last longer.

Furthermore, a few studies have linked these psychological differences to immune system functioning. A particular subset of immune cells called NK cells, thought to form an important defense against cancer, have been found in higher numbers among patients who are optimistic and openly express their anger about being ill (Penedo et al., 2005). And one study of AIDS patients showed that T-cell counts declined more rapidly among those who responded to their disease with repression (similar to the stoic acceptance and helplessness groups in the Greer study), while those who showed a fighting spirit had slower loss of T cells (Solano et al., 1993).

Despite the consistency of these results, two important cautions are in order before you leap to the conclusion that a fighting spirit is the optimum response to any disease. First, some careful studies find no link between depression, stoic acceptance, or helplessness and more rapid death from cancer (e.g., Cassileth, Walsh, & Lusk, 1988; Kung et al., 2006; Richardson, Zarnegar, Bisno, & Levine, 1990). Second, it is not clear that the same psychological response is necessarily appropriate for every disease. Consider heart disease, for example. There is a certain irony in the fact that many of the responses to cancer that appear to be optimum could be considered as reflections of a type A personality. Because having a type A personality constitutes a risk factor for heart disease, a "fighting spirit" response to a diagnosis of advanced heart disease might not be the most desirable. The growing body of research on responses to diseases does confirm, though, that there are connections between psychological defenses or ways of coping and physical functioning, even in the last stages of life.

Another important ingredient in an individual's response to imminent death is the amount of social support he has. Those with positive and supportive relationships describe lower levels of pain and less depression during their final months of illness (Carey, 1974; Hinton, 1975). Such well-supported patients also live longer. For example, both African American and White American heart attack patients who live alone are more likely to have a second heart attack than are those who live with someone else. Similarly, those with significant levels of atherosclerosis live longer if they have a confidant than if they do not (Case, Moss, Case, McDermott, & Eberly, 1992; Williams, 1992).

This link between social support and length of survival has also been found in experimental studies in which patients with equivalent diagnoses and equivalent medical care have

Critical Thinking

1. In what ways is Kübler-Ross's model helpful to health care professionals who work with terminal patients, and in what ways might the model interfere with their responses to the needs of patients?

been randomly assigned either to an experimental group in which they participate in regular support group sessions or to a control group in which they have no such support system. In one study of a group of 86 women with metastatic breast cancer (that is, cancer that had spread beyond the original site), researchers found that the average length of survival was 36.6 months for those who had access to the support group compared with 18.9 months for those in the control group (Spiegel, Bloom, Kraemer, & Gottheil, 1989). Thus, just as social support helps to buffer children and adults from some of the negative effects of many kinds of nonlethal stress, so it seems to perform a similar function for those facing death.

Theoretical Perspectives on Grieving

There are a number of ways of looking at the emotion of grief, but the two that have had the greatest influence on the way psychologists think about grief are Freud's psychoanalytic theory and Bowlby's attachment theory.

Learning Objective 19.10
How does Freud's psychoanalytic theory view grief?

Freud's Psychoanalytic Theory

From the psychoanalytic perspective, the death of a loved one is an emotional trauma. As with any trauma, the ego, or mind, tries to insulate itself from the unpleasant emotions such losses induce through the use of defense mechanisms, including denial and repression. However, Freud believed that defense mechanisms were only temporary devices for dealing with negative emotions. Eventually, he thought, the individual must examine the emotions and their source directly. Otherwise, such emotions lead to the development of physical symptoms and, perhaps, mental illnesses.

Freud's view has been very influential in grief counseling and in popular notions about the necessity of "working through" grief in order to avoid its long-term negative effects. It is generally accepted that bereaved individuals need to talk openly about their loss. Thus, grief counselors often recommend that friends of a bereaved person encourage the person to cry or express grief in other ways.

Psychoanalytically based grief therapy for children often emphasizes the use of defense mechanisms other than denial and repression to cope with grief. Following this approach, therapists sometimes encourage children to express their feelings through art. The idea is that this kind of defense mechanism, known as *sublimation*, will lead to better health outcomes than avoidance of emotions through more negative defense mechanisms (Glazer, 1998). Similarly, some therapists advocate encouraging children to use another defense mechanism, *identification*, to manage their grief. This goal can be accomplished by having the child watch popular films depicting children's grief, such as *The Lion King*; discuss the young characters' feelings; and compare the characters' emotions to their own (Sedney, 1999).

In addition, the psychoanalytic perspective has shaped grief research by characterizing the loss of a loved one as a trauma. An important concept in such research is that the more traumatic the death, the more likely it is to be followed by physical or mental problems. In fact, researchers have found that people who lose loved ones in sudden, tragic ways, such as to a drunk-driving accident or a murder, are more likely to display symptoms of post-traumatic stress disorder (Murphy et al., 1999; Sprang & McNeil, 1998).

Learning Objective 19.11
What are the theories of Bowlby and Sanders regarding grief?

Bowlby's Attachment Theory

John Bowlby and other attachment theorists argue that intense grief reactions are likely to occur at the loss of any person to whom one is attached, whether a partner, a parent, or a child (Bowlby, 1980; Sanders, 1989; Stroebe, 2002). Moreover, their theories predict that the quality of attachment to the loved one should be related in some way to the experience of grief. Research seems to confirm this aspect of their view. The stronger the attachment between a mourner and a lost loved one, the deeper and more prolonged the grief response (van Doorn et al., 1998; Waskowic & Chartier, 2003). By contrast, the death of someone who is part of one's social network but not an intimate confidant or an attachment figure is less likely to trigger an intense emotional reaction (Murrell & Himmelfarb, 1989).

Bowlby proposed four stages of grief, and Catherine Sanders, another attachment theorist, proposed five stages, but as you can see in Table 19.5, the two systems overlap a great deal. In the first period, that of shock or numbness, people say things that reveal their state of mind:

> "I feel so vague. I can't keep my mind on anything for very long." (Bowlby, 1980, p. 47)
>
> "I'm afraid I'm losing my mind. I can't seem to think clearly." (Bowlby, 1980, p. 48)
>
> "It was so strange. I was putting on my makeup, combing my hair, and all the time it was as if I were standing by the door watching myself go through these motions." (Sanders, 1989, p. 56).

In the stage of awareness of loss, or yearning, when anger is a common ingredient, people say things such as "His boss should have known better than to ask him to work so hard." Bowlby suggested that this is equivalent to the behavior observed in young children when temporarily separated from their closest attachment figures; they go from room to room in search of this favored person. Adults who are widowed do some of the same searching—sometimes physically, sometimes mentally.

In the stage of disorganization and despair, the restlessness of the previous period disappears and is replaced by a great lethargy. One 45-year-old whose child had just died described her feelings:

> I can't understand the way I feel. Up to now, I had been feeling restless. I couldn't sleep. I paced and ranted. Now, I have an opposite reaction. I sleep a lot. I feel fatigued and worn out. I don't even want to see the friends who have kept me going. I sit and stare, too exhausted to move. . . . Just when I thought I should be feeling better, I am feeling worse. (Sanders, 1989, p. 73)

Finally, the resolution of the grieving process comes in Bowlby's stage of reorganization. Sanders hypothesized that this stage comprises two separate periods: healing and renewal. The outcome, from both Bowlby's and Sanders's perspectives, is that the grieving person

Table 19.5 Stages of Grief

Stage	Bowlby's Label	Sanders's Label	General Description
1	Numbness	Shock	Characteristic of the first few days after the death of the loved one and occasionally longer; mourner experiences disbelief, confusion, restlessness, feelings of unreality, a sense of helplessness.
2	Yearning	Awareness	The bereaved person tries to recover the lost person; may actively search or wander as if searching; may report that he sees the dead person; mourner feels full of anger, anxiety, guilt, fear, frustration; may sleep poorly and weep often.
3	Disorganization and despair	Conservation/withdrawal	Searching ceases and the loss is accepted, but acceptance of loss brings depression and despair or a sense of helplessness; this stage is often accompanied by great fatigue and a desire to sleep all the time.
4	Reorganization	Healing and renewal	Sanders views this as two periods, Bowlby as only one. Both see this as the period when the individual takes control again. Some forgetting occurs and some sense of hope emerges, along with increased energy, better health, better sleep patterns, and reduced depression.

(*Sources*: Bowlby, 1980; Sanders, 1989.)

begins to be able to maintain control. Sleep patterns return to normal, and a more optimistic outlook is typical.

These descriptions of the grieving process are highly evocative and can be useful in counseling grieving individuals. Discussion of the stages helps those who are grieving communicate with therapists about how they are feeling and describe the kinds of symptoms they are experiencing. Stage approaches also help survivors realize that their emotions and physical symptoms are normal and that the grieving process is complex.

However, as with the concept of stages of dying, there are two important questions about these proposed stages of grieving:

1. Do they really occur in fixed stages?
2. Does everyone feel all these feelings, in whatever sequence?

The answer to both questions, as you'll see, seems to be no.

Learning Objective 19.12

What theories of grief have been proposed by critics of psychoanalytic and attachment theories?

Alternative Perspectives

A growing set of "revisionist" views of grieving gives a rather different picture from that of either Freud or the attachment theorists. First, research suggests that, contrary to psychoanalytic hypotheses, avoiding expressions of grief neither prolongs the experience of grief nor leads inevitably to physical or mental health problems. In fact, at least one study suggests that bereaved individuals who avoid talking about the deceased or their feelings of loss actually experience milder grief and are less likely to suffer long-term effects (Bonanno, Znoj, Siddique, & Horowitz, 1999).

Second, many researchers and theorists find that grieving simply does not occur in fixed stages, with everyone following the same pattern (Wortman & Silver, 1990). There may be common themes, such as anger, guilt, depression, and restlessness, but these do not seem to appear in a fixed order.

One compromise model suggests that each of the key themes in the grieving process has a likely trajectory, as suggested in Figure 19.2 (Jacobs et al., 1987/1988). For example, numbness may be most prominent in the days immediately following the loved one's death. After a few months, the grieving person may feel numb at times, but depression may be a more dominant theme. The basic idea, obviously, is that many themes are present at the same time, but that one or another may dominate, in an approximate sequence. Thus, it may well be that disbelief is highest immediately after the death, and that depression peaks some months later—which makes the process look stagelike, although in fact both elements are present throughout. Some bereaved people might move more quickly and others more slowly through these various emotions.

In contrast, other revisionist theorists and researchers contend that for some adults, grieving simply does not include all these elements. Psychologists Camille Wortman and

Figure 19.2
Jacobs's Model of Grieving

Jacobs offers this model as an alternative to strict stage theories of grieving. At any given moment, many different emotions or themes may be apparent, but each may have a typical trajectory.

(*Source*: Jacobs et al., 1987/1988, Figure 1, p. 43.)

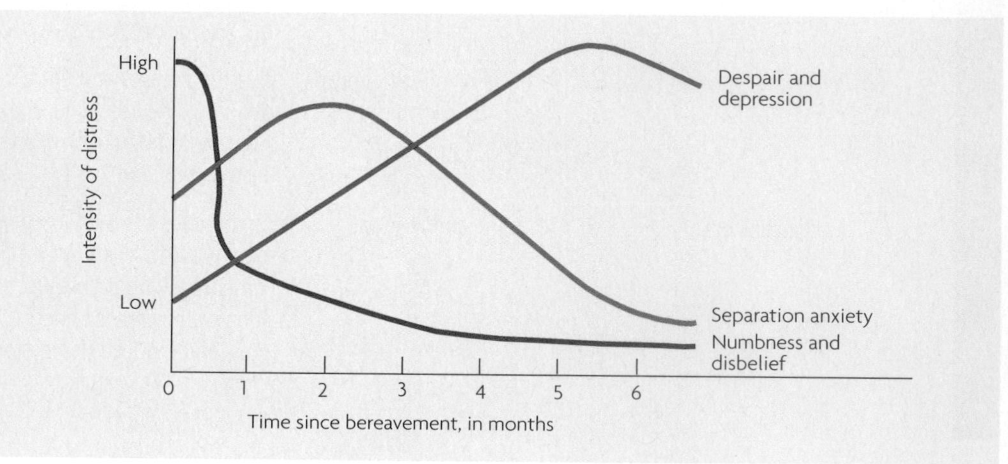

Roxane Silver have amassed an impressive amount of evidence to support such a view (Wortman & Silver, 1989, 1990, 1992; Wortman, Silver, & Kessler, 1993). They dispute the traditional view of grieving expressed in both Freud's and Bowlby's theories. First, Wortman and Silver do not agree that distress is an inevitable response to loss. Second, their research challenges the notion that failure to experience distress is a sign that the individual has not grieved "properly."

Based on their findings, Wortman and Silver conclude that there are at least four distinct patterns of grieving (Wortman & Silver, 1990):

- *Normal.* The person feels great distress immediately following the loss, with relatively rapid recovery.
- *Chronic.* The person's distress continues at a high level over several years.
- *Delayed.* The grieving person feels little distress in the first few months but high levels of distress some months or years later.
- *Absent.* The person feels no notable level of distress either immediately or at any later time.

Contrary to the predictions of stage theories of grief, it turns out that the pattern of absent grief is remarkably common. In Wortman and Silver's own first study, 26% of bereaved participants showed essentially no distress, either immediately after the death or several years later, a pattern confirmed in other research (Levy, Martinkowski, & Derby, 1994; Wortman & Silver, 1990). The least common pattern is delayed grief. Only 1–5% of adults appear to show such a response to loss, while as many as a third show chronic grief. Thus, Wortman and Silver find little support for either aspect of the traditional view: High levels of distress are neither an inevitable nor a necessary aspect of the grieving process. Many adults seem to handle the death of a spouse, a child, or a parent without significant psychological dislocation—although it remains true that, on average, bereaved persons have more depression, less life satisfaction, and a greater risk of illness than the nonbereaved.

The *dual-process model* takes a different approach to grief (Stroebe & Schut, 1999). Psychologists Margaret Stroebe and Henk Schut, developers of the model, propose that bereaved individuals alternate between an emotional state in which they confront their loss and actively grieve (confrontation) and another in which they focus on moving forward with their lives (restoration). In a sense, the restoration phase provides the bereaved with a respite from the emotional turmoil that is characteristic of the confrontation phase. Like Bowlby's model, the dual-process approach suggests that the attachment relationship between the bereaved and the deceased influences the grieving process (Stroebe, Schut, & Stroebe, 2005). But the model also emphasizes the loss of a loved one as analogous to other forms of stress (Stroebe, Folkman, Hansson, & Schut, 2006).

Finally, it's important not to lose sight of the fact that loss can lead to growth. Indeed, the majority of widows say not only that they changed as a result of their husbands' deaths, but that the change was toward greater independence and greater skill (Wortman & Silver, 1990). Like all crises and all major life changes, bereavement can be an opportunity as well as—or instead of—a disabling experience. Which way a person responds is likely to depend very heavily on the patterns established from early childhood: in temperament or personality, in internal working models of attachment and self, in intellectual skills, and in social networks. Ultimately, we respond to death—our own or someone else's—as we have responded to life.

Critical Thinking

1. How can the theories discussed in this section be integrated into a comprehensive explanation of the process of grieving?

The Experience of Grieving

In virtually every culture, the immediate response to a death is some kind of funeral ritual. However, a death ritual is only the first step in the process of **grieving**—the emotional response to a death—which may take months or years to complete.

grieving the emotional response to a death

Learning Objective 19.13

How do funerals and ceremonies help survivors cope with grief?

Psychosocial Functions of Death Rituals

Funerals, wakes, and other death rituals help family members and friends manage their grief by giving them a specific set of roles to play. Like all roles, these include both expected behaviors and prohibited or discouraged behaviors. The content of these roles differs markedly from one culture to the next, but their clarity in most cases gives a shape to the days or weeks immediately following the death of a loved person. Among Tibetan Buddhists, for instance, dead persons are believed to be unaware of their state for the first four days after their deaths. Mourners are expected to pray that they will realize that they are dead soon enough to avoid having to be reborn as another human or in another life form. In American culture, the rituals prescribe what one should wear, who should be called, who should be fed, what demeanor one should show, and far more. Depending on one's ethnic or religious background, one may gather family and friends for a wake or to "sit shiva," a traditional Jewish 7-day period of mourning during which family members stay in the same home and formally mourn a deceased loved one. One may be expected to respond stoically or to wail and tear one's hair. Friends and acquaintances, too, have guiding rules, at least for those first few days. They may bring food, write letters of condolence, offer help, and attend wakes and funerals.

The emotional tone of death rituals varies across cultures. African Americans in the city of New Orleans have a tradition of celebrating the passing of their loved ones with a parade that features upbeat music that reminds mourners that the departed has gone on to a better place.

Death rituals also bring family members together as no other occasion does (with the possible exception of weddings). Frequently, cousins and other distant relatives see one another for the first time in many years at funerals. Such occasions typically inspire shared reminiscences and renew family relationships that have been inactive for a long time. In this way, death rituals can strengthen family ties, clarify the new lines of influence or authority within a family, and "pass the torch" in some way to the next generation. Likewise, funerals help establish deaths as shared milestones for family members—"that was before Grandpa died" or "the last time I saw her was at Grandpa's funeral." A death can become an important organizer of experience that separates the past from the present. Dividing time in this way seems to help survivors cope with grief (Katz & Bartone, 1998).

Death rituals are also designed to help the survivors understand the meaning of death itself, in part by emphasizing the meaning of the life of the person who has died. It is not accidental that most death rituals include testimonials, biographies, and witnessing. By telling the story of a person's life and describing that life's value and meaning, others can more readily accept the person's death.

Finally, death rituals may give some transcendent meaning to death itself by placing it in a philosophical or religious context (Pangt & Lam, 2002). In this way, they provide comfort to the bereaved by offering answers to that inevitable question "Why?"

Learning Objective 19.14

What factors influence the grieving process?

The Process of Grieving

The ritual of a funeral, in whatever form it occurs, can provide structure and comfort in the days immediately following a death. But what happens when that structure is gone? How do people handle the sense of loss? Answering that question requires a look at a number of factors associated with grief.

Age of the Bereaved Children express feelings of grief very much the same way teens and adults do (Auman, 2007). Like adults, children demonstrate grief through sad facial expressions, crying, loss of appetite, and age-appropriate displays of anger such as temper tantrums (Oatley & Jenkins, 1996). Funerals seem to serve the same adaptive function for children as for adults, and most children resolve their feelings of grief within the first year after the loss.

In addition, knowing that a loved one or even a pet is ill and in danger of death helps children cope with the loss in advance, just as it does for those who are older (Jarolmen, 1998).

Although the behavioral aspects of adolescents' grief responses vary little from those of adults, teens may be more likely than children or adults to experience prolonged grief. One study found that more than 20% of a group of high school students who had a friend killed in an accident continued to experience intense feelings of grief 9 months after the death (Dyregrov, Gjestad, Bie Wikander, & Vigerust, 1999). Adolescents may also grieve longer than children or adults for lost siblings; in some cases, teens continue to have problems with grief-related behaviors, such as intrusive thoughts about the deceased, for as long as 2 years after the death of a sibling (Lohan & Murphy, 2001/2002). Other research suggests that adolescent girls whose mothers have died run a particularly high risk of developing long-term, grief-related problems (Lenhardt & McCourt, 2000). Teenagers may also be more likely than adults to experience grief responses to the deaths of celebrities or to idealize peers' suicides.

Adolescents' grief responses are probably related to their general cognitive characteristics. You should remember from Chapters 11 and 12 that adolescents often judge the real world by idealized images. Consequently, a teenager may become caught up in fantasizing about how the world would be different if a friend or loved one had not died. In addition, prolonged grieving among adolescents may be rooted in their tendency to engage in "what if" thinking. This kind of thinking may lead teens to believe that they could have prevented the death and, thus, cause them to develop irrational guilt feelings (Cunningham, 1996).

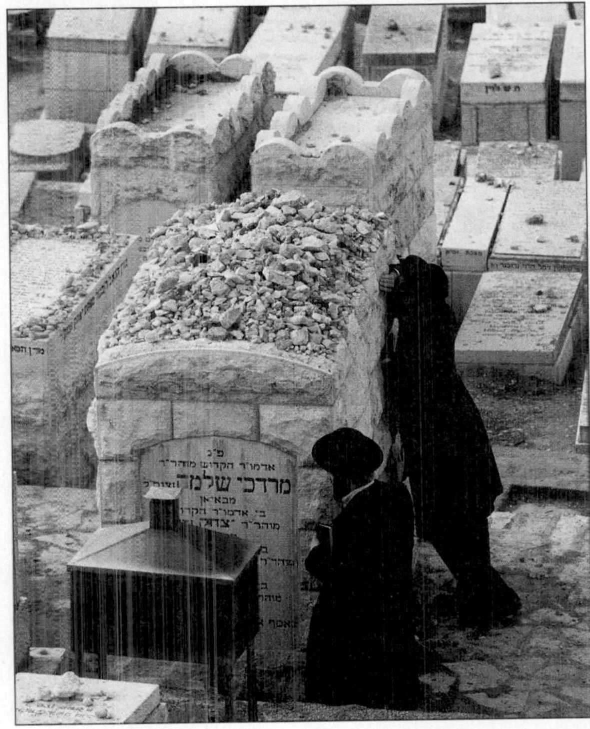

Each culture has its own death rituals. The customarily quiet graveside service in the United States would seem strange to people in many other societies.

Mode of Death How an individual dies contributes to the grief process of those who are in mourning. For example, widows who have cared for spouses during a period of illness prior to death are less likely to become depressed after the death than those whose spouses die suddenly (Carnelley, Wortman, & Kessler, 1999). Grief-related depression seems to emerge during the spouse's illness rather than after the death. The spouse's death is thought of as an escape from suffering for the one who dies and a release from grieving for the caregiver. Similarly, a death that has intrinsic meaning, such as that of a young soldier who dies defending his country, is not necessarily easier to cope with but does provide the bereaved with a sense that the death has not been without purpose (Malkinson & Bar-Tur, 1999). Consequently, mourners have a built-in cognitive coping device—a rational explanation for the death—that allows them to grieve but also protects them from long-term depression.

However, sudden and violent deaths evoke more intense grief responses (Murphy, Johnson, & Lohan, 2003). One study found that 36% of widows and widowers whose spouses had died in accidents or by suicide were suffering from post-traumatic stress symptoms (e.g., nightmares) 2 months after the death, compared to only 10% of widows and widowers whose spouses had died of natural causes (Zisook, Chentsova-Dutton, & Shuchter, 1998). Moreover, almost all of those whose spouses had died unnaturally and who had PTSD symptoms were also depressed.

Death in the context of a natural disaster is also associated with prolonged grieving and development of symptoms of PTSD (Kilic & Ulusoy, 2003). Such events bring to mind the inescapable reality of the fragility of human life. Public memorial services in which the common experiences of survivors are recognized and the differences between controllable and noncontrollable aspects of life are emphasized can help survivors cope with this kind of grief.

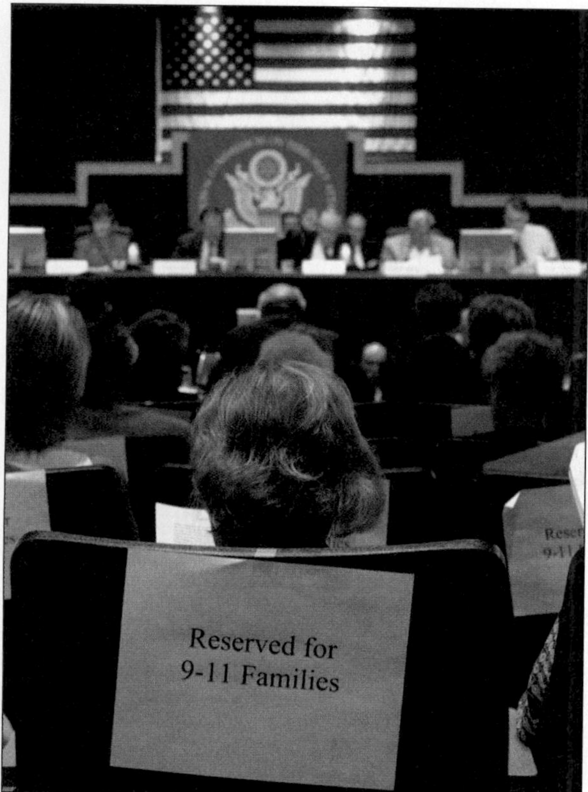

Some September 11 survivors have become involved in political activism geared toward preventing future terrorist attacks.

Public memorials can also be helpful to survivors whose loved ones have died as a result of what might be called "politically motivated" mass murders—such as the 1995 bombing of a federal government office building in Oklahoma City and the terrorist attacks of September 11, 2001 (Shapiro, 2002). Moreover, political activism on the part of survivors aimed at preventing future events of this kind may be helpful to policymakers and also may serve as a coping mechanism for those who engage in it (Shapiro, 2002).

By contrast, the most frustrating aspect of the grieving process for people who have lost a loved one through a violent crime is the inability to find meaning in the event (Currier, Holland, & Neimeyer, 2006). In the initial phases of the grief process, survivors protect themselves against such frustration through cognitive defenses such as denial and by focusing on tasks that are immediately necessary (Goodrum, 2005). Next, survivors often channel their grief and anger into the criminal justice process through which they hope that the perpetrator of the crime will be justly punished. Finally, many survivors become involved in organizations that support crime victims and survivors of murdered loved ones or those that seek to prevent violence (Stetson, 2002).

Finally, suicide is associated with a unique pattern of responses among survivors (Bailley, Kral, & Dunham, 1999). In general, family and close friends of someone who commits suicide experience feelings of rejection and anger. Moreover, their grief over the loss of the loved one is complicated by the feeling that they could or should have done something to prevent the suicide. They are less likely to discuss the loss with other family members or with friends because of their sense that a suicide in the family is a source of shame. For these reasons, suicide survivors may be more likely than others who have lost loved ones to experience long-term negative effects.

Learning Objective 19.15

How does grief affect the physical and mental health of widows and widowers?

Widowhood

The relationship between the deceased and those who are in mourning affects the grieving process. For example, bereaved parents often report that their health is poorer than before a child's death, and many continue to experience intense feelings of sadness for several years (Arbuckle & De Vries, 1995; Malkinson & Bar-Tur, 1999) (see The Real World, page 564). Similarly, children who lose a sibling sometimes worry that thoughts produced by sibling rivalry, such as wishing a brother or sister would die, caused the death (Crehan, 2004). As a general rule, though, the most difficult death to recover from is that of a spouse (Kaslow, 2004) (see the Research Report on page 563).

Widowhood and Physical Health The experience of widowhood appears to have both immediate and longer-term effects on the immune system (Beem et al., 1999; Gallagher-Thompson, Futterman, Farberow, Thompson, & Peterson, 1993; Irwin & Pike, 1993). (The term *widowhood* applies to both men and women; *widow* refers to women and *widower* to men.) In one Norwegian study, researchers measured immune functioning in widows twice, shortly after their husbands' deaths and 1 year later (Lindstrom, 1997). Investigators found that the widows' immune systems were suppressed somewhat immediately after the death but in most cases had returned to normal a year later.

Similarly, a study comparing widows to married women in the Netherlands found that widows' immune responses continued to differ from those of married participants 7 months after the spouses' deaths, even though psychological differences (such as feelings of sadness) between the two groups had disappeared (Beem et al., 1999). Thus, the bereaved may continue to suffer at a biochemical level even after obvious signs of grieving have subsided.

RESEARCH REPORT

Ethnicity and the Widowhood Effect

In celebration of their 50th wedding anniversary, British couple Brian and Betty Eckersley took their children and grandchildren on a vacation to Spain. The day before the family was scheduled to return home, Betty suffered a brain hemorrhage which doctors said was fatal. Her family faced the agonizing decision to discontinue artificial means of maintaining her life. Shortly thereafter, Brian suffered a heart attack. Within hours, both of the Eckersleys had passed away.

Brian Eckersley's heart attack is an extreme example of the *widowhood effect*, a phenomenon in which the death of one spouse is soon followed by the other. It is thought to result from the immune system's response to emotional trauma. However, the widowhood effect varies considerably across ethnic groups in the United States.

Researchers were astonished at the results of a study of the widowhood effect in which the medical records of nearly half a million widows and widowers were examined (Elwert & Christakis, 2006). Consistent with earlier research, the risk of death was elevated by 50% to 60% among White widows and widowers during the first year of bereavement. For their African American counterparts, though, there was no increase in mortality whatsoever among individuals who had lost a spouse. Mortality rates among interracial couples were even more startling. African American widows of White men and White widowers of African American women showed no increase in mortality. By contrast, White widows of African American men and African American widowers of White women were at increased risk of death. Interestingly, too, studies involving Hispanic Americans suggest that the widowhood effect occurs only among Hispanic men (Stimpson et al., 2006).

Researchers hypothesize that a protective factor exists in African American culture that moderates the effects of spousal death on the immune system (Elwert & Christakis, 2006). However, the benefits associated with this factor appear to extend to the White husbands of African American women but not to the White wives of African American men. Thus, some theorists suggest that the factor operates through African American women's traditional kin-keeper role. A similar factor may also protect Hispanic women from the widowhood effect. Ethnic group differences in family support, social networks, religious coping, and other factors among widows and widowers are currently being studied in an effort to find an explanation for this puzzling phenomenon.

Questions for Critical Analysis

1. In Chapter 18, you learned that African American and Hispanic American elders were more likely to share a household with relatives than their White peers. In your view, how does the ethnic group difference in living arrangements contribute to the findings on the widowhood effect?
2. You have also learned that African American and Hispanic American men have shorter average life expectancies than White men do. How might this difference contribute to the absence of the widowhood effect among African American and Hispanic American women?

Moreover, the association between death of a spouse and ensuing illness in the surviving partner may be the result of the effects of grief on the body's defenses against disease agents such as viruses and bacteria.

Widowhood and Mental Health In the year following bereavement, the incidence of depression among widows and widowers rises substantially, though rates of death and disease rise only slightly (Onrust & Cuijpers, 2006; CuReich, Zautra, & Guarnaccia, 1989; Stroebe & Stroebe, 1993). In one important longitudinal study, researchers repeatedly interviewed a sample of 3,000 adults, all age 55 or older at the beginning of the study (Norris & Murrell, 1990). Forty-eight of these adults were widowed during the 2 ½ years of the study, which allowed investigators to look at depression and health status before and immediately after bereavement. They found no differences in physical health between widowed and nonwidowed participants, but they did note a rise in depression among the widowed immediately following the loss and then a decline within a year after bereavement.

However, other researchers have found that older adults whose spouses have died differ in mental health for several years following the death from peers whose spouses are still alive (Bennett, 1997). So it appears that declines in physical and mental health follow bereavement fairly consistently, but how long such effects last may be highly variable. Several factors contribute to this variability.

One such factor is mental health history. Older adults who enter widowhood with a history of depression are *more* likely to experience depression after the death of their spouse (Zisook, Paulus, Shuchter, & Judd 1997). Lack of social support, both actual and perceived, also contributes to variability in depression among widows and widowers (Reed, 1998; Tomita et al., 1997). Moreover, the quality of the relationship of the widow or widower with the deceased spouse is related to depressive symptoms. Perhaps surprisingly, relationships

THE REAL WORLD

When an Infant Dies

Morgan recently lost her two-month-old son to SIDS. After the baby's death, she was determined to continue living as normal a life as possible, despite the overwhelming grief she felt. To that end, she went back to work immediately after the funeral and kept up all of her social activities. She also forced herself to attend family gatherings, even though she feared having to talk about the experience. To her dismay, her co-workers and relatives kept their distance from her, almost as if they didn't know what to say to her about her child's death. Morgan was torn between the relief she felt over not having to talk too much about what had happened and a desperate need for others to somehow acknowledge her loss.

Many parents grieving for a lost infant do not receive adequate support from either their social networks or health professionals (Vaeisaenen, 1998). It is important for those who are in a position to support grieving parents to understand that the grief that follows the death of an infant is no less intense than any other kind of bereavement. In fact, it may be more complex.

When an older child dies, parents have a relationship history and an intimate knowledge of the child's personality on which to build reminiscences. Such cognitive devices help them reorganize their attachment to the lost child so that they are able to release the child psychologically. But with an infant, there is little or no relationship history to draw on. The parents, of course, feel deep emotions of attachment, but the cognitive elements that help parents cope with the loss of a child are absent. For these reasons, bereaved parents of a dead infant often have a greater need for support from family, friends, and health professionals than even they themselves realize (Vaeisaenen, 1998).

Well-intentioned friends or family may pressure the couple to cope with their loss by simply replacing the infant with another one. However, research suggests that starting another pregnancy soon after the loss of an infant doesn't necessarily end either a mother's or a father's grief, although it does tend to protect both against long-term negative effects such as depression (Franche & Bulow, 1999). Moreover, parents may fear that a subsequent child will also die in infancy and may try to avoid becoming emotionally attached to a newborn (Wong, 1993). This could have adverse effects on the whole family.

Health professionals have compiled a few guidelines that can be useful to family members or friends in supporting parents who have lost an infant (Wong, 1993):

- Don't try to force bereaved parents to talk about their grief or the infant if they don't want to.
- Always refer to the deceased infant by name.
- Express your own feelings of loss for the infant, if they are sincere.
- Follow the parents' lead in engaging in reminiscences about the baby's looks or personality.
- Discourage the parents from resorting to drugs or alcohol to manage grief.
- Assure grieving parents that their responses are normal and that it will take time to resolve the emotions associated with losing an infant.
- Don't pressure the parents to "replace" the baby with another one.
- Don't offer rationalizations (e.g., "Your baby's an angel now") that may offend the parents.
- Do offer support for the parents' own rationalizations.
- Be aware that the infant's siblings, even those who are very young, are likely to experience some degree of grief.

Questions for Reflection

1. If you were one of Morgan's co-workers or relatives, how do you think you would behave toward her in everyday situations?
2. What sort of "mental script" could you develop from the recommendations above that would be helpful to friends and relatives of a person who has lost a child?

characterized by emotional distance and conflict are *more* likely to lead to depression than those that were warm (van Doorn, Kasl, Beery, Jacobs, & Prigerson, 1998).

Economic changes accompany the loss of a spouse and add to the overall stress involved in the transition to widowhood. Women typically suffer greater economic losses after the death of a spouse than men do, usually because they lose their husbands' income or pension (Zick & Holden, 2000). However, the household incomes of both widows and widowers are lower than those of married elders (FIFARS, 2006). Thus, the degree to which an individual's economic status changes as a result of a spouse's death is probably another factor that contributes to individual differences in the long-term effects of bereavement.

Pathological Grief Some psychologists argue that **pathological grief**, depression-like symptoms following death of a loved one, should be thought of as a separate disorder from depression (Stroebe et al., 2000). They suggest that individuals who continue to experience grief symptoms such as loss of appetite more than 2 months following loss of a loved one may be developing pathological grief.

pathological grief symptoms of depression brought on by the death of a loved one

Diagnosis and treatment of pathological grief may be important for preventing problems in both mental and physical health among widows and widowers. Researchers have found that survivors whose grief symptoms continue for 6 months or longer are more likely to suffer long-term depression, as well as physical ailments such as cancer and heart disease (Prigerson et al., 1997). Moreover, they continue to show important differences in physical and mental functioning for up to 2 years after their spouse's death.

However, it's important to keep in mind that many aspects of grief are culturally determined. Beliefs about how long mourning should last and how the bereaved should behave vary widely from one culture to another (Braun & Nichols, 1997; Rubin & Schechter, 1997). For example, Orthodox Jewish men traditionally do not shave or trim their beards for 30 days after the death of a family member. Furthermore, mourning traditions among Orthodox Jews require abstaining from entertainment such as attending the theater or seeing movies for an entire year after the death of someone close (Bial, 1971).

Since inattention to grooming and lack of interest in social activities are also sometimes signs of depression, observers who are unfamiliar with Orthodox Jewish mourning practices might conclude that those who follow them are exhibiting pathological rather than normal grieving. Thus, mental health professionals are advised to learn about an individual's cultural beliefs before forming conclusions about grief-related behavior. Likewise, friends, neighbors, and co-workers of someone who is mourning the death of a spouse or other close family member should be careful to interpret any grief-related behaviors within the context of the person's cultural background. Moreover, it is not unusual for nondepressed widows and widowers to express feelings of grief even decades after their spouses have died (Carnelley, Wortman, Bolger, & Burke, 2006).

Sex Differences The death of a spouse appears to be a more negative experience for men than for women, despite the fact that there seem to be no sex differences in the actual grieving process following such a loss (Quigley & Schatz, 1999; Lee & DeMaris, 2007). The risk of death from either natural causes or suicide in the months immediately after widowhood is significantly greater among men than among women (Stroebe & Stroebe, 1993). Depression and suicidal thoughts are also more common in widowers than in widows (Byrne & Raphael, 1999; Chen et al., 1999). Further, men seem to have a more difficult time than women do in returning to the levels of emotional functioning they exhibited before the spouse's death (van Grootheest, Beekman, van Groenou, & Deeg, 1999).

These differences are most often interpreted as yet another sign of the importance of social support. Social activities are very important in the lives of widows. In contrast, researchers have found that widowers withdraw from social activities to a far greater degree than widows do in the months immediately following bereavement (Bennett, 1998).

However, some developmentalists have suggested that activities-oriented studies have led to a stereotype that characterizes widowers as lonely and isolated. In fact, research involving in-depth examinations of widowers' friendships, rather than just their social activities, suggests that social relationships are very important in the lives of men who have lost a spouse (Riggs, 1997). Thus, differences in social involvement may be part of the explanation for sex differences in health and depression following the death of a spouse, but they do not appear to tell the whole story.

The results of a carefully designed longitudinal study of Australian widowers and married men over age 65 suggest that alcohol use may play a role in the greater prevalence of depression among widowers (Byrne, Raphael, & Arnold, 1999). Researchers found that more than twice as many widowers as married men (19% versus 8%) consumed five or more alcoholic drinks per day. Although alcohol may temporarily relieve unpleasant feelings of grief, it is a central nervous system depressant, and prolonged heavy drinking can lead to depression.

Preventing Long-Term Problems Some research suggests that the "talk it out" approach to managing grief can be helpful in preventing grief-related depression, especially when feelings are shared with others who have had similar experiences, in the context of a support group (Francis, 1997). Research also indicates that developing a coherent personal narrative of the events surrounding the spouse's death helps widows and widowers manage grief (Neimeyer, Prigerson, & Davies, 2002; van den Hoonaard, 1999). Participating in support

Critical Thinking

1. Given what you have learned in this section, what kinds of factors would lead you to make different predictions about how long a person who has lost a loved one will grieve?

groups—or even jointly recalling relevant events with close family members—can facilitate the formation of such stories.

Clearly, this kind of psychosocial management of grief requires time. Mental health professionals advise employers that providing bereaved employees (especially those whose spouses have died) with sufficient time off to grieve may be critical to their physical and mental health. In the long run, illness and depression among bereaved workers who return to their jobs too soon may be more costly to employers than providing additional time off (Eyetsemitan, 1998).

SUMMARY

The Experience of Death

Learning Objective 19.1 What are the characteristics of clinical death, brain death, and social death?

- Death is a somewhat nonspecific term. Medical personnel refer to *clinical death* and *brain death; social death* occurs when the deceased person is treated like a corpse by those around him.

Learning Objective 19.2 How do hospice and hospital care differ with respect to their effects on terminally ill patients?

- About half of adults in industrialized countries die in hospitals. Hospice care emphasizes patient and family control of the dying process and palliative care rather than curative treatment. Some studies suggest that patients and families are slightly more satisfied with hospice care than hospital care, but hospice care is also highly burdensome for the caregiver.

The Meaning of Death across the Lifespan

Learning Objective 19.3 What are the characteristics of children's and adolescents' ideas about death?

- Until about age 6 or 7, children do not understand that death is permanent and inevitable and involves loss of function. Teens understand the physical aspects of death much better than children do, but they sometimes have distorted ideas about it, especially their own mortality.

Learning Objective 19.4 How do young, middle-aged, and older adults think about death?

- Many young adults believe they possess unique characteristics that protect them from death. For middle-aged and older adults, death has many possible meanings: a signal of changes in family roles, a transition to another state (such as a life after death), and a loss of opportunity and relationships. Awareness of death may help a person organize her remaining time.

Learning Objective 19.5 What factors are related to fear of death in adults?

- Fear of death appears to peak in mid-life, after which it drops rather sharply. Older adults talk more about death but are less afraid of it. Deeply religious adults are typically less afraid of death.

Learning Objective 19.6 How do adults prepare for death?

- Many adults prepare for death in practical ways, such as by buying life insurance, writing a will, and making a living will. Reminiscence may also serve as preparation. There are some signs of deeper personality changes immediately before death, including more dependence and docility and less emotionality and assertiveness.

The Process of Dying

Learning Objective 19.7 How did Kübler-Ross explain the process of dying?

- Kübler-Ross suggested five stages of dying: denial, anger, bargaining, depression, and acceptance. Research fails to support the hypothesis that all dying adults go through all five stages or that the stages necessarily occur in this order. The emotion most commonly observed is depression.

Learning Objective 19.8 What are some other views of the process of dying?

- Critics of Kübler-Ross suggest that her findings may be culture-specific. They also argue that the process of dying is less stagelike than her theory claims.

Learning Objective 19.9 How do people vary in the ways they adapt to impending death?

- Research with cancer and AIDS patients suggests that those who are most pessimistic and docile in response to diagnosis and treatment have shorter life expectancies. Those who fight hardest, and even display anger, live longer. Dying adults who have better social support, either from family and friends or through specially created support groups, live longer than those who lack such support.

Theoretical Perspectives on Grieving

Learning Objective 19.10 How does Freud's psychoanalytic theory view grief?

- Freud's psychoanalytic theory emphasizes loss as an emotional trauma, the effects of defense mechanisms, and the need to work through feelings of grief.

Learning Objective 19.11 What are the theories of Bowlby and Sanders regarding grief?

- Bowlby's attachment theory views grief as a natural response to the loss of an attachment figure. Attachment theorists suggest that the grief process involves several stages.

Learning Objective 19.12 What theories of grief have been proposed by critics of psychoanalytic and attachment theories?

- Alternative views suggest that neither Freud's nor Bowlby's theory accurately characterizes the grief experience. Responses are more individual than either theory might suggest. The dual-process model suggests that bereaved individuals alternate between confrontation and restoration phases.

The Experience of Grieving

Learning Objective 19.13 How do funerals and ceremonies help survivors cope with grief?

- Funerals and other rituals after death serve important functions, including defining roles for the bereaved, bringing family together, and giving meaning to the deceased's life and death.

Learning Objective 19.14 What factors influence the grieving process?

- Grief responses depend on a number of variables. The age of the bereaved and the mode of death shape the grief process.

Learning Objective 19.15 How does grief affect the physical and mental health of widows and widowers?

- In general, the death of a spouse evokes the most intense and long-lasting grief. Widows and widowers show high levels of illness and death in the months immediately after the death of a spouse, perhaps as a result of the effects of grief on the immune system. Widowers appear to have a more difficult time than widows managing grief.

KEY TERMS

brain death *(p. 542)*
clinical death *(p. 542)*
grieving *(p. 559)*
hospice care *(p. 542)*
palliative care *(p. 543)*
pathological grief *(p. 564)*
social death *(p. 542)*
thanatology *(p. 553)*
unique invulnerability *(p. 546)*

TEST YOURSELF

The Experience of Death

19.1 What form of death has an individual experienced if she has died and been resuscitated?

a. brain death
b. clinical death
c. marginal death
d. social death

19.2 What form of death has an individual experienced if he has survived on life-support systems for a number of years?

a. brain death
b. clinical death
c. primitive death
d. social death

19.3 About half of people in industrialized countries die

a. at home.
b. in relatives' homes.
c. in hospitals.
d. in nursing homes.

19.4 Which of the following is *not* an element of the philosophy of hospice care?

a. Death is normal and should be faced and accepted.
b. Medical care should be palliative, not curative.
c. The patient and the family should control decisions about the patient's care.
d. Treatment should be provided by professionals trained in hospice procedures for palliative care.

The Meaning of Death across the Lifespan

19.5 When they start school, most children seem

a. not to know anything about death.
b. to understand the permanence of death.
c. to engage in magical thinking about death.
d. not to understand the universality of death.

19.6 Most young adults

a. feel that they are invulnerable to death.
b. underestimate the age at which they will die.
c. feel suicidal.
d. are not afraid of death.

19.7 According to research, how would a young adult who has just been told she has six months to live most likely want to spend her remaining time?

a. focusing on her inner life
b. completing unfinished projects and tying up loose ends
c. living as she has been living, with no change in her life
d. spending time with her loved ones

19.8 According to research, how would an older adult who has just been told she has six months to live most likely want to spend her remaining time?

a. focusing on her inner life by praying or meditating
b. making sure that loved ones and survivors are ready for her death
c. completing unfinished business
d. traveling and having exotic adventures

19.9 Which group of people is most afraid of death?

a. young adults
b. middle-aged adults
c. older adults
d. men

19.10 Feelings about death are influenced by all of the following except

a. religious beliefs.
b. age.
c. people's sense of worth.
d. intelligence.

The Process of Dying

19.11 According to Elisabeth Kübler-Ross's model of the psychological stages of dying, what is a necessary stage if an individual is to accept his death?

a. ego integrity
b. depression
c. moratorium
d. resolution of disagreements with loved ones

19.12 An individual who says to her physician "You have made a mistake. I'm not sick!" is most likely in the __________ stage of Kübler-Ross's model of psychological preparation for death.

a. denial
b. defense
c. rejection
d. stoicism

19.13 Which of the following is *not* an accurate statement about criticisms of Kübler-Ross's model of the psychological stages of dying?

a. The model has been criticized for failing to convey clear ideas or meaningful concepts about the process of dying.
b. Kübler-Ross's study lacked methodological rigor, such as information on the ages of the patients studied and the frequency of the observations.
c. Reactions to dying are culturally conditioned, and Kübler-Ross's model may not apply to other cultures.
d. Clinicians and researchers do not agree that all dying persons exhibit the emotions Kübler-Ross identified or that the emotions are experienced in the order specified in the model.

19.14 Of the emotional responses identified in Kübler-Ross's model of the psychological stages of dying, which one is most common among Western patients?

a. anger
b. denial
c. bargaining
d. depression

19.15 Research into the relationship between an individual's emotional response to impending or probable death and the actual outcome suggests, in general, that

a. emotional response to a condition does not affect outcome or survival rate.
b. difficult patients who express their anger and hostility openly die sooner.
c. individuals who question and challenge and have a fighting spirit have a more difficult recovery experience.
d. emotional responses contribute to disease progress.

19.16 How does social support affect terminally ill patients?

a. They experience less pain.
b. They die sooner but more happily.
c. They live longer.
d. They need less medical treatment.

Theoretical Perspectives on Grieving

19.17 Which of the following is *not* a Freudian concept that has influenced grief counseling?

a. the idea that survivors need to talk openly about their loss in order to avoid negative long-term effects
b. the idea that depression is an essential preparation for accepting one's death
c. the use of defense mechanisms to cope with grief
d. the concept of death as a trauma that will have physical or mental consequences for the survivors

19.18 Which of the following is not a pattern of grieving identified by Wortman and Silver?

a. absent

b. balanced

c. chronic

d. delayed

19.19 What form of euthanasia occurs when a physician hastens a person's death by withdrawing the life-support system?

a. active euthanasia

b. altruistic euthanasia

c. assisted suicide euthanasia

d. passive euthanasia

19.20 What form of euthanasia occurs when a physician hastens a patient's death by administering a fatal dose of a drug such as morphine?

a. active euthanasia

b. assisted suicide euthanasia

c. palliative euthanasia

d. resolved suicide

19.21 Where in the world is assisted suicide fully and explicitly legal?

a. nowhere

b. in the Netherlands

c. in Sweden

d. in the countries belonging to the European Union

19.22 According to the dual-process model, mourners in the ___________ phase express the emotions that are associated with the loss of a loved one, while in the ___________ phase they focus on moving forward with their lives.

a. restoration, confrontation

b. confrontation, restoration

c. attachment, relinquishment

d. relinquishment, attachment

The Experience of Grieving

19.23 Which of the following is *not* a psychological function of death rituals?

a. bring family members together

b. helping the survivors understand the meaning of death itself

c. showing others how much the survivors loved the person who died

d. giving some transcendent meaning to death

19.24 Which of the following is *not* an accurate statement about the way widowhood affects physical and mental health?

a. The experience of widowhood has a negative effect on immune system functioning.

b. In the year after bereavement, the incidence of depression among widows and widowers rises significantly.

c. Older adults who enter widowhood with a history of depression are more likely to experience depression after the death of their spouse.

d. Depression is a universal symptom of grief that is unaffected by cultural factors.

19.25 Which of the following is *not* a suggestion for friends and family members supporting parents who have lost an infant?

a. Don't refer to the deceased infant by name.

b. Don't offer rationalizations that may offend the parents.

c. Assure the grieving parents that their responses are normal.

d. Express your own feelings of loss for the infant, if they are sincere.

mydevelopmentlab Study Plan

Are You Ready for the Test?

Students who use the study materials on MyDevelopmentLab report higher grades in the course than those who use the text alone. Here are three easy steps to mastering this chapter and improving your grade…

Step 1

Take the chapter pre-test in MyDevelopmentLab and review your customized Study Plan.

According to attachment theorists, the experience of grief is related to

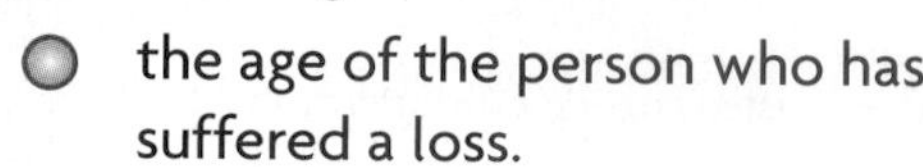

- the age of the person who has suffered a loss.
- whether the bereaved person lived with the person who died.
- whether the bereaved person could identify with the person who died.
- the quality of attachment to the loved one who died.

Step 2

Use MyDevelopmentLab's Multimedia Library to help strengthen your knowledge of the chapter.

Watch: Death and Dying

Learning Objective 19.2
How do hospice and hospital care differ with respect to their effects on terminally ill patients?

81% of students responding to a national user survey wish they had a program like MyDevelopmentLab in other courses.

Watch: Coping with Loss and Grief

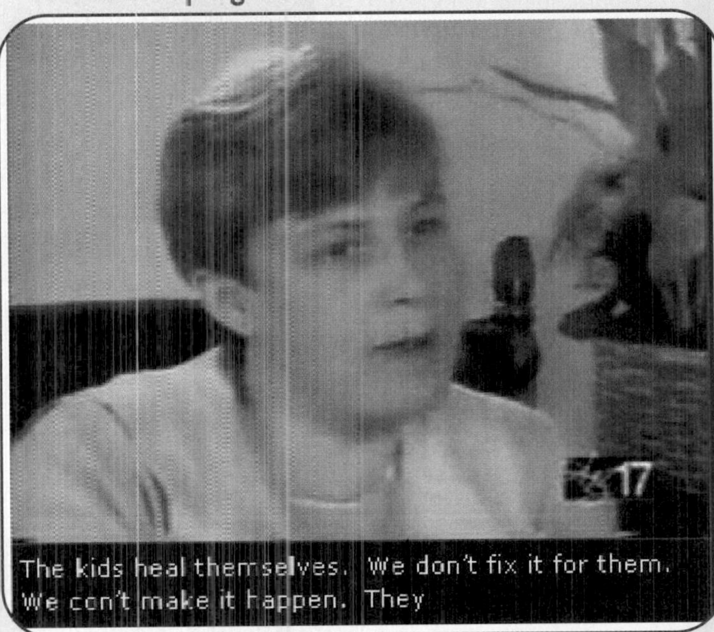

The kids heal themselves. We don't fix it for them. We can't make it happen. They

Learning Objective 19.3

What are the characteristics of children's and adolescents' ideas about death?

Watch: Death, Grief, and Mourning

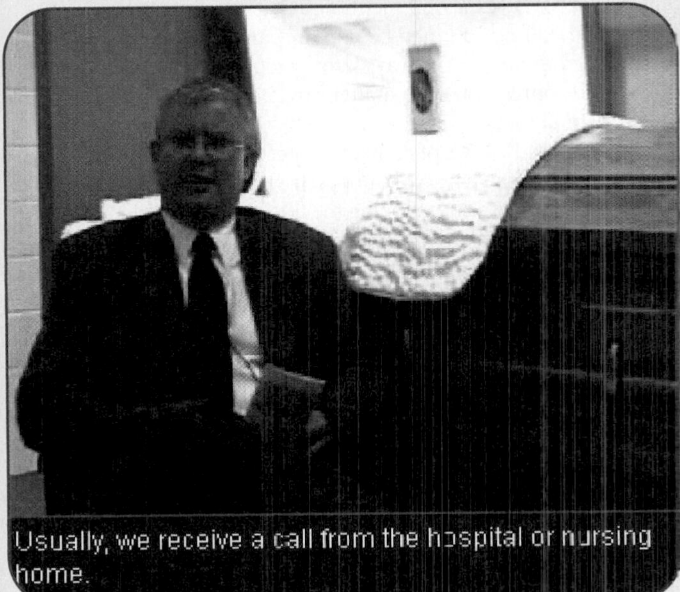

Usually, we receive a call from the hospital or nursing home.

Learning Objective 19.13

How do funerals and ceremonies help survivors cope with grief?

Step 3

Take the chapter post-test and compare your results against the pre-test.

In one influential study, as people got nearer to death, they became

- more emotional, introspective, and aggressive.
- more conventional, docile, dependent, and warm.
- more ambivalent and questioning about the meaning of life.
- less concerned about the wants and needs of others.

POLICY QUESTION

How Should Stem Cell Research Be Funded and Regulated?

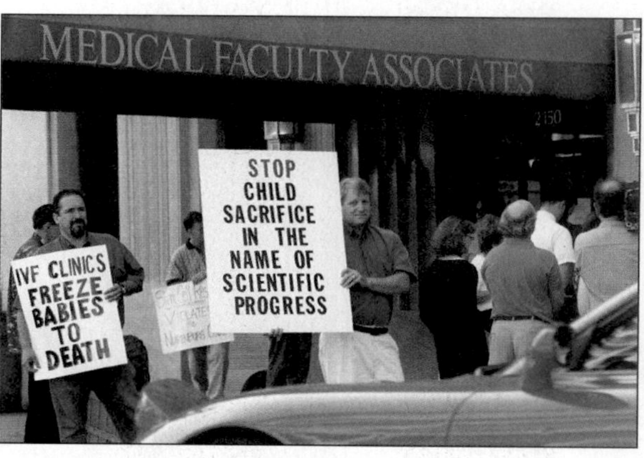

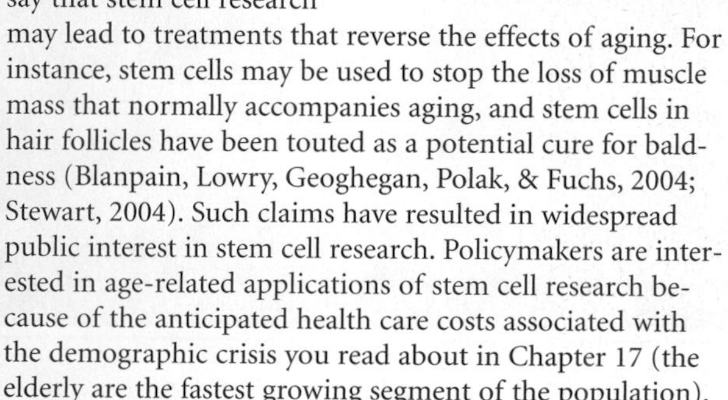

Stem cells are partially developed, unspecialized cells. In response to biochemical signals that scientists don't yet understand, they develop into mature, specialized cells (Stewart, 2004). The potential of stem cells for curing many diseases associated with aging, such as Parkinson's disease and Alzheimer's disease, has received a great deal of media attention in recent years. There are experts who say that stem cell research may lead to treatments that reverse the effects of aging. For instance, stem cells may be used to stop the loss of muscle mass that normally accompanies aging, and stem cells in hair follicles have been touted as a potential cure for baldness (Blanpain, Lowry, Geoghegan, Polak, & Fuchs, 2004; Stewart, 2004). Such claims have resulted in widespread public interest in stem cell research. Policymakers are interested in age-related applications of stem cell research because of the anticipated health care costs associated with the demographic crisis you read about in Chapter 17 (the elderly are the fastest growing segment of the population).

Nevertheless, public policies related to stem cell research are controversial. In 2004, for the first time, both major political parties in the United States included statements on stem cell research in their platforms (Foust, 2004). Before examining the arguments involved in the stem cell research debate, it is essential that you understand a bit about the different kinds of stem cells and the current state of scientific knowledge about how they might be used to treat diseases.

Types of Stem Cells

You should recall from Chapter 3 that a zygote results from the union of a sperm and an egg. The zygote is a kind of stem cell scientists refer to as *totipotent* because it is capable of developing into an entire human being. As the zygote divides, each resulting cell retains the characteristic of totipotentiality until the eight-cell stage is reached. In other words, each of the cells in an eight-cell embryo can develop into an entire human body.

Once the number of cells exceeds eight, each cell can develop into one of the body's 216 different cell types, but none can become an entire human body. Stem cells of this kind are called *pluripotent*. As the embryo develops, cells become committed to specific tissues and lose their pluripotent characteristics. Understanding how pluripotent cells develop into specialized tissues and applying that knowledge to the treatment of disease and injury is the goal of embryonic stem cell research. Such research involves extracting undifferentiated stem cells from embryos and experimenting with them in the laboratory.

Some cells that are committed to a particular kind of tissue retain some degree of plasticity, even though they are not pluripotent. Such cells represent a third kind of stem cell called *multipotent* and are present in the body at all stages of development, including adulthood. For example, multipotent stem cells in bone marrow can become any kind of blood cell the body needs. Likewise, multipotent stem cells in muscle tissue can become muscle cells, fat cells, or connective tissue (Stewart, 2004). When tissues are damaged by injury, disease, or the natural aging process, the body initiates a developmental process through which these multipotent cells mature into precisely the kind of tissue the body needs to repair itself. In the stem cell research debate, when people talk about "adult" stem cells, they are referring to these multipotent cells.

Why Is Stem Cell Research Controversial?

Many people object to embryonic stem cell research because it requires the destruction of a human embryo (Shannon, 2004). These opponents equate destroying an embryo with killing a human being. They argue that destruction of human life is always wrong, regardless of its stage of development and no matter how noble the purpose of such killing is.

In response, advocates of embryonic stem cell research argue that the human embryo is not yet a person, so its destruction is not equivalent to taking the life of a fully developed human being (Shannon, 2004). Furthermore, because embryonic stem cell research involves excess embryos that are created for in vitro fertilization (IVF), many argue that they would be destroyed whether they were used for research or not. Thus, advocates ask, why not use them to benefit others?

However, the debate takes a different turn when the issue of creating embryos strictly for the purpose of research is raised. Many who would endorse using excess IVF embryos for research balk at the idea that human sperm and ova might be joined in a test tube for the sole purpose of experimentation. They argue that leftover embryos from IVF were conceived with the intention of allowing them to develop into fully grown human beings. For this reason, they say, using their tissue to help others is morally acceptable, much like transplanting the organs of an individual who dies into the bodies of others who need them to live.

By contrast, research involving multipotent cells extracted from the tissues of children and/or adults is unhampered by such ethical dilemmas (Stewart, 2004). What is controversial, however, is the degree to which funds ought to be differentially allocated to embryonic and multipotent stem cell research. Some say that most funding should go to embryonic stem cell studies because pluripotent cells hold the best hope for curing diseases. Others argue that money is better spent on furthering scientists' understanding of how the body uses multipotent cells in natural healing processes. Research can be cited in support of both positions.

Can Stem Cells Cure Diseases?

Experts point out that scientists are still years away from knowing whether embryonic stem cells can be used to treat diseases (Stewart, 2004). Experiments have shown that it is possible to extract pluripotent cells from developing embryos and grow them in the laboratory. In fact, a few such cells can turn into millions in a matter of weeks (National Institutes of Health, 2004). Moreover, scientists have learned how to keep them from differentiating into specialized cells. In other words, they know how to maintain the cells' pluripotent characteristics. What isn't known, though, is exactly how to initiate and control specialization.

Recently, however, British scientists succeeded in developing neurons from embryonic stem cells (National Institutes of Health, 2004). These neurons were then implanted in the brains of mice with a condition similar to Parkinson's disease. Remarkably, most of the mice showed improvements in motor function after receiving the laboratory-grown neurons. These findings have been widely cited by advocates for embryonic stem cell research.

However, even the most ardent advocates of embryonic stem cell research warn that much remains to be learned before similar experiments can be carried out with human beings. For one thing, they caution that stem cell transplants, like organ transplants, can be rejected by the body that receives them. Moreover, studies suggest that laboratory-grown cells may be more likely than naturally developed cells to develop into malignant tumors (Stewart, 2004). Consequently, embryonic stem cells cannot be used to treat diseases in human beings until much more is known about how to control the tissue rejection and tumor development processes.

There is no doubt that multipotent, or adult, stem cells, can be used to treat diseases. In fact, bone marrow stem cells have been used in the treatment of blood diseases for decades (Stewart, 2004). Outside the United States, researchers have successfully used adult stem cells to treat diabetes as well (Dolan, 2006). And in recent years, scientists have identified many new adult stem cell "populations"—in muscle tissue, the liver, the brain, the skin, hair follicles, and many other tissues (National Institutes of Health, 2004). Thus, most experts agree that the potential for using multipotent stem cells to treat disease—or even to moderate the effects of aging—is tremendous. Moreover, scientists have recently discovered that some adult stem cells are pluripotent (National Institutes of Health, 2004). Furthermore, scientists have discovered how to alter multipotent adult cells so that they have all the properties of pluripotent embryonic cells (Egli, Rosains, Birkhoff, & Eggan, 2007).

Nevertheless, new tissues grown from multipotent stem cells are unlikely to become a panacea for disease or a fountain of youth. Rejection isn't an issue, of course, when an individual receives new tissue grown from his or her own stem cells. However, the tendency of these cells to develop into malignant tumors is just as great as that of embryonic stem cells. Another difficulty is that genes in the stem cells of individuals who suffer from genetic disorders carry the same defects as those in their fully developed organs. Thus, gene therapy would be required before their stem cells could be used to fight such diseases.

In addition, stem cells extracted from adults' bodies grow much more slowly than those from embryos, and the older adults are, the more slowly their stem cells grow (Stewart, 2004). The slow growth rate of adults' stem cells represents an important obstacle to using them for research. In clinical applications, it might mean that new tissue could not be grown in time to treat a life-threatening disease or injury.

Stem Cell Research Policies

On August 9, 2001, President George W. Bush issued a directive that, with few exceptions, banned the use of U.S. taxpayer dollars for embryonic stem cell research (Office of the White House Press Secretary, 2001). However, this policy left privately funded embryonic stem cell research almost completely unregulated, and the number of private facilities devoted to such research in the United States has increased dramatically since the policy was enacted (Dolan, 2006; Vergano, 2004). Moreover, President Bush's policy encouraged the U.S. Congress to appropriate additional funding for multipotent stem cell research.

By contrast, most other nations in the industrialized world have established policies that favor publicly funded over privately funded embryonic stem cell research (Rosenthal, 2004). To ensure continued funding, researchers must abide by strict ethical guidelines. Further, these nations' policies place a higher priority on embryonic than on multipotent stem cell research.

Your Turn

In summary, stem cell research policy in the United States might be characterized as follows: (1) emphasis on private rather than public funding for embryonic stem cell research, (2) little regulation of privately funded embryonic stem cell research, and (3) prioritization of multipotent over embryonic stem cell research. Other nations' policies could be summarized as follows: (1) emphasis on public rather than private funding for embryonic stem cell research, (2) strict regulation of embryonic stem cell research, and (3) prioritization of embryonic over multipotent stem cell research. Which approach do you think is better? Finding the answers to these questions may help you decide.

- How do organizations for (e.g., the American Medical Association) and against (e.g., U.S. Conference of Catholic Bishops) embryonic stem cell research explain and support their positions?
- How do scientists grow stem cells in the laboratory?
- What are the top five diseases that scientists currently believe are most likely to be helped through stem cell research?
- Other than the treatment of diseases, what applications might there be for stem cell research?

References

ABC News. (2000, August 22). *Poll: Americans like public school.* Retrieved August 23, 2000, from http://www.abcnews.com.

Abele, A., (2005). Goals, gender-related self-concept, and work-life balance in long-term life pursuit: Findings from the Erlangen longitudinal study BELA-E. *Zeitscrift fur Arbeits und Organisationspsychologie, 49*, 176–186.

Abengozar, C., Bueno, B., & Vega, J. (1999). Intervention on attitudes toward death along the life span. *Educational Gerontology, 25*, 435–447.

Abma, J., & Martinez, G. (2006). Childlessness among older women in the United States: Trends and profiles. *Journal of Marriage and Family, 68*, 1045–1056.

Abraham, J. D., & Hansson, R. O. (1995). Successful aging at work: An applied study of selection, optimization, and compensation through impression management. *Journals of Gerontology: Psychological Sciences, 50B*, P94–P103.

Abrams, E. J., Matheson, P. B., Thomas, P. A., Thea, D. M., Krasinski, K., Lambert, G., Shaffer, N., Bamji, M., Hutson, D., Grimm, K., Kaul, A., Bateman, D., Rogers, M., & New York City Perinatal HIV Transmission Collaborative Study Group (1995). Neonatal predictors of infection status and early death among 332 infants at risk of HIV-1 infection monitored prospectively from birth. *Pediatrics, 96*, 451–458.

Accardo, P., Tomazic, T., Fete, T., Heaney, M., Lindsay, R., & Whitman, B. (1997). Maternally reported fetal activity levels and developmental diagnoses. *Clinical Pediatrics, 36*, 279–283.

Ackerman, B., Brown, E., & Izard, C. (2004). The relations between contextual risk, earned income, and the school adjustment of children from economically disadvantaged families. *Developmental Psychology, 40*, 204–216.

Ackerman, S., Zuroff, D., & Moskowitz, D. (2000). Generativity in midlife and young adults: Links to agency, communion and subjective well-being. *Aging and Human Development, 50*, 17–41.

Adams, C. (1991). Qualitative age differences in memory for text: A life-span developmental perspective. *Psychology & Aging, 6*, 323–336.

Adams, M., & Henry, M. (1997). Myths and realities about words and literacy. *School Psychology Review, 26*, 425–436.

Addis, M., & Mahalik, J. (2003). Men, masculinity, and the contexts of help seeking. *American Psychologist, 58*, 5–14.

Adelmann, P. K. (1994). Multiple roles and physical health among older adults: Gender and ethnic comparisons. *Research on Aging, 16*, 142–166.

Adesman, A. R. (1996). Fragile X syndrome. In A. J. Capute & P. J. Accardo (Eds.), *Developmental disabilities in infancy and childhood, Vol. II: The spectrum of developmental disabilities* (pp. 255–269). Baltimore: Paul H. Brookes.

Adkins, V. (1999). Grandparents as a national asset: A brief note. *Activities, Adaptation, & Aging, 24*, 13–18.

Administration for Children and Families. (2006). *Office of Child Support Enforcement Factsheet.* Retrieved June 18, 2007 from www.acf.hhs.gov/opa/fact_sheets/cse_factsheet.html

Administration on Aging. (2003). *A profile of older Americans: 2003.* Retrieved July 31, 2007 from http://www.aoa.gov/prof/Statistics/profile/2003/15.asp.

Agahi, N., Ahacic, K., & Parker, M. (2006). Continuity of leisure participation from middle age to old age. *The Journals of Gerontology Series B: Psychological Sciences and Social Sciences, 61*, S340–S346.

Agnew, J., Dorn, C., & Eden, G. (2004). Effect of intensive training on auditory processing and reading skills. *Brain & Language, 88*, 21–25.

Ahadi, S. A., & Rothbart, M. K. (1994). Temperament, development, and the big five. In C. F. Halverson, Jr., G. A. Kohnstamm, & R. P. Martin (Eds.), *The developing structure of temperament and personality from infancy to adulthood* (pp. 189–207). Hillsdale, NJ: Erlbaum.

Ahituv, A., & Lehman, R. (2004). *Job turnover, wage rates, and marital stability.* Retrieved July 7, 2007 from http://www.urban.org/UploadedPDF/411148_job_turnover.pdf.

Ahmad, G., & Najam, N. (1998). A study of marital adjustment during first transition to parenthood. *Journal of Behavioural Sciences, 9*, 67–86.

Aiken, L. (1997). *Psychological testing and assessment* (9th ed.). Boston: Allyn & Bacon.

Ainsworth, M. D. S., & Marvin, R. S. (1995). On the shaping of attachment theory and research: An interview with Mary D. S. Ainsworth (Fall 1994). *Monographs of the Society for Research in Child Development, 60* (244, Nos. 2–3), 3–21.

Ainsworth, M. D. S., Blehar, M., Waters, E., & Wall, S. (1978). *Patterns of attachment.* Hillsdale, NJ: Erlbaum.

Akers, J., Jones, R., & Coyl, D. (1998). Adolescent friendship pairs: Similarities in identity status development, behaviors, attitudes, and interests. *Journal of Adolescent Research, 13*, 178–201.

Akiyama, H., Antonucci, T., Takahashi, K., & Langfahl, E. (2003). Negative interactions in close relationships across the life span. *Journals of Gerontology, Series B: Psychological Sciences & Social Sciences, 58B*, P70–P79.

Aksu-Koc, A. A., & Slobin, D. I. (1985). The acquisition of Turkish. In D. I. Slobin (Ed.), *The crosslinguistic study of language acquisition: Vol. 1: The data* (pp. 839–878). Hillsdale, NJ: Erlbaum.

Alan Guttmacher Institute. (2004). *U.S. teenage pregnancy statistics with comparative statistics for women aged 20–24.* Retrieved July 9, 2004, from http://www.guttmacher.org/pubs/teen_stats.html.

Alberg, A., Patnaik, J., May, J., Hoffman, S., Gitchelle, J., Comstock, G., & Helzlsouer, K. (2005). Nicotine replacement therapy use among a cohort of smokers. *Journal of Addictive Diseases, 24*, 101–113.

Alexander, G., & Hines, M. (1994). Gender labels and play styles: Their relative contribution to children's selection of playmates: *Child Development, 65*, 869–879.

Allen, C., & Kisilevsky, B. (1999). Fetal behavior in diabetic and nondiabetic pregnant women: An exploratory study. *Developmental Psychobiology, 35*, 69–80.

Allen, K. R., & Pickett, R. S. (1987). Forgotten streams in the family life course: Utilization of qualitative retrospective interviews in the analysis of lifelong single women's family careers. *Journal of Marriage & the Family, 49*, 517–526.

Allen, W., Dreves, R., & Ruhe, J. (1999). Reasons why college-educated women change employment. *Journal of Business & Psychology, 14*, 77–93.

Alsaker, F. D. (1995). Timing of puberty and reactions to pubertal change. In M. Rutter (Ed.), *Psychosocial disturbances in young people: Challenges for prevention* (pp. 37–82). Cambridge, England: Cambridge University Press.

Alsaker, F. D., & Olweus, D. (1992). Stability of global self-evaluations in early adolescence: A cohort longitudinal study. *Journal of Research on Adolescence, 2*, 123–145.

Alster, E. (1997). The effects of extended time on algebra test scores for college students with and without learning disabilities. *Journal of Learning Disabilities, 30*, 222–227.

Alter, J. (June 22, 2007). The case for national service. *Newsweek Online.* Retrieved July 5, 2007 from http://www.msnbc.msn.com/id/19371599/site/newsweek/.

Alvidrez, J., & Weinstein, R. (1999). Early teacher perceptions and later student academic achievement. *Journal of Educational Psychology, 91*, 731–746.

Alzheimer's Association. (2007). *Alzheimer's disease facts and figures.* Retrieved July 31, 2007 from www.alz.org/national/documents/Report_2007FactsAndFigures.pdf.

Amato, P., & Rogers, S. (1999). Do attitudes toward divorce affect marital quality? *Journal of Family Issues, 20*, 69–86.

Amato, P. R. (1993). Children's adjustment to divorce: Theories, hypotheses, and empirical support. *Journal of Marriage & the Family, 55*, 23–38.

Amato, S. (1998). Human genetics and dysmorphy. In R. Behrman & R. Kliegman (Eds.), *Nelson essentials of pediatrics* (3rd ed., pp. 129–146). Philadelphia: W. B. Saunders.

Ambert, A. (2001). *Families in the new millennium.* Boston: Allyn & Bacon.

Ambuel, B. (1995). Adolescents, unintended pregnancy, and abortion: The struggle for a compassionate social policy. *Current Directions in Psychological Science, 4*, 1–5.

Amenedo, E., & Diaz, F. (1998). Aging-related changes in processing of non-target and target stimuli during an auditory oddball task. *Biological Psychology, 48*, 235–267.

Amenedo, E., & Diaz, F. (1999). Aging-related changes in the processing of attended and unattended standard stimuli. *Neuroreport: For Rapid Communication of Neuroscience Research, 10*, 2383–2388.

American Academy of Pediatrics (AAP). (1999). Committee on public education. *Pediatrics, 104*, 341–343.

American Academy of Pediatrics. (1998). Guidance for effective discipline. *Pediatrics, 101*, 723–728.

American Association of Colleges and Universities. (2005). Connecting higher education, public opinion, and public policy. *Policy Matters, 2(9)*. Retrieved June 30, 2007 from http://www.aascu.org/policy_matters/v2_9/default.htm.

American Association of Colleges and Universities. (2006). Student debt burden. *Policy Matters, 3(8)*. Retrieved June 30, 2007 from www.aascu.org/policy_matters/v3_8/default.htm.

American College of Cardiology. (2002). *Ischemic heart disease.* Retrieved July 9, 2007 from http //www.acc.org/media/patient/chd/ischemic.htm.

American College of Obstetrics and Gynecology (ACOG). (2001, December 12). *ACOG addresses latest controversies in obstetrics.* Retrieved April 1, 2004, from http://www.acog.org.

American College of Obstetrics and Gynecology. (2002, November 29). *Rubella vaccination recommendation changes for pregnant women.* Retrieved April 2, 2004, from http://www.acog.org.

American College of Obstetrics and Gynecology. (2004a). *Ethics in obstetrics and gynecology.* Washington, DC: Author.

American College of Obstetrics and Gynecology. (2004b). *Hormone therapy after the WHI: Time to strike a balance.* Retrieved August 26, 2004, from http://www.acog.org.

American Indian Higher Education Consortium. (1999). *Tribal colleges: An introduction.* Alexandria, VA: Author. Retrieved June 15, 2006 from http://www.aihec.org/documents/Research/intro.pdf.

American Psychiatric Association. (2000). *Diagnostic and statistical manual of mental disorders* (4th ed., Text Revision). Washington, DC: Author.

American Psychiatric Association. (2000). *Practice guidelines for eating disorders.* Retrieved January 31, 2005 from www.psych.org.

AmeriCorps.org. (2007). *What is AmeriCorps?* Retrieved July 5, 2007 from http://www.americorps.org/about/ac/index.asp.

Amieva, H., Lentenneur, L., Dartiques, J., Rouch-Leroyer, I., Sourgen, C., D'Alchée-Birée, F., Dib, M., Barberger-Gateau, P., Orgogozo, J., & Fabrigoule, C. (2004). Annual rate and predictors of conversion to dementia in subjects presenting mild cognitive impairment criteria defined according to a population-based study. *Dementia & Geriatric Cognitive Disorders, 18*, 87–93.

Anderson, C., & Dill, K. (2000). Video games and aggressive thoughts, feelings, and behavior in the laboratory and in life. *Journal of Personality & Social Psychology, 78*, 772–790.

Anderson, K. M., Castelli, W. P., & Levy, D. (1987). Cholesterol and mortality: 30 years of follow–up from the Framingham study. *Journal of the American Medical Association, 257*, 2176–2180.

Anderson, R. (1998). Examining language loss in bilingual children. *Electronic Multicultural Journal of Communication Disorders*, 1.

Anderson, S., Dallal, G., & Must, A. (2003). Relative weight and race influence average age at menarche: Results from two nationally representative surveys of U.S. girls studied 25 years apart. *Pediatrics, 111*, 844–850.

Andersson, H. (1996). The Fagan Test of Infant Intelligence: Predictive validity in a random sample. *Psychological Reports, 78*, 1015–1026.

Andrén, S., & Elmstahl, S. (2007). Relationships between income, subjective health, and caregiver burden in caregivers of people with dementia in group living care: A cross-sectional community-based study. *International Journal of Nursing Studies, 44*, 435–446.

Andreou, E., & Metallidou, P. (2004). The relationship of academic and social cognition to behaviour in bullying situations among Greek primary school children. *Educational Psychology, 24*, 27–41.

Andrews, M., Dowling, W., Bartlett, J., & Halpern, A. (1998). Identification of speeded and slowed familiar melodies by younger, middle-aged, and older musicians and nonmusicians. *Psychology & Aging, 13*, 462–471.

Angier, N. (June 9, 1992). Clue to longevity found at chromosome tip. *New York Times*, pp. B5, B9.

Anglin, J. M. (1993). Vocabulary development: A morphological analysis. *Monographs of the Society for Research in Child Development, 58* (Serial No. 238).

Anglin, J. M. (1995, March). *Word learning and the growth of potentially knowable vocabulary.* Paper presented at the biennial meetings of the Society for Research in Child Development, Indianapolis, IN.

Anisfeld, M. (1991). Neonatal imitation. *Developmental Review, 11*, 60–97.

Annett, M. (2003). Do the French and the English differ for hand skill asymmetry? Handedness subgroups in the sample of Doyen and Carlier (2002) and in English schools and universities. *Laterality: Asymmetries of Body, Brain & Cognition, 8*, 233–245.

Annunziato, P. W., & Frenkel, L. M. (1993). The epidemiology of pediatric HIV-1 infection. *Pediatric Annals, 22*, 401–405.

Anthony, J., & Lonigan, C. (2004). The nature of phonological awareness: Converging evidence from four studies of preschool and early grade school children. *Journal of Educational Psychology, 96*, 43–55.

Anthony, J. C., & Aboraya, A. (1992). The epidemiology of selected mental disorders in later life. In J. E. Birren, R. B. Sloane, & G. D. Cohen (Eds.), *Handbook of mental health and aging* (2nd ed., pp. 28–73). San Diego, CA: Academic Press.

Antonucci, T. C. (1990). Social supports and social relationships. In R. H. Bin-stock & L. K. George (Eds.), *Handbook of aging and the social sciences* (3rd ed., pp. 205–226). San Diego, CA: Academic Press.

Antonucci, T., Lansford, J., & Akiyama, H. (2001). Impact of positive and negative aspects of marital relationships and friendships on well-being of older adults. *Applied Developmental Science, 5*, 68–75.

Antrop, I., Roeyers, H., Van Oost, P., & Buysse, A. (2000). Stimulation seeking and hyperactivity in children with ADHD. *Journal of Child Psychology, Psychiatry & Allied Disciplines, 41*, 225–231.

Apgar, V. A. (1953). A proposal for a new method of evaluation of the newborn infant. *Current Research in Anesthesia and Analgesia, 32*, 260–267.

Aranha, M. (1997). Creativity in students and its relation to intelligence and peer perception. *Revista Interamericana de Psicologia, 31*, 309–313.

Arbaugh, J., & Benbunan-Fich, R. (2007). The importance of participant interaction in online environments. *Decision Support Systems, 43*, 853–865.

Arbuckle, N. W., & De Vries, B. (1995). The long-term effects of later life spousal and parental bereavement on personal functioning. *The Gerontologist, 35*, 637–647.

Ardelt, M. (2003). Effects of religion and purpose in life on elders' subjective well-being and attitudes toward death. *Journal of Religious Gerontology, 14*, 55–77.

Ardelt, M., & Koenig, C. (2006). The role of religion for hospice patients and relatively healthy older adults. *Research on Aging, 28*, 184–215.

Arenberg, D. (1983). Memory and learning do decline late in life. In J. E. Birren, J. M. A. Munnichs, H. Thomae, & M. Marios (Eds.), *Aging: A challenge to science and society, Vol. 3: Behavioral sciences and conclusions* (pp. 312–322). New York: Oxford University Press.

Arias, E. (2006) United States life tables, 2003. *National Vital Statistics Reports, 54*, pp. 1–40.

Arluk, S., Swain, D., & Dowling, E. (2003). Childhood obesity's relationship to time spent in sedentary behavior. *Military Medicine, 168*, 583–586.

Armstrong, T. (2003). Effect of moral reconation therapy on the recidivism of youthful offenders: A randomized experiment. *Criminal Justice & Behavior, 30*, 668–687

Arnett, J. (1998). Risk behavior and family role transitions during the twenties. *Journal of Youth & Adolescence, 27*, 301–320.

Arnett, J. (2000). Emerging adulthood: A theory of development from the late teens through the twenties. *American Psychologist, 57*, 774–783.

Arrindell, W., & Luteijn, F. (2000). Similarity between intimate partners for personality traits as related to individual levels of satisfaction with life. *Personality & Individual Differences, 28*, 629–637.

Asbjornsen, A., Obrzut, J., Boliek, C., Myking, E., Holmefjord, A., Reisaeter, S., Klausen, O. & Moller, P. (2005). Impaired auditory attention skills following middle-ear infections. *Child Neuropsychology, 11*, 121–133.

Asendorpf, J. B., Warkentin, V., & Baudonnière, P. (1996). Self-awareness and other-awareness, II: Mirror self-recognition, social contingency awareness, and synchronic imitation. *Developmental Psychology, 32*, 313–321.

Ashkar, P., & Kenny, D. (2007). Moral reasoning of adolescent male offender: Comparison of sexual and nonsexual offenders. *Criminal Justice and Behavior, 34*, 108–118.

Aslin, R. (1987). Motor aspects of visual development in infancy. In N. P. Salapatek & L. Cohen (Eds.), *Handbook of infant perception, Vol. 1: From sensation to perception* (pp. 43–113). Orlando, FL: Academic Press.

Aslin, R., Saffran, J., & Newport, E. (1998). Computation of conditional probability statistics by 8-month-old infants. *Psychological Science, 9*, 321–324.

Asplund, R. (2003). Sleepiness and sleep in elderly persons with tinnitus. *Archives of Gerontology and Geriatrics, 37*, 139–145.

Assibey-Mensah, G. (1997). Role models and youth development: Evidence and lessons from the perceptions of African-American male youth. *Western Journal of Black Studies, 21*, 242–252.

Associated Press. (February 13, 2007). *Pakistan's ruling party introduces bill to prohibit forced marriages.* Retrieved July 5, 2007 from www.startribune.com/722/story/999058.html.

Associated Press. (February 27, 2007). *Overweight 8-year-old sets off child obesity debate in Britain.* Retrieved June 16, 2007 from www.iht.com/articles/ap/2007/02/27/europe/EU-GEN-Britain-Child-Obesity.php

Association of Reproductive Health Professionals (ARHP). (2000). *Mature sex.* Retrieved August 26, 2004, from http://www.ahrp.org/maturesex.

Astington, J., & Jenkins, J. (1999). A longitudinal study of the relation between language and theory-of-mind development. *Developmental Psychology, 35,* 1311–1320.

Astington, J. W., & Jenkins, J. M. (1995, March). *Language and theory of mind: A theoretical review and a longitudinal study.* Paper presented at the biennial meetings of the Society for Research in Child Development, Indianapolis, IN.

Astor, R. (1994). Children's moral reasoning about family and peer violence: The role of provocation and retribution. *Child Development, 65,* 1054–1067.

Atchley, R. (1989). A continuity theory of normal aging. *The Gerontologist, 29,* 183–190.

Attie, I., & Brooks-Gunn, J. (1995). The development of eating regulation across the life span. In D. Cicchetti and D. Cohen (Eds.). *Developmental psychopathology: Risk, disorder, and adaptation.* (pp. 332–368). New York: John Wiley & Sons, Inc.

Attie, I., Brooks-Gunn, J., & Petersen, A. (1990). A developmental perspective on eating disorders and eating problems. In M. Lewis & S. M. Miller (Eds.), *Handbook of developmental psychopathology* (pp. 409–420). New York: Plenum.

Auman, M. (2007). Bereavement support for children. *The Journal of School Nursing, 23,* 34–39.

Austin, S., Ziyadeh, N., Kahn, J., Camargo, C., Colditz, G., & Field, A. (2004). Sexual orientation, weight concerns, and eating-disordered behaviors in adolescent girls and boys. *Journal of the American Academy of Child & Adolescent Psychiatry, 43,* 1115–1123.

Avis, J., & Harris, P. L. (1991). Belief-desire reasoning among Baka children: Evidence for a universal conception of mind. *Child Development, 62,* 460–467.

Aylward, G. (2002). Cognitive and neuropsychological outcomes: More than IQ scores. *Mental Retardation & Developmental Disabilities Research Reviews, 8,* 234–240.

Babiloni, C., Babiloni, F., Carducci, F., Cappa, S., Cincotti, F., Del Percio, C., Miniussi, C., Moretti, D., Rossi, S., Sosta, K., & Rossini, P. (2004). Human cortical rhythms during visual delayed choice reaction time tasks: A high-resolution EEG study on normal aging. *Behavioural Brain Research, 153,* 261–271.

Bach, P., Pham, H., Schrag, D., Tate, R., & Hargraves, L. (2004). Primary care physicians who treat blacks and whites. *New England Journal of Medicine, 351,* 575–584.

Bachman, J., Safron, D., Sy, S., & Schulenberg, J. (2003). Wishing to work: New perspectives on how adolescents' part-time work intensity is linked to educational disengagement, substance use, and other problem behaviours. *International Journal of Behavioral Development, 27,* 301–315.

Bachman, J., Segal, D., Freedman-Doan, P., & O'Malley, P. (2000). Who chooses military service? Correlates of propensity and enlistment in the U.S. Armed Forces. *Military Psychology, 12,* 1–30.

Baddeley, A. (1998). *Human memory: Theory and practice* (Rev. ed.) Boston: Allyn & Bacon.

Badr, H., Acitelli, L., & Taylor, C. (2007). Does couple identity mediate the stress experienced by caregiving spouses. *Psychology & Health, 22,* 211–229.

Baek, H. (2002). A comparative study of moral development of Korean and British children. *Journal of Moral Education, 31,* 373–391.

Bahrick, L., & Lickliter, R. (2000). Intersensory redundancy guides attentional selectivity and perceptual learning in infancy. *Developmental Psychology, 36,* 190–201.

Bailey, J., Brobow, D., Wolfe, M., & Mikach, S. (1995). Sexual orientation of adult sons of gay fathers. *Developmental Psychology, 31,* 124–129.

Bailey, J. M., & Pillard, R. C. (1991). A genetic study of male sexual orientation. *Archives of General Psychiatry, 48,* 1089–1096.

Bailey, J. M., Pillard, R. C., Neale, M. C., & Agyei, Y. (1993). Heritable factors influence sexual orientation in women. *Archives of General Psychiatry, 50,* 217–223.

Bailey, S., & Zvonkovic, A. (2003). Parenting after divorce: Nonresidential parents' perceptions of social and institutional support. *Journal of Divorce & Remarriage, 39,* 59–80.

Baillargeon, R. (1987). Object permanence in very young infants. *Developmental Psychology, 23,* 655–664.

Baillargeon, R. (1994). How do infants learn about the physical world? *Current Directions in Psychological Science, 3,* 133–140.

Baillargeon, R., & DeVos, J. (1991). Object permanence in young infants: Further evidence. *Child Development, 62,* 1227–1246.

Baillargeon, R., Spelke, E. S., & Wasserman, S. (1985). Object permanence in five-month-old infants. *Cognition, 20,* 191–208.

Bailley, S., Kral, M., & Dunham, K. (1999). Survivors of suicide do grieve differently: Empirical support for a common sense proposition. *Suicide & Life-Threatening Behavior, 29,* 256–271.

Baker, D., Jeganathan, K., Cameron, D., Thompson, M., Juneja, S., Kopecka, A., Kumar, R., Jenkins, R., de Groen, P., Roche, P., & van Deursen, J. (2004). BubR1 insufficiency causes early onset of aging-associated phenotypes and infertility in mice. *Nature Genetics, 36,* 744–749.

Baker, J. M. & Zigmond, N. (1995). The meaning and practice of inclusion for students with learning disabilities: Themes and implications from the five cases. *The Journal of Special Education, 29,* 163–180.

Baldwin, D. A. (1995, March). *Understanding relations between constraints and a socio-pragmatic account of meaning acquisition.* Paper presented at the biennial meetings of the Society for Research in Child Development, Indianapolis, IN.

Ball, E. (1997). Phonological awareness: Implications for whole language and emergent literacy programs. *Topics in Language Disorders, 17,* 14–26.

Ball, R. (2006). *Meeting Social Security's long-range shortfall.* Retrieved July 31, 2007 from http://www.tcf.org/Publications/RetirementSecurity/ballplan.pdf.

Baltes, P., & Kunzmann, U. (2004). The two faces of wisdom: Wisdom as a general theory of knowledge and judgment about excellence in mind and virtue vs. wisdom as everyday realization in people and products. *Human Development, 47,* 290–299.

Baltes, P., & Staudinger, U. (2000). Wisdom: A metaheuristic (pragmatic) to orchestrate mind and virtue toward excellence. *American Psychologist, 55,* 122–136.

Baltes, P. B., & Baltes, M. M. (1990). Psychological perspectives on successful aging: The model of selective optimization with compensation. In P. B. Baltes & M. M. Baltes (Eds.), *Successful aging* (pp. 1–34). Cambridge, England: Cambridge University Press.

Baltes, P. B., & Kliegl, R. (1992). Further testing of limits of cognitive plasticity: Negative age differences in a mnemonic skill are robust. *Developmental Psychology, 28,* 121–125.

Baltes, P. B., Reese, H. W., & Lipsitt, L. P. (1980). Life-span developmental psychology. *Annual Review of Psychology, 31,* 65–10.

Bamford, F. N., Bannister, R. P., Benjamin, C. M., Hillier, V. F., Ward, B. S., & Moore, W. M. O. (1990). Sleep in the first year of life. *Developmental Medicine & Child Neurology, 32,* 718–724.

Bandura, A. (1977a). *Social learning theory.* Englewood Cliffs, NJ: Prentice-Hall.

Bandura, A. (1977b). Self-efficacy: Toward a unifying theory of behavioral change. *Psychological Review, 84,* 91–125.

Bandura, A. (1982). The psychology of chance encounters and life paths. *American Psychologist, 37,* 747–755.

Bandura, A. (1986). *Social foundations of thought and action: A social cognitive theory.* Englewood Cliffs, NJ: Prentice-Hall.

Bandura, A. (1989). Social cognitive theory. *Annals of Child Development, 6,* 1–60.

Bandura, A. (1997). *Self-efficacy: The exercise of control.* New York: Freeman.

Bandura, A., Ross, D., & Ross, S. A. (1961). Transmission of aggression through imitation of aggressive models. *Journal of Abnormal & Social Psychology, 63,* 575–582.

Bangerter, A., & Heath, C. (2004). The Mozart effect: Tracking the evolution of a scientific legend. *British Journal of Social Psychology, 43,* 605–623.

Baranchik, A. (2002). Identifying gaps in mathematics preparation that contribute to ethnic, gender, and American/foreign differences in precalculus performance. *Journal of Negro Education, 71,* 253–268.

Barayuga, D. (November 30, 2005). "Ice" addict cleared of killing newborn. Retrieved June 8, 2007 from http://starbulletin.com/2005/11/30/news/story02.html

Barbarin, O. (1999). Social risks and psychological adjustment: A comparison of African American and South African children. *Child Development, 70,* 1348–1359.

Barenboim, C. (1981). The development of person perception in childhood and adolescence: From behavioral comparisons to psychological constructs to psychological comparisons. *Child Development, 52,* 129–144.

Barer, B. (2001). The "grands and greats" of very old black grandmothers. *Journal of Aging Studies, 15,* 1–11.

Barker, J., Morrow, J., & Mitteness, L. (1998). Gender, informal social support networks, and elderly urban African Americans. *Journal of Aging Studies, 12,* 199–222.

Barkin, S., Scheindlin, B., Ip, E., Richardson, I., & Finch, S. (2007). Determinants of parental discipline practices: A national sample from primary care practices. *Clinical Pediatrics, 46,* 64–69.

Barkley, R. (1990). *Attention-deficit hyperactivity disorder.* New York: Guilford Press.

Barlow, J., & Lewandowski, L. (2000, August). *Ten-year longitudinal study of preterm infants: Outcomes and predictors.* Paper presented at the annual meeting of the American Psychological Association, Washington, DC.

Barnard, K. E., Hammond, M. A., Booth, C. L., Bee, H. L., Mitchell, S. K., & Spieker, S. J. (1989). Measurement and meaning of parent-child interaction. In J. J. Morrison, C. Lord, & D. P. Keating (Eds.), *Applied developmental psychology, Vol. 3* (pp. 40–81). San Diego, CA: Academic Press.

Barness, L., & Curran, J. (1996). Nutrition. In R. E. Behrman, R. M. Kliegman, & A. M. Arvin (Eds.), *Nelson's textbook of pediatrics* (15th ed., pp. 141–184). Philadelphia: Saunders.

Barnett, R. (2004). Women and multiple roles: Myths and reality. *Harvard Review of Psychiatry, 12*, 158–164.

Barnett, W. S. (1993). Benefit-cost analysis of preschool education: Findings from a 25-year follow-up. *American Journal of Orthopsychiatry, 63*, 500–508.

Barnett, W. S. (1995). Long-term effects of early childhood programs on cognitive and school outcomes. *The Future of Children, 5* (3), 25–50.

Barr, R., Marrott, H., & Rovee-Collier, C. (2003). The role of sensory preconditioning in memory retrieval by preverbal infants. *Learning & Behavior, 31*, 111–123.

Barrett, H., & Behne, T (2005). Children's understanding of death as the cessation of agency: A test using sleep versus death. *Cognition, 96*, 93–108.

Barron, V., & Menken, K. (2002). *What are the characteristics of the bilingual education and ESL teacher shortage?* National Clearinghouse for English Language Acquisition & Language Instruction Educational Programs Factsheet. Retrieved June 23, 2004, from http://www.ncela.gwu.edu/expert/faq/14shortage.htm.

Barrow, F., Armstrong, M., Vargo, A., & Boothroyd, R. (2007). Understanding the findings of resilience-related research for fostering the development of African American adolescents. *Child and Adolescent Psychiatric Clinics of North America, 16*, 393–413.

Bartholow, B., Bushman, B., & Sestir, M. (2006). Chronic violent video game exposure and desensitization to violence: Behavioral and event-related brain potential data. *Journal of Experimental Social Psychology, 42*, 532–539.

Bartlik, B., & Goldstein, M. (2000, June). Maintaining sexual health after menopause. *Psychiatric Services Journal, 51*, 751–753.

Barusch, A. (1999). Religion, adversity and age: Religious experiences of low-income elderly women. *Journal of Sociology & Social Welfare, 26*, 125–142.

Basham, P. (2001). Home schooling: From the extreme to the mainstream. *Public Policy Sources/The Fraser Institute, 51*. Retrieved June 23, 2004, from http://www.fraserinstitute.ca/admin/books/files/homeschool.pdf.

Bass, D. M. (1985). The hospice ideology and success of hospice care. *Research on Aging, 7*, 307–328.

Basseches, M. (1984). *Dialectical thinking and adult development*. Norwood, NJ: Ablex.

Basseches, M. (1989). Dialectical thinking as an organized whole: Comments on Irwin and Kramer. In M. L. Commons, J. D. Sinnott, F. A. Richards, & C. Armon (Eds.), *Adult development: Vol. 1. Comparisons and applications of developmental models* (pp. 161–178). New York: Praeger.

Bates, E. (1993). Commentary: Comprehension and production in early language development. *Monographs of the Society for Research in Child Development, 58* (3–4, Serial No. 233), 222–242.

Bates, E., Marchman, V., Thal, D., Fenson, L., Dale, P., Reznick, J. S., Reilly, J., & Hartung, J. (1994). Developmental and stylistic variation in the composition of early vocabulary. *Journal of Child Language, 21*, 85–123.

Bates, E., O'Connell, B., & Shore, C. (1987). Language and communication in infancy. In J. D. Osofsky (Ed.), *Handbook of infant development* (2nd ed., pp. 149–203). New York: Wiley.

Bates, J. E. (1989). Applications of temperament concepts. In G. A. Kohnstamm, J. E. Bates, & M. K. Rothbart (Eds.), *Temperament in childhood* (pp. 321–356). Chichester, England: Wiley.

Batten, M., & Oltjenbruns, K. (1999). Adolescent sibling bereavement as a catalyst for spiritual development: A model for understanding. *Death Studies, 23*, 529–546.

Bauer, P., Schwade, J., Wewerka, S., & Delaney, K. (1999). Planning ahead: Goal-directed problem solving by 2-year-olds. *Developmental Psychology, 35*, 1321–1337.

Baugher, R. J., Burger, C., Smith, R., & Wallston, K. (1989/1990). A comparison of terminally ill persons at various time periods to death. *Omega, 20*, 103–115.

Bauminger, N., & Kasari, C. (1999). Brief report: Theory of mind in high-functioning children with autism. *Journal of Autism & Developmental Disorders, 29*, 81–86.

Baumrind, D. (1967). Child care practices anteceding three patterns of preschool behavior. *Genetic Psychology Monographs, 75*, 43–88.

Baumrind, D. (1971). Current patterns of parental authority. *Developmental Psychology Monograph, 4* (1, Part 2).

Baumrind, D. (1972). Socialization and instrumental competence in young children. In W. W. Hartup (Ed.), *The young child: Reviews of research, Vol. 2* (pp. 202–224). Washington, DC: National Association for the Education of Young Children.

Baumrind, D. (1980). New directions in socialization research. *American Psychologist, 35*, 639–652.

Baumrind, D. (1991). Effective parenting during the early adolescent transition. In P. A. Cowan & M. Hetherington (Eds.), *Family transitions* (pp. 111–163). Hillsdale, NJ: Erlbaum.

Bausell, C. (2007). Quality Counts 2007: From cradle to career: Connecting American education from birth to adulthood. *Education Week, 26*, 86–87.

Baxter, J., Shetterly, S., Eby, C., Mason, L., Cortese, C., & Hamman, R. (1998). Social network factors associated with perceived quality of life: The San Luis Valley Health and Aging Study. *Journal of Aging & Health, 10*, 287–310.

Baydar, N., & Brooks-Gunn, J. (1991). Effects of maternal employment and child-care arrangements on preschoolers' cognitive and behavioral outcomes: Evidence from the children of the National Longitudinal Survey of Youth. *Developmental Psychology, 27*, 932–945.

Baydar, N., Brooks-Gunn, J., & Furstenberg, F. F. (1993). Early warning signs of functional illiteracy: Predictors in childhood and adolescence. *Child Development, 64*, 815–829.

Bayley, N. (1969). *Bayley scales of infant development*. New York: Psychological Corporation.

Bayley, N. (1993). *Bayley scales of infant development: Birth to two years*. San Antonio, TX: Psychological Corporation.

Bayley, N. (2006). *Bayley scales of infant and toddler development-Third Edition*. San Antonio, TX: Harcourt Assessment, Inc.

Bearce, K., & Rovee-Collier, C. (2006). Repeated priming increases memory accessibility in infants. *Journal of Experimental Child Psychology, 93*, 357–376

Beaty, L. (1999). Identity development of homosexual youth and parental and familial influences on the coming out process. *Adolescence, 34*, 597–601.

Beaudry, M., Dufour, R., & Marcoux, S. (1995). Relation between infant feeding and infections during the first six months of life. *Journal of Pediatrics, 126*, 191–197.

Bechara, A. (2005). Decision making, impulse control and loss of willpower to resist drugs: A neurocognitive perspective. *Nature Neuroscience, 18*, 1458–1463.

Bee, H. L., Barnard, K. E., Eyres, S. J., Gray, C. A., Hammond, M. A., Spietz, A. L., Snyder, C., & Clark, B. (1982). Prediction of IQ and language skill from perinatal status, child performance, family characteristics, and mother-infant interaction. *Child Development, 53*, 1135–1156.

Beekman, A., Copeland, J., & Prince, M. (1999). Review of community prevalence of depression in later life. *British Journal of Psychiatry, 174*, 307–311.

Beem, E., Hooijkaas, H., Cleriren, M., Schut, H., Garssen, B., Croon, M., Jabaaij, L., Goodkin, K., Wind, H., & de Vries, M. (1999). The immunological and psychological effects of bereavement: Does grief counseling really make a difference? A pilot study. *Psychiatry Research, 85*, 81–93.

Behrend, D., Scofield, J., & Kleinknecht, E. (2001) Beyond fast mapping: Young children's extensions of novel words and novel facts. *Developmental Psychology, 37*, 690–705.

Beilke, J., & Yssel, N. (1999). The chilly climate for students with disabilities in higher education. *College Student Journal, 33*, 364–371.

Bell, J., & Bromnick, R. (2003). The social reality of the imaginary audience: A ground theory approach. *Adolescence, 38*, 205–219.

Bell, L. G., & Bell, D. C. (1982). Family climate and the role of the female adolescent: Determinants of adolescent functioning. *Family Relations, 31*, 519–527.

Bellantoni, M. F., & Blackman, M. R. (1996). Menopause and its consequences. In E. L. Schneider & J. W. Rowe (Eds.), *Handbook of the biology of aging* (4th ed., pp. 415–430). San Diego, CA: Academic Press.

Belsky, J. (1985). Prepared statement on the effects of day care. In Select Committee on Children, Youth, and Families, House of Representatives, 98th Congress, Second Session, *Improving child care services: What can be done?* Washington, DC: U.S. Government Printing Office.

Belsky, J. (1992). Consequences of child care for children's development: A deconstructionist view. In A. Booth (Ed.), *Child care in the 1990s: Trends and consequences* (pp. 83–94). Hillsdale, NJ: Erlbaum.

Belsky, J. (2001). Developmental risks (still) associated with early child care. *Journal of Child Psychology & Psychiatry & Allied Disciplines, 42*, 845–859.

Belsky, J. (2002). Quantity counts: Amount of child care and children's socioemotional development. *Journal of Developmental & Behavioral Pediatrics, 23* 167–170.

Belsky, J., & Rovine, M. (1988). Nonmaternal care in the first year of life and the security of infant-parent attachment. *Child Development, 59*, 157–167.

Belsky, J., Hsieh, K., & Crnic, K. (1996). Infant positive and negative emotionality: One dimension or two? *Developmental Psychology, 32,* 289–298.
Belsky, J., Jaffee, S., Caspi, A., Moffitt, T., & Silva, P. (2003). Intergenerational relationships in young adulthood and their life course, mental health, and personality correlates. *Journal of Family Psychology, 17,* 460–471.
Belsky, J., Lang, M. E., & Rovine, M. (1985). Stability and change in marriage across the transition to parenthood: A second study. *Journal of Marriage & the Family, 47,* 855–865.
Bem, S. (1981). Gender schema theory: A cognitive account of sex-typing. *Psychological Review, 88,* 354–364.
Bem, S. L. (1974). The measurement of psychological androgyny. *Journal of Consulting & Clinical Psychology, 42,* 155–162.
Benbow, C. P. (1988). Sex differences in mathematical reasoning ability in intellectually talented preadolescents: Their nature, effects, and possible causes. *Behavioral & Brain Sciences, 11,* 169–232.
Bender, B. G., Harmon, R. J., Linden, M. G., & Robinson, A. (1995). Psychosocial adaptation of 39 adolescents with sex chromosome abnormalities. *Pediatrics, 96,* 302–308.
Bender, K. (1999). Assessing antidepressant safety in the elderly. *Psychiatric Times, 16.* Retrieved February 7, 2001, from http://www.mhsource.com/pt/p990151.html.
Bendersky, M., & Lewis, M. (1994). Environmental risk, biological risk, and developmental outcome. *Developmental Psychology, 30,* 484–494.
Benedetti, W. (April 20, 2007). *Were video games to blame for Virginia Tech massacre?* Retrieved June 28, 2007 from http://www.msnbc.msn.com/id/18220228/
Benenson, J., & Benarroch, D. (1998). Gender differences in responses to friends' hypothetical greater success. *Journal of Early Adolescence, 18,* 192–208.
Benenson, J. F. (1994). Ages four to six years: Changes in the structures of play networks of girls and boys. *Merrill-Palmer Quarterly, 40,* 478–487.
Bengtson, V., Rosenthal, C., & Burton, L. (1990). Families and aging: Diversity and heterogeneity. In R. H. Binstock & L. K. George (Eds.), *Handbook of aging and the social sciences* (3rd ed., pp. 263–287). San Diego, CA: Academic Press.
Bengtson, V., Rosenthal, C., & Burton, L. (1996). Paradoxes of families and aging. In R. H. Binstock & L. K. George (Eds.), *Handbook of aging and the social sciences* (4th ed., pp. 253–282). San Diego, CA: Academic Press.
Bengtson, V. L., Cuellar, J. B., & Ragan, P. K. (1977). Stratum contrasts and similarities in attitudes toward death. *Journal of Gerontology, 32,* 76–88.
Bennett, M. (1997). A longitudinal study of wellbeing in widowed women. *International Journal of Geriatric Psychiatry, 12,* 61–66.
Bennett, M. (1998). Longitudinal changes in mental and physical health among elderly, recently widowed men. *Mortality, 3,* 265–273.
Benton, J. (2007). Fort Worth charter school in trouble over TAKS cheating. *Dallas Morning New Online.* Retrieved June 25, 2007 from www.dallasnews.com/sharedcontent/dws/dn/latestnews/stories/061507dnmetcheatinglee.3c44589.html
Berg, S. (1996). Aging, behavior, and terminal decline. In J. E. Birren & K. W. Schaie (Eds.), *Handbook of the psychology of aging* (4th ed., pp. 323–337). San Diego, CA: Academic Press.
Bergeman, C. S., Chipuer, H. M., Plomin, R., Pedersen, N. L., McClearn, G. E., Nesselroade, J. R., Costa, P. T., & McCrae, R. R. (1993). Genetic and environmental effects on openness to experience, agreeableness, and conscientiousness: An adoption/twin study. *Journal of Personality, 61,* 159–179.
Bergeson, T., & Trehub, S. (1999). Mothers' singing to infants and preschool children. *Infant Behavior & Development, 22,* 53–64.
Bergman, R. (2002). Why be moral? A conceptual model from developmental psychology. *Human Development, 45,* 104–124.
Berkman, L. F. (1985). The relationship of social networks and social support to morbidity and mortality. In S. Coen & S. L. Syme (Eds.), *Social support and health* (pp. 241–262). Orlando, FL: Academic Press.
Berkman, L. F., & Breslow, L. (1983). *Health and ways of living: The Alameda County Study.* New York: Oxford University Press.
Berliner, D., & Biddle, B. (1997). *The manufactured crisis: Myths, fraud, and the attack on America's public schools.* New York: Addison-Wesley.
Berndt, T. J., & Keefe, K. (1995a). Friends' influence on adolescents' adjustment to school. *Child Development, 66,* 1312–1329.
Berne, L., & Huberman, B. (1996, February). Sexuality education works: Here's proof. *Education Digest,* 25–29.
Bernhard, J., Lefebvre, M., Kilbride, K., Chud, G., & Lange, R. (1998). Troubled relationships in early childhood education: Parent-teacher interactions in ethnoculturally diverse child care settings. *Early Education & Development, 9,* 5–28.
Berninger, V., Abbott, R., Zook, D., Ogier, S., et al. (1999). Early intervention for reading disabilities: Teaching the alphabet principle in a connectionist framework. *Journal of Learning Disabilities, 32,* 491–503.
Berthier, N., DeBlois, S., Poirier, C., Novak, M., & Clifton, R. (2000). Where's the ball? Two- and three-year-olds reason about unseen events. *Developmental Psychology, 36,* 394–401.
Bertram, L., McQueen, M., Mullin, K., Blacker, D., & Tanzi, R. (2007). Systematic meta-analyses of Alzheimer disease genetic association studies: The AlzGene database. *Nature Genetics, 39,* 17–23.
Betancourt, H., & Lopez, S. R. (1993). The study of culture, ethnicity, and race in American psychology. *American Psychologist, 48,* 629–637.
Betancourt, L., Fischer, R., Gianetta, J., Malmud, E., Brodsky, N. & Hurt, H. (1999). Problem-solving ability of inner-city children with and without in utero cocaine exposure. *Journal of Developmental Disabilities, 20,* 418–424.
Bethus, I., Lemaire, V., Lhomme, M., & Goodall, G. (2005). Does prenatal stress effect latent inhibition? It depends on the gender. *Behavioural Brain Research, 158,* 331–338.
Betz, N. E., & Fitzgerald, L. F. (1987). *The career psychology of women.* Orlando, FL: Academic Press.
Beyene, Y., Gilliss, C., & Lee, K. (2007). "I take the good with the bad, and I moisturize": Defying middle age in the new millennium. *Menopause,* 14, 734–741.
Bhatt, R., Wilk, A., Hill, D., & Rovee-Collier, C. (2004). Correlated attributes and categorization in the first half-year of life. *Developmental Psychobiology, 44,* 103–115.
Bial, M. (1971). *Liberal Judaism at home.* New York: Union of American Hebrew Congregations.
Bialystok, E. (1997). Effects of bilingualism and biliteracy on children's emerging concepts of print. *Developmental Psychology, 33.*
Bialystok, E., & Majumder, S. (1998). The relationship between bilingualism and the development of cognitive processes in problem solving. *Applied Psycholinguistics, 19,* 69–85.
Bialystok, E., Majumder, S., & Martin, M. (2003). Developing phonological awareness: Is there a bilingual advantage? *Applied Linguistics, 24,* 27–44.
Bialystok, E., Shenfield, T., & Codd, J. (2000). Languages, scripts, and the environment: Factors in developing concepts of print. *Developmental Psychology, 36,* 66–76.
Biblarz, T. J., Bengtson, V. L., & Bucur, A. (1996). Social mobility across three generations. *Journal of Marriage & the Family, 58,* 188–200.
Bigler, R., & Liben, S. (1993). The role of attitudes and interventions in gender-schematic processing. *Child Development, 61,* 1440–1452.
Billy, J. O. G., Brewster, K. L., & Grady, W. R. (1994). Contextual effects on the sexual behavior of adolescent women. *Journal of Marriage & the Family, 56,* 387–404.
Binet, A., & Simon, T. (1905). Méthodes nouvelles pour le diagnostic du niveau intellectuel des anormaux [New methods for diagnosing the intellectual level of the abnormal]. *L'Anée Psychologique, 11,* 191–244.
Bingham, C. R., Miller, B. C., & Adams, G. R. (1990). Correlates of age at first sexual intercourse in a national sample of young women. *Journal of Adolescent Research, 5,* 18–33.
Birch, D. (1998). The adolescent parent: A fifteen-year longitudinal study of school-age mothers and their children. *International Journal of Adolescent Medicine & Health, 19,* 141–153.
Birren, J. E., & Fisher, L. M. (1995). Aging and speed of behavior: Possible consequences for psychological functioning. *Annual Review of Psychology, 56,* 329–353.
Birren, J. E., & Schroots, J. J. F. (1996). History, concepts, and theory in the psychology of aging. In J. R. Birren & K. W. Schaie (Eds.), *Handbook of the psychology of aging* (4th ed., pp. 3–23). San Diego, CA: Academic Press.
Bish, C., Blanck, H., Serdula, M., Marcus, M., Kohl, H., & Khan, L. (2005). Diet and physical activity behaviors among Americans trying to lose weight: 2000 Behavioral Risk Factor Surveillance System. *Obesity Research, 13,* 596–607.
Biswas, M. K., & Craigo, S. D. (1994). The course and conduct of normal labor and delivery. In A. H. DeCherney & M. L. Pernoll (Eds.), *Current obstetric and gynecologic diagnosis and treatment* (pp. 202–227). Norwalk, CT: Appleton & Lange.
Bittner, S., & Newberger, E. (1981). Pediatric understanding of child abuse and neglect. *Pediatric Review, 2,* 198.
Black, K., & McCartney, K. (1997). Adolescent females' security with parents predicts the quality of peer interactions. *Social Development, 6,* 91–110.
Black, K. A., & McCartney, K. (1995, March). *Associations between adolescent attachment to parents and peer interactions.* Paper presented at the biennial meetings of the Society for Research in Child Development, Indianapolis, IN.
Black, S., Markides, K., & Miller, T. (1998). Correlates of depressive symptomatology among older community-dwelling Mexican Americans: The hispanic EPESE. *Journals of Gerontology, Series B: Psychological Sciences & Social Sciences, 53B,* S198–S208.

Blackman, J. A. (1990). Update on AIDS, CMV, and herpes in young children: Health, developmental, and educational issues. In M. Wolraich & D. K. Routh (Eds.), *Advances in developmental and behavioral pediatrics Vol. 9* (pp. 33–58). London: Jessica Kingsley Publishers.

Blackwell, D., & Lichter, D. (2000). Mate selection among married and cohabiting couples. *Journal of Family Issues, 21*, 275–302.

Blair, S. N., Kohl, H. W., III, Barlow, C. E., Paffenbarger, R. S., Gibbons, L. W., & Macera, C. A. (1995). Changes in physical fitness and all-cause mortality. *Journal of the American Medical Association, 273*, 1093–1098.

Blakemore, J., LaRue, A., Olejnik, A. (1979). Sex-appropriate toy preference and the ability to conceptualize toys as sex-role related. *Developmental Psychology, 15*, 339–340.

Blanchard-Fields, F., Chen, Y., Schocke, M., & Hertzog, C. (1998). Evidence for content-specificity of causal attributions across the adult life span. *Aging, Neuropsychology, & Cognition, 5*, 241–263.

Blau, F. D., & Ferber, M. A. (1991). Career plans and expectations of young women and men: The earnings gap and labor force participation. *The Journal of Human Resources, 26*, 581–607.

Blau, G. (1996). Adolescent depression and suicide. In G. Blau & T. Gullotta (Eds.), *Adolescent dysfunctional behavior: Causes, interventions, and prevention* (pp. 187–205). Newbury Park, CA: Sage.

Blazer, D., Hybels, C., Simonsick, E., & Hanlon, J. (2000). Marked differences in antidepressant use by race in an elderly community sample: 1986–1996. *American Journal of Psychiatry, 157*, 1089–1094.

Blazer, D., Landerman, L., Hays, J., Simonsick, E., & Saunders, W. (1998). Symptoms of depression among community-dwelling elderly African American and White older adults. *Psychological Medicine, 28*, 1311–1320.

Blickstine, I., Jones, C., & Keith, L. (2003). Zygotic-splitting rates after single-embryo transfers in in vitro fertilization. *New England Journal of Medicine, 348*, 2366–2367.

Block, J. (1971). *Lives through time.* Berkeley, CA: Bancroft.

Block, J., & Robins, R W. (1993). A longitudinal study of consistency and change in self-esteem from early adolescence to early adulthood. *Child Development, 64*, 909–923.

Block, S. (March 6, 2006). Few young workers take heed of need to start saving now. *USA Today Online.* Retrieved June 30, 2007 from www.usatoday.com/money/perfi/columnist/block/2006-03-06-young-savings_x.htm.

Bloom, B. L., White, S. W., & Asher, S. J. (1979). Marital disruption as a stressful life event. In C. Levinger & O. C. Moles (Eds.), *Divorce and separation: Context, causes, and consequences* (pp. 184–200). New York: Basic Books.

Bloom, L. (1973). *One word at a time.* The Hague: Mouton.

Bloom, L. (1991). *Language development from two to three.* Cambridge, England: Cambridge University Press.

Bloom, L. (1993). *The transition from infancy to language: Acquiring the power of expression.* Cambridge, England: Cambridge University Press.

Bloom, L. (1997, April). *The child's action drives the interaction.* Paper presented at the biennial meetings of the Society for Research in Child Development, Washington, DC.

Blumberg, J. B. (1996). Status and functional impact of nutrition in older adults. In E. L. Schneider & J. W. Rowe (Eds.), *Handbook of the biology of aging* (4th ed., pp. 393–414). San Diego, CA: Academic Press.

Blumenthal, J. A., Emery, C. F., Madden, D. J., Schniebolk, S., Walsh-Riddle, M., George, L. K., McKee, D. C., Higginbotham, M. B., Cobb, R. R., & Coleman, R. E. (1991). Long-term effects of exercise on physiological functioning in older men and women. *Journals of Gerontology: Psychological Sciences, 46*, P352–361.

Blustein, D., Phillips, S., Jobin-Davis, K., & Finkelberg, S. (1997). A theory-building investigation of the school-to-work transition. *Counseling Psychology, 25*, 364–402.

Bonanno, G., Znoj, H., Siddique, H., & Horowitz, M. (1999). Verbal-autonomic dissociation and adaptation to midlife conjugal loss: A follow-up at 25 months. *Cognitive Therapy & Research, 23*, 605–624.

Bond, L., Braskamp, D., & Roeber, E. (1996). *The status report of the assessment programs in the United States.* Oakbrook, IL: North Central Regional Educational Laboratory. ERIC No. ED 401 333.

Bondevik, M., & Skogstad, A. (1998). The oldest old, ADL, social network, and loneliness. *Western Journal of Nursing Research, 20*, 325–343.

Booth-LaForce, C., Oh, W., Kim, A., Rubin, K., Rose-Krasnor, L., & Burgess, K. (2006). Attachment, self-worth, and peer-group functioning in middle childhood. *Attachment & Human Development, 8*, 309–325.

Borawski, E., Trapl, E., Lovegreen, L., Colabianchi, N., & Block, T. (2005). Effectiveness of abstinence-only intervention in middle school teens. *American Journal of Health Behavior, 29*, 423–434.

Borkowski, M., Hunter, K., & Johnson, C. (2001). White noise and scheduled bedtime routines to reduce infant and childhood sleep disturbances. *Behavior Therapist, 24*, 29–37.

Bornstein, M., Arterberry, M., & Mash, C. (2005). Perceptual development. In M. Bornstein & M. Lamb (Eds). *Developmental science: An advanced textbook* (5th Ed., pp. 283–326). Hillsdale, NJ: Lawrence Erlbaum Associates.

Bornstein, M., Tamis-LeMonda, D., Tal, J., Ludemann, P., Toda, S., Rahn, C., Pecheux, M., Azuma, H., & Vardi, D. (1992). Maternal responsiveness to infants in three societies: The United States, France, and Japan. *Child Development, 63*, 808–821.

Bornstein, M. H. (1992). Perception across the life span. In M. H. Bornstein & M. E. Lamb (Eds.), *Developmental psychology: An advanced textbook* (3rd ed., pp. 155–210). Hillsdale, NJ: Erlbaum.

Bossé, R., Aldwin, C. M., Levenson, M. R., & Workman-Daniels, K. (1991). How stressful is retirement? Findings from the normative aging study. *Journals of Gerontology: Psychological Sciences, 46*, P9–14.

Bosworth, H., Park, K., McQuoid, D., Hays, J., & Steffens, D. (2003). The impact of religious practice and religious coping on geriatric depression. *International Journal of Geriatric Psychiatry, 18*, 905–914.

Bosworth, H., Siegler, I., Brummett, B., Barefoot, J., Williams, R., Clapp-Channing, N., & Mark, D. (2000, August). *Health-related quality of life in a coronary artery sample.* Paper presented at the annual meeting of the American Psychological Association. Washington, DC.

Bouchard, T. J., Jr., & McGue, M. (1981). Familial studies of intelligence: A review. *Science, 212*, 1055–1059.

Bouhuys, A., Flentge, F., Oldehinkel, A., & van den Berg, M. (2004). Potential psychosocial mechanisms linking depression to immune function in elderly subjects. *Psychiatry Research, 127*, 237–245.

Bourreille, C. (1999). Diana/Diana. *Cahiers Jungiens de Psychanalyse, 96*, 75–76.

Bowen, J., Gibson, F., & Hand, P. (2002). Educational outcome at 8 years for children who were born extremely prematurely: A controlled study. *Journal of Pediatrics & Child Health, 38*, 438–444.

Bowerman, M. (1985). Beyond communicative adequacy: From piecemeal knowledge to an integrated system in the child's acquisition of language. In K. E. Nelson (Ed.), *Children's language, Vol. 5* (pp. 369–398). Hillsdale, NJ: Erlbaum.

Bowker, A. (2004). Predicting friendship stability during early adolescence. *Journal of Early Adolescence, 24*, 85–112.

Bowlby, J. (1969). *Attachment and loss, Vol. 1: Attachment.* New York: Basic Books.

Bowlby, J. (1980). *Attachment and loss, Vol. 3: Loss, sadness, and depression.* New York: Basic Books.

Boxall, P., Macky, K., & Rasmussen, E. (2003). Labour turnover and retention in New Zealand: The causes and consequences of leaving and staying with employers. *Asia Pacific Journal of Human Resources, 41*, 195–214.

Boyan, S., & Termini, A. (2005). *The psychotherapist as parent coordinator in high-conflict divorce: Strategies and techniques.* Binghamton, NY: Haworth Clinical Practice Press.

Braam, A., Beekman, A., Deeg, D., Smit, J., & van Tilburg, W. (1997). Religiosity as a protective or prognostic factor of depression in later life: Results from a community survey in the Netherlands. *Longitudinal Aging Study, 96*, 199–205.

Bradbury, K., & Katz, J. (2002). Women's labor market involvement and family income mobility when marriages end. *New England Economic Review, Q4*, 41–74.

Bradley, R. H., Caldwell, B. M., Rock, S. L., Barnard, K. E., Gray, C., Hammond, M. A., Mitchell, S., Siegel, L., Ramey, C. D., Gottfried, A. W., & Johnson, D. L. (1989). Home environment and cognitive development in the first 3 years of life: A collaborative study involving six sites and three ethnic groups in North America. *Developmental Psychology, 25*, 217–235.

Brandon, P. (1999). Determinants of self-care arrangements among school-age children. *Children & Youth Services Review, 21*, 497–520.

Brandon, P., & Hofferth, S. (2003). Determinants of out-of-school childcare arrangements among children in single-mother and two-parent families. *Social Science Research, 32*, 129–147.

Branje, S., Van Lieshout, C., & Gerris, J. (2007). Big Five personality development in adolescence and adulthood. *European Journal of Personality, 21*, 45–62.

Braten, I., & Olaussen, B. (1998). The learning and study strategies of Norwegian first-year college students. *Learning & Individual Differences, 10*, 309–327.

Braun, K., & Nichols, R. (1997). Death and dying in four Asian American cultures: A descriptive study. *Death Studies, 21*, 327–359.

Braveman, N. S. (1987). Immunity and aging immunologic and behavioral perspectives. In M. W. Riley, J. D. Matarazzo, & A. Baum (Eds.), *Perspectives in behavioral medicine: The aging dimension* (pp. 94–124). Hillsdale, NJ: Erlbaum.

Bravo, G., Dubois, M., & Pâquet, M. (2003). Advance directives for health care and research prevalence and correlates. *Alzheimer Disease & Associate Disorders, 17,* 215–222.

Brazelton, T. B. (1984). *Neonatal Behavioral Assessment Scale.* Philadelphia: Lippincott.

Bremner, J. (2002). The nature of imitation by infants. *Infant Behavior & Development, 25,* 65–67.

Brener, N., Hassan, S., & Barrios, L. (1999). Suicidal ideation among college students in the United States. *Journal of Consulting & Clinical Psychology, 67,* 1004–1008.

Brennan, F., & Ireson, J. (1997). Training phonological awareness: A study to evaluate the effects of a program of metalinguistic games in kindergarten. *Reading & Writing, 9,* 241–263.

Brenner, V. (1997). Psychology of computer use: XLVII. Parameters of Internet use. *Psychological Reports, 80,* 879–882.

Brent, B. (2006). What accounts for race and ethnic differences in parental financial transfers to adult children in the United States. *Journal of Family Issues, 27,* 1583–1604.

Breslau, N., & Chilcoat, H. (2000). Psychiatric sequelae of low birth weight at 11 years of age. *Biological Psychiatry, 47,* 1005–1011.

Breslau, N., DelDotto, J. E., Brown, G. G., Kumar, S., Ezhuthachan, S., Hufnagle, K. G., & Peterson, E. L. (1994). A gradient relationship between low birth weight and IQ at age 6 years. *Archives of Pediatric & Adolescent Medicine, 2148,* 377–383.

Breslau, N., Johnson, E., & Lucia, V. (2001). Academic achievement of low birthweight children at age 11: The role of cognitive abilities at school entry. *Journal of Abnormal Child Psychology, 29,* 273–279.

Breslow, L., & Breslow, N. (1993). Health practices and disability: Some evidence from Alameda County. *Preventive Medicine, 22,* 86–95.

Bretscher, M., Rummans, T., Sloan, J., Kaur, J., Bartlett, A., Borkenhagen, L., & Loprinzi, C. (1999). Quality of life in hospice patients: A pilot study. *Psychosomatics, 40,* 309–313.

Bristow, J. (2002). *An anti-independence culture.* Retrieved July 7, 2007 from www.spiked-online.com/Articles/00000006D864.htm.

Britner, S., & Pajares, F. (2006). Sources of science self-efficacy beliefs in middle school students. *Journal of Research in Science Teaching, 43,* 485–499.

Broach, D., & Schroeder, D. (2006). Air traffic control specialist age and en route operational errors. *International Journal of Aviation Psychology, 16,* 363–373.

Brockington, I. (1996). *Motherhood and mental health.* Oxford, England: Oxford University Press.

Brody, E. M., Litvin, S. J., Albert, S. M., & Hoffman, C. J. (1994). Marital status of daughters and patterns of parent care. *Journals of Gerontology: Social Sciences, 49,* S95–103.

Brody, J. E. (1995, October 4). Personal health. *New York Times,* p. B7.

Brody, J. E. (1996, February 28). Good habits outweigh genes as key to a healthy old age. *New York Times,* p. B9.

Brody, N. (1992). *Intelligence* (2nd ed.). San Diego, CA: Academic Press.

Broman, C., Reckase, M., & Freedman-Doan, C. (2006). The role of parenting in drug use among Black, Latino and White adolescents. *Journal of Ethnicity in Substance Abuse, 5,* 39–50.

Bromberger, J., Matthews, K., Schott, L., Brockwell, S., Avis, N., Kravitz, H., Everson-Rose, S., Gold, E., Sowers, M., & Randolph, J. (2007). Depressive symptoms during the menopausal transition: The Study of Women's Health Across the Nation (SWAN). *Journal of Affective Disorders, 103,* 267–272.

Bronfenbrenner, U. (1979). *The ecology of human development.* Cambridge, MA: Harvard University Press.

Bronfenbrenner, U. (1993). The ecology of cognitive development: Research models and fugitive findings. In R. H. Wozniak and K. W. Fischer (Eds.), *Development in context: Acting and thinking in specific environments.* Hillsdale, NJ: Erlbaum.

Bronson, G. W. (1994). Infants' transitions toward adult-like scanning. *Child development, 65,* 1253–1261.

Brooks-Gunn, J. (1987). Pubertal processes and girls' psychological adaptation. In R. M. Lerner & T. T. Foch (Eds.), *Biological-psychosocial interactions in early adolescence* (pp. 123–154). Hillsdale, NJ: Erlbaum.

Brooks-Gunn, J. (1995). Children in families in communities: Risk and intervention in the Bronfenbrenner tradition. In P. Moen, G. H. Elder, Jr., & K. Lüscher (Eds.), *Examining lives in context: Perspectives on the ecology of human development* (pp. 467–519). Washington, DC: American Psychological Association.

Brooks-Gunn, J., & Warren, M. P. (1985). The effects of delayed menarche in different contexts: Dance and nondance students. *Journal of Youth & Adolescence, 13,* 285–300.

Broom, D., D'Souza, R., Rennie, M., Strazdins, L., Butterworth, P., Parslow, R., & Rodgers, B. (2007). The lesser evil: Bad jobs or unemployment? A survey of mid-aged Australians. *Social Science & Medicine, 63,* 575–586.

Brown, A., & Day, J. (1983). Macrorules for summarizing text: The development of expertise. *Journal of Verbal Learning & Verbal Behavior, 22,* 1–14.

Brown, A. S., Jones, E. M., & Davis, T. L. (1995). Age differences in conversational source monitoring. *Psychology & Aging, 10,* 111–122.

Brown, B. (2004). *Homes for a booming market.* Retrieved August 2, 2007 from www.aarp.org/bulletin/yourlife/a2004-08-11-boomingmarket.html.

Brown, B. B. (1990). Peer groups and peer cultures. In S. S. Feldman & G. R. Elliott (Eds.), *At the threshold: The developing adolescent* (pp. 171–196). Cambridge, MA: Harvard University Press.

Brown, B. B., & Huang, B. (1995). Examining parenting practices in different peer contexts: Implications for adolescent trajectories. In L. J. Crockett & A. C. Crouter (Eds.), *Pathways through adolescence* (pp. 151–174). Mahwah, NJ: Erlbaum.

Brown, B. B., Mory, M. S., & Kinney, D. (1994). Casting adolescent crowds in a relational perspective: Caricature, channel, and context. In R. Montemayor, G. R. Adams, & T. P. Gullotta (Eds.), *Personal relationships during adolescence* (pp. 123–167). Thousand Oaks, CA: Sage.

Brown, J., Bakeman, R., Coles, C., Sexson, W., & Demi, A. (1998). Maternal drug use during pregnancy: Are preterm and full-term infants affected differently? *Developmental Psychology, 34,* 540–554.

Brown, L. (2000). *Helicobacter pylori*: Epidemiology and routes of transmission. *Epidemiology Review, 22,* 283–297.

Brown, R. (1973). *A first language: The early stages.* Cambridge, MA: Harvard University Press.

Brown, S. (2003). Relationship quality dynamics of cohabitating unions. *Journal of Family Issues, 24,* 583–601.

Brown, S., & Booth, A. (1996). Cohabitation versus marriage: A comparison of relationship quality. *Journal of Marriage & the Family, 58,* 668–678.

Brown, S., Estroff, J., & Barnewolf, C. (2004). Fetal MRI. *Applied Radiology, 33,* 9–25.

Brown, W., Basil, M., & Bocarnea, M. (2003). Social influence of an international celebrity: Responses to the death of Princess Diana. *Journal of Communication, 53,* 587–605.

Brownell, C. A. (1990). Peer social skills in toddlers: Competencies and constraints illustrated by same-age and mixed-age interaction. *Child Development, 61,* 836–848.

Bryant, P., MacLean, M., & Bradley, L. (1990). Rhyme, language, and children's reading. *Applied Psycholinguistics, 11,* 237–252.

Bryant, P. E., MacLean, M., Bradley, L. L., & Crossland, J. (1990). Rhyme and alliteration, phoneme detection, and learning to read. *Developmental Psychology, 26,* 429–438.

Bryant, S., & Rakowski, W. (1992). Predictors of mortality among elderly African-Americans. *Research on Aging, 14,* 50–67.

Buchanan, C. M., Maccoby, E. E., & Dornbusch, S. M. (1991). Caught between parents: Adolescents' experience in divorced homes. *Child Development, 62,* 1008–1029.

Buchanan, P., & Vardaxis, V. (2003). Sex-related and age-related differences in knee strength of basketball players ages 11–17 years. *Journal of Athletic Training, 38,* 231–237.

Buchbinder, E., & Eisikovits, Z. (2003). Battered women's entrapment in shame: A phenomenological study. *American Journal of Orthopsychiatry, 73,* 355–366.

Buchner, D. M., Beresford, S. A. A., Larson, E. B., LaCroix, A. Z., & Wagner, E. H. (1992). Effects of physical activity on health status in older adults II: Intervention studies. *Annual Review of Public Health, 13,* 469–488.

Bugental, D., & Happaney, K. (2004). Predicting infant maltreatment in low-income families: The interactive effects of maternal attributions and child status at birth. *Developmental Psychology, 40,* 234–243.

Bulcroft, R. A., & Bulcroft, K. A. (1991). The nature and functions of dating in later life. *Research on Aging, 13,* 244–260.

Bullock, M., & Lütkenhaus, P. (1990). Who am I? Self-understanding in toddlers. *Merrill-Palmer Quarterly, 36,* 217–238.

Bumpass, L. L., & Aquilino, W. S. (1995). *A social map of midlife: Family and work over the middle life course.* Report of the MacArthur Foundation research network on successful midlife development, Vero Beach, FL.

Bunton, J. (June 14, 2007). *The best in the nation: Students named Grand Champions of "InvestWrite" essay competition.* Retrieved June 18, 2007 from www.sifma.org/news/46344778.shtml

Bureau of Justice Statistics. (2006). *Drug use: Youth, general population.* Retrieved June 22, 2007 from http://www.ojp.usdoj.gov/bjs/dcf/du.htm

Burgess, S. (1997). The role of shared reading in the development of phonological awareness: A longitudinal study of middle to upper class children. *Early Child Development & Care, 127/128,* 191–199.

Burgess, S. (2005). The preschool home literacy environment provided by teenage mothers. *Early Child Development & Care, 175,* 249–258.

Burke, L., & Follingstad, D. (1999). Violence in lesbian and gay relationships: Theory, prevalence, and correlational factors. *Clinical Psychology Review, 19,* 487–512.

Burkham, D., Lee, V., & Smerdon, B. (1997). Gender and science learning early in high school: Subject matter and laboratory experiences. *American Educational Research Journal, 34,* 297–332.

Burn, S., O'Neil, A., & Nederend, S. (1996). Childhood tomboyishness and adult androgeny. *Sex Roles, 34,* 419–428.

Burnham, H., & Hogervorst, E. (2004). Recognition of facial expressions of emotion by patients with dementia of the Alzheimer type. *Dementia & Geriatric Cognitive Disorders, 18,* 75–79.

Burton, L. (1992). Black grandparents rearing children of drug-addicted parents: Stressors, outcomes, and social service needs. *Gerontologist, 31,* 744–751.

Bus, A., & van IJzendoorn, M. (1999). Phonological awareness and early reading: A meta-analysis of experimental training studies. *Journal of Educational Psychology, 91,* 403–414.

Bushman, B. (2006). Effects of warning and information labels on attraction to television violence in viewers of different ages. *Journal of Applied Social Psychology, 36* 2073–2078.

Bushman, B., & Huesmann, R. (2006). Short-term and long-term effects of violent media on aggression in children and adults. *Archives of Pediatric Adolescent Medicine, 160,* 348–352.

Buss, D. (1999). *Evolutionary psychology.* Boston: Allyn & Bacon.

Buss, D., Abbott, M., Algleitner, A., Ahserian, A., Biaggio, A., et al. (1990). International preferences in selecting mates: A study of 37 cultures. *Journal of Cross-Cultural Psychology, 21,* 5–47.

Bussey, K., & Bandura, A. (1992). Self-regulation mechanisms governing gender development. *Child Development, 63,* 1236–1250.

Butler, R. (1963). The life review: An interpretation of reminiscence in the aged. *Psychiatry: Interpersonal & Biological Processes, 26,* 65–76.

Butler, R. (2002). The life review. *Journal of Geriatric Psychiatry, 35,* 7–10.

Butters, M., Whyte, E., Nebes, R., Begley, A., Dew, M., Mulsant, B., Zmuda, M., Bhalla, R., Meltzer, C., Pollock, B., Reynolds, C., & Becker, J. (2004). Nature and determinants of neuropsychological functioning in late-life depression. *Archives of General Psychiatry, 61,* 587–595.

Buzi, R., Roberts, R., Ross, M., Addy, R., & Markham, C. (2003). The impact of a history of sexual abuse on high-risk sexual behaviors among females attending alternative schools. *Adolescence, 38,* 595–605.

Byrne, G., & Raphael, B. (1999). Depressive symptoms and depressive episodes in recently widowed older men. *International Psychogeriatrics, 11,* 67–74.

Byrne, G., Raphael, G., & Arnold, E. (1999). Alcohol consumption and psychological distress in recently widowed older men. *Australian & New Zealand Journal of Psychiatry, 33,* 740–747.

Byrne, M. (1998). Taking a computational approach to aging: The SPAN theory of working memory. *Psychology & Aging, 13,* 309–322.

Cadwallader, B. (2006). *Woman will plead guilty to raping 12-year-old cousin.* Retrieved June 18, 2007 from www.dispatch.com/dispatch/contentbe/EPIC_shim.php?story=181844

Cahn, D., Marcotte, A., Stern, R., Arruda, J., Akshoomoff, N., & Leshko, I. (1966). The Boston Qualitative Scoring System for the Rey-Osterrieth Complex Figure: A study of children with attention deficit hyperactivity disorder. *Clinical Neuropsychologist, 10,* 397–406.

Cairns, R. B., & Cairns, B. D. (1994). *Lifelines and risks: Pathways of youth in our time.* Cambridge, England: Cambridge University Press.

Calero, M., & Navarro, E. (2007). Cognitive plasticity as a modulating variable on the effects of memory training in elderly persons. *Archives of Clinical Neuropsychology, 22,* 63–72.

Calkins, S., Dedmon, S., Gill, K., Lomax, L., & Johnson, L. (2002). Frustration in infancy: Implications for emotion regulation, physiological processes, and temperament. *Infancy, 3,* 175–197.

Callaghan, T. (1999). Early understanding and production of graphic symbols. *Child Development, 70,* 1314–1324.

Callaghan, T., & Rankin, M. (2002). Emergence of graphic symbol functioning and the question of domain specificity: A longitudinal training study. *Child Development, 73,* 359–376.

Calvert, S., & Kotler, J. (2003). Lessons from children's television: The impact of the Children's Television Act on children's learning. *Applied Developmental Psychology, 24,* 275–335.

Calvert, S., Mahler, B., Zehnder, S., Jenkins, A., & Lee, M. (2003). Gender differences in preadolescent children's online interactions: Symbolic modes of self-presentation and self-expression. *Applied Developmental Psychology, 24,* 627–644.

Camilleri, C., & Malewska-Peyre, H. (1997). Socialization and identity strategies. In J. Berry, P. Dasen, & T. Saraswathi (Eds.), *Handbook of cross-cultural psychology, Vol. 2: Basic processes and human development.* Boston: Allyn & Bacon.

Campbell, A., Shirley, L., & Candy, J. (2004). A longitudinal study of gender-related cognition and behaviour. *Developmental Science, 7,* 1–9.

Campbell, A., Shirley, L., & Caygill, L. (2002). Sex-typed preferences in three domains: Do two-year-olds need cognitive variables? *British Journal of Psychology, 93,* 203–217.

Campbell, F., Ramey, C., Pungello, E., Sparling, J., & Miller-Johnson, S. (2002). Early childhood education: Young adult outcomes from the Abecedarian Project. *Applied Developmental Science, 6,* 42–57.

Campbell, F. A., & Ramey, C. T. (1994). Effects of early intervention on intellectual and academic achievement: A follow-up study of children from low-income families. *Child Development, 65,* 684–698.

Campbell, L., Connidis, I., & Davies, L. (1999). Sibling ties in later life: A social network analysis. *Journal of Family Issues, 20,* 114–148.

Campbell, S. B., Cohn, J. F., Flanagan, C., Popper, S., & Meyers, T. (1992). Course and correlates of postpartum depression during the transition to parenthood. *Development & Psychopathology, 4,* 29–47.

Campisi, J., Dimri, G., & Hara, E. (1996). Control of replicative senescence. In E. L. Schneider & J. W. Rowe (Eds.), *Handbook of the biology of aging* (4th ed., pp. 121–149). San Diego, CA: Academic Press.

Cao, L., Jiao, X., Zuzga, D., Liu, Y., Fong, D., Young, D., & During, M. (2004). VEGF links hippocampal activity with neurogenesis, learning and memory. *Nature Genetics, 36,* 827–835.

Caplan, G. (1964). *Principles of preventive psychiatry.* New York: Basic Books.

Capron, C., & Duyme, M. (1989). Assessment of effects of socio-economic status on IQ in a full cross-fostering study. *Nature, 340,* 552–554.

Capute, A. J., Palmer, F. B., Shapiro, B. K., Wachtel, R. C., Ross, A., & Accardo, P. J. (1984). Primitive reflex profile: A quantification of primitive reflexes in infancy. *Developmental Medicine & Child Neurology, 26,* 375–383.

Carbone, L. (June 19, 2007). Accountability necessary to protect all. *South Florida Sun-Sentinel Online.* Retrieved June 30, 2007 from www.sun-sentinel.com/news/opinion/columnists/sfl-forum20loannbjun19,0,896144.story.

Cardon, R., & Fulker, D. (1991). Sources of continuity in infant predictors of later IQ. *Intelligence, 15,* 279–293.

Carey, R. G. (1974). Living until death: A program of service and research for the terminally ill. *Hospital Progress.* (Reprinted in E. Kübler-Ross [Ed.], *Death: The final stage of growth.* Englewood Cliffs, NJ: Prentice-Hall, 1975.)

Carey, S., & Bartlett, E. (1978). Acquiring a single new word. *Papers & Reports on Child Language Development, 15,* 17–29.

Carlson, E., Sampson, M., & Sroufe, A. (2003). Implications of attachment theory and research for developmental-behavioral pediatrics. *Journal of Developmental & Behavioral Pediatrics, 24,* 364–379.

Carlson, E., Sroufe, A., & Egeland, B. (2004). The construction of experience: A longitudinal study of representation and behavior. *Child Development, 75,* 66–83.

Carlson, E. A., & Sroufe, L. A. (1995). Contribution of attachment theory to developmental psychopathology. In D. Cicchetti & D. J. Conen (Eds.), *Developmental psychopathology, Vol. 1: Theory and methods* (pp. 581–617). New York: Wiley.

Carmeli, E., Reznick, A., Coleman, R., & Carmeli, V. (2000). Muscle strength and mass of lower extremities in relation to functional abilities in elderly adults. *Gerontology, 46,* 249–257.

Carne, L., & Burke, E. (2007). *Cashed-up boomers want it all.* Retrieved July 9, 2007 from www.news.com.au/couriermail/story/0,23739,21559569623272,00.html.

Carnelley, K., Wortman, C., & Kessler, R. (1999). The impact of widowhood on depression: Findings from a prospective survey. *Psychological Medicine, 29,* 1111–1123.

Carnelley, K., Wortman, C., Bolger, N., & Burke, C. (2006). The time course of grief reactions to spousal loss: Evidence from a national probability sample. *Journal of Personality and Social Psychology, 91,* 476–492.

Caron, A. J., & Caron, R. F. (1981). Processing of relational information as an index of infant risk. In S. Friedman & M. Sigman (Eds.), *Preterm birth and psychological development* (pp. 219–240). New York: Academic Press.

Carpenter, S. (2001). Teens' risky behavior is about more than race and family resources. *APA Monitor, 32*, 22–23.

Carrera, M., Kaye, J., Philiber, S., & West, E. (2000). Knowledge about reproduction, contraception, and sexually transmitted infections among young adolescents in American cities. *Social Policy, 30*, 41–50.

Carroll, J., & Snowling, M. (2004). Language and phonological skills in children at high risk of reading difficulties. *Journal of Child Psychology & Psychiatry, 45*, 631–640.

Carstensen, L. L. (1992). Social and emotional patterns in adulthood: Support for socioemotional selectivity theory. *Psychology & Aging, 7*, 331–338.

Carstensen, L. L., Gottman, J. M., & Levenson, R. W. (1995). Emotional behavior in long-term marriage. *Psychology & Aging, 10*, 149.

Cartwright, C. (2006). You want to know how it affected me? Young adults' perceptions of the impact of parental divorce. *Journal of Divorce & Remarriage, 44*, 125–143.

Carver, P., Egan, S., & Perry, D. (2004). Children who question their heterosexuality. *Developmental Psychology, 40*, 43–53.

Carver, R. P. (1990). Intelligence and reading ability in grades 2–12. *Intelligence, 14*, 449–455.

Casas, J. F., & Mosher, M. (1995, March). *Relational and overt aggression in preschool: "You can't come to my birthday party unless . . ."* Paper presented at the biennial meeting of the Society for Research in Child Development, Indianapolis, IN.

Casasola, M., & Cohen, L. (2000). Infants' association of linguistic labels with causal actions. *Developmental Psychology, 36*, 155–168.

Case, R. (1985). *Intellectual development: Birth to adulthood.* New York: Academic Press.

Case, R. (1991). Stages in the development of the young child's first sense of self. *Developmental Review, 11*, 210–230.

Case, R. (1992). *The mind's staircase: Exploring thought and knowledge.* Hillsdale, NJ: Erlbaum.

Case, R. (1997). The development of conceptual structures. In B. Damon (General Ed.) and D. Kuhn & R. S. Siegler (Series Eds.), *Handbook of child psychology, Vol. 2: Cognitive, language, and perceptual development.* New York: Wiley.

Case, R. B., Moss, A. J., Case, N., McDermott, M., & Eberly, S. (1992). Living alone after myocardial infarction: Impact on prognosis. *Journal of the American Medical Association, 267*, 515–519.

Cashon, C., & Cohen, L. (2000). Eight-month-old infants' perceptions of possible and impossible events. *Infancy, 1*, 429–446.

Caslyn, C., Gonzales, P., & Frase, M. (1999). *Highlights from the Third International Mathematics and Science Study.* Washington, DC: National Center for Education Statistics.

Casper, L., & Smith, K. (2002). Dispelling the myths: Self-care, class, and race. *Journal of Family Issues, 23*, 716–727.

Caspi, A. (2000). The child is father of the man: Personality continuities from childhood to adulthood. *Journal of Personality & Social Psychology, 78*, 158–172.

Cassidy, J., & Berlin, L. J. (1994). The insecure/ambivalent pattern of attachment: Theory and research. *Child Development, 65*, 971–991.

Cassileth, B. R., Walsh, W. P., & Lusk, E. J. (1988). Psychosocial correlates of cancer survival: A subsequent report 3 to 8 years after cancer diagnosis. *Journal of Clinical Oncology, 6*, 1753–1759.

Castellino, D., Lerner, J., Lerner, R., & von Eye, A. (1998). Maternal employment and education: Predictors of young adolescent career trajectories. *Applied Developmental Science, 2*, 114–126.

Castellsagué, X., Bosch, X., Muñoz, N., Meijer, C., Shah, K., Sanjosé, S., Eluf-Neto, J., Ngelangel, C., Chicareon, S., Smith, J., Herrero, R., Moreno, V., & Franceschi, F. (2002). Male circumcision, penile human papillomavirus infection, and cervical cancer in female partners. *New England Journal of Medicine, 346*, 1105–1112.

Castle, J., Groothues, C., Bredenkamp, D., Beckett, C., et al. (1999). Effects of qualities of early institutional care on cognitive attainment. *American Journal of Orthopsychiatry, 69*, 424–437.

Castle, N., Engberg, J., & Anderson, R. (2007). Job satisfaction of nursing home administrators and turnover. *Medical Care Research and Review, 64*, 191–211.

Cataletto, M., & Hertz, G. (2005). *Sleeplessness and circadian rhythm disorder.* Retrieved July 31, 2007 from http://www.emedicine.com/neuro/topic655.htm.

Cate, R., & John, O. (2007). Testing models of the structure and development of future time perspective: Maintaining a focus on opportunities in middle age. *Psychology and Aging, 22*, 186–201.

Cato, J., & Canetto, S. (2003). Attitudes and beliefs about suicidal behavior when coming out is the precipitant of the suicidal behavior. *Sex Roles, 49*, 497–505.

Caughy, M. O., DiPietro, J. A., & Strobino, D. M. (1994). Day-care participation as a protective factor in the cognitive development of low-income children. *Child Development, 65*, 457–471.

Cavanaugh, J., & Whitbourne, S. (1999). *Gerontology: An interdisciplinary perspective.* New York: Oxford University Press.

Cavill, S., & Bryden, P. (2003). Development of handedness: Comparison of questionnaire and performance-based measures of preference. *Brain & Cognition, 53*, 149–151.

CBS News Polls. (October 30, 2005). *Poll: Majority believe in ghosts.* Retrieved August 4, 2007 from www.cbsnews.com/stories/2005/10/29/opinion/polls/main994766.shtml.

Ceci, S., & Bronfenbrenner, U. (1985). "Don't forget to take the cupcakes out of the oven": Prospective memory, strategic time-monitoring, and context. *Child Development, 56*, 152–164.

Ceci, S. J., & Bruck, M. (1993). Suggestibility of the child witness: A historical review and synthesis. *Psychological Bulletin, 113*, 403–439.

Center for Education Reform. (2005). *Charter high schools target the dropout epidemic.* Retrieved June 21, 2007 from www.edreform.com/index.cfm?fuseAction=document&documentID=1980

Centers for Disease Control. (1998a). *National diabetes fact sheet.* Retrieved October 11, 2000, from http://www.cdc.gov.

Centers for Disease Control. (1998b). *The role of STD detection and treatment in HIV prevention.* Retrieved September 1, 2000, from http://www.cdc.gov.

Centers for Disease Control. (1998c). Single-year U.S. mortality rates. *National Vital Statistics Reports, 47*, 10, Table 3.

Centers for Disease Control. (2000c). Youth risk behavior surveillance—United States, 1999. *Morbidity & Mortality Weekly Report, 49*, 1–96.

Centers for Disease Control (CDC). (2005). *Birth defects: Frequently asked questions.* Retrieved June 7, 2007 from www.cdc.gov/ncbddd/bd/facts.htm

Centers for Disease Control (CDC). (2006a). *Understanding child maltreatment.* Retrieved June 14, 2007 from www.cdc.gov/ncipc/pub-res/CM Factsheet.pdf

Centers for Disease Control (CDC). (2006b). Youth risk behavior surveillance: United States, 2005. *Morbidity & Mortality Weekly Report, 55*, 1–112.

Centers for Disease Control. (CDC). (2006a). *Sudden Infant Death Syndrome (SIDS): Risk factors.* Retrieved June 8, 2007 from www.cdc.gov/SIDS/riskfactors.htm

Centers for Disease Control (CDC). (2007). *Suicide: Fact sheet.* Retrieved June 22, 2007 from http://www.cdc.gov/ncipc/factsheets/suifacts.htm

Centers for Disease Control and Prevention. (2003a). *About minority health.* Retrieved August 26, 2004, from http://www.cdc.gov/omy/AMH/AMH.htm.

Centers for Disease Control and Prevention. (2003b). *Sexually transmitted disease surveillance, 2002.* Retrieved August 18, 2004, from http://www.cdc.gov/std/stats/natoverview.htm.

Centers for Disease Control and Prevention. (2004). Surveillance summaries. *Morbidity & Mortality Weekly Report, 53*, 2–29.

Centers for Disease Control and Prevention (CDC). (2005). Mental health in the United States: Prevalence of diagnosis and medication treatment for attention-deficit/hyperactivity disorder-United States, 2003. *Morbidity & Mortality Weekly Report, 54*, 842–847.

Centers for Disease Control and Prevention (CDC). (2006a). *HPV Vaccine questions and answers.* Retrieved June 29, 2006 from www.cdc.gov/std/hpv/STDFact-HPV-vaccine.htm#vaccine.

Centers for Disease Control and Prevention (CDC). (2006b). *Sexually transmitted disease surveillance: 2005.* Retrieved July 4, 2007 from www.cdc.gov/std/stats/05pdf/Surv2005.pdf.

Centers for Disease Control and Prevention (CDC). (2007a). *The importance of physical activity.* Retrieved July 4, 2007 from www.cdc.gov/nccdphp/dnpa/physical/importance/index.htm.

Centers for Disease Control and Prevention (CDC). (2007b). *Tips for parents: Ideas and tips to help prevent child overweight.* Retrieved June 19, 2007 from www.cdc.gov/nccdphp/dnpa/obesity/childhood/tips_for_parents.htm

Centers for Disease Control National Immunization Program. (2000, January 21). 2000 childhood immunization schedule. *Morbidity & Mortality Weekly Report, 49*, 35–38.

Centers for Medicare and Medicaid Services (CMS). (2004). *Health care industry market update.* Retrieved September 9, 2004, from http://www.ahca.org/research/cms_market_update_030520.pdf.

Ceponiene, R., Kuchnerenko, E., Fellman, V., Renlund, M., Suominen, K., & Naeaetaenen, R. (2002). Event-related potential features indexing central auditory discrimination by newborns. *Cognitive Brain Research, 13*, 101–113.

Cernoch, J. M., & Porter, R. H. (1985). Recognition of maternal axillary odors by infants. *Child Development, 56*, 1593–1598.

Certain, L., & Kahn, R. (2002). Prevalence, correlates, and trajectory of television viewing among infants and toddlers. *Pediatrics, 109*, 634–642.

Chabris, C. F. (1999). Prelude or requiem for the "Mozart effect"? *Nature, 400*, 826–827.

Chadwick, O., Taylor, E., Taylor, A., Heptinstall, E. et al., (1999). Hyperactivity and reading disability: A longitudinal study of the nature of the association. *Journal of Child Psychology & Psychiatry, 40*, 1039–1050.

Chan, R., Raboy, B., & Patterson, C. (1998). Psychosocial adjustment among children conceived via donor insemination by lesbian and heterosexual mothers. *Child Development, 69*, 443–457.

Chang, L., & Murray, A. (1995, March). *Math performance of 5- and 6-year-olds in Taiwan and the U.S.: Maternal beliefs, expectations, and tutorial assistance.* Paper presented at the biennial meetings of the Society for Research in Child Development, Indianapolis, IN.

Chang, L., Schwartz, D., Dodge, K., & McBride-Chang, C. (2003). Harsh parenting in relation to child emotion regulation and aggression. *Journal of Family Psychology, 17*, 598–606.

Chao, R. (1994). Beyond parental control and authoritarian parenting style: Understanding Chinese parenting through the cultural notion of training. *Child Development, 65*, 1111–1119.

Chapman, J., & Tunmer, W. (1997). A longitudinal study of beginning reading achievement and reading self-concept. *British Journal of Educational Psychology, 67*, 279–291.

Chapman, K., Nicholas, P., & Supramaniam, R. (2006). How much food advertising is there on Australian television? *Health Promotion International, 21*, 172–180.

Charlesworth, W. R. (1992). Darwin and developmental psychology: Past and present. *Developmental Psychology, 28*, 5–16.

Chase-Lansdale, P. L., & Hetherington, E. M. (1990). The impact of divorce on life-span development: Short and long term effects. In P. B. Baltes, D. L. Featherman, & R. M. Lerner (Eds.), *Life-span development and behavior, Vol. 10* (pp. 107–151). Hillsdale, NJ: Erlbaum.

Chase-Lansdale, P. L., Cherlin, A. J., & Kiernan, K. E. (1995). The long-term effects of parental divorce on the mental health of young adults: A developmental perspective. *Child Development, 66*, 1614–1634.

Chasseigne, G., Grau, S., Mullet, E., & Cama, V. (1999). How well do elderly people cope with uncertainty in a learning task? *Acta Psychologica, 103*, 229–238.

Chatlos, J. (1997). Substance use and abuse and the impact on academic difficulties. *Child & Adolescent Clinics of North America, 6*, 545–568.

Chatters, L. M. (1991). Physical health. In J. S. Jackson (Ed.), *Life in black America* (pp. 199–220). Newbury Park, CA: Sage.

Cheay, C., & Rubin, K. (2004). European American and mainland Chinese mothers' responses to aggression and social withdrawal in preschoolers. *International Journal of Behavioral Development, 28*, 83–94.

Cheitlin, M. (2003). Cardiovascular physiology: Changes with aging. *American Journal of Geriatric Cardiology, 12*, 9–13.

Chen, J., Bierhals, A., Prigerson, H., Kasl, S., Mazure, C., & Jacobs, S. (1999). Gender differences in the effects of bereavement-related psychological distress in health outcomes. *Psychological Medicine, 29*, 367–380.

Chen, K., Paick, J., & Ishii, N. (2007). The efficacy and safety of vardenafil in East Asian men with erectile dysfunction. *Journal of Sexual Medicine, 4*, 753–761.

Chen, S. (1997). Child's understanding of secret and friendship development. *Psychological Science (China), 20*, 545.

Chen, X., Rubin, K. H. & Li, Z. (1995). Social functioning and adjustment in Chinese children: A longitudinal study. *Developmental Psychology, 31*, 531–539.

Chen, X., Rubin, K. H., & Sun, Y. (1992). Social reputation and peer relationships in Chinese and Canadian children: A cross-cultural study. *Child Development, 63*, 1336–1343.

Chen, Z. (1999). Ethnic similarities and differences in the association of emotional autonomy and adolescent outcomes: Comparing Euro-American and Asian-American adolescents. *Psychological Reports, 84*, 501–516.

Cheng, G., Xiaoyan, H., & Dajun, Z. (2006). A review of academic self-concept and its relationship with academic achievement. *Psychological Science (China), 29*, 133–136.

Chen-Hafteck, L. (1997). Music and language development in early childhood: Integrating past research in the two domains. *Early Child Development & Care, 130*, 85–97.

Cheour, M., Martynova, O., Naeaetaenen, R., Erkkola, R., Sillanpaeae, M., Kero, P., Raz, A., Kaipio, M., Hiltunen, J., Aaltonen, O., Savela, J., & Haemaelaeinen, H. (2002). Speech sounds learned by sleeping newborns. *Nature, 415*, 599–600.

Cherlin, A. (1992). *Marriage, divorce, remarriage*, Cambridge, MA: Harvard University Press.

Cherlin, A., Chase-Lansdale, P., & McRae, C. (1998). Effects of parental divorce on mental health throughout the life course. *American Sociological Review, 63*, 239–249.

Cherlin, A., & Furstenberg, F. F. (1986). *The new American grandparent.* New York: Basic Books.

Chi, M. T. (1978). Knowledge structure and memory development. In R. S. Siegler (Ed.) *Children's thinking: What develops?* (pp. 73–96). Hillsdale, NJ: Erlbaum.

Chiapin, G., DeAraujo, G., & Wagner, A. (1998). Mother-in-law and daughter-in-law: How is the relationship between these two women? *Psicologia: Reflexao e Critica, 11*, 541–550.

Chiappe, P., & Siegel, L. (1999). Phonological awareness and reading acquisition in English- and Punjabi-speaking Canadian children. *Journal of Educational Psychology, 91*, 20–28.

Chiappe, P., Glaeser, B., & Ferko, D. (2007). Speech perception, vocabulary, and the development of reading skills in English among Korean- and English-speaking children. *Journal of Educational Psychology, 99*, 154–166.

Chickering, A., & Reisser, L. (1993). *Education and identity* (2nd ed.). San Francisco: Jossey-Bass.

Chien, Y., Cheng, J., Liu, M., Yang, H., Hsu, M., Chen, C., & Yang, C. (2001). Serologic markers of Epstein-Barr virus infection and nasopharyngeal carcinoma in Taiwanese men. *New England Journal of Medicine, 345*, 1877–1882.

"Children spend more time playing video games than watching TV, MSU survey shows." (2004, April 4). Retrieved July 23, 2005, from www.newsroom.msu.edu/site/indexer/1943/content.htm.

"China imposes online gaming curbs." (August 25, 2005). Retrieved June 28, 2007 from http://news.bbc.co.uk/1/hi/technology/4183340.stm

Chincotta, D., & Underwood, G. (1997). Estimates, language of schooling and bilingual digit span. *European Journal of Cognitive Psychology, 9*, 325–348.

Chlebowski, R., Hendrix, S., Langer, R., Stefanick, M., Gass, M., Lane, D., Rodabough, R., Gilligan, M., Cyr, M., Thomson, C., Khandekar, J., Petrovitch, H., & McTiernan, A. (2003). Influence of estrogen plus progestin on breast cancer and mammography in healthy postmenopausal women: The Women's Health Initiative randomized trial. *Journal of the American Medical Association, 289*, 3243–3253.

Choi, N. (2003). Nonmarried aging parents' and their adult children's characteristics associated with transitions into and out of intergenerational coresidence. *Journal of Gerontological Social Work, 40*, 7–29.

Choi, N. G. (1991). Racial differences in the determinants of living arrangements of widowed and divorced elderly women. *The Gerontologist, 31*, 496–504.

Choi, S. (2000). Caregiver input in English and Korean: Use of nouns and verbs in book-reading and toy-play contexts. *Journal of Children's Language, 27*, 69–96.

Chong, B., Babcook, C., Salamat, M., Nemzek, W., Kroeker, D., & Ellis, W. (1996). A magnetic resonance template for normal neuronal migration in the fetus. *Neurosurgery, 39*, 110–116.

Chou, C., & Tsai, M. (2007). Gender differences in Taiwan high school students' computer game playing. *Computers in Human Behavior, 23*, 812–824.

Chou, K., Chi, I., & Chow, N. (2004). Sources of income and depression in elderly Hong Kong Chinese: Mediating and moderating effects of social support and financial strain. *Aging & Mental Health, 8*, 212–221.

Chou, K., Chow, N., & Chi, I. (2003). Volunteering aspirations of Hong Kong Chinese soon-to-be-old adults. *Activities, Adaptation, & Aging, 27*, 79–96.

Chow, B., & McBride-Chang, C. (2003). Promoting language and literacy development through parent-child reading in Hong Kong preschoolers. *Early Education & Development, 14*, 233–248.

Choy, Y., Fyer, A., & Lipsitz, J. (2007). Treatment of specific phobia in adults. *Clinical Psychology Review, 27*, 266–286.

Christakis, D., Zimmerman, F., DiGiuseppe, D., & McCarty, C. (2004). Early television exposure and subsequent attentional problems in children. *Pediatrics, 113*, 708–713.

Christensen, C. (1997). Onset, rhymes, and phonemes in learning to read. *Scientific Studies of Reading, 1*, 341–358.

Christensen, H., Henderson, A., Griffiths, K., & Levings, C. (1997). Does aging inevitably lead to declines in cognitive performance? A longitudinal study of elite academics. *Personality & Individual Differences, 23*, 67–78.

Church, M., Eldis, F., Blakley, B., & Bawle, E. (1997). Hearing, language, speech, vestibular, and dento-facial disorders in fetal alcohol syndrome. *Alcoholism: Clinical & Experimental Research, 21*, 227–237.

Ciabattari, T. (2004). Cohabitation and housework: The effects of marital intentions. *Journal of Marriage & the Family, 66*, 118–125.

Ciancio, D., Sadovsky, A., Malabonga, V., Trueblood, L., et al. (1999). Teaching classification and seriation to preschoolers. *Child Study Journal, 29*, 193–205.

Cicchetti, D., Rogosch, F., Maughan, A., Toth, S., & Bruce, J. (2003). False belief understanding in maltreated children. *Development & Psychopathology, 15*, 1067–1091.

Cicirelli, V. (2006). Fear of death in mid-old age. *Journals of Gerontology: Series B: Psychological Sciences and Social Sciences, 61B*, P75–P81.

Cillessen, A., & Mayeux, L. (2004). From censure to reinforcement: Developmental changes in the association between aggression and social status. *Child Development, 75*, 147–163.

Cillessen, A. H. N., van IJzendoorn, H. W., van Lieshout, C. F. M., & Hartup, W. W. (1992). Heterogeneity among peer-rejected boys: Subtypes and stabilities. *Child Development, 63*, 893–905.

Cipriani, G., Bianchetti, A., & Trabucchi, M. (2005). Outcomes of a computer-based cognitive rehabilitation program on Alzheimer's disease patients compared with those on patients affected by mild cognitive impairment. *Archives of Gerontology and Geriatrics, 43*, 327–335.

Clarke, D., & Singh, R. (2005). The influence of pessimistic explanatory style on the relation between stressful life events and hospital doctors' psychological distress. *Social Behavior and Personality, 33*, 259–272.

Clawson, R., & Choate, J. (1999). Explaining participation on a class newsgroup. *Social Science Computer Review, 17*, 455–459.

Cobb, K. (2000, September 3). Breaking in drivers: Texas could join states restricting teens in effort to lower rate of fatal accidents. *Houston Chronicle*, pp. A1, A20.

Coffey, C., Saxton, J., Ratcliff, G., Bryan, R., & Lucke, J. (1999). Relation of education to brain size in normal aging: Implications for the reserve hypothesis. *Neurology, 53*, 189–196.

Cohen, G. (2000). *The creative age: Awakening human potential in the second half of life.* New York: Avon Books.

Cohen, H., Hailpern, S., & Alderman, M. (2004). Glucose-cholesterol interaction magnifies coronary disease risk for hypertensive patients. *Hypertension, 43*, 983.

Cohen, S. (1991). Social supports and physical health: Symptoms, health behaviors, and infectious disease. In E. M. Cummings, A. L. Greene, & K. H. Karraker (Eds.), *Life-span developmental psychology: Perspectives on stress and coping* (pp. 213–234). Hillsdale, NJ: Erlbaum.

Cohen, S. (2006). Aging changes in immunity. *Medline: Medical encyclopedia.* Retrieved www.nlm.nih.gov/medlineplus/ency/article/004008.htm.

Cohen-Kettenis, P., & van Goozen, S. (1997). Sex reassignment of adolescent transsexuals: A follow-up study. *American Academy of Child & Adolescent Psychiatry, 36*, 263–271.

Coie, J., Cillessen, A., Dodge, K., Hubbard, J., et al., (1999). It takes two to fight: A test of relational factors and a method for assessing aggressive dyads. *Developmental Psychology, 35*, 1179–1188.

Coie, J. D., & Cillessen, A. H. N. (1993). Peer rejection: Origins and effects on children's development. *Current Directions in Psychological Science, 2*, 89–92.

Coke, M. (1992). Correlates of life satisfaction among elderly African Americans. *Journals of Gerontology, 47*, P316–P320.

Colby, A., Kohlberg, L., Gibbs, J., & Lieberman, M. (1983). A longitudinal study of moral judgment. *Monographs of the Society for Research in Child Development, 48* (1–2, Serial No. 200).

Cole, M. (1992). Culture in development. In M. H. Bornstein & M. E. Lamb (Eds.), *Developmental psychology: An advanced textbook* (pp. 731–789). Hillsdale, NJ: Erlbaum.

Cole, P., Martin, S., & Dennis, T. (2004). Emotion regulation as a scientific construct: Methodological challenges and directions for child development research. *Child Development, 75*, 317–333.

Coleman, J., Pratt, R., Stoddard, R., Gerstmann, D., & Abel, H. (1997). The effects of the male and female singing and speaking voices on selected physiological and behavioral measures of premature infants in the intensive care unit. *International Journal of Arts Medicine, 5*, 4–11.

Coley, R., & Chase-Lansdale, L. (1998). Adolescent pregnancy and parenthood: Recent evidence and future directions. *American Psychologist, 53*, 152–166.

Collet, J. P., Burtin, P., Gillet, J., Bossard, N., Ducruet, T., & Durr, F. (1994). Risk of infectious diseases in children attending different types of daycare setting. Epicreche Research Group. *Respiration, 61*, 16–19.

Collins, R., Elliott, M., Berry, S., Kanouse, D., Kunkel, D., Hunter, S., & Miu, A. (2004). Watching sex on television predicts adolescent initiation of sexual behavior. *Pediatrics, 114*, 280–289.

Colombo, J. (1993). *Infant cognition: Predicting later intellectual functioning.* Newbury Park, CA: Sage.

Colonia-Willner, R. (1999). Investing in practical intelligence: Ageing and cognitive efficiency among executives. *International Journal of Behavioral Development, 23*, 591–614.

Colwell, J., & Kato, M. (2005). Video game play in British and Japanese adolescents. *Simulation & Gaming, 36*, 518–530.

Commissaris, C., Ponds, R., & Jolles, J. (1998). Subjective forgetfulness in a normal Dutch population: Possibilities of health education and other interventions. *Patient Education & Counseling, 34*, 25–32.

Committee on Infectious Diseases (1996). Recommended childhood immunization schedule. *Pediatrics, 97*, 143–146.

Comninos, A., & Grenyer, B. (2007). The influence of interpersonal factors on the speed of recovery from major depression. *Psychotherapy Research, 17*, 230–239.

Compas, B. E., Ey, S., & Grant, K. E. (1993). Taxonomy, assessment, and diagnosis of depression during adolescence. *Psychological Bulletin, 114*, 323–344.

Condry, J., & Condry, S. (1976). Sex differences: A study in the eye of the beholder. *Child Development, 47*, 812–819.

Conduct Problems Research Group. (2004). The Fast Track experiment: Translating the developmental model into a prevention design. In J. Kupersmidt & K. Dodge (Eds.), *Children's peer relations: From development to intervention.* (pp. 181–208). Washington, DC: American Psychological Association.

Connidis, I. A. (1994). Sibling support in older age. *Journals of Gerontology: Social Sciences, 49*, S309–317.

Connidis, I. A., & Davies, L. (1992). Confidants and companions: Choices in later life. *Journals of Gerontology: Social Sciences, 47*, S115–122.

Connolly, K., & Dalgleish, M. (1989). The emergence of a tool-using skill in infancy. *Developmental Psychology, 25*, 894–912.

Consoletti, A., & Allen, J. (2007). Annual survey of American's charter schools. Retrieved October 21, 2007 from www.edreforn.com/_upload/cer_charter_survey.pdf.

Cook, S., & Heppner, P. (1997). Coping control, problem-solving appraisal, and depressive symptoms during a farm crisis. *Journal of Mental Health Counseling, 19*, 64–77.

Coombs, R. H. (1991). Marital status and personal well-being: A literature review. *Family Relations, 40*, 97–102.

Cooper, A., Putnam, D., Planchon, L., & Boies, S. (1999). Online sexual compulsivity: Getting tangled in the net. *Sexual Addiction & Compulsivity, 6*, 79–104.

Cooper, R. P., & Aslin, R. N. (1994). Developmental differences in infant attention to the spectral properties of infant-directed speech. *Child Development, 65*, 1663–1677.

Coplan, R., Bowker, A., & Cooper, S. (2003). Parenting daily hassles, child temperament and social adjustment in preschool. *Early Childhood Research Quarterly, 18*, 376–395.

Corbet, A., Long, W., Schumacher, R., Gerdes, J., & Cotton, R. (1995). Double-blind developmental evaluation at 1-year corrected age of 597 premature infants with birth weights from 500 to 1350 grams enrolled in three placebo-controlled trials of prophylactic synthetic surfactant. *Journal of Pediatrics, 126*, S5–12.

Cornelius, M., Goldschmidt, L., Day, N., & Larkby, C. (2002). Alcohol, tobacco and marijuana use among pregnant teenagers: 6-year follow-up of offspring growth effects. *Neurotoxicology & Teratology, 24*, 703–710.

Cornwell, A., & Feigenbaum, P. (2006). Sleep biological rhythms in normal infants and those at high risk for SIDS. *Chronobiology International, 23*, 935–961.

Corr, C. A. (1991/1992). A task-based approach to coping with dying. *Omega, 24*, 81–94.

Corrada, M., Brookmeyer, R., & Kawas, C. (1995). Sources of variability in prevalence rates of Alzheimer's disease. *International Journal of Epidemiology, 24*, 1000–1005.

Corsaro, W., Molinari, L., Hadley, K., & Sugioka, H. (2003). Keeping and making friends: Italian children's transition from preschool to elementary school. *Social Psychology Quarterly, 66*, 272–292.

Corso, J. F. (1987). Sensory-perceptual processes and aging. In K. W. Schaie (Ed.), *Annual review of gerontology & geriatrics, Vol. 7* (pp. 29–56). New York: Springer.

Corwin, J., Loury, M., & Gilbert, A. N. (1995). Workplace, age, and sex as mediators of olfactory function: Data from the National Geographic smell survey. *Journals of Gerontology: Psychological Sciences, 50B*, P179–186.

Cosden, M., & McNamara, J. (1997). Self-concept and perceived social support among college students with and without learning disabilities. *Learning Disability Quarterly, 20*, 2–12.

Costello, E., Sung, M., Worthman, C., & Angold, A. (2007). Pubertal maturation and the development of alcohol use and abuse. *Drug and Alcohol Dependence, 88*, S50–S59.

Cotton, L., Bynum, D., & Madhere, S. (1997). Socialization forces and the stability of work values from late adolescence to early adulthood. *Psychological Reports, 80*, 115–124.

Coulthard, H., & Harris, G. (2003). Early food refusal: The role of maternal mood. *Journal of Reproductive & Infant Psychology, 21*, 335–345.
Counts, D. R. (1976/1977). The good death in Kaliai: Preparation for death in western New Britain. *Omega, 7*, 367–372.
Courage, M., & Howe, M. (2002). From infant to child: The dynamics of cognitive change in the second year of life. *Psychological Bulletin, 128*, 250–277.
"Court reverses convictions." (Spring, 2006). *Texas Tech University School of Law Clinic News*, Spring, 2006. Retrieved June 8, 2007 from www.law.ttu.edu/lawWeb/centersprograms/clinics/newsletters/2006_SpringNewsletter.pdf
Coury, D. (2002). Developmental & behavioral pediatrics. In A. Rudolph, R. Kamei, & K. Overby (Eds.), *Rudolph's fundamental of pediatrics* (3rd ed., pp. 110–124). New York: McGraw-Hill.
Cowan, B. R., & Underwood, M. K. (1995, March). *Sugar and spice and everything nice? A developmental investigation of social aggression among girls.* Paper presented at the biennial meetings of the Society for Research in Child Development, Indianapolis, IN.
Cox, M., Garrett, E., & Graham, J. (2004–2005). Death in Disney films: Implications for children's understanding of death. *Omega: Journal of Death and Dying, 50*, 267–280.
Cox, M., Paley, B., Burchinal, M., & Payne, C. (1999). Marital perceptions and interactions across the transition to parenthood. *Journal of Marriage & the Family, 61*, 611–625.
Cramer, D. (1991). Type A behavior pattern, extraversion, neuroticism and psychological distress. *British Journal of Medical Psychology, 64*, 73–83.
Cramer, P. (2000). Defense mechanisms in psychology today. *American Psychologist, 55*, 637–646.
Crehan, G. (2004). The surviving sibling: The effects of sibling death in childhood. *Psychoanalytic Psychotherapy, 18*, 202–219.
Crick, N., & Dodge, K. (1994). A review and reformulation of social information processing mechanisms in children's social adjustment. *Psychological Bulletin, 115*, 74–101.
Crick, N., & Dodge, K. (1996). Social information-processing mechanisms in reactive and proactive aggression. *Child Development, 67*, 993–1002.
Crick, N. R., & Grotpeter, J. K. (1995). Relational aggression, gender, and social-psychological adjustment. *Child Development, 66*, 710–722.
Crittenden, P. M. (1992). Quality of attachment in the preschool years. *Development & Psychopathology, 4*, 209–241.
Crittenden, P. M., Partridge, M. F., & Claussen, A. H. (1991). Family patterns of relationship in normative and dysfunctional families. *Development & Psychopathology 3*, 491–512.
Crncec, R., Wilson, S., & Prior, M. (2006). The cognitive and academic benefits of music to children: Facts and fiction. *Educational Psychology, 26*, 579–594.
Crockenberg, S. (2003). Rescuing the baby from the bathwater: How gender and temperament (may) influence how child care affects child development. *Child Development, 74*, 1034–1038.
Crockenberg, S., & Litman, C. (1990). Autonomy as competence in 2-year-olds: Maternal correlates of child defiance, compliance, and self-assertion. *Developmental Psychology, 26*, 961–971.
Crockenberg, S., Leerkes, E., & Lekka, S. (2007). Pathways from marital aggression to infant emotion regulation: The development of withdrawal in infancy. *Infant Behavior & Development, 30*, 97–113.
Crockett, D. (2003). Critical issues children face in the 2000s. *School Psychology Quarterly, 18*, 446–453.
Crompton, R., Brockmann, M., & Lyonette, C. (2005). Attitudes, women's employment and the domestic division of labour: A cross-national analysis in two waves. *Work, Employment, and Society, 19*, 213–233.
Crone, D., & Whitehurst, G. (1999). Age and schooling effects on emergent literacy and early reading skills. *Journal of Educational Psychology, 91*, 594–603.
Crone, E., van der Molen, M. (2004). Developmental changes in real life decision making: Performance on a gambling task previously shown to depend on the ventromedial prefrontal cortex. *Developmental Neuropsychology, 25*, 251–279.
Crone, E., Wendelken, C., Donohue, S., van Leijenhorst, L., & Bunge, S. (2006). Neurocognitive development of the ability to manipulate information in working memory. *Proceedings for the National Academy of Sciences, 103*, 9315–9320.
Crook, C. (1987). Taste and olfaction. In P. Salapatek & L. Cohen (Eds.), *Handbook of infant perception, Vol. 1: From sensation to perception* (pp. 237–264). Orlando, FL: Academic Press.
Crowell, J. A., & Waters, E. (1995, March). *Is the parent-child relationship a prototype of later love relationships? Studies of attachment and working models of attachment.* Paper presented at the biennial meeting of the Society for Research in Child Development, Indianapolis, IN.
Crowley, B., Hayslip, B., & Hobdy, J. (2003). Psychological hardiness and adjustment to life events in adulthood. *Journal of Adult Development, 10*, 237–248.
Crystal, S., Shae, D., & Krishnaswami, S. (1992). Educational attainment, occupational history, and stratification: Determinants of later-life economic outcomes. *Journals of Gerontology: Social Sciences, 47*, S213–221.
Cuba, L., & Longino, C. F., Jr. (1991). Regional retirement migration: The case of Cape Cod. *Journals of Gerontology: Social Sciences, 46*, S33–42.
Cumming, E. (1975). Engagement with an old theory. *International Journal of Aging & Human Development, 6*, 187–191.
Cumming, E., & Henry, W. E. (1961). *Growing old.* New York: Basic Books.
Cummings, E. M., & Davies, P. T. (1994). Maternal depression and child development. *Journal of Child Psychology & Psychiatry, 35*, 73–112.
Cummings, E. M., Hollenbeck, B., Iannotti, R., Radke-Yarrow, M., & Zahn-Waxler, C. (1986). Early organization of altruism and aggression: Developmental patterns and individual differences. In C. Zahn-Waxler, E. M. Cummings, & R. Iannotti (Eds.), *Altruism and aggression* (pp. 165–188). Cambridge, England: Cambridge University Press.
Cunningham, L. (1996). *Grief and the adolescent.* Newhall, CA: TeenAge Grief, Inc.
Cunningham, W. R., & Haman, K. L. (1992). Intellectual functioning in relation to mental health. In J. E. Birren, R. B. Sloane, & G. D. Cohen (Eds.), *Handbook of mental health and aging* (2nd ed., pp. 340–355). San Diego, CA: Academic Press.
Curran, S., McLanahan, S., & Knab, J. (2003). Does remarriage expand perceptions of kinship support among the elderly? *Social Science Research, 32*, 171–190
Currier, J., Holland, J., & Neimeyer, R. (2006). Sense-making, grief, and the experience of violent loss: Toward a mediational model. *Death Studies, 30*, 403–428
Curry, C. (2002). An approach to clinical genetics. In A. Rudolph, R. Kamei, & K. Overby (Eds.), *Rudolph's fundamentals of pediatrics.* (pp. 184–220). New York: McGraw-Hill.
Curry, P. (2005, December 1). *Reality house: Part two.* Retrieved May 22, 2007 from www.builderonline.com/Industry-news.asp?sectionID=27&articleID=227035
Curyto, K., Chaplesk, E., & Lichtenberg, P. (1999). Prediction of the presence and stability of depression in the Great Lakes Native American elderly. *Journal of Mental Health & Aging, 5*, 323–340.
Cushner, K., McClelland, A., & Safford, P. (1992). *Human diversity in education.* New York: McGraw–Hill.
Cutchin, M., Owen, S., & Chang, P. (2003). Becoming "at home" in assisted living residences: Exploring place integration processes. *Journals of Gerontology, Series B: Psychological & Social Sciences, 58B*, S234–S243.
Cuvo, A. (1974). Incentive level influence on overt rehearsal and free recall as a function of age. *Journal of Experimental Child Psychology, 18*, 167–181.
Da Costa, D., Larouche, J., Dritsa, M., & Brender, W. (2000). Psychosocial correlates of prepartum and postpartum depressed mood. *Journal of Affective Disorders, 59*, 31–40.
Daire, A. (2004). Investigating caregiver distress with the Parental Bonding Instrument (PBI) *Dementia: The International Journal of Social Research & Practice, 3* 83–94.
D'Alton, M. E., & DeCherney, A. H. (1993). Prenatal diagnosis. *New England Journal of Medicine, 328*, 114–118.
Daly, K., & Palkovitz, R. (2004). Guest editorial: Reworking work and family issues for fathers. *Fathering, 2*, 211–213.
Daly, L. E., Kirke, P. N., Molloy, A., Weir, D. G., & Scott, J. M. (1995). Folate levels and neural tube defects: Implications for prevention. *Journal of the American Medical Association, 274*, 1698–1702.
Daly, M., & Wilson, M. (1996). Violence against stepchildren. *Current Directions in Psychological Science, 5*, 77–81.
Daly, S., & Glenwick, D. (2000). Personal adjustment and perceptions of grandchild behavior in custodial grandmothers. *Journal of Clinical Child Psychology, 29*, 108–118.
Dammeijer, P., Schlundt, B., Chenault, M., Manni, J., & Anteunis, l. (2002). Effects of early auditory deprivation and stimulation on auditory brainstem responses in the rat. *Acta Oto-Laryngologica, 122*, 703–708.
Damon, W. (1977). *The social world of the child.* San Francisco: Jossey-Bass.
Damon, W. (1983). The nature of social-cognitive change in the developing child. In W. F. Overton (Ed.), *The relationship between social and cognitive development* (pp. 103–142). Hillsdale, NJ: Erlbaum.
Damon, W., & Hart, D. (1988). *Self understanding in childhood and adolescence.* New York: Cambridge University Press.
Danby, S., & Baker C. (1998). How to be masculine in the block area. *Childhood: A Global Journal of Child Research, 5*, 151–175.
Darlington, R. B. (1991). The long-term effects of model preschool programs. In L. Okagaki & R. J. Sternberg (Eds.), *Directors of development* (pp. 203–215). Hillsdale, NJ: Erlbaum.

Datta, P., Poortinga, Y., & Marcoen, A. (2003). Parent care by Indian and Belgian caregivers in their roles of daughter/daughter-in-law. *Journal of Cross-Cultural Psychology, 34*, 736–749.

Dauringnac, E., Toga, A., Jones, D., Aronen, H., Hommer, D., Jernigan, T., Krystal, J., & Mathalon, D. (2005). Applications of morphometric and diffusion tensor magnetic resonance imaging to the study of brain abnormalities in the alcoholism spectrum. *Alcoholism: Clinical and Experimental Research, 29*, 159–166.

Davenport, E. (1992). *The making of minority scientists and engineers.* Invited address presented at the annual meeting of the American Educational Research Association, San Francisco, CA.

Davey, M., Fish, L., Askew, J., & Robila, M. (2003). Parenting practices and the transmission of ethnic identity. *Journal of Marital & Family Therapy, 29*, 195–208.

Davies, L. (2003). Singlehood: Transitions within a gendered world. *Canadian Journal on Aging, 22*, 343–352.

Davies, P., & Rose, J. (1999). Assessment of cognitive development in adolescents by means of neuropsychological tasks. *Developmental Neuropsychology, 15*, 227–248.

Davis, D. L., Dinse, G. E., & Hoel, D. G. (1994). Decreasing cardiovascular disease and increasing cancer among whites in the United States from 1973 through 1987. *Journal of the American Medical Association, 271*, 431–437.

Davis, T. (2003). *Sacred Womb.* Columbus, OH: Autumn Publishing.

Dawber, T. R., Kannel, W. B., & Lyell, L. P. (1963). An approach to longitudinal studies in a community: The Framingham study. *Annals of the New York Academy of Science, 107*, 539–556.

Dawood, K., Pillard, R., Horvath, C., Revelle, W., & Bailey, J. (2000). Familial aspects of male homosexuality. *Archives of Sexual Behavior, 29*, 155–163.

Dawson, D. A. (1991). Family structure and children's health and well-being: Data from the 1988 National Health Interview Survey on child health. *Journal of Marriage & the Family, 53*, 573–584.

Dawson, J., & Langan, P. (1994). *Murder in families.* Washington, DC: U.S. Department of Justice.

Deakin, J., Aitken, M., Robbins, T., & Sahakian, B. (2004). Risk taking during decision-making in normal volunteers changes with age. *Journal of the International Neurospcyhological Society, 10*, 590–598.

DeBell, M., & Chapman, C. (2006). *Computer and Internet use by students in 2003.* Retrieved June 20, 2007 from http://nces.ed.gov/pubs2006/2006065.pdf

DeCasper, A., & Fifer, W. (1980). Of human bonding: Newborns prefer their mothers' voices. *Science, 208*, 1174–1176.

DeCasper, A. J., & Spence, M. J. (1986). Prenatal maternal speech influences newborns' perception of speech sounds. *Infant Behavior and Development, 9*, 133–150.

DeCasper, A. J., Lecaneut, J., Busnel, M., Granier-DeFerre, C., & Maugeais, R. (1994). Fetal reactions to recurrent maternal speech. *Infant Behavior & Development, 17*, 159–164.

Deci, E., Koestner, R., & Ryan, R. (1999). A meta-analytic review of experiments examining the effects of extrinsic rewards on intrinsic motivation. *Psychological Bulletin, 125*, 627–668.

Deeg, D. J. H., Kardaun, W. P. F., & Fozard, J. L. (1996). Health, behavior, and aging. In J. E. Birren & K. W. Schaie (Eds.), *Handbook of the psychology of aging* (4th ed., pp. 129–149). San Diego, CA: Academic Press.

Degirmencioglu, S., Urberg, K., & Tolson, J. (1998). Adolescent friendship networks: Continuity and change over the school year. *Merrill-Palmer Quarterly, 44*, 313–337.

de Graaf, C., Polet, P., & van Staveren, W. A. (1994). Sensory perception and pleasantness of food flavors in elderly subjects. *Journals of Gerontology: Psychological Sciences, 49*, P93–99.

de Haan, M., Luciana, M., Maslone, S. M., Matheny, L. S., & Richards, M. L. M. (1994). Development, plasticity, and risk: Commentary on Huttenlocher, Pollit and Gorman, and Gottesman and Goldsmith. In C. A. Nelson (Ed.), *The Minnesota Symposia on Child Psychology, Vol. 27* (pp. 161–178). Hillsdale, NJ: Erlbaum.

De Jong, G. F., Wilmoth, J. M., Angel, J. L., & Cornwell, G. T. (1995). Motives and the geographic mobility of very old Americans. *Journals of Gerontology: Social Sciences, 50B*, S395–404.

de Jong, M., & Bus, A. (2002). Quality of book-reading matters for emergent readers: An experiment with the same book in a regular or electronic format. *Journal of Educational Psychology, 94*, 144–155.

de Lacoste, M., Horvath, D., & Woodward, J. (1991). Possible sex differences in the developing human fetal brain. *Journal of Clinical & Experimental Neuropsychology, 13*, 831.

Dellatolas, G., de Agostini, M., Curt, F., Kremin, H., Letierce, A., Maccario, J., & Lellouch, J. (2003). Manual skill, hand skill asymmetry, and cognitive performances in young children. *Laterality: Asymmetries of Body, Brain & Cognition, 8*, 317–338.

DeLoache, J. S. (1995). Early understanding and use of symbols: The model model. *Current Directions in Psychological Science, 4*, 109–113.

DeMaris, A., & Rao, K. V. (1992). Premarital cohabitation and subsequent marital stability in the United States: A reassessment. *Journal of Marriage & the Family, 54*, 178–190.

DeMars, C. (2000). Test stakes and item format interactions. *Applied Measurement in Education, 13*, 55–77.

Demb, H., & Chang, C. (2004). The use of psychostimulants in children with disruptive behavior disorders and developmental disabilities in a community setting. *Mental Health Aspects of Developmental Disabilities, 7*, 26–36.

DeMulder, E., Denham, S., Schmidt, M., & Mitchell, J. (2000). Q-sort assessment of attachment security during the preschool years: Links from home to school. *Developmental Psychology, 36*, 274–282.

Denham, S. (2006). Social-emotional competence as support for school readiness: What is it and how do we assess it? *Early Education and Development, 17*, 57–89.

Denham, S., Blair, K., DeMulder, E., Levitas, J., Sawyer, K., Auerbach-Major, S., & Queenan, P. (2003). Preschool emotional competence: Pathway to social competence. *Child Development, 74*, 238–256.

Dennerstein, L., Dudley, E., & Guthrie, J. (2002). Empty nest or revolving door? A prospective study of women's quality of life in midlife during the phase of children leaving and re-entering the home. *Psychological Medicine, 32*, 545–550.

Denney, N. W. (1982). Aging and cognitive changes. In B. B. Wolman (Ed.), *Handbook of developmental psychology* (pp. 807–827). Englewood Cliffs, NJ: Prentice-Hall.

Denney, N. W. (1984). Model of cognitive development across the life span. *Developmental Review, 4*, 171–191.

Dennis, W. (1960). Causes of retardation among institutional children: Iran. *Journal of Genetic Psychology, 96*, 47–59.

Den Ouden, L., Rijken, M., Brand, R., Verloove-Vanhorick, S. P., & Ruys, J. H. (1991). Is it correct to correct? Developmental milestones in 555 "normal" preterm infants compared with term infants. *Journal of Pediatrics, 118*, 399–404.

DeNavas-Walt, C., Proctor, B., & Lee, C. (2006). *Income, poverty, and health insurance coverage in the United States: 2005.* Retrieved June 20, 2007 from www.census.gov/prod/2006pubs/p60-231.pdf

Denollet, J. (1997). Personality, emotional distress and coronary heart disease. *European Journal of Personality, 11*, 343–357.

DeRegnier, R., Wewerka, S., Georgieff, M., Mattia, F., & Nelson, C. (2002). Influences of postconceptional age and postnatal experience on the development of auditory recognition memory in the newborn infant. *Developmental Psychobiology, 41*, 215–225.

DeSpelder, L. A., & Strickland, A. L. (1983). *The last dance: Encountering death and dying.* Palo Alto, CA: Mayfield.

Detchant, Lord Walton. (1995). Dilemmas of life and death: Part one. *Journal of the Royal Society of Medicine, 88*, 311–315.

Deter, H., & Herzog, W. (1994). Anorexia nervosa in a long-term perspective: Results of the Heidelberg-Mannheim study. *Psychosomatic Medicine, 56*, 20–27.

de Villiers, P. A., & de Villiers, J. G. (1992). Language development. In M. H. Bornstein & M. E. Lamb (Eds.), *Developmental psychology: An advanced textbook* (3rd ed., pp. 337–418). Hillsdale, NJ: Erlbaum.

Dezoete, J., MacArthur, B., & Tuck, B. (2003). Prediction of Bayley and Stanford-Binet scores with a group of very low birthweight children. *Child: Care, Health, & Development, 29*, 367–372.

Diagram Group (1977). *Child's body.* New York: Paddington.

Diamond, A. (1991). Neuropsychological insights into the meaning of object concept development. In S. Carey & R. Gelman (Eds.), *The epigenesis of mind: Essays on biology and cognition* (pp. 67–110). Hillsdale, NJ: Erlbaum.

Diehl, L., Vicary, J., & Deike, R. (1997). Longitudinal trajectories of self-esteem from early to middle adolescence and related psychosocial variables among rural adolescents. *Journal of Research on Adolescence, 7*, 393–411.

Diener, M., & Kim, D. (2004). Maternal and child predictors of preschool children's social competence. *Journal of Applied Developmental Psychology, 25*, 3–24.

Dieni, S., & Rees, S. (2003). Dendritic morphology is altered in hippocampal neurons following prenatal compromise, *55*, 41–52.

Diesendruck, G., & Shatz, M. (2001). Two-year-olds' recognition of hierarchies: Evidence from their interpretation of the semantic relation between object labels. *Cognitive Development, 16*, 577–594.

Dietz, B., Carrozza, M., & Ritchey, P. (2003). Does financial self-efficacy explain gender differences in retirement saving strategies? *Journal of Women & Aging, 15*, 83–96.

Diller, L. (2001). *Defusing the explosive child: The debate between drugs and discipline for raising extremely difficult children.* Retrieved October 3, 2007, from http://cycnet.org/today2001/today010730.html.

DiMario, F. (2002). The nervous system. In A. Rudolph, R. Kamei, & K. Overby (Eds.), *Rudolph's fundamental of pediatrics* (3rd ed., pp. 796–846). New York: McGraw-Hill.

D'Imperio, R., Dubow, E., & Ippolito, M. (2000). Resilient and stress-affected adolescents in an urban setting. *Journal of Clinical Child Psychology, 29*, 129–142.

Dindia, K., & Allen, M. (1992). Sex differences in self-disclosure: A meta-analysis. *Psychological Bulletin, 112*, 106–124.

DiPietro, J., Hodgson, D., Costigan, K., & Johnson, T. (1996). Fetal antecedents of infant temperament. *Child Development, 67*, 2568–2583.

DiPietro, J., Hodgson, D., Costigan, K., Hilton, S., & Johnson, T. (1996). Fetal neurobehavioral development. *Child Development, 67*, 2553–2567.

Dishion, T. J., French, D. C., & Patterson, G. R. (1995). The development and ecology of antisocial behavior. In D. Cicchetti & D. J. Cohen (Eds.), *Developmental psychopathology, Vol. 2: Risk, disorder, and adaptation* (pp. 421–471). New York: Wiley.

Dishion, T. J., Patterson, G. R., Stoolmiller, M., & Skinner, M. L. (1991). Family, school, and behavioral antecedents to early adolescent involvement with antisocial peers. *Developmental Psychology, 27*, 172–180.

Dittmann-Kohli, F., Lachman, M. E., Kliegl, R., & Baltes, P. B. (1991). Effects of cognitive training and testing on intellectual efficacy beliefs in elderly adults. *Journals of Gerontology: Psychological Sciences, 46*, P162–164.

Dobson, A., Brown, W., Ball, J., Powers, J., & McFadden, M. (1999). Women drivers' behaviour, socio-demographic characteristics and accidents. *Accident Analysis & Prevention, 31*, 525–535.

Dockett, S., & Smith, I. (1995, March). *Children's theories of mind and their involvement in complex shared pretense.* Paper presented at the biennial meetings of the Society for Research in Child Development, Indianapolis, IN.

Doctoroff, S. (1997). Sociodramatic script training and peer role prompting: Two tactics to promote and sociodramatic play and peer interaction. *Early Child Development & Care, 136*, 27–43.

Dodge, K. (1993). Social-cognitive mechanisms in the development of conduct disorder and depression. *Annual Review of Psychology, 44*, 559–584.

Dodge, K. A., Pettit, G. S., & Bates, J. E. (1994). Socialization mediators of the relation between socioeconomic status and child conduct problems. *Child Development, 65*, 649–665.

Dolan, K. (July 21, 2006). *Despite Bush veto, stem cell research abounds.* Retrieved August 4, 2007 from http://www.forbes.com/technology/2006/07/21/stem-cell-research-cz_kd_0721stemcell.html.

Dollard, J., Doob, L. W., Miller, N. E., Mowrer, O. H., & Sears, R. R. (1939). *Frustration and aggression.* New Haven, CT: Yale University Press.

Donenberg, G., Emerson, E., Bryant, F., & King, S. (2006). Does substance use moderate the effects of parents and peers on risky sexual behavior? *AIDS Care, 18*, 194–200.

Donnerstein, E., Slaby, R. G., & Eron, L. D. (1994). The mass media and youth aggression. In L. D. Eron, J. H. Gentry, & P. Schlegel (Eds.). *Reason to hope: A psychosocial perspective on violence and youth* (pp. 219–250). Washington, DC: American Psychological Association.

Dornbusch, S. M., Ritter, P. L., Liederman, P. H., Roberts, D. F., & Fraleigh, M. J. (1987). The relation of parenting style to adolescent school performance. *Child Development, 58*, 1244–1257.

Doty, R. L., Shaman, P., Appelbaum, S. L., Bigerson, R., Sikorski, L., & Rosenberg, L. (1984). Smell identification ability: Changes with age. *Science, 226*, 1441–1443.

Downe-Wamboldt, B., & Tamlyn, D. (1997). An international survey of death education trends in faculties of nursing and medicine. *Death Studies, 21*, 177–188.

Downey, D. (2001). Number of siblings and intellectual development: The resource dilution explanation. *American Psychologist, 56*, 497–504.

Doyle, A. B., & Aboud, F. E. (1995). A longitudinal study of white children's racial prejudice as a social-cognitive development. *Merrill-Palmer Quarterly, 41*, 209–228.

Draper, B., Gething, L., Fethney, J., & Winfield, S. (1999). The Senior Psychiatrist Survey III: Attitudes towards personal ageing, life experiences and psychiatric practice. *Australian & New Zealand Journal of Psychiatry, 33*, 717–722.

Drevets, W., Price, J., Simpson, J., Todd, R., Reich, T., Vannier, M., & Raichle, M. (1997). Subgenual prefrontal cortex abnormalities in mood disorders. *Nature, 386*, 824–827.

Droege, K., & Stipek, D. (1993). Children's use of dispositions to predict classmates' behavior. *Developmental Psychology, 29*, 646–654.

Drum, P. (1985). Retention of text information by grade, ability and study. *Discourse Processes, 8*, 21–52.

Due, P., Holstein, B., Lund, R., Modvig, J., & Avlund, K. (1999). Social relations: Network, support and relational strain. *Social Science & Medicine, 48*, 561–673.

Dugan, L., Nagin, D., & Rosenfeld, R. (2003). Do domestic violence services save lives? *National Institute of Justice Journal, 250*, 1–6.

Duncan, C., & Loretto, W. (2004). Never the right age? Gender and age-based discrimination in employment. *Gender, Work & Organization, 26*, 883–900.

Dunn, J. (1994). Experience and understanding of emotions, relationships, and membership in a particular culture. In P. Ekman & R. J. Davidson (Eds.), *The nature of emotion: Fundamental questions* (pp. 352–355). New York: Oxford University Press.

Dunphy, D. C. (1963). The social structure of urban adolescent peer groups. *Sociometry, 26*, 230–246.

Dura, J. R., & Kiecolt-Glaser, J. K. (1991). Family transitions, stress, and health. In P. A. Cowan & M. Hetherington (Eds.), *Family transitions* (pp. 59–76). Hillsdale, NJ: Erlbaum.

Durlak, J. A. (1972). Relationship between attitudes toward life and death among elderly women. *Developmental Psychology, 8*, 146.

Dush, C., Cohan, C. & Amato, P. (2003). The relationship between cohabitation and marital quality and stability: Change across cohorts? *Journal of Marriage & the Family, 65*, 539–549.

Duvall, S., Delquadri, J., & Ward, D. (2004). A preliminary investigation of the effectiveness of homeschool instructional environments for students with attention-deficit/hyperactivity disorder. *School Psychology Review, 33*, 140–158.

Dwyer, J., Allayee, H., Dwyer, K., Fan, J., Wu, H., Mar, R., Lusis, A., & Mehrabian, M. (2004). Arachidonate 5-lipoxygenase promoter genotype, dietary arachidonic acid, and atherosclerosis. *New England Journal of Medicine, 350*, 29–37.

DYG, Inc. (2004). *What grown-ups understand about children: A national benchmark survey.* Retrieved June 15, from www.zerotothree.org/site/DocServer/surveyexecutivesummary.pdf?docID=821&AddInterest=1153

Dyl, J., Kittler, J., Phillips, K., & Hunt, J. (2006). Body dysmorphic disorder and other clinically significant body image concerns in adolescent psychiatric inpatients: Prevalance and clinical characteristics. *Child Psychiatry and Human Development, 36*, 369–382.

Dyregrov, A., Gjestad, R., Bie Wikander, A., & Vigerust, S. (1999). Reactions following the sudden death of a classmate. *Scandinavian Journal of Psychology, 40*, 167–176.

Eagly, A., & Wood, W. (1999). The origins of sex differences in human behavior: Evolved dispositions versus social roles. *American Psychologist, 54*, 408–423.

Eames, M., Ben-Schlomo, Y., & Marmot, M. G. (1993). Social deprivation and premature mortality: Regional comparison across England. *British Medical Journal, 307*, 1097–1102.

Eamon, M., & Mulder, C. (2005). Predicting antisocial behavior among Latino young adolescents: An ecological systems analysis. *American Journal of Orthopsychiatry, 75*, 117–127.

Earles, J. L., & Salthouse, T. A. (1995). Interrelations of age, health, and speed. *Journals of Gerontology: Psychological Sciences, 50B*, P33–41.

Ecalle, J., Magan, A., & Gibert, F. (2007). Class size effects on literacy skills and literacy interest in first grade: A large-scale investigation. *Journal of School Psychology, 44*, 191–209.

Eccles, J., Barber, B., & Jozefowicz, D. (1998). Linking gender to educational, occupational, and recreational choices: Applying the Eccles et al. model of achievement-related choices. In W. B. Swann, Jr., J. H. Langlois, & L. A. Gilbert (Eds.), *Sexism and stereotypes in modern society: The gender science of Janet Spence* (pp. 153–192). Washington, DC: APA Press.

Eccles, J., Jacobs, J., & Harold, R. (1990). Gender role stereotypes, expectancy effects, and parents' socialization of gender differences. *Journal of Social Issues, 46*, 183–201.

Echt, K., Morrell, R., & Park, D. (1998). Effects of age and training formats on basic computer skill acquisition in older adults. *Educational Gerontology, 24*, 3–25.

Eckel, R. (2006). Preventive cardiology by lifestyle intervention: Opportunity and/or challenge? *Circulation, 113*, 2657–2661.

Eckensberger, E., & Zimba, R. (1997). The development of moral judgment. In J. Berry, P. Dasen, & T. Saraswathi (Eds.), *Handbook of cross-cultural psychology, Vol. 2* (pp. 299–328). Boston: Allyn & Bacon.

Education Commission of the States (ECS). (2004). *ECS report to the nation: State implementation of the No Child Left Behind Act.* Retrieved September 21, 2004, from http://www.ecs.org/ecsmain.asp?page=/html/special/nclb/reporttothenation/reporttothenation.htm.

Education Commission of the States (ECS). (2006). *NCLB state assessments: State reading, math, and science assessments aligned to No Child Left*

Behind. Retrieved June 25, 2007 from http://www.ecs.org/clearinghouse/68/35/6835.doc

Education Trust. (1996). *Education watch: The 1996 Education Trust state and national data book.* Washington, DC: Author.

Education Trust. (2004). *College results online: A new tool for school counselors.* Retrieved April 28, 2006 from www2.edtrust.org/NR/rdonlyres/B43D90B7-2264-4060-9F8E-FA7B9566A538/0/college_results_online.pdf.

Egan, S. K., & Perry, D. G. (1998). Does low self-regard invite victimization? *Developmental Psychology, 34,* 299–309.

Egli, D., Rosains, J., Birkhoff, G., & Eggan, K. (2007). Developmental reprogramming after chromosome transfer into mitotic mouse zygotes. *Nature, 447,* 679–685.

Eichorn, D. H., Clausen, J. A., Haan, N., Honzik, M. P., & Mussen, P. H. (Eds.). (1981). *Present and past in middle life.* New York: Academic Press.

Eiden, R., Foote, A., & Schuetze, P. (2007). Maternal cocaine use and caregiving status: Group differences in caregiver and infant risk variables. *Addictive Behaviors, 32,* 465–476.

Einerson, M. (1998). Fame, fortune, and failure: Young girls' moral language surrounding popular culture. *Youth & Society, 30,* 241–257.

Eisenberg, N. (1992). *The caring child.* Cambridge, MA: Harvard University Press.

Eisenberg, N. (2000). Emotion, regulation, and moral development. *Annual Review of Psychology, 51,* 665–697.

Eisenberg, N., Fabes, R. A., Murphy, B., Karbon, M., Smith, M., & Maszk, P. (1996). The relations of children's dispositional empathy-related responding to their emotionality, regulation, and social functioning. *Developmental Psychology, 32,* 195–209.

Eisenberg, N., Fabes, R. A., Murphy, B., Maszk, P., Smith, M., & Karbon, M. (1995). The role of emotionality and regulation in children's social functioning: A longitudinal study. *Child Development, 66,* 1360–1384.

Eisenberg, N., Guthrie, I., Murphy, B., Shepard, S., et al. (1999). Consistency and development of prosocial dispositions: A longitudinal study. *Child Development, 70,* 1360–1372.

Eisenberger, N. (2003). Does rejection hurt? An fMRI study of social exclusion. *Science, 302,* 290–292.

Eisenberger, R., Pierce, W., & Cameron, J. (1999). Effects of reward on intrinsic motivation-negative, neutral, and positive: Comment on Deci, Koestner, and Ryan. *Psychological Bulletin, 125,* 677–691.

Elbedour, S., Baker, A., & Charlesworth, W. (1997). The impact of political violence on moral reasoning in children. *Child Abuse & Neglect, 21,* 1053–1066.

Elder, G. H., Jr. (1974). *Children of the Great Depression.* Chicago: University of Chicago Press.

Elder, G. H., Jr. (1978). Family history and the life course. In T. Hareven (Ed.), *Transitions: The family and the life course in historical perspective* (pp. 17–64). New York: Academic Press.

Elder, G. H., Jr., Liker, J. K., & Cross, C. E. (1984). Parent-child behavior in the Great Depression: Life course and intergenerational influences. In P. B. Baltes & O. G. Brim, Jr. (Eds.), *Life-span development and behavior, Vol. 6* (pp. 111–159). New York: Academic Press.

Electronic Frontiers Australia. (2002). *Internet censorship: Law & policy around the world.* Retrieved June 28, 2007 from www.efa.org.au/Issues/Censor/cens3.html#intro

Eley, T., Liang, H., Plomin, R., Sham, P., Sterne, A., Williamson, R., & Purcell, S. (2004). Parental familial vulnerability, family environment, and their interactions as predictors of depressive symptoms in adolescents. *Journal of the American Academy of Child Psychiatry, 43,* 298–306.

Elizur, Y., & Mintzer, A. (2003). Gay males' intimate relationship quality: The roles of attachment security, gay identity, social support, and income. *Personal Relationships, 10,* 411–435.

Elkind, D. (1967). Egocentrism in adolescence. *Child Development, 38,* 1025–1033.

Ellenbogen, S., & Chamberland, C. (1997). The peer relations of dropouts: A comparative study of at-risk and not at-risk youths. *Journal of Adolescence, 20,* 355–367.

Elliott, D., Mok, D., & Briere, J. (2004). Adult sexual assault: Prevalence, symptomatology, and sex differences in the general population. *Journal of Traumatic Stress, 17,* 203–211.

Ellison, M., Danley, K., Bromberg, C., & Palmer-Erbs, V. (1999). Longitudinal outcome of young adults who participated in a psychiatric vocational rehabilitation program. *Psychiatric Rehabilitation Journal, 22,* 337–341.

Ellsworth, C. P., Muir, D. W., & Hains, S. M. J. (1993). Social competence and person-object differentiation: An analysis of the still-face effect. *Developmental Psychology, 29,* 63–73.

Elwert, F., & Christakis, N. (2006). Widowhood and race. *American Sociological Review, 71,* 16–41.

Emde, R. N., Plomin, R., Robinson, J., Corley, R., DeFries, J., Fulker, D. W., Reznick, J. S., Campos, J., Kagan, J., & Zahn-Waxler, C. (1992). Temperament, emotion, and cognition at fourteen months: The MacArthur longitudinal twin study. *Child Development, 63,* 1437–1455.

Emery, C. F., & Gatz, M. (1990). Psychological and cognitive effects of an exercise program for community-residing older adults. *The Gerontologist, 30,* 184–192.

Emery, R., & Laumann-Billings, L. (1998). An overview of the nature, causes, and consequences of abusive family relationships: Toward differentiating maltreatment and violence. *American Psychologist, 53,* 121–135.

Enright, E. (2004). A house divided. *AARP Magazine.* Retrieved July 7, 2007 from www.aarpmagazine.org/family/Articles/a2004-05-26-mag-divorce.html.

Ensign, J. (1998). *Defying the stereotypes of special education: Homeschool students.* Paper presented at the annual meeting of the American Education Research Association, San Diego, CA.

Entwisle, D. R., & Alexander, K. L. (1990). Beginning school math competence: Minority and majority comparisons. *Child Development, 61,* 454–471.

Ericsson, K. A., & Crutcher, R. J. (1990). The nature of exceptional performance. In P. B. Baltes, D. L. Featherman, & R. M. Lerner (Eds.), *Life-span development and behavior, Vol. 10* (pp. 188–218). Hillsdale, NJ: Erlbaum.

Erikson, E. H. (1950). *Childhood and society.* New York: Norton.

Erikson, E. H. (1959). *Identity and the life cycle.* New York: Norton (reissued, 1980).

Erikson, E. H. (1963). *Childhood and society* (2nd ed.). New York: Norton.

Erikson, E.H. (1980a). *Identity and the life cycle.* New York: Norton (originally published 1959).

Erikson, E. H. (1980b). Themes of adulthood in the Freud-Jung correspondence. In N. J. Smelser & E. Erikson (Eds.), *Themes of work and love in adulthood* (pp. 43–76). Cambridge, MA: Harvard University Press.

Erikson, E. H. (1982). *The life cycle completed.* New York: Norton.

Erikson, E. H., Erikson, J. M., & Kivnick, H. Q. (1986). *Vital involvement in old age.* New York: Norton.

Eron, L. D., Huesmann, L. R., & Zelli, A. (1991). The role of parental variables in the learning of aggression. In D. J. Pepler & K. H. Rubin (Eds.), *The development and treatment of childhood aggression* (pp. 169–188). Hillsdale, NJ: Erlbaum.

Escorihuela, R. M., Tobena, A., & Fernández-Teruel, A. (1994). Environmental enrichment reverses the detrimental action of early inconsistent stimulation and increases the beneficial effects of postnatal handling on shuttlebox learning in adult rats. *Behavioral Brain Research, 61,* 169–173.

Eskes, T. K. A. B. (1992). Home deliveries in the Netherlands-perinatal mortality and morbidity. *International Journal of Gynecology & Obstetrics, 38,* 161–169.

Esposito, K., Giugliano, F., Di Palo, C., Giugliano, G., Marfella, R., D'Andrea, F., D'Armiento, M., & Giugliano, D. (2004). Effect of lifestyle changes on erectile dysfunction in obese men: A randomized controlled trial. *Journal of the American Medical Association, 291,* 2978–2984.

Etaugh, C., & Liss, M. (1992). Home, school, and playroom: Training grounds for adult gender roles. *Sex Roles, 26,* 129–147.

Evans, G. (2004). The environment of childhood poverty. *American Psychologist, 59,* 77–92.

Evans, R., & Erikson, E. (1967). *Dialogue with Erik Erikson.* New York: Harper & Row.

Evans, R. I. (1969). *Dialogue with Erik Erikson.* New York: Dutton.

Ewald, P. (2000). *Plague time.* New York: Free Press.

Ex, C., & Janssens, J. (1998). Maternal influences on daughters' gender role attitudes. *Sex Roles, 38,* 171–186.

Fabes, R. A., Knight, G. P., & Higgins, D. A. (1995, March). *Gender differences in aggression: A meta-analytic reexamination of time and age effects.* Paper presented at the biennial meetings of the Society for Research in Child Development, Indianapolis, IN.

Fabi, M. (2004). Cybersex: The dark side of the force. *International Journal of Applied Psychoanalytic Studies, 1,* 208–209.

Fagan, J. (2000). A theory of intelligence as processing: Implications for society. *Psychology, Public Policy, & Law, 6,* 168–179.

Fagan, J., & Holland, C. (2002). Equal opportunity and racial differences in IQ. *Intelligence, 30,* 361–387.

Fagan, J. F., & Detterman, D. K. (1992). The Fagan Test of Infant Intelligence: A technical summary. *Journal of Applied Developmental Psychology, 13,* 173–193.

Fagan, J. F., & Singer, L. T. (1983). Infant recognition memory as a measure of intelligence. In L. P. Lipsett (Ed.), *Advances in infancy research, Vol. 2* (pp. 31–78). Norwood, NJ: Ablex.

Fagard, J., & Jacquet, A. (1989). Onset of bimanual coordination and symmetry versus asymmetry of movement. *Infant Behavior & Development, 12,* 229–235.

Fagot, B. I., & Hagan, R. (1991). Observations of parent reactions to sex-stereotyped behaviors: Age and sex effects. *Child Development, 62,* 617–628.

Fagot, B. I., & Leinbach, M. D. (1993). Gender-role development in young children: From discrimination to labeling. *Developmental Review, 13,* 205–224.

Fahle, M., & Daum, I. (1997). Visual learning and memory as functions of age. *Neuropsychologia, 35,* 1583–1589.

Fallis, R., & Opotow, S. (2003). Are students failing school or are schools failing students? Class cutting in high school. *Journal of Social Issues, 59,* 103–119.

Fantuzzo, J., Coolahan, K., & Mendez, J. (1998). Contextually relevant validation of peer play constructs with African American Head Start children: Penn Interactive Peer Play Scale. *Early Childhood Research Quarterly, 13,* 411–431.

Fantuzzo, J., Sekino, Y., & Cohen, H. (2004). An examination of the contributions of interactive peer play to salient classroom competencies for urban Head Start children. *Psychology in the Schools, 41,* 323–336.

Fantz, R. L. (1956). A method for studying early visual development. *Perceptual & Motor Skills, 6,* 13–15.

Farmer, T., Estell, D., Leung, M., Trott, H., Bishop, J., & Cairns, B. (2003). Individual characteristics, early adolescent peer affiliations, and school dropout: An examination of aggressive and popular group types. *Journal of School Psychology, 41,* 217–232.

Farnham-Diggory, S. (1992). *The learning-disabled child.* Cambridge, MA: Harvard University Press.

Farver, J. (1996). Aggressive behavior in preschoolers' social networks: Do birds of a feather flock together? *Early Childhood Research Quarterly, 11,* 333–350.

Fearon, I., Hains, S., Muir, D., & Kisilevsky, B. (2002). Development of tactile responses in human preterm and full-term infants from 30 to 40 weeks postconceptional age. *Infancy, 3,* 31–51.

Federal Interagency Forum on Aging-Related Statistics (FIFARS). (2000). *Older Americans 2000: Key indicators of well-being.* Retrieved February 7, 2001, from http://www.agingstats.gov/chartbook2000.

Federal Interagency Forum on Aging-Related Statistics. (FIFARS). (2006). *2006 Older American update: Key indicator of wellness.* Retrieved May 18, 2007 from http://agingstats.gov/agingstatsdotnet/Main_Site/Data/Data_2006.aspx.

Federal Interagency Forum on Child and Family Statistics (FIFCFS). (2000). *America's children: Key national indicators of well-being 2000.* Washington, DC: Author.

Federal Interagency Forum on Child and Family Statistics (FIFCFS). (2005) *America's children in brief: Key national indicators of well-being, 2005.* Retrieved May 18, 2007 from www.childstats.gov/pubs.asp.

Feeney, J. A. (1994). Attachment style, communication patterns, and satisfaction across the life cycle of marriage. *Personal Relationships, 1,* 333–348.

Fein, J., Durbin, D., & Selbst, S. (2002). Injuries & emergencies. In A. Rudolph, R. Kamei, & K. Overby (Eds.), *Rudolph's fundamentals of pediatrics,* (3rd ed., pp. 390–436). New York: McGraw-Hill.

Feldman, D. (2004). Piaget's stages: The unfinished symphony of cognitive development. *New Ideas in Psychology, 22,* 175–231.

Feldman, R. (2003). Paternal socio-psychological factors and infant attachment: The mediating role of synchrony in father-infant interactions. *Infant Behavior & Development, 25,* 221–236.

Feldman, R., & Eidelman, A. (2003). Skin-to-skin contact (kangaroo care) accelerates autonomic and neurobehavioural maturation in preterm infants. *Developmental Medicine & Child Neurology, 45,* 274–281.

Feng, J., Spence, I., & Pratt, J. (2007). Playing an action video game reduces gender differences in spatial cognition. *Psychological Science, 18,* 850–855.

Fenson, L., Dale, P. S., Reznick, J. S., Bates, E., Thal, D. J., & Pethick, S. J. (1994). Variability in early communicative development. *Monographs of the Society for Research in Child Development, 59* (5, Serial No. 242).

Fergusson, D. M., Horwood, L. J., & Lynskey, M. T. (1993). Maternal smoking before and after pregnancy: Effects on behavioral outcomes in middle childhood. *Pediatrics, 92,* 815–822.

Fernald, A., & Kuhl, P. (1987). Acoustic determinants of infant preference for motherese speech. *Infant Behavior & Development, 10,* 279–293.

Fernandez, M. (1997). Domestic violence by extended family members in India. *Journal of Interpersonal Violence, 12,* 433–455.

Field, T. (1995). Psychologically depressed parents. In M. H. Bornstein (Ed.), *Handbook of parenting, Vol. 4: Applied and practical parenting* (pp. 85–99). Mahwah, NJ: Erlbaum

Fielding-Barnsley, R., & Purdie, N. (2003). Early intervention in the home for children at risk of reading failure. *Support for Learning, 18,* 77–82.

Fields, R. B. (1992). Psychosocial response to environment change. In V. B. Van Hasselt & M. Hersen (Eds.), *Handbook of social development: A lifespan perspective* (pp. 503–544). New York: Plenum.

Findlay, L., Girardi, A., & Coplan, R. (2006). Links between empathy, social behavior, and social understanding. *Early Childhood Research Quarterly, 21,* 347–359.

Findling, R., Feeny, N., Stansbrey, R., Delporto-Bedoya, D., & Demeter, C. (2004). Special articles: Treatment of mood disorders in children and adolescents: Somatic treatment for depressive illnesses in children and adolescents. *Psychiatric Clinics of North America, 27,* 113–137.

Fischer, K., & Rose, S. (1994). Dynamic development of coordination of components in brain and behavior: A framework for theory and research. In K. Fischer & G. Dawson (Eds.), *Human behavior and the developing brain* (pp. 3–66). New York: Guilford Press.

Fischer, K. W., & Bidell, T. (1991). Constraining nativist inferences about cognitive capacities. In S. Carey & R. Gelman (Eds.), *The epigenesis of mind: Essays on biology and cognition* (pp. 199–236). Hillsdale, NJ: Erlbaum.

Fish, M., Stifter, C. A., & Belsky, J. (1991). Conditions of continuity and discontinuity in infant negative emotionality: Newborn to five months. *Child Development, 62,* 1525–1537.

Fisher, B., & Specht, D. (1999). Successful aging and creativity in later life. *Journal of Aging Studies, 13,* 457–472.

Fisher, J., Feekery, C., & Rowe-Murray, H. (2002). Nature, severity and correlates of psychological distress in women admitted to a private mother-baby unit. *Journal of Paediatrics & Child Health, 38,* 140–145.

Fitzgerald, B. (1999). Children of lesbian and gay parents: A review of the literature. *Marriage & Family Review, 29,* 57–75.

Fitzgerald, D., & White, K. (2003). Linking children's social worlds: Perspective-taking in parent-child and peer contexts. *Social Behavior & Personality, 31,* 509–522.

Fitzpatrick, J. L., & Silverman, T. (1989). Women's selection of careers in engineering: Do traditional-nontraditional differences still exist? *Journal of Vocational Behavior, 34,* 266–278.

Flannery, D., Vazsonyi, A., Embry, D., Powell, K., Atha, H., Vesterdal, W., & Shenyang, G. (2000, August). *Longitudinal effectiveness of the PeaceBuilders' universal school-based violence prevention program.* Paper presented at the annual meeting of the American Psychological Association, Washington, DC.

Flavell, J. (1963). *The developmental psychology of Jean Piaget.* New York: D. Van Nostrand.

Flavell, J. (1999). Cognitive development: Children's knowledge about the mind. *Annual Review of Psychology, 50,* 21–45.

Flavell, J. H. (1985). *Cognitive development* (2nd ed.). Englewood Cliffs, NJ: Prentice-Hall.

Flavell, J. H. (1986). The development of children's knowledge about the appearance-reality distinction. *American Psychologist, 41,* 418–425.

Flavell, J. H. (1993). Young children's understanding of thinking and consciousness. *Current Directions in Psychological Science, 2,* 40–43.

Flavell, J. H., Everett, B. A., Croft, K., & Flavell, E. R. (1981). Young children's knowledge about visual perception: Further evidence for the Level 1–Level 2 distinction. *Developmental Psychology, 17,* 99–103.

Flavell, J. H., Green, F. L., & Flavell, E. R. (1990). Developmental changes in young children's knowledge about the mind. *Cognitive Development, 5,* 1–27.

Flavell, J. H., Green, F. L., Wahl, K. E., & Flavell, E. R. (1987). The effects of question clarification and memory aids on young children's performance on appearance-reality tasks. *Cognitive Development, 2,* 127–144.

Flavell, J. H., Zhang, X.-D., Zou, H., Dong, Q., & Qi, S. (1983). A comparison of the appearance-reality distinction in the People's Republic of China and the United States. *Cognitive Psychology, 15,* 459–466.

Flom, R., & Bahrick, L. (2007). The development of infant discrimination of affect in multimodal and unimodal stimulation: The role of intersensory redundancy. *Developmental Psychology, 43,* 238–252.

Flood, M. (2007). Exploring the relationship between creativity, depression, and successful aging. *Activities, Adaptation, & Aging, 31,* 55–71.

Flowers, L. (2002). The impact of college racial composition on African American students' academic and social gains: Additional evidence. *Journal of College Student Development, 43,* 403–410.

Flowers, L., & Pascarella, E. (1999). Cognitive effects of college racial composition on African American students after 3 years of college. *Journal of College Student Development, 40,* 669–677.

Floyd, F., & Bakeman, R. (2006). Coming-out across the life course: Implications of age and historical context. *Archives of Sexual Behavior, 35,* 287–297.

Floyd, F., Stein, T., Harter, K., Allison, A., et al. (1999). Gay, lesbian, and bisexual youths: Separation-individuation, parental attitudes, identity consolidation, and well-being. *Journal of Youth & Adolescence, 28,* 705–717.

Flynn, J. (1999). Searching for justice: The discovery of IQ gains over time. *American Psychologist, 54,* 5–20.

Flynn, J. (2003). Movies about intelligence: The limitations of *g. Current Directions in Psychological Science, 12,* 95–99.

Foehr, U. (2006). Media multitasking among American youth: Prevalence, predictors and pairings. Menlo Park, CA: Henry J. Kaiser Foundation. Retrieved June 26, 2007 from http://kff.org/entmedia/upload/7592.pdf

Fokin, V., Ponomareva, N., Androsova, L., & Gavrilova, S. (1997). Interhemispheric asymmetry and neuroimmune modulation in normal aging and Alzheimer's dementias. *Human Physiology, 23,* 284–288.

Foley, D., Monjan, A., Izmirlian, G., Hays, J., & Blazer, D. (1999). Incidence and remission of insomnia among elderly adults in a biracial cohort. *Sleep, 22* (Supplement 2), S373–S378.

Foley, E. (2002). Drug screening and criminal prosecution of pregnant women. *Journal of Obstetric, Gynecologic, & Neonatal Nursing, 31,* 1331.

Folkman, S., & Lazarus, R. (1980). An analysis of coping in a middle-aged community sample. *Journal of Personality and Social Psychology, 70,* 336–348.

Folven, R. J., & Bonvillian, J. D. (1991). The transition from nonreferential to referential language in children acquiring American Sign Language. *Developmental Psychology, 27,* 806–816.

Fonda, S., Clipp, E., & Maddox, G. (2002). Patterns in functioning among residents of an affordable assisted living housing facility. *Gerontologist, 42,* 178–187.

Foorman, B., & Nixon, S. (2006). The influence of public policy on reading research and practice. *Topics in Language Disorders, 26,* 157–171.

Fordham, K., & Stevenson-Hinde, J. (1999). Shyness, friendship quality, and adjustment during middle childhood. *Journal of Child Psychology & Psychiatry & Allied Disciplines, 40,* 757–768.

Forsell, Y., & Winblad, B. (1999). Incidence of major depression in a very elderly population. *Journal of Geriatric Psychiatry, 14,* 368–372.

Forte, C., & Hansvick, C. (1999). Applicant age as a subjective employability factor: A study of workers over and under age fifty. *Journal of Employment Counseling, 36,* 24–34.

Foulder-Hughes, L., & Cooke, L. (2003a). Do mainstream schoolchildren who were born preterm have motor problems? *British Journal of Occupational Therapy, 66,* 9–16.

Foulder-Hughes, L., & Cooke, R. (2003b). Motor, cognitive, and behavioural disorders in children born very preterm. *Developmental Medicine & Child Neurology, 45,* 97–103.

Fouquereau, E., & Baudoin, C. (2002). The Marital Satisfaction Questionnaire for Older Persons: Factor structure in a French sample. *Social Behavior & Personality, 30,* 95–104.

Fourn, L., Ducic, S., & Seguin, L. (1999). Smoking and intrauterine growth retardation in the Republic of Benin. *Journal of Epidemiology & Community Health, 53,* 432–433.

Fox, N., Henderson, H., Rubin, K., Calkins, S., & Schmidt, L. (2001). Continuity and discontinuity of behavioral inhibition and exuberance: Psychophysiological and behavioral influences across the first four years of life. *Child Development, 72,* 1–21.

Fox, N. A., Kimmerly, N. L., & Schafer, W. D. (1991). Attachment to mother/attachment to father: A meta-analysis. *Child Development, 62,* 210–225.

Fozard, J. L. (1990). Vision and hearing in aging. In J. E. Birren & K. W. Schaie (Eds.), *Handbook of the psychology of aging* (3rd ed., pp. 150–171). San Diego, CA: Academic Press.

Fozard, J. L., Metter, E. J., & Brant, L. J. (1990). Next steps in describing aging and disease in longitudinal studies. *Journals of Gerontology: Psychological Sciences, 45,* P116–127.

Franche, R., & Bulow, C. (1999). The impact of a subsequent pregnancy on grief and emotional adjustment following a perinatal loss. *Infant Mental Health Journal, 20,* 175–187.

Francis, L. (1997). Ideology and interpersonal emotion management: Redefining identity in two support groups. *Social Psychology Quarterly, 60,* 153–171.

Francis, P. L., Self, P. A., & Horowitz, F. D. (1987). The behavioral assessment of the neonate: An overview. In J. D. Osofsky (Ed.), *Handbook of infant development* (2nd ed., pp. 723–779). New York: Wiley-Interscience.

Francis-Smythe, J., & Smith, P. (1997). The psychological impact of assessment in a development center. *Human Relations, 50,* 149–167.

Franco, N., & Levitt, M. (1998). The social ecology of middle childhood: Family support, friendship quality, and self-esteem. *Family Relations: Interdisciplinary Journal of Applied Family Studies, 47,* 315–321.

Fransen, M. (2004). Dietary weight loss and exercise for obese adults with knee osteoarthritis: Modest weight loss targets, mild exercise, modest effects. *Arthritis and Rheumatology, 50,* 1366–1369.

Fraser, A. M., Brockert, J. E., & Ward, R. H. (1995). Association of young maternal age with adverse reproductive outcomes. *New England Journal of Medicine, 332,* 1113–1117.

Fredriksen, K., Rhodes, J., Reddy, R., & Way, N. (2004). Sleepless in Chicago: Tracking the effects of adolescent sleep loss during the middle school years. *Child Development, 75,* 84–95.

Freeman, E., Sammel, M., Liu, L., García, C., Nelson, D., & Hollander, L. (2004). Hormones and menopausal status as predictors of depression in women in transition to menopause. *Archives of General Psychiatry, 61,* 62–70.

Freeman, E. W., & Rickels, K. (1993). *Early childbearing: Perspectives of black adolescents on pregnancy, abortion, and contraception.* Newbury Park, CA: Sage.

Frey, K. S., & Ruble, D. N. (1992). Gender constancy and the "cost" of sex-typed behavior: A test of the conflict hypothesis. *Developmental Psychology, 28,* 714–721.

Frick, E., Fegg, M., Tyroller, M., Fischer, N., & Bumeder, I. (2007). Patients' health beliefs and coping prior to autologous peripheral stem cell transplantation. *European Journal of Cancer Care, 16,* 156–163.

Friedman, M., & Rosenman, R. H. (1974). *Type A behavior and your heart.* New York: Knopf.

Frieswijk, N., Buunk, B., Steverink, N., & Slaets, J. (2004). The effect of social comparison information on the life satisfaction of frail older persons. *Psychology & Aging, 19,* 183–190.

Frisch, A., Laufer, N., Danziger, Y., Michaelovsky, E., Leor, S., Carel, C., Stein, D., Fenig, S., Mimouni, M., Apter, A., & Weizman, A. (2001). Association of anorexia nervosa with the high activity allele of the COMT gene: A family-based study in Israeli patients. *Molecular Psychiatry, 6,* 243–245.

Frisch, M., Glimelius, B., van den Brule, A., Wohlfahrt, J., Meijer, C., Walboomers, J., Goldman, S., Svensson, C., Hans-Olov, A., & Melbye, M. (1997). Sexually transmitted infection as a cause of anal cancer. *New England Journal of Medicine, 337,* 1350–1358.

Fryar, C., Hirsch, R., Porter, K., Kottiri, B., Brody, D., & Louis, T. (2007). Drug use and sexual behaviors reported by adults: 1999–2002. *Vital and Health Statistics, 384,* 1–15.

Fuchs, L., Fuchs, D., Karns, K., Hamlett, C., Dutka, S., & Katsaroff, M. (2000). The importance of providing background information on the structure and scoring of performance assessments. *Applied Measurement in Education, 13,* 134.

Fuller, T. L., & Fincham, F. D. (1995). Attachment style in married couples: Relation to current marital functioning, stability over time, and method of assessment. *Personal Relationships, 2,* 17–34.

Fullerton, A., & Wallace, M. (2007). Traversing the flexible turn: US workers' perceptions of job security, 1977–2002. *Social Science Research, 36,* 201–221.

Funk, J., Buchman, D., Jenks, J., & Bechtoldt, H. (2003). Playing violent video games, desensitization, and moral evaluation in children. *Journal of Applied Developmental Psychology, 24,* 413–436.

Funk, J., Buchman, D., Myers, B., & Jenks, J. (2000, August). *Asking the right questions in research on violent electronic games.* Paper presented at the annual meeting of the American Psychological Association, Washington, DC.

Furedi, F. (2003). *The children who won't grow up.* Retrieved July 7, 2007 from www.spiked-online.com/Articles/00000006DE8D.htm.

Furrow, D., & Nelson, K. (1984). Environmental correlates of individual differences in language acquisition. *Journal of Child Language, 11,* 523–534.

Gaillard, W., Hertz-Pannier, L., Mott, S., Barnett, A., LeBihan, D., & Theodore, W. (2000). Functional anatomy of cognitive development: fMRI of verbal fluency in children and adults. *Neurology, 54,* 180–185.

Gajria, M., Jitendra, A., Sood, S., & Sacks, G. (2007). Improving comprehension of expository text in students with LD: A research synthesis. *Journal of Learning Disabilities, 40,* 210–225.

Galambos, N., & Maggs, J. (1991). Out-of-school care of young adolescents and self-reported behavior. *Developmental Psychology, 27,* 644–655.

Galambos, N., Turner, P., & Tilton-Weaver, L. (2005). Chronological and subjective age in emerging adulthood: The crossover effect. *Journal of Adolescent Research, 20,* 538–556.

Galanaki, E. (2004). Teachers and loneliness: The children's perspective. *School Psychology International, 25,* 92–105.

Galassi, J., Gulledge, S., & Cox, N. (1997). Middle school advisories: Retrospect and prospect. *Review of Educational Research, 67,* 301–338.

Gallagher, A., Frith, U., & Snowling, M. (2000). Precursors of literacy delay among children at genetic risk of dyslexia. *Journal of Child Psychology & Psychiatry & Allied Disciplines, 41,* 202–213.

Gallagher, S. K. (1994). Doing their share: Comparing patterns of help given by older and younger adults. *Journal of Marriage & the Family, 56*, 567–578.
Gallagher, W. (1993, May). Midlife myths. *The Atlantic Monthly*, pp. 51–68.
Gallagher-Thompson, D., Futterman, A. Farberow, N., Thompson, L. W., & Peterson, J. (1993). The impact of spousal bereavement on older widows and widowers. In M. S. Stroebe, W. Stroebe, & R. O. Hansson (Eds.), *Handbook of bereavement: Theory, research, and intervention* (pp. 227–239). Cambridge, England: Cambridge University Press.
Gallagher-Thompson, D., Tazeau, Y., & Basilic L. (1997). The relationships of dimensions of acculturation to self-reported depression in older Mexican-American women. *Journal of Clinical Geropsychology, 3*, 123–137.
Gallo, W., Bradley, E., Siegel, M., & Kasl, S. (2000). Health effects of involuntary job loss among older workers: Findings from the health and retirement survey. *Journals of Gerontology, Series B: Psychological Sciences & Social Sciences, 55B*, S131–S140.
Gallup Poll. (2006). *Americans still oppose gay marriage.* Retrieved July 8, 2007 from www.galluppoll.com/content/?ci=22882.
Gana, K., Alaphilippe, D., & Bailly, N. (2004). Positive illusions and mental and physical health in later life. *Aging & Mental Health, 8*, 58–64.
Ganchrow, J. R., Steiner, J. E., & Daher, M. (1983). Neonatal facial expressions in response to different qualities and intensities of gustatory stimuli. *Infant Behavior & Development, 6*, 189–200.
Ganong, L., & Coleman, M. (1994). *Remarried family relationships.* Thousand Oaks, CA: Sage Publications.
Garbarino, J., Dubrow, N., Kostelny, K., & Pardo, C. (1992). *Children in danger: Coping with the consequences of community violence.* San Francisco: Jossey-Bass.
Garcia, G., & Miller, R. (2001). Single-cell analyses reveal two defects in peptide-specific activation of naive T cells from aged mice. *Journal of Immunology, 166*, 3151–3157.
Gardiner, M., Luszcz, M., & Bryan, J. (1997). The manipulation and measurement of task-specific memory self-efficacy in younger and older adults. *International Journal of Behavioral Development, 21*, 209–227.
Gardner, A. (2007). *ADHD drugs need better warnings on heart, psychiatric risks: FDA.* Retrieved June 19, 2007 from www.healthfinder.gov/news/newsstory.asp?docID=602115
Gardner, H. (1983). *Frames of mind: The theory of multiple intelligence.* New York: Basic Books.
Gardner, J., Karmel, B., Freedland, R., Lennon, E., Flory, M., Miroschnichenko, I., Phan, H., Barone, A., & Harm, A. (2006). Arousal, attention, and neurobehavioral assessment in the neonatal period: Implications for intervention and policy. *Journal of Policy and Practice in Intellectual Disabilities, 3*, 22–32.
Garfield, P., Kent, A., Paykel, E., Creighton, F., & Jacobson, R. (2004). Outcome of postpartum disorders: A 10 year follow-up of hospital admissions. *Acta Psychiatrica Scandinavica, 109*, 434–439.
Garmezy, N. (1993). Vulnerability and resilience. In D. C. Funder, R. D. Parke, C. Tomlinson-Keasey, & K. Widaman (Eds.), *Studying lives through time: Personality and development* (pp. 377–398). Washington, DC: American Psychological Association.
Garmezy, N., & Rutter, M. (Eds.). (1983). *Stress, coping, and development in children.* New York: McGraw-Hill.
Garnier, H., Stein, J., & Jacobs, J. (1997). The process of dropping out of high school: A 19-year perspective. *American Educational Research Journal, 34*, 395–419.
Garrison, R. J., Gold, R. S., Wilson, P. W. F., & Kannel, W. B. (1993). Educational attainment and coronary heart disease risk: The Framingham offspring study. *Preventive Medicine, 22*, 54–64.
Gartstein, M., & Rothbart, M. (2003). Studying infant temperament via the revised infant behavior questionnaire. *Infant Behavior & Development, 26*, 64–86.
Gass, K., Jenkins, J., & Dunn, J. (2007). Are sibling relationships protective? A longitudinal study. *Journal of Child Psychology and Psychiatry, 48*, 167–175.
Gathercole, S., Pickering, S., Ambridge, B., & Wearing, H. (2004). The structure of working memory from 4 to 15 years of age. *Developmental Psychology, 40*, 177–190.
Gaultney, J., & Gingras, J. (2005). Fetal rate of behavioral inhibition and preference for novelty during infancy. *Early Human Development, 81*, 379–386.
Gauntlett-Gilbert, J., Keegan, A., & Petrak, J. (2004). Drug-facilitated sexual assault: Cognitive approaches to treating the trauma. *Behavioral & Cognitive Psychotherapy, 32*, 211.
Geary, D., Lin, F., Chen, G., Saults, S., et al. (1999). Contributions of computational fluency to cross-national differences in arithmetical reasoning abilities. *Journal of Educational Psychology, 91*, 716–719.
Geary, D. C., Bow-Thomas, C. C., Fan, L., & Siegler, R. S. (1993). Even before formal instruction, Chinese children outperform American children in mental addition. *Cognitive Development, 8*, 517–529.
Gee, C., & Rhodes, J. (1999). Postpartum transitions in adolescent mothers' romantic and maternal relationships. *Merrill-Palmer Quarterly, 45*, 512–532.
Gee, C., & Rhodes, J. (2003). Adolescent mothers' relationship with their children's biological fathers: Social support, social strain and relationship continuity. *Journal of Family Psychology, 17*, 370–383.
Geers, A., Kosbab, K., Helfer, S., Weiland, P., & Wellman, J. (2007). Further evidence for individual differences in placebo responding: An interactionist perspective. *Journal of Psychosomatic Research, 62*, 563–570.
Gelman, R. (1972). Logical capacity of very young children: Number invariance rules. *Child Development, 43*, 75–90.
Gentile, D., Lynch, P. Linder, J., & Walsh, D. (2004). The effects of violent video game habits on adolescent hostility, aggressive behaviors, and school performance. *Journal of Adolescence, 27*, 5–22.
Georgieff, M. K. (1994). Nutritional deficiencies as developmental risk factors: Commentary on Pollitt and Gorman. In C. A. Nelson (Ed.), *The Minnesota Symposia on Child Development, Vol. 27* (pp. 145–159). Hillsdale, NJ: Erlbaum.
Gerbner tackles "fairness." (1997, February 24). *Electronic media.* Retrieved January 15, 2001, from www.mediascope.org/pubs/ibriefs/dft.html.
Gerhardstein, P., Liu, J., & Rovee-Collier, C. (1998). Perceptual constraints on infant memory retrieval. *Journal of Experimental Child Psychology, 69*, 109–131.
Gesell, A. (1925). *The mental growth of the preschool child.* New York: Macmillan.
Gesser, G., Wong, P. T. P., & Reker, G. T. (1987/1988). Death attitudes across the life-span: The development and validation of the death attitude profile (DAP). *Omega, 18*, 113–128.
Giambra, L. M., Arenberg, D., Zonderman, A. B., Kawas, C., & Costa, P. T., Jr. (1995). Adult life span changes in immediate visual memory and verbal intelligence. *Psychology & Aging, 10*, 123–139.
Gilbertson, M., & Bramlett, R. (1998). Phonological awareness screening to identify at-risk readers: Implications for practitioners. *Language, Speech, & Hearing Services in Schools, 29*, 109–116.
Gill, T., Baker, D., Gottschalk, M., Peduzzi, P., Allore, H., & Byers, A. (2002). A program to prevent functional decline in physically frail, elderly persons who live at home. *Medical Care Research & Review, 60*, 223–247.
Gillies, V., & Lucey, H. (2006). "It's a connection you can't get away from": Brothers, sisters and social capital. *Journal of Youth Studies, 9*, 479–493.
Gilligan, C. (1982). *In a different voice: Psychological theory and women's development.* Cambridge, MA: Harvard University Press.
Gilligan, C., & Wiggins, G. (1987). The origins of morality in early childhood relationships. In J. Kagan & S. Lamb (Eds.), *The emergence of morality in young children* (pp. 277–307). Chicago: University of Chicago Press.
Gilman, E. A., Cheng, K. K., Winter, H. R., & Scragg, R. (1995). Trends in rates and seasonal distribution of sudden infant deaths in England and Wales, 1988–1992. *British Medical Journal, 30*, 631–632.
Glück, J., Bluck, S., Baron, J., & McAdams, D. (2005). The wisdom of experience: Autobiographical narratives across adulthood. *International Journal of Behavioral Development, 29*, 197–208.
Gladue, B. A. (1994). The biopsychology of sexual orientation. *Current Directions in Psychological Science, 3*, 150–154.
Glaser, D. (2000). Child abuse and neglect and the brain-a review. *Journal of Child Psychology & Psychiatry & Allied Disciplines, 41*, 97–116.
Glaser, R., Kiecolt-Glaser, J. K., Bonneau, R. H., Malarkey, W., Kennedy, S., & Hughes, J. (1992). Stress-induced modulation of the immune response to recombinant hepatitis B vaccine. *Psychosomatic Medicine, 54*, 22–29.
Glass, J., & Kilpatrick, B. (1998). Gender comparisons of baby boomers and financial preparation for retirement. *Educational Gerontology, 24*, 719–745.
Glaubke, C., Miller, P., Parker, M., & Espejo, E. (2001). *Fair play: Violence, gender, and race in video games.* Retrieved June 28, 2007 from http://publications.childrennow.org/assets/pdf/cmp/fairplay/fair-play-video-01.pdf
Glazer, H. (1998). Expressions of children's grief: A qualitative study. *International Journal of Play Therapy, 7*, 51–65.
Gleitman, L. R., & Gleitman, H. (1992). A picture is worth a thousand words, but that's the problem: The role of syntax in vocabulary acquisition. *Current Directions in Psychological Science, 1*, 31–35.
Glenn, N. D., & Weaver, C. N. (1985). Age, cohort, and reported job satisfaction in the United States. In A. S. Blau (Ed.), *Current perspectives on aging and the life cycle. A research annual, Vol. 1: Work, retirement and social policy* (pp. 89–110). Greenwich, CT: JAI Press.
Gloger-Tippelt, G., & Huerkamp, M. (1998). Relationship change at the transition to parenthood and security of infant-mother attachment. *International Journal of Behavioral Development, 23*, 633–655.

Gnepp, J., & Chilamkurti, C. (1988). Children's use of personality attributions to predict other people's emotional and behavioral reactions. *Child Development, 50*, 743–754.

Gold, D. P., Andres, D., Etezadi, J., Arbuckle, T., Schwartzman, A., & Chaikelson, J. (1995). Structural equation model of intellectual change and continuity and predictors of intelligence in older men. *Psychology & Aging, 10*, 294–303.

Gold, E., Colvin, A., Avis, N., Bromberger, J., Greendale, G., Powell, L., Sternfeld, B., & Matthews, K. (2006). Longitudinal analysis of the association between vasomotor symptoms and race/ethnicity across the menopausal transition: Study of women's health across the nation. *American Journal of Public Health, 96*, 1225–1235.

Goldberg, A. P., Dengel, D. R., & Hagberg, J. M. (1996). Exercise physiology and aging. In E. L. Schneider & J. W. Rowe (Eds.), *Handbook of the biology of aging* (4th ed., pp. 331–354). San Diego, CA: Academic Press.

Goldberg, W. A. (1990). Marital quality, parental personality, and spousal agreement about perceptions and expectations for children. *Merrill-Palmer Quarterly, 36*, 531–556.

Goldfield, B. A. (1993). Noun bias in maternal speech to one-year-olds. *Journal of Child Language, 20*, 85–99.

Goldfield, B. A., & Reznick, J. S. (1990). Early lexical acquisition: Rate, content, and the vocabulary spurt. *Journal of Child Language, 17*, 171–183.

Golding, J., Emmett, P., & Rogers, I. (1997a). Does breast feeding protect against non-gastric infections? *Early Human Development, 49* (Supp.), S105–S120.

Golding, J., Emmett, P., & Rogers, I. (1997b). Gastroenteritis, diarrhea and breast feeding. *Early Human Development, 49* (Supp.), S83–S103.

Goleman, D. (1995). *Emotional intelligence.* New York: Bantam.

Goleman, D. D., Kaufman, P., & Ray, M. (1992). *The creative spirit.* New York: Dutton.

Golinkoff, R. M., Mervis, C. B., & Hirsh-Pasek, K. (1994). Early object labels: The case for lexical principles. *Journal of Child Language, 21*, 125–155.

Gollan, T., & Silverberg, N. (2001). Tip-of-the-tongue states in Hebrew-English bilinguals. *Bilingualism: Language & Cognition*, 4, 63–83.

Golombok, S., & Fivush, R. (1994). *Gender development.* Cambridge, England: Cambridge University Press.

Golombok, S., & Tasker, F. (1996). Do parents influence the sexual orientation of their children? Findings from a longitudinal study of lesbian families. *Developmental Psychology, 32*, 3–11.

Gonzales, N., Dumka, L., Deardorff, J., Carter, S., & McCray, A. (2004). Preventing poor mental health and school dropout of Mexican American adolescents following the transition to junior high school. *Journal of Adolescent Research, 19*, 113–131.

Gonzalez, J., & Valle, I. (2000). Word identification and reading disorders in the Spanish language. *Journal of Learning Disabilities, 33*, 44–60.

Goodenough, F. L. (1931). *Anger in young children.* Minneapolis: University of Minnesota Press.

Goodman, C. (2007). Family dynamics in three-generation families. *Journal of Family Issues, 28*, 355–379.

Goodrum, S. (2005). The interaction between thoughts and emotions following the news of a loved one's murder. *Omega: Journal of Death and Dying, 51*, 143–160.

Goodsitt, J. V., Morse, P. A., Ver Hoeve, J. N., & Cowan, N. (1984). Infant speech recognition in multisyllabic contexts. *Child Development, 55*, 903–910.

Goossens, L., Beyers, W., Emmen, M., & van Aken, M. (2002). The imaginary audience and personal fable: Factor analyses and concurrent validity of the "New Look" measures. *Journal of Research on Adolescence, 12*, 193–215.

Gotay, N., Giedd, J., Lusk, L., Hayashi, K., Greenstein, D., Vaituzis, A., Nugent, T., Herman, D., Clasen, L., Toga, A., Rapoport, J., & Thompson, P. (2004). Dynamic mapping of human cortical development during childhood through early adulthood. *Proceedings of the National Academy of Science, 101*, 8174–8179.

Gothelf, D., Apter, A., Brand-Gothelf, A., Offer, N., Ofek, H., Tyano, S., & Pfeffer, C. (1998). Death concepts in suicidal adolescents. *Journal of the American Academy of Child & Adolescent Psychiatry, 37*, 1279–1286.

Gottlob, L., & Madden, D. (1999). Age differences in the strategic allocation of visual attention. *Journals of Gerontology: Series B: Psychological Sciences & Social Sciences, 54B*, P165–P172.

Gottman, J. M. (1986). The world of coordinated play: Same- and cross-sex friendship in young children. In J. M. Gottman & J. G. Parker (Eds.), *Conversations of friends: Speculations on affective development* (pp. 139–191). Cambridge, England: Cambridge University Press.

Gottman, J. M. (1994). *Why marriages succeed or fail.* New York: Simon & Schuster.

Gould, E., Reeves, A., Graziano, M., & Gross, C. (1999). Neurogenesis in the neocortex of adult primates. *Science, 286*, 548–552.

Gozalo, P., & Miller, S. (2007). Hospice enrollment and evaluation of its causal effect on hospitalization of dying nursing home patients. *Health Services Research, 42*, 587–610.

Graber, J. A., Brooks-Gunn, J., Paikoff, R. L., & Warren, M. P. (1994). Prediction of eating problems: An 8-year study of adolescent girls. *Developmental Psychology, 30*, 823–834.

Grabowski, L., Call, K., & Mortimer, J. (2001). Global and economic self-efficacy in the educational attainment process. *Social Psychology Quarterly, 64*, 164–197.

Grady, D., Herrington, D., Bittner, V., Blumenthal, R., Davidson, M., Hlatky, M., Hsia, J., Hulley, S., Herd, A., Khan, S., Newby, K., Waters, D., Vittinghoff, E., & Wenger, N. (2002). Cardiovascular disease outcomes during 6.8 years of hormone therapy: Heart and estrogen/progestin replacement study follow-up (HERS II). *Journal of the American Medical Association, 288*, 49–57.

Graham, J., Cohen, R., Zbikowski, S., & Secrist, M. (1998). A longitudinal investigation of race and sex as factors in children's classroom friendship choices. *Child Study Journal, 28*, 245–266.

Graham, S., & Harris, K. (1997). It can be taught, but it does not develop naturally: Myths and realities in writing instruction. *School Psychology Review, 26*, 414–424.

Gralinski, J. H., & Kopp, C. B. (1993). Everyday rules for behavior: Mothers' requests to young children. *Developmental Psychology, 29*, 573–584.

Gralinski-Bakker, J., Hauser, S., Billings, R., Allen, J., Lyons, P., & Melton, G. (2005). Transitioning to adulthood for young adults with mental health issues. *Network on Transitions to Adulthood Policy Brief, 21*, 1–3.

Grant, S., & Langan-Fox, J. (2007). Personality and the occupational stressor-strain relationship: The role of the Big Five. *Journal of Occupational Health Psychology, 112*, 20–33.

Green, R., Cupples, A., Go, R., Benke, K., Edeki, T., Griffith, P., Williams, M., Hipps, Y., Graff-Radford, N., Bachman, D., & Farrer, L. (2002). Risk of dementia among white and African American relatives of patients with Alzheimer's disease. *Journal of the American Medical Association, 287*, 329–336.

Green, S. (2001). Systemic vs. individualistic approaches to bullying. *Journal of the American Medical Association, 286*, 787.

Green, S., Anderson, E., Doyle, E., & Ridelbach, H. (2006). Divorce. In Bear, G., & Minke, K. (Eds.). *Children's needs III: Development, prevention, and intervention.* Washington, DC: National Association of School Psychologists.

Green, S., Pring, L., & Swettenham, J. (2004). An investigation of first-order false belief understanding of children with congenital profound visual impairment. *British Journal of Developmental Psychology, 22*, 1–17.

Greenberg, J., Lewis, S., & Dodd, D. (1999). Overlapping addictions and self-esteem among college men and women. *Addictive Behaviors, 24*, 565–571.

Greenberger, E., & Steinberg, L. (1986). *When teenagers work: The psychological and social costs of adolescent employment.* New York: Basic Books.

Greene, K., Krcmar, M., Rubin, D., Walters, L., & Hale, J. (2002). Elaboration in processing adolescent health messages: The impact of egocentrism and sensation seeking on message processing. *Journal of Communication, 52*, 812–831.

Greenfield, E., & Marks, N. (2007). Continuous participation in voluntary groups as a protective factor for the psychological well-being of adults who develop functional limitations: Evidence from the National Survey of Families and Households. *The Journals of Gerontology Series B: Psychological Sciences and Social Sciences, 62*, S60–S68.

Greenhaus, J., Collins, K., Singh, R., & Parasuraman, S. (1997). Work and family influences on departure from public accounting. *Journal of Vocational Behavior, 50*, 249–270.

Greer, D. S., Mor, V., Morris, J. N., Sherwood, S., Kidder, D., & Birnbaum, H. (1986). An alternative in terminal care: Results of the National Hospice Study. *Journal of Chronic Diseases, 39*, 9–26.

Greer, S. (1991). Psychological response to cancer and survival. *Psychological Medicine, 21*, 43–49.

Greer, S. (1999). Mind-body research in psychooncology. *Advances in Mind-Body Medicine, 15*, 236–244.

Greer, S., Morris, T., & Pettingale, K. W. (1979). Psychological response to breast cancer: Effect on outcome. *Lancet*, 785–787.

Greider, L. (2000, March/April). How not to be a monster-in-law. *Modern Maturity, 43*(2), 56–59, 81.

Griffith, J. (2007). *Aging boomers in the age of anti-aging.* Retrieved July 9, 2007 from www.docshop.com/education/cosmetic/news/baby-boomers/.

Griffiths, M. (1999). Internet addiction: Fact or fiction? *Psychologist, 12,* 246–250.

Griffiths, M. (2003). Internet gambling: Issues, concerns, and recommendations. *CyberPsychology, 6,* 557–568.

Grijalva, T., Nowell, C., & Kerkvliet, J. (2006). Academic honesty and online courses. *College Student Journal, 40,* 180–185.

Grohol, J. (1999). *Internet Addiction Guide.* Retrieved February 3, 2000, from http://www.psychcentral.com/netaddiction.

Groome, L., Mooney, D., Holland, S., Smith, L., Atterbury, J., & Dykman, R. (1999). Behavioral state affects heart rate response to low-intensity sound in human fetuses. *Early Human Development, 54,* 39–54.

Grossman, A. (July 6, 1998). Clairol targets boomers, positions product at high-end: Clairol hair coloring for baby boom generation. *Drug Store News.* Retrieved July 9, 2007 from http://findarticles.com/p/articles/mi_m3374/is_n10_v20/ai_20929372.

Grossman, A., Daugelli, A., & Hershberger, S. (2000). Social support networks of lesbian, gay, and bisexual adults 60 years of age and older. *Journals of Gerontology, Series B: Psychological Sciences & Social Sciences, 55B,* P171–P179.

Grov, C., Bimbi, D., Nanin, J., & Pasrons, J. (2006). Race, ethnicity, gender, and generational factors associated with the coming-out process among gay, lesbian, and bisexual individuals. *Journal of Sex Research, 43,* 115–121.

Grusec, J. (1992). Social learning theory and developmental psychology: The legacies of Robert Sears and Albert Bandura. *Developmental Psychology, 28,* 776–786.

Guerin, D. W., & Gottfried, A. W. (1994b). Temperamental consequences of infant difficultness. *Infant Behavior & Development, 17,* 413–421.

Guesry, P. (1998). The role of nutrition in brain development. *Preventive Medicine, 27,* 189–194.

Guilford, J. (1967). *The nature of human intelligence.* New York: McGraw-Hill.

Gunkel, M., Lusk, E., Wolff, B., & Li, F. (2007). Gender-specific effects at work: An empirical study of four countries. *Gender, Work & Organization, 14,* 56–79.

Gunnar, M. R. (1994). Psychoendocrine studies of temperament and stress in early childhood: Expanding current models. In J. E. Bates & T. D. Wachs (Eds.), *Temperament: Individual differences at the interface of biology and behavior* (pp. 175–198). Washington, DC: American Psychological Association.

Gunter, T., Jackson, J., & Mulder, G. (1998). Priming and aging: An electrophysiological investigation of N400 and recall. *Brain & Language, 65,* 333–355.

Gunther, M. (1955). Instinct and the learning couple. *Lancet, 1,* 575.

Gunther, M. (1961). Infant behavior at the breast. In B. Foss (Ed.), *Determinants of infant behavior* (pp. 37–44). London: Methuen.

Guo, S. F. (1993). Postpartum depression. *Chung-Hua Fu Chan Ko Tsa Chi, 28,* 532–533, 569.

Gur, R., Gunning-Dixon, F., Bilker, W., & Gur, R. (2002). Sex differences in temporo-limbic and frontal brain volumes of healthy adults. *Cerebral Cortex, 12,* 998–1003.

Gur, R. C., Turetsky, B., Matsui, M., Yan, M., Bilker, W., Hughett, P., & Gur, R. E. (1999). Sex differences in brain gray and white matter in healthy young adults: Correlations with cognitive performance. *Journal of Neuroscience, 19,* 4065–4072.

Guralnik, J. M., & Kaplan, G. A. (1989). Predictors of healthy aging: Prospective evidence from the Alameda County Study. *American Journal of Public Health, 79,* 703–708.

Guralnik, J. M., & Paul-Brown, D. (1984). Communicative adjustments during behavior-request episodes among children at different developmental levels. *Child Development, 55,* 911–919.

Guralnik, J. M., Land, K. C., Blazer, D., Fillenbaum, G. G., & Branch, L. G. (1993). Educational status and active life expectancy among older blacks and whites. *New England Journal of Medicine, 329,* 110–116.

Guralnik, J. M., Simonsick, E. M., Ferrucci, L., Glynn, R. J., Berkman, L. F., Blazer, D. G., Scherr, P. A., & Wallace, R. B. (1994). A short physical performance battery assessing lower extremity function: Association with self-reported disability and prediction of mortality and nursing home admission. *Journals of Gerontology: Medical Sciences, 49,* M85–94.

Gurland, B., Wilder, D., Lantiga, R., Stern, Y., Chen, J., Killeffer, E., & Mayeux, R. (1999). Rates of dementia in three ethnoracial groups. *International Journal of Geriatric Psychiatry, 14,* 481–493.

Gurubacharya, B. (May 30, 2007). Man, 71, becomes oldest climber to scale Mount Everest. Retrieved May 30, 2007 from www.chron.com/disp/story.mpl/bizarre/4846481.html.

Guse, L., & Masesar, M. (1999). Quality of life and successful aging in long-term care: Perceptions of residents. *Issues in Mental Health Nursing, 20,* 527–539.

Gustafson, S. B., & Magnusson, D. (1991). *Female life careers: A pattern approach.* Hillsdale, NJ: Erlbaum.

Gutman, L. (2006). How student and parent goal orientations and classroom goal structures influence the math achievement of African Americans during the high school transition. *Contemporary Educational Psychology, 31,* 44–63.

Gzesh, S. M., & Surber, C. F. (1985). Visual perspective-taking skills in children. *Child Development, 56,* 1204–1213.

Hack, M., Taylor, C. B. H., Klein, N., Eiber, R., Schatschneider, C., & Mercuri-Minich, N. (1994). School-age outcomes in children with birth weights under 750 g. *New England Journal of Medicine, 331,* 753–759.

Hagan, J. (1997). Defiance and despair: Subcultural and structural linkages between delinquency and despair in the life course. *Social Forces, 76,* 119–134.

Hagan, J., & Kay, F. (2007). Even lawyers get the blues: Gender, depression, and job satisfaction in legal practice. *Law & Society Review, 41,* 51–78.

Hagedorn, L., Chi, W., Cepeda, R., & McLain, M. (2007). An investigation of critical mass: The role of Latino representation in the success of urban community college students. *Research in Higher Education, 48,* 73–91.

Hagestad, G. O. (1984). The continuous bond: A dynamic, multigenerational perspective on parent-child relations between adults. In M. Perlmutter (Ed.), *Minnesota Symposia on Child Psychology* (pp. 129–158). Hillsdale, NJ: Erlbaum.

Hagestad, G. O. (1985). Continuity and connectedness. In V. L. Bengtson (Ed.), *Grandparenthood* (pp. 31–38). Beverly Hills, CA: Sage.

Hagestad, G. O. (1986). Dimensions of time and the family. *American Behavioral Scientist, 29,* 679–694.

Hagestad, G. O. (1990). Social perspectives on the life course. In R. H. Binstock & L. K. George (Eds.), *Handbook of aging and the social sciences* (3rd ed., pp. 151–168). San Diego, CA: Academic Press.

Hahn, C., Yang, M-S., Yang, M-J., Shih, C., & Lo, H. (2004). Religious attendance and depressive symptoms among community dwelling elderly in Taiwan. *International Journal of Geriatric Psychiatry, 19,* 1148–1154.

Haier, R. J., Chueh, D., Touchette, P., Lott, I., Buchsbaum, M. S., MacMillan, D., Sandman, C., LaCasse, L., & Sosa, E. (1995). Brain size and cerebral glucose metabolic rate in nonspecific mental retardation and Down syndrome. *Intelligence, 20,* 191–210.

Haight, W., Wang, X., Fung, H., Williams, K., et al. (1999). Universal, developmental, and variable aspects of young children's play. *Child Development, 70,* 1477–1488.

Hakansson, G., Salameh, E., & Nettelbladt, U. (2003). Measuring language development in bilingual children: Swedish-Arabic children with and without language impairment. *Linguistics, 41,* 255–288.

Halford, G. S., Maybery, M. T., O'Hare, A. W., & Grant, P. (1994). The development of memory and processing capacity. *Child Development, 65,* 1338–1356.

Hall, D. R., & Zhao, J. Z. (1995). Cohabitation and divorce in Canada: Testing the selectivity hypothesis. *Journal of Marriage & the Family, 57,* 421–427.

Hall, G. (2003, September). Primary elective C-section up 20% from 1999 to 2001. *OB/GYN News.* Retrieved April 1, 2004, from www.imng.com.

Halle, T. (1999). Implicit theories of social interactions: Children's reasoning about the relative importance of gender and friendship in social partner choices. *Merrill-Palmer Quarterly, 45* 445–467.

Hallmark Corporation. (2004). *Wedding facts.* Retrieved August 24, 2004, from http://pressroom.hallmark.com/wedding_facts.html.

Halpern, D. F. (1986). *Sex differences in cognitive abilities.* Hillsdale, NJ: Erlbaum.

Hamberger, K., & Minsky, D. (2000, August). *Evaluation of domestic violence training programs for health care professionals.* Paper presented at the annual meeting of the American Psychological Association. Washington, DC.

Hamilton, C. E. (1995, March). *Continuity and discontinuity of attachment from infancy through adolescence.* Paper presented at the biennial meetings of the Society for Research in Child Development, Indianapolis, IN.

Hammond, M., Landry, S., Swank, P., & Smith, K. (2000). Relation of mothers' affective development history and parenting behavior: Effects on infant medical risk. *American Journal of Orthopsychiatry, 70,* 95–103.

Hampson, S., & Goldberg, L. (2006). A first large cohort study of personality trait stability over the 40 years between elementary school and midlife. *Journal of Personality and Social Psychology, 91,* 763–779.

Handley-Derry, M., Low, J., Burke, S., Waurick, M., Killen, H., & Derrick, E. (1997). Intrapartum fetal asphyxia and the occurrence of minor deficits in 4- to 8-year-old children. *Developmental Medicine & Child Neurology, 39,* 508–514.

Handy, J., & Davy, D. (2007). Gendered ageism: Older women's experience of employment agency practices. *Asia Pacific Journal of Human Resources, 45,* 35–99.

Hank, K. (2005). *Spatial proximity and contacts between elderly parents and their adult children: A European comparison.* Retrieved August 2, 2007 from www.diw.de/deutsch/produkte/publikationen/diskussionspapiere/docs/papers/dp510.pdf.

Hanna, E., & Meltzoff, A. N. (1993). Peer imitation by toddlers in laboratory, home, and day-care contexts: Implications for social learning and memory. *Developmental Psychology, 29,* 701–710.

Hannigan, J., O'Leary-Moore, S., & Berman, R. (2007). Postnatal environmental or experiential amelioration of neurobehavioral effects of perinatal alcohol exposure in rats. *Neuroscience & Biobehavioral Reviews, 31,* 202–211.

Hardy, M. A., & Quadagno, J. (1995). Satisfaction with early retirement: Making choices in the auto industry. *Journals of Gerontology: Social Sciences, 50B,* S217–228.

Haring, M., Hewitt, P., & Flett, G. (2003). Perfectionism, coping, and quality of intimate relationships. *Journal of Marriage & the Family, 65,* 143–158.

Harkness, S. (1998). Time for families. *Anthropology Newsletter, 39,* 1, 4.

Harkness, S., & Super, C. M. (1985). The cultural context of gender segregation in children's peer groups. *Child Development, 56,* 219–224.

Harlow, H., & Zimmerman, R. (1959). Affectional responses in the infant monkey. *Science, 130,* 421–432.

Harris, B., Lovett, L., Newcombe, R. G., Read, G. F., Walker, R., & Riad-Fahmy, D. (1994). Maternity blues and major endocrine changes: Cardiff puerperal mood and hormone study II. *British Medical Journal, 308,* 949–953.

Harris, L. (2003). The status of pregnant women and fetuses in US criminal law. *Journal of the American Medical Association, 289,* 1697–1699.

Harris, P. L. (1989). *Children and emotion: The development of psychological understanding.* Oxford: Blackwell.

Harrison, A., Wilson, M., Pine, C., Chan, S., & Buriel, R. (1990). Family ecologies of ethnic minority children. *Child Development, 61,* 347–362.

Harrist, A., Zaia, A., Bates, J., Dodge, K., & Pettit, G. (1997). Subtypes of social withdrawal in early childhood: Sociometric status and social-cognitive differences across four years. *Child Development, 68,* 278–294.

Hart, B., & Risley, T. R. (1995). *Meaningful differences in the everyday experience of young American children.* Baltimore: Paul H. Brookes.

Hart, C., Olsen, S., Robinson, C., & Mandleco, B. (1997). The development of social and communicative competence in childhood: Review and a model of personal, familial, and extrafamilial processes. *Communication Yearbook, 20,* 305–373.

Hart, D., Mele-McCarthy, J., Pasternack, R., Zimbrich, K., & Parker, D. (2004). Community college: A pathway to success for youth with learning, cognitive, and intellectual disabilities in secondary settings. *Education & Training in Developmental Disabilities, 39,* 54–66.

Hart, S., Jones, N., Field, T., & Lundy, B. (1999). One-year-old infants of intrusive and withdrawn depressed mothers. *Child Psychiatry & Human Development, 30,* 111–120.

Harter, S. (1990). Processes underlying adolescent self-concept formation. In R. Montemayor, G. R. Adams, & T. P. Gullotta (Eds.), *From childhood to adolescence: A transitional period?* (pp. 205–239). Newbury Park, CA: Sage.

Harter, S., & Monsour, A. (1992). Developmental analysis of conflict caused by opposing attributes in the adolescent self-portrait. *Developmental Psychology, 28,* 251–260.

Hartup, W. W. (1974). Aggression in childhood: Developmental perspectives. *American Psychologist, 29,* 336–341.

Hartup, W. W. (1996). The company they keep: Friendships and their developmental significance. *Child Development, 67,* 1–13.

Harvey, A., & Hill, R. (2004). Afrocentric youth and family rites of passage program: Promoting resilience among at-risk African American youths. *Social Work, 49,* 65–74.

Harvey, R., Fletcher, J., & French, D. (2001). Social reasoning: A source of influence on aggression. *Clinical Psychology Review, 21,* 447–469.

Harwood, D., Barker, W., Ownby, R., Bravo, M., Aguero, H., & Duara, R. (2000). Depressive symptoms in Alzheimer's disease: An examination among community-dwelling Cuban American patients. *American Journal of Geriatric Psychiatry, 8,* 84–91.

Hasin, D., Stinson, F., Ogburn, M., & Grant, B. (2007). Prevalence, correlates, disability, and comorbidity of *DSM-IV* alcohol abuse and dependence in the United States. *Archives of General Psychiatry, 64,* 830–842.

Hatano, G. (1990). Toward the cultural psychology of mathematical cognition: Commentary. In H. Stevenson & S. Lee (Eds.), *Contexts of achievement. Monographs of the Society for Research in Child Development, 55* (12, Serial No. 221), 108–115.

Hatchett, S. J., & Jackson, J. S. (1993). African American extended kin systems: An assessment. In H. P. McAdoo (Ed.), *Family ethnicity: Strength in diversity* (pp. 90–108). Newbury Park, CA: Sage.

Hausman, P. B., & Weksler, M. E. (1985). Changes in the immune response with age. In C. E. Finch & E. L. Schneider (Eds.), *Handbook of the biology of aging* (2nd ed., pp. 414–432). New York: Van Nostrand Reinhold.

Hawkins, H. L., Kramer, A. F., & Capaldi, D. (1992). Aging, exercise, and attention. *Psychology & Aging, 7,* 643–653.

Hawkley, L., & Cacioppo, J. (2004). Stress and the aging immune system. *Brain, Behavior, and Immunity, 18,* 114–119.

Hay, D., Payne, A., & Chadwick, A. (2004). Peer relations in childhood. *Journal of Child Psychology & Psychiatry & Allied Disciplines, 45,* 84–108.

Hayflick, L. (1977). The cellular basis for biological aging. In C. E. Finch & L. Hayflick (Eds.), *Handbook of the biology of aging* (pp. 159–186). New York: Van Nostrand Reinhold.

Hayflick, L. (1987). Origins of longevity. In H. R. Warner, R. N. Butler, R. L. Sprott, & E. L. Schneider (Eds.), *Aging, Vol. 31. Modern biological theories of aging* (pp. 21–34). New York: Raven Press.

Hayne, H., & Rovee-Collier, C. (1995). The organization of reactivated memory in infancy. *Child Development, 66,* 893–906.

Hayward, M. D., & Hardy, M. A. (1985). Early retirement processes among older men: Occupational differences. *Research on Aging, 7,* 491–518.

Hayward, M. D., Friedman, S., & Chen, H. (1996). Race inequities in men's retirement. *Journals of Gerontology: Social Sciences, 51B,* S1–10.

Hazan, C., & Shaver, P. (1987). Romantic love conceptualized as an attachment process. *Journal of Personality & Social Psychology, 52,* 511–524.

Hazan, C., Hutt, M., Sturgeon, J., & Bricker, T. (1991, April). *The process of relinquishing parents as attachment figures.* Paper presented at the biennial meetings of the Society for Research in Child Development, Seattle, WA.

Hazelrigg, L. E., & Hardy, M. A. (1995). Older adult migration to the sunbelt: Assessing income and related characteristics of recent migrants. *Research on Aging, 17,* 109–234.

Hazuda, H., Wood, R., Lichtenstein, M., & Espino, D. (1998). Sociocultural status, psychosocial factors, and cognitive functional limitation in elderly Mexican Americans: Findings from the San Antonio Longitudinal Study of Aging. *Journal of Gerontological Social Work, 30,* 99–121.

He, Y., Colantonio, A., & Marshall, V. (2003). Later-life career disruption and self-rated health: An analysis of General Social Survey data. *Canadian Journal on Aging, 22,* 45–57.

Heckhausen, J., & Brim, O. (1997). Perceived problems for self and others: Self-protection by social downgrading throughout adulthood. *Psychology & Aging, 12,* 610–619.

Heidelise, A., Duffy, F., McAnulty, G., Rivkin, M., Vajapeyam, S., Mulkern, R., Warfield, S., Huppi, P., Butler, S., Conneman, N., Fischer, C., & Eichenwald, E. (2004). Early experience alters brain function and structure. *Pediatrics, 113,* 846–857.

Heilbronn, L., de Jonge, L., Frisard, M., DeLany, J., Larson-Meyer, E., Rood, J., Nguyen, T., Martin, C., Volaufova, J., Most, M., Greenway, F., Smith, S., Deutsch, W., Williamson, D., Ravussin, E. (2006). Effect of 6-month calorie restriction on biomarkers of longevity, metabolic adaptation, and oxidative stress in overweight individuals. *Journal of the American Medical Association, 295,* 1539–1548.

Heinicke, C., Goorsky, M., Moscov, S., Dudley, K., Gordon, J., Schneider, C., & Guthrie, D. (2000). Relationship-based intervention with at-risk mothers: Factors affecting variations in outcome. *Infant Mental Health Journal, 21,* 133–155.

Heinonen, K., Raikkonen, K., & Keltikangas-Jarvinen, L. (2003). Maternal perceptions and adolescent self-esteem: A six-year longitudinal study. *Adolescence, 38,* 669–687.

Helson, R., & Klohnen, D. (1998). Affective coloring of personality from young adulthood to midlife. *Personality & Social Psychology Bulletin, 24,* 241–252.

Helson, R., Mitchell, V., & Moane, G. (1984). Personality and patterns of adherence and nonadherence to the social clock. *Journal of Personality & Social Psychology, 46,* 1079–1096.

Henderson, H., Marshall, P., Fox, N., & Rubin, K. (2004). Psychophysiological and behavioral evidence for varying forms and functions of nonsocial behavior in preschoolers. *Child Development, 75,* 236–250.

Henderson, M., Wight, D., Raab, G., Abraham, C., Parkes, A., Scott, S., & Hart, G. (2007). Impact of a theoretically based sex education programme (SHARE) delivered by teachers on NHS registered conceptions and terminations: Final results of cluster randomised trial. *BMJ: British Medical Journal, 334,* 7585.

Hendricks, P., Ditre, J., Drobes, D., & Brandon, T. (2006). The early time course of smoking withdrawal effects. *Psychopharmacology, 187,* 385–396.

Hendrie, H. (2006). Lessons learned from international comparative crosscultural studies on dementia. *American Journal of Geriatric Psychiatry, 14,* 480–488.

Henry, B., Caspi, A., Moffitt, T., Harrington, H., et al. (1999). Staying in school protects boys with poor self-regulation in childhood from later crime: A longitudinal study. *International Journal of Behavioral Development, 23,* 1049–1073.

Henry, B., Caspi, A., Moffitt, T., & Silva, P. (1996). Temperamental and familial predictors of violent and nonviolent criminal convictions: Age 3 to age 18. *Developmental Psychology, 32*, 614–623.

Henry J. Kaiser Family Foundation. (1999). *Sex on TV.* Washington, DC: Author.

Henry J. Kaiser Family Foundation. (2005). *Sex on TV 4.* Retrieved June 21, 2007 from http://www.kff.org/entmedia/entmedia110905pkg.cfm

Henry, J., MacLeod, M. Phillips, L., & Crawford, J. (2004). A meta-analytic review of prospective memory and aging. *Psychology & Aging, 19*, 27–39.

Heppner, M., Fuller, B., & Multon, K. (1998). Adults in involuntary career transition: An analysis of the relationship between the psychological and career domains. *Journal of Career Assessment, 6*, 329–346.

Herbert, J., Gross, J., & Hayne, H. (2006). Age-related changes in deferred imitation between 6 and 9 months of age. *Infant Behavior & Development, 29*, 136–139.

Hermes, S., & Keel, P. (2003). The influence of puberty and ethnicity on awareness and internalization of the thin ideal. *International Journal of Eating Disorders, 33*, 465–467.

Hernandez, D. (1997). Child development and the social demography of childhood. *Child Development, 68*, 149–169.

Hertenstein, M., & Campos, J. (2004). The retention effects of an adult's emotional displays on infant behavior. *Child Development, 75*, 595–613.

Herzog, A. R., House, J. S., & Morgan, J. N. (1991). Relation of work and retirement to health and well-being in older age. *Psychology & Aging, 6*, 202–211.

Hess, E. H. (1972). "Imprinting" in a natural laboratory. *Scientific American, 227*, 24–31.

Hess, T., Bolstad, C., Woodburn, S., & Auman, C. (1999). Trait diagnosticity versus behavioral consistency as determinants of impression change in adulthood. *Psychology & Aging, 14*, 77–89.

Hester, R., Kinsella, G., & Ong, B. (2004). Effect of age on forward and backward span tasks. *Journal of the International Neuropsychological Society, 10*, 475–481.

Hetherington, E. M. (1991a). Presidential address: Families, lies, and videotapes. *Journal of Research on Adolescence, 1*, 323–348.

Hetherington, E. M. (1991b). The role of individual differences and family relationships in children's coping with divorce and remarriage. In P. A. Cowen & M. Hetherington (Eds.), *Family transitions* (pp. 165–194) Hillsdale, NJ: Erlbaum.

Hetherington, E. M., & Stanley-Hagan, M. M. (1995). Parenting in divorced and remarried families. In M. H. Bornstein (Ed.), *Handbook of parenting, Vol. 3: Status and social conditions of parenting* (pp. 233–254). Mahwah, NJ: Erlbaum.

Heun, R., & Bonsignore, M. (2004). No evidence for a genetic relationship between Alzheimer's disease and longevity. *Dementia & Geriatric Cognitive Disorders, 18*, 1–5.

Hill, C. (1999). Fusion and conflict in lesbian relationships. *Feminism & Psychology, 9*, 179–185.

Hill, J., Brooks–Gunn, J., & Waldfogel, J. (2003). Sustained effects of high participation in an early intervention for low-birth-weight premature infants. *Developmental Psychology, 39*, 730–744.

Hill, R. D., Storandt, M., & Malley, M. (1993). The impact of long-term exercise training on psychological function in older adults. *Journals of Gerontology: Psychological Sciences, 48*, P12–17.

Hillebrand, J. (2000). New perspectives on the manipulation of opiate urges and the assessment of cognitive effort associated with opiate urges. *Addictive Behaviors, 25*, 139–143.

Hillen, T., Davies, S., Rudd, A., Kieselbach, T., & Wolfe, C. (2003). Self ratings of health predict functional outcome and recurrence free survival after stroke. *Journal of Epidemiology & Community Health, 57*, 960–966.

Hinde, R. A., Titmus, G., Easton, D., & Tamplin, A. (1985). Incidence of "friendship" and behavior toward strong associates versus nonassociates in preschoolers. *Child Development, 56*, 234–245.

Hinton, J. (1975). The influence of previous personality on reactions to having terminal cancer. *Omega, 6*, 95–111.

Hirdes, J. P., & Strain, L. A. (1995). The balance of exchange in instrumental support with network members outside the household. *Journals of Gerontology: Social Sciences, 50B*, S134–142.

Ho, C., & Bryant, P. (1997). Learning to read Chinese beyond the logographic phase. *Reading Research Quarterly, 32*, 276–289.

Hobbs, J., & Ferth, P. (1993). *The Bounty pregnancy guide.* New York: Bounty Health Care Publishing.

Hodges, E. V. E., Malone, M. J., & Perry, D. G. (1997). Individual risk and social risk as interacting determinants of victimization in the peer group. *Developmental Psychology, 33*, 1032–1039.

Hoeksma, J., Oosterlaan, J., & Schipper, E. (2004). Emotion regulation and the dynamics of feelings: A conceptual and methodological framework. *Child Development, 75*, 354–360.

Hoff, E., Grote, S., Dettmer, S., Hohner, H., & Olos, L. (2005). Work-life balance: Professional and private life arrangement forms of women and men in highly qualified professions. *Zeitscrift für Arbeits und Organisationspsychologie, 49*, 196–207.

Hofferth, S., & Curtin, S. (2006). Parental leave statutes and maternal return to work after childbirth in the United States. *Work and Occupations, 33*, 73–105.

Hoffman, M. (1988). Moral development. In M. Bornstein & M. Lamb (Eds.), *Developmental psychology: An advanced textbook* (2nd ed., pp. 497–548). Hillsdale, NJ: Erlbaum.

Hoffman, M. L. (1982). Development of prosocial motivation: Empathy and guilt. In N. Eisenberg (Ed.), *The development of prosocial behavior* (pp. 281–314). New York: Academic Press.

Hogan, T. D., & Steinnes, D. N. (1994). Toward an understanding of elderly seasonal migration using origin-based household data. *Research on Aging, 16*, 463–475.

Holden, K. C., & Smock, P. J. (1991). The economic costs of marital dissolution: Why do women bear a disproportionate cost? *Annual Review of Sociology, 17*, 51–78.

Holland, J. L. (1973). *Making vocational choices: A theory of careers.* Englewood Cliffs, NJ: Prentice-Hall.

Holland, J. L. (1992). *Making vocational choices: A theory of vocational personalities and work environments* (2nd ed.). Odessa, FL: Psychological Assessment Resources.

Hollander, J. (2004). "I Can Take Care of Myself": The impact of self-defense training on women's lives. *Violence Against Women, 10*, 205–235.

Hollon, S., Thas, M., & Markowitz, J. (2002). Treatment and prevention of depression. *Psychological Science in the Public Interest, 3*, 39–77.

Holmgren, S., Molander, B., & Nilsson, L. (2006). Intelligence and executive functioning in adult age: Effects of sibship size and birth order. *European Journal of Cognitive Psychology, 18*, 138–158.

Holstein, M., & Minkler, M. (2003). Self, society, and the "new gerontology." *Gerontologist, 43*, 787–796.

Home Office Press Office. (2004). *Promoting human rights, respecting individual dignity: New measures to tackle forced marriage.* Retrieved July 5, 2007 from http://press.homeoffice.gov.uk/press-releases/Promoting_Human_Rights,_Respecti?version=1.

Honolulu Star-Bulletin. (August 1, 2003). *Baby Moses' laws can be too hastily enacted.* Retrieved June 18, 2007 from http://starbulletin.com/2003/08/01/editorial/editorials.html

Honzik, M. P. (1986). The role of the family in the development of mental abilities: A 50-year study. In N. Datan, A. L. Greene, & H. W. Reese (Eds.), *Life-span developmental psychology: Intergenerational relations* (pp. 185–210). Hillsdale, NJ: Erlbaum.

Hood, M., & Ellison, R. (2003). Television viewing and change in body fat from preschool to early adolescence: The Framingham Children's Study. *International Journal of Obesity & Related Metabolic Disorders, 27*, 827–833.

Hoppmann, C., & Smith, J. (2007). Long-term adjustment of infertile couples following unsuccessful medical intervention. *International Journal of Aging & Human Development, 64*, 109–127.

Horan, W., Pogge, D., Borgaro, S., & Stokes, J. (1997). Learning and memory in adolescent psychiatric inpatients with major depression: A normative study of the California Verbal Learning Test. *Archives of Clinical Neuropsychology, 12*, 575–584.

Hornbrook, M. C., Stevens, V. J., & Wingfield, D. J. (1994). Preventing falls among community-dwelling older persons: Results from a randomized trial. *The Gerontologist, 34*, 16–23.

Horowitz, A., McLaughlin, J., & White, H. (1998). How the negative and positive aspects of partner relationships affect the mental health of young married people. *Journal of Health & Social Behavior, 39*, 124–136.

Horowitz, F. D. (1990). Developmental models of individual differences. In J. Colombo & J. Fagen (Eds.), *Individual differences in infancy: Reliability, stability, prediction* (pp. 3–18). Hillsdale, NJ: Erlbaum.

Hou, J., Chen, H., & Chen, X. (2005). The relationship of parent-children interaction in the free play session and copy-modeling session with the development of children's behavioral inhibition in Chinese families. *Psychological Science (China), 28*, 820–825.

Houck, G., & Lecuyer-Maus, E. (2004). Maternal limit setting during toddlerhood, delay of gratification and behavior problems at age five. *Infant Mental Health Journal, 25*, 28–46.

House of Commons Work and Pensions Committee. (2006). *Child poverty in the UK.* Retrieved June 20, 2007 from www.publications.parliament.uk/pa/cm200304/cmselect/cmworpen/85/85.pdf.

House, J. A., Kessler, R. C., & Herzog, A. R. (1990). Age, socioeconomic status, and health. *The Milbank Quarterly, 68*, 383–411.

Houseknecht, S. K. (1987). Voluntary childlessness. In M. B. Sussman & S. K. Steinmetz (Eds.), *Handbook of marriage and the family* (pp. 369–395). New York: Plenum.

Houston, D., & Jusczyk, P. (2003). Infants' long-term memory for the sound patterns of words and voices. *Journal of Experimental Psychology: Human Perception & Performance, 29,* 1143–1154.

Hovell, M., Blumberg, E., Sipan, C., Hofstetter, C., Burkham, S., Atkins, C., & Felice, M. (1998). Skills training for pregnancy and AIDS prevention in Anglo and Latino youth. *Journal of Adolescent Health, 23,* 139–149.

Hovell, M., Sipan, C., Blumberg, E., Atkins, C., Hofstetter, C. R., & Kreitner, S. (1994). Family influences on Latino and Anglo adolescents' sexual behavior. *Journal of Marriage & the Family, 56,* 973–986.

Howe, D., & Fearnley, S. (2003). Disorders of attachment in adopted and fostered children: Recognition and treatment. *Clinical Child Psychology & Psychiatry, 8,* 369–387.

Howes, C. (1983). Patterns of friendship. *Child Development, 54,* 1041–1053.

Howes, C. (1987). Social competence with peers in young children: Developmental sequences. *Developmental Review, 7,* 252–272.

Howes, C., & Matheson, C. C. (1992). Sequences in the development of competent play with peers: Social and pretend play. *Developmental Psychology, 28,* 961–974.

Hoyert, D., Heron, M., Murphy, S., & Kung, H. (2006). Deaths: Final data for 2003. *National Vital Statistics Reports, 54,* 1–120.

Hoyert, D. L., & Seltzer, M. M. (1992). Factors related to the well-being and life activities of family caregivers. *Family Relations, 41,* 74–81.

Hu, F., Li, T., Colditz, G., Willet, W., & Manson, J. (2003). Television watching and other sedentary behavior in relation to risk of obesity and type 2 diabetes mellitus in women. *Journal of the American Medical Association, 289,* 1785–1791.

Huang, H., & Hanley, J. (1997). A longitudinal study of phonological awareness, visual skills, and Chinese reading acquisition among first-graders in Taiwan. *International Journal of Behavioral Development, 20,* 249–268.

Hubel, D. H., & Weisel, T. N. (1963). Receptive fields of cells in striate cortex of very young, visually inexperienced kittens. *Journal of Neurophysiology, 26,* 994–1002.

Hudziak, J., van Beijsterveldt, C., Bartels, M., Rietveld, M., Rettew, D., Derks, E., & Boomsma, D. (2003). Individual differences in aggression: Genetic analyses by age, gender, and informant in 3-, 7-, and 10-year-old Dutch twins. *Behavior Genetics, 33,* 575–589.

Huesmann, L. R., Moise, J., Podolski, C. P., & Eron, L. D. (2003). Longitudinal relations between childhood exposure to media violence and adult aggression and violence 1977–1982. *Developmental Psychology, 39(2),* 201–221.

Hughes, S., & Hayman, L. (2007). Cardiovascular risk reduction: The fountain of youth. *Journal of Cardiovascular Nursing, 22,* 84–85.

Hulley, S., Furberg, C., Barrett-Connor, E., Cauley, J., Grady, D., Haskell, W., Knopp, R., Lowery, M., Satterfield, S., Schrott, H., Vittinghoff, E., & Hunninghake, D. (2002). Noncardiovascular disease outcomes during 6.8 years of hormone therapy: Heart and estrogen/progestin replacement study follow-up (HERS II). *Journal of the American Medical Association, 288,* 58–64.

Hultsch, D., Hertzog, C., Small, B., & Dixon, R. (1999). Use it or lose it: Engaged lifestyle as a buffer of cognitive decline in aging? *Psychology & Aging, 14,* 245–263.

Hultsch, D. F., Hertzog, C., Small, B. J., McDonald-Miszczak, L., & Dixon, R. A. (1992). Short-term longitudinal change in cognitive performance in later life. *Psychology & Aging, 7,* 571–584.

Humphrey, N., Curran, A., Morris, E., Farrell, P., & Woods, K. (2007). Emotional intelligence and education: A critical review. *Educational Psychology, 27,* 235–254.

Hunfeld, J., Tempels, A., Passchier, J., Hazebroek, F., et al. (1999). Parental burden and grief one year after the birth of a child with a congenital anomaly. *Journal of Pediatric Psychology, 24,* 515–520.

Hurwitz, E., Gunn, W. J., Pinsky, P. F., & Schonberger, L. B. (1991). Risk of respiratory illness associated with day-care attendance: A nationwide study. *Pediatrics, 87,* 62–69.

Husaini, B., Blasi, A., & Miller, O. (1999). Does public and private religiosity have a moderating effect on depression? A bi-racial study of elders in the American South. *International Journal of Aging & Human Development, 48,* 63–72.

Huston, A. C., & Wright, J. C. (1998). Mass media and children's development. In W. Damon (Ed.), *Handbook of Child Psychology*: Vol. 4. Child Psychology in Practice (5th ed., pp. 999–1058). New York: John Wiley & Sons.

Huth-Bocks, A., Levendosky, A., Bogat, G., & von Eye, A. (2004). The impact of maternal characteristics and contextual variables on infant-mother attachment. *Child Development, 75,* 480–496.

Hutt, S. J., Lenard, H. G., & Prechtl, H. F. R. (1969). Psychophysiological studies in newborn infants. In L. P. Lipsitt & H. W. Reese (Eds.), *Advances in child development and behavior, Vol. 4* (pp. 128–173). New York: Academic Press.

Huttenlocher, J. (1995, April). *Children's language in relation to input.* Paper presented at the biennial meetings of the Society for Research in Child Development, Indianapolis, IN.

Iaquinta, A. (2006). Guided reading: A research-based response to the challenges of early reading instruction. *Early Childhood Education Journal, 33,* 1573–1707.

Idler, E., & Kasl, S. (1997a). Religion among disabled and nondisabled persons I: Cross-sectional patterns in health practices, social activities, and well-being. *Journals of Gerontology, Series B: Psychological Sciences & Social Sciences, 52B,* S294–S305.

Idler, E., & Kasl, S. (1997b). Religion among disabled and nondisabled persons II: Attendance at religious services as a predictor of the course of disability. *Journals of Gerontology, Series B: Psychological Sciences & Social Sciences, 52B,* S306–S316.

Iecovich, E., & Lankri, M. (2002). Title attitudes of elderly persons towards receiving financial support from adult children. *Journal of Aging Studies, 16,* 121–133.

Ingersoll-Dayton, B., Neal, M., Ha, J., & Hammer, L. (2003). Collaboration among siblings providing care for older parents. *Journal of Gerontological Social Work, 40,* 51–66.

Ingoldsby, E., Shaw, D., Owens, E., & Winslow, E. (1999). A longitudinal study of interparental conflict, emotional and behavioral reactivity, and preschoolers' adjustment problems among low-income families. *Journal of Abnormal Child Psychology, 27,* 343–356.

Ingram, D. (1981). Early patterns of grammatical development. In R. E. Stark (Ed.), *Language behavior in infancy and early childhood* (pp. 327–358). New York: Elsevier North-Holland.

Ingrassia, M. (1993, August 2). Daughters of Murphy Brown. *Newsweek,* 58–59.

Irwin, M., & Pike, J. (1993). Bereavement, depressive symptoms, and immune function. In M. S. Stroebe, W. Stroebe, & R. O. Hansson (Eds.), *Handbook of bereavement: Theory, research, and intervention* (pp. 160–171). Cambridge, England: Cambridge University Press.

Isaacowitz, D., Löckenhoff, C., Lane, R., Wright, R., Sechrest, L., Riedel, R., & Costa, P. (2007). Age differences in recognition of emotion in lexical stimuli and facial expressions. *Psychology and Aging, 22,* 147–159.

Isabella, R. A. (1995). The origins of infant-mother attachment: Maternal behavior and infant development. *Annals of Child Development, 10,* 57–81.

Isaksson, K., Johansson, G., Bellaagh, K., & Sjöberg, A. (2004). Work values among the unemployed: Changes over time and some gender differences. *Scandinavian Journal of Psychology, 45,* 207–214.

Itier, R., & Taylor, M. (2004). Face inversion and contrast-reversal effects across development: In contrast to the expertise theory. *Developmental Science, 7,* 246–260.

Iversen, L., & Sabroe, S. (1988). Psychological well-being among unemployed and employed people after a company closedown: A longitudinal study. *Journal of Social Issues, 44,* 141–152.

Ivy, G. O., MacLeod, C. M., Petit, T. L., & Marcus, E. J. (1992). A physiological framework for perceptual and cognitive changes in aging. In F. I. M. Craik & T. A. Salthouse (Eds.), *The handbook of aging and cognition* (pp. 273–314). Hillsdale, NJ: Erlbaum.

Iwashyna, T., & Christakis, N. (2003). Marriage, widowhood, and health-care use. *Social Science & Medicine, 57,* 2137–2147.

Izard, C. E., & Harris, P. (1995). Emotional development and developmental psychopathology. In D. Cicchetti & D. J. Cohen (Eds.), *Developmental psychopathology, Vol. 1: Theory and methods* (pp. 467–503). New York: Wiley.

Izard, C. E., Fantauzzo, C. A., Castle, J. M., Haynes, O. M., Rayias, M. F., & Putnam, P. H. (1995). The ontogeny and significance of infants' facial expressions in the first 9 months of life. *Developmental Psychology, 31,* 997–1013.

Jackson, D., & Mannix, J. (2004). Giving voice to the burden of blame: A feminist study of mothers' experiences of mother blaming. *International Journal of Nursing Practice, 10,* 150–158.

Jackson, D., & Tein, J. (1998). Adolescents' conceptualization of adult roles: Relationships with age, gender, work goal, and maternal employment. *Sex Roles, 38,* 987–1008.

Jackson, L., & Bracken, B. (1998). Relationship between students' social status and global and domain-specific self-concepts. *Journal of School Psychology, 36,* 233–246.

Jacobs, J., Chin, C., & Bleeker, M. (2006). Enduring links: Parents' expectations and their young adult children's gender-typed occupational choices. *Educational Research and Evaluation, 12,* 395–407.

Jacobs, S. C., Kosten, T. R., Kasl, S. V., Ostfeld, A. M., Berkman, L., & Charpentier, P. (1987/1988). Attachment theory and multiple dimensions of grief. *Omega, 18,* 41–52.

Jacobsen, T., & Hofmann, V. (1997). Children's attachment representations: Longitudinal relations to school behavior, and academic competency in middle childhood and adolescence. *Developmental Psychology, 33*, 703–710.

Jacobsen, T., Husa, M., Fendrich, M., Kruesi, M., & Ziegenhain, U. (1997). Children's ability to delay gratification: Longitudinal relations to mother-child attachment. *Journal of Genetic Psychology, 158*, 411–426.

Jacoby, S. (2000, July/August). The fine art of grandparenting. *AARP Bulletin, 413*, 23.

Jadack, R. A., Hyde, J. S., Moore, C. F., & Keller, M. L. (1995). Moral reasoning about sexually transmitted diseases. *Child Development, 66*, 167–177.

Jaglal, S., Weller, I., Mamdani, M., Hawker, G., Kreder, H., Jaakkimainen, L., & Adachi, J. (2005) Population trends in BMD testing, treatment, and hip and wrist fracture rates: Are the hip fracture projections wrong? *Journal of Bone and Mineral Research, 20*, 898–905.

Jahnke, H. C., & Blanchard-Fields, F. (1993). A test of two models of adolescent egocentrism. *Journal of Youth & Adolescence, 22*, 313–326.

Jambunathan, S., & Burts, D. (2003). Comparison of perception of self-competence among five ethnic groups of preschoolers in the U.S. *Early Childhood Education, 173*, 651–660.

James, S. A., Keenan, N. L., & Browning, S. (1992). Socioeconomic status, health behaviors, and health status among blacks. In K. W. Schaie, D. Blazer, & J. M. House (Eds.), *Aging, health behaviors, and health outcomes* (pp. 39–57). Hillsdale, NJ: Erlbaum.

Janosz, M., Le Blanc, M., Boulerice, B., & Tremblay, R. (2000). Predicting different types of school dropouts: A typological approach with two longitudinal samples. *Journal of Educational Psychology, 92*, 171–190.

Jansz, J., & Martens, L. (2005). Gaming at a LAN event: The social context of playing video games. *New Media & Society, 7*, 333–355.

Jarolmen, J. (1998). A comparison of the grief reaction of children and adults: Focusing on pet loss and bereavement. *Omega, 37*, 133–150.

Javo, C., Ronning, J., Heyerdahl, S., & Rudmin, F. (2004). Parenting correlates of child behavior problems in a multiethnic community sample of preschool children in northern Norway. *European Child & Adolescent Psychiatry, 13*, 8–18.

Jendrek, M. (1993). Grandparents who parent their grandchildren: Effects on lifestyle. *Journal of Marriage & the Family, 55*, 609–621.

Jenkins, J. & Buccioni, J. (2000). Children's understanding of marital conflict and the marital relationship. *Journal of Child Psychology & Psychiatry & Allied Disciplines, 41*, 161–168.

Jenkins, J. M., & Astington, J. W. (1996). Cognitive factors and family structure associated with theory of mind development in young children. *Developmental Psychology, 32*, 70–78.

Jenkins, L., Myerson, J., Hale, S., & Fry, A. (1999). Individual and developmental differences in working memory across the life span. *Psychonomic Bulletin & Review, 6*, 28–40.

Jensen, A., & Whang, P. (1994). Speed of accessing arithmetic facts in long-term memory: A comparison of Chinese-American and Anglo-American children. *Contemporary Educational Psychology, 19*, 1–12.

Jerrome, D. (1990). Intimate relationships. In J. Bond & P. Coleman (Eds.), *Aging in society* (pp. 181–208). London: Sage.

Jessor, R. (1992). Risk behavior in adolescence: A psychosocial framework for understanding and action. *Developmental Review, 12*, 374–390.

Jette, A. M. (1996). Disability trends and transitions. In R. H. Binstock & L. K. George (Eds.), *Handbook of aging and the social sciences* (4th ed., pp. 94–116). San Diego, CA: Academic Press.

Jeynes, W. (2007). The impact of parental remarriage on children: A meta-analysis. *Marriage & Family Review, 40*, 75–102.

Jimerson, S. (1999). On the failure of failure: Examining the association between early grade retention and educational and employment outcomes during late adolescence. *Journal of School Psychology, 37*, 243–272.

Jin, Y., Jing, J., Morinaga, R., Miki, K., Su, X., & Chen, X. (2002). A comparative study of theory of mind in Chinese and Japanese children. *Chinese Mental Health Journal, 16*, 446–448.

Jirtle, R., & Weidman, J. (2007). Imprinted and more equal. *American Scientist, 95*, 143–149.

Johansson, B., Hofer, S., Allaire, J., Maldonado-Molina, M., Piccinin, A., Berg, S., Pedersen, N., & McClearn, G. (2004). Change in cognitive capabilities in the oldest old: The effects of proximity to death in genetically related individuals over a 6-year period. *Psychology & Aging, 19*, 145–156.

Johnson, C. L., & Barer, B. M. (1990). Families and networks among older inner-city blacks. *The Gerontologist, 30*, 726–733.

Johnson, E., & Breslau, N. (2000). Increased risk of learning disabilities in low birth weight boys at age 11 years. *Biological Psychiatry, 47*, 490–500.

Johnson, H., Nusbaum, B., Bejarano, A., & Rosen, T. (1999). An ecological approach to development in children with prenatal drug exposure. *American Journal of Orthopsychiatry, 69*, 448–456.

Johnson, J., Vogt, B., Kim, R., Cotman, C., & Head, E. (2004). Isolated executive impairment and associated frontal neuropathology. *Dementia & Geriatric Cognitive Disorders, 17*, 360–367.

Johnson, M. (2003). Development of human brain functions. *Biological Psychiatry, 54*, 1312–1316.

Johnson, T., & Dye, J. (2005). *Indicators of marriage and fertility in the United States from the American Community Survey: 2000 to 2003.* Retrieved July 5, 2007 from www.census.gov/population/www/socdemo/fertility/mar-fert-slides.html.

Johnston, L., O'Malley, Bachman, J., & Schulenberg, J. (2007). *Monitoring the Future: National results on adolescent drug use: Overview of key findings.* (NIH Publication No. 07-6202). Retrieved June 22, 2007 from http://monitoringthefuture.org/pubs/monographs/overview2006.pdf

Jones, C. (November 5, 2004). Issues: 11 states nix gay marriage. Retrieved July 8, 2007 from http://www.usatoday.com/news/politicselections/vote2004/initiative.htm.

Jones, M., & Wheatley J. (1990). Gender differences in teacher-student interactions in science classrooms. *Journal of Research in Science Teaching, 27*, 861–874.

Jones, M. C. (1924). A laboratory study of fear: The case of Peter. *Pedagogical Seminary, 31*, 308–315.

Jones, S., & Zigler, E. (2002). The Mozart effect: Not learning from history. *Journal of Applied Developmental Psychology, 23*, 355–372.

Jorgensen, G. (2006). Kohlberg and Gilligan: Duet or duel? *Journal of Moral Education, 35*, 179–196.

Jorgenson, S. (1993). Adolescent pregnancy and parenting. In T. Gullotta, G. Adams, & R. Montemayor (Eds.), *Adolescent sexuality* (pp. 103–140). Thousand Oaks, CA: Sage Publications.

Jorm, A., Christensen, H., Henderson, A., Jacomb, P., Korten, A., & Mackinnon, A. (1998). Factors associated with successful aging. *Journal of Aging, 17*, 33–37.

Jose, O., & Alfons, V. (2007). Do demographics affect marital satisfaction? *Journal of Sex & Marital Therapy, 33*, 73–85.

Joseph, K., Young, D., Dodds, L., O'Connell, C., Allen, V., Chandra, S., & Allen, A. (2003). Changes in maternal characteristics and obstetric practice and recent increases in primary cesarean delivery. *Obstetrics and Gynecology, 102*, 791–800.

Joseph, R. (2000). Fetal brain behavior and cognitive development. *Developmental Review, 20*, 81–98.

Joshi, M. S., & MacLean, M. (1994). Indian and English children's understanding of the distinction between real and apparent emotion. *Child Development, 65*, 1372–1384.

Josse, D., Thibault, H., Bourdais, C., Mirailles, P., Pireyre, E., Surgal, L., Gerboin-Reyrolles, P., & Chauliac, M. (1999). Iron deficiency and psychomotor development in young children in a child health centre: Assessment with a revised version of the Brunet-Lezine scale. *Approche Neuropsychologique des Apprentissages chez l'Enfant, 11*, 21–27.

Joung, I. M. A., Stronks, K., van de Mheen, H., & Mackenbach, J. P. (1995). Health behaviours explain part of the differences in self reported health associated with partner/marital status in The Netherlands. *Journal of Epidemiology & Community Health, 49*, 482–488.

Juan, E., Blascao, T., Font, A., Doval, E., Sanz, A., Maroto, P., & Pallares, C. (2003). Perception of control and survival in patients with advanced lung cancer referred for palliative treatment. *Ansiedad y Estres, 9*, 1–5.

Judge, T., Bono, J., & Locke, E. (2000). Personality and job satisfaction: The mediating role of job characteristics. *Journal of Applied Psychology, 85*, 237–249.

Judson, T., & Nishimori, T. (2005). Concepts and skills in high school calculus: An examination of a special case in Japan and the United States. *Journal for Research in Mathematics, 36*, 24–43.

Juffer, F., Hoksbergen, R., Riksen-Walraven, J., & Kohnstamm, G. (1997). Early intervention in adoptive families: Supporting maternal sensitive responsiveness, infant-mother attachment, and infant competence. *Journal of Child Psychology & Psychiatry & Allied Disciplines, 38*, 1039–1050.

Juffer, F., & Rosenboom, L., (1997). Infant mother attachment of internationally adopted children in the Netherlands. *International Journal of Behavioral Development, 20*, 93–107.

Jusczyk, P., & Hohne, E. (1997). Infants' memory for spoken words. *Science, 277*.

Jusczyk, P., Houston, D., & Newsome, M. (1999). The beginnings of word segmentation in English-learning infants. *Cognitive Psychology, 39*, 159–207.

Jussim, L., & Eccles, J. (1992). Teacher expectations II: Construction and reflection of student achievement. *Journal of Personality & Social Psychology, 63*, 947–961.

Jutras, S., & Lavoie, J. (1995). Living with an impaired elderly person: The informal caregiver's physical and mental health. *Journal of Aging & Health, 7*, 46–73.

Kafetsios, K. (2007). Work-family conflict and its relationship with job satisfaction and psychological distress: The role of affect at work and gender. *Hellenic Journal of Psychology, 4*, 15–35.

Kagan, J. (1994). *Galen's prophecy.* New York: Basic Books.

Kagan, J., & Herschkowitz, N. (2005). *A young mind in a growing brain.* Hillsdale, NJ: Lawrence Erlbaum.

Kagan, J., Snidman, N., & Arcus, D. (1993). On the temperamental categories of inhibited and uninhibited children. In K. H. Rubin & J. B. Asendorpf (Eds.), *Social withdrawal, inhibition, and shyness in childhood* (pp. 19–28). Hillsdale, NJ: Erlbaum.

Kahana-Kalman, R., & Walker-Andrews, A. (2001). The role of person familiarity in young infants' perception of emotional expressions. *Child Development, 72*, 352–369.

Kail, R. (1990). *The development of memory in children* (3rd ed.). New York: Freeman.

Kail, R. (1991). Processing time declines exponentially during childhood and adolescence. *Developmental Psychology, 27*, 259–266.

Kail, R. (1997). Processing time, imagery, and spatial memory. *Journal of Experimental Child Psychology, 64*, 67–78.

Kail, R., & Hall, L. (1999). Sources of developmental change in children's word-problem performance. *Journal of Educational Psychology, 91*, 660–668.

Kail, R., & Hall, L. K. (1994). Processing speed, naming speed, and reading. *Developmental Psychology, 30*, 949–954.

Kaiser Family Foundation. (2000). *The Family Circle/Kaiser Family Foundation Survey on Health Care and Other Elder Care Issues.* Retrieved July 9, 2007 from www.kff.org/mediapartnerships/loader.cfm?url=/commonspot/security/getfile.cfm&PageID=13426.

Kales, H., Blow, F., Bingham, R., Copeland, L. & Mellow, A. (2000, June). Race and inpatient psychiatric diagnoses among elderly veterans. *Psychiatric Services Journal, 51*, 795–800.

Kalish, R. A. (1985). The social context of death and dying. In R. H. Binstock & E. Shanas (Eds.), *Handbook of aging and the social sciences* (2nd ed., pp. 149–170). New York: Van Nostrand Reinhold.

Kalish, R. A., & Reynolds, D. K. (1976). *Death and ethnicity: A psychocultural study.* Los Angeles: University of Southern California Press (reprinted 1981, Baywood Publishing Co, Farmingdale, NJ).

Kallman, D. A., Plato, C. C., & Tobin, J. D. (1990). The role of muscle loss in the age-related decline of grip strength: Cross-sectional and longitudinal perspectives. *Journals of Gerontology: Medical Sciences, 45*, M82–88.

Kalmijn, M. (2003). Shared friendship networks and the life course: An analysis of survey data on married and cohabiting couples. *Social Networks, 25*, 231–249.

Kalmuss, D. (2004). Nonviolational sex and sexual health. *Archives of Sexual Behavior, 33*, 197–209.

Kane, C. (1998). Differences in family of origin perceptions among African American, Asian American and Hispanic American college students. *Journal of Black Studies, 29*, 93–105.

Kane, R. L., Klein, S. J., Bernstein, L., Rothenberg, R., & Wales, J. (1985). Hospice role in alleviating the emotional stress of terminal patients and their families. *Medical Care, 23*, 189–197.

Kane, R. L., Wales, J., Bernstein, L., Leibowitz, A., & Kaplan, S. (1984). A randomized controlled trial of hospice care. *Lancet*, 890–894.

Kane, T., Staiger, P., & Ricciardelli, L. (2000). Male domestic violence: Attitudes, aggression and interpersonal dependency. *Journal of Interpersonal Violence, 15*, 16–29.

Kannel, W. B., & Gordon, T. (1980). Cardiovascular risk factors in the aged: The Framingham study. In S. G. Haynes & M. Feinleib (Eds.), *Second conference on the epidemiology of aging*, U.S. Department of Health and Human Services NIH Publication No. 80–969 (pp. 65–89). Washington, DC: U.S. Government Printing Office.

Kaplan, G. A. (1992). Health and aging in the Alameda County study. In K. W. Schaie, D. Blazer, & J. M. House (Eds.), *Aging, health behaviors, and health outcomes* (pp. 69–88). Hillsdale, NJ: Erlbaum.

Kaplan, H., & Sadock, B. (1991). *Synopsis of psychiatry* (6th ed.). Baltimore, MD: Williams & Wilkins.

Kaplan, P., Bachorowski, J., Smoski, M., & Zinser, M. (2001). Role of clinical diagnosis and medication use in effects of maternal depression on infant-directed speech. *Infancy, 2*, 537–548.

Kaplan, R. M. (1985). The controversy related to the use of psychological tests. In B. B. Wolman (Ed.), *Handbook of intelligence: Theories, measurements, and applications* (pp. 465–504). New York: Wiley.

Kaplowitz, P., & Oberfield, S. (1999). Reexamination of the age limit for defining when puberty is precocious in girls in the United States: Implications for evaluation and treatment. *Pediatrics, 104*, 936–941.

Karmiloff-Smith, A. (1991). Beyond modularity: Innate constraints and developmental change. In S. Carey & R. Gelman (Eds.), *The epigenesis of mind: Essays on biology and cognition* (pp. 171–197). Hillsdale, NJ: Erlbaum.

Kasen, S., Chen, H., Sneed, J., Crawford, T., & Cohen, P. (2006). Social role and birth cohort influences on gender-linked personality traits in women: A 20-year longitudinal analysis. *Journal of Personality and Social Psychology, 91*, 944–958.

Kaslow, F. (2004). Death of one's partner: The anticipation and the reality. *Professional Psychology: Research & Practice, 35*, 227–233.

Katz, P., & Bartone, P. (1998). Mourning, ritual and recovery after an airline tragedy. *Omega, 36*, 193–200.

Katz, P. A., & Ksansnak, K. R. (1994). Developmental aspects of gender role flexibility and traditionality in middle childhood and adolescence. *Developmental Psychology, 30*, 272–282.

Katz, R., & Wertz, R. (1997). The efficacy of computer-provided reading treatment for chronic aphasic adults. *Journal of Speech & Hearing Research, 40*, 493–507.

Kaufman, G., & Elder, G. (2003). Grandparenting and age identity. *Journal of Aging Studies, 17*, 269–282.

Kaufman, M. (1997). The teratogenic effects of alcohol following exposure during pregnancy, and its influence on the chromosome constitution of the pre-ovulatory egg. *Alcohol & Alcoholism, 32*, 113–128.

Keech, R. (2002). Ophthalmology. In A. Rudolph, R. Kamei, & K. Overby (Eds.), *Rudolph's fundamental of pediatrics* (3rd ed., pp. 847–862). New York: McGraw-Hill.

Keefe, S. E. (1984). Real and ideal extended familism among Mexican Americans and Anglo Americans: On the meaning of "close" family ties. *Human Organization, 43*, 65–70.

Keen, R. (2003). Representation of objects and events: Why do infants look so smart and toddlers look so dumb? *Current Directions in Psychological Science, 12*, 79–83.

Keene, J., Hope, T., Rogers, P., & Elliman, N. (1998). An investigation of satiety in ageing, dementia, and hyperphagia. *International Journal of Eating Disorders, 23*, 409–418.

Keith, P. M. (1981/1982). Perception of time remaining and distance from death. *Omega, 12*, 307–318.

Kellehear, A., & Lewin, T. (1988/1989). Farewells by the dying: A sociological study. *Omega, 19*, 275–292.

Kelleher, C., Friel, S., Gabhainn, S., & Tay, J. (2003). Socio-demographic predictors of self-rated health in the Republic of Ireland: Findings from the National Survey on Lifestyle, Attitudes, and Nutrition, SLAN. *Social Science & Medicine, 57*, 477–486.

Keller, S., Maddock, J., Laforge, R., Velicer, W., & Basler, H. (2007). Binge drinking and health behavior in medical students. *Addictive Behaviors, 32*, 505–515.

Kemmelmeier, M., Wieczorkowska, G., Erb, H., & Burnstein, E. (2002). Individualism, authoritarianism, and attitudes toward assisted death: Cross-cultural, cross-regional, and experimental evidence. *Journal of Applied Social Psychology, 32*, 60–85.

Kendall-Tackett, K., Williams, L., & Finkelhor, D. (1993). Impact of sexual abuse on children: A review and synthesis of recent empirical studies. *Psychological Bulletin, 113*, 164–180.

Kendler, K., Kessler, R., Walters, E., MacLean, C., Neale, M., Health, A., & Eaves, L. (1995). Stressful life events, genetic liability, and onset of an episode of major depression in women. *American Journal of Psychiatry, 152*, 833–842.

Kendler, K., Thornton, L., Gilman, S., & Kessler, R. (2000). Sexual orientation in a U.S. national sample of twin and nontwin sibling pairs. *American Journal of Psychiatry, 157*, 1843–1846.

Kensinger, E., Clarke, R., & Corkin, S. (2003). What neural correlates underlie successful encoding and retrieval? A functional magnetic resonance imaging study using a divided attention paradigm. *Journal of Neuroscience, 23*, 2407–2415.

Kent, L., Doerry, U., Hardy, E., Parmar, R., Gingell, K., Hawai, Z., Kirley, A., Lowe, N., Fitzgerald, M., Gill, M., & Craddock, N. (2002). Evidence that variation at the serotonin transporter gene influences susceptibility to attention deficit hyperactivity disorder (ADHD): Analysis and pooled analysis. *Molecular Psychiatry, 7*, 908–912.

Kercsmar, C. (1998). The respiratory system. In R. Behrman & R. Kliegman (Eds.), *Nelson essentials of pediatrics* (3rd ed). Philadelphia: W. B. Saunders.

Kerns, K., Don, A., Mateer, C., & Streissguth, A. (1997). Cognitive deficits in nonretarded adults with fetal alcohol syndrome. *Journal of Learning Disabilities, 30*, 685–693.

Kerr, C., McDowell, B., & McDonough, S. (2007). The relationship between gross motor function and participation restriction in children with cerebral palsy: An exploratory analysis. *Child: Care, Health and Development, 33*, 22–27.

Keskinen, E., Ota, H., & Katila, A. (1998). Older drivers fail in intersections: Speed discrepancies between older and younger male drivers. *Accident Analysis & Prevention, 30*, 323–330.

Kessler, R., Berglund, P., Demler, O., Jin, R., Merikangas, K., & Walters, E. (2005). Lifetime prevalence and age-of-onset distributions of *DSM-IV* disorders in the national comorbidity survey replication. *Archives of General Psychiatry, 62*, 593–602.

Kessler, R., McGonagle, K., Zhao, S., Nelson, C., Hughes, M., Eshleman, S., Wittchen, H., & Kendler, K. (1994). Lifetime and 12-month prevalence of DSM-III-R psychiatric disorders in the United States: Results from the National Comorbidity Survey. *American Journal of Psychiatry, 51*, 8–19.

Khan, M. (2007). *Emotional and behavioral effects, including addictive potential, of video games: Report of the AMA Council on Science and Public Health.* Retrieved June 28, 2007 from http://www.ama-assn.org/ama1/pub/upload/mm/467/csaph12a07.doc

Khanna, G., & Kapoor, S. (2004). Secular trend in stature and age at menarche among Punjabi Aroras residing in New Delhi, India. *Collegium Antropologicum, 28*, 571–575.

Khlat, M., Sermet, C., & Le Pape, A. (2000). Women's health in relation with their family and work roles: France in the early 1990s. *Social Science & Medicine, 50*, 1807–1825.

Kiecolt-Glaser, J. (2000, August). *Friends, lovers, relaxation, and immunity: How behavior modifies health. Cortisol and the language of love: Text analysis of newlyweds' relationship stories.* Paper presented at the annual meeting of the American Psychological Association. Washington, DC.

Kiecolt-Glaser, J. K., & Glaser, R. (1995). Measurement of immune response. In S. Cohen, R. C. Kessler, & L. U. Gordon (Eds.), *Measuring stress: A guide for health and social scientists* (pp. 213–229). New York: Oxford University Press.

Kiecolt-Glaser, J. K., Glaser, R., Suttleworth, E. E., Dyer, C. S., Ogrocki, F., & Speicher, C. E. (1987). Chronic stress and immunity in family caregivers of Alzheimer's disease patients. *Psychosomatic Medicine, 49*, 523–535.

Kikhavani, S., & Kumar, S. (2005). Life events, coping resources, and depression. *Psychological Studies, 50*, 298–302.

Kilbride, H., Castor, C., Hoffman, E., & Fuger, K. (2000). Thirty-six month outcome of prenatal cocaine exposure for term or near-term infants: Impact of early case management. *Journal of Developmental Pediatrics, 21*, 19–26.

Kilic, C., & Ulusoy, M. (2003). Psychological effects of the November 1999 earthquake in Turkey: An epidemiological study. *Psychiatrica Scandinavica, 108*, 232–238.

Kilpatrick, S. J., & Laros, R. K. (1989). Characteristics of normal labor. *Obstetrics & Gynecology, 74*, 85–87.

Kim, S. (1997). Relationships between young children's day care experience and their attachment relationships with parents and socioemotional behavior problems. *Korean Journal of Child Studies, 18*, 5–18.

Kimm, S., Glynn, N., Kriska, A., Barton, B., Kronsberg, S., Daniels, S., Crawford, P., Sabry, A., & Liu, K. (2002). Decline in physical activity in black girls and white girls during adolescence. *New England Journal of Medicine, 347*, 709–715.

Kinzl, J., Mangweth, B., Traweger, C., & Biebl, W. (1996). Sexual dysfunction in males: Significance of adverse childhood experiences. *Child Abuse & Neglect, 20*, 759–766.

Kirby, P., Biever, J., Martinez, I., & Gomez, J. (2004). Adults returning to school: The impact on family and work. *Journal of Psychology: Interdisciplinary & Applied, 138*, 65–76.

Kirk, S., Gallagher, J., & Anastasiow, N. (1993). *Educating exceptional children* (7th ed.). Boston: Houghton Mifflin.

Kitson, G. C. (1992). *Portrait of divorce: Adjustment to marital breakdown.* New York: Guilford Press.

Kitzan, L., Ferraro, F., Petros, T., & Ludorf, M. (1999). The role of vocabulary ability during visual word recognition in younger and older adults. *Journal of General Psychology, 126*, 6–16.

Klahr, D. (1992). Information-processing approaches to cognitive development. In M. H. Bernstein & M. E. Lamb (Eds.), *Developmental psychology: An advanced textbook* (3rd ed., pp. 273–335). Hillsdale, NJ: Erlbaum.

Kleemeier, R. W. (1962). Intellectual changes in the senium. *Proceedings of the Social Statistics Section of the American Statistics Association, 1*, 290–295.

Klein, A., & Swartz, S. (1996). *Reading Recovery in California: Program overview.* San Francisco: San Francisco Unified School District.

Klenow, D. J., & Bolin, R. C. (1989/1990). Belief in an afterlife: A national survey. *Omega, 20*, 63–74.

Kletzky, O. A., & Borenstein, R. (1987). Vasomotor instability of the menopause. In D. R. Mishell, Jr. (Ed.), *Menopause: Physiology and pharmacology.* (pp. 53–66). Chicago: Year Book Medical Publishers.

Kliegl, R., Smith, J., & Baltes, P. B. (1989). Testing-the-limits and the study of adult age differences in cognitive plasticity of a mnemonic skill. *Developmental Psychology, 25*, 247–256.

Kliegl, R., Smith, J., & Baltes, P. B. (1990). On the locus and process of magnification of age differences during mnemonic training. *Developmental Psychology, 26*, 894–904.

Kliegman, R. (1998). Fetal and neonatal medicine. In R. Behrman & R. Kliegman (Eds.), *Nelson essentials of pediatrics* (3rd ed., pp. 167–225). Philadelphia: W. B. Saunders.

Kline, D. W., & Scialfa, C. T. (1996). Visual and auditory aging. In J. E. Birren & K. W. Schaie (Eds.), *Handbook of the psychology of aging* (4th ed., pp. 181–203). San Diego, CA: Academic Press.

Kline, D. W., Kline, T. J. B., Fozard, J. L., Kosnik, W., Schieber, F., & Sekuler, R. (1992). Vision, aging, and driving: The problem of older drivers. *Journals of Gerontology: Psychological Sciences, 47*, P27–34.

Kline, G., Stanley, S., Markman, H., & Olmos-Gallo, P. (2004). Timing is everything: Pre-engagement cohabitation and increased risk for poor marital outcomes. *Journal of Family Psychology, 18*, 311–318.

Klomsten, A., Skaalvik, E., & Espnes, G. (2004). Physical self-concept and sports: Do gender differences still exist? *Sex Roles: A Journal of Research, 50*, 119–127.

Knox, D., Zusman, M., McGinty, K., & Abowitz, D. (2003). Weddings: Some data on college student perceptions. *College Student Journal, 37*, 197–200.

Kochanek, K., & Martin, J. (2004). *Supplemental analyses of recent trends in infant mortality.* Retrieved April 13, 2004, from http://www.cdc.gov.

Kochanek, K., & Smith, B. (2004). Deaths: Preliminary data for 2002. *National Vital Statistics Report: Volume 52.* Hyattsville, Maryland: National Center for Health Statistics. Retrieved April 13, 2004, from http://www.cdc.gov.

Kochanska, G. (1997a). Multiple pathways to conscience for children with different temperaments: From toddlerhood to age 5. *Developmental Psychology, 33*, 228–240.

Kochanska, G. (1997b). Mutually responsive orientation between mothers and their young: Implications for early socialization. *Child Development, 68*, 94–112.

Kochanska, G., Casey, R., & Fukumoto, A. (1995). Toddlers' sensitivity to standard violations. *Child Development, 66*, 643–656.

Kochanska, G., Murray, K., & Coy, K. (1997). Inhibitory control as a contributor to conscience in childhood: From toddler to early school age. *Child Development, 68*, 263–277.

Kochanska, G., Murray, K., Jacques, T., Koenig, A., Vandegeest, K. (1996). Inhibitory control in young children and its role in emerging internalization. *Child Development, 67*, 490–507.

Koenen, K., Moffitt, T., Poulton, R., Martin, J., & Caspi, A. (2007). Early childhood factors associated with the development of post-traumatic stress disorder: Results from a longitudinal birth cohort. *Psychological Medicine, 37*, 181–192.

Koenig, H. (2007). Religion and depression in older medical inpatients. *American Journal of Geriatric Psychiatry, 15*, 282–291.

Koenig, H., George, L., Hays, J., Larson, D., Cohen, H., & Blazer, D. (1998). The relationship between religious activities and blood pressure in older adults. *International Journal of Psychiatry in Medicine, 28*, 189–213.

Koerner, S., & Kenyon, D. (2007). Understanding "Good Days" and "Bad Days": Emotional and physical reactivity among caregivers for elder relatives. *Family Relations, 56*, 1–11.

Kohlberg, L. (1966). A cognitive-developmental analysis of children's sex-role concepts and attitudes. In E. E. Maccoby (Ed.), *The development of sex differences* (pp. 82–172). Stanford, CA: Stanford University Press.

Kohlberg, L. (1976). Moral stages and moralization: The cognitive developmental approach. In T. Lickona (Ed.), *Moral development and behavior: Theory, research, and social issues* (pp. 31–53). New York: Holt.

Kohlberg, L. (1981). *Essays on moral development, Vol. 1: The philosophy of moral development.* New York: Harper & Row.

Kohlberg, L., & Elfenbein, D. (1975). The development of moral judgments concerning capital punishment. *American Journal of Orthopsychiatry, 54*, 614–640.

Kohlberg, L., & Ullian, D. Z. (1974). Stages in the development of psychosexual concepts and attitudes. In R. C. Friedman, R. M. Richart, & R. L. Vande Wiele (Eds.), *Sex differences in behavior* (pp. 209–222). New York: Wiley.

Kohlberg, L., Levine, C., & Hewer, A. (1983). *Moral stages: A current formulation and a response to critics.* Basel, Switzerland: S. Karger.

Koppenhaver, D., Hendrix, M., & Williams, A. (2007). Toward evidence-based literacy interventions for children with severe and multiple disabilities. *Seminars in Speech & Language, 28*, 79–90.

Korobov, N., & Thorne, A. (2006). Intimacy and distancing: Young men's conversations about romantic relationships. *Journal of Adolescent Research, 21*, 27–55.

Koropeckyj-Cox, T., Pienta, A., & Brown, T. (2007). Women of the 1950s and the "normative" life course: The implications of childlessness, fertility timing, and marital status for psychological well-being in late midlife. *International Journal of Aging & Human Development, 64*, 299–330.

Koskinen, P., Blum, I., Bisson, S., Phillips, S., et al. (2000). Book access, shared reading, and audio models: The effects of supporting the literacy learning of linguistically diverse students in school and at home. *Journal of Educational Psychology, 92*, 23–36.

Kost, K. (1997). The effects of support on the economic well-being of young fathers. *Families in Society, 78*, 370–382.

Koster, A., Bosma, H., Boese van Groenou, M., Kempen, G., Penninx, B., van Eijk, T., & Deeg, D. (2006). Explanations of socioeconomic differences in changes in physical function in older adults: Results from the Longitudinal Aging Study Amsterdam. *BMC Public Health, 6*, 244.

Kozu, J. (1999). Domestic violence in Japan. *American Psychologist, 54*, 50–54.

Krakovsky, M. (2005, February 2). Dubious Mozart effect remains music to many Americans' ears. *Stanford Report.* Retrieved May 3, 2005 from http://newservice.stanford.edu/news/2005/february2/mozart-0202.

Kramer, J., Mungas, D., Reed, B., Wetzel, M., Burnett, M., Miller, B., Weiner, M., & Chui, H. (2007). Longitudinal MRI and cognitive change in healthy elderly.

Krause, N., Ingersoll-Dayton, B., Liang, J., & Sugisawa, H. (1999). Religion, social support, and health among the Japanese elderly. *Journal of Health Behavior & Health Education, 40*, 405–421.

Krebs, D., & Denton, K. (2006). Explanatory limitations of cognitive-developmental approaches to morality. *Psychological Review, 113*, 672–675.

Kressley, K., & Huebschmann, M. (2002). The 21st century campus: Gerontological perspectives. *Educational Gerontology, 28*, 835–851.

Kristensen, P., & Bjerkedal, T. (2007). Explaining the relation between birth order and intelligence. *Science, 316*, 1717.

Kristenson, H., Österling, A., Nilsson, J., & Lindgärde, F. (2002). Alcoholism: Clinical and experimental research. *Alcoholism: Clinical and Experimental Research, 26*, 478–484.

Kronenberg, F. (1994). Hot flashes: Phenomenology, quality of life, and search for treatment options. *Experimental Gerontology, 29*, 319–336.

Krueger-Lebus, S., & Rauchfleisch, U. (1999). Level of contentment in lesbian partnerships with and without children. *System Familie, 12*, 74–79.

Krumm, D. (2001). *Psychology at work: An introduction to industrial/organizational psychology.* New York: Worth Publishers.

Krumrei, E., Coit, C., Martin, S., Fogo, W., & Mahoney, A. (2007). Post-divorce adjustment and social relationships: A meta-analytic review. *Journal of Divorce and Remarriage, 46*, 145–166.

Ku, S., Kang, J., Kim, H., Kim, Y., Jee, B., Suh, C., Choi, Y., Kim, J., Moon, S., & Kim, S. (2006). Age at menarche and its influencing factors in North Korean female refugees. *Human Reproduction, 21*, 833–836.

Kübler-Ross, E. (1969). *On death and dying.* New York: Macmillan.

Kübler-Ross, E. (1974). *Questions and answers on death and dying.* New York: Macmillan.

Kubzansky, L., Cole, S., Kawachi, I., Vokonas, P., & Sparrow, D. (2006). Shared and unique contributions of anger, anxiety, and depression to coronary heart disease: A prospective study in the normative aging study. *Annals of Behavioral Medicine, 31*, 21–29.

Kuhn, D. (1992). Cognitive development. In M. H. Bornstein & M. E. Lamb (Eds.), *Developmental psychology: An advanced textbook* (3rd ed., pp. 211–272). Hillsdale, NJ: Erlbaum.

Kuhn, D., Kohlberg, L., Languer, J., & Haan, N. (1977). The development of formal operations in logical and moral judgment. *Genetic Psychology Monographs, 95*, 97–188.

Kumabe, C. (2006). Factors influencing contemporary Japanese attitudes regarding life and death. *Japanese Journal of Health Psychology, 19*, 20–24.

Kung, S., Rummans, T., Colligan, R., Clark, M., Sloan, J., Novotny, P., & Huntington, J. (2006). Association of optimism-pessimism with quality of life in patients with head and neck and thyroid cancers. *Mayo Clinic Proceedings, 81*, 1545–1552.

Kunin, M. (June 13, 2007). A math lesson on college loans. *New York Times Online.* Retrieved June 20, 3007 from www.nytimes.com/2007/06/13/opinion/13kunin.html?ex=1339387200&en=9a590a02a024a48b&ei=5088&partner=rssnyt&emc=rss.

Kunkel, S. R., & Applebaum, R. A. (1992). Estimating the prevalence of long-term disability for an aging society. *Journals of Gerontology: Social Sciences, 47*, S253–260.

Kurdek, L. (1997). Relation between neuroticism and dimensions of relationship commitment: evidence from gay, lesbian, and heterosexual couples. *Journal of Family Psychology, 11*, 109–124.

Kurdek, L. (1998). Relationship outcomes and their predictors: longitudinal evidence from heterosexual married, gay cohabiting, and lesbian cohabiting couples. *Journal of Marriage & the Family, 60*, 553–568.

Kurdek, L. (2000). The link between sociotropy/autonomy and dimensions of relationship commitment: Evidence from gay and lesbian couples. *Personal Relationships, 7*, 153–164.

Kurdek, L. A. (1995a). Developmental changes in relationship quality in gay and lesbian cohabiting couples. *Developmental Psychology, 31*, 86–94.

Kurdek, L. A. (2003). Differences between gay and lesbian cohabiting couples. *Journal of Social & Personal Relationships, 20*, 411–436.

Kurdek, L. A., & Fine, M. A. (1994). Family acceptance and family control as predictors of adjustment in young adolescents: Linear, curvilinear, or interactive effects? *Child Development, 65*, 1137–1146.

Kurz, A., Erkinjuntti, T., Small, G., Lilienfeld, S., & Damaraju, C. (2003). Long-term safety and cognitive effects of galantamine in the treatment of probable vascular dementia or Alzheimer's disease with cerebrovascular disease. *European Journal of Neurology, 10*, 633–640.

Kushi, L., & Giovannucci, E. (2002). Dietary fat and cancer. *American Journal of Medicine, 113*, 63S–70S.

Kyriacou, D., Anglin, D., Taliaferro, E., Stone, S., Tubb, T., Linden, J., Muelleman, R., Barton, E., & Kraus, J. (1999). Risk factors for injury to women from domestic violence. *New England Journal of Medicine, 341*, 1892–1898.

la Cour, P., Avlund, K., & Schultz-Larsen, K. (2006). Religion and survival in a secular region. A twenty year follow-up of 734 Danish adults born in 1914. *Social Science & Medicine, 62*, 157–164.

Labouvie-Vief, G. (2006). Emerging structures of adult thought. In J. Arnett & J. Tanner (Eds.). *Emerging adults in America: Coming of age in the 21st century* (pp. 59–84). Washington, DC: American Psychological Association.

Lacey, J., Mink, P., Lubin, J., Sherman, M., Troisi, R., Hartge, P., Schatzkin, A., & Schairer, C. (2002). Menopausal hormone replacement therapy and risk of ovarian cancer. *Journal of the American Medical Association, 288*, 334–341.

Lachman, M. (2004). Development in midlife. *Annual Review of Psychology, 55*, 305–331.

Lachman, M., & Weaver, S. (1998). Sociodemographic variations in the sense of control by domain: Findings from the MacArthur studies of midlife. *Psychology & Aging, 13*, 553–562.

La Freniere, P., Strayer, F. F., & Gauthier, R. (1984). The emergence of same-sex affiliative preferences among preschool peers. A developmental/ethological perspective. *Child Development, 55*, 1958–1965.

Laird, R., Pettit, G., Dodge, K., & Bates, J. (1999). Best friendships, group relationships, and antisocial behavior in early adolescence. *Journal of Early Adolescence, 19*, 413–437.

Lakatos, K., Nemoda, Z., Birkas, E., Ronai, Z., Kovacs, E., Ney, K., Toth, I., Sasvari-Szekely, M., & Gervai, J. (2003). Association of D4 dopamine receptor gene and serotonin transporter promoter polymorphisms with infants' response to novelty. *Molecular Psychiatry, 8*, 90–97.

Lam, C., Lam, M., Shek, D., & Tang, V. (2004). Coping with economic disadvantage. A qualitative study of Chinese adolescents from low-income families. *International Journal of Adolescent Medicine and Health, 16*, 343–357.

Lam, R., Pacala, J., & Smith, S. (1997). Factors related to depressive symptoms in an elderly Chinese American sample. *Gerontologist, 17*, 57–70.

Lamb, M., & Lewis, C. (2005). The role of parent-child relationships in child development. In M. Bornstein & M. Lamb (Eds.), *Developmental science: An advanced textbook* (5th ed., pp. 429–468). Hillsdale, NJ: Erlbaum.

Lamb, M. E., Sternberg, K. J., & Prodromidis, M. (1992). Nonmaternal care and the security of infant-mother attachment: A reanalysis of the data. *Infant Behavior & Development, 15*, 71–83.

Lamborn, S. D., Mounts, N. S., Steinberg, L., & Dornbusch, S. M. (1991). Patterns of competence and adjustment among adolescents from authoritative, authoritarian, indulgent, and neglectful families. *Child Development, 62*, 1049–1065.

Lampard, R., & Peggs, K. (1999). Repartnering: The relevance of parenthood and gender to cohabitation and remarriage among the formerly married. *British Journal of Sociology, 50*, 443–465.

Landolt, M., & Dutton, D. (1997). Power and personality: An analysis of gay male intimate abuse. *Sex Roles, 37*, 335–359.

Landry, S., Smith, K., Miller-Loncar, C., & Swank, P. (1997). Predicting cognitive-linguistic and social growth curves from early maternal behaviors in children at varying degrees of biologic risk. *Developmental Psychology, 33*, 1040–1053.

Landry, S. H., Garner, P. W., Swank, P. R., & Baldwin, C. D. (1996). Effects of maternal scaffolding during joint toy play with preterm and full-term infants. *Merrill-Palmer Quarterly, 42*, 177–199.

Langer, G., Arnedt, C., & Sussman, D. (2004). *Primetime Live poll: American sex survey analysis.* Retrieved June 22, 2007 from http://abcnews.go.com/Primetime/PollVault/story?id=156921&page=1

Langlois, J. H., Ritter, J. M., Roggman, L. A., & Vaughn, L. S. (1991). Facial diversity and infant preferences for attractive faces. *Developmental Psychology, 27*, 79–84.

Langlois, J. H., Roggman, L. A., & Rieser-Danner, L. A. (1990). Infants' differential social responses to attractive and unattractive faces. *Developmental Psychology, 26*, 153–159.

Lansdown, R., & Benjamin, G. (1985). The development of the concept of death in children aged 5–9 years. *Child: Care, Health & Development, 11*, 13–30.

Lapsley, D. K. (1993). Toward an integrated theory of adolescent ego development: The "new look" at adolescent egocentrism. *American Journal of Orthopsychiatry, 63*, 562–571.

Larson, R. (2000). Toward a psychology of positive youth development. *American Psychologist, 55*, 170–183.

Larson, R., & Verma, S. (1999). How children and adolescents spend time across the world: Work, play, and developmental opportunities. *Psychological Bulletin, 125*, 701–736.

Larson, R., Mannell, R., & Zuzanek, J. (1986). Daily well-being of older adults with friends and family. *Psychology & Aging, 1*, 117–126.

LaSala, M. (2001). Monogamous or not: Understanding and counseling gay male couples. *Families in Society, 82*, 605–611.

Lau, A., Uba, A., & Lehman, D. (2002). Infectious diseases. In A. Rudolph, R. Kamei, & K. Overby (Eds.), *Rudolph's fundamental of pediatrics* (3rd ed., pp. 289–399). New York: McGraw-Hill.

Laumann, E. O., Gagnon, J. H., Michael, R. T., & Michaels, S. (1994). *The social organization of sexuality: Sexual practices in the United States*. Chicago: University of Chicago Press.

Lauriello, J., McEvoy, J., Rodriguez, S., Bossie, C., & Lasser, R. (2005). Long-acting risperidone vs. placebo in the treatment of hospital inpatients with schizophrenia. *Schizophrenia Research, 72*, 249–258.

Lawrence, R. H., Bennett, J. M., & Markides, K. S. (1992). Perceived intergenerational solidarity and psychological distress among older Mexican Americans. *Journals of Gerontology: Social Sciences, 47*, S55–65.

Lawrence, V., Houghton, S., Douglas, G., Durkin, K., Whiting, K., & Tannock, R. (2004). Children with ADHD: Neuropsychological testing and real-world activities. *Journal of Attention Disorders, 7*, 137–149.

Lawton, L., Silverstein, M., & Bengtson, V. (1994). Affection, social contact, and geographic distance between adult children and their parents. *Journal of Marriage & the Family, 56*, 57–68.

Layton, L., Deeny, K., Tall, G., & Upton, G. (1996). Researching and promoting phonological awareness in the nursery class. *Journal of Research in Reading, 19*, 1–13.

Le, T., & Kato, T. (2006). The role of peer, parent, and culture in risky sexual behavior for Cambodian and Lao/Mien adolescents. *Journal of Adolescent Health, 38*, 288–296.

Leaper, C. (1991). Influence and involvement in children's discourse: Age, gender, and partner effects. *Child Development, 62*, 797–811.

Lederer, J. (2000). Reciprocal teaching of social studies in inclusive elementary classrooms. *Journal of Learning Disabilities, 33*, 91–106.

Lederman, R., & Mian, T. (2003). The Parent-Adolescent Relationship Education (PARE) program: A curriculum for prevention of STDs and pregnancy in middle school youth. *Behavioral Medicine, 29*, 33–41.

Lee, G., & DeMaris, A. (2007). Widowhood, gender, and depression: A longitudinal analysis. *Research on Aging, 29*, 56–72.

Lee, G. R., Seccombe, K., & Shehan, C. L. (1991). Marital status and personal happiness: An analysis of trend data. *Journal of Marriage & the Family, 53*, 839–844.

Lee, I.-M., Hsieh, C., & Paffenbarger, R. S. (1995). Exercise intensity and longevity in men. *Journal of the American Medical Association, 273*, 1179–1184.

Lee, J. (1996). *What your doctor may not tell you about menopause*. New York: Warner Books.

Lee, M., Law, C., & Tam, K. (1999). Parenthood and life satisfaction: A comparison of single and dual-parent families in Hong Kong. *International Social Work, 42*, 139–162.

Lee, S. & Keith, P. (1999). The transition to motherhood of Korean women. *Journal of Comparative Family Studies, 30*, 453–470.

Lee, V. E., Burkham, D. T., Zimiles, H., & Ladewski, B. (1994). Family structure and its effect on behavioral and emotional problems in young adolescents. *Journal of Research on Adolescence, 4*, 405–437.

Legendre, G. (2006). Early child grammars: Qualitative and quantitative analysis of morphosyntactic production. *Cognitive Science, 30*, 803–835.

Legerstee, M., Pomerleau, A., Malcuit, G., & Feider, H. (1987). The development of infants' responses to people and a doll: Implications for research in communication. *Infant Behavior & Development, 10*, 81–95.

Lehman, D., & Nisbett, R. (1990). A longitudinal study of the effects of undergraduate training on reasoning. *Developmental Psychology, 26*, 952–960.

Lemaire, P., & Lecacheur, M. (2004). Five-rule effects in young and older adults' arithmetic: Further evidence for age-related differences in strategy selection. *Current Psychology Letters: Behavior, Brain, & Cognition, 12*. Retrieved from http://cpl.revues.org/document412.html.

Lenhardt, A., & McCourt, B. (2000). Adolescent unresolved grief in response to the death of a mother. *Professional School Counseling, 3*, 189–196.

Leo, R., Narayan, D., Sherry, C., Michalek, C., et al. (1997). Geropsychiatric consultation for African-American and Caucasian patients. *General Hospital Psychiatry, 19*, 216–222.

Lester, D. (1990). The Collett-Lester fear of death scale: The original version and a revision. *Death Studies, 14*, 451–468.

Leve, L. D., & Fagot, B. I. (1995, April). *The influence of attachment style and parenting behavior on children's prosocial behavior with peers.* Paper presented at the biennial meetings of the Society for Research in Child Development, Indianapolis, IN.

Levenson, R. W., Carstensen, L. L., & Gottman, J. M. (1993). Long-term marriage: Age, gender, and satisfaction. *Psychology & Aging, 8*, 301–313.

Levine, J., Pollack, H., & Comfort, M. (2001). Academic and behavioral outcomes among the children of young mothers. *Journal of Marriage & Family, 63*, 355–369.

Levine, L., & Bluck, S. (1997). Experienced and remembered emotional intensity in older adults. *Psychology & Aging, 12*, 514–523.

Levinson, D. J. (1978). *The seasons of a man's life*. New York: Knopf.

Levinson, D. J. (1990). A theory of life structure development in adulthood. In C. N. Alexander & E. J. Langer (Eds.), *Higher stages of human development* (pp. 35–54). New York: Oxford University Press.

Levitt, M. J., Weber, R. A., & Guacci, N. (1993). Convoys of social support: An intergenerational analysis. *Psychology & Aging, 8*, 323–326.

Levy, G. D., & Fivush, R. (1993). Scripts and gender: A new approach for examining gender-role development. *Developmental Review, 13*, 126–146.

Levy, L. H., Martinkowski, K. S., & Derby, J. F. (1994). Differences in patterns of adaptation in conjugal bereavement: Their sources and potential significance. *Omega, 29*, 71–87.

Lewald, J. (2004). Gender-specific hemispheric asymmetry in auditory space perception. *Cognitive Brain Research, 19*, 92–99.

Lewis, C., & Lamb, M. E. Fathers' influences on children's development: The evidence from two-parent families. *European Journal of Psychology of Education, 18*, 211–228.

Lewis, C. C. (1981). How adolescents approach decisions: Changes over grades seven to twelve and policy implications. *Child Development, 52*, 538–544.

Lewis, J., Malow, R., & Ireland, S. (1997). HIV/AIDS in heterosexual college students: A review of a decade of literature. *Journal of American College Health, 45*, 147–158.

Lewis, M. (1990). Social knowledge and social development. *Merrill-Palmer Quarterly, 36*, 93–116.

Lewis, M. (1991). Ways of knowing: Objective self-awareness of consciousness. *Developmental Review, 11*, 231–243.

Lewis, M., & Brooks, J. (1978). Self-knowledge and emotional development. In M. Lewis & L. A. Rosenblum (Eds.), *The development of affect* (pp. 205–226). New York: Plenum.

Lewis, M., Allesandri, S. M., & Sullivan, M. W. (1992). Differences in shame and pride as a function of children's gender and task difficulty. *Child Development, 63*, 630–638.

Lewis, M., Sullivan, M. W., Stanger, C., & Weiss, M. (1989). Self development and self-conscious emotions. *Child Development, 60*, 146–156.

Lewis, M. D. (1993). Early socioemotional predictors of cognitive competence at 4 years. *Developmental Psychology, 29*, 1036–1045.

Li, L., & Seltzer, M. (2003). Parent care, intergenerational relationship quality, and mental health of adult daughters. *Research on Aging, 25*, 484–504.

Li, S., Lindenberger, B., Aschersleben, G., Prinz, W., & Baltes, P. (2004). Transformations in the couplings among intellectual abilities and constituent cognitive processes across the life span. *Psychological Science, 15*, 155–163.

Lieberman, M., Doyle, A., & Markiewicz, D. (1999). Developmental patterns in security of attachment to mother and father in late childhood and early adolescence: Associations with peer relations. *Child Development, 70*, 202–213.

Lieberman, M. A. (1965). Psychological correlates of impending death: Some preliminary observations. *Journal of Gerontology, 20*, 182–190.

Lieberman, M. A., & Coplan, A. S. (1970). Distance from death as a variable in the study of aging. *Developmental Psychology, 2*, 71–84.

Liem, R., & Liem, J. H. (1988). Psychological effects of unemployment on workers and their families. *Journal of Social Issues, 44*, 87–105.

Light, L. L. (1991). Memory and aging: Four hypotheses in search of data. *Annual Review of Psychology, 42*, 333–376.

Li-Grining, C. (2007). Effortful control among low-income preschoolers in three cities: Stability, change, and individual differences. *Developmental Psychology, 43*, 208–221.

Lillard, A. (1998). Ethnopsychologies: Cultural variations in theories of mind. *Psychological Bulletin, 123*, 3–32.
Lillard, A. S., & Flavell, J. H. (1992). Young children's understanding of different mental states. *Developmental Psychology, 28*, 626–634.
Lim, V. (2003). An empirical study of older workers' attitudes towards the retirement experience. *Employee Relations, 25*, 330–346.
Lin, A. (2003). Factors related to attitudes toward death among American and Chinese older adults. *Omega, 47*, 3–23.
Lin, C., Hsiao, C., & Chen, W. (1999). Development of sustained attention assessed using the Continuous Performance Test among children 6–15 years of age. *Journal of Abnormal Child Psychology, 27*, 403–412.
Lincourt, A., Rybash, J., & Hoyer, W. (1998). Aging, working memory, and the development of instance-based retrieval. *Brain & Cognition, 37*, 100–102.
Lindahl, K., Clements, M., & Markman, H. (1997). Predicting marital and parent functioning in dyads and triads: A longitudinal investigation of marital processes. *Journal of Family Psychology, 11*, 139–151.
Lindgren, C., Connelly, C., & Gaspar, H. (1999). Grief in spouse and children caregivers of dementia patients. *Western Journal of Nursing Research, 21*, 521–537.
Lindo, G., & Nordholm, L. (1999). Adaptation strategies, well-being, and activities of daily living among people with low vision. *Journal of Visual Impairment & Blindness, 93*, 434–446.
Lindsay, D. S., & Read, J. D. (1994). Psychotherapy and memory of childhood sexual abuse: A cognitive perspective. *Applied Cognitive Psychology, 8*, 281–338.
Lindstrom, T. (1997). Immunity and somatic health in bereavement. A prospective study of 39 Norwegian widows. *Omega, 35*, 231–241.
Lineweaver, T., & Hertzog, C. (1998). Adults' efficacy and control beliefs regarding memory and aging: Separating general from personal beliefs. *Aging, Neuropsychology, & Cognition, 5*, 264–296.
Linnet, K., Dalsgaard, S., Obel, C., Wisborg, K., Henriksen, T., Rodriquez, A., Kotimaa, A., Moilanen, I., Thomsen, P., Olsen, J., & Jarvelin, M. (2003). Maternal lifestyle factors in pregnancy risk of attention deficit hyperactivity disorder and associated behaviors: Review of the current evidence. *American Journal of Psychiatry, 160*, 1028–1040.
Lippé, R., Perchet, C., & Lassonde, M. (2007). Electrophysical markers of visocortical development. *Cerebral Cortex, 17*, 100–107.
Lippa, R. (2005). *Gender, nature, and nurture.* Hillsdale, NJ: Lawrence Erlbaum Associates.
Lissner, L., Bengtsson, C., Björkelund, C., & Wedel, H. (1996). Physical activity levels and changes in relation to longevity: A prospective study of Swedish women. *American Journal of Epidemiology, 143*, 54–62.
Liu, W., & Aaker, J. (2007). Do you look to the future or focus on today? The impact of life experience on intertemporal decisions. *Organizational Behavior and Human Decision Processes, 102*, 212–225.
Livesley, W. J., & Bromley, D. B. (1973). *Person perception in childhood and adolescence.* London: Wiley.
Livingstone, S., & Helsper, E. (2006). Does advertising literacy mediate the effects of advertising on children? A critical examination of two linked research literatures in relation to obesity and food choice. *Journal of Communication, 56*, 560–584.
Loeb, S., Fuller, B., Kagan, S., & Carrol, B. (2004). Child care in poor communities: Early learning effects of type, quality, and stability. *Child Development, 75*, 47–65.
Loehlin, J. C., Horn, J. M., & Willerman, L. (1994). Differential inheritance of mental abilities in the Texas Adoption Project. *Intelligence, 19*, 325–336.
Lohan, J., & Murphy, S. (2001/2002). Parents' perceptions of adolescent sibling grief responses after an adolescent or young adult child's sudden, violent death. *Omega, 44*, 195–213.
Longino, C. (2003). A first look at retirement migration trends in 2000. *The Gerontologist, 43*, 904–907.
Lopez-Alarcon, M., Villapando, S., & Fajardo, A. (1997). Breast-feeding lowers the frequency and duration of acute respiratory infection and diarrhea in infants under six months of age. *Journal of Nutrition, 127*, 436–443.
Lorant, V., Kunst, A., Huisman, M., Bopp, M., & Mackenbach, J. (2005). *Social Science & Medicine, 60*, 2431–2441.
Lorenz, K. (1935). The companion in the bird's world. The fellow-member of the species as releasing factor of social behavior. *Journal for Ornithology, 83*, 137–213.
Love, J., Harrison, L., Sagi-Schwartz, A., van IJzendoorn, M., Ross, C., Ungerer, J., Raikes, H., Brady-Smith, C., Boller, K., Brooks-Gunn, J., Constantine, J., Kisker, E., Paulsell, D., & Chazan-Cohen, R. (2003). Child care quality matters: How conclusions may vary with context. *Child Development, 74*, 1021–1033.
Low, C., Stanton, A., Thompson, N., Kwan, L., & Ganz, P. (2006). Contextual life stress and coping strategies as predictors of adjustment to breast cancer survivorship. *Annals of Behavioral Medicine, 32*, 235–244.
Lowenstein, D., Acevedo, A., Czaja, S., & Duara, R. (2004). Cognitive rehabilitation of mildly impaired Alzheimer disease patients on cholinesterase inhibitors. *American Journal of Geriatric Psychiatry, 12*, 395–402.
Lubinski, D., & Benbow, C. P. (1992). Gender differences in abilities and preferences among the gifted: Implications for the math-science pipeline. *Current Directions in Psychological Science, 1*, 61–66.
Lundh, W., & Gyllang, C. (1993). Use of the Edinburgh Postnatal Depression Scale in some Swedish child health care centres. *Scandinavian Journal of Caring Sciences, 7*, 149–154.
Luster, T., & McAdoo, H. P. (1995). Factors related to self-esteem among African American youths: A secondary analysis of the High/Scope Perry Preschool data. *Journal of Research on Adolescence, 5*, 451–467.
Lutfey, K., & Maynard, D. (1998). Bad news in oncology: How physician and patient talk about death and dying without using those words. *Social Psychology Quarterly, 61*, 321–341.
Luthar, S. S., & Zigler, E. (1992). Intelligence and social competence among high-risk adolescents. *Development & Psychopathology, 4*, 287–299.
Lyons, N. P. (1983). Two perspectives: On self, relationships, and morality. *Harvard Educational Review, 53*, 125–145.
Lytton, H., & Romney, D. M. (1991). Parents' differential socialization of boys and girls: A meta-analysis. *Psychological Bulletin, 109*, 267–296.
Maas, H. S., & Kuypers, J. A. (1974). *From thirty to seventy.* San Francisco: Jossey-Bass.
Maccoby, E., & Jacklin, C. (1974). *The psychology of sex differences.* Stanford, CA: Stanford University Press.
Maccoby, E., & Lewis, C. (2003). Less day care or different day care? *Child Development, 74*, 1069–1075.
Maccoby, E. E. (1980). *Social development: Psychological growth and the parent-child relationship.* New York: Harcourt Brace Jovanovich.
Maccoby, E. E. (1988). Gender as a social category. *Developmental Psychology, 24*, 755–765.
Maccoby, E. E. (1990). Gender and relationships: A developmental account. *American Psychologist, 45*, 513–520.
Maccoby, E. E. (1995). The two sexes and their social systems. In P. Moen, G. H. Elder, Jr., & K. Lüscher (Eds.), *Examining lives in context: Perspectives on the ecology of human development* (pp. 347–364). Washington, DC: American Psychological Association.
Maccoby, E. E., & Jacklin, C. N. (1987). Gender segregation in childhood. In H. W. Reese (Ed.), *Advances in child development and behavior, Vol. 20* (pp. 239–288). Orlando, FL: Academic Press.
Maccoby, E. E., & Martin, J. A. (1983). Socialization in the context of the family: Parent-child interaction. In E. M. Hetherington (Ed.), *Handbook of child psychology: Socialization, personality, & social development, Vol. 4* (pp. 1–102). New York: Wiley.
MacDorman, M., & Atkinson, J. (1999, July 30). Infant mortality statistics from the 1997 period. Linked birth/infant death data set. *National Vital Statistics Reports, 47*(23), 1–24.
Mackey, E., & La Greca, A. (2007). Adolescents' eating, exercise, and weight control behaviors: Does peer crowd affiliation play a role? *Journal of Pediatric Psychology, 32*, 13–23.
Mackintosh, N. (2007). Review of race differences in intelligence: An evolutionary hypothesis. *Intelligence, 35*, 94–96.
Macrae, C., & Bodenhausen, G. (2000). Social cognition: Thinking categorically about others. *Annual Review of Psychology, 51*, 93–120.
MacRae, H. (1992). Fictive kin as a component of the social networks of older people. *Research on Aging, 14*, 226–247.
Madan-Swain, A., Brown, R., Foster, M., Verga, R., et al. (2000). Identity in adolescent survivors of childhood cancer. *Journal of Pediatric Psychology, 25*, 105–115.
Madison, C., Johnson, J., Seikel, J., Arnold, M., & Schultheis, L. (1998). Comparative study of the phonology of preschool children prenatally exposed to cocaine and multiple drugs and non-exposed children. *Journal of Communication Disorders, 31*, 231–244.
Magarey, A., Daniels, l., Boulton, T., & Cockington, R. (2003). Predicting obesity in early adulthood from childhood and parental obesity. *International Journal of Obesity & Related Metabolic Disorders, 27*, 505–513.
Maguire, M., & Dunn, J. (1997). Friendships in early childhood and social understanding. *International Journal of Behavioral Development, 21*, 669–686.
Main, M., & Hesse, E. (1990). Parents' unresolved traumatic experiences are related to infant disorganized attachment status: Is frightened and/or frightening parental behavior the linking mechanism? In M. T. Green-

berg, D. Cicchetti, & E. M. Cummings (Eds.), *Attachment in the preschool years: Theory, research, and intervention* (pp. 161–182). Chicago: University of Chicago Press.

Main, M., & Solomon, J. (1990). Procedures for identifying infants as disorganized/disoriented during the Ainsworth Strange Situation. In M. T. Greenberg, D. Cicchetti, & E. M. Cummings (Eds.), *Attachment in the preschool years: Theory, research, and intervention* (pp. 121–160). Chicago: University of Chicago Press.

Maitel, S., Dromi, E., Sagi, A., & Bornstein, M. (2000). The Hebrew Communicative Development Inventory: Language-specific properties and cross-linguistic generalizations. *Journal of Child Language, 27*, 43–67.

Maki, P., Veijola, J., Rantakallio, P., Jokelainen, J., Jones, P., & Isohanni, M. (2004). Schizophrenia in the offspring of antenatally depressed mothers: A 31-year follow-up of the Northern Finland 1966 Birth Cohort. *Schizophrenia Research, 66*, 79–81.

Malabonga, V., & Pasnak, R. (2002). Hierarchical categorization by bilingual Latino children: Does a basic-level bias exist? *Genetic, Social, & General Psychology Monographs, 128*, 409–441.

Malina, R. M. (1990). Physical growth and performance during the transition years. In R. Montemayor, G. R. Adams, & T. P. Gullotta (Eds.), *From childhood to adolescence: A transitional period?* (pp. 41–62). Newbury Park, CA: Sage.

Malinosky-Rummell, R., & Hansen, D. (1993). Long-term consequences of childhood physical abuse. *Psychological Bulletin, 114*, 68–79.

Malkinson, R., & Bar-Tur, L., (1999). The aging of grief in Israel: A perspective of bereaved parents. *Death Studies, 23*, 413–431.

Mallet, P., Apostolidis, T., & Paty, B. (1997). The development of gender schemata about heterosexual and homosexual others during adolescence. *Journal of General Psychology, 124*, 91–104.

Malo, J., & Tremblay, R. (1997). The impact of parental alcoholism and maternal social position on boys' school adjustment, pubertal maturation and sexual behavior: A test of two competing hypotheses. *Journal of Child Psychology & Psychiatry & Allied Disciplines, 38*, 187–197.

Malvern, J., & Robertson, G. (2007). First video game banned in Britain puts player in role of sadistic killer. *Times of London Online.* Retrieved June 28, 2007 from http://technology.timesonline.co.uk/tol/news/tech_and_web/gadgets_and_gaming/article1957433.ece

Mäntylä, T. (1994). Remembering to remember: Adult age differences in prospective memory. *Journals of Gerontology: Psychological Sciences, 49*, P276–282.

Manzoli, L., Villari, P., Pironec, G., & Boccia, A. (2007). Marital status and mortality in the elderly: A systematic review and meta-analysis. *Social Science & Medicine, 64*, 77–94.

Mao, H. (2003). The relationship between voluntary employer changes and perceived job stress in Taiwan. *International Journal of Stress Management, 10*, 75–85.

Maratsos, M. (1983). Some current issues in the study of the acquisition o f grammar. In J. H. Flavell & E. M. Markman (Eds.), *Handbook of child psychology: Cognitive development* (pp. 707–786). New York: Wiley.

Maratsos, M. (2000). More overregularizations after all: New data and discussion of Marcus, Pinker, Ullman, Hollander, Rosen, & Xu. *Journal of Child Language, 27*, 183–212.

March of Dimes. (2004). *Environmental risks and pregnancy.* Retrieved September, 21, 2004, from http://www.marchofdimes.com/professionals/681_9146.asp.

Marcia, J. E. (1966). Development and validation of ego identity status. *Journal of Personality & Social Psychology, 3*, 551–558.

Marcia, J. E. (1980). Identity in adolescence. In J. Adelson (Ed.), *Handbook of adolescent psychology* (pp. 159–187). New York: Wiley.

Marcovitch, S., Goldberg, S., Gold, A., & Washington, J. (1997). Determinants of behavioural problems in Romanian children adopted in Ontario. *International Journal of Behavioral Development, 20*, 17–31.

Marcus, R. F. (1986). Naturalistic observation of cooperation, helping, and sharing and their association with empathy and affect. In C. Zahn-Waxler, E. M. Cummings, & R. Iannotti (Eds.), *Altruism and aggression: Biological and social origins* (pp. 256–279). Cambridge, England: Cambridge University Press.

Marean, G. C., Werner, L. A., & Kuhl, P. K. (1992). Vowel categorization by very young infants. *Developmental Psychology, 28*, 396–405.

Margolin, G., & Gordis, E. (2000). The effects of family and community violence on children. *Annual Review of Psychology, 51*, 445–479.

Market Wire. (2003). *Research from Quality Planning Corporation shows elderly drivers involved in more accidents, fewer violations than younger drivers.* Retrieved July 31, 2007 from http://findarticles.com/p/articles/mi_pwwi/is_200309/ai_mark4461I0727.

Markey, C., Markey, P., & Tinsley, B. (2003). Personality, puberty, and preadolescent girls' risky behaviors: Examining the predictive value of the Five-Factor Model of personality. *Journal of Research in Personality, 37*, 405–419.

Markides, K. S., & Lee, D. J. (1991). Predictors of health status in middle-aged and older Mexican Americans. *Journals of Gerontology: Social Sciences, 46*, S243–249.

Markman, E. M. (1992). Constraints on word learning: Speculations about their nature, origins, and domain specificity. In M. R. Gunnar & M. Maratsos (Eds.), *Minnesota Symposia on Child Psychology, Vol. 25* (pp. 59–101). Hillsdale, NJ: Erlbaum.

Marks, N., & Lamberg, J. (1998). Marital status continuity and change among young and midlife adults. *Journal of Family Issues, 19*, 652–686.

Marsh, H., Craven, R., & Debus, R. (1999). Separation of competency and affect components of multiple dimensions of academic self-concept: A developmental perspective. *Merrill-Palmer Quarterly, 45*, 567–601.

Marshall, N., Coll, C., Marx, F., McCartney, K., Keefe, N., & Ruh, J. (1997). After-school time and children's behavioral adjustment. *Merrill-Palmer Quarterly, 43*, 497–514.

Marshall, V. W. (1975). Age and awareness of finitude in developmental gerontology. *Omega, 6*, 113–129.

Marshall, V. W., & Levy, J. A. (1990). Aging and dying. In R. H. Binstock & L. K. George (Eds.), *Handbook of aging and the social sciences* (3rd ed., pp. 245–260). San Diego, CA: Academic Press.

Marsiglio, W., & Donnelly, D. (1991). Sexual relations in later life: A national study of married persons. *Journals of Gerontology: Social Sciences, 46*, S338–344.

Martin, C., & Ruble, D. (2002). Cognitive theories of early gender development. *Psychological Bulletin, 128*, 903–933.

Martin, C. L. (1991). The role of cognition in understanding gender effects. In H. W. Reese (Ed.), *Advances in child development and behavior, Vol. 23* (pp. 113–150). San Diego, CA: Academic Press.

Martin, C. L. (1993). New directions for investigating children's gender knowledge. *Developmental Review, 13*, 184–204.

Martin, C. L., & Halverson, C. F., Jr. (1981). A schematic processing model of sex typing and stereotyping in children. *Child Development, 52*, 1119–1134.

Martin, C. L., & Little, J. K. (1990). The relation of gender understanding to children's sex-typed preferences and gender stereotypes. *Child Development, 61*, 1427–1439.

Martin, C. L., Wood, C. H., & Little, J. K. (1990). The development of gender stereotype components. *Child Development, 61*, 1891–1904.

Martin, J. (1995). Birth characteristics for Asian or Pacific Islander subgroups, 1992. *Monthly Vital Statistics Report, 43* (10, Supplement).

Martin, J., & D'Augelli, A. (2003). How lonely are gay and lesbian youth? *Psychological Reports, 93*, 486.

Martin, J., & Nguyen, D. (2004). Anthropometric analysis of homosexuals and heterosexuals: Implications for early hormone exposure. *Hormones & Behavior, 45*, 31–39.

Martin, J., Hamilton, B., Sutton, P., Ventura, S., Menacker, F., & Kirmeyer, S. (2006). Births: Final data for 2004. *National Vital Statistics Reports, 55*, 1–102.

Martin, J., Hamilton, B., Sutton, P., Ventura, S., Menacker, F., & Munson, M. (2005). Births: Final data for 2003. *National Vital Statistics Reports, 54*, 1–116.

Martin, R., Annis, S., Darling, L., Wadley, V., Harrell, L., & Marson, D. (2003). Loss of calculation abilities in patients with mild and moderate Alzheimer disease. *Archives of Neurology, 60*, 1585–1589.

Martin, R., Noyes, J., Wisenbaker, J. & Huttunen, M. (1999). Prediction of early childhood negative emotionality and inhibition from maternal distress during pregnancy. *Merrill-Palmer Quarterly, 45*, 370–391.

Martin, R. P., Wisenbaker, J., & Huttunen, M. (1994). Review of factor analytic studies of temperament measures based on the Thomas-Chess structural model: Implications for the Big Five. In C. F. Halverson, Jr., G. A. Kohnstamm, & R. P. Martin (Eds.), *The developing structure of temperament and personality from infancy to adulthood* (pp. 157–172). Hillsdale, NJ: Erlbaum.

Martinez-Schallmoser, L., Telleen, S., & MacMullen, N. (2003). Effect of social support and acculturation on postpartum depression in Mexican American women. *Journal of Transcultural Nursing, 14*, 329–338.

Martorano, S. C. (1977). A developmental analysis of performance on Piaget's formal operations tasks. *Developmental Psychology, 13*, 666–672.

Maruyama, M., Arai, H., Ootsuki, M., Okamura, N., Matsui, T., Sasaki, H., Yamazaki, T., & Kaneta, T. (2003). Biomarkers in subjects with amnestic mild cognitive impairment. *Journal of the American Geriatrics Society, 51*, 1671–1672.

Masataka, N. (1999). Preference for infant-directed singing in 2-day-old hearing infants of deaf parents. *Developmental Psychology, 35*, 1001–1005.

Mascolo, M. F., & Fischer, K. W. (1995). Developmental transformations in appraisals for pride, shame, and guilt. In J. P. Tangney & K. W. Fischer (Eds.), *Self-conscious emotions: The psychology of shame, guilt, embarrassment, and pride* (pp. 64–113). New York: Guilford Press.

Mason, B., Goodman, A., Chabac, S., & Lehert, P. (2006). Effect of oral acamprosate on abstinence in patients with alcohol dependence in a double-blind, placebo-controlled trial: The role of patient motivation. *Journal of Psychiatric Research, 40*, 383–393.

Mason, M., & Chuang, S. (2001). Culturally-based after-school arts programming for low-income urban children: Adaptive and preventive effects. *Journal of Primary Prevention, 22*, 45–54.

Massachusetts Department of Education. (2000). *Charter school initiative.* Retrieved February 29, 2000, from http://www.doe.mass.edu/cs.

Mast, B., Azar, A., MacNeill, S., & Lichtenberg, P. (2004). Depression and activities of daily living predict rehospitalization within 6 months of discharge from geriatric rehabilitation. *Rehabilitation Psychology, 49*, 219–223.

Masten, A., & Coatsworth, D. (1998). The development of competence in favorable and unfavorable environments: Lessons from research on successful children. *American Psychologist, 53*, 205–220.

Masten, A. S., Best, K. M., & Garmezy, N. (1990). Resilience and development: Contributions from the study of children who overcome adversity. *Development & Psychopathology, 2*, 425–444.

Maszk, P., Eisenberg, N., & Guthrie, I. (1999). Relations of children's social status to their emotionality and regulation: A short-term longitudinal study. *Merrill-Palmer Quarterly, 454*, 468–492.

Mathew, A., & Cook, M. (1990). The control of reaching movements by young infants. *Child Development, 61*, 1238–1257.

Matthews, T. (2005). Racial/ethnic disparities in infant mortality: United States, 1995–2002. *Morbidity & Mortality Weekly Report, 54*, 553–556.

Mattson, S., & Riley, E. (1999). Implicit and explicit memory functioning in children with heavy prenatal alcohol exposure. *Journal of the International Neuropsychological Society, 5*, 462–471.

Mattson, S., Riley, E., Gramling, L., Delis, D., & Jones, K. (1998). Neuropsychological comparison of alcohol-exposed children with or without physical features of fetal alcohol syndrome. *Neuropsychology, 12*, 146–153.

Mature Market Institute. (2004). *The future of retirement living.* Retrieved September 9, 2004, from www.metlife.com/WPSAssets/18620262201089823697V1FFuture%20of%20Retirement%20Living.pdf.

Maughan, B., Pickles, A., & Quinton, D. (1995). Parental hostility, childhood behavior, and adult social functioning. In J. McCord (Ed.), *Coercion and punishment in long-term perspectives* (pp. 34–58). Cambridge, England: Cambridge University Press.

Mauldin, J. (2005). *The new retirement model.* Retrieved July 7, 2007 from www.agewave.com/media_files/ota.htm.

Maurer, D., & Maurer, C. (1988). *The world of the newborn.* New York: Basic Books.

Mayes, L., Cicchetti, D., Acharyya, S., & Zhang, H. (2003). Developmental trajectories of cocaine-and-other-drug-exposed and non-cocaine-exposed children. *Journal of Developmental & Behavioral Pediatrics, 24*, 323–335.

Mayeux, L., & Cillissen, A. (2003). Development of social problem solving in early childhood: Stability, change, and associations with social competence. *Journal of Genetic Psychology, 164*, 153–173.

Maylor, D., Vousden, J., & Brown, D. (1999). Adult age differences in short-term memory for serial order: Data and a model. *Psychology & Aging, 14*, 572–594.

Maylor, E. (1998). Changes in event-based prospective memory across adulthood. *Aging, Neuropsychology, & Cognition, 5*, 107–128.

Maylor, E. A. (1993). Aging and forgetting in prospective and retrospective memory tasks. *Psychology & Aging, 8*, 420–428.

Mayo Clinic. (2005). *Dietary fiber: An essential part of a healthy diet.* Retrieved July 4, 2007 from www.mayoclinic.com/health/fiber/NU00033.

Mayo Clinic. (2006). *STD quiz: What you don't know can hurt you.* Retrieved July 3, 2006 from http://mayoclinic.cm/health/stds/QZ00037.

Mayringer, H., & Wimmer, H. (2000). Pseudoname learning by German-speaking children with dyslexia: Evidence for a phonological learning deficit. *Journal of Experimental Child Psychology, 75*, 116–133.

Mayseless, O., & Scharf, M. (2007). Adolescents' attachment representations and their capacity for intimacy in close relationships. *Journal of Research on Adolescence, 17*, 23–50.

McAdams, D., & Pals, J. (2006). A new Big Five: Fundamental principles for an integrative science of personality. *American Psychologist, 61*, 204–217.

McAlister, A., & Peterson, C. (2006). Mental playmates: Siblings, executive functioning and theory of mind. *British Journal of Developmental Psychology, 24*, 733–751.

McAllister, D., Kaplan, B., Edworthy, S., Martin, L., et al. (1997). The influence of systemic lupus erythematosus on fetal development: Cognitive, behavioral, and health trends. *Journal of the International Neurological Society, 3*, 370–376.

McBride-Chang, C. (1998). The development of invented spelling. *Early Education & Development, 9*, 147–160.

McBride-Chang, C., & Ho, C. (2000). Developmental issues in Chinese children's character acquisition. *Journal of Educational Psychology, 92*, 50–55.

McBride-Chang, C., Shu, H., Zhou, C., & Wagner, R. (2004). Morphological awareness uniquely predicts young children's Chinese character recognition. *Journal of Educational Psychology, 96*, 743–751.

McCall, B., Cavanaugh, M., Arvey, R., & Taubman, P. (1997). Genetic influences on job and occupational switching. *Journal of Vocational Behavior, 50*, 60–77.

McCall, R. B. (1993). Developmental functions for general mental performance. In D. K. Detterman (Ed.), *Current topics in human intelligence, Vol. 3: Individual differences and cognition* (pp. 3–30). Norwood, NJ: Ablex.

McClure, E. (2000). A meta-analytic review of sex differences in facial expression processing and their development in infants, children, and adolescents. *Psychological Bulletin, 126*, 242–453.

McCoy, N. (1998). Methodological problems in the study of sexuality and the menopause. *Maturitas, 29*, 51–60.

McCrae, R., Costa, P., Ostendord, F., & Angleitner, A. (2000). Nature over nurture: Temperament, personality, and life span development. *Journal of Personality & Social Psychology, 78*, 173–186.

McCune, L. (1995). A normative study of representational play at the transition to language. *Developmental Psychology, 31*, 198–206.

McDonald, L. (2004, April 28). China may grow old before it gets rich. *Sydney Morning Herald.* Retrieved September 10, 2004, from http://www.smh.com.au/articles/2004/04/27/1082831569621.html?from=storyrhs&oneclick=true.

McDonald, P. L., & Wanner, R. A. (1990). *Retirement in Canada.* Toronto: Butterworths.

McElree, B., Jia, G., & Litvak, A. (2000). The time course of conceptual processing in three bilingual populations. *Journal of Memory & Language, 42*, 229–254.

McElwain, A., Korabik, K., & Rosin, H. (2005). An examination of gender differences in work-family conflict. *Canadian Journal of Behavioural Science, 37*, 283–298.

McFalls, J. A., Jr. (1990). The risks of reproductive impairment in the later years of childbearing. *Annual Review of Sociology, 16*, 491–519.

McFarlane, J., & Malecha, A. (2005). Sexual assault among intimate: Frequency, consequences and treatments. Retrieved July 3, 2007 from www.ncjrs.gov/pdffiles1/nij/grants/211678.pdf.

McFayden-Ketchumm, S., Bates, J., Dodge, K., & Pettit, G. (1996). Patterns of change in early childhood aggressive-disruptive behavior: Gender differences in predictions from early coercive and affectionate mother-child interactions. *Child Development, 67*, 2417–2433.

McGrath, M., & Sullivan, M. (2002). Birth weight, neonatal morbidities, and school age outcomes in full-term and preterm infants. *Issues in Comprehensive Pediatric Nursing, 25*, 231–254.

McGregor, K., Sheng., L., & Smith, B. (2005). The precocious two-year-old: Status of the lexicon and links to the grammar. *Journal of Child Language, 32*, 563–585.

McHale, S., Crouter, A., & Tucker, C. (1999). Family context and gender role socialization in middle childhood: Comparing girls to boys and sisters to brothers. *Child Development, 70*, 990–1004.

McHugh, M. (2005). Understanding gender and intimate partner abuse. *Sex Roles: A Journal of Research, 52*, 717–724.

McIntosh, B. R., & Danigelis, N. L. (1995). Race, gender, and the relevance of productive activity for elders' affect. *Journals of Gerontology: Social Sciences, 50B*, S229–239.

McKelvie, P., & Low, J. (2002). Listening to Mozart does not improve children's spatial ability: Final curtains for the Mozart effect. *British Journal of Developmental Psychology, 20*, 241–258.

McLanahan, S., & Sandefur, G. (1994). *Growing up with a single parent: What hurts, what helps.* Cambridge, MA: Harvard University Press.

McLoyd, V. (1998). Socioeconomic disadvantage and child development. *American Psychologist, 53*, 185–204.

McLoyd, V., & Wilson, L. (1991). The strain of living poor: Parenting, social support, and child mental health. In A. C. Huston (Ed.), *Children in* poverty: Child development and public policy (pp. 105–135). Cambridge, England: Cambridge University Press.

McMaster, F., & Kusumaker, V. (2004). MRI study of the pituitary gland in adolescent depression. *Journal of Psychiatric Research, 38*, 231–236.

McNeal, C., & Amato, P. (1998). Parents' marital violence: Long-term consequences for children. *Journal of Family Issues, 19*, 123–139.

Mead, S., & Fisk, A. (1998). Measuring skill acquisition and retention with an ATM simulator: The need for age-specific training. *Human Factors, 40*, 516–523.

Mediascope Press. (1999). *Substance use in popular movies and music*/Issue Brief Series. Studio City, CA: Mediascope Inc.

Mediascope Press. (2000). *Teens, sex and the media*/Issue Brief Series. Studio City, CA: Mediascope Inc.

Meeus, W., Dekovic, M., & Iedema, J. (1997). Unemployment and identity in adolescence: A social comparison perspective. *Career Development Quarterly, 45*, 369–380.

Mehta, K. (1997). The impact of religious beliefs and practices on aging: A cross-cultural comparison. *Journal of Aging Studies, 11*, 101–114.

Meisenhelder, J., & Chandler, E. (2000). Faith, prayer, and health outcomes in elderly Native Americans. *Clinical Nursing Research, 9*, 191–203.

Melby, J. N., & Conger, R. D. (1996). Parental behaviors and adolescent academic performance: A longitudinal analysis. *Journal of Research on Adolescence, 6*, 113–137.

Melot, A., & Houde, O. (1998). Categorization and theories of mind: The case of the appearance/reality distinction. *Cahiers de Psychologie Cognitive/Current Psychology of Cognition, 17*, 71–93.

Melson, G., Peet, S., & Sparks, C. (1991). Children's attachments to their pets: Links to socioemotional development. *Children's Environmental Quarterly, 8*, 55–65.

Meltzoff, A. N. (1995). Understanding the intentions of others: Re-enactment of intended acts by 18-month-old children. *Developmental Psychology, 31*, 838–850.

Meltzoff, A. N., & Moore, M. K. (1977). Imitation of facial and manual gestures by human neonates. *Science, 198*, 75–78.

Menaghan, E. G., & Lieberman, M. A. (1986). Changes in depression following divorce: A panel study. *Journal of Marriage & the Family, 48*, 319–328.

Meredith, K., & Rassa, G. (1999). Aligning the levels of awareness with the stages of grieving. *Journal of Cognitive Rehabilitation, 17*, 10–12.

Merikangas, K. R., & Angst, J. (1995). The challenge of depressive disorders in adolescence. In M. Rutter (Ed.), *Psychosocial disturbances in young people: Challenges for prevention* (pp. 131–165). Cambridge, England: Cambridge University Press.

Merrick, J., & Morad, M. (2002). Adolescent pregnancy in Israel. *International Journal of Adolescent Medicine, 14*, 161–164.

Merson, M. (2006). The HIV/AIDS pandemic at 25: The global response. *New England Journal of Medicine, 354*, 2414–2417.

Meyer, C., & Oberman, M. (with White, K., Rone, M., Batra, P., & Proano, T.) (2001). *Mothers who kill their children: Understanding the acts of moms from Susan Smith to the "Prom Mom."* New York: New York University Press.

Meyer, M. (1998). Perceptual differences in fetal alcohol syndrome affect boys performing a modeling task. *Perceptual & Motor Skills, 87*, 784–786.

Meyer-Bahlburg, H. F. L., Ehrhardt, A. A., Rosen, L. R., Gruen, R. S., Veridiano, N. P., Vann, F. H., & Neuwalder, H. F. (1995). Prenatal estrogens and the development of homosexual orientation. *Developmental Psychology, 31*, 12–21.

Michael, R. T., Gagnon, J. H., Laumann, E. O., & Kolata, G. (1994). *Sex in America.* Boston: Little, Brown.

Miech, R., & Shanahan, M. (2000). Socioeconomic status and depression over the life course. *Journal of Health & Social Behavior, 41*, 162–176.

Miller, B., Benson, B., & Galbraith, K. (2001). Family relationships and adolescent pregnancy risk: A research synthesis. *Developmental Review, 21*, 1–38.

Miller, B., Norton, M., Curtis, T., Hill, E., Schvaneveldt, P., & Young, M. (1998). The timing of sexual intercourse among adolescents: Family, peer, and other antecedents: Erratum. *Youth & Society, 29*, 390.

Miller, B. C., & Moore, K. A. (1990). Adolescent sexual behavior, pregnancy, and parenting: Research through the 1980s. *Journal of Marriage & the Family, 52*, 1025–1044.

Miller, P., Eisenberg, N., Fabes, R., & Shell, R. (1996). Relations of moral reasoning and vicarious emotion to young children's prosocial behavior toward peers and adults. *Developmental Psychology, 29*, 3–18.

Miller, P., Wang, S., Sandel, T., & Cho, G. (2002). Self-esteem as folk theory: A comparison of European American and Taiwanese mothers' beliefs. *Science & Practice, 2*, 209–239.

Miller, T. Q., Turner, C. W., Tindale, R. S., Posavac, E. J., & Dugoni, B. L. (1991). Reasons for the trend toward null findings in research on Type A behavior. *Psychological Bulletin, 110*, 469–495.

Mills, D., Coffey-Corina, S., & Neville, H. (1994). Variability in cerebral organization during primary language acquisition. In G. Dawson & K. Fischer (Eds.) *Human behavior and the developing brain.* New York: Guilford Press.

Min, J. (2004, August 31). South Korea to introduce filial piety bill. *Straits Times Interactive.* Retrieved September 10, 2004, from http://straitstimes.asia1.com.sg/eyeoneastasia/story/0,4395,270186,00.html.

Minkler, M., & Fadem, P. (2002). "Successful aging": A disability perspective. *Journal of Disability Policy Studies, 12*, 229–235.

Minkler, M., Fuller-Thomson, E., & Guralnik, J. (2006). *New England Journal of Medicine, 355*, 695–703.

Mischel, W. (1966). A social learning view of sex differences in behavior. In E. E. Maccoby (Ed.), *The development of sex differences* (pp. 56–81). Stanford, CA: Stanford University Press.

Mischel, W. (1970). Sex typing and socialization. In P. H. Mussen (Ed.), *Carmichael's manual of child psychology, Vol. 2* (pp. 3–72). New York: Wiley.

Mitchell, P. R., & Kent, R. D. (1990). Phonetic variation in multisyllable babbling. *Journal of Child Language, 17*, 247–265.

Moen, P., & Erickson, M. A. (1995). Linked lives: A transgenerational approach to resilience. In P. Moen, G. H. Elder, Jr., & K. Lüscher (Eds.), *Examining lives in context: Perspectives on the ecology of human development* (pp. 169–210). Washington, DC: American Psychological Association.

Mohan, J. (2006). Cardiac psychology. *Journal of the Indian Academy of Applied Psychology, 32*, 214–220.

Mohanty, A. & Perregaux, C. (1997). Language acquisition and bilingualism. In J. Berry, P. Dasen, & T. Saraswath (Eds.), *Handbook of cross-cultural psychology, Vol. 2.* Boston: Allyn & Bacon.

Mohsin, M., Wong, F., Bauman, A., & Bai, J. (2003). Maternal and neonatal factors influencing premature birth and low birth weight in Australia. *Journal of Biosocial Science, 35*, 161–174.

Monarch, E., Saykin, A., & Flashman, L. (2004). Neuropsychological impairment in borderline personality disorder. *Psychiatric Clinics of North America, 27*, 67–82.

Monk, C., Webb, S., & Nelson, C. (2001). Prenatal neurobiological development: Molecular mechanisms and anatomical change. *Developmental Neuropsychology, 19*, 211–236.

Monroy, T. (2000, March 15). Boomers alter economics. *Interactive Week.* Retrieved March 21, 2000, from http://www.ZDNet.com.

Montemayor, R., & Eisen, M. (1977). The development of self-conceptions from childhood to adolescence. *Developmental Psychology, 13*, 314–319.

Montero, I., & De Dios, M. (2006). Vygotsky was right: An experimental approach to the relationship between private speech and task performance. *Estudios de Psicologia, 27*, 175–189.

Moon, C., & Fifer, W. P. (1990). Syllables as signals for 2-day-old infants. *Infant Behavior & Development, 13*, 377–390.

Mooney, L., Knox, D., & Schacht, C. (2000a). *Social problems.* Belmont, CA: Wadsworth.

Mooney, L., Knox, D., & Schacht, C. (2000b). *Understanding social problems* (2nd ed.). Thousand Oaks, CA: Wadsworth.

Moore, C. (2007). Maternal behavior, infant development, and the question of developmental resources. *Developmental Psychobiology, 49*, 45–53.

Moore, C., Barresi, J., & Thompson, C. (1998). The cognitive basis of future-oriented prosocial behavior. *Social Development, 7*, 198–218.

Moore, K. L., & Persaud, T. V. N. (1993). *The developing human: Clinically oriented embryology* (5th ed.). Philadelphia: Saunders.

Mor, V. (1987). *Hospice care systems: Structure, process, costs, and outcome.* New York: Springer.

Mor, V., Greer, D. S., & Kastenbaum, R. (Eds.). (1988). *The hospice experiment.* Baltimore, MD: Johns Hopkins University Press.

Morfei, M., Hooker, K., Carpenter, J., Mix, C., & Blakeley, E. (2004). Agentic and communal generative behavior in four areas of adult life: Implications for psychological well-being. *Adult Development, 11*, 55–58.

Morgan, B., Finan, A., Yarnold, R., Petersen, S., Horsfield, M., Rickett, A., & Wailoo, M. (2002). Assessment of infant physiology and neuronal development using magnetic resonance imaging. *Child: Care, Health, & Development, 28*, 7–10.

Morgan, C., Covington, J., Geisler, M., Polich, J., & Murphy, C. (1997). Olfactory event-related potentials: Older males demonstrate the greatest deficits. *Electroencephalography & Clinical Neurophysiology, 104*, 351–358.

Morgan, D. G. (1992). Neurochemical changes with aging: Predisposition towards age-related mental disorders. In J. E. Birren, R. B. Sloane, & G. D. Cohen (Eds.), *Handbook of mental health and aging* (2nd ed., pp. 175–200). San Diego, CA: Academic Press.

Morgan, J. L. (1994). Converging measures of speech segmentation in preverbal infants. *Infant Behavior & Development, 17*, 389–403.

Morgan, L. A. (1991). *After marriage ends: Economic consequences for midlife women.* Newbury Park, CA: Sage.

Mork, J., Lie, K., Glattre, E., Clark, S., Hallmans, G., Jellum, E., Koskela, P., Moller, B., Pukkala, E., Schiller, J., Wang, Z., Youngman, L., Lehtinen, M., & Dillner, J. (2001). Human papillomavirus infection as a risk factor for squamous-cell carcumoma of the head and neck. *New England Journal of Medicine, 344*, 1125–1131.

Morrissette, P. (1999). Post-traumatic stress disorder in child sexual abuse: Diagnostic and treatment considerations. *Child & Youth Care Forum, 28*, 205–219.

Morrongiello, B. A. (1988). Infants' localization of sounds along the horizontal axis: Estimates of minimum audible angle. *Developmental Psychology, 24*, 8–13.

Morrongiello, B. A., Fenwick, K. D., & Chance, G. (1990). Sound localization acuity in very young infants: An observer-based testing procedure. *Developmental Psychology, 24*, 75–84.

Morrow, D., Menard, W., Ridolfo, H., Stine-Morrow, E., Teller, T., & Bryant, D. (2003). Expertise, cognitive ability, and age effects on pilot communication. *International Journal of Aviation Psychology, 13*, 345–371.

Morse, P. A., & Cowan, N. (1982). Infant auditory and speech perception. In T. M. Field, A. Houston, H. C. Quay, L. Troll, & G. E. Finley (Eds.), *Review of human development* (pp. 32–61). New York: Wiley.

Mortimer, J., & Harley, C. (2002). The quality of work and youth mental health. *Work & Occupations, 29*, 166–197.

Mortimer, J., Zimmer-Gembeck, M., Holmes, M., & Shanahan, M. (2002). The process of occupational decision making: Patterns during the transition to adulthood. *Journal of Vocational Behavior, 61*, 439–465.

Mortimer, J. T., & Finch, M. D. (1996). Work, family, and adolescent development. In J. T. Mortimer & M. D. Finch (Eds.), *Adolescents, work, and family: An intergenerational developmental analysis* (pp. 1–24. Thousand Oaks, CA: Sage.

Mortimer, J. T., Finch, M. D., Dennehy, K., Lee, C., & Beebe, T. (1995, March). *Work experience in adolescence.* Paper presented at the biennial meetings of the Society for Research in Child Development, Indianapolis, IN.

Mosher, W. D. (1987). Infertility: Why business is booming. *American Demography*, June, 42–43.

Mosher, W. D., & Pratt, W. F. (1987). Fecundity, infertility, and reproductive health in the United States, 1982. *Vital Health Statistics, 23 (14).*

Mounts, N. S., & Steinberg, L. (1995). An ecological analysis of peer influence on adolescent grade point average and drug use. *Developmental Psychology, 31*, 915–922.

Mueller, K., & Yoder, J. (1999). Stigmatization of non-normative family size status. *Sex Roles, 41*, 901–919.

Mullins, L. C., & Mushel, M. (1992). The existence and emotional closeness of relationships with children, friends, and spouses. The effect on loneliness among older persons. *Research on Aging, 14*, 448–470.

Munroe, R. H., Shimmin, H. S., & Munroe, R. L. (1984). Gender understanding and sex role preference in four cultures. *Developmental Psychology, 20*, 673–682.

Murnen, S., Smolak, L., Mills, J., & Good, L. (2003). Thin, sexy women and strong, muscular men: Grade-school children's responses to objectified images of women and men. *Sex Roles, 49*, 427–437.

Murphy, K., Hanrahan, P., & Luchins, D. (1997). A survey of grief and bereavement in nursing homes: The importance of hospice grief and bereavement for the end-stage Alzheimer's disease patient and family. *Journal of the American Geriatrics Society, 45*, 1104–1107.

Murphy, S., Braun, T., Tillery, L., Cain, K., Johnson, L., & Beaton, R. (1999). PTSD among bereaved parents following the violent deaths of their 12- to 28-year-old children: A longitudinal prospective analysis. *Journal of Traumatic Stress, 12*, 273–291.

Murphy, S., Johnson, L., & Lohan, J. (2003). Finding meaning in a child's violent death: A five-year propective analysis of parents' personal narratives and empirical data. *Death Studies, 27*, 381–404.

Murray, B. (1998, June). Dipping math scores heat up debate over math teaching. *APA Monitor, 29*, 34–35.

Murray, J., Liotti, M., Ingmundson, P., Mayberg, H., Pu U., Zamarripa, F., Liu, Y., Woldorff, M., Gao, J., & Fox, P. (2006). Children's brain activations while viewing televised violence revealed by MRO. *Media Psychology, 8*, 25–37.

Murray, L., Sinclair, D., Cooper, P., Ducournau, P., et al. (1999). The socio-emotional development of 5-year-old children of postnatally depressed mothers. *Journal of Child Psychology & Psychiatry & Allied Disciplines, 40*, 1259–1271.

Murrell, S. A., & Himmelfarb, S. (1989). Effects of attachment bereavement and pre-event conditions on subsequent depressive symptoms in older adults. *Psychology & Aging, 4*, 166–172.

Musick, M., Koenig, H., Hays, J., & Cohen, H. (1998). Religious activity and depression among community-dwelling elderly persons with cancer: The moderating effect of race. *Journals of Gerontology, Series B: Psychological Sciences & Social Sciences, 53B*, S218–S227.

Mutch, L., Leyland, A., & McGee, A. (1993). Patterns of neuropsychological function in a low-birth-weight population. *Developmental Medicine & Child Neurology, 35*, 943–956.

Muzi, M. (2000). *The experience of parenting.* Upper Saddle River, NJ: Prentice Hall.

Nagamine, S. (1999). Interpersonal conflict situations: Adolescents' negotiation processes using an interpersonal negotiation strategy model: Adolescents' relations with their parents and friends. *Japanese Journal of Educational Psychology, 47*, 218–228.

Nagumey, A., Reich, J., & Newsom, J. (2004). Gender moderates the effects of independence and dependence desires during the social support process. *Psychology & Aging, 19*, 215–218.

Nagy, W., Berninger, V., Abbott, R., Vaughan, K., & Vermeulen, K. (2004). Relationship of morphology and other language skills to literacy skills in at-risk second-grade readers and at-risk fourth-grade writers. *Journal of Educational Psychology, 96*, 730–742.

Namka, L. (2002). *What the research literature says about corporal punishment.* Retrieved June 15, 2007 from http://www.angriesout.com/parents10.htm

Narvaez, D. (1998). The influence of moral schemas on the reconstruction of moral narratives in eighth graders and college students. *Journal of Educational Psychology, 90*, 13–24.

National Cancer Institute (NCI). (2000). *Questions and answers about smoking cessation.* Retrieved July 4, 2007 from www.cancer.gov/cancertopics/factsheet/Tobacco/cessation.

National Cancer Institute. (2006). *Breast cancer and the environment research centers chart new territory.* Retrieved June 21, 2007 from http://www.nci.nih.gov/ncicancerbulletin/NCI_Cancer_Bulletin_081506/page9

National Center for Chronic Disease Prevention and Health Promotion. (2000). *Obesity epidemic increases dramatically in the United States.* Retrieved August 23, 2000, from http://www.cdc.gov.

National Center for Education Statistics (NCES). (1997). *Condition of education/1997.* Washington, DC: U.S. Department of Education.

National Center for Education Statistics (NCES). (2004). *A matter of degrees.* Retrieved April 28, 2006 from www2.edtrust.org/NR/rdonlyres/11B4283F-104E-4511-B0CA-1D3023231157/0/highered.pdf.

National Center for Education Statistics (NCES). (2006). *Digest of education statistics 2005.* (NCES 2006-030). Retrieved June 22, 2007 from http://nces.ed.gov/programs/digest/d05/

National Center for Education Statistics (NCES). (2006). *How many students with disabilities receive services?* Retrieved June 19, 2007 from http://nces.ed.gov/fastfacts/display.asp?id=64

National Center for Education Statistics (NCES). (2006a). *2005 Reading Results.* Retrieved May 18, 2007 from http://nces.ed.gov/nationsreportcard/nrc/reading_math_2005/s0002.asp?printver=

National Center for Education Statistics (NCES). (2006b). *2005 Math Results.* Retrieved May 18, 2007 from http://nces.ed.gov/nationsreportcard/nrc/reading_math_2005/s0017.asp?printver=

National Center for Education Statistics (NCES). (2007). *The condition of education.* Retrieved July 3, 2007 from http://nces.ed.gov/programs/coe/2007/pdf/08_2007.pdf.

National Center for Education Statistics. (1998). *Digest of educational statistics.* Washington, DC: Author.

National Center for Education Statistics. (2003a). *The nation's report card: Mathematics highlights 2003.* Washington, DC: U.S. Department of Education, NCES 2004–451.

National Center for Education Statistics. (2003b). *The nation's report card: Reading highlights 2003.* Washington, DC: U.S. Department of Education, NCES 2004–452.

National Center for Health Statistics (NCHS). (2005). *Health, United States, 2005.* Retrieved July 5, 2007 from www.cdc.gov/nchs/data/hus/hus05.pdf#053.

National Center for Health Statistics (NCHS). (2005). *Health, United States, 2005.* Retrieved July 31, 2007 from www.cdc.gov/NCHS/data/hus/hus05.pdf#summary.

National Center for Health Statistics (NCHS). (2006). *Health, United States, 2006.* Hyattsville, MD: Author.

National Center for Health Statistics (NCHS). (2006). *Health, United States 2006.* Retrieved July 6, 2007 from www.cdc.gov/nchs/hus.htm.

National Center for Health Statistics (NCHS). (2006). *Health, United States, 2006.* Retrieved July 31, 2007 from http://www.cdc.gov/nchs/data/hus/hus06.pdf#027.

National Center for Health Statistics (NCHS). (2007). *Prevalence of overweight among children and adolescents: United States 2003–2004.* Retrieved June 19, 2007 from www.cdc.gov/nchs/products/pubs/pubd/hestats/overweight/overwght_child_03.htm

National Center for Health Statistics. (1999, September 14). Trends in twin and triplet births: 1980–1997. *National Vital Statistics Reports.*

National Center for Health Statistics. (2000a). *CDC growth charts.* Retrieved August 23, 2000, from http://www.cdc.gov/nchs.

National Center for Health Statistics. (2003). *Births: Final data for 2002.* Retrieved June 18, 2004, from http://www.cdc.gov/nchs/pressroom/3facts/teenbirth.htm.

National Center for Health Statistics. (NCHS). (2007). *Deaths by place of death, age, race, and sex: United States, 1999–2004.* Retrieved August 3, 2007 from www.cdc.gov/nchs/datawh/statab/unpubd/mortabs/gmwk309_10.htm.

National Center for Injury Prevention and Control (NCIPC). (2000). *Fact book for the year 2000.* Washington, DC: Author.

National Center for Injury Prevention and Control (NCIPC). (2006). *Intimate partner violence.* Retrieved July 3, 2007 from www.cdc.gov/ncipc/factsheets/ipvfacts.htm.

National Center for Injury Prevention and Control (NCIPC). (2007). *Suicide* Retrieved July 3, 2007 from www.cdc.gov/ncipc/factsheets/suifacts.htm

National Clearinghouse for English Language Acquisition and Language Instruction Educational Programs (NCELA). (2002). *The growing numbers of limited English proficient students.* Retrieved June 23, 2004, from http://www.ncela.gwu.edu/policy/states/stateposter.pdf.

National Health Interview Survey (NHIS). (2002). Prevalence of visual impairment and selected eye diseases among person aged ≥ 50 years with and without diabetes, United States, 2002. *Morbidity and Mortality Weekly Report, 53,* 1069–1071.

National Institute of Child Health and Human Development (NICHD) Early Child Care Research Network. (1998). The effects of infant child care on mother-infant attachment security: Results of the NICHD study of early child care. *Child Development, 68,* 860–879.

National Institute of Child Health and Human Development Early Child Care Research Network. (1999). Chronicity of maternal depressive symptoms, maternal sensitivity, and child functioning at 36 months. *Developmental Psychology, 35,* 1297–1310.

National Institute of Child Health and Human Development Early Child Care Research Network. (2003). Does amount of time spent in child care predict socioemotional adjustment during the transition to kindergarten? *Child Development, 74,* 976–1005.

National Institute of Child Health and Human Development (NICHD) Early Child Care Research Network. (2004b). Are child developmental outcomes related to before- and after-school care arrangements? Results from the NICHD Study of Early Child Care. *Child Development, 75,* 280–295.

National Institute of Mental Health (NIMH). (2001). *The numbers count: Mental disorders in America.* NIMH Report No. 01-4584). Washington DC: Author.

National Institute on Aging (NIA). (2000a). *Depression: A serious but treatable illness.* Retrieved February 7, 2001, from http://www.nih.gov/nia.

National Institute on Aging. (2000b). *Sexuality in later life.* Retrieved February 7, 2001, from http://www.nih.gov/nia.

National Middle School Association (NMSA). (2004). *Small schools and small learning communities.* Retrieved June 22, 2007 from http://www.nmsa.org/AboutNMSA/PositionStatements/SmallSchools/tabid/293/Default.aspx

National Vital Statistics System. (2006). *Death rates by 10-year age groups: United States and each state 2004.* Retrieved July 9, 2007 from www.cdc.gov/nchs/data/statab/mortfinal2004_worktable23r.pdf.

Naude, H., & Pretorius, E. (2003). Investigating the effects of asthma medication on the cognitive and psychosocial functioning of primary school children with asthma. *Early Child Development & Care, 173,* 699–709.

Neild, R., & Balfanz, R. (2006). An extreme degree of difficulty: The educational demographics of urban neighborhood high schools. *Journal of Education for Students Placed at Risk, 11,* 123–141.

Neill, M. (1998). *High stakes tests do not improve student learning.* Retrieved October 21, 1998, from http://www.fairtest.org.

Neill, M. (2000). Too much harmful testing? *Educational Measurement: Issues & Practice, 16,* 57–58.

Neimeyer, R., Prigerson, H., & Davies, B. (2002). Mourning and meaning. *American Behavioral Scientist, 46,* 235–251.

Neisser, U., Boodoo, G., Bouchard, T. J., Jr., Boykin, A. W., Brody, N., Ceci, S. J., Halpern, D. F., Loehlin, J. C., Perloff, R., Sternberg, R. J., & Urbina, S. (1996). Intelligence: Knowns and unknowns. *American Psychologist, 51,* 77–101.

Neitzel, C., & Stright, A. (2003). Mothers' scaffolding of children's problem solving: Establishing a foundation of academic self-regulatory competence. *Journal of Family Psychology, 17,* 147–159.

Nelson, E. A., & Dannefer, D. (1992). Aged heterogeneity: Fact or fiction? The fate of diversity in gerontological research. *The Gerontologist, 32,* 17–23.

Nelson, H. (2004). Commonly used types of postmenopausal estrogen for treatment of hot flashes: Scientific review. *Journal of the American Medical Association, 291,* 1610–1620.

Nelson, H., Humphrey, L., Nygren, P., Teutsch, S., & Allan, J. (2002). Postmenopausal hormone replacement therapy: Scientific review. *Journal of the American Medical Association, 288,* 872–881.

Nelson, K. (1973). Structure and strategy in learning to talk. *Monographs of the Society for Research in Child Development, 38* (Serial No. 149).

Nelson, K. (1977). Facilitating children's syntax acquisition. *Developmental Psychology, 13,* 101–107.

Nelson, M. E., Fiatarone, M. A., Morganti, C. M., Trice, I., Greenberg, R. A., & Evans, W. J. (1994). Effects of high-intensity strength training on multiple risk factors for osteoporotic fractures. *Journal of the American Medical Association, 272,* 1909–1914.

Nelson, S. (1980). Factors influencing young children's use of motives and outcomes as moral criteria. *Child Development, 51,* 823–829.

Neshat-Doost, H., Taghavi, M., Moradi, A., Yule, W., & Dalgleish, T. (1998). Memory for emotional trait adjectives in clinically depressed youth. *Journal of Abnormal Psychology, 107,* 642–650.

Neugarten, B. L. (1970). Dynamics of transition of middle age to old age. *Journal of Geriatric Psychiatry, 4,* 71–87.

Neugarten, B. L. (1979). Time, age, and the life cycle. *American Journal of Psychiatry, 136,* 887–894.

Neugebauer, R., Hoek, H., & Susser, E. (1999). Prenatal exposure to wartime famine and development of antisocial personal disorder in early adulthood. *Journal of the American Medical Association, 282,* 455–462.

Neumark-Sztainer, D., Wall, M., Eisenberg, M., Story, M., & Hannan, P. (2006). Overweight status and weight control behaviors in adolescents: Longitudinal and secular trends from 1999 to 2004. *Preventive Medicine, 43,* 52–59.

Newcomb, A. F., & Bagwell, C. L. (1995). Children's friendship relations: A meta-analytic review. *Psychological Bulletin, 117,* 306–347.

Newcomb, A. F., Bukowski, W. M., & Pattee, L. (1993). Children's peer relations: A meta-analytic review of popular, rejected, neglected, controversial, and average sociometric status. *Psychological Bulletin, 113,* 99–128.

Newman, D., Caspi, A., Moffitt, T., & Silva, P. (1997). Antecedents of adult interpersonal functioning: Effects of individual differences in age 3 temperament. *Developmental Psychology, 33,* 206–217.

Ng, A., Ying, P., Phillips, D., & Lee, W. (2002). Persistence and challenges to filial piety and informal support of older persons in a modern Chinese society: A case study in Tuen Mun, Hong Kong. *Journal of Aging Studies, 16,* 135–153.

Ng, B., & Wiemer-Hastings, P. (2005). Addiction to the internet and online gaming. *Cyberpsychological Behavior, 8,* 110–113.

Ni, Y. (1998). Cognitive structure, content knowledge, and classificatory reasoning. *Journal of Genetic Psychology, 159,* 280–296.

NICHD Early Child Care Research Network. (2006). Child-care effect sizes for the NICHD Study of Early Child Care and Youth Development. *American Psychologist, 61,* 99–116.

Nichols, A. (2006). *Understanding recent changes in child poverty.* Retrieved June 20, 2007 from http://www.urbaninstitute.org/UploadedPDF/311356_A71.pdf

Nichols, D., & Melov, S. (2004). The aging cell. *Aging, 3,* 1474–1497.

Nicholson, J. (1998). Inborn errors of metabolism. In R. Behrman & R. Kliegman (Eds.), *Nelson essentials of pediatrics* (3rd ed., pp. 147–166). Philadelphia: W. B. Saunders.

Nicholson, R., Houle, T., Rhudy, J., & Norton, P. (2007). Psychological risk factors in headache. *Headache: The Journal of Head and Face Pain, 47,* 413–425.

Nicklaus, S., Boggio, V., & Issanchou, S. (2005). Gustatory perceptions in children. *Archives of Pediatrics, 12,* 579–584.

Niesse, M. (2007). *Lawmakers considering 'safe haven' for newborns.* Retrieved June 18, 2007 from http://the.honoluluadvertiser.com/article/2007/Apr/22/br/br5241960337.html

Nightingale, E. O., & Goodman, M. (1990). *Before birth. Prenatal testing for genetic disease.* Cambridge, MA: Harvard University Press.

Nijhuis, J. (2003). Fetal behavior. *Neurobiology of Aging, 24,* S41–S46.

Nilsson, E., Gillberg, C., Gillberg, I., & Rastam, M. (1999). Ten-year follow-up of adolescent-onset anorexia nervosa: Personality disorders. *Journal of the American Academy of Child & Adolescent Psychiatry, 38,* 1389–1395.

Nilsson, L., Baeckman, L., Erngrund, K., & Nyberg, L. (1997). The Betula prospective cohort study: Memory, health, and aging. *Aging, Neuropsychology, & Cognition, 4,* 1–32.

Nilsson, S., Johansson, B., Takkinen, S., Berg, S., Zarit, S., McClearn, G., & Melander, A. (2003). Does aspirin protect against Alzheimer's dementia? *European Journal of Clinical Pharmacology, 59,* 313–319.

Nisan, M., & Kohlberg, L. (1982). Universality and variation in moral judgment: A longitudinal and cross-sectional study in Turkey. *Child Development, 53,* 865–876.

Niska, K., Snyder, M., & Lia-Hoagberg, B. (1998). Family ritual facilitates adaptation to parenthood. *Public Health Nursing, 15,* 329–337.

Noldon, D., & Sedlacek, W. (1998). Gender differences in attitudes, skills, and behaviors among academically talented university freshmen. *Roeper Review, 21,* 106–109.

Nolen-Hoeksema, S., & Girgus, J. S. (1994). The emergence of gender differences in depression during adolescence. *Psychological Bulletin, 115,* 424–443.

Norboru, T. (1997). A developmental study of wordplay in preschool children: The Japanese game of "Shiritori." *Japanese Journal of Developmental Psychology, 8,* 42–52.

Norman, S., Norman, G., Rossi, J., & Prochaska, J. (2006). Identifying high- and low-success smoking cessation subgroups using signal detection analysis. *Addictive Behaviors, 31,* 31–41.

Norris, F. H., & Murrell, S. A. (1990). Social support, life events, and stress as modifiers of adjustment to bereavement by older adults. *Psychology & Aging, 5,* 429–436.

Norton, A. J. (1983). Family life cycle: 1980. *Journal of Marriage & the Family, 45,* 267–275.

Norwood, T. H., Smith, J. R., & Stein, G. H. (1990). Aging at the cellular level: The human fibroblastlike cell model. In E. R. Schneider & J. W. Rowe (Eds.), *Handbook of the biology of aging* (3rd ed., pp. 131–154). San Diego, CA: Academic Press.

Nucci, L., & Smetana, J. (1996). Mothers' concepts of young children's areas of personal freedom. *Child Development, 67,* 1870–1886.

Nussbaum, A., & Steele, C. (2007). Situational disengagement and persistence in the face of adversity. *Journal of Experimental Social Psychology, 43,* 127–134.

Oates, J. (1998). Risk factors for infant attrition and low engagement in experiments and free-play. *Infant Behavior & Development, 21,* 569.

Oates, M., Cox, J., Neema, S., Asten, P., Glangeaud-Freudenthal, N., Figueiredo, B., Gorman, L., Hacking, S., Hirst, E., Kammerer, M., Klier, C., Seneviratne, G., Smith, M., Sutter-Dallay, A., Valoriani, V., Wickberg, B., & Yoshida, K. (2004). Postnatal depression across countries and cultures: A qualitative study. *British Journal of Psychiatry, 184* (Supp. 146), s10–s16.

Oatley, K., & Jenkins, J. (1996). *Understanding emotions.* Cambridge, MA: Blackwell Publishers.

Öberg, P., & Tornstam, L. (2001). Youthfulness and fitness: Identity ideals for all ages? *Journal of Aging & Identity, 6,* 15–29.

O'Beirne, H., & Moore, C. (1995, March). *Attachment and sexual behavior in adolescence.* Paper presented at the biennial meetings of the Society for Research in Child Development, Indianapolis, IN.

O'Brien, C. (1996). Recent developments in the pharmacotherapy of substance abuse. *Journal of Consulting and Clinical Psychology, 64,* 677–686.

O'Brien, M. (1992). Gender identity and sex roles. In V. B. Van Hasselt & M. Hersen (Eds.), *Handbook of social development: A lifespan perspective* (pp. 325–345). New York: Plenum.

O'Connor, B. P. (1995). Identity development and perceived parental behavior as sources of adolescent egocentrism. *Journal of Youth & Adolescence, 24,* 205–227.

O'Connor, N. J., Manson, J. E., O'Connor, G. T., & Buring, J. E. (1995). Psychosocial risk factors and nonfatal myocardial infarction. *Circulation, 92,* 1458–1464.

O'Connor, T., Bredenkamp, D., & Rutter, M. (1999). Attachment disturbances and disorders in children exposed to early severe deprivation. *Infant Mental Health Journal, 20,* 10–29.

Office of Educational Research and Improvement (OERI). (1998). *The educational system in Japan: Case study findings.* Washington, DC: U.S. Department of Education.

Offord, D. R., Boyle, M. H., & Racine, Y. A. (1991). The epidemiology of antisocial behavior in childhood and adolescence. In D. J. Pepler & K. H. Rubin (Eds.), *The development and treatment of childhood aggression* (pp. 31–54). Hillsdale, NJ: Erlbaum.

Ofiesh, N., Hughes, C., & Scott, S. (2004). Extended test time and postsecondary students with learning disabilities: A model for decision making. *Learning Disabilities Research & Practice, 19,* 57–70.

Ofstedal, M., Zimmer, Z., & Lin, H. (1999). A comparison of correlates of cognitive functioning in older persons in Taiwan and the United States. *Journals of Gerontology, Series B: Psychological Sciences & Social Sciences. 54B,* S291–S301.

Ogbu, J. (1990). Cultural models, identity and literacy. In J. W. Stigler, R. A. Shweder, & G. Hendt (Eds.), *Cultural psychology: Essays on comparative human development* (pp. 520–541). Hillsdale, NJ: Erlbaum.

Oggins, J. (2003). Topics of marital disagreement among African-American and Euro-American newlyweds. *Psychological Reports, 92,* 419–425.

O'Hara, M. W., Schlechte, J. A., Lewis, D. A., & Varner, M. W. (1992). Controlled prospective study of postpartum mood disorders: Psychological, environmental, and hormonal variables. *Journal of Abnormal Psychology, 100,* 63–73.

Okwumabua, J., Baker, F., Wong, S., & Pilgram, B. (1997). Characteristics of depressive symptoms in elderly urban and rural African Americans. *Journal of Gerontology, 52A,* M241–M246.

O'Leary, A. (1990). Stress, emotion, and human immune function. *Psychological Bulletin, 108,* 363–382.

O'Leary, S., Slep, A. S., & Reid, M. (1999). A longitudinal study of mothers' overreactive discipline and toddlers' externalizing behavior. *Journal of Abnormal Child Psychology, 27,* 331–341.

Olin, J., & Zelinski, E. (1997). Age differences in calibration of comprehension. *Educational Gerontology, 23,* 67–77.

Oller, D., Cobo-Lewis, A., & Eilers, R. (1998). Phonological translation in bilingual and monolingual children. *Applied Psycholinguistics, 19,* 259–278.

Oller, D. K. (1981). Infant vocalizations: Exploration and reflectivity. In R. E. Stark (Ed.), *Language behavior in infancy and early childhood* (pp. 85–104). New York: Elsevier North-Holland.

Olsen, J., Weed, S., Nielsen, A., & Jensen, L. (1992). Student evaluation of sex education programs advocating abstinence. *Adolescence, 27,* 380.

Olson, H., Feldman, J., Streissguth, A., Sampson, P., & Bookstein, F. (1998). Neuropsychological deficits in adolescents with fetal alcohol syndrome: Clinical findings. *Alcoholism: Clinical & Experimental Research, 22,* 1998–2012.

Olson, M., Krantz, D., Kelsey, S., Pepine, C., Sopko, G., Handberg, E., Rogers, W., Gierach, G., McClure, C., & Merz, C. (2005). Hostility scores are associated with increased risk of cardiovascular events in women undergoing coronary angiography: A report from the NHLBI-sponsored WISE study. *Psychosomatic Medicine, 67,* 546–552.

Olson, S. L., Bates, J. E., & Kaskie, B. (1992). Caregiver-infant interaction antecedents of children's school-age cognitive ability. *Merrill-Palmer Quarterly, 38,* 309–330.

Olweus, D. (1995). Bullying or peer abuse at school: Facts and intervention. *Current Directions in Psychological Science, 4,* 196–200.

Oman, D., Thoresen, C., & McMahon, K. (1999). Volunteerism and mortality among the community-dwelling elderly. *Journal of Health Psychology, 4,* 301–316.

Omiya, A., & Uchida, N. (2002). The development of children's thinking strategies: The retrieval of alternatives based on the categorization with conditional reasoning tasks. *Japanese Journal of Psychology, 73,* 10–17.

Ompad, D., Strathdee, S., Celentano, D., Latkin, C., Poduska, J., Kellam, S., & Ialongo, N. (2006). Predictors of early initiation of vaginal and oral sex among urban young adults in Baltimore, Maryland. *Archives of Sexual Behavior, 35,* 53–65.

O'Neill, D. K., Astington, J. W., & Flavell, J. H. (1992). Young children's understanding of the role that sensory experiences play in knowledge acquisition. *Child Development, 63,* 474–490.

Onen, S., Onen, F., Mangeon, J., Abidi, H., Courpron, P., & Schmidt, J. (2005). Alcohol abuse and dependence in elderly emergency department patients. *Archives of Gerontology and Geriatrics, 41,* 191–200.

Onrust, S., & Cuijpers, P. (2006). Mood and anxiety disorders in widowhood: A systematic review. *Aging & Mental Health, 10,* 327–334.

Operario, D., Adler, N., & Williams, D. (2004). Subjective social status: reliability and predictive utility for global health. *Psychology & Health, 19,* 237–246.

Organization of Teratology Information Specialists. (2005). *Acetaminophen and pregnancy.* Retrieved June 7, 2007 from www.otispregnancy.org/pdf/acetaminophen.pdf

Ornish, D. (1990). *Dr. Dean Ornish's program for reversing heart disease.* New York: Random House.

Ornoy, A. (2002). The effects of alcohol and illicit drugs on the human embryo and fetus. *Israel Journal of Psychiatry & Related Sciences, 39*, 120–132.

Orth-Gomér, K., Rosengren, A., & Wilhelmsen, L. (1993). Lack of social support and incidence of coronary heart disease in middle-aged Swedish men. *Psychosomatic Medicine, 55*, 37–43.

Orwoll, L., & Perlmutter, M. (1990). The study of wise persons: Integrating a personality perspective. In R. J. Sternberg (Ed.), *Wisdom: Its nature, origins, and development* (pp. 160–180). Cambridge, England: Cambridge University Press.

Osofsky, J. D. (1995). The effects of exposure to violence on young children. *American Psychologist, 50*, 782–788.

Osofsky, J. D., Hann, D. M., & Peebles, C. (1993). Adolescent parenthood: Risks and opportunities for mothers and infants. In C. H. Zeanah, Jr. (Ed.), *Handbook of infant mental health* (pp. 106–119). New York: Guilford Press.

Ostoja, E., McCrone, E., Lehn, L., Reed, T., & Sroufe, L. A. (1995, March). *Representations of close relationships in adolescence: Longitudinal antecedents from infancy through childhood.* Paper presented at the biennial meetings of the Society for Research in Child Development, Indianapolis, IN.

Ostrom, T., Carpenter, S., Sedikides, C., & Li, F. (1993). Differential processing of in-group and out-group information. *Journal of Personality & Social Psychology, 64*, 21–34.

O'Sullivan, M. (November 9, 2006). 7 US states ban gay marriage, South Dakota overturns abortion ban. Retrieved July 8, 2007 from www.voanews.com/english/archive/2006-11/CR-OSULLIVAN-BALLOT-MEASURES.cfm.

Overby, K. (2002). Pediatric health supervision. In A. Rudolph, R. Kamei, & K. Overby (Eds.), *Rudolph's fundamental of pediatrics* (3rd ed., pp. 1–69). New York: McGraw-Hill.

Overmeyer, S., & Taylor, E. (1999). Principles of treatment for hyperkinetic disorder: Practice approaches for the U.K. *Journal of Child Psychology & Psychiatry & Allied Disciplines, 40*, 1147–1157.

Owen, P. (1998). Fears of Hispanic and Anglo children: Real-world fears in the 1990s. *Hispanic Journal of Behavioral Sciences, 20*, 483–491.

Owens, G., Crowell, J. A., Pan, H., Treboux, D., O'Connor, E., & Waters, E. (1995). The prototype hypothesis and the origins of attachment working models: Adult relationships with parents and romantic partners. *Monographs of the Society for Research in Child Development, 60* (244, No. 2–3), 216–233.

Paarlberg, K., Vingerhoets, A. J., Passchier, J., Dekker, G., & van Geign, H. (1995). Psychosocial factors and pregnancy outcome: A review with emphasis on methodological issues. *Journal of Psychosomatic Research, 39*, 563–595.

Paden, S. L., & Buehler, C. (1995). Coping with the dual-income lifestyle. *Journal of Marriage & the Family, 57*, 101–110.

Paffenbarger, R. S., Hyde, R. T., Wing, A. L., & Hsieh, C. (1987). Physical activity, all-cause mortality, and longevity of college alumni. *New England Journal of Medicine, 314*, 605–613.

Pagani, L., Boulerice, B., Tremblay, R., & Vitaro, F. (1997). Behavioural development in children of divorce and remarriage. *Journal of Child Psychology & Psychiatry & Allied Disciplines, 38*, 769–781.

Painter, M., & Bergman, I. (1998). Neurology. In R. Behrman & R. Kliegman (Eds.), *Nelson essentials of pediatrics* (3rd ed., pp. 694–745). Philadelphia: W. B. Saunders.

Palacios, M. (2004). *Investing in human capital: A capital market's approach to student funding.* Cambridge, U.K.: Cambridge University Press.

Paley, V. (1986). *Mollie is three: Growing up in school.* Chicago: University of Chicago Press.

Palla, B., & Litt, I. R. (1988). Medical complications of eating disorders in adolescents. *Pediatrics, 81*, 613–623.

Palmer, K. (June 22, 2007). Student loan reform: What to expect. *U.S. News Online.* Retrieved June 30, 2007 from www.usnews.com/usnews/biztech/articles/070622/22studentloan.htm?s_cid=rss 22 studentloan.htm.

Palmore, E. (1981). *Social patterns in normal aging: Findings from the Duke Longitudinal Study.* Durham, NC: Duke University Press.

Palmore, E. B. (1990). *Ageism: Negative and positive.* New York: Springer.

Palmore, E. B., Burchett, B. M., Fillenbaum, G. G., George, L. K., & Wallman, L. M. (1985). *Retirement. Causes and consequences.* New York: Springer.

Pang, T., & Lam, C. (2002). The widowers' bereavement process and death rituals: Hong Kong experiences. *Illness, Crisis, & Loss, 10*, 294–303.

Parent, S., Tillman, G., Jule, A., Skakkebaek, N., Toppari, J., & Bourguignon, J. (2003). The timing of normal puberty and the age limits of sexual precocity: Variations around the world, secular trends, and changes after migration. *Endocrine Review, 24*, 668–693.

Parke, R. (2004). The Society for Research in Child Development at 70: Progress and promise. *Child Development, 75*, 1–24.

Parke, R. D., & Tinsley, B. R. (1981). The father's role in infancy: Determinants of involvement in caregiving and play. In M. E. Lamb (Ed.), *The role of the father in child development* (2nd ed., pp. 429–458). New York: Wiley.

Parmelee, A. H., Jr., Wenner, W. H., & Schulz, H. R. (1964). Infant sleep patterns from birth to 16 weeks of age. *Journal of Pediatrics, 65*, 576–582.

Parnes, H. S., & Sommers, D. G. (1994). Shunning retirement: Work experience of men in their seventies and early eighties. *Journals of Gerontology: Social Sciences, 49*, S117–124.

Parrila, R., Kirby, J., & McQuarrie, L. (2004). Articulation rate, naming speed, verbal short-term memory, and phonological awareness: Longitudinal predictors of early reading development? *Scientific Studies of Reading, 8*, 3–26.

Parten, M. (1932). Social participation among preschool children. *Journal of Abnormal and Social Psychology, 27*, 243–269.

Pascalis, O., de Schonen, S., Morton, J., Derulle, C., & Fabre-Grenet, M. (1995). Mother's face recognition by neonates: A replication and extension. *Infant Behavior and Development, 18*, 79–85.

Pascarella, E. (1999). The development of critical thinking: Does college make a difference? *Journal of College Student Development, 40*, 562–569.

Pascarella, E., & Terenzi, P. (1991). *How college affects students: Findings and insights from twenty years of research.* San Francisco: Jossey-Bass.

Patterson, C. (2006). Children of lesbian and gay parents. *Current Directions in Psychological Science, 15*, 241–244.

Patterson, G. R. (1980). Mothers: The unacknowledged victims. *Monographs of the Society for Research in Child Development, 45* (Serial No. 186).

Patterson, G. R., Capaldi, D., & Bank, L. (1991). An early starter model for predicting delinquency. In D. J. Pepler & K. H. Rubin (Eds.), *The development and treatment of childhood aggression* (pp. 139–168). Hillsdale, NJ: Erlbaum.

Patterson, G. R., DeBarsyshe, B. D., & Ramsey, E. (1989). A developmental perspective on antisocial behavior. *American Psychologist, 44*, 329–335.

Patterson, J. (1998). Expressive vocabulary of bilingual toddlers: Preliminary findings. *Multicultural Electronic Journal of Communication Disorders, 1.* Retrieved April 11, 2001, from www.asha.ucf.edu/patterson.html.

Pauen, S. (2002). The global-to-basic level shift in infants' categorical thinking: First evidence from a longitudinal study. *International Journal of Behavioral Development, 26*, 492–499.

Payley, A. (April 19, 2007). Democrat demands student loan reform. *Washington Post Online.* Retrieved June 20, 3007 from http://www.washingtonpost.com/wp-dyn/content/article/2007/04/18/AR2007041802358.html.

Pearman, E. Elliott, T., & Aborn, L. (2004). Transition Services Model: Partnership for student success. *Education & Training in Developmental Disabilities, 39*, 26–34.

Pearsall, N., Skipper, J., & Mintzes, J. (1997). Knowledge restructuring in the life sciences: A longitudinal study of conceptual change in biology. *Science Education, 81*, 193–215.

Pearson, J., Hunter, A., & Cook, J. (1997). Grandmother involvement in child caregiving in an urban community. *Gerontologist, 37*, 650–657.

Pedersen, N. L., & Harris, J. R. (1990). Developmental behavioral genetics and successful aging. In P. B. Baltes & M. M. Baltes (Eds.), *Successful aging* (pp. 359–380). Cambridge, England: Cambridge University Press.

Pederson, D. R., & Moran, G. (1995). A categorical description of infant-mother relationships in the home and its relation to Q-sort measures of infant-mother interaction. *Monographs of the Society for Research in Child Development, 60* (244, Nos. 2–3), 111–132.

Pederson, D. R., Moran, G., Sitko, C., Campbell, K., Ghesquire, K., & Acton, H. (1990). Maternal sensitivity and the security of infant-mother attachment: A Q-sort study. *Child Development, 61*, 1974–1983.

Pediatric Nutrition Surveillance. (2005). *National summary of health indicators.* Retrieved June 14, 2007, from www.cdc.gov/pednss/pednss_tables/pdf/national_table2.pdf

Pedlow, R., Sanson, A., Prior, M., & Oberklaid, F. (1993). Stability of maternally reported temperament from infancy to 8 years. *Developmental Psychology, 29*, 998–1007.

Pegg, J. E., Werker, J. F., & McLeod, P. J. (1992). Preference for infant-directed over adult-directed speech: Evidence from 7-week-old infants. *Infant Behavior & Development, 15*, 325–345.

Peigneux, P., & van der Linden, M. (1999). Influence of ageing and educational level on the prevalence of body-part-as-objects in normal subjects. *Journal of Clinical & Experimental Neuropsychology, 21*, 547–552.

Peisner-Feinberg, E. S. (1995, March). *Developmental outcomes and the relationship to quality of child care experiences.* Paper presented at the biennial meetings of the Society for Research in Child Development, Indianapolis, IN.

Pelletier, L., Dion, S., & Levesque, C. (2004). Can self-determination help protect women against sociocultural influences about body image and reduce their risk of experiencing bulimic symptoms? *Journal of Social & Clinical Psychology, 23*, 61–88.

Pelligrini, A., & Smith, P. (1998). Physical activity play: The nature and function of a neglected aspect of play. *Child Development, 69*, 577–598.

Penedo, F., Dahn, J., Kinsinger, D., Antoni, M., Molton, I., Gonzalez, J., Fletcher, M., Roos, B., Carver, C., & Schneiderman, N. (2005). Anger suppression mediates the relationship between optimism and natural killer cell cytotoxicity in men treated for localized prostate cancer. *Journal of Psychosomatic Research, 60*, 423–427.

Peoples, C. E., Fagan, J. F., III, & Drotar, D. (1995). The influence of race on 3-year-old children's performance on the Stanford-Binet: Fourth edition. *Intelligence, 21*, 69–82.

Peplau, L. A. (1991). Lesbian and gay relationships. In J. C. Gonsiorek & J. D. Weinrich (Eds.), *Homosexuality: Research implications for public policy* (pp. 177–196). Newbury Park, CA: Sage.

Pereverzeva, M., Hui-Lin Chien, S., Palmer, J., & Teller, D. (2002). Infant photometry: Are mean adult isoluminance values a sufficient approximation to individual infant values? *Vision Research, 42*, 1639–1649.

Perho, H., & Korhonen, M. (1999). Coping in work and marriage at the onset of middle age. *Psykologia, 34*, 115–127.

Perry, W. (1968). *Forms of intellectual and ethical development in the college years.* New York: Holt, Rinehart & Winston.

Pesonen, A., Raikkonen, K., Strandberg, T., Kelitikangas-Jarvinen, & L., Jarvenpaa, A. (2004). Insecure adult attachment style and depressive symptoms: Implications for parental perceptions of infant temperament. *Infant Mental Health Journal, 25*, 99–116.

Petersen, A. C., Compas, B. E., Brooks-Gunn, J., Stemmler, M., Ey, S., & Grant, K. E. (1993). Depression in adolescence. *American Psychologist, 48*, 155–168.

Peterson, B. (2002). Longitudinal analysis of midlife generativity, intergenerational roles, and caregiving. *Psychology & Aging, 17*, 161–168.

Peterson, B. (2006). Generativity and successful parenting: An analysis of young adult outcomes. *Journal of Personality, 74*, 847–869.

Peterson, C. (1999). Grandfathers' and grandmothers' satisfaction with the grandparenting role: Seeking new answers to old questions. *International Journal of Aging & Human Development, 49*, 61–78.

Peterson, C., & Siegal, M. (1999). Representing inner worlds: Theory of mind in autistic, deaf, and normal hearing children. *Psychological Science, 10*, 126–129.

Peterson, C. C., & Siegal, M. (1995). Deafness, conversation and theory of mind. *Journal of Child Psychology & Psychiatry, 36*, 459–474.

Peterson, L., Ewigman, B., & Kivlahan, C. (1993). Judgments regarding appropriate child supervision to prevent injury: The role of environmental risk and child age. *Child Development, 64*, 934–950.

Petitto, L., Katerelos, M., Levy, B., Gauna, K., Tetreault, K., & Ferraro, V. (2001). Bilingual signed and spoken language from birth: Implications for the mechanisms underlying early bilingual language acquisition. *Journal of Child Language, 28*, 453–496.

Petitto, L. A. (1988). "Language" in the prelinguistic child. In F. S. Kessell (Ed.), *The development of language and language researchers: Essays in honor of Roger Brown* (pp. 187–222). Hillsdale, NJ: Erlbaum.

Pettingale, K. W., Morris, T., Greer, S., & Haybittle, J. L. (1985). Mental attitudes to cancer: An additional prognostic factor. *Lancet*, 85.

Pettit, G., Laird, R., Bates, J., & Dodge, K. (1997). Patterns of after-school care in middle childhood: Risk factors and developmental outcomes. *Merrill-Palmer Quarterly, 43*, 515–538.

Pettit, G. S., Clawson, M. A., Dodge, K. A., & Bates, J. E. (1996). Stability and change in peer-rejected status: The role of child behavior, parenting, and family ecology. *Merrill-Palmer Quarterly, 42*, 295–318.

Pezdek, K., Blandon-Gitlin, I., & Moore, C. (2003). Children's face recognition memory: More evidence for the cross-race effect. *Journal of Applied Psychology, 88*, 760–763.

Phelps, L., Wallace, N., & Bontrager, A. (1997). Risk factors in early child development: Is prenatal cocaine/polydrug exposure a key variable? *Psychology in the Schools, 34*, 245–252.

Phillips, A., Wellman, H., & Spelke, E. (2002). Infants' ability to connect gaze and emotional expression to intentional action. *Cognition, 85*, 53–78.

Phillips, D., Schwean, V., & Saklofske, D. (1997). Treatment effect of a school-based cognitive-behavioral program for aggressive children. *Canadian Journal of School Psychology, 13*, 60–67.

Phillips, S. K., Bruce, S. A., Newton, D., & Woledge, R. C. (1992). The weakness of old age is not due to failure of muscle activation. *Journals of Gerontology: Medical Sciences, 47*, M45–49.

Phillipsen, L. (1999). Associations between age, gender, and group acceptance and three components of friendship quality. *Journal of Early Adolescence, 19*, 438–464.

Phinney, J., Romero, I., Nava, M., & Huang, D. (2001). The role of language, parents, and peers in ethnic identity among adolescents in immigrant families. *Journal of Youth & Adolescence, 30*, 135–153.

Phinney, J. S. (1990). Ethnic identity in adolescents and adults: Review of research. *Psychological Bulletin, 108*, 499–514.

Phinney, J. S., & Rosenthal, D. A. (1992). Ethnic identity in adolescence: Process, context, and outcome. In G. R. Adams, T. P. Gullotta, & R. Montemayor (Eds.), *Adolescent identity formation* (pp. 145–172). Newbury Park, CA: Sage.

Piaget, J. (1932). *The moral judgment of the child.* New York: Macmillan.

Piaget, J. (1952). *The origins of intelligence in children.* New York: International Universities Press.

Piaget, J. (1954). *The construction of reality in the child.* New York: Basic Books. (Originally published 1937.)

Piaget, J. (1962). *Play, dreams, and imitation in childhood.* New York: W. W. Norton.

Piaget, J. (1965). *The moral judgment of the child.* New York: Free Press.

Piaget, J. (1970). Piaget's theory. In P. H. Mussen (Ed.), *Carmichael's manual of child psychology* (Vol. 1, 3rd ed.) (pp. 703–732). New York: Wiley.

Piaget, J. (1977). *The development of thought: Equilibration of cognitive structures.* New York: Viking.

Piaget, J., & Inhelder, B. (1959). *La gènese des structures logiques élémentaires: Classifications et sériations [The origin of elementary logical structures: Classification and seriation].* Neuchâtel, Switzerland: Delachaux et Niestlé.

Piaget, J., & Inhelder, B. (1969). *The psychology of the child.* New York: Basic Books.

Pianta, R. C., & Egeland, B. (1994). Predictors of instability in children's mental test performance at 24, 48, and 96 months. *Intelligence, 18*, 145–163.

Pickens, J. (1994). Perception of auditory-visual distance relations by 5-month-old infants. *Developmental Psychology, 30*, 537–544.

Pickering, L., Granoff, D., Erickson, J., Masor, M., Cordle, C., Schaller, J., Winship, T., Paule, C., & Hilty, M. (1998). Modulation of the immune system by human milk and infant formula containing nucleotides. *Pediatrics, 101*, 242–249.

Pierce, L. (2001). Caring and expressions of spirituality by urban caregivers of people with stroke in African American families. *Qualitative Health Research, 11*, 339–352.

Pierce, M., & Leon, D. (2005). Age at menarche and adult BMI in the Aberdeen children of the 1950s cohort study. *American Journal of Clinical Nutrition, 82*, 733–739.

Pillard, R. C., & Bailey, J. M. (1995). A biologic perspective on sexual orientation. *The Psychiatric Clinics of North America, 18*(1), 71–84.

Pillemer, K., & Finkelhor, D. (1988). The prevalence of elder abuse: A random sample survey. *The Gerontologist, 28*, 51–58.

Pillemer, K., & Suitor, J. J. (1990). Prevention of elder abuse. In R. Ammerman & M. Hersen (Eds.), *Treatment of family violence: A sourcebook* (pp. 406–422). New York: Wiley.

Pillow, B. (1999). Children's understanding of inferential knowledge. *Journal of Genetic Psychology, 160*, 419–428.

Pine, J. M., Lieven, E. V. M., & Rowland, C. F. (1997). Stylistic variation at the "single-word" stage: Relations between maternal speech characteristics and children's vocabulary composition and usage. *Child Development, 68*, 807–819.

Pinker, S. (1994). *The language instinct: How the mind creates language.* New York: HarperCollins.

Pinker, S. (2002). *The Blank Slate.* New York: Viking.

Pinquart, M., & Soerensen, S. (2000). Influences of socioeconomic status, social network, and competence on subjective well-being in later life: A meta-analysis. *Psychology & Aging, 15*, 187–224.

Pinquart, M., & Sorensen, S. (2006a). Gender differences in caregiver stressors, social resources, and health: An updated meta-analysis. *Journals of Gerontology: Series B: Psychological Sciences and Social Sciences, 61B*, P33–P45.

Pinquart, M., & Sorensen, S. (2006b). Helping caregivers of persons with dementia: Which interventions work and how large are their effects? *International Geriatrics, 18*, 577–595.

Plaud, J., Plaud, D., & von Duvillard, S. (1999). Human behavioral momentum in a sample of older adults. *Journal of General Psychology, 126*, 165–175.

Plomin, R. (1990). *Nature and nurture: An introduction to behavior genetics.* Pacific Grove, CA: Brooks/Cole.

Plomin, R., & McClearn, G. E. (1990). Human behavioral genetics of aging. In J. E. Birren & K. W. Schaie (Eds.), *Handbook of the psychology of aging* (3rd ed., pp. 67–79). San Diego, CA: Academic Press.

Plomin, R., & Rende, R. (1991). Human behavioral genetics. *Annual Review of Psychology, 42*, 161–190.

Plomin, R., Emde, R. N., Braungart, J. M., Campos, J., Corley, R., Fulker, D. W., Kagan, J., Reznick, J. S., Robinson, J., Zahn-Waxler, C., & DeFries, J. C. (1993). Genetic change and continuity from fourteen to twenty months: The MacArthur longitudinal twin study. *Child Development, 64*, 1354–1376.

Plomin, R., Reiss, D., Hetherington, E. M., & Howe, G. W. (1994). Nature and nurture: Genetic contributions to measures of the family environment. *Developmental Psychology, 30*, 32–43.

Polka, L., & Werker, J. F. (1994). Developmental changes in perception of non-native vowel contrasts. *Journal of Experimental Psychology: Human Perception & Performance, 20*, 421–435.

Pollack, J. M. (1979/1980). Correlates of death anxiety: A review of empirical studies. *Omega, 10*, 97–121.

Pollitt, E., & Gorman, K. S. (1994). Nutritional deficiencies as developmental risk factors. In C. A. Nelson (Ed.), *The Minnesota Symposia on Child Development, Vol. 27* (pp. 121–144). Hillsdale, NJ: Erlbaum.

Pomerantz, E., & Ruble, D. (1998). The role of maternal control in the development of sex differences in child self-evaluative factors. *Child Development, 69*, 458–478.

Ponds, R., Commissaris, K., & Jolles, J. (1997). Prevalence and covariates of subjective forgetfulness in a normal population in the Netherlands. *International Journal of Aging and Human Development, 45*, 207–221.

Population Resource Center. (2004). *Latina teen pregnancy: Problems and prevention.* Retrieved October 27, 2004, from http://www.prcdc.org/summaries/latinapreg04/latinapreg04.html.

Portnoi, V. (1999). Progressing from disease prevention to health promotion. *Journal of the American Medical Association, 282*, 1813.

Posada, G., Gao, Y., Wu, F., Posada, R., Tascon, M., Schöelmerich, A., Sagi, A., Kondo-Ikemura, K., Haaland, W., & Synnevaag, B. (1995). The secure-base phenomenon across cultures: Children's behavior, mothers' preferences, and experts' concepts. *Monographs of the Society for Research in Child Development, 60* (244, Nos. 2–3), 27–48.

Posner, J., & Vandell, D. (1994). Low-income children's after-school care: Are there beneficial effects of after-school programs? *Child Development, 65*, 440–456.

Postrado, L., & Nicholson, H. (1992). Effectiveness in delaying the initiation of sexual intercourse in girls aged 12–14. *Youth in Society, 23*, 356–379.

Poulin, F., & Boivin, M. (1999). Proactive and reactive aggression and boys' friendship quality in mainstream classrooms. *Journal of Emotional & Behavioral Disorders, 7*, 168–177.

Poulin, F., & Boivin, M. (2000). The role of proactive and reactive aggression in the formation and development of boys' friendships. *Developmental Psychology, 36*, 233–240.

Poulson, C. L., Nunes, L. R. D., & Warren, S. F. (1989). Imitation in infancy: A critical review. In H. W. Reese (Ed.), *Advances in child development and behavior, Vol. 22* (pp. 272–298). San Diego, CA: Academic Press.

Powell, R. (May 31, 2006). *The $400 billion income shortfall: Baby-boomer women have tougher road to retirement.* Retrieved August 2, 2007 from www.marketwatch.com/News/Story/Story.aspx?guid=%7B107BAF88-C68D-473E-B022-6C3533D216AD%7D.

Powlishta, K. K. (1995). Intergroup processes in childhood: Social categorization and sex role development. *Developmental Psychology, 31*, 781–788.

Prager, E. (1998). Men and meaning in later life. *Journal of Clinical Geropsychology, 4*, 191–203.

Prat-Sala, M., Shillcock, R., & Sorace, A. (2000). Animacy effects on the production of object-dislocated descriptions by Catalan-speaking children. *Journal of Child Language, 27*, 97–117.

Pratt, M., Arnold, M., & Pratt, A. (1999). Predicting adolescent moral reasoning from family climate: A longitudinal study. *Journal of Early Adolescence, 19*, 148–175.

Prechtl, H. F. R., & Beintema, D. J. (1964). *The neurological examination of the full-term newborn infant: Clinics in Developmental Medicine, 12.* London: Heinemann.

Premack, D. (1959). Toward empirical behavior laws: I. Positive reinforcement. *Psychological Review, 66*, 219–233.

Prentice, A. (1994). Extended breast-feeding and growth in rural China. *Nutrition Reviews, 52*, 144–146.

Prepavessis, H., Cameron, L., Baldi, J., Robinson, S., Borrie, K., Harper, T., & Grove, J. (2007). The effects of exercise and nicotine replacement therapy on smoking rates in women. *Addictive Behaviors, 32*, 1416–1432.

Pressley, M., & Dennis-Rounds, J. (1980). Transfer of a mnemonic keyword strategy at two age levels. *Journal of Educational Psychology, 72*, 575–582.

Pressley, M., & Wharton-McDonald, R. (1997). Skilled comprehension and its development through instruction. *School Psychology Review, 26*, 448–466.

Pressman, E., DiPietro, J., Costigan, K., Shupe, A., & Johnson, T. (1998). Fetal neurobehavioral development: Associations with socioeconomic class and fetal sex. *Developmental Psychobiology, 33*, 79–91.

Price, C., & Kunz, J. (2003). Rethinking the paradigm of juvenile delinquency as related to divorce. *Journal of Divorce & Remarriage, 39*, 109–133.

Prigerson, H., Bierhals, A., Kasl, S., Reynolds, C., et al. (1997). Traumatic grief as a risk factor for mental and physical morbidity. *American Journal of Psychiatry, 154* 516–623.

Prigerson, H., Bridge, J., Maciejewski, P., Beery, L., Rosenheck, R., Jacobs, S., Bierhals, A., Kupfer, D., & Brent, D. (1999). Influence of traumatic grief on suicidal ideation among young adults. *American Journal of Psychiatry, 156*, 1994–1995.

Prince, A. (1998). Infectious diseases. In R. Behrman & R. Kliegman (Eds.), *Nelson essentials of pediatrics* (3rd ed., pp. 315–418). Philadelphia: W. B. Saunders.

Prinstein, M., & La Greca, A. (1999). Links between mothers' and children's social competence and associations with maternal adjustment. *Journal of Clinical Child Psychology, 28*, 197–210.

Provasi, J., Dubon, C., & Bloch, H. (2001). Do 9- and 12-month-olds learn means-ends relation by observing? *Infant Behavior & Development, 24*, 195–213.

Public Agenda, Inc. (2004b). *Right to die: People's chief concerns.* Retrieved September 12, 2004, from http://www.publicagenda.org.

Public Agenda, Inc. (2007). *Issue guides: Social Security overview.* Retrieved July 31, 2007 from http://publicagenda.org/issues/overview.cfm?issue_type=ss.

Public Health Agency of Canada. (2006). *Hearing loss info-sheet for seniors.* Retrieved July 6, 2007 from www.phac-aspc.gc.ca/seniors-aines/pubs/info_sheets/hearing_loss/index.htm.

Pulkkinen, L. (1982). Self-control and continuity from childhood to late adolescence. In P. Baltes & O. G. Brim, Jr. (Eds.), *Life span development and behavior, Vol. 4* (pp. 64–107). New York: Academic Press.

Purnine, D., & Carey, M. (1998). Age and gender differences in sexual behavior preferences: A follow-up report. *Journal of Sex & Marital Therapy, 24*, 93–102.

Purugganan, O., Stein, R., Johnson Silver, E., & Benenson, B. (2003). Exposure to violence and psychosocial adjustment among urban school-aged children. *Journal of Developmental & Behavioral Pediatrics, 24*, 424–430.

Pynoos, H., Steinberg, A., & Wraith, R. (1995). A developmental model of childhood traumatic stress. In D. Cicchetti & D. Cohen (Eds.), *Developmental psychopathology, Vol 2: Risk, disorder, and adaptation.* New York: Wiley.

Qi, C., & Kaiser, A. (2003). Behavior problems of preschool children from low-income families: Review of the literature. *Early Childhood Special Education, 23*, 188–216.

Quick, H., & Moen, P. (1998). Gender, employment and retirement quality: A life course approach to the differential experiences of men and women. *Journal of Occupational Health Psychology, 3*, 44–64.

Quigley, D., & Schatz, M. (1999). Men and women and their responses in spousal bereavement. *Hospice Journal, 14*, 65–78.

Raaijmakers, Q., Verbogt, T., & Vollebergh, W. (1998). Moral reasoning and political beliefs of Dutch adolescents and young adults. *Journal of Social Issues, 54*, 531–546.

Rabasca, L. (1999, October). Ultra-thin magazine models found to have little negative effect on adolescent girls. *APA Monitor Online 30.* Retrieved January 16, 2001 from http://www.apa.org/monitor/oct99.

Rabinowitz, P. (2000). Noise-induced hearing loss. *American Family Physician, 61*, 1053.

Radmacher, K., & Azmitia, M. (2006). Are there gendered pathways to intimacy in early adolescents' and emerging adults' friendships? *Journal of Adolescent Research, 21*, 415–448.

Raffaelli, M., & Ontai, L. (2004). Gender socialization in Latino/a families: Results from two retrospective studies. *Sex Roles, 50*, 287–299.

Ragnarsdottir, H., Simonsen, H., & Plunkett, K. (1999). The acquisition of past tense morphology in Icelandic and Norwegian children: An experimental study. *Journal of Child Language, 26*, 577–618.

Rahman, A., Lovel, H., Bunn, J., Igbal, A., & Harrington, R. (2004). Mothers' mental health and infant growth: A case-control study from Rawalpindi, Pakistan. *Child: Care, Health, & Development, 30*, 21–27.

Rahman, O., Strauss, J., Gertler, P., Ashley, D., & Fox, K. (1994). Gender differences in adult health: An international comparison. *The Gerontologist, 34*, 463–469.

Rahman, Q., & Wilson, G. (2003a). Born gay? The psychobiology of human sexual orientation. *Personality and Individual Differences, 34*, 1337–1382.

Raj, A., & Silverman, J. (2002). Intimate partner violence against South-Asian women in Greater Boston. *Journal of American Medical Women's Association, 57*, 111–114.

Raja, M. (2006). The diagnosis of Asperger's syndrome. *Directions in Psychiatry, 26*, 89–104.

Ramey, C., & Ramey, S. (1998). Early intervention and early experience. *American Psychologist, 53,* 109–120.

Ramey, C. T. (1992). High-risk children and IQ: Altering intergenerational patterns. *Intelligence, 16,* 239–256.

Ramey, C. T. (1993). A rejoinder to Spitz's critique of the Abecedarian experiment. *Intelligence, 17,* 25–30.

Ramey, C. T., & Campbell, F. A. (1987). The Carolina Abecedarian Project: An educational experiment concerning human malleability. In J. J. Gallagher & C. T. Ramey (Eds.), *The malleability of children* (pp. 127–140). Baltimore: Paul H. Brookes.

Ramrattan, R., Wolfs, R., Panda-Jonas, S., Jonas, J., Bakker, D., Pols, H., Hofman, A., & de Jong, P. (2001). Prevalence and causes of visual field loss in the elderly and associations with impairment in daily functioning. *Archives of Ophthalmology, 119,* 1874–1875.

Ramsay, D., & Woods, S. (1997). Biological consequences of drug administration: Implications for acute and chronic tolerance. *Psychological Review, 104,* 170–193.

Randall, K. (2007). Examining the relationship between burnout and age among Anglican clergy in England and Wales. *Mental Health, Religion, & Culture, 10,* 39–46.

Rao, G., & Rao, S. (1997). Sector and age differences in productivity. *Social Science International, 13,* 51–56.

Raskind, M. A., & Peskind, E. R. (1992). Alzheimer's disease and other dementing disorders. In J. E. Birren, R. B. Sloane, & G. D. Cohen (Eds.), *Handbook of mental health and aging* (2nd ed., pp. 478–515). San Diego, CA: Academic Press.

Rattaz, C., Goubet, N., & Bullinger, A. (2005). The calming effect of a familiar odor on full-term newborns. *Journal of Developmental & Behavioral Pediatrics, 26,* 86–92.

Rauscher, F. H., Shaw, G. L., & Ky, K. N. (1993). Music and spatial task performance. *Nature, 365,* 611.

Ray, B. (1999). *Home schooling on the threshold: A survey of research at the dawn of the new millennium.* Washington, DC: Home Education Research Institute.

Raz, N., & Rodrigue, K. (2006). Differential aging of the brain: Patterns, cognitive correlates and modifiers. *Neuroscience and Biobehavioral Reviews, 30,* 730–748.

Raz, N., Lindenberger, U., Rodrigue, K., Kennedy, K., Head, D., Williamson, A., Dahle, C., Gerstorf, D., & Acker, J. (2006). Regional brain changes in aging healthy adults: General trends, individual differences and modifiers. *Cerebral Cortex, 15,* 1679–1689.

Raz, N., Rodrigue, K., Kennedy, K., & Acker, J. (2007). Vascular health and longitudinal changes in brain and cognition in middle-aged and older adults. *Neuropsychology, 21,* 149–157.

Recker, R., Lappe, J., Davies, M., & Heaney, R. (2000). Characterization of perimenopausal bone loss: A prospective study. *Journal of Bone and Mineral Research, 15,* 1965–1973.

Reed, G. M., Kemeny, M. E., Taylor, S. E., Wang, H. J., & Visscher, B. R. (1994). Realistic acceptance as a predictor of decreased survival time in gay men with AIDS. *Health Psychology, 13,* 299–307.

Reed, M. (1998). Predicting grief symptomatology among the suddenly bereaved. *Suicide & Life-Threatening Behavior, 28,* 285–301.

Reich, J. W., Zautra, A. J., & Guarnaccia, C. A. (1989). Effects of disability and bereavement on the mental health and recovery of older adults. *Psychology & Aging, 4,* 57–65.

Reichle, B., & Gefke, M. (1998). Justice of conjugal divisions of labor—you can't always get what you want. *Social Justice Research, 11,* 271–287.

Reid, P., & Roberts, S. (2006). Gaining options: A mathematics program for potentially talented at risk adolescent girls. *Merrill-Palmer Quarterly, 52,* 288–304.

Reiman, E. E., Webster, J., Myers, A., Hardy, J., Dunckley, T., Zismann, V., Joshipura, K., Pearson, J., Hu-Lince, D., Juentelman, M., Craig, D., Coon, K., Liang, W., Herbert, R., Beach, T., Rohrer, K., Zhao, A., Grover, A., Heward, C., Ravid, R., Rogers, J., Hutton, M., Melquist, S., Peterson, R., Alexander, G., Caselli, R., Kukull, W., Papassotiropoulos, A., & Staphan, D. (2007). GAB2 alleles modify Alzheimer's risk in ApoE 4 carriers. *Neuron, 54,* 713–720.

Reiner, W., & Gearheardt, J. (2004). Discordant sexual identity in some genetic males with cloacal extrophy assigned to female sex at birth. *The New England Journal of Medicine, 350,* 333–341.

Reisman, J. E. (1987). Touch, motion, and proprioception. In P. Salapatek & L. Cohen (Eds.), *Handbook of infant perception, Vol. 1: From sensation to perception* (pp. 265–304). Orlando, FL: Academic Press.

Reiss, D. (1998). Mechanisms linking genetic and social influences in adolescent development: Beginning a collaborative search. *Current Directions in Psychological Science, 6,* 100–105.

Remafedi, G., French, S., Story, M., Resnick, M., & Blum, R. (1998). The relationship between suicide risk and sexual orientation: Results of a population-based study. *American Journal of Public Health, 88,* 57–60.

Remafedi, G., Resnick, M., Blum, R., & Harris, L. (1998). Demography of sexual orientation in adolescents. *Pediatrics, 89,* 714–721.

Remsberg, K., Demerath, E., Schubert, C., Chumlea, W., Sun, S., & Siervoge, R. (2004). Early menarche and the development of cardiovascular disease risk factors in adolescent girls: The Fels Longitudinal Study. *Journal of Clinical Endocrinology & Metabolism, 90,* 2718–2724.

Rendell, P., & Thomson, D. (1999). Aging and prospective memory: Differences between naturalistic and laboratory tasks. *Journals of Gerontology, 54B,* P256–P269.

Repetto, P., Caldwell, C., & Zimmerman, M. (2004). Trajectories of depressive symptoms among high risk African-American adolescents. *Journal of Adolescent Health, 35,* 468–477.

Reskin, B. (1993). Sex segregation in the workplace. *Annual Review of Sociology, 19,* 241–270.

Reynolds, C. R., & Brown, R. T. (Eds.). (1984). *Perspectives on bias in mental testing.* New York: Plenum.

Reynolds, M., Schieve, L., Martin, J., Jeng, G., & Macaluso, M. (2003). Trends in multiple births conceived using assisted reproductive technology, United States, 1997–2000. *Pediatrics, 111,* 1159–1162.

Rhodes, J., van Praag, H., Jeffrey, S., Girard, I., Mitchell, G., Garland, T., & Gage, F. (2003). Exercise increases hippocampal neurogenesis to high levels but does not improve spatial learning in mice bred for increased voluntary wheel running. *Behavioral Neuroscience, 117,* 1006–1016.

Rholes, W. S., & Ruble, D. N. (1984). Children's understanding of dispositional characteristics of others. *Child Development, 55,* 550–560.

Richardson, G., Conroy, M., & Day, N. (1996). Prenatal cocaine exposure: Effects on the development of school-aged children. *Neurotoxicology & Teratology, 18,* 627–634.

Richardson, J. L., Zarnegar, Z., Bisno, B., & Levine, A. (1990). Psychosocial status at initiation of cancer treatment and survival. *Journal of Psychosomatic Research, 34,* 189–201.

Riegle-Crumb, C., Farkas, G., & Muller, C. (2006). The role of gender and friendship in advanced course taking. *Sociology of Education, 79,* 206–228.

Rieker, P., & Bird, C. (2005). Rethinking gender differences in health: Why we need to integrate social and biological perspectives. *The Journals of Gerontology Series B: Psychological Sciences and Social Sciences, 60,* S40–S47.

Ries, L., Melbert, D., Krapcho, M., Mariotto, A., Miller, B, Feuer, E., Clegg, L., Horner, M., Howlader, N., Eisner, M., Reichman, M., Edwards, B. (2007). *SEER cancer statistics review.* Retrieved July 6, 2007 from http://seer.cancer.gov/csr/1975_2004/.

Riggs, A. (1997). Men, friends, and widowhood: Towards successful aging. *Australian Journal on Ageing, 16,* 182–185.

Rinaldi, P., Polidori, M., Metastasio, A., Mariani, E., Mattioli, P., Cherubini, A., Catani, M., Cecchetti, R., Senin, U., & Mecocci, P. (2003). Plasma antioxidants are similarly depleted in mild cognitive impairment and in Alzheimer's disease. *Neurobiology of Aging, 24,* 915–919.

Rique, J., & Camino, C. (1997). Consistency and inconsistency in adolescents' moral reasoning. *International Journal of Behavioral Development, 21,* 813–836.

Ritter, M. (November 15, 2005). The science of hair loss, and some hope. *LiveScience.com.* Retrieved July 9, 2007 from www.livescience.com/health/ap_051115_balding.html.

Robbins, A. (2001). *Quarterlife crisis: How to get your head around your twenties.* New York: Penguin Putnam.

Roberts, R. E., & Sobhan, M. (1992). Symptoms of depression in adolescence: A comparison of Anglo, African, and Hispanic Americans. *Journal of Youth & Adolescence, 21,* 639–651.

Robins, R., Caspi, A., & Moffitt, T. (2000). Two personalities, one relationship: Both partners' personality traits shape the quality of their relationship. *Journal of Personality & Social Psychology, 79,* 251–259.

Robinson, N., Lanzi, R., Weinberg, R., Ramey, S., & Ramey, C. (2002). Family factors associated with high academic competence in former Head Start children at third grade. *Gifted Child Quarterly, 46,* 278–290.

Robinson-Whelen, S., & Kiecolt-Glaser, N. (1997). The importance of social versus temporal comparison appraisals among older adults. *Journal of Applied Social Psychology, 27,* 959–966.

Rock, A., Trainor, L., & Addison, T. (1999). Distinctive messages in infant-directed lullabies and play songs. *Developmental Psychology, 35,* 527–534.

Rockwood, K., & Stadnyk, K. (1994). The prevalence of dementia in the elderly: A review. *Canadian Journal of Psychiatry, 29,* 253–257.

Roderick, M., & Camburn, E. (1999). Risk and recovery from course failure in the early years of high school. *American Educational Research Journal, 36*, 303–343.

Rodkin, P., Farmer, T., Pearl, R., & Van Acker, R. (2000). Heterogeneity of popular boys: Antisocial and prosocial configurations. *Developmental Psychology, 36*, 14–24.

Rodrigo, M., Janssens, J., & Ceballos, E. (1999). Do children's perceptions and attributions mediate the effects of mothers' child rearing actions? *Journal of Family Psychology, 13*, 508–522.

Rodstrom, K., Bengtsson, C., Milsom, I., Lissner, L., Sundh, V., & Bjourkelund, C. (2003). Evidence for a secular trend in menopausal age: A population study of women in Gothenburg. *Menopause, 10*, 538–543.

Roehling, P., Roehling, M., & Moen, P. (2001). The relationship between work-life policies and practices and employee loyalty: A life course perspective. *Journal of Family & Economic Issues, 22*, 141–170.

Roer-Strier, D., & Rivlis, M. (1998). Timetable of psychological and behavioural autonomy expectations among parents from Israel and the former Soviet Union. *International Journal of Psychology, 33*, 123–135.

Rogers, J. L., Rowe, D. C., & May, K. (1994). DF analysis of NLSY IQ/Achievement data: Nonshared environmental influences. *Intelligence, 19*, 157–177.

Rogers, R. L., Meyer, J. S., & Mortel, K. F. (1990). After reaching retirement age physical activity sustains cerebral perfusion and cognition. *Journal of the American Geriatric Society, 38*, 123–128.

Rogoff, B. (1990). *Apprenticeship in thinking: Cognitive development in social contexts.* New York: Oxford University Press.

Rogosch, F., Cicchetti, D., & Aber, J. (1995). The role of child maltreatment in early deviations in cognitive and affective processing abilities and later peer relationship problems. *Development & Psychopathology, 7*, 591–609.

Roisman, G., Masten, A., Coatsworth, J., & Tellegen, A. (2004). Salient and emerging developmental tasks in the transition to adulthood. *Child Development, 75*, 123–133.

Rollins, B. C., & Feldman, H. (1970). Marital satisfaction over the family life cycle. *Journal of Marriage & the Family, 32*, 20–27.

Rolls, E. (2000). Memory systems in the brain. *Annual Review of Psychology, 51*, 599–630.

Romano, L. (May 16, 2006). Online degree programs take off. *Washington Post Online.* Retrieved July 2, 2007 from www.washingtonpost.com/wp-dyn/content/article/2006/05/15/AR2006051501496.html.

Romi, S., & Kohan, E. (2004). Wilderness programs: Principles, possibilities and opportunities for intervention with dropout adolescents. *Child & Youth Care Forum, 33*, 115–136.

Rosander, K., & von Hofsten, C. (2004). Infants' emerging ability to represent occluded object motion. *Cognition, 91*, 1–22.

Rosario, M., Schrimshaw, E., & Hunter, J. (2004). Ethnic/racial differences in the coming-out process of lesbian, gay, and bisexual youths: A comparison of sexual identity development over time. *Cultural Diversity and Ethnic Minority Psychology, 10*, 215–228.

Rosario, M., Schrimshaw, E., Hunter, J., & Braun, L. (2006). Sexual identity development among lesbian, gay, and bisexual youths: Consistency and change over time. *Journal of Sex Research, 43*, 46–58.

Rose, A., & Asher, S. (2004). Children's strategies and goals in response to help-giving and help-seeking tasks within a friendship. *Child Development, 75*, 749–763.

Rose, R. J. (1995). Genes and human behavior. *Annual Review of Psychology, 56*, 625–654.

Rose, S., Feldman, J., & Jankowski, J. (2004). Infant visual recognition memory. *Developmental Review, 24*, 74–100.

Rose, S. A., & Feldman, J. F. (1995). Prediction of IQ and specific cognitive abilities at 11 years from infancy measures. *Developmental Psychology, 31*, 685–696.

Rose, S. A., & Ruff, H. A. (1987). Cross-modal abilities in human infants. In J. D. Osofsky (Ed.), *Handbook of infant development* (2nd ed., pp. 318–362). New York: Wiley-Interscience.

Rosenberg, M. (1986). Self-concept from middle childhood through adolescence. In J. Suls & A. G. Greenwald (Eds.), *Psychological perspectives on the self* (Vol. 3) (pp. 107–136). Hillsdale, NJ: Erlbaum.

Rosenberg, M. (2003). Recognizing gay, lesbian, and transgender teens in a child and adolescent psychiatry practice. *Journal of the American Academy of Child and Adolescent Psychiatry, 42*, 1517–1521.

Rosenblith, J. F. (1992). *In the beginning* (2nd ed.). Thousand Oaks, CA: Sage.

Rosenkrantz, S., Aronson, S., & Huston, A. (2004). Mother-infant relationship in single, cohabiting, and married families: A case for marriage? *Journal of Family Psychology, 18*, 5–18.

Rosenman, R. H., & Friedman, M. (1983). Relationship of Type A behavior pattern to coronary heart disease. In H. Selye (Ed.), *Selye's guide to stress research* (Vol. 2) (pp. 47–106). New York: Scientific and Academic Editions.

Rosenthal, C. J., Matthews, S. H., & Marshall, V. W. (1989). Is parent care normative? The experiences of a sample of middle-aged women. *Research on Aging, 11*, 244–260.

Rosenthal, J., Rodewald, L., McCauley, M., Berman, S., Irigoyen, M., Sawyer, M., Yusuf, H., Davis, R., & Kalton, G. (2004). Immunization coverage levels among 19- to 35-month-old children in 4 diverse, medically under-served areas of the United States. *Pediatrics, 113*, e296–e302.

Rosenthal, R. (1994). Interpersonal expectancy effects: A 30-year perspective. *Current Directions in Psychological Science, 3*, 176–179.

Rosenthal, S., & Gitelman, S. (2002). Endocrinology. In A. Rudolph, R. Kamei, & K. Overby (Eds.) *Rudolph's fundamentals of pediatrics* (3rd Ed.). New York: McGraw-Hill (pp. 747–795).

Rosenthal, S., Lewis, L., Succop, P., & Burklow, K. (1997). Adolescent girls' perceived prevalence of sexually transmitted diseases and condom use. *Journal of Developmental & Behavioral Pediatrics, 18*, 158–161.

Ross, C. E. (1995). Reconceptualizing marital status as a continuum of social attachment. *Journal of Marriage & the Family, 57*, 129–140.

Ross, H., Ross, M., Stein, N., & Trabasso, T. (2006). How siblings resolve their conflicts: The importance of first offers, planning, and limited opposition. *Child Development, 77*, 1730–1745.

Rossouw, J., Anderson, G., Prentice, R., LaCroix, A., Kooperberg, C., Stefanick, M., Jackson, R., Beresford, S., Howard, B., Johnson, K., Kotchen, J., & Ockene, J. (2002). Risks and benefits of estrogen plus progestin in healthy postmenopausal women: Principal results from the Women's Health Initiative randomized controlled trial. *Journal of the American Medical Association, 288*, 321–333.

Rossow, I., & Amundsen, A. (1997). Alcohol abuse and mortality: A 40-year prospective study of Norwegian conscripts. *Social Science & Medicine, 44*, 261–267.

Rostosky, S., Owens, G., & Zimmerman, R., & Riggle, E. D. (2003). Associations among sexual attraction status, school belonging, and alcohol and marijuana use in rural high school students. *Journal of Adolescence, 26*, 741–751.

Roth, M. (2003). Validation of the Arnett Inventory of Sensation Seeking (AISS): Efficiency to predict the willingness towards occupational change, and affection by social desirability. *Personality & Individual Differences, 35*, 1307–1314.

Rothbard, J. C., & Shaver, P. R. (1994). Continuity of attachment across the life span. In M. B. Sperling & W. H. Berman (Eds.), *Attachment in adults. Clinical and developmental perspectives* (pp. 31–71). New York: Guilford Press.

Rothbart, M., Ahadi, S., & Evans, D. (2000). Temperament and personality: Origins and outcomes. *Journal of Personality & Social Psychology, 78*, 122–135.

Rothbart, M. K., Derryberry, D., & Posner, M. I. (1994). A psychobiological approach to the development of temperament. In J. E. Bates & T. D. Wachs (Eds.), *Temperament. Individual differences at the interface of biology and behavior* (pp. 83–116). Washington, DC: American Psychological Association.

Roux, A., Merkin, S., Arnett, D., Chambless, L., Massing, M., Nieto, J., Sorlie, P., Szklo, M., Tyroler, H., & Watson, R. (2001). Neighborhood of residence and incidence of coronary heart disease. *New England Journal of Medicine, 345*, 99–106.

Rovee-Collier, C. (1993). The capacity for long-term memory in infancy. *Current Directions in Psychological Science, 2*, 130–135.

Rowe, D. (2002). IQ, birth weight, and number of sexual partners in White, African American, and mixed race adolescents. *Population & Environment: A Journal of Interdisciplinary Studies, 23*, 513–524.

Rowe, J., & Kahn, R. (1998). *Successful aging.* New York: Pantheon.

Rowland, D., & Tai, W. (2003). A review of plant-derived and herbal approaches to the treatment of sexual dysfunctions. *Journal of Sex & Marital Therapy, 29*, 185–205.

Roy, E., Bryden, P., & Cavill, S. (2003). Hand differences in pegboard performance through development. *Brain & Cognition, 53*, 315–317.

Roy, P., Rutter, M., & Pickles, A. (2000). Institutional care: Risk from family background or pattern of rearing. *Journal of Child Psychology & Psychiatry & Allied Disciplines, 41*, 139–149.

Rubin, K., Burgess, K., & Hastings, P. (2002). Stability and social-behavioral consequences of toddlers' inhibited temperament and parenting behaviors. *Child Development, 73*, 483–495.

Rubin, K. Burgess, K., Dwyer, K., & Hastings, P. (2003). Predicting preschoolers' externalizing behaviors from toddler temperament, conflict, and maternal negativity. *Developmental Psychology, 39*, 164–176.

Rubin, K. H., Fein, G. G., & Vandenberg, B. (1983). Play. In E. M. Hetherington (Ed.), *Handbook of child psychology: Socialization, personality, and social development* (Vol. 4) (pp. 693–774). New York: Wiley.

Rubin, K. H., Hymel, S., Mills, R. S. L., & Rose-Krasnor, L. (1991). Conceptualizing different developmental pathways to and from social isolation in childhood. In D. Cicchetti & S. L. Toth (Eds.), *Internalizing and externalizing expressions of dysfunction: Rochester Symposium on Developmental Psychopathology* (Vol. 2) (pp. 91–122). Hillsdale, NJ: Erlbaum.

Rubin, S., & Schechter, N. (1997). Exploring the social construction of bereavement: Perceptions of adjustment and recovery in bereaved men. *American Journal of Orthopsychiatry, 67*, 279–289.

Rubinstein, R. L. (1986). *Singular paths: Old men living alone.* New York: Columbia University Press.

Ruble, D., & Dweck, C. (1995). Self-conceptions, person conceptions, and their development. In N. Eisenberg (Ed.), *Social development.* Thousand Oaks, CA: Sage.

Ruble, D. N. (1987). The acquisition of self-knowledge: A self-socialization perspective. In N. Eisenberg (Ed.), *Contemporary topics in developmental psychology* (pp. 243–270). New York: Wiley-Interscience.

Rudd, M., Viney, L., & Preston, C. (1999). The grief experienced by spousal caregivers of dementia patients: The role of place of care of patient and gender of caregiver. *International Journal of Aging & Human Development, 48*, 217–240.

Rushton, J., & Jensen, A. (2006). The totality of available evidence shows the race IQ gap still remains. *Psychological Science, 17*, 921–922.

Rushton, J., & Rushton, E. (2003). Brain size, IQ, and racial-group differences: Evidence from musculoskeletal traits. *Intelligence, 31*, 139–155.

Rushton, J., Skuy, M., & Fridjhon, P. (2003). Performance on Raven's Advanced Progressive Matrices by African, East Indian, and White engineering students in South Africa. *Intelligence, 31*, 123–137.

Rutter, M. (1987). Continuities and discontinuities from infancy. In J. D. Osofsky (Ed.), *Handbook of infant development* (2nd ed.) (pp. 1256–1296). New York: Wiley-Interscience.

Rutter, M., Dunn, J., Plomin, R., Simonoff, E., Pickles, A., Maughan, B., Ormel, J., Meyer, J., & Eaves, L. (1997). Integrating nature and nurture: Implications of person-environment correlations and interactions for developmental psychopathology. *Development & Psychopathology, 9*, 335–364.

Rys, G., & Bear, G. (1997). Relational aggression and peer relations: Gender and developmental issues. *Merrill-Palmer Quarterly, 43*, 87–106.

Saavedra, M., Ramirez, A., & Contreras, C. (1997). Interactive interviews between elders and children: A possible procedure for improving affective state in the elderly. *Psiquiatricay Psicologica de America Latina, 43*, 63–66.

Sackett, P., Hardison, C., & Cullen, M. (2004a). On interpreting stereotype threat as accounting for African American–White differences on cognitive tests. *American Psychologist, 59*, 7–13.

Sackett, P., Hardison, C., & Cullen, M. (2004b). On the value of correcting mischaracterizations of stereotype threat research. *American Psychologist, 59*, 38–49.

Saewyc, E., Bearinger, L., Heinz, P., Blum, R., & Resnick, M. (1998). Gender differences in health and risk behaviors among bisexual and homosexual adolescents. *Journal of Adolescent Health, 23*, 181–188.

Safren, S., & Heimberg, R. (1999). Depression, hopelessness, suicidality, and related factors in sexual minority and heterosexual adolescents. *Journal of Consulting & Clinical Psychology, 67*, 859–866.

Sak, U., & Maker, C. (2006). Developmental variation in children's creative mathematical thinking as a function of schooling, age, and knowledge. *Creativity Research, 18*, 279–291.

Salthouse, T. (2004). What and when of cognitive aging. *Current Directions in Psychological Science, 13*, 140–144.

Salthouse, T. A. (1991). *Theoretical perspectives on cognitive aging.* Hillsdale, NJ: Erlbaum.

Salthouse, T. A. (1993). Speed mediation of adult age differences in cognition. *Developmental Psychology, 29*, 722–738.

Saluja, G., Iachan, R., Scheidt, P., Overpeck, M., Sun, W., & Giedd, J. (2004). Prevalence of and risk factors for depressive symptoms among young adolescents. *Archives of Pediatric & Adolescent Medicine, 158*, 760–765.

Sammartino, F. J. (1987). The effect of health on retirement. *Social Security Bulletin, 50* (2), 31–47.

Sampson, R. J., & Laub, J. H. (1994). Urban poverty and the family context of delinquency: A new look at structure and process in a classic study. *Child Development, 65*, 523–540.

Samuels, S., & Flor, R. (1997). The importance of automaticity for developing expertise in reading. *Reading & Writing Quarterly: Overcoming Learning Difficulties, 13*, 107–121.

Sanchez, B., Reyes, O., & Singh, J. (2006). A qualitative examination of the relationships that serve a mentoring function for Mexican American older adolescents. *Cultural Diversity & Ethnic Minority Psychology, 12*, 615–631.

Sanders, C. M. (1989). *Grief: The mourning after.* New York: Wiley-Interscience.

Sandman, C., Wadhwa, P., Chicz-DeMet, A., Porto, M., & Garite, T. (1999). Maternal corticotropin-releasing hormone and habituation in the human fetus. *Developmental Psychobiology, 34*, 163–173.

Sandman, C., Wadhwa, P., Hetrick, W., Porto, M., & Peeke, H. (1997). Human fetal heart rate dishabituation between thirty and thirty-two weeks. *Child Development, 68*, 1031–1040.

Sandnabba, N., & Ahlberg, C. (1999). Parents' attitudes and expectations about children's cross-gender behavior. *Sex Roles, 40*, 249–263.

Sands, L. P., & Meredith, W. (1992). Blood pressure and intellectual functioning in late midlife. *Journals of Gerontology: Psychological Sciences, 47*, P81–84.

Sands, L. P., Terry, H., & Meredith, W. (1989). Change and stability in adult intellectual functioning assessed by Wechsler item responses. *Psychology & Aging, 4*, 79–87.

Sandvig, C. (2006). The Internet at play: Child users of public internet connections. *Journal of Computer-Mediated Communication, 11*, 932–956.

Sanford, K., & Madill, L. (2006). Resistance through video game play: It's a boy thing. *Canadian Journal of Education, 29*, 287–306.

Santelli, J., Ott, M., Lyon, M., Rogers, J., Summers, D., & Schleifer, R. (2006). Abstinence and abstinence-only education: A review of U.S. policies and programs. *Journal of Adolescent Health, 38*, 72–81.

Sanz, A., Pamplona, R., & Barja, G. (2006). Is the mitochondrial free radial theory of aging intact? *Antioxidants and Redox Signaling, 8*, 582–599.

Saslari, S., & Zhang, W. (2006). Kin keepers and good providers: Influence of gender socialization on well-being among USA birth cohorts. *Aging & Mental Health, 10*, 485–496.

Sattler, J. (2001). *Assessment of children: Cognitive applications.* San Diego, CA: Jerome M. Sattler Publishers, Inc.

Saucier, M. (2004). Midlife and beyond: Issues for aging women. *Journal of Counseling & Development, 82*, 420–425.

Saudino, K. J., & Plomin, R. (1997). Cognitive and temperamental mediators of genetic contributions to the home environment during infancy. *Merrill-Palmer Quarterly, 43*, 1–23.

Savage, M., & Holcomb, D. (1999). Adolescent female athletes' sexual risk-taking behaviors. *Journal of Youth & Adolescence, 28*, 583–594.

Savage, S., & Gauvain, M. (1998). Parental beliefs and children's everyday planning in European-American and Latino families. *Journal of Applied Developmental Psychology, 19*, 319–340.

Savin-Williams, R., & Ream, G. (2003). Suicide attempts among sexual-minority male youth. *Journal of Clinical Child & Adolescent Psychology, 32*, 509–522.

Sax, L., & Bryant, A. (2006). The impact of college on sex-atypical career choices of men and women. *Journal of Vocational Behavior, 68*, 52–63.

Sax, L., Lindholm, J., Astin, A., Korn, W., & Mahoney, K. (2002). *The American freshman: National norms for fall 2002.* Los Angeles, CA: Higher Education Research Institute UCLA.

Scarr, S. (1997). Why child care has little impact on most children's development. *Current Directions in Psychological Science, 6*, 143–147.

Scarr, S., & McCartney, K. (1983). How people make their own environments: A theory of genotype/environment effects. *Child Development, 54*, 424–435.

Scarr, S., & Weinberg, R. A. (1983). The Minnesota adoption studies: Genetic differences and malleability. *Child Development, 54*, 260–267.

Scarr, S., Weinberg, R. A., & Waldman, I. D. (1993). IQ correlations in transracial adoptive families. *Intelligence, 17*, 541–555.

Schadt, D. (1997). The relationship of type to developmental issues of midlife women: Implications for counseling. *Journal of Psychological Type, 43*, 12–21.

Schaffer, H., & Emerson, P. (1964). The development of social attachments in infancy. *Monographs of the Society for Research in Child Development, 29* (3, Serial No. 94).

Schaie, K. W. (1983). The Seattle longitudinal study: A 21-year exploration of psychometric intelligence in adulthood. In K. W. Schaie (Ed.), *Longitudinal studies of adult psychological development* (pp. 64–135). New York: Guilford Press.

Schaie, K. W., Nguyen, H., Willis, S., Dutta, R., & Yue, G. (2001). Environmental factors as a conceptual framework for examining cognitive performance in Chinese adults. *International Journal of Behavioral Development, 25*, 193–202.

Schaie, W., & Willis, S. (2005). *Mind alert: Intellectual functioning in adulthood: Growth, maintenance, decline, and modifiability.* Lecture presented at the Joint Conference of the American Society on Aging and the National Council on Aging as part of the Mind-Alert Program. Retrieved June 10, 2006 from http://geron.psu.edu/sls/publications/MindAlert.pdf.

Schatschneider, C., Fletcher, J., Francis, D., Carlson, C., & Foorman, B. (2004). Kindergarten prediction of reading skills: A longitudinal comparative analysis. *Journal of Educational Psychology, 96*, 265–282.

Schatschneider, C., Francis, D., Foorman, B., Fletcher, J., & Mehta, P. (1999). The dimensionality of phonological awareness: An application of item response theory. *Journal of Educational Psychology, 91*, 439–449.

Scheibel, A. B. (1992). Structural changes in the aging brain. In J. E. Birren, R. B. Sloane, & G. D. Cohen (Eds.), *Handbook of mental health and aging* (2nd ed., pp. 147–174). San Diego, CA: Academic Press.

Scheibel, A. B. (1996). Structural and functional changes in the aging brain. In J. E. Birren & K. W. Schaie (Eds.), *Handbook of the psychology of aging* (4th ed., pp. 105–128). San Diego, CA: Academic Press.

Scheidt, R., Humpherys, D., & Yorgason, J. (1999). Successful aging: What's not to like? *Journal of Applied Gerontology, 18*, 277–282.

Scheier, M. F., Matthews, K. A., Owens, J. F., Magovern, G. J., Lefebvre, S., Abbott, R. A., & Carver, C. S. (1989). Dispositional optimism and recovery from coronary artery bypass surgery: The beneficial effects on physical and psychological well-being. *Journal of Personality & Social Psychology, 57*, 1024–1040.

Schieber, F. (1992). Aging and the senses. In J. E. Birren, R. B. Sloane, & G. D. Cohen (Eds.), *Handbook of mental health and aging* (2nd ed., pp. 252–306). San Diego, CA: Academic Press.

Schieve, L., Peterson, H., Meikle, S., Jeng, G., Danel, I., Burnett, N., & Wilcox, L. (1999). Birth rates and multiple-birth risk using in vitro fertilization. *Journal of the American Medical Association, 282*, 1832–1838.

Schmidt, M., DeMulder, E., & Denham, S. (2002). Kindergarten social-emotional competence: Developmental predictors and psychosocial implications. *Early Child Development & Care, 172*, 451–461.

Schmitt, D., Shackelford, T., & Buss, D. (2001). Are men really more "oriented" toward short-term mating than women? A critical review of theory and research. *Psychology, Evolution, & Gender, 3*, 211–239.

Schneider, B., Hieshima, J. A., Lee, S., & Plank, S. (1994). East-Asian academic success in the United States: Family, school, and community explanations. In P. M. Greenfield & R. R. Cocking (Eds.), *Cross-cultural roots of minority child development* (pp. 323–350). Hillsdale, NJ: Erlbaum.

Schneider, M. (2004). The intersection of mental and physical health in older Mexican Americans. *Hispanic Journal of Behavioral Sciences, 26*, 333–355.

Scholle, S., Buranosky, R., Hanusa, B., Ranieri, L., Dowd, K., & Valappil, B. (2003). Routine screening for intimate partner violence in an obstetrics and gynecology clinic. *American Journal of Public Health, 93*, 1070–1072.

Schonert-Reichl, K. (1999). Relations of peer acceptance, friendship adjustment, and social behavior to moral reasoning during early adolescence. *Journal of Early Adolescence, 19*, 249–279.

Schraf, M., & Hertz-Lazarowitz, R. (2003). Social networks in the school context: Effects of culture and gender. *Journal of Social & Personal Relationships, 20*, 843–858.

Schreiber, M., Lutz, K., Schweizer, A., Kalveram, K., & Jaencke, L., (1998). Development and evaluation of an interactive computer-based training as a rehabilitation tool for dementia. *Psychologische Beitraege, 40*, 85–102.

Schreiber, M., Schweizer, A., Lutz, K., Kalveram, K., & Jaencke, L. (1999). Potential of an interactive computer-based training in the rehabilitation of dementia. An initial study. *Neuropsychological Rehabilitation, 9*, 155–167.

Schuler, M., & Nair, P. (1999). Frequency of maternal cocaine use during pregnancy and infant neurobehavioral outcome. *Journal of Pediatric Psychology, 24*, 511–514.

Schuler, M., Nair, P., & Black, M. (2002). Ongoing maternal drug use, parenting attitudes, and a home intervention: Effects on mother-child interaction at 18 months. *Journal of Developmental & Behavioral Pediatrics, 23*, 87–94.

Schull, W., & Otake, M. (1997). Cognitive function and prenatal exposure to ionizing radiation. *Teratology, 59*, 222–226.

Schultz, N. R., Jr., Elias, M. F., Robbins, M. A., Streeten, D. H. P., & Blakeman, N. (1986). A longitudinal comparison of hypertensives and normotensives on the Wechsler Adult Intelligence Scale: Initial findings. *Journal of Gerontology, 41*, 169–175.

Schulz, R., Visintainer, P., & Williamson, G. M. (1990). Psychiatric and physical morbidity effects of caregiving. *Journals of Gerontology: Psychological Sciences, 45*, 181–191.

Schuster, C. (1997). Condom use behavior: An assessment of United States college students' health education needs. *International Quarterly of Community Health Education, 17*, 237–254.

Schvaneveldt, P., Miller, B., Berry, E. & Lee, T. (2001). Academic goals, achievement, and age at first sexual intercourse: Longitudinal, bidirectional influences. *Adolescence, 36*, 767–787.

Schwartz, R. M., Anastasia, M. L., Scanlon, J. W., & Kellogg, R. J. (1994). Effect of surfactant on morbidity, mortality, and resource use in newborn infants weighing 500 to 1500 g. *New England Journal of Medicine, 330*, 1476–1480.

Schwebel, D., Rosen, C., & Singer, J. (1999). Preschoolers' pretend play and theory of mind: The role of jointly constructed pretence. *British Journal of Developmental Psychology, 17*, 333–348.

Schweizer, T., Schnegg, M., & Berzborn, S. (1998). Personal networks and social support in a multiethnic community of southern California. *Social Networks, 20*, 1–21.

Scott, J. (1998). Hematology. In R. Behrman & R. Kliegman (Eds.), *Nelson essentials of pediatrics* (3rd ed., pp. 545–582). Philadelphia: W. B. Saunders.

Sebanc, A. (2003). The friendship features of preschool children: Links with prosocial behavior and aggression. *Social Development, 12*, 249–268.

Sedney, M. (1999). Children's grief narratives in popular films. *Omega, 39*, 314–324.

Segatto, B., & Di Filippo, L. (2003). Vita relazionale ed emozioni nelle coppie in fase di pensionamento e/o nido vuoto. *Eta Evolutiva, 74*, 5–20.

Seidman, A. (2005). Minority student retention: Resources for practitioners. In G. Gaither (Ed.) *Minority retention: What works?* (pp. 7–24). San Francisco, CA: Jossey-Bass.

Seifer, R., Schiller, M., Sameroff, A. J., Resnick, S., & Riordan, K. (1996). Attachment, maternal sensitivity, and infant temperament during the first year of life. *Developmental Psychology, 32*, 12–25.

Sellers, A., Burns, W., & Guyrke, J. (2002). Differences in young children's IQs on the Wechsler Preschool and Primary Scale of Intelligence-Revised as a function of stratification variables. *Neuropsychology, 9*, 65–73.

Selman, R. L. (1980). *The growth of interpersonal understanding*. New York: Academic Press.

Semrud-Clikeman, M., Nielsen, K., Clinton, A., Sylvester, L., et al. (1999). An intervention approach for children with teacher- and parent-identified attentional difficulties. *Journal of Learning Disabilities, 32*, 581–590.

Senchak, M., Leonard, K., & Greene, B. (1998). Alcohol use among college students as a function of their typical social drinking context. *Psychology of Addictive Behaviors, 12*, 62–70.

Seo, S. (2006). A study of infant developmental outcome with a sample of Korean working mothers of infants in poverty: Implications for early intervention programs. *Early Childhood Education Journal, 33*, 253–260.

Serbin, L., Poulin-Dubois, D., Colbourne, K., Sen, M., & Eichstedt, J. (2001). Gender stereotyping in infancy: Visual preferences for and knowledge of gender-stereotyped toys in the second year. *International Journal of Behavioral Development, 25*, 7–15.

Serbin, L. A., Powlishta, K. K., & Gulko, J. (1993). The development of sex typing in middle childhood. *Monographs of the Society for Research in Child Development, 58* (2, Serial No. 232).

Serdula, M. K., Ivery, D., Coates, R. J., Freedman, D. S., Williamson, D. F., & Byers, T. (1993). Do obese children become obese adults? A review of the literature. *Preventive Medicine, 22*, 167–177.

Segerstrom, S., Taylor, S., Kemeny, M., & Fahey, J. (1998). Optimism is associated with mood, coping, and immune change in response to stress. *Journal of Personality and Social Psychology, 74*, 1646–1655.

Serpell, R., & Hatano, G. (1997). Education, schooling, and literacy. In J. Berry, P. Dasen, & T. Saraswathi (Eds.), *Handbook of cross-cultural psychology, Vol. 2: Basic processes and human development*. Needham Heights, MA: Allyn & Bacon.

Shapiro, E. (2002). Family bereavement after collective trauma: Private suffering, public meanings, and cultural contexts. *Journal of Systemic Therapies, 21*, 81–92.

Share, D., & Leiken, M. (2004). Language impairment at school entry and later reading disability: Connections at lexical versus supralexical levels of reading. *Scientific Studies of Reading, 8*, 87–110.

Sharma, S., Monsen, R., & Gary, B. (1997). Comparison of attitudes toward death and dying among nursing majors and other college students. *Omega, 34*, 219–232.

Sharma, V., & Sharma, A. (1997). Adolescent boys in Gujrat, India: Their sexual behavior and their knowledge of acquired immunodeficiency syndrome and other sexually transmitted diseases. *Journal of Developmental & Behavioral Pediatrics, 18*, 399–404.

Sharpe, D., Hermsen, J., & Billings, J. (2002). Gender differences in use of alternative full-time work arrangements by married workers. *Family & Consumer Sciences Research Journal, 31*, 78–111.

Sher, L. (2004). Type D personality, cortisol and cardiac disease. *Australian and New Zealand Journal of Psychiatry, 38*, 652–653.

Sherman, A., Lansford, J., & Volling, B. (2006). Sibling relationships and best friendships in young adulthood: Warmth, conflict, and well-being. *Personal Relationships, 13*, 151–165.

Shneidman, E. S. (1980). *Voices of death.* New York: Harper & Row.

Shneidman, E. S. (1983). *Deaths of man.* New York: Jason Aronson.

Shore, C. (1986). Combinatorial play, conceptual development, and early multiword speech. *Developmental Psychology, 22*, 184–190.

Shu, H., Anderson, R., & Wu, N. (2000). Phonetic awareness: Knowledge of orthography-phonology relationships in the character acquisition of Chinese children. *Journal of Educational Psychology, 92*, 56–62.

Shumaker, S., Legault, C., Rapp, S., Thal, L., Wallace, R., Ockene, J., Hendrix, S., Jones, B., Assaf, A., Jackson, R., Kotchen, J., Wassertheil-Smoller, S., & Wactawski-Wende, J. (2003). Estrogen plus progestin and the incidence of dementia and mild cognitive impairment in postmenopausal women: The Women's Health Initiative memory study: A randomized controlled trial. *Journal of the American Medical Association, 289*, 2651–2662.

Sicotte, C., & Stemberger, R. (1999). Do children with PDDNOS have a theory of mind? *Journal of Autism & Developmental Disorders, 29*, 225–233.

Siegel, B. (1996). Is the emperor wearing clothes? Social policy and the empirical support for full inclusion of children with disabilities in the preschool and early elementary grades. *Social Policy Report, Society for Research in Child Development, 10(2–3)*, 2–17.

Siegler, I. C. (1983). Psychological aspects of the Duke Longitudinal Studies. In K. W. Schaie (Ed.), *Longitudinal studies of adult psychological development* (pp. 136–190). New York: Guilford Press.

Siegler, R., & Chen, Z. (2002). Development of rules and strategies: Balancing the old and the new. *Journal of Experimental Child Psychology, 81*, 446–457.

Sigman, M., Neumann, C., Carter, E., Cattle, D. J., D'Souza, S., & Bwibo, N. (1988). Home interactions and the development of Embu toddlers in Kenya. *Child Development, 59*, 1251–1261.

Sijuwade, P. (2003). A comparative study of family characteristics of Anglo American and Asian American high achievers. *Journal of Applied Social Psychology, 33*, 445–454.

Silver, J. (2003). *Movie day at the Supreme Court or "I know it when I see it": A history of the definition of obscenity.* Retrieved June 28, 2007 from http://library.findlaw.com/2003/May/15/132747.html

Silver, M., Newell, K., Brady, C., Hedley-White, E., & Perls, T. (2002). Distinguishing between neurodegenerative disease and disease-free aging: Correlating neuropsychological evaluations and neuropathological studies in centenarians. *Psychosomatic Medicine, 64*, 493–501.

Silverman, J., Ciresi, G., Smith, C., Marin, D., & Schnaider-Beeri, M. (2005). Variability of familial risk of Alzheimer's disease across the late life span. *Archives of General Psychiatry, 62*, 565–573.

Silverstein, M., & Long, J. (1998). Trajectories of grandparents' perceived solidarity with adult grandchildren: A growth curve analysis over 23 years. *Journal of Marriage & the Family, 60*, 912–923.

Simoneau, G. G., & Liebowitz, H. W. (1996). Posture, gait, and falls. In J. E. Birren & K. W. Schaie (Eds.), *Handbook of the psychology of aging* (4th ed., pp. 204–217). San Diego, CA: Academic Press.

Simons, R. L., Robertson, J. F., & Downs, W. R. (1989). The nature of the association between parental rejection and delinquent behavior. *Journal of Youth & Adolescence, 18*, 297–309.

Simonton, D. (2000). Creativity: Cognitive, personal, developmental, and social aspects. *American Psychologist, 55*, 151–158.

Simonton, D. K. (1991). Career landmarks in science: Individual differences and interdisciplinary contrasts. *Developmental Psychology, 27*, 119–130.

Simpkins, S., Davis-Kean, P., & Eccles, J. (2006). Math and science motivation: A longitudinal examination of the links between choices and beliefs. *Developmental Psychology, 42*, 70–83.

Sims, M., Hutchins, T., & Taylor, M. (1997). Conflict as social interaction: Building relationship skills in child care settings. *Child & Youth Care Forum, 26*, 247–260.

Singh, I. (2004). Doing their jobs: Mothering with Ritalin in a culture of mother-blame. *Social Science & Medicine, 59*, 1193–1205.

Singh, S., & Darroch, J. (2000). Adolescent pregnancy and childbearing: Levels and trends in industrialized countries. *Family Planning Perspectives, 32*, 14–23.

Skaalvik, E., & Valas, H. (1999). Relations among achievement, self-concept and motivation in mathematics and language arts: A longitudinal study. *Journal of Experimental Education, 67*, 135–149.

Skinner, B. F. (1953). *Science and human behavior.* New York: Macmillan.

Skinner, B. F. (1957). *Verbal behavior.* New York: Prentice Hall.

Skinner, B. F. (1980). The experimental analysis of operant behavior: A history. In R. W. Riebes & K. Salzinger (Eds.), *Psychology: Theoretical-historical perspectives.* New York: Academic Press.

Skoe, E., Hansen, K., Morch, W., Bakke, I., Hoffman, T., Larsen, B., & Aasheim, M. (1999). Care-based moral reasoning in Norwegian and Canadian early adolescents: A cross-national comparison. *Journal of Early Adolescence, 19*, 280–291.

Skoumal, R., Chen, J., Kula, K., Breza, J., Calomfirescu, N., Basson, B., & Kocrnicky, V. (2004). Efficacy and treatment satisfaction with on-demand tadalafil (Cialis) in men with erectile dysfunction. *European Urology, 46*, 362–369.

Skwarchuk, S., & Anglin, J. (2002). Children's acquisition of the English cardinal number words: A special case of vocabulary development. *Journal of Educational Psychology, 97*, 107–125.

Slaby, R. G., & Frey, K. S. (1975). Development of gender constancy and selective attention to same-sex models. *Child Development, 46*, 849–856.

Slater, A. (1995). Individual differences in infancy and later IQ. *Journal of Child Psychology & Psychiatry, 36*, 69–112.

Slaughter, V., & Lyons, M. (2003). Learning about life and death in early childhood. *Cognitive Psychology, 46*, 1–30.

Slaughter, Va. (2005). Young children's understanding of death. *Australian Psychologist, 40*, 179–186.

Slobin, D. I. (1985a). Introduction: Why study acquisition crosslinguistically? In D. I. Slobin (Ed.), *The crosslinguistic study of language acquisition, Vol. 1: The data* (pp. 3–24). Hillsdale, NJ: Erlbaum.

Slobin, D. I. (1985b). Crosslinguistic evidence for the language-making capacity. In D. I. Slobin (Ed.), *The crosslinguistic study of language acquisition, Vol. 2: Theoretical issues* (pp. 1157–1256). Hillsdale, NJ: Erlbaum.

Slobounov, S., Moss, S., Slobounova, E., & Newell, K. (1998). Aging and time to instability in posture. *Journals of Gerontology, Series A: Biological Sciences & Medical Sciences, 53A*, B71–B78.

Small, S. A., & Luster, T. (1994). Adolescent sexual activity: An ecological, risk-factor approach. *Journal of Marriage & the Family, 56*, 181–192.

Smeeding, T. M. (1990). Economic status of the elderly. In R. H. Binstock & L. K. George (Eds.), *Handbook of aging and the social sciences* (3rd ed., pp. 362–381). San Diego, CA: Academic Press.

Smetana, J., Schlagman, N., & Adams, P. (1993). Preschool children's judgments about hypothetical and actual transgressions. *Child Development, 64*, 202–214.

Smetana, J. G., Killen, M., & Turiel, E. (1991). Children's reasoning about interpersonal and moral conflicts. *Child Development, 62*, 629–644.

Smith, D., & Moen, P. (2004). Retirement satisfaction for retirees and their spouses: Do gender and the retirement decision-making process matter? *Journal of Family Issues, 25*, 262–285.

Smith, L., Fagan, J., & Ulvund, S. (2002). The relation of recognition memory in infancy and parental socioeconomic status to later intellectual competence. *Intelligence, 30*, 247–259.

Smith, M., Sharit, J., & Czaja, S. (1999). Aging, motor control, and the performance of computer mouse tasks. *Human Factors, 41*, 389–396.

Smith, P., Smees, R., & Pelligrini, A. (2004). Play fighting and real fighting: Using video playback methodology with young children. *Aggressive Behavior, 30*, 164–173.

Smith, P., White, J., & Holland, L. (2003). A longitudinal perspective on dating violence among adolescent and college-age women. *American Journal of Public Health, 93*, 1104–1109.

Smith, S., Howard, J., & Monroe, A. (1998). An analysis of child behavior problems in adoptions in difficulty. *Journal of Social Service Research, 24*, 61–84.

Smith, T. (2004). *Greece to face Euro court over video game ban.* Retrieved June 28, 2007 from www.theregister.co.uk/2004/10/14/greek_game_ban_to_court/

Smith, Y., van Goozen, S., Kuiper, A., & Cohen-Kettenis, P. (2005). Sex reassignment: Outcomes and predictors of treatment for adolescent and adult transsexuals. *Psychological Medicine, 35*, 89–99.

Smock, P. J. (1993). The economic costs of marital disruption for young women over the past two decades. *Demography, 30*, 353–371.

Smokowski, P., Mann, E., Reynolds, A., & Fraser, M. (2004). Childhood risk and protective factors and late adolescent adjustment in inner city minority youth. *Children and Youth Services Review, 26*, 63–91.

Snarey, J. (1995). In communitarian voice: The sociological expansion of Kohlbergian theory, research, and practice. In W. M. Kurtines & J. L. Gerwitz (Eds.), *Moral development: An introdution* (pp. 109–134). Boston: Allyn & Bacon.

Snarey, J., Son, L., Kuehne, V. S., Hauser, S., & Vaillant, G. (1987). The role of parenting in men's psychosocial development: A longitudinal study of early adulthood infertility and midlife generativity. *Developmental Psychology, 23*, 593–603.

Snarey, J. R. (1985). Cross-cultural universality of social-moral development: A critical review of Kohlbergian research. *Psychological Bulletin, 97*, 202–232.

Snarey, J. R., Reimer, J., & Kohlberg, L. (1985). Development of social-moral reasoning among kibbutz adolescents: A longitudinal cross-sectional study. *Developmental Psychology, 21*, 3–17.

Snow, C. E. (1997, April). *Cross-domain connections and social class differences: Two challenges to nonenvironmentalist views of language development.* Paper presented at the biennial meetings of the Society for Research in Child Development, Washington, DC.

Snyder, C. (1997). Unique invulnerability: A classroom demonstration in estimating personal mortality. *Teaching of Psychology, 24*, 197–199.

Society for Assisted Reproductive Technology. (2004). *Guidelines on number of embryos transferred: Committee report.* Retrieved August 18, 2004, from http://www.sart.org.

Soken, N., & Pick, A. (1999). Infants' perception of dynamic affective expressions: Do infants distinguish specific expressions? *Child Development 70*, 1275–1282.

Sola, A., Rogido, M., & Partridge, J. (2002). The perinatal period. In A. Rudolph, R. Kamei, & K. Overby (Eds.), *Rudolph's fundamental of pediatrics* (3rd ed., pp. 125–183). New York: McGraw-Hill.

Solano, L., Costa, M., Salvati, S., Coda, R., Aiuti, F., Mezzaroma, I., & Bertini, M. (1993). Psychosocial factors and clinical evolution in HIV-1 infection: A longitudinal study. *Journal of Psychosomatic Research, 37*, 39–51.

Soldo, B. J., Wolf, D. A., & Agree, E. M. (1990). Family, households, and care arrangements of frail older women: A structural analysis. *Journals of Gerontology: Social Sciences, 45*, S238–249.

Solomon, S., Rothblum, E., & Balsam, K. (2004). Pioneers in partnership: Lesbian and gay male couples in civil unions compared with those not in civil unions and married heterosexual siblings. *Journal of Family Psychology, 18*, 275–286.

Somers, M. D. (1993). A comparison of voluntarily childfree adults and parents. *Journal of Marriage & the Family, 55*, 643–650.

Sommer, B., Avis, N., Meyer, P., Ory, M., Madden, T., Kagawa-Singer, M., Mouton, C., Rasor, N., & Adler, S. (1999). Attitudes toward menopause and aging across ethnic/racial groups. *American Psychosomatic Society, 61*, 868–875.

Soori, H., & Bhopal, R. (2002). Parental permission for children's independent outdoor activities: Implications for injury prevention. *European Journal of Public Health, 12*, 104–109.

Sophian, C. (1995). Representation and reasoning in early numerical development: Counting, conservation, and comparisons between sets. *Child Development, 66*, 559–577.

Sorlie, P. D., Backlund, E., & Keller, J. B. (1995). U.S. mortality by economic, demographic, and social characteristics: The National Longitudinal Mortality Study. *American Journal of Public Health, 85*, 949–956.

Sotelo, M., & Sangrador, J. (1999). Correlations of self-ratings of attitude towards violent groups with measures of personality, self-esteem, and moral reasoning. *Psychological Reports, 84*, 558–560.

Sowell, E., Peterson, B., Thompson, P., Welcome, S., Henkenius, A., & Toga, A. (2003). Mapping cortical change across the human life span. *Nature Neuroscience, 6*, 309–315.

Spelke, E. S. (1979). Exploring audible and visible events in infancy. In A. D. Pick (Ed.), *Perception and its development: A tribute to Eleanor J. Gibson* (pp. 221–236). Hillsdale, NJ: Erlbaum.

Spelke, E. S. (1982). Perceptual knowledge of objects in infancy. In J. Mehler, E. C. T. Walker, & M. Garrett (Eds.), *Perspectives on mental representation* (pp. 409–430). Hillsdale, NJ: Erlbaum.

Spelke, E. S. (1991). Physical knowledge in infancy: Reflections on Piaget's theory. In S. Carey & R. Gelman (Eds.), *The epigenesis of mind: Essays on biology and cognition* (pp. 133–169). Hillsdale, NJ: Erlbaum.

Spelke, E. S., von Hofsten, C., & Kestenbaum, R. (1989). Object perception in infancy: Interaction of spatial and kinetic information for object boundaries. *Developmental Psychology, 25*, 185–196.

Spiegel, D., Bloom, J. R., Kraemer, H. C., & Gottheil, E. (1989, October 14). Effect of psychosocial treatment on survival of patients with metastatic breast cancer. *Lancet*, 888–901.

Spieler, D., & Griffin, Z. (2006). The influence of age on the time course of word preparation in multiword utterances. *Language and Cognitive Processes, 21*, 291–321.

Spiers, P. S., & Guntheroth, W. G. (1994). Recommendations to avoid the prone sleeping position and recent statistics for Sudden Infant Death Syndrome in the United States. *Archives of Pediatric & Adolescent Medicine, 148*, 141–146.

Spokane, A., & Cruza-Guet, M. (2005). Holland's theory of vocational personalities in work environments. In S. Brown & R. Lent (Eds.). *Career development and counseling: putting theory and research to work* (pp. 24–41). Hoboken, NJ: John Wiley & Sons.

Sprang, G., & McNeil, J. (1998). Post-homicide reactions: Grief, mourning and post-traumatic stress disorder following a drunk driving fatality. *Omega, 37*, 41–58.

Spreen, O., Risser, A., & Edgell, D. (1995). *Developmental neuropsychology.* New York: Oxford University Press.

Srivastava, S., John, O., Gosling, S., & Potter, J. (2003). Development of personality in early and middle adulthood: Set like plaster or persistent change? *Journal of Personality and Social Psychology, 84*, 1041–1053.

Sroufe, L. A., Carlson, E., & Schulman, S. (1993). Individuals in relationships: Development from infancy through adolescence. In D. C. Funder, R. D. Parke, C. Tomlinson-Keasey, & K. Widaman (Eds.), *Studying lives through time: Personality and development* (pp. 315–342). Washington, DC: American Psychological Association.

St. James-Roberts, I., Bowyer, J., Varghese, S., & Sawdon, J. (1994). Infant crying patterns in Manila and London. *Child: Care, Health & Development, 20*, 323–337.

St. Pierre, T., Mark, M., Kaltreider, D., & Aikin, K. (1995). A 27-month evaluation of a sexual activity prevention program in boys and girls clubs across the nation. *Family Relations, 44*, 69–77.

Stack, S. (1992a). The effect of divorce on suicide in Finland: A time series analysis. *Journal of Marriage & the Family, 54*, 636–642.

Stack, S. (1992b). The effect of divorce on suicide in Japan: A time series analysis, 1950–1980. *Journal of Marriage & the Family, 54*, 327–334.

Stack, S., & Wasserman, I. (1993). Marital status, alcohol consumption, and suicide: An analysis of national data. *Journal of Marriage & the Family, 55*, 1018–1024.

Stainback, S., & Stainback, W. (1985). The merger of special and regular education: Can it be done? A response to Lieberman and Mesinger. *Exceptional Children, 51*, 517–521.

Stallworth, J., & Lennon, J. (2003). An interview with Dr. Lester Breslow: A pioneer in chronic disease prevention and health behavior intervention shares insights from his professional and personal experiences. *American Journal of Public Health, 93*, 1803–1805.

Stambrook, M., & Parker, K. C. H. (1987). The development of the concept of death in childhood: A review of the literature. *Merrill-Palmer Quarterly, 33*, 133–158.

Stanford, E. P., Happersett, C. J., Morton, D. J., Molgaard, C. A., & Peddecord, K. M. (1991). Early retirement and functional impairment from a multi-ethnic perspective. *Research on Aging, 13*, 5–38.

Stattin, H., & Klackenberg-Larsson, I. (1993). Early language and intelligence development and their relationship to future criminal behavior. *Journal of Abnormal Psychology, 102*, 369–378.

Steele, C., & Aronson, J. (1995). Stereotype threat and the intellectual test performance of African Americans. *Journal of Personality & Social Psychology, 69*, 797–811.

Steele, C., & Aronson, J. (2004). Stereotype threat does not live by Steele and Aronson (1995) alone. *American Psychologist, 59*, 47–48.

Steele, J., & Mayes, S. (1995). Handedness and directional asymmetry in the long bones of the human upper limb. *International Journal of Osteoarchaeology, 5*, 39–49.

Steele, K. M., Bass, K. E., & Crook, M. D. (1999). The mystery of the Mozart effect: Failure to replicate. *Psychological Science, 10*, 366–369.

Steele, M., Hodges, J., Kaniuk, J., Hillman, S., & Henderson, K. (2003). Attachment representations and adoption: Associations between maternal states of mind and emotion narratives in previously maltreated children. *Journal of Child Psychotherapy, 29*, 187–205.

Steffens, D., Artigues, D., Ornstein, K., & Krishnan, K. (1997). A review of racial differences in geriatric depression: Implications for care and clinical research. *Journal of the National Medical Association, 89*, 731–736.

Stein, C., Wemmerus, V., Ward, M., Gaines, M., Freeberg, A., & Jewell, T. (1998). "Because they're my parents": An intergenerational study of felt obligation and parental caregiving. *Journal of Marriage & the Family, 60*, 611–622.

Stein, G. (2004). Improving our care at life's end: Making a difference. *Health & Social Work, 29*, 77–79.

Steinberg, L. (1986). Latchkey children and susceptibility to peer pressure: An ecological analysis. *Developmental Psychology, 22*, 433–439.

Steinberg, L., Blatt-Eisengart, I., & Cauffman, E. (2006). Patterns of competence and adjustment among adolescents from authoritative, authoritarian, indulgent, and neglectful homes: A replication in a sample of serious juvenile offenders. *Journal of Research on Adolescence, 16*, 47–58.

Steinberg, L., Elmen, J. D., & Mounts, N. S. (1989). Authoritative parenting, psychosocial maturity, and academic success among adolescents. *Child Development, 60*, 1424–1436.

Steinberg, L., Fletcher, A., & Darling, N. (1994). Parental monitoring and peer influences on adolescent substance use. *Pediatrics, 93,* 1060–1064.

Steinberg, L., Lamborn, S. D., Dornbusch, S. M., & Darling, N. (1992). Impact of parenting practices on adolescent achievement: Authoritative parenting, school involvement, and encouragement to succeed. *Child Development, 63,* 1266–1281.

Steinberg, L., Mounts, N. S., Lamborn, S. D., & Dornbusch, S. D. (1991). Authoritative parenting and adolescent adjustment across varied ecological niches. *Journal of Research on Adolescence, 1,* 19–36.

Steiner, J. E. (1979). Human facial expressions in response to taste and smell stimulation. In H. W. Reese & L. P. Lipsitt (Eds.), *Advances in child development and behavior, Vol. 13* (pp. 257–296). New York: Academic Press.

Steinhauser, K., Christakis, N., Clipp, E., McNeilly, M., Grambow, S., Parker, J., & Tulsky, J. (2001). Preparing for the end of life: Preferences of patients, families, physicians, and other care providers. *Journal of Pain & Symptom Management, 22,* 727–737.

Sternberg, R. (1988). *The triarchic mind: A new theory of intelligence.* New York: Viking Press.

Sternberg, R. (2002). A broad view of intelligence: The theory of successful intelligence. *Consulting Psychology Journal: Practice and Research, 55,* 139–154.

Sternberg, R., & Grigorenko, E. (2006). Cultural intelligence and successful intelligence. *Group & Organization Management, 31,* 37–39.

Sternberg, R., Wagner, R., Williams, W., & Horvath, J. (1995). Testing common sense. *American Psychologist, 50,* 912–927.

Sternberg, R. J. (1987). Liking versus loving: A comparative evaluation of theories. *Psychological Bulletin, 102,* 331–345.

Sternberg, R. J., & Wagner, R. K. (1993). The g-ocentric view of intelligence and job performance is wrong. *Current Directions in Psychological Science, 2,* 1–5.

Stetson, B. (2002). *Living victims, stolen lives: Parents of murdered children speak to American about death value, and meaning.* New York: Baywood Publishing Company.

Stevenson, H. (1994). Moving away from stereotypes and preconceptions: Students and their education in East Asia and the United States. In P. M. Greenfield & R. R. Cocking (Eds.), *Cross-cultural roots of minority child development* (pp. 315–322). Hillsdale, NJ: Erlbaum.

Stevenson, H. W., & Lee, S. (1990). Contexts of achievement: A study of American, Chinese, and Japanese children. *Monographs of the Society for Research in Child Development, 55* (1–2, Serial No. 221).

Stevenson, H. W., Lee, S., Chen, C., Lummis, M., Stigler, J., Fan, L., & Ge, F. (1990). Mathematics achievement of children in China and the United States. *Child Development, 61,* 1053–1066.

Stewart, S., Pearson, S., Luke, C., & Horowitz, J. (1998). Effects of home-based intervention on unplanned readmissions and out-of-hospital deaths. *Journal of the American Geriatrics Society, 46,* 174–180.

Stigler, J. W., & Stevenson, H. W. (1991). How Asian teachers polish each lesson to perfection. *American Educator* (Spring), 12–20, 43–47.

Stigler, J. W., Lee, S., & Stevenson, H. W. (1987). Mathematics classrooms in Japan, Taiwan, and the United States. *Child Development, 58,* 1272–1285.

Stilberg, J., San Miguel, V., Murelle, E., Prom, E., Bates, J., Canino, G., Egger, H., & Eaves, L. (2005). Genetic environmental influences on temperament in the first year of life: The Puerto Rico Infant Twin Study (PRINTS). *Twin Research and Human Genetics, 8,* 328–336.

Stimpson, J., Kuo, Y., Ray, L., Raji, M., & Peek, K. (2006). Risk of mortality related to widowhood in older Mexican Americans. *Annals of Epidemiology, 17,* 313–319.

Stipek, D., Gralinski, J., & Kopp, C. (1990). Self-concept development in the toddler years. *Developmental Psychology, 26,* 972–977.

Stolarova, M., Whitney, H., Webb, S., deRegnier, R., Georgieff, M., & Nelson, C. (2003). Electrophysiological brain responses of six-month-old low risk premature infants. *Infancy, 4,* 437–450.

Stoller, E. P., Forster, L. E., & Duniho, T. S. (1992). Systems of parent care within sibling networks. *Research on Aging, 14,* 28–49.

Stormshak, E., Bierman, K., McMahon, R., Lengua, L., et al. (2000). Parenting practices and child disruptive behavior problems in early elementary school. *Journal of Clinical Child Psychology, 29,* 17–29.

Strawbridge, W. J., Camacho, T. C., Cohen, R. D., & Kaplan, G. A. (1993). Gender differences in factors associated with change in physical functioning in old age: A 6-year longitudinal study. *The Gerontologist, 33,* 603–609.

Strayer, J., & Roberts, W. (2004). Empathy and observed anger and aggression in five-year-olds. *Social Development, 13,* 1–13.

Streissguth, A. P., Aase, J. M., Clarren, S. K., Randels, S. P., LaDue, R. A., & Smith, D. F. (1991). Fetal alcohol syndrome in adolescents and adults. *Journal of the American Medical Association, 265,* 1961–1967.

Striano, T., & Rochat, P. (1999). Developmental link between dyadic and triadic social competence in infancy. *British Journal of Developmental Psychology, 17,* 551–562.

Stroebe, M., & Schut, H. (1999). The dual process model of coping with bereavement: Rationale and description. *Death Studies, 23,* 1–28.

Stroebe, M., Folkman, S., Hansson, R., & Schut, H. (2006). The prediction of bereavement outcome: Development of an integrative risk factor framework. *Social Science & Medicine, 63,* 2440–2451.

Stroebe, M., Schut, H., & Stroebe, W. (2005). Attachment in coping with bereavement: A theoretical integration. *Review of General Psychology, 9,* 48–66.

Stroebe, M., van Son, M., Stroebe, W., Kleber, R., Schut, H., & van den Bout, J. (2000). On the classification and diagnosis of pathological grief. *Clinical Psychology Review, 20,* 57–75.

Stroebe, M. S., & Stroebe, W. (1993). The mortality of bereavement: A review. In M. S. Stroebe, W. Stroebe, & R. O. Hansson (Eds.), *Handbook of bereavement: Theory, research, and intervention* (pp. 175–195). Cambridge, England: Cambridge University Press.

Stroganova, T., Posikera, I., Pushina, N., & Orekhova, E. (2003). Lateralization of motor functions in early human ontogeny. *Human Physiology, 29,* 48–58.

Stroud, R. (2004). The strain of the occasional athlete. *Orthopedic Technology Review, 6.* Retrieved July 4, 2007 from www.orthopedictechreview.com/issues/mayjun04/pg24.htm.

Stull, D. E., & Hatch, L. R. (1984). Unravelling the effects of multiple life changes. *Research on Aging, 6,* 560–571.

Stunkard, A. J., Harris, J. R., Pedersen, N. L., & McClearn, G. E. (1990). The body-mass index of twins who have been reared apart. *New England Journal of Medicine, 322,* 1483–1487.

Sturm, J., & Seery, C. (2007). Speech and articulatory rate of school-aged children in conversation and narrative contexts. *Language, Speech, and Hearing Services in Schools, 38,* 47–59.

Sue, S., & Okazaki, S. (1990). Asian-American educational achievements: A phenomenon in search of an explanation. *American Psychologist, 45,* 913–920.

Sugisawa, H., Liang, J., & Liu, X. (1994). Social networks, social support, and mortality among older people in Japan. *Journals of Gerontology: Social Sciences, 49,* S3–13.

Sulkes, S. (1998). Developmental and behavioral pediatrics. In R. Behrman & R. Kliegman (Eds.), *Nelson essentials of pediatrics* (3rd ed., pp. 1–55). Philadelphia: W. B. Saunders.

Sullivan, K., Zaitchik, D., & Tager-Flusberg, H. (1994). Preschoolers can attribute second-order beliefs. *Developmental Psychology, 30,* 395–402.

Sullivan, M., Ormel, J., Kempen, G., & Tymstra, T. (1998). Beliefs concerning death, dying, and hastening death among older, functionally impaired Dutch adults: A one-year longitudinal study. *Journal of the American Geriatrics Society, 46,* 1251–1257.

Super, D. (1990). A life-span, life-space approach to career development. In D. Brown & L. Brooks (Eds.). *Applying contemporary theories to practice.* (2nd ed.) (pp. 197–261). The Jossey-Bass management series and the Jossey-Bass social and behavioral science series. San Francisco, CA: Jossey-Bass.

Suryadevara, V., Storey, S., Aronow, W., & Ahn, C. (2003). Association of abnormal serum lipids in elderly persons with atherosclerotic vascular disease and dementia, atherosclerotic vascular disease without dementia, dementia without atherosclerotic vascular disease, and no dementia or atherosclerotic vascular disease. *Journals of Gerontology, Series A: Biological Sciences & Medical Sciences, 58A,* 859–861.

Susman, E. J., Inoff-Germain, G., Nottelmann, E. D., Loriaux, D. L., Cutler, G. B., Jr., & Chrousos, G. P. (1987). Hormones, emotional dispositions, and aggressive attributes in young adolescents. *Child Development, 58,* 1114–1134.

Susser, E., & Lin, S. (1992). Schizophrenia after prenatal exposure to the Dutch hunger winter of 1944–45. *Archives of General Psychiatry, 49,* 983–988.

Sutton, P., & Munson., M. (2004). Births, marriages, divorces, and deaths: Provisional data for January 2004. *National Vital Statistics Reports; 53,* 1–6.

Suzuki, L., & Aronson, J. (2005). The cultural malleability of intelligence and its impact on the racial/ethnic hierarchy. *Psychology, Public Policy, & Law, 11,* 320–327.

Svrakic, N., Svrakic, D., & Cloninger, C. (1996). A general quantitative theory of personality development: Fundamentals of a self-organizing psychobiological complex. *Development & Psychopathology, 8,* 247–272.

Swanson, L., & Kim, K. (2007). Working memory, short-term memory, and naming speed as predictors of children's mathematical performance. *Intelligence, 35,* 151–168.

Sweeting, H., & West, P. (2002). Gender differences in weight related concerns in early to late adolescence. *Journal of Family Issues, 23*, 728–747.

Swendsen, J., & Mazure, C. (2000). Life stress as a risk factor for postpartum depression: Current research and methodological issues. *Clinical Psychology, 7*, 17–31.

Swensen, C. H., Eskew, R. W., & Kohlhepp, K. A. (1981). Stage of family life cycle, ego development, and the marriage relationship. *Journal of Marriage & the Family, 43*, 841–853.

Symister, P., & Friend, R. (2003). The influence of social support and problematic support on optimism and depression in chronic illness: A prospective study evaluating self-esteem as a mediator. *Health Psychology, 22*, 123–129.

Syska, E., Schmidt, R., & Schubert, J. (2004). The time of palatal fusion in mice: A factor of strain susceptibility to teratogens. *Journal of Craniomascillofacial Surgery, 32*, 2–4.

Szabo, A., & Underwood, J. (2004). Cybercheats: Is information and communication technology fuelling academic dishonesty? *Active Learning in Higher Education, 5*, 180–199.

Szinovacz, M., & Davey, A. (2005). Retirement and marital decision making: Effects on retirement satisfaction. *Journal of Marriage and Family, 67*, 387–398.

Tadmor, C. (2004). Preventive intervention for children with cancer and their families at the end-of-life. *Journal of Primary Prevention, 24*, 311–323.

Taga, K., Markey, C., Friedman, H. (2006). A longitudinal investigation of associations between boys' pubertal timing and adult behavioral health and well-being. *Journal of Youth and Adolescence, 35*, 401–411.

Tait, M., Padgett, M. Y., & Baldwin, T. T. (1989). Job and life satisfaction: A reevaluation of the strength of the relationship and gender effects as a function of the date of the study. *Journal of Applied Psychology, 74*, 502–507.

Takahashi, K., Tamura, J., & Tokoro, M. (1997). Patterns of social relationships and psychological well-being among the elderly. *International Journal of Behavioral Development, 21*, 417–430.

Takata, T. (1999). Development process of independent and interdependent self-construal in Japanese culture: Cross-cultural and cross-sectional analyses. *Japanese Journal of Educational Psychology, 47*, 480–489.

Takei, W. (2001). How do deaf infants attain first signs? *Developmental Science, 4*, 71–78.

Talan, J. (1998, October 28). Possible genetic link found for right-handedness, not for left. *Seattle Times.*

Talbott, M. (1998). Older widows' attitudes towards men and remarriage. *Journal of Aging Studies, 12*, 429–449.

Tanner, J. M. (1990). *Fetus into man: Physical growth from conception to maturity.* Cambridge, MA: Harvard University Press.

Tan-Niam, C., Wood, D., & O'Malley, C. (1998). A cross-cultural perspective on children's theories of mind and social interaction. *Early Child Development & Care, 144*, 55–67.

Tapanya, S., Nicki, R., & Jarusawad, O. (1997). Worry and intrinsic/extrinsic religious orientation among Buddhist (Thai) and Christian (Canadian) elderly persons. *International Journal of Aging and Human Development, 44*, 73–83.

Tardif, T., & Wellman, H. (2000). Acquisition of mental state language in Mandarin- and Cantonese-speaking children. *Developmental Psychology, 36*, 25–43.

Tardif, T., So, C., & Kaciroti, N. (2007). Language and false belief: Evidence for general, not specific, effects in Cantonese-speaking preschoolers. *Developmental Psychology, 43*, 318–340.

Tasbihsazan, R., Nettelbeck, T., & Kirby, N. (2003). Predictive validity of the Fagan Test of Infant Intelligence. *British Journal of Developmental Psychology, 21*, 585–597.

Task Force on Sudden Infant Death Syndrome. (2005). The changing concept of Sudden Infant Death Syndrome: Diagnostic coding shifts, controversies regarding the sleeping environment, and new variables to consider in reducing risk. *Pediatrics, 116*, 1245–1255.

Taveras, E., Li, R., Grummer-Strawn, L., Richardson, M., Marshall, R., Rêgo, V., Miroshnik, I., & Lieu, T. (2004). Opinions and practices of clinicians associated with continuation of exclusive breastfeeding, *Pediatrics, 113*, e283–e290.

Taylor, L., & Gaskin-Laniyan, N. (2007). Sexual assault in abusive relationships. *National Institute of Justice Journal, 256*, 1–3.

Taylor, P., Funk, C., & Clark, A. (2007). *Generation gap in values, behaviors: As marriage and parenthood drift apart, public is concerned about social impact.* Pew Research Center. Retrieved July 5, 2007 from http://pewresearch.org/assets/social/pdf/Marriage.pdf.

Taylor, P., Funk, C., Craighill, P., & Kennedy, C. (2006). *Families drawn together by communication revolution.* Retrieved August 2, 2007 from http://pewresearch.org/assets/social/pdf/FamilyBonds.pdf.

Taylor, P. J., & Kopelman, M. D. (1984). Amnesia for criminal offenses. *Psychological Medicine, 14*, 481–588.

Teachman, J. (2003). Premarital sex, premarital cohabitation and the risk of subsequent marital dissolution among women. *Journal of Marriage & the Family, 65*, 444–455.

Teilmann, G., Pedersen, C., Jensen, T., Skakkebaek, N., & Juul, A. (2005). Prevalence of precocious pubertal development in Denmark: An epidemiologic study based on national registries. *Pediatrics, 116*, 1323–1328.

Temko, N. (2005). *Anti-bullying protests force policy u-turn.* Retrieved June 20, 2007 from www.guardian.co.uk/child/story/0,7369,1557999,00.html

Temoshok, L. (1987). Personality, coping style, emotion and cancer: Towards an integrative model. *Cancer Surveys, 6*, 545–567.

Terashima, K., Mikami, A., Tachibana, N., Kumano-Go, T., Teshima, Y., Sugita, Y., & Takeda, M. (2004). Sleep characteristics of menopausal insomnia: A polysomnographic study. *Psychiatry & Clinical Neurosciences, 58*, 179–185.

Terman, L. (1916). *The measurement of intelligence.* Boston: Houghton Mifflin.

Terman, L., & Merrill, M. A. (1937). *Measuring intelligence: A guide to the administration of the new revised Stanford-Binet tests.* Boston: Houghton Mifflin.

Terrisse, B. (2000). *The resilient child: Theoretical perspectives and a review of the literature.* Paper presented to the Council of Ministers of Education, Canada. Ottawa, Ontario, April, 2000.

Tershakovec, A. & Stallings, V. (1998). Pediatric nutrition and nutritional disorders. In R. Behrman & R. Kliegman (Eds.), *Nelson essentials of pediatrics* (3rd ed.). Philadelphia: W. B. Saunders.

Tervo, S., Kivipelto, M., Hänninen, T., Vanhanen, M., Hallikainen, M., Mannermaa, A., & Soininen, H. (2004). Incidence and risk factors for mild cognitive impairment: A population-based three-year follow-up study of cognitively healthy elderly subjects. *Dementia & Geriatric Cognitive Disorders, 17*, 196–203.

Tessier, R., Cristo, M., Velez, S., Giron, M., Line, N., Figueroa de Calume, Z., Ruiz-Palaez, J., & Charpak, N. (2003). Kangaroo mother care: A method for protecting high-risk low-birth-weight and premature infants against developmental delay. *Infant Behavior & Development, 26*, 384–397.

Teti, D. M., Gelfand, D. M., Messinger, D. S., & Isabella, R. (1995). Maternal depression and the quality of early attachment: An examination of infants, preschoolers, and their mothers. *Developmental Psychology, 31*, 364–376.

Thal, D., & Bates, E. (1990). Continuity and variation in early language development. In J. Colombo & J. Fagen (Eds.), *Individual differences in infancy: Reliability, stability, prediction* (pp. 359–385). Hillsdale, NJ: Erlbaum.

Thal, D., Tobias, S., & Morrison, D. (1991). Language and gesture in late talkers: A 1-year follow-up. *Journal of Speech & Hearing Research, 34*, 604–612.

Thapar, A., Fowler, T., Rice, F., Scourfield, J., van den Bree, M., Thomas, H., Harold, G., & Hay, D. (2003). Maternal smoking during pregnancy and attention deficit hyperactivity disorder symptoms in offspring. *American Journal of Psychiatry, 160*, 1985–1989.

Tharenou, P. (1999). Is there a link between family structures and women's and men's managerial career advancement? *Journal of Organizational Behavior, 20*, 837–863.

Tharp, R. G., & Gallimore, R. (1988). *Rousing minds to life.* New York: Cambridge University Press.

Thelen, E. (1995). Motor development: A new synthesis. *American Psychologist, 50*, 79–95.

Thelen, E. (1996). Motor development: A new synthesis. *American Psychologist, 50*, 79–95.

Thelen, E., & Adolph, K. E. (1992). Arnold L. Gesell: The paradox of nature and nurture. *Developmental Psychology, 28*, 368–380.

Thierer, A. (2003). *Regulating video games: Parents or Uncle Sam?* Retrieved June 28, 2007 from www.cato.org/pub_display.php?pub_id=3167

Thobaben, M., & Duncan, R. (2003). Domestic elder abuse by health care providers. *Home Health Care Management & Practice, 15*, 168–169.

Thomas, A., & Chess, S. (1977). *Temperament and development.* New York: Brunner/Mazel.

Thomas, C., Benzeval, M., & Stansfeld, S. (2007). Psychological distress after employment transitions: The role of subjective financial position as a mediator. *Journal of Epidemiology & Community Health, 61*, 48–52.

Thomas, D., Townsend, T., & Belgrave, F. (2003). The influence of cultural and racial identification on the psychosocial adjustment of inner-city African American children in school. *American Journal of Community Psychology, 32*, 217–228.

Thomas, J., Yan, J., & Stelmach, G. (2000). Movement substructures change as a function of practice in children and adults. *Journal of Experimental Child Psychology, 75*, 228–244.

Thomas, L. (2003, June). Marriage insurance: Will you be married 'til death do you part? *The Washingtonian.* Retrieved August 24, 2004, from http://www.washingtonian.com/weddings/insurance.html.

Thomas, M. (2000). *Comparing theories of development* (5th ed.). Pacific Grove, CA: Brooks/Cole.

Thomas, R. M. (Ed.). (1990). *The encyclopedia of human development and education: Theory, research, and studies.* Oxford, England: Pergamon Press.

Thompson, B., Brough, P., & Schmidt, H. (2006). Supervisor and subordinate work-family values: Does similarity make a difference? *International Journal of Stress Management, 13*, 45–63.

Thompson, L., Fagan, J., & Fulker, D. (1991). Longitudinal prediction of specific cognitive abilities from infant novelty preference. *Child Development, 62*, 530–538.

Thompson, R., & Goodvin, R. (2005). The individual child: Temperament, emotion, self, and personality. In M. Bornstein & M. Lamb (Eds.) *Developmental science: An advanced textbook* (5th edition). Hillsdale, NJ: Lawrence Erlbaum.

Thompson, W., & Lande, R. (2007). Alcoholism. Retrieved July 2, 2007 from www.emedicine.com/med/topic98.htm.

Thomson, E., & Colella, U. (1992). Cohabitation and marital stability: Quality or commitment? *Journal of Marriage & the Family, 54*, 259–267.

Thorn, A., & Gathercole, S. (1999). Language-specific knowledge and short-term memory in bilingual and non-bilingual children. *Quarterly Journal of Experimental Psychology: Human Experimental Psychology, 52A*, 303–324.

Thorne, B. (1986). Girls and boys together . . . but mostly apart: Gender arrangements in elementary schools. In W. W. Hartup & Z. Rubin (Eds.), *Relationships and development* (pp. 167–184). Hillsdale, NJ: Erlbaum.

Thorpe, M., Pittenger, D., & Reed, B. (1999). Cheating the researcher: A study of the relation between personality measures and self-reported cheating. *College Student Journal, 33*, 49–59.

Thorslund, M., & Lundberg, O. (1994). Health and inequalities among the oldest old. *Journal of Aging & Health, 6*, 51–69.

Thorson, J. A., & Powell, F. C. (1990). Meanings of death and intrinsic religiosity. *Journal of Clinical Psychology, 46*, 379–390.

Thorson, J. A., & Powell, F. C. (1992). A revised death anxiety scale. *Death Studies, 16*, 507–521.

Thun, M., Peto, R., Lopez, A., Monaco, J., Henley, S., Heath, C., & Doll, R. (1997). Alcohol consumption and mortality among middle-aged and elderly U.S. adults. *New England Journal of Medicine, 337*, 1705–1714.

Tice, R. R., & Setlow, R. B. (1985). DNA repair and replication in aging organisms and cells. In C. E. Finch & E. L. Schneider (Eds.), *Handbook of the biology of aging* (2nd ed., pp. 173–224). New York: Van Nostrand Reinhold.

Tiedemann, J. (2000). Parents' gender stereotypes and teachers' beliefs as predictors of children's concept of their mathematical ability in elementary school. *Journal of Educational Psychology, 92*, 144–151.

Tippeconnic, J. (2003). The use of academic achievement tests and measurements with American Indian and Alaska Native students. *Eric Digest Online.* Retrieved June 25, 2007 from www.ericdigests.org/2005-2/tests.html

Todd, R. D., Swarzenski, B., Rossi, P. G., & Visconti, P. (1995). Structural and functional development of the human brain. In D. Cicchetti & D. J. Cohen (Eds.), *Developmental psychopathology: Vol. 1. Theory and methods* (pp. 161–194). New York: Wiley.

Tomasello, M. (1999). *The cultural origins of human cognition.* Cambridge, MA: Harvard University Press.

Tomassini, C., Kalogirou, S., Grundy, E., Fokkema, T., Martikainen, P., van Groenou, M., & Karisto, A. (2004). Contacts between elderly parents and their children in four European countries: Current patterns and future prospects. *European Journal of Ageing, 1*, 54–63.

Tomblin, J., Smith, E., & Zhang, X. (1997). Epidemiology of specific language impairment: Prenatal and perinatal risk factors. *Journal of Communication Disorders, 30*, 325–344.

Tomita, T., Ohta, Y., Ogawa, K., Sugiyama, H., Kagami, N., & Agari, I. (1997). Grief process and strategies of psychological helping: A review. *Japanese Journal of Counseling Science, 30*, 49–67.

Tomlinson-Keasey, C., Eisert, D. C., Kahle, L. R., Hardy-Brown, K., & Keasey, B. (1979). The structure of concrete operational thought. *Child Development, 50*, 1153–1163.

Toomela, A. (1999). Drawing development: Stages in the representation of a cube and a cylinder. *Child Development, 70*, 1141–1150.

Torbert, K. (2000). Japan's new material girls: "Parasite singles" put off marriage for good life. *Washington Post.* p. A01.

Torgerson, D., & Bell-Syer, S. (2001). Hormone replacement therapy and prevention of nonvertebral fractures: A meta-analysis of randomized trials. *Journal of the American Medical Association, 285*, 2891–2897.

Torgerson, D., Thomas, R., Campbell, M., & Reid, D. (1997). Alcohol consumption and age of maternal menopause are associated with menopause onset. *Maturitas, 26*, 21–25.

Torgesen, J., Wagner, R., Rashotte, C., Rose, E., et al. (1999). Preventing reading failure in young children with phonological processing disabilities: Group and individual responses to instruction. *Journal of Educational Psychology, 91*, 594–603.

Tortora, G., & Grabowski, S. (1993). *Principles of anatomy and physiology.* New York: HarperCollins.

Trainor, L., Clark, E., Huntley, A., & Adams, B. (1997). The acoustic basis of preferences for infant-directed singing. *Infant Behavior & Development, 20*, 383–396.

Trautner, H., Gervai, J., & Nemeth, R. (2003). Appearance-reality distinction and development of gender constancy understanding in children. *International Journal of Behavioral Development, 27*, 275–283.

Trehub, S., Unyk, A., Kamenetsky, S., Hill, D., et al. (1997). Mothers' and fathers' singing to infants. *Developmental Psychology, 33*, 500–507.

Trehub, S. E., & Rabinovitch, M. S. (1972). Auditory-linguistic sensitivity in early infancy. *Developmental Psychology, 6*, 74–77.

Trentin, G. (2004). E-learning and the third age. *Journal of Computer Assisted Learning, 20*, 21–30.

Trivers, R. (1972). Parental investment and sexual selection. In B. Campbell (Ed.), *Sexual selection and the descent of man: 1871–1971* (pp. 136–179). Chicago: Aldine.

Tronick, E. Z., Morelli, G. A., & Ivey, P. K. (1992). The Efe forager infant and toddler's pattern of social relationships: Multiple and simultaneous. *Developmental Psychology, 28*, 568–577.

Trosclair, A., Husten, C., Pederson, L., & Dhillon, I. (2002). Cigarette smoking among adults: United States, 2000. *Morbidity & Mortality Weekly Report, 51*, 642–645.

Truluck, J., & Courtenay, B. (1999). Learning style preferences among older adults. *Educational Gerontology, 25*, 221–236.

Tsang, P. (1998). Age, attention, expertise, and time-sharing performance. *Psychology & Aging, 13*, 323–347.

Tsang, W., & Hui-Chan, C. (2003). Effects of Tai Chi on joint proprioception and stability limits in elderly subjects. *Medicine & Science in Sports & Exercise, 35*, 1962–1971.

Tsang, W., & Hui-Chan, C. (2004). Effects of exercise on joint sense. *Medicine and Science in Sports and Exercise, 36*, 658–667.

Tsuya, N. O., & Martin, L. G. (1992). Living arrangements of elderly Japanese and attitudes toward inheritance. *Journals of Gerontology: Social Sciences, 47*, S45–54.

Turic, D., Robinson, L., Duke, M., Morris, D. W., Webb, V., Hamshere, M., Milham, C., Hopkin, E., Pound, K., Fernando, S., Grierson, A., Easton, M., Williams, N., Van Den Bree, M., Chowdhury, R., Gruen, J., Krawczak, M., Owen, M. J., O'Donovan, M. C., & Williams, J. (2004). Linkage disequilibrium mapping provides further evidence of a gene for reading disability on chromosome 6p21.3–22. *Molecular Psychiatry, 8*, 176–185.

Twenge, J., Campbell, W., & Foster, C. (2003). Parenthood and marital satisfaction: A meta-analytic review. *Journal of Marriage & the Family, 65*, 574–583.

Tyler-Smith, K. (2006). Early attrition among first time learners: A review of factors that contribute to drop-out, withdrawal, and non-completion rates of adult learners undertaking learning programmes. *Journal of Online Learning and Teaching, 2 (2).* Retrieved July 2, 2007 from http://jolt.merlot.org/Vol2_No2_TylerSmith.htm.

Tylka, T. (2004). The relation between body dissatisfaction and eating disorder symptomatology: An analysis of moderating variables. *Journal of Counseling Psychology, 51*, 178–191.

Udell, J., Fischer, M., Brookhart, M., Solomon, D., & Choudhry, N. (2006). Effect of the Women's Health Initiative on osteoporosis therapy and expenditure in Medicaid. *Journal of Bone and Mineral Research, 21*, 765–771.

Uecker, A., & Nadel, L. (1996). Spatial locations gone awry: Object and spatial memory deficits in children with fetal alcohol syndrome. *Neuropsychologia, 34*, 209–223.

Uemura, N., Okamoto, S., Yamamoto, S., Matsumura, N., Yamaguchi, S., Yamakido, M., Taniyama, K., Sasaki, N., & Schlemper, R. (2001). *Helicobacter pylori* infection and the development of gastric cancer. *New England Journal of Medicine, 345*, 784–789.

Uhlenberg, P., Cooney, T., & Boyd, R. (1990). Divorce for women after midlife. *Journals of Gerontology: Social Sciences, 45*, S3–11.

Umetsu, D. (1998). Immunology and allergy. In R. Behrman & R. Kleigman (Eds.), *Nelson essentials of pediatrics* (3rd ed.). Philadelphia: W. B. Saunders.

Underwood, M. (1997). Peer social status and children's understanding of the expression and control of positive and negative emotions. *Merrill-Palmer Quarterly, 43*, 610–634.

Underwood, M. K., Coie, J. D., & Herbsman, C. R. (1992). Display rules for anger and aggression in school-age children. *Child Development, 63*, 366–380.

Underwood, M. K., Kupersmidt, J. B., & Coie, J. D. (1996). Childhood peer sociometric status and aggression as predictors of adolescent childbearing. *Journal of Research on Adolescence, 6*, 201–224.

Ungerer, J. A., & Sigman, M. (1984). The relation of play and sensorimotor behavior to language in the second year. *Child Development, 55*, 1448–1455.

Uno, D., Florsheim, P., & Uchino, B. (1998). Psychosocial mechanisms underlying quality of parenting among Mexican-American and White adolescent mothers. *Journal of Youth & Adolescence, 27*, 585–605.

Updegraff, K., & Obeidallah, D. (1999). Young adolescents' patterns of involvement with siblings and friends. *Social Development, 8*, 52–69.

Urban, J., Carlson, E., Egeland, B., & Sroufe, L. A. (1991). Patterns of individual adaptation across childhood. *Development and Psychopathology, 3*, 445–460.

Urberg, K., Degirmencioglu, S., & Tolson, J. (1998). Adolescent friendship selection and termination: The role of similarity. *Journal of Social & Personal Relationships, 15*, 703–710.

U.S. Bureau of Labor Statistics. (2005). *Women in the labor force: a Databook.* Retrieved July 28, 2006, from http://www.bls.gov/cps/wlf-databook2005.htm.

U.S. Bureau of the Census. (1994). *Statistical abstract of the United States: 1994.* Washington, DC: U.S. Government Printing Office.

U.S. Bureau of the Census. (1995a). *Sixty-five plus in the United States.* Statistical Brief. Washington, DC: U.S. Government Printing Office.

U.S. Bureau of the Census. (1997). *Statistical abstract of the United States: 1997.* Washington, DC: U.S. Government Printing Office.

U.S. Bureau of the Census. (1998). *Statistical abstract of the United States: 1998.* Washington, DC: U.S. Government Printing Office.

U.S. Bureau of the Census. (1999). *Current population survey: March 1960 to 1999.* Washington, DC: U.S. Government Printing Office.

U.S. Bureau of the Census. (2001). *Statistical abstract of the United States: 2001.* Washington, DC: U.S. Government Printing Office.

U.S. Bureau of the Census. (2003a). *Statistical abstract of the United States: 2003.* Washington, DC: U.S. Government Printing Office.

U.S. Bureau of the Census. (2003b). *Married-couple and unmarried-partner households: 2000.* Retrieved August 18, 2004, from http://www.census.gov.

U.S. Census Bureau. (2002). *Current population survey.* Retrieved August 3, 2007 from http://www.census.gov/population/socdemo/race/black/ppl-164/tab16.pdf.

U.S. Census Bureau. (2006). *2005 American community survey.* Retrieved November 19, 2006 from www.census.gov/acs/www/index.html.

U.S. Department of Education. (2004). *No Child Left Behind: Introduction.* Retrieved September 21, 2004, from http://www.ed.gov/print/nclb/overview/intro/index.html.

U.S. Department of Health and Human Services. (1998b). *National initiative to eliminate racial and ethnic disparities in health: Cardiovascular disease.* Retrieved October 11, 2000, from http://www.raceandhealth.omhrc.gov.

U.S. Department of Health and Human Services. (1998c). *National initiative to eliminate racial and ethnic disparities in health: Diabetes.* Retrieved October 11, 2000, from http://www.raceandhealth.omhrc.gov.

U.S. Department of Health and Human Services. (2007). *Choosing long-term care.* Retrieved August 2, 2007 from http://www.ahrq.gov/consumer/qnt/qntltc.htm.

Ushikubo, M. (1998). A study of factors facilitating and inhibiting the willingness of the institutionalized disabled elderly for rehabilitation: A United States-Japanese comparison. *Journal of Cross-Cultural Gerontology, 13*, 127–157.

Uylings, H. (2006). Development of the human cortex and the concept of "critical" or "sensitive" periods. *Language Learning, 56*, 59–90.

Vachon, M. (1998). Psychosocial needs of patients and families. *Journal of Palliative Care, 14*, 49–56.

Vaeisaenen, L. (1998). Family grief and recovery process when a baby dies. *Psychiatria Fennica, 29*, 163–174.

Vaillant, G. (2002). *Aging well: Surprising guideposts to a happier life from the landmark Harvard Study of Adult Development.* New York: Little, Brown & Company.

Vaillant, G. E. (1977). *Adaptation to life: How the best and brightest came of age.* Boston: Little, Brown.

Vaillant, G. E. (1991). The association of ancestral longevity with successful aging. *Journals of Gerontology: Psychological Sciences, 46*, P292–298.

Valdez-Menchaca, M. C., & Whitehurst, G. J. (1992). Accelerating language development through picture book reading: A systematic extension to Mexican day care. *Developmental Psychology, 28*, 1106–1114.

Valenza, E., Leo, I., Gava, L., & Simion, F. (2006). Perceptual completion in newborn human infants. *Child Development, 77*, 1810–1821.

van Beijsterveldt, C., Bartels, M., Hudziak, J., & Boomsma, D. (2003). Causes of stability of aggression from early childhood to adolescence: A longitudinal genetic analysis in Dutch twins. *Behavior Genetics, 33*, 591–605.

Van Beijsterveldt, T. Hudziak, J., & Boomsma, D. (2005). Short- and long-term effects of child care on problem behaviors in a Dutch sample of twins. *Twin Research and Human Genetics, 8*, 250–258.

Van Boxtel, M., Paas, F., Houx, P., Adam, J., Teeken, J., & Jolles, J. (1997). Aerobic capacity and cognitive performance in a cross-sectional aging study. *Medicine & Science in Sports & Exercise, 29*, 1357–1365.

van den Boom, D. (1995). Do first-year intervention effects endure? Follow-up during toddlerhood of a sample of Dutch irritable infants. *Child Development, 66*, 1798–1816.

van den Boom, D. C. (1994). The influence of temperament and mothering on attachment and exploration: An experimental manipulation of sensitive responsiveness among lower-class mothers with irritable infants. *Child Development, 65*, 1457–1477.

Van den Broek, P., Lynch, J., Naslund, J., Ievers-Landis, C., & Verduin, K. (2004). The development of comprehension of main ideas in narratives: Evidence from the selection of titles. *Journal of Educational Psychology, 96*, 707–718.

van den Hoonaard, D. (1999). "No regrets": Widows' stories about the last days of their husbands' lives. *Journal of Aging Studies, 13*, 59–72.

van der Molen, M., Molenaar, P. (1994). Cognitive psychophysiology: A window to cognitive development and brain maturation. In G. Dawson & K. Fischer (Eds.), *Human behavior and the developing brain* (pp. 456–492). New York: Guilford Press.

van Doorn, C., Kasl, S., Beery, L., Jacobs, S., & Prigerson, H. (1998). The influence of marital quality and attachment styles on traumatic grief and depressive symptoms. *Journal of Nervous & Mental Disease, 186*, 566–573.

van Doornen, L., Snieder, H., & Boomsma, D. (1998). Serum lipids and cardiovascular reactivity to stress. *Biological Psychology, 47*, 279–297.

van Grootheest, D., Beekman, A., van Groenou, M., & Deeg, D. (1999). Sex differences in depression after widowhood: Do men suffer more? *Social Psychiatry & Psychiatric Epidemiology, 34*, 391–398.

van IJzendoorn, M. (2005). Attachment at an early age (0–5) and its impact on children's development. In Centres of Excellence for Children's Well-Being (Eds.), *Encyclopedia on Early Childhood Development.* Retrieved June 13, 2007, from www.excellence-earlychildhood.ca/documents/van_IJzendoornANGxp.pdf

van IJzendoorn, M. H. (1995). Adult attachment representations, parental responsiveness, and infant attachment: A meta-analysis on the predictive validity of the Adult Attachment Interview. *Psychological Bulletin, 117*, 387–403.

van IJzendoorn, M. H., & Kroonenberg, P. M. (1988). Cross-cultural patterns of attachment: A meta-analysis of the Strange Situation. *Child Development, 59*, 147–156.

Van Lange, P., DeBruin, E., Otten, W., & Joireman, J. (1997). Development of prosocial, individualistic, and competitive orientations: Theory and preliminary evidence. *Journal of Personality & Social Psychology, 73*, 733–746.

Van Solinge, H. (2007). Health change in retirement: A longitudinal study among older workers in the Netherlands. *Research on Aging, 29*, 225–256.

van Wormer, K., & McKinney, R. (2003). What schools can do to help gay/lesbian/bisexual youth: A harm reduction approach. *Adolescence, 38*, 409–420.

Vandewater, E., Shim, M., & Caplovitz, A. (2004). Linking obesity and activity level with children's television and video game use. *Journal of Adolescence, 27*, 71–85.

Varady, K., & Hellerstein, M. (2007). Alternative-day fasting and chronic disease prevention: A review of human and animal trials. *American Journal of Clinical Nutrition, 86*, 7–13.

Varea, C., Bernis, C., Montero, P., Arias, S. Barroso, A., & Gonzalez, B. (2000). Secular trend and intrapopulational variation in age at menopause in Spanish women. *Journal of Biosocial Science, 32*, 383–393.

Vartanian, L. (2000). Revisiting the imaginary audience and personal fable constructs of adolescent egocentrism: A conceptual review. *Adolescence, 35*, 639–661.

Vartanian, L. (2001). Adolescents' reactions to hypothetical peer group conversations: Evidence for an imaginary audience? *Adolescence, 36,* 347–380.

Vartanian, L. R. (1997). Separation-individuation, social support, and adolescent egocentrism: An exploratory study. *Journal of Early Adolescence, 17,* 245–270.

Vartanian, L. R., & Powlishta, K. K. (1996). A longitudinal examination of the social-cognitive foundations of adolescent egocentrism. *Journal of Early Adolescence, 16,* 157–178.

Vedder, R. (2004). *Going broke by degree: Why college costs too much.* Washington, DC: American Enterprise Institute Press.

Vega, W. A. (1990). Hispanic families in the 1980s: A decade of research. *Journal of Marriage & the Family, 52,* 1015–1024.

Venkatraman, M. M. (1995). A cross-cultural study of the subjective wellbeing of married elderly persons in the United States and India. *Journals of Gerontology: Social Sciences, 50B,* S35–44.

Verbrugge, L. M. (1989). Gender, aging, and health. In K. S. Markides (Ed.), *Aging and health* (pp. 23–78). Newbury Park, CA: Sage.

Verbrugge, L. M., & Wingard, D. L. (1987). Sex differentials in health and mortality. *Women & Health, 12,* 103–145.

Verbrugge, L. M., Lepkowski, J. M., & Konkol, L. L. (1991). Levels of disability among U.S. adults with arthritis. *Journals of Gerontology: Social Sciences, 46,* S71–83.

Verhaeghen, P., & Marcoen, A. (1993). Memory aging as a general phenomenon: Episodic recall of older adults is a function of episodic recall of young adults. *Psychology & Aging, 8,* 380–388.

Verhaeghen, P., Marcoen, A., & Goossens, L. (1992). Improving memory performance in the aged through mnemonic training: A meta-analytic study. *Psychology & Aging, 7,* 242–251.

Verhulst, F., & Versluis-Den Bieman, H. (1995). Development course of problem behaviors in adolescent adoptees. *Journal of the American Academy of Child & Adolescent Psychiatry, 34,* 151–159.

Verkooijen, K., de Vries, N., & Nielsen, G. (2007). Youth crowds and substance use: The impact of perceived group norm and multiple group identification. *Psychology of Addictive Behaviors, 21,* 55–61.

Vermeer, H., & van IJzendoorn, M. (2006). Children's elevated cortisol levels at daycare. *Early Childhood Research Quarterly, 21,* 390–401.

Veroff, J., Douvan, E., & Kulka, R. A. (1981). *The inner American: A self-portrait from 1957 to 1976.* New York: Basic Books.

Viadero, D. (2007). Teachers say NCLB has changed classroom practice. *Education Week, 26,* 6.

Vig, E., & Pearlman, R. (2003). Quality of life while dying: A qualitative study of terminally ill older men. *Journal of the American Geriatrics Society, 51,* 1595–1601.

Vikat, A., Rimpela, A., Kosunen, E., & Rimpela, M. (2002). Sociodemographic differences in the occurrence of teenage pregnancies in Finland in 1987–1998: A follow up study. *Journal of Epidemiology & Community Health, 56,* 659–670.

Ville, I., & Khlat, M. (2007). Meaning and coherence of self and health: An approach based on narratives of life events. *Social Science & Medicine, 64,* 1001–1014.

Viner, R. (2002). Is puberty getting earlier in girls? *Archives of Disease in Childhood, 86,* 8–10.

Vinokur, A. D., & van Ryn, M. (1993). Social support and undermining in close relationships: Their independent effects on the mental health of unemployed persons. *Journal of Personality & Social Psychology, 65,* 350–359.

Visscher, W., Feder, M., Burns, A., Brady, T., & Bray, R. (2003). The impact of smoking and other substance use by urban women on the birthweight of their infants. *Substance Use & Misuse, 38,* 1063–1093.

Vitaro, F., Tremblay, R., Kerr, M., Pagani, L., & Bukowski, W. (1997). Disruptiveness, friends' characteristics, and delinquency in early adolescence: A test of two competing models of development. *Child Development, 68,* 676–689.

Vogin, J. (2005). *Taking medication while pregnant.* Retrieved June 7, 2007 from http://www.medicinenet.com/script/main/art.asp?articlekey=51639

Volz, J. (2000). Successful aging: The second 50. *Monitor, 31,* 24–28.

Voyer, D., Voyer, S., & Bryden, M. P. (1995). Magnitude of sex differences in spatial abilities: A meta-analysis and consideration of critical variables. *Psychological Bulletin, 117,* 250–270.

Vuchinich, S., Bank, L., & Patterson, G. R. (1992). Parenting, peers, and the stability of antisocial behavior in preadolescent boys. *Developmental Psychology, 28,* 510–521.

Vuorenkoski, L., Kuure, O., Moilanen, I., & Peninkilampi, V. (2000). Bilingualism, school achievement, and mental wellbeing: A follow-up study of return migrant children. *Journal of Child Psychology & Psychiatry & Allied Disciplines, 41,* 261–266.

Waggoner, G. (2000). The new grandparents: What they buy, what they think. *Modern Maturity, 43,* 85, 91.

Walden, T. A. (1991). Infant social referencing. In J. Garber & K. A. Dodge (Eds.), *The development of emotion regulation and dysregulation* (pp. 69–88). Cambridge, England: Cambridge University Press.

Walker, H., Messinger, D., Fogel, A., & Karns, J. (1992). Social and communicative development in infancy. In V. B. V. Hasselt & M. Hersen (Eds.), *Handbook of social development: A lifespan perspective* (pp. 157–181). New York: Plenum.

Walker, L. J. (1989). A longitudinal study of moral reasoning. *Child Development, 60,* 157–160.

Walker, L. J., de Vries, B., & Trevethan, S. D. (1987). Moral stages and moral orientations in real-life and hypothetical dilemmas. *Child Development, 58,* 842–858.

Walker-Andrews, A., & Kahana-Kalman, R. (1999). The understanding of pretence across the second year of life. *British Journal of Developmental Psychology, 17,* 523–536.

Walker-Andrews, A. S. (1997). Infants' perception of expressive behaviors: Differentiation of multimodal information. *Psychological Bulletin, 121,* 437–456.

Walker-Andrews, A. S., & Lennon, E. (1991). Infants' discrimination of vocal expressions: Contributions of auditory and visual information. *Infant Behavior & Development, 14,* 131–142.

Waller, A., Dennis, F., Brodie, J., & Cairns, A. (1998). Evaluating the use of TalksBac, a predictive communication device for nonfluent adults with aphasia. *International Journal of Language & Communication Disorders, 33,* 45–70.

Wallerstein, J., & Lewis, J. (1998). The long-term impact of divorce on children: A first report from a 25-year study. *Family & Conciliation Courts Review, 36,* 368–383.

Walls, C. T., & Zarit, S. H. (1991). Informal support from black churches and the well-being of elderly blacks. *The Gerontologist, 31,* 490–495.

Walton, G. E., Bower, N. J. A., & Bower, T. G. R. (1992). Recognition of familiar faces by newborns. *Infant Behavior & Development, 15,* 265–269.

Walusinski, O., Kurjak, A., Andonotopo, W., & Azumendi, G. (2005). Fetal yawning: A behavior's birth with 4D US revealed. *The Ultrasound Review of Obstetrics & Gynecology, 5,* 210–217.

Wang, C., & Phinney, J. (1998). Differences in child rearing attitudes between immigrant Chinese mothers and Anglo-American mothers. *Early Development & Parenting, 7,* 181–189.

Wang, X., Dow-Edwards, D., Anderson, V., Minkoff, H., & Hurd, Y. (2004). In utero marijuana exposure associated with abnormal amygdala dopamine D-sub-2 gene expression in the human fetus. *Biological Psychiatry, 56,* 909–915.

Wang, Y. (2002). Is obesity associated with early sexual maturation? A comparison of the association in American boys versus girls. *Pediatrics, 110,* 903–910.

Wang, Y., & Lobstein, T. (2006). Worldwide trends in childhood overweight and obesity. *International Journal of Pediatric Obesity, 1,* 11–25.

Wang, Y., & Ollendick, T. (2001). A cross-cultural and developmental analysis of self-esteem in Chinese and Western children. *Clinical Child & Family Psychology Review, 4,* 253–271.

Wark, G. R., & Krebs, D. L. (1996). Gender and dilemma differences in real-life moral judgment. *Developmental Psychology, 32,* 220–230.

Warr, P., Jackson, P., & Banks, M. (1988). Unemployment and mental health: Some British studies. *Journal of Social Issues, 44,* 47–68.

Warren, S., Gunnar, M., Kagan, J., Anders, T., Simmens, S., Rones, M., Wease, S., Aron, E., Dahl, R., & Sroufe, A. (2003). Maternal panic disorder: Infant temperament, neurophysiology, and parenting behaviors. *Journal of the American Academy of Child & Adolescent Psychiatry, 42,* 814–825.

Wartner, U. B., Grossman, K., Fremmer-Bombik, E., & Suess, G. (1994). Attachment patterns at age six in south Germany: Predictability from infancy and implications for preschool behavior. *Child Development, 65,* 1014–1027.

Waskowic, T., & Chartier, B. (2003). Attachment and the experience of grief following the loss of a spouse. *Omega, 47,* 77–91.

Watamura, S., Donzella, B., Alwin, J., & Gunnar, M. (2003). Morning-to-afternoon increases in cortisol concentrations for infants and toddlers at child care: Age differences and behavioral correlates. *Child Development, 74,* 1006–1020.

Waters, E., Treboux, D., Crowell, J., Merrick, S., & Albersheim, L. (1995, March). *From the Strange Situation to the Adult Attachment Interview: A*

20-year longitudinal study of attachment security in infancy and early adulthood. Paper presented at the biennial meetings of the Society for Research in Child Development, Indianapolis, IN.

Watson, A., Nixon, C., Wilson, A., & Capage, L. (1999). Social interaction skills and theory of mind in young children. *Developmental Psychology, 35,* 386–391.

Watson, J. (1997). Grandmothering across the lifespan. *Journal of Gerontological Social Work, 28,* 45–62.

Watson, J. B. (1930). *Behaviorism.* New York: Norton.

Waxman, S. R., & Kosowski, T. D. (1990). Nouns mark category relations: Toddlers' and preschoolers' word-learning biases. *Child Development, 61,* 1461–1473.

Weaver, J. (1999). Gerontology education: A new paradigm for the 21st century. *Educational Gerontology, 25,* 479–490.

Webster, J., & McCall, M. (1999). Reminiscence functions across adulthood: A replication and extension. *Journal of Adult Development, 6,* 73–85.

Webster, M. L., Thompson, J. M., Mitchell, E. A., & Werry, J. S. (1994). Postnatal depression in a community cohort. *Australian & New Zealand Journal of Psychiatry, 28,* 42–49.

Webster-Stratton, C., & Reid, M. (2003). Treating conduct problems and strengthening social and emotional competence in young children: The Dina Dinosaur treatment program. *Journal of Emotional & Behavioral Disorders, 11,* 130–143.

Wechsler, H., Davenport, A., Dowdall, G., Moeykens, B., & Castillo, S. (1994). Health and behavioral consequences of binge drinking in college. *Journal of the American Medical Association, 272,* 1672–1677.

Wechsler, H., Dowdall, G., Maenner, G., Gledhill-Hoyt, J., & Lee, H. (1998). Changes in binge drinking and related problems among American college students between 1993 and 1997. *Journal of American College Health, 47,* 57–68.

Wee, C., Hamel, N., Davis, R., & Phillips, R. (2004). Assessing the value of weight loss among primary care patients. *Journal of General Internal Medicine, 19,* 1206–1211.

Weeks, J. (2004). Same-sex partnerships. *Feminism & Psychology, 14,* 158–164.

Weinberg, R. A. (1989). Intelligence and IQ: Landmark issues and great debates. *American Psychologist, 44,* 98–104.

Weinberg, R. A., Scarr, S., & Waldman, I. D. (1992). The Minnesota transracial adoption study: A follow-up of IQ test performance. *Intelligence, 16,* 117–135.

Weindrich, D., Jennen-Steinmetz, C., Laucht, M., & Schmidt, M. (2003). Late sequelae of low birthweight: Mediators of poor school performance at 11 years. *Developmental Medicine & Child Neurology, 45,* 463–469.

Weinfield, N., & Egeland, B. (2004). Continuity, discontinuity, and coherence in attachment from infancy to late adolescence: Sequelae of organization and disorganization. *Attachment & Human Development, 6,* 73–97.

Weisner, T., & Wilson-Mitchell, J. (1990). Nonconventional family lifestyles and sex typing in six-year olds. *Child Development, 62,* 1915–1933.

Weiss, R., Dziura, J., Burgert, T., Tamborlane, W., Tasali, S., Yeckel, C., Allen, K., Lopes, M., Savoye, M., Morrison, J., Sherwin, R., & Caprio, S. (2004). Obesity and the metabolic syndrome in children and adolescents. *New England Journal of Medicine, 350,* 2362–2374.

Welch-Ross, M. (1997). Mother-child participation in conversation about the past: Relationships to preschoolers' theory of mind. *Developmental Psychology, 33,* 618–629.

Welford, A. T. (1993). The gerontological balance sheet. In J. Cerella, J. Rybash, W. Hoyer, & M. L. Commons (Eds.), *Adult information processing: Limits on loss* (pp. 3–10). San Diego, CA: Academic Press.

Wellman, H., Cross, D., & Watson, J. (2001). Meta-analysis of theory-of-mind development: The truth about false belief. *Child Development, 72,* 655–684.

Wellman, H. M. (1982). The foundations of knowledge: Concept development in the young child. In S. G. Moore & C. C. Cooper (Eds.), *The young child: Reviews of research, Vol. 3* (pp. 115–134). Washington, DC: National Association for the Education of Young Children.

Wentzel, K. R., & Asher, S. R. (1995). The academic lives of neglected, rejected, popular, and controversial children. *Child Development, 66,* 754–763.

Werker, J., Pons, F., Dietrich, C., Kajikawa, S., Fais, L., & Amano, S. (2007). Infant directed speech supports phonetic category learning in English and Japanese. *Cognition, 103,* 147–162.

Werker, J. F., Pegg, J. E., & McLeod, P. J. (1994). A cross-language investigation of infant preference for infant-directed communication. *Infant Behavior & Development, 17,* 323–333.

Werner, E. E. (1995). Resilience in development. *Current Directions in Psychological Science, 4,* 81–85.

Werner, E. E., & Smith, R. S. (1992). *Overcoming the odds: High risk children from birth to adulthood.* Ithaca, NY: Cornell University Press.

Werner, L. A., & Gillenwater, J. M. (1990). Pure-tone sensitivity of 2- to 5-week-old infants. *Infant Behavior & Development, 13,* 355–375.

West, R. L., & Crook, T. H. (1990). Age differences in everyday memory: Laboratory analogues of telephone number recall. *Psychology & Aging, 5,* 520–529.

Westerhof, G., Katzko, M., Dittmann-Kohli, F., & Hayslip, B. (2001). Life contexts and health-related selves in old age: Perspectives from the United States, India and Congo/Zaire. *Journal of Aging Studies, 15,* 105–126.

Wharton, A., & Blair-Loy, M. (2006). Long work hours and family life: A cross-national study of employees' concerns. *Journal of Family Issues, 27,* 415–436.

Whitam, F. L., Diamond, M., & Martin, J. (1993). Homosexual orientation in twins: A report on 61 pairs and three triplet sets. *Archives of Sexual Behavior, 22,* 187–206.

White, M., Wilson, M., Elander, G., & Persson, B. (1999). The Swedish family: Transition to parenthood. *Scandinavian Journal of Caring Sciences, 13,* 171–176.

White, W. H. (1992). G. Stanley Hall: From philosophy to developmental psychology. *Developmental Psychology, 28,* 25–34.

Whitehurst, G. J., Arnold, D. S., Epstein, J. N., Angell, A. L., Smith, M., & Fischel, J. E. (1994). A picture book reading intervention in day care and home for children from low-income families. *Developmental Psychology, 30,* 679–689.

Whitehurst, G. J., Falco, F. L., Lonigan, C. J., Fischel, J. E., DeBaryshe, B. D., Valdez-Menchaca, M. C., & Caulfield, M. (1988). Accelerating language development through picture book reading. *Developmental Psychology, 24,* 552–559.

Whitehurst, G. J., Fischel, J. E., Crone, D. A., & Nania, O. (1995, March). *First year outcomes of a clinical trial of an emergent literacy intervention in Head Start homes and classrooms.* Paper presented at the biennial meetings of the Society for Research in Child Development, Indianapolis, IN.

White-Traut, R., Nelson, M., Silvestri, J., Vasan, U., Littau, S., Meleedy-Rey, P., Gu, G., & Patel, M. (2002). Effect of auditory, tactile, visual, and vestibular intervention on length of stay, alertness, and feeding progression in preterm infants. *Developmental Medicine & Child Neurology, 44,* 91–97.

Whitfield, J. (2007). Semi-identical twins discovered. *Nature, 13,* 520–521.

Wich, B. K., & Carnes, M. (1995). Menopause and the aging female reproductive system. *Endocrinology & Metabolism Clinics of North America, 24,* 273–295.

Wicki, W. (1999). The impact of family resources and satisfaction with division of labour on coping and worries after the birth of the first child. *International Journal of Behavioral Development, 23,* 431–456.

Wiederman, M., & Allgeier, E. (1992). Gender differences in mate selection criteria: Sociobiological or socioeconomic explanation? *Ethology & Sociobiology, 13,* 115–124.

Wiehe, V. (2003). Empathy and narcissism in a sample of child abuse perpetrators and a comparison sample of foster parents. *Child Abuse & Neglect, 27,* 541–555.

Wigfield, A., Eccles, J. S., MacIver, D., Reuman, D. A., & Midgley, C. (1991). Transitions during early adolescence: Changes in children's domain-specific self-perceptions and general self-esteem across the transition to junior high school. *Developmental Psychology, 27,* 552–565.

Wilde, C. (2000). The new workplace: Telework programs are on the rise. *Information Week, 781,* 189.

Williams, D. R. (1992). Social structure and the health behaviors of blacks. In K. W. Schaie, D. Blazer, & J. S. House (Eds.), *Aging, health behaviors, and health outcomes* (pp. 59–64). Hillsdale, NJ: Erlbaum.

Williams, J. E., & Best, D. L. (1990). *Measuring sex stereotypes: A multination study* (rev. ed.). Newbury Park, CA: Sage.

Williams-Mbengue, N. (2003). *Safe havens for abandoned infants.* Retrieved June 18, 2007 from www.ncsl.org/programs/cyf/slr268.htm

Wilmore, J., Stanforth, P., Gagnon, J., Rice, T., Mandel, S., Leon, A., Rao, D., Skinner, J., & Bouchard, C. (2001). Cardiac output and stroke volume changes with endurance training: The HERITAGE Family Study. *Medical Science & Sports Exercise, 33,* 99–106.

Wilson, H., & Donenberg, G. (2004). Quality of parent communication about sex and its relationship to risky sexual behavior among youth in psychiatric care: A pilot study. *Journal of Child Psychology & Psychiatry & Allied Disciplines, 45,* 387–395.

Wilson, W. J. (1995). Jobless ghettos and the social outcome of youngsters. In P. Moen, G. H. Elder, Jr., & K. Lüscher (Eds.), *Examining lives in context: Perspectives on the ecology of human development* (pp. 527–543). Washington, DC: American Psychological Association.

Wiltenburg, M. (2003). *Safe haven.* Retrieved June 18, 2007 from www.csmonitor.com/2003/0724/p14s02-lifp.html

Wimmer, H., Mayringer, H., & Landerl, K. (1998). Poor reading: A deficit in skill-automatization or a phonological deficit? *Scientific Studies of Reading, 2,* 321–340.

Winter, B., Breitenstein, C., Mooren, F., Voelker, K., Fobker, M., Lechtermann, A., Krueger, K., Fromme, A., Korsukewitz, C., Floel, A., & Knecht, S. (2007). High impact running improves learning. *Neurobiology of Learning and Memory, 87,* 597–609.

Winter, L., Lawton, M., Casten, R., & Sando, R. (2000). The relationship between external events and affect states in older people. *International Journal of Aging & Human Development, 50,* 85–96.

Winter, R. (1999). A Biblical and theological view of grief and bereavement. *Journal of Psychology & Christianity, 18,* 367–379.

Wintre, M., & Yaffe, M. (2000). First-year students' adjustment to university life as a function of relationships with parents. *Journal of Adolescent Research, 15,* 9–37.

Wolfle, L., & List, J. (2004). Locus of control is fairly stable over time but does change as a result of natural events, such as the acquisition of college education. *Structural Equation Modeling, 11,* 244–260.

Wolfram, G. (2005). Making college more expensive: The unintended consequences of federal tuition aid. *Policy Analysis, 531.* Retrieved June 20, 2007 from www.cato.org/pubs/pas/pa531.pdf.

Wong, C., & Tang, C. (2004). Coming out experiences and psychological distress of Chinese homosexual men in Hong Kong. *Archives of Sexual Behavior, 33,* 149–157.

Wong, D. (1993). *Whaley & Wong's essentials of pediatric nursing.* St. Louis, MO: Mosby-Yearbook, Inc.

Wong, M., Shapiro, M., Boscardin, J., & Ettner, S. (2002). Contribution of major diseases to disparities in mortality. *New England Journal of Medicine, 347,* 1585–1592.

Woo, M., & Oei, T. (2006). The MMPI-2 gender-masculine and gender-feminine scales: Gender roles as predictors of psychological health in clinical patients. *International Journal of Psychology, 41,* 413–422.

Wood, C., & Terrell, C. (1998). Pre-school phonological awareness and subsequent literacy development. *Educational Psychology, 18,* 253–274.

Woolley, M., & Grogan-Kaylor, A. (2006). Protective family factors in the context of neighborhood: Promoting positive school outcomes. *Family Relations, 55,* 93–104.

World Health Organization (WHO). (2006). *The world health report 2006.* Retrieved July 6, 2007 from www.who.int/whr/2006/en/index.html.

World Health Organization. (2000). *Violence against women.* Retrieved September 1, 2000, from http://www.who.int.

Worrell, F. (1997). Predicting successful or non-successful at-risk status using demographic risk factors. *High School Journal, 81,* 46–53.

Wortman, C. B., & Silver, R. C. (1989). The myths of coping with loss. *Journal of Consulting & Clinical Psychology, 57,* 349–357.

Wortman, C. B., & Silver, R. C. (1990). Successful mastery of bereavement and widowhood: A life course perspective. In P. B. Baltes & M. M. Baltes (Eds.), *Successful aging: Perspectives from the behavioral sciences* (pp. 225–264). New York: Cambridge University Press.

Wortman, C. B., & Silver, R. C. (1992). Reconsidering assumptions about coping with loss: An overview of current research. In L. Montada, S. Filipp, & M. J. Lerner (Eds.), *Life crises and experiences of loss in adulthood* (pp. 341–365). Hillsdale, NJ: Erlbaum.

Wortman, C. B., Silver, R. C., & Kessler, R. C. (1993). The meaning of loss and adjustment to bereavement. In M. S. Stroebe, W. Stroebe, & R. O. Hansson (Eds.), *Handbook of bereavement* (pp. 349–366). Cambridge, England: Cambridge University Press.

Wright, C., & Birks, E. (2000). Risk factors for failure to thrive: A population-based survey. *Child: Care, Health & Development, 26,* 5–16.

Wright, T., & Bonett, D. (2007). Job satisfaction and psychological well-being as nonadditive predictors of workplace turnover. *Journal of Management, 33,* 141–160.

Writing Group for the Women's Health Initiative Investigators. (2002). Risks and benefits of estrogen plus progestin in healthy postmenopausal women: Principal results from the Women's Health Initiative randomized controlled trial. *Journal of the American Medical Association, 288,* 321–333.

Wu, T., Mendola, P., & Buck, G. (2002). Ethnic differences in the presence of secondary sex characteristics and menarche among U.S. girls: The Third National Health and Nutrition Examination Survey, 1988–1994.

Wu, Z., & Penning, M. (1997). Marital instability after midlife. *Journal of Family Issues, 18,* 459–478.

Wyatt, G., Axelrod, J., Chin, D., Carmona, J., & Loeb, T. (2000). Examining patterns of vulnerability to domestic violence among African American women. *Violence Against Women, 6,* 495–514.

Xie, H., Cairns, R., & Cairns, B. (1999). Social networks and configurations in inner-city schools: Aggression, popularity, and implications for students with EBD. *Journal of Emotional & Behavioral Disorders, 7,* 147–155.

Yang, H., Lu, S., Liaw, Y., You, S., Sun, C., Wang, L., Hsiao, C., Chen, P., Chen, D., & Chen, C. (2002). Hepatitis B/e antigen and the risk of hepatocellular carcinoma. *New England Journal of Medicine, 347,* 168–174.

Yellowlees, P., & Marks, S. (2007). Problematic internet use of internet addiction? *Computers in Human Behavior, 23,* 1447–1453.

Yirmiya, N., & Shulman, C. (1996). Seriation, conservation, and theory of mind abilities in individuals with autism, individuals with mental retardation, and normally developing children. *Child Development, 67,* 2045–2059.

Yirmiya, N., Eriel, O., Shaked, M., & Solomonica-Levi, D. (1998). Meta-analyses comparing theory of mind abilities of individuals with autism, individuals with mental retardation, and normally developing individuals. *Psychological Bulletin, 124,* 283–307.

Yirmiya, N., Solomonica-Levi, D., Shulman, C., & Pilowsky, T. (1996). Theory of mind abilities in individuals with autism, Down syndrome, and mental retardation of unknown etiology: The role of age and intelligence. *Journal of Child Psychology & Psychiatry & Allied Disciplines, 37,* 1003–1014.

Yonas, A., & Owsley, C. (1987). Development of visual space perception. In P. Salpatek & L. Cohen (Eds.), *Handbook of infant perception, Vol. 2: From perception to cognition* (pp. 80–122). Orlando, FL: Academic Press.

Yonas, A., Elieff, C., & Arterberry, M. (2002). Emergence of sensitivity to pictorial depth cues: Charting development in individual infants. *Infant Behavior & Development, 25,* 495–514.

Yordanova, J., Kolev, V., & Basar, E. (1998). EEG theta and frontal alpha oscillations during auditory processing change with aging. *Electroencephalography & Clinical Neurophysiology: Evoked Potentials, 108,* 497–505.

Young, C. (2002). *New look at "deadbeat dads."* Retrieved June 16, 2007 from www.reason.com/news/printer/31886.html.

Young, J., & Rodgers, R. (1997). A model of radical career change in the context of psychosocial development. *Journal of Career Assessment, 5,* 167–182.

Young, S., Fox, N., & Zahn-Waxler, C. (1999). The relations between temperament and empathy in 2-year-olds. *Developmental Psychology, 35,* 1189–1197.

YouthBuild/Boston. (2000). *Program report.* Retrieved February 29, 2000, from http://www.doe.mass.edu/cs.www/cs.youthbuild.html.

Yuill, N. (1997). English children as personality theorists: Accounts of the modifiability, development, and origin of traits. *Genetic, Social & General Psychology Monographs, 123,* 5–26.

Yurgelun-Todd, D., Killgore, W., & Young, A. (2002). Sex differences in cerebral tissue volume and cognitive performance during adolescence. *Psychological Reports, 91,* 743–757.

Zahn-Waxler, C., & Radke-Yarrow, M. (1982). The development of altruism: Alternative research strategies. In N. Eisenberg (Ed.), *The development of prosocial behavior* (pp. 109–138). New York: Academic Press.

Zahn-Waxler, C., Radke-Yarrow, M., Wagner, E., & Chapman, M. (1992). Development of concern for others. *Developmental Psychology, 28,* 126–136.

Zakriski, A., & Coie, J. (1996). A comparison of aggressive-rejected and nonaggressive-rejected children's interpretation of self-directed and other-directed rejection. *Child Development, 67,* 1048–1070.

Zamboni, B. (2006). Therapeutic considerations in working with the family, friends, and partners of transgendered individuals. *The Family Journal, 14,* 174–179.

Zelazo, N. A., Zelazo, P. R., Cohen, K. M., & Zelazo, P. D. (1993). Specificity of practice effects on elementary neuromotor patterns. *Developmental Psychology, 29,* 686–691.

Zelazo, P., Helwig, C., & Lau, A. (1996). Intention, act, and outcome in behavioral prediction and moral judgment. *Child Development, 67,* 2478–2492.

Zelinski, E., & Burnight, K. (1997). Sixteen-year longitudinal and time lag changes in memory and cognition in older adults. *Psychology & Aging, 12,* 503–513.

Zelinski, E. M., Gilewski, M. J., & Schaie, K. W. (1993). Individual differences in cross-sectional and 3-year longitudinal memory performance across the adult life span. *Psychology & Aging, 8,* 176–186.

Zhang, R., & Yu, Y. (2002). A study of children's coordinational ability for outcome and intention information. *Psychological Science* (China), *25,* 527–530.

Zhou, L., Dawson, M., Herr, C., & Stukas, S. (2004). American and Chinese college students' predictions of people's occupations, housework responsibilities, and hobbies as a function of cultural and gender influences. *Sex Roles, 50*, 463.

Zhou, M., Yao, L., & Xu, J. (2002). Studied the influence of Taoist education on the subjective well-being of the elderly. *Chinese Mental Health Journal, 16*, 175–176.

Zhou, Z., & Boehm, A. (2004). American and Chinese children's understanding of basic relational concepts in directions. *Psychology in the Schools, 41*, 261–272.

Zick, C., & Holden, K. (2000). An assessment of the wealth holdings of recent widows. *Journal of Gerontology, 55B*, S90–S97.

Zigler, E., & Finn-Stevenson, M. (1993). *Children in a changing world: Developmental and social issues.* Pacific Grove, CA: Brooks/Cole.

Zigler, E., & Hodapp, R. M. (1991). Behavioral functioning in individuals with mental retardation. *Annual Review of Psychology, 42*, 29–50.

Zigler, E., & Styfco, S. J. (1993). Using research and theory to justify and inform Head Start expansion. *Social Policy Report, Society for Research in Child Development, VII* (2), 1–21.

Zimmer, Z., Hickey, T., & Searle, M. S. (1995). Activity participation and well-being among older people with arthritis. *The Gerontologist, 35*, 463–471.

Zimmer-Gembeck, M. (1999). Stability, change and individual differences in involvement with friends and romantic partners among adolescent females. *Journal of Youth & Adolescence, 28*, 419–438.

Zimmerman, C. (2000). The development of scientific reasoning skills. *Developmental Review, 20*, 99–149.

Zimmerman, M., Copeland, L., Shope, J., & Dielman, T. (1997). A longitudinal study of self-esteem: Implications for adolescent development. *Journal of Youth & Adolescence, 26*, 117–141.

Zimmerman, S., Scott, A., Park, N., Hall, S., Wetherby, M., Gruber-Baldini, A., & Morgan, L. (2003). Social engagement and its relationship to service provision in residential care and assisted living. *Social Work Research, 27*, 6–18.

Zisook, S., Chentsova-Dutton, Y., & Shuchter, S. (1998). PTSD following bereavement. *Annals of Clinical Psychiatry, 10*, 157–163.

Zisook, S., Paulus, M., Shuchter, S., & Judd, L. (1997). The many faces of depression following spousal bereavement. *Journal of Affective Disorders, 45*, 85–94.

Zola, S., & Squire, L. (2003). Genetics of childhood disorders: Learning and memory: Multiple memory systems. *Journal of the American Academy of Child and Adolescent Psychiatry, 42*, 504–506.

Zucker, A., Ostrove, J., & Stewart A. (2002). College-educated women's personality development in adulthood: Perceptions and age differences. *Psychology & Aging, 17*, 236–244.

Zunker, V. (1994). *Career Counseling.* Pacific Grove, CA: Brooks/Cole.

Zunzunegui, M., Alvarado, B., Del Ser, T., & Otero, A. (2003). Social networks, social integration, and social engagement determine cognitive decline in community-dwelling Spanish older adults. *Journals of Gerontology, Series B: Psychological Sciences & Social Sciences, 58B*, S93–S100.

Zysset, S., Schroeter, M., Neumann, J., & von Cramon, D. (2007). Stroop interference, hemodynamic response and aging: An event-related fMRI study. *Neurobiology of Aging, 28*, 937–946.

Glossary

ability goals (p. 328) goals based on a desire to be superior to others

accommodation (p. 37) changing a scheme as a result of some new information

achievement test (p. 259) a test designed to assess specific information learned in school

activities of daily living (ADLs) (p. 487) self-help tasks such as bathing, dressing, and using the toilet

activity theory (p. 514) the idea that it is normal and healthy for older adults to try to remain as active as possible for as long as possible

adaptive reflexes (p. 99) reflexes, such as sucking, that help newborns survive

adolescence (p. 307) the transitional period between childhood and adulthood

ageism (p. 8) a prejudicial view of older adults that characterizes them in negative ways

aggression (p. 232) behavior intended to harm another person or an object

aging in place (p. 520) living in a non-institutional environment, to which modifications have been made to accommodate an older adult's needs

alcoholism (p. 448) physical and psychological dependence on alcohol

Alzheimer's disease (p. 496) a very severe form of dementia, the cause of which is unknown

amenity move (p. 532) post-retirement move away from kin to a location that has some desirable feature, such as year-round warm weather

amnion (p. 66) fluid-filled sac in which the fetus floats until just before it is born

analytical style (p. 263) a tendency to focus on the details of a task

anorexia nervosa (p. 321) an eating disorder characterized by self-starvation

A-not-B error (p. 124) substage 4 infants' tendency to look for an object in the place where it was last seen (position A) rather than in the place to which they have seen a researcher move it (position B)

anoxia (p. 84) oxygen deprivation experienced by a fetus during labor and/or delivery

assimilation (p. 36) the process of using a scheme to make sense of an event or experience

association areas (p. 247) parts of the brain where sensory, motor, and intellectual functions are linked

assortative mating (homogamy) (p. 409) sociologists' term for the tendency to mate with someone who has traits similar to one's own

asthma (p. 248) a chronic lung disease, characterized by sudden, potentially fatal attacks of breathing difficulty

atherosclerosis (p. 443) narrowing of the arteries caused by deposits of a fatty substance called plaque

at-risk-for-overweight (p. 249) a child whose BMI is between the 85th and 95th percentiles

attachment (p. 150) the emotional tie to a parent experienced by an infant, from which the child derives security

attachment theory (p. 148) the view that infants are biologically predisposed to form emotional bonds with caregivers and that the characteristics of those bonds shape later social and personality development

attention-deficit hyperactivity disorder (ADHD) (p. 268) a mental disorder that causes children to have difficulty attending to and completing tasks

atypical development (p. 9) development that deviates from the typical developmental pathway in a direction that is harmful to the individual

auditory acuity (p. 108) how well one can hear

authoritarian parenting style (p. 221) a style of parenting that is low in nurturance and communication, but high in control and maturity demands

authoritative parenting style (p. 221) a style of parenting that is high in nurturance, maturity demands, control, and communication

automaticity (p. 254) the ability to recall information from long-term memory without using short-term memory capacity

avoidant couples (p. 413) partners who agree to disagree and who minimize conflict by avoiding each other

axons (p. 68) Tail-like extensions of neurons

babbling (p. 134) the repetitive vocalizing of consonant-vowel combinations by an infant

balanced approach (p. 257) reading instruction that combines explicit phonics instruction with other strategies for helping children acquire literacy

Bayley Scales of Infant Development (p. 140) the best-known and most widely used test of infant "intelligence"

behavior genetics (p. 41) the study of the role of heredity in individual differences

behaviorism (p. 32) the view that defines development in terms of behavior changes caused by environmental influences

bilingual education (p. 258) an approach to second-language education in which children receive instruction in two different languages

bioecological theory (p. 43) Bronfenbrenner's theory that explains development in terms of relationships between individuals and their environments, or interconnected contexts

BMI-for-age (p. 248) comparison of an individual child's BMI against established norms for his or her age group and sex

brain death (p. 542) the point at which vital signs, including brain activity, are absent and resuscitation is no longer possible

bulimia nervosa (p. 321) an eating disorder characterized by binge eating and purging

burnout (p. 471) lack of energy, exhaustion, and pessimism that results from chronic stress

cardiovascular disease (CVD) (p. 443) a set of disease processes in the heart and circulatory system

career development (p. 423) the process of adapting to the workplace, managing career transitions, and pursuing goals through employment

caregiver burden (p. 470) a term for the cumulative negative effects of caring for an elderly or disabled person

case study (p. 12) an in-depth examination of a single individual

cell body (p. 67) The part of a neuron that contains the cell body and is the site of vital cell functions

centration (p. 185) the young child's tendency to think of the world in terms of one variable at a time

cephalocaudal pattern (p. 64) growth that proceeds from the head downward

cesarean section (c-section) (p. 82) delivery of an infant through incisions in the abdominal and uterine walls

chromosomes (p. 55) strings of genetic material in the nuclei of cells

class inclusion (p. 253) the understanding that subordinate classes are included in larger, superordinate classes

classical conditioning (p. 32) learning that results from the association of stimuli

climacteric (p. 437) the term used to describe the adult period during which reproductive capacity declines or is lost

clinical death (p. 542) a period during which vital signs are absent but resuscitation is still possible

clique (p. 360) four to six young people who appear to be strongly attached to one another

cognitive domain (p. 5) changes in thinking, memory, problem-solving, and other intellectual skills

cognitive theories (p. 36) theories that emphasize mental processes in development, such as logic and memory

cohort effects (p. 15) findings that are the result of historical factors to which one age group in a cross-sectional study has been exposed

colic (p. 100) an infant behavior pattern involving intense daily bouts of crying totaling 3 or more hours a day

companionate relationships (p. 468) relationships in which grandparents have frequent contact and warm interactions with grandchildren

compensatory (kinship) migration (p. 532) a move to a location near family or friends that happens when an elder requires frequent help because of a disability or disease

concrete operational stage (p. 251) Piaget's third stage of cognitive development, during which children construct schemes that enable them to think logically about objects and events in the real world

conservation (p. 185) the understanding that matter can change in appearance without changing in quantity

continuity theory (p. 515) the idea that older adults adapt life-long interests and activities to the limitations imposed upon them by physical aging

control group (p. 14) the group in an experiment that receives either no special treatment or a neutral treatment

conventional morality (p. 351) in Kohlberg's theory, the level of moral reasoning in which judgments are based on rules or norms of a group to which the person belongs

cooing (p. 134) making repetitive vowel sounds, particularly the *uuu* sound

corpus callosum (p. 178) the membrane that connects the right and left hemispheres of the cerebral cortex

correlation (p. 13) a relationship between two variables that can be expressed as a number ranging from −1.00 to +1.00

creativity (p. 453) the ability to produce original, appropriate, and valuable ideas and/or solutions to problems

critical period (p. 8) a specific period in development when an organism is especially sensitive to the presence (or absence) of some particular kind of experience

cross-gender behavior (p. 219) behavior that is atypical for one's own sex but typical for the opposite sex

cross-linking (p. 493) the formation of undesirable bonds between proteins or fats

cross-sectional design (p. 14) a research design in which groups of people of different ages are compared

crowd (p. 360) a combination of cliques, which includes both males and females

crystallized intelligence (p. 393) knowledge and judgment acquired through education and experience

decentration (p. 251) thinking that takes multiple variables into account

deductive logic (p. 252) a type of reasoning, based on hypothetical premises, that requires predicting a specific outcome from a general principle

deferred imitation (p. 124) imitation that occurs in the absence of the model who first demonstrated it

delinquency (p. 356) antisocial behavior that includes law-breaking

dementia (p. 496) a neurological disorder involving problems with memory and thinking that affect an individual's emotional, social, and physical functioning

dendrites (p. 68) Branchlike protrusions from the cell bodies of neurons

deoxyribonucleic acid (DNA) (p. 55) chemical material that makes up chromosomes and genes

dependent variable (p. 14) the characteristic or behavior that is expected to be affected by the independent variable

dialectical thought (p. 391) a form of thought involving recognition and acceptance of paradox and uncertainty

disengagement theory (p. 515) the theory that it is normal and healthy for older adults to scale down their social lives and to separate themselves from others to a certain degree

dishabituation (p. 109) responding to a somewhat familiar stimulus as if it were new

dominant-recessive pattern (p. 57) pattern of inheritance in which a single dominant gene influences a person's phenotype but two recessive genes are necessary to produce an associated trait

dynamic systems theory (p. 101) the view that several factors interact to influence development

dyslexia (p. 266) problems in reading or the inability to read

eclecticism (p. 47) the use of multiple theoretical perspectives to explain and study human development

ego (p. 27) according to Freud, the thinking element of personality

ego integrity (p. 513) the feeling that one's life has been worthwhile

egocentrism (p. 183) the young child's belief that everyone sees and experiences the world the way she does

embryonic stage (p. 66) the second stage of prenatal development, from week 2 through week 8, during which the embryo's organ systems form

emerging adulthood (p. 407) the period from the late teens to early twenties when individuals explore options prior to committing to adult roles

emotional regulation (p. 212) the ability to control emotional states and emotion-related behavior

empathy (p. 213) the ability to identify with another person's emotional state

empiricists (p. 113) theorists who argue that perceptual abilities are learned

English-as-a-second-language (ESL) program (p. 258) an approach to second-language education in which children attend English classes for part of the day and receive most of their academic instruction in English

episodic memories (p. 452) recollections of personal events

equilibration (p. 37) the process of balancing assimilation and accommodation to create schemes that fit the environment

ethnic identity (p. 347) a sense of belonging to an ethnic group

ethnography (p. 17) a detailed description of a single culture or context

ethology (p. 42) a perspective on development that emphasizes genetically determined survival behaviors presumed to have evolved through natural selection

excessive weight gain (p. 248) a pattern in which children gain more weight in a year than is appropriate for their age and height

executive processes (p. 255) information-processing skills that involve devising and carrying out strategies for remembering and solving problems

experiment (p. 13) a study that tests a causal hypothesis

experimental group (p. 14) the group in an experiment that receives the treatment the experimenter thinks will produce a particular effect

expressive language (p. 135) the ability to use sounds, signs, or symbols to communicate meaning

expressive style (p. 137) a style of word learning characterized by low rates of nounlike terms and high use of personal-social words and phrases

extended family (p. 230) a social network of grandparents, aunts, uncles, cousins, and so on

extinction (p. 33) the gradual elimination of a behavior through repeated nonreinforcement

false belief principle (p. 187) an understanding that enables a child to look at a situation from another person's point of view and determine what kind of information will cause that person to have a false belief

fast-mapping (p. 191) the ability to categorically link new words to real-world referents

fetal stage (p. 67) the third stage of prenatal development, from week 9 to birth, during which growth and organ refinement take place

fluid intelligence (p. 393) the aspect of intelligence that reflects fundamental biological processes and does not depend on specific experiences

foreclosure (p. 342) in Marcia's theory, the identity status of a person who has made a commitment without having gone through a crisis; the person has simply accepted a parentally or culturally defined commitment

formal operational stage (p. 324) the fourth of Piaget's stages, during which adolescents learn to reason logically about abstract concepts

frail elderly (p. 488) older adults whose physical and/or mental impairments are so extensive that they cannot care for themselves

free radicals (p. 493) molecules or atoms that possess an unpaired electron

gametes (p. 55) cells that unite at conception (ova in females; sperm in males)

gender (p. 214) the psychological and social associates and implications of biological sex

gender constancy (p. 215) the understanding that gender is a component of the self that is not altered by external appearance

gender identity (p. 216) the ability to correctly label oneself and others as male or female

gender role identity (p. 346) the gender-related aspects of the psychological self

gender schema theory (p. 215) an information-processing approach to gender concept development that asserts that people use a schema for each gender to process information about themselves and others

gender stability (p. 216) the understanding that gender is a stable, life-long characteristic

generativity (p. 462) a sense that one is making a valuable contribution to society by bringing up children or mentoring younger people in some way

genes (p. 55) pieces of genetic material that control or influence traits

genotype (p. 57) the unique genetic blueprint of each individual

germinal stage (p. 66) the first stage of prenatal development, beginning at conception and ending at implantation (approximately 2 weeks)

gerontology (p. 485) the scientific study of aging

glial cells (p. 69) The "glue" that holds neurons together to give form to the structures of the nervous system

gonads (p. 55) sex glands (ovaries in females; testes in males)

goodness-of-fit (p. 160) the degree to which an infant's temperament is adaptable to his or her environment, and vice versa

grieving (p. 559) the emotional response to a death

habituation (p. 109) a decline in attention that occurs because a stimulus has become familiar

handedness (p. 179) a strong preference for using one hand or the other that develops between 3 and 5 years of age

Hayflick limit (p. 493) the genetically programmed time limit to which each species is theoretically proposed to be subject, after which cells no longer have any capacity to replicate themselves accurately

hippocampus (p. 179) a brain structure that is important in learning

holophrases (p. 136) combinations of gestures and single words that convey more meaning than just the word alone

hospice care (p. 542) an approach to care for the terminally ill that emphasizes individual and family control of the process of dying

hostile aggression (p. 233) aggression used to hurt another person or gain an advantage

hostile/detached couples (p. 413) partners who fight regularly, rarely look at each other and lack affection and support

hostile/engaged couples (p. 413) partners who have frequent arguments and lack the balancing effect of humor and affection

human development (p. 2) the scientific study of age-related changes in behavior, thinking, emotion, and personality

hypertension (p. 447) elevated blood pressure

hypothetico-deductive reasoning (p. 324) the ability to derive conclusions from hypothetical premises

id (p. 27) in Freud's theory, the part of the personality that comprises a person's basic sexual and aggressive impulses; it contains the libido and motivates a person to seek pleasure and avoid pain

identity (p. 341) an understanding of one's unique characteristics and how they have been, are, and will be manifested across ages, situations, and social roles

identity achievement (p. 342) in Marcia's theory, the identity status achieved by a person who has been through a crisis and reached a commitment to ideological or occupational goals

identity crisis (p. 341) Erikson's term for the psychological state of emotional turmoil that arises when an adolescent's sense of self becomes "unglued" so that a new, more mature sense of self can be achieved

identity diffusion (p. 342) in Marcia's theory, the identity status of a person who is not in the midst of a crisis and who has made no commitment

identity versus role confusion (p. 341) in Erikson's theory, the stage during which adolescents attain a sense of who they are

imaginary audience (p. 326) an internalized set of behavioral standards usually derived from a teenager's peer group

implantation (p. 66) attachment of the blastocyst to the uterine wall

inclusive education (p. 268) general term for education programs in which children with disabilities are taught in regular classrooms

independent variable (p. 14) the presumed causal element in an experiment

inductive discipline (p. 223) a discipline strategy in which parents explain to children why a punished behavior is wrong

inductive logic (p. 252) a type of reasoning in which general principles are inferred from specific experiences

infant mortality (p. 104) death within the first year of life

infant-directed speech (p. 132) the simplified, higher-pitched speech that adults use with infants and young children

inflections (p. 136) additions to words that change their meaning (e.g., the *s* in toys, the *ed* in waited)

information-processing theory (p. 39) a theoretical perspective that uses the computer as a model to explain how the mind manages information

insecure/ambivalent attachment (p. 152) a pattern of attachment in which the infant shows little exploratory behavior, is greatly upset when separated from the mother, and is not reassured by her return or efforts to comfort him

insecure/avoidant attachment (p. 152) a pattern of attachment in which an infant avoids contact with the parent and shows no preference for the parent over other people

insecure/disorganized attachment (p. 152) a pattern of attachment in which an infant seems confused or apprehensive and shows contradictory behavior, such as moving toward the mother while looking away from her

institutional migration (p. 532) a move to an institution such as a nursing home that is necessitated by a disability

instrumental activities of daily living (IADLs) (p. 487) more intellectually demanding daily living tasks such as doing housework, cooking, and managing money

instrumental aggression (p. 233) aggression used to gain or damage an object

intelligence (p. 140) the ability to take in information and use it to adapt to the environment

intelligence quotient (IQ) (p. 194) the ratio of mental age to chronological age; also, a general term for any kind of score derived from an intelligence test

interactionists (p. 131) theorists who argue that language development is a subprocess of general cognitive development and is influenced by both internal and external factors

intermodal perception (p. 113) formation of a single perception of a stimulus that is based on information from two or more senses

intimacy (p. 405) the capacity to engage in a supportive, affectionate relationship without losing one's own sense of self

intimacy versus isolation (p. 405) Erikson's early adulthood stage, in which an individual must find a life partner or supportive friends in order to avoid social isolation

intimate partner abuse (p. 382) physical acts or other behavior intended to intimidate or harm an intimate partner

invented spelling (p. 193) a strategy young children with good phonological awareness skills use when they write

involved relationships (p. 468) relationships in which grandparents are directly involved in the everyday care of grandchildren or have close emotional ties with them

kin-keeper (p. 420) a family role, usually occupied by a woman, which includes responsibility for maintaining family and friendship relationships

laboratory observation (p. 12) observation of behavior under controlled conditions

language acquisition device (LAD) (p. 131) an innate language processor, theorized by Chomsky, that contains the basic grammatical structure of all human language

lateralization (p. 178) the process through which brain functions are divided between the two hemispheres of the cerebral cortex

learning disability (p. 266) a disorder in which a child has difficulty mastering a specific academic skill, even though she possesses normal intelligence and no physical or sensory handicaps

learning theories (p. 32) theories that assert that development results from an accumulation of experiences

life events approach (p. 463) a theoretical perspective on middle adulthood that focuses on normative and non-normative events and how adults in this age group respond to them

life review (p. 514) evaluative process in which elders make judgments about past behavior

life structure (p. 406) in Levinson's theory, the underlying pattern or design of a person's life at a given time, which includes roles, relationships, and behavior patterns

lifespan perspective (p. 4) the current view of developmentalists that important changes occur throughout the entire human lifespan and that these changes must be interpreted in terms of the culture and context in which they occur; thus, interdisciplinary research is critical to understanding human development

limbic system (p. 374) the part of the brain that regulates emotional responses

locus of control (p. 380) a set of beliefs about the causes of events

longitudinal design (p. 14) a research design in which people in a single group are studied at different times in their lives

low birth weight (LBW) (p. 85) newborn weight below 5.5 pounds

maturation (p. 4) the gradual unfolding of a genetically programmed sequential pattern of change

maximum oxygen uptake (VO_2 max) (p. 376) a measure of the body's ability to take in and transport oxygen to various body organs

mean length of utterance (MLU) (p. 137) the average number of meaningful units in a sentence

means-end behavior (p. 123) purposeful behavior carried out in pursuit of a specific goal

memory strategies (p. 255) learned methods for remembering information

menarche (p. 310) the beginning of menstrual cycles

menopause (p. 437) the cessation of monthly menstrual cycles in middle-aged women

metacognition (p. 190) knowledge about how the mind thinks and the ability to control and reflect on one's own thought processes

metamemory (p. 190) knowledge about how memory works and the ability to control and reflect on one's own memory function

moral realism stage (p. 284) the first of Piaget's stages of moral development, in which children believe rules are inflexible

moral relativism stage (p. 285) the second of Piaget's stages of moral development, in which children understand that many rules can be changed through social agreement

moratorium (p. 342) in Marcia's theory, the identity status of a person who is in a crisis but who has made no commitment

multi-factorial inheritance (p. 59) inheritance affected by both genes and the environment

multi-infarct dementia (p. 498) a form of dementia caused by one or more strokes

myelinization (p. 93) a process in neuronal development in which sheaths made of a substance called myelin gradually cover individual axons and electrically insulate them from one another to improve the conductivity of the nerve

naming explosion (p. 136) the period when toddlers experience rapid vocabulary growth, typically beginning between 16 and 24 months

nativists (p. 113) theorists who claim that perceptual abilities are inborn

naturalistic observation (p. 12) the process of studying people in their normal environments

nature-nurture debate (p. 6) the debate about the relative contributions of biological processes and experiential factors to development

neonate (p. 84) term for babies between birth and 1 month of age

neo-Piagetian theory (p. 39) an approach that uses information-processing principles to explain the developmental stages identified by Piaget

neurons (p. 66) specialized cells of the nervous system

niche-picking (p. 159) the process of selecting experiences on the basis of temperament

nonnormative changes (p. 8) changes that result from unique, unshared events

nontraditional post-secondary student (p. 394) a student who either attends college part-time or delays enrollment after high school graduation

normative age-graded changes (p. 7) changes that are common to every member of a species

normative history-graded changes (p. 8) changes that occur in most members of a cohort as a result of factors at work during a specific, well-defined historical period

norms (p. 4) average ages at which developmental milestones are reached

object concept (p. 126) an infant's understanding of the nature of objects and how they behave

object permanence (p. 123) the understanding that objects continue to exist when they can't be seen

objective (categorical) self (p. 160) the toddler's understanding that she or he is defined by various categories such as gender or qualities such as shyness

observational learning (p. 34) , or modeling learning that results from seeing a model reinforced or punished for a behavior

operant conditioning (p. 33) learning to repeat or stop behaviors because of their consequences

operational efficiency (p. 189) a neo-Piagetian term that refers to the maximum number of schemes that can be processed in working memory at one time

organogenesis (p. 66) process of organ development

osteoporosis (p. 440) loss of bone mass with age, resulting in more brittle and porous bones

overregularization (p. 192) attachment of regular inflections to irregular words such as the substitution of "goed" for "went"

overweight (p. 249) a child whose BMI is at the 95th percentile

palliative care (p. 543) a form of care for the terminally ill that focuses on relieving patients' pain, rather than curing their diseases

parental investment theory (p. 408) the theory that sex differences in mate preferences and mating behavior are based on the different amounts of time and effort men and women must invest in childrearing

parenting styles (p. 220) the characteristic strategies that parents use to manage children's behavior.

pathological grief (p. 564) symptoms of depression brought on by the death of a loved one

pelvic inflammatory disease (p. 381) an infection of the female reproductive tract that may result from a sexually transmitted disease and can lead to infertility

perimenopausal phase (p. 438) the stage of menopause during which estrogen and progesterone levels are erratic, menstrual cycles may be very irregular, and women begin to experience symptoms such as hot flashes

permissive parenting style (p. 221) a style of parenting that is high in nurturance and low in maturity demands, control, and communication

person perception (p. 209) the ability to classify others according to categories such as age, gender, and race

personal fable (p. 325) the belief that the events of one's life are controlled by a mentally constructed autobiography

personality (p. 157) a pattern of responding to people and objects in the environment

personality disorder (p. 387) an inflexible pattern of behavior that leads to difficulty in social, educational, and occupational functioning

phenotype (p. 57) an individual's particular set of observed characteristics

phobia (p. 387) an irrational fear of an object, a person, a place, or a situation

phonological awareness (p. 193) children's understanding of the sound patterns of the language they are acquiring

physical domain (p. 5) changes in the size, shape, and characteristics of the body

pituitary gland (p. 309) gland that triggers other glands to release hormones

placenta (p. 66) specialized organ that allows substances to be transferred from mother to embryo and from embryo to mother, without their blood mixing

plasticity (p. 96) the ability of the brain to change in response to experience

polygenic inheritance (p. 58) pattern of inheritance in which many genes influence a trait

population (p. 13) the entire group that is of interest to a researcher

postconventional morality (p. 352) in Kohlberg's theory, the level of moral reasoning in which judgments are based on an integration of individual rights and the needs of society

postformal thought (p. 391) types of thinking that are associated with a hypothesized fifth stage of cognitive development

postmenopausal phase (p. 438) the last stage of menopause beginning when a woman has had no menstrual periods for a year or more

post-secondary education (p. 393) any kind of formal educational experience that follows high school

preconventional morality (p. 351) in Kohlberg's theory, the level of moral reasoning in which judgments are based on authorities outside the self

preference technique (p. 109) a research method in which a researcher keeps track of how long a baby looks at each of two objects shown

premenopausal phase (p. 438) the stage of menopause during which estrogen levels fall somewhat, menstrual periods are less regular, and anovulatory cycles begin to occur

preoperational stage (p. 183) Piaget's second stage of cognitive development, during which children become proficient in the use of symbols in thinking and communicating but still have difficulty thinking logically

presbycusis (p. 442) normal loss of hearing with aging, especially of high-frequency tones

presbyopia (p. 441) normal loss of visual acuity with aging, especially the ability to focus the eyes on near objects

primary aging (senescence) (p. 372) age-related physical changes that have a biological basis and are universally shared and inevitable

primary circular reactions (p. 122) Piaget's phrase to describe a baby's simple repetitive actions in substage 2 of the sensorimotor stage, organized around the baby's own body

primary sex characteristics (p. 310) the sex organs: ovaries, uterus, and vagina in the female; testes and penis in the male

primitive reflexes (p. 99) reflexes, controlled by "primitive" parts of the brain, that disappear during the first year of life

processing efficiency (p. 254) the ability to make efficient use of short-term memory capacity

programmed senescence theory (p. 493) the view that age-related declines are the result of species-specific genes for aging

prosocial behavior (p. 234) behavior intended to help another person

proximodistal pattern (p. 66) growth that proceeds from the middle of the body outward

pruning (p. 96) the process of eliminating unused synapses

psychoanalytic theories (p. 27) theories proposing that developmental change happens because of the influence of internal drives and emotions on behavior

psychological self (p. 280) an understanding of one's stable, internal traits

psychosexual stages (p. 28) Freud's five stages of personality development through which children move in a fixed sequence determined by maturation; the libido is centered in a different body part in each stage

psychosocial stages (p. 30) Erikson's eight stages, or crises, of personality development in which inner instincts interact with outer cultural and social demands to shape personality

puberty **(p. 309)** collective term for the physical changes which culminate in sexual maturity

punishment **(p. 33)** anything that follows a behavior and causes it to stop

qualitative change **(p. 7)** a change in kind or type

quality of work-life (QWL) movement **(p. 424)** An approach to reducing work-related stress by basing job and workplace design on analyses of the quality of employee experiences in an organization.

quantitative change **(p. 7)** a change in amount

reaction range **(p. 198)** a range, established by one's genes, between upper and lower boundaries for traits such as intelligence; one's environment determines where, within those limits, one will be

receptive language **(p. 134)** comprehension of spoken language

reciprocal determinism **(p. 279)** Bandura's model in which personal, behavioral, and environmental factors interact to influence personality development

referential style **(p. 139)** a style of word learning characterized by emphasis on things and people and their naming and description

reflective judgment **(p. 391)** the ability to identify the underlying assumptions of differing perspective on controversial issues

reinforcement **(p. 33)** anything that follows a behavior and causes it to be repeated

relational aggression **(p. 290)** aggression aimed at damaging another person's self-esteem or peer relationships, such as by ostracism or threats of ostracism, cruel gossiping, or facial expressions of disdain

relational style **(p. 263)** a tendency to ignore the details of a task in order to focus on the "big picture"

relative right-left orientation **(p. 247)** the ability to identify right and left from multiple perspectives

relativism **(p. 391)** the idea that some propositions cannot be adequately described as either true or false

religious coping **(p. 518)** the tendency to turn to religious beliefs and institutions for support in times of difficulty

reminiscence **(p. 514)** reflecting on past experience

remote relationships **(p. 468)** relationships in which grandparents do not see their grandchildren often

research ethics **(p. 18)** the guidelines researchers follow to protect the rights of animals used in research and humans who participate in studies

retaliatory aggression **(p. 291)** aggression to get back at someone who has hurt you

reticular formation **(p. 98)** the part of the brain that regulates attention

reversibility **(p. 252)** the understanding that both physical actions and mental operations can be reversed

role conflict **(p. 464)** any situation in which two or more roles are at least partially incompatible, either because they call for different behaviors or because their separate demands add up to more hours than there are in the day

role-taking **(p. 353)** the ability to look at a situation from another person's perspective

sample **(p. 13)** subset of a group that is of interest to a researcher who participate in a study

satiety **(p. 495)** the feeling of fullness that follows a meal

schematic learning **(p. 129)** organization of experiences into expectancies, called schemas, which enable infants to distinguish between familiar and unfamiliar stimuli

scheme **(p. 36)** in Piaget's theory, an internal cognitive structure that provides an individual with a procedure to use in a specific circumstance

schizophrenia **(p. 388)** a serious mental disorder characterized by disturbances of thought such as delusions and hallucinations

secondary aging **(p. 372)** age-related changes that are due to environmental influences, poor health habits, or disease

secondary circular reactions **(p. 123)** repetitive actions in substage 3 of the sensorimotor period, oriented around external objects

secondary sex characteristics **(p. 310)** body parts such as breasts in females and pubic hair in both sexes

secular trend **(p. 311)** a change that occurs in developing nations when nutrition and health improve—for example, the decline in average age of menarche and the increase in average height for both children and adults that happened between the mid-18th and mid-19th centuries in Western countries

secure attachment **(p. 152)** a pattern of attachment in which an infant readily separates from the parent, seeks proximity when stressed, and uses the parent as a safe base for exploration

selective attention **(p. 247)** the ability to focus cognitive activity on the important elements of a problem or situation

selective optimization with compensation **(p. 450)** the process of balancing the gains and losses associated with aging

self-care children **(p. 293)** children who are at home by themselves after school for an hour or more each day

self-efficacy **(p. 281)** belief in one's capacity to cause an intended event to occur or to perform a task

self-esteem **(p. 281)** a global evaluation of one's own worth

self-regulation **(p. 286)** children's ability to conform to parental standards of behavior without direct supervision

semantic memories **(p. 452)** general knowledge

semiotic (symbolic) function **(p. 183)** the understanding that one object or behavior can represent another

sensitive period **(p. 8)** a span of months or years during which a child may be particularly responsive to specific forms of experience or particularly influenced by their absence

sensorimotor stage **(p. 122)** Piaget's first stage of development, in which infants use information from their senses and motor actions to learn about the world

separation anxiety **(p. 152)** expressions of discomfort, such as crying, when separated from an attachment figure

sequential design **(p. 14)** a research design that combines cross-sectional and longitudinal examinations of development

sex-typed behavior **(p. 218)** different patterns of behavior exhibited by boys and girls

sexual violence **(p. 385)** the use of physical coercion to force a person to engage in a sexual act against his or her will

short-term storage space (STSS) **(p. 189)** neo-Piagetian theorist Robbie Case's term for the working memory

social clock **(p. 8)** a set of age norms defining a sequence of life experiences that is considered normal in a given culture and that all individuals in that culture are expected to follow

social death **(p. 542)** the point at which family members and medical personnel treat the deceased person as a corpse

social domain **(p. 5)** change in variables that are associated with the relationship of an individual to others

social referencing **(p. 152)** an infant's use of others' facial expressions as a guide to his or her own emotions

social role theory **(p. 409)** the idea that sex differences in mate preferences and mating behavior are adaptations to gender roles

social skills **(p. 231)** a set of behaviors that usually lead to being accepted as a play partner or friend by peers

social status **(p. 292)** an individual child's classification as popular, rejected, or neglected

social-cognitive theory **(p. 208)** the theoretical perspective that asserts that social and personality development in early childhood is related to improvements in the cognitive domain

sociobiology **(p. 43)** the study of society using the methods and concepts of biology; when used by developmentalists, an approach that emphasizes genes that aid group survival

sociocultural theory (p. 38) Vygotsky's view that complex forms of thinking have their origins in social interactions rather than in an individual's private explorations

spatial cognition (p. 247) the ability to infer rules from and make predictions about the movement of objects in space

spatial perception (p. 247) the ability to identify and act on relationships between objects in space

stages (p. 7) qualitatively distinct periods of development

stranger anxiety (p. 152) expressions of discomfort, such as clinging to the mother, in the presence of strangers

subjective self (p. 160) an infant's awareness that she or he is a separate person who endures through time and space and can act on the environment

substance abuse (p. 389) a pattern of behavior in which a person continues to use a substance even though it interferes with psychological, occupational, educational, and social functioning

successful aging (p. 516) the term gerontologists use to describe maintaining one's physical health, mental abilities, social competence, and overall satisfaction with one's life as one ages

sudden infant death syndrome (SIDS) (p. 105) a phenomenon in which an apparently healthy infant dies suddenly and unexpectedly

superego (p. 27) Freud's term for the part of personality that is the moral judge

survey (p. 12) data collection method in which participants respond to questions

synapses (p. 67,96) Tiny spaces across which neural impulses flow from one neuron to the next

synaptic plasticity (p. 490) the redundancy in the nervous system that ensures that it is nearly always possible for a nerve impulse to move from one neuron to another or from a neuron to another type of cell (e.g., a muscle cell)

synaptogenesis (p. 96) the process of synapse development

synchrony (p. 150) a mutual, interlocking pattern of attachment behaviors shared by a parent and child

systematic problem-solving (p. 324) the process of finding a solution to a problem by testing single factors

task goals (p. 328) goals based on a desire for self-improvement

telegraphic speech (p. 136) simple two-word sentences that usually include a noun and a verb

telomere (p. 493) a string of repetitive DNA at the tip of each chromosome in the body that appears to serve as a kind of timekeeping mechanism

temperament (p. 157) inborn predispositions, such as activity level, that form the foundations of personality

teratogens (p. 70) substances, such as viruses and drugs, that can cause birth defects

terminal drop hypothesis (p. 494) the hypothesis that mental and physical functioning decline drastically only in the few years immediately preceding death

tertiary circular reactions (p. 123) The deliberate experimentation with variations of previous actions that occurs in substage 5 of the sensorimotor period

thanatology (p. 553) the scientific study of death and dying

theory of mind (p. 187) a set of ideas constructed by a child or adult to explain other people's ideas, beliefs, desires, and behavior

tinnitus (p. 491) persistent ringing in the ears

tracking (p. 107) the smooth movements of the eye used to follow the track of a moving object

traditional post-secondary student (p. 394) a student who attends college full-time immediately after graduating from high school

trait (p. 278) a stable pattern of responding to situations

transgendered (p. 317) a person whose psychological gender is the opposite of his or her biological sex

umbilical cord (p. 66) organ that connects the embryo to the placenta

uninvolved parenting style (p. 221) a style of parenting that is low in nurturance, maturity demands, control, and communication

unique invulnerability (p. 546) the belief that bad things, including death, happen only to others

validating couples (p. 412) partners who express mutual respect, even in disagreements, and are good listeners

viability (p. 67) ability of the fetus to survive outside the womb

violation of expectations method (p. 126) a research strategy in which researchers move an object in one way after having taught an infant to expect it to move in another

visual acuity (p. 107) how well one can see details at a distance

volatile couples (p. 412) partners who argue a lot and don't listen well, but still have more positive than negative interactions

volunteerism (p. 517) performance of unpaid work for altruistic motives

wisdom (p. 505) a cognitive characteristic that includes accumulated knowledge and the ability to apply that knowledge to practical problems of living, popularly thought to be more commonly found in older adults

work-life balance (p. 424) the interactive influences among employees' work and non-work roles

zygote (p. 55) single cell created when sperm and ovum unite

Name Index

L

Subject Index

E

S

X

Y

Z

Photo Credits

p. 1, Copyright © Ariel Skelley/Blend Images/Getty Images; p. 3, Courtesy of Denise Boyd; p. 4, Copyright © AMNH Special Collections; p. 5, Copyright © Joe Raedle/Getty Images; p. 8, Copyright © ALAN ODDIE/Photo Edit-All rights reserved; p. 10, Copyright © WoodyStock/Alamy; p. 12, Copyright © Laura Dwight/Photo Edit-All rights reserved; p. 17, Copyright © Michael Doolittle/The Image Works; p. 25, Copyright © Huy Lam/First Light/Getty Images; p. 29, Copyright © Peter M. Fisher/Corbis; p. 33, Copyright © Ken Heyman-Woodfin Camp; p. 34, Copyright © Kathy Sloane/Photo Researchers, Inc.; p. 34, Copyright © LWA-Dann Tardif/CORBIS; p. 36, Copyright © Bill Anderson/Photo Researchers, Inc.; p. 37, Copyright © Tim Brown/Stone/Getty Images; p. 37, Copyright © T. Lindfors/Lindfors Photography; p. 38, Copyright © David Young-Wolff/Photo Edit-All rights reserved; p. 39, Copyright © Nina Leen/Getty Images/Time Life Pictures; p. 43, Copyright © Jose Luis Pelaez, Inc./CORBIS; p. 53, Copyright © RCWW, Inc./RCWW, Inc./Corbis; p. 54, Copyright © Michael Clancy; p. 55, Copyright © Biophoto Associates/Photo Researchers, Inc.; p. 56, Copyright © Addenbrookes Hospital/ Photo Researchers, Inc.; p. 56, Copyright © Addenbrookes Hospital/Photo Researchers, Inc.; p. 62, Copyright © Mark Richards/Photo Edit-All rights reserved; p. 64, Copyright © stockbyte/Getty Images; p. 65, Courtesy of Profs. P.M. Motta & J. Van Blerkom/Photo Researchers, Inc.; p. 65, Copyright © Lennart Nilsson/Albert Bonniers Forlag AB; p. 65, Copyright © Claude Edelmann/Photo Researchers, Inc.; p. 65, Copyright © Claude Edelmann/Photo Researchers, Inc.; p. 65, Courtesy of James Stevenson/Photo Researchers, Inc.; p. 65, Copyright © Petit Format/Photo Researchers, Inc.; p. 68, Courtesy of Dr. Olivier Walusinski, www.yawning.info; p. 68, Reprinted with permission of Anderson Publishing Ltd. from Brown, S.D., Estroff, J.A. & Barnewolt, C.E. (2004). Fetal MRI. *Applied Radiology*, *33*(2), pp 9-25, Fig. 2. Copyright © Anderson Publishing Ltd.; p. 72, Copyright © 2000 George Steinmetz; p. 75, Copyright © REALITATEA TV/AFP/Getty Images; p. 78, Copyright © Keith Brofsky/Getty Images; p. 80, Copyright © Sean Sprague/Stock Boston; p. 80, Copyright © Margaret Miller/Photo Researchers, Inc.; p. 82, Copyright © Purestock/Getty Images; p. 86, Copyright © Jonathan Nourok/Photo Edit-All rights reserved; p. 92, Courtesy of U.S. Department of Health and Human Services ; p. 94, Copyright © Craig Holmes/Alamy; p. 97, Copyright © Elizabeth Crews/The Image Works; p. 99, Copyright © Richard Meats/Getty Images; p. 101, Copyright © Myrleen Cate/PhotoEdit Inc.; p. 101, Copyright © Laura Dwight/Photo Edit-All rights reserved; p. 101, Copyright © Myrleen Ferguson Cate/Photo Edit-All rights reserved; p. 103, Copyright © Photo Network/Alamy; p. 107, Copyright © Jonathan Nourok/Photo Edit-All rights reserved; p. 109, From Steiner, J. E., "Human Facial Expressions in Response to Taste and Smell Stimulation," in *Advances in Child Development and Behavior*, Vol. 13, H.W. Reese and L.P. Lipsitt, eds. Copyright © 1979 by Academic Press. By permission; p. 110, Copyright © Mark Richards/Photo Edit-All rights reserved; p. 112, Copyright © Elizabeth Crews/The Image Works; p. 113, Copyright © Laura Dwight/Mira.com; p. 120, Copyright © JUPITERIMAGES/Brand X/Alamy; p. 121, Copyright © The Granger Collection, New York; p. 121, Copyright © Maria Zarnayova/isifa/Getty Images; p. 123, Copyright © Laura Dwight/Photo Edit-All rights reserved; p. 124, Copyright © thislife pictures/Alamy; p. 125, Copyright © Picture Partners/Alamy; p. 125, From Meltzoff & Moore, SCIENCE 198:75 (1977). Reprinted with permission from AAAS; p. 129, Copyright © Michael Newman/Photo Edit-All rights reserved; p. 130, Courtesy of Carolyn Rovee-Collier; p. 134, Copyright © Laura Dwight Photography; p. 146, Copyright © Tetra Images/Getty Images; p. 148, Copyright © Martin Rogers, Woodfin Camp & Associates, Inc.; p. 150, Copyright © Lynne J. Weinstein, Woodfin Camp & Associates, Inc.; p. 151, Copyright © Laura Dwight/Photo Edit-All rights reserved; p. 151, Copyright © Laura Dwight/Photo Edit-All rights reserved; p. 159, Copyright © Gabe Palmer/CORBIS; p. 160, Copyright © Joseph Pobereskin/Getty Images; p. 161, Copyright © Laurance Monneret/Stone/Getty Images; p. 163, Copyright © Syracuse Newspapers/Dick Blume/The Image Works; p. 173, Copyright © AP Photo/Steven Senne; p. 175, Copyright © David Young-Wolff/Photo Edit-All rights reserved; p. 177, Copyright © D. Hurst/Alamy; p. 180, Copyright © Steve Rubin/The Image Works; p. 184, Copyright © Stock Connection Distribution/Alamy; p. 184, Photo courtesy of Jerry and Denise Boyd. Used with permission; p. 184, Copyright © Stock Connection Blue/Alamy; p. 187, Copyright © Spencer Grant/Photo Edit-All rights reserved; p. 192, Copyright © Will Faller; p. 196, Copyright © Paul Conklin/Photo Edit-All rights reserved; p. 206, Copyright © Esbin-Anderson/The Image Works; p. 208, Copyright © Larry Williams/CORBIS; p. 212, Copyright © Chris Knapton/Alamy; p. 217, Copyright © Mary Kate Denny/Photo Edit-All rights reserved; p. 217, Copyright © Sunstar/Photo Researchers, Inc.; p. 219, Copyright © AGB Photo/Alamy; p. 219, Copyright © Sue Ann Miller/Stone/Getty Images; p. 220, Copyright © Ben Blankenburg/Corbis; p. 226, Copyright © Rayes/Digital Vision/Getty Images; p. 227, Copyright © Tom & Dee Ann McCarthy/Corbis; p. 229, Copyright © Cindy Charles/Photo Edit-All rights reserved; p. 229, Copyright © Rachel Epstein/Photo Edit-All rights reserved; p. 231, Copyright © Myrleen Ferguson Cate/Photo Edit-All rights reserved; p. 234, Copyright © Danita Delimont/Alamy; p. 242, Copyright © David Young-Wolff/Photo Edit-All rights reserved; p. 243, Copyright © Mitch Wojnarowicz/Amsterdam Recorder/The Image Works; p. 244, Copyright © JUPITERIMAGES/Polka Dot/Alamy; p. 246, Copyright © Cindy Charles/Photo Edit-All rights reserved; p. 249, Copyright © Michael Newman/Photo Edit-All rights reserved; p. 250, Copyright © Comedy Central/Courtesy: Everett Collection; p. 255, Copyright © Alistair Berg/Digital Vision/Getty Images; p. 257, Copyright © A. Ramey, Woodfin Camp & Associates, Inc.; p. 257, Copyright © Joseph Sohm/Visions of America/Corbis; p. 257, Photographer: Shehzad Noorani-Woodfin Camp; p. 263, Copyright © Dimitri Vervitsiotis/Digital Vision/Getty Images; p. 264, Copyright © Andy Sacks/Stone/Getty Images; p. 269, Copyright © Michael Newman/Photo Edit-All

…; p. 276, Copyright © Michael Newman/Photo Edit-…erved; p. 282, Copyright © David Young-Wolff/… All rights reserved; p. 284, Copyright © Michael … Photo Edit-All rights reserved; p. 287, Copyright …el Newman/Photo Edit-All rights reserved; … Copyright © Rolf Bruderer/CORBIS; p. 289, Copyright …ry Kate Denny/Photo Edit-All rights reserved; …89, Copyright © Eastcott/Momatiuk/The Image Works ; …292, Copyright © Bill Aron/Photo Edit-All rights reserved; …. 294, Copyright © Stewart Cohen/Taxi/Getty Images; p. 295, Copyright © Mario Tama/Getty Images; p. 296, Copyright © Corbis RF/Alamy; p. 306, Copyright © Larry Kolvoord/The Image Works ; p. 309, Copyright © David Young-Wolff/Photo Edit-All rights reserved; p. 312, Copyright © LWA-Dann Tardif/CORBIS; p. 313, Photo: Joel Warren/Copyright © Disney Channel/Courtesy Everett Collection; p. 314, Copyright © Maria Taglienti-Molinari/Brand X/Corbis ; p. 321, Copyright © Tony Freeman/Photo Edit-All rights reserved; p. 324, Copyright © James Shaffer/Photo Edit-All rights reserved; p. 329, Copyright © AP Photo/Daniel R. Patmore; p. 331, Copyright © Will & Deni McIntyre/Photo Researchers, Inc; p. 339, Copyright © Adrian Sherratt/Alamy; p. 340, Copyright © Adams Picture Library t/a apl/Alamy; p. 343, Copyright © Bill Aron/Photo Edit-All rights reserved; p. 343, Copyright © Carl & Ann Purcell/CORBIS; p. 347, Copyright © Myrleen Ferguson Cate/Photo Edit-All rights reserved; p. 348, Copyright © Kris Timken/Blend Images/Getty Images; p. 348, Copyright © Will & Deni McIntyre/Corbis; p. 352, Copyright © Bettmann/CORBIS; p. 356, Copyright © John Neubauer/Photo Edit-All rights reserved; p. 359, Copyright © Penny Tweedie/Stone/Getty Images; p. 360, Copyright © David Young-Wolff/Stone/Getty Images; p. 368, Copyright © Dwayne Newton/Photo Edit-All rights reserved; p. 370, Copyright © John Eder/Taxi/Getty Images; p. 374, Copyright © Mark Richards/Photo Edit-All rights reserved.; p. 377, Courtesy of Lisa McClellan; p. 379, Copyright © Timothy Shonnard/Getty Images; p. 379, Copyright © Gary Conner/Photo Edit-All rights reserved; p. 383, Copyright © Jonathan Nourok/Photo Edit-All rights reserved; p. 391, Copyright © Jeff Greenberg/Photo Edit-All rights reserved; p. 395, Copyright © image100/Corbis; p. 403, Copyright © Jose Luis Pelaez, Inc./CORBIS; p. 405, Copyright © Simon Marcus/Corbis; p. 405, Copyright © Gallo Images-Hayley Baxter/Getty Images; p. 410, Copyright © Allan Hall Photography. Used with permission; p. 410, Copyright © JUPITERIMAGES/Brand X/Alamy; p. 415, Copyright © Ghislain & Marie David de Lossy/The Image Bank/Getty Images; p. 416, Copyright © Brian Bailey/Stone/Getty Images; p. 417, Copyright © JUPITERIMAGES/Thinkstock/Alamy; p. 421, Copyright © Mark Wilson/Getty Images; p. 422, Copyright © Jack Hollingsworth/Stockbyte/Getty Images; p. 424, Copyright © James Levin/Getty Images; p. 425, Copyright © Rolf Bruderer/CORBIS; p. 425, Copyright © Rob Crandal/The Image Works; p. 432, Copyright © Jeff Greenberg/Alamy; p. 434, Copyright © American Images Inc./Getty Images; p. 437, Copyright © Rhoda Sidney/The Image Works; p. 441, Copyright © David Madison/Stone/Getty Images; p. 442, Copyright © Myrleen Ferguson Cate/Photo Edit-All rights reserved; p. 445, Copyright © Tim Boyles/Getty Images; p. 447, Courtesy EIF Foundation/Diabetesaware.com; p. 450, Copyright © Tom Stewart/CORBIS; p. 452, Copyright © Jeff Greenberg/The Image Works; p. 460, Copyright © Kevin Dodge/Corbis; p. 462, Copyright © ShapeShifters/Iconica/Getty Images; p. 464, Copyright © Manuel Balce Ceneta/AP Photo; p. 465, Copyright © Jeff Greenberg/Photo Edit-All rights reserved; p. 465, Copyright © David Young-Wolff/Photo Edit-All rights reserved; p. 467, Copyright © Sean Justice/Corbis; p. 467, Copyright © Jack Monnier/Stone/Getty Images; p. 468, Copyright © HBO/WORLDWIDE PANTS INC/THE KOBAL COLLECTION; p. 469, Copyright © Michael Newman/Photo Edit-All rights reserved; p. 472, Copyright © Ronnie Kaufman/Corbis; p. 474, Copyright © AP Photo/Sara D. Davis; p. 475, Copyright © Thinkstock/Corbis; p. 481, Copyright © Darren McCollester/Getty Images; p. 482, Copyright © AP Photo/Nancy Palmieri; p. 483, Copyright © Digital Vision/Alamy; p. 484, Amy Snyder, Copyright © Exploratorium, www.exploratorium.edu; p. 486, Copyright © Mark Richards/Photo Edit-All rights reserved; p. 489, Copyright © VisionsofAmerica/Joe Sohm/Getty Images; p. 491, Copyright © Steve Mason/Getty Images; p. 494, Copyright © Tom Prettyman/Photo Edit-All rights reserved; p. 500, Copyright © Stewart Cohen/Pam Ostrow/Blend Images/Corbis; p. 501, Copyright © Mario Tama/Getty Images; p. 501, Copyright © Ellen Senisi/The Image Works; p. 502, Copyright © A. Ramey/Photo Edit-All rights reserved; p. 506, Copyright © David Young-Wolff/Getty Images; p. 512, Copyright © JLP/Jose L. Pelaez/CORBIS; p. 515, Copyright © Frank Siteman; p. 517, Copyright © Stock Connection Blue/Alamy; p. 519, Copyright © Michael Newman/Photo Edit-All rights reserved; p. 520, Copyright © Erin Moroney LaBelle/The Image Works ; p. 522, Copyright © Michael Newman/Photo Edit-All rights reserved; p. 523, Copyright © Paul Barton/CORBIS; p. 525, Copyright © David Young-Wolff/Photo Edit-All rights reserved; p. 526, Copyright © Michael Newman/Photo Edit-All rights reserved; p. 527, Copyright © Michael L. Abramson/Woodfin Camp & Associates; p. 532, Copyright © A. Ramey/Photo Edit-All rights reserved; p. 533, Copyright © Don Smetzer/Stone/Getty Images; p. 533, Copyright © Tom Carter/Photo Edit-All rights reserved; p. 533, Copyright © David Young-Wolff/Photo Edit-All rights reserved; p. 540, Copyright © AP Photo/Lucy Pemoni; p. 544, Copyright © Bill Aron/Photo Edit-All rights reserved; p. 545, Copyright © Lawrence Migdale/Stone/Getty Images; p. 546, Copyright © Bradley Kanaris/Getty Images; p. 552, Copyright © Zigy Kaluzny/Stone/Getty Images; p. 553, Copyright © AP Photo/Charles Bennett; p. 560, Copyright © Philip Gould/CORBIS; p. 561, Copyright © Michael Weisbrot and family/Stock Boston, LLC.; p. 561, Photo: Copyright © A. Ramey/Stock Boston, LLC.; p. 562, Copyright © AP Photo/Evan Vucci; p. 572, Copyright © AP Photo/Kamenko Pajic; p. 573, Copyright © AP Photo/David Adame.

Test Yourself Answer Keys

CHAPTER 1

1.1 b
1.2 a
1.3 lifespan perspective
1.4 plasticity
1.5 cognitive
1.6 prenatal = conception; birth
infancy = birth; language
early childhood = language; school entrance
middle childhood = school entrance; puberty
adolescence = puberty; attainment of legal adulthood
early adulthood = attainment of legal adulthood; age 40
middle adulthood = age 40; age 60
late adulthood = age 60; death
1.7 a
1.8 c
1.9 d
1.10 d
1.11 b
1.12 normative age-graded = walking
normative history-graded = effects of the Great Depression
nonnormative = genetic characteristics
1.13 a
1.14 a
1.15 c
1.16 a
1.17 c
1.18 c
1.19 b
1.20 d
1.21 (1) e (2) d (3) c (4) g (5) b (6) f (7) a (8) h
1.22 d
1.23 a

CHAPTER 2

2.1 c
2.2 d
2.3 c
2.4 d
2.5 (1) Freud; (2) Erikson; (3) Freud; (4) Freud; (5) Freud; (6) Erikson; (7) Erikson
2.6 a
2.7 reinforcement; punishment
2.8 b
2.9 b
2.10 b
2.11 c
2.12 c
2.13 a
2.14 d
2.15 short-term memories
2.16 b
2.17 c
2.18 ethology
2.19 sociobiology
2.20 a
2.21 a
2.22 d
2.23 b
2.24 a
2.25 c
2.26 eclecticism

CHAPTER 3

3.1 b
3.2 a
3.3 a
3.4 d
3.5 d
3.6 b
3.7 a
3.8 c
3.9 c
3.10 a
3.11 b
3.12 b
3.13 d
3.14 c
3.15 d
3.16 a
3.17 d
3.18 c
3.19 a
3.20 b
3.21 d
3.22 b
3.23 b
3.24 a
3.25 d

CHAPTER 4

4.1 b
4.2 b
4.3 c
4.4 a
4.5 b
4.6 a
4.7 d
4.8 b
4.9 c
4.10 d
4.11 c
4.12 a
4.13 b
4.14 b
4.15 a
4.16 d
4.17 c
4.18 b
4.19 a
4.20 b
4.21 d
4.22 d
4.23 b
4.24 a
4.25 a

CHAPTER 5

5.1 a
5.2 c
5.3 c
5.4 a
5.5 b
5.6 d
5.7 b
5.8 a
5.9 d
5.10 c
5.11 b
5.12 d
5.13 d
5.14 d
5.15 c
5.16 c
5.17 b
5.18 c
5.19 c
5.20 b
5.21 b
5.22 a
5.23 a
5.24 b

CHAPTER 6

6.1 d
6.2 d
6.3 c
6.4 a
6.5 c
6.6 b
6.7 b
6.8 c
6.9 a
6.10 a
6.11 d
6.12 b
6.13 b
6.14 c
6.15 b
6.16 d
6.17 b
6.18 a
6.19 d
6.20 c
6.21 d
6.22 c
6.23 b

CHAPTER 7

7.1 b
7.2 a
7.3 b
7.4 b
7.5 d
7.6 c
7.7 a
7.8 d
7.9 d
7.10 b
7.11 b
7.12 a
7.13 a
7.14 c
7.15 d
7.16 d
7.17 c
7.18 a
7.19 b
7.20 d
7.21 b
7.22 a
7.23 b
7.24 d
7.25 c

CHAPTER 8

8.1 a
8.2 d
8.3 d
8.4 b
8.5 a
8.6 a
8.7 c
8.8 b
8.9 b
8.10 b
8.11 d
8.12 d
8.13 a
8.14 b
8.15 c
8.16 b
8.17 c
8.18 d
8.19 c
8.20 c
8.21 d
8.22 a
8.23 a
8.24 d
8.25 c

CHAPTER 9

9.1 b	9.7 b	9.13 c	9.19 b
9.2 a	9.8 a	9.14 d	9.20 c
9.3 c	9.9 d	9.15 b	9.21 a
9.4 a	9.10 c	9.16 c	9.22 a
9.5 b	9.11 b	9.17 d	9.23 d
9.6 a	9.12 d	9.18 a	9.24 c

CHAPTER 10

10.1 c	10.7 c	10.13 c	10.19 c
10.2 b	10.8 d	10.14 b	10.20 d
10.3 d	10.9 b	10.15 d	10.21 b
10.4 b	10.10 b	10.16 c	10.22 b
10.5 b	10.11 d	10.17 d	10.23 b
10.6 d	10.12 a	10.18 a	

CHAPTER 11

11.1 b	11.8 b	11.15 d	11.22 b
11.2 a	11.9 b	11.16 a	11.23 b
11.3 d	11.10 d	11.17 d	11.24 c
11.4 b	11.11 d	11.18 b	11.25 a
11.5 d	11.12 c	11.19 c	11.26 b
11.6 d	11.13 b	11.20 b	11.27 d
11.7 c	11.14 d	11.21 a	

CHAPTER 12

12.1 d	12.7 a	12.13 d	12.19 b
12.2 c	12.8 c	12.14 b	12.20 b
12.3 c	12.9 b	12.15 c	12.21 d
12.4 a	12.10 c	12.16 d	12.22 b
12.5 d	12.11 d	12.17 c	
12.6 c	12.12 d	12.18 a	

CHAPTER 13

13.1 a	13.8 a	13.15 b	13.22 b
13.2 b	13.9 b	13.16 b	13.23 a
13.3 d	13.10 b	13.17 d	13.24 b
13.4 d	13.11 d	13.18 a	13.25 a
13.5 c	13.12 b	13.19 b	
13.6 a	13.13 b	13.20 d	
13.7 b	13.14 c	13.21 b	

CHAPTER 14

14.1 a	14.7 b	14.13 b	14.19 d
14.2 d	14.8 c	14.14 d	14.20 b
14.3 b	14.9 b	14.15 a	14.21 d
14.4 b	14.10 c	14.16 c	14.22 b
14.5 a	14.11 a	14.17 c	14.23 d
14.6 d	14.12 a	14.18 c	

CHAPTER 15

15.1 b	15.7 c	15.13 b	15.19 a
15.2 c	15.8 b	15.14 b	15.20 c
15.3 a	15.9 b	15.15 d	15.21 d
15.4 a	15.10 d	15.16 a	15.22 c
15.5 d	15.11 a	15.17 a	15.23 c
15.6 b	15.12 a	15.18 c	

CHAPTER 16

16.1 b	16.6 c	16.11 a	16.16 a
16.2 a	16.7 c	16.12 d	16.17 b
16.3 a	16.8 b	16.13 b	16.18 a
16.4 b	16.9 d	16.14 a	16.19 a
16.5 d	16.10 b	16.15 b	16.20 d

CHAPTER 17

17.1 a	17.7 d	17.13 a	17.19 b
17.2 d	17.8 d	17.14 b	17.20 c
17.3 d	17.9 c	17.15 c	17.21 b
17.4 c	17.10 b	17.16 a	17.22 d
17.5 c	17.11 b	17.17 d	
17.6 c	17.12 c	17.18 a	

CHAPTER 18

18.1 c	18.7 b	18.13 d	18.19 c
18.2 a	18.8 a	18.14 b	18.20 d
18.3 c	18.9 b	18.15 b	18.21 b
18.4 b	18.10 d	18.16 d	18.22 c
18.5 b	18.11 c	18.17 b	18.23 c
18.6 c	18.12 c	18.18 d	

CHAPTER 19

19.1 b	19.8 a	19.15 d	19.22 b
19.2 a	19.9 b	19.16 c	19.23 c
19.3 c	19.10 d	19.17 b	19.24 d
19.4 d	19.11 b	19.18 b	19.25 a
19.5 b	19.12 a	19.19 d	
19.6 a	19.13 a	19.20 a	
19.7 d	19.14 d	19.21 b	